T0189689

Lecture Notes in Computer Science 12365

More information about this series at http://www.springer.com/series/7412

Andrea Vedaldi · Horst Bischof ·
Thomas Brox · Jan-Michael Frahm (Eds.)

Computer Vision – ECCV 2020

16th European Conference
Glasgow, UK, August 23–28, 2020
Proceedings, Part XX

Springer

Editors
Andrea Vedaldi 🆔
University of Oxford
Oxford, UK

Horst Bischof 🆔
Graz University of Technology
Graz, Austria

Thomas Brox 🆔
University of Freiburg
Freiburg im Breisgau, Germany

Jan-Michael Frahm
University of North Carolina at Chapel Hill
Chapel Hill, NC, USA

ISSN 0302-9743 ISSN 1611-3349 (electronic)
Lecture Notes in Computer Science
ISBN 978-3-030-58564-8 ISBN 978-3-030-58565-5 (eBook)
https://doi.org/10.1007/978-3-030-58565-5

LNCS Sublibrary: SL6 – Image Processing, Computer Vision, Pattern Recognition, and Graphics

This Springer imprint is published by the registered company Springer Nature Switzerland AG
The registered company address is: Gewerbestrasse 11, 6330 Cham, Switzerland

Foreword

Hosting the European Conference on Computer Vision (ECCV 2020) was certainly an exciting journey. From the 2016 plan to hold it at the Edinburgh International Conference Centre (hosting 1,800 delegates) to the 2018 plan to hold it at Glasgow's Scottish Exhibition Centre (up to 6,000 delegates), we finally ended with moving online because of the COVID-19 outbreak. While possibly having fewer delegates than expected because of the online format, ECCV 2020 still had over 3,100 registered participants.

Although online, the conference delivered most of the activities expected at a face-to-face conference: peer-reviewed papers, industrial exhibitors, demonstrations, and messaging between delegates. In addition to the main technical sessions, the conference included a strong program of satellite events with 16 tutorials and 44 workshops.

Furthermore, the online conference format enabled new conference features. Every paper had an associated teaser video and a longer full presentation video. Along with the papers and slides from the videos, all these materials were available the week before the conference. This allowed delegates to become familiar with the paper content and be ready for the live interaction with the authors during the conference week. The live event consisted of brief presentations by the oral and spotlight authors and industrial sponsors. Question and answer sessions for all papers were timed to occur twice so delegates from around the world had convenient access to the authors.

As with ECCV 2018, authors' draft versions of the papers appeared online with open access, now on both the Computer Vision Foundation (CVF) and the European Computer Vision Association (ECVA) websites. An archival publication arrangement was put in place with the cooperation of Springer. SpringerLink hosts the final version of the papers with further improvements, such as activating reference links and supplementary materials. These two approaches benefit all potential readers: a version available freely for all researchers, and an authoritative and citable version with additional benefits for SpringerLink subscribers. We thank Alfred Hofmann and Aliaksandr Birukou from Springer for helping to negotiate this agreement, which we expect will continue for future versions of ECCV.

August 2020

Vittorio Ferrari
Bob Fisher
Cordelia Schmid
Emanuele Trucco

Preface

Welcome to the proceedings of the European Conference on Computer Vision (ECCV 2020). This is a unique edition of ECCV in many ways. Due to the COVID-19 pandemic, this is the first time the conference was held online, in a virtual format. This was also the first time the conference relied exclusively on the Open Review platform to manage the review process. Despite these challenges ECCV is thriving. The conference received 5,150 valid paper submissions, of which 1,360 were accepted for publication (27%) and, of those, 160 were presented as spotlights (3%) and 104 as orals (2%). This amounts to more than twice the number of submissions to ECCV 2018 (2,439). Furthermore, CVPR, the largest conference on computer vision, received 5,850 submissions this year, meaning that ECCV is now 87% the size of CVPR in terms of submissions. By comparison, in 2018 the size of ECCV was only 73% of CVPR.

The review model was similar to previous editions of ECCV; in particular, it was double blind in the sense that the authors did not know the name of the reviewers and vice versa. Furthermore, each conference submission was held confidentially, and was only publicly revealed if and once accepted for publication. Each paper received at least three reviews, totalling more than 15,000 reviews. Handling the review process at this scale was a significant challenge. In order to ensure that each submission received as fair and high-quality reviews as possible, we recruited 2,830 reviewers (a 130% increase with reference to 2018) and 207 area chairs (a 60% increase). The area chairs were selected based on their technical expertise and reputation, largely among people that served as area chair in previous top computer vision and machine learning conferences (ECCV, ICCV, CVPR, NeurIPS, etc.). Reviewers were similarly invited from previous conferences. We also encouraged experienced area chairs to suggest additional chairs and reviewers in the initial phase of recruiting.

Despite doubling the number of submissions, the reviewer load was slightly reduced from 2018, from a maximum of 8 papers down to 7 (with some reviewers offering to handle 6 papers plus an emergency review). The area chair load increased slightly, from 18 papers on average to 22 papers on average.

Conflicts of interest between authors, area chairs, and reviewers were handled largely automatically by the Open Review platform via their curated list of user profiles. Many authors submitting to ECCV already had a profile in Open Review. We set a paper registration deadline one week before the paper submission deadline in order to encourage all missing authors to register and create their Open Review profiles well on time (in practice, we allowed authors to create/change papers arbitrarily until the submission deadline). Except for minor issues with users creating duplicate profiles, this allowed us to easily and quickly identify institutional conflicts, and avoid them, while matching papers to area chairs and reviewers.

Papers were matched to area chairs based on: an affinity score computed by the Open Review platform, which is based on paper titles and abstracts, and an affinity score computed by the Toronto Paper Matching System (TPMS), which is based on the paper's full text, the area chair bids for individual papers, load balancing, and conflict avoidance. Open Review provides the program chairs a convenient web interface to experiment with different configurations of the matching algorithm. The chosen configuration resulted in about 50% of the assigned papers to be highly ranked by the area chair bids, and 50% to be ranked in the middle, with very few low bids assigned.

Assignments to reviewers were similar, with two differences. First, there was a maximum of 7 papers assigned to each reviewer. Second, area chairs recommended up to seven reviewers per paper, providing another highly-weighed term to the affinity scores used for matching.

The assignment of papers to area chairs was smooth. However, it was more difficult to find suitable reviewers for all papers. Having a ratio of 5.6 papers per reviewer with a maximum load of 7 (due to emergency reviewer commitment), which did not allow for much wiggle room in order to also satisfy conflict and expertise constraints. We received some complaints from reviewers who did not feel qualified to review specific papers and we reassigned them wherever possible. However, the large scale of the conference, the many constraints, and the fact that a large fraction of such complaints arrived very late in the review process made this process very difficult and not all complaints could be addressed.

Reviewers had six weeks to complete their assignments. Possibly due to COVID-19 or the fact that the NeurIPS deadline was moved closer to the review deadline, a record 30% of the reviews were still missing after the deadline. By comparison, ECCV 2018 experienced only 10% missing reviews at this stage of the process. In the subsequent week, area chairs chased the missing reviews intensely, found replacement reviewers in their own team, and managed to reach 10% missing reviews. Eventually, we could provide almost all reviews (more than 99.9%) with a delay of only a couple of days on the initial schedule by a significant use of emergency reviews. If this trend is confirmed, it might be a major challenge to run a smooth review process in future editions of ECCV. The community must reconsider prioritization of the time spent on paper writing (the number of submissions increased a lot despite COVID-19) and time spent on paper reviewing (the number of reviews delivered in time decreased a lot presumably due to COVID-19 or NeurIPS deadline). With this imbalance the peer-review system that ensures the quality of our top conferences may break soon.

Reviewers submitted their reviews independently. In the reviews, they had the opportunity to ask questions to the authors to be addressed in the rebuttal. However, reviewers were told not to request any significant new experiment. Using the Open Review interface, authors could provide an answer to each individual review, but were also allowed to cross-reference reviews and responses in their answers. Rather than PDF files, we allowed the use of formatted text for the rebuttal. The rebuttal and initial reviews were then made visible to all reviewers and the primary area chair for a given paper. The area chair encouraged and moderated the reviewer discussion. During the discussions, reviewers were invited to reach a consensus and possibly adjust their ratings as a result of the discussion and of the evidence in the rebuttal.

After the discussion period ended, most reviewers entered a final rating and recommendation, although in many cases this did not differ from their initial recommendation. Based on the updated reviews and discussion, the primary area chair then made a preliminary decision to accept or reject the paper and wrote a justification for it (meta-review). Except for cases where the outcome of this process was absolutely clear (as indicated by the three reviewers and primary area chairs all recommending clear rejection), the decision was then examined and potentially challenged by a secondary area chair. This led to further discussion and overturning a small number of preliminary decisions. Needless to say, there was no in-person area chair meeting, which would have been impossible due to COVID-19.

Area chairs were invited to observe the consensus of the reviewers whenever possible and use extreme caution in overturning a clear consensus to accept or reject a paper. If an area chair still decided to do so, she/he was asked to clearly justify it in the meta-review and to explicitly obtain the agreement of the secondary area chair. In practice, very few papers were rejected after being confidently accepted by the reviewers.

This was the first time Open Review was used as the main platform to run ECCV. In 2018, the program chairs used CMT3 for the user-facing interface and Open Review internally, for matching and conflict resolution. Since it is clearly preferable to only use a single platform, this year we switched to using Open Review in full. The experience was largely positive. The platform is highly-configurable, scalable, and open source. Being written in Python, it is easy to write scripts to extract data programmatically. The paper matching and conflict resolution algorithms and interfaces are top-notch, also due to the excellent author profiles in the platform. Naturally, there were a few kinks along the way due to the fact that the ECCV Open Review configuration was created from scratch for this event and it differs in substantial ways from many other Open Review conferences. However, the Open Review development and support team did a fantastic job in helping us to get the configuration right and to address issues in a timely manner as they unavoidably occurred. We cannot thank them enough for the tremendous effort they put into this project.

Finally, we would like to thank everyone involved in making ECCV 2020 possible in these very strange and difficult times. This starts with our authors, followed by the area chairs and reviewers, who ran the review process at an unprecedented scale. The whole Open Review team (and in particular Melisa Bok, Mohit Unyal, Carlos Mondragon Chapa, and Celeste Martinez Gomez) worked incredibly hard for the entire duration of the process. We would also like to thank René Vidal for contributing to the adoption of Open Review. Our thanks also go to Laurent Charling for TPMS and to the program chairs of ICML, ICLR, and NeurIPS for cross checking double submissions. We thank the website chair, Giovanni Farinella, and the CPI team (in particular Ashley Cook, Miriam Verdon, Nicola McGrane, and Sharon Kerr) for promptly adding material to the website as needed in the various phases of the process. Finally, we thank the publication chairs, Albert Ali Salah, Hamdi Dibeklioglu, Metehan Doyran, Henry Howard-Jenkins, Victor Prisacariu, Siyu Tang, and Gul Varol, who managed to compile these substantial proceedings in an exceedingly compressed schedule. We express our thanks to the ECVA team, in particular Kristina Scherbaum for allowing open access of the proceedings. We thank Alfred Hofmann from Springer who again serve as the publisher. Finally, we thank the other chairs of ECCV 2020, including in particular the general chairs for very useful feedback with the handling of the program.

August 2020

Andrea Vedaldi
Horst Bischof
Thomas Brox
Jan-Michael Frahm

Organization

General Chairs

Vittorio Ferrari	Google Research, Switzerland
Bob Fisher	University of Edinburgh, UK
Cordelia Schmid	Google and Inria, France
Emanuele Trucco	University of Dundee, UK

Program Chairs

Andrea Vedaldi	University of Oxford, UK
Horst Bischof	Graz University of Technology, Austria
Thomas Brox	University of Freiburg, Germany
Jan-Michael Frahm	University of North Carolina, USA

Industrial Liaison Chairs

Jim Ashe	University of Edinburgh, UK
Helmut Grabner	Zurich University of Applied Sciences, Switzerland
Diane Larlus	NAVER LABS Europe, France
Cristian Novotny	University of Edinburgh, UK

Local Arrangement Chairs

Yvan Petillot	Heriot-Watt University, UK
Paul Siebert	University of Glasgow, UK

Academic Demonstration Chair

Thomas Mensink	Google Research and University of Amsterdam, The Netherlands

Poster Chair

Stephen Mckenna	University of Dundee, UK

Technology Chair

Gerardo Aragon Camarasa	University of Glasgow, UK

Tutorial Chairs

Carlo Colombo   University of Florence, Italy
Sotirios Tsaftaris   University of Edinburgh, UK

Publication Chairs

Albert Ali Salah   Utrecht University, The Netherlands
Hamdi Dibeklioglu   Bilkent University, Turkey
Metehan Doyran   Utrecht University, The Netherlands
Henry Howard-Jenkins   University of Oxford, UK
Victor Adrian Prisacariu   University of Oxford, UK
Siyu Tang   ETH Zurich, Switzerland
Gul Varol   University of Oxford, UK

Website Chair

Giovanni Maria Farinella   University of Catania, Italy

Workshops Chairs

Adrien Bartoli   University of Clermont Auvergne, France
Andrea Fusiello   University of Udine, Italy

Area Chairs

Lourdes Agapito   University College London, UK
Zeynep Akata   University of Tübingen, Germany
Karteek Alahari   Inria, France
Antonis Argyros   University of Crete, Greece
Hossein Azizpour   KTH Royal Institute of Technology, Sweden
Joao P. Barreto   Universidade de Coimbra, Portugal
Alexander C. Berg   University of North Carolina at Chapel Hill, USA
Matthew B. Blaschko   KU Leuven, Belgium
Lubomir D. Bourdev   WaveOne, Inc., USA
Edmond Boyer   Inria, France
Yuri Boykov   University of Waterloo, Canada
Gabriel Brostow   University College London, UK
Michael S. Brown   National University of Singapore, Singapore
Jianfei Cai   Monash University, Australia
Barbara Caputo   Politecnico di Torino, Italy
Ayan Chakrabarti   Washington University, St. Louis, USA
Tat-Jen Cham   Nanyang Technological University, Singapore
Manmohan Chandraker   University of California, San Diego, USA
Rama Chellappa   Johns Hopkins University, USA
Liang-Chieh Chen   Google, USA

Yung-Yu Chuang   National Taiwan University, Taiwan
Ondrej Chum   Czech Technical University in Prague, Czech Republic
Brian Clipp   Kitware, USA
John Collomosse   University of Surrey and Adobe Research, UK
Jason J. Corso   University of Michigan, USA
David J. Crandall   Indiana University, USA
Daniel Cremers   University of California, Los Angeles, USA
Fabio Cuzzolin   Oxford Brookes University, UK
Jifeng Dai   SenseTime, SAR China
Kostas Daniilidis   University of Pennsylvania, USA
Andrew Davison   Imperial College London, UK
Alessio Del Bue   Fondazione Istituto Italiano di Tecnologia, Italy
Jia Deng   Princeton University, USA
Alexey Dosovitskiy   Google, Germany
Matthijs Douze   Facebook, France
Enrique Dunn   Stevens Institute of Technology, USA
Irfan Essa   Georgia Institute of Technology and Google, USA
Giovanni Maria Farinella   University of Catania, Italy
Ryan Farrell   Brigham Young University, USA
Paolo Favaro   University of Bern, Switzerland
Rogerio Feris   International Business Machines, USA
Cornelia Fermuller   University of Maryland, College Park, USA
David J. Fleet   Vector Institute, Canada
Friedrich Fraundorfer   DLR, Austria
Mario Fritz   CISPA Helmholtz Center for Information Security,
                           Germany
Pascal Fua   EPFL (Swiss Federal Institute of Technology
                           Lausanne), Switzerland
Yasutaka Furukawa   Simon Fraser University, Canada
Li Fuxin   Oregon State University, USA
Efstratios Gavves   University of Amsterdam, The Netherlands
Peter Vincent Gehler   Amazon, USA
Theo Gevers   University of Amsterdam, The Netherlands
Ross Girshick   Facebook AI Research, USA
Boqing Gong   Google, USA
Stephen Gould   Australian National University, Australia
Jinwei Gu   SenseTime Research, USA
Abhinav Gupta   Facebook, USA
Bohyung Han   Seoul National University, South Korea
Bharath Hariharan   Cornell University, USA
Tal Hassner   Facebook AI Research, USA
Xuming He   Australian National University, Australia
Joao F. Henriques   University of Oxford, UK
Adrian Hilton   University of Surrey, UK
Minh Hoai   Stony Brooks, State University of New York, USA
Derek Hoiem   University of Illinois Urbana-Champaign, USA

Timothy Hospedales	University of Edinburgh and Samsung, UK
Gang Hua	Wormpex AI Research, USA
Slobodan Ilic	Siemens AG, Germany
Hiroshi Ishikawa	Waseda University, Japan
Jiaya Jia	The Chinese University of Hong Kong, SAR China
Hailin Jin	Adobe Research, USA
Justin Johnson	University of Michigan, USA
Frederic Jurie	University of Caen Normandie, France
Fredrik Kahl	Chalmers University, Sweden
Sing Bing Kang	Zillow, USA
Gunhee Kim	Seoul National University, South Korea
Junmo Kim	Korea Advanced Institute of Science and Technology, South Korea
Tae-Kyun Kim	Imperial College London, UK
Ron Kimmel	Technion-Israel Institute of Technology, Israel
Alexander Kirillov	Facebook AI Research, USA
Kris Kitani	Carnegie Mellon University, USA
Iasonas Kokkinos	Ariel AI, UK
Vladlen Koltun	Intel Labs, USA
Nikos Komodakis	Ecole des Ponts ParisTech, France
Piotr Koniusz	Australian National University, Australia
M. Pawan Kumar	University of Oxford, UK
Kyros Kutulakos	University of Toronto, Canada
Christoph Lampert	IST Austria, Austria
Ivan Laptev	Inria, France
Diane Larlus	NAVER LABS Europe, France
Laura Leal-Taixe	Technical University Munich, Germany
Honglak Lee	Google and University of Michigan, USA
Joon-Young Lee	Adobe Research, USA
Kyoung Mu Lee	Seoul National University, South Korea
Seungyong Lee	POSTECH, South Korea
Yong Jae Lee	University of California, Davis, USA
Bastian Leibe	RWTH Aachen University, Germany
Victor Lempitsky	Samsung, Russia
Ales Leonardis	University of Birmingham, UK
Marius Leordeanu	Institute of Mathematics of the Romanian Academy, Romania
Vincent Lepetit	ENPC ParisTech, France
Hongdong Li	The Australian National University, Australia
Xi Li	Zhejiang University, China
Yin Li	University of Wisconsin-Madison, USA
Zicheng Liao	Zhejiang University, China
Jongwoo Lim	Hanyang University, South Korea
Stephen Lin	Microsoft Research Asia, China
Yen-Yu Lin	National Chiao Tung University, Taiwan, China
Zhe Lin	Adobe Research, USA

Haibin Ling	Stony Brooks, State University of New York, USA
Jiaying Liu	Peking University, China
Ming-Yu Liu	NVIDIA, USA
Si Liu	Beihang University, China
Xiaoming Liu	Michigan State University, USA
Huchuan Lu	Dalian University of Technology, China
Simon Lucey	Carnegie Mellon University, USA
Jiebo Luo	University of Rochester, USA
Julien Mairal	Inria, France
Michael Maire	University of Chicago, USA
Subhransu Maji	University of Massachusetts, Amherst, USA
Yasushi Makihara	Osaka University, Japan
Jiri Matas	Czech Technical University in Prague, Czech Republic
Yasuyuki Matsushita	Osaka University, Japan
Philippos Mordohai	Stevens Institute of Technology, USA
Vittorio Murino	University of Verona, Italy
Naila Murray	NAVER LABS Europe, France
Hajime Nagahara	Osaka University, Japan
P. J. Narayanan	International Institute of Information Technology (IIIT), Hyderabad, India
Nassir Navab	Technical University of Munich, Germany
Natalia Neverova	Facebook AI Research, France
Matthias Niessner	Technical University of Munich, Germany
Jean-Marc Odobez	Idiap Research Institute and Swiss Federal Institute of Technology Lausanne, Switzerland
Francesca Odone	Università di Genova, Italy
Takeshi Oishi	The University of Tokyo, Tokyo Institute of Technology, Japan
Vicente Ordonez	University of Virginia, USA
Manohar Paluri	Facebook AI Research, USA
Maja Pantic	Imperial College London, UK
In Kyu Park	Inha University, South Korea
Ioannis Patras	Queen Mary University of London, UK
Patrick Perez	Valeo, France
Bryan A. Plummer	Boston University, USA
Thomas Pock	Graz University of Technology, Austria
Marc Pollefeys	ETH Zurich and Microsoft MR & AI Zurich Lab, Switzerland
Jean Ponce	Inria, France
Gerard Pons-Moll	MPII, Saarland Informatics Campus, Germany
Jordi Pont-Tuset	Google, Switzerland
James Matthew Rehg	Georgia Institute of Technology, USA
Ian Reid	University of Adelaide, Australia
Olaf Ronneberger	DeepMind London, UK
Stefan Roth	TU Darmstadt, Germany
Bryan Russell	Adobe Research, USA

Mathieu Salzmann	EPFL, Switzerland
Dimitris Samaras	Stony Brook University, USA
Imari Sato	National Institute of Informatics (NII), Japan
Yoichi Sato	The University of Tokyo, Japan
Torsten Sattler	Czech Technical University in Prague, Czech Republic
Daniel Scharstein	Middlebury College, USA
Bernt Schiele	MPII, Saarland Informatics Campus, Germany
Julia A. Schnabel	King's College London, UK
Nicu Sebe	University of Trento, Italy
Greg Shakhnarovich	Toyota Technological Institute at Chicago, USA
Humphrey Shi	University of Oregon, USA
Jianbo Shi	University of Pennsylvania, USA
Jianping Shi	SenseTime, China
Leonid Sigal	University of British Columbia, Canada
Cees Snoek	University of Amsterdam, The Netherlands
Richard Souvenir	Temple University, USA
Hao Su	University of California, San Diego, USA
Akihiro Sugimoto	National Institute of Informatics (NII), Japan
Jian Sun	Megvii Technology, China
Jian Sun	Xi'an Jiaotong University, China
Chris Sweeney	Facebook Reality Labs, USA
Yu-wing Tai	Kuaishou Technology, China
Chi-Keung Tang	The Hong Kong University of Science and Technology, SAR China
Radu Timofte	ETH Zurich, Switzerland
Sinisa Todorovic	Oregon State University, USA
Giorgos Tolias	Czech Technical University in Prague, Czech Republic
Carlo Tomasi	Duke University, USA
Tatiana Tommasi	Politecnico di Torino, Italy
Lorenzo Torresani	Facebook AI Research and Dartmouth College, USA
Alexander Toshev	Google, USA
Zhuowen Tu	University of California, San Diego, USA
Tinne Tuytelaars	KU Leuven, Belgium
Jasper Uijlings	Google, Switzerland
Nuno Vasconcelos	University of California, San Diego, USA
Olga Veksler	University of Waterloo, Canada
Rene Vidal	Johns Hopkins University, USA
Gang Wang	Alibaba Group, China
Jingdong Wang	Microsoft Research Asia, China
Yizhou Wang	Peking University, China
Lior Wolf	Facebook AI Research and Tel Aviv University, Israel
Jianxin Wu	Nanjing University, China
Tao Xiang	University of Surrey, UK
Saining Xie	Facebook AI Research, USA
Ming-Hsuan Yang	University of California at Merced and Google, USA
Ruigang Yang	University of Kentucky, USA

Kwang Moo Yi	University of Victoria, Canada
Zhaozheng Yin	Stony Brook, State University of New York, USA
Chang D. Yoo	Korea Advanced Institute of Science and Technology, South Korea
Shaodi You	University of Amsterdam, The Netherlands
Jingyi Yu	ShanghaiTech University, China
Stella Yu	University of California, Berkeley, and ICSI, USA
Stefanos Zafeiriou	Imperial College London, UK
Hongbin Zha	Peking University, China
Tianzhu Zhang	University of Science and Technology of China, China
Liang Zheng	Australian National University, Australia
Todd E. Zickler	Harvard University, USA
Andrew Zisserman	University of Oxford, UK

Technical Program Committee

Sathyanarayanan
 N. Aakur
Wael Abd Almgaeed
Abdelrahman
 Abdelhamed
Abdullah Abuolaim
Supreeth Achar
Hanno Ackermann
Ehsan Adeli
Triantafyllos Afouras
Sameer Agarwal
Aishwarya Agrawal
Harsh Agrawal
Pulkit Agrawal
Antonio Agudo
Eirikur Agustsson
Karim Ahmed
Byeongjoo Ahn
Unaiza Ahsan
Thalaiyasingam Ajanthan
Kenan E. Ak
Emre Akbas
Naveed Akhtar
Derya Akkaynak
Yagiz Aksoy
Ziad Al-Halah
Xavier Alameda-Pineda
Jean-Baptiste Alayrac

Samuel Albanie
Shadi Albarqouni
Cenek Albl
Hassan Abu Alhaija
Daniel Aliaga
Mohammad
 S. Aliakbarian
Rahaf Aljundi
Thiemo Alldieck
Jon Almazan
Jose M. Alvarez
Senjian An
Saket Anand
Codruta Ancuti
Cosmin Ancuti
Peter Anderson
Juan Andrade-Cetto
Alexander Andreopoulos
Misha Andriluka
Dragomir Anguelov
Rushil Anirudh
Michel Antunes
Oisin Mac Aodha
Srikar Appalaraju
Relja Arandjelovic
Nikita Araslanov
Andre Araujo
Helder Araujo

Pablo Arbelaez
Shervin Ardeshir
Sercan O. Arik
Anil Armagan
Anurag Arnab
Chetan Arora
Federica Arrigoni
Mathieu Aubry
Shai Avidan
Angelica I. Aviles-Rivero
Yannis Avrithis
Ismail Ben Ayed
Shekoofeh Azizi
Ioan Andrei Bârsan
Artem Babenko
Deepak Babu Sam
Seung-Hwan Baek
Seungryul Baek
Andrew D. Bagdanov
Shai Bagon
Yuval Bahat
Junjie Bai
Song Bai
Xiang Bai
Yalong Bai
Yancheng Bai
Peter Bajcsy
Slawomir Bak

Mahsa Baktashmotlagh
Kavita Bala
Yogesh Balaji
Guha Balakrishnan
V. N. Balasubramanian
Federico Baldassarre
Vassileios Balntas
Shurjo Banerjee
Aayush Bansal
Ankan Bansal
Jianmin Bao
Linchao Bao
Wenbo Bao
Yingze Bao
Akash Bapat
Md Jawadul Hasan Bappy
Fabien Baradel
Lorenzo Baraldi
Daniel Barath
Adrian Barbu
Kobus Barnard
Nick Barnes
Francisco Barranco
Jonathan T. Barron
Arslan Basharat
Chaim Baskin
Anil S. Baslamisli
Jorge Batista
Kayhan Batmanghelich
Konstantinos Batsos
David Bau
Luis Baumela
Christoph Baur
Eduardo
   Bayro-Corrochano
Paul Beardsley
Jan Bednavr'ik
Oscar Beijbom
Philippe Bekaert
Esube Bekele
Vasileios Belagiannis
Ohad Ben-Shahar
Abhijit Bendale
Róger Bermúdez-Chacón
Maxim Berman
Jesus Bermudez-cameo

Florian Bernard
Stefano Berretti
Marcelo Bertalmio
Gedas Bertasius
Cigdem Beyan
Lucas Beyer
Vijayakumar Bhagavatula
Arjun Nitin Bhagoji
Apratim Bhattacharyya
Binod Bhattarai
Sai Bi
Jia-Wang Bian
Simone Bianco
Adel Bibi
Tolga Birdal
Tom Bishop
Soma Biswas
Mårten Björkman
Volker Blanz
Vishnu Boddeti
Navaneeth Bodla
Simion-Vlad Bogolin
Xavier Boix
Piotr Bojanowski
Timo Bolkart
Guido Borghi
Larbi Boubchir
Guillaume Bourmaud
Adrien Bousseau
Thierry Bouwmans
Richard Bowden
Hakan Boyraz
Mathieu Brédif
Samarth Brahmbhatt
Steve Branson
Nikolas Brasch
Biagio Brattoli
Ernesto Brau
Toby P. Breckon
Francois Bremond
Jesus Briales
Sofia Broomé
Marcus A. Brubaker
Luc Brun
Silvia Bucci
Shyamal Buch

Pradeep Buddharaju
Uta Buechler
Mai Bui
Tu Bui
Adrian Bulat
Giedrius T. Burachas
Elena Burceanu
Xavier P. Burgos-Artizzu
Kaylee Burns
Andrei Bursuc
Benjamin Busam
Wonmin Byeon
Zoya Bylinskii
Sergi Caelles
Jianrui Cai
Minjie Cai
Yujun Cai
Zhaowei Cai
Zhipeng Cai
Juan C. Caicedo
Simone Calderara
Necati Cihan Camgoz
Dylan Campbell
Octavia Camps
Jiale Cao
Kaidi Cao
Liangliang Cao
Xiangyong Cao
Xiaochun Cao
Yang Cao
Yu Cao
Yue Cao
Zhangjie Cao
Luca Carlone
Mathilde Caron
Dan Casas
Thomas J. Cashman
Umberto Castellani
Lluis Castrejon
Jacopo Cavazza
Fabio Cermelli
Hakan Cevikalp
Menglei Chai
Ishani Chakraborty
Rudrasis Chakraborty
Antoni B. Chan

Kwok-Ping Chan
Siddhartha Chandra
Sharat Chandran
Arjun Chandrasekaran
Angel X. Chang
Che-Han Chang
Hong Chang
Hyun Sung Chang
Hyung Jin Chang
Jianlong Chang
Ju Yong Chang
Ming-Ching Chang
Simyung Chang
Xiaojun Chang
Yu-Wei Chao
Devendra S. Chaplot
Arslan Chaudhry
Rizwan A. Chaudhry
Can Chen
Chang Chen
Chao Chen
Chen Chen
Chu-Song Chen
Dapeng Chen
Dong Chen
Dongdong Chen
Guanying Chen
Hongge Chen
Hsin-yi Chen
Huaijin Chen
Hwann-Tzong Chen
Jianbo Chen
Jianhui Chen
Jiansheng Chen
Jiaxin Chen
Jie Chen
Jun-Cheng Chen
Kan Chen
Kevin Chen
Lin Chen
Long Chen
Min-Hung Chen
Qifeng Chen
Shi Chen
Shixing Chen
Tianshui Chen

Weifeng Chen
Weikai Chen
Xi Chen
Xiaohan Chen
Xiaozhi Chen
Xilin Chen
Xingyu Chen
Xinlei Chen
Xinyun Chen
Yi-Ting Chen
Yilun Chen
Ying-Cong Chen
Yinpeng Chen
Yiran Chen
Yu Chen
Yu-Sheng Chen
Yuhua Chen
Yun-Chun Chen
Yunpeng Chen
Yuntao Chen
Zhuoyuan Chen
Zitian Chen
Anchieh Cheng
Bowen Cheng
Erkang Cheng
Gong Cheng
Guangliang Cheng
Jingchun Cheng
Jun Cheng
Li Cheng
Ming-Ming Cheng
Yu Cheng
Ziang Cheng
Anoop Cherian
Dmitry Chetverikov
Ngai-man Cheung
William Cheung
Ajad Chhatkuli
Naoki Chiba
Benjamin Chidester
Han-pang Chiu
Mang Tik Chiu
Wei-Chen Chiu
Donghyeon Cho
Hojin Cho
Minsu Cho

Nam Ik Cho
Tim Cho
Tae Eun Choe
Chiho Choi
Edward Choi
Inchang Choi
Jinsoo Choi
Jonghyun Choi
Jongwon Choi
Yukyung Choi
Hisham Cholakkal
Eunji Chong
Jaegul Choo
Christopher Choy
Hang Chu
Peng Chu
Wen-Sheng Chu
Albert Chung
Joon Son Chung
Hai Ci
Safa Cicek
Ramazan G. Cinbis
Arridhana Ciptadi
Javier Civera
James J. Clark
Ronald Clark
Felipe Codevilla
Michael Cogswell
Andrea Cohen
Maxwell D. Collins
Carlo Colombo
Yang Cong
Adria R. Continente
Marcella Cornia
John Richard Corring
Darren Cosker
Dragos Costea
Garrison W. Cottrell
Florent Couzinie-Devy
Marco Cristani
Ioana Croitoru
James L. Crowley
Jiequan Cui
Zhaopeng Cui
Ross Cutler
Antonio D'Innocente

Rozenn Dahyot
Bo Dai
Dengxin Dai
Hang Dai
Longquan Dai
Shuyang Dai
Xiyang Dai
Yuchao Dai
Adrian V. Dalca
Dima Damen
Bharath B. Damodaran
Kristin Dana
Martin Danelljan
Zheng Dang
Zachary Alan Daniels
Donald G. Dansereau
Abhishek Das
Samyak Datta
Achal Dave
Titas De
Rodrigo de Bem
Teo de Campos
Raoul de Charette
Shalini De Mello
Joseph DeGol
Herve Delingette
Haowen Deng
Jiankang Deng
Weijian Deng
Zhiwei Deng
Joachim Denzler
Konstantinos G. Derpanis
Aditya Deshpande
Frederic Devernay
Somdip Dey
Arturo Deza
Abhinav Dhall
Helisa Dhamo
Vikas Dhiman
Fillipe Dias Moreira
    de Souza
Ali Diba
Ferran Diego
Guiguang Ding
Henghui Ding
Jian Ding

Mingyu Ding
Xinghao Ding
Zhengming Ding
Robert DiPietro
Cosimo Distante
Ajay Divakaran
Mandar Dixit
Abdelaziz Djelouah
Thanh-Toan Do
Jose Dolz
Bo Dong
Chao Dong
Jiangxin Dong
Weiming Dong
Weisheng Dong
Xingping Dong
Xuanyi Dong
Yinpeng Dong
Gianfranco Doretto
Hazel Doughty
Hassen Drira
Bertram Drost
Dawei Du
Ye Duan
Yueqi Duan
Abhimanyu Dubey
Anastasia Dubrovina
Stefan Duffner
Chi Nhan Duong
Thibaut Durand
Zoran Duric
Iulia Duta
Debidatta Dwibedi
Benjamin Eckart
Marc Eder
Marzieh Edraki
Alexei A. Efros
Kiana Ehsani
Hazm Kemal Ekenel
James H. Elder
Mohamed Elgharib
Shireen Elhabian
Ehsan Elhamifar
Mohamed Elhoseiny
Ian Endres
N. Benjamin Erichson

Jan Ernst
Sergio Escalera
Francisco Escolano
Victor Escorcia
Carlos Esteves
Francisco J. Estrada
Bin Fan
Chenyou Fan
Deng-Ping Fan
Haoqi Fan
Hehe Fan
Heng Fan
Kai Fan
Lijie Fan
Linxi Fan
Quanfu Fan
Shaojing Fan
Xiaochuan Fan
Xin Fan
Yuchen Fan
Sean Fanello
Hao-Shu Fang
Haoyang Fang
Kuan Fang
Yi Fang
Yuming Fang
Azade Farshad
Alireza Fathi
Raanan Fattal
Joao Fayad
Xiaohan Fei
Christoph Feichtenhofer
Michael Felsberg
Chen Feng
Jiashi Feng
Junyi Feng
Mengyang Feng
Qianli Feng
Zhenhua Feng
Michele Fenzi
Andras Ferencz
Martin Fergie
Basura Fernando
Ethan Fetaya
Michael Firman
John W. Fisher

Matthew Fisher
Boris Flach
Corneliu Florea
Wolfgang Foerstner
David Fofi
Gian Luca Foresti
Per-Erik Forssen
David Fouhey
Katerina Fragkiadaki
Victor Fragoso
Jean-Sébastien Franco
Ohad Fried
Iuri Frosio
Cheng-Yang Fu
Huazhu Fu
Jianlong Fu
Jingjing Fu
Xueyang Fu
Yanwei Fu
Ying Fu
Yun Fu
Olac Fuentes
Kent Fujiwara
Takuya Funatomi
Christopher Funk
Thomas Funkhouser
Antonino Furnari
Ryo Furukawa
Erik Gärtner
Raghudeep Gadde
Matheus Gadelha
Vandit Gajjar
Trevor Gale
Juergen Gall
Mathias Gallardo
Guillermo Gallego
Orazio Gallo
Chuang Gan
Zhe Gan
Madan Ravi Ganesh
Aditya Ganeshan
Siddha Ganju
Bin-Bin Gao
Changxin Gao
Feng Gao
Hongchang Gao

Jin Gao
Jiyang Gao
Junbin Gao
Katelyn Gao
Lin Gao
Mingfei Gao
Ruiqi Gao
Ruohan Gao
Shenghua Gao
Yuan Gao
Yue Gao
Noa Garcia
Alberto Garcia-Garcia
Guillermo
   Garcia-Hernando
Jacob R. Gardner
Animesh Garg
Kshitiz Garg
Rahul Garg
Ravi Garg
Philip N. Garner
Kirill Gavrilyuk
Paul Gay
Shiming Ge
Weifeng Ge
Baris Gecer
Xin Geng
Kyle Genova
Stamatios Georgoulis
Bernard Ghanem
Michael Gharbi
Kamran Ghasedi
Golnaz Ghiasi
Arnab Ghosh
Partha Ghosh
Silvio Giancola
Andrew Gilbert
Rohit Girdhar
Xavier Giro-i-Nieto
Thomas Gittings
Ioannis Gkioulekas
Clement Godard
Vaibhava Goel
Bastian Goldluecke
Lluis Gomez
Nuno Gonçalves

Dong Gong
Ke Gong
Mingming Gong
Abel Gonzalez-Garcia
Ariel Gordon
Daniel Gordon
Paulo Gotardo
Venu Madhav Govindu
Ankit Goyal
Priya Goyal
Raghav Goyal
Benjamin Graham
Douglas Gray
Brent A. Griffin
Etienne Grossmann
David Gu
Jiayuan Gu
Jiuxiang Gu
Lin Gu
Qiao Gu
Shuhang Gu
Jose J. Guerrero
Paul Guerrero
Jie Gui
Jean-Yves Guillemaut
Riza Alp Guler
Erhan Gundogdu
Fatma Guney
Guodong Guo
Kaiwen Guo
Qi Guo
Sheng Guo
Shi Guo
Tiantong Guo
Xiaojie Guo
Yijie Guo
Yiluan Guo
Yuanfang Guo
Yulan Guo
Agrim Gupta
Ankush Gupta
Mohit Gupta
Saurabh Gupta
Tanmay Gupta
Danna Gurari
Abner Guzman-Rivera

JunYoung Gwak
Michael Gygli
Jung-Woo Ha
Simon Hadfield
Isma Hadji
Bjoern Haefner
Taeyoung Hahn
Levente Hajder
Peter Hall
Emanuela Haller
Stefan Haller
Bumsub Ham
Abdullah Hamdi
Dongyoon Han
Hu Han
Jungong Han
Junwei Han
Kai Han
Tian Han
Xiaoguang Han
Xintong Han
Yahong Han
Ankur Handa
Zekun Hao
Albert Haque
Tatsuya Harada
Mehrtash Harandi
Adam W. Harley
Mahmudul Hasan
Atsushi Hashimoto
Ali Hatamizadeh
Munawar Hayat
Dongliang He
Jingrui He
Junfeng He
Kaiming He
Kun He
Lei He
Pan He
Ran He
Shengfeng He
Tong He
Weipeng He
Xuming He
Yang He
Yihui He

Zhihai He
Chinmay Hegde
Janne Heikkila
Mattias P. Heinrich
Stéphane Herbin
Alexander Hermans
Luis Herranz
John R. Hershey
Aaron Hertzmann
Roei Herzig
Anders Heyden
Steven Hickson
Otmar Hilliges
Tomas Hodan
Judy Hoffman
Michael Hofmann
Yannick Hold-Geoffroy
Namdar Homayounfar
Sina Honari
Richang Hong
Seunghoon Hong
Xiaopeng Hong
Yi Hong
Hidekata Hontani
Anthony Hoogs
Yedid Hoshen
Mir Rayat Imtiaz Hossain
Junhui Hou
Le Hou
Lu Hou
Tingbo Hou
Wei-Lin Hsiao
Cheng-Chun Hsu
Gee-Sern Jison Hsu
Kuang-jui Hsu
Changbo Hu
Di Hu
Guosheng Hu
Han Hu
Hao Hu
Hexiang Hu
Hou-Ning Hu
Jie Hu
Junlin Hu
Nan Hu
Ping Hu

Ronghang Hu
Xiaowei Hu
Yinlin Hu
Yuan-Ting Hu
Zhe Hu
Binh-Son Hua
Yang Hua
Bingyao Huang
Di Huang
Dong Huang
Fay Huang
Haibin Huang
Haozhi Huang
Heng Huang
Huaibo Huang
Jia-Bin Huang
Jing Huang
Jingwei Huang
Kaizhu Huang
Lei Huang
Qiangui Huang
Qiaoying Huang
Qingqiu Huang
Qixing Huang
Shaoli Huang
Sheng Huang
Siyuan Huang
Weilin Huang
Wenbing Huang
Xiangru Huang
Xun Huang
Yan Huang
Yifei Huang
Yue Huang
Zhiwu Huang
Zilong Huang
Minyoung Huh
Zhuo Hui
Matthias B. Hullin
Martin Humenberger
Wei-Chih Hung
Zhouyuan Huo
Junhwa Hur
Noureldien Hussein
Jyh-Jing Hwang
Seong Jae Hwang

Sung Ju Hwang
Ichiro Ide
Ivo Ihrke
Daiki Ikami
Satoshi Ikehata
Nazli Ikizler-Cinbis
Sunghoon Im
Yani Ioannou
Radu Tudor Ionescu
Umar Iqbal
Go Irie
Ahmet Iscen
Md Amirul Islam
Vamsi Ithapu
Nathan Jacobs
Arpit Jain
Himalaya Jain
Suyog Jain
Stuart James
Won-Dong Jang
Yunseok Jang
Ronnachai Jaroensri
Dinesh Jayaraman
Sadeep Jayasumana
Suren Jayasuriya
Herve Jegou
Simon Jenni
Hae-Gon Jeon
Yunho Jeon
Koteswar R. Jerripothula
Hueihan Jhuang
I-hong Jhuo
Dinghuang Ji
Hui Ji
Jingwei Ji
Pan Ji
Yanli Ji
Baoxiong Jia
Kui Jia
Xu Jia
Chiyu Max Jiang
Haiyong Jiang
Hao Jiang
Huaizu Jiang
Huajie Jiang
Ke Jiang

Lai Jiang
Li Jiang
Lu Jiang
Ming Jiang
Peng Jiang
Shuqiang Jiang
Wei Jiang
Xudong Jiang
Zhuolin Jiang
Jianbo Jiao
Zequn Jie
Dakai Jin
Kyong Hwan Jin
Lianwen Jin
SouYoung Jin
Xiaojie Jin
Xin Jin
Nebojsa Jojic
Alexis Joly
Michael Jeffrey Jones
Hanbyul Joo
Jungseock Joo
Kyungdon Joo
Ajjen Joshi
Shantanu H. Joshi
Da-Cheng Juan
Marco Körner
Kevin Köser
Asim Kadav
Christine Kaeser-Chen
Kushal Kafle
Dagmar Kainmueller
Ioannis A. Kakadiaris
Zdenek Kalal
Nima Kalantari
Yannis Kalantidis
Mahdi M. Kalayeh
Anmol Kalia
Sinan Kalkan
Vicky Kalogeiton
Ashwin Kalyan
Joni-kristian Kamarainen
Gerda Kamberova
Chandra Kambhamettu
Martin Kampel
Meina Kan

Christopher Kanan
Kenichi Kanatani
Angjoo Kanazawa
Atsushi Kanehira
Takuhiro Kaneko
Asako Kanezaki
Bingyi Kang
Di Kang
Sunghun Kang
Zhao Kang
Vadim Kantorov
Abhishek Kar
Amlan Kar
Theofanis Karaletsos
Leonid Karlinsky
Kevin Karsch
Angelos Katharopoulos
Isinsu Katircioglu
Hiroharu Kato
Zoltan Kato
Dotan Kaufman
Jan Kautz
Rei Kawakami
Qiuhong Ke
Wadim Kehl
Petr Kellnhofer
Aniruddha Kembhavi
Cem Keskin
Margret Keuper
Daniel Keysers
Ashkan Khakzar
Fahad Khan
Naeemullah Khan
Salman Khan
Siddhesh Khandelwal
Rawal Khirodkar
Anna Khoreva
Tejas Khot
Parmeshwar Khurd
Hadi Kiapour
Joe Kileel
Chanho Kim
Dahun Kim
Edward Kim
Eunwoo Kim
Han-ul Kim

Hansung Kim
Heewon Kim
Hyo Jin Kim
Hyunwoo J. Kim
Jinkyu Kim
Jiwon Kim
Jongmin Kim
Junsik Kim
Junyeong Kim
Min H. Kim
Namil Kim
Pyojin Kim
Seon Joo Kim
Seong Tae Kim
Seungryong Kim
Sungwoong Kim
Tae Hyun Kim
Vladimir Kim
Won Hwa Kim
Yonghyun Kim
Benjamin Kimia
Akisato Kimura
Pieter-Jan Kindermans
Zsolt Kira
Itaru Kitahara
Hedvig Kjellstrom
Jan Knopp
Takumi Kobayashi
Erich Kobler
Parker Koch
Reinhard Koch
Elyor Kodirov
Amir Kolaman
Nicholas Kolkin
Dimitrios Kollias
Stefanos Kollias
Soheil Kolouri
Adams Wai-Kin Kong
Naejin Kong
Shu Kong
Tao Kong
Yu Kong
Yoshinori Konishi
Daniil Kononenko
Theodora Kontogianni
Simon Korman

Adam Kortylewski
Jana Kosecka
Jean Kossaifi
Satwik Kottur
Rigas Kouskouridas
Adriana Kovashka
Rama Kovvuri
Adarsh Kowdle
Jedrzej Kozerawski
Mateusz Kozinski
Philipp Kraehenbuehl
Gregory Kramida
Josip Krapac
Dmitry Kravchenko
Ranjay Krishna
Pavel Krsek
Alexander Krull
Jakob Kruse
Hiroyuki Kubo
Hilde Kuehne
Jason Kuen
Andreas Kuhn
Arjan Kuijper
Zuzana Kukelova
Ajay Kumar
Amit Kumar
Avinash Kumar
Suryansh Kumar
Vijay Kumar
Kaustav Kundu
Weicheng Kuo
Nojun Kwak
Suha Kwak
Junseok Kwon
Nikolaos Kyriazis
Zorah Lähner
Ankit Laddha
Florent Lafarge
Jean Lahoud
Kevin Lai
Shang-Hong Lai
Wei-Sheng Lai
Yu-Kun Lai
Iro Laina
Antony Lam
John Wheatley Lambert

Xiangyuan lan
Xu Lan
Charis Lanaras
Georg Langs
Oswald Lanz
Dong Lao
Yizhen Lao
Agata Lapedriza
Gustav Larsson
Viktor Larsson
Katrin Lasinger
Christoph Lassner
Longin Jan Latecki
Stéphane Lathuilière
Rynson Lau
Hei Law
Justin Lazarow
Svetlana Lazebnik
Hieu Le
Huu Le
Ngan Hoang Le
Trung-Nghia Le
Vuong Le
Colin Lea
Erik Learned-Miller
Chen-Yu Lee
Gim Hee Lee
Hsin-Ying Lee
Hyungtae Lee
Jae-Han Lee
Jimmy Addison Lee
Joonseok Lee
Kibok Lee
Kuang-Huei Lee
Kwonjoon Lee
Minsik Lee
Sang-chul Lee
Seungkyu Lee
Soochan Lee
Stefan Lee
Taehee Lee
Andreas Lehrmann
Jie Lei
Peng Lei
Matthew Joseph Leotta
Wee Kheng Leow

Gil Levi
Evgeny Levinkov
Aviad Levis
Jose Lezama
Ang Li
Bin Li
Bing Li
Boyi Li
Changsheng Li
Chao Li
Chen Li
Cheng Li
Chenglong Li
Chi Li
Chun-Guang Li
Chun-Liang Li
Chunyuan Li
Dong Li
Guanbin Li
Hao Li
Haoxiang Li
Hongsheng Li
Hongyang Li
Houqiang Li
Huibin Li
Jia Li
Jianan Li
Jianguo Li
Junnan Li
Junxuan Li
Kai Li
Ke Li
Kejie Li
Kunpeng Li
Lerenhan Li
Li Erran Li
Mengtian Li
Mu Li
Peihua Li
Peiyi Li
Ping Li
Qi Li
Qing Li
Ruiyu Li
Ruoteng Li
Shaozi Li

Sheng Li
Shiwei Li
Shuang Li
Siyang Li
Stan Z. Li
Tianye Li
Wei Li
Weixin Li
Wen Li
Wenbo Li
Xiaomeng Li
Xin Li
Xiu Li
Xuelong Li
Xueting Li
Yan Li
Yandong Li
Yanghao Li
Yehao Li
Yi Li
Yijun Li
Yikang LI
Yining Li
Yongjie Li
Yu Li
Yu-Jhe Li
Yunpeng Li
Yunsheng Li
Yunzhu Li
Zhe Li
Zhen Li
Zhengqi Li
Zhenyang Li
Zhuwen Li
Dongze Lian
Xiaochen Lian
Zhouhui Lian
Chen Liang
Jie Liang
Ming Liang
Paul Pu Liang
Pengpeng Liang
Shu Liang
Wei Liang
Jing Liao
Minghui Liao

Renjie Liao
Shengcai Liao
Shuai Liao
Yiyi Liao
Ser-Nam Lim
Chen-Hsuan Lin
Chung-Ching Lin
Dahua Lin
Ji Lin
Kevin Lin
Tianwei Lin
Tsung-Yi Lin
Tsung-Yu Lin
Wei-An Lin
Weiyao Lin
Yen-Chen Lin
Yuewei Lin
David B. Lindell
Drew Linsley
Krzysztof Lis
Roee Litman
Jim Little
An-An Liu
Bo Liu
Buyu Liu
Chao Liu
Chen Liu
Cheng-lin Liu
Chenxi Liu
Dong Liu
Feng Liu
Guilin Liu
Haomiao Liu
Heshan Liu
Hong Liu
Ji Liu
Jingen Liu
Jun Liu
Lanlan Liu
Li Liu
Liu Liu
Mengyuan Liu
Miaomiao Liu
Nian Liu
Ping Liu
Risheng Liu

Sheng Liu
Shu Liu
Shuaicheng Liu
Sifei Liu
Siqi Liu
Siying Liu
Songtao Liu
Ting Liu
Tongliang Liu
Tyng-Luh Liu
Wanquan Liu
Wei Liu
Weiyang Liu
Weizhe Liu
Wenyu Liu
Wu Liu
Xialei Liu
Xianglong Liu
Xiaodong Liu
Xiaofeng Liu
Xihui Liu
Xingyu Liu
Xinwang Liu
Xuanqing Liu
Xuebo Liu
Yang Liu
Yaojie Liu
Yebin Liu
Yen-Cheng Liu
Yiming Liu
Yu Liu
Yu-Shen Liu
Yufan Liu
Yun Liu
Zheng Liu
Zhijian Liu
Zhuang Liu
Zichuan Liu
Ziwei Liu
Zongyi Liu
Stephan Liwicki
Liliana Lo Presti
Chengjiang Long
Fuchen Long
Mingsheng Long
Xiang Long

Yang Long
Charles T. Loop
Antonio Lopez
Roberto J. Lopez-Sastre
Javier Lorenzo-Navarro
Manolis Lourakis
Boyu Lu
Canyi Lu
Feng Lu
Guoyu Lu
Hongtao Lu
Jiajun Lu
Jiasen Lu
Jiwen Lu
Kaiyue Lu
Le Lu
Shao-Ping Lu
Shijian Lu
Xiankai Lu
Xin Lu
Yao Lu
Yiping Lu
Yongxi Lu
Yongyi Lu
Zhiwu Lu
Fujun Luan
Benjamin E. Lundell
Hao Luo
Jian-Hao Luo
Ruotian Luo
Weixin Luo
Wenhan Luo
Wenjie Luo
Yan Luo
Zelun Luo
Zixin Luo
Khoa Luu
Zhaoyang Lv
Pengyuan Lyu
Thomas Möllenhoff
Matthias Müller
Bingpeng Ma
Chih-Yao Ma
Chongyang Ma
Huimin Ma
Jiayi Ma

K. T. Ma
Ke Ma
Lin Ma
Liqian Ma
Shugao Ma
Wei-Chiu Ma
Xiaojian Ma
Xingjun Ma
Zhanyu Ma
Zheng Ma
Radek Jakob Mackowiak
Ludovic Magerand
Shweta Mahajan
Siddharth Mahendran
Long Mai
Ameesh Makadia
Oscar Mendez Maldonado
Mateusz Malinowski
Yury Malkov
Arun Mallya
Dipu Manandhar
Massimiliano Mancini
Fabian Manhardt
Kevis-kokitsi Maninis
Varun Manjunatha
Junhua Mao
Xudong Mao
Alina Marcu
Edgar Margffoy-Tuay
Dmitrii Marin
Manuel J. Marin-Jimenez
Kenneth Marino
Niki Martinel
Julieta Martinez
Jonathan Masci
Tomohiro Mashita
Iacopo Masi
David Masip
Daniela Massiceti
Stefan Mathe
Yusuke Matsui
Tetsu Matsukawa
Iain A. Matthews
Kevin James Matzen
Bruce Allen Maxwell
Stephen Maybank

Helmut Mayer
Amir Mazaheri
David McAllester
Steven McDonagh
Stephen J. Mckenna
Roey Mechrez
Prakhar Mehrotra
Christopher Mei
Xue Mei
Paulo R. S. Mendonca
Lili Meng
Zibo Meng
Thomas Mensink
Bjoern Menze
Michele Merler
Kourosh Meshgi
Pascal Mettes
Christopher Metzler
Liang Mi
Qiguang Miao
Xin Miao
Tomer Michaeli
Frank Michel
Antoine Miech
Krystian Mikolajczyk
Peyman Milanfar
Ben Mildenhall
Gregor Miller
Fausto Milletari
Dongbo Min
Kyle Min
Pedro Miraldo
Dmytro Mishkin
Anand Mishra
Ashish Mishra
Ishan Misra
Niluthpol C. Mithun
Kaushik Mitra
Niloy Mitra
Anton Mitrokhin
Ikuhisa Mitsugami
Anurag Mittal
Kaichun Mo
Zhipeng Mo
Davide Modolo
Michael Moeller

Pritish Mohapatra
Pavlo Molchanov
Davide Moltisanti
Pascal Monasse
Mathew Monfort
Aron Monszpart
Sean Moran
Vlad I. Morariu
Francesc Moreno-Noguer
Pietro Morerio
Stylianos Moschoglou
Yael Moses
Roozbeh Mottaghi
Pierre Moulon
Arsalan Mousavian
Yadong Mu
Yasuhiro Mukaigawa
Lopamudra Mukherjee
Yusuke Mukuta
Ravi Teja Mullapudi
Mario Enrique Munich
Zachary Murez
Ana C. Murillo
J. Krishna Murthy
Damien Muselet
Armin Mustafa
Siva Karthik Mustikovela
Carlo Dal Mutto
Moin Nabi
Varun K. Nagaraja
Tushar Nagarajan
Arsha Nagrani
Seungjun Nah
Nikhil Naik
Yoshikatsu Nakajima
Yuta Nakashima
Atsushi Nakazawa
Seonghyeon Nam
Vinay P. Namboodiri
Medhini Narasimhan
Srinivasa Narasimhan
Sanath Narayan
Erickson Rangel
    Nascimento
Jacinto Nascimento
Tayyab Naseer

Lakshmanan Nataraj
Neda Nategh
Nelson Isao Nauata
Fernando Navarro
Shah Nawaz
Lukas Neumann
Ram Nevatia
Alejandro Newell
Shawn Newsam
Joe Yue-Hei Ng
Trung Thanh Ngo
Duc Thanh Nguyen
Lam M. Nguyen
Phuc Xuan Nguyen
Thuong Nguyen Canh
Mihalis Nicolaou
Andrei Liviu Nicolicioiu
Xuecheng Nie
Michael Niemeyer
Simon Niklaus
Christophoros Nikou
David Nilsson
Jifeng Ning
Yuval Nirkin
Li Niu
Yuzhen Niu
Zhenxing Niu
Shohei Nobuhara
Nicoletta Noceti
Hyeonwoo Noh
Junhyug Noh
Mehdi Noroozi
Sotiris Nousias
Valsamis Ntouskos
Matthew O'Toole
Peter Ochs
Ferda Ofli
Seong Joon Oh
Seoung Wug Oh
Iason Oikonomidis
Utkarsh Ojha
Takahiro Okabe
Takayuki Okatani
Fumio Okura
Aude Oliva
Kyle Olszewski

Björn Ommer
Mohamed Omran
Elisabeta Oneata
Michael Opitz
Jose Oramas
Tribhuvanesh Orekondy
Shaul Oron
Sergio Orts-Escolano
Ivan Oseledets
Aljosa Osep
Magnus Oskarsson
Anton Osokin
Martin R. Oswald
Wanli Ouyang
Andrew Owens
Mete Ozay
Mustafa Ozuysal
Eduardo Pérez-Pellitero
Gautam Pai
Dipan Kumar Pal
P. H. Pamplona Savarese
Jinshan Pan
Junting Pan
Xingang Pan
Yingwei Pan
Yannis Panagakis
Rameswar Panda
Guan Pang
Jiahao Pang
Jiangmiao Pang
Tianyu Pang
Sharath Pankanti
Nicolas Papadakis
Dim Papadopoulos
George Papandreou
Toufiq Parag
Shaifali Parashar
Sarah Parisot
Eunhyeok Park
Hyun Soo Park
Jaesik Park
Min-Gyu Park
Taesung Park
Alvaro Parra
C. Alejandro Parraga
Despoina Paschalidou

Nikolaos Passalis
Vishal Patel
Viorica Patraucean
Badri Narayana Patro
Danda Pani Paudel
Sujoy Paul
Georgios Pavlakos
Ioannis Pavlidis
Vladimir Pavlovic
Nick Pears
Kim Steenstrup Pedersen
Selen Pehlivan
Shmuel Peleg
Chao Peng
Houwen Peng
Wen-Hsiao Peng
Xi Peng
Xiaojiang Peng
Xingchao Peng
Yuxin Peng
Federico Perazzi
Juan Camilo Perez
Vishwanath Peri
Federico Pernici
Luca Del Pero
Florent Perronnin
Stavros Petridis
Henning Petzka
Patrick Peursum
Michael Pfeiffer
Hanspeter Pfister
Roman Pflugfelder
Minh Tri Pham
Yongri Piao
David Picard
Tomasz Pieciak
A. J. Piergiovanni
Andrea Pilzer
Pedro O. Pinheiro
Silvia Laura Pintea
Lerrel Pinto
Axel Pinz
Robinson Piramuthu
Fiora Pirri
Leonid Pishchulin
Francesco Pittaluga

Daniel Pizarro
Tobias Plötz
Mirco Planamente
Matteo Poggi
Moacir A. Ponti
Parita Pooj
Fatih Porikli
Horst Possegger
Omid Poursaeed
Ameya Prabhu
Viraj Uday Prabhu
Dilip Prasad
Brian L. Price
True Price
Maria Priisalu
Veronique Prinet
Victor Adrian Prisacariu
Jan Prokaj
Sergey Prokudin
Nicolas Pugeault
Xavier Puig
Albert Pumarola
Pulak Purkait
Senthil Purushwalkam
Charles R. Qi
Hang Qi
Haozhi Qi
Lu Qi
Mengshi Qi
Siyuan Qi
Xiaojuan Qi
Yuankai Qi
Shengju Qian
Xuelin Qian
Siyuan Qiao
Yu Qiao
Jie Qin
Qiang Qiu
Weichao Qiu
Zhaofan Qiu
Kha Gia Quach
Yuhui Quan
Yvain Queau
Julian Quiroga
Faisal Qureshi
Mahdi Rad

Filip Radenovic
Petia Radeva
Venkatesh
  B. Radhakrishnan
Ilija Radosavovic
Noha Radwan
Rahul Raguram
Tanzila Rahman
Amit Raj
Ajit Rajwade
Kandan Ramakrishnan
Santhosh
  K. Ramakrishnan
Srikumar Ramalingam
Ravi Ramamoorthi
Vasili Ramanishka
Ramprasaath R. Selvaraju
Francois Rameau
Visvanathan Ramesh
Santu Rana
Rene Ranftl
Anand Rangarajan
Anurag Ranjan
Viresh Ranjan
Yongming Rao
Carolina Raposo
Vivek Rathod
Sathya N. Ravi
Avinash Ravichandran
Tammy Riklin Raviv
Daniel Rebain
Sylvestre-Alvise Rebuffi
N. Dinesh Reddy
Timo Rehfeld
Paolo Remagnino
Konstantinos Rematas
Edoardo Remelli
Dongwei Ren
Haibing Ren
Jian Ren
Jimmy Ren
Mengye Ren
Weihong Ren
Wenqi Ren
Zhile Ren
Zhongzheng Ren

Zhou Ren
Vijay Rengarajan
Md A. Reza
Farzaneh Rezaeianaran
Hamed R. Tavakoli
Nicholas Rhinehart
Helge Rhodin
Elisa Ricci
Alexander Richard
Eitan Richardson
Elad Richardson
Christian Richardt
Stephan Richter
Gernot Riegler
Daniel Ritchie
Tobias Ritschel
Samuel Rivera
Yong Man Ro
Richard Roberts
Joseph Robinson
Ignacio Rocco
Mrigank Rochan
Emanuele Rodolà
Mikel D. Rodriguez
Giorgio Roffo
Grégory Rogez
Gemma Roig
Javier Romero
Xuejian Rong
Yu Rong
Amir Rosenfeld
Bodo Rosenhahn
Guy Rosman
Arun Ross
Paolo Rota
Peter M. Roth
Anastasios Roussos
Anirban Roy
Sebastien Roy
Aruni RoyChowdhury
Artem Rozantsev
Ognjen Rudovic
Daniel Rueckert
Adria Ruiz
Javier Ruiz-del-solar
Christian Rupprecht

Chris Russell
Dan Ruta
Jongbin Ryu
Ömer Sümer
Alexandre Sablayrolles
Faraz Saeedan
Ryusuke Sagawa
Christos Sagonas
Tonmoy Saikia
Hideo Saito
Kuniaki Saito
Shunsuke Saito
Shunta Saito
Ken Sakurada
Joaquin Salas
Fatemeh Sadat Saleh
Mahdi Saleh
Pouya Samangouei
Leo Sampaio
  Ferraz Ribeiro
Artsiom Olegovich
  Sanakoyeu
Enrique Sanchez
Patsorn Sangkloy
Anush Sankaran
Aswin Sankaranarayanan
Swami Sankaranarayanan
Rodrigo Santa Cruz
Amartya Sanyal
Archana Sapkota
Nikolaos Sarafianos
Jun Sato
Shin'ichi Satoh
Hosnieh Sattar
Arman Savran
Manolis Savva
Alexander Sax
Hanno Scharr
Simone Schaub-Meyer
Konrad Schindler
Dmitrij Schlesinger
Uwe Schmidt
Dirk Schnieders
Björn Schuller
Samuel Schulter
Idan Schwartz

William Robson Schwartz
Alex Schwing
Sinisa Segvic
Lorenzo Seidenari
Pradeep Sen
Ozan Sener
Soumyadip Sengupta
Arda Senocak
Mojtaba Seyedhosseini
Shishir Shah
Shital Shah
Sohil Atul Shah
Tamar Rott Shaham
Huasong Shan
Qi Shan
Shiguang Shan
Jing Shao
Roman Shapovalov
Gaurav Sharma
Vivek Sharma
Viktoriia Sharmanska
Dongyu She
Sumit Shekhar
Evan Shelhamer
Chengyao Shen
Chunhua Shen
Falong Shen
Jie Shen
Li Shen
Liyue Shen
Shuhan Shen
Tianwei Shen
Wei Shen
William B. Shen
Yantao Shen
Ying Shen
Yiru Shen
Yujun Shen
Yuming Shen
Zhiqiang Shen
Ziyi Shen
Lu Sheng
Yu Sheng
Rakshith Shetty
Baoguang Shi
Guangming Shi

Hailin Shi
Miaojing Shi
Yemin Shi
Zhenmei Shi
Zhiyuan Shi
Kevin Jonathan Shih
Shiliang Shiliang
Hyunjung Shim
Atsushi Shimada
Nobutaka Shimada
Daeyun Shin
Young Min Shin
Koichi Shinoda
Konstantin Shmelkov
Michael Zheng Shou
Abhinav Shrivastava
Tianmin Shu
Zhixin Shu
Hong-Han Shuai
Pushkar Shukla
Christian Siagian
Mennatullah M. Siam
Kaleem Siddiqi
Karan Sikka
Jae-Young Sim
Christian Simon
Martin Simonovsky
Dheeraj Singaraju
Bharat Singh
Gurkirt Singh
Krishna Kumar Singh
Maneesh Kumar Singh
Richa Singh
Saurabh Singh
Suriya Singh
Vikas Singh
Sudipta N. Sinha
Vincent Sitzmann
Josef Sivic
Gregory Slabaugh
Miroslava Slavcheva
Ron Slossberg
Brandon Smith
Kevin Smith
Vladimir Smutny
Noah Snavely

Roger
   D. Soberanis-Mukul
Kihyuk Sohn
Francesco Solera
Eric Sommerlade
Sanghyun Son
Byung Cheol Song
Chunfeng Song
Dongjin Song
Jiaming Song
Jie Song
Jifei Song
Jingkuan Song
Mingli Song
Shiyu Song
Shuran Song
Xiao Song
Yafei Song
Yale Song
Yang Song
Yi-Zhe Song
Yibing Song
Humberto Sossa
Cesar de Souza
Adrian Spurr
Srinath Sridhar
Suraj Srinivas
Pratul P. Srinivasan
Anuj Srivastava
Tania Stathaki
Christopher Stauffer
Simon Stent
Rainer Stiefelhagen
Pierre Stock
Julian Straub
Jonathan C. Stroud
Joerg Stueckler
Jan Stuehmer
David Stutz
Chi Su
Hang Su
Jong-Chyi Su
Shuochen Su
Yu-Chuan Su
Ramanathan Subramanian
Yusuke Sugano

Masanori Suganuma
Yumin Suh
Mohammed Suhail
Yao Sui
Heung-Il Suk
Josephine Sullivan
Baochen Sun
Chen Sun
Chong Sun
Deqing Sun
Jin Sun
Liang Sun
Lin Sun
Qianru Sun
Shao-Hua Sun
Shuyang Sun
Weiwei Sun
Wenxiu Sun
Xiaoshuai Sun
Xiaoxiao Sun
Xingyuan Sun
Yifan Sun
Zhun Sun
Sabine Susstrunk
David Suter
Supasorn Suwajanakorn
Tomas Svoboda
Eran Swears
Paul Swoboda
Attila Szabo
Richard Szeliski
Duy-Nguyen Ta
Andrea Tagliasacchi
Yuichi Taguchi
Ying Tai
Keita Takahashi
Kouske Takahashi
Jun Takamatsu
Hugues Talbot
Toru Tamaki
Chaowei Tan
Fuwen Tan
Mingkui Tan
Mingxing Tan
Qingyang Tan
Robby T. Tan

Xiaoyang Tan
Kenichiro Tanaka
Masayuki Tanaka
Chang Tang
Chengzhou Tang
Danhang Tang
Ming Tang
Peng Tang
Qingming Tang
Wei Tang
Xu Tang
Yansong Tang
Youbao Tang
Yuxing Tang
Zhiqiang Tang
Tatsunori Taniai
Junli Tao
Xin Tao
Makarand Tapaswi
Jean-Philippe Tarel
Lyne Tchapmi
Zachary Teed
Bugra Tekin
Damien Teney
Ayush Tewari
Christian Theobalt
Christopher Thomas
Diego Thomas
Jim Thomas
Rajat Mani Thomas
Xinmei Tian
Yapeng Tian
Yingli Tian
Yonglong Tian
Zhi Tian
Zhuotao Tian
Kinh Tieu
Joseph Tighe
Massimo Tistarelli
Matthew Toews
Carl Toft
Pavel Tokmakov
Federico Tombari
Chetan Tonde
Yan Tong
Alessio Tonioni

Andrea Torsello
Fabio Tosi
Du Tran
Luan Tran
Ngoc-Trung Tran
Quan Hung Tran
Truyen Tran
Rudolph Triebel
Martin Trimmel
Shashank Tripathi
Subarna Tripathi
Leonardo Trujillo
Eduard Trulls
Tomasz Trzcinski
Sam Tsai
Yi-Hsuan Tsai
Hung-Yu Tseng
Stavros Tsogkas
Aggeliki Tsoli
Devis Tuia
Shubham Tulsiani
Sergey Tulyakov
Frederick Tung
Tony Tung
Daniyar Turmukhambetov
Ambrish Tyagi
Radim Tylecek
Christos Tzelepis
Georgios Tzimiropoulos
Dimitrios Tzionas
Seiichi Uchida
Norimichi Ukita
Dmitry Ulyanov
Martin Urschler
Yoshitaka Ushiku
Ben Usman
Alexander Vakhitov
Julien P. C. Valentin
Jack Valmadre
Ernest Valveny
Joost van de Weijer
Jan van Gemert
Koen Van Leemput
Gul Varol
Sebastiano Vascon
M. Alex O. Vasilescu

Subeesh Vasu
Mayank Vatsa
David Vazquez
Javier Vazquez-Corral
Ashok Veeraraghavan
Erik Velasco-Salido
Raviteja Vemulapalli
Jonathan Ventura
Manisha Verma
Roberto Vezzani
Ruben Villegas
Minh Vo
MinhDuc Vo
Nam Vo
Michele Volpi
Riccardo Volpi
Carl Vondrick
Konstantinos Vougioukas
Tuan-Hung Vu
Sven Wachsmuth
Neal Wadhwa
Catherine Wah
Jacob C. Walker
Thomas S. A. Wallis
Chengde Wan
Jun Wan
Liang Wan
Renjie Wan
Baoyuan Wang
Boyu Wang
Cheng Wang
Chu Wang
Chuan Wang
Chunyu Wang
Dequan Wang
Di Wang
Dilin Wang
Dong Wang
Fang Wang
Guanzhi Wang
Guoyin Wang
Hanzi Wang
Hao Wang
He Wang
Heng Wang
Hongcheng Wang

Hongxing Wang
Hua Wang
Jian Wang
Jingbo Wang
Jinglu Wang
Jingya Wang
Jinjun Wang
Jinqiao Wang
Jue Wang
Ke Wang
Keze Wang
Le Wang
Lei Wang
Lezi Wang
Li Wang
Liang Wang
Lijun Wang
Limin Wang
Linwei Wang
Lizhi Wang
Mengjiao Wang
Mingzhe Wang
Minsi Wang
Naiyan Wang
Nannan Wang
Ning Wang
Oliver Wang
Pei Wang
Peng Wang
Pichao Wang
Qi Wang
Qian Wang
Qiaosong Wang
Qifei Wang
Qilong Wang
Qing Wang
Qingzhong Wang
Quan Wang
Rui Wang
Ruiping Wang
Ruixing Wang
Shangfei Wang
Shenlong Wang
Shiyao Wang
Shuhui Wang
Song Wang

Tao Wang
Tianlu Wang
Tiantian Wang
Ting-chun Wang
Tingwu Wang
Wei Wang
Weiyue Wang
Wenguan Wang
Wenlin Wang
Wenqi Wang
Xiang Wang
Xiaobo Wang
Xiaofang Wang
Xiaoling Wang
Xiaolong Wang
Xiaosong Wang
Xiaoyu Wang
Xin Eric Wang
Xinchao Wang
Xinggang Wang
Xintao Wang
Yali Wang
Yan Wang
Yang Wang
Yangang Wang
Yaxing Wang
Yi Wang
Yida Wang
Yilin Wang
Yiming Wang
Yisen Wang
Yongtao Wang
Yu-Xiong Wang
Yue Wang
Yujiang Wang
Yunbo Wang
Yunhe Wang
Zengmao Wang
Zhangyang Wang
Zhaowen Wang
Zhe Wang
Zhecan Wang
Zheng Wang
Zhixiang Wang
Zilei Wang
Jianqiao Wangni

Anne S. Wannenwetsch
Jan Dirk Wegner
Scott Wehrwein
Donglai Wei
Kaixuan Wei
Longhui Wei
Pengxu Wei
Ping Wei
Qi Wei
Shih-En Wei
Xing Wei
Yunchao Wei
Zijun Wei
Jerod Weinman
Michael Weinmann
Philippe Weinzaepfel
Yair Weiss
Bihan Wen
Longyin Wen
Wei Wen
Junwu Weng
Tsui-Wei Weng
Xinshuo Weng
Eric Wengrowski
Tomas Werner
Gordon Wetzstein
Tobias Weyand
Patrick Wieschollek
Maggie Wigness
Erik Wijmans
Richard Wildes
Olivia Wiles
Chris Williams
Williem Williem
Kyle Wilson
Calden Wloka
Nicolai Wojke
Christian Wolf
Yongkang Wong
Sanghyun Woo
Scott Workman
Baoyuan Wu
Bichen Wu
Chao-Yuan Wu
Huikai Wu
Jiajun Wu

Jialin Wu
Jiaxiang Wu
Jiqing Wu
Jonathan Wu
Lifang Wu
Qi Wu
Qiang Wu
Ruizheng Wu
Shangzhe Wu
Shun-Cheng Wu
Tianfu Wu
Wayne Wu
Wenxuan Wu
Xiao Wu
Xiaohe Wu
Xinxiao Wu
Yang Wu
Yi Wu
Yiming Wu
Ying Nian Wu
Yue Wu
Zheng Wu
Zhenyu Wu
Zhirong Wu
Zuxuan Wu
Stefanie Wuhrer
Jonas Wulff
Changqun Xia
Fangting Xia
Fei Xia
Gui-Song Xia
Lu Xia
Xide Xia
Yin Xia
Yingce Xia
Yongqin Xian
Lei Xiang
Shiming Xiang
Bin Xiao
Fanyi Xiao
Guobao Xiao
Huaxin Xiao
Taihong Xiao
Tete Xiao
Tong Xiao
Wang Xiao

Yang Xiao
Cihang Xie
Guosen Xie
Jianwen Xie
Lingxi Xie
Sirui Xie
Weidi Xie
Wenxuan Xie
Xiaohua Xie
Fuyong Xing
Jun Xing
Junliang Xing
Bo Xiong
Peixi Xiong
Yu Xiong
Yuanjun Xiong
Zhiwei Xiong
Chang Xu
Chenliang Xu
Dan Xu
Danfei Xu
Hang Xu
Hongteng Xu
Huijuan Xu
Jingwei Xu
Jun Xu
Kai Xu
Mengmeng Xu
Mingze Xu
Qianqian Xu
Ran Xu
Weijian Xu
Xiangyu Xu
Xiaogang Xu
Xing Xu
Xun Xu
Yanyu Xu
Yichao Xu
Yong Xu
Yongchao Xu
Yuanlu Xu
Zenglin Xu
Zheng Xu
Chuhui Xue
Jia Xue
Nan Xue

Tianfan Xue
Xiangyang Xue
Abhay Yadav
Yasushi Yagi
I. Zeki Yalniz
Kota Yamaguchi
Toshihiko Yamasaki
Takayoshi Yamashita
Junchi Yan
Ke Yan
Qingan Yan
Sijie Yan
Xinchen Yan
Yan Yan
Yichao Yan
Zhicheng Yan
Keiji Yanai
Bin Yang
Ceyuan Yang
Dawei Yang
Dong Yang
Fan Yang
Guandao Yang
Guorun Yang
Haichuan Yang
Hao Yang
Jianwei Yang
Jiaolong Yang
Jie Yang
Jing Yang
Kaiyu Yang
Linjie Yang
Meng Yang
Michael Ying Yang
Nan Yang
Shuai Yang
Shuo Yang
Tianyu Yang
Tien-Ju Yang
Tsun-Yi Yang
Wei Yang
Wenhan Yang
Xiao Yang
Xiaodong Yang
Xin Yang
Yan Yang

Yanchao Yang
Yee Hong Yang
Yezhou Yang
Zhenheng Yang
Anbang Yao
Angela Yao
Cong Yao
Jian Yao
Li Yao
Ting Yao
Yao Yao
Zhewei Yao
Chengxi Ye
Jianbo Ye
Keren Ye
Linwei Ye
Mang Ye
Mao Ye
Qi Ye
Qixiang Ye
Mei-Chen Yeh
Raymond Yeh
Yu-Ying Yeh
Sai-Kit Yeung
Serena Yeung
Kwang Moo Yi
Li Yi
Renjiao Yi
Alper Yilmaz
Junho Yim
Lijun Yin
Weidong Yin
Xi Yin
Zhichao Yin
Tatsuya Yokota
Ryo Yonetani
Donggeun Yoo
Jae Shin Yoon
Ju Hong Yoon
Sung-eui Yoon
Laurent Younes
Changqian Yu
Fisher Yu
Gang Yu
Jiahui Yu
Kaicheng Yu

Ke Yu
Lequan Yu
Ning Yu
Qian Yu
Ronald Yu
Ruichi Yu
Shoou-I Yu
Tao Yu
Tianshu Yu
Xiang Yu
Xin Yu
Xiyu Yu
Youngjae Yu
Yu Yu
Zhiding Yu
Chunfeng Yuan
Ganzhao Yuan
Jinwei Yuan
Lu Yuan
Quan Yuan
Shanxin Yuan
Tongtong Yuan
Wenjia Yuan
Ye Yuan
Yuan Yuan
Yuhui Yuan
Huanjing Yue
Xiangyu Yue
Ersin Yumer
Sergey Zagoruyko
Egor Zakharov
Amir Zamir
Andrei Zanfir
Mihai Zanfir
Pablo Zegers
Bernhard Zeisl
John S. Zelek
Niclas Zeller
Huayi Zeng
Jiabei Zeng
Wenjun Zeng
Yu Zeng
Xiaohua Zhai
Fangneng Zhan
Huangying Zhan
Kun Zhan

Xiaohang Zhan
Baochang Zhang
Bowen Zhang
Cecilia Zhang
Changqing Zhang
Chao Zhang
Chengquan Zhang
Chi Zhang
Chongyang Zhang
Dingwen Zhang
Dong Zhang
Feihu Zhang
Hang Zhang
Hanwang Zhang
Hao Zhang
He Zhang
Hongguang Zhang
Hua Zhang
Ji Zhang
Jianguo Zhang
Jianming Zhang
Jiawei Zhang
Jie Zhang
Jing Zhang
Juyong Zhang
Kai Zhang
Kaipeng Zhang
Ke Zhang
Le Zhang
Lei Zhang
Li Zhang
Lihe Zhang
Linguang Zhang
Lu Zhang
Mi Zhang
Mingda Zhang
Peng Zhang
Pingping Zhang
Qian Zhang
Qilin Zhang
Quanshi Zhang
Richard Zhang
Rui Zhang
Runze Zhang
Shengping Zhang
Shifeng Zhang

Shuai Zhang
Songyang Zhang
Tao Zhang
Ting Zhang
Tong Zhang
Wayne Zhang
Wei Zhang
Weizhong Zhang
Wenwei Zhang
Xiangyu Zhang
Xiaolin Zhang
Xiaopeng Zhang
Xiaoqin Zhang
Xiuming Zhang
Ya Zhang
Yang Zhang
Yimin Zhang
Yinda Zhang
Ying Zhang
Yongfei Zhang
Yu Zhang
Yulun Zhang
Yunhua Zhang
Yuting Zhang
Zhanpeng Zhang
Zhao Zhang
Zhaoxiang Zhang
Zhen Zhang
Zheng Zhang
Zhifei Zhang
Zhijin Zhang
Zhishuai Zhang
Ziming Zhang
Bo Zhao
Chen Zhao
Fang Zhao
Haiyu Zhao
Han Zhao
Hang Zhao
Hengshuang Zhao
Jian Zhao
Kai Zhao
Liang Zhao
Long Zhao
Qian Zhao
Qibin Zhao

Qijun Zhao
Rui Zhao
Shenglin Zhao
Sicheng Zhao
Tianyi Zhao
Wenda Zhao
Xiangyun Zhao
Xin Zhao
Yang Zhao
Yue Zhao
Zhichen Zhao
Zijing Zhao
Xiantong Zhen
Chuanxia Zheng
Feng Zheng
Haiyong Zheng
Jia Zheng
Kang Zheng
Shuai Kyle Zheng
Wei-Shi Zheng
Yinqiang Zheng
Zerong Zheng
Zhedong Zheng
Zilong Zheng
Bineng Zhong
Fangwei Zhong
Guangyu Zhong
Yiran Zhong
Yujie Zhong
Zhun Zhong
Chunluan Zhou
Huiyu Zhou
Jiahuan Zhou
Jun Zhou
Lei Zhou
Luowei Zhou
Luping Zhou
Mo Zhou
Ning Zhou
Pan Zhou
Peng Zhou
Qianyi Zhou
S. Kevin Zhou
Sanping Zhou
Wengang Zhou
Xingyi Zhou

Yanzhao Zhou
Yi Zhou
Yin Zhou
Yipin Zhou
Yuyin Zhou
Zihan Zhou
Alex Zihao Zhu
Chenchen Zhu
Feng Zhu
Guangming Zhu
Ji Zhu
Jun-Yan Zhu
Lei Zhu
Linchao Zhu
Rui Zhu
Shizhan Zhu
Tyler Lixuan Zhu

Wei Zhu
Xiangyu Zhu
Xinge Zhu
Xizhou Zhu
Yanjun Zhu
Yi Zhu
Yixin Zhu
Yizhe Zhu
Yousong Zhu
Zhe Zhu
Zhen Zhu
Zheng Zhu
Zhenyao Zhu
Zhihui Zhu
Zhuotun Zhu
Bingbing Zhuang
Wei Zhuo

Christian Zimmermann
Karel Zimmermann
Larry Zitnick
Mohammadreza
   Zolfaghari
Maria Zontak
Daniel Zoran
Changqing Zou
Chuhang Zou
Danping Zou
Qi Zou
Yang Zou
Yuliang Zou
Georgios Zoumpourlis
Wangmeng Zuo
Xinxin Zuo

Additional Reviewers

Victoria Fernandez
   Abrevaya
Maya Aghaei
Allam Allam
Christine
   Allen-Blanchette
Nicolas Aziere
Assia Benbihi
Neha Bhargava
Bharat Lal Bhatnagar
Joanna Bitton
Judy Borowski
Amine Bourki
Romain Brégier
Tali Brayer
Sebastian Bujwid
Andrea Burns
Yun-Hao Cao
Yuning Chai
Xiaojun Chang
Bo Chen
Shuo Chen
Zhixiang Chen
Junsuk Choe
Hung-Kuo Chu

Jonathan P. Crall
Kenan Dai
Lucas Deecke
Karan Desai
Prithviraj Dhar
Jing Dong
Wei Dong
Turan Kaan Elgin
Francis Engelmann
Erik Englesson
Fartash Faghri
Zicong Fan
Yang Fu
Risheek Garrepalli
Yifan Ge
Marco Godi
Helmut Grabner
Shuxuan Guo
Jianfeng He
Zhezhi He
Samitha Herath
Chih-Hui Ho
Yicong Hong
Vincent Tao Hu
Julio Hurtado

Jaedong Hwang
Andrey Ignatov
Muhammad
   Abdullah Jamal
Saumya Jetley
Meiguang Jin
Jeff Johnson
Minsoo Kang
Saeed Khorram
Mohammad Rami Koujan
Nilesh Kulkarni
Sudhakar Kumawat
Abdelhak Lemkhenter
Alexander Levine
Jiachen Li
Jing Li
Jun Li
Yi Li
Liang Liao
Ruochen Liao
Tzu-Heng Lin
Phillip Lippe
Bao-di Liu
Bo Liu
Fangchen Liu

Hanxiao Liu
Hongyu Liu
Huidong Liu
Miao Liu
Xinxin Liu
Yongfei Liu
Yu-Lun Liu
Amir Livne
Tiange Luo
Wei Ma
Xiaoxuan Ma
Ioannis Marras
Georg Martius
Effrosyni Mavroudi
Tim Meinhardt
Givi Meishvili
Meng Meng
Zihang Meng
Zhongqi Miao
Gyeongsik Moon
Khoi Nguyen
Yung-Kyun Noh
Antonio Norelli
Jaeyoo Park
Alexander Pashevich
Mandela Patrick
Mary Phuong
Bingqiao Qian
Yu Qiao
Zhen Qiao
Sai Saketh Rambhatla
Aniket Roy
Amelie Royer
Parikshit Vishwas
  Sakurikar
Mark Sandler
Mert Bülent Sarıyıldız
Tanner Schmidt
Anshul B. Shah

Ketul Shah
Rajvi Shah
Hengcan Shi
Xiangxi Shi
Yujiao Shi
William A. P. Smith
Guoxian Song
Robin Strudel
Abby Stylianou
Xinwei Sun
Reuben Tan
Qingyi Tao
Kedar S. Tatwawadi
Anh Tuan Tran
Son Dinh Tran
Eleni Triantafillou
Aristeidis Tsitiridis
Md Zasim Uddin
Andrea Vedaldi
Evangelos Ververas
Vidit Vidit
Paul Voigtlaender
Bo Wan
Huanyu Wang
Huiyu Wang
Junqiu Wang
Pengxiao Wang
Tai Wang
Xinyao Wang
Tomoki Watanabe
Mark Weber
Xi Wei
Botong Wu
James Wu
Jiamin Wu
Rujie Wu
Yu Wu
Rongchang Xie
Wei Xiong

Yunyang Xiong
An Xu
Chi Xu
Yinghao Xu
Fei Xue
Tingyun Yan
Zike Yan
Chao Yang
Heran Yang
Ren Yang
Wenfei Yang
Xu Yang
Rajeev Yasarla
Shaokai Ye
Yufei Ye
Kun Yi
Haichao Yu
Hanchao Yu
Ruixuan Yu
Liangzhe Yuan
Chen-Lin Zhang
Fandong Zhang
Tianyi Zhang
Yang Zhang
Yiyi Zhang
Yongshun Zhang
Yu Zhang
Zhiwei Zhang
Jiaojiao Zhao
Yipu Zhao
Xingjian Zhen
Haizhong Zheng
Tiancheng Zhi
Chengju Zhou
Hao Zhou
Hao Zhu
Alexander Zimin

Contents – Part XX

The Average Mixing Kernel Signature

Luca Cosmo[1,2], Giorgia Minello[3], Michael Bronstein[2,4,5], Luca Rossi[6(✉)],
and Andrea Torsello[3]

[1] Sapienza University of Rome, Rome, Italy
[2] University of Lugano, Lugano, Switzerland
[3] Università Ca' Foscari Venezia, Venice, Italy
[4] Imperial College London, London, UK
[5] Twitter, London, UK
[6] Queen Mary University of London, London, UK
luca.rossi@qmul.ac.uk

Abstract. We introduce the Average Mixing Kernel Signature (AMKS), a novel signature for points on non-rigid three-dimensional shapes based on the average mixing kernel and continuous-time quantum walks. The average mixing kernel holds information on the average transition probabilities of a quantum walk between each pair of vertices of the mesh until a time T. We define the AMKS by decomposing the spectral contributions of the kernel into several bands, allowing us to limit the influence of noise-dominated high-frequency components and obtain a more descriptive signature. We also show through a perturbation theory analysis of the kernel that choosing a finite stopping time T leads to noise and deformation robustness for the AMKS. We perform an extensive experimental evaluation on two widely used shape matching datasets under varying level of noise, showing that the AMKS outperforms two state-of-the-art descriptors, namely the Heat Kernel Signature (HKS) and the similarly quantum-walk based Wave Kernel Signature (WKS).

Keywords: Shape representation · Shape analysis · Quantum walks

1 Introduction

A central ingredient in shape analysis, with applications that range from shape correspondence [9,10,14,24,25,35] to shape segmentation [1,16], is the computation of a signature (also known as descriptor or feature descriptor) that effectively characterizes the local and global geometric information around each point on a shape's surface. In this context, an effective descriptor is one that accurately

L. Cosmo and G. Minello—Equal contribution.

Electronic supplementary material The online version of this chapter (https://doi.org/10.1007/978-3-030-58565-5_1) contains supplementary material, which is available to authorized users.

© Springer Nature Switzerland AG 2020
A. Vedaldi et al. (Eds.): ECCV 2020, LNCS 12365, pp. 1–17, 2020.
https://doi.org/10.1007/978-3-030-58565-5_1

(a) $T = 1$ (b) $T = 10^2$ (c) $T = 10^4$

Fig. 1. The average transition probability of a quantum walk from one point to the rest of the shape for increasing values of the stopping time T (left to right). More (less) intense shades of red correspond to higher (lower) probability. This is the information in the row of the average mixing matrix (Eq. 9) indexed by the starting point. Note the presence of grey bands when $T = 1$ (corresponding to points with zero probability of being visited) which are a result of the interference effects typical of quantum walks. (Color figure online)

characterizes each point while remaining invariant to rigid transformations, stable against non-rigid ones, and robust to various sources of noise.

Despite a flurry of descriptors introduced in the past years, spectral-based descriptors remain among the most popular type of descriptors [2,5,7,31,33]. These rely on the analysis of the eigenvalues and eigenfunctions of the Laplace-Beltrami operator. Examples include two widely used state-of-the-art spectral signatures, the Heat Kernel Signature (HKS) [33] and the Wave Kernel Signature (WKS) [2]. The common idea underpinning these signatures is that of filtering the frequency information, where low and high frequencies capture global and local topological information respectively, with the latter being more discriminative but also easily affected by noise.

The HKS and the WKS are based on analyzing the shape through similarly defined yet profoundly different physical processes, namely heat diffusion and wavefunction evolution. On a discrete domain these correspond to continuous-time random walks and continuous-time quantum walks [17], respectively. Both processes are similar in that they explore the vertices and edges of the mesh representing the discrete approximation of the shape surface. However apparently subtle differences in their mathematical formulation lead to significantly different behaviors, with the emergence of quantum effects resulting in a superior ability to characterize the underlying structure with respect to classical walks. This is not only demonstrated in shape analysis by the WKS being more discriminative than the HKS for shape matching, but also in a variety of other domains, including graph theory [12,29] and machine learning [3,22,27,28].

In this paper, we propose a novel signature for points on non-rigid three-dimensional shapes based on continuous-time quantum walks. Given a mesh representing the discrete approximation of a shape surface, we define a continuous-time quantum walk over the vertices and edges of the mesh and we let the walker explore the structure until a stopping time T is reached. We compute the average mixing kernel holding the average transition probabilities between each pair of vertices of the mesh. This is the continuous version of the average mixing matrix of Godsil [15] and it's effectively the quantum analogue of the heat kernel under-pinning the signature of Sun et al. [33]. We show using perturbation theory that the choice of a finite time T (as opposed to letting the quantum particle explore the shape surface for an infinite time [2]) is crucial to achieve increased robustness against noise and deformation. We then propose to decompose the spectral contributions to the average mixing kernel into several bands. This in turn has the effect of both limiting the influence of noise-dominated high-frequency components as well as creating a more descriptive signature as a function of the energy levels. Finally, we use the diagonal information of this band-pass filtered kernel sampled at different temporal evolution steps to compute the proposed Average Mixing Kernel Signature (AMKS).

An extensive set of experiments shows that the AMKS outperforms state-of-the-art signatures like the HKS and the WKS. Our key findings include:

- when compared to the WKS, we theoretically show that our method increases the robustness to noise by accounting for the noise-induced mixing of the Laplace-Beltrami operator eigenspaces (see the Supplementary Material);
- we show that under Gaussian noise ($\sigma = 0.02$) the proposed AMKS shows an improvement of up to 10% wrt to the WKS, in terms of hit rate;
- when computing the point-wise correspondences between pairs of shapes, we observe an improvement of the geodesic error of up to 4% wrt to the WKS;
- despite the additional need to compute the mixing components wrt the WKS, the AMKS can be fully written in terms of matrix operations and efficiently computed (see the Supplementary Material);
- the computational complexity of the AMKS is linear in the number of vertices of the mesh and energy levels, and quadratic in the dimension of the truncated eigenbase, resulting in an overall computational time that is comparable with that of the WKS.

In [26] Rossi et al. introduced another structural signature based on the average mixing matrix (AMMS) for the analysis of graphs. However, we stress that our work significantly differs from [26] in several key aspects:

- the AMMS is defined on graphs of limited size with long-range connections where using all the spectral range is important. The AMKS is defined on manifold structures where structural information is found at low bandwidths while high bandwidths are dominated by noise. Directly applying the AMMS to our problem would lead to a computationally infeasible, noise-dominated signature where we cannot focus on the energy levels of interest. One way of reducing the computational cost of the AMMS would have been truncating the spectrum, however this would not have led to the quantum-mechanically feasible process one which our framework is based;
- in the AMMS the sampling is done over the time domain, as opposed to the energy domain in the AMKS;
- while a limited empirical analysis suggests that the AMMS is robust to structural noise, we perform the first theoretical analysis of the noise-robustness resulting from the average mixing matrix use, revealing that the mixing factors naturally account for the noise-induced mixing of eigenspaces;

- while there is no analysis of the computational complexity of the AMMS in [26], here we perform a thorough complexity as well as runtime analysis of the AMKS in addition to showing that its computation can be fully expressed in terms of matrix operations;
- finally, as the application domains and communities of interest of the AMMS and AMKS are different, in this paper we perform an entirely separate and more extensive set of experiments.

2   Related Work

Spectral signatures aim to characterize a shape by analyzing the eigenvalues and eigenfunctions of the Laplace-Beltrami operator [19,23]. Based on this key idea, Rustamov [31] introduced the Global Point Signature (GPS), where each point of a mesh is characterized by a vector computed from the scaled eigenfunctions of the Laplace-Beltrami operator evaluated at that point.

While GPS is a global signature and thus lacks the ability to perform partial matching, the Heat Kernel Signature (HKS) of Sun et al. [33] and its scale-invariant version [7] addressed this shortcoming by allowing to capture multi-scale information around each point of a shape. This in turn is achieved by analyzing a heat diffusion process over the shape surface at different time-scales. From a signal processing point of view, the HKS can be seen as performing a low-pass filtering of the spectral information parametrized by the diffusion time t. As a result, its value is dominated by global shape properties, while it fails to accurately capture the highly discriminative small-scale information that is crucial in matching applications.

The Wave Kernel Signature (WKS) [2], on the other hand, solves this issue by acting as a band-pass filter that better separates the frequency information related to different spatial scales. To this end, the authors define a quantum system where a particle explores the shape surface under the Schrödinger equation. This is intimately connected to our approach, however, as explained in Sect. 4 and in the Supplementary Material, there are some stark differences between the two methods which result in a more accurate and noise resilient descriptor.

Learning-based signatures have recently emerged as alternatives to spectral-based signatures, although the latter remain widely used due to their efficacy and ease of computation. Litman and Bronstein [20] introduced a family of spectral descriptors that generalizes the HKS and the WKS and they propose a learning scheme to construct the optimal descriptor for a given task. Corman et al. [8] learn optimal descriptors from a given set of shape correspondences. In particular, they use a functional maps representation where spectral signatures (e.g.., HKS or WKS) are used as probe functions that are meant to constraint the degree of deformation between corresponding points.

In [13] Fang et al. use a deep autoencoder to construct a global descriptor for shape retrieval. In this framework, one of the first processing steps is the extraction of the HKS, which is then fed to the autoencoder itself. Masci et al. [21] extend CNNs to non-Euclidean manifolds, where a local geodesic patch is defined around each point and a filter is convolved with vertex-level functions (e.g.., HKS and WKS). Huang et al. [16], on the other hand, omit this pre-processing step by designing a 2D convolutional neural network (CNN) architecture where each point on the shape surface is rendered using multi-scale 2D images.

Presenting a comprehensive review of spectral- and learning-based signatures is beyond the scope of this paper, so we refer the reader to the spectral-based signatures review of Masci et al. [21] and the survey of Rostami et al. on data-driven signatures [30]. Finally, we would like to stress that while learning-based descriptors are gaining increasing popularity in the literature, particularly due to the success of CNNs in computer vision, spectral-based signatures are still often used as the first processing step in a modern (deep) learning framework [16,30].

3 Quantum Mechanical Background

In this section we introduce the quantum mechanical concepts underpinning our signature, i.e., continuous-time quantum walks and the average mixing kernel.

3.1 Quantum Walks and the Schrödinger equation

Let M denote the manifold representing the shape surface. The state of a quantum particle at time t is given by the wave function $\psi(t)$, defined as an element of the Hilbert space of functions mapping points on the surface of M to $\mathbb{C}$, such that the squared modulus $|\psi(t)|^2$ is a real number and the integral of this quantity over M is unity. In other words, the squared modulus of the wave function is interpreted as the probability of the quantum walker being located at a certain point on M at time t.

The Dirac notation (also known as *bra-ket* notation) is a standard notation used for describing quantum states, where a *ket* vector $|a\rangle$ denotes a pure quantum state and is a complex valued column vector of unit Euclidean length, in a n-dimensional Hilbert space. Its conjugate transpose is a *bra* (row) vector, denoted as $\langle a|$. As a result, the inner product between two states $|a\rangle$ and $|b\rangle$ is written $\langle a | b \rangle$, while their outer product is $|a\rangle \langle b|$. With this notation to hand, on a discrete domain, the state of the walker at time t is denoted as

$$|\psi(t)\rangle = \sum_{u \in V} \alpha_u(t) |u\rangle, \tag{1}$$

where $|u\rangle$ denotes the state corresponding to the vertex u and $\alpha_u(t) \in \mathbb{C}$ is its amplitude. Moreover, we have that $\alpha_u(t)\alpha_u^*(t)$ is the probability that at time t the walker is at the vertex u, and thus $\sum_{u \in V} \alpha_u(t)\alpha_u^*(t) = 1$ and $\alpha_u(t)\alpha_u^*(t) \in [0,1]$, for all $u \in V$, $t \in \mathbb{R}^+$ (where $\alpha_u^*(t)$ is the complex conjugate of $\alpha_u(t)$).

The evolution of the walker is governed by the Schrödinger equation

$$\frac{\partial}{\partial t} |\psi(t)\rangle = -i\Delta_M |\psi(t)\rangle, \tag{2}$$

where the Laplace-Beltrami operator plays the role of a time-independent Hamiltonian, i.e., the operator that accounts for the total energy of the system. The solution to this equation is given by

$$|\psi(t)\rangle = U(t)|\psi(0)\rangle, \qquad (3)$$

where $U(t) = e^{-it\Delta_M}$ is a unitary operator. Similarly to the heat operator, $U(t)$ shares the same eigenvectors of Δ_M and for each eigenvalue λ of Δ_M there exists a corresponding eigenvalue of $U(t)$.

Measuring Quantities in Quantum Mechanics. Consider a quantum system in a state $|\psi\rangle$. While in classical mechanics an observable (i.e., a measurable physical quantity) is a real-valued function of the system state, in quantum mechanics an observable is a self-adjoint operator acting on $|\psi\rangle$, such that the possible outcomes of an observation correspond to the eigenvalues of the associated self-adjoint operator. In this context, observing a state corresponds to performing a projective measurement of $|\psi\rangle$. Given the observable O and its spectral decomposition $O = \sum_\lambda \lambda P_\lambda$, where P_λ is the projector on the subspace spanned by the eigenvalue λ, the outcome λ is observed with probability $p(\lambda) = \langle\psi| P_\lambda |\psi\rangle$. Notably, the state of the quantum system changes after the measurement and becomes $|\bar{\psi}\rangle = P_\lambda |\psi\rangle / ||P_\lambda |\psi\rangle||$ where $|| |\psi\rangle || = \sqrt{\langle\psi|\psi\rangle}$ denotes the norm of the vector $|\psi\rangle$.

3.2   Average Mixing Matrix

In [15] Godsil introduces the concept of mixing matrix $M_G(t) = (m_{uv})$ as the probability that a quantum walker starting at node v is observed at node u at time t. Given the eigenvalues λ of the Hamiltonian and the associated projectors P_λ, the unitary operator inducing the quantum walk can be rewritten as

$$U(t) = \sum_{\lambda \in \Lambda} e^{-i\lambda t} P_\lambda, \qquad (4)$$

where Λ is the set of unique eigenvalues. We can then write the mixing kernel in terms of the Schur-Hadamard product (also known as element-wise product) of the projectors

$$M_G(t) = \sum_{\lambda_1 \in \Lambda} \sum_{\lambda_2 \in \Lambda} e^{-i(\lambda_1 - \lambda_2)t} P_{\lambda_1} \circ P_{\lambda_2}. \qquad (5)$$

Recall that, while in the classical case the probability distribution induced by a random walk converges to a steady state, this does not happen in the quantum case. However, we can enforce convergence by taking a time-average even if $U(t)$ is norm-preserving. Let us define the average mixing kernel [15] at time T as

$$\widehat{M}_{G;T} = \frac{1}{T} \int_0^T M_G(t)\, dt = \sum_{\lambda_1 \in \Lambda} \sum_{\lambda_2 \in \Lambda} P_{\lambda_1} \circ P_{\lambda_2} \frac{1}{T} \int_0^T e^{-i(\lambda_1 - \lambda_2)t}\, dt, \qquad (6)$$

which has solution

$$\widehat{M}_{G;T} = \sum_{\lambda_1 \in \Lambda} \sum_{\lambda_2 \in \Lambda} P_{\lambda_1} \circ P_{\lambda_2} \frac{i(1 - e^{iT(\lambda_2 - \lambda_1)})}{T(\lambda_2 - \lambda_1)}. \tag{7}$$

In the limit $T \to \infty$, Eq. 7 becomes

$$\widehat{M}_{G;\infty} = \sum_{\lambda \in \tilde{\Lambda}} P_{\lambda} \circ P_{\lambda}, \tag{8}$$

where $\tilde{\Lambda}$ is the set of distinct eigenvalues of the Hamiltonian.

Finally, we note that the average mixing kernel can be rewritten as

$$\begin{aligned}
\widehat{M}_{G;T} &= \sum_{\lambda_1 \in \Lambda} \sum_{\lambda_2 \in \Lambda} P_{\lambda_1} \circ P_{\lambda_2} \frac{i(1 - e^{iT(\lambda_2 - \lambda_1)})}{T(\lambda_2 - \lambda_1)} \\
&= \sum_{\lambda_1 \in \Lambda} \sum_{\lambda_2 \in \Lambda} P_{\lambda_1} \circ P_{\lambda_2} \frac{i - i\cos(T(\lambda_2 - \lambda_1)) + \sin(T(\lambda_2 - \lambda_1))}{T(\lambda_2 - \lambda_1)} \\
&= \sum_{\lambda_1 \in \Lambda} \sum_{\lambda_2 \in \Lambda} P_{\lambda_1} \circ P_{\lambda_2} \operatorname{sinc}(T(\lambda_2 - \lambda_1)), \tag{9}
\end{aligned}$$

where $\operatorname{sinc}(x) = \frac{\sin(x)}{x}$ is the unnormalized sinc function. In Sect. 4 we will show that the noise robustness of our signature is closely related to the rate of mixing of the eigenspaces given by the sinc component when we take a finite time average (Eq. 9) instead of an infinite time one (Eq. 8). Figure 1 shows the entries of the average mixing matrix computed according to Eq. 9 on a mesh of n vertices sampled from an underlying shape and for different choices of the stopping time T.

4 Average Mixing Kernel Signature

The average mixing matrix provides observation probabilities on node j for a particle starting on node i. In doing so it integrates contributions at all energy levels. In order to construct a signature we decompose the spectral contributions to the matrix into several bands so as to both limit the influence of the noise-dominated high-frequency components and create a more descriptive signature as a function of energy level, as first proposed by Aubry et al. [2]. We do this selectively reducing the spectral components at frequency λ according to an amplitude $f_E(\lambda)$ for a given target energy level E, obtaining the band-filtered average mixing matrix

$$AMM(E) = \sum_{\lambda_1} \sum_{\lambda_2} P_{\lambda_1} \circ P_{\lambda_2} \operatorname{sinc}(T(\lambda_2 - \lambda_1)) f_E(\lambda_1) f_E(\lambda_2), \tag{10}$$

where, following Aubry et al. [2], $f_E(\lambda) = e^{\frac{-(E - \log \lambda)^2}{2\sigma^2}}$, with E being a band parameter as in the WKS.

Table 1. Average percentage of correspondences ± standard error on the nearest 0.1% neighbours in the descriptor space for the AMKS (for increasing stopping time T, columns 1 to 13) and the WKS (last column) over a subset of the TOSCA (top) and FAUST (bottom) datasets with added Gaussian noise (η) to the vertex positions (rows). The highest value for each row is highlighted in bold.

$\eta\backslash T$	0.005	0.01	0.2	0.5	0.8	1	1.2	1.5	1.8	2	2.5	1000	WKS
0	36.8±2.1	36.8±2.1	**37.1±2.1**	36.9±2.1	36.3±2.1	35.8±2.1	35.4±2.0	34.7±2.0	34.2±2.0	33.7±1.9	32.6±1.9	27.8±1.6	33.0±1.6
0.01	27.9±1.4	27.9±1.4	28.2±1.4	**28.3±1.4**	28.0±1.4	27.7±1.4	27.3±1.4	26.9±1.4	26.5±1.4	26.2±1.4	25.5±1.3	21.9±1.2	24.9±1.2
0.015	20.1±1.1	20.1±1.1	20.5±1.1	**20.5±1.0**	20.3±1.0	20.0±1.0	19.8±1.0	19.6±1.0	19.5±1.0	19.1±0.9	18.8±0.9	16.6±0.8	17.6±0.8
0.02	14.1±0.8	14.1±0.8	**14.5±0.8**	14.5±0.8	14.2±0.8	14.1±0.8	14.0±0.7	13.8±0.7	13.7±0.7	13.5±0.7	13.2±0.7	11.8±0.6	11.8±0.6

$\eta\backslash T$	0.005	0.01	0.2	0.5	0.8	1	1.2	1.5	1.8	2	2.5	1000	WKS
0	53.3±2.4	53.3±2.4	53.7±2.4	**53.8±2.5**	53.4±2.5	53.2±2.4	52.6±2.5	51.4±2.4	50.8±2.4	50.3±2.4	49.2±2.5	40.7±2.5	47.0±2.5
0.01	33.9±1.1	33.9±1.1	34.2±1.1	34.7±1.2	35.3±1.2	**35.4±1.2**	35.1±1.2	34.7±1.1	34.1±1.1	33.7±1.1	32.9±1.1	24.3±1.0	29.5±1.0
0.015	19.3±0.6	19.3±0.6	19.6±0.6	19.9±0.6	20.4±0.7	**20.4±0.6**	20.3±0.6	20.1±0.6	19.6±0.6	19.3±0.6	18.7±0.6	15.0±0.8	18.1±0.8
0.02	10.8±0.4	10.8±0.4	10.7±0.4	10.8±0.5	11.0±0.4	**11.1±0.5**	11.0±0.5	10.8±0.5	10.5±0.5	10.2±0.4	10.0±0.4	8.8±0.4	10.5±0.4

Quantum-mechanically, this is equivalent to the introduction of a filter or an annihilation process that eliminates from the ensemble walkers at energy-eigenstate μ with rate $1 - f_E(\mu)$ just before the final observation on the vertex basis $|i\rangle$. This is equivalent to an observation on the states images of the projectors P_μ and $I - P_\mu$, with $\frac{1-f_E(\mu)}{\langle j|P_\mu|j\rangle}$ being the probability that the particle starting at node j is discarded from the ensemble if observed in P_μ.

After annihilation, the ensemble at time t of the particle starting from j is

$$\sum_{\lambda_1}\sum_{\lambda_2} e^{-i(\lambda_1-\lambda_2)t}\Big(I - \sum_{\mu_1}(1 - f_E(\mu_1))P_{\mu_1}\Big)\Big(P_{\lambda_1}|j\rangle\langle j|P_{\lambda_2}\Big)$$

$$\Big(I - \sum_{\mu_2}(1 - f_E(\mu_2))P_{\mu_2}\Big)$$

$$= \sum_{\lambda_1}\sum_{\lambda_2} e^{-i(\lambda_1-\lambda_2)t} f_E(\lambda_1)f_E(\lambda_2)\Big(P_{\lambda_1}|j\rangle\langle j|P_{\lambda_2}\Big), \qquad (11)$$

resulting, after time integration, in the band-filtered average mixing matrix (Eq. 10). To obtain the descriptor, we take the self-propagation, i.e., the probability that a particle in state u is still observed in u after the evolution, as a function of the energy level E and normalized so that the integral over all energies is 1, i.e.,

$$AMKS_u(E) = \frac{AMM(E)_{uu}}{\sum_{\lambda_1,\lambda_2} f_E(\lambda_1)f_E(\lambda_2)}. \qquad (12)$$

There are some clear similarities with the WKS, namely the fact that it is based on the evolution of a quantum system under the Schrödinger equation, the time average is taken to move towards a steady-state distribution, and the fact that we adopt the same energy band-filtering over which the signature is defined. However, there are some stark differences as well. First, band-filtering is not determined by an initial state, like in WKS, but it is posed as a pre-measurement process on the particle ensemble, similar to adding filters in front of a light detector. This is not only cleaner, but physically much easier to implement.

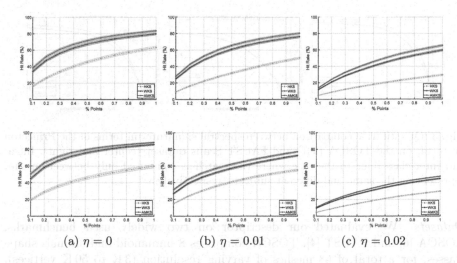

(a) $\eta = 0$ (b) $\eta = 0.01$ (c) $\eta = 0.02$

Fig. 2. Quantitative comparison of the match performance of different descriptors (HKS, WKS, and AMKS) on TOSCA (top) and FAUST (bottom) using the CMC curve ± standard error, considering an increasing percentage of nearest points in the descriptor space (x-axis) and with increasing level of Gaussian noise (left to right).

A consequence is that we map initial to final states, thus defining a kernel as in HKS, in contrast with WKS that maps energy bands to point distributions. This potentially offers better localization and opens the possibility to a more descriptive signature. Mathematically the way the kernel is defined is different also in the infinite-time limit: while WKS is fundamentally a function of the square of the entries of the eigenvectors of the Laplace-Beltrami operator, our signature results in their fourth power. This in turn creates a more distinctive descriptor while at the same time flattening small and possibly noise-induced variations. Finally, instead of taking the infinite-time average of the evolution of a single particle, we look at the statistical behavior of the finite time average of an ensemble of particles. This in turn can be shown to increase the robustness to noise as it imposes a mixing of the eigenspaces at a rate similar to the effect of noise (see the Supplementary Material).

5   Experiments

In this section we present quantitative and qualitative analysis testing the performance of our descriptor with respect to two alternative state-of-the-art spectral signatures, the WKS [2] and the scaled HKS [33], as these represent two of the most successful and used non-learned descriptors for deformable shapes. We omit the comparison with the AMMS [26] doe to its performance in this domain. Indeed, the AMMS was introduced to work on graphs of limited size and with long-range connections and, as we observed, its poor performance in the shape domain is further exacerbated by the need to truncate the spectrum.

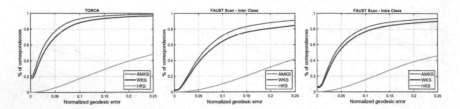

Fig. 3. Quantitative comparison between spectral signatures in terms of the Princeton protocol, on the TOSCA (left) and FAUST Scans dataset (center and right). Intra- and inter-class refer to the case where the match is computed only between meshes representing the same and different subjects, respectively.

Datasets. We evaluated our descriptor on two widely used benchmarks, TOSCA [6] and FAUST [4]. TOSCA comprises 8 humanoid and animals shape classes, for a total of 68 meshes of varying resolution (3 K to 50 K vertices). FAUST (both the real scans and synthetic version) consists of scanned human shapes in different poses. In total, there are 10 human subjects, each in 10 different poses, for a total of 100 meshes. In the next experiments, we refer to the synthetic version, unless specified otherwise. In both datasets, all shapes have been remeshed to 5 K vertices by iterative pair contractions and re-scaled to unit area.

Setting. We used the cotangent scheme approximation of the Laplace-Beltrami operator. Unless otherwise specified, we considered $k = 100$ eigenvectors of the Laplacian and a descriptor size of $d = 100$ in all methods. The choice of diffusion time will be discussed later. For the settings specific to the HKS and the WKS, we refer the reader to [33] and [2], respectively. It should be noted that our method requires setting the same number of parameters as the HKS and the WKS, with the exception of an additional time parameter. For the energy we use the same range as the WKS (we refer the reader to [2]). The time parameter is extensively discussed in the next subsection, where we show that the AMKS is not particularly sensitive to its value provided that it sits within a certain range.

Distance. We adopted the distance proposed by Aubry et al. in [2], here denoted as L^1_{KS}. Given two shapes $\mathcal{X}$ and $\mathcal{Y}$, in order to compare the descriptors for two points $x \in \mathcal{X}$ and $y \in \mathcal{Y}$ we measure their distance as

$$L^1_{KS}(x,y) = \sum_i^d \left| \frac{KS(x)_i - KS(y)_i}{KS(x)_i + KS(y)_i} \right|, \tag{13}$$

where $KS(\cdot)$ is the feature descriptor vector for a given point.

Metrics. We used two measures to evaluate the signatures. First, we made use of the Cumulative Match Characteristic (CMC) measure to estimate the probability of finding a correct correspondence among the p-nearest neighbours in

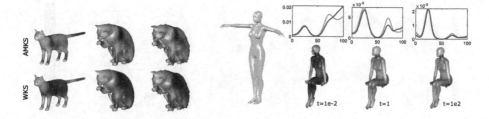

Fig. 4. The two figures show the distance in the descriptor space between a given point (red dot) and all the other points of the shape where the blue color corresponds to smaller distances. The *left* figure shows the behaviour of our AMKS at increasing noise levels, compared with WKS. The *right* figure shows the AMKS of the same point on different shapes, at increasing times $t = 0.01, 1, 100$. Each plot above the sitting shape shows the behaviour of two signatures: the green curve belongs to the shape in reference pose whereas the red curve represents the sitting shape. (Color figure online)

the descriptor space. The probability (hit rate), is calculated as the percentage of correct matches in the p-nearest neighbours. We average the hit rate for all points across all pairs of shapes at increasing values of p. The resulting CMC curve is then a monotonically increasing function of p.

The second measure is the Princeton protocol [18], also known as correspondence accuracy, which captures the proximity of predicted corresponding points to ground-truth ones in terms of geodesic distance on the surface. It counts the percentage of matches that are below a certain distance from the ground-truth correspondence. Given a pair of shapes and an input feature descriptor over a point on one of the shapes, we find the closest point on the other shape in descriptor space. Then we calculate the geodesic distance between its position over the surface and the position of the ground-truth corresponding point. In particular, given a match $(x, y) \in \mathcal{X} \times \mathcal{Y}$, and the ground-truth correspondence (x, y^*), the normalized geodesic error is $\epsilon(x) = d_{\mathcal{Y}}(y, y^*)/\text{area}(\mathcal{Y})^{0.5}$.

5.1 Choice of Time

In order to show how the choice of the diffusion time affects the performance of our descriptor, we performed some tests over two subsets of shapes from the two datasets. Table 1 shows the hit ratio of our descriptor on the nearest 0.1% of points in descriptor space. In particular, we explore how the performance changes as noise and time increase. In addition, we compare the results to those obtained with the WKS, noting that the WKS is time-independent. For the TOSCA dataset, we used 7 classes (wolf excluded) for a total of 28 pairs, whereas for FAUST we used 10 pairs. A pair consists of a class reference shape, in canonical pose, and another shape of the same class in a different pose. When adding noise, the reference shape is first rescaled, then Gaussian noise is added to the vertex positions and finally the shape is rescaled again.

Fig. 5. Qualitative comparison between WKS and AMKS on shapes from the TOSCA dataset. For each point of the surface we show the normalized geodesic error between the closest descriptor on the corresponding *reference shape* and the ground truth correspondence (or its symmetric one). The AMKS improves the overall matching quality.

It is worth noting that a) the hit rate of the AMKS is almost always superior to that of the WKS and b) the optimal times are different in the two datasets. More specifically, in the FAUST dataset the optimal performance of the AMKS is reached at slightly higher times when compared to TOSCA. Indeed, in the TOSCA dataset there is a stronger mixing of eigenvectors as it exhibits smaller deviations from isometry (see the perturbation analysis in the Supplementary Material for a discussion of the link between the stopping time T and the noise-induced mixing of the eigenspaces). Note however that the performance of the signature is fairly stable on a relatively wide interval around $T = 0.5$, implying that fine-tuning this parameter is not crucial. This optimal range in turn is a consequence of Weyl's law and the eigenvalues normalization that follows from normalizing all shapes to have unit area. Consequently, in order to avoid leaving free parameters and to ensure a fair comparison, in the next experiments we set $T = 0.5$ for both the TOSCA and FAUST datasets.

5.2   Quantitative Evaluation

We now compare our signature with that of the WKS and the HKS in the context of shape matching following the CMC and Princeton protocols.

Descriptor Robustness. The first quantitative comparison of the matching performance is shown in Fig. 2. Each plot shows the CMC curve of our method compared to those of the other spectral signatures, for varying levels of Gaussian noise (left to right, $\eta = 0, 0.01, 0.02$) and $T = 0.5$ (time of our signature). Here the y-axis is the hit rate (note that the plots were drawn by averaging the hit rate of all pairs of shapes for each dataset) and the x-axis defines the p-nearest neighbours (in percentage) in the descriptor space. Our approach clearly outperforms the alternatives, with the difference becoming larger as the noise increases. This is more evident in the TOSCA dataset, as it exhibits smaller deviations from isometry. This in turn shows the noise robustness of our signature.

Point-Wise Correspondence. In this experiment, we use the three signatures (HKS, WKS, and AMKS) to compute point-wise correspondences between pairs of shapes by taking the nearest neighbour in descriptor space. In Fig. 3 we show the results following the previously described Princeton protocol. As expected, our method shows the largest improvement on the TOSCA and FAUST inter-class datasets, which contain stronger non-isometric deformations.

Point Classification. One of the most used methods to train a neural network to perform the task of shape matching is to cast it as a classification task, where corresponding points on different shapes belong to the same class and there are as many classes as the number of points per shape. We used our descriptor as input to one of the state-of-the-art architectures for deep learning on shapes, FeastNet [34]. We used the code provided by authors, with the translation invariant single-scale network architecture proposed in the paper. The first 80 FAUST shapes have been used for training, the remaining 20 for test.

Table 2 shows the accuracy after training the network with different descriptors as input. We compare against WKS, the local rigid descriptor SHOT [32], and using just XYZ coordinates of points as input. We can see how the network is able to exploit the higher descriptivity of AMKS in order to achieve better classification accuracy. Note that, while training directly on XYZ coordinates allows to achieve the same accuracy, the performance rapidly decreases if we allow shapes to undergo a random rotation (i.e., ROT(XYZ)) since neither the XYZ coordinates nor the network are intrinsically invariant to this transformation.

Table 2. Classification accuracy of FeastNet trained with different input descriptors.

	XYZ	ROT(XYZ)	SHOT	WKS	AMKS
FeastNet	86%	50%	63%	80%	86%

5.3   Qualitative Evaluation

On the left side of Fig. 4 we contrast the behaviour of the AMKS and the WKS, showing the distance in descriptor space of a given point from the other points of the shape. We can see that our descriptor is more informative showing a more peaked distribution around the correct match, even in the presence of high levels of Gaussian noise. We employ the same type of visualization in the right side of Fig. 4. Here we can observe the behaviour of AMKS as the stopping time varies. By increasing the stopping time, the rate at which eigenspaces are mixed decreases, resulting in flatter and less descriptive signatures, while for very short times the signature varies significantly on the high energy bands. Hence, the optimal choice of the diffusion time is a key factor in the trade-off between descriptiveness and sensitivity of the signature.

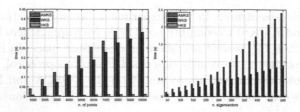

Fig. 6. Running times comparison wrt number of points (left) and eigenvectors (right).

Finally, in Fig. 5 we show some qualitative examples illustrating the normalized geodesic error, where we compare our results with those obtained with the WKS on a selection of shapes from the TOSCA dataset. The lower presence of coloured spots for the AMKS suggests a better matching quality.

5.4   Runtime Analysis

The computational complexity of our descriptor, without considering the spectral decomposition, is $\mathcal{O}(dnk^2)$ with n being the number of points of the mesh, k the dimension of the truncated eigenbase, and d the number of energy levels (see the Supplementary Material).[1] Here we perform an experimental evaluation of the running time needed to compute the AMKS. To this end, we implement our method in MATLAB and we run the code on a desktop workstation with 16 GB of RAM and Intel i7 8600 processor. Since the eigendecomposition is a common step in all the compared methods, we ignore it when measuring the running time. In Fig. 6 we show the time needed to compute each descriptor, averaged over 100 executions. In the left plot, we fix the number of eigenvalues to 100 and let the number of points vary between 1 k and 10 k, while in the right plot we keep 5 k points and increase the number of eigenvectors from 50 to 500.

As expected, introducing the mixing factor results in a slightly higher running time while the computational complexity remains linear in the number of points. On the other hand, we introduce a quadratic complexity with respect to the number of eigenvalues. Note, however, that in the range of number of eigenvectors normally used in spectral shape retrieval and matching tasks (<200) the behaviour is almost linear and that for a higher number of eigenvectors the main bottleneck is the spectral decomposition of the Laplace-Beltrami operator.

6   Conclusions

We have proposed a spectral signature for points on non-rigid three-dimensional shapes based on continuous-time quantum walks and the average mixing matrix holding the transition probabilities between each pair of vertices of a mesh. We

---

[1] https://github.com/lcosmo/amks-descriptor.

have shown both theoretically and experimentally that our signature is robust to noise, outperforming both the HKS and the WKS on a shape matching task. Future work will look into the application of our signature on different problems, including partial correspondences [11,25], point clouds, and shape segmentation.

Acknowledgements. Luca Cosmo was supported by the ERC Starting Grant No. 802554 (SPECGEO) and the ERC Consolidator grant No. 724228 (LEMAN).

References

1. Aubry, M., Schlickewei, U., Cremers, D.: Pose-consistent 3D shape segmentation based on a quantum mechanical feature descriptor. In: Mester, R., Felsberg, M. (eds.) DAGM 2011. LNCS, vol. 6835, pp. 122–131. Springer, Heidelberg (2011). https://doi.org/10.1007/978-3-642-23123-0_13
2. Aubry, M., Schlickewei, U., Cremers, D.: The wave kernel signature: a quantum mechanical approach to shape analysis. In: 2011 IEEE International Conference on Computer Vision Workshops (ICCV Workshops), pp. 1626–1633. IEEE (2011)
3. Bai, L., Rossi, L., Torsello, A., Hancock, E.R.: A quantum Jensen-Shannon graph kernel for unattributed graphs. Pattern Recogn. **48**(2), 344–355 (2015)
4. Bogo, F., Romero, J., Loper, M., Black, M.J.: Faust: dataset and evaluation for 3D mesh registration. In: Proceedings of the IEEE Conference on Computer Vision and Pattern Recognition, pp. 3794–3801 (2014)
5. Boscaini, D., Masci, J., Rodolà, E., Bronstein, M.M., Cremers, D.: Anisotropic diffusion descriptors. Comput. Graph. Forum **35**, 431–441 (2016). Wiley Online Library
6. Bronstein, A.M., Bronstein, M.M., Kimmel, R.: Numerical Geometry of Non-Rigid Shapes. Springer, New York (2008)
7. Bronstein, M.M., Kokkinos, I.: Scale-invariant heat kernel signatures for non-rigid shape recognition. In: 2010 IEEE Computer Society Conference on Computer Vision and Pattern Recognition, pp. 1704–1711. IEEE (2010)
8. Corman, É., Ovsjanikov, M., Chambolle, A.: Supervised descriptor learning for non-rigid shape matching. In: Agapito, L., Bronstein, M.M., Rother, C. (eds.) ECCV 2014. LNCS, vol. 8928, pp. 283–298. Springer, Cham (2015). https://doi.org/10.1007/978-3-319-16220-1_20
9. Cosmo, L., Rodola, E., Albarelli, A., Mémoli, F., Cremers, D.: Consistent partial matching of shape collections via sparse modeling. Comput. Graph. Forum **36**, 209–221 (2017). Wiley Online Library
10. Cosmo, L., Rodolà, E., Bronstein, M.M., Torsello, A., Cremers, D., Sahillioglu, Y.: Shrec'16: partial matching of deformable shapes. In: Proceedings of the 3DOR, vol. 2(9), p. 12 (2016)
11. Cosmo, L., Rodola, E., Masci, J., Torsello, A., Bronstein, M.M.: Matching deformable objects in clutter. In: 2016 Fourth International Conference on 3D Vision (3DV), pp. 1–10. IEEE (2016)
12. Emms, D., Severini, S., Wilson, R.C., Hancock, E.R.: Coined quantum walks lift the cospectrality of graphs and trees. Pattern Recogn. **42**(9), 1988–2002 (2009)
13. Fang, Y., Xie, J., Dai, G., Wang, M., Zhu, F., Xu, T., Wong, E.: 3D deep shape descriptor. In: Proceedings of the IEEE Conference on Computer Vision and Pattern Recognition, pp. 2319–2328 (2015)

14. Gasparetto, A., Minello, G., Torsello, A.: Non-parametric spectral model for shape retrieval. In: 2015 International Conference on 3D Vision, pp. 344–352. IEEE (2015)
15. Godsil, C.: Average mixing of continuous quantum walks. J. Comb. Theor. Ser. A **120**(7), 1649–1662 (2013)
16. Huang, H., Kalogerakis, E., Chaudhuri, S., Ceylan, D., Kim, V.G., Yumer, E.: Learning local shape descriptors from part correspondences with multiview convolutional networks. ACM Trans. Graph. (TOG) **37**(1), 6 (2018)
17. Kempe, J.: Quantum random walks: an introductory overview. Contemp. Phys. **44**(4), 307–327 (2003)
18. Kim, V.G., Lipman, Y., Funkhouser, T.: Blended intrinsic maps. ACM Trans. Graph. (TOG) **30**, 79 (2011). ACM
19. Levy, B.: Laplace-Beltrami eigenfunctions towards an algorithm that "understands" geometry. In: IEEE International Conference on Shape Modeling and Applications 2006 (SMI 2006), p. 13. IEEE (2006)
20. Litman, R., Bronstein, A.M.: Learning spectral descriptors for deformable shape correspondence. IEEE Trans. Pattern Anal. Mach. Intell. **36**(1), 171–180 (2013)
21. Masci, J., Boscaini, D., Bronstein, M., Vandergheynst, P.: Geodesic convolutional neural networks on Riemannian manifolds. In: Proceedings of the IEEE International Conference on Computer Vision Workshops, pp. 37–45 (2015)
22. Minello, G., Rossi, L., Torsello, A.: Can a quantum walk tell which is which? A study of quantum walk-based graph similarity. Entropy **21**(3), 328 (2019)
23. Reuter, M., Wolter, F.E., Peinecke, N.: Laplace-spectra as fingerprints for shape matching. In: Proceedings of the 2005 ACM Symposium on Solid and Physical Modeling, pp. 101–106. ACM (2005)
24. Rodola, E., et al.: Shrec'17: deformable shape retrieval with missing parts. In: Proceedings of the Eurographics Workshop on 3D Object Retrieval, Lisbon, Portugal, pp. 23–24 (2017)
25. Rodolà, E., Cosmo, L., Bronstein, M.M., Torsello, A., Cremers, D.: Partial functional correspondence. Comput. Graph. Forum **36**, 222–236 (2017). Wiley Online Library
26. Rossi, L., Severini, S., Torsello, A.: The average mixing matrix signature. In: Robles-Kelly, A., Loog, M., Biggio, B., Escolano, F., Wilson, R. (eds.) S+SSPR 2016. LNCS, vol. 10029, pp. 474–484. Springer, Cham (2016). https://doi.org/10.1007/978-3-319-49055-7_42
27. Rossi, L., Torsello, A., Hancock, E.R.: A continuous-time quantum walk kernel for unattributed graphs. In: Kropatsch, W.G., Artner, N.M., Haxhimusa, Y., Jiang, X. (eds.) GbRPR 2013. LNCS, vol. 7877, pp. 101–110. Springer, Heidelberg (2013). https://doi.org/10.1007/978-3-642-38221-5_11
28. Rossi, L., Torsello, A., Hancock, E.R.: Measuring graph similarity through continuous-time quantum walks and the quantum Jensen-Shannon divergence. Phys. Rev. E **91**(2), 022815 (2015)
29. Rossi, L., Torsello, A., Hancock, E.R., Wilson, R.C.: Characterizing graph symmetries through quantum Jensen-Shannon divergence. Phys. Rev. E **88**(3), 032806 (2013)
30. Rostami, R., Bashiri, F.S., Rostami, B., Yu, Z.: A survey on data-driven 3D shape descriptors. Comput. Graph. Forum **38**, 356–393 (2019). Wiley Online Library
31. Rustamov, R.M.: Laplace-Beltrami eigenfunctions for deformation invariant shape representation. In: Proceedings of the Fifth Eurographics Symposium on Geometry Processing, pp. 225–233. Eurographics Association (2007)
32. Salti, S., Tombari, F., di Stefano, L.: Shot: unique signatures of histograms for surface and texture description. Comput. Vis. Image Underst. **125**, 251–264 (2014)

33. Sun, J., Ovsjanikov, M., Guibas, L.: A concise and provably informative multi-scale signature based on heat diffusion. Comput. Graph. Forum **28**, 1383–1392 (2009). Wiley Online Library
34. Verma, N., Boyer, E., Verbeek, J.: Feastnet: feature-steered graph convolutions for 3D shape analysis. In: The IEEE Conference on Computer Vision and Pattern Recognition (CVPR), June 2018
35. Vestner, M., et al.: Efficient deformable shape correspondence via kernel matching. In: 2017 International Conference on 3D Vision (3DV), pp. 517–526. IEEE (2017)

BCNet: Learning Body and Cloth Shape from a Single Image

Boyi Jiang[1], Juyong Zhang[1(✉)], Yang Hong[1], Jinhao Luo[1], Ligang Liu[1],
and Hujun Bao[2]

[1] University of Science and Technology of China, Hefei, China
juyong@ustc.edu.cn
[2] State Key Lab of CAD&CG, Zhejiang University, Hangzhou, China

Abstract. In this paper, we consider the problem to automatically reconstruct garment and body shapes from a single near-front view RGB image. To this end, we propose a layered garment representation on top of SMPL and novelly make the skinning weight of garment independent of the body mesh, which significantly improves the expression ability of our garment model. Compared with existing methods, our method can support more garment categories and recover more accurate geometry. To train our model, we construct two large scale datasets with ground truth body and garment geometries as well as paired color images. Compared with single mesh or non-parametric representation, our method can achieve more flexible control with separate meshes, makes applications like re-pose, garment transfer, and garment texture mapping possible.

Keywords: Clothed body reconstruction · 3D garment shape · 3D body shape · Skinning weight

1 Introduction

Applications like virtual try-on, VR/AR, and entertainment need detailed and accurate reconstruction of both body and dressed garments with simple input like color image. However, the variety of body shapes, postures and garment categories, makes it a very challenging problem. A simulation-based method [52] explores this problem, but their solution is dedicated and time-consuming. In this paper, we aim to automatically reconstruct both body and cloth shapes from just a single near-front view image, utilizing the powerful fitting ability of the deep neural network.

In recent years, body shape reconstruction from images has made significant progress [23,24,29,36]. A common way is to infer the shape and pose parameter of a statistical body model, like SMPL [32]. These methods are robust for different posture, but the reconstructed geometry is constrained to be within the model space, which can not capture the complex cloth shape.

Electronic supplementary material The online version of this chapter (https://doi.org/10.1007/978-3-030-58565-5_2) contains supplementary material, which is available to authorized users.

© Springer Nature Switzerland AG 2020
A. Vedaldi et al. (Eds.): ECCV 2020, LNCS 12365, pp. 18–35, 2020.
https://doi.org/10.1007/978-3-030-58565-5_2

To infer detailed geometry beyond body shape, some non-parametric representations have been proposed [35,43,46,57]. These non-parametric representations based on voxel and implicit function can recover arbitrary shapes. However, voxel representation is hard to recover shape details due to their large memory consumption for high resolution. Although implicit representation is more memory efficient, it may generate infeasible results like broken arms. Moreover, the lack of semantic information limits their applications like garment transfer.

Expanding the representation ability of the statistical model of body shape is another solution. Several prior works [3,4,7,38] utilize the vertex displacements of body shape represented by SMPL to represent garment geometry. Under this configuration, tight garments can be reconstructed. However, this representation cannot recover the feature of garment edges. More importantly, binding garments with SMPL points causes the problem that garments have the same skinning weights and connectivity with SMPL. Therefore, large scale displacements of loose garments may cause artifacts because of inappropriate skinning weights. More importantly, garments like skirts which have a different topology with body shape, are beyond the representation range.

Like Bhatnagar et al. [7], we train a model to reconstruct body mesh and layered garment meshes separately. The difference in input is that our method only requires a single RGB image and no additional semantic information and body rough A-pose constrain. Another difference is that our garment mesh is not bound with the body mesh, and can reconstruct more garment categories. To this end, we address three major challenges: learning a shared skinning weight network for all garments, garment detail inference, and dataset construction. Our method supports six garment categories, including upper garment, pants, and skirts with short and long templates for each type. For all garment types, we train a network to predict skinning weights related to SMPL's skeleton. For each type, we use graph convolution to recover the details. To train the model, a dataset with various RGB images and their corresponding body and cloth shapes is needed. However, there is no available public datasets that satisfy our demands. Instead, for each type of garment, we design different sizes of clothes dressed on different SMPL neutral bodies and repose these clothes to various postures utilizing a physics engine. Besides, a commercial 3D human dataset with high-definition texture is added to increase the diversity of training data.

Our method can infer both body and garment shapes from a single image with different poses, and also supports loose garment types, like skirts. Based on the reconstruction results by our method, applications like garments and poses transferring between different images can be achieved. In summary, the contributions of this work include the following aspects:

- We present a novel garment representation on top of SMPL and a neural network-based method to reconstruct the shapes of body and garment from a single near-front viewpoint color image.
- Rather than binding the skinning weight of garment with body mesh, we propose a generic skinning weights generating network, which enables our approach to support garments with different topologies.

- We design a complete algorithm pipeline for dressed SMPL body data construction with different types of garments. The constructed dataset, including synthetic images and clothed body shapes, will be publicly available.

2   Related Work

Template-Free Clothed Human Estimation. Some non-parametric methods based on voxel or implicit function have been proposed to address the complex topology of garments. BodyNet [46] directly infers a voxel representation of clothed bodies with a deep network. Due to the large memory cost for high resolution, high-frequency details are often missed. Jackson *et al.* [20] reconstruct the shape of humans via volumetric regression and show the ability to output fine-scale details. Zheng *et al.* [57] infer clothed body volume representation with an initial aligned SMPL body, and combine image features to enhance reconstruction details. Natsume *et al.* [35] propose a reconstruction method based on a multi-view framework using synthesizing new silhouettes from a single image. More recently, [43] proposes a promising clothed body reconstruction network using a memory-efficient implicit representation. Template-free methods do not utilize the human body prior to obtain complex topology modeling ability, at the cost of lacking semantic information and control of reconstructed results.

Template-Based Clothed Human Estimation. Based on human body statistical model [5,21,32], many works can estimate naked body shape from image [9,14,23,27,36,38,54]. For better representation ability, a displacement vector is added for each vertex. [1–3] adopt this strategy to reconstruct clothed body with skin-tight garment. Alldieck *et al.* [4] estimate detailed normal and vector displacement on the UV map, which leads to finer-scale details. Zhu *et al.* [59] model fine-scale details by adding free-form 3D deformation on top of parametric model. Instead of using a single surface to represent both garment and body, [7] separates SMPL mesh to represent upper garment and pant independently, leading to more flexible control. However, binding garment vertices to body model strictly restricts the topology of support garment categories, and it is hard to represent more loose garment types, such as skirts. [39,55] also use separate body and garment templates to register clothed body motion sequences.

Garment Dataset Construction. BUFF [56] supplies high-quality 4D scans of clothed bodies, but it only has 5 subjects and 2 suits for each subject. Lahner *et al.* [26] collect high-quality 4D scans of garments, but the method leaves out body reconstruction, and their dataset is not publicly available. Recently, [7] constructs a training dataset with garment and body shapes from real scan data, but the training dataset is also unavailable. Moreover, many prior works generate ground truth dataset based on physics-based simulation [12,17,28,29, 40,44,49]. [28,29] dress SMPL bodies and construct more truthful images than SURREAL [47]. [49] simulates three types of garment and dress them on neutral

SMPL bodies to learn garments design from sketches. All mentioned datasets do not meet our requirements. Therefore, we build a dataset containing a variety of garments and body types with different sizes and postures.

Garment Deformation Representation. How to represent the deformation of a garment is also related to our work. De Aguiar *et al.* [13] represent the garment dynamic dressed on a specific virtual avatar with a linear combination of pre-computed multiple deformations. DRAPE [17] regresses garment deformation from body shape with a technique derived from SCAPE [5]. Xu *et al.* [50] combine rotation and translation weights to approximate the non-local and non-linear clothing deformation and introduce a pose sensitive rigging scheme. Lahner *et al.* [26] recover high-frequency garment details from a normal map created from Generative Adversarial Network. Yang *et al.* [51] model garments with different connectivity based on a body template and use PCA to parameterize garment deformation. Santesteban *et al.* [44] propose to deform base garment conditioned on body parameters and then add high-frequency wrinkles.

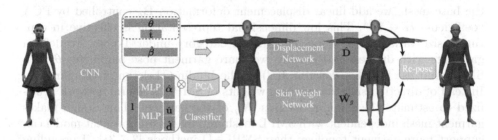

Fig. 1. The architecture of our proposed network. The CNN encodes image into latent feature, then we get reconstructed SMPL parameters $\hat{\beta}$, $\hat{\theta}$, $\hat{t}$ and shared garment latent feature l with respective FC layers. From l, we reconstruct garment shape parameter $\hat{\alpha}$ and garment type scores $\{\hat{u}, \hat{d}\}$ for upper and lower garment separately. With the classifier, $\hat{\alpha}$ and $\hat{\beta}$, we reconstruct neutral clothed body. Followed a displacement network and skinning weight network, we predict garment vertex displacements and skinning weights separately. Finally, utilizing predicted pose parameters $\hat{\theta}$, $\hat{t}$ and $\hat{W}_g$, we re-pose neutral body and garments with displacements to reference posture.

3   Algorithm

The target of this work is to automatically reconstruct both body and cloth shapes from a single near-front view image. Our model currently supports six garment categories and can be easily extended to other new types. In the following, we first describe our garment representation model. Then, we introduce our network structure and training loss design.

3.1 Garment Model

We use SMPL [32] as our parametric human body model. SMPL is a function which maps shape parameters $\beta \in \mathbb{R}^{10}$ and pose parameters $\theta \in \mathbb{R}^{72}$ to a body mesh $\mathbf{M}_b(\beta, \theta) \in \mathbb{R}^{3|\mathcal{V}_b|}$, where $\mathcal{V}_b$ is SMPL mesh vertices set. The mapping can be summarized as the following equation:

$$\mathbf{M}_b(\beta, \theta) = W(\mathbf{T}_b(\beta, \theta), \mathbf{J}(\beta), \theta, \mathbf{W}_b), \quad \mathbf{T}_b(\beta, \theta) = \mathbf{B} + \mathbf{B}_s\beta + \mathbf{B}_p\theta, \quad (1)$$

where SMPL applies linear displacement bases $\mathbf{B}_s$ and $\mathbf{B}_p$ on a T-posed template mesh $\mathbf{B}$, and then utilize standard skeleton skinning operation W to get posed body mesh. $\mathbf{J}(\beta) \in \mathbb{R}^{24 \times 3}$ is SMPL body's neutral skeleton and $\mathbf{W}_b \in \mathbb{R}^{|\mathcal{V}_b| \times 24}$ is the skinning weights of each vertex of SMPL.

As most clothes follow the deformations of the body, we compute our garment mesh $\mathbf{M}_g \in \mathbb{R}^{3|\mathcal{V}_g|}$ similarly based on the skin deformation of SMPL:

$$\mathbf{M}_g(\alpha, \beta, \theta, \mathbf{D}) = W(\mathbf{T}_g(\alpha, \mathbf{D}), \mathbf{J}(\beta), \theta, \mathbf{W}_g(\alpha, \beta)), \quad \mathbf{T}_g(\alpha, \mathbf{D}) = \mathbf{G} + \mathbf{B}_g\alpha + \mathbf{D}. \tag{2}$$

For each garment category, a T-posed template mesh $\mathbf{G}$ is defined. On top of the base mesh, we add linear displacement deformation $\mathbf{B}_g$ controlled by PCA coefficients $\alpha \in \mathbb{R}^{64}$. This low dimensional representation is effective in capturing size variations of a specific garment category under T-pose. To deform garments with dressed SMPL body, we share garment pose parameter θ with SMPL and use SMPL's skeleton $\mathbf{J}(\beta)$ as the binding skeleton of the garment. Instead of directly using the skinning weights of SMPL, a neural network is utilized to estimate the skinning weights $\mathbf{W}_g$ of the garment. This design makes garment mesh independent with SMPL mesh and makes our garment model can support more garment topology than SMPL+D methods [3,7,38], if providing corresponding garment training data. To capture variations caused by different pose and interaction between clothing and body, we add a high-frequency displacement $\mathbf{D} \in \mathbb{R}^{3|\mathcal{V}_g|}$ for vertices of the clothing. In this paper, for the conciseness of writing symbol, we denote the displacement directly as $\mathbf{D}$ instead of a function of latent dependent variables, such as α, θ.

3.2 Image to Dressed Body

Given a near-front view RGB image depicting a posed subject dressed on specific garments, our model estimates its body shape, pose parameters and global translation with $\hat{\beta} \in \mathbb{R}^{10}, \hat{\theta} \in \mathbb{R}^{72}, \hat{t} \in \mathbb{R}^3$ and the garment parameters $\hat{\alpha} \in \mathbb{R}^{64}$ and $\hat{\mathbf{D}}$. Our model mainly consists of four modules: image encoder, classification module, skinning weight network, and displacement network. Figure 1 shows our algorithm pipeline, and we will discuss the details of the last two modules.

Our image encoder uses the feature extraction of ResNet-18 [19] and average pooling the final feature map to 8×8 size. From the map, a fully connected layer is used to get the latent feature. Then, four fully connected layers are used to predict shape parameters $\hat{\beta}$, pose parameters $\hat{\theta}$, translation $\hat{t}$ and shared garment latent feature $l \in \mathbb{R}^{256}$. For pose parameters, instead of directly predicting the axis-angle representation parameters $\hat{\boldsymbol{\theta}}$, we predict vectorized rotation matrices $R(\hat{\boldsymbol{\theta}}) \in \mathbb{R}^{24 \times 9}$ of all joints, where R is the Rodrigues rotation transformation. This strategy makes training more stable and continuous [27,37,38].

From shared garment latent $\mathbf{l}$, two fully connected layers are used to predict upper and lower garment classify scores $\hat{\mathbf{u}} \in \mathbb{R}^2$ and $\hat{\mathbf{d}} \in \mathbb{R}^4$ separately. Then, we concatenate $\hat{\boldsymbol{\beta}}$ and $\mathbf{l}$ as input of a two-layer Multi-layer perceptron(MLP) [41] to predict neutral garment shape parameters $\hat{\boldsymbol{\alpha}}$. After that, utilizing skinning weight and displacement networks, we get garment skinning weights $\hat{\mathbf{W}}_g$ and high-frequency displacements $\hat{\mathbf{D}}$, respectively. Finally, with predicted pose parameters, we can reconstruct the body shapes and dressed garments together.

3.3   Skinning Weight Network

It is an open problem to estimate skinning weights for an arbitrary character given a binding skeleton hierarchy. Recently, Liu et al. [30] proposed the first generic network to infer the skinning weights of various characters binding to the mutative skeleton hierarchy. Inspired by [30], we design our skinning weight network to infer weights for neutral garments, and the network makes weights computation fast, differentiable and garment type independent.

Our network predicts the skinning weights of a specific neutral garment $\mathbf{T}_g(\hat{\boldsymbol{\alpha}}, \mathbf{0})$ binding to the skeleton $\mathbf{J}$ of corresponding neutral SMPL body $\mathbf{T}_b(\hat{\boldsymbol{\beta}}, \mathbf{0})$. We compute all distances of each vertex of $\mathbf{T}_g(\hat{\boldsymbol{\alpha}}, \mathbf{0})$ to each joint point of $\mathbf{J}$. Then, the coordinate, normal, and distances of each vertex of $\mathbf{T}_g(\hat{\boldsymbol{\alpha}}, \mathbf{0})$ are concatenated as the input feature for the network, and it computes the weights for all vertices. Our network uses MLP to change the vertex feature dimension and utilizes standard Residual Block [19] to extract features. Besides, we use graph convolution to aggregate the neighborhood information. In order to make our network applicable to different garment categories, we use GAT [48] graph convolution, whose filter weight learning is independent of mesh connectivity, and the weight is determined by the input feature on vertices only. This characteristic makes our network based on GAT suitable for different garment types. The architecture details can be found in the supplementary.

3.4   Displacement Network

The shape structure of the garment can be well reconstructed based on the PCA coefficients $\boldsymbol{\alpha}$. However, high-frequency details, such as folds caused by different pose, are beyond the representation ability of the linear model. We train a displacement network to regress the displacement of each garment vertex on top of the base mesh. For the displacement, we use a similar network structure with the skinning weight network. To improve the regression ability, we train an independent network for each garment category rather than a general network for all types. Moreover, we use spiral graph convolution [10] for each garment category, which has state-of-the-art regression ability for meshes with the same connectivity. To capture high frequency information, we project each vertex of deformed base garment $\mathbf{M}_g(\hat{\alpha}, \hat{\beta}, \hat{\theta}, \mathbf{0})$ on the image, and crop the 32×32 patch centered on the projected vertex. Then, for each vertex, we use a shared MLP to encode its patch into a latent feature, and concatenate the feature with shared garment latent l, predicted SMPL shape parameter $\hat{\beta}$, garment shape parameter $\hat{\alpha}$ as well as its coordinate, normal and skinning transformation together as its input feature for the displacement network. The details of the neural network are given in the supplementary.

3.5 Loss Function

With our constructed dataset, ground truth shape and pose parameters are available for all training data, thus it is natural to adopt supervised training. In this part, we denote predicted $\mathbf{M}_g(\hat{\alpha}, \hat{\beta}, \hat{\theta}, \hat{\mathbf{D}})$ and $\mathbf{M}_b(\hat{\beta}, \hat{\theta}))$ as $\hat{\mathbf{M}}_g$ and $\hat{\mathbf{M}}_b$ separately. In the following, we will give the details on how to design the loss terms.

Losses on Shape Parameters. We directly adopt the MSE between predicted and ground truth shape parameters. The loss for SMPL body parameters and garment parameters are separately defined as:

$$L_{Bp} = \|\hat{\beta} - \beta\|_2^2 + \|R(\hat{\theta}) - R(\theta)\|_2^2 + \|\hat{t} - t\|_2^2, \quad L_{Gp} = \|\hat{\alpha} - \alpha\|_2^2. \quad (3)$$

Losses on Geometry. We supervise reconstructed geometries and joints with ground truth data. J_B is the mapping to output posed 3D joints of SMPL body $\mathbf{M}_b$.

– Losses on reconstructed garment geometry and reconstructed body joints are separately defined as:

$$L_G = \|\hat{\mathbf{M}}_g - \mathbf{M}_g\|_2^2, \quad L_{J3D} = \|J_B(\hat{\mathbf{M}}_b) - J_B(\mathbf{M}_b)\|_2^2. \quad (4)$$

– Losses on displacements $\mathbf{D}$. To improve detail reconstruction ability, we use ℓ_1 loss for each vertex of $\mathbf{D}$ and ℓ_2 loss on laplacian coordinates of $\mathbf{D}$. $\mathcal{L}$ represents the laplacian coordinates mapping from a 3D mesh.

$$L_{D1} = |\hat{\mathbf{D}} - \mathbf{D}|, \quad L_{D2} = \|\mathcal{L}(\hat{\mathbf{D}}) - \mathcal{L}(\mathbf{D})\|_2^2. \quad (5)$$

Losses of Projection. We use Π to represent the camera projection of 3D geometries. All our training data share a common camera intrinsic matrix. The loss of body projections and garment projections are separately defined as:

$$L_{B2D} = \|\Pi(\hat{\mathbf{M}}_b) - \Pi(\mathbf{M}_b)\|_2^2, \quad L_{G2D} = \|\Pi(\hat{\mathbf{M}}_g) - \Pi(\mathbf{M}_g)\|_2^2. \quad (6)$$

Losses of Classification. We use standard softmax loss to penalize the classification error of $\hat{u}$ and $\hat{d}$ relative to ground truth garment types.

Losses of Interpenetration. During training, inferred garments and body are easy to occur interpenetration. We use a simple yet effective interpenetration term inspired by [18] to alleviate this problem:

$$L_{int}(\mathbf{P}, \mathbf{Q}) = \sum_{\{i,j\} \in \mathcal{C}(\mathbf{P}, \mathbf{Q})} ReLU(-\mathbf{n}_{\mathbf{q}_j}^T (\mathbf{p}_i - \mathbf{q}_j))/N, \tag{7}$$

where $\mathbf{P}, \mathbf{Q}$ are two interpenetrated meshes. $\mathcal{C}(\mathbf{P}, \mathbf{Q})$ represents the valid corresponding pairs between $\mathbf{P}$ and $\mathbf{Q}$, and these pairs are filtered based on distances and normal angles. This loss penalizes vertex $\mathbf{p}_i$ that is inside the local plane defined by its corresponding point $\mathbf{q}_j$ and its normal $\mathbf{n}_{\mathbf{q}_j}$. We use this loss on reconstructed neutral garments and body as well as posed garments and body separately:

$$L_{inters} = L_{int}(T_g(\hat{\boldsymbol{\alpha}}, \mathbf{0}), T_b(\hat{\boldsymbol{\beta}}, \mathbf{0})) + L_{int}(\hat{\mathbf{M}}_g, \hat{\mathbf{M}}_b) \tag{8}$$

Loss of Skinning Weight Network. As discussed in [30], the weight vector $\{\omega_{ij} | j \in |J(\boldsymbol{\beta})|\}$ of $\mathbf{W}_g$ is a selection of different bones with different probabilities. We use the Kullback-Leibler divergence loss to measure the distance between predicted weights distribution $\hat{\omega}_{ij}$ and ground truth distribution ω_{ij}:

$$L_{ws} = \sum_{i=1}^{|\mathcal{V}_g|} \sum_{j=1}^{24} \hat{\omega}_{ij} (\log \frac{\hat{\omega}_{ij}}{\omega_{ij}}). \tag{9}$$

To train the whole network, we first train the skinning weight network with loss in Eq. (9), and then train other parts together by fixing the skinning weight network.

4 Dataset Construction

4.1 Skinning Weight Dataset

To train our skinning weight network, we need some neutral garments with ground truth skinning weights. Our network training adapts to any weight calculation method. For simpleness, we compute garment weights from the dressed SMPL body.

For vertex $\mathbf{p}_i$ of the garment, we select K vertices from dressed body mesh, based on distance, normal angle, and segmentation prior. Segmentation prior is some information we can utilize, such as corresponding vertices of right trouser leg must belong to the right leg of body mesh. From selected K vertices of body, we average their skinning weights with IDW(inverse distance weighting) as the skinning weight of $\mathbf{p}_i$. After all vertices' weights have been computed, we apply Laplacian smoothing [45] to remove noises and artifacts.

With this method, for all garment types, we construct a skinning weights dataset, which includes 48000 neutral garments for training, and 6467 for test.

4.2   Synthetic Dataset Construction

As there does not exist publicly available dataset containing pairs of the color image and corresponding body and cloth shapes, we construct the dataset with a physics-based simulation method. The dataset construction process can be divided into four steps: sewing pattern design, neutral garment synthesis, posed garment simulation and rendering. [49] proposed a novel method to synthesize neutral garments. We extend their method to support more garment types and posed garments generation.

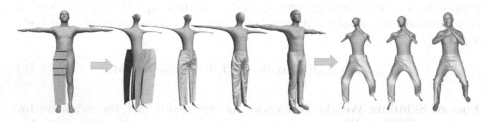

Fig. 2. Our synthesis process of a pant. First, we generate a random sewing pattern based on neutral body type. Then, we stitch the pattern on the skeleton and inflate the skeleton to its original shape to generate the neutral pant. Finally, we skinning deform the skeleton and neutral pant to a posture, and simulate the final pant with gravity by inflating the posed skeleton.

As shown in Fig. 2, we first design the pant sewing pattern based on body type. Then, around the neutral skeleton, we connect the sewing lines of the front and back pattern and shorten the length gradually. The sewing lines are stitched together after all lengths of the sewing line are less than a threshold. To simulate the realistic result of the garment draped on the neutral body, we inflate the skeleton and add gravity. For posed garment simulation, we deform the neutral garment to target pose with generated skinning weights and inflate the body and add gravity to simulate the posed garment. In this work, we assume that both the human body and the garment are in a statically stable state. Therefore, we sample discrete pose instead of simulating the whole motion sequence.

After generating the garment shapes, the synthetic images are rendered by following the methods in [28,29,47]. By randomly selecting body textures from SURREAL [47], garment textures from Fabrics [22] and DTD [11], background images from Places365-Standard dataset [58] and global illumination from hundreds HDR images, we can render near-front view dressed body images with abundant variations.

We implement the abovementioned pipeline using the simulator NvFlex[15] and Blender[8]. We utilize 3048 body shape of SPRING dataset [53], and randomly generate neutral clothes dressed on them. For posed garment, we select 55 motion sequences from CMU Mocap [34], whose poses have been converted to SMPL pose parameters with MoSh [31]. For each motion sequence, we randomly

Fig. 3. Some examples from our synthetic dataset(left three) and HD texture dataset(right three).

select 10 different persons with 4 sets of different clothing separately and sample pose parameters every 30 frames. Finally, we get 168602 dressed bodies as training data and 8874 as test data. The left part of Fig. 3 shows several examples of our synthetic images.

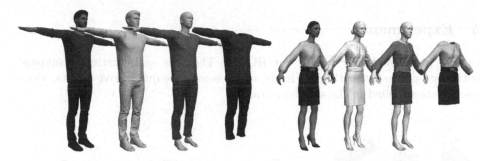

Fig. 4. Two examples of rigged avatar registration. We show the scanned meshes with and without texture, reconstructed geometries and garment with texture in each group.

4.3   HD Texture Dataset

Although synthetic samples are visually realistic, they still have a noticeable domain difference with real images. Therefore, we process another dataset with high-definition (HD) textures. We purchase 104 and 181 rigged avatar from RenderPeople [42] and Axyz [6], respectively. These avatars have high-quality geometry and realistic texture. We use Mixamo [33] to drive avatars and get about 89425 posed meshes as training data and 4386 as test data. The abovementioned rendering pipeline is used to produce high-quality images, and the right part of Fig. 3 shows some examples. Because the body and clothes part of the scanned mesh are not separated, and the connectivities of scanned meshes are not consistent, we need to process these meshes to our representation via the following two steps.

Rigged Registration. For a rigged mesh with A- or T-pose, we segment it to garment and skin parts. We optimize garment shape parameters α, displacements $\mathbf{D}$, body parameters β, θ and translation $\mathbf{t}$ to register our representation to the avatar. We penalize the point-to-plane distance for both reconstructed garment and body. And we use Eq. (7) to reduce the interpenetration among them. To get a size matching garment, we adopt the rendered silhouette loss utilizing [25]. And we add ℓ_2 regular term for garment and body parameters. With this pipeline, we reconstruct all garments and body shapes of rigged avatars, and we extract texture for each garment. Figure 4 shows two examples.

Posed Registration. After we finish the rigged avatar reconstruction, we initialize our posed model optimization with rigged reconstruction parameters and optimize pose parameters θ and translation $\mathbf{t}$ first. And then, we fine-tune all parameters to get final posed reconstruct results.

5   Experiments

In this part, we first evaluate our BCNet. Then we quantitatively compare with state-of-the-art methods. Finally, we present some qualitative results. More results are supplied in the supplementary.

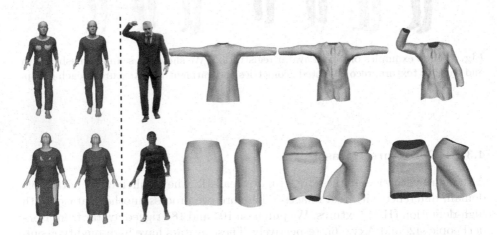

Fig. 5. The left shows the ablation study for interpenetration loss. The examples demonstrate that the interpenetration term in Eq. (7) alleviates the collision problem. The right shows our predicted displacement results. For each example, We present the base mesh, mesh with displacement and reposed mesh, respectively. The first example captures detail geometry on top of the base mesh, and the second one recovers large scale deformation for the skirt caused by leg movement. For better visualization, we show two viewpoints for the second result.

Table 1. The MED (cm) between predicted and ground truth shapes on our test dataset. For garments, we report errors with (gray) and without (white) displacement module, respectively.

Dataset	Shirt	Pant	Skirt	Body
Synthetic	0.91	0.75	0.87	1.57
	1.72	1.59	2.46	
HD	1.71	1.42	1.65	2.93
texture	1.97	1.72	1.87	

Table 2. The errors (cm) on BUFF rough A-pose dataset (gray) and Digital Wardrobe dataset (white).

Methods	Upper	Lower	Total	Chamfer
MGN-opt-8	1.63	1.91	1.82	1.91
MGN-8	1.78	2.13	1.99	2.08
Octopus-opt-8	1.40	**1.35**	**1.31**	1.41
Octopus-8	1.54	1.74	1.70	1.76
Ours	**1.07**	**1.35**	1.35	**1.34**
PIFu	1.59	**1.37**	1.85	**1.61**
DeepHuman	2.38	2.46	3.15	2.98
Ours	**1.44**	1.78	**1.80**	1.77

5.1   Analysis of BCNet

Our Test Set. We test our predicted errors on Synthetic and HD Texture test set, respectively. Table 1 shows the mean Euclidean distance(MED) of reconstructed shapes after Procrustes transformation and ground truth shapes.

Skinning Weight Network. We test the reconstruction ability of the skinning weight network on our test dataset. For each garment, we reconstruct its skinning weights with our network. The average ℓ_1 reconstruction error on the whole test set is 6.5×10^{-4}. Then, we sample 20 poses from the Mocap dataset and deform the neutral clothes to the posture with our predicted weights and ground truth weights separately. The average MED of reposed mesh for all garment types is 0.43mm. These results demonstrate that our skinning weight network can reach very high accuracy. More details are given in supplementary.

Interpenetration. Our network infers human body and layered garments mesh separately, which brings better flexibility but at the cost of introducing more complex interactions between body and garments. Interpenetration is a common unreal phenomenon which is very easy to perceive by a human. Therefore, it is quite necessary to process interpenetration between these meshes. We propose an interpenetration term in Eq. (7) to alleviate this problem, and an ablation study on this term is shown in the left of Fig. 5. We can see that the interpenetration loss is beneficial to alleviate the interpenetration problem.

Displacement Network. Garment PCA shape parameter α can represent the garment structure, while it can not represent the detailed shape of a specific garment and large scale deformations caused by pose and gravity for loose garments. We train our non-linear displacement network to expand the representation ability. The result of ablation study on displacement network is given in Table 1, we can observe that the displacement network greatly improves the reconstruction

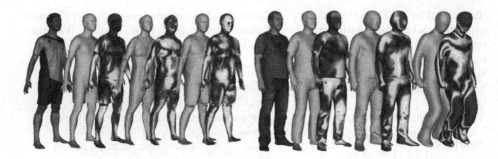

Fig. 6. Error maps on BUFF(left part) and MGN(right part). From left to right, we show the GT mesh, results of ours, Octopus-opt-8, MGN-opt-8 for the BUFF example, and results of ours, PIFu, DeepHuman for the MGN example(red means $\geq$ 4cm). (Color figure online)

accuracy. In the right part of Fig. 5, we show two examples of our displacement results. We present input image, base garment $\mathbf{T}_g(\boldsymbol{\alpha}, \mathbf{0})$, the garment with predicted displacement $\mathbf{T}_g(\boldsymbol{\alpha}, \mathbf{D})$ and final reposed garment $\mathbf{M}_g(\boldsymbol{\alpha}, \boldsymbol{\beta}, \boldsymbol{\theta}, \mathbf{D})$ for each result. In the first row, we show an example of predicted displacement capturing detailed geometry, such as tie and suit boundary line. In the second row, we show large scale deformations on a skirt caused by bending leg motion, and we use two viewpoints to show the deformation results.

5.2 Quantitative Comparison.

We test our reconstruction accuracy on two public data sets, BUFF [56] and Digit Wardrobe(DW) [7]. We segment the ground truth scan mesh into upper, lower garment and body parts, and compute error for garments and whole clothed bodies separately. Because our model predicts separate body and garment meshes, we extract the outer surface of all meshes as the proxy to do registration and error computing for a fair comparison. We measure the average point-to-surface Euclidean distance(P2S) in cm from the ground truth to predicted surface for upper, lower garments, and the whole surface. We also compute the Chamfer distance [43] between the reconstructed and the ground truth surfaces.

BUFF Dataset. We compare the reconstruction accuracy of our method with SMPL+D based methods octopus [38] and MGN [7]. By default, their methods require multi-view semantic segmentation images and 2D joints of a clothed body under rough A-pose as inputs, and post-optimization is applied to refine the results. Therefore, we select 21 rough A-pose data from BUFF [56] as our test set. Table 2 shows our results, and their results of 8 perspective inputs with and without optimization, respectively. Although the input of our method only needs one image, our method can get better numerical results than theirs without post-optimization, and an equivalent result with Octopus with optimization. The post-optimization is time-consuming and takes several seconds and several minutes for Octopus and MGN, respectively. For MGN, we manually modified some segmentation error of PGN [16] to refine their results. In the left part of Fig. 6, we show an example of our result and their results with post-optimization. Some unnatural folds are introduced in the post-optimization step of MGN while our method does not have this problem.

DW Dataset. Digital Wardrobe [7] includes registered clothed body meshes with real texture under more general posture. We use 94 meshes to compare with non-parametric methods PIFu [43] and DeepHuman [57][1]. Table 2 shows the results. For PIFu with single image input, our method can get similar reconstruction accuracy. However, the reconstructed results by PIFu combine both shapes in one mesh without semantic information, while our method can fully control the predicted separate body and cloth meshes. The results of DeepHuman tend to bend the leg, which introduces large errors for this dataset. The right part of Fig. 6 shows an example of the results.

Fig. 7. The left part: reconstructed body and garment shapes by our method on four images of our test set. The right part: qualitative comparison between the results of MGN [7] without post-optimization and ours. In each group, the input image, result of MGN, and ours are displayed respectively.

5.3 Qualitative Results

In this following, we show some visual results of our method and the comparison with MGN. As our method can reconstruct the body and garments separately, garment transfer between two input images can be achieved. Some garment transfer results are given in the supplementary.

---

[1] We did not test [7,38] on this dataset as most of the samples are not A-pose.

Reconstruction Quality. In the left part of Fig. 7, we present our reconstructed body and garments shapes on several test images. Our method can recover accurate body posture and capture the garment geometry to some extent from a single input image. Thanks to our separated garment representation with adaptive skinning weights, we can reconstruct plausible shape for loose garments with large edges.

Comparison with MGN. As a template-based method, MGN [7] is the most relevant prior method with ours. MGN represents garment by binding the garment to SMPL vertices and uses a mask to select valid vertices for a specific garment type. MGN needs multi semantic segmentation images as input and constrains the posture to rough A-pose. Besides, MGN needs a time-consuming post-optimization step to refine the predicted result. Differently, Our method only requires one frontal view image with arbitrary posture and directly produces the final results from the network. In the right part of Fig. 7, we show two qualitative comparisons with MGN. Our method can generate more accurate body shape and size of garments, while the results of MGN without post-optimization have similar shapes for different inputs and lack garment details.

6   Conclusion

We introduced BCNet, a novel method to automatically reconstruct both body and garment shapes from a single RGB image. Rather than binding garment with SMPL like prior SMPL+D based representation, our proposed model can produce layered garments with different topology and skinning weights, which makes BCNet a model capable of jointly reconstructing body and loose garment, like skirts. To train BCNet, we designed a complete algorithm pipeline to generate clothed body data. Experiments demonstrated that our method can generate comparable or better reconstruction results compared with state-of-the-art methods, while allowing more flexible controls such as garment transfer. Our constructed dataset and our proposed BCNet would push a step for the research on digitizing human.

References

1. Alldieck, T., Magnor, M., Bhatnagar, B.L., Theobalt, C., Pons-Moll, G.: Learning to reconstruct people in clothing from a single RGB camera. In: IEEE Conference on Computer Vision and Pattern Recognition (CVPR), pp. 1175–1186 (2019)
2. Alldieck, T., Magnor, M., Xu, W., Theobalt, C., Pons-Moll, G.: Detailed human avatars from monocular video. In: International Conference on 3D Vision (3DV), pp. 98–109. IEEE (2018)
3. Alldieck, T., Magnor, M., Xu, W., Theobalt, C., Pons-Moll, G.: Video based reconstruction of 3d people models. In: IEEE Conference on Computer Vision and Pattern Recognition (CVPR), pp. 8387–8397 (2018)

4. Alldieck, T., Pons-Moll, G., Theobalt, C., Magnor, M.: Tex2shape: detailed full human body geometry from a single image. In: IEEE International Conference on Computer Vision (ICCV) (2019)
5. Anguelov, D., Srinivasan, P., Koller, D., Thrun, S., Rodgers, J., Davis, J.: Scape: shape completion and animation of people. In: ACM Transactions on Graphics (TOG), vol. 24, pp. 408–416. ACM (2005)
6. axyz (2019). https://secure.axyz-design.com/
7. Bhatnagar, B.L., Tiwari, G., Theobalt, C., Pons-Moll, G.: Multi-garment net: learning to dress 3D people from images. In: IEEE International Conference on Computer Vision (ICCV) (2019)
8. Blender (2019). https://www.blender.org/
9. Bogo, F., Kanazawa, A., Lassner, C., Gehler, P., Romero, J., Black, M.J.: Keep it SMPL: automatic estimation of 3D human pose and shape from a single image. In: Leibe, B., Matas, J., Sebe, N., Welling, M. (eds.) ECCV 2016. LNCS, vol. 9909, pp. 561–578. Springer, Cham (2016). https://doi.org/10.1007/978-3-319-46454-1_34
10. Bouritsas, G., Bokhnyak, S., Ploumpis, S., Bronstein, M., Zafeiriou, S.: Neural 3D morphable models: spiral convolutional networks for 3D shape representation learning and generation. In: Proceedings of the IEEE International Conference on Computer Vision, pp. 7213–7222 (2019)
11. Cimpoi, M., Maji, S., Kokkinos, I., Mohamed, S., Vedaldi, A.: Describing textures in the wild. In: IEEE Conference on Computer Vision and Pattern Recognition (CVPR), pp. 3606–3613 (2014)
12. Daněřek, R., Dibra, E., Öztireli, C., Ziegler, R., Gross, M.: Deepgarment: 3D garment shape estimation from a single image. In: Computer Graphics Forum, vol. 36, pp. 269–280. Wiley Online Library (2017)
13. De Aguiar, E., Sigal, L., Treuille, A., Hodgins, J.K.: Stable spaces for real-time clothing. ACM Trans. Graph. (TOG) 29(4), 1–9 (2010)
14. Dibra, E., Jain, H., Oztireli, C., Ziegler, R., Gross, M.: Human shape from silhouettes using generative HKS descriptors and cross-modal neural networks. In: IEEE Conference on Computer Vision and Pattern Recognition (CVPR), pp. 4826–4836 (2017)
15. Flex, N.: 2019. https://developer.nvidia.com/flex/
16. Gong, K., Liang, X., Li, Y., Chen, Y., Yang, M., Lin, L.: Instance-level human parsing via part grouping network. In: Proceedings of the European Conference on Computer Vision (ECCV), pp. 770–785 (2018)
17. Guan, P., Reiss, L., Hirshberg, D.A., Weiss, A., Black, M.J.: Drape: dressing any person. ACM Trans. Graph. (TOG) 31(4), 1–35 (2012)
18. Gundogdu, E., Constantin, V., Seifoddini, A., Dang, M., Salzmann, M., Fua, P.: Garnet: A two-stream network for fast and accurate 3D cloth draping. In: IEEE International Conference on Computer Vision (ICCV), pp. 8739–8748 (2019)
19. He, K., Zhang, X., Ren, S., Sun, J.: Deep residual learning for image recognition. In: IEEE Conference on Computer Vision and Pattern Recognition (CVPR), pp. 770–778 (2016)
20. Jackson, A.S., Manafas, C., Tzimiropoulos, G.: 3D human body reconstruction from a single image via volumetric regression. In: European Conference on Computer Vision (ECCV), (2018)
21. Jiang, B., Zhang, J., Cai, J., Zheng, J.: Learning 3D human body embedding. arXiv preprint arXiv:1905.05622 (2019)

22. Kampouris, C., Zafeiriou, S., Ghosh, A., Malassiotis, S.: Fine-grained material classification using micro-geometry and reflectance. In: Leibe, B., Matas, J., Sebe, N., Welling, M. (eds.) ECCV 2016. LNCS, vol. 9909, pp. 778–792. Springer, Cham (2016). https://doi.org/10.1007/978-3-319-46454-1_47

23. Kanazawa, A., Black, M.J., Jacobs, D.W., Malik, J.: End-to-end recovery of human shape and pose. In: IEEE Conference on Computer Vision and Pattern Recognition (CVPR), pp. 7122–7131 (2018)

24. Kanazawa, A., Zhang, J.Y., Felsen, P., Malik, J.: Learning 3D human dynamics from video. In: IEEE Conference on Computer Vision and Pattern Recognition (CVPR), pp. 5614–5623 (2019)

25. Kato, H., Ushiku, Y., Harada, T.: Neural 3d mesh renderer. In: IEEE Conference on Computer Vision and Pattern Recognition (CVPR), pp. 3907–3916 (2018)

26. Lahner, Z., Cremers, D., Tung, T.: Deepwrinkles: accurate and realistic clothing modeling. In: Proceedings of the European Conference on Computer Vision (ECCV), pp. 667–684 (2018)

27. Lassner, C., Romero, J., Kiefel, M., Bogo, F., Black, M.J., Gehler, P.V.: Unite the people: Closing the loop between 3D and 2D human representations. In: IEEE Conference on Computer Vision and Pattern Recognition (CVPR), pp. 6050–6059 (2017)

28. Liang, J., Lin, M.C.: Shape-aware human pose and shape reconstruction using multi-view images. In: The IEEE International Conference on Computer Vision (ICCV) (2019)

29. Liu, J., Akhtar, N., Mian, A.: Temporally coherent full 3D mesh human pose recovery from monocular video. arXiv preprint arXiv:1906.00161 (2019)

30. Liu, L., Zheng, Y., Tang, D., Yuan, Y., Fan, C., Zhou, K.: Neuroskinning: automatic skin binding for production characters with deep graph networks. ACM Trans. Graph. (TOG) 38(4), 114 (2019)

31. Loper, M., Mahmood, N., Black, M.J.: Mosh: motion and shape capture from sparse markers. ACM Trans. Graph. (TOG) 33(6), 220 (2014)

32. Loper, M., Mahmood, N., Romero, J., Pons-Moll, G., Black, M.J.: Smpl: a skinned multi-person linear model. ACM Trans. Graph. (TOG) 34(6), 248 (2015)

33. Mixamo (2019). https://www.mixamo.com/

34. Mocap, C.: 2019. http://mocap.cs.cmu.edu/

35. Natsume, R., Saito, S., Huang, Z., Chen, W., Ma, C., Li, H., Morishima, S.: Siclope: silhouette-based clothed people. In: IEEE Conference on Computer Vision and Pattern Recognition (CVPR), pp. 4480–4490 (2019)

36. Omran, M., Lassner, C., Pons-Moll, G., Gehler, P., Schiele, B.: Neural body fitting: unifying deep learning and model based human pose and shape estimation. In: International Conference on 3D Vision (3DV), pp. 484–494. IEEE (2018)

37. Pavlakos, G., et al.: Expressive body capture: 3D hands, face, and body from a single image. In: IEEE Conference on Computer Vision and Pattern Recognition (CVPR), pp. 10975–10985 (2019)

38. Pavlakos, G., Zhu, L., Zhou, X., Daniilidis, K.: Learning to estimate 3D human pose and shape from a single color image. In: IEEE Conference on Computer Vision and Pattern Recognition (CVPR), pp. 459–468 (2018)

39. Pons-Moll, G., Pujades, S., Hu, S., Black, M.J.: Clothcap: seamless 4D clothing capture and retargeting. ACM Trans. Graph. (TOG) 36(4), 1–15 (2017)

40. Pumarola, A., Sanchez, J., Choi, G., Sanfeliu, A., Moreno-Noguer, F.: 3D people: modeling the geometry of dressed humans. In: IEEE International Conference on Computer Vision (ICCV) (2019)

41. Qi, C.R., Su, H., Mo, K., Guibas, L.J.: Pointnet: deep learning on point sets for 3D classification and segmentation. In: IEEE Conference on Computer Vision and Pattern Recognition (CVPR), pp. 652–660 (2017)
42. Renderpeople (2019). https://renderpeople.com/3d-people
43. Saito, S., Huang, Z., Natsume, R., Morishima, S., Kanazawa, A., Li, H.: Pifu: pixel-aligned implicit function for high-resolution clothed human digitization. In: IEEE International Conference on Computer Vision (ICCV) (2019)
44. Santesteban, I., Otaduy, M.A., Casas, D.: Learning-based animation of clothing for virtual try-on. In: Computer Graphics Forum, vol. 38, pp. 355–366. Wiley Online Library (2019)
45. Sorkine, O.: Laplacian mesh processing. In: Eurographics - State of the Art Reports, pp. 53–70 (2005)
46. Varol, G., et al.: Bodynet: volumetric inference of 3D human body shapes. In: European Conference on Computer Vision (ECCV), pp. 20–36 (2018)
47. Varol, G., et al.: Learning from synthetic humans. In: IEEE Conference on Computer Vision and Pattern Recognition (CVPR), pp. 109–117 (2017)
48. Velickovic, P., Cucurull, G., Casanova, A., Romero, A., Liò, P., Bengio, Y.: Graph attention networks. In: International Conference on Learning Representations, ICLR (2018)
49. Wang, T.Y., Ceylan, D., Popovic, J., Mitra, N.J.: Learning a shared shape space for multimodal garment design. ACM Trans. Graph. (TOG) 37(6), 203:1–203:13 (2018)
50. Xu, W., Umentani, N., Chao, Q., Mao, J., Jin, X., Tong, X.: Sensitivity-optimized rigging for example-based real-time clothing synthesis. ACM Trans. Graph. (TOG) 33(4), 107 (2014)
51. Yang, J., Franco, J.S., Hétroy-Wheeler, F., Wuhrer, S.: Analyzing clothing layer deformation statistics of 3D human motions. In: Proceedings of the European Conference on Computer Vision (ECCV), pp. 237–253 (2018)
52. Yang, S., et al.: Physics-inspired garment recovery from a single-view image. ACM Trans. Graph. (TOG) 37(5), 170 (2018)
53. Yang, Y., Yu, Y., Zhou, Y., Du, S., Davis, J., Yang, R.: Semantic parametric reshaping of human body models. In: International Conference on 3D Vision (3DV), vol. 2, pp. 41–48. IEEE (2014)
54. Yao, P., Fang, Z., Wu, F., Feng, Y., Li, J.: Densebody: directly regressing dense 3D human pose and shape from a single color image. arXiv preprint arXiv:1903.10153 (2019)
55. Yu, T., et al.: Simulcap: Single-view human performance capture with cloth simulation. arXiv preprint arXiv:1903.06323 (2019)
56. Zhang, C., Pujades, S., Black, M.J., Pons-Moll, G.: Detailed, accurate, human shape estimation from clothed 3D scan sequences. In: IEEE Conference on Computer Vision and Pattern Recognition (CVPR), pp. 4191–4200 (2017)
57. Zheng, Z., Yu, T., Wei, Y., Dai, Q., Liu, Y.: Deephuman: 3D human reconstruction from a single image. In: IEEE International Conference on Computer Vision (ICCV) (2019)
58. Zhou, B., Lapedriza, A., Khosla, A., Oliva, A., Torralba, A.: Places: a 10 million image database for scene recognition. IEEE Trans. Pattern Anal. Mach. Intell. 40(6), 1452–1464 (2017)
59. Zhu, H., Zuo, X., Wang, S., Cao, X., Yang, R.: Detailed human shape estimation from a single image by hierarchical mesh deformation. In: IEEE Conference on Computer Vision and Pattern Recognition (CVPR), pp. 4491–4500 (2019)

Self-supervised Keypoint Correspondences for Multi-person Pose Estimation and Tracking in Videos

Umer Rafi[1], Andreas Doering[1(✉)], Bastian Leibe[2], and Juergen Gall[1]

[1] University of Bonn, Bonn, Germany
doering@iai.uni-bonn.de
[2] RWTH Aachen, Aachen, Germany

Abstract. Video annotation is expensive and time consuming. Consequently, datasets for multi-person pose estimation and tracking are less diverse and have more sparse annotations compared to large scale image datasets for human pose estimation. This makes it challenging to learn deep learning based models for associating keypoints across frames that are robust to nuisance factors such as motion blur and occlusions for the task of multi-person pose tracking. To address this issue, we propose an approach that relies on keypoint correspondences for associating persons in videos. Instead of training the network for estimating keypoint correspondences on video data, it is trained on a large scale image dataset for human pose estimation using self-supervision. Combined with a top-down framework for human pose estimation, we use keypoint correspondences to (i) recover missed pose detections and to (ii) associate pose detections across video frames. Our approach achieves state-of-the-art results for multi-frame pose estimation and multi-person pose tracking on the PoseTrack 2017 and 2018 datasets.

1 Introduction

Human pose estimation is a very active research field in computer vision that is relevant for many applications like computer games, security, sports, and autonomous driving. Over the years, the human pose estimation models have been greatly improved [4,7,12,23,25,32,42] due to the availability of large scale image datasets for human pose estimation [2,27,41]. More recently, researchers started to tackle the more challenging problem of multi-person pose tracking [19,20,38,42,46].

In multi-person pose tracking, the goal is to estimate human poses in all frames of a video and associate them over time. However, video annotations are

---

U. Rafi and A. Doering—Equal contribution.

Electronic supplementary material The online version of this chapter (https://doi.org/10.1007/978-3-030-58565-5_3) contains supplementary material, which is available to authorized users.

A. Vedaldi et al. (Eds.): ECCV 2020, LNCS 12365, pp. 36–52, 2020.
https://doi.org/10.1007/978-3-030-58565-5_3

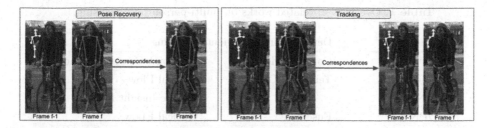

Fig. 1. Our contributions: (Left) We use keypoint correspondences to recover missed pose detections by using the temporal context of the previous frame. (Right) We use keypoint correspondences to associate detected and recovered pose detections for the task of multi-person pose tracking.

costly and time consuming. Consequently, recently proposed video datasets [1] are less diverse and are sparsely annotated as compared to large scale image datasets for human pose estimation [27,41]. This makes it challenging to learn deep networks for associating human keypoints across frames that are robust to nuisance factors such as motion blur, fast motions, and occlusions as they occur in videos.

State-of-the-art approaches [14,38,42] rely on optical flow or person re-identification [46] in order to track the persons. Both approaches, however, have disadvantages. Optical flow fails if a person becomes occluded which results in a lost track. While person re-identification allows to associate persons even if they disappeared for a long time, it remains difficult to associate partially occluded persons with person re-identification models that operate on bounding boxes of the full person. Moreover, the limited annotations in pose tracking datasets require to train the models on additional datasets for person re-identification.

We therefore propose to learn a network that infers keypoint correspondences for multiple persons. The correspondence network comprises a Siamese matching module that takes a frame with estimated human poses as input and estimates the corresponding poses for a second frame. Such an approach has the advantage that it is not limited to a fixed temporal frame distance, and it allows to track persons when they are partially occluded. Our goal is to utilize keypoint correspondences to recover missed poses of a top-down human pose estimator, e.g., due to partial occlusion, and to utilize keypoint correspondences for multi-person tracking. The challenge, however, is to train such a network due to the sparsely annotated video datasets. In fact, in this work we consider the extreme case where the network is not trained on any video data or a dataset where identities of persons are annotated. Instead we show that such a network can be trained on an image dataset for multi-person pose estimation [27]. Besides of the human pose annotations, which are anyway needed to train the human pose estimator, the approach does not require any additional supervision. In order to improve the keypoint associations, we propose an additional refinement module that refines the affinity maps of the Siamese matching module.

Table 1. Overview of related works on multi-person pose tracking.

Method	Detection improvement	Tracking
Ours	Correspondences	Keypoint Correspondences
HRNet [38]	Temporal OKS	Optical Flow
POINet [36]	-	Ovonic Insight Net
MDPN [14]	Ensemble	Optical FLow
LightTrack [33]	Ensemble/BBox Prop	GCN
ProTracker [13]	-	IoU
STAF [35]	-	ST Fields
ST Embeddings [21]	-	ST Embeddings
JointFlow [11]	-	Flow Fields

To summarize, the contributions of the paper are:

- We propose an approach for multi-frame pose estimation and multi-person pose tracking that relies on self-supervised keypoint correspondences which are learned from a large scale image dataset with human pose annotations.
- Combined with a top-down pose estimation framework, we use keypoint correspondences in two ways as illustrated in Fig. 1: We use keypoint correspondences to (i) recover pose detections that have been missed by the top-down pose estimation framework and to (ii) associate detected and recovered poses in different frames of a video.
- We evaluate the approach on the PoseTrack 2017 and 2018 datasets for the tasks of multi-frame pose estimation and multi-person pose tracking. Our approach achieves state-of-the-art results without using any additional training data except of [27] for the proposed correspondence network.

2 Related Work

Multi-person Pose Estimation. Multi-person pose estimation can be categorized into top-down and bottom-up approaches. Bottom-up based methods [7,16,23,30,32] first detect all person keypoints simultaneously and then associate them to their corresponding person instances. For example, Chao *et al.* [7] predict part affinity fields which provide information about the location and orientation of the limbs. For the association, a greedy approach is used. More recently, Kocabas *et al.* [23] propose to detect bounding boxes and pose keypoints within the same neural network. In the first stage, bounding box predictions are used to crop from predicted keypoint heatmaps. As a second stage, a pose residual module is proposed, which regresses the respective keypoint locations of each person instance.

Top-down methods [8,25,29,31,42,44,44] utilize person detectors and estimate the pose on each image crop individually. In contrast to bottom-up methods, top-down approaches do not suffer from scale variations. For example, Xiao *et al.* [42] propose a simple yet strong model based on a ResNet152 [17] and achieve state-of-the-art performance by replacing the last fully connected layer by three transposed convolutions. Li *et al.* [25] propose an information propagation procedure within a multi-stage architecture based on four ResNet50 networks [17] with coarse-to-fine supervision.

Multi-frame Pose Estimation. In video data, such as PoseTrack [1], related works [4,14,43] leverage temporal information of neighboring frames to increase robustness against fast motions, occlusion, and motion blur. Xiu *et al.* [43] and Guo *et al.* [14] utilize optical flow to warp preceding frames into the current frame. Recently, Bertasius *et al.* [4] propose a feature warping method based on deformable convolutions to warp pose heatmaps from preceding and subsequent frames into the current frame. While they show that they are able to learn from sparse video annotations, they do not address multi-person pose tracking.

Multi-person Pose Tracking. Early works for multi-person pose tracking [19,20] build spatio-temporal graphs which are solved by integer linear programming. Since such approaches are computationally expensive, researchers reduced the task to bipartite graphs which are solved in a greedy fashion [11,13,14,21, 33,35,36,38,43]. Girdhar *et al.* [13] propose a 3D Mask R-CNN [16] to generate person tubelets for tracking which are associated greedily. More recent works [14,38,42,46] incorporate temporal information by using optical flow. Xiao *et al.* [42] rely on optical flow to recover missed person detections and propose an optical-flow based similarity metric for tracking. In contrast, Zhang *et al.* [46] builds on [13] and propose an adapted Mask R-CNN [16] with a greedy bounding box generation strategy. Furthermore, optical flow and a person re-identification module are combined for tracking. Jin *et al.* [21] perform multi-person pose estimation and tracking within a unified framework based on human pose embeddings. Table 1 provides a summary of the contributions of the recent related works.

Correspondences. In recent years, deep learning has been successfully applied to the task of correspondence matching [9,15,22], including the task of visual object tracking (VOT) [5,24,47,48]. All of the above approaches establish correspondences at object level. In contrast, our approach establishes correspondences at instance level. Moreover, VOT tasks assume a ground truth object location for the first frame, which is in contrast to the task of pose tracking.

Self-supervised Learning. Self-supervised learning approaches [26,40] have been proposed for establishing correspondences at patch and keypoints level from videos. However, these approaches use videos for learning and process a single set of keypoints or patch at a time. In contrast, our approach establishes correspondences for multiple instances and is trained on single images.

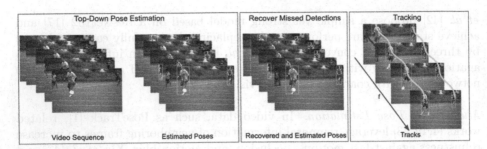

Fig. 2. Given a sequence of frames, we detect a set of person bounding boxes and perform top-down pose estimation. Our proposed method uses keypoint correspondences to (i) recover missed detections and (ii) to associate detected and recovered poses to perform tracking. The entire framework does not require any video data for training since the network for estimating keypoint correspondences is trained on single images using self-supervision.

3   Method Overview

In this work, we propose a multi-person pose tracking framework that is robust to motion blur and severe occlusions, even though it does not need any video data for training. As it is illustrated in Fig. 2, we first estimate for each frame the human poses and then track them. For multi-person human pose estimation, we utilize an off-the-shelf object detector [6] to obtain a set of bounding boxes for the persons in each frame. For each bounding box, we then perform multi-person pose estimation in a top-down fashion by training an adapted GoogleNet [39], which we will discuss in Sect. 6.1.

In order to be robust to motion blur and severe occlusions, we do not use optical flow in contrast to previous works like [42]. Instead we propose a network that estimates for a given frame with estimated keypoints the locations of the keypoints in another frame. We use this network for recovering human poses that have been missed by the top-down pose estimation framework as described in Sect. 5.1 and for associating detected and recovered poses across the video as described in Sect. 5.2.

The main challenge for the keypoint correspondence network is the handling of occluded keypoints and the limited amount of densely annotated video data. In order to address these issues, we do not train the network on video data, but on single images using self-supervision. In this way, we can simulate disappearing keypoints by truncation and leverage large scale image dataset like MS-COCO [27] for tracking. We will first describe the keypoint correspondence network in Sect. 4 and then discuss the tracking framework in Sect. 5.

4   Keypoint Correspondence Network

Given two images I_1 and I_2 with keypoints $\{j^p\}_{1:N_p}$ for all persons p in image I_1, our goal is to find the corresponding keypoints in I_2. Towards this end, we

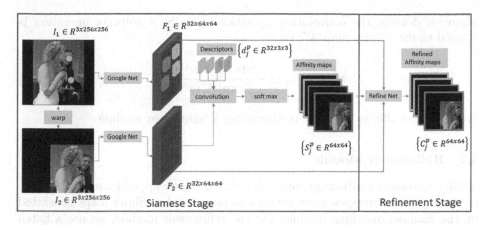

Fig. 3. Keypoint correspondence network. The Siamese network takes images I_1 and I_2 and keypoints $\{j^p\}_{1:N_p}$ for all persons p in image I_1 as input and generates the feature maps F_1 and F_2, respectively. The keypoints of the different persons are shown in green and yellow, respectively. For each keypoint, a descriptor d_j^p is extracted from F_1 and convolved with the feature map F_2 to generate an affinity map S_j^p. In order to improve the affinity maps for each person, the refinement network takes F_1, F_2 and the affinity maps S_j^p for person p as input and generates refined affinity maps C_j^p.

use a Siamese network as shown in Fig. 3 which estimates for each keypoint an affinity map. The affinity maps are further improved by the refinement module, which is described in Sect. 4.2.

4.1   Siamese Matching Module

The keypoint correspondence network consists of a Siamese network. Each branch in the Siamese network is a batch normalized GoogleNet up to layer 17 with shared parameters [39]. The Siamese network takes an image pair (I_1, I_2) and keypoints $\{j^p\}_{1:N_p}$ for persons $p \in \{1,\ldots,P\}$ in the image I_1 as input. During training, I_2 is generated by applying a randomly sampled affine warp to I_1. In this way, we do not need any annotated correspondences during training or pairs of images, but train the network on single images with annotated poses. We use an image resolution of 256×256 for both images.

The Siamese network generates features $F_1 \in \mathbb{R}^{32 \times 64 \times 64}$ and $F_2 \in \mathbb{R}^{32 \times 64 \times 64}$ for images I_1 and I_2, respectively. The features are then pixel-wise l_2 normalized and local descriptors $d_j^p \in R^{32 \times 3 \times 3}$ are generated for each keypoint j^p by extracting squared patches around the spatial position of a keypoint in the feature maps F_1.

Given a local descriptor d_j^p, we compute its affinity map A_j^p over all pixels $x = \{1,\ldots,64\}$ and $y = \{1,\ldots,64\}$ in F_2 as:

$$A_j^p = d_j^p \circledast F_2 \tag{1}$$

where ⊛ denotes the convolution operation. Finally, a softmax operation is applied to the affinity map A_j^p, i.e.,

$$S_j^p(x, y) = \frac{\exp(A_j^p(x, y))}{\sum_{x', y'} \exp(A_j^p(x', y'))}. \tag{2}$$

We refine the affinity maps S_j^p further using a refinement module.

4.2 Refinement Module

Similar to related multi-stage approaches [7,10,23], we append a second module to the keypoint correspondence network to improve the affinity maps generated by the Siamese matching module. For the refinement module, we use a batch normalized GoogleNet from layer 3 till layer 17. The refinement module concatenates F_1, F_2, and the affinity maps $\{S_j^p\}_{1:N_p}$ for a single person p and refines the affinity maps, which we denote by $C_j^p \in \mathbb{R}^{64 \times 64}$. The refinement module is therefore applied to the affinity maps for all persons $p \in \{1, \ldots, P\}$. Before we describe in Sect. 5 how we will use the affinity maps for tracking C_j^p, we describe how the keypoint correspondence network is trained.

4.3 Training

Since we train our network using self-supervision, we train it using a single image I_1 with annotated poses. We generate a second image I_2 by applying a randomly sampled affine warp to I_1. We then generate the ground-truth affinity map G_j^p for a keypoint j^p belonging to person p as:

$$G_j^p(x, y) = \begin{cases} 1 & \text{if } x = \hat{x}_j^p \text{ and } y = \hat{y}_j^p, \\ 0 & \text{otherwise}, \end{cases} \tag{3}$$

where $(\hat{x}_j^p, \hat{y}_j^p)$ is the spatial position of the ground-truth correspondence for keypoint j^p in image I_2, which we know from the affine transformation. As illustrated in Fig. 3, not all corresponding keypoints are present in image I_2. In this case, the ground-truth affinity map is zero and predicting a corresponding keypoint is therefore penalized.

During training, we minimize the binary cross entropy loss between the predicted affinity maps S_j^p and C_j^p and the ground-truth affinity map G_j^p:

$$\min_\theta \sum_{x, y} - \left(G_j^p \log(S_j^p) + (1 - G_j^p)(1 - \log(S_j^p)) \right), \tag{4}$$

$$\min_\theta \sum_{x, y} - \left(G_j^p \log(C_j^p) + (1 - G_j^p)(1 - \log(C_j^p)) \right), \tag{5}$$

where θ are the parameters of the keypoint correspondence framework.

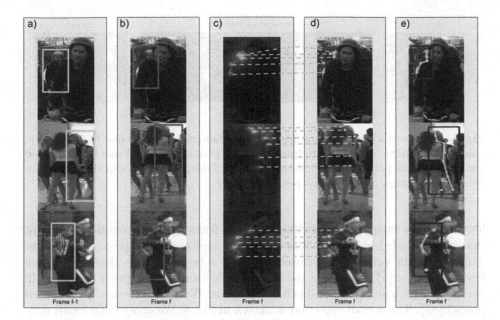

Fig. 4. Recovering missed detections. (a) Person detected by the top-down pose estimation framework in frame $f-1$. (b) Person missed by the top down pose estimation framework in frame f due to occlusion. (c) Keypoint affinity maps of the missed person from frame $f-1$ to frame f. (d) Corresponding keypoints in frame f. (e) Estimated bounding box from the corresponding keypoints and the recovered pose.

5 Multi-person Pose Tracking

We use the keypoint correspondence network in two ways. First, we use it to recover human poses that have been missed by the frame-wise top-down multi-person pose estimation step, which will be described in Sect. 5.1. Second, we use keypoint correspondences for tracking poses across frames of the video as described in Sect. 5.2.

5.1 Recover Missed Detections

For a given frame f, we first detect the human poses in the frame using the top-down multi-person pose estimator described in Sect. 6.1. While the person detector [6] performs well, it fails in situations with overlapping persons and motion blur. Consequently, the human pose is not estimated in these cases. Examples are shown in Fig. 4(b).

Given the detected human poses $J_{f-1}^p = \{j_{f-1}^p\}$ for persons $p \in \{1, \ldots, P\}$ in frame $f-1$, we compute the corresponding refined affinity maps $C^p = \{C_j^p\}$ by using the keypoint correspondence network. For each keypoint j_{f-1}^p, we then get the corresponding keypoint $\bar{j}_f^p$ in frame f by taking the argmax of C_j^p and mapping it to the image resolution. Since the resolution of the affinity maps is

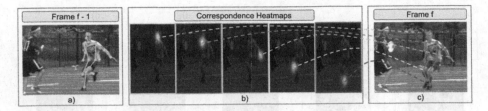

Fig. 5. Pose to track association. (a) A tracked human pose till frame $f-1$. (b) Keypoint affinity maps of the track to frame f. (c) A pose instance of frame f. The dashed lines indicate the position of each detected joint of the pose instance in the correspondence affinity maps of the tracked pose in frame $f-1$.

lower than the image resolution and since the frame f might contain a keypoint that was occluded in the previous frame, we reestimate the propagated poses. This is done by computing for each person p a bounding box that encloses all keypoints $\bar{J}_f^p = \{\bar{j}_f^p\}$ and using the human pose estimation network described in Sect. 6.1 to get a new pose for this bounding box. We denote the newly estimated poses by $\hat{J}_f^p$. The overall procedure is shown in Fig. 4. We apply OKS based non-maximum suppression [42] to discard redundant poses.

5.2   Tracking

Given detected and recovered poses, we need to link them across video frames to obtain tracks of human poses. Tracking can be seen as a data association problem over estimated poses. Previously, the problem has been approached using bipartite graph matching [13] or greedy approaches [11,38,42]. In this work, we greedily associate estimated poses over time by using the keypoint correspondences. We initialize tracks on the first frame and then associate new candidate poses to intial tracks one frame at a time.

Formally, our goal is to assign pose instances $\{B_f^p\} = \{J_f^p\} \cup \{\hat{J}_f^p\}$ in frame f for persons $p \in \{1, \ldots P\}$ to tracks $\{T_{f-1}^q\}$ till frame $f-1$ for persons $q \in \{1, \ldots Q\}$. Towards this end, we measure the similarity between a pose instance B_f^p and a track T_{f-1}^q as:

$$S(T_{f-1}^q, B_f^p) = \frac{\sum_{j=1}^{N_q} C_j^q(j_f^p) \cdot \mathbb{I}_{C_j^q(j_f^p) > \tau_{corr}}}{\sum_{j=1}^{N_q} \mathbb{I}_{C_j^q(j_f^p) > \tau_{corr}}}, \qquad (6)$$

where C_j^q is the affinity map of the keypoint j in track T_{f-1}^q for frame f. The affinity map is computed by the network described in Sect. 4. $C_j^q(j_f^p)$ is the confidence value in the affinity map C_j^q at the location of the joint j_f^p for person p in frame f. N_q is the number of detected joints. An example is shown in Fig. 5. We only consider j_f^p if its affinity is above τ_{corr}. If a pose B_f^p cannot be matched to a track T_{f-1}^q, a new track is initiated.

6   Experiments and Results

We evaluate our approach on the Posetrack 2017 and 2018 datasets [1]. The datasets have 292 and 593 videos for training and 214 and 375 videos for evaluation, respectively. We evaluate multi-frame pose estimation and tracking results using the mAP and MOTA evaluation metrics.

6.1   Implementation Details

We provide additional implementation details for our top-down pose estimation and keypoint correspondence network below.

Top-down Pose Estimation. We use a top-down framework for frame level pose estimation. We use cascade R-CNN [6] for person detection and extract crops of size 384×288 around detected persons as input to our pose estimation framework, which consists of two stages. Each stage is a batch normalized GoogleNet [39]. The backbone in the first stage consists of layer 1 to layer 17 while the second backbone consists of layer 3 to layer 17 only. Both stages predict pose heatmaps and joint offset maps for the cropped person as in [46]. We use the pose heatmaps in combination with the joint offsets from the second stage as our pose detections. The number of parameters (39.5 M) of our model is significantly lower compared to related works such as FlowTrack [42] (63.6 M) or EOGN [46] (60.3 M).

We train the pose estimation framework on the MS-COCO dataset [27] for 260 epochs with a base learning rate of $1e^{-3}$. The learning rate is reduced to $1e^{-4}$ after 200 epochs. During training we apply random flippings and rotations to input crops. We finetune the pose estimation framework on the PoseTrack 2017 dataset [1] for 12 epochs. The learning rate is further reduced to $1e^{-5}$ after epoch 7.

Keypoint Correspondence Network. We perform module-wise training. We first train the Siamese module. We then fix the Siamese module and train the refinement module. Both modules are trained for 100 epochs with base learning rate of $1e^{-4}$ reduced to $1e^{-5}$ after 50 epochs. We generate a second image for each training image by applying random translations, rotations, and flippings to the first image. The keypoint correspondence network is trained only on the MS-COCO dataset [27]. We did not observe any improvements in our tracking results by finetuning the correspondence model on the PoseTrack dataset. Training only on the PoseTrack dataset yielded sub-optimal tracking results since PoseTrack is sparsely annotated and contains far less person instances than MS-COCO.

6.2   Baselines

We compare our keypoint correspondence tracking to different standard tracking baselines for multi-person pose tracking as reported in Table 2. To measure the performance of each baseline, we report the number of identity switches and the MOTA score. For a fair comparison, we replace the keypoint correspondences

Table 2. Comparison with tracking baselines on the PoseTrack 2017 validation set. For the comparison, the detected poses based on ground-truth bounding boxes (GT Boxes) or detected bounding boxes are the same for each approach. Correspondence based tracking consistently improves MOTA compared to the baselines and significantly reduces the number of identity switches (IDSW).

Tracking method	GT Boxes	IDSW	MOTA
OKS	✓	6582	65.9
Optical Flow	✓	4419	68.4
Re-ID	✓	4164	67.1
Correspondences	✓	3583	70.5
OKS	✗	7207	60.4
Optical Flow	✗	5611	66.7
Re-ID	✗	4589	64.1
Correspondences	✗	3632	67.9

in our framework by different baselines. For all experiments, we use the same detected poses using either ground truth or detected bounding boxes.

OKS. OKS without taking the motion of the poses into account has been proposed in [42]. OKS measures the similarity between two poses and is independent of their appearance. It is not robust to large motion, occlusion, and large temporal offsets. This is reflected in Table 2 as this baseline achieves the lowest performance.

Optical Flow. Optical flow is a temporal baseline that has been proposed in [42]. We use optical flow to warp the poses from the previous frame to the current frame. We then apply OKS for associating the warped poses with candidate poses in the current frame. We use the pre-trained PWC-net [37] as done in [37] for a fair comparison. Optical flow clearly outperforms OKS and achieves superior MOTA of 68.4 and 66.7 for GT and detected bounding boxes, respectively.

Person Re-id. Compared to optical flow and OKS, person re-identification is more robust to larger temporal offsets and large motion. However, the achieved results indicate that person re-identification operating on the bounding boxes performs sub-optimally under the frequent partial occlusions in the PoseTrack datasets. For our experiments, we use the pre-trained re-identification model from [28]. Re-identification based tracking achieves MOTA scores of 67.1 and 64.1 for GT and detected bounding boxes, respectively.

The results show that correspondence based tracking (1) achieves a consistent improvement over the baselines for ground-truth and detected bounding boxes with MOTA scores of 70.5 and 67.9, respectively, and (2) significantly reduces the number of identity switches. Compared to optical flow, correspondences are more robust to partial occlusions, motion blur, and large motions. A qualitative comparison is provided in Sect. 6.5.

Table 3. Effect of joint detection threshold and pose recovery on mAP and MOTA for the PoseTrack 2018 validation set. The results are shown for (left) detected poses only and (right) detected and recovered poses. As expected, recovering missed detections improves both MOTA and mAP. A good trade-off between mAP and MOTA is achieved by the joint detection threshold 0.3.

Joint threshold	mAP	MOTA	Joint threshold	mAP	MOTA
Detected Poses Only			Detected and Recovered Poses.		
0.0	80.1	48.1	0	82.0	48.1
0.1	79.7	63.3	0.1	81.4	64.1
0.2	78.9	66.1	0.2	80.5	67.2
0.3	**77.7**	**67.6**	**0.3**	**79.2**	**68.8**
0.4	75.9	68.0	0.4	77.2	69.2
0.5	73.1	67.1	0.5	74.2	68.2

Table 4. Comparison to the state-of-the-art on the PoseTrack 2017 and 2018 validation set for multi-frame pose estimation.

Dataset	Method	Head	Shoulder	Elbow	Wrist	Hip	Knee	Ankle	mAP
PoseTrack 17 Val Set	DetectNTrack [13]	72.8	75.6	65.3	54.3	63.5	60.9	51.8	64.1
	PoseFlow [43]	66.7	73.3	68.3	61.1	67.5	67.0	61.3	66.5
	FlowTrack [42]	81.7	83.4	80.0	72.4	75.3	74.8	67.1	76.7
	HRNet [38]	82.1	83.6	80.4	73.3	75.5	75.3	68.5	77.3
	MDPN [14]	85.2	88.5	83.9	78.0	82.4	80.5	73.6	80.7
	PoseWarper [4]	81.4	88.3	83.9	78.0	82.4	!80.5	73.6	**81.2**
	Ours	86.1	87.0	83.4	76.4	77.3	79.2	73.3	80.8
PoseTrack 18 Val Set	PoseFlow [43]	63.9	78.7	77.4	71.0	73.7	73.0	69.7	71.9
	MDPN [14]	75.4	81.2	79.0	74.1	72.4	73.0	69.9	75.0
	PoseWarper [4]	79.9	86.3	82.4	77.5	79.8	78.8	73.2	79.7
	Ours	86.0	87.3	84.8	78.3	79.1	81.1	75.6	**82.0**

6.3 Effect of Joint Detection Threshold and Pose Recovery

We evaluate the impact of different joint detection thresholds on mAP and MOTA for the PoseTrack 2018 dataset as shown in Table 3. Since mAP does not penalize false-positive keypoints, thresholding decreases the pose estimation performance by discarding low confident joints. Vice versa, joint thresholding results in cleaner tracks and improves the tracking performance, as MOTA penalizes false-positive keypoint detections. A good trade-off between mAP and MOTA is achieved for the joint detection threshold 0.3 resulting in mAP and MOTA of 77.7 and 67.6, respectively.

While on the left hand side of Table 3 we report the results without recovering missed detections as described in Sect. 5.1, the table on the right hand side

Table 5. Comparison to the state-of-the-art on the PoseTrack 2017 and 2018 validation and test sets. Approaches marked with $^+$ use additional external training data. Approaches marked with * do not report results on the official test set

	Approach	mAP	MOTA		Approach	mAP	MOTA
PoseTrack 17 val set	STEmbedding [21]*	77.0	71.8	PoseTrack 18 val set	**Ours + Merge**	**79.2**	**69.1**
	EOGN [46]	76.7	70.1		Ours	79.2	68.8
	PGPT [3]	77.2	68.4		MIPAL [18]	74.6	65.7
	Ours + Merge	**78.0**	**68.3**		LightTrack [33]	71.2	64.9
	Ours	78.0	67.9		Miracle$^+$ [45]	80.9	64.0
	POINet [36]	-	65.9		OpenSVAI [34]	69.7	62.4
	HRNet [38]	77.3	-		STAF [35]	70.4	60.9
	FlowTrack [42]	76.7	65.4				
PoseTrack 17 test set	EOGN [46]	74.8	61.1	PoseTrack 18 test set	MSRA$^+$	74.0	61.4
	PGPT [3]	72.6	60.2		ALG$^+$	74.9	60.8
	Ours + Merge	**74.2**	**60.0**		**Ours + Merge**	**74.4**	**60.7**
	POINet [36]	72.5	58.4		Miracle$^+$ [45]	70.9	57.4
	LightTrack [33]	66.8	58.0		MIPAL [18]	67.8	54.9
	HRNet [38]	75.0	58.0		CV-Human	64.7	54.5
	FlowTrack	74.6	57.8				

shows the impact on mAP and MOTA if missed detections are recovered. The recovering of missed detections improves the accuracy for all thresholds. For the joint detection threshold 0.3, mAP and MOTA are further improved to 79.2 and 68.8, respectively.

6.4   Comparison with State-of-the-Art Methods

We compare to the state-of-the-art for multi-frame pose estimation and multi-person pose tracking on the PoseTrack 2017 and 2018 datasets.

Multi-frame Pose Estimation. For the task of multi-frame pose estimation, we compare to the state-of-the-art on the PoseTrack 2017 and 2018 validation sets, respectively. Although our correspondences are trained without using any video data, our approach outperforms the recently proposed PoseWrapper [4] approach on the PoseTrack 2018 validation set with mAP of 82.0 and achieves very competitive mAP on the PoseTrack 2017 validation set with mAP of 80.8 as shown in Table 4.

Multi-person Pose Tracking. We compare our tracking approach with the state-of-the-art for multi-person pose tracking on the PoseTrack 2017 and 2018 validation sets and leaderboards. In addition, we perform a post-processing step in which we merge broken tracks similar to the recovery of missed detections described in Sect. 5.1. This further improves the tracking performance. For further details we refer to the supplementary material.

We submitted our results to the PoseTrack 2017 and 2018 test servers, respectively. Our approach achieves top scoring MOTA of 60.0 on the PoseTrack 2017 leaderboard without any bells and whistles as shown in Table 5. Our tracking

Fig. 6. Qualitative comparison between optical flow and correspondences for the task of pose warping under occlusion, motion blur, and large motion. (a) Query pose in frame f. (b) Warped pose using optical flow. (c) Warped pose using correspondences. In contrast to optical flow, the correspondences warp the poses correctly despite of occlusions, motion blur, or large motion.

performance is on-par with state-of-the-art approaches on the PoseTrack 2017 validation set.

Similarly, we achieve top scoring MOTA of 69.1 on the PoseTrack 2018 validation set as shown in Table 5. Our tracking results are very competitive to the winning entries on the PoseTrack 2018 leaderboard although the winning entries use additional training data.

6.5 Qualitative Results

We qualitatively compare optical flow and correspondences for the task of pose warping under motion blur, occlusions, and large motion in Fig. 6. While the column on the left hand side shows the query pose in frame f. The columns in the middle and on the right hand side show the warped poses generated by optical flow or correspondences, respectively. In contrast to optical flow, our approach is robust to occlusion and fast human or camera motion. Our approach, however, has also some limitations. For instance, we observe that we obtain sometimes two tracks for the same person if the person detector provides two or more bounding boxes for a person like one bounding box for the upper body and one bounding box for the full body. Examples of failure cases are shown in the supplementary material.

7 Conclusion

In this work, we have proposed a self-supervised keypoint correspondence framework for the tasks of multi-frame pose estimation and multi-person pose tracking. The proposed keypoint correspondence framework solves two tasks: (1) recovering missed detections and (2) associating human poses across video frames for the task of multi-person pose tracking. The proposed approach based on keypoint correspondences outperforms the state-of-the-art for the tasks of multi-frame pose estimation and multi-person pose tracking on the PoseTrack 2017 and 2018 datasets.

Acknowledgment. The work has been funded by the Deutsche Forschungsgemeinschaft (DFG, German Research Foundation) GA 1927/8-1 and the ERC Starting Grant ARCA (677650).

References

1. Andriluka, M., et al.: PoseTrack: a benchmark for human pose estimation and tracking. In: CVPR (2018)
2. Andriluka, M., Pishchulin, L., Gehler, P., Schiele, B.: 2D human pose estimation: new benchmark and state of the art analysis. In: CVPR (2014)
3. Bao, Q., Liu, W., Cheng, Y., Zhou, B., Mei, T.: Pose-guided tracking-by-detection: Robust multi-person pose tracking. IEEE Trans. Multimedia (2020)
4. Bertasius, G., Feichtenhofer, C., Tran, D., Shi, J., Torresani, L.: Learning temporal pose estimation from sparsely-labeled videos. In: NeurIPS (2019)
5. Bertinetto, L., Valmadre, J., Henriques, J.F., Vedaldi, A., Torr, P.H.S.: Fully-convolutional Siamese networks for object tracking. In: Hua, G., Jégou, H. (eds.) ECCV 2016. LNCS, vol. 9914, pp. 850–865. Springer, Cham (2016). https://doi.org/10.1007/978-3-319-48881-3_56
6. Cai, Z., Vasconcelos, N.: Cascade R-CNN: delving into high quality object detection. In: CVPR (2017)
7. Cao, Z., Simon, T., Wei, S.E., Sheikh, Y.: Realtime multi-person 2D pose estimation using part affinity fields. In: CVPR (2017)
8. Chen, Y., Wang, Z., Peng, Y., Zhang, Z., Yu, G., Sun, J.: Cascaded pyramid network for multi-person pose estimation. In: CVPR (2018)
9. Choy, C., Gwak, J., Savarese, S., Chandraker, M.: Universal correspondence network. In: NIPS (2016)
10. Dantone, M., Gall, J., Leistner, C., van Gool, L.: Body parts dependent joint regressors for human pose estimation in still images. TPAMI (2014)
11. Doering, A., Iqbal, U., Gall, J.: Joint flow: Temporal flow fields for multi person tracking. In: BMVC (2018)
12. Felzenszwalb, P.F., Huttenlocher, D.P.: Pictorial structures for object recognition. IJCV (2005)
13. Girdhar, R., Gkioxari, G., Torresani, L., Paluri, M., Tran, D.: Detect-and-track: efficient pose estimation in videos. In: CVPR (2018)
14. Guo, H., Tang, T., Luo, G., Chen, R., Lu, Y., Wen, L.: Multi-domain pose network for multi-person pose estimation and tracking. In: CVPR (2018)
15. Han, K., Rezende, R., Ham, B., Wong, K.Y., Cho, M., Schmid, C., Ponce., J.: Scnet: learning semantic correspondence. In: ICCV (2017)

16. He, K., Gkioxari, G., Dollár, P., Girshick, R.B.: Mask R-CNN. In: ICCV (2017)
17. He, K., Zhang, X., Ren, S., Sun, J.: Deep residual learning for image recognition. In: CVPR (2016)
18. Hwang, J., Lee, J., Park, S., Kwak, N.: Pose estimator and tracker using temporal flow maps for limbs. In: IJCNN (2019)
19. Insafutdinov, E., et al.: ArtTrack: articulated multi-person tracking in the wild. In: CVPR (2017)
20. Iqbal, U., Milan, A., Gall, J.: Posetrack: Joint multi-person pose estimation and tracking. In: CVPR (2017)
21. Jin, S., Liu, W., Ouyang, W., Qian, C.: Multi-person articulated tracking with spatial and temporal embeddings. In: CVPR (2019)
22. Kim, S., Min, D., Ham, B., Jeon, S., Lin, S., Sohn, K.: Fully convolutional self-similarity for dense semantic correspondence. In: CVPR (2017)
23. Kocabas, M., Karagoz, S., Akbas, E.: MultiPoseNet: fast multi-person pose estimation using pose residual network. In: Ferrari, V., Hebert, M., Sminchisescu, C., Weiss, Y. (eds.) ECCV 2018. LNCS, vol. 11215, pp. 437–453. Springer, Cham (2018). https://doi.org/10.1007/978-3-030-01252-6_26
24. Li, B., Yan, J., Wu, W., Zhu, Z., Hu, X.: High performance visual tracking with Siamese region proposal network. In: CVPR (2018)
25. Li, W., et al.: Rethinking on multi-stage networks for human pose estimation. arXiv preprint (2019)
26. Li, X., Liu, S., Mello, S.D., Wang, X., Kautz, J., Yang, M.H.: Joint-task self-supervised learning for temporal correspondence. In: NeurIPS (2019)
27. Lin, T.-Y., et al.: Microsoft COCO: common objects in context. In: Fleet, D., Pajdla, T., Schiele, B., Tuytelaars, T. (eds.) ECCV 2014. LNCS, vol. 8693, pp. 740–755. Springer, Cham (2014). https://doi.org/10.1007/978-3-319-10602-1_48
28. Luo, H., Gu, Y., Liao, X., Lai, S., Jiang, W.: Bag of tricks and a strong baseline for deep person re-identification. In: CVPR Workshop (2019)
29. Moon, G., Chang, J.Y., Lee, K.M.: Multi-scale aggregation R-CNN for 2D multi-person pose estimation. In: CVPR Workshop (2019)
30. Newell, A., Huang, Z., Deng, J.: Associative embedding: end-to-end learning for joint detection and grouping. In: NIPS (2017)
31. Newell, A., Yang, K., Deng, J.: Stacked hourglass networks for human pose estimation. In: Leibe, B., Matas, J., Sebe, N., Welling, M. (eds.) ECCV 2016. LNCS, vol. 9912, pp. 483–499. Springer, Cham (2016). https://doi.org/10.1007/978-3-319-46484-8_29
32. Nie, X., Feng, J., Xing, J., Yan, S.: Generative partition networks for multi-person pose estimation. In: ECCV (2018)
33. Ning, G., Huang, H.: Lighttrack: a generic framework for online top-down human pose tracking. arXiv preprint (2019)
34. Ning, G., Liu, P., Fan, X., Zhang, C.: A top-down approach to articulated human pose estimation and tracking. In: Leal-Taixé, L., Roth, S. (eds.) ECCV 2018. LNCS, vol. 11130, pp. 227–234. Springer, Cham (2019). https://doi.org/10.1007/978-3-030-11012-3_20
35. Raaj, Y., Idrees, H., Hidalgo, G., Sheikh, Y.: Efficient online multi-person 2D pose tracking with recurrent spatio-temporal affinity fields. In: CVPR (2019)
36. Ruan, W., Liu, W., Bao, Q., Chen, J., Cheng, Y., Mei, T.: POINet: pose-guided ovonic insight network for multi-person pose tracking. In: International Conference on Multimedia (2019)
37. Sun, D., Yang, X., Liu, M.Y., Kautz, J.: PWC-Net: CNNs for optical flow using pyramid, warping, and cost volume. In: CVPR (2018)

38. Sun, K., Xiao, B., Liu, D., Wang, J.: Deep high-resolution representation learning for human pose estimation. In: CVPR (2019)
39. Szegedy, C., et al.: Going deeper with convolutions. In: CVPR (2015)
40. Wang, X., Jabri, A., Efros, A.A.: Learning correspondence from the cycle-consistency of time. In: CVPR (2019)
41. Wu, J., et al.: AI challenger: a large-scale dataset for going deeper in image understanding. arXiv preprint (2017)
42. Xiao, B., Wu, H., Wei, Y.: Simple baselines for human pose estimation and tracking. In: Ferrari, V., Hebert, M., Sminchisescu, C., Weiss, Y. (eds.) ECCV 2018. LNCS, vol. 11210, pp. 472–487. Springer, Cham (2018). https://doi.org/10.1007/978-3-030-01231-1_29
43. Xiu, Y., Li, J., Wang, H., Fang, Y., Lu, C.: Pose Flow: Efficient online pose tracking. In: BMVC (2018)
44. Yang, W., Li, S., Ouyang, W., Li, H., Wang, X.: Learning feature pyramids for human pose estimation. In: ICCV (2017)
45. Yu, D., Su, K., Sun, J., Wang, C.: Multi-person pose estimation for pose tracking with enhanced cascaded pyramid network. In: Leal-Taixé, L., Roth, S. (eds.) ECCV 2018. LNCS, vol. 11130, pp. 221–226. Springer, Cham (2019). https://doi.org/10.1007/978-3-030-11012-3_19
46. Zhang, R., et al.: Exploiting offset-guided network for pose estimation and tracking. In: CVPR (2019)
47. Zhang, Z., Peng, H., Wang, Q.: Deeper and wider Siamese networks for real-time visual tracking. In: CVPR (2019)
48. Zhu, Z., Wang, Q., Li, B., Wu, W., Yan, J., Hu, W.: Distractor-aware Siamese networks for visual object tracking. In: Ferrari, V., Hebert, M., Sminchisescu, C., Weiss, Y. (eds.) ECCV 2018. LNCS, vol. 11213, pp. 103–119. Springer, Cham (2018). https://doi.org/10.1007/978-3-030-01240-3_7

Interactive Multi-dimension Modulation with Dynamic Controllable Residual Learning for Image Restoration

Jingwen He[1,2], Chao Dong[1,2], and Yu Qiao[1,2(✉)]

[1] ShenZhen Key Lab of Computer Vision and Pattern Recognition,
SIAT-SenseTime Joint Lab, Shenzhen Institutes of Advanced Technology,
Chinese Academy of Sciences, Beijing, China
{jw.he,chao.dong,yu.qiao}@siat.ac.cn
[2] SIAT Branch, Shenzhen Institute of Artificial Intelligence and Robotics for Society,
Shenzhen, China

Abstract. Interactive image restoration aims to generate restored images by adjusting a controlling coefficient which determines the restoration level. Previous works are restricted in modulating image with a single coefficient. However, real images always contain multiple types of degradation, which cannot be well determined by one coefficient. To make a step forward, this paper presents a new problem setup, called multi-dimension (MD) modulation, which aims at modulating output effects across multiple degradation types and levels. Compared with the previous single-dimension (SD) modulation, the MD is setup to handle multiple degradations adaptively and relief unbalanced learning problem in different degradations. We also propose a deep architecture - CResMD with newly introduced controllable residual connections for multi-dimension modulation. Specifically, we add a controlling variable on the conventional residual connection to allow a weighted summation of input and residual. The values of these weights are generated by another condition network. We further propose a new data sampling strategy based on beta distribution to balance different degradation types and levels. With corrupted image and degradation information as inputs, the network can output the corresponding restored image. By tweaking the condition vector, users can control the output effects in MD space at test time. Extensive experiments demonstrate that the proposed CResMD achieve excellent performance on both SD and MD modulation tasks. Code is available at https://github.com/hejingwenhejingwen/CResMD.

J. He and C. Dong—The first two authors are co-first authors.

Electronic supplementary material The online version of this chapter (https://doi.org/10.1007/978-3-030-58565-5_4) contains supplementary material, which is available to authorized users.

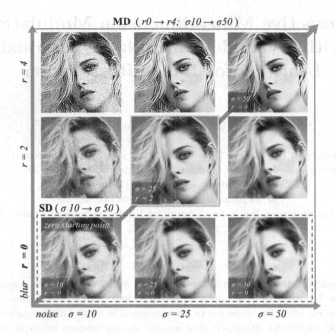

Fig. 1. Two-dimension (2D) modulation for a corrupted image with blur $r2$+noise $\sigma25$. When the blur level is fixed to $r0$, we can only modulate the denoising effect ($\sigma10 \rightarrow \sigma50$), which is a typical single dimension (SD) modulation. In multi-dimension (MD) modulation, the users are allowed to modulate both the deblurring and denoising levels.

1   Introduction

Conventional deep learning methods for image restoration (e.g., image denoising, deblurring and super resolution) learn a deterministic mapping from the degraded image space to the natural image space. For a given input, most of these methods can only generate a fixed output with a pre-determined restoration level. In other words, they lack the flexibility to alter the output effects according to different users' flavors. This flexibility is essential in many image processing applications, such as photo editing, where users desire to adjust the restoration level/strength continuously by a sliding bar. To adapt conventional deep models to real scenarios, several recent works investigate the use of additional branches to tune imagery effects, such as AdaFM [7], CFSNet [20], Dynamic-Net [17], DNI [21], and Decouple-Learning [5]. The outputs of their networks can be interactively controlled by a single variable at test-time, without retraining on new datasets. They can generate continuous restoration results between the pre-defined "start level" and "end level" (e.g., JPEG quality $q40 \rightarrow q10$).

These pioneer modulation works assume that the input image has only a single degradation type, such as noise or blur, thus the modulation lies in one dimension. However, the real-world scenarios are more complicated than the above assumptions. Specifically, real images usually contain multiple types of degradations, e.g., noise, blur, compression, etc. [18,22]. Then the users will need separate buttons to control each of them. The solution is far beyond adding more controllable parameters. As these degradations are coupled together, altering a single degradation will introduce new artifacts that do not belong to the pre-defined degradation types. We denote this problem as multi-dimension (MD) modulation for image restoration. Compared with single-dimension (SD) modulation, MD modulation has the following three major differences/difficulties.

Joint Modulation. MD modulation aims to remove the effects of individual degradations as well as their combinations. Different types of degradations are coherently related. Removing one type of degradation could unavoidably affect the other degradations. It is highly challenging to decouple different degradations and modulate each of them separately. This can be illustrated in Fig. 1. When we only adjust the noise level, the outputs should contain less noise but with fixed deblurring effects. All restored images should also be natural-looking and artifacts-free.

Zero Starting Point. In image restoration, the degradation level for modulation can be zero, indicating that the input does not contain the corresponding type of degradation. We call these zero starting points (e,g, $[0, a]$, $[a, 0]$, $[0, 0]$). When the input image has no degradation, restoration algorithm is expected to perform identity mapping. However, this poses challenges for existing SD restoration networks, which usually have information loss in forward processing. Thus it is hard to directly extend current SD methods to the MD task. Please refer to Related Work for details.

Unbalanced Learning. As there are different degradation types with a large range of degradation levels, the pixel-wise loss (e.g., MSE) will be severely unbalanced for different inputs. For instance, given an input image, the MSE for its blurry version and noisy version could have different orders of magnitude. Furthermore, as the degradation level starts from 0, the MSE can be pretty small around zero points. When we collect these different kinds of data as a training batch, the updating mechanism will favor the patches with large losses and ignore those with small ones. This phenomenon will result in inferior performance on mild degradations.

To address the aforementioned problems, we propose the first MD modulation framework with dynamic Controllable Residual learning, called CResMD. This is based on a novel use of residual connection. In conventional ResNet [8], the original input and its residual are combined by direct addition. In our settings, we reformulate it as a weighted sum – "$output = input + residual \times \alpha$", where α is the summation weight. If we add a global residual connection and set $\alpha = 0$, the output will be exactly the input. Then we can realize a special case of "*zero starting point*"—identity mapping. In addition, we can also add more local residual connections on building blocks. The underlying assumption is that the building blocks have their unique functions. When we enable some blocks and disable the others, the network can deal with different degradations.

Therefore, the *"joint modulation"* can also be achieved by dynamically altering the weights α. We further propose a condition network that accepts the degradation type/level as inputs and generates the weight α for each controllable residual connection. During training, the base network and the condition network are jointly optimized. To further alleviate *"unbalanced learning"*, we adopt a new data sampling strategy based on beta distribution. The key idea is to sample more mild degradations than severe ones.

To verify the effectiveness of the proposed methods, we conduct extensive experiments on 2D and 3D modulation for deblurring, denoising and JPEG debloking. We have also made comparisons with SD methods (e.g., AdaFM [7], CFSNet [20], DNI [21]) on SD tasks. Experimental results show that the proposed CResMD could realize MD modulation with high accuracy, and achieve superior performance to existing approaches on SD tasks with much less (0.16%) additional parameters

2   Related Work

Image Restoration. Deep learning methods have been widely used in image restoration problems, and most of them focus on a specific restoration task, such as denoising, deblurring, super-resolution and compression artifacts reduction [2–4,11–13,24]. Here we review some recent works that are designed to handle a wide range of degradation types or levels. Zhang et al. [24] propose DnCNN to deal with different levels of Gaussian noise. Then, Guo et al. [6] attempt to estimate a noise map to improve the denoising performance in real-world applications. Different from these task-specific methods, Yu et al. [22] aim to restore images corrupted with combined distortions with unknown degradation levels by exploiting the effectiveness of reinforcement learning. Later on, they propose a multi-path CNN [23] that can dynamically determine the appropriate route for different image regions. In addition, the work in [18] utilizes the attention mechanism to select the proper operations in different layers based on the input itself. However, these fixed networks cannot be modulated to meet various application requirements.

Modulation. We briefly review four representative SD methods—AdaFM [7], CFSNet [20], Dynamic-Net [17] and DNI [21]. As a common property, all these methods train a couple of networks on two related objectives, and achieve the intermediate results at test time. The main differences lie on the network structure and the modulation strategy. In the first three works, they decompose the model into a main branch and a tuning branch. AdaFM adopts feature modulation filters after each convolution layer. CFSNet uses a side-by-side network upon the main branch and couples their results after each residual block. Dynamic-Net adds modulation blocks directly after some convolution layers. During training, only the tuning branch is optimized to another objective. Due to this finetuning strategy, the modulation could only happen between two objectives. DNI interpolates all network parameters, thus has the flexibility to do MD modulation. However, the linear interpolation strategy of DNI cannot achieve high accuracy

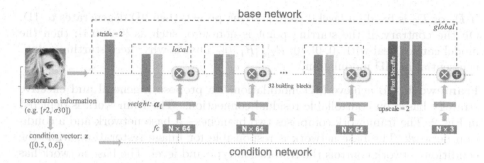

Fig. 2. Framework of CResMD, consisting of two branches: base network and condition network. The base network deals with image restoration, while the condition network generates the weights α for the cotrollable residual connections. The condition network contains several fully-connected layers and accepts the normalized restoration information as input. The building block (green) can be replaced by any existing block like residual attention block [19] or dense block [10]. (Color figure online)

Fig. 3. Different levels of restoration effects by setting different weights α on global residual. When $\alpha = 1$, the network outputs the restored image. To achieve identity mapping, we set $\alpha = 0$ to disable the residual branch.

(PSNR/SSIM) for image restoration tasks. In contrast, CResMD adopts the joint training strategy with much fewer additional parameters. It could achieve MD as well as SD modulation.

3 Method

Problem Formulation. We first give the formulation of multi-dimension (MD) modulation. Suppose there are N degradation types $\{D_j\}_{j=1}^{N}$. For each degradation D_j, there is a degradation range $[0, R_j]$. Our goal is to build a restoration model that accepts the degraded image together with desired restoration information as inputs and generates the restored image. The restoration information (corresponding to the degradation type/level) will act like tool bars, which can be interactively modulated during testing. We use a two-dimension (2D) example to illustrate the modulation process. As shown in Fig. 1, there are two separate bars to control the blur level D_1 and noise level D_2. The modulation space is a square 2D space, spreading from $[0,0]$ to $[R_1, R_2]$. We can fix D_1 and change D_2, then the modulation trajectory is a horizontal line. We can also modulate D_1 and D_2 simultaneously, then the trajectory will become a diagonal line.

If D_1 or D_2 is fixed on level 0 (zero starting point), then 2D degenerates to 1D. On the contrary, if the starting point is non-zero, such as [0.2, 0.1], then the model cannot deal with [0, 0], [0, R_2], [R_1, 0]. That is why "zero starting point" is essential in MD modulation.

Framework. To achieve MD modulation, we propose a general and effective strategy based on controllable residual connections. The framework is depicted in Fig. 2. The framework comprises two branches—a base network and a condition network. The base network is responsible for image restoration, while the condition network controls the restoration type and level. The base network has a general form with downsampling/upsampling layers at two ends and several building blocks in the middle. The building block can be residual block [8], recurrent block [9], dense block [10], and etc. This structure is widely adopted in advanced image restoration models [6,11,12,24,25]. The only difference comes from the additional "controllable residual connections", shown as blue and green dash lines in Fig. 2. These residual connections are controlled by the condition network. Take any degradation type/level as input, the condition network will first convert them into a condition vector, then generate the weights α for controllable residual connections. At inference time, we can modulate the degradation level/type – $\{D_i\}_{i=1}^N$, then the model can generate continuous restoration results.

Controllable Residual Connection. The proposed controllable residual connection comes from the standard residual connection, thus it is essential to review the general form of residual connection. Denote X and Y as the input and output feature maps. Then the residual connection can be represented as

$$Y = f(X, W_i) + X, \tag{1}$$

where $f(X, W_i)$ refers to the residual feature maps and $f(\cdot)$ is the mapping function. While in our controllable residual connection, we add a tunable variable α to control the summation weight. The formulation becomes

$$Y = f(X, W_i) \times \alpha + X, \tag{2}$$

where α has the same dimension as the number of feature maps. This simple change gives residual connection two different properties. First, through tuning the variable α from 0 to 1, the output Y will change continuously from X to $f(X, W_i) + X$. Second, the residual part can be fairly skipped by setting $\alpha = 0$. We can add the following two types of controllable residual connections.

(1) Global connection – X, Y are input/output images. The initial motivation of adding global connection is to handle the extreme case of zero starting point, where all degradation levels are zero. Generally, it is hard for a conventional neural network to perform identity mapping and image restoration simultaneously. However, with the help of global connection, the identity mapping can be easily realized by setting $\alpha = 0$. Furthermore, when we change the values of α, the output will exhibit different levels of restoration effects. This

phenomenon is illustrated in Fig. 3, where the input image is degraded by noise+blur and the intermediate results are obtained by using different α.

(2) Local connection – X, Y are input/output feature maps. If the imagery effects can be affected by a simple variable, we can also control the feature maps to achieve more complicated transformation. A reasonable idea is to add local residual connection on each function unit, which is responsible for specific degradation. By disabling/suppressing some function units, we can deal with different degradations. However, it is almost impossible to decouple these degradations and define a clear function for each block. Thus we roughly group some basic building blocks and add controllable residual connections. The minimum function unit consists of a single building block. Experiments in Fig. 7 show that more local residual connections achieve better performance at the cost of more controlling variables. More analyses can be found in Sect. 4.4.

Condition Network. We further propose a condition network that accepts the degradation type/level as input and generates the weight α for each controllable residual connection. As each degradation has its own range, we should first encode the degradation information into a condition vector. Specifically, we linearly map each degradation level to a value within the range $[0, 1]$, and concatenate those values to a vector z. Then the condition vector is passed through the condition network, which can be a stack of fully-connected layers (see Fig. 2).

Data Sampling Strategy. Data sampling is an important issue for MD modulation. As the training images contain various degradation types/levels, the training loss will be severely biased. If we uniformly sample these data, then the optimization will easily ignore the patches with small MSE values, and the performance of mild degradations cannot be guaranteed. To alleviate the unbalanced learning problem, we sample the degradation levels for each degradation type based on the beta distribution:

$$g(z, \alpha, \beta) = \frac{1}{B(\alpha, \beta)} z^{\alpha-1}(1-z)^{\beta-1}. \tag{3}$$

As shown in Fig. 4, a larger value of α is associated with a steeper curve, indicating that the sampled degradation levels are inclined to the mild degradations. In our experiments, α and β are set to 0.5 and 1, respectively. We also compare the results of different sampling curves in Sect. 4.4.

Training and Testing. The training strategy is straightforward. We generate the training data with different degradations and their combinations by random sampling, and encode the degradation information into the condition vector (range $[0, 1]$). Note that the training data is artificially generated, thus the degradation information is known during training. The model takes both the corrupted image and the condition vector as inputs. The original clean image is used as ground truth. The joint training based on L1 loss will enable different restoration effects under different condition vectors.

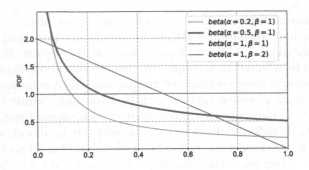

Fig. 4. Beta distribution.

In the testing stage, the degradation information is unknown, thus the users can modify the elements of the condition vector to obtain various restoration results. In other words, the condition vector refers to the restoration strength and performs like sliding bars. For example, given a corrupted image with blur level $r = 2$ (range $[0, 4]$) and noise level $\sigma = 30$ (range $[0, 50]$), the users are free to modulate the denoising/debluring bars (condition vector) with any sequence or simultaneously, and finally find the best choice at around $[2/4, 30/50]$.

Discussion. The proposed CResMD is a simple yet effective method that is specially designed for MD modulation. In comparison, existing SD methods cannot be directly extended to the MD task, mainly for two reasons. (1) The training strategy determines that their modulation trajectory cannot span across the 2D space. Specifically, their models generally have a main branch and a tuning branch. The main brunch is trained for the first objective, and the tuning brunch is fine-tuned on another objective. Thus the modulation trajectory is a line connecting two objectives. Even we use multiple parameters, the modulation trajectory will become a diagonal line instead of a 2D space. For example, if the start level is $[0.1, 0.1]$ and the end level is $[1, 1]$, the model can deal with $[0.5, 0.5]$ but not $[0.4, 0.6]$. In order to achieve joint modulation, we cannot just use degradations on the start and end levels, but should consider all combinations of degradations between two ends. (2) The network structure prevents them from realizing "zero starting point". For example, if the start level is $[0, 0]$, the main branch will perform identity mapping (output=input). Then it is hard to adapt this network to another objective only by modulating intermediate features. That is why we propose to use skip/residual connection with controllable parameters.

4 Experiments

4.1 Implementation Details

We first describe the network architectures. For the base network, we adopt the standard residual block as the building block, which consists of two convolution layers and a ReLU activation layer. There are 32 building blocks, of which each convolution layers have 64 filters with kernel size 3×3. In order to save computation, we use strided convolution to downsample the features to half size. The last upsampling module uses a pixel-shuffle [16] layer followed by two convolution layers. Note that the first and last convolution layers are not followed by ReLU activation. We add a local controllable residual connection on each building block. For the condition network, we use a single fully-connected layer to output a 64-dimension vector α for each local controllable residual connection. In total, there are 32 layers for 32 local connections and 1 layer for the global connection.

To ease the burden of evaluation, we conduct most experiments and ablation studies on 2D modulation. To demonstrate the generalization ability, we conduct an additional experiment on 3D modulation at last. In 2D experiments, we adopt two widely-used degradation types – Gaussian blur and Gaussian noise. JPEG compression is further added in the 3D experiment.

The training dataset is DIV2K[1], and the test datasets are CBSD68 [14] and LIVE1 [15]. The training images are cropped into 64×64 sub-images. To generate corrupted input images, we employ mixed distortions on the training data. In particular, blur, noise and JPEG are sequentially added to the training images with random levels. For Gaussian blur, the range of kernel width is set to $r \in [0, 4]$, and the kernel size is fixed to 21×21. The covariance range of Gaussian noise is $\sigma \in [0, 50]$, and the quality range of JPEG compression is $q \in [100, 10]$. We sample the degradations with stride of 0.1, 1, and 2 for blur, noise, and JPEG compression, respectively.

These training images are further divided into two groups, one with individual degradations and the other with degradation combinations. To augment the training data, we perform horizontal flipping and 90-degree rotation. To obtain more images with mild degradations, we force the sampling to obey beta distribution, where α and β are set to 0.5 and 1, respectively. The mini-batch size is set to 16. The L1 loss is adopted as the loss function. During the training process, the learning rate is initialized as 5×10^{-4}, and is decayed by a factor of 2 after 2×10^5 iterations. All experiments run 1×10^6 iterations. We use PyTorch framework and train all models on NVIDIA 1080Ti GPUs.

4.2 Complexity Analysis

The proposed CResMD is extremely light-weight, contributing to less than 4.2 k parameters. As the additional parameters come from the condition network, the number of introduced parameters in 2D modulation is calculated as $32 \times 2 \times 64 + 2 \times 3 = 4102$. Note that the base network contains 32 building blocks with parameters around 2.5 M, CResMD only comprises 0.16% of entire model. In contrast, the tuning blocks in AdaFM and CFSNet account for 4% and 110% of the total parameters of the base network, respectively. Another appealing property is that the computation cost of condition network is a constant, as there are no spatial or convolution operations. In other words, the computation burden is nearly negligible for a large input image.

Table 1. 2D experiments evaluated on CBSD68 [14]. The PSNR distances within 0.2 dB are shown in bold. Lower is better.

	One degradation						Two degradations					
blur r	1	2	4	0	0	0	1	1	2	2	4	4
noise σ	0	0	0	15	30	50	15	50	15	50	15	50
upper bound	39.07	30.24	26.91	34.12	30.56	28.21	29.11	26.07	26.30	24.55	24.08	23.03
CResMD	38.38	30.09	26.53	33.97	30.43	28.06	29.00	25.96	26.24	24.48	24.03	22.95
PSNR distance	0.69	**0.15**	0.38	**0.15**	**0.13**	**0.15**	**0.11**	**0.11**	**0.06**	**0.07**	**0.05**	**0.08**

4.3 Performance Evaluation

To evaluate the modulation performance, we follow AdaFM [7] and use PSNR distance. Specifically, if we want to evaluate the performance on D_1, D_2, then we train a baseline model using the architecture of the base network on D_1, D_2. This baseline model can be regarded as an upper bound. With the ground truth images, we can calculate PSNR of CResMD and the baseline model respectively. Their PSNR distance is used as the evaluation metric (lower is better).

2D Modulation. First, we evaluate the 2D modulation performance of the proposed method. The quantitative results[1] of different degradations on CBSD68 dataset are provided in Table 1. We can observe different trends for different degradation types. For two degradations, the PSNR distances are all below 0.2 dB, indicating a high modulation accuracy. For one degradation, where there are zero starting points, the performance will slightly decrease. Furthermore, blur generally leads to higher PSNR distances than noise. The largest PSNR distance appears in $r1$, which is a starting point as well as a mild degradation. Nevertheless, its absolute PSNR value is more than 38 dB, thus the restoration quality is still acceptable. We further show qualitative results in Fig. 8, where all images exhibit smooth transition effects.

Comparison with SD Methods. As the state-of-the-art methods are all proposed for SD modulation, we can only compare with them on single degradation types. We want to show that even trained for MD modulation, CResMD can still achieve excellent performance on all SD tasks. Specifically, we compare with DNI, AdaFM, and CFSNet on deblurring, starting from $r2$ to $r4$. Deblurring is harder than denoising, thus could show more apparent differences. To re-implement their models, we first train a base network on the start level $r2$. Then we finetune (1) the whole network in DNI, (2) the AdaFM layers with kernel size 5×5 in AdaFM, (3) the parallel tuning blocks and coefficient network in CFSNet, to the end level $r4$. To obtain the deblurring results between $r2$ and $r4$, we interpolate the networks of two ends with stride 0.01. For CResMD, we directly use the deblurring results in the 2D experiments (Table 1).

From Fig. 5, we observe that our method significantly outperforms the others in almost all intermediate points. In particular, the SD methods tend to yield

---

[1] Results on more datasets can be found in supplementary file.

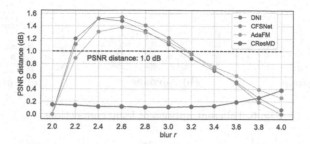

Fig. 5. Quantitative comparison with SD methods on CBSD68 data set in PSNR.

Table 2. The effectiveness of global connection. Results are evaluated by PSNR.

blur r	0	0	0.5	1	0.5	0.5	1
noise σ	0	5	0	0	5	15	5
CBSD68 w/o	71.39	40.21	52.70	38.04	37.80	32.31	31.48
w	$+\infty$	40.33	53.17	38.38	37.92	32.44	31.63
gain	$+\infty$	0.12	0.47	0.34	0.12	0.13	0.15
LIVE1 w/o	64.17	39.79	51.22	38.38	37.71	32.51	31.65
w	$+\infty$	39.99	52.21	38.85	37.89	32.69	31.86
gain	$+\infty$	0.20	0.99	0.47	0.18	0.18	0.21

high PSNR distances (> 1.0 dB) on tasks $r2.2 \sim r3.0$. It is not surprising that they perform perfect at two ends as they are trained and finetuned on these points. This trend also holds for denoising, but with much smaller distances. All these results demonstrate the effectiveness of our proposed method in SD modulation. Results of deblurring $r1 \rightarrow r4$, denoising $\sigma5 \rightarrow \sigma50$ and $\sigma15 \rightarrow \sigma50$ can be found in the supplementary file.

4.4 Ablation Study

Effectiveness of Global Connection. The global connection is initially designed to handle the problem of zero starting point. In general, it is hard for a conventional network to deal with both identity mapping and image restoration at the same time. With the proposed controllable global connection, we can ideally turn off the residual branch by setting $\alpha = 0$. To evaluate its effectiveness, we conduct a straightforward comparison experiment by just removing the global connection. This new model is trained under the same setting as CResMD. As for testing, we only select those mild degradations, such as blur $r < 1$ and noise $\sigma < 15$. It is clear that the model with controllable global connection could achieve better performance on all mild degradations as we can see from Table 2.

Effectiveness of Local Connection. Here we test the influence of the number of local connections. In particular, we group some basic building blocks

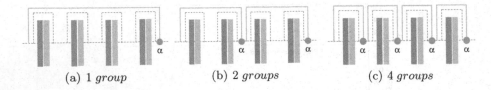

(a) 1 *group*   (b) 2 *groups*   (c) 4 *groups*

Fig. 6. Different options of local connections.

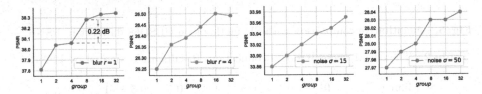

Fig. 7. Performance under different local connections evaluated by CBSD68 dataset.

as a function unit and add controllable residual connection. All the building blocks are divided into 1, 2, 4, 8, 16 and 32 groups (the details are illustrated in Fig. 6). They are evaluated in 2D modulation on CBSD68 dataset. The results are depicted in Fig. 7. Obviously, more groups or local connections could lead to better performance. Particularly, we also observe a sharp leap (0.22 dB) in deblurring $r1$ (from 4 to 8 local connections), indicating that at least 8 local connections are required. In contrast, results on denoising tasks are less significant, where the PSNR distance between 1 and 32 local connections is less than 0.1 dB in denoising $\sigma15$ and $\sigma50$.

Effectiveness of Data Sampling. After analysis of the proposed network structures, we then investigate different data sampling strategies. As mentioned in Sect. 3.4, appropriate data sampling strategies could help alleviate the unbalanced learning problem. To validate this comment, we conduct a set of controlled experiments with different sampling curves, which can be generated using different parameters of beta distribution in Function (3). To be specific, the most commonly used strategy is uniform sampling, corresponding to the green horizontal line in Fig. 4. We can generate this curve by setting β and α to 1. Similarly, we can further set α, β to be (0.5, 1.0), (0.2, 1.0) and (1.0, 2.0) to generate linear and non-linear curves, shown in Fig. 4. Then we train four CResMDs on different training datasets with the above sampling strategies. Results are shown in Table 3, where we use uniform sampling ($\alpha = 1, \beta = 1$) as our baseline and calculate the PSNR distances with other strategies. Obviously, when we sample more data on mild degradations, the performance will significantly improve. Furthermore, the PSNR increases on some degradation levels generally comes at the cost of the decrease on the others. For instance, in deblurring $r = 1$, $\alpha = 1.0, \beta = 2.0$ and $\alpha = 0.2, \beta = 1.0$ reach the highest performance, but also get severe degradation in $r4$. As a better trade-off, we select the setting $\alpha = 0.5$, $\beta = 1.0$ for our CResMD, which stably improves most degradation levels.

Table 3. Performance under different sampling curves evaluated on LIVE1 [15]. results are given in PSNR.

blur r	1	2	4	0	0	0	1	2	4	Total
noise σ	0	0	0	5	30	50	5	30	50	
$\alpha = 1.0, \beta = 1.0$	38.66	30.01	**26.26**	39.90	30.63	28.24	31.78	24.97	**22.58**	
$\alpha = 0.5, \beta = 1.0$	38.85	30.03	26.14	39.99	30.65	28.25	31.86	24.98	22.56	
(CResMD)	+0.19	+0.02	−0.12	+0.09	+0.02	**+0.01**	+0.08	+0.01	−0.02	**+0.28**
$\alpha = 0.2, \beta = 1.0$	38.94	29.98	26.07	39.97	30.55	28.10	31.68	24.85	22.39	
	+0.28	−0.03	−0.19	+0.07	−0.08	−0.14	−0.10	−0.12	−0.19	−0.50
$\alpha = 1.0, \beta = 2.0$	38.93	30.08	25.80	40.00	30.66	28.24	31.90	24.99	22.50	
	+0.27	**+0.07**	−0.46	**+0.10**	**+0.03**	+0.00	**+0.12**	**+0.02**	−0.08	+0.07

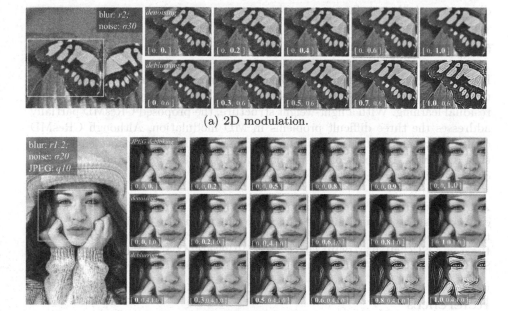

(a) 2D modulation.

(b) 3D modulation.

Fig. 8. Qualitative results of MD modulation. In each row, we only change one factor with other factors fixed. We arrive at the best choice in the yellow box. **Better view in zoom and color.** (Color figure online)

Generalization to 3D Modulation. In the above experiments, we mainly use 2D modulation for illustration. Our method can be easily extended to higher dimension cases. Here we show a 3D modulation example with three degradation types: blur, noise and JPEG compression. Note that in JPEG compression, the zero starting point is not quality 100 but quality ∞, thus we extend the JPEG range as $\{\infty, [100, 10]\}$. In 2D modulation, there is only one degradation combination—noise+blur. However, in 3D, the number increases to 4, including noise+blur, noise+JPEG, blur+JPEG and noise+blur+JPEG. Then the difficulty also improves dramatically. Nevertheless, our method can handle this situation by simply setting the dimension of the condition vector to 3. All the other network structures and training strategy remain the same. The results can be found in the supplementary file. We can observe that most PSNR distances are below 0.3 dB, indicating a good modulation accuracy. Compared with 2D modulation, the performance on single degradations decreases a little bit, which is mainly due to the insufficient training data. We also show some qualitative results in Fig. 8, where we modulate one factor and fix the others.

Experimentally, more degradation types (>3) require larger datasets/ networks, and the performance on individual tasks will also degrade. Considering that there are not so many degradation types in real-world scenarios, our method can deal with most cases of image restoration tasks. We leave the higher dimension problem to future research.

5   Conclusion

In this work, we first present the multi-dimension modulation problem for image restoration, and propose an efficient framework based on dynamic controllable residual learning. With a light-weight structure, the proposed CResMD partially addresses the three difficult problems in MD modulation. Although CResMD could realize modulation across multiple domains, the performance can be further improved. The controlling method can be more accurate and diverse. We encourage future research on better solutions.

Acknowledgement. This work is partially supported by the National Natural Science Foundation of China (61906184), Science and Technology Service Network Initiative of Chinese Academy of Sciences (KFJ-STS-QYZX-092), Shenzhen Basic Research Program (JSGG20180507182100698, CXB201104220032A), the Joint Lab of CAS-HK, Shenzhen Institute of Artificial Intelligence and Robotics for Society.

References

1. Agustsson, E., Timofte, R.: Ntire 2017 challenge on single image super-resolution: dataset and study. In: Proceedings of the IEEE Conference on Computer Vision and Pattern Recognition Workshops, pp. 126–135 (2017)
2. Dong, C., Deng, Y., Change Loy, C., Tang, X.: Compression artifacts reduction by a deep convolutional network. In: Proceedings of the IEEE International Conference on Computer Vision, pp. 576–584 (2015)
3. Dong, C., Loy, C.C., He, K., Tang, X.: Image super-resolution using deep convolutional networks. IEEE Trans. Pattern Anal. Mach. Intell. **38**(2), 295–307 (2015)
4. Dong, C., Loy, C.C., Tang, X.: Accelerating the super-resolution convolutional neural network. In: Leibe, B., Matas, J., Sebe, N., Welling, M. (eds.) ECCV 2016. LNCS, vol. 9906, pp. 391–407. Springer, Cham (2016). https://doi.org/10.1007/978-3-319-46475-6_25
5. Fan, Q., Chen, D., Yuan, L., Hua, G., Yu, N., Chen, B.: Decouple learning for parameterized image operators (2018)

6. Guo, S., Yan, Z., Zhang, K., Zuo, W., Zhang, L.: Toward convolutional blind denoising of real photographs. In: 2019 IEEE Conference on Computer Vision and Pattern Recognition (CVPR) (2019)
7. He, J., Dong, C., Qiao, Y.: Modulating image restoration with continual levels via adaptive feature modification layers. In: The IEEE Conference on Computer Vision and Pattern Recognition (CVPR), June 2019
8. He, K., Zhang, X., Ren, S., Sun, J.: Deep residual learning for image recognition. arXiv preprint arXiv:1512.03385 (2015)
9. Hochreiter, S., Schmidhuber, J.: Long short-term memory. Neural Comput. **9**(8), 1735–1780 (1997)
10. Huang, G., Liu, Z., Van Der Maaten, L., Weinberger, K.Q.: Densely connected convolutional networks. In: Proceedings of the IEEE Conference on Computer Vision and Pattern Recognition, pp. 4700–4708 (2017)
11. Ledig, C., et al.: Photo-realistic single image super-resolution using a generative adversarial network. In: Proceedings of the IEEE Conference on Computer Vision and Pattern Recognition, pp. 4681–4690 (2017)
12. Lim, B., Son, S., Kim, H., Nah, S., Mu Lee, K.: Enhanced deep residual networks for single image super-resolution. In: Proceedings of the IEEE Conference on Computer Vision and Pattern Recognition Workshops, pp. 136–144 (2017)
13. Zhang, W., Liu, Y., Dong, C., Qiao, Y.: RankSRGAN: generative adversarial networks with ranker for image super-resolution. In: Proceedings of the IEEE/CVF International Conference on Computer Vision (ICCV), October 2019
14. Roth, S., Black, M.J.: Fields of experts: a framework for learning image priors. In: 2005 IEEE Computer Society Conference on Computer Vision and Pattern Recognition (CVPR 2005), vol. 2, pp. 860–867. IEEE (2005)
15. Sheikh, H.R., Sabir, M.F., Bovik, A.C.: A statistical evaluation of recent full reference image quality assessment algorithms. IEEE Trans. Image Process. **15**(11), 3440–3451 (2006)
16. Shi, W., et al.: Real-time single image and video super-resolution using an efficient sub-pixel convolutional neural network. In: Proceedings of the IEEE Conference on Computer Vision and Pattern Recognition, pp. 1874–1883 (2016)
17. Shoshan, A., Mechrez, R., Zelnik-Manor, L.: Dynamic-net: tuning the objective without re-training for synthesis tasks. In: The IEEE International Conference on Computer Vision (ICCV), October 2019
18. Suganuma, M., Liu, X., Okatani, T.: Attention-based adaptive selection of operations for image restoration in the presence of unknown combined distortions. In: The IEEE Conference on Computer Vision and Pattern Recognition (CVPR), June 2019
19. Wang, F., et al.: Residual attention network for image classification. In: The IEEE Conference on Computer Vision and Pattern Recognition (CVPR), July 2017
20. Wang, W., Guo, R., Tian, Y., Yang, W.: CFSNet: toward a controllable feature space for image restoration. In: The IEEE International Conference on Computer Vision (ICCV), October 2019
21. Wang, X., Yu, K., Dong, C., Tang, X., Loy, C.C.: Deep network interpolation for continuous imagery effect transition. In: Proceedings of the IEEE Conference on Computer Vision and Pattern Recognition, pp. 1692–1701 (2019)
22. Yu, K., Dong, C., Lin, L., Loy, C.C.: Crafting a toolchain for image restoration by deep reinforcement learning. In: Proceedings of IEEE Conference on Computer Vision and Pattern Recognition, pp. 2443–2452 (2018)
23. Yu, K., Wang, X., Dong, C., Tang, X., Loy, C.C.: Path-restore: learning network path selection for image restoration. arXiv preprint arXiv:1904.10343 (2019)

24. Zhang, K., Zuo, W., Chen, Y., Meng, D., Zhang, L.: Beyond a Gaussian denoiser: Residual learning of deep CNN for image denoising. IEEE Trans. Image Process. **26**(7), 3142–3155 (2017)
25. Zhang, Y., Tian, Y., Kong, Y., Zhong, B., Fu, Y.: Residual dense network for image super-resolution. In: The IEEE Conference on Computer Vision and Pattern Recognition (CVPR), June 2018

Polysemy Deciphering Network for Human-Object Interaction Detection

Xubin Zhong[1], Changxing Ding[1(✉)], Xian Qu[1], and Dacheng Tao[2]

[1] School of Electronic and Information Engineering, South China University
of Technology, Guangzhou, China
{eexubin,eequxian971017}@mail.scut.edu.cn, chxding@scut.edu.cn
[2] UBTECH Sydney AI Centre, School of Computer Science, Faculty of Engineering,
The University of Sydney, Darlington, NSW 2008, Australia
dacheng.tao@sydney.edu.au

Abstract. Human-Object Interaction (HOI) detection is important in human-centric scene understanding. Existing works typically assume that the same verb in different HOI categories has similar visual characteristics, while ignoring the diverse semantic meanings of the verb. To address this issue, in this paper, we propose a novel Polysemy Deciphering Network (PD-Net), which decodes the visual polysemy of verbs for HOI detection in three ways. First, PD-Net augments human pose and spatial features for HOI detection using language priors, enabling the verb classifiers to receive language hints that reduce the intra-class variation of the same verb. Second, we introduce a novel Polysemy Attention Module (PAM) that guides PD-Net to make decisions based on more important feature types according to the language priors. Finally, the above two strategies are applied to two types of classifiers for verb recognition, i.e., object-shared and object-specific verb classifiers, whose combination further relieves the verb polysemy problem. By deciphering the visual polysemy of verbs, we achieve the best performance on both HICO-DET and V-COCO datasets. In particular, PD-Net outperforms state-of-the-art approaches by 3.81% mAP in the Known-Object evaluation mode of HICO-DET. Code of PD-Net is available at https://github.com/MuchHair/PD-Net.

Keywords: Human-object interaction · Verb polysemy · Attention model

1 Introduction

In recent years, researchers working in the field of computer vision have paid increasing attention to scene understanding tasks [1,2,5,12,18,28]. As human beings are often central to real-world scenes, Human-Object Interaction (HOI)

Electronic supplementary material The online version of this chapter (https://doi.org/10.1007/978-3-030-58565-5_5) contains supplementary material, which is available to authorized users.

© Springer Nature Switzerland AG 2020
A. Vedaldi et al. (Eds.): ECCV 2020, LNCS 12365, pp. 69–85, 2020.
https://doi.org/10.1007/978-3-030-58565-5_5

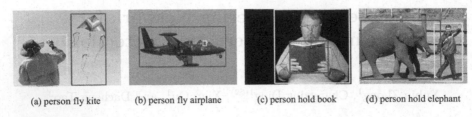

(a) person fly kite   (b) person fly airplane   (c) person hold book   (d) person hold elephant

Fig. 1. Examples reflecting the polysemy problem of the same verb. (a) and (b) illustrate HOI examples of "fly". (c) and (d) present HOI examples of "hold".

detection has become a fundamental problem in scene understanding. HOI detection not only involves identifying the classes and locations of objects in the images, but also the interactions (verbs) between each human-object pair. As shown in Fig. 1, an interaction between a human-object pair can be represented by a triplet *<person verb object>*, herein referred to as one HOI category. One human-object pair may comprise multiple triplets, e.g. *<person fly airplane>* and *<person sit on airplane>* (see Fig. 1(b)). Therefore, HOI detection requires multi-label verb classification for each human-object pair.

The HOI detection task is, however, challenging [4,9]. One major reason is that verbs can be polysemic. As illustrated in Fig. 1, a verb may present substantially different semantic meanings and visual characteristics with respect to different objects. This semantic difference can be very large, resulting in the importance of the same type of visual feature varies dramatically as the objects of interest change. For example, the human pose plays a vital role in describing *<person fly kite>* in Fig. 1(a). However, human pose is invisible and therefore useless for characterizing *<person fly airplane>* in Fig. 1(b). Another example can be found in Fig. 1(c) and (d), here both *<person hold book>* and *<person hold elephant>* pay attention to the spatial feature, i.e. the relative location between two bounding boxes, however, their spatial features are extremely different. Therefore, verb polysemy is a significant challenge in HOI detection.

The verb polysemy problem is relatively underexplored and sometimes even ignored in existing works [9,14,16,27,29]. Most contemporary approaches assume that the same verb in different HOI categories have similar visual characteristics, so design object-shared verb classifiers. However, due to the polysemic nature of the verbs, a dramatic semantic gap may exist for the same verb across different HOI categories. Chao *et al.* [4] constructed object-specific verb classifiers for each HOI category, which can overcome the polysemy problem for HOI categories with large training data. However, this approach lacks few- and zero-shot learning abilities for HOI categories with small training data.

Accordingly, in this paper, we propose a novel Polysemy Deciphering Network (PD-Net) that addresses the verb polysemy problem in three ways. First, as illustrated in Fig. 2, PD-Net transforms the multi-label verb classifications for each human-object pair into a set of binary classification problems, where each binary classifier is used for one verb category identification, respectively.

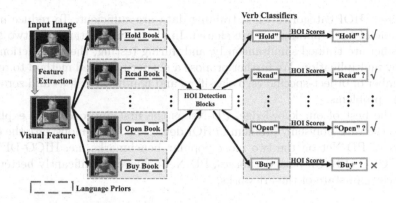

Fig. 2. Visual features of each human-object pair are duplicated multiple times so that the pose and spatial features can be augmented using different language priors. Under the guidance of language priors, polysemy-sensing visual feature of the same verbs can be generated. To reduce the number of duplicated human-object pairs, meaningless HOI categories are ignored, e.g. $<person\,eat\,book>$ and $<person\,ride\,book>$. Meaningful and common HOI categories are available in each popular HOI detection database.

The binary classifiers share parameters expect for the final layers for binary prediction. Therefore, their total model size is equal to one common multi-label verb classifier. The main difference between the binary classifiers lies in their input human pose and spatial features. More specifically, we augment the two features of each human-object pair with language priors, respectively. These language priors are word embeddings of phrases composed of one verb and one object. The object class is predicted by the Faster R-CNN [24] backbone model; the verb is the one to be determined by one specific binary verb classifier. Our motivation is that both pose and spatial features are vague and varied dramatically for the same verb, as illustrated in Fig. 1. By concatenating the language priors, the classifiers receive hints to reduce the intra-class variation of the same verb for the pose and spatial features.

Moreover, we design a novel Polysemy Attention Module (PAM) that produces attention scores based on the above language priors to dynamically fuse four feature types for each binary classifier: human appearance, object appearance, human pose, and spatial features. The language priors provide hints as to the importance of the features for each HOI category. For example, human pose feature is discriminative when the language prior is "fly kite" (Fig. 1(a)); but is less useful when the language prior is "fly airplane" (Fig. 1(b)). Therefore, PAM deciphers the verb polysemy problem by highlighting more important features for each HOI category.

The above two strategies can be applied to both object-shared and object-specific verb classifiers. We further promote the performance of PD-Net by fusing the two types of classifiers. The classifiers are complementary, as the first can reduce the class imbalance problem for HOI categories with a small sample size, while the second is better able to capture the semantic gap of the same verb in different HOI categories when training data are sufficient. To reduce model size, some of their parameters are shared. In the training stage, the two types of classifier are trained simultaneously, and during testing, their predictions are fused by multiplication. We further propose a clustering-based method to reduce the number of object-specific verb classifiers and handle their few- and zero-shot learning problems.

To the best of our knowledge, PD-Net is the first approach that explicitly handles the verb polysemy problem in HOI detection. We demonstrate the effectiveness of PD-Net on the two most popular benchmarks, i.e. HICO-DET [4] and VCOCO [13]. On both databases, PD-Net achieves significantly better performance than state-of-the-art works.

2   Related Works

Human-Object Interaction Detection. HOI detection performs multi-label verb classification for each human-object pair, meaning that multiple verbs may be used to describe the interaction between the same human-object pair. Depending on the order of verb classification and target object association, existing approaches in HOI detection can be divided into two main sets of methods. The first set of methods infer the verbs performed by one person, then associate each verb of the person with the target objects in the image. Multiple target object association approaches have been proposed. For example, Shen et al. [25] proposed an approach based on the value of object detection scores. Gkioxari et al. [11] fit a distribution density function of the target object locations based on the human appearance feature. Qi et al. [23] adopted a graph parsing network to associate the target objects. Zhou et al. [35] constructed graph models that highlight the importance of the link between object and human body parts.

The second category of methods first pair each human instance with all object instances as candidates, then recognize the verb for each candidate pair [14]. For example, Xu et al. [32] constructed a graph neural network for verb classification. Xu et al. [31] utilized the gaze and intention of human to assist HOI detection. Li et al. [16] introduced a Transferable Interactiveness Network to exclude candidate pairs without interactions. Wan et al. [27] employed human pose as cues [6,7] to obtain important human part features for verb classification. Wang et al. [29] extracted context-aware human and object appearance features in order to promote HOI detection performance. Peyre et al. [22] constructed a multi-stream model that projects the visual features and word embeddings into a joint space, which is powerful for detecting unseen HOI categories.

The Exploitation of Language Priors. Language priors have been successfully utilized in many computer vision tasks, including Scene Graph Generation [18,19,30], Image Captioning [3,15,33,34] and Visual Question Answering [10,20,26]. Moreover, there are several works that have also adopted language priors for HOI detection [22,32]. They improve HOI detection by exploiting the correlation between similar verbs or HOI categories with the help of language

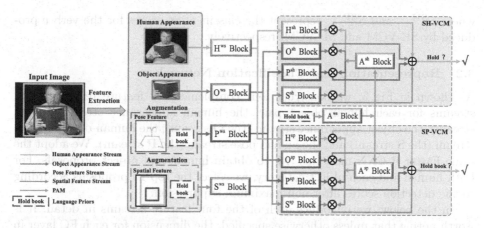

Fig. 3. Overview of the Polysemy Deciphering Network. In the interests of simplicity, only one binary object-shared classifier for "hold" and one binary object-specific classifier for "hold book" are illustrated. $\mathbf{A}^{ws}$, $\mathbf{A}^{sh}$, and $\mathbf{A}^{sp}$ are blocks for the PAM module. $\mathbf{H}^{ws}$, $\mathbf{O}^{ws}$, $\mathbf{P}^{ws}$, and $\mathbf{S}^{ws}$ are blocks shared by SH-VCM and SP-VCM. The superscript "ws" denotes "weight sharing". $\mathbf{H}^{sh}$ ($\mathbf{H}^{sp}$), $\mathbf{O}^{sh}$ ($\mathbf{O}^{sp}$), $\mathbf{P}^{sh}$ ($\mathbf{P}^{sp}$) and $\mathbf{S}^{sh}$ ($\mathbf{S}^{sp}$) are blocks in SH-VCM (SP-VCM). The binary classification scores from $\mathbf{H}^{sh}$ ($\mathbf{H}^{sp}$), $\mathbf{O}^{sh}$ ($\mathbf{O}^{sp}$), $\mathbf{P}^{sh}$ ($\mathbf{P}^{sp}$) and $\mathbf{S}^{sh}$ ($\mathbf{S}^{sp}$) are fused by attention scores produced by PAM. $\otimes$ and $\oplus$ denote the element-wise multiplication and addition operations, respectively.

priors. However, these works do not employ language priors to solve the verb polysemy problem.

3 Our Method

3.1 Overview

Given an image, we obtain human and object proposals using Faster R-CNN [24]. Each human proposal h and object proposal o will be paired as a candidate for verb classification. PD-Net produces a set of verb classification scores for each candidate pair. As shown in Fig. 2, we first transform the multi-label verb classification into a set of binary classification problems. Moreover, as illustrated in Fig. 3, in order to overcome the verb polysemy problem, PD-Net performs HOI detection by combining Language Prior Augmentation (LPA), Polysemy Attention Module (PAM), Object-SHared Verb Classification Module (SH-VCM), and Object-SPecific Verb Classification Module (SP-VCM). SH-VCM and SP-VCM contain a set of object-shared binary classifiers and object-specific binary classifiers, respectively.

The identification score produced by PD-Net for the verb v in the HOI category (h, o, v) can be denoted as $\mathcal{S}^{\mathbf{PD}}_{(h,o,v)}$:

$$\mathcal{S}^{\mathbf{PD}}_{(h,o,v)} = \mathcal{S}^{\mathbf{SH}}_{(h,o,v)} \times \mathcal{S}^{\mathbf{SP}}_{(h,o,v)}, \tag{1}$$

where $S^{SH}_{(h,o,v)}$ and $S^{SP}_{(h,o,v)}$ represent the classification scores for the verb v produced by SH-VCM and SP-VCM, respectively.

3.2 Representation and Classification Networks

As shown in Fig. 3, we construct four complementary feature representation streams for each human-object pair: the human appearance stream (the **H** stream), the object appearance stream (the **O** stream), the human-object spatial stream (the **S** stream) and the human pose stream (the **P** stream). We adopt the same Faster R-CNN model as [14] to obtain human and object proposals. For both human and each object category, we select the top 10 proposals according to the detection scores after non-maximum suppression.

In the below, we introduce each of the four feature streams in detail. It is worth noting that unless otherwise specified, the dimension for each FC layer in the following is set as the dimension of its input feature vector in the interests of simplicity.

Human Appearance Stream. Input feature of the **H** stream is a 2048-dimensional vector for each human proposal. We adopt the same way as [14] to obtain this feature vector from Faster R-CNN. This feature vector passes through three blocks for verb classification: $\mathbf{H}^{ws}$, $\mathbf{H}^{sh}$ in SH-VCM, and $\mathbf{H}^{sp}$ in SP-VCM. $\mathbf{H}^{ws}$ is realized by one FC layer, which is followed by one batch normalization (BN) layer and one ReLU layer. $\mathbf{H}^{sh}$ includes only one K_V-dimensional FC layer, where K_V denotes the number of verb categories. Each element of this layer's output denotes the prediction of one binary classifier according to the **H** stream feature. $\mathbf{H}^{sp}$ includes two FC layers; the first of these is followed by one BN layer and one ReLU layer. The dimension of the second one is K_T, which represents the number of meaningful HOI categories provided by each HOI dataset [4,13]. It is worth noting that K_V and K_T equals to the number of binary classifiers in SH-VCM and SP-VCM, respectively.

Object Appearance Stream. For the **O** stream, the model structure and the way in which features are constructed are the same as for the **H** stream. Feature vectors for the **O** stream pass through three blocks for verb classification: $\mathbf{O}^{ws}$, $\mathbf{O}^{sh}$ in SH-VCM, and $\mathbf{O}^{sp}$ in SP-VCM.

Spatial Feature Stream. Following [14], we encode a 42-dimensional spatial feature vector using the bounding box coordinates of one human-object pair. As illustrated in Fig. 1, spatial features are vague and vary dramatically for the same verb. By transforming the multi-label verb classifier into a set of binary classifiers, the same spatial feature can be augmented using different language priors to generate polysemy-sensing feature of each specific verb, as shown in Fig. 2. We concatenate this spatial feature with a 600-dimensional word embedding of two words. One word denotes the verb to be identified and the other one is the detected object. Word embeddings are generated using the word2vec tool [21]. Features for this stream pass through three blocks: $\mathbf{S}^{ws}$, $\mathbf{S}^{sh}$ in SH-VCM, and $\mathbf{S}^{sp}$ in SP-VCM. $\mathbf{S}^{ws}$ includes two FC layers. $\mathbf{S}^{sh}$ is a K_V-dimensional FC layer. $\mathbf{S}^{sp}$ incorporates two FC layers; the dimension of the last one is K_T.

Human Pose Feature Stream. We use a pose estimation model [8] to obtain the coordinates of 17 keypoints for each human instance. Following [14], the human keypoints and the bounding box coordinates of object proposal are then encoded into a 272-dimensional pose feature vector. To generate polysemy-sensing features, we use the same strategy as the **S** stream to augment the pose feature with word embeddings. Features for this stream pass through three blocks: $\mathbf{P}^{ws}$, $\mathbf{P}^{sh}$ in SH-VCM, and $\mathbf{P}^{sp}$ in SP-VCM. The structure for each of these blocks is the same as its counterpart in the **S** stream.

It is worth noting that LPA is not applied to human and object appearance features. This is because they are redundant and thus require no further augmentation. In comparisons, the pose and spatial features are simply encoded using box or keypoint coordinates. Therefore, they are insufficient in information.

3.3 Polysemy Attention Module

As mentioned in Sect. 1, one major challenge posed by the verb polysemy problem is that the relative importance of each of the four feature streams to identifying the same verb may vary dramatically as the objects change. As shown in Fig. 1, the human appearance and pose features are important for detecting $<person\,fly\,kite>$; by contrast, these features are almost invisible and therefore less useful for detecting $<person\,fly\,airplane>$.

Therefore, we propose PAM to generate attention scores that dynamically fuse the predictions of the four feature streams. In more detail, we use the same 600-dimensional word embedding (e.g. "hold book") as in Sect. 3.2. PAM can be used for both SH-VCM and SP-VCM, and its structure is very simple. As illustrated in Fig. 3, PAM incorporates three blocks: $\mathbf{A}^{ws}$, $\mathbf{A}^{sh}$, and $\mathbf{A}^{sp}$. The $\mathbf{A}^{ws}$ block is shared by SH-VCM and SP-VCM in order to reduce the number of parameters. The $\mathbf{A}^{ws}$ block is composed of two 600-dimensional FC layers. $\mathbf{A}^{sh}$ is for SH-VCM only and includes only one four-dimensional FC layer. $\mathbf{A}^{sp}$ is for SP-VCM only and includes two FC layers, the dimensions of which are 600 and 4, respectively. The output of the two four-dimensional FC layers are processed by the sigmoid activation function and then used as attention scores for SH-VCM and SP-VCM, respectively. In this way, the role of important features with respect to the language prior is highlighted, while that of less useful features is suppressed.

Given one human-object pair (h, o), the identification score for one specific verb v obtained by the corresponding binary classifier in SH-VCM can be denoted as $\mathcal{S}^{\mathbf{SH}}_{(h,o,v)}$:

$$\mathcal{S}^{\mathbf{SH}}_{(h,o,v)} = \sigma\Big(\sum_{i\in\{\mathbf{H},\mathbf{O},\mathbf{P},\mathbf{S}\}} a^{\mathbf{sh}}_{(i,o,v)} s^{\mathbf{sh}}_{(i,o,v)} \Big), \tag{2}$$

where i denotes one feature stream, while $a^{\mathbf{sh}}_{(i,o,v)}$ is the attention score generated by PAM for the i-th feature stream. $s^{\mathbf{sh}}_{(i,o,v)}$ is the verb prediction score generated by the i-th feature stream. $\sigma(\cdot)$ represents the sigmoid activation function.

3.4 Object-SPecific Verb Classification Module

Since the verb polysemy problem is essentially caused by the change of objects, SP-VCM is introduced to construct a binary classifier for each meaningful HOI category. Meaningful and common HOI categories are provided by each popular HOI detection database, e.g. HICO-DET [4] and V-COCO [13]. Meaningless HOI categories, e.g. *<person read bicycle>* and *<person open bicycle>*, are not considered in HOI detection. The input features for SH-VCM and SP-VCM are identical. The four feature streams for each binary classifier in SP-VCM are also fused using the attention scores produced by PAM. In theory, SP-VCM will be better at solving the polysemy problem than SH-VCM, provided that each HOI category has sufficient training data; however, due to the class imbalance problem, only limited training data is available for many HOI categories. Therefore, we propose to combine SH-VCM and SP-VCM for verb classification purposes. In addition, some of their layers are shared between them, i.e. $\mathbf{H}^{ws}$, $\mathbf{O}^{ws}$, $\mathbf{P}^{ws}$, and $\mathbf{S}^{ws}$, to reduce the overfitting risk of SP-VCM on detecting HOI categories that have limited training data. In the experiments section, we prove that in the absence of this parameter sharing, the naive combination of SH-VCM and SP-VCM achieves worse performance on detecting HOI categories which have limited training data.

Given one human-object pair (h, o), the identification score for one specific verb v obtained by the corresponding binary classifier in SP-VCM can be denoted as $\mathcal{S}^{\mathbf{SP}}_{(h,o,v)}$:

$$\mathcal{S}^{\mathbf{SP}}_{(h,o,v)} = \sigma\Big(\sum_{i \in \{\mathbf{H},\mathbf{O},\mathbf{P},\mathbf{S}\}} a^{\mathbf{sp}}_{(i,o,v)} s^{\mathbf{sp}}_{(i,o,v)} \Big), \qquad (3)$$

where i denotes one feature stream. $a^{\mathbf{sp}}_{(i,o,v)}$ and $s^{\mathbf{sp}}_{(i,o,v)}$ represent the attention score and the verb identification score for the i-th feature stream, respectively.

3.5 Clustering-Based SP-VCM

If we assume that the number of object categories is $|O|$ and the number of verb categories is $|V|$, the total number of their combinations is therefore $|O| \times |V|$, which is usually very large. Accordingly, SP-VCM may include many binary classifiers, even if we remove meaningless HOI categories. In the following, we propose a clustering-based method, named CSP-VCM, aiming at reducing the number of binary classifiers in SP-VCM.

The main motivation for this step is that some HOI categories with the same verb are semantically similar [2,22], e.g. *<person hold elephant>*, *<person hold horse>* and *<person hold cow>*; therefore, they can share the same object-specific classifier. In this way, the number of binary classifiers in CSP-VCM is reduced. In more detail, we first obtain all meaningful and common HOI categories for each verb. The number of meaningful HOI categories that include the verb v is indicated by O_v. Next, we use the K-means method to cluster the HOI categories with the same verb v into C_v clusters according to the cosine distance between the word embeddings of objects. We empirically set C_v of each verb as a rounded number of the square root of O_v. This clustering strategy is also capable of handling the few- and zero-shot learning problems of SP-VCM. For example, a new HOI category $<person\,hold\,sheep>$ during testing can share the same classifier with HOI categories that have similar semantic meanings, e.g. $<person\,hold\,horse>$.

3.6   Training and Testing

Training. PD-Net can be viewed as a multi-task network. Its loss for the identification of the verb v in one HOI category (h, v, o) is represented as follows:

$$\mathcal{L}_{(h,o,v)} = \mathcal{L}^{\mathbf{SH}}(\mathcal{S}^{\mathbf{SH}}_{(h,o,v)}, l_v) + \mathcal{L}^{\mathbf{SP}}(\mathcal{S}^{\mathbf{SP}}_{(h,o,v)}, l_v), \qquad (4)$$

where $\mathcal{L}^{\mathbf{SH}}$ and $\mathcal{L}^{\mathbf{SP}}$ represent the loss of the corresponding binary classifiers in SH-VCM and SP-VCM, respectively. The loss functions of all binary classifiers are realized by binary cross-entropy loss. l_v denotes a binary label ($l_v \in \{0, 1\}$).

Testing. During testing, we use the same method as that in the training stage to obtain language priors: the object category in the prior is predicted by Faster R-CNN (rather than the ground-truth); the verb category in the prior varies for each binary classifier of the verb. Finally, the prediction score for one HOI category (h, v, o) is represented as follows:

$$\mathcal{S}^{\mathbf{HOI}}_{(h,o,v)} = \mathcal{S}_h \times \mathcal{S}_o \times \mathcal{S}^{\mathbf{PD}}_{(h,o,v)} \times \mathcal{S}^{\mathbf{I}}_{(h,o)}, \qquad (5)$$

where $\mathcal{S}_h$ and $\mathcal{S}_o$ are the detection scores of human and object proposals, respectively. $\mathcal{S}^{\mathbf{I}}_{(h,o)}$ denotes the detection score generated by a pre-trained Interactiveness Network (INet) [16], which can suppress pairs that contain no interaction. In the experiments section, we demonstrate that INet slightly promotes the performance of PD-Net.

4   Experiments

4.1   Datasets and Metrics

Datasets. HICO-DET [4] and V-COCO [13] are the two most popular benchmarks for HOI detection. HICO-DET is a large-scale dataset, containing 47,776 images in total. Of these, 38,118 images are assigned to the training set, while the remaining 9568 images are used as the testing set. There are 117 verb categories, 80 object categories, and 600 common HOI categories overall. Moreover, these 600 HOI categories are divided into 138 rare and 462 non-rare categories. Each rare HOI category contains less than 10 training samples. V-COCO [13] is a subset of MS-COCO [17], including 2533, 2867, and 4946 images for training, validation and testing, respectively. Each human instance is annotated with binary labels for 26 action categories.

Metrics. According to the official protocols [4,13], mean average precision (mAP) is used as the evaluation metric for HOI detection. On both HOI datasets, a positive human-object pair must meet the following two requirements: (1) the predicted HOI category must be the same type as the ground truth; (2) both the human and object proposals must have an Intersection over Union (IoU) with the ground truth proposals of more than 0.5. Moreover, there are two modes of mAP in HICO-DET, namely the **Default** (DT) mode and the **Known-Object** (KO) mode. In the DT mode, we calculate the average precision (AP) for each HOI category in all testing images. In the KO mode, as the categories of objects in all images are known, we need only to compute the AP for each HOI category from images containing the interested object; therefore, the KO mode can better reflect the verb classification ability. Finally, for V-COCO, the role mAP [13] (AP_{role}) is used for evaluation.

4.2 Implementation Details

We adopt the same Faster R-CNN model as [14] for object detection and object feature extraction. To facilitate fair comparison with the majority of existing works [11,14,16,23], we fix parameters of the feature extraction backbone on both datasets. The ratio between positive and negative HOI candidate pairs is set to 1:1000, while the output layer dimensions of K_V and K_T are set to 117 (24) and 600 (234), respectively in HICO-DET (V-COCO). For CSP-VCM, K_T is reduced from 600 (234) to 187 (45) in HICO-DET (V-COCO).

We adopt a two-step training strategy. First, we train all blocks in PD-Net for 6 epochs. Second, we fix those parameters that are shared between SH-VCM and SP-VCM, and fine-tune only their exclusive parameters for 2 epochs. Adam is used to optimize PD-Net with a learning rate of 1e-3 (1e-4) on HICO-DET (V-COCO). During testing, we rank the HOI candidate pairs by their detection scores (according to Equation (5)) and calculate mAP for evaluation purposes.

4.3 Ablation Studies

In this subsection, we perform ablation studies to demonstrate the effectiveness of each of the components in PD-Net on HICO-DET [4]. Experimental results are summarized in Table 1 and Table 2.

Language Prior Augmentation. LPA is used to provide hints for the classifier to reduce the intra-class variation of the pose and spatial features by augmenting them with language priors. When LPA is incorporated, SH-VCM is promoted by 0.42% and 0.73% mAP in the DT and KO modes, respectively (in Table 1).

Polysemy Attention Module. PAM is designed to decipher the verb polysemy by assigning larger weights to the important feature types for each HOI category. As shown in Table 1, under the guidance of PAM, the performance of SH-VCM is improved significantly by 1.10% and 1.34% respectively in the two evaluation modes. We further equip SH-VCM with both LPA and PAM, after which the mAP in the DT (KO) mode is promoted from 17.31% (22.40%) to

18.77% (24.04%). Moreover, the combination of LPA and PAM can improve the performance of SP-VCM by 1.04% (0.84%) in the terms of DT (KO) mAP.

Table 1. Ablation studies of LPA, PAM, CSP-VCM, and INet. Full refers to the evaluation with the mAP metric on all 600 HOI categories of the HICO-DET database.

Method	DT (Full)	KO (Full)
SH-VCM	17.31	22.40
SP-VCM	17.45	22.07
SH-VCM + LPA	17.73	23.13
SH-VCM + PAM	18.41	23.74
SH-VCM + LPA + PAM	18.77	24.04
SP-VCM + LPA + PAM	18.49	22.91
CSP-VCM + LPA + PAM	18.88	23.68
SH-VCM + SP-VCM + LPA + PAM	19.69	24.35
SH-VCM + SP-VCM + LPA + PAM + INet	20.20	24.22

Table 2. Ablation studies of PD-Net on Full, Rare, and Non-Rare HOI categories.

Method	DT Mode		
	Full	Rare	Non-rare
SH-VCM + SP-VCM + LPA + PAM + INet	20.20	14.08	22.03
SH-VCM + CSP-VCM + LPA + PAM + INet	20.22	14.59	21.90
PD-Net	19.99	14.95	21.50

Combination of SH-VCM and SP-VCM. We also naively combine the HOI detection scores from the separately trained SH-VCM+LPA+PAM and SP-HCM+LPA+PAM models, meaning that the two models share no parameters except for their backbone. As shown in Table 1, their combination outperforms both SH-VCM+LPA+PAM and SP-VCM+LPA+PAM in both the DT and KO modes. These experimental results clearly demonstrate that the two classifiers are complementary and significant to overcoming the verb polysemy problem.

When INet is integrated, the mAP in DT mode is promoted by 0.51%. However, the mAP in the KO mode decreases by 0.13%. This is because INet can suppress candidate pairs that have no interaction, which are typically caused by the incorrect or redundant object proposals. In comparison, KO mode is less affected by object detection errors; therefore, PD-Net can achieve high performance without the assist from INet in this mode. This experiment demonstrates that the strong performance of PD-Net is primarily due to its excellent verb classification ability.

Clustering-Based SP-VCM. As shown in Table 2, the combination of CSP-VCM+LPA+PAM and SH-VCM+LPA+PAM also achieves good performance of 20.22% mAP in the DT Full mode. It outperforms the combination of SP-VCM+LPA+PAM and SH-VCM+LPA+PAM on rare HOI categories by 0.51%. Performance promotion on the rare HOI categories is obtained by sharing verb classifiers with semantically similar HOI categories. These experimental results demonstrate that CSP-VCM is effective in reducing the number of object-specific classifiers and handling their few-shot learning problems in SP-VCM.

The Weight Sharing Strategy. PD-Net shares the weights of some blocks between SH-VCM and SP-VCM. As shown in Table 2, on full HOI categories, this strategy is less effective than the naive combination between SH-VCM and SP-VCM. However, with the weight sharing strategy, PD-Net achieves far better performance on rare HOI categories with a margin of 0.87% in terms of mAP. This experiment justifies the weight sharing strategy in PD-Net.

Table 3. Performance comparisons on HICO-DET. ‡ denotes the methods that adopt exactly the same object detector and feature extraction backbone as PD-Net.

Method	DT Mode			KO mode		
	Full	Rare	Non-rare	Full	Rare	Non-rare
Shen et al. [25]	6.46	4.24	7.12	-	-	-
HO-RCNN [4]	7.81	5.37	8.54	10.41	8.94	10.85
InteractNet [11]	9.94	7.16	10.77	-	-	-
GPNN [23]	13.11	9.34	14.23	-	-	-
Xu et al. [32]	14.70	13.26	15.13	-	-	-
iCAN [9]	14.84	10.45	16.15	16.26	11.33	17.73
Wang et al. [29]	16.24	11.16	17.75	17.73	12.78	19.21
No-Frills‡ [14]	17.18	12.45	18.68	-	-	-
TIN [16]	17.22	13.51	18.32	19.38	15.38	20.57
RPNN [35]	17.35	12.78	18.71	-	-	-
PMFNet [27]	17.46	15.65	18.00	20.34	17.47	21.20
Peyre et al. [22]	19.40	14.60	20.90	-	-	-
Our baseline (SH-VCM)	17.31	12.09	18.86	22.40	16.48	24.17
PD-Net	**19.99**	14.95	**21.50**	**24.15**	**18.06**	**25.97**
PD-Net†	**20.81**	**15.90**	**22.28**	**24.78**	**18.88**	**26.54**

Table 4. Performance comparisons on V-COCO. ‡ denotes the methods that adopt exactly the same object detector and feature extraction backbone.

Methods	AP_{role}
Gupta *et al.* [11,13]	31.8
InteractNet [11]	40.0
GPNN [23]	44.0
iCAN [9]	45.3
Xu *et al.* [32]	45.9
Wang *et al.* [29]	47.3
RPNN [35]	47.5
Baseline of PMFNet [27]	48.6
TIN [16]	48.7
PMFNet° [27]	50.9
PMFNet‡ [27]	52.0
Our baseline (SH-VCM)	48.2
PD-Net	51.6
PD-Net‡	**52.6**

4.4   Comparisons with State-of-the-Art Methods

In this subsection, we compare the performance of PD-Net with state-of-the-art methods. Experimental results are summarized in Table 3 and Table 4.

HICO-DET. PD-Net outperforms all state-of-the-art methods by considerable margins. In particular, with the same Faster R-CNN model, PD-Net outperforms No-Frills [14] by 2.81%, 2.50%, and 2.82% in mAP on the full, rare and non-rare HOI categories of the DT mode respectively. PD-Net outperforms state-of-the-art approaches by 3.81% mAP in the KO mode. We also observe that the performance of PD-Net can be further promoted by fusing another classifier that is based only on the human appearance feature. Similar to [22,32], the same 600-dimensional word embedding used in LPA and PAM is projected to a new feature space by two FC layers, the dimensions of which are 1024 and 2048 respectively. The inner product between the human appearance feature and that of the word embedding produces the score for one verb binary classifier. During testing, this score is fused with the original score of PD-Net via multiplication for HOI detection. This fused model is denoted as PD-Net[†]. As shown in Table 3, PD-Net[†] outperforms state-of-the-art methods by 1.41% in the DT mode.

V-COCO. Following [27], we add an union-box appearance stream on both our baseline and PD-Net. This stream extracts appearance features from the union bounding boxes composed of human-object proposal pairs. As shown in Table 4, PD-Net achieves 51.6% in mAP and outperforms our baseline by a large margin of 3.4%. The best performance on V-COCO was achieved by PMFNet [27] with

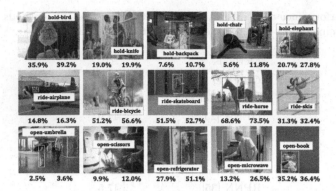

Fig. 4. Visualization of PD-Net's advantage in deciphering the verb polysemy problem. We randomly select three verbs affected by the polysemy problem: "hold" (top row), "ride" (middle row), and "open" (bottom row). The green number and red number denote the AP of SH-VCM and PD-Net respectively for the same HOI category. (Color figure online)

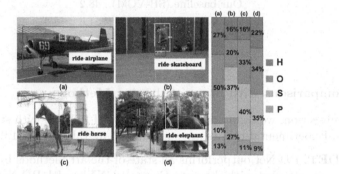

Fig. 5. Attention scores produced by PAM on four types of features. HOI categories in this figure have the same verb ("ride"). **H**, **O**, **S** and **P** denote human appearance, object appearance, spatial feature, and human pose feature respectively.

52% in mAP, which is slightly better than PD-Net. The following two details may be helpful in the implementation of PMFNet. First, PMFNet fine-tuned the Feature Pyramid Network (FPN) component of its feature extraction backbone on V-COCO. Second, it adopted human part features [27]. Therefore, we further compare PD-Net with PMFNet using two more fair settings in Table 4. First, we fix the FPN component in PMFNet according to the code released by the authors (denoted as PMFNet°) and re-train the model. PD-Net outperforms PMFNet° by 0.7%. Second, we adopt the same feature extraction backbone and the five feature streams as described in [27] for PD-Net. The contributions in this paper remain unchanged. This model is denoted as PD-Net‡ in Table 4. It is shown that PD-Net‡ outperforms PMFNet by 0.6%. The above experiments justify the effectiveness of PD-Net.

4.5   Qualitative Visualization Results

Figure 4 visualizes PD-Net's advantage in deciphering the polysemy problem of verbs on HICO-DET. The performance gain by PD-Net compared with SH-VCM reaches 23.2% in AP for the "open refrigerator" category.

Figure 5 illustrates attention scores produced by PAM for four types of features on HICO-DET. HOI categories in this figure share the verb "ride", but differ dramatically in semantic meanings. The "person" proposal in Fig. 5(a) is very small and severely occluded while the "airplane" proposal is very large; thus, object appearance feature is much more important for verb classification than the human appearance feature. In Fig. 5(b), both the spatial feature and human pose feature play important roles in determining the verb. Attention scores for Fig. 5(c) and (d) are similar, as <person ride horse> and <person ride elephant> are indeed close in semantics. More qualitative visualization results on the V-COCO database are provided in the supplementary file.

5   Conclusions

The verb polysemy problem is relatively underexplored and sometimes even ignored in existing works for HOI detection. In this paper, we propose a novel model, named PD-Net, which significantly mitigates the challenging verb polysemy problems for HOI detection through the use of three key components: LPA, PAM, and the combination of SH-VCM with SP-VCM. Exhaustive ablation studies are performed to demonstrate the effectiveness of these three components. Finally, the effectiveness of PD-Net for decoding the verb polysemy is demonstrated on the two most popular datasets for HOI detection.

Acknowledgement. Changxing Ding is the corresponding author. This work was supported by the NSF of China under Grant 61702193, the Science and Technology Program of Guangzhou under Grant 201804010272, the Program for Guangdong Introducing Innovative and Entrepreneurial Teams under Grant 2017ZT07X183, the Fundamental Research Funds for the Central Universities of China under Grant 2019JQ01, and ARC FL-170100117.

References

1. Ashual, O., Wolf, L.: Specifying object attributes and relations in interactive scene generation. In: ICCV (2019)
2. Bansal, A., Rambhatla, S.S., Shrivastava, A., Chellappa, R.: Detecting human-object interactions via functional generalization. arXiv preprint arXiv:1904.03181 (2019)
3. Cadene, R., Ben-Younes, H., Cord, M., Thome, N.: MUREL: multimodal relational reasoning for visual question answering. In: CVPR (2019)
4. Chao, Y.W., Liu, Y., Liu, X., Zeng, H., Deng, J.: Learning to detect human-object interactions. In: WACV (2018)

5. Chen, T., Yu, W., Chen, R., Lin, L.: Knowledge-embedded routing network for scene graph generation. In: CVPR (2019)
6. Chen, Y., Wang, Z., Peng, Y., Zhang, Z., Yu, G., Sun, J.: Cascaded pyramid network for multi-person pose estimation. In: CVPR (2018)
7. Fang, H.-S., Cao, J., Tai, Y.-W., Lu, C.: Pairwise body-part attention for recognizing human-object interactions. In: Ferrari, V., Hebert, M., Sminchisescu, C., Weiss, Y. (eds.) ECCV 2018. LNCS, vol. 11214, pp. 52–68. Springer, Cham (2018). https://doi.org/10.1007/978-3-030-01249-6_4
8. Fang, H.S., Xie, S., Tai, Y.W., Lu, C.: RMPE: regional multi-person pose estimation. In: ICCV (2017)
9. Gao, C., Zou, Y., Huang, J.B.: iCAN: instance-centric attention network for human-object interaction detection. In: BMVC (2018)
10. Gao, P., et al.: Dynamic fusion with intra-and inter-modality attention flow for visual question answering. In: CVPR (2019)
11. Gkioxari, G., Girshick, R., Dollár, P., He, K.: Detecting and recognizing human-object interactions. In: CVPR (2018)
12. Gu, J., Zhao, H., Lin, Z., Li, S., Cai, J., Ling, M.: Scene graph generation with external knowledge and image reconstruction. In: CVPR (2019)
13. Gupta, S., Malik, J.: Visual semantic role labeling. arXiv preprint arXiv:1505.04474 (2015)
14. Gupta, T., Schwing, A., Hoiem, D.: No-frills human-object interaction detection: Factorization, layout encodings, and training techniques. In: ICCV (2019)
15. He, S., Tavakoli, H.R., Borji, A., Pugeault, N.: Human attention in image captioning: dataset and analysis. In: ICCV (2019)
16. Li, Y.L., et al.: Transferable interactiveness knowledge for human-object interaction detection. In: CVPR (2019)
17. Lin, T.-Y., et al.: Microsoft COCO: common objects in context. In: Fleet, D., Pajdla, T., Schiele, B., Tuytelaars, T. (eds.) ECCV 2014. LNCS, vol. 8693, pp. 740–755. Springer, Cham (2014). https://doi.org/10.1007/978-3-319-10602-1_48
18. Lin, X., Ding, C., Zeng, J., Tao, D.: GPS-Net: graph property sensing network for scene graph generation. In: CVPR (2020)
19. Lu, C., Krishna, R., Bernstein, M., Fei-Fei, L.: Visual relationship detection with language priors. In: Leibe, B., Matas, J., Sebe, N., Welling, M. (eds.) ECCV 2016. LNCS, vol. 9905, pp. 852–869. Springer, Cham (2016). https://doi.org/10.1007/978-3-319-46448-0_51
20. Marino, K., Rastegari, M., Farhadi, A., Mottaghi, R.: OK-VQA: a visual question answering benchmark requiring external knowledge. In: CVPR (2019)
21. Mikolov, T., Sutskever, I., Chen, K., Corrado, G.S., Dean, J.: Distributed representations of words and phrases and their compositionality. In: NIPS (2013)
22. Peyre, J., Laptev, I., Schmid, C., Sivic, J.: Detecting unseen visual relations using analogies. In: ICCV (2019)
23. Qi, S., Wang, W., Jia, B., Shen, J., Zhu, S.-C.: Learning human-object interactions by graph parsing neural networks. In: Ferrari, V., Hebert, M., Sminchisescu, C., Weiss, Y. (eds.) ECCV 2018. LNCS, vol. 11213, pp. 407–423. Springer, Cham (2018). https://doi.org/10.1007/978-3-030-01240-3_25
24. Ren, S., He, K., Girshick, R., Sun, J.: Faster R-CNN: towards real-time object detection with region proposal networks. In: NIPS (2015)
25. Shen, L., Yeung, S., Hoffman, J., Mori, G., Li, F.F.: Scaling human-object interaction recognition through zero-shot learning. In: WACV (2018)
26. Shrestha, R., Kafle, K., Kanan, C.: Answer them all! toward universal visual question answering models. In: CVPR (2019)

27. Wan, B., Zhou, D., Liu, Y., Li, R., He, X.: Pose-aware multi-level feature network for human object interaction detection. In: ICCV (2019)
28. Wan, H., Luo, Y., Peng, B., Zheng, W.S.: Representation learning for scene graph completion via jointly structural and visual embedding. In: IJCAI (2018)
29. Wang, T., et al.: Deep contextual attention for human-object interaction detection. In: ICCV (2019)
30. Wang, W., Wang, R., Shan, S., Chen, X.: Exploring context and visual pattern of relationship for scene graph generation. In: CVPR (2019)
31. Xu, B., Li, J., Wong, Y., Zhao, Q., Kankanhalli, M.S.: Interact as you intend: intention-driven human-object interaction detection. IEEE Trans. Multimed., 1 (2019). https://doi.org/10.1109/TMM.2019.2943753
32. Xu, B., Wong, Y., Li, J., Zhao, Q., Kankanhalli, M.S.: Learning to detect human-object interactions with knowledge. In: CVPR (2019)
33. Yang, X., Tang, K., Zhang, H., Cai, J.: Auto-encoding scene graphs for image captioning. In: CVPR (2019)
34. Yao, T., Pan, Y., Li, Y., Mei, T.: Hierarchy parsing for image captioning. arXiv preprint arXiv:1909.03918 (2019)
35. Zhou, P., Chi, M.: Relation parsing neural network for human-object interaction detection. In: ICCV (2019)

PODNet: Pooled Outputs Distillation for Small-Tasks Incremental Learning

Arthur Douillard[1,2(✉)], Matthieu Cord[2,3], Charles Ollion[1], Thomas Robert[1], and Eduardo Valle[4]

[1] Heuritech, Paris, France
{arthur.douillard,charles.ollion,thomas.robert}@heuritech.com
[2] Sorbonne University, Paris, France
matthieu.cord@sorbonne-universite.fr
[3] Valeo.ai, Paris, France
[4] University of Campinas, Campinas, Brazil
dovalle@dca.fee.unicamp.br

Abstract. Lifelong learning has attracted much attention, but existing works still struggle to fight catastrophic forgetting and accumulate knowledge over long stretches of incremental learning. In this work, we propose PODNet, a model inspired by representation learning. By carefully balancing the compromise between remembering the old classes and learning new ones, PODNet fights catastrophic forgetting, even over very long runs of small incremental tasks – a setting so far unexplored by current works. PODNet innovates on existing art with an efficient spatial-based distillation-loss applied throughout the model and a representation comprising multiple proxy vectors for each class. We validate those innovations thoroughly, comparing PODNet with three state-of-the-art models on three datasets: CIFAR100, ImageNet100, and ImageNet1000. Our results showcase a significant advantage of PODNet over existing art, with accuracy gains of 12.10, 6.51, and 2.85 percentage points, respectively.

Keywords: Incremental-learning · Representation-learning pooling

1 Introduction

Lifelong machine learning [7,31,34] focuses on models that accumulate and refine knowledge over large timespans. Incremental learning – the ability to aggregate different learning objectives seen over time into a coherent whole – is paramount to those models. To achieve incremental learning, models must fight *catastrophic forgetting* [7,31] of previous knowledge. Lifelong and incremental learning have attracted much attention in the past few years, but existing works still struggle

Electronic supplementary material The online version of this chapter (https://doi.org/10.1007/978-3-030-58565-5_6) contains supplementary material, which is available to authorized users.

© Springer Nature Switzerland AG 2020
A. Vedaldi et al. (Eds.): ECCV 2020, LNCS 12365, pp. 86–102, 2020.
https://doi.org/10.1007/978-3-030-58565-5_6

to preserve acquired knowledge over many cycles of short incremental learning steps[1].

We will focus on image classifiers, which are ordinarily trained once on a fixed set of classes. In *incremental learning*, however, the classifier must learn the classes by steps, in training cycles called *tasks*. At each task, we expose the classifier to a new set of classes. Incremental learning would reduce trivially to ordinary classification if we were allowed to store all training samples, but we are imposed a limited *memory*: a maximum number of samples for previously learned classes. This limitation is motivated by practical applications, in which privacy issues, or storage and computing limitations prevent us from simply retraining the entire model for each new task [21,22]. Furthermore, incremental learning is different from transfer learning in that we aim to have good performance in both old and new classes.

To overcome catastrophic forgetting, different approaches have been proposed: reusing a limited amount of previous training data [3,30]; learning to generate the training data [15,33]; extending the architecture for new phases of data [20,36]; using a sub-network for each phase [6,10]; or constraining the model divergence as it evolves [1,3,16,21,23,30].

In this work, we propose PODNet, approaching incremental learning as representation learning, with a distillation loss that constrains the evolution of the representation. By carefully balancing the compromise between remembering the old classes and learning new ones, we learn a representation that fights catastrophic forgetting, remaining stable over long runs of small incremental tasks. Our model innovates on existing art with (1) an *efficient spatial-based* distillation-loss applied *throughout the model*; and (2) as a refinement, a representation comprising multiple proxy vectors for each class, resulting in a more flexible representation.

In this paper, we first present the existing state of the art (Sect. 2), which we close by detailing our contributions. We then describe our model (Sect. 3), and evaluate it in an extensive set of experiments (Sect. 4) on CIFAR100, ImageNet100, and ImageNet1000, including ablation studies assessing each contribution, and extensive comparisons with existing methods.

2   Related Work

To approach the problem of incremental learning, consider a single incremental task: one has a classifier already trained over a set of old classes and must adapt it to learn a set of new classes. To perform that single task, we will consider: (1) the data/class representation model; (2) the set of constraints to prevent catastrophic forgetting; (3) the experimental context (including the constraints over the memory for previous training data) for which to design the model.

---

[1] Code is available at: github.com/arthurdouillard/incremental_learning.pytorch.

Data/Class Representation Model. Representation learning was already implicitly present in iCaRL [30]: it introduced the Nearest Mean Exemplars (NME) strategy which averages the outputs of the deep convolutional network to create a single proxy feature vector per class that are then used by a nearest-neighbor classifier predict the final classes. Hou et al. [13] adopted this method and also introduced another, named CNN, which uses the output class probabilities to classify incoming samples, freezing (during training) the classifier weights associated with old classes, and then fine-tuning them on an under-sampled dataset.

Hou et al. [13], in the method called here UCIR, made representation learning explicit, by noticing that the limited memory imposed a severe imbalance on the training samples available for the old and for the new classes. To overcome that difficulty, they designed a metric-learning model instead of a classification model. That strategy is often used in few-shot learning [8] because of its robustness to few data. Because classical metric architectures require special training sampling (e.g., semi-hard sampling for triplets), Hou et al. chose instead to redesign the classifier's last layer of their model to use the cosine similarity [25].

Model Constraints to Prevent Catastrophic Forgetting. Constraining the model's evolution to prevent forgetting is a fruitful idea proposed by several methods [1,3,16,21,23,30]. Preventing the model's parameters from diverging too much forces it to remember the old classes, but care must be taken to still allow it to learn the new ones. We call this balance the *rigidity-plasticity trade-off*.

Existing art on knowledge distillation/compression [12] was an important source of inspiration for constraints on models. The goal is to distill a large trained model (called teacher) into a new smaller model (called student). The distillation loss forces the features of the student to approach those of its teacher. In our case, the student is the current model and the teacher—with same capacity—is its version at the previous task. Zagoruyko and Komodakis [17] investigated attention-based distillation for image classifiers, by pooling the intermediate features of convolutional networks into attention maps, then used in their distillation losses. Li and Hoiem [21]—and several authors after them [3,30,35]—used a binary cross-entropy between the output probabilities by the models. Hou et al. [13], used instead *Less-Forget*, a cosine-similarity constraint on the flat feature embeddings after the global average pooling. Dhar et al. [5] proposed to constrain the gradient-based attentions generated by GradCam [32], a visualization method. Wu et al. [35] proposed BiC, an algorithm oriented towards large-scale datasets, which employs a small linear model learned on validation data to recalibrate the output probabilities before applying a distillation loss.

Experimental Context. A critical component of incremental learning is the convention used for the memory storing samples of previous data. An usual convention is to consider a fixed amount of samples allowed in that memory, as illustrated in Fig. 1.

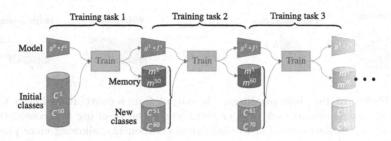

Fig. 1. Training protocol for incremental learning. At each training task we learn a new set of classes, and the model must retain knowledge about *all* classes. The model is allowed a *limited* memory of samples of old classes.

Still, there are two experimental protocols for such fixed-sample convention: we may either use the memory budget at will (M_{total}), or add a constraint on the number of samples per class for the old classes (M_{per}). When $M_{\text{total}} = M_{\text{per}} \times \#$ *of classes*, both settings have equivalent *final* memory size, but the latter, that we adopt, is much more challenging since early tasks cannot benefit from the full memory size. *The granularity of the increments* is another critical element: with a fixed number of classes, increasing the number of tasks decreases the number of classes per task. More tasks imply stronger forgetting of the earliest classes, and pushing that number creates a challenging protocol, so far unexplored by existing art. Hou et al. evaluate at most 10 tasks on CIFAR100, while we propose as much as 50 tasks.

Finally, to score the experiments, Rebuffi et al. [30] proposed a global metric that they called **average incremental accuracy**, taking into account the entire history of the run, averaging the accuracy at the end of each task (including the first).

Contributions. As seen, associating representation learning to model constraints is a particularly fruitful idea for incremental learning, but requires carefully balancing the goals of rigidity (to avoid catastrophic forgetting) and plasticity (to learn new classes).

Employing a distillation-based loss to constrain the evolution of the representation has also resulted in leading results [5,13,35,37]. Our model improves existing art by employing a *novel and efficient spatial-based* distillation loss, which we are able to apply *throughout the model*.

Implicit or explicit proxy vectors representing each class inside the models have lead to state of the art results [13,30]. Our model extends that idea allowing for *multiple proxy vectors* per class, resulting in a more flexible representation.

3   Model

Formally, we learn the model in T *tasks*, task t comprising a set of new classes C_N^t, and a set of old classes C_O^t, and aiming at classifying all seen classes $C_O^t \cup C_N^t$.

Fig. 2. Different possible poolings. The output from a convolutional layer $\mathbf{h}^t_{\ell,c,w,h}$ may be pooled (summed over) one or more axes. The resulting loss considers only the pooled activations instead of the individual components, allowing more plasticity across the pooled axes.

Between tasks, the new set C^t_O will be set to $C^{t-1}_O \cup C^{t-1}_N$, but the amount of training samples from C^t_O (called *memory*) is constrained to exactly M_{per} samples per class, while all training samples in the dataset are allowed for the classes in C^t_N, as shown in Fig. 1. The resulting imbalance, if unmanaged, leads to *catastrophic forgetting* [7,31], i.e., learning the new classes at the cost of forgetting the old ones.

Our base model is a deep convolutional network $\hat{\mathbf{y}} = g(f(\mathbf{x}))$, where $\mathbf{x}$ is the input image, $\mathbf{y}$ is the output vector of class probabilities, $\mathbf{h} = f(\mathbf{x})$ is the "feature extraction" part of the network (all layers up to the next-to-last), $\hat{\mathbf{y}} = g(\mathbf{h})$ is the final classification layer, and $\mathbf{h}$ is the final embedding of the network before classification (Fig. 3). The superscript t denotes the model learned at task $t : f^t$, g^t, $\mathbf{h}^t$, etc.

3.1   POD: Pooled Outputs Distillation Loss

Constraining the evolution of the weights is crucial to reduce forgetting. Each new task t learns a new (student) model, whose weights are not only initialized with those of the previous (teacher) model, but also constrained by a distillation loss. That loss must be carefully balanced to prevent forgetting (rigidity), while allowing the learning of new classes (plasticity).

To this goal, we propose a set of constraints we call **Pooled Outputs Distillation (POD)**, applied not only over the final embedding output by $\mathbf{h}^t = f^t(\mathbf{x})$, but also over the output of its intermediate layers $\mathbf{h}^t_\ell = f^t_\ell(\mathbf{x})$ (where by notation overloading $f^t_\ell(\mathbf{x}) \equiv f^t_\ell \circ \ldots \circ f^t_1(\mathbf{x})$, and thus $f^t(\mathbf{x}) \equiv f^t_L \ldots \circ f^t_\ell \circ \ldots f^t_1(\mathbf{x})$).

The convolutional layers of the network output tensors $\mathbf{h}^t_\ell$ with components $\mathbf{h}^t_{\ell,c,w,h}$, where c stands for channel (filter), and $w \times h$ for column and row of the spatial coordinates. The loss used by POD may pool (sum over) one or several of those indexes, more aggressive poolings (Fig. 2) providing more freedom, and thus, plasticity: the lowest possible plasticity imposes an exact similarity between the previous and current model while higher plasticity relaxes the similarity definition.

Pooling is an important operation in Computer Vision, with a strong theoretical motivation. In the past, pooling has been introduced to obtain invariant representations [19,24]. Here, the justification is similar, but the goal is different: as we will see, the pooled indexes are aggregated in the proposed loss, allowing *plasticity*. Instead of the model acquiring invariance to the input image, the desired loss acquires invariance to model evolution, and thus, representation. The proposed pooling-based formalism has two advantages: first, it organizes disparately proposed distillation losses into a neat, general formalism. Second, as we will see, it allowed us to propose novel distillation losses, with better plasticity-rigidity compromises. Those topics are explored next.

Pooling of Convolutional Outputs. As explained before, POD constrains the output of each intermediate convolutional layer $\mathbf{h}^t_{\ell,c,w,h} = f^t_\ell(\cdot)$ (in practice, each stage of a ResNet [11]). As a reminder, c is the channel and $w \times h$ are the spatial coordinates. All POD variants use the Euclidean distance of ℓ^2-normalize tensors, here noted as $\|\cdot - \cdot\|$. They differ on the type of pooling applied before that distance is computed. On one extreme, one can apply no pooling at all, resulting in the most strict loss, the most rigid constrains, and the lowest plasticity:

$$\mathcal{L}_{\text{POD-pixel}}(\mathbf{h}^{t-1}_\ell, \mathbf{h}^t_\ell) = \sum_{c=1}^{C}\sum_{w=1}^{W}\sum_{h=1}^{H}\left\|\mathbf{h}^{t-1}_{\ell,c,w,h} - \mathbf{h}^t_{\ell,c,w,h}\right\|^2 . \tag{1}$$

By pooling the channels, one preserves only the spatial coordinates, resulting in a more permissive loss, allowing the activations to reorganize across the channels, but penalizing global changes of those activations across the space,

$$\mathcal{L}_{\text{POD-channel}}(\mathbf{h}^{t-1}_\ell, \mathbf{h}^t_\ell) = \sum_{w=1}^{W}\sum_{h=1}^{H}\left\|\sum_{c=1}^{C}\mathbf{h}^{t-1}_{\ell,c,w,h} - \sum_{c=1}^{C}\mathbf{h}^t_{\ell,c,w,h}\right\|^2 ; \tag{2}$$

or, contrarily, by pooling the space (equivalent, up to a factor, to a Global Average Pooling), one preserves *only* the channels:

$$\mathcal{L}_{\text{POD-gap}}(\mathbf{h}^{t-1}_\ell, \mathbf{h}^t_\ell) = \sum_{c=1}^{C}\left\|\sum_{w=1}^{W}\sum_{h=1}^{H}\mathbf{h}^{t-1}_{\ell,c,w,h} - \sum_{w=1}^{W}\sum_{h=1}^{H}\mathbf{h}^t_{\ell,c,w,h}\right\|^2 . \tag{3}$$

Note that the only difference between the variants is in the position of the summation. For example, contrast equations Eqs. 1 and 2: in the former the differences are computed between activation pixels, and then totaled; in the latter, first the channel axis is flattened, then the differences are computed, resulting in a more permissive loss.

We can trade a little plasticity for rigidity, with less aggressive pooling by aggregating statistics across just one of the spatial dimensions:

$$\mathcal{L}_{\text{POD-width}}(\mathbf{h}^{t-1}_\ell, \mathbf{h}^t_\ell) = \sum_{c=1}^{C}\sum_{h=1}^{H}\left\|\sum_{w=1}^{W}\mathbf{h}^{t-1}_{\ell,c,w,h} - \sum_{w=1}^{W}\mathbf{h}^t_{\ell,c,w,h}\right\|^2 ; \tag{4}$$

or, likewise, for the vertical dimension, resulting in POD-height. Each of those variants measure the distribution of activation pixels across their respective axis. These two complementary intermediate statistics can be further combined together:

$$\mathcal{L}_{\text{POD-spatial}}(\mathbf{h}_\ell^{t-1}, \mathbf{h}_\ell^t) = \mathcal{L}_{\text{POD-width}}(\mathbf{h}_\ell^{t-1}, \mathbf{h}_\ell^t) + \mathcal{L}_{\text{POD-height}}(\mathbf{h}_\ell^{t-1}, \mathbf{h}_\ell^t). \qquad (5)$$

$\mathcal{L}_{\text{POD-spatial}}$ is minimal when the average statistics over the dataset, on both width and height axes, are similar for the previous and current model. It brings the right balance between being too rigid (Eq. 1) and being too permissive (Eqs. 2 and 3).

Constraining the Final Embedding. After the convolutional layers, the network, by design, flattens the spatial coordinates, and the formalism above needs adjustment, as a summation over w and h is no longer possible. Instead, we set a flat constraint on the final embedding $\mathbf{h}^t = f^t(\mathbf{x})$:

$$\mathcal{L}_{\text{POD-flat}}(\mathbf{h}^{t-1}, \mathbf{h}^t) = \left\| \mathbf{h}^{t-1} - \mathbf{h}^t \right\|^2. \qquad (6)$$

Combining the Losses, Analysis. The final POD loss combines the two components:

$$\mathcal{L}_{\text{POD-final}}(\mathbf{x}) = \frac{\lambda_c}{L-1} \sum_{\ell=1}^{L-1} \mathcal{L}_{\text{POD-spatial}}\left(f_\ell^{t-1}(\mathbf{x}), f_\ell^t(\mathbf{x})\right)$$
$$+ \lambda_f \mathcal{L}_{\text{POD-flat}}\left(f^{t-1}(\mathbf{x}), f^t(\mathbf{x})\right). \qquad (7)$$

The hyperparameters λ_c and λ_f are necessary to balance the two terms, due to the different nature of the intermediate outputs (spatial and flat).

As mentioned, the strategy above generalizes disparate propositions existing both in the literature of incremental learning, and elsewhere. When $\lambda_c = 0$, it reduces to the cosine constraint of *Less-Forget*, proposed by Hou et al. for incremental learning, which constrains only the final embedding [13]. When $\lambda_f = 0$ and POD-spatial is replaced by POD-pixel, it suggests the Perceptual Features loss, proposed for style transfer [14]. When $\lambda_f = 0$ and POD-spatial is replaced by POD-channel, the strategy hints at the loss proposed by Komodakis et al. [17] to allow distillation across different networks, a situation in which the channel pooling responds to the very practical need to allow the comparison of architectures with different number of channels.

As we will see in our evaluations of pooling strategies (Subsect. 4.2), what proved optimal was a completely novel idea, POD-spatial, combining two poolings, each of which flattens one of the spatial coordinates. That relatively rigid strategy (channels and one of the spatial coordinates are considered in each half of the loss) makes intuitive sense in our context, which is *small-task* incremental learning, and thus where we expect a slow drift of the model across a single task.

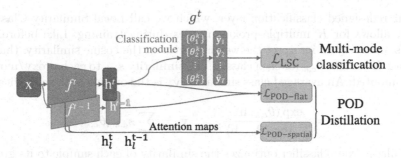

Fig. 3. Overview of PODNet: the distillation loss POD prevent excessive model drift by constraining intermediate outputs of the ConvNet f and the LSC classifier g learns a more expressive multi-modal representation.

3.2 Local Similarity Classifier

Hou et al. [13] observed that the class imbalance of incremental learning have concrete manifestations on the parameters of the final layer on classifiers, namely the weights for the over-represented (new) classes becoming much larger than those for the underrepresented (old) classes. To overcome this issue, their method (called here UCIR) ℓ^2-normalizes both the weights and the activations, which corresponds to taking the cosine similarity instead of the dot product. For each class c, their last layer becomes

$$\hat{\mathbf{y}}_c = \frac{\exp\left(\eta\langle\boldsymbol{\theta}_c, \mathbf{h}\rangle\right)}{\sum_i \exp\left(\eta\langle\boldsymbol{\theta}_i, \mathbf{h}\rangle\right)}, \tag{8}$$

where $\boldsymbol{\theta}_c$ are the last-layer weights for class c, η is a learned scaling parameter, and $\langle\cdot, \cdot\rangle$ is the cosine similarity.

However, this strategy optimizes a *global similarity*: its training objective increases the similarity between the extracted features and their associated weights. For each class, the normalized weight vector acts as a *single* proxy [26], towards which the learning procedure pushes all samples in the class.

We observed that such global strategy is hard to optimize in an incremental setting. To avoid forgetting, the distillation losses (Subsect. 3.1) tries to keep the final embedding $\mathbf{h}$ consistent through time so that the class proxies stay relevant for the classifier. Unfortunately catastrophic forgetting, while alleviated by current methods, is not solved and thus the distribution of $\mathbf{h}$ may change. The cosine classifier is very sensitive to those changes as it models a unique majority mode through its class proxies.

Local Similarity Classifier. The problem above lead us to amend the classification layer during training, in order to consider multiple proxies/modes per class. A shift in the distribution of $\mathbf{h}$ will have less impact on the classifier as more modes are covered.

Our redesigned classification layer, which we call Local Similarity Classifier (LSC), allows for K multiple proxies/modes during training. Like before, the proxies are a way to interpret the weight vector in the cosine similarity, thus we allow for K vectors $\boldsymbol{\theta}_{c,k}$ for each class c. The similarity $s_{c,k}$ to each proxy/mode is first computed. An averaged class similarity $\hat{\mathbf{y}}_c$ is the output of the classification layer:

$$s_{c,k} = \frac{\exp \langle \boldsymbol{\theta}_{c,k}, \mathbf{h} \rangle}{\sum_i \exp \langle \boldsymbol{\theta}_{c,i}, \mathbf{h} \rangle}, \qquad \hat{\mathbf{y}}_c = \sum_k s_{c,k} \langle \boldsymbol{\theta}_{c,k}, \mathbf{h} \rangle. \tag{9}$$

The multi-proxies classifier optimizes the similarity of each sample to its ground truth class representation and minimizes all others. A simple cross-entropy loss would work, but we found empirically that the NCA loss [9,26] converged faster. We added to the original loss a hinge $[\cdot]_+$ to keep it bounded, and a small margin δ to enforce stronger class separation, resulting in the final formulation:

$$\mathcal{L}_{\text{LSC}} = \left[-\log \frac{\exp \left(\eta (\hat{\mathbf{y}}_y - \delta) \right)}{\sum_{i \neq y} \exp \eta \hat{\mathbf{y}}_i} \right]_+. \tag{10}$$

Weight Initialization for New Classes. The incremental learning setting imposes detecting new classes at each new task t. New weights $\{\boldsymbol{\theta}_{c,k} \mid \forall c \in C_N^t, \forall k \in 1...K\}$ must be added to predict them. We could initialize them randomly, but the class-agnostic features of the ConvNet f, extracted by the model trained so far offer a better prior. Thus, we employ a generalization of Imprinted Weights [28] procedure to multiple modes: for each new class c, we extract the features of its training samples, use a k-means algorithm to split them into K clusters, and use the centroids of those clusters as initial values for $\boldsymbol{\theta}_{c,k}$. This procedure ensures mode diversity at the beginning of a new task and resulted in a one percentage point improvement on CIFAR100 [18].

3.3 Complete Model Formulation

Our model has the classical structure of a convolutional network $f(\cdot)$ acting as a features extractor, and a classifier $g(\cdot)$ producing a score per class. We introduced two innovations to this model: (1) our main contribution is a novel distillation loss (POD) applied all over the ConvNet, from the spatial features $\mathbf{h}_\ell$ to the final flat embedding $\mathbf{h}$; (2) as further refinement we propose that the classifier learns a multi-modal representation that explicitly keeps multiple proxy vectors per class, increasing the model expressiveness and thus making it less sensible to shift in the distribution of $\mathbf{h}$. The final loss for current model $g^t \circ f^t$, i.e., the model trained for task t, is simply their addition $\mathcal{L}_{\{f^t;g^t\}} = \mathcal{L}_{\text{LSC}} + \mathcal{L}_{\text{POD-final}}$.

4 Experiments

We compare our technique (PODNet) with three state-of-the-art models. Those models are particularly comparable to ours since they all employ a sample memory with a fixed capacity. Both iCaRL [30] and UCIR [13] use the same inference method – *Nearest-Mean-Examplars* (NME), although UCIR also proposes a second inference method based on the classifier probabilities (called here UCIR-CNN). We evaluate PODNet with both inference methods for a small scale dataset, and the later for larger scale datasets. BiC [35], while not focused on representation learning, is specially designed to be effective on large scale datasets, and thus provided an interesting baseline.

Datasets. We employ three images datasets – extensively used in the literature of incremental learning – for our experiments: CIFAR100 [18], ImageNet100 [4, 13,35], and ImageNet1000 [4]. ImageNet100 is a subset of ImageNet1000 with only 100 classes, randomly sampled from the original 1000.

Protocol. We validate our model and the compared baselines using the challenging protocol introduced by Hou et al. [13]: we start by training the models on half the classes (i.e., 50 for CIFAR100 and ImageNet100, and 500 for ImageNet1000). Then the classes are added incrementally in steps. We divide the remaining classes equally among the steps, e.g., for CIFAR100 we could have 5 steps of 10 classes or 50 steps of 1 class. Note that a training of 50 steps is actually made of 51 different tasks: the initial training followed by the incremental steps. Models are evaluated after each step on *all the classes seen until then*. To facilitate comparison, the accuracies at the end of each step are averaged into a unique score called *average incremental accuracy* [30]. If not specified otherwise, the average incremental accuracy is the score reported in all our results.

Following Hou et al. [13], for all datasets, and all compared models, we limit the memory M_{per} to 20 images per old class. For results with different memory settings, refer to Subsect. 4.2.

Implementation Details. For fair comparison, all compared models employ the same ConvNet backbone: ResNet-32 for CIFAR100, and ResNet-18 for ImageNet. We remove the ReLU activation at the last block of each ResNet end-of-stage to provide a signed input to POD (Subsect. 3.1). We implemented our method (called here PODNet) in PyTorch [27]. We compare both ours and UCIR's implementation [13] of iCaRL. Results of UCIR come from the implementation of Hou et al. [13]. We provide their reported results and also run their code ourselves. We used our implementation of BiC in order to compare with the same backbone. We sample our memory images using *herding selection* [30] and perform the inference with two different methods: the *Nearest-Mean-Examplars* (NME) proposed for iCarl, and also adopted on one of the variants of UCIR [13], and the "CNN" method introduced for UCIR (see Sect. 2). Please see the supplementary materials for the full implementation details.

4.1   Quantitative Results

The comparisons with all the state of the art are tabulated in Table 1 for CIFAR100 and Table 2 for ImageNet100 and ImageNet1000. All tables shows

Table 1. Average incremental accuracy for PODNet *vs.* state of the art. We run experiments three times (random class orders) on CIFAR100 and report averages ± standard deviations. Models with an asterisk * are reported directly from Hou et al. [13]

New classes per step	CIFAR100			
	50 steps	25 steps	10 steps	5 steps
	1	2	5	10
iCaRL * [30]	—	—	52.57	57.17
iCaRL	44.20 ± 0.98	50.60 ± 1.06	53.78 ± 1.16	58.08 ± 0.59
BiC [35]	47.09 ± 1.48	48.96 ± 1.03	53.21 ± 1.01	56.86 ± 0.46
UCIR (NME) * [13]	—	—	60.12	63.12
UCIR (NME) [13]	48.57 ± 0.37	56.82 ± 0.19	60.83 ± 0.70	63.63 ± 0.87
UCIR (CNN) * [13]	—	—	60.18	63.42
UCIR (CNN) [13]	49.30 ± 0.32	57.57 ± 0.23	61.22 ± 0.69	64.01 ± 0.91
PODNet (NME)	**61.40 ± 0.68**	**62.71 ± 1.26**	**64.03 ± 1.30**	**64.48 ± 1.32**
PODNet (CNN)	**57.98 ± 0.46**	**60.72 ± 1.36**	**63.19 ± 1.16**	**64.83 ± 0.98**

the average incremental accuracy for each considered models with various number of steps on the incremental learning run. The "New classes per step" row shows the amount of new classes introduced per task.

CIFAR100. We run our comparisons on 5, 10, 25, and 50 steps with respectively 10, 5, 2, and 1 classes per step. We created three random class orders to ran each experiment thrice, reporting averages and standard deviations. For CIFAR100 only, we evaluated our model with two different kind of inference: NME and CNN. With both methods, our model surpasses all previous state of the art models on all steps. Moreover, our model relative improvement grows as the number the steps increases, surpassing existing models by 0.82, 2.81, 5.14, and 12.1 percent points (*p.p.*) for respectively 5, 10, 25, and 50 steps. Larger numbers of steps imply stronger forgetting; those results confirm that PODNet manages to reduce drastically the said forgetting. While PODNet with NME has the largest gain, PODNet with CNN also outperforms the previous state of the art by up to 8.68*p.p.* See Fig. 4 for a plot of the incremental accuracies on this dataset. In the extreme setting of 50 increments of 1 class (Fig. 4a), our model showcases large differences, with slow degradation ("*gradual forgetting*" [7]) due to forgetting throughout the run, while the other models show a quick performance collapse ("*catastrophic forgetting*") at the start of the run.

ImageNet100. We run our comparisons on 5, 10, 25, and 50 steps with respectively 10, 5, 2, and 1 classes per step. For both ImageNet100, and ImageNet1000 we report only PODNet with CNN, as the kNN-based NME classifier did not generalize as well to larger-scale datasets. With the more complex images of

Table 2. Average incremental accuracy, PODNet *vs.* state of the art. Models with an asterisk * are reported directly from Hou et al. [13]

New classes per step	ImageNet100				Imagenet1000	
	50 steps	25 steps	10 steps	5 steps	10 steps	5 steps
	1	2	5	10	50	100
iCaRL* [30]	—	—	59.53	65.04	46.72	51.36
iCaRL [30]	54.97	54.56	60.90	65.56	—	—
BiC [35]	46.49	59.65	65.14	68.97	44.31	45.72
UCIR (NME)* [13]	—	—	66.16	68.43	59.92	61.56
UCIR (NME) [13]	55.44	60.81	65.83	69.07	—	—
UCIR (CNN)* [13]	—	—	68.09	70.47	61.28	64.34
UCIR (CNN) [13]	57.25	62.94	67.82	71.04	—	—
PODNet (CNN)	**62.48**	**68.31**	**74.33**	**75.54**	**64.13**	**66.95**
	± 0.59	± 2.45	± 0.93	± 0.26		

ImageNet100, our model also outperforms the state of the art on all tested runs, by up to $6.51 p.p.$

ImageNet1000. This dataset is the most challenging, with much greater image complexity than CIFAR100, and ten times the number of classes as ImageNet100. We evaluate the models in 5 and 10 steps, and results confirm the consistent improvement of PODNet against existing arts by up to $2.85 p.p.$

4.2 Further Analysis and Ablation Studies

Ablation Studies. Our model has two components: the distillation loss POD and the LSC classifier. An ablation study showcasing the contribution of each component is displayed in Table 3a: each additional component improves the model performance. We evaluate every ablation on CIFAR100 with 50 steps of 1 new class each. The reported metric is the average incremental accuracy. The table shows that our novel method of constraining the whole ConvNet is beneficial. Furthermore applying only POD-spatial still beats the previous state of the art by a significant margin. Using both POD-spatial and POD-flat then further increases results with a large gain. We also compare the results with the Cosine classifier [13, 25] against the Local Similarity Classifier (LSC) with NCA loss. Finally, we add LSC-CE: our classifier with multi-mode but with a simple cross-entropy loss instead of our modified NCA loss. This version brings to mind SoftTriple [29] and Infinited Mixture Prototypes [2], used in the different context of few-shot learning. The latter only considers the closest mode of each class in its class assignment, while LSC considers all modes of a class, thus, taking into account the intra-class variance. That allows LSC to decrease class similarity

Table 3. Ablation studies performed on CIFAR100 with 50 steps. We report the average incremental accuracy.

(a) Comparison of the performance of the model when disabling parts of the complete PODNet loss

Classifier	POD-flat	POD-spatial	NME	CNN
Cosine			40.76	37.93
Cosine	✓		48.03	46.73
Cosine		✓	54.32	57.27
Cosine	✓	✓	56.69	55.72
LSC-CE	✓	✓	59.86	57.45
LSC			41.56	40.76
LSC	✓		53.29	52.98
LSC		✓	**61.42**	57.64
LSC	✓	✓	61.40	**57.98**

(b) Comparison of distillation losses based on intermediary features. All losses evaluated with POD-flat

Loss	NME	CNN
None	53.29	52.98
POD-pixels	49.74	52.34
POD-channels	57.21	54.64
POD-gap	58.80	55.95
POD-width	60.92	57.51
POD-height	60.64	57.50
POD-spatial	**61.40**	**57.98**
GradCam [5]	54.13	52.48
Perceptual style [14]	51.01	52.25

when intra-class variance is high (which could signal a lack of confidence in the class).

Spatial-Based Distillation. We apply our distillation loss POD differently for the flat final embedding $\mathbf{h}$ (POD-flat) and the ConvNet's intermediate features maps $\mathbf{h}_\ell$ (POD-spatial). We designed and evaluated several alternative for the latter whose results are shown in Table 3b. Refer to Sect. 3.1 and Fig. 2 for their definition. All losses are evaluated with POD-flat. "*None*" is using only POD-flat. Overall, we see that not using pooling results in bad performance (POD-pixels). Our final loss, POD-spatial, surpasses all others by taking advantages of the statistics aggregated from both spatial axis. For the sake of completeness we also included losses not designed by us: GradCam distillation [5] and Perceptual Style [14]. The former uses a gradient-based attention while the later – used for style transfer – computes a gram matrix for each channel.

Forgetting and Plasticity Balance. Forgetting can be drastically reduced by imposing a high factor on the distillation losses. Unfortunately, it will also degrade the capacity (its *plasticity*) to learn new classes. When POD-spatial is added on top of POD-flat, we manage to increase the oldest classes performance (+7 percentage points) while the newest classes performance were barely reduced ($-0.2p.p.$). Because our loss POD-spatial constraints only statistics, it is less stringent than a loss based on exact pixels values as POD-pixel. The latter hurts the newest classes ($-2p.p.$) for a smaller improvement of old classes ($+5p.p.$). Furthermore our experiments confirmed that LSC reduced the sensibility of the model to distribution shift, as the performance it brings was localized on the old classes.

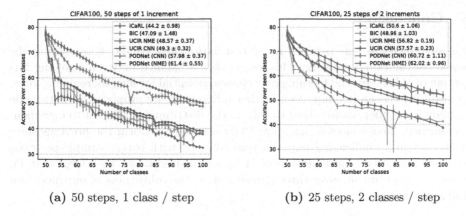

(a) 50 steps, 1 class / step   (b) 25 steps, 2 classes / step

Fig. 4. Incremental Accuracy on CIFAR100 over three orders for two different step sizes. The legend reports the average incremental accuracy.

Table 4. Effect of the memory size per class M_{per} on the models performance. Results from CIFAR100 with 50 steps, we report the average incremental accuracy

M_{per}	5	10	**20**	50	100	200
iCaRL [30]	16.44	28.57	44.20	48.29	54.10	57.82
BiC [35]	20.84	21.97	47.09	55.01	62.23	**67.47**
UCIR (NME) [13]	21.81	41.92	48.57	56.09	60.31	64.24
UCIR (CNN) [13]	22.17	42.70	49.30	57.02	61.37	65.99
PODNet (NME)	**48.37**	**57.20**	**61.40**	62.27	63.14	63.63
PODNet (CNN)	35.59	48.54	57.98	**63.69**	**66.48**	**67.62**

Robustness of Our Model. While previous results showed that PODNet improved significantly over the state-of-the-arts, we wish here to demonstrate here the robustness of our model to various factors. In Table 4, we compared how PODNet behaves against the baseline when the memory size per class M_{per} changes: PODNet improvements increase as the memory size decrease, up to a gain of $26.20 p.p.$ with NME (resp. $13.42 p.p.$ for CNN) with $M_{per} = 5$. Notice that by default, the memory size is 20 in Subsect. 4.1. We also compared our model against baselines with a more flexible memory $M_{total} = 2000$ [30,35], and with various initial task size (by default it is 50 on CIFAR100). In the former case, models benefit from a larger memory per class in the early tasks. In the later case, models initialization is worse because of a smaller initial task size. In these settings very different from Sect. 4.1, PODNet still outperformed significantly the compared models, proving the robustness of our model. The full results of those experiments can be found in the supplementary material.

5   Conclusion

We introduced in this paper a novel distillation loss (POD) constraining the whole convolutional network. This loss strikes a balance between reducing forgetting of old classes and learning new classes, essential for long incremental runs, by carefully chosen pooling. As a further refinement, we proposed a multi-mode similarity classifier, more robust to shift in the distribution inherent to incremental learning. Those innovations allow PODNet to outperform the previous state of the art in a challenging experimental context, with severe sample-per-class memory limitation, and long runs of many small-sized tasks, by a large margin. Extensive experiments over three datasets show the robustness of our model on different settings.

Acknowledgement. E. Valle is funded by FAPESP grant 2019/05018-1 and CNPq grants 424958/2016-3 and 311905/2017-0. This work was performed using HPC resources from GENCI–IDRIS (Grant 2019-AD011011588). We also wish to thanks Estelle Thou for the helpful discussion.

References

1. Aljundi, R., Babiloni, F., Elhoseiny, M., Rohrbach, M., Tuytelaars, T.: Memory aware synapses: learning what (not) to forget. In: Proceedings of the IEEE European Conference on Computer Vision (ECCV) (2018)
2. Allen, K., Shelhamer, E., Shin, H., Tenenbaum, J.: Infinite mixture prototypes for few-shot learning. In: International Conference on Machine Learning (ICML) (2019)
3. Castro, F.M., Marín-Jiménez, M.J., Guil, N., Schmid, C., Alahari, K.: End-to-end incremental learning. In: Proceedings of the IEEE European Conference on Computer Vision (ECCV) (2018)
4. Deng, J., Dong, W., Socher, R., Li, L.J., Li, K., Fei-Fei, L.: ImageNet: a large-scale hierarchical image database. In: Proceedings of the IEEE Conference on Computer Vision and Pattern Recognition (CVPR) (2009)
5. Dhar, P., Singh, R.V., Peng, K.C., Wu, Z., Chellappa, R.: Learning without memorizing. In: Proceedings of the IEEE Conference on Computer Vision and Pattern Recognition (CVPR) (2019)
6. Fernando, C., et al.: PathNet: evolution channels gradient descent in super neural networks. arXiv preprint library (2017)
7. French, R.: Catastrophic forgetting in connectionist networks. Trends Cogn. Sci. **3**(4), 128–135 (1999)
8. Gidaris, S., Komodakis, N.: Dynamic few-shot visual learning without forgetting. In: Proceedings of the IEEE Conference on Computer Vision and Pattern Recognition (CVPR) (2018)
9. Goldberger, J., Hinton, G.E., Roweis, S.T., Salakhutdinov, R.R.: Neighbourhood components analysis. In: Advances in Neural Information Processing Systems (NeurIPS) (2005)
10. Golkar, S., Kagan, M., Cho, K.: Continual learning via neural pruning. In: Advances in Neural Information Processing Systems (NeurIPS), Neuro AI Workshop (2019)

11. He, K., Zhang, X., Ren, S., Sun, J.: Deep residual learning for image recognition. In: Proceedings of the IEEE Conference on Computer Vision and Pattern Recognition (CVPR) (2016)

12. Hinton, G., Vinyals, O., Dean, J.: Distilling the knowledge in a neural network. In: Advances in Neural Information Processing Systems (NeurIPS), Deep Learning and Representation Learning Workshop (2015)

13. Hou, S., Pan, X., Change Loy, C., Wang, Z., Lin, D.: Learning a unified classifier incrementally via rebalancing. In: Proceedings of the IEEE Conference on Computer Vision and Pattern Recognition (CVPR) (2019)

14. Johnson, J., Alahi, A., Fei-Fei, L.: Perceptual losses for real-time style transfer and super-resolution. In: Proceedings of the IEEE European Conference on Computer Vision (ECCV) (2016)

15. Kemker, R., Kanan, C.: FearNet: Brain-inspired model for incremental learning. In: Proceedings of the International Conference on Learning Representations (ICLR) (2018)

16. Kirkpatrick, J., et al.: Overcoming catastrophic forgetting in neural networks. In: Proceedings of the National Academy of Sciences (2017)

17. Komodakis, N., Zagoruyko, S.: Paying more attention to attention: improving the performance of convolutional neural networks via attention transfer. In: Proceedings of the International Conference on Learning Representations (ICLR) (2017)

18. Krizhevsky, A., Hinton, G.: Learning multiple layers of features from tiny images. Technical report (2009)

19. Lazebnik, S., Schmid, C., Ponce, J.: Beyond bags of features: spatial pyramid matching for recognizing natural scene categories. Object Categorization: Computer and Human Vision Perspectives. Cambridge University Press (2006)

20. Li, X., Zhou, Y., Wu, T., Socher, R., Xiong, C.: Learn to grow: a continual structure learning framework for overcoming catastrophic forgetting (2019)

21. Li, Z., Hoiem, D.: Learning without forgetting. In: Proceedings of the IEEE European Conference on Computer Vision (ECCV) (2016)

22. Lomonaco, V., Maltoni, D.: CORe50: a new dataset and benchmark for continuous object recognition. In: Annual Conference on Robot Learning (2017)

23. Lopez-Paz, D., Ranzato, M.: Gradient episodic memory for continual learning. In: Guyon, I., Luxburg, U.V., Bengio, S., Wallach, H., Fergus, R., Vishwanathan, S., Garnett, R. (eds.) Advances in Neural Information Processing Systems (NeurIPS) (2017)

24. Lowe, D.G.: Object recognition from local scale-invariant features. In: Proceedings of the IEEE International Conference on Computer Vision (ICCV) (1999)

25. Luo, C., Zhan, J., Xue, X., Wang, L., Ren, R., Yang, Q.: Cosine normalization: Using cosine similarity instead of dot product in neural networks. In: International Conference on Artificial Neural Networks (2018)

26. Movshovitz-Attias, Y., Toshev, A., Leung, T.K., Ioffe, S., Singh, S.: No fuss distance metric learning using proxies. In: Proceedings of the IEEE International Conference on Computer Vision (ICCV) (2017)

27. Paszke, A., et al.: Automatic differentiation in PyTorch. In: Advances in Neural Information Processing Systems (NeurIPS), Autodiff Workshop (2017)

28. Qi, H., Brown, M., Lowe, D.G.: Low-shot learning with imprinted weights. In: Proceedings of the IEEE Conference on Computer Vision and Pattern Recognition (CVPR) (2018)

29. Qian, Q., Shang, L., Sun, B., Hu, J., Li, H., Jin, R.: SoftTriple loss: deep metric learning without triplet sampling. In: Proceedings of the IEEE International Conference on Computer Vision (ICCV) (2019)

30. Rebuffi, S.A., Kolesnikov, A., Sperl, G., Lampert, C.H.: iCaRL: incremental classifier and representation learning. In: Proceedings of the IEEE Conference on Computer Vision and Pattern Recognition (CVPR) (2017)
31. Robins, A.: Catastrophic forgetting, rehearsal and pseudorehearsal. Connection Sci. **7**, 123–146 (1995)
32. Selvaraju, R.R., Cogswell, M., Das, A., Vedantam, R., Parikh, D., Batra, D.: Grad-CAM: visual explanations from deep networks via gradient-based localization. In: Proceedings of the IEEE International Conference on Computer Vision (ICCV) (2017)
33. Shin, H., Lee, J.K., Kim, J., Kim, J.: Continual learning with deep generative replay. In: Advances in Neural Information Processing Systems (NeurIPS) (2017)
34. Thrun, S.: Lifelong learning algorithms. In: Thrun, S., Pratt, L. (eds.) Learning to Learn, pp. 181–209. Springer, Boston, MA (1998). https://doi.org/10.1007/978-1-4615-5529-2_8
35. Wu, Y., et al.: Large scale incremental learning. In: Proceedings of the IEEE Conference on Computer Vision and Pattern Recognition (CVPR) (2019)
36. Yoon, J., Yang, E., Lee, J., Hwang, S.J.: Lifelong learning with dynamically expandable networks. In: Proceedings of the International Conference on Learning Representations (ICLR) (2018)
37. Zhou, P., Mai, L., Zhang, J., Xu, N., Wu, Z., Davis, L.S.: M2KD: multi-model and multi-level knowledge distillation for incremental learning. arXiv preprint library (2019)

Learning Graph-Convolutional Representations for Point Cloud Denoising

Francesca Pistilli⬤, Giulia Fracastoro⬤, Diego Valsesia(✉)⬤,
and Enrico Magli⬤

Politecnico di Torino, Turin, Italy
francesca.pistilli@polito.it

Abstract. Point clouds are an increasingly relevant data type but they are often corrupted by noise. We propose a deep neural network based on graph-convolutional layers that can elegantly deal with the permutation-invariance problem encountered by learning-based point cloud processing methods. The network is fully-convolutional and can build complex hierarchies of features by dynamically constructing neighborhood graphs from similarity among the high-dimensional feature representations of the points. When coupled with a loss promoting proximity to the ideal surface, the proposed approach significantly outperforms state-of-the-art methods on a variety of metrics. In particular, it is able to improve in terms of Chamfer measure and of quality of the surface normals that can be estimated from the denoised data. We also show that it is especially robust both at high noise levels and in presence of structured noise such as the one encountered in real LiDAR scans.

Keywords: Point cloud · Denoising · Graph neural network

1 Introduction

A point cloud is a geometric data type consisting in an unordered collection of 3D points representing samples of 2D surfaces of physical objects or entire scenes. Point clouds are becoming increasingly popular due to the availability of instruments such as LiDARs and the interest in exploiting the richness of the geometric representation in challenging applications such as autonomous driving. However, the acquisition process is imperfect and a significant amount of noise typically affects the raw point clouds. Therefore, point cloud denoising methods are of paramount importance to improve the performance of various downstream tasks such as shape matching, surface reconstruction, object segmentation and more.

Traditional model-based techniques [1–6] have typically focused on fitting a surface to the noisy data. Such techniques work well in low-noise settings but they usually suffer from oversmoothing, especially in presence of high amounts

© Springer Nature Switzerland AG 2020
A. Vedaldi et al. (Eds.): ECCV 2020, LNCS 12365, pp. 103–118, 2020.
https://doi.org/10.1007/978-3-030-58565-5_7

of noise or geometries with sharp edges. Given the success of learning-based methods, in particular those exploiting deep neural networks, in a wide variety of tasks, including image denoising and restoration problems [7–9], a few works have recently started exploring point cloud denoising with deep neural networks. The most challenging problems in processing point clouds are the lack of a regular domain, such as a grid, and the fact that a point cloud is just a set of points and any permutation of them still represents the same data. Any learning-based method must therefore learn a *permutation-invariant* function that can deal with data defined on an irregular domain. This is a significant challenge that point cloud processing algorithms tackled by either approximating the irregular domain with a grid, e.g. by building voxels, or building a permutation-invariant function as a composition of operations acting on single points (e.g., size-1 convolution) and a globally symmetric function (e.g., a max pool) as done by PointNet [10]. Neither of these solutions is completely satisfactory. The former introduces an undesirable approximation, while the latter lacks the expressiveness of convolutional neural networks (CNN) where the convolution operation extracts features that are localized as functions of the neighborhood of a pixel and features of features are assembled in a hierarchical manner by means of multiple layers, progressively expanding the receptive field. Recently, graph convolution [11] has emerged as an elegant way to build operators that are intrinsically permutation-invariant and defined on irregular domains, while also exploiting some of the useful properties of traditional convolution, such as localization and compositionality of the features as well as efficient weight reuse. In particular, spatial-domain definitions of graph convolution have been recently applied in several problems involving point clouds such as classification [12], segmentation [13], shape completion [14] and generation [15]. Notably, the point cloud denoising problem has yet to be addressed with graph-convolutional neural networks.

In this paper, we propose a deep graph-convolutional neural network for denoising of point cloud geometry. The proposed architecture has an elegant fully-convolutional behavior that, by design, can build hierarchies of local or non-local features to effectively regularize the denoising problem. This is in contrast with other methods in the literature that typically work on fixed-size patches or apply global operations [16,17]. Moreover, dynamic computation of the graph from similarities among the high-dimensional feature-space representations of the points allows to uncover more complex latent correlations than defining neighborhoods in the noisy 3D space. Extensive experimental results show a significant improvement over state-of-the-art methods, especially in the challenging conditions of high noise levels. The proposed approach is also robust to structured noise distributions such as the ones encountered in real LiDAR acquisitions.

2   Related Work

The literature on 3D point cloud denoising is vast and it can be subdivided into four categories: local surface fitting methods [1–6], sparsity-based methods [18–20], graph-based methods [21–23], and learning-based methods [16,17,24,25].

Among the methods belonging to the first category, the moving least squares (MLS) approach [1] and its robust extensions [2,3] are the most widely used. Other surface fitting methods have also been proposed for point cloud denoising, such as jet fitting [6] or parameterization-free local projector operator (LOP) [4,5]. These methods achieve remarkable performance at low levels of noise, but they suffer from over-smoothing when the noise level is high [26].

A second class of point cloud denoising methods [18–20] is based on sparse representations. In this case, the denoising procedure is composed of two minimization problems with sparsity constraints, where the first one estimates the surface normals and then the second one uses them in order to update the point positions. However, at high levels of noise the normal estimation can be very poor, leading to over-smoothing or over-sharpening [19].

Another approach for point cloud denoising is derived from the theory of graph signal processing [27]. These methods [21–23] first define a graph whose nodes are the points of the point cloud. Then, graph total variation (GTV)-based regularization methods are applied for denoising. These techniques have proved to achieve very strong performance when the noise level is low. Instead, at high noise levels, the graph construction can become unstable, negatively affecting the denoising performance.

In the last years, learning-based methods [16,17,24,25], especially the ones based on deep learning, have been gaining attention. Extending convolutional neural networks to point cloud data is not straightforward, due to the irregular positioning of the points in the space. However, in the context of shape classification and segmentation, many methods have recently been proposed specifically to handle point cloud data. PointNet [10] is one of the most relevant works in this field, where each point is processed independently before applying a global aggregation. Recently, a few methods proposed to extend the approach of PointNet to point cloud denoising. PointCleanNet [16] uses an approach similar to PointNet in order to estimate correction vectors for the points in the noisy point cloud. Instead, in [17] the authors use a neural network similar to PointNet to estimate a reference plane for each noisy point and then they obtain the denoised point cloud by projecting the noisy point onto the corresponding reference plane. Also PointProNet [25] performs point cloud denoising by employing an architecture similar to PointNet in order to estimate the local directions of the surface. However, the main drawback of these techniques based on PointNet is that they work on individual points and then apply a global symmetric aggregation function, but they do not exploit the local structure of the neighborhood. PointCleanNet addresses this issue by taking as input local patches instead of the entire point cloud. However, this solution is still limited by the fact that the network cannot learn hierarchical feature representations, like standard CNNs.

Graph-convolutional networks have shown promising performance on tasks such as segmentation and classification. In particular, DGCNN [13] first introduced the idea of a dynamic graph update in the hidden layers of a graph-convolutional network. However, the denoising problem is significantly different from the classification and segmentation tasks addressed in [13], that rely more on global features instead of localized representations. In particular, there are several design choices that make DGCNN unsuitable for point cloud denoising: the spatial transformer block is not useful for denoising since it seeks a canonical global representation, whereas denoising is mostly concerned with local representations of point neighborhoods and also significantly increases the computational complexity for large point clouds; the graph convolution operation uses a max operator in the aggregation, which is unstable in presence of noise; the specific graph convolution definition is also less general than the one presented in this paper, which allows to implement adaptive filters where the aggregation weights are dependent on the feature vectors instead of being fixed as in [13], as well as incorporating an edge attention term which is especially important in presence of noise because it promotes a lowpass behavior by penalizing edges with large feature variations.

3   Proposed Method

In this section we present the proposed Graph-convolutional Point Denoising Network (GPDNet), i.e., a deep neural network architecture to denoise the geometry of point clouds based on graph-convolutional layers. The focus of the paper is to investigate the potential of graph convolution as a simple and elegant way of dealing with the permutation invariance problem encountered when processing point clouds. For this reason, we focus on analyzing the network in a discriminative learning setting where a clean reference is available and it is perturbed with white Gaussian noise. We refer the reader to [24] for a technique to train any point cloud denoising network in an unsupervised fashion only using noisy data.

3.1   Architecture

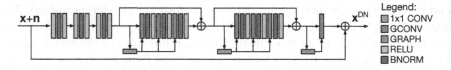

Fig. 1. GPDNet: graph-convolutional point cloud denoising network.

An overview of the architecture of GPDNet is shown in Fig. 1. At a high level, it is a residual network that estimates the noise component of the input point cloud, which has been shown [7] to be easier than directly cleaning the data. A first block is composed of three single-point convolutions that gradually transform the 3D space into an F-dimensional feature space. Then a cascade of two residual blocks is used, having an input-output skip connection to reduce vanishing gradient issues. Each residual block is composed of three graph-convolutional layers.

The graph is computed by selecting the k nearest neighbors to each point in terms of Euclidean distances in the feature space. Notice that the graph construction is dynamic, i.e., it is updated after every residual block but shared among the graph convolutional layers inside the block to limit computational complexity. Dynamic construction of a similarity graph has been shown to induce more powerful feature representations [13,15] and, in the context of a residual denoising network, it progressively uncovers the latent correlations that have not yet been eliminated. Intuitively, dynamic graph construction is preferable over building the graph in the noisy 3D space as neighborhoods might be strongly perturbed at high noise variances, leading to unstable or sub-optimal neighbor assignments. All layers are interleaved with batch normalization which stabilizes training, especially in presence of Gaussian noise. Finally, the last graph-convolutional layer projects the features back to the 3D space.

3.2   Graph-Convolutional Layer

The core of the proposed architecture is the graph-convolutional layer. Graph convolution is a generalization of convolution to data that are defined over the nodes of a general graph rather than a grid. Multiple definitions of graph convolution have been proposed to capture salient properties of classical convolution, notably localization and weight reuse. In this paper, we use a modified version of the Edge-Conditioned Convolution (ECC) [12] to address vanishing gradient and over-parameterization. In particular, we use some of the approximations introduced in [28] in the context of image denoising.

The graph-convolutional layer has two inputs: a tensor representing a feature vector for each point, and a graph where nodes are points and edges represent similarities between points. The output feature vector $\mathbf{h}_i^{l+1} \in \mathbb{R}^{F^l}$ of point i at layer l is computed by performing a weighted aggregation over its neighborhood $\mathcal{N}_i^l$ as defined by the graph:

$$\mathbf{h}_i^{l+1} = \mathbf{W}^l \mathbf{h}_i^l + \sum_{j \in \mathcal{N}_i^l} \gamma^{l,j \to i} \frac{\sum_{t=1}^r \omega_t^{j \to i} \phi_t^{j \to i} \psi_t^{j \to i^T} \mathbf{h}_j^l}{|\mathcal{N}_i^l|}. \tag{1}$$

The weights include a self-loop matrix $\mathbf{W}^l \in \mathbb{R}^{F^{l+1} \times F^l}$ which is shared among all points. The other weights in the aggregation, i.e., vectors $\phi_t^{j \to i} \in \mathbb{R}^{F^{l+1}}$, $\psi_t^{j \to i} \in \mathbb{R}^{F^l}$ and scalar $\omega_t^{j \to i}$ are computed as functions of the difference between the feature vector of point i and point j, i.e., $\phi_t^{j \to i}, \psi_t^{j \to i}, \omega_t^{j \to i} = \mathcal{F}(\mathbf{h}_i^l - \mathbf{h}_j^l)$. This function is implemented as a multilayer perceptron (MLP) with two layers, where the final fully-connected layer can be approximated by means of a stack of circulant matrices since the number of free parameters would otherwise be very large. The value r is a hyperparameter setting the maximum rank of the aggregation weight matrix obtained by explicitly computing $\sum_{t=1}^r \omega_t^{j \to i} \phi_t^{j \to i} \psi_t^{j \to i^T}$, again to reduce the number of parameters and memory requirements of the aggregation operation. The parameter $\gamma^{l,j \to i}$ is a scalar edge attention term which exponentially depends on the Euclidean distance between feature vectors across an edge:

$$\gamma^{l,j \to i} = \exp\left(-\|\mathbf{h}_i^l - \mathbf{h}_j^l\|_2^2 / \delta\right), \tag{2}$$

being δ a decay hyperparameter.

This definition of graph convolution has some advantages over alternative definitions such as GraphSAGE [29], FeastNet [30] or DGCNN [13]. In particular, the aggregation weights are functions of feature differences making the filtering operation performed by the graph-convolutional layer *adaptive*. Moreover, since the function is implemented as an MLP, it can be more general than a fixed function with some learnable parameters.

The graph is constructed by searching for the k-nearest neighbors of each point in terms of Euclidean distance between their feature vectors. To limit complexity, a search area of predefined size, centered around the point, is defined, e.g., as a fixed number of neighbors in the noisy 3D space (see Fig. 4 for a visual representation of the search area and feature space neighborhoods).

We remark that GPDNet is fully-convolutional thanks to the graph convolution operation. By fully-convolutional we mean that the output feature vector of each point at a given layer is obtained as a multi-point aggregation of the feature vectors of neighboring points in the previous layer, thus building complex hierarchies of aggregations. This is in contrast with PointCleanNet [16] which works by processing each patch independently to estimate the denoised version of the central point. That approach does not create hierarchies of features obtained by successive multi-point aggregations, as in a classical CNN. The graph-convolutional structure recovers this behavior and can learn more powerful feature spaces.

3.3   Loss Functions

We consider two loss functions to train the proposed method in a supervised setting. The first one is the mean squared error (MSE) between the denoised point cloud $\hat{\mathbf{x}}$ and its noiseless ground truth $\mathbf{x}$, i.e.:

$$L_{\mathrm{MSE}} = \frac{1}{N} \sum_{i=1}^{N} \|\hat{\mathbf{x}}_i - \mathbf{x}_i\|_2^2 \tag{3}$$

being N the number of points in the point cloud. This is the most natural choice in presence of Gaussian noise. However, it does not exploit prior knowledge about the distribution of points. In fact, it does not use the fact that the points may lie on a surface and therefore the tangential component of the noise is not as relevant as the normal component.

This property can be incorporated by regularizing the MSE loss with a term measuring the distance of the denoised point from the ground truth surface. Such measure can be approximated by the proximity to surface metric which computes the distance between the denoised point and the closest ground truth point. The loss function (MSE-SP) then becomes:

$$L_{\mathrm{MSE-SP}} = \frac{1}{N} \sum_{i=1}^{N} \left[\|\hat{\mathbf{x}}_i - \mathbf{x}_i\|_2^2 + \lambda \min_j \|\hat{\mathbf{x}}_i - \mathbf{x}_j\|_2^2 \right] \tag{4}$$

for a regularization hyperparameter λ. Other works also considered proximity to surface in the loss function. Notably, PointCleanNet [16] uses a loss that combines the proximity to surface with a dual term measuring the distance between a ground truth point and the closest denoised point. This is done to ensure that the denoised points do not collapse into filament structures. We found that using the MSE to enforce this property provides better results.

4 Experimental Results

In this section an experimental evaluation against state-of-the-art approaches as well as an analysis of the proposed technique is performed. Code is available[1].

4.1 Experimental Setting

The training and test set are created selecting post-processed subsets of ShapeNet [31] repository. This database is composed by 3D models of 55 object categories, each one described by a collection of meshes. Before utilization, the data has to be sampled and normalized. First we sample 30720 uniformly distributed points for each model, then we rescale the obtained point clouds normalizing their diameter in order to ensure that data are at the same scale. More than 100000 patches of 1024 points each are randomly selected from the point clouds to create the training set, taking point clouds from all the categories except 10 reserved for the test set. Each patch is created by randomly selecting a point from a point cloud and collecting its 1023 closest points. The test set is constituted by 100 point clouds taken from ten different categories: airplane, bench, car, chair, lamp, pillow, rifle, sofa, speaker, table. We randomly select ten models from each category and sample 30720 uniformly distributed points from each model.

GPDNet is trained for a fixed noise variance for approximately 700000 iterations, each one characterized by a batch size of 16. The number of features used for all the layers is 99, except for the first three single-point convolutional layers where the number of features is gradually increased from 33 to 66 and finally to 99. The Adam optimizer has been employed with a fixed learning rate equal to 10^{-4}. Concerning the graph-convolutional implementation, the rank r for the low-rank approximation is set to 11, 3 circulant rows are considered for the construction of the circulant matrix, and $\delta = 10$. During testing, GPDNet takes as input the whole point cloud and a search area is associated to each point of the

---

[1] https://github.com/diegovalsesia/GPDNet.

point cloud, wherein the neighbors are searched and identified. Unless otherwise stated, 16 nearest neighbors in terms of Euclidean distances are used for graph construction.

4.2   Comparisons with State-of-the-Art

In this section the proposed method is compared with state-of-the-art methods for point cloud denoising. As described in Sect. 2, different categories of point cloud denoising methods are present in the literature. In the experiments, we take into account at least one algorithm from each category. APSS [3] and RIMLS [2] are well-known MLS-based surface fitting methods and they were tested using the MeshLab software [32]. AWLOP [5] is another surface fitting method and it was implemented using the software released by the authors. MRPCA [20] is a sparsity-based method and it was implemented using the code provided by the authors. GLR [21] is one of the most promising works belonging to the graph-based category and it was implemented using the code provided by the authors. PointCleanNet (PCN) [16] is one of the most recent learning-based methods and its code is publicly available. In order to ensure a fair comparison, PointCleanNet was retrained with additive Gaussian noise at a specific standard deviation, instead of using the blind model released by the authors. We also include a modified version of DGCNN [13] as an additional baseline. This modified version replaces the segmentation head with a single-point convolution to regress the point displacement.

As metric to evaluate the performance of the proposed method, we compute the Chamfer measure, also called Cloud-to-Cloud (C2C) distance. This metric is widely utilized in point cloud denoising, because it computes an average distance of the denoised points from the original surface. First, the mean distance between each denoised point and its closest ground truth point is computed, then the one between each ground truth point and its closest denoised point. The Chamfer measure is then their average:

$$\text{C2C} = \frac{1}{2N}\left[\sum_{i=1}^{N}\min_{j}\|\hat{\mathbf{x}}_i - \mathbf{x}_j\|_2^2 + \sum_{j=1}^{N}\min_{i}\|\hat{\mathbf{x}}_i - \mathbf{x}_j\|_2^2\right]. \tag{5}$$

The results of the experiments at different noise levels are reported in Table 1. As described in Sect. 3.3, in the proposed network we consider two different loss functions obtaining two versions of the proposed method, namely GPDNet MSE and GPDNet MSE-SP. It is clearly visible that both versions of the proposed method significantly outperform state-of-the-art methods, especially at medium and high levels of noise, as shown in Table 1 with $\sigma = 0.015$ and $\sigma = 0.02$. Instead, at low noise level the other algorithms become more competitive and the performance gap decreases, but the proposed method still obtains the best results in the majority of the categories. This can be explained by the fact that most of the other methods involves surface reconstruction or normal estimation, operations that cannot be computed with sufficient accuracy at high levels of noise. Instead, the proposed method directly estimates the denoised point cloud.

In addition, it can be observed from Table 1 that the GPDNet MSE-SP version is particularly effective at high levels of noise, outperforming GPDNet MSE in almost all the categories. This behavior can be explained by the regularizing effect of the surface distance component of the loss, which is especially useful at high noise variance due to the fact that it can incorporate more prior knowledge about the data. The performance difference between the two variants decreases at low noise levels. It is worth noting that DGCNN shows poor performance for the reasons explained in Sect. 2, being originally designed for classification or segmentation. This is in line with the results presented in the PointClean-Net paper [16] where the authors also show the poor denoising performance of DGCNN, and highlights the importance of the design in this paper, which is tailored to the denosing task.

We also consider another metric for a quantitative assessment of the denoised point clouds. In particular, we assess whether an off-the-shelf algorithm for surface normal estimation can produce more accurate normals when provided with point clouds denoised by the proposed method. Since surface normals are widely used in many applications, we believe that measuring their quality when extracted from the denoised data is a relevant metric for the characterization of a denoiser. In this experiment we consider a different test set, composed of 5 well-known point clouds: Armadillo, Bunny, Column, Galera and Tortuga. The change of dataset is motivated by the availability of ground truth normals for these point clouds. For every denoising method considered in the comparison, we compute the unoriented normal vector of each point in the denoised point cloud. The standard algorithm employed for the normal estimation is the built-in MAT-LAB function, which is based on principal component analysis. We compute the unoriented normal angle error (UNAE) as

$$
\text{UNAE} = \frac{1}{N} \sum_{i=1}^{N} \arccos\left[1 - \frac{1}{2} \min\left(\|\hat{\mathbf{n}}_{i*} - \mathbf{n}_i\|_2^2, \|\hat{\mathbf{n}}_{i*} + \mathbf{n}_i\|_2^2 \right) \right],
\tag{6}
$$

where $\mathbf{n}_i$ is the groud-truth normal vector at $\mathbf{x}_i$ and $\hat{\mathbf{n}}_{i*}$ is the estimated normal vector at the denoised point closest to $\mathbf{x}_i$. Table 2 reports the average error across the five test point clouds. A minimum error of 6.44 degrees is measured since the MATLAB algorithm introduces a non-zero estimation error in the computation of the normals, as can be seen from the first column of Table 2. The error on the noisy data is 31.13, 32.77 and 33.77 degrees respectively. It can be observed that the proposed denoising method, in particular the version with only MSE as loss function, increases the accuracy of the normal estimation, outperforming the state-of-the-art at each noise level considered. It is also interesting to notice that learning-based methods are more stable to noise than model-based methods as their performance degrades more gracefully for increasing noise variance.

Figure 2 shows qualitative results at a medium noise level by presenting the denoised point cloud for each method. The surface distance of each point is visualized in the figure to understand the position of the denoised points with respect to the ground truth. The root mean square value of the surface distance

Table 1. Chamfer measure ($\times 10^{-6}$), 16-NN, N = Noisy.

Class	N	DGCNN [13]	APSS [3]	RIMLS [2]	AWLOP [5]	MRPCA [20]	GLR [21]	PCN [16]	GPD MSE	GPD MSE-SP
$\sigma = 0.01$										
airp.	50	44.82	28.22	39.73	31.27	28.19	19.56	26.36	**17.22**	17.58
bench	49	38.70	26.97	32.76	34.08	32.93	20.43	27.64	**19.33**	19.80
car	64	60.47	47.73	55.56	54.21	44.33	42.22	75.34	**38.09**	38.14
chair	61	59.69	37.31	45.65	47.91	38.41	34.98	55.10	**29.50**	29.69
lamp	60	52.54	24.57	34.02	35.23	31.51	19.67	20.58	**16.17**	17.15
pill.	70	64.28	**15.64**	21.23	46.36	23.95	17.59	21.07	17.11	19.04
rifle	39	26.99	36.01	49.37	27.79	23.49	15.84	15.09	14.45	**14.00**
sofa	70	65.05	**22.27**	28.04	53.08	32.14	30.88	43.36	25.87	27.21
speak.	74	68.72	**26.50**	30.19	58.92	47.57	40.78	76.09	34.87	35.81
table	56	50.17	27.45	32.63	41.26	34.78	27.12	43.02	**24.27**	24.64
$\sigma = 0.015$										
airp.	98	84.40	86.42	106.33	73.32	67.39	36.76	35.27	28.47	**27.62**
bench	95	64.76	75.51	91.93	82.04	70.05	32.19	30.10	28.72	**26.96**
car	102	93.43	72.56	103.52	93.38	69.88	55.92	92.23	52.92	**51.77**
chair	105	94.4 5	81.47	104.38	92.47	73.45	48.62	69.18	46.28	**43.73**
lamp	121	112.06	65.79	82.40	88.78	77.09	39.93	30.59	**27.37**	28.60
pill.	133	113.32	22.74	42.54	112.54	73.67	31.38	29.02	**23.32**	27.25
rifle	80	61.04	92.14	110.51	69.35	55.65	31.81	**21.45**	28.43	22.48
sofa	121	99.63	42.80	69.92	107.58	72.62	51.12	61.15	**40.10**	42.04
speak.	123	114.12	46.45	58.28	110.29	77.95	53.75	87.68	**49.20**	49.57
table	104	84.95	62.64	78.21	89.33	70.87	37.94	43.88	36.06	**33.89**
$\sigma = 0.02$										
airp.	162	127.44	175.68	186.24	145.94	123.71	90.55	74.17	45.96	**42.30**
bench	162	99.36	166.85	182.42	157.29	127.51	83.99	90.34	41.24	**36.77**
car	149	113.94	141.69	167.78	145.51	109.49	77.56	160.08	72.06	**67.43**
chair	163	132.91	160.01	155.38	158.12	122.70	79.85	145.56	67.91	**60.16**
lamp	204	153.02	178.08	198.22	187.31	146.41	109.24	85.31	45.21	**44.60**
pill.	216	190.32	164.83	196.53	206.14	150.65	85.86	92.84	**34.47**	38.58
rifle	144	131.91	195.68	176.07	144.22	105.87	89.19	71.57	43.07	**29.55**
sofa	184	155.51	166.34	190.91	178.93	133.98	89.31	144.72	**62.58**	65.06
speak.	186	136.72	138.80	162.34	180.45	126.17	84.37	160.26	66.57	**63.40**
table	168	115.00	171.25	179.81	162.36	125.72	78.06	102.17	50.47	**44.80**

Table 2. Unoriented normal angle error (degrees), 16-NN.

σ	DGCNN [13]	APSS [3]	RIMLS [2]	AWLOP [5]	MRPCA [20]	GLR [21]	PCN [16]	GPDNet MSE	GPDNet MSE-SP
0.01	30.83	22.60	24.52	29.79	31.40	21.90	26.85	**20.11**	22.33
0.015	32.52	31.83	37.35	32.17	39.97	25.99	27.54	**21.16**	24.46
0.02	32.31	42.42	45.86	33.41	42.45	31.30	28.65	**22.78**	27.06

Fig. 2. Denosing results for $\sigma = 0.015$. Color represents distance to surface (red is high, blue is low). Top left to bottom right: clean point cloud, DGCNN (RMSD = 0.0091), APSS (0.0123), RIMLS (0.0127), AWLOP (0.0106), MRPCA (0.0096), GLR (0.0070), PointCleanNet (0.0065), GPDNet MSE (0.0060), GPDNet MSE-SP (0.0062). (Color figure online)

(RMSD) can be computed as:

$$\text{RMSD} = \sqrt{\frac{1}{N} \sum_{i=1}^{N} \min_j \|\hat{\mathbf{x}}_i - \mathbf{x}_j\|_2^2}. \tag{7}$$

It can be seen that on average both versions of our method provide lower points-surface distance and that the shape of the reconstructed point cloud is more similar to the original one. Figure 3 shows another qualitative comparison, displaying the unoriented normal estimation error for each denoised point. It can be seen that GPDNet, especially the MSE variant, provides lower normal estimation errors, highlighting the higher quality of the denoised point cloud.

4.3 Ablation Studies

Table 3. Fixed vs. dynamic graph, $\sigma = 0.015$, 8-NN.

	GPDNet	MSE	GPDNet	MSE-SP
	Dynamic	Fixed	Dynamic	Fixed
C2C ($\times 10^{-6}$)	**35.68**	37.00	**36.99**	38.45
UNAE (degrees)	**23.56**	23.75	**26.29**	26.65

We study the behavior of GPDNet in terms of a few design choices. In particular, we first investigate the impact of dynamic graph computation, i.e., updating the graph from the hidden feature space as in Fig. 1, as opposed to a fixed graph construction where neighbors are identified in the noisy 3D space and used for all graph-convolutional layers. Table 3 shows that dynamic graph update provides improved performance thanks to refined neighbor selection.

We also study the impact of neighborhood size on the overall performance. Selecting a larger number of neighbors for graph convolution increases the size

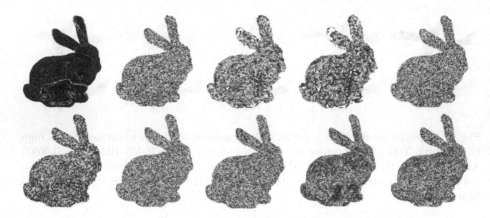

Fig. 3. Denosing results for $\sigma = 0.015$. Color is per-point UNAE (red is high, blue is low). Top left to bottom right: clean point cloud (UNAE = 3.75°), DGCNN (29.73°), APSS (26.29°), RIMLS (33.63°), AWLOP (29.18°), MRPCA (37.50°), GLR (22.08°), PointCleanNet (23.63°), GPDNet MSE (16.62°), GPDNet MSE-SP (23.11°). (Color figure online)

of the receptive field and can help denoise smooth areas in the point cloud by capturing more context, at the price of losing some localization and increased computational complexity. This is related to results on image denoising [33], where it is known that the optimal size of the receptive field depends on the noise variance. Table 4 shows that increasing the number of neighbors is beneficial, up to a saturation point. We also see that the impact of a larger receptive field is more significant for the GPDNet MSE-SP variant.

Table 4. Number of neighbors.

			4-NN	8-NN	16-NN	24-NN
C2C ($\times 10^{-6}$)	$\sigma = 0.01$	GPDNet MSE	28.27	24.43	**23.69**	23.84
		GPDNet MSE-SP	30.38	25.54	24.31	24.44
	$\sigma = 0.015$	GPDNet MSE	40.46	35.68	36.09	36.67
		GPDNet MSE-SP	46.05	36.99	**35.39**	35.80
	$\sigma = 0.02$	GPDNet MSE	58.88	50.34	52.96	55.45
		GPDNet MSE-SP	64.63	51.82	**49.26**	50.43
UNAE (degrees)	$\sigma = 0.01$	GPDNet MSE	27.22	22.51	**20.11**	20.89
		GPDNet MSE-SP	29.04	24.10	22.33	22.16
	$\sigma = 0.015$	GPDNet MSE	28.03	23.56	**21.16**	21.18
		GPDNet MSE-SP	31.31	26.29	24.46	23.80
	$\sigma = 0.02$	GPDNet MSE	31.09	25.67	**22.78**	22.98
		GPDNet MSE-SP	32.00	28.81	27.06	26.92

4.4   Feature Analysis

Fig. 4. Receptive field (green) and search area (black) of a point (red) for the output of the three graph-convolutional layers of the second residual block of the network with respect to the input of the first graph-convolutional layer in the block. Effective receptive field size: 16, 65, 189 points. (Color figure online)

We analyze the characteristics of the receptive field, i.e., the set of points whose feature vectors influence the features of a specific point, induced by the graph convolutional layers. In Fig. 4 we show an example of the receptive field of a single point for the output of the graph convolutional layers of a residual block with respect to the input of the residual block. The visualization is on the denoised point cloud. We observe that the receptive field is quite localized in the 3D space and its size increases as the number of layers increases. It is interesting to note that, since the graph is dynamically constructed in the feature space, the points of the receptive field are not just the spatially closest ones but they are also among the ones with similar shape characteristics. For example, in Fig. 4 the considered point is on the lower side of the chair stretcher and all the points of the receptive field belong to the same part of the surface.

In order to better analyze this non-local property of the receptive field we measure its radius in the 3D space and compare it to a fixed graph construction where the neighbors are determined by proximity in the noisy 3D space. Figure 5 shows the radius of the receptive field of each point at the output of a residual block with respect to the input of the residual block. The radius is evaluated as the 90 percentile Euclidean distance in the 3D space on the clean point cloud (90 percentile is used since the maximum might be an unstable metric). It can be noticed that when using the dynamic graph construction the radius is only slightly larger in the first residual block but can be significantly larger in the second one. This can be interpreted as the feature space building and exploiting more and more non-local features with patterns similar to those in Fig. 4.

4.5   Structured Noise

In order to check if the proposed architecture can generalize beyond white Gaussian noise, we train it on a simulated LiDAR dataset. We simulate scanning the

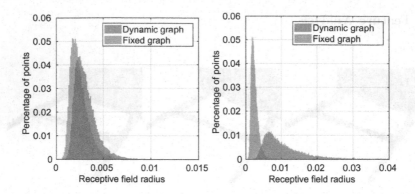

Fig. 5. Radius of receptive field of points at the output of residual block with respect to its input. Left: first residual block. Right: second residual block. Neighbor selection in the noisy 3D space for fixed graph and in the feature space for dynamic graph. Radius is measured as the 90 percentile Euclidean distance to the points in the receptive field on the clean 3D point cloud. (Color figure online)

Table 5. Velodyne scan structured noise, RMSD, 8-NN.

Noisy	PointCleanNet	**GPDNet MSE**	**GPDNet MSE-SP**
0.1447	0.0966	0.0664	**0.0602**

Shapenet objects with a Velodyne HDL-64E scanner using the Blensor software [34]. Two sources of noise are considered for the acquisition process: a laser distance bias with Gaussian distribution and a per-ray Gaussian noise. We set both distributions to be zero-mean and with a standard deviation equal to 1% of the longest side of the object bounding box. We also retrained PointCleanNet on the simulated data for comparison with a state-of-the-art model. Table 5 shows that the results follow those on white Gaussian noise, with the proposed method improving over PointCleanNet. RMSD is used as metric instead of the Chamfer measure since it is better suited to when points are not uniformly distributed.

5   Conclusions

In this paper, we have presented a new graph-convolutional neural network targeted for point cloud denoising. Thanks to the graph-convolutional layers, the proposed architecture is fully convolutional and can learn hierarchies of features, showing a behaviour similar to standard CNNs. The experimental results show that the proposed method provides a significant improvement over state-of-the-art techniques. In particular, the proposed method is robust to high level of noise and structured noise distributions, such as those observed in real LiDAR scans.

References

1. Alexa, M., Behr, J., Cohen-Or, D., Fleishman, S., Levin, D., Silva, C.T.: Computing and rendering point set surfaces. IEEE Trans. Vis. Comput. Graph. **9**(1), 3–15 (2003)
2. Öztireli, A.C., Guennebaud, G., Gross, M.: Feature preserving point set surfaces based on non-linear kernel regression. In: Computer Graphics Forum, vol. 28, pp. 493–501. Wiley Online Library (2009)
3. Guennebaud, G., Gross, M.: Algebraic point set surfaces. ACM Trans. Graph. (TOG) **26**, 23-es (2007)
4. Lipman, Y., Cohen-Or, D., Levin, D., Tal-Ezer, H.: Parameterization-free projection for geometry reconstruction. ACM Trans. Graph. (TOG) **26**, 22-es (2007)
5. Huang, H., Wu, S., Gong, M., Cohen-Or, D., Ascher, U., Zhang, H.R.: Edge-aware point set resampling. ACM Trans. Graph. (TOG) **32**(1), 1–12 (2013). Article no. 9
6. Cazals, F., Pouget, M.: Estimating differential quantities using polynomial fitting of osculating jets. Comput. Aided Geom. Des. **22**(2), 121–146 (2005)
7. Zhang, K., Zuo, W., Chen, Y., Meng, D., Zhang, L.: Beyond a Gaussian denoiser: residual learning of deep CNN for image denoising. IEEE Trans. Image Process. **26**(7), 3142–3155 (2017)
8. Liu, D., Wen, B., Fan, Y., Loy, C.C., Huang, T.S.: Non-local recurrent network for image restoration. In: Advances in Neural Information Processing Systems, pp. 1673–1682 (2018)
9. Valsesia, D., Fracastoro, G., Magli, E.: Image denoising with graph-convolutional neural networks. In: 2019 IEEE International Conference on Image Processing (ICIP), pp. 2399–2403 (September 2019)
10. Qi, C.R., Su, H., Mo, K., Guibas, L.J.: PointNet: deep learning on point sets for 3D classification and segmentation. In: Proceedings of the IEEE Conference on Computer Vision and Pattern Recognition, pp. 652–660 (2017)
11. Bronstein, M.M., Bruna, J., LeCun, Y., Szlam, A., Vandergheynst, P.: Geometric deep learning: going beyond Euclidean data. IEEE Sig. Process. Mag. **34**(4), 18–42 (2017)
12. Simonovsky, M., Komodakis, N.: Dynamic edge-conditioned filters in convolutional neural networks on graphs. In: IEEE Conference on Computer Vision and Pattern Recognition (CVPR), pp. 29–38 (July 2017)
13. Wang, Y., Sun, Y., Liu, Z., Sarma, S.E., Bronstein, M.M., Solomon, J.M.: Dynamic graph CNN for learning on point clouds. ACM Trans. Graph. (TOG) **38**(5), 1–12 (2019). Article no. 146
14. Litany, O., Bronstein, A., Bronstein, M., Makadia, A.: Deformable shape completion with graph convolutional autoencoders. In: Proceedings of the IEEE Conference on Computer Vision and Pattern Recognition, pp. 1886–1895 (2018)
15. Valsesia, D., Fracastoro, G., Magli, E.: Learning localized generative models for 3D point clouds via graph convolution. In: International Conference on Learning Representations, ICLR 2019 (2019)
16. Rakotosaona, M.J., La Barbera, V., Guerrero, P., Mitra, N.J., Ovsjanikov, M.: PointCleanNet: learning to denoise and remove outliers from dense point clouds. In: Computer Graphics Forum. Wiley Online Library (2019)
17. Duan, C., Chen, S., Kovacevic, J.: 3D point cloud denoising via deep neural network based local surface estimation. In: 2019 IEEE International Conference on Acoustics, Speech and Signal Processing (ICASSP), pp. 8553–8557. IEEE (2019)

18. Avron, H., Sharf, A., Greif, C., Cohen-Or, D.: l1-sparse reconstruction of sharp point set surfaces. ACM Trans. Graph. (TOG) **29**(5), 1–12 (2010). Article no. 135
19. Sun, Y., Schaefer, S., Wang, W.: Denoising point sets via l0 minimization. Comput. Aided Geom. Des. **35**, 2–15 (2015)
20. Mattei, E., Castrodad, A.: Point cloud denoising via moving RPCA. In: Computer Graphics Forum, vol. 36, pp. 123–137. Wiley Online Library (2017)
21. Zeng, J., Cheung, G., Ng, M., Pang, J., Yang, C.: 3D point cloud denoising using graph Laplacian regularization of a low dimensional manifold model. arXiv preprint arXiv:1803.07252 (2018)
22. Dinesh, C., Cheung, G., Bajic, I.V.: 3D Point Cloud Denoising via Bipartite Graph Approximation and Reweighted Graph Laplacian. arXiv preprint arXiv:1812.07711 (2018)
23. Schoenenberger, Y., Paratte, J., Vandergheynst, P.: Graph-based denoising for time-varying point clouds. In: 3DTV-Conference: The True Vision-Capture, Transmission and Display of 3D Video (3DTV-CON), vol. 2015, pp. 1–4. IEEE (2015)
24. Hermosilla, P., Ritschel, T., Ropinski, T.: Total Denoising: Unsupervised Learning of 3D Point Cloud Cleaning. arXiv preprint arXiv:1904.07615 (2019)
25. Roveri, R., Öztireli, A.C., Pandele, I., Gross, M.: PointProNets: consolidation of point clouds with convolutional neural networks. In: Computer Graphics Forum, vol. 37, pp. 87–99. Wiley Online Library (2018)
26. Han, X.F., Jin, J.S., Wang, M.J., Jiang, W., Gao, L., Xiao, L.: A review of algorithms for filtering the 3D point cloud. Sig. Process. Image Commun. **57**, 103–112 (2017)
27. Shuman, D.I., Narang, S.K., Frossard, P., Ortega, A., Vandergheynst, P.: The emerging field of signal processing on graphs: extending high-dimensional data analysis to networks and other irregular domains. IEEE Sig. Process. Mag. **30**(3), 83–98 (2013)
28. Valsesia, D., Fracastoro, G., Magli, E.: Deep Graph-Convolutional Image Denoising. arXiv preprint arXiv:1907.08448 (2019)
29. Hamilton, W., Ying, Z., Leskovec, J.: Inductive representation learning on large graphs. In: Advances in Neural Information Processing Systems, pp. 1024–1034 (2017)
30. Verma, N., Boyer, E., Verbeek, J.: FeaStNet: feature-steered graph convolutions for 3D shape analysis. In: Proceedings of the IEEE Conference on Computer Vision and Pattern Recognition, pp. 2598–2606 (2018)
31. Chang, A.X., et al.: ShapeNet: An Information-Rich 3D Model Repository. Technical report. arXiv:1512.03012 [cs.GR], Stanford University – Princeton University – Toyota Technological Institute at Chicago (2015)
32. Cignoni, P., Callieri, M., Corsini, M., Dellepiane, M., Ganovelli, F., Ranzuglia, G.: MeshLab: an open-source mesh processing tool. In: Scarano, V., Chiara, R.D., Erra, U. (eds.) Eurographics Italian Chapter Conference. The Eurographics Association (2008)
33. Burger, H.C., Schuler, C.J., Harmeling, S.: Image denoising: can plain neural networks compete with BM3D? In: IEEE Conference on Computer Vision and Pattern Recognition, vol. 2012, pp. 2392–2399. IEEE (2012)
34. Gschwandtner, M., Kwitt, R., Uhl, A., Pree, W.: BlenSor: blender sensor simulation toolbox. In: Bebis, G., et al. (eds.) ISVC 2011. LNCS, vol. 6939, pp. 199–208. Springer, Heidelberg (2011). https://doi.org/10.1007/978-3-642-24031-7_20

Semantic Line Detection Using Mirror Attention and Comparative Ranking and Matching

Dongkwon Jin[iD], Jun-Tae Lee[iD], and Chang-Su Kim[✉][iD]

School of Electrical Engineering, Korea University, Seoul, Korea
{dongkwonjin,jtlee}@mcl.korea.ac.kr, changsukim@korea.ac.kr

Abstract. A novel algorithm to detect semantic lines is proposed in this paper. We develop three networks: detection network with mirror attention (D-Net) and comparative ranking and matching networks (R-Net and M-Net). D-Net extracts semantic lines by exploiting rich contextual information. To this end, we design the mirror attention module. Then, through pairwise comparisons of extracted semantic lines, we iteratively select the most semantic line and remove redundant ones overlapping with the selected one. For the pairwise comparisons, we develop R-Net and M-Net in the Siamese architecture. Experiments demonstrate that the proposed algorithm outperforms the conventional semantic line detector significantly. Moreover, we apply the proposed algorithm to detect two important kinds of semantic lines successfully: dominant parallel lines and reflection symmetry axes. Our codes are available at https://github.com/dongkwonjin/Semantic-Line-DRM.

Keywords: Semantic lines · Line detection · Attention · Ranking · Matching

1 Introduction

A *semantic line* [28] can be roughly defined as a dominant line, separating different semantic regions in a scene, which is reasonably approximated by an end-to-end straight line, as exemplified in Fig. 1.

Fig. 1. Examples of various semantic lines.

Electronic supplementary material The online version of this chapter (https://doi.org/10.1007/978-3-030-58565-5_8) contains supplementary material, which is available to authorized users.

© Springer Nature Switzerland AG 2020
A. Vedaldi et al. (Eds.): ECCV 2020, LNCS 12365, pp. 119–135, 2020.
https://doi.org/10.1007/978-3-030-58565-5_8

| Semantic line detection (D-Net) | ❯ | Comparative ranking and matching (R-Net and M-Net) |

Fig. 2. Illustration of the proposed DRM algorithm: First, D-Net extracts semantic lines (orange). Second, R-Net selects the most semantic line (yellow). Third, M-Net removes redundant lines overlapping with the selected one. The second and third steps are iteratively applied. In this example, three semantic lines are selected. The first one is called the primary semantic line (dashed red). (Color figure online)

Semantic lines are essential components in high-level image understanding [15,19,20,29,55,57]. In photography, photographic composition rules, such as horizontal, diagonal, and symmetric ones, are described by semantic lines [15,29]. Under perspective projection, dominant parallel lines in the 3D world are projected to semantic lines in 2D images, intersecting at vanishing points and conveying depth impressions [57]. Also, in autonomous driving systems [19,20], the boundaries of road lanes, sidewalks, or crosswalks are important semantic lines. However, it is difficult to detect semantic lines, which are often unobvious and implied by complex boundaries of semantic regions.

Although many techniques have been developed to detect lines by exploiting low-level cues [3,11,34,45] or deep features [23,49,56], they extract many short (possibly noisy) line segments or rather obvious lines in man-made environments. Also, several attempts [27,48,52] have been made to detect unobvious horizon lines. However, horizons are just a specific type of semantic lines. Recently, SLNet, which is a general semantic line detector, was proposed in [28]. Although SLNet provides promising results, it tends to detect many redundant lines near the boundaries of semantic regions.

In this paper, we propose a novel semantic line detection algorithm, called DRM, which consists of three networks: detection network with mirror attention (D-Net) and comparative ranking and matching networks (R-Net and M-Net). In Fig. 2, D-Net first extracts semantic lines by classifying and regressing candidate lines. For effective detection, we design the mirror attention module and the region pooling layer in D-Net. Then, by comparing semantic lines in pairs, R-Net selects the most semantic line and M-Net removes redundant lines overlapping with the selected one. This comparative ranking and matching process is performed iteratively. In Fig. 2, three iterations are performed to yield three semantic lines. Experimental results demonstrate that the proposed DRM algorithm outperforms the conventional SLNet [28] significantly.

This work has the following major contributions:

- We develop D-Net to detect semantic lines, in which the mirror attention module and the region pooling layer extract discriminate features effectively.
- We propose two Siamese networks, R-Net and M-Net, for pairwise ranking and matching of semantic lines.

- We construct a challenging dataset (SEL_Hard) of semantic lines, which are highly implied in cluttered scenes.[1]
- We also apply the proposed algorithm to two important line detection tasks: dominant parallel lines and reflection symmetry axes.

2   Related Work

2.1   Line Detection

Lines are geometrically important cues to describe the layouts or structural information of images. In line segment detection [3,11,34,45], many short line segments are detected using low-level cues (e.g. image gradients). However, this approach may not discriminate meaningful lines from noisy ones. To utilize higher-level cues, deep learning methods have been proposed [23,40,49,56]. In [23], two networks were used to predict, respectively, a line heat map and junctions in man-made environments. Then, the wireframe, summarizing the scene, was obtained by connecting the junctions based on the heat map. In [56], a network verified whether a candidate line was salient or not, where the candidate was also generated by connecting two junctions. In [49], the line segment detection was posed as the dual problem of region coloring to address local ambiguity and class imbalance. In [40], a network was trained to yield the coordinates of a bounding box, whose diagonal was the resultant line segment. However, these methods [23,40,49,56] detect rather obvious lines in man-made environments.

Meanwhile, several methods [12,28,48,52] have been developed to detect implied lines. In [48], horizon lines were directly estimated by CNNs, without requiring geometric constraints. In [52], horizons were detected similarly to [48], but their locations were refined by exploiting vanishing points. In [12], soft labels of horizon line parameters were used to train the regression network. In [28], the first semantic line detector was proposed, which can detect general, semantically meaningful lines. Semantic lines, located near the boundaries of semantic regions, represent the layout and composition of an image, even when the boundaries are not straight lines.

2.2   Attention Mechanisms in CNNs

Human visual system pays more attention to salient parts of a scene for efficiency [10,24]. Similarly, attempts have been made to bias the processing resource of a neural network towards more informative parts of input data [4,43,50,51]. Also, attention mechanisms have been developed to improve the representation power of convolutional layers in CNN-based vision tasks [22,35,46,47,53]. In [46], Wang et al. adopted an encoder-decoder structure to obtain a pixel-wise attention mask of a convolutional feature map. In [22], to address the interdependencies of filter responses, Hu et al. used the average-pooled feature at each channel to compute the channel-wise attention. In [35,47], this channel-wise

---

[1] SEL_Hard is available at https://github.com/dongkwonjin/Semantic-Line-DRM.

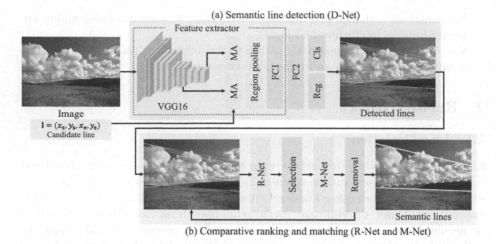

(a) Semantic line detection (D-Net)

(b) Comparative ranking and matching (R-Net and M-Net)

Fig. 3. An overview of the proposed algorithm: (a) D-Net detects semantic lines, by classifying and regressing candidate lines, based on mirror attention (MA). (b) R-Net selects the most meaningful semantic line and M-Net removes redundant lines alternately through pairwise comparisons.

attention module has been modified to obtain both spatial and channel-wise attention. In [25], multiple attention maps were obtained from intermediate convolutional layers, and then the ensemble of those maps was applied to the last layer. In [53], Zhao and Wu applied spatial attention to lower layers to focus on local details and channel-wise attention to higher layers to capture contextual cues.

2.3 Metric Learning and Order Learning

Metric learning [38,39] constructs an appropriate feature embedding space, where similar objects are located tightly while dissimilar objects are far from one another. In contrast, in order learning [30], embedded features are ordered according to the ranks or priorities of objects. Both the similarity and order relationships depend on target applications and are implicitly defined by user-provided examples. Accordingly, the learned metric is useful for matching similar objects, *e.g.*, in image retrieval [17,21], person re-identification [7,13], and few-shot learning [41,44]. On the other hand, the learned order can be used to rank or sort objects, as done in image quality assessment [26,31], object detection [37,42], and age estimation [5,6].

3   Proposed Algorithm

We propose a novel semantic line detection algorithm, called DRM, which is composed of three networks: D-Net, R-Net, and M-Net. Figure 3 is an overview

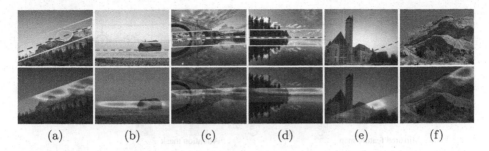

(a)   (b)   (c)   (d)   (e)   (f)

Fig. 4. [Top] A semantic (or candidate) line is shown in red, while two regions producing the line are in cyan and yellow. [Bottom] The attention mask is color-coded: red and blue depict big and small values. Note that the two regions are semantically different from each other in (a) and (b) and symmetric in (c) and (d). In (e) and (f), the candidate lines are not semantic. (Color figure online)

of the proposed DRM algorithm. First, we generate candidate lines by connecting two points, uniformly sampled on image boundaries [28]. Second, D-Net extracts semantic lines by classifying and regressing the candidate lines. For discriminative feature extraction, we design the mirror attention module and the region pooling layer. Third, through pairwise comparisons, we iteratively select the most meaningful semantic line and remove the other semantic lines overlapping with the selected one. For this purpose, we develop R-Net and M-Net in the Siamese architecture.

3.1 D-Net: Semantic Line Detection with Mirror Attention

Mirror Attention: A semantic line separates a region into two distinct subregions. Those two regions can be semantically different as in Fig. 4(a), (b), or symmetric around the line as in Fig. 4(c), (d). In the former case, if a region is mirrored along the line, it should contain quite different objects from the other region. In the latter case, it should be almost identical with the other region. To summarize, the line is semantic because of the mirrored dissimilarity (heterogeneity of two regions) or mirrored similarity (symmetry). Based on this observation, we develop the mirror attention module in Fig. 5. Given a feature map, the mirror attention module generates an attention mask, which is then used to reweight the feature map to make it more discriminative.

We apply the mirror attention module to a convolutional feature map $X = [X^1, X^2, \ldots, X^C] \in \mathbb{R}^{H \times W \times C}$, where H, W, and C denote the height, the width, and the number of channels. Since pixels near a candidate line are more relevant for semantic line detection, we first obtain a weighted feature map $Y = [Y^1, Y^2, \ldots, Y^C] \in \mathbb{R}^{H \times W \times C}$, where $X^c(k)$ for pixel k is weighted by

$$Y^c(k) = \omega(d_k) \times X^c(k). \tag{1}$$

Here, d_k is the distance of pixel k from the candidate line and $\omega(\cdot)$ is the Gaussian weighting function.

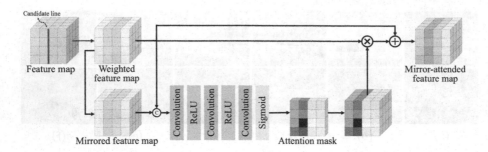

Fig. 5. Illustration of the mirror attention process.

To analyze the mirror relationships around the candidate line, we obtain the mirrored feature map $\tilde{Y}$ by flipping Y across the line. If a flipped pixel is outside the feature map, it is set to zero. Then, we concatenate Y and $\tilde{Y}$ and obtain an initial mask $A_0 \in \mathbb{R}^{H \times W}$ by

$$A_0 = f_0([Y, \tilde{Y}]) \tag{2}$$

where f_0 is a convolutional layer using a single filter of size $n \times n \times 2C$. We set n to 3 empirically. To increase the receptive field and capture the semantics from a wider region, we use two more convolution layers to yield $A_2 = f_2(f_1(A_0))$, where f_1 or f_2 uses a single filter of size $(2n+1) \times (2n+1) \times 1$. Finally, we obtain the attention mask $A = \sigma(A_2)$ where $\sigma(\cdot)$ is the sigmoid activation function.

We apply the mirror attention module to two deep layers of D-Net, as shown in Fig. 3. The attention mask may over-suppress the values in the weighted feature map Y. To prevent this, we adopt the residual attention scheme [46]. More specifically, we obtain the attended feature map $Y_{\text{att}} = [Y_{\text{att}}^1, Y_{\text{att}}^2, \ldots, Y_{\text{att}}^C]$, where Y_{att}^c is given by

$$Y_{\text{att}}^c = (1 + A) \otimes Y^c \tag{3}$$

for each $1 \leq c \leq C$.

Figure 4 shows examples of attention masks. In Fig. 4(a)–(d), there are roughly two semantic regions around the candidate line. We see that one region is attended with small weights, while the other with big weights. Thus, the feature difference between the two regions is emphasized, facilitating the semantic line detection. Note that the mirror attention module is trained in an end-to-end manner such that emphasizing masks are generated in both cases of mirrored dissimilarity (Fig. 4(a) or (b)) and mirrored similarity (Fig. 4(c) or (d)). On the other hand, in Fig. 4(e) or (f), a less informative mask is generated because the candidate line is not semantic.

Region Pooling: Whereas the conventional algorithm [28] uses a line pooling layer, we design a region pooling layer to extract more discriminated features from the mirror-attended feature map Y_{att}. We set two adjacent regions $\mathcal{U}$ and $\mathcal{V}$ along the candidate line, which contain pixels whose distances from the line are less than a threshold, respectively. Then, we aggregate the regional information of $\mathcal{U}$ and $\mathcal{V}$ into $\mathbf{u}$ and $\mathbf{v} \in \mathbb{R}^C$;

$$\mathbf{u} = \frac{1}{|\mathcal{U}|} \sum_{k \in \mathcal{U}} Y_{\text{att}}(k) \quad \text{and} \quad \mathbf{v} = \frac{1}{|\mathcal{V}|} \sum_{k \in \mathcal{V}} Y_{\text{att}}(k). \tag{4}$$

Then, $\mathbf{u}$ and $\mathbf{v}$ are concatenated to form the feature vector of the candidate line.

D-Net Architecture: We plug the proposed mirror attention module and region pooling layer into the classification-regression framework of [28]. Hence, D-Net takes an image and a candidate line, parameterized by $\mathbf{l} = (x_s, y_s, x_e, y_e)$, and yields classification and regression results. Figure 3(a) shows its architecture. We use the 13 convolution layers of VGG16 [36] as the backbone, and implement two mirror attention modules after Conv10 and Conv13, respectively. From each mirror-attended feature map, the region pooling layer extracts the feature vector. The two vectors are concatenated and fed into fully connected layers FC1 and FC2. Finally, D-Net branches into two parallel output layers: one for classifying the candidate line (Cls), and the other for computing regression offsets for the line parameters (Reg). Cls computes the softmax vector $\mathbf{p} = (p, q)$, where p is the probability that the candidate line $\mathbf{l}$ is semantic. Reg outputs a line offset $\Delta \mathbf{l}$. When $p > 0.5$, D-Net declares that the regressed line $\mathbf{l} + \Delta \mathbf{l}$ is semantic.

To train D-Net, when a candidate line is annotated by $\bar{\mathbf{p}}$ and $\Delta \bar{\mathbf{l}}$, we minimize the loss

$$L(\mathbf{p}, \bar{\mathbf{p}}, \Delta \mathbf{l}, \Delta \bar{\mathbf{l}}) = L_{\text{cls}}(\mathbf{p}, \bar{\mathbf{p}}) + \lambda L_{\text{reg}}(\Delta \mathbf{l}, \Delta \bar{\mathbf{l}}) \tag{5}$$

where $L_{\text{cls}}(\mathbf{p}, \bar{\mathbf{p}})$ and $L_{\text{reg}}(\Delta \mathbf{l}, \Delta \bar{\mathbf{l}})$ are the classification loss and the regression loss, respectively, and λ is a balancing parameter. L_{cls} is the cross-entropy loss over the two classes (semantic and non-semantic). $L_{\text{reg}}(\Delta \mathbf{l}, \Delta \bar{\mathbf{l}}) = \eta(\Delta \mathbf{l} - \Delta \bar{\mathbf{l}})$, where η is the smooth L_1 loss [18].

3.2   R-Net and M-Net: Comparative Ranking and Matching

Note that D-Net detects many semantic lines from densely sampled candidate lines, as illustrated in Fig. 2. Since each candidate is tested independently, semantically identical lines are detected closely. For example, in Fig. 2, there are three groups, each of which contains semantically identical lines. From each group, we select the most reliable line, while removing the other redundant ones. To this end, we develop the comparative ranking and matching networks, referred to as R-Net and M-Net, respectively. Given a pair of semantic lines, R-Net finds which one is more reliable and M-Net determines whether they are semantically identical or not. Thus, R-Net is related to *priority* in order learning [30], while M-Net is to *similarity* in metric learning [38, 39].

Both R-Net and M-Net are implemented as binary classifiers in the Siamese architecture. Figure 6 shows R-Net, which yields a softmax probability vector $\mathbf{p}^{\text{r}} = (p^{\text{r}}, q^{\text{r}})$. Here, p^{r} or q^{r} is the probability that line i is more reliable or less reliable than line j, respectively. Since D-Net is well-trained for semantic line

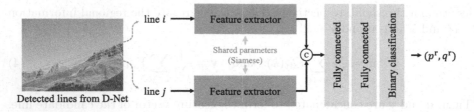

Fig. 6. Siamese architecture for R-Net: Given a pair of detected lines from D-Net, R-Net decides whether one line is more reliable or less reliable than the other.

detection, we truncate it before the FC2 layer and use it as the feature extractor of R-Net. Then, the features of the two lines are concatenated, propagated into two fully connected layers, and categorized into one of the binary classes. The cross-entropy loss is used to train R-Net. Also, M-Net is implemented in the same way as R-Net, except that it yields a softmax vector $\mathbf{p}^m = (p^m, q^m)$, where p^m or q^m is the probability that the two lines are semantically identical or not, respectively.

Using R-Net and M-Net, we perform the selection and removal of semantic lines alternately. At step t, we measure the reliability of each semantic line. Specifically, the reliability r_i of semantic line i is defined as

$$r_i = \sum_{j=1,\, j \neq i}^{N_t} p_{ij}^r \qquad (6)$$

where N_t is the number of available semantic lines at step t, and p_{ij}^r is the probability that line i is more reliable than line j. Then, we select the most reliable line i^* by

$$i^* = \arg\max_i r_i. \qquad (7)$$

We then remove the lines that are semantically identical with line i^*. Specifically, line j is removed if the matching probability $p_{i^*j}^m$ from M-Net is higher than 0.5. We iteratively perform the alternate selection and removal until $N_t = 0$. In the example of Fig. 2, three iterations are performed to select the three resultant lines. The firstly selected line is called the primary line.

We configure the training data for R-Net and M-Net as follows. Note that a detected semantic line is declared to be correct if its mean intersection over union (mIoU) ratio with the ground-truth is higher than 0.85 [28]. After training D-Net on the SEL dataset [28], we use the correctly detected semantic lines in the training images to train R-Net and M-Net. For R-Net, a ground-truth semantic line and one of its detection results are used as an input pair. To encode the one-hot vector $\bar{\mathbf{p}}^r = (\bar{p}^r, \bar{q}^r)$, the ground-truth line is used as the more reliable one than the detection result. For M-Net, we use two detected lines as input. To encode $\bar{\mathbf{p}}^m = (\bar{p}^m, \bar{q}^m)$, if the two lines correspond to the same ground-truth, they are regarded as semantically identical.

4   Experimental Results

4.1   Datasets

SEL: The semantic line (SEL) dataset [28] contains 1,750 outdoor images in total, which are split into 1,575 training and 175 testing images. Each semantic line is annotated by the coordinates of the two end-points on an image boundary. If an image has a single dominant line, it is set as the ground truth primary semantic line. If an image has multiple semantic lines, the line with the best rank by human annotators is set as the ground-truth primary line, and the others as additional ground-truth semantic lines. In SEL, 61% of the images contain multiple semantic lines.

SEL_Hard: In addition to the SEL dataset, we construct a more challenging test dataset, called SEL_Hard. Its semantic lines are more implied (or less obvious), are more severely occluded, and are in more cluttered scenes. We collect 300 images from the ADE20K image segmentation dataset [54], manually annotate semantic lines, and then also select primary lines. Notice that SEL_Hard is constructed for testing semantic line detectors and is not used for training them. The supplemental document describes the annotation process in detail and provides example images.

4.2   Semantic Line Detection Results

We assess primary and multiple semantic line detection performances on the SEL and SEL_Hard datasets.

We measure the accuracy for primary semantic line detection and the precision and recall rates for multiple semantic line detection, based on the mIoU metric [28]. A semantic line is regarded as correctly detected if its mIoU score with the ground-truth is greater than a threshold τ. Then, the accuracy of the primary semantic line detection is defined as

$$\text{Accuracy} = \frac{N_c}{N} \tag{8}$$

where N_c is the number of the test images whose primary semantic lines are correctly detected, and N is the number of all test images. For the multiple semantic line detection, the precision and the recall are computed by

$$\text{Precision} = \frac{N_l}{N_l + N_e}, \quad \text{Recall} = \frac{N_l}{N_l + N_m} \tag{9}$$

where N_l is the number of correctly detected semantic lines, N_e is the number of false positives, and N_m is the number of false negatives.

Figure 7 compares the accuracy, precision, and recall curves of the proposed DRM algorithm and the conventional SLNet algorithm [28] on the SEL dataset. The proposed DRM outperforms SLNet in all three curves in the entire range of

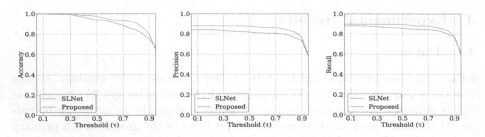

Fig. 7. Comparison of the accuracy, precision, and recall curves of the proposed DRM and the conventional SLNet in terms of the threshold τ on the SEL dataset.

Table 1. Comparison of the AUC scores (%) on the SEL and SEL_Hard datasets.

	SEL			SEL_Hard		
	AUC_A	AUC_P	AUC_R	AUC_A	AUC_P	AUC_R
SLNet	92.00	80.44	83.50	73.59	74.22	70.68
Proposed DRM	94.54	85.44	87.16	80.68	87.19	77.69

the threshold τ. Table 1 reports the area under curve (AUC) performances of the accuracy, precision, and recall curves in Fig. 7, which are denoted by AUC_A, AUC_P, and AUC_R, respectively. DRM provides higher AUC_A, AUC_P, and AUC_R than SLNet by 2.54, 5.00, and 3.66, respectively. Table 1 also compares the performances on SEL_Hard. For this comparison as well, we use the same DRM and SLNet, which are trained using the training images in the SEL dataset. Since SEL_Hard consists of more challenging images, the performances are lower than those on SEL. Nevertheless, on SEL_Hard, DRM outperforms SLNet by significant margins 7.09, 12.97, and 7.01 in terms of AUC_A, AUC_P, and AUC_R, respectively.

Figure 8 compares detection results qualitatively. Compared to SLNet, the proposed DRM detects implied, as well as obvious, semantic lines more precisely. Also, DRM suppresses redundant lines more effectively. More detection results are available in the supplemental document.

4.3   Ablation Studies

We conduct ablation studies to analyze the efficacy of the proposed D-Net, R-Net, and M-Net on the SEL dataset.

Efficacy of Mirror Attention Model: Table 2 compares the performances of several ablated methods. First, to demonstrate the impacts of the mirror attention module in D-Net, we do not use the comparative ranking and matching (R-Net and M-Net). Instead, we adopt the non-maximum suppression (NMS) scheme in [28], which removes overlapped semantic lines based on low-level edge features. Method i uses no attention module. Method ii uses the attention module

Fig. 8. Comparison of semantic line detection results. The left two images are from SEL, and the other three from SEL_Hard. Primary and multiple semantic lines are depicted in dashed red and solid yellow, respectively. (Color figure online)

Table 2. The ablation studies in terms of the mirror attention module and comparative ranking and matching. AUC scores (%) of primary and multiple semantic line detection are compared on the SEL dataset.

		AUC_A	AUC_P	AUC_R
i	D-Net(without attention)+NMS	92.48	83.37	84.76
ii	D-Net(with attention, no flipped feature map)+NMS	93.24	81.33	84.86
iii	D-Net(with spatial-channel attention)+NMS	92.85	81.74	85.84
iv	D-Net(with mirror attention)+NMS	93.38	83.98	86.23
v	D-Net(with mirror attention)+R-Net+M-Net	94.54	85.44	87.16

in Fig. 5 but without concatenating a flipped feature map. Method iii replaces the mirror attention module with the spatial-channel attention in [47]. As compared with no attention in i, the two attention schemes in ii and iii improve the accuracy and recall scores but lower the precision score. On the contrary, the proposed mirror attention model in iv improves all three scores and also outperforms the two alternative schemes in ii and iii. Also, by comparing iv with ii, we see that the mirroring of feature maps across semantic lines is effective for emphasizing informative regions. More specifically, the mirroring improves AUC_A, AUC_P, and AUC_R by 0.14, 2.65, and 1.37, respectively.

Efficacy of R-Net and M-Net: By comparing methods iv and v, we see that the proposed DRM algorithm provides 1.16, 1.46 and 0.93 higher AUC_A, AUC_P, and AUC_R scores, by employing R-Net and M-Net instead of NMS. This indicates that the proposed comparative ranking and matching is an effective approach to select reliable semantic lines and remove redundant ones.

Fig. 9. Detection results of dominant parallel lines. For reference, the ground-truth vanishing points are depicted by red cross symbols. (Color figure online)

Table 3. AUC_A scores (%) in the dominant parallel line detection, according to the number K of detected lines.

K	1	2	3	4	5
SLNet [28]	46.83	41.73	38.58	37.22	36.44
D-Net+NMS	52.62	48.93	46.24	44.71	43.30
Proposed	56.31	54.36	52.42	51.17	50.72

5 Applications

We apply the proposed DRM algorithm to detect two kinds of semantically important lines: dominant parallel lines and reflection symmetry axes.

5.1 Dominant Parallel Lines

When projected onto a 2D image, dominant parallel lines in the 3D world convey depth impressions, intersecting at a vanishing point (VP) [57]. Despite researches on the VP detection [55,57], a single VP is less informative for conveying the depth information than those projected parallel lines are. Hence, we apply the proposed DRM algorithm to detect dominant parallel lines in a 2D image. We first extract semantic lines using D-Net. To this end, D-Net is trained to detect semantic lines passing through VPs. Next, using R-Net, the primary semantic line is selected. In this application, M-Net is trained to declare a pair of lines, which are parallel in the 3D space, as 'matched.' Then, we repeatedly select the semantic line yielding the highest 'matched' score to the primary semantic line. To avoid overlapping, we remove the semantic lines whose mIoUs with an already selected one are greater than 0.85 after each selection.

We assess the proposed algorithm on the AVA landscape dataset [57]. It contains 2,275 training and 275 test landscape images. For each image, a dominant

Table 4. Comparison of AA scores (%) for the dominant VP detection.

	AA1°	AA2°	AA10°
Zhou *et al.* [57]	18.5	33.0	60.0
NeurVPS [55]	**19.6**	**35.9**	65.9
Proposed	8.6	22.9	**68.3**

VP and two dominant parallel lines are annotated. We declare a detected line as correct, when its distance to the ground-truth VP is smaller than a threshold. Then, we compute AUC_A scores by varying the threshold. Table 3 compares the AUC_A scores of the conventional SLNet [28], 'D-Net+NMS,' and the proposed algorithm according to the number K of detected lines in each image. As more lines are selected in an image, the accuracy score is lowered. However, for every K, D-Net+NMS outperforms SLNet, which indicates that D-Net detects dominant parallel lines more precisely. Moreover, by employing R-Net and M-Net, the proposed algorithm further improves the performances. Figure 9 shows that the proposed algorithm detects dominant lines that pass through VPs accurately.

Next, we detect a VP as the intersecting point of the first two selected lines. Table 4 compares this VP detection scheme with the existing methods[55,57]. Angle accuracies AA1°, AA2°, AA10° are used as the performance metrics, as done in [55]. Two performances of NeurVPS are reported in [55]. Table 4 includes their accuracies when the same training data as the proposed algorithm are used. Note that the proposed algorithm focuses on the detection of dominant lines and provides VPs as side results. In contrast, the existing methods are tailored for the VP detection. Therefore, when the tolerance angles are small (1° or 2°), the proposed algorithm yields poorer accuracies than the existing methods. However, when the tolerance angle is 10°, the proposed algorithm outperforms them. This indicates that the proposed algorithm can detect rough locations of VPs with a high recall rate, although it lacks the precision of the existing methods.

5.2   Reflection Symmetry Axes

Reflection symmetry is a common, but important visual property in various scenes, such as landscapes and man-made structures [32]. However, since reflection symmetry axes are often highly implied or even invisible, their detection should exploit semantic regions around the axes. Accordingly, we train the proposed algorithm to detect the reflection symmetry axis of an image as the primary semantic line. More specifically, we train D-Net to extract symmetry axes as semantic lines, and R-Net to prioritize those axes among the detected lines. We empirically find that the Gaussian weighting in (1) and the residual attention in (3) are less effective in this task. Hence, we exclude those operations from the mirror attention module in Fig. 5. Then, we extract semantic lines using D-Net, and choose the most reliable one as the symmetry axis via (7) using R-Net.

Fig. 10. Detection results of symmetry axes. The ground-truth axes are in red, the detection results of Loy and Eklundh [33] are in green, and those of the proposed algorithm are in yellow. (Color figure online)

Table 5. Comparison of AUC_A scores (%) of the symmetry axis detection.

	ICCV	NYU	SYM_Hard
Cicconet et al. [8]	80.80	82.85	68.99
Elawady et al. [14]	87.24	83.83	73.90
Cicconet et al. [9]	87.38	87.64	81.04
Loy & Eklundh [33]	89.77	90.85	81.99
Proposed	**90.60**	**92.78**	**84.73**

We test the proposed algorithm on three datasets: ICCV [16], NYU [9], and SYM_Hard. ICCV provides 100 training and 96 test images, and NYU contains 176 test images. In SYM_Hard, we collect 45 images from photo sharing websites [1,2], each of which includes a reflection symmetry axis. The axis is implied, and the neighboring regions are not exactly symmetric. Thus, its detection is challenging. Since the proposed algorithm detects symmetry axes as primary lines, we compare the proposed algorithm with the existing methods [8,9,14,33] using the AUC_A metric. We train the proposed algorithm using the ICCV training images and use it to assess the performances on all three datasets. Table 5 compares the results. On ICCV, NYU, and SYM_Hard, the proposed algorithm outperforms the existing methods by at least 0.83, 1.93, and 2.74, respectively. Figure 10 compares detection results of the proposed algorithm with those of Loy and Eklundh [33]. The proposed algorithm detects symmetry axes more robustly. More experimental results are available in the supplemental document.

6   Conclusions

We proposed a novel semantic line detector using D-Net, R-Net, and M-Net. First, D-Net extracts semantic lines using the mirror attention module. Second, R-Net selects the most semantic line through ranking. Third, M-Net removes redundant lines overlapping with the selected one through matching. The second and third steps are alternately performed to yield reliable semantic lines as output. Experimental results demonstrated that the proposed DRM algorithm outperforms the conventional SLNet significantly. Moreover, it was shown that the proposed algorithm can be applied to successfully detect two important kinds of semantic lines: dominant parallel lines and reflection symmetry axes.

Acknowledgement. This work was supported in part by the Agency for Defense Development (ADD) and Defense Acquisition Program Administration (DAPA) of Korea under grant UC160016FD and in part by the National Research Foundation of Korea (NRF) through the Korea Government (MSIP) under grant NRF-2018R1A2B3003896.

References

1. Flickr. https://www.flickr.com/
2. GoogleImage. https://www.google.com/
3. Akinlar, C., Topal, C.: EDLines: a real-time line segment detector with a false detection control. Pattern Recogn. Lett. **32**(13), 1633–1642 (2011)
4. Bahdanau, D., Cho, K., Bengio, Y.: Neural machine translation by jointly learning to align and translate. In: Proceedings of ICLR (2015)
5. Chen, S., Zhang, C., Dong, M.: Deep age estimation: from classification to ranking. IEEE Trans. Multimedia **20**(8), 2209–2222 (2017)
6. Chen, S., Zhang, C., Dong, M., Le, J., Rao, M.: Using ranking-CNN for age estimation. In: Proceedings of IEEE CVPR (2017)
7. Chu, R., Sun, Y., Li, Y., Liu, Z., Zhang, C., Wei, Y.: Vehicle re-identification with viewpoint-aware metric learning. In: Proceedings of IEEE ICCV (2019)
8. Cicconet, M., Birodkar, V., Lund, M., Werman, M., Geiger, D.: A convolutional approach to reflection symmetry. Pattern Recogn. Lett. **95**, 44–50 (2017)
9. Cicconet, M., Hildebrand, D.G., Elliott, H.: Finding mirror symmetry via registration and optimal symmetric pairwise assignment of curves: algorithm and results. In: Proceedings of IEEE ICCV Workshops (2017)
10. Corbetta, M., Shulman, G.L.: Control of goal-directed and stimulus-driven attention in the brain. Nat. Rev. Neurosci. **3**(3), 201–215 (2002)
11. Desolneux, A., Moisan, L., Morel, J.M.: Meaningful alignments. Int. J. Comput. Vis. **40**(1), 7–23 (2000)
12. Diaz, R., Marathe, A.: Soft labels for ordinal regression. In: Proceedings of IEEE CVPR (2019)
13. Ding, S., Lin, L., Wang, G., Chao, H.: Deep feature learning with relative distance comparison for person re-identification. Pattern Recogn. **48**(10), 2993–3003 (2015)
14. Elawady, M., Ducottet, C., Alata, O., Barat, C., Colantoni, P.: Wavelet-based reflection symmetry detection via textural and color histograms. In: Proceedings of IEEE ICCV Workshops (2017)
15. Freeman, M.: The Photographer's Eye: Composition and Design for Better Digital Photos. Focal Press, Waltham (2007)
16. Funk, C., et al.: 2017 ICCV Challenge: Detecting symmetry in the wild. In: Proceedings of IEEE ICCV (2017)
17. Gao, X., Hoi, S.C., Zhang, Y., Wan, J., Li, J.: SOML: sparse online metric learning with application to image retrieval. In: Proceedings of AAAI (2014)
18. Girshick, R.: Fast R-CNN. In: Proceedings of IEEE ICCV (2015)
19. Guo, C., Yamabe, T., Mita, S.: Robust road boundary estimation for intelligent vehicles in challenging scenarios based on a semantic graph. In: Intelligent Vehicles Symposium. IEEE (2012)
20. Hillel, A.B., Lerner, R., Levi, D., Raz, G.: Recent progress in road and lane detection: a survey. Mach. Vis. Appl. **25**(3), 727–745 (2014)

21. Hoi, S.C., Liu, W., Chang, S.F.: Semi-supervised distance metric learning for collaborative image retrieval and clustering. ACM Trans. Multimed. Comput. Commun. Appl. **6**(3), 1–26 (2010)
22. Hu, J., Shen, L., Sun, G.: Squeeze-and-excitation networks. In: Proceedings of IEEE CVPR (2018)
23. Huang, K., Wang, Y., Zhou, Z., Ding, T., Gao, S., Ma, Y.: Learning to parse wireframes in images of man-made environments. In: Proceedings of IEEE CVPR (2018)
24. Itti, L., Koch, C., Niebur, E.: A model of saliency-based visual attention for rapid scene analysis. IEEE Trans. Pattern Anal. Mach. Intell. **20**(11), 1254–1259 (1998)
25. Jetley, S., Lord, N.A., Lee, N., Torr, P.H.S.: Learn to pay attention. In: Proceedings of ICLR (2018)
26. Kong, S., Shen, X., Lin, Z., Mech, R., Fowlkes, C.: Photo aesthetics ranking network with attributes and content adaptation. In: Proceedings of ECCV (2016)
27. Koo, H.I., Cho, N.I.: Skew estimation of natural images based on a salient line detector. J. Electron. Imaging **22**(1), 013020 (2013)
28. Lee, J.T., Kim, H.U., Lee, C., Kim, C.S.: Semantic line detection and its applications. In: Proceedings of IEEE ICCV (2017)
29. Lee, J.T., Kim, H.U., Lee, C., Kim, C.S.: Photographic composition classification and dominant geometric element detection for outdoor scenes. J. Vis. Commun. Image Represent. **55**, 91–105 (2018)
30. Lim, K., Shin, N.H., Lee, Y.Y., Kim, C.S.: Order learning and its application to age estimation. In: Proceedings of ICLR (2020)
31. Liu, X., van de Weijer, J., Bagdanov, A.D.: RankIQA: learning from rankings for no-reference image quality assessment. In: Proceedings of IEEE ICCV (2017)
32. Liu, Y., Hel-Or, H., Kaplan, C.S., Van Gool, L.: Computational symmetry in computer vision and computer graphics. Found. Trends Comput. Graph. Vision **5**(1–2), 1–195 (2010)
33. Loy, G., Eklundh, J.O.: Detecting symmetry and symmetric constellations of features. In: Proceedings of ECCV (2006)
34. Matas, J., Galambos, C., Kittler, J.: Robust detection of lines using the progressive probabilistic hough transform. Comput. Vis. Image Understand. **78**(1), 119–137 (2000)
35. Park, J., Woo, S., Lee, J., Kweon, I.S.: BAM: bottleneck attention module. In: Proceedings of BMVC (2018)
36. Simonyan, K., Zisserman, A.: Very deep convolutional networks for large-scale image recognition. In: Proceedings of ICLR (2015)
37. Singh, K.K., Lee, Y.J.: You reap what you sow: using videos to generate high precision object proposals for weakly-supervised object detection. In: Proceedings of IEEE CVPR (2019)
38. Sohn, K.: Improved deep metric learning with multi-class n-pair loss objective. In: Proceedings of NIPS (2016)
39. Song, O.H., Xiang, Y., Jegelka, S., Savarese, S.: Deep metric learning via lifted structured feature embedding. In: Proceedings IEEE CVPR (2016)
40. Sun, Y., Han, X., Sun, K.: Sem-LSD: A learning-based semantic line segment detector. arXiv preprint arXiv:1909.06591 (2019)
41. Sung, F., Yang, Y., Zhang, L., Xiang, T., Torr, P.H., Hospedales, T.M.: Learning to compare: relation network for few-shot learning. In: Proceedings of IEEE CVPR (2018)
42. Tan, Z., Nie, X., Qian, Q., Li, N., Li, H.: Learning to rank proposals for object detection. In: Proceedings of IEEE ICCV (2019)

43. Vaswani, A., et al.: Attention is all you need. In: Proceedings of NIPS (2017)
44. Vinyals, O., Blundell, C., Lillicrap, T., kavukcuoglu, k., Wierstra, D.: Matching networks for one shot learning. In: Proceedings of NIPS (2016)
45. Von Gioi, R.G., Jakubowicz, J., Morel, J.M., Randall, G.: LSD: a fast line segment detector with a false detection control. IEEE Trans. Pattern Anal. Mach. Intell. **32**(4), 722–732 (2008)
46. Wang, F., et al.: Residual attention network for image classification. In: Proceedings of IEEE CVPR (2017)
47. Woo, S., Park, J., Lee, J.Y., Kweon, I.S.: CBAM: convolutional block attention module. In: Proceedings of ECCV (2018)
48. Workman, S., Zhai, M., Jacobs, N.: Horizon lines in the wild. In: Proceedings of BMVC (2016)
49. Xue, N., Bai, S., Wang, F., Xia, G.S., Wu, T., Zhang, L.: Learning attraction field representation for robust line segment detection. In: Proceedings of IEEE CVPR (2019)
50. Yu, A.W., et al.: QANet: combining local convolution with global self-attention for reading comprehension. In: Proceedings of ICLR (2018)
51. Zambaldi, V., et al.: Deep reinforcement learning with relational inductive biases. In: Proceedings of ICLR (2019)
52. Zhai, M., Workman, S., Jacobs, N.: Detecting vanishing points using global image context in a non-manhattan world. In: Proceedings of IEEE CVPR (2016)
53. Zhao, T., Wu, X.: Pyramid feature attention network for saliency detection. In: Proceedings of IEEE CVPR (2019)
54. Zhou, B., Zhao, H., Puig, X., Fidler, S., Barriuso, A., Torralba, A.: Scene parsing through ADE2020K dataset. In: Proceedings of IEEE CVPR (2017)
55. Zhou, Y., Qi, H., Huang, J., Ma, Y.: NeurVPS: neural vanishing point scanning via conic convolution. In: Proc. NIPS (2019)
56. Zhou, Y., Qi, H., Ma, Y.: End-to-end wireframe parsing. In: Proceedings of IEEE ICCV (2019)
57. Zhou, Z., Farhat, F., Wang, J.Z.: Detecting dominant vanishing points in natural scenes with application to composition-sensitive image retrieval. IEEE Trans. Multimedia **19**(12), 2651–2665 (2017)

A Differentiable Recurrent Surface
for Asynchronous Event-Based Data

Marco Cannici[✉], Marco Ciccone, Andrea Romanoni, and Matteo Matteucci

Politecnico di Milano, Milan, Italy
{marco.cannici,marco.ciccone,andrea.romanoni,matteo.matteucci}@polimi.it

Abstract. Dynamic Vision Sensors (DVSs) asynchronously stream events in correspondence of pixels subject to brightness changes. Differently from classic vision devices, they produce a sparse representation of the scene. Therefore, to apply standard computer vision algorithms, events need to be integrated into a frame or event-surface. This is usually attained through hand-crafted grids that reconstruct the frame using ad-hoc heuristics. In this paper, we propose Matrix-LSTM, a grid of Long Short-Term Memory (LSTM) cells that efficiently process events and learn end-to-end task-dependent event-surfaces. Compared to existing reconstruction approaches, our learned event-surface shows good flexibility and expressiveness on optical flow estimation on the MVSEC benchmark and it improves the state-of-the-art of event-based object classification on the N-Cars dataset.

Keywords: Event-based vision · Representation learning · LSTM · Classification · Optical flow

1 Introduction

Event-based cameras, such as dynamic vision sensors (DVSs) [2,17,25,29], are bio-inspired devices that attempt to emulate the efficient data-driven communication mechanisms of the brain. Unlike conventional frame-based active pixel sensors (APS), which capture the scene at a predefined and constant framerate, these devices are composed of independent pixels that output sequences of asynchronous events, efficiently encoding pixel-level brightness changes caused by moving objects. This results in a sensor having a very high dynamic range (>120 dB) and high temporal resolution (in the order of microseconds), matched with low power consumption and minimal delay. All these characteristics are key features in challenging scenarios involving fast movements (e.g., drones or

---

A. Romanoni—Work done prior to Amazon involvement of the author and does not reflect views of the Amazon company.

Electronic supplementary material The online version of this chapter (https://doi.org/10.1007/978-3-030-58565-5_9) contains supplementary material, which is available to authorized users.

© Springer Nature Switzerland AG 2020
A. Vedaldi et al. (Eds.): ECCV 2020, LNCS 12365, pp. 136–152, 2020.
https://doi.org/10.1007/978-3-030-58565-5_9

moving cars), and abrupt brightness changes (e.g., when exiting a dark tunnel in a car). However, novel methods and hardware architectures need to be specifically designed to exploit these advantages and leverage their potential in complex tasks. Event-cameras only provide a timed sequence of changes that is not directly compatible with computer vision systems which typically work on frames.

Driven by the great success of frame-based deep learning architectures, that learn representations directly from standard APS signals, research in event-based processing is now focusing on how to effectively aggregate event information in grid-based representations which can be directly used, for instance, by convolutional deep learning models. Nevertheless, finding the best mechanism to extract information from event streams is not trivial. Multiple solutions have indeed emerged during the past few years, mostly employing hand-crafted mechanisms to accumulate events. Examples of such representations are mechanisms relying on exponential [6,15,31] and linear [4,6] decays, "event-surfaces" storing the timestamp of the last received event in each pixel and extensions of such mechanism making use of memory cells [31] and voxel-grids [26,36].

Only very recently deep learning techniques have been applied to learn such surfaces in a data-driven manner [10]. In this paper, we focus on this recent trend in event-based processing, and propose a mechanism to efficiently apply a Long Short-Term Memory (LSTM) network [12] as a convolutional filter over the 2D stream of events in order to accumulate pixel information through time and build 2D event representations. The reconstruction mechanism is end-to-end differentiable, meaning that it can be jointly trained with state-of-the-art frame-based architectures to learn event-surfaces specifically tailored for the task at hand. Most importantly, the mechanism specifically focuses on preserving sparsity during computation, enabling the reconstruction process to only focus on pixels receiving events and without requiring events to be densified in a dense tensor during the intermediate feature extraction steps, process that is otherwise necessary when applying standard computer vision approaches, such as ConvLSTM [30], in most of the cases.

Substituting hand-crafted event-surfaces with our trainable layer in state-of-the-art architectures improves their performance substantially without requiring particular effort in hyper-parameter tuning, enabling researchers to exploit event information effectively. The contributions of the paper are summarized as follows:

- We propose Matrix-LSTM, a task-independent mechanism to extract grid-like event representations from asynchronous streams of events. The framework is end-to-end differentiable, it can be used as input of any existing frame-based state-of-the-art architecture and jointly trained to extract the best representation from the events.
- Replacing input representations with a Matrix-LSTM layer in existing architectures, we show that it improves the state-of-the-art on event-based object classification on N-CARS [31] by 3.3% and performs better than hand-crafted features on N-Caltech101 [23]. Finally, it improves optical flow estimation on

the MVSEC benchmark [37] up to 30.76% over hand-crafted features [37] and up to 23.07% over end-to-end differentiable ones [10].
- We developed custom CUDA kernels, both in PyTorch [32] and Tensor-Flow [1], to efficiently aggregate events by position and perform a convolution-like operation on the stream of events using an LSTM as a convolutional filter[1].

2   Related Work

Event cameras provide outstanding advantages over ordinary devices in terms of time resolution and dynamic range. However, their potentialities are still unlocked, mainly due to the difficulty of building good representations from a sparser, asynchronous and much more rough source of information compared to frame-based data. In this section, we give a brief overview of related works, focusing on representations for event-based data and highlighting the differences and similarities with our work. We refer the reader to [8] for a thorough overview.

Hand-Crafted Representations. Several hand-crafted event representations have been proposed over the years, ranging from biologically inspired, such as those used in Spiking Neural Networks [19], to more structured ones. Recently, the concept of *time-surface* was introduced [15,20], in which 2D surfaces are obtained by keeping track of the timestamp of the last event occurred in each location and by associating each event with features computed applying exponential kernels on the surface. An extension of these methods, called HATS [31], employs memory cells that retain temporal information from past events. Instead of building the surface using just the last event, too sensitive to noise, HATS uses a fixed-length memory. Histograms are then extracted from the surface and a SVM classifier is finally used for prediction. The use of a memory to compute the event-surface closely relates HATS with the solution presented in this paper. Crucially, the accumulation procedure employed in HATS is hand-crafted, while our work is end-to-end trainable thanks to a grid of LSTM cells [12], which enable to learn a better accumulation strategy directly from data.

In [36], the authors propose the EV-FlowNet network for optical flow estimation together with a new time-surface variant. Events of different polarities are kept separate to build a four-channel grid containing the number of events occurred in each location besides temporal information. A similar representation has also been used in [34]. To improve the temporal resolution of such representations, [38] suggests to discretize time into consecutive bins and accumulate events into a voxel-grid through a linearly weighted accumulation similar to bilinear interpolation. A similar time discretization has also been used in Events-to-Video [26], where the event representation is used within a recurrent-convolutional architecture to produce realistic video reconstructions of event sequences. Despite being slower, the quality of reconstructed frames closely

---

[1] Code available at https://marcocannici.github.io/matrixlstm.

resembles actual gray-scale frames, allowing the method to take full advantage from transferring feature representations trained on natural images.

End-to-End Representations. Most closely related to the current work, [10] learns a dense representation end-to-end directly from raw events. A multi-layer perceptron (MLP) is used to implement a trilinear filter that produces a voxel-grid of temporal features. The event time information of each event is encoded using the MLP network and the value obtained from events occurring in the same spatial location are summed up together to build the final feature. A look-up table is then used, after training, to speed-up the procedure. Events are processed independently as elements of a set, disregarding their sequentiality and preventing the network to modulate the information based on previous events. Our method, instead, by leveraging the memory mechanism of LSTM cells, can integrate information conditioned on the current state and can decide how much each event is relevant to perform the task, and how much information to retain from past events. A recent trend in event-based processing is studying mechanisms that do not require to construct intermediate explicit dense representations to perform the task at hand [3,28,33]. Among these, [22] uses a variant of the LSTM network, called PhasedLSTM, to learn the precise timings of events. While it integrates the events sequentially as in our work, PhasedL-STM employs a single cell on the entire stream of events and can be used only on very simple tasks [5]. The model, indeed, does not maintain the input spatial structure and condenses the 2D stream of events into a single feature vector, preventing the network to be used as input to standard CNNs. Finally, although it has never been adopted with event-based cameras, we also mention here the ConvLSTM [30] network, a convolutional variant of the LSTM that has previously been applied on several end-to-end prediction tasks. Despite its similarity with our method, since both implement the notion of convolution to LSTM cells, ConvLSTM is not straightforward to apply to sparse event-based streams and requires the input to be densified into frames before processing. This involves building very sparse frames of simultaneous events, mostly filled with padding, or dense frames containing uncorrelated events. Our formulation, instead, preserves sparsity during computation and does not require events to be densified, even when large receptive fields are considered.

3   Method

Event-based cameras are vision sensors composed of pixels able to work independently. Each pixel has its own exposure time and it is free to fire independently by producing an event as soon as it detects a significant change in brightness. Unlike conventional devices, no rolling shutter is used, instead, an asynchronous stream of events is generated describing what has changed in the scene. Each event e_i is a tuple $e_i = (x_i, y_i, t_i, p_i)$ specifying the time t_i, the location $(x, y)_i$ (within a $H \times W$ space) and the polarity $p_i \in \{-1, 1\}$ of the change (brightness increase or decrease). Therefore, given a time interval τ (i.e., the sample length), the set of events produced by the camera can be described as a sequence

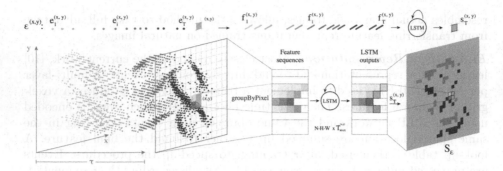

Fig. 1. Overview of Matrix-LSTM (figure adapted from [22]). Events in each pixel are first associated to a set of features $f_i^{(x,y)}$, and then processed by the LSTM. The last output, $s_T^{(x,y)}$, is finally used to construct $\mathcal{S}_\mathcal{E}$. *GroupByPixel* is shown here on a single sample ($N = 1$) highlighting a 2×2 pixel region. Colors refer to pixel locations while intensity indicates time. For clarity, the features dimension is not shown in the figure (Color figure online)

$\mathcal{E} = \{(x_i, y_i, t_i, p_i) \mid t_i \in \tau\}$, ordered by the event timestamp. In principle, multiple events could be generated at the same timestamp. However, the grid representation of the events at a fixed timestamp t is likely to be very sparse, hence, an integrating procedure is necessary to reconstruct a dense representation $\mathcal{S}_\mathcal{E}$ before being processed by conventional frame-based algorithms.

Note that, in this work, we do not aim to reconstruct a frame that resembles the actual scene, such as a grey-scale or RGB image [26,27], but instead to extract task-aware features regardless of their appearance. In the following, *"surface"*, *"reconstruction"* and *"representation"* are used with this meaning.

3.1   Matrix-LSTM

Analogously to [10], our goal is to learn end-to-end a fully parametric mapping $\mathcal{M} : \mathcal{E} \rightarrow \mathcal{S}_\mathcal{E} \in \mathbb{R}^{H \times W \times C}$, between the event sequence and the corresponding dense representation, providing the best features for the task to optimize.

In this work, we propose to implement $\mathcal{M}$ as an $H \times W$ *matrix of LSTM cells* [12] (see Fig. 1). Let's define the ordered sequence of events $\mathcal{E}^{(x,y)}$ produced by the pixel (x, y) during interval τ as $\mathcal{E}^{(x,y)} = \{(x_i, y_i, t_i, p_i) \mid t_i \in \tau, x_i = x, y_i = y\} \subset \mathcal{E}$, and its length as $T^{(x,y)} = |\mathcal{E}^{(x,y)}|$, which may potentially be different for each location (x, y). A set of features $f_i^{(x,y)} \in \mathbb{R}^F$ is first computed for each event occurring at location (x, y), typically the polarity and one or multiple temporal features (see Sect. 4). At each location (x, y), an $LSTM^{(x,y)}$ cell then processes these features asynchronously, keeping track of the current integration state and condensing all events into a single output vector $s^{(x,y)} \in \mathbb{R}^C$. In particular, at each time t, the $LSTM^{(x,y)}$ cell produces an intermediate representation $s_t^{(x,y)}$. Once all the events are processed, the last output of the LSTM cell compresses the dynamics of the entire sequence $\mathcal{E}^{(x,y)}$ into a fixed-length vector $s_T^{(x,y)}$ that can be used as pixel feature (here we dropped the superscript $^{(x,y)}$ from T for readability). The final surface $\mathcal{S}_{\mathcal{E}}$ is finally built by collecting all LSTMs final outputs $s_T^{(x,y)}$ into a dense tensor of shape $H \times W \times C$. A fixed all-zeros output is used where the set of events $\mathcal{E}^{(x,y)}$ is empty.

Temporal Bins. Taking inspiration from previous methods [10,26,38] that discretize time into temporal bins, we also propose a variant of Matrix-LSTM that operates on successive time windows. Given a fixed number of bins B, the original event sequence is split into B consecutive windows $\mathcal{E}_{\tau_1}, \mathcal{E}_{\tau_2}, \ldots, \mathcal{E}_{\tau_B}$. Each sequence is processed independently, i.e., the output of each LSTM at the end of each interval is used to construct a surface $\mathcal{S}_{\mathcal{E}_b}$ and the LSTMs state is re-initialized before the next sub-sequence starts. This gives rise of B different reconstructions $\mathcal{S}_{\mathcal{E}_b}$ that are concatenated to form the final surface $\mathcal{S}_{\mathcal{E}} \in \mathbb{R}^{H \times W \times B \cdot C}$. In this formulation, the LSTM input features $f_i^{(x,y)}$ usually contain both global temporal features (i.e., w.r.t. the original uncut sequence) and relative features (i.e., the event position in the sub-sequence). Although LSTMs should be able to retain memory over very long periods, we found that discretizing time into intervals helps , especially in tasks requiring precise time information such as optical flow estimation (see Sect. 4.2). A self-attention module [13] is then optionally applied on the reconstructed surface to correlate intervals (see Sect. 4.1).

Parameters Sharing. Inspired by the convolution operation defined on images, we designed Matrix-LSTM to enjoy translation invariance. This is implemented by sharing the parameters across all the LSTM cells, as in a convolutional kernel. Sharing parameters not only drastically reduces the number of parameters in the network, but it also allows us to transfer a learned transformation to higher or lower resolutions as in fully-convolutional networks [18].

We highlight that such an interpretation of the Matrix-LSTM functioning also fits the framework proposed in [10], in which popular event densification mechanisms are rephrased as kernel convolutions on the *event field*, i.e., a discretized four-dimensional manifold spanning x and y, and the time and polarity dimensions. We finally report that this formulation is equivalent to a 1×1 ConvLSTM [30] applied on a dense tensor where events are stacked in pixel locations by arrival order. However, as reported in Sect. 4.1, this formulation has better space and time performance on sparse event sequences. Moreover, in the next section, an extension to larger receptive fields with better accuracy performance on asynchronous event data compared to ConvLSTM, is also proposed.

Receptive Field Size. As in a conventional convolution operation, Matrix-LSTM can be convolved on the input space using different strides and kernel dimensions. In particular, given a receptive field of size $K_H \times K_W$, each LSTM cell processes a local neighborhood of asynchronous events $\mathcal{E}^{(x,y)} = \{(x_i, y_i, t_i, p_i) \mid t_i \in \tau, |x - x_i| < K_W - 1, |y - y_i| < K_H - 1\}$. Events features are computed as in the original formulation, however, an additional coordinate feature (p_x, p_y) is also added specifying the relative position of each event within the receptive field. Coordinate features are range-normalized in such a way that an event occurring in the top-left pixel of the receptive field has feature $(0,0)$, whereas one occurring in the bottom-right position has features $(1,1)$. Events belonging to multiple receptive fields (e.g., when the LSTM is convolved with a stride 1×1 and receptive field greater then 1×1) are processed multiple times, independently.

Implementation. The convolution-like operation described in the previous section can be implemented efficiently by means of two carefully designed event grouping operations. Rather than replicating the LSTM unit multiple times on each spatial location, a single recurrent unit is applied over different $\mathcal{E}^{(x,y)}$ sequences in parallel. This requires a reshape operation, i.e., *groupByPixel*, that splits events based on their pixel location maintaining the events relative ordering within each sub-sequence. A similar procedure, i.e., *groupByTime*, is employed to efficiently split events into consecutive temporal windows without making use of expensive masking operations. An example of the *groupByPixel* operation is provided in Fig. 1 while implementation details of both operations, implemented as custom CUDA kernels, are provided in the supplementary materials. We finally highlight that these operations are not specific to Matrix-LSTM, since grouping events by pixel index is a common operation in event-based processing, and could indeed benefit other implementations making use of GPUs.

4   Evaluation

We test the proposed mechanism on two different tasks: object classification (see Sect. 4.1) and optical flow estimation (see Sect. 4.2), where the network is required to extract effective temporal features. We evaluated the goodness of Matrix-LSTM features indirectly: a state-of-the-art architecture is taken as a reference and the proposed method is evaluated in terms of the gain in performance obtained by replacing the network representation with a Matrix-LSTM.

4.1   Object Classification

We evaluated the model on the classification task using two publicly available event-based collections, namely the N-Cars [31] and the N-Caltech101 [23] datasets, which represent to date the most complex benchmarks for event-based classification. N-Cars is a collection of urban scenes recordings (lasting 100ms each) captured with a DVS sensor and showing two object categories: cars and urban background. The dataset comes already split into $7,940$ car and $7,482$ background training samples, and $4,396$ car and $4,211$ background testing samples. The N-Caltech101 collection is an event-based conversion of the popular Caltech-101 [16] dataset obtained by moving an event-based camera in front of a still monitor showing one of the original RGB images. Like the original version, the dataset contains objects from 101 classes distributed amongst $8,246$ samples.

Network Architectures. We used two network configurations to test Matrix-LSTM on both datasets, namely the classifier used in Events-to-Video [26], and the one used to evaluate the EST [10] reconstruction. Both are based on

Table 1. Results on N-Cars: **(a)** ResNet18–Ev2Vid, variable time encoding, and normalization; **(b)** ResNet18–EST, variable time encoding and number of bins

(a)

ResNet Norm	ts absolute	ts relative	delay relative
	95.22 ± 0.41%	94.77 ± 1.01%	95.40 ± 0.59%
✓	**95.75 ± 0.27%**	95.32 ± 0.85%	**95.80 ± 0.53%**

(b)

		1 bin	2 bins	9 bins
delay	glob+loc	-	92.68 ± 1.23%	92.32 ± 1.02%
	local	92.64 ± 1.21%	92.35 ± 0.83%	92.67 ± 0.90%
ts	ts glob+loc	-	**93.46 ± 0.84%**	93.21 ± 0.49%
	local	92.65 ± 0.78%	92.75 ± 1.38%	93.12 ± 0.68%

ResNet [11] backbones and pre-trained on ImageNet [7]. Events-to-Video [26] uses a ResNet18 configuration maintaining the first 3 channels convolution (since reconstructed images are RGB) while adding an extra fully-connected layer to account for the different number of classes in both N-Calthec101 and N-Cars (we refer to this configuration as *ResNet–Ev2Vid*). EST [10] instead uses a ResNet34 backbone and replaces both the first and last layers respectively, with a convolution matching the input features, and a fully-connected layer with the proper number of neurons (we refer to this configuration as *ResNet–EST*).

To perform a fair comparison we replicated the two settings, using the same number of channels in the event representation (although we also tried different channel values) and data augmentation procedures (random horizontal flips and crops of 224 × 224 pixels). We perform early stopping on a validation set in all experiments, using 20% of the training on N-Cars and using the splits provided by the EST official code repository [9] for N-Caltech101. ADAM [14] was used as optimizer for all experiments with a learning rate of 10^{-4}. Finally, we use a batch size of 64 and a constant learning rate on N-Cars in both configurations. On N-Caltech101, instead, we use a batch size of 16 while decaying the learning rate by a factor of 0.8 after each epoch when testing on *ResNet–Ev2Vid*, and a batch size of 100 with no decay with the *ResNet–EST* setup. Finally, to perform a robust evaluation, we compute the mean and standard deviation values using five different seeds in all the experiments reported in this section.

Results. The empirical evaluation is organized as it follows for both *ResNet–Ev2Vid* and *ResNet–EST*. We always perform hyper-parameters search using ResNet18 on N-Cars, being faster to train and thus allowing to explore a larger parameter space. We then select the best configuration to train the remaining architectures, i.e., ResNet34 on N-Cars and both variants on N-Caltech101.

Matrix-LSTM + ResNet-Ev2Vid. We start out with the *ResNet–Ev2Vid* baseline (setting up the Matrix-LSTM to output 3 channels) by identifying the optimal time feature to provide as input to the LSTM, as reported in Table 1a. We distinguish between *ts* and *delay* features and between *absolute* and *relative* scope. The first distinction refers to the type of time encoding, i.e., the timestamp of each event in the case of *ts* feature, or the delay between an event and the previous one in case of *delay*. Time features are always range-normalized between 0 and 1, with the scope distinction differentiating if the normalization takes place before splitting events into pixels (*absolute* feature) or after (*relative* feature).

Table 2. Results on N-Cars with ResNet18–EST: **(a)** *polarity + global ts + local ts* encoding, optional SELayer and variable number of bins; **(b)** *polarity + global ts + local ts* encoding, SELayer and variable number of channels

SE	2 bins	4 bins	9 bins	16 bins
	93.46 ± 0.84%	92.68 ± 0.62%	93.21 ± 0,49%	92.01 ± 0.45%
✓	93.71 ± 0.93%	92.90 ± 0.62%	93.30 ± 0,47%	92.44 ± 0.43%

(a)

	Channels		
bins	4	8	16
1	93.88 ± 0.87%	93.60 ± 0.30%	94.37 ± 0.40%
2	93.05 ± 0.92%	93.97 ± 0.52%	94.09 ± 0.29%
bins	4	7	8
9	92.42 ± 0.65%	93.56 ± 0.46%	93.49 ± 0.84%

(b)

In the case of *ts, absolute* means that the first and last events in the sequence have time feature 0 and 1, respectively, regardless of their position, whereas *relative* means that the previous condition holds for each position (x, y). Note that we only consider relative delays since it is only meaningful to compute them between events of the same pixel. Finally, we always add the polarity, obtaining a 2-value feature $f_i^{(x,y)}$. *Delay relative* and *ts absolute* are those providing the best results, with *ts relative* having higher variance. We select *delay relative* as the best configuration. In Table 1a we also show the effect of applying the same frame normalization used while pre-training the ResNet backbone on ImageNet al.so to the Matrix-LSTM output. While performing normalization makes sense when training images are very similar to those used in pre-training, as in Events-to-Video [26], we found out that in our case, where no constraint is imposed on the appearance of reconstructions, this does not improve the performance.

Matrix-LSTM + ResNet-EST. We continue the experiments on N-Cars by considering *ResNet–EST* as baseline, where we explore the effect of using bins, i.e., intervals, on the quality of Matrix-LSTM surfaces. Since multiple intervals are involved, we distinguish between *global* and *local* temporal features. The first type is computed on the original sequence $\mathcal{E}$, before splitting events into intervals, whereas the latter locally, within the interval scope $\mathcal{E}_{T_b}$. For local features we consider the best options we identified on ResNet-Ev2Vid, namely *delay relative* and *ts absolute*, while we only consider *ts* as global feature since a global delay loses meaning after interval splitting. Results are reported in Table 1b where values for single bin are missing since there is no distinction between *global* and *local* scope. Adding a global feature consistently improves performance. This can indeed help the LSTM network in performing integration conditioned on a global timescale and thus enabling the extraction of temporal consistent features. We use *global ts + local ts* features in next experiments, since this provides better performance and reduced variance, and always add the polarity feature.

The next set of experiments was designed to select the optimal number of bins, searching for the best $B = 2, 4, 9, 16$ as done in EST, while using a fixed *polarity + global ts + local ts* configuration. In these experiments, we also make use of the SELayer [13], a self-attention operation specifically designed to correlate channels. Being the number of channels limited, we always use a reduction factor of 1. Please refer to the paper [13] for more details. As reported in Table 2a, adding the layer consistently improves performance. We explain this by noticing

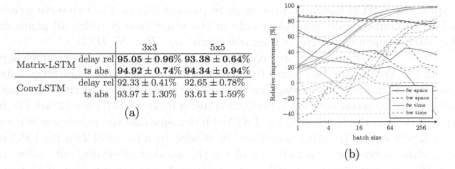

		3x3	5x5
Matrix-LSTM	delay rel	95.05 ± 0.96%	93.38 ± 0.64%
	ts abs	94.92 ± 0.74%	94.34 ± 0.94%
ConvLSTM	delay rel	92.33 ± 0.41%	92.65 ± 0.78%
	ts abs	93.97 ± 1.30%	93.61 ± 1.59%

(a)

(b)

Fig. 2. (a) Comparison between Matrix-LSTM and ConvLSTM on N-Cars. (b) Space and time relative improvements of Matrix-LSTM over ConvLSTM as a function of input density (from 10% to 100% with 30% steps). Colors refer to different density, from low density (dark colors) to high density (light colors) (Color figure online)

that surfaces computed on successive intervals are naturally correlated and, thus, explicitly modeling this behavior helps in extracting richer features. Finally, we perform the last set of experiments to select the Matrix-LSTM hidden size (which also controls the number of output channels). Results are reported in Table 2b. Note that we only consider $4, 7, 8$ channels with 9 bins to limit the total number of channels after concatenation.

Matrix-LSTM vs. ConvLSTM. In Table 2a we compare Matrix-LSTM with ConvLSTM [30] for different choices of kernel size on the N-Cars [31] dataset using the Ev2Vid–ResNet18 backbone. When using ConvLSTM, events are densified in a volume $\tilde{\mathcal{E}}_{dense}$ of shape $N \times T_{max}^{(x,y)} \times H \times W \times F$. Matrix-LSTM performs better on all configurations, despite achieving worst performance than the 1×1 Matrix-LSTM best configuration in Table 1a. Event surfaces produced by the Matrix-LSTM layer are indeed more blurry with larger receptive fields and this may prevent the subsequent ResNet backbone from extracting effective features. Using a 1×1 kernel enables to focus on temporal information while the subsequent convolutional layers deal with spatial correlation.

ConvLSTM, instead, does not properly handle asynchronous data when large receptive fields are considered, and this may explains the performance difference with Matrix-LSTM. Indeed, since pixels at different locations most often fire at different times and with different frequencies, the $\tilde{\mathcal{E}}_{dense}[n, i, :, :, :]$ slice processed by the ConvLSTM in each iteration does not contain all simultaneous events. Using a large ConvLSTM receptive field means to compare a neighborhood of events occurred at different timestamps and therefore not necessarily correlated. Contrary to ConvLSTM, Matrix-LSTM allows for a greater flexibility when large receptive fields are considered since the original events arrival order is preserved and we do not require events to be densified during intermediate steps. We do not compare the two LSTMs on the 1×1 configuration since, when using $\tilde{\mathcal{E}}_{dense}$ as input to ConvLSTM, the two configurations compute the same transformation, despite ConvLSTM having to process more padded values. The two settings are indeed computationally equivalent only in the worst case in which all pixels in the batch happen to receive at least one event (i.e., $P = N \cdot H \cdot W$).

The 1×1 configurations are compared in terms of space and time efficiency in Fig. 2b. We use the two layers to extract a 224×224 frame from artificially generated events with increasing density, i.e., the ratio of pixels receiving at least one event. The reconstruction is performed using PyTorch [32] on a 12 GB Titan Xp, by varying the batch size, the LSTM hidden size and the number of events in each active pixel (starting from 1 and increasing by a factor of 2 for the hidden size, while increasing by a factor of 10 for the number of events, until allowed by GPU memory constraints). We compute the relative improvement of Matrix-LSTM in terms of sample reconstruction time and peak processing space (i.e., excluding model and input space) during both forward and backward passes, and finally aggregate the results by batch size computing the mean improvement over all the trials. Matrix-LSTM performs better than ConvLSTM on prediction time, with the time efficiency improving as the batch size increases, while worst than ConvLSTM on memory efficiency in very dense surfaces ($>70\%$ density). However, this situation is quite uncommon in event-cameras since they only generate events when brightness changes are detected. Uniform parts of the scene that remain unchanged, despite the camera movement, do not appear in the event stream. For instance, the background sky and road in MVSEC [37] make *outdoor_day* sequences only have an average 10% of active pixels.

Discussion. Results of the top performing configurations for both *ResNet-Ev2Vid* and *ResNet-EST* variants on both N-Cars and N-Caltech101 are reported in Table 3. We use *relative delay* with *ResNet-Ev2Vid* and *global ts + local ts* with *ResNet-EST*. Through an extensive evaluation, we show that using Matrix-LSTM representation as input to the baseline networks and training them jointly improves performance by a good margin. Indeed, using the ResNet34-Ev2Vid setup, our solution sets a new state-of-the-art on N-Cars, even surpassing the Events-to-Video model that was trained to extract realistic reconstructions. The same does not happen on N-Caltech101, whose performance usually greatly depends on pre-training also on the original image-based version, and where Events-to-Video has therefore advantage. Despite this, our model only performs 0.9% worse than the baseline. On the ResNet-EST configuration, the model performs consistently better on N-Cars, while slightly worse on N-Caltech101 on most configurations. However, we remark that search for the best configuration was indeed performed on N-Cars, while a hyper-parameter search directly performed on N-Caltech101 would have probably lead to better results.

4.2   Optical Flow Prediction

For the evaluation of optical flow prediction we used the MVSEC [37] suite. Fusing event-data with lidar, IMU, motion capture and GPS sources, MVSEC is the first event-based dataset to provide a solid benchmark in real urban conditions. The dataset provides ground truth information for depth and vehicle

Table 3. Matrix-LSTM best configurations compared to state-of-the-art

Method	Classifier	Channels (bins)	N-Cars	N-Caltech101
H-First [24]	Spike-based	-	56.1	0.54
HOTS [15]	Histogram similarity	-	62.4	21.0
Gabor-SNN [31]	SVM	-	78.9	19.6
HATS [31]	SVM	-	90.2	64.2
	ResNet34–EST [10]	-	90.9	69.1
	ResNet18–Ev2Vid [26]	-	90.4	70.0
Ev2Vid [26]	ResNet18–Ev2Vid	3	91.0	**86.6**
Matrix-LSTM (Ours)	ResNet18–Ev2Vid	3 (1)	**95.80 ± 0.53**	84.12 ± 0.84
	ResNet34–Ev2Vid	3 (1)	**95.65 ± 0.46**	85.72 ± 0.37
EST [10]	ResNet34–EST	2 (9)	92.5	81.7
	ResNet34–EST	2 (16)	92.3	83.7
Matrix-LSTM (Ours)	ResNet18–EST	16 (1)	**94.37 ± 0.40**	81.24 ± 1.31
	ResNet34–EST	16 (1)	**94.31 ± 0.43**	78.98 ± 0.54
	ResNet18–EST	16 (2)	94.09 ± 0.29	83.42 ± 0.80
	ResNet34–EST	16 (2)	94.31 ± 0.44	80.45 ± 0.55
	ResNet18–EST	2 (16)	**92.58 ± 0.68**	**84.31 ± 0.59**
	ResNet34–EST	2 (16)	92.15 ± 0.73	83.50 ± 1.24

pose and was later extended in [36] with optical flow information extracted from depth-maps. The dataset has been recorded on a range of different vehicles and features both indoor and outdoor scenarios and different lighting conditions.

Network Architecture. We used the EV-FlowNet [36] architecture as reference model. To perform a fair comparison between Matrix-LSTM and the original hand-crafted features, we built our model on top of its publicly available code-base [35]. The code contains few minor upgrades over the paper version, which we made sure to remove as reported in the supplementary materials.

The original network uses a 4-channels event-surface, collecting in pairs of separate channels based on the event polarity, the timestamp of the most recent event, and the number of events occurred in every spatial location. We replaced this representation with a Matrix-LSTM making use of 4 output channels, as well. We trained the model on the *outdoor_day1* and *outdoor_day2* sequences for 300,000 iterations, as in the original paper. We used the ADAM optimizer with batch size 8, and an initial learning rate of 10^{-5}, exponentially decayed every 4 epochs by a factor of 0.8. We noticed that EV-FlowNet is quite unstable at higher learning rates, while Matrix-LSTM could benefit from larger rates, so we multiply its learning rate, i.e., the Matrix-LSTM gradients, by a factor of 10 during training. Test was performed on a separate set of recordings, namely *indoor_flying1*, *indoor_flying2* and *indoor_flying3*, which are visually different from the training data. The network performance is measured in terms of average endpoint error (AEE), defined as the distance between the endpoints of the predicted and ground truth flow vectors. In addition, as proposed in the KITTI benchmark [21] and as done in [36], we report the percentage of outliers, namely points with endpoint error greater than 3 pixels and 5% of the magnitude ground truth vector. Finally, following the procedure used in [36], we only report the error computed in spatial locations where at least one event was generated.

Table 4. Optical flow estimation on MVSEC

Method		indoor_flying1		indoor_flying2		indoor_flying3	
		AEE	%Outlier	AEE	%Outlier	AEE	%Outlier
Two-Channel Image [20]		1.21	4.49	2.03	22.8	1.84	17.7
EV-FlowNet [36]		1.03	2.20	1.72	15.1	1.53	11.9
Voxel Grid [38]		0.96	1.47	1.65	14.6	1.45	11.4
EST [10]	Exp. kernel	0.96	1.27	1.58	10.5	1.40	9.44
	Learnt kernel	0.97	0.91	1.38	8.20	1.43	6.47
Matrix-LSTM (Ours)	1 bin	1.017	2.071	1.642	13.88	1.432	10.44
	2 bins	**0.829**	**0.471**	**1.194**	**5.341**	**1.083**	**4.390**
	4 bins	0.969	1.781	1.505	11.63	1.507	12.97
	8 bins	0.881	0.672	1.292	6.594	1.181	5.389
	2 bins + SELayer	**0.821**	**0.534**	**1.191**	**5.590**	**1.077**	**4.805**

Results. In the previous classification experiments, we observed that the type of temporal features and the number of bins play an important role in extracting effective representations. We expect time resolution to be a key factor of performance in optical flow, hence, we focus here on measuring how different interval choices impact on the flow prediction. We decided to always use the *polarity + global ts + local ts* configuration, which worked well on N-Cars while considering different bin setups. Results are reported in Table 4.

As performed on classification, we study the effect of adding a SELayer on the best performing configuration. Correlating the intervals slightly improves the AEE metric in all test sequences but increases the number of outliers. As expected, varying the number of bins has a great impact on performance. The AEE metric, indeed, greatly reduces by simply considering two intervals instead of one. Interestingly, we achieved the best performance by considering only 2 intervals, as adding more bins hurts performance. We believe this behavior resides on the nature of optical flow prediction, where the network is implicitly asked to compare two distinct temporal instants. This configuration consistently improves the baseline up to 30.76% on *indoor_flying2*, highlighting the capability of the Matrix-LSTM to adapt also to low-level tasks.

4.3   Time Performance Analysis

We compared the time performance of Matrix-LSTM with other event representations following EST [10] and HATS [31] evaluation procedure. In Table 3b we report the time required to compute features on a sample averaged over the whole N-Cars training dataset for both ResNet–Ev2Vid and ResNet–EST configurations. Our surface achieves similar time performance than both HATS and EST, performing only ~2 ms slower than EST on the same setting (9 bins

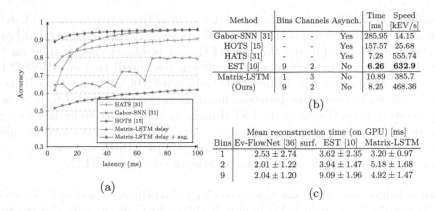

Fig. 3. (a) Accuracy as a function of latency (adapted from [31]). (b) Average sample computation time on N-Cars and number of events processed per second. (c) Average time to reconstruct the event surface in MVSEC test sequences

and 2 channels). Similarly, in Table 3c, we compute the mean surface recon-struct time for MVSEC *indoor_flying* test sequences. While EST can exploit parallel batch computation of events within the same sample, since each event feature is processed independently, Matrix-LSTM relies on sequential computa-tion to reconstruct the surface. The custom CUDA kernels we designed, however, enable bins and pixel sequences to be processed in parallel, drastically reducing the processing time. Please, refer to the additional materials for more details. All evaluations are performed with PyTorch on a GeForce GTX 1080Ti GPU.

In Fig. 3a we analyze the accuracy-vs-latency trade-off on the N-Cars dataset, as proposed in [31], using the ResNet18-Ev2Vid configuration. While the perfor-mance of the model, trained on 100 ms sequences, significantly drops when very few milliseconds of events are considered, the proposed method still shows good generalization, achieving better performance than the baselines when more than 20 ms of events are used. However, fixing the performance loss on small latencies is just a matter of training augmentation: by randomly cropping sequences to variable lengths (from 5 ms to 100 ms), our method consistently improves the baselines, dynamically adapting to sequences of different lengths.

5   Conclusion

We proposed Matrix-LSTM, an effective method for learning dense event repre-sentations from event-based data. By modeling the reconstruction with a spa-tially shared LSTM we obtained a fully differentiable procedure that can be trained end-to-end to extract the event representation that best fits the task at hand. Focusing on efficiently handling asynchronous data, Matrix-LSTM pre-serves sparsity during computation and surpasses other popular LSTM variants on space and time efficiency when processing sparse inputs. In this regard, we proposed an efficient implementation of the method that exploits parallel batch-wise computation and demonstrated the effectiveness of the Matrix-LSTM layer on multiple tasks, improving the state-of-the-art of object classification on N-Cars by 3.3% and the performance on optical flow prediction on MVSEC by up to 23.07% over previous differentiable techniques [10]. Although we only integrate windows of events, the proposed mechanism can be extended to process a continuous streams thanks to the LSTM memory that is able to update its representation as soon as a new event arrives. As a future line of research, we plan to explore the use of Matrix-LSTM for more complex tasks such as gray-scale frame reconstruction [26], ego-motion and depth estimation [34,38].

Acknowledgments. We thank Alex Zihao Zhu for his help on replicating Ev-FlowNet results and the ISPL group at Politecnico di Milano for GPU support. This research is supported from project TEINVEIN, CUP: E96D17000110009 - Call "Accordi per la Ricerca e l'Innovazione", cofunded by POR FESR 2014-2020 (Regional Operational Programme, European Regional Development Fund).

References

1. Abadi, M., et al.: TensorFlow: a system for large-scale machine learning. In: 12th USENIX Symposium on Operating Systems Design and Implementation, OSDI 2016, pp. 265–283 (2016)
2. Berner, R., Brandli, C., Yang, M., Liu, S.C., Delbruck, T.: A 240×180 10mW 12us latency sparse-output vision sensor for mobile applications. In: 2013 Symposium on VLSI Circuits, pp. C186–C187. IEEE (2013)
3. Bi, Y., Chadha, A., Abbas, A., Bourtsoulatze, E., Andreopoulos, Y.: Graph-based object classification for neuromorphic vision sensing. In: Proceedings of the IEEE International Conference on Computer Vision, pp. 491–501 (2019)
4. Cannici, M., Ciccone, M., Romanoni, A., Matteucci, M.: Asynchronous convolutional networks for object detection in neuromorphic cameras. In: Proceedings of the IEEE Conference on Computer Vision and Pattern Recognition Workshops (2019)
5. Cannici, M., Ciccone, M., Romanoni, A., Matteucci, M.: Attention mechanisms for object recognition with event-based cameras. In: 2019 IEEE Winter Conference on Applications of Computer Vision (WACV), pp. 1127–1136. IEEE (2019)
6. Cohen, G.K.: Event-Based Feature Detection, Recognition and Classification. Theses, Université Pierre et Marie Curie - Paris VI (September 2016)
7. Deng, J., Dong, W., Socher, R., Li, L.J., Li, K., Fei-Fei, L.: ImageNet: a large-scale hierarchical image database. In: 2009 IEEE Conference on Computer Vision and Pattern Recognition, pp. 248–255. IEEE (2009)
8. Gallego, G., et al.: Event-based vision: A survey. arXiv preprint arXiv:1904.08405 (2019)
9. Gehrig, D., Loquercio, A., Derpanis, K.G., Scaramuzza, D.: End-to-end learning of representations for asynchronous event-based data. https://github.com/uzh-rpg/rpg_event_representation_learning
10. Gehrig, D., Loquercio, A., Derpanis, K.G., Scaramuzza, D.: End-to-end learning of representations for asynchronous event-based data. In: IEEE International Conference of Computer Vision (ICCV) (October 2019)

11. He, K., Zhang, X., Ren, S., Sun, J.: Deep residual learning for image recognition. In: Proceedings of the IEEE Conference on Computer Vision and Pattern Recognition, pp. 770–778 (2016)
12. Hochreiter, S., Schmidhuber, J.: Long short-term memory. Neural Comput. 9(8), 1735–1780 (1997)
13. Hu, J., Shen, L., Sun, G.: Squeeze-and-excitation networks. In: Proceedings of the IEEE Conference on Computer Vision and Pattern Recognition, pp. 7132–7141 (2018)
14. Kingma, D.P., Ba, J.: Adam: a method for stochastic optimization. In: International Conference on Learning Representations (ICLR) (2015)
15. Lagorce, X., Orchard, G., Galluppi, F., Shi, B.E., Benosman, R.B.: HOTS: a hierarchy of event-based time-surfaces for pattern recognition. IEEE Trans. Pattern Anal. Mach. Intell. 39(7), 1346–1359 (2016)
16. Fei-Fei, L., Fergus, R., Perona, P.: One-shot learning of object categories. IEEE Trans. Pattern Anal. Mach. Intell. 28(4), 594–611 (2006)
17. Lichtsteiner, P., Posch, C., Delbruck, T.: A 128×128 120 db 15μs latency asynchronous temporal contrast vision sensor. IEEE J. Solid-State Circ. 43(2), 566–576 (2008)
18. Long, J., Shelhamer, E., Darrell, T.: Fully convolutional networks for semantic segmentation. In: The IEEE Conference on Computer Vision and Pattern Recognition (CVPR) (June 2015)
19. Maass, W.: Networks of spiking neurons: the third generation of neural network models. Neural Netw. 10(9), 1659–1671 (1997)
20. Maqueda, A.I., Loquercio, A., Gallego, G., García, N., Scaramuzza, D.: Event-based vision meets deep learning on steering prediction for self-driving cars. In: Proceedings of the IEEE Conference on Computer Vision and Pattern Recognition, pp. 5419–5427 (2018)
21. Menze, M., Geiger, A.: Object scene flow for autonomous vehicles. In: Conference on Computer Vision and Pattern Recognition (CVPR) (2015)
22. Neil, D., Pfeiffer, M., Liu, S.C.: Phased LSTM: accelerating recurrent network training for long or event-based sequences. In: Advances in Neural Information Processing Systems, pp. 3882–3890 (2016)
23. Orchard, G., Jayawant, A., Cohen, G.K., Thakor, N.: Converting static image datasets to spiking neuromorphic datasets using saccades. Front. Neurosci. 9, 437 (2015)
24. Orchard, G., Meyer, C., Etienne-Cummings, R., Posch, C., Thakor, N., Benosman, R.: HFirst: a temporal approach to object recognition. IEEE Trans. Pattern Anal. Mach. Intell. 37(10), 2028–2040 (2015)
25. Posch, C., Serrano-Gotarredona, T., Linares-Barranco, B., Delbruck, T.: Retinomorphic event-based vision sensors: bioinspired cameras with spiking output. Proc. IEEE 102(10), 1470–1484 (2014)
26. Rebecq, H., Ranftl, R., Koltun, V., Scaramuzza, D.: Events-to-video: bringing modern computer vision to event cameras. In: Proceedings of the IEEE Conference on Computer Vision and Pattern Recognition, pp. 3857–3866 (2019)
27. Scheerlinck, C., Rebecq, H., Stoffregen, T., Barnes, N., Mahony, R., Scaramuzza, D.: CED: color event camera dataset. In: Proceedings of the IEEE Conference on Computer Vision and Pattern Recognition Workshops (2019)
28. Sekikawa, Y., Hara, K., Saito, H.: EventNet: asynchronous recursive event processing. In: Proceedings of the IEEE Conference on Computer Vision and Pattern Recognition, pp. 3887–3896 (2019)

29. Serrano-Gotarredona, T., Linares-Barranco, B.: A 128×128 1.5% contrast sensitivity 0.9% FPN 3μs latency 4 mW asynchronous frame-free dynamic vision sensor using transimpedance preamplifiers. IEEE J. Solid-State Circ. **48**(3), 827–838 (2013)
30. SHI, X., Chen, Z., Wang, H., Yeung, D.Y., Wong, W., WOO, W.: Convolutional LSTM network: a machine learning approach for precipitation nowcasting. In: Cortes, C., Lawrence, N.D., Lee, D.D., Sugiyama, M., Garnett, R. (eds.) Advances in Neural Information Processing Systems, vol. 28, pp. 802–810. Curran Associates, Inc. (2015)
31. Sironi, A., Brambilla, M., Bourdis, N., Lagorce, X., Benosman, R.: HATS: histograms of averaged time surfaces for robust event-based object classification. In: Proceedings of the IEEE Conference on Computer Vision and Pattern Recognition, pp. 1731–1740 (2018)
32. Steiner, B., et al.: PyTorch: an imperative style, high-performance deep learning library. In: Advances in Neural Information Processing Systems, vol. 32 (2019)
33. Wang, Q., Zhang, Y., Yuan, J., Lu, Y.: Space-time event clouds for gesture recognition: from RGB cameras to event cameras. In: 2019 IEEE Winter Conference on Applications of Computer Vision (WACV), pp. 1826–1835. IEEE (2019)
34. Ye, C., Mitrokhin, A., Fermüller, C., Yorke, J.A., Aloimonos, Y.: Unsupervised learning of dense optical flow, depth and egomotion from sparse event data. arXiv preprint arXiv:1809.08625 (2018)
35. Zhu, A., Yuan, L., Chaney, K., Daniilidis, K.: EV-FlowNet: Self-supervised optical flow estimation for event-based cameras. https://github.com/daniilidis-group/EV-FlowNet
36. Zhu, A., Yuan, L., Chaney, K., Daniilidis, K.: EV-FlowNet: self-supervised optical flow estimation for event-based cameras. In: Proceedings of Robotics: Science and Systems, Pittsburgh, Pennsylvania (June 2018)
37. Zhu, A.Z., Thakur, D., Özaslan, T., Pfrommer, B., Kumar, V., Daniilidis, K.: The multivehicle stereo event camera dataset: an event camera dataset for 3D perception. IEEE Robot. Autom. Lett. **3**(3), 2032–2039 (2018)
38. Zhu, A.Z., Yuan, L., Chaney, K., Daniilidis, K.: Unsupervised event-based learning of optical flow, depth, and egomotion. In: Proceedings of the IEEE Conference on Computer Vision and Pattern Recognition, pp. 989–997 (2019)

Fine-Grained Visual Classification via Progressive Multi-granularity Training of Jigsaw Patches

Ruoyi Du[1], Dongliang Chang[1], Ayan Kumar Bhunia[2], Jiyang Xie[1],
Zhanyu Ma[1](✉), Yi-Zhe Song[2], and Jun Guo[1]

[1] Pattern Recognition and Intelligent System Laboratory, School of Artificial
Intelligence, Beijing University of Posts and Telecommunications, Beijing, China
{beiyoudry,changdongliang,xiejiyang2013,mazhanyu,guojun}@bupt.edu.cn
[2] SketchX, CVSSP, University of Surrey, Guildford, UK
{a.bhunia,y.song}@surrey.ac.uk

Abstract. Fine-grained visual classification (FGVC) is much more challenging than traditional classification tasks due to the inherently subtle
intra-class object variations. Recent works are mainly part-driven (either
explicitly or implicitly), with the assumption that fine-grained information naturally rests within the parts. In this paper, we take a different
stance, and show that part operations are not strictly necessary – the key
lies with encouraging the network to learn at different granularities and
progressively fusing multi-granularity features together. In particular, we
propose: (i) a progressive training strategy that effectively fuses features
from different granularities, and (ii) a random jigsaw patch generator
that encourages the network to learn features at specific granularities.
We evaluate on several standard FGVC benchmark datasets, and show
the proposed method consistently outperforms existing alternatives or
delivers competitive results. The code is available at https://github.com/
PRIS-CV/PMG-Progressive-Multi-Granularity-Training.

1 Introduction

Fine-grained visual classification (FGVC) aims at identifying sub-classes of a
given object category, *e.g.*, different species of birds, and models of cars and
aircrafts. It is a much more challenging problem than traditional classification
due to the inherently subtle intra-class object variations amongst sub-categories.
Most effective solutions to date rely on extracting fine-grained feature representations at local discriminative regions, either by explicitly detecting semantic
parts [11,12,38,39,41] or implicitly via saliency localization [4,10,25,33]. It follows that such locally discriminative features are collectively fused to perform
final classification.

Electronic supplementary material The online version of this chapter (https://
doi.org/10.1007/978-3-030-58565-5_10) contains supplementary material, which is
available to authorized users.

© Springer Nature Switzerland AG 2020
A. Vedaldi et al. (Eds.): ECCV 2020, LNCS 12365, pp. 153–168, 2020.
https://doi.org/10.1007/978-3-030-58565-5_10

Early work mostly finds discriminative regions with the assistance of manual annotations [2,16,21,37,40]. However, human annotations are difficult to obtain, and can often be error-prone resulting in performance degradations [41]. Research focus has consequently shifted to training models in a weakly-supervised manner given only category labels [4,26,33,38,41]. Success behind these models can be largely attributed to being able to locate more discriminative local regions for downstream classification. However little or no effort has been made towards (i) at which granularities are these local regions most discriminative, e.g., head or beak of a bird, and (ii) how can information across different granularities be fused together to classification accuracy, e.g., can do head and beak work together.

Information cross various granularities is however helpful for avoiding the effect of large intra-class variations. For example, experts sometimes need to identify a bird using *both* the overall structure of a bird's head, and finer details such as the shape of its beak. That is, it is often not sufficient to identify discriminative parts, but also how these parts interact amongst each other in a complementary manner. Very recent research has focused on the "zooming-in" factor [11,39], i.e., not just identifying parts, but also focusing on the truly discriminative regions within each part (e.g., the beak, more than the head). Yet these methods mostly focuses on a few parts and ignores others as zooming in beyond simple fusion. More importantly, they do not consider how features from different zoomed-in parts can be fused together in a synergistic manner. Different to these approaches, we further argue that, one not only needs to identify parts and their most discriminative granularities, but meanwhile how parts at different granularities can be effectively merged.

In this paper, we take an alternative stance towards fine-grained classification. We do not explicitly, nor implicitly attempt to mine fine-grained feature representations from parts (or their zoomed-in versions). Instead, we approach the problem with the hypothesis that the fine-grained discriminative information lies *naturally* within different visual granularities – it is all about encouraging the network to learn at different granularities and simultaneously fusing multi-granularity features together. This can be better explained by Fig. 1.

More specifically, we propose a consolidated framework that accommodates part granularity learning and cross-granularity feature fusion simultaneously. This is achieved through two components that work synergistically with each other: (i) a progressive training strategy that effectively fuses features from different granularities, and (ii) a random jigsaw patch generator that encourages the network to learn features at specific granularities. Note that we refrain from using "scale" since we do not apply Gaussian blur filters on image patches, rather we evenly divide and shuffle image patches to form different granularity levels.

As the first contribution, we propose a multi-granularity progressive training framework to learn the complementary information across different granularities. This differs significantly to prior art where parts are first detected, and later fused in an ad-hoc manner. Our progressive framework works in steps during training, where at each step the training focuses on cultivating granularity-specific

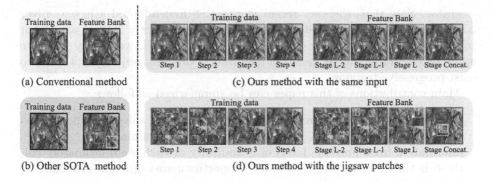

Fig. 1. Illustration of features learned by general methods (a and b) and our proposed method (c and d). (a) Traditional convolution neural networks trained with cross entropy (CE) loss tend to find the most discriminative parts. (b) Other state-of-the-art methods focus on how to find more discriminative parts. (c) Our proposed progressive training (Here we use last three stages for explanation.) gradually locates discriminative information from low stages to deeper stages. And features extracted from all trained stages are concatenated together to ensure complementary relationships are fully explored, which is represented by "Stage Concat." (d) With assistance of jigsaw puzzle generator the granularity of parts learned at each step are restricted inside patches.

information with a corresponding stage of the network. We start with finer granularities which are more stable, gradually move onto coarser ones, which avoids the confusion made by large intra-class variations that appear in large regions. On its own, this is akin to a "zooming out" operation, where the network would focus on a local region, then zoom out a larger patch surrounding this local region, and finish when we reach the whole image. More specifically, when each training step ends, the parameters trained at the current step will pass onto the next training as its parameter initialization. This passing operation essentially enables the network to mine information of larger granularity based on the region learned in its previous training step. Features extracted from all stages are concatenated only at the last step to further ensure complementary relationships are fully explored.

However, applying progressive training naively would not benefit fine-grained feature learning. This is because the multi-granularity information learned via progressive training may tend to focus on the similar region. As the second contribution, we tackle this problem by introducing a jigsaw puzzle generator to form different granularity levels at each training step, and only the last step is still trained with original images. This effectively encourage the model to operate on patch-level, where patch sizes are specific to a particular granularity. It essentially forces each stage of the network to focus on local patches other than holistically across the entire image, therefore learning information specific to a given granularity level. This effect is demonstrated in Fig. 1 and the Fig. 2 illustrates the learning process of progressive training with the jigsaw puzzle generator. Note that, the very recent work of [4] first adopted a jigsaw solver to solve for fine-grained classification. We differ significantly in that we do not employ jigsaw solver as part of feature learning. Instead, we simply generate jigsaw patches randomly as means of introducing different object parts levels to assist progressive training.

Main contributions of this paper can be summarized as follows:

1. We propose a novel progressive training strategy to solve for fine-grained visual classification (FGVC). It operates in different training steps, and fuses information from previous levels of granularity at each step, ultimately cultivating the inherent complementary properties across different granularities for fine-grained feature learning.
2. We adapt a simple yet effective jigsaw puzzle generator to form images with different levels of granularity. This allows the network to focus on different "scales" of features as per prior work.
3. The proposed Progressive Multi-Granularity (PMG) Training framework obtains state-of-the-art or competitive performances on three standard FGVC benchmark datasets.

2   Related Work

2.1   Fine-Grained Classification

Recent studies on FGVC have moved from strongly-supervised scenario with additional annotations *e.g.*, bounding box [2,16,21,37,40], to weakly-supervised conditions with only category labels [11,12,22,36,38,39,41,42].

In the weakly-supervised configuration, recent studies mainly focus on locating the most discriminative parts, more complementary parts, and parts of various granularities. However, few considered how to fuse information from these discriminative parts together. Current fusion techniques can be roughly divided into two categories. The first category conducts predictions based on different parts and then directly combines their probabilities together. For example, Zhang et al. [39] trained several networks focusing on features of different granularities to produce diverse prediction distributions, and then weighted their results before combining them together. The other group concatenate features extracted from different parts together for next prediction [11,12,38,41]. Fu et al. [11] found region detection and fine-grained feature learning can reinforce each other, and built a series of networks which located discriminative regions for the next network while conducting predictions. With similar motivation, Zheng et al. [41] jointly learned part proposals and the feature representations on each part, and located various discriminative parts before prediction. Both of them train a fully-connected fusion layer to fuse features extracted from different parts. Ge et al. [12] went one step further by fusing features from complementary object parts with two LSTMs stacked together.

Fusing features from different parts is still a challenging problem with limited efforts. In this work, we tackle it based on the intrinsic characteristics of fine-grained objects: although with large intra-class variation, the subtle details exhibit stability at local regions. Hence, instead of locating discriminative parts first, we guide the network to learn features from small granularity to large granularity progressively.

2.2 Image Splitting Operations

Splitting an image into pieces with the same size has been utilized for various task in prior art. Amongst them, one typical solution is to solve the jigsaw puzzle [6,31]. It can also go one step further by adopting the jigsaw puzzle solution as the initialization to a weakly-supervised network, which leads to better transformation performance [35]. This helps the network to exploit the spatial relationship of local image regions. In one-shot learning, image splitting operation was used for data augmentation [5], which split two images and exchanged patches across to generate new training ones. In more recent research, DCL [4] first adopted image splitting operation for FGVC, who destructed images to emphasize local details and then reconstructed them to learn semantic correlation among local regions. However, it split images with the same size during the whole training process, which made it difficult to exploit multi-granularity regions. In this work, we apply a jigsaw puzzle generator to restrict the granularity of learned regions at each training step.

2.3 Progressive Training

Progressive training methodology was originally proposed for generative adversarial networks [18], where it started with low-resolution images, and then progressively increased the resolution by adding new layers to the network. Instead of learning information from all scales, this strategy allows the network to discover large-scale structure of the image distribution and then shift attention to increasingly finer scale details. Recently, progressive training strategy has been widely utilized for generation tasks [1,19,29,34], since it can simplify the information propagation within the network by intermediate supervision.

For FGVC, the fusion of multi-granularity information is critical to the model performance. In this work, we adopt the idea of progressive training to design a single network that can learn these information with a series of training stages. The input images are firstly split into small patches to train low-level layers of the model. Then the number of patches are progressively increased and the corresponding high-level layers are added and trained. Most of the existing work with progressive training are focusing on the task of sample generation. To the best of our knowledge, this has not been attempted before for the task of FGVC.

3   Approach

In this section, we present our proposed Progressive Multi-Granularity (PMG) training framework. We encourage the model to learn stable fine-grained information in the shallower layers, and gradually focus on learning more abstracted

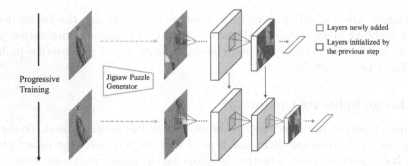

Fig. 2. The illustration of the progressive training process. The network is trained from shallow stages with smaller patches to deeper stages with larger patches. At the end of each training step, the parameter from current step will initialize the parameter of following step. This enables the network to further mine information of larger granularity based on the detail knowledge learned in the previous training step.

information of larger granularity in the deeper layers as the training progresses. Please refer to Fig. 2.

3.1 Progressive Training

Network Architecture. Our network design for progressive training is generic and could be implemented on the top of any state-of-the-art backbone feature extractors, like Resnet [14]. Let F be our backbone feature extractor, which has L stages. The output feature-map from any intermediate stage is represented as $F^l \in \mathbb{R}^{H_l \times W_l \times C_l}$, where H_l, W_l, C_l are the height, width and number of channels of the feature map at l-th stage, and $l = \{1, 2, \ldots, L\}$. Here, our objective is to impose classification loss on the feature-map extracted at different intermediate stages. Hence, in addition to F, we introduce convolution block H_{conv}^l that takes l-th intermediate stage output F^l as input and reduces it to a vector representation $V^l = H_{conv}^l(F^l)$. Thereafter, a classification module H_{class}^l consisting of two fully-connected layers with Batchnorm [17] and Elu[7] non-linearity, corresponding to l-th stage, predicts the probability distribution over the classes as $y^l = H_{class}^l(V^l)$. Here, we consider last S stages: $l = L, L - 1, \ldots, L - S + 1$. Finally, we concatenate the output from the last S stages as

$$V^{concat} = \text{concat}[V^{L-S+1}, \ldots, V^{L-1}, V^L] \tag{1}$$

This is followed by an additional classification module $y^{concat} = H_{class}^{concat}(V^{concat})$

Training Process. During training, each iteration contains $S + 1$ steps where low-level stages of the model are trained first and new stages are progressively added. Since the receptive field and representation ability of low-level stages are limited, the network will be forced to first exploit discriminative information from local details (*i.e.* object textures). Directly training the whole network intends

---

Algorithm 1. Progressive Training

Training data set D, Training data for a batch d, Training label for a batch y.

for $epoch \in [0, epoch\_num)$ **do**

    for $b \in [0, batch\_num)$ **do**

        $d, y \Leftarrow$ batch b of D

        for $l \in [L - S + 1, L]$ **do**

            $n \Leftarrow 2^{L-l+1}$

            $V^l \Leftarrow H_{conv}^l(F^l(P(d, n)))$

            $y^l \Leftarrow H_{class}^l(V^l)$

            $\mathscr{L}_l \Leftarrow \alpha \times \mathscr{L}_{CE}(y^l, y)$

            Backprop($\mathscr{L}_l$)

        end for

        $V^{concat} = \text{concat}[V^{L-S+1}, \ldots, V^{L-1}, V^L]$

        $y^{concat} = H_{class}^{concat}(V^{concat})$

        $\mathscr{L}_{concat} \Leftarrow \beta \times \mathscr{L}_{CE}(y^{concat}, y)$

        Backprop($\mathscr{L}_{concat}$)

    end for

end for

---

to learn all the granularities simultaneously. In contrast to that, step-wise incremental training naturally allows the model to mine discriminative information from local details to global structures when the features are gradually sent into higher stages.

For training, we compute cross entropy (CE) loss $\mathscr{L}_{CE}$ between the ground truth label y and the predicted output from every stage.

At each iteration, a batch of data d will be used for $S + 1$ steps, and we only train one stage's output at each step in sequence. It needs to be clear that all parameters are used in the current prediction will be optimized, even they may have been updated in the previous steps, and this can help all stages in the model working together.

3.2   Jigsaw Puzzle Generator

Jigsaw Puzzle solving [35] has been found to be suitable for self-supervised task in representation learning. On the contrary, we borrow the notion of Jigsaw Puzzle to generate input images for different steps of progressive training. The objective is to devise different granularity regions and force the model to learn information specific to the corresponding granularity level at each training step. Given an input image $d \in R^{3 \times W \times H}$, we equally split it into $n \times n$ patches which have $3 \times \frac{W}{n} \times \frac{H}{n}$ dimensions. Then, the patches are shuffled randomly and merged together into a new image $P(d, n)$. Here, the granularities of patches are controlled by the hyper-parameter n.

Regarding the choice of hyper-parameter n for each stage, two conditions needs to be satisfied: (i) the size of the patches should be smaller than the receptive field of the corresponding stage, otherwise, the performance of the jigsaw

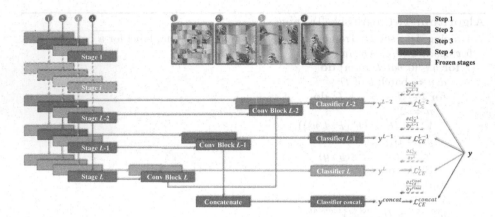

Fig. 3. The training procedure of the progressive training strategy which consists of $S + 1$ steps at each iteration (Here $S = 3$ for explanation). The *Conv Block* represents the combination of two convolution layers and a max pooling layer, and *Classifier* represent two fully connected layers with a softmax layer at the end. At each iteration, the training data are augmented by the jigsaw generator and sequentially fed into the network by $S + 1$ steps. In our training process, the hyper-parameter n is 2^{L-l+1} for the lth stage. At each step, the output from the corresponding classifier will be used for loss computation and parameter updating.

puzzle generator will be reduced; (ii) the patch size should increase proportionately with the increase of the receptive fields of the stages. Usually, the receptive field of each stage is approximately double than that of the last stage. Hence, we set n as 2^{L-l+1} for the lth stage's output.

During training, a batch of training data d will first be augmented to several jigsaw puzzle generator-processed batches, obtaining $P(d, n)$. All the jigsaw puzzle generator-processed batches share the same label y. Then, for the lth stage's output y^l, we input the batch $P(d, n), n = 2^{L-l+1}$, and optimize all the parameters used in this propagation. Figure 3 illustrates the whole progressive training process with the jigsaw puzzle generator step by step.

It should be clarified that the jigsaw puzzle generator cannot always guarantee the completeness of all the parts which are smaller than the size of the patch, because they still have chances of getting split. However, it should not be a bad news for model training, since we adopt random cropping which is a standard data augmentation strategy before the jigsaw puzzle generator and leads to the result that parts with appropriate granularities, which are split at this iteration due to the jigsaw puzzle generator, will not be always split in other iterations. Hence, it brings an additional advantage of forcing our model to find more discriminative parts at the specific granularity level.

3.3   Inference

At the inference phase, we merely input the original images into the trained model and the jigsaw puzzle generator is unnecessary. If we only use y^{concat} for prediction, the FC layers for the other three stages can be removed which leads to less computational budget. In this case, the final result C_1 can be expressed as

$$C_1 = argmax(y^{concat}). \tag{2}$$

However, the prediction from a single stage with information of a specific granularity is unique and complementary, which leads to a better performance when we simply combine all outputs together with equal weights. The multi-output combined prediction C_2 can be written as

$$C_2 = argmax(\sum_{l=L-S+1}^{L} y^l + y^{concat}). \tag{3}$$

4   Experimental Results and Discussion

In this section, we evaluate the performance of the proposed method on three ne-grained image classification datasets: CUB-200-2011 (CUB) [32], Stanford Cars (CAR) [20], and FGVC-Aircraft (AIR) [27]. Firstly, the implementation details are introduced in Sect. 4.1. Subsequently, the classification accuracy comparisons with other state-of-the-art methods are provided in Sect. 4.2. In order to illustrate the advantages of different components and design choices in our method, a comprehensive ablation study and a visualization are provided in Sect. 4.3 and 4.5. Besides, the discussion about the hyper-parameter selection and the fusion techniques are provided in Sect. 4.4.

4.1   Implementation Details

We perform all experiments using PyTorch [28] with version higher than 1.3 over a cluster of GTX 2080 GPUs. The proposed method is evaluated on the widely used backbone networks: VGG16 [30] and ResNet50 [14], which means the total number of stages $L = 5$. For the best performance, we set $S = 3$, $\alpha = 1$, and $\beta = 2$. The category labels of the images are the only annotations used for training. The input images are resized to a xed size of 550×550 and randomly cropped into 448×448, and random horizontal ip is applied for data augmentation when we train the model. During testing, the input images are resized to a xed size of 550×550 and cropped from center into 448×448. All the above settings are standard in the literatures.

We use stochastic gradient descent (SGD) optimizer and batch normalization as the regularizer. Meanwhile, the learning rates of the convolution layers and the FC layers newly added by us are initialized as 0.002 and reduced by following the cosine annealing schedule [24]. The learning rates of the pre-trained convolution layers are maintained as $1/10$ of those of the newly added layers. For all the aforementioned models, we train them for up to 200 epochs with batch size as 16 and used a weight decay as 0.0005 and a momentum as 0.9.

Table 1. Comparison with other state-of-the-art methods.

Method	Base model	CUB (%)	CAR (%)	AIR (%)
FT VGG (CVPR18) [33]	VGG16	77.8	84.9	84.8
FT ResNet (CVPR18) [33]	ResNet50	84.1	91.7	88.5
B-CNN (ICCV15) [23]	VGG16	84.1	91.3	84.1
KP (CVPR17) [8]	VGG16	86.2	92.4	86.9
RA-CNN (ICCV17) [11]	VGG19	85.3	92.5	-
MA-CNN (ICCV17) [41]	VGG19	86.5	92.8	89.9
PC (ECCV18) [10]	DenseNet161	86.9	92.9	89.2
DFL (CVPR18) [33]	ResNet50	87.4	93.1	91.7
NTS-Net (ECCV18) [38]	ResNet50	87.5	93.9	91.4
MC-Loss (TIP20) [3]	ResNet50	87.3	93.7	92.6
DCL (CVPR19) [4]	ResNet50	87.8	94.5	<u>93.0</u>
MGE-CNN (ICCV19) [39]	ResNet50	88.5	93.9	-
S3N (ICCV19) [9]	ResNet50	88.5	94.7	92.8
Stacked LSTM (CVPR19) [12]	ResNet50	**90.4**	-	-
PMG	VGG16	88.2	94.2	92.4
PMG (combined accuracy)	VGG16	88.8	94.3	92.7
PMG	ResNet50	88.9	<u>95.0</u>	92.8
PMG (combined accuracy)	ResNet50	<u>89.6</u>	**95.1**	**93.4**

Table 2. The p-value of one-sample Student's t-tests between combined accuracies of our method and methods with close performances on three datasets. The proposed method has statistically significant difference from a referred technique if the corresponding p-value is smaller than 0.05

Method	CUB	CAR	AIR
DCL (CVPR19) [4]	6.4e−07	2.5e−06	2.2e−05
MGE-CNN (ICCV19) [39]	8.7e−06	1.5e−07	-
S3N (ICCV19) [9]	4.3e−06	1.4e−05	4.5e−06

4.2 Comparisons with State-of-the-Art Methods

The comparisons of our method with other state-of-the-art methods on CUB-200-2011, Stanford Cars, and FGVC-Aircraft are presented in Table 1. Both the accuracy of the single output C_1 and the combined output C_2 are listed. In addition, we run our method 5 times with random initialization and conduct a one-sample Student's t-test to confirm the significance of our results in Table 2. Results show that our improvement is statistically significant with significance level 0.05.

CUB-200-2011. We achieve a competitive result on this dataset in a much easier experimental procedure, since only single feed-forward propagation through one network is needed during testing. Our method outperforms RA-CNN [11] and MGE-CNN [39] by 4.3% and 1.1%, even though they build several different networks to learn information of various granularities. They train the classification of each network separately and then combine their information for testing, which proofs our advantage of exploiting multi-granularity information gradually in one network. Besides, even Stacked LSTM [12] obtains better performance than our method, it is a two phase algorithm that requires Mask-RCNN [13] and CPF to offer complementary object parts and then uses bi-directional LSTM [15] for classification, which leads to longer inference time and more computation budget.

Stanford Cars. Our method achieves state-of-the-art performance with Resnet50 as the base model. Since the performance of y^{concat} is good enough, the improvement of combining multi-stage outputs is not obvious. The result of our method surpasses PC [10] even it acquires great performance gains by adopting more advanced backbone network $i.e.$ DenseNet161. For MA-CNN [41] and NTS-Net [38] which first locate several different discriminative parts to combine feature extracted from each of them for final classification. We outperform them by a large margin of 2.3% and 1.2%, respectively.

FGVC-Aircraft. On this task, the multi-output combined result of our method also achieves the state-of-the-art performance. Although S3N [9] finds both discriminative parts and complementary parts for feature extraction, and applies additional inhomogeneous transform to highlight these parts, we still outperform it by 0.6% with the same backbone network ResNet50, and show competitive result even when we adopt VGG16 as the base model.

4.3   Ablation Study

We conduct ablation studies to understand the effectiveness of the progressive training strategy and the jigsaw puzzle generator. We choose CUB-200-2011 dataset for experiments and ResNet50 as the backbone network, which means the total number of stages L is 5. We first design different runs with the number of stages used for output S increasing from 1 to 5 and no jigsaw puzzle generator, as shown in Table 3. The y^{concat} is kept for all runs and number of steps is $S+1$. It is clear that the increasing of S boosts the model performance significantly when $S < 4$. However, we also notice the accuracy starts to decrease when $S = 4$. The possible reason is that the low stage layers are mainly focus on the class-irrelevant features, but the additional supervision will force it to distill class-relevant information and then affect the overall performance.

In Table 3, we also report the results of our method with the jigsaw puzzle generator. The hyper-parameter n of the jigsaw puzzle generator for l^{th} stage follows the pattern that $n = 2^{L-l+1}$. It is obvious that the jigsaw puzzle generator

Table 3. The performances of the proposed method by using different hyper-parameter s with/without the jigsaw puzzle generator.

S,n	Accuracy (%)	Combined accuracy (%)
1,{1,1}	86.3	86.5
2,{1,1,1}	87.6	88.0
3,{1,1,1,1}	**88.3**	**88.7**
4,{1,1,1,1,1}	87.8	88.5
5,{1,1,1,1,1,1}	87.7	88.3
1,{2,1}	86.9	86.9
2,{4,2,1}	88.5	88.7
3,{8,4,2,1}	**88.9**	**89.6**
4,{16,8,4,2,1}	88.0	88.5
5,{32,16,8,4,2,1}	87.2	87.7

Table 4. The combined accuracies of our method with different α and β.

α, β	CUB(%)	CAR(%)	AIR(%)
$1, \frac{1}{3}$	88.6	94.5	92.8
$1, \frac{1}{2}$	88.9	94.7	92.8
1,1	89.2	95.0	93.1
1,2	**89.6**	**95.1**	**93.4**
1,3	89.1	**95.1**	93.2

improves the model performance on the basis of progressive training when $S < 4$. When $S = 4$, the model with the jigsaw puzzle generator does not show any advantages, and when $S = 5$ the jigsaw puzzle generator lowers the model performance. This is because when $n > 8$ the split patches are too small to keep meaningful information, which instigates confusion in the model training.

According to the above analysis, progressive training is beneficial for fine-grained classification task when we choose appropriate S. In such a case, the jigsaw puzzle generator can further improve the performance.

4.4   Discussions

The Choice of Hyper-parameter (α and β). In our training procedure, the first S steps and the last step are trained for different goals: learning features with increasing granularity as the network going deeper, and learning correlations between multi-granularity features. Hence, we introduce two hyper-parameter α and β to adjust their training loss. The model performances with different choice of α and β are listed in Table 4. When we keep $\alpha = 1$, it can be observed that the accuracy increases and then decreases as β changes. And the model achieves the best performance on both three datasets when $\beta = 2$.

Table 5. The comparison between our fusion technique and the other manners.

Fusion technique	Combined accuracy(%)
Four Networks Separately	87.7
One network non-progressively	89.1
One network progressively	**89.6**

Fusion of Multi-granularity Information. In the experiments, we generate images contain multi-granularity information via jigsaw puzzle generator with $n = \{8, 4, 2, 1\}$, and fused these information with one network in a progressive manner. In order to demonstrate the advantage of the fusion strategy under the same configuration, we conduct two experiment on (i) training four different networks with generated images where $n = \{8, 4, 2, 1\}$ separately and concatenating their features for final classification with a fully connected fusion layer, which is similar to the fusion technique used in RA-CNN [11], and (ii) training a model with same architecture as ours but back-propagating the losses of four outputs in one step. We choose CUB-200-2011 dataset for experiments with ResNet50 as the base model and the results are listed in Table 5. The performance of four networks trained separately is higher than a lot of state-of-the-art methods but our method still outperforms it by a large margin, which indicates the effectiveness of our fusion technique. When we back-propagate losses of four outputs in one step, which means multi-granularity information is learnt simultaneously, the performance clearly drops even the other configurations are unchanged. Hence, the unique advantage of progressively learning multi-granularity information is significant.

4.5 Visualization

In order to demonstrate the achievement of our motivation, we apply the Grad-CAM to visualize the last three stages' convolution layers of both our method and the baseline model. Columns (a)–(c) in Fig. 4 are visualization of the convolution layers from the third to the fifth stage of our model's backbone network, which are supervised by the jigsaw puzzle generator-processed images with $n = \{8, 4, 2\}$ sequentially. It is shown in column (a) that the model concentrates on discriminative parts of small granularity at the third stage like bird eyes and small pattern or texture of birds' feathers. And when it comes to column (c), the fifth stage of the model pays attention to parts of larger granularity. The visualization result demonstrates that our model truly gives predictions based on discriminative parts from small granularity to large granularity gradually.

When compared with the activation map of the baseline model, our model shows more meaningful concentration on the target object, while the baseline model only shows the correct attention at the last stage. This difference indicates that the intermediate supervision of progressive training can help the model distill useful information at low-level stages. Besides, we find the baseline model

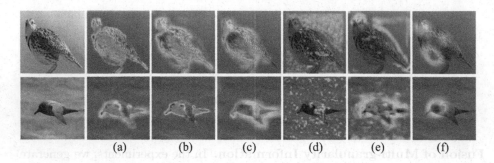

Fig. 4. Activation map of selected results on the CUB dataset with the Resnet50 as the base model. Columns (a)–(c) and (d)–(f) are visualizations of the last three stages' convolution layers of our model and the baseline model, respectively.

usually only concentrates on one or two parts of the object at the last stage. However, the attention regions of our method nearly cover the whole object at each stage, which indicates that jigsaw puzzle generator-processed images can force the model to learn more discriminative parts at each granularity level.

5   Conclusions

In this paper, we approached the problem of fine-grained visual classification from a rather unconventional perspective – we do not explicitly nor implicitly mine for object parts, instead we show fine-grained features can be extracted by learning across granularities and effectively fusing multi-granularity features. Our method can be trained end-to-end without additional manual annotations other than category labels, and only needs one network with one feed-forward pass during testing. We conducted experiments on three widely used fine-grained datasets, and obtained state-of-the-art performance on two of them while being competitive on the other.

Acknowledgement. This work was supported in part by the National Key R&D Program of China under Grant 2019YFF0303300 and under Subject II No. 2019YFF0303302, in part by the National Natural Science Foundation of China under Grant 61773071, 61922015, and U19B2036, in part by Beijing Academy of Artificial Intelligence (BAAI) under Grant BAAI2020ZJ0204, in part by the Beijing Nova Program Interdisciplinary Cooperation Project under Grant Z191100001119140, in part by the National Science and Technology Major Program of the Ministry of Science and Technology under Grant 2018ZX03001031, in part by the Key Program of Beijing Municipal Natural Science Foundation under Grant L172030, in part by MoE-CMCC Artificial Intelligence Project No. MCM20190701, in part by the scholarship from China Scholarship Council (CSC) under Grant CSC No. 201906470049, and in part by the BUPT Excellent Ph.D. Students Foundation No. CX2020105 and No. CX2019109.

References

1. Ahn, N., Kang, B., Sohn, K.A.: Image super-resolution via progressive cascading residual network. In: CVPR Workshops (2018)
2. Berg, T., Belhumeur, P.: Poof: part-based one-vs.-one features for fine-grained categorization, face verification, and attribute estimation. In: CVPR (2013)
3. Chang, D., et al.: The devil is in the channels: mutual-channel loss for fine-grained image classification. IEEE Trans. Image Process. **29**, 4683–4695 (2020)
4. Chen, Y., Bai, Y., Zhang, W., Mei, T.: Destruction and construction learning for fine-grained image recognition. In: CVPR (2019)
5. Chen, Z., Fu, Y., Chen, K., Jiang, Y.G.: Image block augmentation for one-shot learning. In: AAAI (2019)
6. Cho, T.S., Avidan, S., Freeman, W.T.: A probabilistic image jigsaw puzzle solver. In: CVPR (2010)
7. Clevert, D.A., Unterthiner, T., Hochreiter, S.: Fast and accurate deep network learning by exponential linear units (ELUs). arXiv preprint arXiv:1511.07289 (2015)
8. Cui, Y., Zhou, F., Wang, J., Liu, X., Lin, Y., Belongie, S.: Kernel pooling for convolutional neural networks. In: CVPR (2017)
9. Ding, Y., Zhou, Y., Zhu, Y., Ye, Q., Jiao, J.: Selective sparse sampling for fine-grained image recognition. In: ICCV (2019)
10. Dubey, A., Gupta, O., Guo, P., Raskar, R., Farrell, R., Naik, N.: Pairwise confusion for fine-grained visual classification. In: Ferrari, V., Hebert, M., Sminchisescu, C., Weiss, Y. (eds.) ECCV 2018. LNCS, vol. 11216. Springer, Cham (2018). https://doi.org/10.1007/978-3-030-01258-8_5
11. Fu, J., Zheng, H., Mei, T.: Look closer to see better: recurrent attention convolutional neural network for fine-grained image recognition. In: CVPR (2017)
12. Ge, W., Lin, X., Yu, Y.: Weakly supervised complementary parts models for fine-grained image classification from the bottom up. In: CVPR (2019)
13. He, K., Gkioxari, G., Dollár, P., Girshick, R.: Mask R-CNN. In: ICCV (2017)
14. He, K., Zhang, X., Ren, S., Sun, J.: Deep residual learning for image recognition. In: CVPR (2016)
15. Hochreiter, S., Schmidhuber, J.: Long short-term memory. Neural Comput. **9**(8), 1735–1780 (1997)
16. Huang, S., Xu, Z., Tao, D., Zhang, Y.: Part-stacked CNN for fine-grained visual categorization. In: CVPR (2016)
17. Ioffe, S., Szegedy, C.: Batch normalization: Accelerating deep network training by reducing internal covariate shift. In: ICML (2015)
18. Karras, T., Aila, T., Laine, S., Lehtinen, J.: Progressive growing of GANs for improved quality, stability, and variation. arXiv preprint arXiv:1710.10196 (2017)
19. Karras, T., Laine, S., Aila, T.: A style-based generator architecture for generative adversarial networks. In: CVPR (2019)
20. Krause, J., Stark, M., Deng, J., Fei-Fei, L.: 3D object representations for fine-grained categorization. In: ICCV Workshops (2013)
21. Lei, J., Duan, J., Wu, F., Ling, N., Hou, C.: Fast mode decision based on grayscale similarity and inter-view correlation for depth map coding in 3D-HEVC. IEEE Trans. Circ. Syst. Video Technol. **28**(3), 706–718 (2016)
22. Li, X., Yu, L., Chang, D., Ma, Z., Cao, J.: Dual cross-entropy loss for small-sample fine-grained vehicle classification. IEEE Trans. Veh. Technol. **68**(5), 4204–4212 (2019)

23. Lin, T.Y., RoyChowdhury, A., Maji, S.: Bilinear CNN models for fine-grained visual recognition. In: ICCV (2015)
24. Loshchilov, I., Hutter, F.: SGDR: Stochastic gradient descent with warm restarts. arXiv preprint arXiv:1608.03983 (2016)
25. Luo, W., et al.: Cross-X learning for fine-grained visual categorization. In: ICCV (2019)
26. Ma, Z., et al.: Fine-grained vehicle classification with channel max pooling modified CNNs. IEEE Trans. Veh. Technol. 68(4), 3224–3233 (2019)
27. Maji, S., Rahtu, E., Kannala, J., Blaschko, M., Vedaldi, A.: Fine-grained visual classification of aircraft. arXiv preprint arXiv:1306.5151 (2013)
28. Paszke, A., et al.: Automatic differentiation in PyTorch (2017)
29. Shaham, T.R., Dekel, T., Michaeli, T.: Singan: Learning a generative model from a single natural image. In: ICCV (2019)
30. Simonyan, K., Zisserman, A.: Very deep convolutional networks for large-scale image recognition. arXiv preprint arXiv:1409.1556 (2014)
31. Son, K., Hays, J., Cooper, D.B.: Solving square jigsaw puzzles with loop constraints. In: Fleet, D., Pajdla, T., Schiele, B., Tuytelaars, T. (eds.) ECCV 2014. LNCS, vol. 8694, pp. 32–46. Springer, Cham (2014). https://doi.org/10.1007/978-3-319-10599-4_3
32. Wah, C., Branson, S., Welinder, P., Perona, P., Belongie, S.: The Caltech-UCSD Birds-200-2011 dataset (2011)
33. Wang, Y., Morariu, V.I., Davis, L.S.: Learning a discriminative filter bank within a CNN for fine-grained recognition. In: CVPR (2018)
34. Wang, Y., Perazzi, F., McWilliams, B., Sorkine-Hornung, A., Sorkine-Hornung, O., Schroers, C.: A fully progressive approach to single-image super-resolution. In: CVPR Workshops (2018)
35. Wei, C., et al.: Iterative reorganization with weak spatial constraints: solving arbitrary jigsaw puzzles for unsupervised representation learning. In: CVPR (2019)
36. Wei, K., Yang, M., Wang, H., Deng, C., Liu, X.: Adversarial fine-grained composition learning for unseen attribute-object recognition. In: ICCV (2019)
37. Xie, L., Tian, Q., Hong, R., Yan, S., Zhang, B.: Hierarchical part matching for fine-grained visual categorization. In: ICCV (2013)
38. Yang, Z., Luo, T., Wang, D., Hu, Z., Gao, J., Wang, L.: Learning to navigate for fine-grained classification. In: Ferrari, V., Hebert, M., Sminchisescu, C., Weiss, Y. (eds.) Computer Vision – ECCV 2018. LNCS, vol. 11218, pp. 438–454. Springer, Cham (2018). https://doi.org/10.1007/978-3-030-01264-9_26
39. Zhang, L., Huang, S., Liu, W., Tao, D.: Learning a mixture of granularity-specific experts for fine-grained categorization. In: ICCV (2019)
40. Zhang, N., Donahue, J., Girshick, R., Darrell, T.: Part-based R-CNNs for fine-grained category detection. In: Fleet, D., Pajdla, T., Schiele, B., Tuytelaars, T. (eds.) ECCV 2014. LNCS, vol. 8689, pp. 834–849. Springer, Cham (2014). https://doi.org/10.1007/978-3-319-10590-1_54
41. Zheng, H., Fu, J., Mei, T., Luo, J.: Learning multi-attention convolutional neural network for fine-grained image recognition. In: ICCV (2017)
42. Zheng, Y., Chang, D., Xie, J., Ma, Z.: IU-Module: intersection and union module for fine-grained visual classification. In: ICME (2020)

LiteFlowNet3: Resolving Correspondence Ambiguity for More Accurate Optical Flow Estimation

Tak-Wai Hui[1]([⊠]) and Chen Change Loy[2]

[1] The Chinese University of Hong Kong, Hong Kong, China
twhui@ie.cuhk.edu.hk
[2] Nanyang Technological University, Singapore, Singapore
ccloy@ntu.edu.sg
https://github.com/twhui/LiteFlowNet3

Abstract. Deep learning approaches have achieved great success in addressing the problem of optical flow estimation. The keys to success lie in the use of cost volume and coarse-to-fine flow inference. However, the matching problem becomes ill-posed when partially occluded or homogeneous regions exist in images. This causes a cost volume to contain outliers and affects the flow decoding from it. Besides, the coarse-to-fine flow inference demands an accurate flow initialization. Ambiguous correspondence yields erroneous flow fields and affects the flow inferences in subsequent levels. In this paper, we introduce LiteFlowNet3, a deep network consisting of two specialized modules, to address the above challenges. (1) We ameliorate the issue of outliers in the cost volume by amending each cost vector through an adaptive modulation prior to the flow decoding. (2) We further improve the flow accuracy by exploring local flow consistency. To this end, each inaccurate optical flow is replaced with an accurate one from a nearby position through a novel warping of the flow field. LiteFlowNet3 not only achieves promising results on public benchmarks but also has a small model size and a fast runtime.

1 Introduction

Optical flow estimation is a classical problem in computer vision. It is widely used in many applications such as motion tracking, action recognition, video segmentation, 3D reconstruction, and more. With the advancement of deep learning, many research works have attempted to address the problem by using convolutional neural networks (CNNs) [10–13,18,27,28,31,32]. The majority of the CNNs belongs to the 2-frame method that infers a flow field from an image pair. Particularly, LiteFlowNet [10] and PWC-Net [27] are the first CNNs to propose using the feature warping and cost volume at multiple pyramid levels in a coarse-to-fine estimation. This greatly reduces the number of model parameters from

---

Electronic supplementary material The online version of this chapter (https://doi.org/10.1007/978-3-030-58565-5_11) contains supplementary material, which is available to authorized users.

© Springer Nature Switzerland AG 2020
A. Vedaldi et al. (Eds.): ECCV 2020, LNCS 12365, pp. 169–184, 2020.
https://doi.org/10.1007/978-3-030-58565-5_11

160M in FlowNet2 [13] to 5.37M in LiteFlowNet and 8.75M in PWC-Net while accurate flow estimation is still maintained.

One of the keys to success for the lightweight optical flow CNNs is the use of cost volume for establishing correspondence at each pyramid level. However, a cost volume is easily corrupted by ambiguous feature matching [17,26,30]. This causes flow fields that are decoded from the cost volume to become unreliable. The underlying reasons for the existence of ambiguous matching are twofold. First, when given a pair of images, it is impossible for a feature point in the first image to find the corresponding point in the second image, when the latter is occluded. Second, ambiguous correspondence is inevitable in homogeneous regions (*e.g.,* shadows, sky, and walls) of images. Another key to success for the optical flow CNNs is to infer flow fields using a coarse-to-fine framework. However, this approach highly demands an accurate flow initialization from the preceding pyramid level. Once ambiguous correspondence exists, erroneous optical flow is generated and propagates to subsequent levels.

To address the aforementioned challenges, we attempt to make correspondence across images less ambiguous and in turn improves the accuracy of optical flow CNNs by introducing the following specialized CNN modules:

Cost Volume Modulation. Ambiguous feature matching causes outliers to exist in a cost volume. Inaccurate cost vectors need to be amended to allow the correct flow decoding. To deal with occlusions, earlier work improves the matching process by using the offset-centered matching windows [17]. A cost volume is filtered to remove outliers prior to the correspondence decoding [26,30]. However, existing optical flow CNNs [11–13,18,28,31,32] infer optical flow from a cost volume using convolutions without explicitly addressing the issue of outliers. We propose to amend each cost vector in the cost volume by using an adaptive affine transformation. A confidence map that pinpoints the locations of unreliable flow is used to facilitate the generation of transformation parameters.

Flow Field Deformation. When the correspondence problem becomes ill-posed, it is very difficult to find correct matching pairs. Local flow consistency and co-occurrence between flow boundaries and intensity edges are commonly used as the clues to regularize flow fields in conventional methods [29,33]. The two principles are also adopted in recent optical flow CNNs [10–12]. We propose a novel technique to further improve the flow accuracy by using the clue from local flow consistency. Intuitively, we replace each inaccurate optical flow with an accurate one from a nearby position having similar feature vectors. The replacement is achieved by a meta-warping of the flow field in accordance with a computed displacement field (similar to optical flow but the displacement field no longer represents correspondence). We compute the displacement field by using a confidence-guided decoding from an auto-correlation cost volume.

In this work, we make the first attempt to use cost volume modulation and flow field deformation in optical flow CNNs. We extend our previous work (Lite-FlowNet2 [11]) by incorporating the proposed modules for addressing the aforementioned challenges. LiteFlowNet3 achieves promising performance in the 2-frame method. It outperforms VCN-small [31], IRR-PWC [12], PWC-Net+ [28], and LiteFlowNet2 on Sintel and KITTI. Even though SelFlow [18] (a multi-frame method) and HD³ [32] use extra training data, LiteFlowNet3 outperforms SelFlow on Sintel clean and KITTI while it performs better than HD³ on Sintel, KITTI 2012, and KITTI 2015 (in foreground region). LiteFlowNet3 does not suffer from the artifact problem on real-world images as HD³, while being 7.7 times smaller in model size and 2.2 times faster in runtime.

2 Related Work

Variational Approach. Since the pioneering work of Horn and Schunck [8], the variational approach has been widely studied for optical flow estimation. Brox et al. address the problem of illumination change across images by introducing the gradient constancy assumption [3]. Brox et al. [3] and Papenberg et al. [23] propose the use of image warping in minimizing an energy functional. Bailer et al. propose Flow Fields [1], which is a searching-based method. Optical flow is computed by a numerical optimization with multiple propagations and random searches. In EpicFlow [25], Revaud et al. use sparse flows as an initialization and then interpolate them to a dense flow field by fitting a local affine model at each pixel based on nearby matches. The affine parameters are computed as the least-square solution of an over-determined system. Unlike EpicFlow, we use an adaptive affine transformation to amend a cost volume. The transformation parameters are implicitly generated in the CNN instead.

Cost Volume Approach. Kang et al. address the problem of ambiguous matching by using the offset-centered windows and select a subset of neighboring image frames to perform matching dynamically [17]. Rhemann et al. propose to filter a cost volume using an edge-preserving filter [26]. In DCFlow [30], Xu et al. exploit regularity in a cost volume and improve the optical flow accuracy by adapting the semi-global matching. With the inspiration of improving cost volume from the above conventional methods, we propose to modulate each cost vector in the cost volume by using an affine transformation prior to the flow decoding. The transformation parameters are adaptively constructed to suit different cost vectors. In particular, DCFlow combines the interpolation in EpicFlow [25] with a complementary scheme to convert a sparse correspondence to a dense one. On the contrary, LiteFlowNet3 applies an affine transformation to all elements in the cost volume but not to sparse correspondence.

Unsupervised and Self-supervised Optical Flow Estimation. To avoid annotating labels, Meister et al. propose a framework that uses the difference between synthesized and real images for unsupervised training [21]. Liu et al. propose SelFlow that distills reliable flow estimations from non-occluded pixels in a large dataset using self-supervised training [18]. It also uses multiple frames and fine-tunes the self-supervised model in supervised training for improving the flow accuracy further. Unlike the above works, we focus on supervised learning. Even though LiteFlowNet3 is a 2-frame method and trained on a much smaller dataset, it still outperforms SelFlow on Sintel clean and KITTI.

Supervised Learning of Optical Flow. Dosovitskiy et al. develop FlowNet [6], the first optical flow CNN. Mayer et al. extend FlowNet to estimate disparity and scene flow [20]. In FlowNet2 [13], Ilg et al. improve the flow accuracy of FlowNet by cascading several variants of it. However, the model size is increased to over 160M parameters and it also demands a high computation time. Ranjan et al. develop a compact network SPyNet [24], but the accuracy is not comparable to FlowNet2. Our LiteFlowNet [10], which consists of the cascaded flow inference and flow regularization, has a small model size (5.37M) and comparable performance as FlowNet2. We then develop LiteFlowNet2 for more accurate flow accuracy and faster runtime [11]. LiteFlowNet3 is built upon LiteFlowNet2 with the incorporation of cost volume modulation and flow field deformation for improving the flow accuracy further. A concurrent work to Lite-FlowNet is PWC-Net [27], which proposes using the feature warping and cost volume as LiteFlowNet. Sun et al. then develop PWC-Net+ by improving the training protocol [28]. Ilg et al. extend FlowNet2 to FlowNet3 with the joint learning of occlusion and optical flow [14]. In Devon [19], Lu et al. perform feature matching that is governed by an external flow field. On the contrary, our displacement field is used to deform optical flow but not to facilitate feature matching. Hur et al. propose IRR-PWC [12], which improves PWC-Net by adopting the flow regularization from LiteFlowNet as well as introducing the occlusion decoder and weight sharing. Yin et al. introduce HD^3 for learning a probabilistic pixel correspondence [32], but it requires pre-training on ImageNet. While LiteFlowNet3 learns a flow confidence implicitly but not computed from the probabilistic estimation. Despite HD^3 uses extra training data and 7.7 times more parameters, LiteFlowNet3 outperforms HD^3 on Sintel, KITTI 2012, and KITTI 2015 (in foreground region). LiteFlowNet3 outperforms VCN-small [31] even though the model sizes are similar. Comparing to deformable convolution [5], we perform deformation on flow fields but not on feature maps. Our deformation aims to replace each inaccurate optical flow with an accurate one from a nearby position in the flow field, while deformable convolution aims to augment spatial sampling.

3   LiteFlowNet3

Feature matching becomes ill-posed in homogeneous and partially occluded regions as one-to-multiple correspondence occurs for the first case while one-to-none correspondence occurs for the second case. Duplicate of image structure (so-called "ghosting effect") is inevitable whenever warping is applied to images [15]. The same also applies to feature maps. In coarse-to-fine estimation, erroneous optical flow resulting from the preceding level affects the subsequent flow inferences. To address the above challenges, we develop two specialized CNN modules: *Cost volume Modulation* (CM) and *Flow field Deformation* (FD). We demonstrate the applicability of the modules on LiteFlowNet2 [11]. The resulting network is named as LiteFlowNet3. Figure 1 illustrates a simplified overview of the network architecture. FD is used to refine the previous flow estimate before

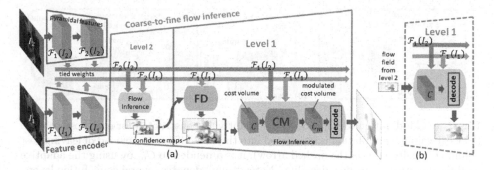

Fig. 1. (a) A simplified overview of LiteFlowNet3. Flow field deformation (FD) and cost volume modulation (CM) together with confidence maps are incorporated into LiteFlowNet3. For the ease of presentation, only a 2-level encoder-decoder structure is shown. The proposed modules are applicable to other levels but not limited to level 1. (b) The optical flow inference in LiteFlowNet2 [11].

it is used as a flow initialization in the current pyramid level. In flow inference, the cost volume is amended by CM prior to the flow decoding.

3.1 Preliminaries

We first provide a concise description on the construction of cost volume in optical flow CNNs. Suppose a pair of images I_1 (at time $t = 1$) and I_2 (at time $t = 2$) is given. We convert I_1 and I_2 respectively into pyramidal feature maps $\mathcal{F}_1$ and $\mathcal{F}_2$ through a feature encoder. We denote $\mathbf{x}$ as a point in the rectangular domain $\Omega \subset \mathbb{R}^2$. Correspondence between I_1 and I_2 is established by computing the dot product between two high-level feature vectors in the individual feature maps $\mathcal{F}_1$ and $\mathcal{F}_2$ as follows [6]:

$$c(\mathbf{x}; D) = \mathcal{F}_1(\mathbf{x}) \cdot \mathcal{F}_2(\mathbf{x}')/N, \tag{1}$$

where D is the maximum matching radius, $c(\mathbf{x}; D)$ (a 3D column vector with length $2D + 1$) is the collection of matching costs between feature vectors $\mathcal{F}_1(\mathbf{x})$ and $\mathcal{F}_2(\mathbf{x}')$ for all possible $\mathbf{x}'$ such that $\|\mathbf{x} - \mathbf{x}'\|_\infty = D$, and N is the length of the feature vector. Cost volume C is constructed by aggregating all $c(\mathbf{x}; D)$ into a 3D grid. Flow decoding is then performed on C using convolutions (or native winner-takes-all approach [17]). The resulting flow field $\mathbf{u} : \Omega \rightarrow \mathbb{R}^2$ provides the dense correspondence from I_1 to I_2. In the following, we will omit variable D that indicates the maximum matching radius for brevity and use $c(\mathbf{x})$ to represent the cost vector at $\mathbf{x}$. When we discuss operations in a pyramid level, the same operations are applicable to other levels.

3.2 Cost Volume Modulation

Given a pair of images, the existence of partial occlusion and homogeneous regions makes the establishment of correspondence very challenging. This situation also occurs on feature space because simply transforming images into

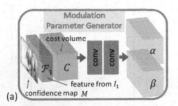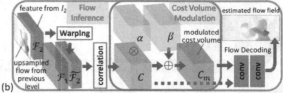

Fig. 2. (a) Modulation tensors (α, β) are adaptively constructed for each cost volume. (b) Cost volume modulation is integrated into the flow inference. Instead of leaving cost volume C unaltered (via the dashed arrow), it is amended to C_m by using the adaptive modulation prior to the flow decoding. Note: "conv" denotes several convolution layers.

feature maps does not resolve the correspondence ambiguity. In this way, a cost volume is corrupted and the subsequent flow decoding is seriously affected. Conventional methods [26, 30] address the above problem by filtering a cost volume prior to the decoding. But there has not been any existing works to address this problem for optical flow CNNs. Some studies [2, 10, 12] have revealed that applying feature-driven convolutions on feature space is an effective approach to influence the feed-forward behavior of a network since the filter weights are adaptively constructed. Therefore, we devise to filter outliers in a cost volume by using an adaptive modulation. We will show that our modulation approach is not only effective in improving the flow accuracy but also parameter-efficient.

An overview of cost volume modulation is illustrated in Fig. 2b. At a pyramid level, each cost vector $c(\mathbf{x})$ in cost volume C is adaptively modulated by an affine transformation $(\alpha(\mathbf{x}), \beta(\mathbf{x}))$ as follows:

$$c_m(\mathbf{x}) = \alpha(\mathbf{x}) \otimes c(\mathbf{x}) \oplus \beta(\mathbf{x}), \tag{2}$$

where $c_m(\mathbf{x})$ is the modulated cost vector, "$\otimes$" and "$\oplus$" denote element-wise multiplication and addition, respectively. The dimension of the modulated cost volume is same as the original. This property allows cost volume modulation to be jointly used and trained with an existing network without major changes made to the original network architecture.

To have an efficient computation, the affine parameters $\{\alpha(\mathbf{x}), \beta(\mathbf{x})\}, \forall \mathbf{x} \in \Omega$, are generated altogether in the form of modulation tensors (α, β) having the same dimension as C. As shown in Fig. 2a, we use cost volume C, feature $\mathcal{F}_1$ from the encoder, and confidence map M at the same pyramid level as the inputs to the modulation parameter generator. The confidence map is introduced to facilitate the generation of modulation parameters. Specifically, $M(\mathbf{x})$ pinpoints the probability of having an accurate optical flow at $\mathbf{x}$ in the associated flow field. The confidence map is constructed by introducing an additional output in the preceding optical flow decoder. A sigmoid function is used to constrain its values to $[0, 1]$. We train the confidence map using a L2 loss with the ground-truth label $M_{gt}(\mathbf{x})$ as follows:

$$M_{gt}(\mathbf{x}) = \mathrm{e}^{-\|\mathbf{u}_{gt}(\mathbf{x}) - \mathbf{u}(\mathbf{x})\|^2}, \tag{3}$$

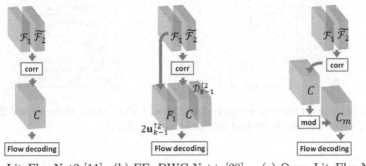

(a) NO: LiteFlowNet2 [11]   (b) FF: PWC-Net+ [28]   (c) Ours: LiteFlowNet3

Fig. 3. Augmenting a cost volume under different configurations. (a) NO, (b) FF, and (c) Our solution: Cost volume C is modulated to C_m by using an adaptive affine transformation prior to the flow decoding. Note: "corr" and "mod" denote correlation and modulation, respectively. Correlation is performed on $\mathcal{F}_1$ and warped $\mathcal{F}_2$ (i.e., $\widetilde{\mathcal{F}_2}$).

Table 1. Average end-point error (AEE) and model size of different models trained on FlyingChairs under different augmentations of cost volume.

Augmentations	NO	FF	Ours
Features of I_1	✗	✓	✗
Flow field	✗	✓	✗
Modulation	✗	✗	✓
Number of model parameters (M)	**6.42**	7.16	7.18
Sintel clean (training set)	2.71	2.70	**2.65**
Sintel final (training set)	4.14	4.20	**4.02**
KITTI 2012 (training set)	4.20	4.28	**3.95**
KITTI 2015 (training set)	11.12	11.30	**10.65**

where $\mathbf{u}_{gt}(\mathbf{x})$ is the ground truth of $\mathbf{u}(\mathbf{x})$. An example of predicted confidence maps will be provided in Sect. 4.2.

Discussion. In the literature, there are two major approaches to infer a flow field from a cost volume as shown in Fig. 3. The first approach (Fig. 3a) is to perform flow decoding directly on the cost volume without any augmentation [10,11]. This is similar to the conventional winner-takes-all approach [17] except using convolutions for yielding flow fields rather than argument of the minimum. The second approach (Fig. 3b) feed-forwards the pyramidal features $\mathcal{F}_1$ from the feature encoder [27,28]. It also feed-forwards the upsampled flow field ($2\mathbf{u}_{k-1}^{\uparrow 2}$) and features ($\mathcal{D}_{k-1}^{\uparrow 2}$) from the previous flow decoder (at level $k-1$). Flow decoding is then performed on the concatenation. Our approach (Fig. 3c) is to perform modulation on the cost volume prior to the flow decoding. The effectiveness of the above approaches has not been studied in the literature. Here, we use Lite-

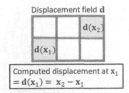
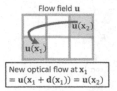

Fig. 4. Replacing an inaccurate optical flow $\mathbf{u}(\mathbf{x}_1)$ with an accurate optical flow $\mathbf{u}(\mathbf{x}_2)$ through a meta-warping governed by displacement $\mathbf{d}(\mathbf{x}_1)$.

FlowNet2 [11] as the backbone architecture and train all the models from scratch on FlyingChairs dataset [6]. Table 1 summarizes the results of our evaluation. Even though FF needs 11.5% more model parameters than NO, it attains lower flow accuracy. On the contrary, our modulation approach that has just 0.28% more parameters than FF outperforms the compared methods on all the benchmarks, especially KITTI 2012 and KITTI 2015. This indicates that a large CNN model does not always perform better than a smaller one.

3.3   Flow Field Deformation

In coarse-to-fine flow estimation, a flow estimate from the preceding decoder is used as a flow initialization for the subsequent decoder. This highly demands the previous estimate to be accurate. Otherwise, erroneous optical flow is propagated to subsequent levels and affects the flow inference. Using cost volume modulation alone is not able to address this problem. We explore local flow consistency [29, 33] and propose to use a meta-warping for improving the flow accuracy.

Intuitively, we refine a given flow field by replacing each inaccurate optical flow with an accurate one from a nearby position using the principle of local flow consistency. As shown in Fig. 4, suppose an optical flow $\mathbf{u}(\mathbf{x}_1)$ is inaccurate. With some prior knowledge, 1) a nearby optical flow $\mathbf{u}(\mathbf{x}_2)$ such that $\mathbf{x}_2 = \mathbf{x}_1 + \mathbf{d}(\mathbf{x}_1)$ is known to be accurate as indicated by a confidence map; 2) the pyramidal features of I_1 at $\mathbf{x}_1$ and $\mathbf{x}_2$ are similar $i.e.,$ $\mathcal{F}_1(\mathbf{x}_1) \sim \mathcal{F}_1(\mathbf{x}_2)$ as indicated by an auto-correlation cost volume. Since image points that have similar feature vectors have similar optical flow in a neighborhood, we replace $\mathbf{u}(\mathbf{x}_1)$ with a clone of $\mathbf{u}(\mathbf{x}_2)$.

The previous analysis is just for a single flow vector. To cover the whole flow field, we need to find a displacement vector for every position in the flow field. In other words, we need to have a displacement field for guiding the meta-warping of flow field. We use a warping mechanism that is similar to image [13] and feature warpings [10, 27]. The differences are that our meta-warping is limited to two channels and the physical meaning of the introduced displacement field no longer represents correspondence across images.

An overview of flow field deformation is illustrated in Fig. 5b. At a pyramid level, we replace $\mathbf{u}(\mathbf{x})$ with an neighboring optical flow by warping of $\mathbf{u}(\mathbf{x})$ in

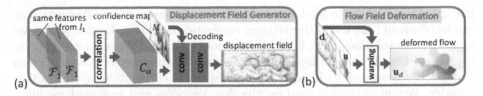

Fig. 5. (a) Displacement field **d** is constructed according to auto-correlation cost volume C_a and confidence map M. (b) Flow field **u** is warped to $\mathbf{u}_d$ in accordance to **d**. Flow deformation is performed before **u** is used as an initialization for the flow inference. Note: "conv" denotes several convolution layers.

accordance to the computed displacement $\mathbf{d}(\mathbf{x})$ as follows:

$$\mathbf{u}_d(\mathbf{x}) = \mathbf{u}\left(\mathbf{x} + \mathbf{d}(\mathbf{x})\right). \tag{4}$$

In particular, not every optical flow needs an amendment. Suppose $\mathbf{u}(\mathbf{x_0})$ is very accurate, then no flow warping is required *i.e.*, $\mathbf{d}(\mathbf{x_0}) \sim \mathbf{0}$.

To generate the displacement field, the location of image point having similar feature as the targeted image point needs to be found. This is accomplished by decoding from an auto-correlation cost volume. The procedure is similar to flow decoding from a normal cost volume [6]. As shown in Fig. 5a, we first measure the feature similarity of targeted point at **x** and its surrounding points at $\mathbf{x}'$ by computing auto-correlation cost vector $c_a(\mathbf{x}; D)$ between features $\mathcal{F}_1(\mathbf{x})$ and $\mathcal{F}_1(\mathbf{x}')$ as follows:

$$c_a(\mathbf{x}; D) = \mathcal{F}_1(\mathbf{x}) \cdot \mathcal{F}_1(\mathbf{x}')/N, \tag{5}$$

where D is the maximum matching radius, **x** and $\mathbf{x}'$ are constrained by $\|\mathbf{x} - \mathbf{x}'\|_\infty = D$, and N is the length of the feature vector. The above equation is identical to Eq. (1) except using features from I_1 only. Auto-correlation cost volume C_a is then built by aggregating all cost vectors into a 3D grid.

To avoid trivial solution, confidence map M associated with flow field **u** that is constructed by the preceding flow decoder (same as the one presented in Sect. 3.2) is used to guide the decoding of displacement from C_a. As shown in Fig. 5a, we use cost volume C_a for the auto-correlation of $\mathcal{F}_1$ and confidence map M at the same pyramid level as the inputs to the displacement field generator. Rather than flow decoding from the cost volume as the normal descriptor matching [6], our displacement decoding is performed on the auto-correlation cost volume and is guided by the confidence map.

4 Experiments

Network Details. LiteFlowNet3 is built upon LiteFlowNet2 [11]. Flow inference is performed from levels 6 to 3 (and 2) with the given image resolution as level 1. Flow field deformation is applied prior to the cascaded flow inference while cost volume modulation is applied in the descriptor matching unit. We do not apply the modules to level 6 as no significant improvement on flow accuracy can be observed (and level 2 due to large computational load). Each module uses four 3×3 convolution layers followed by a leaky rectified linear unit except to use a 5×5 filter in the last layer at levels 4 and 3. Confidence of flow prediction is implicitly generated by introducing an additional convolution layer in a flow decoder. Weight sharing is used on the flow decoders and proposed modules. This variant is denoted by the suffix "S".

Training Details. For a fair comparison, we use the same training sets as other optical flow CNNs in the literature [6,10–13,19,24,27,28,31]. We use the same training protocol (including data augmentation and batch size) as Lite-FlowNet2 [11]. We first train LiteFlowNet2 on FlyingChairs dataset [6] using the stage-wise training procedure [11]. We then integrate brand new modules, cost volume deformation and flow field modulation, into LiteFlowNet2 to form LiteFlowNet3. The newly introduced CNN modules are trained with a learning rate of 1e-4 while the other components are trained with a reduced learning rate of 2e-5 for 300K iterations. We then fine-tune the whole network on FlyingThings3D [20] with a learning rate 5e-6 for 500K iterations. Finally, we fine-tune LiteFlowNet3 respectively on a mixture of Sintel [4] and KITTI [22], and KITTI training sets with a learning rate 5e-5 for 600K iterations. The two models are also re-trained with reduced learning rates and iterations same as LiteFlowNet2.

4.1 Results

We evaluate LiteFlowNet3 on the popular optical flow benchmarks including Sintel clean and final passes [4], KITTI 2012 [7], and KITTI 2015 [22]. We report average end-point error (AEE) for all the benchmarks unless otherwise explicitly specified. More results are available in the supplementary material [9].

Preliminary Discussion. The majority of optical flow CNNs including Lite-FlowNet3 are 2-frame methods and use the same datasets for training. However, HD^3 [32] is pre-trained on ImageNet (>10M images). SelFlow [18] uses Sintel movie (~10K images) and multi-view extensions of KITTI (>20K images) for self-supervised training. SENSE [16] uses SceneFlow dataset [20] (>39K images) for pre-training. While SelFlow also uses more than two frames to boost the flow accuracy. Therefore, their evaluations are not directly comparable to the majority of the optical flow CNNs in the literature.

Quantitative Results. Table 2 summarizes the AEE results of LiteFlowNet3 and the state-of-the-art methods on the public benchmarks. With the exception of HD^3 [32], SelFlow [18], and SENSE [16], all the compared CNN models are trained on the same datasets and are the 2-frame method. Thanks to the cost volume modulation and flow field deformation, LiteFlowNet3 outperforms these CNN models including the recent state-of-the-art methods IRR-PWC [12] and VCN-small [31] on both Sintel and KITTI benchmarks. Despite the recent state-of-the-art methods HD^3 and SelFlow (a multi-frame method) use extra training data, LiteFlowNet3 outperforms HD^3 on Sintel, KITTI 2012, and KITTI 2015

Table 2. AEE results on the public benchmarks. (Notes: The values in parentheses are the results of the networks on the data they were trained on, and hence are not directly comparable to the others. The best in each category is in bold and the second best is underlined. For KITTI 2012, "All" (or "Noc") represents the average end-point error in total (or non-occluded areas). For KITTI 2015, "Fl-all" (or "-fg") represents the percentage of outliers averaged over all (or foreground) pixels. Inliers are defined as end-point error < 3 pixels or 5%. [†]Using additional training sets. [‡]A multi-frame method.)

Method	Sintel Clean		Sintel Final		KITTI 2012			KITTI 2015			
	train	test	train	test	train	test (All)	test (Noc)	train	train (Fl-all)	test (Fl-fg)	test (Fl-all)
FlowNetS [6]	(3.66)	6.96	(4.44)	7.76	7.52	9.1	-	-	-	-	-
FlowNetC [6]	(3.78)	6.85	(5.28)	8.51	8.79	-	-	-	-	-	-
FlowNet2 [13]	(1.45)	4.16	(2.19)	5.74	(1.43)	1.8	1.0	(2.36)	(8.88%)	8.75%	11.48%
FlowNet3 [14]	(1.47)	4.35	(2.12)	5.67	(1.19)	-	-	(1.79)	-	-	8.60%
SPyNet [24]	(3.17)	6.64	(4.32)	8.36	3.36	4.1	2.0	-	-	43.62%	35.07%
Devon [19]	-	4.34	-	6.35	-	2.6	1.3	-	-	19.49%	14.31%
PWC-Net [27]	(2.02)	4.39	(2.08)	5.04	(1.45)	1.7	0.9	(2.16)	(9.80%)	9.31%	9.60%
PWC-Net+ [28]	(1.71)	3.45	(2.34)	4.60	(0.99)	1.4	0.8	(1.47)	(7.59%)	7.88%	7.72%
IRR-PWC [12]	(1.92)	3.84	(2.51)	4.58	-	1.6	0.9	(1.63)	(5.32%)	7.52%	7.65%
SENSE [16][†]	(1.54)	3.60	(2.05)	4.86	(1.18)	1.5	-	(2.05)	(9.69%)	9.33%	8.16%
HD[3] [32][†]	(1.70)	4.79	(1.17)	4.67	(0.81)	1.4	0.7	(1.31)	(4.10%)	9.02%	6.55%
SelFlow [18][†,‡]	(1.68)	3.75	(1.77)	4.26	(0.76)	1.5	0.9	(1.18)	-	12.48%	8.42%
VCN-small [31]	(1.84)	3.26	(2.44)	4.73	-	-	-	(1.41)	(5.5%)	-	7.74%
LiteFlowNet [10]	(1.35)	4.54	(1.78)	5.38	(1.05)	1.6	0.8	(1.62)	(5.58%)	7.99%	9.38%
LiteFlowNet2 [11]	(1.30)	3.48	(1.62)	4.69	(0.95)	1.4	0.7	(1.33)	(4.32%)	7.64%	7.62%
LiteFlowNet3	(1.32)	**2.99**	(1.76)	4.45	(0.91)	1.3	0.7	(1.26)	(3.82%)	7.75%	7.34%
LiteFlowNet3-S	(1.43)	3.03	(1.90)	4.53	(0.94)	1.3	0.7	(1.39)	(4.35%)	**6.96%**	7.22%

(Fl-fg). Our model also performs better than SelFlow on Sintel clean and KITTI. It should be noted that LiteFlowNet3 has a smaller model size and a faster run-time than HD[3] and VCN [31] (a larger variant of VCN-small). We also perform evaluation by dividing AEE into matched and unmatched regions (error over regions that are visible in adjacent frames or only in one of two adjacent frames, respectively). As revealed in Table 3, LiteFlowNet3 achieves the best results on both matched and unmatched regions. Particularly, there is a large improvement on unmatched regions comparing to LiteFlowNet2. This indicates that the proposed modules are effective in addressing correspondence ambiguity.

Qualitative Results. Examples of optical flow predictions on Sintel and KITTI are shown in Figs. 6 and 7, respectively. AEE evaluated on the respective training sets is also provided. For Sintel, the flow fields resulting from LiteFlowNet3 contain less artifacts when comparing with the other state-of-the-art methods. As shown in the second row of Fig. 7, a portion of optical flow over the road fence cannot be recovered by LiteFlowNet2 [11]. On the contrary, it is fully recovered by HD[3] [32] and LiteFlowNet3. Flow bleeding is observed over the road signs for LiteFlowNet2 as illustrated in the third and fourth rows of Fig. 7 while HD[3] and LiteFlowNet3 do not have such a problem. Despite HD[3] is pre-trained on

Table 3. AEE results on the testing sets of Sintel. (Note: [†]Using additional training sets.)

Models	All		Matched		Unmatched	
	Clean	Final	Clean	Final	Clean	Final
FlowNet2 [13]	4.16	5.74	1.56	2.75	25.40	30.11
Devon [19]	4.34	6.35	1.74	3.23	25.58	31.78
PWC-Net+ [28]	3.45	4.60	1.41	2.25	20.12	23.70
IRR-PWC [12]	3.84	4.58	1.47	2.15	23.22	24.36
SENSE [16][†]	3.60	4.86	1.38	2.30	21.75	25.73
HD^3 [32][†]	4.79	4.67	1.62	2.17	30.63	24.99
LiteFlowNet2 [11]	3.48	4.69	1.33	2.25	20.64	24.57
LiteFlowNet3	**2.99**	**4.45**	**1.15**	**2.09**	**18.08**	**23.68**

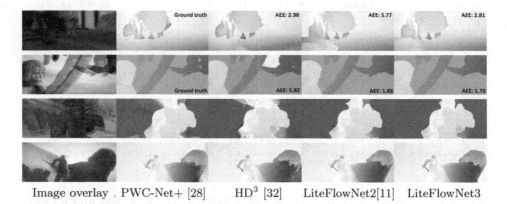

Image overlay   PWC-Net+ [28]   HD^3 [32]   LiteFlowNet2[11]   LiteFlowNet3

Fig. 6. Examples of flow fields on Sintel training set (Clean pass: first row, Final pass: second row) and testing set (Clean pass: third row, Final pass: forth row).

ImageNet and uses 7.7 times more model parameters than LiteFlowNet3, there are serious artifacts on the generated flow fields as shown in the second column of Fig. 7. The above observations suggest that LiteFlowNet3 incorporating the cost volume modulation and flow field deformation is effective in generating optical flow with high accuracy and less artifacts.

Runtime and Model Size. We measure runtime using a Sintel image pair (1024 × 436) on a machine equipped with Intel Xeon E5 2.2 GHz and NVIDIA GTX 1080. Timing is averaged over 100 runs. LiteFlowNet3 needs 59 ms for computation and has 5.2M parameters. When weight sharing is not used, the model size is 7.5M. The runtimes of the state-of-the-art 2-frame methods HD^3 [32] and IRR-PWC [12] are 128 ms and 180 ms, respectively. While HD^3 and IRR-PWC have 39.9M and 6.4M parameters, respectively.

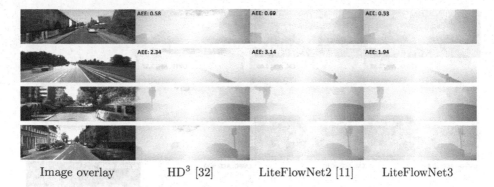

Image overlay   HD³ [32]   LiteFlowNet2 [11]   LiteFlowNet3

Fig. 7. Examples of flow fields on KITTI training set (2012: first row, 2015: second row) and testing set (2012: third row, 2015: fourth row).

Table 4. AEE results of variants of LiteFlowNet3 having some of the components disabled. (Note: The symbol "-" indicates that confidence map is not being used.)

Settings	NO	CM-	CMFD-	CM	CMFD
Cost Volume Modulation	✗	✓	✓	✓	✓
Flow Field Deformation	✗	✗	✓	✗	✓
Confidence map	✗	✗	✗	✓	✓
Sintel clean (training set)	2.78	2.66	2.63	2.65	**2.59**
Sintel final (training set)	4.14	4.09	4.06	4.02	**3.91**
KITTI 2012 (training set)	4.11	4.02	4.06	3.95	**3.88**
KITTI 2015 (training set)	11.31	11.01	10.97	10.65	**10.40**

4.2 Ablation Study

To study the role of each proposed component in LiteFlowNet3, we disable some of the components and train the resulting variants on FlyingChairs. The evaluation results on the public benchmarks are summarized in Table 4 and examples of flow fields are illustrated in Fig. 8.

Cost Volume Modulation and Flow Deformation. As revealed in Table 4, when only cost volume modulation (CM) is incorporated to LiteFlowNet3, it performs better than its counterpart (NO) neither using modulation nor deformation on all the benchmarks, especially KITTI 2015. When both of cost volume modulation and flow field formation (CMFD) are utilized, it outperforms the others and achieves in a large improvement on KITTI 2015. Examples of visual performance are demonstrated in Fig. 8. For Sintel, we can observe a large discrepancy in flow color of the human arm between NO and ground truth. On the contrary, flow color is close to ground truth when CM and CMFD are enabled. Particularly, the green artifact is successfully removed in CMFD. In the example of KITTI, the car's windshield and triangle road sign in NO are not completely

Fig. 8. Examples of flow fields on Sintel Final (top two rows) and KITTI 2015 (bottom two rows) generated by different variants of LiteFlowNet3. Note: NO = No proposed modules are used, CM = **C**ost Volume **M**odulation, CMFD = **C**ost Volume **M**odulation and **F**low Field **D**eformation, and the suffix "-" indicates that confidence map is not being used. (Color figure online)

(a) Confidence map (b) Original flow field   (c) Displacement   (d) Deformed flow

Fig. 9. An example of flow field deformation. The darker a pixel in the confidence map, the more chance the associated optical flow is not correct.

filled with correct optical flow. In comparison with CM, the missed flow can be recovered using CMFD only. This indicates that flow field deformation is more efficient in "hole filling" than cost volume modulation.

Confidence Map. Variants CM and CMFD, as revealed in Table 4, perform better than their counterparts CM- and CMFD- with confidence map disabled. For the example of Sintel in Fig. 8, the green artifact is greatly reduced when comparing CM- with CM. Optical flow of the human arm is partially disappeared in CMFD-, while it is recovered in CMFD. The corresponding confidence map is illustrated in Fig. 9a. It indicates that optical flow near the human arm is highly unreliable. Similar phenomenon can also be observed in the example of KITTI. Through pinpointing the flow correctness, the use of confidence map facilitates both cost volume modulation and flow field deformation.

Displacement Field. As shown in Fig. 9c, the active region of the displacement field (having strong color intensity) is well-coincided with the active region of the confidence map (having strong darkness, so indicating high probability of being incorrect flow) in Fig. 9a. The deformed flow field in Fig. 9d has not only less artifacts but also sharper motion boundaries and a lower AEE when comparing to the flow field without meta-warping in Fig. 9b.

5   Conclusion

Correspondence ambiguity is a common problem in optical flow estimation. Ambiguous feature matching causes outliers to exist in a cost volume and in turn affects the decoding of flow from it. Besides, erroneous optical flow can be propagated to subsequent pyramid levels. We propose to amend the cost volume prior to the flow decoding. This is accomplished by modulating each cost vector through an adaptive affine transformation. We further improve the flow accuracy by replacing each inaccurate optical flow with an accurate one from a nearby position through a meta-warping governed by a displacement field. We also propose to use a confidence map to facilitate the generation of modulation parameters and displacement field. LiteFlowNet3, which incorporates the cost volume modulation and flow field deformation, not only demonstrates promising performance on public benchmarks but also has a small model size and a fast runtime.

References

1. Bailer, C., Taetz, B., Stricker, D.: Flow fields: dense correspondence fields for highly accurate large displacement optical flow estimation. In: ICCV, pp. 4015–4023 (2015)
2. Brabandere, B.D., Jia, X., Tuytelaars, T., Gool, L.V.: Dynamic filter networks. In: NIPS (2016)
3. Brox, T., Bruhn, A., Papenberg, N., Weickert, J.: High accuracy optical flow estimation based on a theory for warping. In: Pajdla, T., Matas, J. (eds.) ECCV 2004. LNCS, vol. 3024, pp. 25–36. Springer, Heidelberg (2004). https://doi.org/10.1007/978-3-540-24673-2_3
4. Butler, D.J., Wulff, J., Stanley, G.B., Black, M.J.: A naturalistic open source movie for optical flow evaluation. In: Fitzgibbon, A., Lazebnik, S., Perona, P., Sato, Y., Schmid, C. (eds.) ECCV 2012. LNCS, vol. 7577, pp. 611–625. Springer, Heidelberg (2012). https://doi.org/10.1007/978-3-642-33783-3_44
5. Dai, J., et al.: Deformable convolutional networks. In: ICCV, pp. 764–773 (2017)
6. Dosovitskiy, A., et al.: FlowNet: learning optical flow with convolutional networks. In: ICCV, pp. 2758–2766 (2015)
7. Geiger, A., Lenz, P., Urtasun, R.: Are we ready for autonomous driving? In: CVPR, pp. 3354–3361 (2012)
8. Horn, B.K.P., Schunck, B.G.: Determining optical flow. Aritif. Intell. **17**, 185–203 (1981)
9. Hui, T.W., Loy, C.C.: Supplementary material for LiteFlowNet3: resolving correspondence ambiguity for more accurate optical flow estimation (2020)
10. Hui, T.W., Tang, X., Loy, C.C.: LiteFlowNet: a lightweight convolutional neural network for optical flow estimation. In: CVPR, pp. 8981–8989 (2018)
11. Hui, T.W., Tang, X., Loy, C.C.: A lightweight optical flow CNN - revisiting data fidelity and regularization. TPAMI (2020). https://doi.org/10.1109/TPAMI.2020.2976928
12. Hur, J., Roth, S.: Iterative residual refinement for joint optical flow and occlusion estimation. In: CVPR, pp. 5754–5763 (2019)

13. Ilg, E., Mayer, N., Saikia, T., Keuper, M., Dosovitskiy, A., Brox, T.: FlowNet2.0: evolution of optical flow estimation with deep networks. In: CVPR, pp. 2462–2470 (2017)
14. Ilg, E., Saikia, T., Keuper, M., Brox, T.: Occlusions, motion and depth boundaries with a generic network for disparity, optical flow or scene flow estimation. In: Ferrari, V., Hebert, M., Sminchisescu, C., Weiss, Y. (eds.) ECCV 2018. LNCS, vol. 11216. Springer, Cham (2018). https://doi.org/10.1007/978-3-030-01258-8_38
15. Janai, J., Güney, F., Ranjan, A., Black, M., Geiger, A.: Unsupervised learning of multi-frame optical flow with occlusions. In: Ferrari, V., Hebert, M., Sminchisescu, C., Weiss, Y. (eds.) ECCV 2018. LNCS, vol. 11220, pp. 713–731. Springer, Cham (2018). https://doi.org/10.1007/978-3-030-01270-0_42
16. Jiang, H., Sun, D., Jampani, V., Lv, Z., Learned-Miller, E., Kautz, J.: SENSE: a shared encoder network for scene-flow estimation. In: ICCV, pp. 3195–3204 (2019)
17. Kang, S.B., Szeliski, R., Chai, J.: Handling occlusions in dense multi-view stereo. In: CVPR, pp. 103–110 (2001)
18. Liu, P., Lyu, M., King, I., Xu, J.: SelFlow: self-supervised learning of optical flow. In: CVPR, pp. 4566–4575 (2019)
19. Lu, Y., Valmadre, J., Wang, H., Kannala, J., Harandi, M., Torr, P.H.S.: Devon: deformable volume network for learning optical flow. In: Leal-Taixé, L., Roth, S. (eds.) ECCV 2018. LNCS, vol. 11134, pp. 673–677. Springer, Cham (2019). https://doi.org/10.1007/978-3-030-11024-6_50
20. Mayer, N., et al.: A large dataset to train convolutional networks for disparity, optical flow, and scene flow estimation. In: CVPR, pp. 4040–4048 (2016)
21. Meister, S., Hur, J., Roth, S.: UnFlow: unsupervised learning of opticalflow with a bidirectional census loss. In: AAAI, pp. 7251–7259 (2018)
22. Menze, M., Geiger, A.: Object scene flow for autonomous vehicles. In: CVPR, pp. 3061–3070 (2015)
23. Papenberg, N., Bruhn, A., Brox, T., Didas, S., Weickert, J.: Highly accurate optic flow computation with theoretically justified warping. IJCV **67**(2), 141–158 (2006)
24. Ranjan, A., Black, M.J.: Optical flow estimation using a spatial pyramid network. In: CVPR, pp. 4161–4170 (2017)
25. Revaud, J., Weinzaepfel, P., Harchaoui, Z., Schmid, C.: EpicFlow: edge-preserving interpolation of correspondences for optical flow. In: CVPR, pp. 1164–1172 (2015)
26. Rhemann, C., Hosni, A., Bleyer, M., Rother, C., Gelautz, M.: Fast cost-volume filtering for visual correspondence and beyond. In: CVPR, pp. 3017–3024 (2011)
27. Sun, D., Yang, X., Liu, M.Y., Kautz, J.: PWC-Net: CNNs for optical flow using pyramid, warping, and cost volume. In: CVPR, pp. 8934–8943 (2018)
28. Sun, D., Yang, X., Liu, M.Y., Kautz, J.: Models matter, so does training: an empirical study of CNNs for optical flow estimation. TPAMI (2019). https://doi.org/10.1109/TPAMI.2019.2894353
29. Werlberger, M., Trobin, W., Pock, T., Wedel, A., Cremers, D., Bischof, H.: Anisotropic Huber-L^1 optical flow. In: BMVC (2009)
30. Xu, J., Ranftl, R., Koltun, V.: Accurate optical flow via direct cost volume processings. In: CVPR, pp. 1289–1297 (2017)
31. Yang, G., Ramanan, D.: Volumetric correspondence networks for optical flow. In: NeurIPS (2019)
32. Yin, Z., Darrell, T., Yu, F.: Hierarchical discrete distribution decomposition for match density estimation. In: CVPR, pp. 6044–6053 (2019)
33. Zimmer, H., Bruhn, A., Weickert, J.: Optic flow in harmony. IJCV **93**(3), 368–388 (2011). https://doi.org/10.1007/s11263-011-0422-6

Microscopy Image Restoration with Deep Wiener-Kolmogorov Filters

Valeriya Pronina[1]([⊠]), Filippos Kokkinos[2], Dmitry V. Dylov[1],
and Stamatios Lefkimmiatis[3]

[1] Skolkovo Institute of Science and Technology, Moscow, Russia
Valeriya.Pronina@skoltech.ru
[2] University College London, London, UK
[3] Q.bio Inc., Redwood City, USA

Abstract. Microscopy is a powerful visualization tool in biology, enabling the study of cells, tissues, and the fundamental biological processes; yet, the observed images typically suffer from blur and background noise. In this work, we propose a unifying framework of algorithms for Gaussian image deblurring and denoising. These algorithms are based on deep learning techniques for the design of learnable regularizers integrated into the Wiener-Kolmogorov filter. Our extensive experimentation line showcases that the proposed approach achieves a superior quality of image reconstruction and surpasses the solutions that rely either on deep learning or on optimization schemes alone. Augmented with the variance stabilizing transformation, the proposed reconstruction pipeline can also be successfully applied to the problem of Poisson image deblurring, surpassing the state-of-the-art methods. Moreover, several variants of the proposed framework demonstrate competitive performance at low computational complexity, which is of high importance for real-time imaging applications.

Keywords: Deblurring · Denoising · Learnable regularizers · Microscopy deblurring · Wiener filter

1 Introduction

Microscopes are widely used in biological and medical research, allowing the study of organic and inorganic substances at the minuscule scale. The observed microscopy images, however, suffer from the following two inherent distortions: a blur of detail caused by the resolution limit of a microscope, and a background noise introduced by the imperfections of the imaging system as a whole and by the image-recording sensor in particular. Both of these traits not only distort the perception of the detail in the image but also influence the quantitative analysis of its content [14,33].

Electronic supplementary material The online version of this chapter (https://doi.org/10.1007/978-3-030-58565-5_12) contains supplementary material, which is available to authorized users.

A. Vedaldi et al. (Eds.): ECCV 2020, LNCS 12365, pp. 185–201, 2020.
https://doi.org/10.1007/978-3-030-58565-5_12

Mathematically, the image formation process can be described by the operation of convolution, where the underlying image is convolved with the point spread function of the microscope [17, 39]. Two fluorescence microscopy imaging systems – widefield and confocal – are very popular among biologists. In the case of widefield microscopy, the entire specimen is exposed to a uniform light source. Here, the intensity of the illuminating light is high and the noise statistics of the recorded image can be approximated by the Gaussian distribution [47]. On the contrary, the confocal microscopes rely on point-by-point imaging of the specimen thanks to an aperture (pin-hole) installed in the microscope's optical system to block the out-of-focus signal. This improves the resolution but limits the numerical aperture of the microscope, effectively reducing the number of photons captured by the imaging detector. A more appropriate approximation for the noise in such low-photon images is the Poisson distribution [47].

While general deconvolution problems require estimation of a blurring kernel, in microscopy, the precise PSF measurement is a simpler problem since it can be accomplished using nano-scale beads that act as a Dirac input [38]. For this reason, in our work we do not address the problem of PSF estimation.

Restoration of microscopy images is an ill-posed inverse problem where a unique solution does not exist [17]. One, therefore, needs to constrain the space of solutions in order to obtain a statistically or a physically meaningful one. A popular approach for doing that follows the variational formulation of the problem, where the restored image is obtained as the minimizer of an objective function [12] with the aid of calculus of variations. This objective function comprises two terms: the data fidelity term that measures the proximity between the obtained measurements and the solution, and the regularization term that integrates prior information about the expected solution. There are several methods focused on the development of an effective regularization scheme for the image restoration, e.g., the Hyper-Laplacian priors [22], the non-local means [10], the shrinkage fields [37], and others.

With the advent of deep learning, many inverse problems have been successfully approached with Fully Convolutional Neural Networks (FCNNs) [32, 41] which can learn a mapping between the measured image and its expected reconstruction. Furthermore, a series of works have incorporated deep learning for the regularization purposes in a wide range of image restoration problems [20, 23–25, 49, 50]. Such a regularization paradigm, in turn, has allowed to surpass the performance of the one-shot methods relying on FCNN; however, none of these techniques have been tested on microscopy related deblurring problems.

In this work, we present a joint denoising and deblurring framework for microscopy images, which comprises a collection of methods that leverage the advantages of both the classical schemes for optimization, and the deep learning approaches for regularization. We develop an extensive set of techniques for handling the image prior information, by using both shallow and deep learning for parametrization. The proposed framework entails the following steps:

– First, a regularizer is formed as a group of learnable kernels and is deployed to every image identically.

- Second, an intuitive extension is further examined with the group of kernels being predicted *per image* using a compact FCNN as a Kernel Prediction Network (KPN).
- The same kernel-predicting approach is then probed in *per pixel* evaluation, with the KPN predicting the appropriate regularizer for each spatial location in the image.
- The last step consists of approximating the entire regularization function with a neural network, which is then employed in an iterative manner.

The developed methods outperform solutions based either on optimization schemes alone or the solutions based merely on deep learning techniques. Exploiting both the classical optimization and the deep learning methodologies, the proposed approaches are intrinsically ready for fine-tuning the trade-off between the computational efficiency and the accuracy of image reconstruction.

2   Related Work

Deconvolution in the presence of noise is generally considered a challenging task, and it has attracted significant attention by the research community. The simplest deconvolution approach consists in estimation of the maximum likelihood under the assumption of the statistical model of the observed data. The main drawback of this approach is the amplification of the measurement noise. One common way to avoid this hurdle is to add the regularization term to penalize the values of the solution.

One of the well-known classical methods for image deblurring and denoising, the Wiener-Kolmogorov filter, or Wiener filter [43, 46], is derived as a maximum likelihood estimator under the assumption of Gaussian noise. It uses the Tikhonov regularization functional to incorporate prior knowledge about the expected solution. Wiener filter also retrieves the minimum mean squared error estimate and it has established itself as a fast deconvolution algorithm [4,9,51] due to its closed-form solution in the Fourier domain. Recently, the Wiener filter became a part of methods such as PURE-LET [27] and SURE-LET [51], performing deconvolution with a piece-wise thresholding under wavelet coefficients regularization.

Another well-known method for image deblurring is the Richardson-Lucy algorithm, which is derived as a maximum-likelihood estimator under the assumption of Poisson noise [29,35]. Richardson-Lucy algorithm is a common method for tackling problems of image deblurring and denoising in microscopy and it is mostly used with Tikhonov and total-variation regularization [15].

In order to drive the solution of the optimization problem towards a subset of physically plausible image reconstructions, many researchers have resorted to hand-crafted regularization schemes. For example, Krishnan *et al.* in [22] propose to use hyper-Laplacian penalty functions, while in [7] a method using non-local regularization constraint is proposed for image deblurring and denoising.

With the advent of deep learning, nearly all image restoration methods were revisited from a learnable perspective with great success. Being widely used in many research areas, including the biomedical field, a plethora of neural network approaches have been proposed for denoising [32], demosaicking [21], and super-resolution [41]. Deep learning methods are also applied in image deblurring, e.g., in [16], where a CNN is used for restoring images corrupted with various visual artifacts, and in [13], where a parametric CNN model was used to enhance a shape-based artifact elimination. Xu *et al.* in [48] proposed a CNN that learns the deconvolution operation for natural images in a supervised manner. A step into combining traditional optimization schemes with deep learning is made in [37] by using iterative FFT-based deconvolution with learnable regularization filters, weights and shrinkage functions. A similar approach was introduced by [49], where the authors proposed to learn horizontal and vertical image gradient filters. Zhang *et al.* in [50] developed a trainable denoiser prior that is then integrated into a model-based optimization method. Finally, in [6] the authors propose to learn a prior that represents a Gaussian-smoothed version of the natural image distribution.

3   Problem Formulation

3.1   Image Formation in Microscopy

The image formation process can be described by the observation model

$$\mathbf{y} = \mathbf{Kx} + \mathbf{n}, \tag{1}$$

where $\mathbf{y} \in \mathbb{R}^N$ corresponds to the observed image, $\mathbf{K} \in \mathbb{R}^{N \times N}$ is the matrix corresponding to the point spread function (PSF), $\mathbf{x} \in \mathbb{R}^N$ is the underlying image that we aim to restore and $\mathbf{n} \sim \mathcal{N}(0, \sigma^2)$ denotes noise, which is assumed to follow i.i.d Gaussian distribution. While $\mathbf{x}$ and $\mathbf{y}$ are two dimensional images, for the sake of mathematical derivations, we assume that they have been raster scanned using a lexicographical order, and they correspond to vectors of N dimensions.

3.2   Regularization

Deconvolution being an image restoration task is an ill-posed inverse problem, which implies that a unique solution does not exist. In general, such problems can be addressed following a variational approach. Note that the name of this approach comes from the field of calculus of variations, where the basic problem is to find minima or maxima of a functional using the variations – small changes in functions or functionals (variational derivatives). In our case, the solution of the variational approach $\hat{\mathbf{x}}$ is obtained by minimizing the objective function

$$\hat{\mathbf{x}} = \underset{\mathbf{x}}{\arg\min} \underbrace{\frac{1}{2}||\mathbf{y} - \mathbf{Kx}||_2^2 + \lambda r(\mathbf{x})}_{\mathbf{J}(\mathbf{x})}. \tag{2}$$

Here the first term corresponds to the data fidelity term, which measures the proximity of the solution to the observation, while the second one corresponds to the regularizer that models any prior knowledge one might have about the ground-truth image. The parameter λ is a trade-off coefficient that determines the contribution of the regularizer into the estimation of the solution. A list of popular regularizers contains Tikhonov [42] and TV functionals [36] which have been widely used in a plethora of image restoration tasks, including deconvolution problems [15]. However, in this work we attempt to incorporate prior information learned directly from available training data in a supervised manner with the inclusion of deep learning strategies.

4 Proposed Approach

4.1 Learnable Regularization Kernels

First, we start from the observation that in most of the modern methods for image restoration the regularization term is formed as

$$r(\mathbf{x}) = \sum_{d=1}^{D} \rho_d(\mathbf{g}_d * \mathbf{x}), \qquad (3)$$

where $\mathbf{g}_d$ are typically linear filters and $\rho_d(\cdot)$ is a set of penalty functions, acting on the filters outputs [22]. In this work, we explicitly set the penalty function to be the squared ℓ_2 norm, leading to a Tikhonov regularizer [42]

$$r(\mathbf{x}) = \sum_{d=1}^{D} ||\mathbf{g}_d * \mathbf{x}||_2^2 = \sum_{d=1}^{D} ||\mathbf{G}_d \mathbf{x}||_2^2, \qquad (4)$$

where $\mathbf{g}_d$ are learnable convolution kernels and $\mathbf{G}_d \in \mathbb{R}^{N \times N}$ are convolution matrices, corresponding to these kernels. This specific choice of the penalty function allows us to obtain the solution of (2) in the closed-form

$$\hat{\mathbf{x}} = (\mathbf{K}^\top \mathbf{K} + \lambda \sum_{d=1}^{D} \mathbf{G}_d^\top \mathbf{G}_d)^{-1} \mathbf{K}^\top \mathbf{y}, \qquad (5)$$

which corresponds to the Wiener-Kolmogorov filter. Here $\mathbf{K}^\top$ and $\mathbf{G}_d^\top$ are the adjoint matrices of $\mathbf{K}$ and $\mathbf{G}_d$, respectively. To obtain the solution of Eq. (5) one has first to perform the inversion of a huge matrix which can be very slow in practice or even intractable. However, the supremacy of the Wiener filter lies in its FFT-based inference, which renders it a fast and efficient method and allows to restore the underlying signal at a low computational complexity. Specifically, under the assumption of periodic image boundary conditions, the degradation matrix $\mathbf{K}$ and convolution matrix $\mathbf{G}_d$ are circulant real matrices and thus, they can be diagonalized in the Fourier domain as

$$\mathbf{K} = \mathbf{F}^H \mathbf{D_K} \mathbf{F}, \quad \mathbf{D_K} = \mathbf{F} \mathbf{S_K} \mathbf{P_K} \mathbf{k}; \quad \mathbf{G}_d = \mathbf{F}^H \mathbf{D}_{\mathbf{G}_d} \mathbf{F}, \quad \mathbf{D}_{\mathbf{G}_d} = \mathbf{F} \mathbf{S}_{\mathbf{G}d} \mathbf{P}_{\mathbf{G}d} \mathbf{g}_d. \quad (6)$$

Here $\mathbf{F} \in \mathbb{C}^{N \times N}$ is the Fourier (DFT) matrix, $\mathbf{F}^H \in \mathbb{C}^{N \times N}$ is its inverse, $\mathbf{D_K}$, $\mathbf{D}_{\mathbf{G}_d} \in \mathbb{C}^{N \times N}$ are diagonal matrices, $\mathbf{S_K}, \mathbf{S}_{\mathbf{G}d} \in \mathbb{R}^{N \times N}$ are the corresponding circulant shift operators, $\mathbf{P_K} \in \mathbb{R}^{N \times M}, \mathbf{P}_{\mathbf{G}d} \in \mathbb{R}^{N \times Ld}$ are the corresponding zero-padding operators, $\mathbf{k} \in \mathbb{R}^M$ is the blurring kernel and $\mathbf{g}_d \in \mathbb{R}^{Ld}$ is a regularization convolution kernel. We also consider the trade-off coefficient λ to be equal to e^α in all experiments to ensure the positivity of the regularization weight. Based on the above, the one-shot solution of Eq. (5) is

$$\hat{\mathbf{x}} = \mathbf{F}^H \left(\frac{\mathbf{D}_\mathbf{K}^* \mathbf{F} \mathbf{y}}{|\mathbf{D}_\mathbf{K}|^2 + e^\alpha \sum_{d=1}^{D} |\mathbf{D}_{\mathbf{G}d}|^2} \right), \tag{7}$$

where $\mathbf{D}_\mathbf{K}^*$ is the Hermitian transpose of $\mathbf{D}_\mathbf{K}$ and the division is applied in an element-wise fashion. The method is depicted in Fig. 1a and hereafter we refer to it as WF-K. To obtain the solution in this form, we firstly employ a group of D learnable kernels $\mathbf{g}_d$ of size $K \times K$ which are initialized using a two-dimensional discrete cosine transform (DCT) frequency basis; a common choice in image processing since it has shown the ability to extract useful prior image information. We also consider α to be a learnable parameter in all proposed regularization schemes in order for the trade-off coefficient value to be tuned alongside the learnable kernels during the training process.

4.2   Prediction of Regularization Kernels

A critical drawback of the standard Wiener method lies in the way the group of kernels is formulated. In detail, the learnable group is global which means that all kernels are applied on every image identically without any dependency on the underlying content. To remedy this situation, we propose the content-driven WF-KPN method that predicts per image the group of kernels that need to be used for regularization. In this framework, the solution of a Wiener filter yields the same form as presented in Eq. (7), but unlike the previous approach, the convolution kernels $\mathbf{g}_d$, that form the diagonal matrix $\mathbf{D}_{\mathbf{G}d}$ in Eq. (6), are now predicted from a Kernel Prediction Network (KPN) [32] as shown in Fig. 1b.

For the Kernel Prediction Network we select a compact customized UNet architecture with nearly 470 k parameters that receives the distorted input $\mathbf{y}$ and produces an output with $K^2 D$ channels and the same spatial resolution as the input. Unlike the traditional UNet, we perform global average pooling in the spatial dimension on the output of the last layer, which is then reshaped into a stack of $D \times K \times K$ regularization kernels. Here D is the number of kernels and $K \times K$ is the support size. In all our experiments, we set $D = 8$ and $K = 3$. We also use instance normalization [44] after each convolutional layer to normalize weights for each image independently. In this way, the KPN predicts D content dependent regularization kernels of size $K \times K$ for each image, that then under the assumption of periodic boundary conditions form the diagonal matrix $\mathbf{D}_{\mathbf{G}_d}$ in Eq. (6). After that, the resulting diagonal matrices $\mathbf{D}_{\mathbf{G}_d}$ are incorporated into the solution of the Wiener filter according to Eq. (7).

The proposed models WF-K and WF-KPN involve learning of the trade-off coefficient α and regularization kernels $\mathbf{g}_d$ in a supervised manner via means of back-propagation of a loss function. While the loss function we are minimizing during training is real-valued, the solution in Eq. (7) involves complex quantities and therefore we cannot perform back-propagation by solely relying on

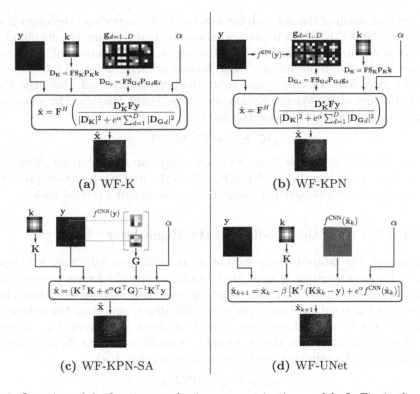

Fig. 1. Overview of the four proposed prior parametrization models. In Fig. 1a the one-shot Wiener filter with learnable kernels is depicted, while in Fig. 1b the same filter with predictable kernels is presented. In Fig. 1c the scheme incorporating prediction of per-pixel regularization kernels into Wiener filter is shown. The proposed iterative scheme which combines Wiener filtering with the approximation of regularization with a CNN is visualized in Fig. 1d

layers currently available in existing deep-learning libraries. For this reason we have implemented our own customized layers which depend on the analytical derivations of the gradients of the solution $\hat{\mathbf{x}}$ w.r.t. the trainable parameters. All analytical derivations of the necessary gradients are provided in the supplementary material.

4.3 Prediction of Spatially Adaptive Regularization Kernels

While the prediction of global regularization kernels per image provides the appealing property of content adaptation, we further extend WF-KPN to be both spatially and content adaptive. This is achieved by predicting for each image a different regularization kernel per-pixel and hence the method is dubbed as WF-KPN-SA. For this extension, we modify the UNet of Sect. 4.2 to predict a kernel per spatial location of an image. Unlike WF-KPN, the output of the network has K^2 channels and the same size as the input. We empirically found that normalization of the network hinders the performance and therefore it was removed in all WF-KPN-SA related experiments. Furthermore, the output of the network is reshaped into spatially adaptive regularization kernels of size $K \times K$ for each pixel of an input image. These kernels are then unfolded into a matrix $\mathbf{G}$ which now does not correspond to a circulant matrix, and, thus, the FFT-based inference of the Wiener-Kolmogorov filter is not feasible. The solution of the restoration problem has now the form of

$$\hat{\mathbf{x}} = (\mathbf{K}^\top \mathbf{K} + e^\alpha \mathbf{G}^\top \mathbf{G})^{-1} \mathbf{K}^\top \mathbf{y} \tag{8}$$

and the calculation of $\hat{\mathbf{x}}$ is done using the conjugate gradient algorithm [40]. To the best of our knowledge, WF-KPN-SA is the first method that predicts a spatially varying regularizer per image for inverse imaging related tasks.

4.4   Prediction of the Gradient of the Regularizer

Finally, with the desire to fully exploit deep learning capabilities, we employ a CNN for parametrizing a prior that would be specific for each image and, thus, completely content adaptive. This way we do not make assumptions about the form of the regularization term as we did above, and thus, the solution of Eq. (2) cannot be derived anymore in a closed-form expression. One common way to solve Eq. (2) in this case is to apply a gradient descent [8] optimization algorithm to find a minimizer of the objective function $\mathbf{J}(\mathbf{x})$,

$$\hat{\mathbf{x}}_{k+1} = \hat{\mathbf{x}}_k - \beta \nabla \mathbf{J}(\mathbf{x}). \tag{9}$$

Here $\hat{\mathbf{x}}_{k+1}$ is the solution of Eq. (2) that is updated after each iteration k of the gradient descent scheme and β is the learning rate defining the speed of the algorithm. Introducing the objective function $\mathbf{J}(\mathbf{x})$, defined according to Eq. (2), into Eq. (9), we obtain the solution of the gradient descent scheme,

$$\hat{\mathbf{x}}_{k+1} = \hat{\mathbf{x}}_k - \beta \left[\mathbf{K}^\top (\mathbf{K}\hat{\mathbf{x}}_k - \mathbf{y}) + e^\alpha f^{\mathrm{CNN}}(\hat{\mathbf{x}}_k) \right]. \tag{10}$$

Here we parametrize the gradient of the regularizer with the CNN, $\nabla \mathbf{r}(\hat{\mathbf{x}}_k) = f^{\mathrm{CNN}}(\hat{\mathbf{x}}_k)$. For the prediction of the gradient of a regularizer we employ the UNet architecture that was defined in Sect. 4.2. Unlike WF-KPN and WF-KPN-SA, we do not modify the original UNet architecture, and in this case the network receives a distorted image $\mathbf{y}$ as an input and maps it to an output with the same resolution and number of channels as the input. We also use instance normalization after each convolutional layer to normalize weights for each image independently. Although this method does not exactly fit into the family of Wiener-Kolmogorov filters, it belongs to the general idea of reconstruction by regularization. Thus, to remain consistent across all the methods starting from Eq. (2), this method is hereafter referred to as WF-UNet and it is depicted in Fig. 1d. The number of gradient descent iterations for WF-UNet is set to be equal to 10. We also consider the step size β to be a learnable parameter in order for the gradient descent speed to be tuned during the training process.

We stress that the proposed methods, WF-KPN, WF-KPN-SA and WF-UNet, share a UNet with almost identical architecture to have approximately the same number of trainable parameters that allows for fair comparison between the models. Furthermore, the selected network architecture is relatively compact, which in return allows the development of methods capable of deblurring an image in milliseconds. The architecture of the implemented UNet is described in the supplementary material.

Further, we apply the edge tapering technique [34] to mitigate the boundary issues that arise from the Wiener filter due to the periodic boundary assumption.

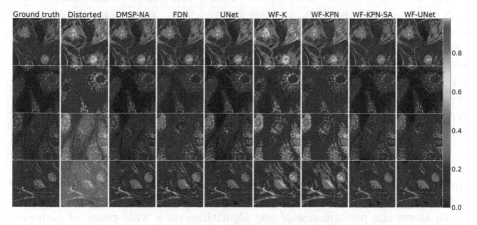

Fig. 2. Restoration of microscopy images degraded by PSF and Gaussian noise with standard deviation equal to 0.005, 0.01, 0.05, 0.1, respectively, from top to bottom. All images are originally grayscale but a different colormap is used to better highlight the differences among the various reconstructions.

5   Network Training

5.1   Dataset

Since there is a lack of a deconvolution dataset, comprising of microscopy images perturbed by Gaussian noise, we create training pairs of ground-truth and distorted with blur and noise images using the Fluorescence Microscopy Denoising (FMD) dataset [52] and a dataset that is used in cell segmentation of microscopy images [3]. To create a large set of reference images, we take the ground-truth images from both datasets and crop each image into patches of size 256×256. After, all patches that contain no information about cells are discarded by comparing the mean value of a patch with the mean value of the original image. Note that all ground-truth images as well as resulting distorted images are grayscale.

To produce blurred versions of the ground-truth images we create 35 different 2D PSFs of sizes 7×7, 9×9, 11×11 and 13×13 by altering the index of refraction of the media, the numerical aperture, the pixel size and the excitation wavelength using the ImageJ plugins Diffraction PSF 3D [2] and PSF Generator [1] with the Richards & Wolf optical model. In detail, 25 PSFs are reserved for training, 5 for

Table 1. PSNR and SSIM comparisons on Gaussian image deblurring for five noise levels. In all tables, we highlight the best result in bold and underline the second best result.

| | STD | | | | | | | | | |
| | 0.001 | | 0.005 | | 0.01 | | 0.05 | | 0.1 | |
	PSNR	SSIM	PSNR	SSIM	PSNR	SSIM	PSNR	SSIM	PSNR	SSIM
Input	36.23	.8955	35.37	.8791	33.93	.8339	26.03	.3858	21.14	.1718
IRCNN [50]	33.33	.8604	36.88	.8972	36.80	.9013	32.44	.7932	28.95	.6835
FDN [23]	<u>40.31</u>	**.9424**	38.61	.9239	37.33	.9086	33.50	.8406	30.49	.7550
DMSP-NA [6]	**40.44**	.9402	**39.16**	**.9290**	<u>37.73</u>	<u>.9123</u>	<u>34.31</u>	<u>.8589</u>	32.19	.8312
DMSP-NB [6]	40.27	<u>.9411</u>	37.23	.9027	36.59	.8930	34.29	.8582	32.20	<u>.8313</u>
UNet	37.73	.9177	37.27	.9136	36.64	.9064	34.04	.8556	<u>32.40</u>	.8187
WF-K	35.66	.8849	35.61	.8834	35.45	.8787	32.74	.7950	29.27	.6835
WF-KPN	38.72	.9253	37.98	.9176	36.80	.9028	32.33	.8022	29.20	.7259
WF-KPN-SA	39.86	.9390	<u>38.76</u>	<u>.9275</u>	**37.81**	**.9157**	**34.58**	**.8688**	**32.60**	**.8363**
WF-UNet	38.08	.9102	37.55	.9053	36.77	.8966	33.89	.8442	32.01	.8096

validation and the rest for testing purposes. Notably, all PSFs $\mathbf{k}$ are normalized such that $\sum_i k_i = 1$, which is a realistic assumption in optics [15].

To assess the performance of our algorithms on a wide range of Gaussian noise levels, all images are scaled in the range of $[0, 1]$, then blurred with a PSF and finally perturbed with i.i.d. Gaussian noise with standard deviation from the set $(0.001, 0.005, 0.01, 0.05, 0.1)$.

The resulting dataset, which contains 1405 pairs of ground-truth and distorted images, is split into 975 training, 200 validation and 230 testing samples. During training, a ground-truth sample is convolved with a randomly chosen blur kernel from the 25 training PSFs, and subsequently Gaussian noise with a randomly selected standard deviation from the set presented above is added to the blurred image.

5.2 Training Details

All proposed methods are trained in an end-to-end fashion to minimize the ℓ_1 loss function between the output and the ground-truth image as well as the gradients of the aforementioned entities

$$\mathcal{L} = ||\hat{\mathbf{x}} - \mathbf{x}||_1 + ||\nabla\hat{\mathbf{x}} - \nabla\mathbf{x}||_1. \tag{11}$$

It has been reported that training with the ℓ_1 loss function yields images with sharper edges [53]. Also, by incorporating a gradient based loss alongside the pixel-wise loss, we obtain models that are capable of reconstructing the sharp details of the underlying images. All proposed methods are optimized using Adam [19] with a learning rate 10^{-3}. For all methods, except the WF-KPN-SA, we use batch size equal to 25 and train the models for 300 epochs. For the WF-KPN-SA network, due to memory-related limitations, we set the batch size to be equal to 3. The Python source code of the proposed methods can be downloaded at https://github.com/vpronina/DeepWienerRestoration.

5.3   Evaluation

To evaluate the performance of all algorithms on each noise level, we use 230 ground-truth images that are convolved with the 5 PSFs reserved for testing purposes. Note that the held-out PSFs were not seen during training to explore the generalization ability of the methods to unknown blurring kernels. Finally, the noisy observation of a blurry image is produced by adding Gaussian noise with each standard deviation from the set (0.001, 0.005, 0.01, 0.05, 0.1). In detail, we get 1150 test samples in total, combined into 5 test sets of different noise levels which allows the thorough comparison of the performance of our algorithms on each noise level separately.

We compare our proposed algorithms with three state-of-the-art algorithms for deblurring images distorted by Gaussian noise: IRCNN [50], FDN [23] and DMSP [6]. The latter was considered in two implementations – noise-blind, or noise-adaptive (NA), and noise-aware, or non-blind (NB). We also provide a CNN baseline which is a UNet with almost the same architecture and number of parameters as the one used for the parametrization of the regularization gradient. For this instance of UNet we use batch normalization layers instead of instance normalization. This way we get a valid comparison and we are able to investigate if the combination of a standard optimization scheme and a deep learning approach will help to achieve good restoration results and surpass those obtained by employing solely a deep learning based algorithm. For assessing the methods performance we use the standard peak signal-to-noise ratio (PSNR) and the structural similarity index (SSIM [45]) metrics. Comparisons of all the methods runtime was conducted on a computer with an Intel Core i7-8750H CPU and a NVIDIA GeForce GTX 1080Ti GPU.

6   Results

We evaluate all methods on the developed test set across all different noise ranges, as described in Sect. 5.3. The results presented in Table 1 show that our proposed spatially adaptive method WF-KPN-SA surpasses in performance all competing state-of-the-art methods except in the very low noise cases. The performance over the deep learning based competing methods FDN [23], IRCNN [50] and DMSP [6] ranges from nearly 0.1 in the low noise regime to 0.4 dB for high noise. Only in the case of very low noise the previous state-of-the-art methods provide better reconstruction quality than WF-KPN-SA. However, we stress that, as well as DMSP-NA, our methods are noise-blind, while IRCNN, FDN and DMSP-NB are noise-aware, with the oracle noise standard deviation being explicitly provided as an input.

Furthermore, we find that Wiener Filter (WF-K) with the learnable regularization filters yields satisfactory reconstruction quality and perform only slightly

Table 2. Runtime of several deconvolution algorithms for processing an image with the spatial dimensions of 256×256. All times were calculated using the publicly available implementations and the reported benchmarks are the average of 10 runs.

	CPU, ms	GPU, ms		CPU, ms	GPU, ms		CPU, ms	GPU, ms
GILAM [11]	4155.9	–	DMSP [6]	79656.0	19707.7	WF-KPN	45.4	7.7
HSPIRAL [26]	5828.8	–	IRCNN [50]	7890.7	–	WF-KPN-SA	1382.9	187.2
PURE-LET [27]	211.3	–	UNet	32.4	**2.8**	WF-UNet	354.1	39.8
FDN [23]	34542.1	36.6	WF-K	**5.6**	4.6			

worse than several deep learning methods for a fraction of its computational complexity. A detailed benchmark of computational time for all methods presented in our work can be found in Table 2. As presented in Fig. 2, WF-K and WF-KPN methods tend to miss sharp details in the restored images, while WF-KPN-SA and WF-UNet al.low the restoration of fine image details.

7   Poisson Image Deblurring

As an extension, all developed methods are applied in the case of confocal microscopy, where as it was mentioned in Sect. 1 the intensity of the light illuminating the sample is very small and thus the noise statistics obey the Poisson distribution. One notable property of the Poisson distribution is that the mean and variance of the random variable are not independent, i.e. $\text{mean}(\mathbf{y}) = \text{var}(\mathbf{y})$. As such, the image formation model is formulated as $\mathbf{y} = \mathcal{P}(\mathbf{Kx})$ where $\mathcal{P}$ denotes the Poisson noise distorting the image. One successful way to perform deconvolution and denoising in the presence of Poisson noise is to first apply a variance stabilizing transformation (VST) [31] which transforms a variable from the Poisson distribution into one from the Gaussian. This allows to borrow the ample apparatus of the well-studied methods derived for Gaussian statistics. This approach has been successfully applied in the literature [18,28,31,52] to solve the Poissonian restoration problem using Gaussian denoising algorithms.

In our work we explore a similar approach and make use of the widely known VST, the Anscombe transform [5], which is applied on the distorted observation

$$\mathbf{y} \to 2\sqrt{\mathbf{y} + \frac{3}{8}}. \tag{12}$$

The Anscombe transform aims to stabilize the data variance to be approximately unity. After the transformation, the data can be viewed as a signal-independent Gaussian process with unit variance, and therefore the Wiener filter, which is derived from Gaussian statistics, can be directly applied. Once the deconvolved solution, denoted as $\hat{\mathbf{x}}$, is obtained, an inverse Anscombe transform is applied to return the data to its original domain. Applying the simple algebraic inverse usually results in a biased estimate of the output. To mitigate the bias in the case of photon-limited imaging the exact unbiased inverse transformation should

Table 3. PSNR and SSIM comparisons on Poisson image deblurring for six different noise levels. Methods that were not able to produce meaningful results due to numerical instability issues are marked with N/A.

	PEAK										
	1		2		5		10		25		50	
	PSNR	SSIM	PSNR	SSIM	PSNR	SSIM	PSNR	SSIM	PSNR	SSIM	PSNR	SSIM
Input	10.93	.0981	13.22	.1105	16.67	.1639	19.45	.2425	23.21	.3930	26.00	.5247
GILAM [11]	24.57	.4977	25.66	.6350	26.64	.5451	28.24	.6304	29.92	.6975	30.97	.7463
HSPIRAL [26]	23.18	.4101	26.54	.5809	30.18	.7576	31.94	.8229	33.39	.8578	34.38	.8729
PURE-LET [27]	26.18	.7318	26.44	.7494	26.77	.7612	27.67	.7799	28.77	.8065	28.77	.8114
FDN [23]	N/A	N/A	N/A	N/A	N/A	N/A	N/A	N/A	N/A	N/A	31.16	.8176
DMSP-NA [6]	16.07	0.4243	18.86	.5648	23.80	.7126	27.76	.7880	31.74	.8490	33.65	.8770
DMSP-NB [6]	10.86	.2079	12.97	.2761	20.49	.5691	26.12	.7356	30.25	.8136	33.01	.8633
IRCNN [50]	6.81	.0902	11.67	.1809	17.37	.3695	22.14	.5323	29.46	.8038	33.10	.8660
UNet	28.50	.7916	29.79	.8143	31.47	.8428	32.72	.8633	34.20	.8871	35.17	.9008
WF-K	25.81	.5821	27.85	.6947	29.94	.7888	31.13	.8288	32.06	.8557	32.43	.8654
WF-KPN	27.09	.7503	28.19	.7811	29.89	.8177	31.34	.8460	33.22	.8770	34.50	.8945
WF-KPN-SA	28.80	.7949	30.12	.8185	31.72	.8468	32.92	.8672	34.48	.8909	35.60	.9056
WF-UNet	**29.04**	**.8005**	**30.27**	**.8220**	**31.83**	**.8492**	**33.06**	**.8694**	**34.59**	**.8928**	**35.67**	**.9069**

be used, whose closed-form approximation [30] is

$$\hat{x} \rightarrow \left(\frac{\hat{x}}{2}\right)^2 - \frac{1}{8} + \frac{1}{4}\sqrt{\frac{3}{2}}\hat{x}^{-1} - \frac{11}{8}\hat{x}^{-2} + \frac{5}{8}\sqrt{\frac{3}{2}}\hat{x}^{-3}. \tag{13}$$

Data Preparation and Results. To assess the performance of our algorithms on the task of Poisson image deblurring, we retrain our models using the VST and the exact unbiased inverse transformation included into the pipeline. The Anscombe transform is applied on the input image y as described in Eq. (12) before being fed into any of the proposed models of Sect. 4. Accordingly, the restored signal $\hat{x}$ from any of the proposed models is transformed back using the exact unbiased version of the inverse transformation, presented in Eq. (13), in order to recover the final solution. For this task we use the same dataset as the one used for the evaluation of the Gaussian deblurring. We create 35 2D PSFs of size 5×5 to simulate confocal microscope pinhole with the ImageJ Diffraction PSF 3D plugin [1]. We again use 25 PSFs for training purposes, 5 for validation and 5 for test. To simulate various SNR values of Poisson noise, we use the prior art approach [11,26] and scale the ground-truth images to have a maximum intensity of $(1, 2, 5, 10, 25, 50)$. Poisson noise is signal dependent with local $SNR = \sqrt{y_i}$, where y_i denotes the underlying image intensity at position i, therefore by increasing the maximum intensity of an image, the amount of noise decreases and vice versa. Furthermore, it is long known fact that images with large mean value and perturbed with Poisson noise follow approximately a normal, or Gaussian distribution, and therefore methods based on Gaussian statistics might work equally well. Scaling the ground-truth images to have various ranges of maximum intensities aims to cover a wide gamut of noise levels, including the ones that belong to approximately a Gaussian distribution.

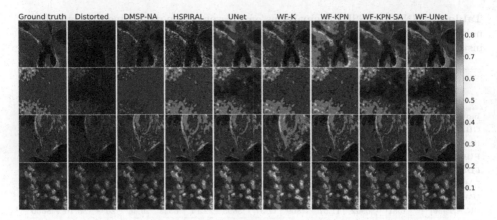

Fig. 3. Restoration of microscopy images scaled to have peak intensities equal to 1, 5, 10, 25, respectively from top to bottom and degraded by PSF and Poisson noise. All images are originally grayscale, but a different colormap is used to better highlight the differences among the various reconstructions.

During training, a ground-truth sample is rescaled to a randomly chosen maximum intensity from the range mentioned above. Then the sample is convolved with a randomly chosen blur kernel from the 25 training PSFs, and after that the noisy observation is produced from the blurred image. We follow the same strategy as in Sect. 5.3 to produce blurred and noisy images for the test set.

We compare the proposed algorithms with the non-blind deblurring algorithms, developed for Poisson distribution: GILAM [11], HSPIRAL [26] and PURE-LET [27]. We also include the aforementioned state-of-the-art methods for Gaussian image deblurring into the comparison by applying the VST to the distorted data and the exact unbiased transformation to the result of the restorations. Table 3 and Fig. 3 clearly show that WF-UNet outperforms the other approaches at most of the noise levels, which is especially important on the low intensity peak values where the Poisson noise is stronger. WF-KPN-SA shows comparable to WF-UNet performance being only marginaly inferior. Overall, WF-UNet and WF-KPN-SA show good quantitative improvement from nearly 2.6 dB to 5.8 dB over the previous state-of-the-art methods on the low intensity peaks and from nearly 1.2 dB to 7 dB on the high intensity peaks. Moreover, Fig. 3 demonstrates that, despite the good quantitative improvement, WF-K and WF-KPN struggle to reconstruct the fine details in the images, while the reconstructions generated by WF-KPN-SA and WF-UNet are very accurate.

8   Conclusion

In this work, we proposed a series of methods based on the Wiener-Kolmogorov filtering technique for dealing with the problem of Gaussian and Poisson image deblurring. We introduced three novel ways to parametrize the image priors, including a new approach of regularization with kernel predictions obtained by a neural network. Our extensive experimentation line showcased that our proposed framework based on the prediction of a regularizer achieves superior quality of image reconstruction and surpasses the solutions that rely either on deep learning or on optimization schemes alone. Finally, several of our proposed algorithms demonstrate low computational complexity, without sacrificing the accuracy of image restoration. Being fast and accurate, the proposed framework paves the way towards real-time microscopy image restoration.

References

1. PSF Generator. http://bigwww.cpfl.ch/algorithms/psfgenerator/#ref. Accessed 25 Feb 2020
2. Diffraction PSF 3D. https://www.optinav.info/Diffraction-PSF-3D.htm. Accessed 30 May 2019
3. Al-Kofahi, Y., Zaltsman, A.B., Graves, R.M., Marshall, W., Rusu, M.: A deep learning-based algorithm for 2-D cell segmentation in microscopy images. BMC Bioinform. **19** (2018)
4. AL-Qinani, I.H.: Deblurring image and removing noise from medical images for cancerous diseases using a wiener filter. IRJET **8**(4), 2354–2365 (2017)
5. Anscombe, F.J.: The transformation of Poisson, binomial and negative-binomial data. Biometrika **35**(3–4), 246–254 (1948)
6. Arjomand Bigdeli, S., Zwicker, M., Favaro, P., Jin, M.: Deep mean-shift priors for image restoration. In: Guyon, I., et al. (eds.) Advances in Neural Information Processing Systems 30, pp. 763–772. Curran Associates, Inc. (2017)
7. van Beek, P., Yang, J., Yamamoto, S., Ueda, Y.: Image deblurring and denoising with non-local regularization constraint. In: Information Processing and Communications, vol. 7543, January 2010
8. Bertsekas, D.P.: Nonlinear Programming, 2nd edn. (1999)
9. Boyat, A.K., Joshi, B.K.: Image denoising using wavelet transform and Wiener filter based on log energy distribution over Poisson-Gaussian noise model, pp. 1–6 (2014)
10. Buades, A., Coll, B., Morel, J.: A non-local algorithm for image denoising. In: 2005 IEEE Computer Society Conference on Computer Vision and Pattern Recognition (CVPR), vol. 2, pp. 60–65 (2005)
11. Chen, D.Q.: Regularized generalized inverse accelerating linearized alternating minimization algorithm for frame-based Poissonian image deblurring. SIAM J. Imaging Sci. **7**, 716–739 (2014)
12. Chen, K.: Introduction to variational image-processing models and applications. Int. J. Comput. Math. **90**, 1–8 (2013)
13. Chowdhury, A., et al.: Blood vessel characterization using virtual 3D models and convolutional neural networks in fluorescence microscopy. In: 2017 IEEE 14th International Symposium on Biomedical Imaging (ISBI), pp. 629–632. IEEE (2017)
14. Conchello, J.A., Lichtman, J.W.: Fluorescence microscopy. Nat. Methods **2**(12), 910–919 (2005)
15. Dey, N., et al.: Richardson-Lucy algorithm with total variation regularization for 3D confocal microscope deconvolution. Microsc. Res. Tech. **69**, 4 (2006)

16. Eigen, D., Krishnan, D., Fergus, R.: Restoring an image taken through a window covered with dirt or rain. In: 2013 IEEE International Conference on Computer Vision, pp. 633–640 (2013)
17. Evangelista, V., Barsanti, L., Passarelli, V., Gualtieri, P.: From cells to proteins: imaging nature across dimensions. In: Proceedings of the NATO Advanced Study Institute, Pisa, Italy (2005)
18. Foi, A., Trimeche, M., Katkovnik, V., Egiazarian, K.: Practical Poissonian-Gaussian noise modeling and fitting for single-image raw-data. IEEE Trans. Image Process. **17**(10), 1737–1754 (2008)
19. Kingma, D.P., Ba, J.: Adam: a method for stochastic optimization. CoRR abs/1412.6980 (2014)
20. Kokkinos, F., Lefkimmiatis, S.: Deep image demosaicking using a cascade of convolutional residual denoising networks. In: Ferrari, V., Hebert, M., Sminchisescu, C., Weiss, Y. (eds.) Computer Vision – ECCV 2018. LNCS, vol. 11218, pp. 317–333. Springer, Cham (2018). https://doi.org/10.1007/978-3-030-01264-9_19
21. Kokkinos, F., Lefkimmiatis, S.: Iterative joint image demosaicking and denoising using a residual denoising network. IEEE Trans. Image Process. **PP**, 1 (2019)
22. Krishnan, D., Fergus, R.: Fast image deconvolution using hyper-laplacian priors. In: Bengio, Y., Schuurmans, D., Lafferty, J.D., Williams, C.K.I., Culotta, A. (eds.) Advances in Neural Information Processing Systems 22, pp. 1033–1041. Curran Associates, Inc. (2009)
23. Kruse, J., Rother, C., Schmidt, U.: Learning to push the limits of efficient FFT-based image deconvolution. In: 2017 IEEE International Conference on Computer Vision (ICCV), pp. 4596–4604 (2017)
24. Lefkimmiatis, S.: Universal denoising networks: a novel CNN architecture for image denoising. In: Proceedings of the CVPR, June 2018
25. Lefkimmiatis, S.: Non-local color image denoising with convolutional neural networks, pp. 5882–5891 (2017)
26. Lefkimmiatis, S., Unser, M.: Poisson image reconstruction with Hessian Schatten-norm regularization. IEEE Trans. Image Process. **22**, 4314–4327 (2013)
27. Li, J., Luisier, F., Blu, T.: PURE-LET image deconvolution. IEEE Trans. Image Process. **27**(1), 92–105 (2018)
28. Lu, H., Cheng, J.H., Han, G., Li, L., Liang, Z.: 3D distance-weighted Wiener filter for Poisson noise reduction in sinogram space for SPECT imaging. In: Antonuk, L.E., Yaffe, M.J. (eds.) Medical Imaging 2001: Physics of Medical Imaging, vol. 4320, pp. 905–913. International Society for Optics and Photonics, SPIE (2001)
29. Lucy, L.B.: An iterative technique for the rectification of observed distributions. Astron. J. **79**, 745–754 (1974)
30. Makitalo, M., Foi, A.: A closed-form approximation of the exact unbiased inverse of the Anscombe variance-stabilizing transformation. IEEE Trans. Image Process. **20**(9), 2697–2698 (2011)
31. Makitalo, M., Foi, A.: Optimal inversion of the generalized Anscombe transformation for Poisson-Gaussian noise. IEEE Trans. Image Process. **22**(1), 91–103 (2013)
32. Mildenhall, B., Barron, J.T., Chen, J., Sharlet, D., Ng, R., Carroll, R.: Burst denoising with kernel prediction networks, pp. 2502–2510 (2018)
33. de Monvel, J.B., Calvez, S.L., Ulfendahl, M.: Image restoration for confocal microscopy: improving the limits of deconvolution, with application to the visualization of the mammalian hearing organ. Biophys. J. **80**(5), 2455–70 (2001)
34. Reeves, S.J.: Fast image restoration without boundary artifacts. IEEE Trans. Image Process. **14**(10), 1448–1453 (2005)

35. Richardson, W.H.: Bayesian-based iterative method of image restoration∗. J. Opt. Soc. Am. **62**(1), 55–59 (1972)
36. Rudin, L.I., Osher, S., Fatemi, E.: Nonlinear Total Variation Based Noise Removal Algorithms. Elsevier North-Holland Inc., USA (1992)
37. Schmidt, U., Roth, S.: Shrinkage fields for effective image restoration. In: 2014 IEEE Conference on Computer Vision and Pattern Recognition, pp. 2774–2781 (2014)
38. Shaw, P.J., Rawlins, D.J.: The point-spread function of a confocal microscope: its measurement and use in deconvolution of 3-D data. J. Microsc. **163**(2), 151–165 (1991)
39. Sheppard, C., Wilson, T.: Image formation in confocal scanning microscopes. Optik - Int. J. Light Electron Opt. **55**, 331–342 (1980)
40. Shewchuk, J.R.: An introduction to the conjugate gradient method without the agonizing pain. Technical report, USA (1994)
41. Tao, X., Gao, H., Liao, R., Wang, J., Jia, J.: Detail-revealing deep video super-resolution. In: 2017 IEEE International Conference on Computer Vision (ICCV), pp. 4482–4490 (2017)
42. Tikhonov, A.N.: Solution of incorrectly formulated problems and the regularization method. Soviet Math. Dokl. **4**, 1035–1038 (1963)
43. Tintner, G., Kailath, T.: Linear least-squares estimation (1980)
44. Ulyanov, D., Vedaldi, A., Lempitsky, S.V.: Instance normalization: the missing ingredient for fast stylization. arXiv: 1607.08022. Computer Vision and Pattern Recognition (2016)
45. Wang, Z., Bovik, A.C., Sheikh, H.R., Simoncelli, E.P.: Image quality assessment: from error visibility to structural similarity. IEEE Trans. Image Process. **13**, 600–612 (2004)
46. Wiener, N.: The Extrapolation, Interpolation and Smoothing of Stationary Time Series, with Engineering Applications. Wiley, New York (1949)
47. Wu, Q., Merchant, F., Castleman, K.: Microscope Image Processing. Elsevier (2010)
48. Xu, L., Ren, J.S., Liu, C., Jia, J.: Deep convolutional neural network for image deconvolution. In: Ghahramani, Z., Welling, M., Cortes, C., Lawrence, N.D., Weinberger, K.Q. (eds.) Advances in Neural Information Processing Systems 27, pp. 1790–1798. Curran Associates, Inc. (2014)
49. Zhang, J., Pan, J., Lai, W., Lau, R.W.H., Yang, M.: Learning fully convolutional networks for iterative non-blind deconvolution. In: 2017 IEEE Conference on Computer Vision and Pattern Recognition (CVPR), pp. 6969–6977 (2017)
50. Zhang, K., Zuo, W., Gu, S., Zhang, L.: Learning deep CNN denoiser prior for image restoration. In: 2017 IEEE Conference on Computer Vision and Pattern Recognition (CVPR), pp. 2808–2817 (2017)
51. Zhang, X.: An effective SURE-based Wiener filter for image denoising. In: Liang, Q., Mu, J., Wang, W., Zhang, B. (eds.) CSPS 2016. LNEE, vol. 423, pp. 889–895. Springer, Singapore (2018). https://doi.org/10.1007/978-981-10-3229-5_96
52. Zhang, Y., et al.: A Poisson-Gaussian denoising dataset with real fluorescence microscopy images. In: 2019 IEEE Conference on Computer Vision and Pattern Recognition (2019)
53. Zhao, H., Gallo, O., Frosio, I., Kautz, J.: Loss functions for image restoration with neural networks. IEEE Trans. Comput. Imaging **3**, 47–57 (2017)

ScanRefer: 3D Object Localization in RGB-D Scans Using Natural Language

Dave Zhenyu Chen[1]([✉]), Angel X. Chang[2], and Matthias Nießner[1]

[1] Technical University of Munich, Munich, Germany
zhenyu.chen@tum.de
[2] Simon Fraser University, Burnaby, Canada

Abstract. We introduce the task of 3D object localization in RGB-D scans using natural language descriptions. As input, we assume a point cloud of a scanned 3D scene along with a free-form description of a specified target object. To address this task, we propose **ScanRefer**, learning a fused descriptor from 3D object proposals and encoded sentence embeddings. This fused descriptor correlates language expressions with geometric features, enabling regression of the 3D bounding box of a target object. We also introduce the ScanRefer dataset, containing $51,583$ descriptions of $11,046$ objects from 800 ScanNet [8] scenes. ScanRefer is the first large-scale effort to perform object localization via natural language expression directly in 3D (Code: https://daveredrum.github.io/ScanRefer/).

1 Introduction

In recent years, there has been tremendous progress in both semantic understanding and localization of objects in 2D images from natural language (also known as visual grounding). Datasets such as ReferIt [27], RefCOCO [70], and Flickr30K Entities [46] have enabled the development of various methods for visual grounding in 2D [21,22,38]. However, these methods and datasets are restricted to 2D images, where object localization fails to capture the true 3D extent of an object (see Fig. 1, left). This is a limitation for applications ranging from assistive robots to AR/VR agents where understanding the global 3D context and the physical size is important, e.g., finding objects in large spaces, interacting with them, and understanding their spatial relationships. Early work by Kong et al. [30] looked at coreference in 3D, but was limited to single-view RGB-D images.

In this work, we address these shortcomings by proposing the task of object localization using natural language directly in 3D space. Specifically, we develop a neural network architecture that localizes objects in 3D point clouds given natural language descriptions referring to the underlying objects; i.e., for a given text

Electronic supplementary material The online version of this chapter (https://doi.org/10.1007/978-3-030-58565-5_13) contains supplementary material, which is available to authorized users.

© Springer Nature Switzerland AG 2020
A. Vedaldi et al. (Eds.): ECCV 2020, LNCS 12365, pp. 202–221, 2020.
https://doi.org/10.1007/978-3-030-58565-5_13

Fig. 1. We introduce the task of object localization in 3D scenes using natural language. Given as input a 3D scene and a natural language expression, we predict the bounding box for the target 3D object (right). The counterpart 2D task (left) does not capture the physical extent of the 3D objects.

description in a 3D scene, we predict a corresponding 3D bounding box matching the best-described object. To facilitate the task, we collect the ScanRefer dataset, which provides natural language descriptions for RGB-D scans in Scan-Net [8]. In total, we acquire 51, 583 descriptions of 11, 046 objects. To the best of our knowledge, our ScanRefer dataset is the first large-scale effort that combines 3D scene semantics and free-form descriptions. In summary, our contributions are as follows:

- We introduce the task of localizing objects in 3D environments using natural language descriptions.
- We provide the ScanRefer dataset containing 51, 583 human-written free-form descriptions of 11, 046 objects in 3D scans.
- We propose a neural network architecture for localization based on language descriptions that directly fuses features from 2D images and language expressions with 3D point cloud features.
- We show that our end-to-end method outperforms the best 2D visual grounding method that simply backprojects its 2D predictions to 3D by a significant margin (9.04 Acc@0.5IoU vs. 22.39 Acc@0.5IoU).

2   Related Work

Grounding Referring Expressions in Images. There has been much work connecting images to natural language descriptions across tasks such as image captioning [25,26,58,63], text-to-image retrieval [24,60], and visual grounding [22,38,69]. The task of visual grounding (with variants also known as referring expression comprehension or phrase localization) is to localize a region described by a given referring expression, the query. Localization can be specified by a 2D bounding box [27,38,46] or a segmentation mask [21], with the input description being short phrases [27,46] or more complex descriptions [38].

Table 1. Comparison of referring expression datasets in terms of the number of objects (#objects), number of expressions (#expressions), average lengths of the expressions, data format and the 3D context.

Dataset	#objects	#expressions	AvgLeng	Data format	3D context
ReferIt [27]	96,654	130,364	3.51	Image	–
RefCOCO [70]	50,000	142,209	3.50	Image	–
Google RefExp [38]	49,820	95,010	8.40	Image	–
SUN-Spot [40]	3,245	7,990	14.04	Image	Depth
REVERIE [51]	4,140	21,702	18.00	Image	Panoramic image
ScanRefer (ours)	**11,046**	**51,583**	**20.27**	**3D scan**	**Depth, size, location, etc.**

Recently, Acharya et al. [1] proposed visual query detection where the input is a question. The focus of our work is to lift this task to 3D, focusing on complex descriptions that can localize an unique object in a scene.

Existing methods focus on predicting 2D bounding boxes [11,22,36,45,54, 59,60,69,70] and some predict segmentation masks [5,21,32,34,39,68]. A two-stage pipeline is common, where first an object detector, either unsupervised [73] or pretrained [53], is used to propose regions of interest, and then the regions are ranked by similarity to the query, with the highest scoring region provided as the final output. Other methods address the referring expression task with a single stage end-to-end network [21,42,67]. There are also approaches that incorporate syntax [16,35], use graph attention networks [61,65,66], speaker-listener models [38,71], weakly supervised methods [10,62,72] or tackle zero-shot settings for unseen nouns [55].

However, all these methods operate on 2D image datasets [27,46,70]. A recent dataset [40] integrates RGB-D images but lacks the complete 3D context beyond a single image. Qi et al. [51] study referring expressions in an embodied setting, where semantic annotations are projected from 3D to 2D bounding boxes on images observed by an agent. Our contribution is to lift NLP tasks to 3D by introducing the first large-scale effort that couples free-form descriptions to objects in 3D scans. Table 1 summarizes the difference between our ScanRefer dataset and existing 2D datasets.

Object Detection in 3D. Recent work on 3D object detection on volumetric grids [12,18,19,31,41] has been applied to several 3D RGB-D datasets [3,8,57]. As an alternative to regular grids, point-based methods, such as PointNet [49] or PointNet++ [50], have been used as backbones for 3D detection and/or object instance segmentation [13,64]. Recently, Qi et al. [48] introduced VoteNet, a 3D object detection method for point clouds based on Hough Voting [20]. Our

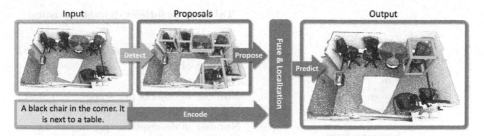

Fig. 2. Our task: ScanRefer takes as input a 3D scene point cloud and a description of an object in the scene, and predicts the object bounding box.

Fig. 3. Our data collection pipeline. The annotator writes a description for the focused object in the scene. Then, a verifier selects the objects that match the description. The selected object is compared with the target object to check that it can be uniquely identified by the description.

approach extracts geometric features in a similar fashion, but backprojects 2D feature information since the color signal is useful for describing 3D objects with natural language.

3D Vision and Language. Vision and language research is gaining popularity in image domains (e.g., image captioning [25,37,58,63], image-text matching [14, 15,23,29,33], and text-to-image generation [15,52,56]), but there is little work on vision and language in 3D. Chen et al. [6] learn a joint embedding of 3D shapes from ShapeNet [4] and corresponding natural language descriptions. Achlioptas et al. [2] disambiguate between different objects using language. Recent work has started to investigate grounding of language to 3D by identifying 3D bounding boxes of target objects for simple arrangements of primitive shapes of different colors [47]. Instead of focusing on isolated objects, we consider large 3D RGB-D reconstructions that are typical in semantic 3D scene understanding. A closely related work by Kong et al. [30] studied the problem of coreference in text description of single-view RGB-D images of scenes, where they aimed to connect noun phrases in a scene description to 3D bounding boxes of objects.

3   Task

We introduce the task of object localization in 3D scenes using natural language (Fig. 2). The input is a 3D scene and free-form text describing an object in the

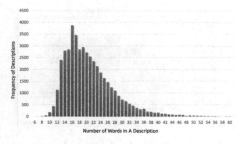

Fig. 4. Description lengths

Table 2. ScanRefer dataset statistics.

Number of descriptions	51,583
Number of scenes	800
Number of objects	11,046
Number of objects per scene	13.81
Number of descriptions per scene	64.48
Number of descriptions per object	4.67
Size of vocabulary	4,197
Average length of descriptions	20.27

| (a) | (b) | (c) | (d) | (e) |

Fig. 5. Word clouds of terms for (a) object names (b) colors (c) shapes (d) sizes, and (e) spatial relations for the ScanRefer dataset. Bigger fonts indicate more frequent terms in the descriptions.

scene. The scene is represented as a point cloud with additional features such as colors and normals for each point. The goal is to predict the 3D bounding box of the object that matches the input description.

4   Dataset

The ScanRefer dataset is based on ScanNet [8] which is composed of 1,613 RGB-D scans taken in 806 unique indoor environments. We provide 5 descriptions for each object in each scene, focusing on complete coverage of all objects that are present in the reconstruction. Here, we summarize the annotation process and statistics of our dataset (see supplement for more details).

4.1   Data Collection

We deploy a web-based annotation interface on Amazon Mechanical Turk (AMT) to collect object descriptions in the ScanNet scenes. The annotation pipeline consists of two stages: i) description collection, and ii) verification (Fig. 3). From each scene, we select objects to annotate by restricting to indoor furniture categories and excluding structural objects such as "Floor" and "Wall". We manually check the selected objects are recognizable and filter out objects with reconstructions that are too incomplete or hard to identify.

Annotation. The 3D web-based UI shows each object in context. The workers see all objects other than the target object faded out and a set of captured image frames to compensate for incomplete details in the reconstructions. The initial viewpoint is random but includes the target object. Camera controls allow for adjusting the camera view to better examine the target object. We ask the annotator to describe the appearance of the target and its spatial location relative to other objects. To ensure the descriptions are informative, we require the annotator to provide at least two full sentences. We batch and randomize the tasks so that each object is described by five different workers.

Verification. We recruit trained workers (students) to verify that the descriptions are discriminative and correct. Verifiers are shown the 3D scene and a description, and are asked to select the objects (potentially multiple) in the scene that match the description. Descriptions that result in the wrong object or multiple objects are filtered out. Verifiers also correct spelling and wording issues in the description when necessary. We filter out 2,823 invalid descriptions that do not match the target objects and fix writing issues for 2,129 descriptions.

4.2 Dataset Statistics

We collected 51,583 descriptions for 800 ScanNet scenes[1]. On average, there are 13.81 objects, 64.48 descriptions per scene, and 4.67 descriptions per object after filtering (see Table 2 for basic statistics, Table 3 for sample descriptions, and Fig. 4 for the distribution of the description lengths). The descriptions are complex and diverse, covering over 250 types of common indoor objects, and exhibiting interesting linguistic phenomena. Due to the complexity of the descriptions, one of the key challenges of our task is to determine what parts of the description describe the target object, and what parts describe neighboring objects. Among those descriptions, 41,034 mention object attributes such as color, shape, size, etc. We find that many people use spatial language (98.7%), color (74.7%), and shape terms (64.9%). In contrast, only 14.2% of the descriptions convey size information. Figure 5 shows commonly used object names and attributes. Table 3 shows interesting expressions, including comparatives ("taller") and superlatives ("the biggest one"), as well as phrases involving ordinals such as "third from the wall". Overall, there are 672 and 2,734 descriptions with comparative and superlative phrases. We provide more detailed statistics in the supplement.

5   Method

Our architecture consists of two main modules: 1) detection & encoding; 2) fusion & localization (Fig. 6). The detection & encoding module encodes the input point cloud and description, and outputs the object proposals and the language embedding, which are fed into the fusion module to mask out invalid object proposals and produce the fused features. Finally, the object proposal with the highest confidence predicted by the localization module is chosen as the final output.

---

[1] 6 scenes are excluded since they do not contain any objects to describe.

Table 3. Examples from our dataset illustrating different types of phrases such as attributes (1–8) and parts (5), comparatives (4), superlatives (5), intra-class spatial relations (6), inter-class spatial relations (7) and ordinal numbers (8).

1.	There is a brown wooden chair placed right against the wall
2.	This is a triangular shape table. The table is near the armchair
3.	The little nightstand. The nightstand is on the right of the bed
4.	This is a short trash can. It is in front of a taller trash can
5.	The couch is the biggest one below the picture. The couch has three seats and is brown
6.	This is a gray desk chair. This chair is the last one on the side closest to the open door
7.	The kitchen counter is covering the lower cabinets. The kitchen counter is under the upper cabinets that are mounted above
8.	This is a round bar stool. It is third from the wall

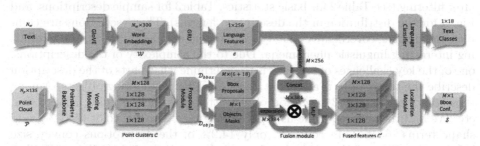

Fig. 6. ScanRefer architecture: The PointNet++ [50] backbone takes as input a point cloud and aggregates it to high-level point feature maps, which are then clustered and fused as object proposals by a voting module similar to Qi et al. [48]. Object proposals are masked by the objectness predictions, and then fused with the sentence embedding of the input descriptions, which is obtained by a GloVE [44] + GRU [7] embedding. In addition, an extra language-to-object classifier serves as a proxy loss. We apply a softmax function in the localization module to output the confidence scores for the object proposals.

5.1 Data Representations

Point Clouds. We randomly sample N_P vertices of one scan from ScanNet as the input point cloud $\mathcal{P} = \{(p_i, f_i)\}$, where $p_i \in \mathcal{R}^3$ represents the point coordinates in 3D space and f_i stands for additional point features such as colors and normals. Note that the point coordinates p_i provides only geometrical information and does not contain other visual information such as color and texture. Since descriptions of objects do refer to attributes such as color and texture, we incorporate visual appearance by adapting the feature projection scheme in Dai et al. [9] to project multi-view image features $v_i \in \mathcal{R}^{128}$ to the point cloud. The image features are extracted using a pre-trained ENet [43]. Following Qi et al. [48], we also append the height of the point from the ground and normals to the new point features $f_i' \in \mathcal{R}^{135}$. The final point cloud data is prepared offline as $\mathcal{P}' = \{(p_i, f_i')\} \in \mathcal{R}^{N_P \times 135}$. We set N_P to $40,000$ in our experiments.

Descriptions. We tokenize the input description with SpaCy [17] and the N_W tokens to 300-dimensional word embedding vectors $\mathcal{W} = \{w_j\} \in \mathcal{R}^{N_W \times 300}$ using pretrained GloVE word embeddings [44].

5.2 Network Architecture

Our method takes as input the preprocessed point cloud $\mathcal{P}'$ and the word embedding sequence $\mathcal{W}$ representing the input description and outputs the 3D bounding box for the proposal which is most likely referred to by the input description. Conceptually, our localization pipeline consists of the following four stages: detection, encoding, fusion and localization.

Detection. As the first step in our network, we detect all probable objects in the given point cloud. To construct our detection module, we adapt the Point-Net++ [50] backbone and the voting module in Qi et al. [48] to process the point cloud input and aggregate all object candidates to individual clusters. The output from the voting module is a set of point clusters $\mathcal{C} \in \mathcal{R}^{M \times 128}$ representing all object proposals with enriched point features, where M is the upper bound of the number of proposals. Next, the proposal module takes in the point clusters and processes those clusters to predict the objectness mask $\mathcal{D}_{objn} \in \mathcal{R}^{M \times 1}$ and the axis-aligned bounding boxes $\mathcal{D}_{bbox} \in \mathcal{R}^{M \times (6+18)}$ for all M proposals, where each $\mathcal{D}_{bbox}^i = (c_x, c_y, c_z, r_x, r_y, r_z, l)$ consists of the box center c, the box lengths r and a vector $l \in \mathcal{R}^{18}$ representing the semantic predictions.

Encoding. The sequences of word embedding vectors of the input description are fed into a GRU cell [7] to aggregate the textual information. We take the final hidden state $e \in \mathcal{R}^{256}$ of the GRU cell as the final language embedding.

Fusion. The outputs from the previous detection and encoding modules are fed into the fusion module (orange block in Fig. 6, see supplemental for details) to integrate the point features together with the language embeddings. Specifically, each feature vector $c_i \in \mathcal{R}^{128}$ in the point cluster $\mathcal{C}$ is concatenated with the language embedding $e \in \mathcal{R}^{256}$ as the extended feature vector, which is then masked by the predicted objectness mask $\mathcal{D}_{objn}^i \in \{0, 1\}$ and fused by a multi-layer perceptron as the final fused cluster features $\mathcal{C}' = \{c_i'\} \in \mathcal{R}^{M \times 128}$.

Localization. The localization module aims to predict which of the proposed bounding boxes corresponds to the description. Point clusters with fused cluster features $\mathcal{C}' = \{c_i'\}$ are processed by a single layer perceptron to produce the raw scores of how likely each box is the target box. We use a softmax function to squash all the raw scores into the interval of $[0,1]$ as the localization confidences $S = \{s_i\} \in \mathcal{R}^{M \times 1}$ for the proposed M bounding boxes.

5.3 Loss Function

Localization Loss. For the predicted localization confidence $s_i \in [0,1]$ for object proposal $\mathcal{D}^i_{\text{bbox}}$, the target label is represented as $t_i \in \{0,1\}$. Following the strategy of Yang et al. [67], we set the label t_j for the jth box that has the highest IoU score with the ground truth box as 1 and others as 0. We then use a cross-entropy loss as the localization loss $\mathcal{L}_{\text{loc}} = -\sum_{i=1}^{M} t_i \log(s_i)$.

Object Detection Loss. We use the same detection loss $\mathcal{L}_{det}$ as introduced in Qi et al. [48] for object proposals $\mathcal{D}^i_{\text{bbox}}$ and $\mathcal{D}^i_{\text{objn}}$: $\mathcal{L}_{\text{det}} = \mathcal{L}_{\text{vote-reg}} + 0.5\mathcal{L}_{\text{objn-cls}} + \mathcal{L}_{\text{box}} + 0.1\mathcal{L}_{\text{sem-cls}}$, where $\mathcal{L}_{\text{vote-reg}}$, $\mathcal{L}_{\text{objn-cls}}$, $\mathcal{L}_{\text{box}}$ and $\mathcal{L}_{\text{sem-cls}}$ represent the vote regression loss (defined in Qi et al. [48]), the objectness binary classification loss, box regression loss and the semantic classification loss for the 18 ScanNet benchmark classes, respectively. We ignore the bounding box orientations in our task and simplify $\mathcal{L}_{\text{box}}$ as $\mathcal{L}_{\text{box}} = \mathcal{L}_{\text{center-reg}} + 0.1\mathcal{L}_{\text{size-cls}} + \mathcal{L}_{\text{size-reg}}$, where $\mathcal{L}_{\text{center-reg}}$, $\mathcal{L}_{\text{size-cls}}$ and $\mathcal{L}_{\text{size-reg}}$ are used for regressing the box center, classifying the box size and regressing the box size, respectively. We refer readers to Qi et al. [48] for more details.

Language to Object Classification Loss. To further supervise the training, we include an object classification loss based on the input description. We consider the 18 ScanNet benchmark classes (excluding the label "Floor" and "Wall"). The language to object classification loss $\mathcal{L}_{\text{cls}}$ is a multi-class cross-entropy loss.

Final Loss. The final loss is a linear combination of the localization loss, object detection loss and the language to object classification loss: $\mathcal{L} = \alpha\mathcal{L}_{\text{loc}} + \beta\mathcal{L}_{\text{det}} + \gamma\mathcal{L}_{\text{cls}}$, where α, β and γ are the weights for the individual loss terms. After fine-tuning on the validation split, we set those weights to 1, 10, and 10 in our experiments to ensure the loss terms are roughly of the same magnitude.

5.4 Training and Inference

Training. During training, the detection and encoding modules propose object candidates as point clusters, which are then fed into the fusion and localization modules to fuse the features from the previous module and predict the final bounding boxes. We train the detection backbone end-to-end with the detection loss. In the localization module, we use a softmax function to compress the raw scores to $[0,1]$. The higher the predicted confidence is, the more likely the proposal will be chosen as output. To filter out invalid object proposals, we use the predicted objectness mask to ensure that only positive proposals are taken into account. We set the maximum number of proposals M to 256 in practice.

Inference. Since there can be overlapping detections, we apply a non-maximum suppression module to suppress those overlapping proposals in the inference step. The remaining object proposals are fed into the localization module to predict the final score for each proposal. The number of object proposals is less than the upper bound M in the training step.

Implementation Details. We implement our architecture using PyTorch and train the model end-to-end using ADAM [28] with a learning rate of 1e−3. We train the model for roughly 130,000 iterations until convergence. To avoid overfitting, we set the weight decay factor to 1e−5 and apply data augmentations to our training data. For point clouds, we apply rotation about all three axes by a random angle in $[-5°, 5°]$ and randomly translate the point cloud within 0.5 meters in all directions. We rotate around all axes (not just up), since the ground alignment in ScanNet is imperfect.

6 Experiments

Train/Val/Test Split. Following the official ScanNet [8] split, we split our data into train/val/test sets with 36,665, 9,508 and 5,410 samples respectively, ensuring disjoint scenes for each split. Results and analysis are conducted on the val split (except for results in Table 4 bottom). The test set is hidden and will be reserved for the ScanRefer benchmark.

Metric. To evaluate the performance of our method, we measure the thresholded accuracy where the positive predictions have higher intersection over union (IoU) with the ground truths than the thresholds. Similar to work with 2D images, we use Acc@kIoU as our metric, where the threshold value k for IoU is set to 0.25 and 0.5 in our experiments.

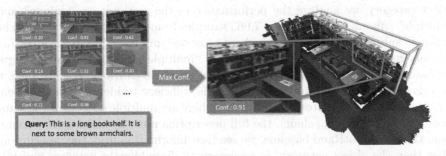

Fig. 7. Object localization in an image using a 2D grounding method and back-projecting the result to the 3D scene (blue box) vs. directly localizing in the 3D scene (green box). Grounding in 2D images suffers from the limited view of a single frame, which results in inaccurate 3D bounding boxes. (Color figure online)

Baselines. We design several baselines by 1) evaluating our language localization module on ground truth bounding boxes, 2) adapting 3D object detectors, and 3) adapting 2D referring methods to 3D using back-projection.

OracleCatRand & OracleRefer: To examine the difficulty of our task, we use an oracle with ground truth bounding boxes of objects, and predict the box by simply selecting a random box that matches the object category (OracleCatRand) or our trained fusion and localization modules (OracleRefer).

VoteNetRand & VoteNetBest: From the predicted object proposals of the VoteNet backbone [48], we select one of the bounding box proposals, either by selecting a box randomly with the correct semantic class label (VoteNetRand) or the best matching box given the ground truth (VoteNetBest). VoteNetBest provides an upper bound on how well the object detection component works for our task, while VoteNetRand provides a measure of whether additional information beyond the semantic label is required.

SCRC & One-Stage: 2D image baselines for referring expression comprehension by extending SCRC [22] and One-stage [67] to 3D using back-projection. Since 2D referring expression methods operate on a single image frame, we construct a 2D training set by using the recorded camera pose associated with each annotation to retrieve the frame from the scan video with the closest camera pose. At inference time, we sample frames from the scans (using every 20th frame) and predict the target 2D bounding boxes in each frame. We then select the 2D bounding box with the highest confidence score from the bounding box candidates and project it to 3D using the depth map for that frame (see Fig. 7).

Ours: We compare our full end-to-end model against using a pretrained VoteNet backbone with a trained GRU [7] for selecting a matching bounding box.

6.1   Task Difficulty

To understand how informative the input description is beyond capturing the object category, we analyze the performance of the methods on "unique" and "multiple" subsets with 1,875 and 7,663 samples from val split, respectively. The "unique" subset contains samples where only one unique object from a certain category matches the description, while the "multiple" subset contains ambiguous cases where there are multiple objects of the same category. For instance, if there is only one refrigerator in a scene, it is sufficient to identify that the sentence refers to a refrigerator. In contrast, if there are multiple objects of the same category in a scene (e.g., chair), the full description must be taken into account. From the OracleCatRand baseline, we see that information from the description, other than the object category, is necessary to disambiguate between multiple objects (see Table 4 Acc@0.5IoU multiple). From the OracleRefer baseline, we see that using our fused language module, we are able to improve beyond over selecting a random object of the same category (multiple Acc@0.5IoU increases from 17.84% to 32.00%), but we often fail to identify the correct object category (unique Acc@0.5IoU drops from 100.0% to 73.55%).

Table 4. Comparison of localization results obtained by our ScanRefer and baseline models. We measure percentage of predictions whose IoU with the ground truth boxes are greater than 0.25 and 0.5. We also report scores on "unique" and "multiple" subsets; unique means that there is only a single object of its class in the scene. We outperform all baselines by a significant margin.

	Unique		Multiple		Overall	
	Acc@0.25	Acc@0.5	Acc@0.25	Acc@0.5	Acc@0.25	Acc@0.5
OracleCatRand (GT boxes + RandCat)	100.00	100.00	18.09	17.84	29.99	29.76
OracleRefer (GT boxes + GRU)	74.09	73.55	32.57	32.00	40.63	40.06
VoteNetRand (VoteNet [48] + RandCat)	34.34	19.35	5.73	2.81	10.00	5.28
VoteNetBest (VoteNet [48] + Best)	88.85	85.50	46.63	46.42	55.10	54.33
SCRC [22] + backproj	24.03	9.22	17.77	5.97	18.70	6.45
One-stage [67] + backproj	29.32	22.82	18.72	6.49	20.38	9.04
Ours (VoteNet [48] + GRU)	55.09	37.66	26.37	16.03	32.49	20.53
Ours (end-to-end)	**63.04**	**39.95**	**28.91**	**18.17**	**35.53**	**22.39**
Test results (ScanRefer benchmark)						
OracleRefer (GT boxes + GRU)	72.37	71.84	31.81	31.26	39.69	39.13
VoteNetBest (VoteNet [48] + Best)	86.78	83.85	45.54	45.33	53.82	53.07
Ours (VoteNet [48] + GRU)	57.67	36.96	28.31	15.16	34.90	20.05
Ours (end-to-end)	**62.90**	**40.31**	**30.88**	**16.54**	**38.06**	**21.87**

6.2   Quantitative Analysis

We evaluate the performance of our model against baselines on the val and the hidden test split of ScanRefer which serves as the ScanRefer benchmark (see Table 4). Note that for all results using Ours and VoteNet for object proposal, we take the average of 5 differently seeded subsamplings (of seed points and vote points) during inference (see supplemental for more details on experimental variance). Training the detection backbone jointly with the localization module (end-to-end) leads to a better performance when compared to the model trained separately (VoteNet [48] + GRU). However, as the accuracy gap between VoteNetBest and ours (end-to-end) indicates, there is still room for improving the match between language inputs and the visual signals. For the val split, we also include additional experiments on the 2D baselines and a comparison with VoteNetRand. With just category information, VoteNetRand is able to perform relatively well on the "unique" subset, but has trouble identifying the correct object in the "multiple" case. However, the gap between the VoteNetRand and OracleCatRand for the "unique" case shows that 3D object detection still need to be improved. Our method is able to improve over the bounding box predic-

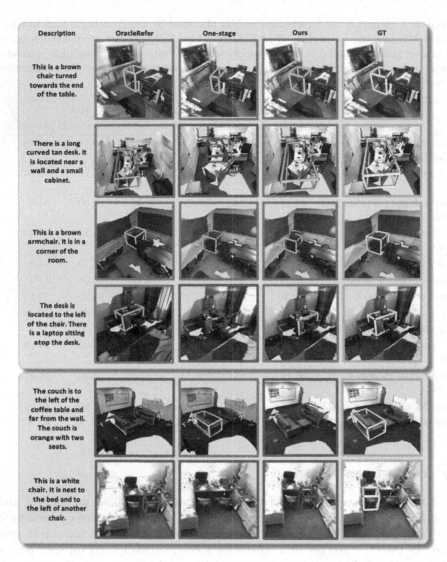

Fig. 8. Qualitative results from baseline methods and ScanRefer. Predicted boxes are marked green if they have an IoU score higher than 0.5, otherwise they are marked red. We show examples where our method produced good predictions (blue block) as well as failure cases (orange block). Image best viewed in color. (Color figure online)

tions from VoteNetRand, and leverages additional information in the description to differentiate between ambiguous objects. It adapts better to the 3D context compared to the 2D methods (SCRC and One-stage) which is limited by the view of a single frame (see Fig. 7 and Fig. 8).

Table 5. Ablation study with different features. We measure the percentages of predictions whose IoU with the ground truth boxes are greater than 0.25 and 0.5. Unique means that there is only a single object of its class in the scene.

	Unique		Multiple		Overall	
	Acc@0.25	Acc@0.5	Acc@0.25	Acc@0.5	Acc@0.25	Acc@0.5
Ours (xyz)	50.83	31.81	24.38	13.98	29.51	17.43
Ours (xyz+rgb)	51.22	32.09	24.50	14.51	29.68	17.92
Ours (xyz+rgb+normals)	54.24	33.71	25.44	15.53	31.05	19.05
Ours (xyz+multiview)	56.69	35.32	25.83	14.26	31.63	19.75
Ours (xyz+multiview+normals)	55.27	35.51	25.95	16.29	31.64	20.02
Ours (xyz+lobjcls)	58.92	35.01	28.27	16.99	34.21	20.49
Ours (xyz+rgb+lobjcls)	60.11	37.89	27.21	16.49	33.59	20.65
Ours (xyz+rgb+normals+lobjcls)	60.54	39.19	26.95	16.69	33.47	21.06
Ours (xyz+multiview+lobjcls)	61.16	39.02	26.49	16.69	34.71	21.87
Ours (xyz+multiview+normals+lobjcls)	**63.04**	**39.95**	**28.91**	**18.17**	**35.53**	**22.39**

6.3 Qualitative Analysis

Figure 8 shows results produced by OracleRefer, One-stage, and our method. The successful localization cases in the green boxes show our architecture can handle the semantic correlation between the scene contexts and the textual descriptions. In contrast, even provided with a pool of ground truth proposals, OracleRefer sometimes still fails to predict correct bounding boxes, while One-stage is limited by the single view and hence cannot produce accurate bounding boxes in 3D space. The failure case of OracleRefer suggests that our fusion & localization module can still be improved. Some failure cases of our method are displayed in the orange block in Fig. 8, indicating that our architecture cannot handle all spatial relations to distinguish between ambiguous objects.

6.4 Ablation Studies

We conduct an ablation study on our model to examine what components and point cloud features contribute to the performance (see Table 5).

Does a Language-Based Object Classifier Help? To show the effectiveness of the extra supervision on input descriptions, we conduct an experiment with the language to object classifier (+lobjcls) and without. Architectures with a language to object classifier outperform ones without it. This indicates that it is helpful to predict the category of the target object based on the input description.

Do Colors Help? We compare our method trained with the geometry and multi-view image features (xyz+multiview+lobjcls) with a model trained with only geometry (xyz+lobjcls) and one trained with RGB values from the reconstructed meshes (xyz+rgb+lobjcls). ScanRefer trained with geometry and preprocessed multi-view image features outperforms the other two models. The performance of models with color information are higher than those that use only geometry.

Do Other Features Help? We include normals from the ScanNet meshes to the input point cloud features and compare performance against networks trained without them. The additional 3D information improves performance. Our architecture trained with geometry, multi-view features, and normals (xyz+multiview+ normals+lobjcls) achieves the best performance among all ablations.

7   Conclusion

In this work, we introduce the task of localizing a target object in a 3D point cloud using natural language descriptions. We collect the ScanReferdataset which contains 51,583 unique descriptions for 11,046 objects from 800 ScanNet [8] scenes. We propose an end-to-end method for localizing an object with a free-formed description as reference, which first proposes point clusters of interest and then matches them to the embeddings of the input sentence. Our architecture is capable of learning the semantic similarities of the given contexts and regressing the bounding boxes for the target objects. Overall, we hope that our new dataset and method will enable future research in the 3D visual language field.

Acknowledgements. We would like to thank the expert annotators Josefina Manieu Seguel and Rinu Shaji Mariam, all anonymous workers on Amazon Mechanical Turk and the student volunteers (Akshit Sharma, Yue Ruan, Ali Gholami, Yasaman Etesam, Leon Kochiev, Sonia Raychaudhuri) at Simon Fraser University for their efforts in building the ScanRefer dataset, and Akshit Sharma for helping with statistics and figures. This work is funded by Google (AugmentedPerception), the ERC Starting Grant Scan2CAD (804724), and a Google Faculty Award. We would also like to thank the support of the TUM-IAS Rudolf Mößbauer and Hans Fischer Fellowships (Focus Group Visual Computing), as well as the German Research Foundation (DFG) under the Grant *Making Machine Learning on Static and Dynamic 3D Data Practical*. Angel X. Chang is supported by the Canada CIFAR AI Chair program. Finally, we thank Angela Dai for the video voice-over.

References

1. Acharya, M., Jariwala, K., Kanan, C.: VQD: visual query detection in natural scenes. In: Proceedings of the Conference of the North American Chapter of the Association for Computational Linguistics (NAACL) (2019)
2. Achlioptas, P., Fan, J., Hawkins, R.X., Goodman, N.D., Guibas, L.J.: ShapeGlot: learning language for shape differentiation. In: Proceedings of the International Conference on Computer Vision (ICCV) (2019)
3. Chang, A., et al.: Matterport3D: learning from RGB-D data in indoor environments. In: Proceedings of the International Conference on 3D Vision (3DV) (2017)
4. Chang, A.X., et al.: ShapeNet: an information-rich 3D model repository. arXiv preprint arXiv:1512.03012 (2015)

5. Chen, D.J., Jia, S., Lo, Y.C., Chen, H.T., Liu, T.L.: See-through-text grouping for referring image segmentation. In: Proceedings of the IEEE International Conference on Computer Vision, pp. 7454–7463 (2019)
6. Chen, K., Choy, C.B., Savva, M., Chang, A.X., Funkhouser, T., Savarese, S.: Text2Shape: generating shapes from natural language by learning joint embeddings. In: Jawahar, C.V., Li, H., Mori, G., Schindler, K. (eds.) ACCV 2018. LNCS, vol. 11363, pp. 100–116. Springer, Cham (2019). https://doi.org/10.1007/978-3-030-20893-6_7
7. Chung, J., Gulcehre, C., Cho, K., Bengio, Y.: Empirical evaluation of gated recurrent neural networks on sequence modeling. arXiv preprint arXiv:1412.3555 (2014)
8. Dai, A., Chang, A.X., Savva, M., Halber, M., Funkhouser, T., Nießner, M.: ScanNet: Richly-annotated 3D reconstructions of indoor scenes. In: Proceedings of the Computer Vision and Pattern Recognition (CVPR) (2017)
9. Dai, A., Nießner, M.: 3DMV: joint 3D-multi-view prediction for 3D semantic scene segmentation. In: Ferrari, V., Hebert, M., Sminchisescu, C., Weiss, Y. (eds.) ECCV 2018. LNCS, vol. 11214, pp. 458–474. Springer, Cham (2018). https://doi.org/10.1007/978-3-030-01249-6_28
10. Datta, S., Sikka, K., Roy, A., Ahuja, K., Parikh, D., Divakaran, A.: Align2Ground: weakly supervised phrase grounding guided by image-caption alignment. In: Proceedings of the IEEE International Conference on Computer Vision (2019)
11. Dogan, P., Sigal, L., Gross, M.: Neural sequential phrase grounding (SeqGROUND). In: Proceedings of the IEEE Conference on Computer Vision and Pattern Recognition, pp. 4175–4184 (2019)
12. Elich, C., Engelmann, F., Schult, J., Kontogianni, T., Leibe, B.: 3D-BEVIS: birds-eye-view instance segmentation. arXiv preprint arXiv:1904.02199 (2019)
13. Engelmann, F., Kontogianni, T., Leibe, B.: Dilated point convolutions: on the receptive field of point convolutions. arXiv preprint arXiv:1907.12046 (2019)
14. Feng, F., Wang, X., Li, R.: Cross-modal retrieval with correspondence autoencoder. In: Proceedings of the 22nd ACM International Conference on Multimedia, pp. 7–16. ACM (2014)
15. Gu, J., Cai, J., Joty, S.R., Niu, L., Wang, G.: Look, imagine and match: improving textual-visual cross-modal retrieval with generative models. In: Proceedings of the IEEE Conference on Computer Vision and Pattern Recognition, pp. 7181–7189 (2018)
16. Hong, R., Liu, D., Mo, X., He, X., Zhang, H.: Learning to compose and reason with language tree structures for visual grounding. IEEE Trans. Pattern Anal. Mach. Intell. (2019)
17. Honnibal, M., Montani, I.: spaCy 2: natural language understanding with Bloom embeddings, convolutional neural networks and incremental parsing (2017, to appear)
18. Hou, J., Dai, A., Nießner, M.: 3D-SIC: 3D semantic instance completion for RGB-D scans. arXiv preprint arXiv:1904.12012 (2019)
19. Hou, J., Dai, A., Nießner, M.: 3D-SIS: 3D semantic instance segmentation of RGB-D scans. In: Proceedings of the IEEE Conference on Computer Vision and Pattern Recognition, pp. 4421–4430 (2019)
20. Hough, P.V.: Machine analysis of bubble chamber pictures. In: Conference Proceedings, vol. 590914, pp. 554–558 (1959)
21. Hu, R., Rohrbach, M., Darrell, T.: Segmentation from natural language expressions. In: Leibe, B., Matas, J., Sebe, N., Welling, M. (eds.) ECCV 2016. LNCS, vol. 9905, pp. 108–124. Springer, Cham (2016). https://doi.org/10.1007/978-3-319-46448-0_7

22. Hu, R., Xu, H., Rohrbach, M., Feng, J., Saenko, K., Darrell, T.: Natural language object retrieval. In: Proceedings of the IEEE Conference on Computer Vision and Pattern Recognition, pp. 4555–4564 (2016)
23. Huang, Y., Wang, W., Wang, L.: Instance-aware image and sentence matching with selective multimodal LSTM. In: Proceedings of the IEEE Conference on Computer Vision and Pattern Recognition, pp. 2310–2318 (2017)
24. Huang, Y., Wu, Q., Song, C., Wang, L.: Learning semantic concepts and order for image and sentence matching. In: Proceedings of the IEEE Conference on Computer Vision and Pattern Recognition, pp. 6163–6171 (2018)
25. Karpathy, A., Fei-Fei, L.: Deep visual-semantic alignments for generating image descriptions. In: Proceedings of the IEEE Conference on Computer Vision and Pattern Recognition, pp. 3128–3137 (2015)
26. Karpathy, A., Joulin, A., Fei-Fei, L.: Deep fragment embeddings for bidirectional image sentence mapping. In: Advances in Neural Information Processing Systems, pp. 1889–1897 (2014)
27. Kazemzadeh, S., Ordonez, V., Matten, M., Berg, T.: ReferItGame: referring to objects in photographs of natural scenes. In: Proceedings of the 2014 Conference on Empirical Methods in Natural Language Processing (EMNLP), pp. 787–798 (2014)
28. Kingma, D.P., Ba, J.: Adam: a method for stochastic optimization. arXiv preprint arXiv:1412.6980 (2014)
29. Kiros, R., Salakhutdinov, R., Zemel, R.S.: Unifying visual-semantic embeddings with multimodal neural language models. arXiv preprint arXiv:1411.2539 (2014)
30. Kong, C., Lin, D., Bansal, M., Urtasun, R., Fidler, S.: What are you talking about? Text-to-image coreference. In: Proceedings of the IEEE Conference on Computer Vision and Pattern Recognition, pp. 3558–3565 (2014)
31. Lahoud, J., Ghanem, B., Pollefeys, M., Oswald, M.R.: 3D instance segmentation via multi-task metric learning. arXiv preprint arXiv:1906.08650 (2019)
32. Li, R., et al.: Referring image segmentation via recurrent refinement networks. In: Proceedings of the IEEE Conference on Computer Vision and Pattern Recognition, pp. 5745–5753 (2018)
33. Li, S., Xiao, T., Li, H., Yang, W., Wang, X.: Identity-aware textual-visual matching with latent co-attention. In: Proceedings of the IEEE International Conference on Computer Vision, pp. 1890–1899 (2017)
34. Liu, C., Lin, Z., Shen, X., Yang, J., Lu, X., Yuille, A.: Recurrent multimodal interaction for referring image segmentation. In: Proceedings of the IEEE International Conference on Computer Vision, pp. 1271–1280 (2017)
35. Liu, D., Zhang, H., Wu, F., Zha, Z.J.: Learning to assemble neural module tree networks for visual grounding. In: Proceedings of the IEEE International Conference on Computer Vision, pp. 4673–4682 (2019)
36. Liu, X., Wang, Z., Shao, J., Wang, X., Li, H.: Improving referring expression grounding with cross-modal attention-guided erasing. In: Proceedings of the IEEE Conference on Computer Vision and Pattern Recognition, pp. 1950–1959 (2019)
37. Lu, J., Xiong, C., Parikh, D., Socher, R.: Knowing when to look: adaptive attention via a visual sentinel for image captioning. In: Proceedings of the IEEE Conference on Computer Vision and Pattern Recognition, pp. 375–383 (2017)
38. Mao, J., Huang, J., Toshev, A., Camburu, O., Yuille, A.L., Murphy, K.: Generation and comprehension of unambiguous object descriptions. In: Proceedings of the IEEE Conference on Computer Vision and Pattern Recognition, pp. 11–20 (2016)

39. Margffoy-Tuay, E., Pérez, J.C., Botero, E., Arbeláez, P.: Dynamic multimodal instance segmentation guided by natural language queries. In: Ferrari, V., Hebert, M., Sminchisescu, C., Weiss, Y. (eds.) ECCV 2018. LNCS, vol. 11215, pp. 656–672. Springer, Cham (2018). https://doi.org/10.1007/978-3-030-01252-6_39

40. Mauceri, C., Palmer, M., Heckman, C.: SUN-Spot: an RGB-D dataset with spatial referring expressions. In: Proceedings of the IEEE International Conference on Computer Vision Workshops (2019)

41. Narita, G., Seno, T., Ishikawa, T., Kaji, Y.: PanopticFusion: online volumetric semantic mapping at the level of stuff and things. arXiv preprint arXiv:1903.01177 (2019)

42. Nguyen, A., Do, T.T., Reid, I., Caldwell, D.G., Tsagarakis, N.G.: Object captioning and retrieval with natural language. arXiv preprint arXiv:1803.06152 (2018)

43. Paszke, A., Chaurasia, A., Kim, S., Culurciello, E.: ENet: a deep neural network architecture for real-time semantic segmentation. arXiv preprint arXiv:1606.02147 (2016)

44. Pennington, J., Socher, R., Manning, C.: Glove: global vectors for word representation. In: Proceedings of the 2014 Conference on Empirical Methods in Natural Language Processing (EMNLP), pp. 1532–1543 (2014)

45. Plummer, B.A., Kordas, P., Kiapour, M.H., Zheng, S., Piramuthu, R., Lazebnik, S.: Conditional image-text embedding networks. In: Ferrari, V., Hebert, M., Sminchisescu, C., Weiss, Y. (eds.) ECCV 2018. LNCS, vol. 11216, pp. 258–274. Springer, Cham (2018). https://doi.org/10.1007/978-3-030-01258-8_16

46. Plummer, B.A., Wang, L., Cervantes, C.M., Caicedo, J.C., Hockenmaier, J., Lazebnik, S.: Flickr30k entities: collecting region-to-phrase correspondences for richer image-to-sentence models. In: Proceedings of the IEEE International Conference on Computer Vision, pp. 2641–2649 (2015)

47. Prabhudesai, M., Tung, H.Y.F., Javed, S.A., Sieb, M., Harley, A.W., Fragkiadaki, K.: Embodied language grounding with implicit 3D visual feature representations. arXiv preprint arXiv:1910.01210 (2019)

48. Qi, C.R., Litany, O., He, K., Guibas, L.J.: Deep hough voting for 3D object detection in point clouds. In: Proceedings of the IEEE International Conference on Computer Vision (2019)

49. Qi, C.R., Su, H., Mo, K., Guibas, L.J.: PointNet: deep learning on point sets for 3D classification and segmentation. In: Proceedings of the IEEE Conference on Computer Vision and Pattern Recognition, pp. 652–660 (2017)

50. Qi, C.R., Yi, L., Su, H., Guibas, L.J.: PointNet++: deep hierarchical feature learning on point sets in a metric space. In: Advances in Neural Information Processing Systems, pp. 5099–5108 (2017)

51. Qi, Y., Wu, Q., Anderson, P., Liu, M., Shen, C., van den Hengel, A.: REVERIE: remote embodied visual referring expression in real indoor environments. In: Proceedings of the IEEE Conference on Computer Vision and Pattern Recognition (2020)

52. Reed, S., Akata, Z., Yan, X., Logeswaran, L., Schiele, B., Lee, H.: Generative adversarial text to image synthesis. arXiv preprint arXiv:1605.05396 (2016)

53. Ren, S., He, K., Girshick, R., Sun, J.: Faster R-CNN: towards real-time object detection with region proposal networks. In: Advances in Neural Information Processing Systems, pp. 91–99 (2015)

54. Rohrbach, A., Rohrbach, M., Hu, R., Darrell, T., Schiele, B.: Grounding of textual phrases in images by reconstruction. In: Leibe, B., Matas, J., Sebe, N., Welling, M. (eds.) ECCV 2016. LNCS, vol. 9905, pp. 817–834. Springer, Cham (2016). https://doi.org/10.1007/978-3-319-46448-0_49

55. Sadhu, A., Chen, K., Nevatia, R.: Zero-shot grounding of objects from natural language queries. In: Proceedings of the IEEE International Conference on Computer Vision, pp. 4694–4703 (2019)
56. Sharma, S., Suhubdy, D., Michalski, V., Kahou, S.E., Bengio, Y.: Chat-Painter: improving text to image generation using dialogue. arXiv preprint arXiv:1802.08216 (2018)
57. Song, S., Lichtenberg, S.P., Xiao, J.: SUN RGB-D: a RGB-D scene understanding benchmark suite. In: Proceedings of the IEEE Conference on Computer Vision and Pattern Recognition, pp. 567–576 (2015)
58. Vinyals, O., Toshev, A., Bengio, S., Erhan, D.: Show and tell: a neural image caption generator. In: Proceedings of the IEEE Conference on Computer Vision and Pattern Recognition, pp. 3156–3164 (2015)
59. Wang, L., Li, Y., Huang, J., Lazebnik, S.: Learning two-branch neural networks for image-text matching tasks. IEEE Trans. Pattern Anal. Mach. Intell. **41**(2), 394–407 (2018)
60. Wang, L., Li, Y., Lazebnik, S.: Learning deep structure-preserving image-text embeddings. In: Proceedings of the IEEE Conference on Computer Vision and Pattern Recognition, pp. 5005–5013 (2016)
61. Wang, P., Wu, Q., Cao, J., Shen, C., Gao, L., van den Hengel, A.: Neighbourhood watch: referring expression comprehension via language-guided graph attention networks. In: Proceedings of the IEEE Conference on Computer Vision and Pattern Recognition, pp. 1960–1968 (2019)
62. Xiao, F., Sigal, L., Jae Lee, Y.: Weakly-supervised visual grounding of phrases with linguistic structures. In: Proceedings of the IEEE Conference on Computer Vision and Pattern Recognition, pp. 5945–5954 (2017)
63. Xu, K., et al.: Show, attend and tell: neural image caption generation with visual attention. In: International Conference on Machine Learning, pp. 2048–2057 (2015)
64. Yang, B., et al.: Learning object bounding boxes for 3D instance segmentation on point clouds. arXiv preprint arXiv:1906.01140 (2019)
65. Yang, S., Li, G., Yu, Y.: Cross-modal relationship inference for grounding referring expressions. In: Proceedings of the IEEE Conference on Computer Vision and Pattern Recognition, pp. 4145–4154 (2019)
66. Yang, S., Li, G., Yu, Y.: Dynamic graph attention for referring expression comprehension. In: Proceedings of the IEEE International Conference on Computer Vision, pp. 4644–4653 (2019)
67. Yang, Z., Gong, B., Wang, L., Huang, W., Yu, D., Luo, J.: A fast and accurate one-stage approach to visual grounding. In: Proceedings of the IEEE International Conference on Computer Vision, pp. 4683–4693 (2019)
68. Ye, L., Rochan, M., Liu, Z., Wang, Y.: Cross-modal self-attention network for referring image segmentation. In: Proceedings of the IEEE Conference on Computer Vision and Pattern Recognition, pp. 10502–10511 (2019)
69. Yu, L., et al.: MAttNet: modular attention network for referring expression comprehension. In: Proceedings of the IEEE Conference on Computer Vision and Pattern Recognition, pp. 1307–1315 (2018)
70. Yu, L., Poirson, P., Yang, S., Berg, A.C., Berg, T.L.: Modeling context in referring expressions. In: Leibe, B., Matas, J., Sebe, N., Welling, M. (eds.) ECCV 2016. LNCS, vol. 9906, pp. 69–85. Springer, Cham (2016). https://doi.org/10.1007/978-3-319-46475-6_5
71. Yu, L., Tan, H., Bansal, M., Berg, T.L.: A joint speaker-listener-reinforcer model for referring expressions. In: Proceedings of the IEEE Conference on Computer Vision and Pattern Recognition, pp. 7282–7290 (2017)

72. Zhao, F., Li, J., Zhao, J., Feng, J.: Weakly supervised phrase localization with multi-scale anchored transformer network. In: Proceedings of the IEEE Conference on Computer Vision and Pattern Recognition, pp. 5696–5705 (2018)
73. Zitnick, C.L., Dollár, P.: Edge boxes: locating object proposals from edges. In: Fleet, D., Pajdla, T., Schiele, B., Tuytelaars, T. (eds.) ECCV 2014. LNCS, vol. 8693, pp. 391–405. Springer, Cham (2014). https://doi.org/10.1007/978-3-319-10602-1_26

JSENet: Joint Semantic Segmentation and Edge Detection Network for 3D Point Clouds

Zeyu Hu[1]([✉])[iD], Mingmin Zhen[1][iD], Xuyang Bai[1][iD], Hongbo Fu[2][iD],
and Chiew-lan Tai[1][iD]

[1] Hong Kong University of Science and Technology, Kowloon, Hong Kong
{zhuam,mzhen,xbaiad,taicl}@cse.ust.hk
[2] City University of Hong Kong, Kowloon Tong, Hong Kong
hongbofu@cityu.edu.hk

Abstract. Semantic segmentation and semantic edge detection can be seen as two dual problems with close relationships in computer vision. Despite the fast evolution of learning-based 3D semantic segmentation methods, little attention has been drawn to the learning of 3D semantic edge detectors, even less to a joint learning method for the two tasks. In this paper, we tackle the 3D semantic edge detection task for the first time and present a new two-stream fully-convolutional network that jointly performs the two tasks. In particular, we design a joint refinement module that explicitly wires region information and edge information to improve the performances of both tasks. Further, we propose a novel loss function that encourages the network to produce semantic segmentation results with better boundaries. Extensive evaluations on S3DIS and ScanNet datasets show that our method achieves on par or better performance than the state-of-the-art methods for semantic segmentation and outperforms the baseline methods for semantic edge detection. Code release: https://github.com/hzykent/JSENet.

Keywords: Semantic segmentation · Semantic edge detection · 3D point clouds · 3D scene understanding

1 Introduction

Semantic segmentation (SS) and semantic edge detection (SED) are two fundamental problems for scene understanding. The former aims to parse a scene and assign a class label to each pixel in images or each point in 3D point clouds. The latter focuses on detecting edge pixels or edge points and classifying each of them to one or more classes. Interestingly, the SS and the SED tasks can be seen as two dual problems with even interchangeable outputs in an ideal case

Electronic supplementary material The online version of this chapter (https://doi.org/10.1007/978-3-030-58565-5_14) contains supplementary material, which is available to authorized users.

© Springer Nature Switzerland AG 2020
A. Vedaldi et al. (Eds.): ECCV 2020, LNCS 12365, pp. 222–239, 2020.
https://doi.org/10.1007/978-3-030-58565-5_14

Fig. 1. (Left) Point cloud of a real-world scene from S3DIS [12]; (Middle) Semantic segmentation point (SSP) mask; (Right) Semantic edge point (SEP) map. For visualization, we paint an edge point to the color of one of its class labels. (Color figure online)

(see Fig. 1). While SS has been extensively studied in both 2D and 3D [1–7], SED has only been explored in 2D [8–11], to our best knowledge.

There are strong motivations to address both problems in a joint learning framework. On one hand, previous SS models tend to struggle in edge areas since these areas constitute only a small part of the whole scene and thus have little effect on the supervision during training [13,14]. Performing the complementary SED task simultaneously may help the network sharpen the boundaries of the predicted SS results [15]. On the other hand, existing SED models are easily affected by non-semantic edges in the scene [8,11], while a trained SS model is less sensitive to those edges [16]. Information from the SS model thus may help SED models suppress network activations on the non-semantic edges. Despite the close relationships of the two tasks, there is no existing work tackling them jointly as far as we know.

Although not focusing on the SS and the SED tasks, in 2D, several existing works have already made fruitful attempts at proposing joint learning methods for complementary segmentation and edge detection tasks [2,14,15,17–20]. These works often treat the two tasks naïvely by sharing parts of their networks and limit the interactions between them to the feature domain. Predicted segmentation masks and edge maps are used only for loss calculation and do not contribute to each other. Strong links between the outputs of the two tasks are not fully exploited.

In this work, we introduce the task of SED into the 3D field and propose *JSENet*, a new 3D fully-convolutional network (FCN) for joint SS and SED. The proposed network consists of two streams and a joint refinement module on top of them. Specifically, we use a classical encoder-decoder FCN for SS in one stream, which outputs semantic segmentation point (SSP) masks, and add an SED stream outputting semantic edge point (SEP) maps in parallel. The key to our architecture is the lightweight joint refinement module. It takes the output SSP masks and SEP maps as inputs and jointly refines them by explicitly exploiting the duality between them. Moreover, we further propose a novel loss function to encourage the predicted SSP masks to better align with the ground truth semantic edges.

To summarize, our contributions are threefold:

1. We introduce the task of SED into the 3D field and design an FCN-based architecture with enhanced feature extraction and hierarchical supervision to generate precise semantic edges.
2. We propose a novel framework for joint learning of SS and SED, named JSENet, with an effective lightweight joint refinement module that brings improvements by explicitly exploiting the duality between the two tasks.
3. We propose a dual semantic edge loss, which encourages the network to produce SS results with finer boundaries.

To build our FCN network in 3D, we resort to KPConv [21], a recently proposed kernel-based convolution method for point clouds, for its state-of-the-art performance and ease of implementation. We conduct extensive experiments to demonstrate the effectiveness of our method. Since there is no existing 3D SED dataset, we construct a new 3D SED benchmark using S3DIS [12] and ScanNet [7] datasets. We achieve state-of-the-art performance for the SS task with IoU scores of 67.7% on S3DIS Area-5 and 69.9% on ScanNet test set. For the SED task, our method outperforms the baseline methods by a large margin.

2   Related Work

2.1   3D Semantic Segmentation

Based on different data representations, 3D SS methods can be roughly divided into three categories: multiview image-based, voxel-based, and point-based. Our method falls into the point-based category.

Although the *multiview image-based* methods easily benefit from the success of 2D CNN [22,23], for SS, they suffer from occluded surfaces and density variations, and rely heavily on viewpoint selection. Based on powerful 3D CNN [24–30], *voxel-based* methods achieve the best performance on several 3D SS datasets, but they need intensive computation power.

Compared with the previously mentioned methods, *point-based* methods suffer less from information loss and thus achieve high point-level accuracy with less computation power consumption [5,6]. They can be generally classified into four categories: neighboring feature pooling [31–34], graph construction [35–38], attention-based aggregation [39], and kernel-based convolution [21,40–46]. Among all the point-based methods, the recently proposed kernel-based method KPConv [21] achieves the best performance for efficient 3D convolution. Thus, we adopt KPConv to build our backbone and refinement network.

2.2   2D Semantic Edge Detection

Learning-based SED dates back to the early work of Prasad et al. [47]. Later, Hariharan et al. [48] introduced the first Semantic Boundaries Dataset. After the dawn of deep learning, the HFL method [49] builds a two-stage prediction process by using two deep CNNs for edge localization and classification, respectively. More recently, CASENet [8] extended the CNN-based class-agnostic edge detector HED [50] to a class-aware semantic edge detector by combining low- and high-level features with a multi-label loss function for supervision. Later, several follow-up works [9–11,51] improved CASENet by adding diverse deep supervision and reducing annotation noises.

In 2D images, semantic edges of different classes are weakly related since they are essentially occlusion boundaries of projected objects. Based on this observation, 2D SED methods treat SED of different classes as independent binary classification problems and utilize structures that limit the interaction between different classes like group convolution modules. Unlike the ones in 2D, semantic edges in 3D are physical boundaries of objects and thus are highly related to each other. In this work, we study the problem of 3D SED for the first time. We adopt from 2D methods the idea of extracting enhanced features and construct a network that does not limit the interaction between different classes.

2.3 Joint Learning of Segmentation and Edge Detection

For 2D images, several works have explored the idea of combining networks for complementary segmentation and edge detection tasks to improve the learning efficiency, prediction accuracy, and generalization ability [2,14,15,17–20].

To be more specific, for salient object detection, researchers have exploited the duality between the binary segmentation and *class-agnostic* edge detection tasks [15,20]. As for SS, such *class-agnostic* edges are used to build semantic segmentation masks with finer boundaries [2,14,17–19]. In contrast, we tackle the problem of joint learning for SS and *class-aware* SED. Furthermore, unlike previous works, which limit the interactions between segmentation and edge detection to the sharing of features and network structures, our method exploits the close relationship between SSP masks and SEP maps.

3 JSENet

In this section, we present our JSENet architecture for the joint learning of SS and class-aware SED. As depicted in Fig. 2, our architecture consists of two streams of networks with a shared feature encoder and followed by a joint refinement module. The first stream of the network, the SS stream, is a standard encoder-decoder FCN for SS using the same structure as presented in KPConv [21]. The second stream, the SED stream, is another FCN with enhanced feature extraction and hierarchical supervision. We then fuse the outputs from the two streams using our carefully designed joint refinement module to produce refined SSP masks and refined SEP maps. Next, we will describe each of the modules in detail and then explain the supervisions used for joint learning.

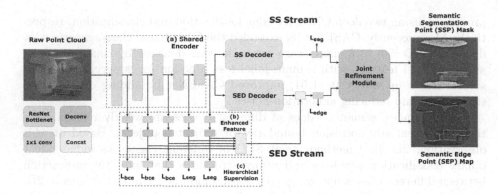

Fig. 2. JSENet architecture. Our architecture consists of two main streams. The SS stream can be any fully-convolutional network for SS. The SED stream extracts enhanced features through a skip-layer structure and is supervised by multiple loss functions. A joint refinement module later combines the information from the two streams and outputs refined SSP masks and SEP maps.

3.1   Semantic Segmentation Stream

We denote the SS stream as $\mathcal{S}_\theta(\mathcal{P})$ with parameters θ, taking a point cloud $\mathcal{P} \in \mathbb{R}^{N \times 6}(x, y, z, r, g, b)$ with N points as input and outputting an SSP mask. More specifically, for a segmentation prediction of K semantic classes, it outputs a categorical distribution $s \in \mathbb{R}^{N \times K}$: $s(p|\mathcal{P}, \theta)$ representing the probability of point p belonging to each of the K classes. We supervise this stream with the standard multi-class cross-entropy loss (L_{seg} in Fig. 2). The SS stream can be any feedforward 3D fully-convolutional SS network such as InterpCNNs [46] and SSCNs [29]. In this work, we adopt KPConv [21] and use it as our backbone network for its efficient convolution operation and ability to build complex network structures. There are two types of KPConv: rigid and deformable. We use the rigid version in this work for its better convergence performance. In order to demonstrate the improvements introduced by joint learning, we use the same structure as described in KPConv.

3.2   Semantic Edge Detection Stream

We denote the SED stream as $\mathcal{E}_\phi(\mathcal{P})$ with parameters ϕ, taking a point cloud $\mathcal{P}$ with N points as input and outputting SEP maps. For K defined semantic categories, this stream outputs K SEP maps $\{e_1, ..., e_K\}$, each having the same size as $\mathcal{P}$ with one channel. We denote $e_k(p|\mathcal{P}, \phi)$ as the network output, which indicates the computed edge probability of the k-th semantic category at point p. Note that one point may belong to multiple categories.

The SED stream shares the same feature encoder with the SS stream to force the network to prefer representations with a better generalization ability for both tasks. Our backbone is an FCN-based structure. However, one major drawback of an FCN-based structure is the loss in spatial information of the output after

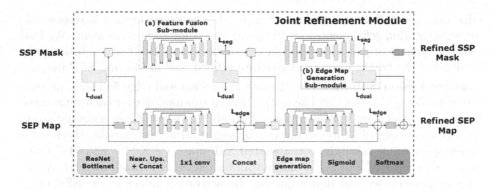

Fig. 3. Illustration of the joint refinement module, which consists of two branches.

propagating through several alternated convolutional and pooling layers. This drawback would harm the localization performance, which is essential for our SED task. Besides, according to the findings of CASENet [8], the low-level features of CNN-based encoder are not suitable for semantic classification (due to the limited receptive fields) but are able to help augment top classifications by suppressing non-edge activations and providing detailed edge localization information. Based on these observations, we propose to extract enhanced features with hierarchical supervisions to alleviate the problem of spatial information loss and offer richer semantic cues for final classification.

Enhanced Feature Extraction. In detail, we extract the feature maps generated by the layers of the shared encoder (Fig. 2(a)). We then reduce the numbers of their feature channels and deconvolve them to the size of the input point cloud. The features of different layers participate and augment the final SED through a skip-layer architecture, as shown in Fig. 2(b).

Hierarchical Supervision. As shown in Fig. 2(c), from the extracted feature maps of the first three layers, we generate binary edge point maps indicating the probability of points belonging to the semantic edges of any classes. From the last two layers, we generate two SSP masks. All binary edge point maps are supervised by the weighted binary cross-entropy loss (L_{bce}) using ground-truth (GT) binary edges obtained from the GT SSP masks. The two SSP masks are supervised by the standard multi-class cross-entropy loss (L_{seg}). The output SEP maps of the SED stream are supervised by a weighted multi-label loss (L_{edge}) following the idea from CASENet [8]. We will give details about different loss functions in Sect. 3.4.

3.3 Joint Refinement Module

We denote the joint refinement module as $\mathcal{R}_\gamma(s, e_1, ..., e_K)$ with parameters γ, taking as input the SSP mask s coming from the SS stream and the SEP maps $\{e_1, ..., e_K\}$ generated by the SED stream. As shown in Fig. 3, we construct a two-branch structure with simple feature fusion sub-modules (Fig. 3(a)) and novel edge map generation sub-modules (Fig. 3(b)). The upper branch is responsible for segmentation refinement, and the lower one is for edge refinement. We feed different joint features (described in detail below) to the feature fusion sub-modules of the two branches and generate refined SSP masks and SEP maps.

Feature Fusion Sub-Module. To fuse the region and edge features, we construct two simple U-Net [52] like feature fusion sub-modules for each refinement branch. In detail, each feature fusion sub-module consists of five encoding layers with channel sizes of 32 for all layers. For segmentation refinement, the feature fusion sub-module takes the concatenated SSP mask $s \in \mathbb{R}^{N \times K}$ and SEP maps $\{e_1, ..., e_K\}$ ($e_i \in \mathbb{R}^N$) as input and outputs a refined SSP mask directly. As for edge refinement, we find that adjusting the activation values of the SEP maps is more effective than asking the neural network to output refined SEP maps naïvely. Thus, we put the unrefined SEP maps through a sigmoid operation and concatenate them with the edge activation point maps $\{a_1, ..., a_K\}$ ($a_i \in \mathbb{R}^N$) generated by the edge map generation sub-module. The concatenated features are then fed to the feature fusion sub-module to generate auxiliary point maps, which are added to the unrefined SEP maps to adjust the edge activation values.

Edge Map Generation Sub-Module. In order to exploit the duality between two tasks, we design an edge map generation sub-module to convert an SSP mask to edge activation point maps. More formally, we denote the edge map generation sub-module as $\mathcal{G}(s)$, which takes a categorical distribution $s \in \mathbb{R}^{N \times K}$ as input and outputs edge activation point maps $\{a_1, ..., a_K\}$ ($a_i \in \mathbb{R}^N$), where $a_i(p)$ is a potential that represents whether a particular point p belongs to the semantic boundary of the i-th class. It is computed by taking a spatial derivative on the segmentation output as follows:

$$a_i = col_i(|M * Softmax(s) - Softmax(s)|), \tag{1}$$

where col_i denotes the i-th column and M denotes the Mean filter, which takes neighboring points within a small radius. As illustrated in Fig. 4, the i-th column of the output tensor of a softmax operation represents an activation point mask for class_i, where a higher value indicates a higher probability of belonging to class_i. On this mask, points near to the boundaries of class_i will have neighbors with activation values of significant differences, and points far from the boundaries will have neighbors with similar activation values. Thus, after the mean filtering and subtraction, points nearer to the predicted boundaries will have larger activation values. The converted edge activation point maps are fed to the edge refinement branch and utilized for loss calculation as well.

Supervisions. For supervision, the output SSP masks are supervised by the multi-class cross-entropy loss (L_{seg}), and the output SEP maps are supervised by the weighted multi-label loss (L_{edge}). Additionally, we supervise the generated edge activation point maps with our proposed dual semantic edge loss (L_{dual}) to encourage the predicted SS results to align with the GT semantic edges correctly (see Sect. 3.4). After refinement, the final output SSP mask is normalized by a softmax operation. The final output SEP maps are normalized by a sigmoid operation and added element-wise with the final edge activation point maps.

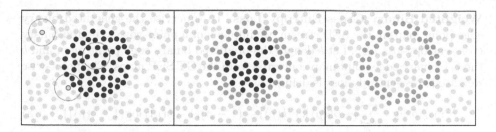

Fig. 4. Illustration of the edge map generation process on 2D points. (Left) An activation point mask, with dark colors representing high activation values. Three red points represent three different situations: far from the activated region, near the boundary, and within the activated region. (Middle) The activation point mask after the mean filtering; (Right) The generated edge activation point map. (Color figure online)

3.4 Joint Multi-task Learning

The key to joint learning of the SS and the SED tasks is to design a proper supervision signal. The total loss is formulated as:

$$L_{total} = \lambda_0 L_{seg} + \lambda_1 L_{edge} + \lambda_2 L_{bce} + \lambda_3 L_{dual}. \tag{2}$$

During training, λ_0 is set to the number of semantic classes to balance the influences of the two tasks. The other weights are set to 1. We describe in detail all the loss functions used for supervision in our framework below.

Multi-class Cross-Entropy Loss. We use a standard multi-class cross-entropy loss, which denoted as L_{seg}, on a predicted SSP mask s:

$$L_{seg}(\hat{s}, s) = -\sum_k \sum_p \hat{s}_k(p) \log(s_k(p)), \tag{3}$$

where $\hat{s} \in \mathbb{R}^{N \times K}$ denotes GT semantic labels in a one-hot form.

Weighted Multi-label Loss. Following the idea proposed in CASENet [8], we address the SED problem for a point cloud by a multi-label learning framework and implement a point-wise weighted multi-label loss L_{edge}. Suppose an input point cloud $\mathcal{P}$ has K SEP maps $\{e_1, ..., e_K\}$ ($e_i \in \mathbb{R}^N$) predicted by the network and K label point maps $\{\hat{e}_1, ..., \hat{e}_K\}$ ($\hat{e}_i \in \mathbb{R}^N$), where $\hat{e}_k$ is a binary point map indicating the ground truth of the k-th class semantic edges. The point-wise weighted multi-label loss L_{edge} is formulated as:

$$L_{edge}(\{\hat{e}_1, ..., \hat{e}_K\}, \{e_1, ..., e_K\}) = \sum_k \sum_p \{-\beta_k \hat{e}_k(p) \log(e_k(p))$$
$$- (1 - \beta_k)(1 - \hat{e}_k(p)) \log(1 - e_k(p))\}, \tag{4}$$

where β_k is the percentage of non-edge points in the point cloud of the k-th class to account for the skewness of sample numbers.

Weighted Binary Cross-Entropy Loss. To supervise the generated binary edge point maps in the SED stream, we implement a point-wise weighted binary cross-entropy loss L_{bce}. Let b denote the predicted binary edge point map, and $\hat{b}$ the GT binary edge point map converted from the GT SEP maps. The point-wise weighted cross-entropy loss is defined as:

$$L_{bce}(\hat{b}, b) = \sum_p \{-\beta \hat{b}(p) \log(b(p)) - (1 - \beta)(1 - \hat{b}(p)) \log(1 - b(p))\}, \quad (5)$$

where β is the percentage of non-edge points among all classes.

Dual Semantic Edge Loss. As mentioned above, inspired by the duality between SS and SED, we design an edge map generation sub-module to convert the predicted SSP mask $s \in \mathbb{R}^{N \times K}$ to edge activation point maps $\{a_1, ..., a_K\}$ $(a_i \in \mathbb{R}^N)$(c.f., Eq. 1). In a similar way, we can compute GT edge activation point maps $\{\hat{a}_1, ..., \hat{a}_K\}$ from the GT semantic labels $\hat{s}$:

$$\hat{a}_i = col_i(|M * One\_hot(\hat{s}) - One\_hot(\hat{s})|). \quad (6)$$

Note that the softmax operation for predicted SSP mask s is changed to the one-hot encoding operation for GT semantic labels $\hat{s}$. Taking the converted GT edge activation point maps, we can define the loss function as follows:

$$L_{dual}(\{\hat{a}_1, ..., \hat{a}_K\}, \{a_1, ..., a_K\}) = \sum_k \sum_p \beta(|\hat{a}_k(p) - a_k(p)|), \quad (7)$$

where β is the same weight as above. Intuitively, the network will get penalized when there are mismatches on edge points. It is worth noting that the loss function will not be dominated by the non-edge points since the calculated loss values on these points are zeros or very small numbers. The above dual loss is naturally differentiable and exploits the duality between SS and SED.

4   Experiments

To demonstrate the effectiveness of our proposed method, we now present various experiments conducted on the S3DIS [12] and ScanNet[7] datasets, for which GT SSP masks are available and we can generate GT SEP maps from them easily. We first introduce the dataset preparation and evaluation metrics in Sect. 4.1, and then present the implementation details for reproduction in Sect. 4.2. We report the results of our ablation studies in Sect. 4.3, and the results on the S3DIS and ScanNet datasets in Sect. 4.4.

4.1   Datasets and Metrics

We use S3DIS [12] and ScanNet [7] datasets for our experiments. There are two reasons for choosing these datasets: 1) they are both of high quality and 2) semantic edges are better defined on indoor data: compared to existing 3D outdoor datasets, in indoor scenes, more detailed semantic labels are defined and objects are more densely connected. The S3DIS dataset consists of 3D point clouds for six large-scale indoor areas captured from three different buildings. It has around 273 million points annotated with 13 semantic classes. The ScanNet dataset includes 1513 training scenes and 100 test scenes in a mesh format, all annotated with 20 semantic classes, for online benchmarking.

To generate the GT SEP maps, for S3DIS, we directly check the neighbors within a $2cm$ radius of each point in the dataset. For a specific point, if it has neighbors with different semantic labels, we label it as an edge point of all the semantic classes that appear in its neighborhood. As for the ScanNet dataset, following the work of KPConv [21], we first rasterize the training meshes by uniformly sampling points on the faces of meshes and then downsample the generated point clouds with $1cm$ grids. We use these point clouds for training and generate the GT SEP maps using the same way as described for the S3DIS dataset. During testing, we project the semantic edge labels to the vertices of the original meshes and test directly on meshes.

To evaluate the performance of SS and SED, we adopt the standard mean intersection over union (mIoU) for SS and use the mean maximum F-measure (MF) at the optimal dataset scale (ODS) for SED following the works in 2D [8–11]. We generate thicker edges for point clouds than for images since a point cloud is much sparser than an image. Since we have thicker edges, the localization tolerance used in the 2D case is not introduced to our evaluation.

4.2   Implementation Details

In this section, we discuss the implementation details for our experiments. JSENet is coded in Python and TensorFlow. All the experiments are conducted on a PC with 8 Intel(R) i7-7700 CPUs and a single GeForce GTX 1080Ti GPU.

Training. Since the 3D scenes in both datasets are of huge size, we randomly sample spheres with 2 m radius in the training set and augment them with Gaussian noise, random scaling, and random rotation. Following the settings in KPConv, the input point clouds are downsampled with a grid size of 4 cm. In all our experiments, unless explicitly stated otherwise, we use a Momentum gradient descent optimizer with a momentum of 0.98 and an initial learning rate of 0.01. The learning rate is scheduled to decrease exponentially. In particular, it is divided by 10 for every 100 epochs. Although the framework is end-to-end trainable, in order to clearly demonstrate the efficacy of the proposed joint refinement module, we first train our network without the joint refinement module for 350 epochs and then optimize the joint refinement module alone with the other parts fixed for 150 epochs.

Testing. Similar to the training process, during testing, we sample spheres with $2m$ radius from the testing set regularly and ensure each point to be sampled for multiple times. The predicted probabilities for each point are averaged through a voting scheme [21]. All predicted values are projected to the original point clouds (S3DIS) or meshes (ScanNet) for evaluation.

Table 1. Ablation experiments of network structures on S3DIS Area-5. **SEDS**: semantic edge detection stream; **EFE**: enhanced feature extraction; **HS**: hierarchical supervision; **SSS**: semantic segmentation stream; **JRM**: joint refinement module. The results in some cells (with '-') are not available, since the corresponding models perform either SS or SED.

0	SEDS	EFE	HS	SSS	JRM	mIoU (%)	mMF (ODS)(%)
1	✓	✓	✓	✓	✓	67.7	31.0
2	✓	✓	✓	✓		66.2	30.5
3				✓		64.7	-
4	✓	✓	✓			-	30.2
5	✓	✓				-	29.9
6	✓					-	29.4

4.3   Ablation Study

In this section, we compare the performances of JSENet under different settings on the S3DIS dataset since it is originally presented in a point cloud format and all semantic labels are available. Following the common setting [3,5,21,30,37, 53,54], we use Area-5 as a test scene and train our network on the other scenes. All experiments are conducted keeping all hyperparameters the same.

Network Structures. In Table 1, we evaluate the effectiveness of each component of our method. For the SS task, as shown in the table (Row 3), the performance of training our SS stream alone is 64.7% in terms of mIoU. Our SS stream shares the same architecture with KPConv and the reported score of KPConv is 65.4% in their paper. By naïvely combining the SS stream and the SED stream, we can improve the SS task by 1.5% (Row 2). From the joint refinement module, we further gain about 1.5% (Row 1) improvement in performance. We achieve about 3% improvement comparing to training our SS stream alone and still more than 2% improvement comparing to the result reported in KPConv.

For the SED task, it can be seen from the table that the performance of training the SED stream alone without the enhanced feature extraction and hierarchical supervision is 29.4% (Row 6) in terms of mMF (ODS). We gain about 0.5% and 0.3% improvements in performance from the enhanced feature extraction (Row 5) and hierarchical supervision (Row 4), respectively. Naïvely combining the SS stream and the SED stream brings a further improvement of 0.3% (Row 2) in terms of mMF. By adding the joint refinement module, we can further improve the SED task by 0.5% (Row 1).

Choice of Loss Functions for Hierarchical Supervision. To justify our choices of the loss functions in the SED stream for hierarchical supervision, we test the performances of SED using different settings of supervision. As shown in Table 2, if all hierarchical supervisions are removed, the performance of our

Table 2. (a) Comparison of different supervision choices for SED. (b) Effects of the dual semantic edge loss in terms of boundary quality (F-score).

(a)

Method	mMF (ODS) (%)
L_{bce} for all five layers	30.1
L_{seg} for all five layers	30.1
No hierarchical supervision	29.9
L_{bce} for first three, L_{seg} for last two	30.2

(b)

Method	F-score (%)
JSENet w/o dual loss	22.7
JSENet	23.1

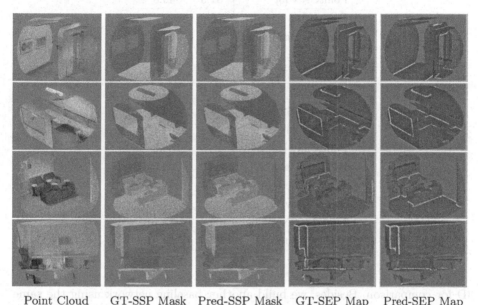

Point Cloud   GT-SSP Mask   Pred-SSP Mask   GT-SEP Map   Pred-SEP Map

Fig. 5. Qualitative results on S3DIS Area-5. For better visualization, we thickened all the semantic edges.

SED model will decrease by 0.3%. Among all the choices listed in the table, the one used in our network achieves the best result.

Efficacy of Dual Semantic Edge Loss. We further showcase the effects of the dual semantic edge loss in terms of F-score for edge alignment of the predicted SSP masks in Table 2. We train our network without the dual semantic edge losses for the edge map generation sub-modules as the baseline. It is shown that the dual semantic edge losses bring an improvement of 0.4% in terms of F-score.

4.4 Results on S3DIS & ScanNet Datasets

To compare JSENet with the state-of-the-arts, for SS, we choose the latest methods [3–5, 29, 30, 37, 42, 53–64] with reported results on the S3DIS or the ScanNet datasets as our baselines. For SED, since we cannot find any existing solutions in 3D, we extend CASENet [8], which is the state-of-the-art method for 2D SED to

Table 3. mIoU scores (%) of semantic segmentation task.

Method	S3DIS	ScanNet
TangentConv [54]	52.6	43.8
RNN Fusion [55]	53.4	-
SPGraph [56]	58.0	-
FCPN [57]	-	44.7
PointCNN [3]	57.3	45.8
ParamConv [58]	58.3	-
PanopticFusion [59]	-	52.9
TextureNet [60]	-	56.6
SPH3D-GCN [61]	59.5	61.0
HPEIN [37]	61.9	61.8
MCCNN [62]	-	63.3
MVPNet [4]	62.4	64.1
PointConv [42]	-	66.6
KPConv rigid [21]	65.4	68.6
KPConv deform [21]	67.1	68.4
SparseConvNet [29]	-	72.5
MinkowskiNet [30]	65.4	**73.6**
JSENet (ours)	**67.7**	69.9

3D for comparison. Besides, we build another baseline network using the same structure as the one presented in KPConv with a changed output layer.

For the S3DIS dataset, we use the same *train-test* splitting setting as in Sect. 4.3. For the ScanNet dataset, since it is built for online benchmarking, the GT semantic labels for its test set are not available. Thus, for the SS task, we train our network using the 1513 training scenes and report the testing results on the 100 test scenes following the common setting. To evaluate the task of SED, as explained in Sect. 4.1, we obtain semantic edge labels from the training set and divide the 1513 training scenes into a new training set with 1201 scenes and a new test set with 312 scenes following the *train-val* splitting file offered by ScanNet. All the compared networks for SED are trained on the new training set and tested on the new test set. Qualitative results are shown in Fig. 5. Complexity comparison and more qualitative results can be found in **supplementary**.

Results of SS Task. The results for the SS task are reported in Table 3. The detailed IoU scores of each class for the S3DIS dataset can be found in the supplementary. The details for the ScanNet dataset can be found on the Scan-Net benchmarking website.[1] For the S3DIS dataset, JSENet achieves a 67.7% mIoU score and outperforms all the baseline methods. For the ScanNet dataset,

---

[1] http://kaldir.vc.in.tum.de/scannet_benchmark/semantic_label_3d.

Table 4. MF (ODS) scores (%) of semantic edge detection on S3DIS Area-5.

Method	Mean	Ceil	Floor	Wall	Beam	Col	Wind	Door	Chair	Table	Book	Sofa	Board	Clut
CASENet [8]	27.1	**46.5**	**49.0**	33.3	0.2	21.9	12.6	22.6	36.9	33.6	21.8	25.1	22.6	26.1
KPConv [21]	29.4	43.7	41.8	36.4	0.2	23.6	**13.4**	29.7	**39.8**	**37.3**	26.6	29.4	29.2	31.3
JSENet (ours)	**31.0**	44.5	43.2	**38.8**	0.2	**24.1**	13.2	**36.7**	37.7	36.3	**29.1**	**34.0**	**33.3**	**32.4**

Table 5. MF (ODS) scores (%) of semantic edge detection on ScanNet val set.

Method	mean	bath	bed	bksf	cab	chair	cntr	curt	desk	door	floor	othr	pic	ref	show	sink	sofa	tab	toil	wall	wind
CASENet [8]	32.3	38.2	55.9	29.9	36.0	36.0	36.8	28.1	28.5	19.1	26.6	25.1	32.2	28.6	26.6	23.9	19.0	45.7	27.1	54.6	27.4
KPConv [21]	34.8	40.5	**55.9**	33.6	**38.5**	39.3	38.0	32.9	31.2	22.0	25.1	28.5	36.2	30.8	30.9	22.7	22.8	46.5	33.3	**55.2**	32.3
JSENet (ours)	**37.3**	**43.8**	55.8	**35.9**	38.2	**41.0**	**40.8**	**34.5**	**35.9**	**25.5**	**28.7**	**29.5**	**37.3**	36.2	31.7	28.1	28.3	48.5	35.6	53.2	**37.8**

JSENet ranks third with a 69.9% mIoU score. The first two (i.e., SparseConvNet and MinkowskiNet) are two voxel-based methods that require intense computation power. Compared to other point-based methods, JSENet achieves the best performance and consistently outperforms the results of KPConv.

Results of SED Task. We present the results for the SED task in Tables 4 and 5. It can be seen that our method outperforms the two baseline methods on both datasets. We find that the extended CASENet architecture performs worse than KPConv with the changed output layer. This result supports our previous argument (Sect. 2.2) that 3D semantic edges have stronger relevance between different classes (since they are physical boundaries of objects and the 2D semantic edges are occlusion boundaries of projected objects), and thus the network designs that enforce limitations between interactions of different classes would harm the edge detection performance.

5 Conclusions

In this paper, we proposed a joint semantic segmentation and semantic edge detection network (JSENet), which is a new two-stream fully-convolutional architecture with a lightweight joint refinement module that explicitly wires region information and edge information for output refinement. We constructed a two-branch structure with simple feature fusion sub-modules and novel edge map generation sub-modules for the joint refinement module and designed the dual semantic edge loss that encourages the network to produce sharper predictions around object boundaries. Our experiments show that JSENet is an effective architecture that produces SSP masks and SEP maps of high qualities. JSENet achieves the state-of-the-art results on the challenging S3DIS and Scan-Net datasets, significantly improving over strong baselines. For future works, one straightforward direction is to explore the potential of joint improvement of these two tasks in the 2D field. Moreover, we notice that our SED method is easily affected by the noises in the GT labels introduced by human annotation. We believe that future works with special treatments on the misaligned GT semantic edges will further improve the performance of the SED task.

Acknowledgements. This work is supported by Hong Kong RGC GRF 16206819, 16203518 and Centre for Applied Computing and Interactive Media (ACIM) of School of Creative Media, City University of Hong Kong.

References

1. Long, J., Shelhamer, E., Darrell, T.: Fully convolutional networks for semantic segmentation. In: Proceedings of the IEEE Conference on Computer Vision and Pattern Recognition, pp. 3431–3440 (2015)
2. Takikawa, T., Acuna, D., Jampani, V., Fidler, S.: Gated-SCNN: Gated shape CNNs for semantic segmentation. In: Proceedings of the IEEE International Conference on Computer Vision, pp. 5229–5238 (2019)
3. Li, Y., Bu, R., Sun, M., Wu, W., Di, X., Chen, B.: PointCNN: convolution on x-transformed points. In: Advances in Neural Information Processing Systems, pp. 820–830 (2018)
4. Jaritz, M., Gu, J., Su, H.: Multi-view pointnet for 3D scene understanding. In: Proceedings of the IEEE International Conference on Computer Vision Workshops (2019)
5. Qi, C.R., Su, H., Mo, K., Guibas, L.J.: Pointnet: deep learning on point sets for 3D classification and segmentation. In: Proceedings of the IEEE Conference on Computer Vision and Pattern Recognition, pp. 652–660 (2017)
6. Qi, C.R., Yi, L., Su, H., Guibas, L.J.: Pointnet++: deep hierarchical feature learning on point sets in a metric space. In: Advances in Neural Information Processing Systems, pp. 5099–5108 (2017)
7. Dai, A., Chang, A.X., Savva, M., Halber, M., Funkhouser, T., Nießner, M.: Scannet: richly-annotated 3D reconstructions of indoor scenes. In: Proceedings of the Computer Vision and Pattern Recognition (CVPR). IEEE (2017)
8. Yu, Z., Feng, C., Liu, M.Y., Ramalingam, S.: Casenet: deep category-aware semantic edge detection. In: Proceedings of the IEEE Conference on Computer Vision and Pattern Recognition, pp. 5964–5973 (2017)
9. Liu, Y., Cheng, M.M., Fan, D.P., Zhang, L., Bian, J., Tao, D.: Semantic edge detection with diverse deep supervision (2018)
10. Yu, Z., et al.: Simultaneous edge alignment and learning. In: Ferrari, V., Hebert, M., Sminchisescu, C., Weiss, Y. (eds.) ECCV 2018. LNCS, vol. 11207, pp. 400–417. Springer, Cham (2018). https://doi.org/10.1007/978-3-030-01219-9_24
11. Acuna, D., Kar, A., Fidler, S.: Devil is in the edges: learning semantic boundaries from noisy annotations. In: Proceedings of the IEEE Conference on Computer Vision and Pattern Recognition, pp. 11075–11083 (2019)
12. Armeni, I., et al.: 3D semantic parsing of large-scale indoor spaces. In: Proceedings of the IEEE International Conference on Computer Vision and Pattern Recognition (2016)
13. Zhao, H., Shi, J., Qi, X., Wang, X., Jia, J.: Pyramid scene parsing network. In: Proceedings of the IEEE Conference on Computer Vision and Pattern Recognition, pp. 2881–2890 (2017)
14. Lin, G., Milan, A., Shen, C., Reid, I.: Refinenet: multi-path refinement networks for high-resolution semantic segmentation. In: Proceedings of the IEEE Conference on Computer Vision and Pattern Recognition, pp. 1925–1934 (2017)
15. Wu, Z., Su, L., Huang, Q.: Stacked cross refinement network for edge-aware salient object detection. In: Proceedings of the IEEE International Conference on Computer Vision, pp. 7264–7273 (2019)

16. Yu, C., Wang, J., Peng, C., Gao, C., Yu, G., Sang, N.: Learning a discriminative feature network for semantic segmentation. In: Proceedings of the IEEE Conference on Computer Vision and Pattern Recognition, pp. 1857–1866 (2018)

17. Cheng, D., Meng, G., Xiang, S., Pan, C.: Fusionnet: edge aware deep convolutional networks for semantic segmentation of remote sensing harbor images. IEEE J. Sel. Top. Appl. Earth Obs. Remote Sens. **10**(12), 5769–5783 (2017)

18. Bertasius, G., Shi, J., Torresani, L.: Semantic segmentation with boundary neural fields. In: Proceedings of the IEEE Conference on Computer Vision and Pattern Recognition, pp. 3602–3610 (2016)

19. Peng, C., Zhang, X., Yu, G., Luo, G., Sun, J.: Large kernel matters-improve semantic segmentation by global convolutional network. In: Proceedings of the IEEE Conference on Computer Vision and Pattern Recognition, pp. 4353–4361 (2017)

20. Su, J., Li, J., Zhang, Y., Xia, C., Tian, Y.: Selectivity or invariance: boundary-aware salient object detection. In: Proceedings of the IEEE International Conference on Computer Vision, pp. 3799–3808 (2019)

21. Thomas, H., Qi, C.R., Deschaud, J.E., Marcotegui, B., Goulette, F., Guibas, L.J.: KPConv: flexible and deformable convolution for point clouds. In: Proceedings of the IEEE International Conference on Computer Vision, pp. 6411–6420 (2019)

22. Boulch, A., Le Saux, B., Audebert, N.: Unstructured point cloud semantic labeling using deep segmentation networks. 3DOR **2**, 7 (2017)

23. Lawin, F.J., Danelljan, M., Tosteberg, P., Bhat, G., Khan, F.S., Felsberg, M.: Deep projective 3D semantic segmentation. In: Felsberg, M., Heyden, A., Krüger, N. (eds.) CAIP 2017. LNCS, vol. 10424, pp. 95–107. Springer, Cham (2017). https://doi.org/10.1007/978-3-319-64689-3_8

24. Roynard, X., Deschaud, J.E., Goulette, F.: Classification of point cloud scenes with multiscale voxel deep network. arXiv preprint arXiv:1804.03583 (2018)

25. Ben-Shabat, Y., Lindenbaum, M., Fischer, A.: 3DMFV: three-dimensional point cloud classification in real-time using convolutional neural networks. IEEE Rob. Autom. Lett. **3**(4), 3145–3152 (2018)

26. Le, T., Duan, Y.: Pointgrid: a deep network for 3D shape understanding. In: Proceedings of the IEEE Conference on Computer Vision and Pattern Recognition, pp. 9204–9214 (2018)

27. Meng, H.Y., Gao, L., Lai, Y., Manocha, D.: VV-Net: voxel VAE net with group convolutions for point cloud segmentation (2018)

28. Riegler, G., Osman Ulusoy, A., Geiger, A.: Octnet: learning deep 3D representations at high resolutions. In: Proceedings of the IEEE Conference on Computer Vision and Pattern Recognition, pp. 3577–3586 (2017)

29. Graham, B., Engelcke, M., van der Maaten, L.: 3D semantic segmentation with submanifold sparse convolutional networks. In: Proceedings of the IEEE Conference on Computer Vision and Pattern Recognition, pp. 9224–9232 (2018)

30. Choy, C., Gwak, J., Savarese, S.: 4D spatio-temporal convnets: Minkowski convolutional neural networks. In: 2019 IEEE/CVF Conference on Computer Vision and Pattern Recognition (CVPR), June 2019

31. Li, J., Chen, B.M., Hee Lee, G.: So-net: self-organizing network for point cloud analysis. In: Proceedings of the IEEE Conference on Computer Vision and Pattern Recognition, pp. 9397–9406 (2018)

32. Huang, Q., Wang, W., Neumann, U.: Recurrent slice networks for 3D segmentation of point clouds. In: 2018 IEEE/CVF Conference on Computer Vision and Pattern Recognition, June 2018

33. Zhao, H., Jiang, L., Fu, C.W., Jia, J.: Pointweb: enhancing local neighborhood features for point cloud processing. In: Proceedings of the IEEE Conference on Computer Vision and Pattern Recognition, pp. 5565–5573 (2019)
34. Zhang, Z., Hua, B.S., Yeung, S.K.: Shellnet: efficient point cloud convolutional neural networks using concentric shells statistics. In: Proceedings of the IEEE International Conference on Computer Vision, pp. 1607–1616 (2019)
35. Wang, Y., Sun, Y., Liu, Z., Sarma, S.E., Bronstein, M.M., Solomon, J.M.: Dynamic graph CNN for learning on point clouds. ACM Trans. Graph. (TOG) **38**(5), 1–12 (2019)
36. Wang, L., Huang, Y., Hou, Y., Zhang, S., Shan, J.: Graph attention convolution for point cloud semantic segmentation. In: Proceedings of the IEEE Conference on Computer Vision and Pattern Recognition, pp. 10296–10305 (2019)
37. Jiang, L., Zhao, H., Liu, S., Shen, X., Fu, C.W., Jia, J.: Hierarchical point-edge interaction network for point cloud semantic segmentation. In: Proceedings of the IEEE International Conference on Computer Vision, pp. 10433–10441 (2019)
38. Liu, J., Ni, B., Li, C., Yang, J., Tian, Q.: Dynamic points agglomeration for hierarchical point sets learning. In: Proceedings of the IEEE International Conference on Computer Vision, pp. 7546–7555 (2019)
39. Xie, S., Liu, S., Chen, Z., Tu, Z.: Attentional shapecontextnet for point cloud recognition. In: Proceedings of the IEEE Conference on Computer Vision and Pattern Recognition, pp. 4606–4615 (2018)
40. Su, H., et al.: Splatnet: sparse lattice networks for point cloud processing. In: 2018 IEEE/CVF Conference on Computer Vision and Pattern Recognition, June 2018
41. Hua, B.S., Tran, M.K., Yeung, S.K.: Pointwise convolutional neural networks. In: Proceedings of the IEEE Conference on Computer Vision and Pattern Recognition, pp. 984–993 (2018)
42. Wu, W., Qi, Z., Fuxin, L.: Pointconv: deep convolutional networks on 3D point clouds. In: Proceedings of the IEEE Conference on Computer Vision and Pattern Recognition, pp. 9621–9630 (2019)
43. Lei, H., Akhtar, N., Mian, A.: Octree guided CNN with spherical kernels for 3D point clouds. In: 2019 IEEE/CVF Conference on Computer Vision and Pattern Recognition (CVPR), June 2019
44. Komarichev, A., Zhong, Z., Hua, J.: A-CNN: annularly convolutional neural networks on point clouds. In: 2019 IEEE/CVF Conference on Computer Vision and Pattern Recognition (CVPR), June 2019
45. Lan, S., Yu, R., Yu, G., Davis, L.S.: Modeling local geometric structure of 3D point clouds using geo-CNN. In: 2019 IEEE/CVF Conference on Computer Vision and Pattern Recognition (CVPR), June 2019
46. Mao, J., Wang, X., Li, H.: Interpolated convolutional networks for 3D point cloud understanding. In: Proceedings of the IEEE International Conference on Computer Vision, pp. 1578–1587 (2019)
47. Prasad, M., Zisserman, A., Fitzgibbon, A., Kumar, M.P., Torr, P.H.S.: Learning class-specific edges for object detection and segmentation. In: Kalra, P.K., Peleg, S. (eds.) ICVGIP 2006. LNCS, vol. 4338, pp. 94–105. Springer, Heidelberg (2006). https://doi.org/10.1007/11949619_9
48. Hariharan, B., Arbeláez, P., Bourdev, L., Maji, S., Malik, J.: Semantic contours from inverse detectors. In: 2011 International Conference on Computer Vision, pp. 991–998. IEEE (2011)

49. Bertasius, G., Shi, J., Torresani, L.: High-for-low and low-for-high: Efficient boundary detection from deep object features and its applications to high-level vision. In: 2015 IEEE International Conference on Computer Vision (ICCV), December 2015

50. Xie, S., Tu, Z.: Holistically-nested edge detection. In: Proceedings of the IEEE International Conference on Computer Vision, pp. 1395–1403 (2015)

51. Hu, Y., Zou, Y., Feng, J.: Panoptic edge detection (2019)

52. Ronneberger, O., Fischer, P., Brox, T.: U-Net: convolutional networks for biomedical image segmentation. In: Navab, N., Hornegger, J., Wells, W.M., Frangi, A.F. (eds.) MICCAI 2015. LNCS, vol. 9351, pp. 234–241. Springer, Cham (2015). https://doi.org/10.1007/978-3-319-24574-4_28

53. Tchapmi, L., Choy, C., Armeni, I., Gwak, J., Savarese, S.: Segcloud: semantic segmentation of 3D point clouds. In: International Conference on 3D Vision (3DV), pp. 537–547. IEEE (2017)

54. Tatarchenko, M., Park, J., Koltun, V., Zhou, Q.Y.: Tangent convolutions for dense prediction in 3D. In: Proceedings of the IEEE Conference on Computer Vision and Pattern Recognition, pp. 3887–3896 (2018)

55. Ye, X., Li, J., Huang, H., Du, L., Zhang, X.: 3D recurrent neural networks with context fusion for point cloud semantic segmentation. In: Ferrari, V., Hebert, M., Sminchisescu, C., Weiss, Y. (eds.) ECCV 2018. LNCS, vol. 11211, pp. 415–430. Springer, Cham (2018). https://doi.org/10.1007/978-3-030-01234-2_25

56. Landrieu, L., Simonovsky, M.: Large-scale point cloud semantic segmentation with superpoint graphs. In: Proceedings of the IEEE Conference on Computer Vision and Pattern Recognition, pp. 4558–4567 (2018)

57. Rethage, D., Wald, J., Sturm, J., Navab, N., Tombari, F.: Fully-convolutional point networks for large-scale point clouds. In: Ferrari, V., Hebert, M., Sminchisescu, C., Weiss, Y. (eds.) ECCV 2018. LNCS, vol. 11208, pp. 625–640. Springer, Cham (2018). https://doi.org/10.1007/978-3-030-01225-0_37

58. Wang, S., Suo, S., Ma, W.C., Pokrovsky, A., Urtasun, R.: Deep parametric continuous convolutional neural networks. In: Proceedings of the IEEE Conference on Computer Vision and Pattern Recognition, pp. 2589–2597 (2018)

59. Narita, G., Seno, T., Ishikawa, T., Kaji, Y.: Panopticfusion: online volumetric semantic mapping at the level of stuff and things. arXiv preprint arXiv:1903.01177 (2019)

60. Huang, J., Zhang, H., Yi, L., Funkhouser, T., Nießner, M., Guibas, L.J.: Texturenet: consistent local parametrizations for learning from high-resolution signals on meshes. In: Proceedings of the IEEE Conference on Computer Vision and Pattern Recognition, pp. 4440–4449 (2019)

61. Lei, H., Akhtar, N., Mian, A.: Spherical kernel for efficient graph convolution on 3D point clouds. arXiv preprint arXiv:1909.09287 (2019)

62. Hermosilla, P., Ritschel, T., Vázquez, P.P., Vinacua, À., Ropinski, T.: Monte Carlo convolution for learning on non-uniformly sampled point clouds. ACM Trans. Graph. (TOG) 37(6), 1–12 (2018)

63. Su, H., et al.: Splatnet: sparse lattice networks for point cloud processing. In: Proceedings of the IEEE Conference on Computer Vision and Pattern Recognition, pp. 2530–2539 (2018)

64. Zhang, C., Luo, W., Urtasun, R.: Efficient convolutions for real-time semantic segmentation of 3D point clouds. In: 2018 International Conference on 3D Vision (3DV), pp. 399–408. IEEE (2018)

Motion-Excited Sampler: Video Adversarial Attack with Sparked Prior

Hu Zhang[1(✉)], Linchao Zhu[1], Yi Zhu[2], and Yi Yang[1]

[1] ReLER, University of Technology Sydney, Ultimo, NSW, Australia
Hu.Zhang-1@student.uts.edu.au, zhulinchao7@gmail.com, Yi.Yang@uts.edu.au
[2] Amazon Web Services, Seattle, USA
yzaws@amazon.com

Abstract. Deep neural networks are known to be susceptible to adversarial noise, which is tiny and imperceptible perturbation. Most of previous works on adversarial attack mainly focus on image models, while the vulnerability of video models is less explored. In this paper, we aim to attack video models by utilizing intrinsic movement pattern and regional relative motion among video frames. We propose an effective motion-excited sampler to obtain motion-aware noise prior, which we term as sparked prior. Our sparked prior underlines frame correlations and utilizes video dynamics via relative motion. By using the sparked prior in gradient estimation, we can successfully attack a variety of video classification models with fewer number of queries. Extensive experimental results on four benchmark datasets validate the efficacy of our proposed method.

Keywords: Video adversarial attack · Video motion · Noise sampler

1 Introduction

Despite the superior performance achieved in a variety of computer vision tasks, i.e., image classification [12], object detection [25], segmentation [4,11], Deep Neural Networks (DNNs) are shown to be susceptible to adversarial attacks that a well-trained DNN classifier may make severe mistakes due to a single invisible perturbation on a benign input and suffer dramatic performance degradation. To investigate the vulnerability and robustness of DNNs, many effective attack methods have been proposed on image models. They either consider a white-box attack setting where the adversary can always get the full access to the model including exact gradients of given input, or a black-box one, in which the structure and parameters of the model are blocked that the attacker can only access the (*input, output*) pair through queries.

Electronic supplementary material The online version of this chapter (https://doi.org/10.1007/978-3-030-58565-5_15) contains supplementary material, which is available to authorized users.

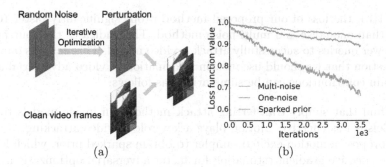

(a)   (b)

Fig. 1. (a) A pipeline of generating adversarial examples to attack a video model. (b) Loss curve comparison: i) Multi-noise: sample noise prior individually for each frame; ii) One-noise: sample one noise prior for all frames; iii) Sparked prior (ours): sample one noise prior for all frames and sparked by motion information. Loss is computed in attacking an I3D model on Kinetics-400 dataset. The lower loss indicates the better attacking performance. Our proposed sparked prior clearly outperforms (i) and (ii) in terms of attacking video models. The figure is best viewed in color. (Color figure online)

DNNs have also been widely applied in video tasks, such as video action recognition [18,31], video object detection [37], video segmentation [32], video inpainting [19] etc. However, limited work has been done on attacking video models. A standard pipeline of video adversarial attack is shown in Fig. 1(a). Specially designed perturbations are estimated from prior, which normally is random noise, and imposed on the clean video frames to generate the adversarial examples. The goal is using the adversarial examples to trick the model into giving a wrong prediction. Most literature [21,34] focuses on the white-box attack setting and simply transfer the methods used in image domain to video domain. Recently [17] proposes a black box attack method, which simply decodes a video into frames and transfers gradients from a pretrained image model for each frame. All the aforementioned methods ignore the intrinsic difference between images and videos, e.g., the extra temporal dimension. This naturally leads to a question: should we use motion information in video adversarial attack?

In this work, we propose to use motion information for black-box attack on video models. In each optimization step, instead of directly using random noise as prior, we first generate a motion map (i.e., motion vector or optical flow) between frames and construct a motion-excited sampler. The random noise will then be selected by the sampler to obtain motion-aware noise for gradient estimation, which we term as sparked prior. In the end, we feed the original video frames and the sparked prior to gradient estimator and use the estimated gradients to iteratively update the video. To show the effectiveness of using motion information, we perform a proof-of-concept comparison to two baselines. One is initializing noises separately for each frame extending [14] (multi-noise), the other is initializing one noise and replicating it across all video frames (one-noise). We use the training loss curve to reflect the effectiveness of video attack methods, in which the loss measures the distance to a fake label. As we can see in Fig. 1(b), the loss of our proposed method drops significantly faster (orange curve) than one-noise and multi-noise method. This indicates that our method takes fewer queries to successfully attack a video model. This answers our previous question that we should use motion information in video adversarial attack. Our main contributions can be summarized as follows:

– We find that simply transferring attack methods on image models to video models is less effective. Motion plays a key role in video attacking.
– We propose a motion-excited sampler to obtain sparked prior, which leads to more effective gradient estimation for faster adversarial optimization.
– We perform thorough experiments on four video action recognition datasets against two kinds of models and show the efficacy of our proposed algorithm.

2   Related Work

Adversarial Attack. Adversarial examples have been well studied on image models. [28] first shows that an adversarial sample, computed by imposing small noise on the original image, could lead to a wrong prediction. By defining a number of new losses, [1] demonstrates that previous defense methods do not significantly increase the robustness of neural networks. [23] first studies the black-box attack in image model by leveraging the transferability of adversarial examples, however, their success rate is rather limited. [13] extends Natural Evolutionary Strategies (NES) to do gradient estimation and [14] proposes to use time and data-dependent priors to reduce queries in black-box image attack. More recently, [6] proposes a meta-based method for query-efficient attack on image models.

However, limited work have been done on attacking video models. In terms of white-box attack, [34] proposes to investigate the sparsity of adversarial perturbations and their propagation across video frames. [21] leverages a Generative Adversarial Network (GAN) to account for temporal correlations and generate adversarial samples for a real-time video classification system. [15] focuses on attacking the motion stream in a two-stream video classifier by extending [9]. [5] proposes to append a few dummy frames to attack different networks by optimizing specially designed loss. The first black-box video attack method is proposed in [17], where they utilize the ImageNet pretrained models to generate a tentative gradient for each video frame and use NES to rectify it. More recently, [35] and [38] focus on sparse perturbations only on the selected frames and regions, instead of the whole video.

Our work is different from [17] because we leverage the motion information directly in generating adversarial videos. We do not utilize the ImageNet pretrained models to generate gradient for each video frame. Our work is also different from [35,38] in terms of both problem setting and evaluation metric. We follow the setting of [17] to treat the entire video as integrity, instead of attacking the video model from the perspective of frame difference in a sparse attack setting. We use attack success rate and consumed queries to evaluate our method instead of mean absolute perturbation. By using our proposed motion-aware sparked prior, we can successfully attack a number of video classification models using much fewer queries.

Video Action Recognition. Recent methods for video action recognition can be categorized into two families depending on how they reason motion information, i.e., 3D Convolutional Neural Networks (CNNs) [2,7,16,29,33,39] and two-stream networks [8,22,26,31,41]. 3D CNNs simply extend 2D filters to 3D filters in order to learn spatio-temporal representations directly from videos. Since early 3D models [16,29] are hard to train, many follow-up work have been proposed [2,7,24,30]. Two-stream methods [26] train two separate networks, a spatial stream given input of RGB images and a temporal stream given input of stacked optical flow images. An early [8] or late [31] fusion is then performed to combine the results and make a final prediction. Optical flow information has also been found beneficial in few-shot video classification [40]. Although 3D CNNs and two-stream networks are two different family of methods, they are not mutually exclusive and can be combined together. All aforementioned methods indicate the importance of motion information in video understanding.

Based on this observation, we believe motion information should benefit video adversarial attack. We thus propose the motion-excited sampler to generate a better prior for gradient estimation in a black-box attack setting. By incorporating motion information, our method shows superior attack performance on four benchmark datasets against two widely adopted video classification models.

3   Method

3.1   Problem Formulation

We consider a standard video action recognition task for attacking. Suppose the given videos have an underlying distribution denoted as $\mathcal{X}$, sample $x \in \mathbb{R}^{V \times H \times W \times C}$ and its corresponding label $y \in \{1, 2, \ldots, K\}$ are a pair in $\mathcal{X}$, where V, H, W, C denote the number of video frames, height, width and channels of each frame respectively. K represents the number of categories. We denote DNN model as function f_θ, where θ represents the model's parameters. The goal of a black-box adversarial attack is to find an adversarial example x_{adv} with imperceivable difference from x to fail the target model f_θ through querying the target model multiple times. It can be mathematically formulated as:

$$\arg\min_{x_{adv}} L(f_\theta(x_{adv}), y)$$
$$\text{s.t. } \|x_{adv}^i - x^i\| \leq \kappa, i = 0, 1, \ldots, V-1 \tag{1}$$
$$\#\text{queries} \leq Q$$

Here i is the video frame index, starting from 0 to $V-1$. $\|\cdot\|$ denotes the ℓ_p norm that measures how much perturbation is imposed, and κ indicates the maximum perturbations allowed. $f_\theta(x)$ is the returned logits or probability by the target

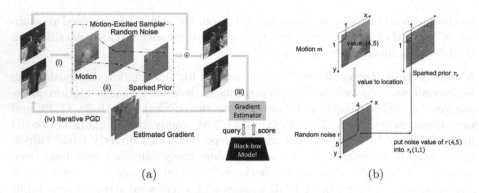

(a)   (b)

Fig. 2. (a): Overview of our framework for black-box video attack. i) Compute motion maps from given video frames; ii) Generate sparked prior from random noise by the proposed motion-excited sampler; iii) Estimate gradients by querying the black-box video model; iv) Use the estimated gradient to perform iterative projected gradient descent (PGD) optimization on the video. **(b)**: Illustration of Motion-Excited Sampler.

model f_θ when given an input video x. The loss function $L(f_\theta(x_{adv}), y)$ measures the degree of certainty for the input x_{adv} maintaining true class y. For simplicity, we shorten the loss function as $L(x_{adv}, y)$ in the rest of the paper since model parameters θ remain unchanged. The goal is to minimize the certainty and successfully fool the classification model. The first constraint enforces high similarity between clean video x and its adversarial version x_{adv}. The second constraint imposes a fixed budget Q for the number of queries used in the optimization. Hence, the fewer queries required for adversarial video and the higher overall success rate within κ perturbation, the better the attack method. The overview of our method is shown in Fig. 2(a).

3.2   Motion Map Generation

In order to incorporate motion information for video adversarial attack, we need to find an appropriate motion representation. There are two widely adopted motion representations in video analysis domain [26,31], motion vector and optical flow. Both of them can reflect the pixel intensity changes between two adjacent video frames. In this work, we adopt the accumulated motion vector [36] and the TVL1 flow [3] as the motion representation. We first describe accumulated motion vector as below.

Most modern codecs in video compression divide video into several intervals and split frames into I-frames (intracoded frames) and P-frames (predictive frames). Here, we denote the number of intervals as N and the length of an interval as T. In each interval, the first frame is I-frame and the rest $T-1$ are P-frames. The accumulated motion vector is formulated as the motion vector of each P-frame, that can trace back to the initial I-frame instead of depending on previous P-frames. Suppose the accumulated motion vector in frame t of interval

n is denoted as $m^{(t,n)} \in \mathbb{R}^{H \times W \times 2}$ and each pixel value at location i in $m^{(t,n)}$ can be computed as:

$$m_i^{(t,n)} = i - \mathcal{B}_i^{(t,n)}, 1 \leq t \leq T - 1, 0 \leq n \leq N - 1 \qquad (2)$$

where $\mathcal{B}_i^{(t,n)}$ represents the location traced back to initial I-frame from t-th frame in interval n. We refer the readers to [36] for more details.

For an interval with T frames, we can obtain $T - 1$ accumulated motion vectors. We only choose the last one $m^{(T-1,n)}$ since it traces all the way back to the I-frame in this interval and is most motion-informative. We abbreviate $m^{(T-1,n)}$ as $m^{(n)}$ and thus, we have a set of N accumulated motion vectors for the whole video, denoted as $\mathcal{M} = \{m^{(0)}, m^{(1)}, \ldots, m^{(N-1)}\}$.

Optical flow is a motion representation that is similar to motion vector with the same dimension $\mathbb{R}^{H \times W \times 2}$. It also contains spatial details but is not directly available in compressed videos. Here we use TVL1 algorithm [3] to compute the flow given its wide adoption in video-related applications [2,7,31]. We apply the same strategy as motion vectors to select optical flow and will also obtain N flow vectors. The set of flow vectors is also denoted as $\mathcal{M}$ for simplicity.

3.3 Motion-Excited Sampler

In a black-box setting, random noise is normally employed in generating adversarial examples. However, as stated before in Fig. 1(b), direct usage of random noise is not promising in video attack. To tackle this problem, we propose to involve motion information in the process of generating adversarial examples, and thus propose motion-excited sampler.

First, we define the operation of motion-excited sampler (ME-Sampler) as

$$r_s = \text{ME-SAMPLER}(r, m), \qquad (3)$$

where $r \in \mathbb{R}^{V \times H \times W \times 3}$ denotes the initial random noise, motion maps $m \in \mathbb{R}^{V \times H \times W \times 2}$ are selected with replacement from set $\mathcal{M}$ introduced in Sect. 3.2. $r_s \in \mathbb{R}^{V \times H \times W \times 3}$ will be the transformed motion-aware noise, which we term as **sparked prior** afterwards.

To be specific, we use the motion-excited sampler to "warp" the random noise by motion. It is not just rearranging the pixels in the random noise, but constructing a completely new prior given the motion information. For simplicity, we only consider the operation for one frame here. It is straightforward to extend to the case of multiple frames. Without abuse of notation, we still use r, r_s, m for clarification in this section.

At the i-th location of the motion map m, we denote the motion vector value as $p_i \in \mathbb{R}^2$ and its coordinate is denoted (x_i, y_i), i.e., $p_i = m[x_i, y_i]$. Here, $p_i = (u_i, v_i)$ has two values, which indicate the horizontal and vertical relative movements, respectively. When computing the value of position (x_i, y_i) in sparked prior r_s, (u_i, v_i) will serve as the new coordinates for searching in

---

Algorithm 1. GRAD-EST(x, y, g, loop): Estimate $\ell(g) = -\nabla_g \langle \nabla_x L(x,y), g \rangle$.

Input: video x, its label y, number of frame of video x is V. initialized g, interval t for sampling new motion map, δ for loss variation and ϵ for approximation.

1: **if** loop % t = 0 **then**
2:    motion map $m_1, m_2, \ldots, m_{V-1}$ are chosen from $\mathcal{M} = \{m^{(0)}, m^{(1)}, \ldots, m^{(N-1)}\}$ with replacement and are concatenated to be m;
3: **end if**
4: $r \leftarrow \mathcal{N}(0, I)$;
5: $r_s = $ ME-SAMPLER(r, m);
6: $w_1 = g + \delta r_s$;
7: $w_2 = g - \delta r_s$;
8: $\ell(w_1) = -\langle \nabla_x L(x,y), w_1 \rangle \approx \frac{L(x,y) - L(x + \epsilon \cdot w_1, y)}{\epsilon}$;
9: $\ell(w_2) = -\langle \nabla_x L(x,y), w_2 \rangle \approx \frac{L(x,y) - L(x + \epsilon \cdot w_2, y)}{\epsilon}$;
10: $\Delta = \frac{L(x + \epsilon w_2, y) - L(x + \epsilon w_1, y)}{\delta \epsilon} r_s$;

Output: Δ.

---

original random noise. The corresponding noise value of $r[u_i, v_i]$ will be assigned as the value in $r_s[x_i, y_i]$. Thus, we have:

$$(u_i, v_i) = m[x_i, y_i],$$
$$r_s[x_i, y_i] = r[u_i, v_i]. \tag{4}$$

We give a simplified example in Fig. 2(b) to show how our motion-excited sampler works. To determine pixel value located in $(1,1)$ of r_s, we first get motion value $(4,5)$ from motion map m at its $(1,1)$ location. We then select pixel value located in $(4,5)$ of r and put its value into location $(1,1)$ of r_s.

Generally speaking, sparked prior is still a noise map. Note that, initial noise is completely random and irrelevant to the input video. With motion-excited sampler (operation in Eq. 4 and Fig. 2(b)), pixels with the same movements will have the same noise values in sparked prior. Then, sparked prior connects different pixels on the basis of motion map and is thus block-wised. Compared to the initial noise which is completely random, sparked prior is more informative and relevant to the video because of the incorporated motion information. It thus helps to guide the direction of estimated gradients towards attacking video models in a black-box setting and enhances the overall performance.

3.4   Gradient Estimation and Optimization

Once we have the sparked prior, we incorporate it with the input video and feed them to the black-box model to estimate the gradients. We consider ℓ_{inf} noise in our paper following [17], but our framework also applies to other norms.

Similar to [14], rather than directly estimating the gradient $\nabla_x L(x,y)$ for generating adversarial video, we perform iterative updating to search. The new loss function designed for such optimization is,

$$\ell(g) = -\langle \nabla_x L(x,y), g \rangle, \tag{5}$$

$\nabla_x L(x, y)$ is the groundtruth gradient we desire and g is the gradient to be estimated. An intuitive observation from this loss function is that iterative minimization of Eq. 5 will drive our estimated gradient g closer to the true gradient.

We denote Δ to be the gradient $\nabla_g \ell(g)$ of loss $\ell(g)$. We perform a two-query estimation to the expectation and apply the authentic sampling to get

$$\Delta = \frac{\ell(g + \delta r_s) - \ell(g - \delta r_s)}{\delta} r_s, \tag{6}$$

where δ is a small number adjusting the magnitude of loss variation. By substituting Eq. (5) to Eq. (6), we have

$$\Delta = \frac{\langle \nabla_x L(x, y), g - \delta r_s \rangle - \langle \nabla_x L(x, y), g + \delta r_s \rangle}{\delta} r_s. \tag{7}$$

In the context of finite difference method, we notice, given the function L at a point x in the direction of vector g, the directional derivative $\langle \nabla L(x, y), g \rangle$ can be transferred as:

$$\langle \nabla_x L(x, y), g \rangle \approx \frac{L(x + \epsilon g, y) - L(x, y)}{\epsilon}, \tag{8}$$

ϵ is a small constant for approximation. By combining Eq. (7)–(8), we have,

$$\Delta = \frac{L(x + \epsilon w_2, y) - L(x + \epsilon w_1, y)}{\delta \epsilon} r_s, \tag{9}$$

with $w_1 = g + \delta r_s$ and $w_2 = g - \delta r_s$. The resulting algorithm for generating gradient for g is shown in Algorithm 1.

Once we have Algorithm 1, we can use it to update estimated gradient and optimize the adversarial video. To be specific, in iteration t, Δ_t is returned by Algorithm 1. We update g_t by simply applying one-step gradient descent: $g_t = g_{t-1} - \eta \Delta_t$, η is a hyperparameter to update g_t. The updated g_t is the gradient we want to use for generating adversarial videos. Finally, we combine our estimated g_t with projection gradient descent (PGD) to translate our gradient estimation algorithm into an efficient video adversarial attack method. The detailed procedure is shown in Algorithm 2, in which $\arg\max[f_\theta(x_t)]$ returns top predicted class label, $\mathrm{CLIP}(\cdot)$ constrain the updated video x_t close to the original video x_0, where $x_0 - \kappa$ is the lower bound and $x_0 + \kappa$ the upper bound. κ is the noise constraint in Eq. (1).

3.5 Loss Function

Different from applying cross-entropy loss directly, we adopt the idea in [1] and design a logits-based loss. Here, the logits returned from the black-box model is denoted as $l \in \mathbb{R}^K$, where K is the number of classes. We denote the class of largest value in logits l as y, the largest logits value is l_y. The final loss can be obtained as $L = \max(l_y - \max_{k \neq y} l_k, 0)$. Minimizing L is expected to confuse the model with the second most confident class prediction so that our adversarial attack could succeed.

Algorithm 2. Adversarial Example Optimization for ℓ_{inf} norm perturbations.

Input: original video x, its label y, learning rate h for updating adversarial video.

1: $x_0 \leftarrow x$, initially estimated $g_0 \leftarrow 0$, initial loop $t = 1$;
2: **while** $\arg\max[f_\theta(x_t)] = y$ **do**
3:     $\Delta_t = \text{GRAD-EST}(x_{t-1}, y, g_{t-1}, t-1)$;
4:     $g_t = g_{t-1} - \eta\Delta_t$;
5:     $x_t = x_{t-1} - h \cdot sign(g_t)$;
6:     $x_t = \text{CLIP}(x_t, x_0 - \kappa, x_0 + \kappa)$;
7:     $t = t + 1$;
8: **end while**
Output: x_t.

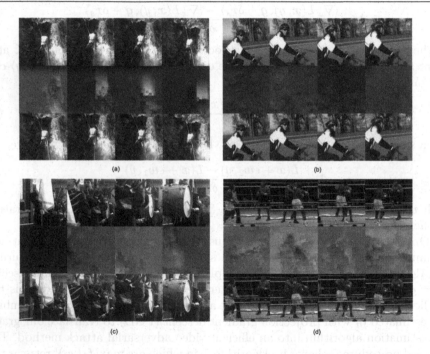

Fig. 3. Examples of motion vectors in generating adversarial samples. In (a)–(d), the first row is the original video frame, the second row is the motion vector and the third row is generated adversarial video frame. a) Kinetics-400 on I3D: Abseling → Rock climbing; b) UCF-101 on I3D: Biking → Walking with dog; c) Kinetics-400 on TSN: Playing bagpipes → Playing accordion; d) UCF-101 on TSN: Punching → Lunges.

4 Experiments

4.1 Experimental Setting

Datasets. We perform video attack on four video action recognition datasets: UCF-101 [27], HMDB-51 [20], Kinetics-400 [18] and Something-Something V2 [10]. UCF-101 consists of 13,200 videos spanned over 101 action classes.

Table 1. Test accuracy (%) of the video models.

Model	Kinetics-400	UCF-101	HMDB-51	SthSth-V2
I3D	70.11	93.55	68.30	50.25
TSN2D	68.87	86.04	54.83	35.11

HMDB-51 includes 6,766 videos in 51 classes. Kinetics-400 is a large-scale dataset which has around 300K videos in 400 classes. Something-Something V2 is a recent crowd-sourced video dataset on human-object interaction that needs more temporal reasoning. It contains 220,847 video clips in 174 classes. For notation simplicity, we use SthSth-V2 to represent Something-Something V2.

Video Models. We choose two video action recognition models, I3D [18] and TSN2D [31], as our black-box models. For I3D training on Kinetics-400 and SthSth-V2, we train it from ImageNet initialized weights. For I3D training on UCF-101 and HMDB-51, we train it with Kinetics-400 pretrained parameters as initialization. For TSN2D training, we use ImageNet initialized weights on all four datasets. The test accuracy of two models can be found in Table 1.

Attack Setting. We perform both untargeted and targeted attack under limited queries. Untargeted attack requires the given video to be misclassified to any wrong label and targeted attack requires classifying it to a specific label. For each dataset, we randomly select one video from each category following the setting in [17]. All attacked videos are correctly classified by the black-box model. We impose ℓ_{inf} noise on video frames whose pixels are normalized to 0–1. We constrain the maximum perturbation $\kappa = 0.03$, maximal queries $Q = 60,000$ for untargeted attack and $\kappa = 0.05$, $Q = 200,000$ for targeted attack. If one video is failed to attack within these constraints, we record its consumed queries as Q.

Evaluation Metric. We use the average number of queries (ANQ) required in generating effective adversarial examples and the attack success rate (SR). ANQ measures the average number of queries consumed in attacking across all videos and SR shows the overall success rate in attacking within query budget Q. A smaller ANQ and higher SR is preferred. For now, there is not a balanced metric that takes both ANQ and SR into account.

4.2 Comparison to State-of-the-Art

We report the effectiveness of our proposed method in Table 2. We present the results of leveraging two kinds of motion representations: Motion Vector (MV) and Optical Flow (OF) in our proposed method. In comparison, we first show the attacking performance of V-BAD [17] under our video models since V-BAD is the only directly comparable method. We also extend two image attack methods [13, 14] as strong baselines to video to demonstrate the advantage of using motion information. They are denoted as E-NES and E-Bandits respectively and their attacking results are shown in Table 2.

Table 2. Untargeted attacks on SthSth-V2, HMDB-51, Kinetics-400, UCF-101. The attacked models are I3D and TSN2D. "ME-Sampler" denotes the results of our method. "OF" denotes Optical Flow. "MV" denotes Motion Vector.

Dataset/model	Method	I3D		TSN2D	
		ANQ	SR (%)	ANQ	SR (%)
SthSth-V2	E-NES [13]	11,552	86.96	1,698	99.41
	E-Bandits [14]	968	100.0	435	99.41
	V-BAD [17]	7,239	97.70	495	100.0
	ME-Sampler (OF)	735	98.90	315	100.0
	ME-Sampler (MV)	**592**	**100.0**	**244**	**100.0**
HMDB-51	E-NES [13]	13,237	84.31	19,407	76.47
	E-Bandits [14]	4,549	99.80	4,261	100.0
	V-BAD [17]	5,064	100.0	2,405	100.0
	ME-Sampler (OF)	**3,306**	**100.0**	842	100.0
	ME-Sampler (MV)	3,915	100.0	**831**	**100.0**
Kinetics-400	E-NES [13]	11,423	89.30	20,698	71.93
	E-Bandits [14]	3,697	99.00	6,149	97.50
	V-BAD [17]	4,047	**99.75**	2,623	99.75
	ME-Sampler (OF)	3,415	99.30	2,631	98.80
	ME-Sampler (MV)	**2,717**	99.00	**1,715**	**99.75**
UCF-101	E-NES [13]	23,531	69.23	41,328	34.65
	E-Bandits [14]	10,590	89.10	24,890	66.33
	V-BAD [17]	8,819	97.03	17,638	91.09
	ME-Sampler (OF)	6,101	96.00	6,598	97.00
	ME-Sampler (MV)	**4,748**	**98.02**	**5,353**	**99.00**

Overall, our method using motion information achieves promising results on different datasets and models. On SthSth-V2 and HMDB-51, we even achieve 100% SR. On Kinetics-400 and UCF-101, we also get over 97% SR. The number of queries used in attacking is also encouraging. One observation worth noticing is that it only takes hundreds of queries to completely break the models on SthSth-V2. For the rest of models, we just consume slightly more queries. To analyze this, we observe that models consuming slightly more queries often have higher recognition accuracy from Table 1. From this result, we conclude that a model is likely to be more robust if its performance on the clean video is better.

In terms of using motion vector and optical flow, we find that motion vector outperforms optical flow in most cases, e.g., the number of queries used 5,353 (MV) vs 6,598 (OF) on UCF-101 against TSN2D. The reason is that motion vector always has a clearer motion region since it is computed by a small block of size 16 × 16. However, optical flow is always pixel-wisely calculated. It is not difficult to imagine that when the region used for describing is relatively larger, it

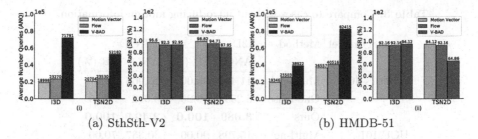

(a) SthSth-V2   (b) HMDB-51

Fig. 4. (a): Comparisons of targeted attack on SthSth-V2 with V-BAD: i) Average queries consumed by I3D and TSN2D; ii) Success rate achieved by I3D and TSN2D. (b): Comparisons of targeted attack on HMDB-51 with V-BAD: i) Average queries consumed by I3D and TSN2D; ii) Success rate achieved by I3D and TSN2D.

is easier and more accurate to portray the overall motion. When only considering each pixel, the movement is likely to be lost in tracking and make some mistakes.

Compared to E-NES and E-Bandits, we achieve better results, either on consumed queries or success rate, e.g., when attacking a TSN2D model on UCF-101, our success rate is 99.00%, which is much higher than 34.65% for E-NES and 66.33% for E-Bandits. The query 5,353 is also much smaller than 41,328 and 24,890. When compared to V-BAD, our method requires much fewer queries. For example, we save at least 1,758 queries on HMDB-51 against I3D models. Meanwhile, we achieve better success rate 100.0% vs 97.70% on SthSth-V2.

Finally, we show the visualizations of adversarial frames on Kinetics-400 and UCF-101 in Fig. 3. We note that the generated video has little difference from the original one but can lead to a failed prediction. More visualization can be found in the supplementary materials.

4.3 Targeted Attack

In this section, we report the results of targeted attack on dataset HMDB-51 and SthSth-V2 in Fig. 4. For dataset SthSth-V2 from Fig. 4(a), our method consumes less than 25,000 queries using either motion vector or optical flow. However, it costs V-BAD 71,791 against I3D model and 52,182 against TSN2D model. The success rate is about 6% higher in TSN2D model but with much fewer queries. For dataset HMDB-51 against I3D from Fig. 4(b), we also outperform V-BAD by saving more than 10,000 queries and achieve comparable success rate. For TSN2D, we only require half of the queries as V-BAD consumes but achieve a much higher success rate meanwhile, i.e., 92.16% vs 64.86%.

Combining with the untargeted results, we conclude that our method is more effective in generating adversarial videos than the comparing baselines.

4.4 Ablation Study

In this section, we first show the necessity of motion maps and then demonstrate that it is the movement pattern in the motion map that contributes to the

Table 3. Compare to cases without introducing motion information.

Dataset/model	Method	I3D		TSN2D	
		ANQ	SR (%)	ANQ	SR (%)
Kinetics-400	Multi-noise	11,416	95.00	15,966	89.87
	One-noise	8,258	96.25	8,392	96.25
	Ours	**3,089**	**100.0**	**2,494**	**100.0**
UCF-101	Multi-noise	15,798	90.00	30,337	70.00
	One-noise	22,908	93.33	16,620	90.00
	Ours	**6,876**	**100.0**	**8,399**	**100.0**

Table 4. Comparison of motion map with two handcrafted maps.

Dataset/model	Method	I3D		TSN2D	
		ANQ	SR (%)	ANQ	SR (%)
Kinetics-400	U-Sample	10,250	96.25	9,166	96.20
	S-Vaule	8,610	98.75	8,429	96.20
	Our	**3,089**	**100.0**	**2,494**	**100.0**
UCF-101	U-Sample	13,773	93.33	17,718	83.33
	S-Vaule	11,471	96.67	17,116	86.67
	Our	**6,876**	**100.0**	**8,399**	**100.0**

attacking. We also study the effect of different losses. Experiments in this section are conducted on a subset of 30 randomly selected categories from UCF-101 and 80 from Kinetics-400 by following the setting in [17].

The Necessity of Motion Maps. As mentioned in Sect. 1, we show motion is indeed important for the attack and evaluate two cases without using motion maps: 1) Multi-noise: Directly introducing random noise for each frame independently; 2) One-noise: Introducing only one random noise and replicated to all frames. The results are in Table 3. The results show that methods without using motion are likely to spend more queries and suffer a lower success rate. For example, on UCF-101 against I3D model, 'Multi-noise' consumes queries more than twice as our result and the success rate is 10% lower. Such big gaps between methods without motion and ours indicate that our designed mechanism to utilize motion maps plays an important role in directing effective gradient generation for an improved search of adversarial videos.

Why Motion Maps Helps? Here, we further replace the motion map with two handcrafted maps to reveal that the intrinsic movement pattern in a motion map matters. We show that without the correct movement pattern, the attacking performance drops significantly even using the same operation in Eq. 4.

We first define a binary map $\mathcal{R}$ whose pixel values are 1 when the corresponding pixels in original motion map are nonzero, the rest pixel values are set

Table 5. Comparison of losses based on Cross-Entropy, Probability, Logits.

Dataset/model	Method	I3D		TSN2D	
		ANQ	SR (%)	ANQ	SR (%)
Kinetics-400	Cross-Entropy	3,452	98.75	2,248	100.0
	Probability	3,089	100.0	2,494	100.0
	Logits	**2,423**	**100.0**	**1,780**	**100.0**
UCF-101	Cross-Entropy	17,362	80.00	17,992	73.26
	Probability	13,217	90.00	14,842	81.19
	Logits	**6,876**	**100.0**	**6,182**	**100.0**

as 0 and then define the two new maps here. "Uniformly Sample" (U-Sample): A map $\mathcal{U}$ is created whose pixel values are uniformly sampled from $[0, 1]$ and scaled to $[-50,50]$. Binary map $\mathcal{R}$ and $\mathcal{U}$ are multiplied together to replace original motion map. "Sequenced Value" (S-Value): A map $\mathcal{S}$ whose pixel values are ranged in order starting from 0, 1, 2 from left to right and from top to bottom. Binary map $\mathcal{R}$ and $\mathcal{S}$ are multiplied together replace original motion map.

The results are in Table 4. We first notice that 'S-Value' slightly outperforms 'U-Sample'. For example, on Kinetics-400 against I3D, 'S-Value' saves more than 1,000 queries but gets 2% higher success rate. We analyze the reason to be the gradual change of pixel values in 'S-Value', rather than irregular change. As for our method, on UCF-101 against TSN2D, 9,319 queries are saved and 16.77% higher success rate is obtained when compared to 'U-sample'. Through such comparison, we conclude that the movement pattern in motion map is the key factor to improve the attacking performance.

Comparison of Different Losses. We study the effect of three different losses for optimization here: cross-entropy loss, logits-based in Sect. 3.5. We further transfer logits l to probability p by Softmax and construct probability-based loss: $L = \max(\sum_k p_k - \max_{k \neq y} p_k, 0)$, y is the class with the largest probability value. From the results in Table 5, we conclude that logits-based loss always performs better while the other two are less effective. We also observe that Kinetics-400 is less restrictive to the selection of optimization loss, compared to UCF-101.

5   Conclusion

In this paper, we study the black-box adversarial attack on video models. We find that direct transfer of attack methods from image to video is less effective and hypothesize motion information in videos plays a big role in misleading video action recognition models. We thus propose a motion-excited sampler to generate sparked prior and obtain significantly better attack performance. We perform extensive ablation studies to reveal that movement pattern matters in attacking. We hope that our work will give a new direction to study adversarial attack on video models and some insight into the difference between videos and images.

Acknowledgement. This work is partially supported by ARC DP200100938. Hu Zhang (No. 201706340188) is partially supported by the Chinese Scholarship Council.

References

1. Carlini, N., Wagner, D.: Towards evaluating the robustness of neural networks. In: 2017 IEEE Symposium on Security and Privacy (SP), pp. 39–57. IEEE (2017)
2. Carreira, J., Zisserman, A.: Quo vadis, action recognition? A new model and the kinetics dataset. In: Proceedings of the IEEE Conference on Computer Vision and Pattern Recognition, pp. 6299–6308 (2017)
3. Chambolle, A.: An algorithm for total variation minimization and applications. J. Math. Imaging Vis. **20**(1–2), 89–97 (2004)
4. Chen, L.-C., Zhu, Y., Papandreou, G., Schroff, F., Adam, H.: Encoder-decoder with Atrous separable convolution for semantic image segmentation. In: Ferrari, V., Hebert, M., Sminchisescu, C., Weiss, Y. (eds.) ECCV 2018. LNCS, vol. 11211, pp. 833–851. Springer, Cham (2018). https://doi.org/10.1007/978-3-030-01234-2_49
5. Chen, Z., Xie, L., Pang, S., He, Y., Tian, Q.: Appending adversarial frames for universal video attack. arXiv preprint arXiv:1912.04538 (2019)
6. Du, J., Zhang, H., Zhou, J.T., Yang, Y., Feng, J.: Query-efficient meta attack to deep neural networks. In: International Conference on Learning Representations (2020). https://openreview.net/forum?id=Skxd6gSYDS
7. Feichtenhofer, C., Fan, H., Malik, J., He, K.: SlowFast networks for video recognition. In: International Conference on Computer Vision (ICCV) (2019)
8. Feichtenhofer, C., Pinz, A., Zisserman, A.: Convolutional two-stream network fusion for video action recognition. In: Proceedings of the IEEE Conference on Computer Vision and Pattern Recognition (CVPR) (2016)
9. Goodfellow, I., Shlens, J., Szegedy, C.: Explaining and harnessing adversarial examples. In: International Conference on Learning Representations (2015). http://arxiv.org/abs/1412.6572
10. Goyal, R., et al.: The "something something" video database for learning and evaluating visual common sense. In: ICCV, vol. 1, p. 3 (2017)
11. He, K., Gkioxari, G., Dollár, P., Girshick, R.: Mask R-CNN. In: Proceedings of the IEEE International Conference on Computer Vision (2017)
12. He, K., Zhang, X., Ren, S., Sun, J.: Deep residual learning for image recognition. In: Proceedings of the IEEE Conference on Computer Vision and Pattern Recognition (2016)
13. Ilyas, A., Engstrom, L., Athalye, A., Lin, J.: Black-box adversarial attacks with limited queries and information. In: International Conference on Machine Learning, pp. 2137–2146 (2018)
14. Ilyas, A., Engstrom, L., Madry, A.: Prior convictions: Black-box adversarial attacks with bandits and priors. arXiv preprint arXiv:1807.07978 (2018)
15. Inkawhich, N., Inkawhich, M., Chen, Y., Li, H.: Adversarial attacks for optical flow-based action recognition classifiers. arXiv preprint arXiv:1811.11875 (2018)
16. Ji, S., Xu, W., Yang, M., Yu, K.: 3D convolutional neural networks for human action recognition. IEEE Trans. Pattern Anal. Mach. Intell. **35**(1), 221–231 (2012)

17. Jiang, L., Ma, X., Chen, S., Bailey, J., Jiang, Y.G.: Black-box adversarial attacks on video recognition models. In: Proceedings of the 27th ACM International Conference on Multimedia, pp. 864–872 (2019)
18. Kay, W., et al.: The kinetics human action video dataset. arXiv preprint arXiv:1705.06950 (2017)
19. Kim, D., Woo, S., Lee, J.Y., So Kweon, I.: Deep video inpainting. In: Proceedings of the IEEE Conference on Computer Vision and Pattern Recognition, pp. 5792–5801 (2019)
20. Kuehne, H., Jhuang, H., Garrote, E., Poggio, T., Serre, T.: HMDB: a large video database for human motion recognition. In: 2011 International Conference on Computer Vision, pp. 2556–2563. IEEE (2011)
21. Li, S., et al.: Adversarial perturbations against real-time video classification systems. arXiv preprint arXiv:1807.00458 (2018)
22. Lin, J., Gan, C., Han, S.: TSM: temporal shift module for efficient video understanding. In: Proceedings of the IEEE International Conference on Computer Vision (2019)
23. Papernot, N., McDaniel, P., Goodfellow, I., Jha, S., Celik, Z.B., Swami, A.: Practical black-box attacks against machine learning. In: Proceedings of the 2017 ACM on Asia Conference on Computer and Communications Security, pp. 506–519. ACM (2017)
24. Qiu, Z., Yao, T., Mei, T.: Learning spatio-temporal representation with pseudo-3D residual networks. In: International Conference on Computer Vision (ICCV) (2017)
25. Ren, S., He, K., Girshick, R., Sun, J.: Faster R-CNN: towards real-time object detection with region proposal networks. In: Advances in Neural Information Processing Systems (NeurIPS) (2015)
26. Simonyan, K., Zisserman, A.: Two-stream convolutional networks for action recognition in videos. In: Advances in Neural Information Processing Systems, pp. 568–576 (2014)
27. Soomro, K., Zamir, A.R., Shah, M.: Ucf101: A dataset of 101 human actions classes from videos in the wild. arXiv preprint arXiv:1212.0402 (2012)
28. Szegedy, C., et al.: Intriguing properties of neural networks. arXiv preprint arXiv:1312.6199 (2013)
29. Tran, D., Bourdev, L., Fergus, R., Torresani, L., Paluri, M.: Learning spatiotemporal features with 3D convolutional networks. In: Proceedings of the IEEE International Conference on Computer Vision, pp. 4489–4497 (2015)
30. Tran, D., Wang, H., Torresani, L., Ray, J., LeCun, Y., Paluri, M.: A closer look at spatiotemporal convolutions for action recognition. In: Proceedings of the IEEE Conference on Computer Vision and Pattern Recognition (CVPR) (2018)
31. Wang, L., et al.: Temporal segment networks: towards good practices for deep action recognition. In: Leibe, B., Matas, J., Sebe, N., Welling, M. (eds.) ECCV 2016. LNCS, vol. 9912, pp. 20–36. Springer, Cham (2016). https://doi.org/10.1007/978-3-319-46484-8_2
32. Wang, Q., Zhang, L., Bertinetto, L., Hu, W., Torr, P.H.: Fast online object tracking and segmentation: a unifying approach. In: Proceedings of the IEEE Conference on Computer Vision and Pattern Recognition (2019)
33. Wang, X., Girshick, R., Gupta, A., He, K.: Non-local neural networks. In: Proceedings of the IEEE Conference on Computer Vision and Pattern Recognition (CVPR) (2018)
34. Wei, X., Zhu, J., Su, H.: Sparse adversarial perturbations for videos. arXiv preprint arXiv:1803.02536 (2018)

35. Wei, Z., et al.: Heuristic black-box adversarial attacks on video recognition models. arXiv preprint arXiv:1911.09449 (2019)
36. Wu, C.Y., et al.: Compressed video action recognition. In: Proceedings of the IEEE Conference on Computer Vision and Pattern Recognition, pp. 6026–6035 (2018)
37. Wu, H., Chen, Y., Wang, N., Zhang, Z.: Sequence level semantics aggregation for video object detection. In: Proceedings of the IEEE International Conference on Computer Vision (2019)
38. Yan, H., Wei, X., Li, B.: Sparse black-box video attack with reinforcement learning. arXiv preprint arXiv:2001.03754 (2020)
39. Zhu, L., Tran, D., Sevilla-Lara, L., Yang, Y., Feiszli, M., Wang, H.: Faster recurrent networks for efficient video classification. In: AAAI (2020)
40. Zhu, L., Yang, Y.: Label independent memory for semi-supervised few-shot video classification. IEEE Trans. Pattern Anal. Mach. Intell. (2020). https://doi.org/10.1109/TPAMI.2020.3007511
41. Zhu, Y., Lan, Z., Newsam, S., Hauptmann, A.: Hidden two-stream convolutional networks for action recognition. In: Jawahar, C.V., Li, H., Mori, G., Schindler, K. (eds.) ACCV 2018. LNCS, vol. 11363, pp. 363–378. Springer, Cham (2019). https://doi.org/10.1007/978-3-030-20893-6_23

An Inference Algorithm for Multi-label MRF-MAP Problems with Clique Size 100

Ishant Shanu[1(✉)], Siddhant Bharti[1(✉)], Chetan Arora[2(✉)], and S. N. Maheshwari[2(✉)]

[1] Indraprastha Institute of Information Technology, Delhi, India
ishants@iiitd.ac.in, sbharti51@gmail.com
[2] Indian Institute of Technology, Delhi, India
{chetan,snm}@cse.iitd.ac.in

Abstract. In this paper, we propose an algorithm for optimal solutions to submodular higher order multi-label MRF-MAP energy functions which can handle practical computer vision problems with up to 16 labels and cliques of size 100. The algorithm uses a transformation which transforms a multi-label problem to a 2-label problem on a much larger clique. Earlier algorithms based on this transformation could not handle problems larger than 16 labels on cliques of size 4. The proposed algorithm optimizes the resultant 2-label problem using the submodular polyhedron based Min Norm Point algorithm. The task is challenging because the state space of the transformed problem has a very large number of invalid states. For polyhedral based algorithms the presence of invalid states poses a challenge as apart from numerical instability, the transformation also increases the dimension of the polyhedral space making the straightforward use of known algorithms impractical. The approach reported in this paper allows us to bypass the large costs associated with invalid configurations, resulting in a stable, practical, optimal and efficient inference algorithm that, in our experiments, gives high quality outputs on problems like pixel-wise object segmentation and stereo matching.

Keywords: Submodular minimization · Discrete optimization · Hybrid methods · MRF-MAP · Image segmentation

1 Introduction

Many problems in computer vision can be formulated as pixel labeling problems, in which each pixel $p \in \mathcal{P}$ needs to be assigned a label $l_p \in \mathcal{L}$. Finding the joint labeling configuration, $l_{\mathcal{P}}$, over all pixels, with maximum posterior probability can then be formulated as a MRF-MAP inference problem

---

Electronic supplementary material The online version of this chapter (https://doi.org/10.1007/978-3-030-58565-5_16) contains supplementary material, which is available to authorized users.

© Springer Nature Switzerland AG 2020
A. Vedaldi et al. (Eds.): ECCV 2020, LNCS 12365, pp. 257–274, 2020.
https://doi.org/10.1007/978-3-030-58565-5_16

[25,48]. The formulation involves solving the following optimization problem: $l_{\mathcal{P}}^* = \arg\min_{l_{\mathcal{P}} \in \mathcal{L}^{|\mathcal{P}|}} \sum_{c \in \mathcal{C}} f_c(l_c)$. Here, c, also called a *clique*, is defined as a set of pixels whose labels are contextually dependent on each other. A labeling configuration on a clique c is denoted as l_c, $\mathcal{P}$ denotes the set of all pixels and $\mathcal{C}$ denotes the set of all cliques. The *order* of the MRF-MAP problem is considered as one less than the size of the maximal clique, $k = \max_{c \in \mathcal{C}} |c|$. Each term, $f_c(l_c)$, also called the *clique potential*, measures the cost of the labeling configuration l_c of a clique c, depending on how consistent the labeling is with respect to the observation and prior knowledge.

Optimal inference problem, in general, is NP hard even for first order MRFs. Therefore, researchers have explored approximate solutions to the inference problem for first order [9,28,32,52] as well as higher order MRFs [7,33,50]. Another line of research has been to identify sub-classes of clique potentials which model vision problems well and for which optimal inference algorithms can be devised with polynomial time complexity. The MRF-MAP problems with *submodular* clique potentials is one such popular sub-class [2,11,32], which is also the focus of this paper.

Use of higher-order cliques in an MRF-MAP problem is important because it has been established that they can capture more complex dependencies between pixels thereby significantly improving the quality of a labeling solution [21,26,33, 40,41,46,51,53]. Our experiments also show improvement over state of the art techniques based on the deep neural networks. Note that MRF-MAP formulation allows one to use the output of deep neural networks as the likelihood term in the objective function. Therefore, performing posterior inference, even using the manually defined priors, helps exploit the problem structure, and improves performance further.

Inference algorithms for higher-order MRF-MAP with general clique potentials output approximate solutions, and are generally based on either message passing/dual decomposition [18,31,33,37,38,47,49] or reduction to first-order potentials frameworks [10,12,15,19,21,24,32,39,41]. The focus of this paper is on developing optimal inference algorithm for multi-label, submodular, higher-order MRF-MAP problems.

One approach to handle multi-label potentials is to use encodings [2,20,53] to convert a multi-label problem to an equivalent 2-label problem while preserving submodularity. However there are some practical challenges. For a multi-label problem of order k with m labels, the encoding blows the problem to cliques of size mk and exploding the size of the solution space to 2^{mk} [2]. Note that only m^k of the 2^{mk} binary configurations resulting from the encoding correspond to the original m^k labeling configurations. The rest are *invalid* in the problem context. Note that if potentials for invalid states are kept very large and those for valid states the same as in the original multi-label version, the minimum is always among the valid states.

The use of Block Co-ordinate Descent (BCD) based techniques to handle the Min Norm Point polyhedral algorithm [45,46] is also possible in principle for such transformed problems. But the encoding based transformations pose new challenges. As explained in the next section, these techniques maintain the current feasible base vector as a convex combination of a set of extreme bases. For the 2-label problems arising out of encoding multi-label versions, some of the values in the extreme bases can correspond to energy of the invalid states. Giving a large or effectively an infinite value to the invalid states creates numerical challenges in maintaining/updating these convex combinations. Also, encoding increases the size of the cliques by m times, which increases the dimensions of the polyhedral space to an extent that cannot be handled by the algorithm in [46].

The main contribution of this paper is to show that there is enough structure in the submodular polyhedron to handle invalid extreme bases arising out of converted 2-label problems efficiently. The proposed algorithm raises the bar significantly in that using it we can handle multi-label MRF-MAP problems with 16 labels, and clique size upto 100. In comparison the current state of the art [2] can only work with cliques of size up to 4.

At this stage we would like to contrast out mapping technique with that of [29], which has exploited the linear relationship between a tree and order in labels, to map multi-label submodular functions to the more general class of tree based $L^{\natural}$-convex functions. However, these algorithms have high degree polynomial time complexity (based on [22,35,36]), limiting them to be of theoretical interest only. Our focus on the other hand is to extend the frontiers of practical optimal algorithms.

Finally, we would like to point out that when the case for higher-order potential was first made, the then existing algorithms could only work with small cliques. Solutions were approximate and potentials many times were decomposable [26,33,41]. It is only with [45] and [46] that experiments could be done with cliques of size 100 or larger. Experiments reported in [46] established that quality of object segmentation improves with larger clique sizes [46]. We extend that exercise further here by focusing on quality of multi object segmentation as a function of clique size.

2   Background

We briefly describe the basic terminology and results from *submodular function minimization* (SFM) literature required to follow the discussion in this paper. We direct the reader to [44] for more details. The objective of a SFM problem is to find a minimizer set, $S^* = \min_{S \subseteq \mathcal{V}} f(S)$ of a submodular function f, where $\mathcal{V}$ is the set of all the elements. W.l.o.g. we assume $f(\phi) = 0$. We associate two polyhedra in $\mathbb{R}^{|\mathcal{V}|}$ with f, the *submodular polyhedron*, $P(f)$, and the *base polyhedron*, $B(f)$, such that

$$P(f) = \{x \mid x \in \mathbb{R}^{|\mathcal{V}|}, \ \forall\, U \subseteq \mathcal{V} : x(U) \leq f(U)\}, \text{ and}$$
$$B(f) = \{x \mid x \in P(f), x(\mathcal{V}) = f(\mathcal{V})\},$$

where $x(v)$ denotes the element at index v in the vector x, and $x(U) = \sum_{v \in U} x(v)$. A vector in the base polyhedron $B(f)$ is called a *base*, and an extreme point of $B(f)$ is called an *extreme base*. *Edmond's greedy algorithm* gives a procedure to create an extreme base, $b^{\prec}$, given a total order $\prec$ of elements of $\mathcal{V}$ such that $\prec : v_1 \prec \ldots \prec v_n$, where $n = |\mathcal{V}|$. Denoting the first k elements in the ordered set $\{v_1, \ldots, v_k, \ldots, v_n\}$ by $k_{\prec}$, the algorithm initializes the first element as $b^{\prec}(1) = f(\{v_1\})$ and rest of the elements as $b^{\prec}(k) = f(k_{\prec}) - f((k-1)_{\prec})$. There is a one to one mapping between an ordering of the elements, and an extreme base. The *Min Max Theorem*, states that $\max\{x^-(\mathcal{V}) \mid x \in B(f)\} = \min\{f(U) \mid U \subseteq \mathcal{V}\}$. Here, $x^-(\mathcal{V})$ gives the sum of negative elements of x.

The min-norm equivalence result shows that $\arg\max_{x \in B(f)} x^-(\mathcal{V}) = \arg\min_{x \in B(f)} \|x\|_2$. Fujishige and Isotani's [14] *Min Norm Point* (MNP) algorithm uses the equivalence and solves the problem using Wolfe's algorithm [13]. The algorithm has been shown empirically to be the fastest among all base polyhedron based algorithms [23,46]. The algorithm maintains a set of extreme bases, $\{b^{\prec i}\}$, and a minimum norm base vector, x, in their convex hull, s.t.:

$$x = \sum_i \lambda_i b^{\prec i} \quad \lambda_i \geq 0, \text{ and } \sum_i \lambda_i = 1. \tag{1}$$

At a high level, an iteration in the MNP/Wolfe's algorithm comprises of two stages. In the first stage, given the current base vector, x, an extreme base, q, that minimizes $x^\mathsf{T} q$ is added to the current set. The algorithm terminates in case $\|x\| = x^\mathsf{T} q$. Otherwise it finds a new x, with smaller norm, in the convex hull of the updated set of extreme bases.

The MRF-MAP inference problem can be seen as minimizing a sum of submodular functions [30,46]. Shanu et al. [46] have suggested a block coordinate descent framework to implement the Min Norm Point algorithm in the sum of submodular functions environment when cliques are large. A very broad overview of that scheme is as follows.

With each f_c, the submodular clique potential of clique c, one can associate a base polyhedron such that:

$$B(f_c) := \left\{ y_c \in \mathbb{R}^{|c|} \mid y_c(U) \leq f_c(U), \ \forall U \subseteq c \ ; \ y_c(c) = f_c(c) \right\}. \tag{2}$$

The following results [46] relate a base vector x of function f, and a set of base vectors y_c of a f_c:

Lemma 1. *Let $x(S) = \sum_c y_c(c \cap S)$ where each y_c belongs to base polyhedra $B(f_c)$. Then the vector x belongs to base polyhedron $B(f)$.*

Lemma 2. *Let x be a vector belonging to the base polyhedron $B(f)$. Then, x can be expressed as the sum: $x(S) = \sum_c y_c(S \cap c)$, where each y_c belongs to the submodular polyhedron $B(f_c)$ i.e., $y_c \in B(f_c) \ \forall$ c.*

The block coordinate descent approach based on the results requires each block to represent a base vector y_c as defined above (c.f. [46]). Note that a base vector y_c is of dimension $|c|$ (clique size), whereas a base x is of dimension $|\mathcal{V}|$ (number of pixels in an image). Since $|c| \ll |\mathcal{V}|$, minimizing the norm of y_c over its submodular polyhedron $B(f_c)$ is much more efficient than minimizing the norm of x by just applying the MNP algorithm. However, for reasons already given and discussed in the Introduction, the algorithm based on the above fails to converge on multi-label submodular MRF-MAP problems when transformed to a 2-label MRF-MAP problems using an extension of the encoding given in [2] that preserves submodularity.

We now show how these problems can be overcome by performing block coordinate descent over two blocks: one block has convex combination of only extreme bases corresponding to valid states and the other has the convex combination of extreme bases corresponding to the invalid states. The block corresponding to valid states is small enough for the traditional MNP algorithm to output optimal solutions. For the larger block corresponding to the invalid states we develop a flow based algorithm to find a vector with minimum ℓ_2 norm. This results in an algorithm which is numerically stable and practically efficient.

3   Properties of the Multi-label to 2-Label Transformation

Let F be a multi-label submodular function defined over the set of n pixels $\mathcal{P}$. Let X and Y stand for the n-tuples of parameters. Let $\vee$ and $\wedge$ be max and min operators and let $(X \vee Y), (X \wedge Y)$ denote the n-tuples resulting from element wise application of the max and min operators over n-tuples X and Y. F is called submodular if:

$$F(X) + F(Y) \geq F(X \vee Y) + F(X \wedge Y). \tag{3}$$

We now summarize the transformation to convert a multi-label to a 2-label problem as suggested in [2,20]. Consider an *unordered* set of pixels $\mathcal{P} = \{p_1, \ldots, p_i, \ldots, p_n\}$, and an *ordered* set of labels $\mathcal{L} = \{1, \ldots, m\}$. To save the notation clutter, whenever obvious, we denote a pixel simply using variables p, q without the subscript index.

Definition 1 (Binary Encoding). *The encoding $\mathcal{E} : \mathcal{L} \to \mathbb{B}^m$ maps a label $i \in \mathcal{L}$ to a m dimensional binary vector such that its first $m - i$ elements are 0 and the remaining elements are 1.*

For example, $\mathcal{E}(1) = (0, \ldots, 0, 0, 1)$, and $\mathcal{E}(2) = (0, \ldots, 0, 1, 1)$. Let us denote the encoded label vector corresponding to a pixel p_i as $\gamma_i = (p_i^1, \ldots, p_i^m), p_i^j \in \{0, 1\}$. We denote by $\Gamma \in \mathbb{B}^{mn}$, the vector obtained by concatenating all encoded vectors $\gamma : \Gamma = (\gamma_1, \ldots, \gamma_i, \ldots, \gamma_n)$. The vector Γ represents encoding of labeling configuration over all the pixels. We also define a *universal set* containing all elements of $\Gamma : \mathcal{V} = \{p_1^1, \ldots, p_1^m, \ldots, p_n^1, \ldots, p_n^m\}$.

Definition 2 (Universal Ordering). *Assuming an arbitrary ordering among the pixels, the universal ordering, defines a total ordering of the elements p_i^j, $i \in \mathcal{Z}_{1:n}, j \in \mathcal{Z}_{1:m}$:*

$$\prec_0 : p_1^1 \prec \cdots \prec p_1^m \prec \cdots \prec p_n^1 \cdots \prec p_n^m.$$

We denote by $S \subseteq \mathcal{V}$, called *state*, set of all the elements, p_i^j of Γ labeled as 1. Note that there are 2^{mn} possible states, however only m^n of them correspond to valid Γ vector obtained by encoding labeling configurations over the pixels. We call such states as *valid states*. If label of a pixel p_i is denoted as $l_i \in \mathcal{L}$, a valid state may be represented as: $S = \{\mathcal{E}(l_1), \ldots, \mathcal{E}(l_i), \ldots, \mathcal{E}(l_n)\}$. Similarly $S_p = \{\mathcal{E}(l_p)\}$ includes elements corresponding to pixel p.

Definition 3 (Valid Ordering/Extreme Base). *An ordering $\prec$ is called a valid ordering, if for any $p_i^j, p_i^k \in \mathcal{V}$, $j > k \Rightarrow p_i^j \prec p_i^k$. An extreme base $b^\prec$ is called a valid extreme base, if it corresponds to a valid ordering.*

The states, orderings or extreme-bases which are not valid are called *invalid*. We denote the set of all valid states by $\mathcal{S}$.

Definition 4 (Covering State, Minimal Covering State). *For an arbitrary state, S, a valid state, $\hat{S} \in \mathcal{S}$, is called covering if $S \subseteq \hat{S}$. There may be multiple covering states corresponding to a S. The one with the smallest cardinality among them is referred to as the minimal covering state, and is denoted by $\overline{S}$. There is a unique minimal covering state corresponding to any S. For a valid state $S = \overline{S}$.*

We are now ready to show that the above transformation can be used to define a binary set function which is not only submodular but is also identical to the multi-label submodular function on valid states. We encode the multi-label function to a submodular pseudo-Boolean function f defined over set $\mathcal{V}$ of size mn as follows:

Definition 5 (The Extended Binary Set Function).

$$f(S) = \begin{cases} F(\ldots, l_i, \ldots), & \text{if } S = \{\ldots, \mathcal{E}(l_i), \ldots\} \\ f(\overline{S}) + (|\overline{S}| - |S|)L & \text{otherwise} \end{cases}$$

Here $l_i \in \mathcal{L}$ is label of pixel p_i, and $L \gg M = [\max_{S \in \mathcal{S}} f(S) - \min_{S \in \mathcal{S}} f(S)]$.

It is easy to see that $f(S)$ can also be defined as follows:

Definition 6 (The Extended Binary Set Function: Alternate Definition).

$$f(S) = f(\overline{S}) + \sum_{p \in \mathcal{P}} (|\overline{S}_p| - |S_p|)L, \tag{4}$$

where $\overline{S}_p \subset \overline{S}$, and $S_p \subset S$ are the subsets containing elements corresponding to pixel p in $\overline{S}$ and S respectively.

Theorem 1. *The extended binary set function f, as given by Definition 5, is submodular, and $\min f(\cdot) = \min F(\cdot)$.*

To prevent the breaking of thought flow, and due to restrictions on length, the detailed proof of this theorem as well as those following are given in the supplementary material.

The reader may, at this stage, wonder whether it is at all possible to limit to working only with the valid states in the submodular mode, perhaps using one-hot encoding as in [53]. The answer is no, since in a one-hot encoding the set of all valid states is not a ring family [34], and hence the encoded function is not submodular.

Note that in the proposed encoding, any value of $L \gg M$, keeps the function, f, submodular. However, as we show later, choosing such a large value of L, makes the contribution of some extreme bases very small causing precision issues in the computation. We also show that including those extreme bases with very small contribution is extremely important for achieving the optimal inference. The major contribution of this paper is in showing that one can perform an efficient inference bypassing L altogether. Therefore, the use of L is merely conceptual in our framework. There is no impact of actual value of L on the algorithm's performance.

4 Representing Invalid Extreme Bases

In the discussion that follows, we refer to any scalar as _small_ or _finite_ if its absolute value is $\ll L$, and _large_ or _infinite_ if the absolute value is $\propto L$. We write Eq. (1) as:

$$x = x_v + x_i = \sum_{b^{\prec j} \in R} \lambda_j b^{\prec j} + \sum_{b^{\prec i} \in Q} \lambda_i b^{\prec i}. \tag{5}$$

Here, R and Q are the sets of valid and invalid extreme bases, and x_v, and x_i, their contribution in x respectively. It is easy to see that, all the elements of x_i must be much smaller than L [1]. We first focus on the relationship between λ and L in the block of invalid extreme bases.

Lemma 3. _For any element, e, of an invalid extreme base, $b^{\prec} : b^{\prec}(e) = a_e L + b_e$, where $|a_e|, |b_e| \ll L$ and $a_e \in I$._

Lemma 4. _Consider two base vectors x_1 and x_2 such that $\|x_1\|^2, \|x_2\|^2 < |\mathcal{V}|M^2$. If $x_2 = (1-\lambda)x_1 + \lambda b^{\prec}$ and $b^{\prec}$ is an invalid extreme base, then $\lambda \leq |\mathcal{V}|\frac{M}{L}$._

Conceptually, Lemma 3 shows that all elements of an invalid extreme base are either small or are proportional to L (and not proportional to, say L^2, or other higher powers of L). Whereas, Lemma 4 shows that since $\mathcal{V}$ and M are effectively constants, λ the multiplicative factor associated with in the contribution of invalid extreme bases, λ is proportional to $1/L$. Therefore, for $L \approx \infty$, the value

---

[1] We start the algorithm with a valid extreme base, where the condition is satisfied. In all further iterations the norm of x decreases monotonically, and the condition continues to remain satisfied.

of $\lambda \approx 0$. However, it is important to note that the value of $\lambda b^{\prec}(e)$, is always finite. It is easy to see that, whenever $a_e = 0$, $\lambda b^{\prec}(e) \approx 0$, and when $a_e \neq 0$, the L present in the $b^{\prec}(e)$ and $1/L$ present in λ cancel each other, leading to a finite contribution. The argument as given above motivates our overall approach in this paper that, for a numerically stable norm minimization algorithm, focus should be on manipulating the finite valued product $\lambda b^{\prec}$, and not the individual λ and $b^{\prec}(e)$. We show in the following sections that this is indeed possible.

We start by showing that it is possible to find a small set of what we call *elementary* invalid extreme bases whose linear combination contains as a subset the space of vectors x_i as given in Eq. (5). Crucial to doing this is the notion of *canonical orderings*.

4.1   Canonical Ordering and Its Properties

In an arbitrary, valid or invalid, ordering $\prec$ consider two adjacent elements u and v such that $u \prec v$. We term swapping of order locally between u and v in $\prec$ as an *exchange operation*. The operation will result in a new ordering $\prec_{\text{new}}$ such that u and v are still adjacent but $v \prec_{\text{new}} u$.

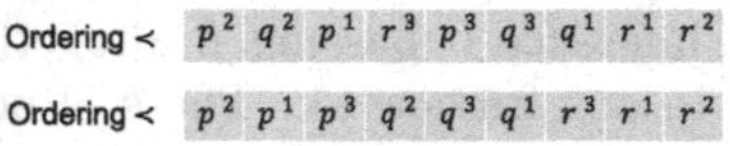

Ordering $<$ $\boxed{p^2 \; q^2 \; p^1 \; r^3 \; p^3 \; q^3 \; q^1 \; r^1 \; r^2}$

Canonical Ordering $<$ $\boxed{p^2 \; p^1 \; p^3 \; q^2 \; q^3 \; q^1 \; r^3 \; r^1 \; r^2}$

Fig. 1. Top: An ordering of elements in $\mathcal{P} = \{p, q, r\}$, for a label of size 3. Bottom: Corresponding canonical ordering.

Consider a strategy in which starting with $\prec$ we carry out exchange operations till all the elements corresponding to a pixel come together, and repeat this for all pixels. Note that we do not change the relative ordering between elements corresponding to the same pixel. We call the resultant ordering the *canonical* form of the original ordering $\prec$ and denote it by $\overline{\prec}$. The corresponding extreme base is called *canonical extreme base*. Note that there can be multiple canonical forms of an ordering. Figure 1 contains an example of an arbitrary ordering and one of its canonical orderings. We emphasize here that there may be more than one canonical orderings corresponding to $\prec$.

Note that a valid (invalid) ordering leads to a valid (invalid) canonical ordering. For any p^j and p^k, in a valid canonical ordering, if $j = k + 1$, then p^j, p^k are adjacent in the ordering and $p^k \overline{\prec} p^j$. Further, a canonical ordering is agnostic to any relative order among pixels. For example, for pixels p and q, a canonical ordering only requires that all elements of p (or q) are contiguous. An ordering in which elements corresponding to p come before those of q will define a different canonical ordering from the one in which the relative ordering of elements of p and q is vice-versa. In general a canonical ordering $\overline{\prec}$ corresponding to a $\prec$ can be any one of the possible canonical orderings.

Lemma 5. *Let $\prec$ be an invalid ordering and $\overline{\prec}$ be its canonical ordering. Then,* $b^{\prec}(e) - b^{\overline{\prec}}(e) \ll L, \forall e \in \mathcal{V}$.

The above result serves to indicate that by changing an invalid extreme base to canonical one, the change in value of any element of the extreme base is much less than L. Therefore, due to Lemma 4, one can conclude that the contribution of an invalid extreme base or its canonical extreme base in a base vector is going to be the same.

Lemma 6. *For a canonical invalid ordering $\precsim$, let p^i and p^j be two adjacent elements corresponding to a pixel p, s.t. $p^i \precsim p^j$. Let $\precsim_p^{i,j}$ be the ordering obtained by swapping p^i and p^j. Then: $b^{\precsim_p^{i,j}} - b^{\precsim} = (\chi_p^j - \chi_p^i)(aL + b)$, where χ_p^i is an indicator vector for the element p^i, and $a, b \ll L$.*

Lemma 6 relates the two extreme bases when one pair of their elements is swapped. It is useful to note that in a valid extreme base all elements have small values. With each swap in an invalid canonical ordering we either move the canonical ordering towards validity or away from it. In each swap the change in the value of an element is proportional to L (positive or negative). Since conversion of an invalid canonical ordering to a valid one may involve swaps between a number of elements, the extreme base corresponding to the invalid ordering will contain multiple elements with values proportional to L. The special cases are the ones in which only one swap has been done. In these cases there will be only two elements with values proportional to L (positive and negative). We show that using such extreme bases as the basis to represent canonical invalid extreme bases. In the next section we show that it is indeed possible.

4.2 Elementary Invalid Extreme Base

Definition 7 (Elementary Invalid Extreme Base). *The ordering obtained by swapping two elements p^j and p^{j+1}, corresponding to a pixel p, in a canonical valid ordering, is called an elementary invalid ordering. Its corresponding extreme base is called elementary invalid extreme base, and is denoted as $b^{\precsim_p^j}$.*

Lemma 7. *Consider an elementary invalid extreme base $b^{\precsim_p^i}$, obtained by swapping two adjacent elements (p^{i+1}, p^i) in the universal ordering, $\prec_0$ (Def. 2). Then: $b^{\precsim_p^i} - b^{\prec_0} = (\chi_p^i - \chi_p^{i+1})(L + b)$, where $b^{\prec_0}$ is the valid extreme base corresponding to $\prec_0$.*

Lemma 8. *An invalid canonical extreme base, $b^{\precsim}$, can be represented as a linear combination of elementary invalid extreme base vectors such that: $b^{\precsim} = \sum_{p \in \mathcal{P}} \sum_{i=1}^{m-1} \alpha_p^i b^{\precsim_p^i} + \Lambda$, where $0 < \alpha_p^i \ll L$, and Λ is a vector with all its elements much smaller than L.*

Due to Lemma 5, the above result is also true for representing the invalid extreme bases (and not only the canonical ones), with a different Λ. Lemma 7 allows us to further simplify the result of Lemma 8 to the following:

Lemma 9 (Invalid Extreme Base Representation). *An invalid extreme base can be represented as $b^{\precsim} = \sum_{p \in \mathcal{P}} \sum_{i=1}^{m-1} \alpha_p^i L(\chi_p^i - \chi_p^{i+1}) + \Lambda$, where χ_p^i is an indicator vector corresponding to element p^i, $0 < \alpha_p^i \ll L$, and Λ is some vector whose all elements are $\ll L$.*

Recall from Eq. (5): $x = x_v + x_i$, where $x_v = \sum_{b^{\prec j} \in R} \lambda_j b^{\prec j}$, and $x_i = \sum_{b^{\prec i} \in Q} \lambda_i b^{\prec i}$. Using Lemma 9 to replace the second term, and noting that $L \approx \infty \Rightarrow \lambda_i \approx 0$, and $\sum \lambda_j \approx 1$, one observes that the term $\sum_{b^{\prec i} \in Q} \lambda_i \Lambda_i$ in the expansion can be made smaller than the precision constant by increasing the value of L ($\lambda < |\mathcal{V}|M/L$ by Lemma 4) and can be dropped. As one of the final theoretical results of this paper, we can show the following:

Theorem 2 (Main Result).

$$\sum_{\forall b^{\prec i} \in Q} \lambda_i b^{\prec i} = \sum_{p \in \mathcal{P}} \sum_{k=1}^{m-1} \beta_p^k L(\chi_p^k - \chi_p^{k+1}), \tag{6}$$

where $\lambda_i \geq 0$, $\beta_p^k = \sum_{b_i \in Q} \alpha_p^k \lambda_i$.

Note that the above result incorporates _all_ the invalid extreme bases, not merely the ones involved in the representation of base vector x in any iteration of MNP. Using the result in Eq. (5), we get: $\|x\|^2 = \left\| \sum_{b^{\prec j} \in R} \lambda_j b^{\prec j} + \sum_{p \in \mathcal{P}} \sum_{k=1}^{m-1} \beta_p^k L(\chi_p^k - \chi_p^{k+1}) \right\|^2$.

5 The Multi-label Hybrid Algorithm

In this section we give the algorithm for minimizing the norm of the base vector corresponding to a single clique in the original MRF-MAP problem, where the pseudo-Boolean function is generated from encoding the multi-label function. For solving the overall MRF-MAP problem with multiple cliques, the proposed algorithm can be used in the inner loop of the BCD strategy as suggested in [46].

Theorem (2) opens up the possibility of minimizing $\|x\|^2$ for a single clique using the BCD strategy. We will have two blocks. The first block, called the _valid block_, is a convex combination of valid extreme bases $b^{\prec j}$, where standard MNP algorithm can be used to optimize the block. The other block, called the _invalid block_, corresponds to the sum of the mn

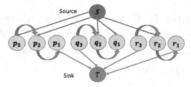

Fig. 2. Flow graph corresponding to the exchange operations for optimizing the block containing invalid extreme bases.

terms of type: $\beta_p^k L(\chi_p^k - \chi_p^{k+1})$, representing the invalid extreme bases. For minimizing the norm of the overall base vector using the invalid block, we hold the contribution from the valid block, x_v, constant[2]. Each vector $\beta_p^k L(\chi_p^k - \chi_p^{k+1})$ may be looked upon as capturing the β_p^k increase/decrease due to the exchange operation between the two adjacent elements which define an elementary extreme base. This exchange operation can be viewed as flow of $\beta_p^k L$ from the element

---

[2] Recall that we start from a valid extreme base. Therefore, at initialization $x = x_v$.

Algorithm 1. Computing Min ℓ_2 Norm from the Flow Output

Input: Vector e the output of the max flow algorithm.
Output: The transformed vector e with minimum ℓ_2 norm.

1: **for** $\forall p \in \mathcal{P}$ **do**
2:     **for** $i = 2 : m$ **do**
3:         **repeat**
4:             Find smallest k, $i \geq k \geq 1$, such that
                $e(p^i) > e(p^{i-1}) = e(p^{i-2}) \cdots = e(p^k)$ or
                $e(p^i) = e(p^{i-1}) = e(p^{i-2}) \cdots = e(p^{k+1}) > e(p^k)$;
5:             Set $e(p^i), e(p^{i-1}), \ldots, e(p^k)$ equal to av_k,
                where av_k is the average of $e(p^i), e(p^{i-1}), \ldots, e(p^k)$;
6:         **until** $e(p^{k+1}) \leq e(p^k)$
7:     **end for**
8: **end for**

---

p^{k+1} to p^k. We model the optimization problem for the invalid block using a flow graph whose nodes consists of $\{p^k \mid p \in \mathcal{P}, 1 \leq k \leq m-1\} \cup \{s, t\}$. We add two type of edges:

- **Type 1:** If $x_v(p^k)$, corresponding to the valid block contribution, is > 0, then we add a directed edge from $s \rightarrow p^k$, else we add the edge from $p^k \rightarrow t$ with capacity $x_v(p^k)$.
- **Type 2:** The directed edges p^{k+1} to p^k, $1 \leq k \leq (m-1)$ with capacity $|\mathcal{V}|M$ to ensure that the capacity is at least as large as $\beta_p^k L$: much larger than any permissible value of $x_v(p^k)$. Thus, any feasible flow augmentation in a path from from s to t can saturate only the first or the last edge in the augmenting path (i.e. the edge emanating from s or the edge incident at t in the path).

Figure 2 is an example of a flow graph for 3 pixel and 3 label problem. Since the starting state is x_v the "initial flow" prior to pushing flow for flow maximization requires setting flow in a type 1 edge incident at p^k equal to the value of $x_v(p^k)$ and that in type 2 edges as 0. This is because sum of flow on all edges incident at a node may be looked upon as the value of the corresponding element in the base vector[3]. In effect initially there are non zero excesses on the non s, t nodes in the flow graph defined as the sum of net in-flow on all edges incident at a node. The excess at node p_k is denoted by $e(p_k)$. Max flow state can be looked upon as that resulting from repeatedly sending flow from a positive excess vertex to a negative excess vertex till that is no more possible. Values in the optimal base vector (optimal subject to the given x_v) at the end of this iteration will be the excesses at nodes when max flow state has been reached.

5.1   Computing Min ℓ_2 Norm by Flow

Since there is no edge between any two nodes corresponding to different pixels max flow can be calculated independently for each pixel. When max flow state

---

[3] We refer the reader to [45] for details about the flow to base vector correspondence.

is reached in the flow graph associated with a pixel, a vertex which still has a negative excess will be to the left of vertices with positive excess (planar flow graph laid out as in Fig. 2) otherwise flow could be pushed from a positive excess vertex to a negative excess vertex.

Note that the optimal base vector is not unique. Consider two adjacent vertices, p^{k+1} and p^k, in the flow graph when the max flow state has been reached. If $e(p^{k+1})$ is larger than $e(p^k)$ then increasing the flow in the edge from p^{k+1} to p^k by δ decreases $e(p^{k+1})$ by δ and increases $e(p^k)$ by δ. The result of this "exchange operation" is to create another optimal base vector but with a smaller ℓ_2 norm.

An optimal base vector with minimum ℓ_2 norm will correspond to the max flow state in the flow graph in which $e(p^{k+1}) \leq e(p^k)$ for all adjacent pairs of type 2 vertices. If this is not so then there would exist at least a pair $e(p^{k+1})$ and $e(p^k)$ such that $e(p^{k+1}) > e(p^k)$. Doing an exchange operation between p^{k+1} and p^k involving setting $e(p^{k+1})$ and $e(p^k)$ to the average of the old values will create a new optimal base vector with lower value of the ℓ_2 norm. Algorithm 1 gives an efficient procedure to transform the optimal base vector outputted by the max flow algorithm to one with minimum ℓ_2 norm. Note that the proposed algorithm simply updates the base vector in one pass without any explicit flow pushing. In contrast, the corresponding algorithm for general flow graphs given in [45] requires $O(n \log n)$ additional max flow iterations over an n vertex flow graph.

5.2   Overall Algorithm

The proposed Multi-label Hybrid (MLHybrid) algorithm is quite similar to the algorithm in [46] in its over all structure. Just like [46], we also create blocks corresponding to each clique, and optimize each block independently (taking the contribution of other blocks as suggested in [46]) in an overall block coordinate descent strategy. The only difference between SoSMNP and MLHybrid is the way we optimize one block. While SoSMNP uses standard MNP, we optimize using a special technique, as outlined in previous section, with (sub)blocks of valid and invalid extreme bases, within each block/clique. Hence, the convergence and correctness of overall algorithm follows from block coordinate descent similar to [46]. What we need to show is that for a single clique/block, the algorithmic strategy of alternating between valid and invalid blocks converges to the optimal for that clique/block.

Recall that in a standard MNP algorithm iteration, given the current base vector x, an extreme base q, that minimizes $x^\mathsf{T} q$ is added to the current set. Hence, steps to convergence of MNP is bounded by the number of extreme bases that may be added. In our case we have shown in the Supplementary Section that when we start with a valid extreme base, the extreme base generated in the valid block after using the latest contribution from the invalid block, will come out to be a valid extreme base. This implies that the number of iterations involving invalid blocks can not exceed the number of valid extreme bases added as in the standard MNP algorithm. This ensures convergence of the optimization

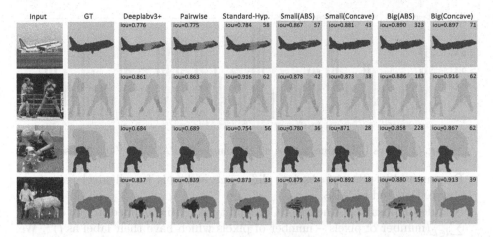

Fig. 3. Pixel-wise object segmentation comparison. Input images from the Pascal VOC dataset.

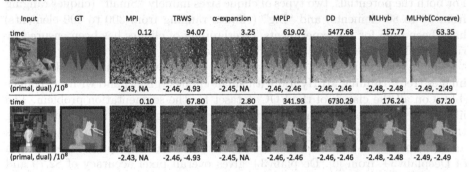

Fig. 4. Stereo matching problem. Input images from the Middlebury dataset.

step for each block. The formal convergence proof for the MLHybrid algorithm is given in the Supplementary Section.

The correctness of our optimization for each block follows from the fact that the optimization for valid blocks proceeds in the standard way, and results in a new extreme base given the current base vector. The correctness of the optimization step of the invalid block, which finds a minimum norm base vector given a valid block, has already been explained in the previous section.

6 Experiments

We have experimented with pixel-wise object segmentation and stereo correspondence problems. All experiments have been conducted on a computer with Intel Core i7 CPU, 8 GB of RAM running Windows 10. Implementation of our algorithm is in C++ (https://github.com/ishantshanu/ML-Minnorm). For the segmentation experiments, the input images are from Pascal VOC dataset [8] with a small amount of Gaussian noise added. We have experimented with two types of submodular clique potentials:

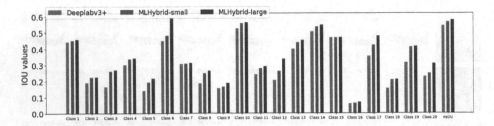

Fig. 5. Shows IOU values across all the classes of PASCAL VOC dataset.

- Decomposable: Sum of absolute difference of labels for all pixel pairs in a clique. Denoted by ABS.
- Non-decomposable: Concave-of-Cardinality potential defined in [53] as: $\sum_{l \in \mathcal{L}}$(number of pixels − number of pixels which have their label as l)$^{\alpha}$. We have used $\alpha = 0.5$ in our experiments.

For both the potentials, two types of clique sizes namely "Small" (cliques ranging from 60 to 80 elements) and "Big" (cliques ranging from 300 to 400 elements) have been used for the experiments. Overlapping of cliques has been ensured by running SLIC algorithm [1] with different seeds.

Figure 5 shows the IOU values as bars for Deeplabv3+ [6] fine-tuned on noisy images (red), running MLHybrid with small cliques (green) and with big cliques (blue) on all the classes of the VOC dataset for the segmentation problem. The likelihood of a label on each pixel, required for our algorithm, is estimated using the scaled score from the Deeplabv3+. The scaling factors are specific to labels and are the hyper-parameters in our algorithm. We use the pre-trained version of Deeplabv3+ from [6]. Deeplabv3+ gives overall pixel accuracy of 82.79 and with MLHybrid we get pixel accuracy of 84.07 and 85.11 respectively for small and big cliques. Mean IOU values (three bars at the right end) are 0.544, 0.566, and 0.579 respectively. MLHybrid has been run with non-decomposable clique potentials and the same standard fixed hyper parameters on the VOC dataset.

The performance of MLHybrid improves with fine tuning of hyper parameters. Figure 3 shows the visual results on four pictures from the data set when the hyper parameters have been tuned. To show the extent of improvement we have also included in Fig. 3 the MlHybrid output with the standard hyper parameters (standard-hyp). We have also included the IOU values in the images (upper left hand corner) corresponding to Deeplabv3+, MlHybrid (Big(concave)) run with standard and fine tuned hyper parameters respectively. For all the four images IOU values hover around 0.9 when MLHybrid is run with big cliques and concave potentials. Run time for MLhybrid in seconds are shown at the upper right corner of the respective images. Deeplabv3+ takes approximately 0.5 seconds per image excluding the training time. Hyper parameters for α-expansion running on pairwise cliques (4th column in Fig. 3) are the optimized parameters used for MLHybrid as are the likelihood labels for the pixels.

Note that the quality of output is distinctly better for the non-decomposable concave potential in comparison to the decomposable ABS potential for both

Small and Big clique configurations. The output for Big(Concave) matches the ground truth significantly. The time taken for concave potentials is distinctly less than ABS potentials for the same size and number of cliques. This difference is because the number of iterations taken for convergence is proportionately less for non-decomposable potentials. It is reasonable to infer that the segmentation quality improves with clique size. Since for large cliques, potentials will need to be predefined and not learnt, designing clique potentials calls for further investigation. Also, since fine tuning of hyper parameters improves quality of segmentation results significantly an area of research with high pay off is how to automate the process of fine tuning the hyper parameters for the segmentation problem.

For stereo correspondence, the images are from Middelbury dataset [42] and are of size 200×200. The cliques are generated, as earlier, using SLIC algorithm. Label likelihood is calculated using Birchfield/Tomasi cost given in [3]. There are 16 disparity labels considered and clique potential used is the same as for the segmentation problem. Figure 4 shows the output. We have compared with implementations of Max Product Inference (MPI) [27], TRWS [28], MPLP [16], α-expansion [4] available in Darwin framework [17]. We use the pair wise absolute difference of labels potential with a pixel covered by maximum of four cliques. Other than α-expansion, other methods could not handle pairwise potentials emanating out of all pairs of variables in a clique of size 50 or larger. Primal/Dual values are shown below the images and their corresponding running times on the top.

Our final experiments are to show efficacy of convergence of the MLHybrid algorithm. Table 1 shows the performance of SOS-MNP [46] on the extended pseudo-boolean submodular function. Since [46] do not bypass L

Table 1. Primal dual for SoS-MNP [46] for different values of L.

$L =$	10^9	10^{11}	10^{13}	10^{15}
Primal	$1.26(10^{15})$	$1.26(10^{17})$	$-1.75(10^8)$	$-1.77(10^8)$
Dual	$-5.37(10^8)$	$-5.37(10^8)$	$-5.58(10^8)$	$-5.60(10^8)$

therefore we run it for different values of L. Note that primal and dual do not converge even when the value of L is as large as 10^{15} after running the algorithm for approximately 50 min. SOS-MNP not only takes huge amount of time but do not even converge to the right point.

In contrast Fig. 6 shows the convergence performance of the MLHybrid algorithm for solving a stereo problem on the sawtooth sample with sum of absolute difference potential. The figure shows that on the same potential function and same problem size, time taken for effective convergence by the MLHybrid algorithm is only around 28 seconds. It must be pointed out that one of the factors contributing to speed gain is the way invalid extreme bases are being handled. The flow

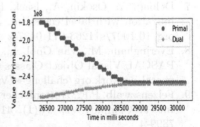

Fig. 6. Convergence of MLHybrid.

graph created at each iteration handles a fixed number of (only $n(m-1)$) elementary extreme bases which span the space of all invalid extreme bases. The run-time at each iteration is essentially independent of the number of invalid extreme bases added by Wolfe's algorithm.

7   Conclusions

In this paper, we have proposed a new efficient inference algorithm for higher-order multi-label MRF-MAP problems, which enables obtaining optimal solution to such problems when potentials are submodular, and even when the cliques are of size upto 100 (for a 16 label problem). This has been made possible by exploiting the structure of the potentials used to make the extension function submodular. The min ℓ_2 norm solution to the block of invalid extreme bases can be found by max flow techniques on a particularly simple flow graph. What takes a series of max flow iterations in [45] requires only two linear time passes on the resultant flow graph.

References

1. Achanta, R., Shaji, A., Smith, K., Lucchi, A., Fua, P., Süsstrunk, S.: SLIC superpixels compared to state-of-the-art superpixel methods. PAMI **34**(11), 2274–2282 (2012)
2. Arora, C., Maheshwari, S.: Multi label generic cuts: optimal inference in multi label multi clique MRF-MAP problems. In: CVPR, pp. 1346–1353 (2014)
3. Birchfield, S., Tomasi, C.: A pixel dissimilarity measure that is insensitive to image sampling. PAMI **20**(4), 401–406 (1998)
4. Boykov, Y., Veksler, O., Zabih, R.: Fast approximate energy minimization via graph cuts. IEEE Trans. Pattern Anal. Mach. Intell. **23**(11), 1222–1239 (2001)
5. Chakrabarty, D., Jain, P., Kothari, P.: Provable submodular minimization using Wolfe's algorithm. In: NIPS, pp. 802–809 (2014)
6. Chen, L.-C., Zhu, Y., Papandreou, G., Schroff, F., Adam, H.: Encoder-decoder with atrous separable convolution for semantic image segmentation. In: Ferrari, V., Hebert, M., Sminchisescu, C., Weiss, Y. (eds.) ECCV 2018. LNCS, vol. 11211, pp. 833–851. Springer, Cham (2018). https://doi.org/10.1007/978-3-030-01234-2_49
7. Delong, A., Osokin, A., Isack, H.N., Boykov, Y.: Fast approximate energy minimization with label costs. Int. J. Comput. Vis. **96**(1), 1–27 (2012). https://doi.org/10.1007/s11263-011-0437-z
8. Everingham, M., Van Gool, L., Williams, C.K.I., Winn, J., Zisserman, A.: The PASCAL Visual Object Classes Challenge 2012 (VOC2012) Results. http://www.pascal-network.org/challenges/VOC/voc2012/workshop/index.html
9. Felzenszwalb, P.F., Huttenlocher, D.P.: Efficient belief propagation for early vision. Int. J. Comput. Vis. **70**(1), 41–54 (2006). https://doi.org/10.1007/s11263-006-7899-4
10. Fix, A., Gruber, A., Boros, E., Zabih, R.: A graph cut algorithm for higher-order Markov random fields. In: ICCV, pp. 1020–1027 (2011)
11. Fix, A., Wang, C., Zabih, R.: A primal-dual algorithm for higher-order multilabel Markov random fields. In: CVPR, pp. 1138–1145 (2014)

12. Freedman, D., Drineas, P.: Energy minimization via graph cuts: settling what is possible. In: CVPR, pp. 939–946 (2005)
13. Fujishige, S., Hayashi, T., Isotani, S.: The minimum-norm-point algorithm applied to submodular function minimization and linear programming (2006)
14. Fujishige, S., Isotani, S.: A submodular function minimization algorithm based on the minimum-norm base. Pac. J. Optim. **7**, 3–17 (2011)
15. Gallagher, A.C., Batra, D., Parikh, D.: Inference for order reduction in Markov random fields. In: CVPR, pp. 1857–1864 (2011)
16. Globerson, A., Jaakkola, T.S.: Fixing max-product: convergent message passing algorithms for map LP-relaxations. In: NIPS, pp. 553–560 (2008)
17. Gould, S.: Darwin: a framework for machine learning and computer vision research and development. JMLR **13**(Dec), 3533–3537 (2012)
18. Hazan, T., Shashua, A.: Norm-product belief propagation: primal-dual message-passing for approximate inference. Inf. Theory **56**(12), 6294–6316 (2010)
19. Ishikawa, H.: Higher-order clique reduction without auxiliary variables. In: CVPR, pp. 1362–1369 (2014)
20. Ishikawa, H.: Exact optimization for Markov random fields with convex priors. PAMI **25**(10), 1333–1336 (2003)
21. Ishikawa, H.: Transformation of general binary MRF minimization to the first-order case. TPAMI **33**(6), 1234–1249 (2011)
22. Iwata, S., Fleischer, L., Fujishige, S.: A combinatorial strongly polynomial algorithm for minimizing submodular functions. JACM **48**(4), 761–777 (2001)
23. Jegelka, S., Bach, F., Sra, S.: Reflection methods for user-friendly submodular optimization. In: NIPS, pp. 1313–1321 (2013)
24. Kahl, F., Strandmark, P.: Generalized roof duality for pseudo-Boolean optimization. In: ICCV, pp. 255–262 (2011)
25. Kappes, J.H., et al.: A comparative study of modern inference techniques for structured discrete energy minimization problems. IJCV **115**(2), 155–184 (2015). https://doi.org/10.1007/s11263-015-0809-x
26. Kohli, P., Torr, P.H., et al.: Robust higher order potentials for enforcing label consistency. IJCV **82**(3), 302–324 (2009). https://doi.org/10.1007/s11263-008-0202-0
27. Koller, D., Friedman, N., Bach, F.: Probabilistic Graphical Models: Principles and Techniques. MIT Press, Cambridge (2009)
28. Kolmogorov, V.: Convergent tree-reweighted message passing for energy minimization. PAMI **28**(10), 1568–1583 (2006)
29. Kolmogorov, V.: Submodularity on a tree: unifying $L^\natural$-convex and bisubmodular functions. In: Murlak, F., Sankowski, P. (eds.) MFCS 2011. LNCS, vol. 6907, pp. 400–411. Springer, Heidelberg (2011). https://doi.org/10.1007/978-3-642-22993-0_37
30. Kolmogorov, V.: Minimizing a sum of submodular functions. Discrete Appl. Math. **160**(15), 2246–2258 (2012)
31. Kolmogorov, V.: A new look at reweighted message passing. TPAMI **37**(5), 919–930 (2015)
32. Kolmogorov, V., Zabin, R.: What energy functions can be minimized via graph cuts? TPAMI **26**(2), 147–159 (2004)
33. Komodakis, N., Paragios, N.: Beyond pairwise energies: efficient optimization for higher-order MRFs. In: 2009 IEEE Conference on Computer Vision and Pattern Recognition. CVPR 2009, pp. 2985–2992. IEEE (2009)
34. McCormick, S.T.: Submodular function minimization (2005)

35. Murota, K.: On steepest descent algorithms for discrete convex functions. SIAM J. Optim. **14**(3), 699–707 (2004)
36. Orlin, J.B.: A faster strongly polynomial time algorithm for submodular function minimization. Math. Program. **118**(2), 237–251 (2009). https://doi.org/10.1007/s10107-007-0189-2
37. Pearl, J.: Probabilistic Reasoning in Intelligent Systems: Networks of Plausible Inference. Morgan Kaufmann, Burlington (2014)
38. Potetz, B., Lee, T.S.: Efficient belief propagation for higher-order cliques using linear constraint nodes. CVIU **112**(1), 39–54 (2008)
39. Ramalingam, S., Russell, C., Ladicky, L., Torr, P.H.: Efficient minimization of higher order submodular functions using monotonic Boolean functions. arXiv preprint arXiv:1109.2304 (2011)
40. Roth, S., Black, M.J.: Fields of experts. IJCV **82**(2), 205–229 (2009). https://doi.org/10.1007/s11263-008-0197-6
41. Rother, C., Kohli, P., Feng, W., Jia, J.: Minimizing sparse higher order energy functions of discrete variables. In: CVPR, pp. 1382–1389 (2009)
42. Scharstein, D., Szeliski, R.: A taxonomy and evaluation of dense two-frame stereo correspondence algorithms. IJCV **47**(1–3), 7–42 (2002). https://doi.org/10.1023/A:1014573219977
43. Schrijver, A.: A combinatorial algorithm minimizing submodular functions in strongly polynomial time. J. Comb. Theory Ser. B **80**(2), 346–355 (2000)
44. Schrijver, A.: Combinatorial Optimization: Polyhedra and Efficiency, vol. 24. Springer, Heidelberg (2003)
45. Shanu, I., Arora, C., Maheshwari, S.: Inference in higher order MRF-map problems with small and large cliques. In: CVPR, pp. 7883–7891 (2018)
46. Shanu, I., Arora, C., Singla, P.: Min norm point algorithm for higher order MRF-MAP inference. In: CVPR, pp. 5365–5374 (2016)
47. Sontag, D., Globerson, A., Jaakkola, T.: Introduction to dual decomposition for inference. Optim. Mach. Learn. **1**, 219–254 (2011)
48. Szeliski, R., et al.: A comparative study of energy minimization methods for Markov random fields with smoothness-based priors. TPAMI **30**(6), 1068–1080 (2008)
49. Tarlow, D., Givoni, I.E., Zemel, R.S.: HOP-MAP: efficient message passing with high order potentials. In: AISTATS (2010)
50. Windheuser, T., Ishikawa, H., Cremers, D.: Generalized roof duality for multi-label optimization: optimal lower bounds and persistency. In: Fitzgibbon, A., Lazebnik, S., Perona, P., Sato, Y., Schmid, C. (eds.) ECCV 2012. LNCS, vol. 7577, pp. 400–413. Springer, Heidelberg (2012). https://doi.org/10.1007/978-3-642-33783-3_29
51. Woodford, O., Torr, P., Reid, I., Fitzgibbon, A.: Global stereo reconstruction under second order smoothness priors. In: CVPR, pp. 1–8 (2008)
52. Yedidia, J.S., Freeman, W.T., Weiss, Y.: Generalized belief propagation. In: Advances in Neural Information Processing Systems, pp. 689–695 (2001)
53. Zhang, J., Djolonga, J., Krause, A.: Higher-order inference for multi-class log-supermodular models. In: Proceedings of the IEEE International Conference on Computer Vision, pp. 1859–1867 (2015)

Dual Refinement Underwater Object Detection Network

Baojie Fan[1]($\boxtimes$), Wei Chen[1], Yang Cong[2], and Jiandong Tian[2]

[1] College of Automation and College of Artificial Intelligence,
Nanjing University of Posts and Telecommunications, Nanjing 210023, China
jobfbj@gmail.com, no1chenwei@gmail.com
[2] Shenyang Institute of Automation (SIA), Chinese Academy of Sciences,
Shenyang 110016, China
{congyang,tianjd}@sia.cn

Abstract. Due to the complex underwater environment, underwater imaging often encounters some problems such as blur, scale variation, color shift, and texture distortion. Generic detection algorithms can not work well when we use them directly in the underwater scene. To address these problems, we propose an underwater detection framework with feature enhancement and anchor refinement. It has a composite connection backbone to boost the feature representation and introduces a receptive field augmentation module to exploit multi-scale contextual features. The developed underwater object detection framework also provides a prediction refinement scheme according to six prediction layers, it can refine multi-scale features to better align with anchors by learning from offsets, which solve the problem of sample imbalance to a certain extent. We also construct a new underwater detection dataset, denoted as UWD, which has more than 10,000 train-val and test underwater images. The extensive experiments on PASCAL VOC and UWD demonstrate the favorable performance of the proposed underwater detection framework against the states-of-the-arts methods in terms of accuracy and robustness. Source code and models are available at: https://github.com/Peterchen111/FERNet.

Keywords: Underwater object detection · Feature enhancement · Anchor refinement · Underwater dataset

1 Introduction

At present, underwater robots are used in many fields, such as underwater target capture, underwater investigation, and underwater search. As the key technology of underwater robots, underwater object detection still faces severe challenges (e.g., blur, texture distortion, imbalanced illumination, etc.). The above issues restrict the development of underwater robot object detection.

B. Fan and W. Chen—The first two authors contribute equally to this work.

© Springer Nature Switzerland AG 2020
A. Vedaldi et al. (Eds.): ECCV 2020, LNCS 12365, pp. 275–291, 2020.
https://doi.org/10.1007/978-3-030-58565-5_17

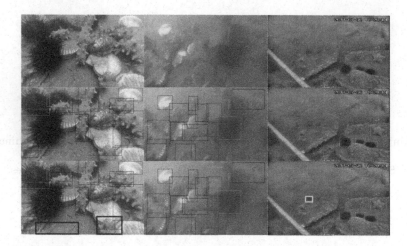

Fig. 1. Comparison of the baseline and our algorithm. (Best viewed in color and with zoom in) The upper part is the original test image. The middle part is the detection result of the baseline and the lower part is the result of our algorithm, the areas with obvious contrast are marked by bold lines. (Color figure online)

In recent years, generic object detection based on Convolutional Neural Network (CNN) [30] occupies a dominant position in object detection research. The mainstream object detectors can be divided into two categories: (1) the one-stage object detectors [18,24,25] and (2) the two-stage object detectors [6,11,23,26]. One-stage object detectors can directly localize objects by matching the large number of prior boxes, which been densely sampling on the input image at different scales and ratios. This method has a strong advantage in efficiency, but accuracy is usually low. In contrast, two-stage detectors can obtain more accurate results by generating object proposals first and then further calculate classification scores and regression bounding-box. In this work, we will focus on a one-stage object detection framework.

To deal with some real-time object detection tasks, a variety of one-stage object detection methods [15,18,24,36] have been introduced. In these methods, the Single Shot Multi-box Detector (SSD) [18] gains popularity because of its excellent performance and high speed. The standard SSD framework uses VGG16 [27]as backbone and adds a series of extra layers at the end of it. These additional layers and several former convolutional layers are used to predict the objects. Due to the use of a pyramid structure [1,14,22], each prediction layer conducts independent predictions with a specific scale in the standard SSD. SSD possesses high detection efficiency, but its accuracy performance still behind modern two-stage detectors.

During our research, we find that when many superior generic object detection frameworks are directly applied to the underwater task, they can hardly maintain high accuracy and robustness (Fig. 1). For example, Faster-RCNN [26] is affected by the invariance of the CNN scale. It is difficult to deal with the problem of scale variation under the water. Due to the existence of the Regional Proposal Network (RPN), it can hardly meet the real-time requirements. SSD [18] can detect at a high speed, but there will be a problem of missing detection for small and blur objects under the water. Despite generic object detectors encounter some problems, they still have inspiration for the detection research in the underwater scene. Most approaches [1,15,36] adopt a top-down pyramid representation, which injects high-level semantic information into a high-resolution feature map to solve the scale problem. To process the occlusions problem, the data augmentation method called Mix up [35] becomes popular. This method can simulate occlusion samples during the training phase, thereby enhancing the ability of the model to discriminate occluded objects. In this work, we are devoted to improving a generic one-stage object detection algorithm to adapt it in underwater detection tasks.

Motivated by the works above, we propose a one-stage underwater object detection algorithm named **FERNet**. Our contributions are mainly as follows:

- To deal with blurring and texture distortion problems in underwater dataset, we introduce a Composite Connection Backbone (CCB) to enhance the feature representation, rather than finding a brand-new deeper backbone.
- To solve the problem of scale variation and sample imbalance, we introduce a Receptive Field Augmentation Module (RFAM) to enrich multi-scale contextual features and provide the Prediction Refinement Scheme (PRS) to align features with anchors.
- We have collected and integrated a large number of relevant images from the Internet, then form a brand-new UnderWater Dataset.

To sum up, we integrate and expand the existing underwater dataset. In the algorithm, we connect two pre-trained backbones to enhance feature extraction capabilities. The combination of the top-down pyramid structure and the receptive field enhancement module can instill multi-scale semantic features into the network. We also introduce RFAM to enrich multi-scale contextual features. Finally, PRS first performs binary classification to distinguish fore-background and then conducts preliminary localization. Afterward, refining previous results to get the final classification scores and bounding-box regression.

2   Related Work

One-Stage Object Detection. The current mainstream one-stage detectors have mostly followed the work based on YOLO [24] or SSD [18]. YOLO uses a forward convolutional network directly to predict object categories and locations on the dense feature map. It is the first work to achieve end-to-end detection. On this basis, there are many developments [25,31] in the follow-up. Different from YOLO, SSD introduces anchors and dense multi-scale feature maps into one-stage object detectors. It uses a pyramidal hierarchical structure to do prediction. Through this structure, the shallow texture information and deep semantic information can be combined to make the network achieve stronger representation capabilities. Meanwhile, the dense anchor boxes also bring the overwhelming easy background samples, which limit the accuracy of one-stage object detectors. To solve this problem, RetinaNet [15] utilizes a novelty loss function named Focal Loss to down-weight the contribution of easy samples and makes network focus on the difficult samples. RefineDet [36] proposes a cascade prediction method to remove the background anchors in advance and then refine the anchors to boost detection performance. FCOS [29] uses the anchor-free method, which fundamentally avoids the impact of dense anchors.

Underwater Detection and Its Challenges. Underwater object detection [10,12,21] is generally achieved by sonar, laser and camera. The sonar is sensitive to the geometric information of the object, but can only show the difference in the distance between scanning points. It always omits other factors (e.g. visual characteristics). The laser can provide high performance to accurately model underwater objects but too expensive. In contrast, the camera is low cost and it can catch more types of visual information with high temporal and spatial resolution. Certain prominent objects can be identified by color, texture, and contour visual features. With the development of computer vision and underwater robots, vision-based underwater object detection [2,4,5,13] becomes more and more popular.

The images obtained by underwater cameras often have problems like low contrast, distorted texture, and uneven illumination. Besides, affected by living habits, underwater creatures are densely distributed and vary in size. The camera acquisition will encounter serious occlusion and scale variation problems, which pose a challenge to CNNs with scale invariance. To deal with these problems. Lv *et al.* [20] proposes a weakly supervised object detection method, which improves the accuracy by the strategy of weak fitting the foreground-background segmentation network first and refining proposals. Considerable accuracy has been achieved by this method, but it is difficult to achieve real-time performance due to the deep feature extraction network. Lin *et al.* [16] improves Faster-RCNN and proposes an enhanced strategy called Roimix to simulate overlapping and occluded objects in the training phase. This method endows the model stronger generalization ability and improves the accuracy in the occlusion scene. However, the performance of this data augmentation strategy on the one-stage detector is limited. Different from the above research, we hope to improve the one-stage underwater detector through a structural method.

Methods for Anchor Refinement. The accuracy of traditional one-stage detectors is often inferior to two-stage detectors. The main reason is that two-stage detectors have a fine-tuning process for the initial anchors but this process is omitted in one-stage detectors. Therefore, a large number of anchors caused the problem of anchor imbalance. In order to solve this problem, RefineDet [36] uses two-stage regression to get more refined results. It filters out a large number of negative anchors through the first time classification so that the positive and negative samples can be balanced, and then refines anchors based on the first time regression to obtain more accurate results. Although RefineDet can perform regression and classification of multiple stages, the features of different stages

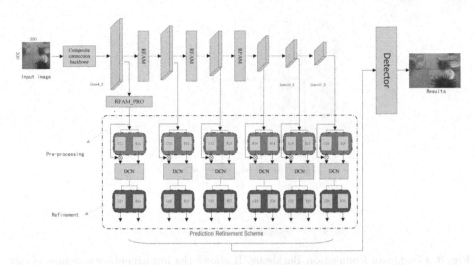

Fig. 2. Overall architecture of our framework. It specifically shows the down-sampling process after conv4_3, the composite connection backbone, the receptive field enhancement module and the prediction refinement scheme. (C_{1x}, R_{1x}) represents the results of the pre-processing phase and (C_{2x}, R_{2x}) represents the final result after the refinement process.

are the same. In fact, the anchors have changed after the first regression, and subsequent operations should rely more on the updated anchor. Therefore, Align-Det [3] learns the offset before and after the regression through the Deformable Convolution Network (DCN) [7], thereby solving the problem of feature misalignment to a certain extent. Reppoints [33] uses weak supervision to locate key points and predict their offsets, which is used as the offsets of DCN to convolution the original feature map so that the features are aligned with the object area.

3   Method

Our improved underwater object detection algorithm is based on standard SSD structure, which consists of the following components (see Fig. 2): **(1)** Composite Connection Backbone (CCB); **(2)** Receptive Field Augmentation Module (RFAM); **(3)** Prediction Refinement Scheme (PRS). The composite connection backbone network combines two common backbones. With the purpose of reducing time costs in searching for a new powerful backbone, we make up two existing backbones by a new way of composite connection to maximize the potential of them. The combined powerful feature extraction network has a stronger ability to represent the detailed features of the underwater object, which mainly deals with underwater blur problems. The RFAM is used to process the extracted information. Through RFAM, the reception field can be increased by individual kernels in different dilation rate and the multi-scale contextual features are

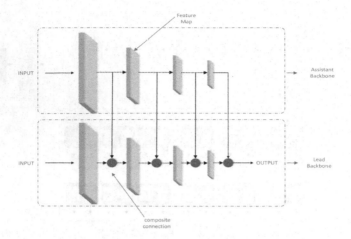

Fig. 3. Composite Connection Backbone. It shows the implementation details of our composite connection. The ⊕ means the fusion of two different features. In fact, we only have three layers of composite connection in actual use.

better expanded, which makes the information involved in prediction more discriminative. Our prediction refinement scheme is used to perform regression and classification operations on the prediction anchors. This scheme can both refine the anchors and features. In this step, PRS can roughly distinguish the foreground and background, giving the location on the whole, and then refine the anchors to get the final improvement results.

As we can see in the overall architecture, we utilize the new structure of composite connection to replace the VGG16 in the original standard SSD, and the input image size is 300 × 300. After the backbone, RFAM is interspersed between extra layers of standard SSD. In PRS, we use DCN to correct the offset of anchors after the first classification and regression, the outputs of DCN guide the second classification and regression and finally output the more accurate results.

3.1 Composite Connection Backbone

The underwater dataset has severe blurring and texture distortion problems. These problems often make it difficult for some networks to extract key feature information and affect the discrimination ability of the classifier. To this end, a feature extraction network with stronger representation capabilities is desperately needed. We first rule out the use of deeper feature extraction backbones, as this would slow down the speed of the one-stage detector, but redesigning a new and effective structure is difficult and time-consuming. So we explored the relationship between the extracted features of different backbones. Inspired by CBNet [19], we combine the existing characteristic backbone networks and get more performance than the single backbone.

The proposed composite connection backbone is shown in Fig. 3. The whole new backbone is divided into two parts: the lead backbone and the assistant backbone. The lead backbone still uses the standard VGG16 structure, and we use ResNet50 structure as the assistant backbone. Our proposed method is to replace the original backbone network with a composite connection form of these two basic backbones. In the assistant backbone, the result of each stage can be regarded as a higher-level feature. The output of each feature level is a part of the lead backbone input and flows to the parallel phase of subsequent backbones. In this way, multiple high-level and low-level features are fused to generate richer feature representations. This process can be expressed as:

$$F_{out} = F_l \oplus F_a \tag{1}$$

$$F_{OUT} = \varepsilon(F_{out}) \tag{2}$$

where $\oplus$ is the process of feature fusion, F_l denotes the output features of the lead backbone at the current stage and F_a denotes the output features of the assistant backbone, we use F_{out} to show the results of feature fusion and F_{OUT} is used as the input value of the next layer in the lead backbone. The process from F_{out} to F_{OUT} goes through the channel adjustment. As is shown in Eq. 2, ε work as a convolution operation of 1×1. In theory, we can use this kind of composite connection method at each layer of the backbone, and our experiment only uses one of the most basic and useful composite connection methods. In fact, the connection between the lead backbone and the assistant backbone can be designed more complicated. We can also select feature layers of different sizes on the lead backbone and the assistant backbone, and bilinearly interpolate to the same size for the composite connection. This shows that our composite connection method is not limited by the size of the feature size. In order to simplify the operation, we select 150×150, 75×75, and 38×38 characteristic layers on the lead backbone, which corresponds to the output of three layers of ResNet50.

3.2   Receptive Field Augmentation Module

Figure 4 shows the receptive field augmentation module we introduced, which reproduces the work of RFB [17]. In order to imitate the design idea of ResNext [32] and the Inception structure [28], RFAM has multiple branches structure. First, the multiple branches of structure processes input data in parallel. Each branch is composed of 1×1 convolution and several other simple convolutions with different kernel sizes, and finally, each branch forms a structure similar to the bottleneck. The convolution kernel size of each branch changes slightly, which is conducive to capture the multi-scale contextual information. Aiming to expand the receptive field, we use the dilated convolution [34] with different dilation rate to enhance the multi-scale features, then the features of multiple branches are fused, after that, we use 1×1 convolution to adjust the channel size. Finally, we also simulate the residual structure using the shortcut connection method, weighting the input and feature fusion results, then obtain the

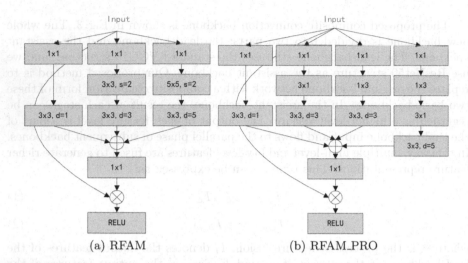

(a) RFAM   (b) RFAM_PRO

Fig. 4. Receptive Field Augmentation Module. RFAM is used alternately in the down-sampling layer to expand the receptive field of the feature map. RFAM_PRO is used on shallow feature maps to help detect small objects.

final output through ReLU. To adapt to a variety of situations, we proposed two RFAM structures, RFAM and RFAM_PRO. RFAM_PRO has more branches than RFAM and use many small convolution kernels, which is friendly to small object detection. RFAM_PRO replaces a 5×5 convolution with two superimposed 3×3 convolution. This can reduce the number of parameters to decrease the computational complexity, and increase the nonlinearity of the model. Furthermore, we replace the original 3×3 convolution with a 1×3 convolution and 3×1 convolution. The whole process of RFAM can be expressed by Eq. 3:

$$X_{out} = \tau(X_{in} \otimes \epsilon(Br1 \oplus Br2 \oplus Br3) \times scale) \tag{3}$$

here X_{in} represents the input feature, Br1, Br2, and Br3 denote the output of three branches, $\oplus$ is the operation of feature fusion. We use ϵ to represent the process of adjusting the number of channels through 1×1 convolution, the value of scale is the weight of linear operation in shortcut, here we take 0.1. $\otimes$ represents the element-wise addition, and finally, τ is the activation function of ReLU.

3.3   Prediction Refinement Scheme

Our prediction refinement scheme mainly includes two steps: Pre-processing and Refinement. As shown in Fig. 2, this process uses two-step treatment to refine the prediction of object's locations and sizes, which is good for the challenging underwater scenarios, especially for the small objects. The prediction refinement scheme mainly performs initial binary classification and regression in the pre-processing stage, and then the refinement module obtains the final result based on the pre-processing results. The main process will be explained in detail below. Different from RefineDet [36], our prediction refinement scheme uses six feature prediction layers for refinement. Moreover, PRS can aggregate important features through a designed attention mechanism and refine anchors by learning from offsets. We will confirm the advantages of our structure through later experiments.

Pre-processing: In the pre-processing phase, the prediction value obtained by the Receptive Field Enhancement Module (RFAM) and the extra layer is processed first. In Fig. 2, starting from the last layer conv4_3 of the composite connection backbone, downsampling through the additional layers of the standard SSD and the RFAM to reach the size required by the prediction layer. What is special is that conv4_3 is followed by an RFAM_PRO to strengthen the detection ability of shallow features to small objects. We believe that adding RFAM_PRO to large-scale feature maps can fully extract the semantic information of high-resolution feature maps, so operating on high-resolution feature maps is conducive to the detection of the small underwater objects. Finally, binary classification and box regression are performed on the information of the six enhanced feature layers. Filter the obvious background first in preparation for the refinement module. The output C_{1x} is used to distinguish the foreground and background. R_{1x} includes four important values, which are used to locate the anchors.

Refinement: In this stage, we perform the max-pooling operation along the channel axis for the pre-processing result C_{1x} and then carry out the Sigmoid function to gain better features. The result of this process is recorded as S_{1x}. S_{1x} obtained through max-pooling and Sigmoid operations can highlight the position of the object, which is used to enhance the result X_{out} of six prediction layers. S_{1x} and X_{out} are multiplied element by element and then added to X_{out}. The result is recorded as X_{end}. Generally speaking, we replace the RefineDet's TCB module with an attention mechanism module, making the network pay more attention to the object itself. This process can be expressed by Eq. 4:

$$X_{end} = (X_{out} \odot S_{1x}) \otimes X_{out} \qquad (4)$$

where $\odot$ is element-wise multiplication, $\otimes$ means element-wise addition, and X_{end} denotes the amount of enhancement of existing foreground position information. In the previous R_{1x} regression, four output values are obtained: $\triangle x$, $\triangle y$, $\triangle h$ and $\triangle w$. The first two values ($\triangle x$, $\triangle y$) represent the spatial offsets of the center point of the anchor and the last two values ($\triangle h$, $\triangle w$) represent the offsets of the size. To align features, we fine-tune the anchor frame through the DCN. Specifically, we compute the kernel offsets by $\triangle x$ and $\triangle y$ in location offsets layers, which combine with the X_{end} as the input of DCN. We also use dilated convolution in deformable convolution to enhance the semantic relevance of context. About the classification and regression in the refinement stage, C_{2x} no longer simply performs binary classification but performs multiple classification tasks. We gain the final positioning result R_{2x} through the output of DCN.

On the whole, in order to obtain more fine-grained positioning results, we adopt a strategy similar to RefineDet. We apply DCN to this process and the results of the pre-processing stage are used to calculate the feature offsets and then send to DCN to align the features. The refinement phase is fine-tuned for the best results.

4   Experiments

We perform experiments on PASCAL VOC 2007 [9] and UWD. Mean Average Precision (mAP) is adopted for the evaluation metric. Our underwater object detection algorithm has the advantages of strong feature extraction capabilities, multi-scale detection, and anchor refinement to solve the underwater issues, below we will focus on three parts: implementation details, detection performance, and ablation experiment. Our algorithm is mainly oriented to the underwater environment, so the experimental result of the UWD is used as the main evaluation criteria. To verify the feasibility of the framework, we also performed experiments on PASCAL VOC 2007 benchmarks.

4.1   Implementation Details

Our framework utilizes the composite connection of VGG16 and ResNet50 as the backbone. Both VGG16 and ResNet50 are pre-trained on ImageNet [8]. About the experiments on two datasets, we keep the consistent initial experiment settings and choose the same optimizer (SGD). Our six prediction branches of PRS use the anchor scale of [6, 6, 6, 6, 4, 4] and aspect ratio of 2:3 and 2:2. During the training phase, we adopt a warm-up strategy. The learning rate of the first six epochs is randomly selected between 10^{-6} and 4×10^{-3}, and gradually approach the basic learning rate 0.002. After that, it decreases ten times each time. The PASCAL VOC 2007 and underwater dataset decrease to the lowest learning rate at the last 10 epochs respectively. Non-maximum Suppression (NMS) with Intersection over Union (IoU) threshold 0.5 is adopted for post-processing. To simulate the occlusion problem in the underwater environment, we also add a random erasing strategy to the data augmentation during the training session. In our experiments, PASCAL VOC 2007 and underwater dataset were trained for 160 epochs and the batch size was set to 32. Besides, we used two Nvidia RTX2080Ti for training, our code is based on the deep learning framework of PyTorch.

4.2   Detection Performance

PASCAL VOC 2007: In order to verify the rationality of our underwater detection framework, we perform experiments on the PASCAL VOC 2007 dataset and compared it with the general detection methods in existing papers. We both perform experiments with input sizes of 300 × 300 and 512 × 512. Table 1 shows the test results of PASCAL VOC 2007. We can see that our algorithm achieves

Table 1. Results on PASCAL VOC 2007 testset, trained on 07 and 12 train-val dataset. VGG16* represents our composite connection backbone.

Method	Backbone	Input size	mAP
Two-Stage Detectors:			
Faster RCNN	VGG16	1000 × 600	73.2
Faster RCNN	ResNet101	1000 × 600	76.4
MR-CNN	VGG16	1000 × 600	78.2
R-FCN	ResNet101	1000 × 600	80.5
CoupleNet	ResNet101	1000 × 600	82.7
Single-Stage Detectors:			
SSD300	VGG16	300 × 300	77.2
YOLO	GoogleNet	448 × 448	63.4
YOLOV2	DarkNet-19	544 × 544	78.6
RON320++	VGG16	320 × 320	76.6
DSSD321	ResNet101	321 × 321	78.6
RefineDet320	VGG16	320 × 320	80.0
DES300	VGG16	300 × 300	79.7
DFPR300	VGG16	300 × 300	79.6
RFBNet300	VGG16	300 × 300	80.5
EFIPNet	VGG16	300 × 300	80.4
FERNet (Ours)	VGG16*	300 × 300	80.2
SSD512	VGG16	512 × 512	79.5
DSSD512	ResNet101	513 × 513	81.5
DES512	VGG16	512 × 512	81.7
RefineDet512	VGG16	512 × 512	81.8
DFPR512	VGG16	512 × 512	81.1
EFIPNet512	VGG16	512 × 512	81.8
RFBNet512	VGG16	512 × 512	82.1
FERNet (Ours)	VGG16*	512 × 512	81.0

the result of 80.2 mAP on PASCAL VOC 2007, leading most of the one-stage detectors, and even surpassing most two-stage detection algorithms. However, from the data in Table 1, the accuracy of our algorithm has not reached the state of art. The main reasons may be as follows: Firstly, the PASCAL VOC 2007 has a few cases of blurred, occlusion, and scale variation, so our algorithm doesn't improve much. Secondly, the detection accuracy fluctuates due to the influence of hardware equipment and the Anaconda environment. For example, we use RFBNet source code for training, and the detection accuracy can only reach 80.0 mAP. Our algorithm is 0.2 mAP higher than the RFBNet. Compared with RefineDet, although it has only a 0.2 map improvement, our input size is

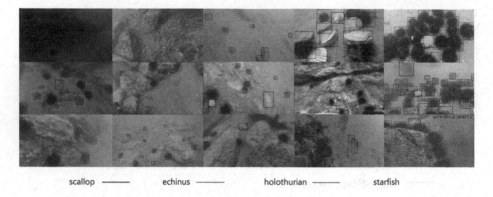

scallop ——— echinus ——— holothurian ——— starfish

Fig. 5. Qualitative detection results of our detector on UWD dataset. Each color of an anchor belongs to an object class.

300×300, which is less than 320×320 of the RefineDet input size. Our methods can save computing resources and time while still achieving accuracy improvements. In a word, the result in Table 1 demonstrates that despite our detection framework does not reach the current best accuracy, it can still maintain a high detection level in general object detection.

UWD: We comprehensively evaluate our method on the UnderWater Dataset (UWD). We collect and integrated relevant underwater pictures on the Internet, and perform manual data annotation through Label Image[1] to expand the URPC dataset[2], and finally form our dataset. Our underwater dataset contains 10 thousand train-val and test images, it contains four classes: holothurian, echinus, scallop, and starfish. In the experiments, we use the same network structure and parameter settings like that in the PASCAL VOC experiment and make the result of RFBNet as the baseline. Table 2 shows that the accuracy of the baseline algorithm on UWD can only reach 60 mAP, but FERNet can reach an accuracy of 74.2 mAP. Compared with the baseline algorithm, our algorithm has improved by nearly 14.5% points on the UWD dataset. The algorithm has certain feasibility when dealing with complex underwater environments.

Figure 5 is the detection result of our underwater detection framework on the UWD dataset. Four classes of holothurian, echinus, scallop, and starfish are marked by blue, red, black, and yellow boxes. As is shown from the image, our detection framework can maintain a high performance when facing problems like underwater occlusion, blur, color shift, and uneven lighting.

4.3 Ablation Experiment

In this part, we will perform ablation experiments on various functional blocks of FERNet to verify their effectiveness. We gradually add functional modules

---

[1] Datasets Annotation Tool. https://github.com/tzutalin/labelImg.
[2] Underwater Robot Picking Contest. http://www.cnurpc.org/.

Table 2. Detection results on underwater dataset UWD. The baseline represents the result of RFBNet. RE represents the trick of random-erasing. FERNet$^+$ represents that we use focal loss on the basis of FERNet, FERNet* means we use VGG16 with BN as our lead backbone. The above results are obtained by experiments on images with an input size of 300 × 300.

Method	mAP	CCB	RE	Focal loss	PRS	Holothurain	Echinus	Scallop	Starfish
Baseline(BL)	60.0					56.0	77.1	35.9	71.2
BL+C	63.8	√				63.4	78.3	38.2	75.3
BL+F	63.2			√		60.2	79.0	38.1	75.4
BL+C+F	66.6	√		√		61.9	83.3	42.9	78.5
BL+C+R+F	66.7	√	√	√		62.1	83.5	42.7	78.6
FERNet	**74.2**	√	√		√	**71.4**	**91.5**	**52.2**	82.0
FERNet$^+$	73.0	√	√	√	√	71.1	90.8	48	**82.2**
FERNet*	73.0	√	√		√	68.3	90.7	51.2	81.8

Table 3. Ablation experiments on the number of prediction layers. The results of PASCAL VOC and UWD show that six prediction layers are better than that of four.

Datasets	Num	mAP
PASCAL VOC	4	79.8
PASCAL VOC	6	**80.2**
UWD	4	73.3
UWD	6	**74.2**

based on the baseline to observe the changes in the results. Besides, we also added some tricks like random erasing and BatchNormalization to participate in comparing the results.

Rationality of Three Functional Modules. In order to prove the rationality of these functional blocks proposed in this paper, we have carefully designed multiple comparative experiments as shown in Table 2. We gradually add them to observe the changes in the experimental results. Firstly, we added the Composite Connection Block (CCB) module to the baseline algorithm. We can see that a single composite connection function block can provide 3.8 mAP gains. To maximize the potential of a single composite connection block module, we use tricks of Random-Erasing [37] and focal loss, which can finally achieve a gain of 6.7 mAP compared to the baseline algorithm. Secondly, we continue to increase the functional modules of the prediction refinement scheme (PRS) on this basis and reach the best accuracy of 74.2 mAP. The process above can prove the rationality of our proposed functional modules.

BatchNorm in Backbone. BatchNorm is widely used to enable fast and stable training of deep neural networks [38]. To investigate whether BatchNorm has an improvement on the backbone, we add the BatchNorm operation to each convolution layer in the VGG16 network, denoted as FERNet[*]. As shown in Table 2, FERNet[*] only gain the accuracy of 73.0 mAP, 1.2 mAP lower than VGG16 without BatchNorm. This indicates that the BatchNormalization layer does not significantly improve the accuracy of our algorithm.

Number of the Prediction Layers. Our refinement module is inspired by the RefineDet and it is similar but essentially different. The selection and design details of our prediction layers have been explained before. The ablation experiment here is mainly to analyze the rationality of the number of the prediction layers. We know that in RefineDet, the author selected four feature layers for prediction, and confirm that the selection of the four layers can achieve the best accuracy. In our experiments, we believe that small feature maps are also necessary to preserve, because, for our underwater dataset, high-level semantic information can help us identify something more detailed and benefit for those blurry and distorted image detection. Therefore, we perform another small ablation experiment on selecting the number of prediction layers in our experiment. We use four prediction layer structures and six prediction layer structures for experiments. Table 3 proves that six prediction layers are better than four prediction layers on both UWD and PASCAL VOC 2007 datasets.

In summary, the experiments above show that all the functional modules we proposed have a significant improvement in detection accuracy, especially the PRS. On this basis, we find that using PRS with focal loss together can not get accuracy improvement, probably because Online Hard Example Mining (OHEM) has been used in PRS. Strangely, the improvement of our algorithm on PASCAL VOC 2007 is not obvious. We guess that it is because the PASCAL VOC 2007 dataset rarely has blur, scale variation, and occlusion problems.

5   Conclusion

In this paper, we analyze the challenging problems which affect the performance of object detection in the underwater environment. To address these issues, we propose a one-stage underwater detection framework named FERNet. We combine existing feature extraction backbones by the form of a composite connection to propose a backbone with stronger feature expression capabilities. Further, we introduce the receptive field enhancement module, which is used to enrich the receptive field, expand multi-scale contextual features, and boost the discrimination ability of the entire detection network. Finally, we utilize the prediction refinement scheme to align the features with anchors to deal with the problem of sample imbalance and feature misalignment to some extent. Experiments show that our detection algorithm has great improvements compared to the baseline algorithm on the underwater dataset.

Acknowledgments. This work is supported by the Ministry of Science and Technology of the People's Republic of China (2019YFB1310300), National Natural Science Foundation of China (No. 61876092), State Key Laboratory of Robotics (No. 2019-O07) and State Key Laboratory of Integrated Service Network (ISN20-08).

References

1. Cao, J., Pang, Y., Li, X.: Triply supervised decoder networks for joint detection and segmentation. In: Proceedings of the IEEE Conference on Computer Vision and Pattern Recognition, pp. 7392–7401 (2019)
2. Chen, X., Lu, Y., Wu, Z., Yu, J., Wen, L.: Reveal of domain effect: how visual restoration contributes to object detection in aquatic scenes. arXiv. Computer Vision and Pattern Recognition (2020)
3. Chen, Y., Han, C., Wang, N., Zhang, Z.: Revisiting feature alignment for one-stage object detection. arXiv preprint arXiv:1908.01570 (2019)
4. Chen, Z., Zhang, Z., Dai, F., Bu, Y., Wang, H.: Monocular vision-based underwater object detection. Sensors 17(8), 1784 (2017)
5. Cong, Y., Fan, B., Hou, D., Fan, H., Liu, K., Luo, J.: Novel event analysis for human-machine collaborative underwater exploration. Pattern Recogn. 96, 106967 (2019)
6. Dai, J., Li, Y., He, K., Sun, J.: R-FCN: object detection via region-based fully convolutional networks. In: Advances in Neural Information Processing Systems, pp. 379–387 (2016)
7. Dai, J., et al.: Deformable convolutional networks. In: Proceedings of the IEEE International Conference on Computer Vision, pp. 764–773 (2017)
8. Deng, J., Dong, W., Socher, R., Li, L.J., Li, K., Fei-Fei, L.: ImageNet: a large-scale hierarchical image database. In: 2009 IEEE Conference on Computer Vision and Pattern Recognition, pp. 248–255. IEEE (2009)
9. Everingham, M., Van Gool, L., Williams, C.K., Winn, J., Zisserman, A.: The pascal visual object classes (VOC) challenge. Int. J. Comput. Vis. 88(2), 303–338 (2010). https://doi.org/10.1007/s11263-009-0275-4
10. Galceran, E., Djapic, V., Carreras, M., Williams, D.P.: A real-time underwater object detection algorithm for multi-beam forward looking sonar. IFAC Proc. Vol. 45(5), 306–311 (2012)
11. He, K., Gkioxari, G., Dollár, P., Girshick, R.: Mask R-CNN. In: Proceedings of the IEEE International Conference on Computer Vision, pp. 2961–2969 (2017)
12. Henriksen, L.: Real-time underwater object detection based on an electrically scanned high-resolution sonar. In: Proceedings of IEEE Symposium on Autonomous Underwater Vehicle Technology (AUV 1994), pp. 99–104. IEEE (1995)
13. Li, C., Anwar, S., Porikli, F.: Underwater scene prior inspired deep underwater image and video enhancement. Pattern Recogn. 98, 107038 (2020)
14. Lin, T.Y., Dollár, P., Girshick, R., He, K., Hariharan, B., Belongie, S.: Feature pyramid networks for object detection. In: Proceedings of the IEEE Conference on Computer Vision and Pattern Recognition, pp. 2117–2125 (2017)
15. Lin, T.Y., Goyal, P., Girshick, R., He, K., Dollár, P.: Focal loss for dense object detection. In: Proceedings of the IEEE International Conference on Computer Vision, pp. 2980–2988 (2017)
16. Lin, W.H., Zhong, J.X., Liu, S., Li, T., Li, G.: RoIMix: proposal-fusion among multiple images for underwater object detection. arXiv preprint arXiv:1911.03029 (2019)
17. Liu, S., Huang, D., Wang, Y.: Receptive field block net for accurate and fast object detection. arXiv preprint arXiv:1711.07767 (2017)
18. Liu, W., et al.: SSD: single shot MultiBox detector. In: Leibe, B., Matas, J., Sebe, N., Welling, M. (eds.) ECCV 2016. LNCS, vol. 9905, pp. 21–37. Springer, Cham (2016). https://doi.org/10.1007/978-3-319-46448-0_2

19. Liu, Y., et al.: CBNet: a novel composite backbone network architecture for object detection. arXiv preprint arXiv:1909.03625 (2019)
20. Lv, X., Wang, A., Liu, Q., Sun, J., Zhang, S.: Proposal-refined weakly supervised object detection in underwater images. In: Zhao, Y., Barnes, N., Chen, B., Westermann, R., Kong, X., Lin, C. (eds.) ICIG 2019. LNCS, vol. 11901, pp. 418–428. Springer, Cham (2019). https://doi.org/10.1007/978-3-030-34120-6_34
21. Mullen, L.J., et al.: Modulated laser line scanner for enhanced underwater imaging. In: Airborne and In-Water Underwater Imaging, vol. 3761, pp. 2–9. International Society for Optics and Photonics (1999)
22. Pang, Y., Wang, T., Anwer, R.M., Khan, F.S., Shao, L.: Efficient featurized image pyramid network for single shot detector. In: Proceedings of the IEEE Conference on Computer Vision and Pattern Recognition, pp. 7336–7344 (2019)
23. Purkait, P., Zhao, C., Zach, C.: SPP-Net: deep absolute pose regression with synthetic views. arXiv preprint arXiv:1712.03452 (2017)
24. Redmon, J., Farhadi, A.: YOLO9000: better, faster, stronger. In: Proceedings of the IEEE Conference on Computer Vision and Pattern Recognition, pp. 7263–7271 (2017)
25. Redmon, J., Farhadi, A.: YOLOv3: an incremental improvement. arXiv preprint arXiv:1804.02767 (2018)
26. Ren, S., He, K., Girshick, R., Sun, J.: Faster R-CNN: towards real-time object detection with region proposal networks. In: Advances in Neural Information Processing Systems, pp. 91–99 (2015)
27. Simonyan, K., Zisserman, A.: Very deep convolutional networks for large-scale image recognition (2014)
28. Szegedy, C., Ioffe, S., Vanhoucke, V., Alemi, A.A.: Inception-v4, Inception-ResNet and the impact of residual connections on learning. In: Thirty-First AAAI Conference on Artificial Intelligence (2017)
29. Tian, Z., Shen, C., Chen, H., He, T.: FCOS: fully convolutional one-stage object detection. In: Proceedings of the IEEE International Conference on Computer Vision, pp. 9627–9636 (2019)
30. Touretzky, D.S., Mozer, M.C., Hasselmo, M.E.: Advances in Neural Information Processing Systems 8: Proceedings of the 1995 Conference, vol. 8. MIT Press, Cambridge (1996)
31. Wong, A., Famuori, M., Shafiee, M.J., Li, F., Chwyl, B., Chung, J.: YOLO Nano: a highly compact you only look once convolutional neural network for object detection. arXiv preprint arXiv:1910.01271 (2019)
32. Xie, S., Girshick, R., Dollár, P., Tu, Z., He, K.: Aggregated residual transformations for deep neural networks. In: Proceedings of the IEEE Conference on Computer Vision and Pattern Recognition, pp. 1492–1500 (2017)
33. Yang, Z., Liu, S., Hu, H., Wang, L., Lin, S.: RepPoints: point set representation for object detection, pp. 9657–9666 (2019)
34. Yu, F., Koltun, V.: Multi-scale context aggregation by dilated convolutions. arXiv preprint arXiv:1511.07122 (2015)
35. Zhang, H., Cisse, M., Dauphin, Y.N., Lopez-Paz, D.: Mixup: beyond empirical risk minimization. arXiv preprint arXiv:1710.09412 (2017)

36. Zhang, S., Wen, L., Bian, X., Lei, Z., Li, S.Z.: Single-shot refinement neural network for object detection. In: Proceedings of the IEEE Conference on Computer Vision and Pattern Recognition, pp. 4203–4212 (2018)
37. Zhong, Z., Zheng, L., Kang, G., Li, S., Yang, Y.: Random erasing data augmentation. arXiv preprint arXiv:1708.04896 (2017)
38. Zhu, R., et al.: ScratchDet: training single-shot object detectors from scratch. In: Proceedings of the IEEE Conference on Computer Vision and Pattern Recognition, pp. 2268–2277 (2019)

Multiple Sound Sources Localization
from Coarse to Fine

Rui Qian[1], Di Hu[2], Heinrich Dinkel[1], Mengyue Wu[1], Ning Xu[3],
and Weiyao Lin[1(✉)]

[1] Shanghai Jiao Tong University, Shanghai, China
{qrui9911,richman,mengyuewu,wylin}@sjtu.edu.cn
[2] Baidu Research, Beijing, China
hudi04@baidu.com
[3] Adobe Research, San Jose, USA
nxu@adobe.com

Abstract. How to visually localize multiple sound sources in uncon-strained videos is a formidable problem, especially when lack of the pairwise sound-object annotations. To solve this problem, we develop a two-stage audiovisual learning framework that disentangles audio and visual representations of different categories from complex scenes, then performs cross-modal feature alignment in a coarse-to-fine manner. Our model achieves state-of-the-art results on public dataset of localization, as well as considerable performance on multi-source sound localization in complex scenes. We then employ the localization results for sound sep-aration and obtain comparable performance to existing methods. These outcomes demonstrate our model's ability in effectively aligning sounds with specific visual sources. Code is available at https://github.com/shvdiwnkozbw/Multi-Source-Sound-Localization.

Keywords: Sound localization · Audiovisual alignment · Complex scene

1 Introduction

Humans usually perceive the world through information in different modalities, e.g., vision and hearing. By leveraging the relevance and complementary between audio and vision, humans can clearly distinguish different sound sources and infer which object is making sound. In contrast, machines have been proven capable of separately processing audio and visual information using deep neural networks. But can they benefit from joint audiovisual learning?

Works in recent years mainly focus on establishing multi-modal relationship based on temporally synchronized audio and visual signals [1,3,17,19]. This syn-chronization in video-level becomes the correspondence that is whether audio

Electronic supplementary material The online version of this chapter (https://doi.org/10.1007/978-3-030-58565-5_18) contains supplementary material, which is available to authorized users.

A. Vedaldi et al. (Eds.): ECCV 2020, LNCS 12365, pp. 292–308, 2020.
https://doi.org/10.1007/978-3-030-58565-5_18

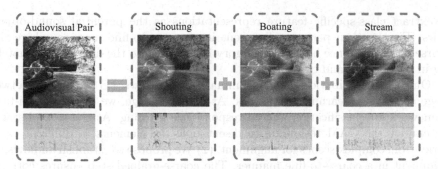

Fig. 1. Our model separates a complex audiovisual scene into several simple scenes. The figure shows the input audiovisual pair majorly consists of three elements: a man shouting, sound of boating from the boat and paddle, sound of a water stream. This disentanglement simplifies a complex scenario and generates several one-to-one audiovisual associations.

and visual signals originate from the same video, which works effectively for simple scenes [2,18], i.e., the single-source conditions. However, in unconstrained videos, various sounds are usually mixed, where the video-level supervision is too coarse to provide the precise alignment between each sound and visual source pair. To tackle this problem, [15,16] establish audiovisual clusters to associate sound-object pairs, but require to pre-determine the number of clusters, which becomes difficult in an unconstrained scenario, thus greatly affects alignment performance.

Some works further apply audiovisual learning into a series of downstream tasks (e.g., sound localization, sound separation) and exhibit promising performance [10,16,18,22,24,29,31]. Regarding previous works on sound localization, [2,18,24] mainly focus on simple scenes, usually unable to find source specific objects from mixed audio, while [6,7,9] employ stereo audio as prior, which contains location information but is difficult to obtain. Additionally, existing evaluation pipelines also lack the ability to measure sound localization performance in multi-source scenarios. For sound separation, [29] uses the entire coarse visual scene as guidance, while [5,10,28] rely on extra motion or detection results to improve performance.

To sum up, existing dominant methods mostly lack the ability to analyze complex audiovisual scenes, and fail to effectively utilize the latent alignment between sound and visual source pairs in unconstrained videos. This is because there are majorly two challenges in complex audiovisual scene analysis: one is how to distinguish different sound-sources, the other is how to ensure the established sound-object alignment is fairly satisfactory without one-to-one annotations. To address these challenges, we develop a two-stage audiovisual learning framework. At the first stage, we employ a multi-task framework consisting of classification and audiovisual correspondence to provide the reference of audiovisual content for the second stage. At the second stage, based on the classification predictions, we use the operation of *Class Activation Mapping* (CAM) [4,23,30] to extract class-specific feature representations as the potential sound-object pairs (Fig. 1), then perform alignment in a coarse-to-fine manner, where the coarse correspondence based on category is evolved into the fine-grained matching in both video- and category-level.

Our main contributions can be summarized as follows: (1) We develop a two-stage audiovisual learning framework. At the first stage, we employ multi-task framework for classification and correspondence learning. At the second stage, we employ the CAM technique to disentangle the elements of different categories from complex scenes for alignment. (2) We propose to establish audiovisual alignment in a coarse-to-fine manner. The coarse-grained step ensures correctness of correspondence in category level, while the fine-grained one establishes video- and category-based sound-object association. (3) We achieve state-of-the-art results on public sound localization dataset. In the multi-source conditions, according to our proposed class-specific localization metric, our method shows considerable performance compared with several baselines. Besides, the object representation obtained from localization provides valuable visual reference for sound separation.

2   Related Work

Audiovisual Correspondence. Although most audiovisual datasets consist of unlabelled videos, the natural correspondence between sound and vision provides essential supervision for audiovisual learning [1–3,18,19]. [3,19] introduced a method to learn feature representation of one modality with supervision from the other in a teacher-student manner. Arandjelovic and Zisserman [1] viewed audiovisual correspondence (AVC) as the supervision for audiovisual representation learning. [18] adopted temporal synchronization as self-supervision signal to correlate audiovisual content. But these methods mostly fail to process complex scene with multiple sound sources. Hu et al. [15,16] used clustering to associate latent sound-object pairs, but its performance greatly relies on pre-defined number of clusterings. Our multi-task framework simultaneously treats unimodal content label and audiovisual correspondence as supervision, then performs class-specific audiovisual alignment under complex scenes.

Sound Localization in Visual Scenes. Recent methods for localizing sound in visual context mainly focus on joint modeling of audio and visual modalities [2,15,18,24,27–29]. In [2,18], authors performed sound localization through audiovisual correspondences. [24] proposed an attention mechanism to capture primary areas in a semi-supervised or unsupervised setting. Tian et al. [27] leveraged audio-guided visual attention and temporal alignment to find semantic regions corresponding to sound sources. Hu et al. [15,16] established audiovisual clustering to localize sound makers. Zhao et al. [28,29] employed a self-supervised framework to simultaneously achieve sound separation and visual grounding. Although [28,29] can separate sound given visual sound source, they require single-source samples to achieve mix-and-separate training. In contrast, our model is directly trained on unconstrained videos, and can precisely localize visual source of different sounds in complex scenes.

CAM for Weakly-Supervised Localization. CAM was proposed by Zhou et al. [30] to localize objects with only holistic image labels. This approach employs a weighted sum of the global average pooled features at the last convolutional layer to generate class-specific saliency maps, but can only be applied to fully-convolutional networks due to modification of network architectures. To generalize CAM and improve visual explanations for convolutional networks, Grad-CAM [23] and Grad-CAM++ [4] were proposed. These two gradient-based methods can achieve weakly-supervised localization with arbitrary off-the-shelf CNN architectures and require no re-training.

Some previous works on audiovisual learning have adopted CAM or similar methods to localize sound producers [2,18,29]. Arandjelovic et al. [2] performed max pooling on predicted score map over all spatial grids, and used obtained correspondence score for training on AVC task. Owens et al. [18] adopted audiovisual synchronization as training supervision, and employed CAM to measure the likelihood of a patch to be sound source. However, they only use CAM at the final step to measure the relationship between two modalities. Our method employs CAM to disentangle audio and visual features of different sounding objects, achieving fine-grained audiovisual alignment.

3   Approach

Our two-stage framework is illustrated in Fig. 2. At the first stage, we employ multi-task learning for classification and video-level audiovisual correspondence. At the second stage, the audiovisual feature maps and classification predictions are fed into Grad-CAM [23] module to disentangle class-specific features on both modalities, based on which we employ valid representations to perform fine-grained audiovisual alignment.

3.1   Multi-task Training Framework

Given audio and visual (image) messages $\{a_i, v_i\}$ from i-th video, we can obtain the category labels from annotated video tags or predictions of pretrained models, as well as the natural audiovisual correspondence. To leverage these two types of supervision, we employ a multi-task learning model. This model consists of audio and visual learning backbones, classification network and an audiovisual correspondence network, as shown in Fig. 2. Specifically, we adopt CRNN [25], composed of 2D convolutions and a GRU, to process audio spectrograms, and use ResNet-18 [13] to extract deep features from video frames.

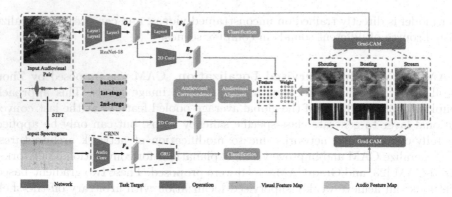

Fig. 2. An overview of our two-stage audiovisual learning framework. At the first stage, our model extracts deep features from the audio and visual streams, then performs classification and video-level correspondence. At the second stage, our model disentangles representations of different classes and implements a fine-grained audiovisual alignment.

Classification on Two Modalities. To perform classification with audio and visual messages $\{a_i, v_i\}$, we adopt video tags or predicted pseudo labels from pretrained models as supervision. Considering the sound-object alignment to be established, we employ the same categories for both modalities. We denote C as the number of class and c as the c-th class.

Considering there are multiple sound sources contained in the video, multi-label binary cross entropy loss is considered for classification:

$$L_{cls} = \mathcal{H}_{bce}(\boldsymbol{y}_{a_i}, \boldsymbol{p}_{a_i}) + \mathcal{H}_{bce}(\boldsymbol{y}_{v_i}, \boldsymbol{p}_{v_i}), \tag{1}$$

where $\mathcal{H}_{bce}$ is the binary cross-entropy loss for multi-label classification, $\boldsymbol{y}$ and $\boldsymbol{p}$ are the annotated class labels and corresponding predicted probability respectively, $\boldsymbol{y} \in \{0, 1\}^C$, $\boldsymbol{p} \in [0, 1]^C$.

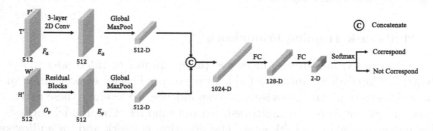

Fig. 3. Details for audiovisual correspondence learning network. For audio stream, the 3-layer 2D convolutions are listed as: (1) $3 \times 1 \times 512$, with dilation 2 on time dimension, (2) $1 \times 2 \times 512$, with stride 2 on frequency dimension, (3) $3 \times 1 \times 512$, each followed with a batch normalization layer and ReLU activation. For visual stream. the layer settings for residual blocks are the same as layer4 in ResNet-18, but the weights are not shared.

Audiovisual Correspondence Learning. Similar to [1], audiovisual correspondence learning is viewed as a two-class classification problem, i.e., corresponding or not. And the network shown in Fig. 3 is employed for achieving this learning task. Specifically, we take audio features before GRU in CRNN and visual outputs from layer3 of ResNet-18 as inputs[1], i.e., F_a and O_v in Fig. 2. Through a series of convolution and pooling operation in Fig. 3, we can get 512-D audio and visual features. Then, these two 512-D features are concatenated into one 1024-D vector and passed through two fully-connected layers of 1024-128-2. The 2-D output with softmax regression aims to determine whether audio and vision correspond.

$\{a_i, v_i\}$ from $i\text{-}th$ video are viewed as corresponding pair, then we random select a different video j and use its image v_j to construct mis-corresponding pair $\{a_i, v_j\}$. The learning objective can be written as:

$$L_{avc} = \mathcal{H}_{cce}(\boldsymbol{\delta}, \boldsymbol{q}), \tag{2}$$

where $\mathcal{H}_{cce}$ is the categorical cross entropy loss, $\boldsymbol{q} \in [0, 1]^2$ is the predicted output, $\boldsymbol{\delta}$ is the class indicator, $\boldsymbol{\delta} = (0, 1)$ for correspondence while $\boldsymbol{\delta} = (1, 0)$ for not. For multi-task learning, we take L_{mul} as final loss function, λ is the hyperparameter of weighting:

$$L_{mul} = L_{cls} + \lambda L_{avc}. \tag{3}$$

After training with multi-task objective, we could achieve coarse-grained audiovisual correspondence in the category level.

3.2   Audiovisual Feature Alignment

In this section, we propose to disentangle feature representations of different categories based on the classification predictions and implement fine-grained audiovisual alignment with the video- and category-based sound-object association.

Disentangle Features by Grad-CAM. Inspired by [4,23,30], CAM method can generate class-specific localization maps, which measures the importance of each spatial grid on the feature map to specific categories, through classification task. Hence, it is feasible for us to disentangle feature representations of different classes based on the predictions in Sect. 3.1.

Specifically, we leverage the operation of Grad-CAM [23] to perform disentanglement. For simplicity, we use $r \in \{a, v\}$ to represent audio or visual modality. Given the feature map activations of the last convolutional layer, F_r, and the

---

[1] We choose F_a and O_v for two reasons: we can obtain more fine-grained local features and achieve easier training process.

output of classification branch without activation for class c, $\hat{p}_r^c$, we calculate the class-specific map W_r^c, i.e.,

$$W_r^c = \text{Grad-CAM}(F_r, \hat{p}_r^c). \tag{4}$$

Then we take class-specific map W_r^c, i.e., the visualized heatmap in Fig. 2, as weights to perform weighted global pooling over the feature map $E_r(u, v)$ to obtain class-aware representation[2], where u and v are the map entries. That is:

$$f_r^c = \frac{\sum_{u,v} E_r(u, v) W_r^c(u, v)}{\sum_{u,v} W_r^c(u, v)}. \tag{5}$$

Finally, we get C 512-D vectors as the feature representation of all the categories. And $\{f_{a_i}^m | m = 1, 2, ..., C\}$ and $\{f_{v_i}^n | n = 1, 2, ..., C\}$ are as the set of audio and visual class-specific feature representations for i-th video. We use them for fine-grained feature alignment in next step.

Fine-Grained Audiovisual Alignment. To effectively establish audiovisual alignment with disentangled features, there are potentially two ways. One is to treat all audio and visual features of the same class in a batch as positive pairs for alignment, the other is to only take pairs of the same class from the same video as positive. As each category contains various entities (e.g., the human category contains audio and visual patterns of baby, sportsman, old man etc.), in order to reduce the interference among different entities, we choose the latter one to acquire the positive pairs with higher quality.

To effectively compare the class-specific audio and visual representation, i.e., $f_{a_i}^m$ and $f_{v_j}^n$, we project them into a shared embedding space via two fully-connected layers of 512-1024-128 followed with $L2$ normalization, respectively. Then we compare the projected features with Euclidean distance,

$$D(f_{a_i}^m, f_{v_j}^n) = ||g_a(f_{a_i}^m) - g_v(f_{v_j}^n)||_2, \tag{6}$$

where g_a and g_v are the fully-connected layers for audio and visual modalities, respectively. We then adopt contrastive loss [12] to implement sound-object alignment. The loss function is written as[3]

$$L_{ava} = \sum_{i,j=1}^{N} \sum_{m} \sum_{n} (\delta_{i=j}^{m=n} D^2(f_{a_i}^m, f_{v_j}^n) + \tag{7}$$

$$(1 - \delta_{i=j}^{m=n}) max(\Delta - D(f_{a_i}^m, f_{v_j}^n), 0)^2),$$

where $\delta_{i=j}^{m=n}$ indicates whether the audiovisual pair is positive, i.e., $\delta_{i=j}^{m=n} = 1$ when $i = j$ and $m = n$, otherwise 0. Δ is a margin hyper-parameter.

---

[2] We find that directly using F_r with the weights W_r^c is difficult to perform alignment objective, but by performing weighted pooling on E_r, we achieve easier training and faster convergence.

[3] In practice, a threshold over all the class predictions is considered to select valid categories.

3.3 Sound Localization and Its Application in Separation

In this section, we use our method to visually localize sounds, and adopt localization results as object representation to guide sound separation.

Visual Localization of Sounds. In this task, we aim to visually localize sounds by generating source-aware localization maps. To leverage the established alignment to associate sounds with objects, the visual feature map E_{v_i} of testing image is firstly projected into the shared embedding space via g_v in Eq. 6, then compared with the disentangled c-th class audio features $f_{a_i}^c$ through Eq. 8,

$$K_i^c(u, v) = -||g_a(f_{a_i}^c) - g_v(E_{v_i})(u, v)||_2. \tag{8}$$

Note that g_v in Eq. 8 is transformed into 1×1 convolutions with parameters unchanged. The obtained $K_i^c \in \mathbb{R}^{U \times V}$ reveals how likely a specific region in the visual scene v_i is the c-th visual source of sound a_i. Then, K_i^c is normalized and resized to the original image size to be the final localization maps for sound source in the c-th class. Further, the localization results with class label can be used to evaluate sound localization performance in multi-source conditions.

Sound Source Separation. To evaluate the effectiveness of our sound localization results, we use localized objects to guide sound separation. To generate the visual source guidance for the sound belonging to c-th class, we perform weighted global pooling over the feature map E_{v_i} w.r.t. the localized visual source K_i^c, similar to Eq. 5. Then, following [29], we adopt the same mix-and-separate learning framework, and take U-Net [21] to process mixed audio spectrogram, where the visual representation of object in [29] is replaced by our automatically determined visual source guidance. Finally, the output of masked spectrogram w.r.t. the visual source is converted into audio waveform via inverse short-time Fourier transform. More details about the processing can be found in [29].

4 Experiments

4.1 Datasets

SoundNet-Flickr. This dataset was proposed in [3], containing over 2 million unconstrained videos from Flickr. Following [1,24], we adopt one 5-s audio clip and its corresponding image as an audiovisual pair, and no extra supervision is used for training. For quantitative evaluation of sound localization, the human-annotated subset of SoundNet-Flickr [24] is adopted. In our setting, a random subset of 10k pairs is used for training, and 250 annotated pairs for testing.

AudioSet. AudioSet consists of mainly 10-s video clips, many containing multiple sound sources, divided into 632 event categories. Following [8,10], we only consider sounds from 15 musical instruments extracted from the "unbalanced" split for training and from the "balanced" split for testing. Since this subset provides musical scenes with multiple sound sources, some of poor quality, it is proper and also challenging for multi-source sound localization evaluation. We extract video frames at 1 fps, and employ the well-trained Faster RCNN detector w.r.t. these 15 instruments [10] to provide object locations (bounding boxes), which is then used as the evaluation reference for the sound localization. Finally, we get 96,414 10-s clips for training, and 4503 ones for testing[4].

MUSIC. MUSIC dataset consists of 685 untrimmed videos, with 536 musical solo and 149 duet, containing 11 categories of musical instrument. Since this dataset contains less noise and cleaner than AudioSet, it is more proper to train sound separation models. Following [29], we set the first/second video of each category as validation/test set, and use the rest for training. But some videos have been removed on YouTube, we finally get 474 solo and 105 duet videos in total.

4.2 Implementation Details

Our audiovisual learning model is implemented in PyTorch. We pretrain CRNN [25] and ResNet-18 [13] model as audio and visual feature extractors. The CRNN is pretrained on a subset of the unbalanced AudioSet corpus, encompassing 700k audio-clips out of the available 2 Million. The ResNet-18 is pretrained on ImageNet.

For all experiments, if not specially mentioned, we sample the audio at 22.05 kHz and convert it to log-mel spectrogram (LMS) [14], obtaining 64 frequency bins from a window of 40 ms every 20 ms using the librosa framework. Regarding visual input, we resize the image to $256 \times 256 \times 3$. Our model is optimized in a two-stage manner. First, we set λ to 1 and train the multi-task model w.r.t. Eq. 3 in Sect. 3.1. Then, we jointly optimize the entire network w.r.t. Eq. 3 and Eq. 7. The model is trained by SGD optimizer with momentum 0.9 and starting learning rate 1×10^{-3}. We set learning rate for two backbones to 1×10^{-4}. The learning rate is decreased by 0.1 every 20 epochs.

4.3 Sound Localization

Sound Localization on SoundNet-Flickr. In this section, we adopt audiovisual pairs from SoundNet-Flickr [3] for training and evaluation. The videos in this dataset are completely unconstrained and noisy, thus very challenging to localize sound sources. As there are no video tags available, we adopt the

---

[4] Since AudioSet only provides clip-level audio labels, we can only ensure that labelled sounds appear in the clip. Thus we adopt the whole 10-s audio clip with one randomly selected frame from video as a pair.

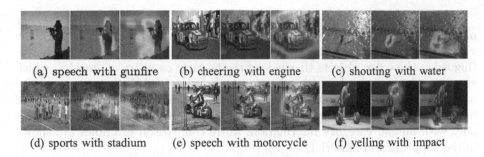

(a) speech with gunfire   (b) cheering with engine   (c) shouting with water

(d) sports with stadium   (e) speech with motorcycle   (f) yelling with impact

Fig. 4. We visualize the localization maps corresponding to different elements contained in the mixed sounds of two sources. The results qualitatively demonstrate our model's performance in multi-source sound localization.

(a) playing violin   (b) yelling sound

Fig. 5. We compare violin and human yelling sound localization results of our model and CAM output of corresponding category, images in each subfigure are listed as: original image, localization result of our method, and result of CAM.

first-level labels in AudioSet [11] of 7 categories (human sounds, music, animal, sounds of things, natural sounds, source-ambiguous sounds, and environment) as final classification target. We correlate ImageNet labels with these 7 categories by using the similarity of word embeddings [20] and conditional probabilities between labels of these two datasets, more details on this are in the supplemental materials. The pseudo labels are generated based on the prediction of pretrained CRNN and ResNet-18 model. For evaluation, we disentangle class-specific features on audio stream and localize corresponding sound source on each spatial grid of visual feature maps.

To effectively present our model's ability of category-level disentanglement and fine-grained alignment, we visualize video frames with localization maps in Fig. 4. Unlike [24] which inputs different types of audio to demonstrate interactive sound localization, we input a mixed audio containing multiple sources to generate class-specific localization responses. For example, in Fig. 4(a), when input audio clip contains human speaking and sound of gunfire, our model automatically separates these two parts and respectively highlights the person and gun area. Besides sounds with clear visual sources, for source-ambiguous sound like impact, our model accurately captures the contact surface as shown in Fig. 4(f). More examples are shown in the supplemental material.

The comparison between our model and CAM is shown in Fig. 5. First, our method can generally associate sounds with specific sources. In Fig. 5(a), the violin is making sound while the piano is silent, and our method accurately distinguishes these two objects that belong to the same category of "music", which surpasses the category-based localization technique of CAM. Second, compared with CAM, Fig. 5(b) shows that our model can precisely localize the position of human by listening to the yelling sound but CAM somewhat fails to achieve this only with human category information. More comparison examples are shown in the supplemental material.

Further we implement quantitative evaluation on 249 pairs from human annotated subset of SoundNet-Flickr [24]. Consensus Intersection over Union (cIoU) and Area Under Curve (AUC) [24] are employed as evaluation metrics. To evaluate the localization response to the entire audio, we perform weighted summation over valid categories as final localization map, where the weights are the normalized predicted probabilities. Table 1 shows the results for different methods, all of which are trained in an unsupervised manner. Despite that most audiovisual pairs in test set are of single-source, our model still outperforms Attention [24] and DMC [15] by a large margin, and is slightly better than CAVL [16]. But note that CAVL is trained on single-source videos while our model is trained on unconstrained ones, which poses greater challenge in the joint audiovisual learning. This result demonstrates that our fine-grained alignment effectively facilitates audiovisual learning with unconstrained videos. Due to limited computing resources, we did not try very large training data size like 144K as [24], but the result on 20K training data has shown the performance is increased with the number of training data.

Table 1. Quantitative localization results on SoundNet-Flickr subset, cIoU and AUC are reported (results of other methods are directly reported from [16]).

Methods	cIoU@0.5	AUC
Random	7.2	30.7
Attention 10K [24]	43.6	44.9
DMC AudioSet [15]	41.6	45.2
CAVL AudioSet [16]	50.0	49.2
Ours 10K	**52.2**	**49.6**
Ours 20K	53.8	50.6

Multi-source Localization on AudioSet. Since existing methods of sound localization evaluation are mainly for single-source scenes, We propose a quantitative evaluation pipeline for multi-source sound localization in complex scenes. We adopt a subset of AudioSet covering 15 musical instruments for training and testing.

To evaluate the model's ability of separating sounds of different instruments and aligning them with corresponding visual sources, we use cIoU and AUC metric in a class-aware manner. Different from class-agnostic score map used in [24], our method uses the detected bounding boxes of Faster RCNN to indicate the localization of sounding objects[5], each box is labelled as one specific category of music instruments, i.e., $C = 15$ on this dataset. Next, we calculate cIoU scores (e.g., with threshold 0.5) on each valid sound source and take an average. Final cIoU_class on each frame can be calculated by

$$\text{cIoU\_class} = \frac{\sum_{c=1}^{C} \theta_c cIoU_c}{\sum_{c=1}^{C} \theta_c}, \tag{9}$$

where c indicates the class index of instruments, $\theta_c = 1$ if instrument of class c makes sounds, otherwise 0. In this way, only when the model is able to establish class-specific association between sounds and objects, the evaluation score of cIoU_class will become high.

Table 2. Quantitative localization results on AudioSet of different difficulty levels. The cIoU_class threshold is 0.5 for level-1 and level-2, but 0.3 for level-3. Note that †AVC method is evaluated in a class-agnostic way.

Methods	level-1		level-2		level-3	
	cIoU_class	AUC	cIoU_class	AUC	cIoU_class@0.3	AUC
†AVC	24.8	32.0	4.27	23.6	5.3	14.9
Multi-task	20.6	29.5	2.37	17.4	10.5	17.8
Ours	**32.8**	**38.3**	**6.16**	**23.9**	**21.1**	**22.0**

To clearly present the effectiveness of our audiovisual alignment, we further divide the testing set into different difficulty levels based on the number of categories of sounding instruments, which results in 4,273 pairs of single-source (level-1), 211 pairs of two-source (level-2) and 19 pairs of three-source (level-3). As our model is a two-stage learning method, consisting of multi-task learning and fine-grained alignment, to validate the contribution of each of them, we conduct an ablation study with two baselines. The two baselines are (1) AVC: only using video-level audiovisual correspondence for training and inferring the sound locations in a class-agnostic way. (2) multi-task learning: using both of classification and audiovisual correspondence for training and inferring the sound locations with the coarse-grained audiovisual correspondence. Table 2 shows the localization results on different difficulty levels. Note that, as AVC method is not provided with any category information, we evaluate it in a class-agnostic way. From the results, we have several observations. First, using AVC to localize sound in a class-agnostic way is effective with limited sound sources,

---

[5] We have filtered out those silent detected objects.

but fails when more objects make sounds. This is because the video-level correspondence is too coarse to provide sound-object association in complex scenes. Second, although AVC takes a much looser evaluation metric of class-agnostic, it is still worse than the multi-task method on level-3, which reveals introduced classification helps to distinguish sounds of different sources. Third, our method with audiovisual alignment significantly outperforms two baselines and is robust on all difficulty levels. It demonstrates that our feature disentanglement and fine-grained alignment is effective to establish one-to-one association in both single-source and multi-source scenes.

We visualize some localization maps for the scenes in level-2 w.r.t. three different methods: AVC, Multi-task and Ours in Fig. 6. It is clear that our method can generally associate sounds with specific instruments. For example, our method precisely focuses on the tiny area where the flute locates, while the other two associate flute sound with visual object of harp.

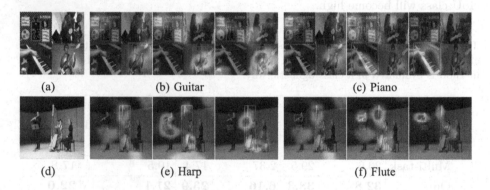

(a)   (b) Guitar   (c) Piano

(d)   (e) Harp   (f) Flute

Fig. 6. We visualize some examples in AudioSet level-2. The localization maps in each subfigure are listed from left to right: AVC, Multi-task, Ours. The green boxes are detection results of Faster RCNN. (Color figure online)

4.4   Sound Separation

In this task, we use localized objects as visual guidance to perform sound source separation, and evaluate it on MUSIC dataset. Following [29], we sub-sample it at 11kHz, and randomly crop 6-s clips to generate 256×256 spectrograms with log-frequency projection as input, then feed to U-Net. To acquire effective visual guidance of sound source, we use clip-level audio tags for classification and perform audiovisual alignment within the contained 11 instruments. Then the visual representation of sound source is generated to guide source separation.

To precisely evaluate the separation performance, we adopt three metrics of Signal-to-Distortion Ratio (SDR), Signal-to-Interference Ratio (SIR) and Signal-to-Artifact Ratio (SAR), where higher is better for all [10,29]. Table 3 shows separation results under different training conditions, where Single-Source means training with only solo videos, while Multi-Source refers to training with both solo and duet videos. We compare three different learning settings, the first is to directly use weights output by Grad-CAM as prediction mask, and the latter two are using audio and visual representation as guidance. The separation performance with Grad-CAM output weight is relatively poor, because it is of very low resolution, far from enough precise for sound separation. As for audio representations, since they are disentangled from mixed spectrogram by weighted pooling (Eq. 5), it is only slightly better than Grad-CAM but still not enough to represent a specific instrument. But when using visual representation as guidance, our model achieves comparable results on all three metrics. It demonstrates that our sound localization results contribute to effective visual representation of specific sound sources. Note that our model is trained with fewer audiovisual pairs compared to other methods, and [10] adopts an additional detector to extract sound source but which is not necessary for our model. To further validate the efficacy of our approach in multi-source scenes, our model is also trained with duet videos. The results reveal that our model can capture useful information in complex scenes to establish cross-modal association.

Table 3. Sound source separation results on MUSIC dataset. We report performance when training only on single-source (solo) videos and multi-source (solo+duet) videos as [10]. Note that SAR only captures absence of artifacts, and can be high even if separation of poor quality.

Methods	Single-source			Multi-source		
	SDR	SIR	SAR	SDR	SIR	SAR
NMF-MFCC [26]	0.92	5.68	5.84	0.92	5.68	5.84
AV-Mix-Sep [8]	3.16	6.74	8.89	3.23	7.01	9.14
Sound-of-Pixels [29]	7.30	11.90	11.90	6.05	9.81	12.40
Co-Separation [10]	7.38	13.70	10.80	7.64	13.80	11.30
CAVL [16]	6.59	10.10	12.56	6.78	10.62	12.19
Ours Grad-CAM	−2.78	−0.01	7.79	−2.49	0.08	8.34
Ours Audio	−1.16	0.33	11.11	−0.97	0.43	11.02
Ours Visual	6.53	12.15	11.31	6.57	11.90	10.78

5   Conclusions

In this work, we present an audiovisual learning framework which automatically disentangles audio and visual representations of different categories from complex scenes, and performs feature alignment in a coarse-to-fine manner. We further propose a novel evaluation pipeline for multi-source sound localization to demonstrate the superiority of our model. And our model shows promising performance on sound localization in complex scenes with multiple sound sources, as well as on sound source separation.

In future, to better distinguish different sounds and objects, we would like to introduce more categories into classification task. In this way, we are able to establish more precise sound-object association.

Acknowledgement. The paper is supported in part by the following grants: China Major Project for New Generation of AI Grant (No.2018AAA0100400), National Natural Science Foundation of China (No. 61971277, No. 61901265).

References

1. Arandjelovic, R., Zisserman, A.: Look, listen and learn. In: 2017 IEEE International Conference on Computer Vision (ICCV), pp. 609–617, October 2017. https://doi.org/10.1109/ICCV.2017.73
2. Arandjelović, R., Zisserman, A.: Objects that sound. In: Ferrari, V., Hebert, M., Sminchisescu, C., Weiss, Y. (eds.) ECCV 2018. LNCS, vol. 11205, pp. 451–466. Springer, Cham (2018). https://doi.org/10.1007/978-3-030-01246-5_27
3. Aytar, Y., Vondrick, C., Torralba, A.: SoundNet: learning sound representations from unlabeled video. In: Lee, D.D., Sugiyama, M., Luxburg, U.V., Guyon, I., Garnett, R. (eds.) Advances in Neural Information Processing Systems 29, pp. 892–900. Curran Associates, Inc. (2016). http://papers.nips.cc/paper/6146-soundnet-learning-sound-representations-from-unlabeled-video.pdf
4. Chattopadhay, A., Sarkar, A., Howlader, P., Balasubramanian, V.N.: Grad-CAM++: generalized gradient-based visual explanations for deep convolutional networks. In: 2018 IEEE Winter Conference on Applications of Computer Vision (WACV), pp. 839–847, March 2018. https://doi.org/10.1109/WACV.2018.00097
5. Gan, C., Huang, D., Zhao, H., Tenenbaum, J.B., Torralba, A.: Music gesture for visual sound separation. In: Proceedings of the IEEE/CVF Conference on Computer Vision and Pattern Recognition, pp. 10478–10487 (2020)
6. Gan, C., Zhang, Y., Wu, J., Gong, B., Tenenbaum, J.B.: Look, listen, and act: towards audio-visual embodied navigation. arXiv preprint arXiv:1912.11684 (2019)
7. Gan, C., Zhao, H., Chen, P., Cox, D., Torralba, A.: Self-supervised moving vehicle tracking with stereo sound. In: Proceedings of the IEEE International Conference on Computer Vision, pp. 7053–7062 (2019)
8. Gao, R., Feris, R., Grauman, K.: Learning to separate object sounds by watching unlabeled video. In: Ferrari, V., Hebert, M., Sminchisescu, C., Weiss, Y. (eds.) ECCV 2018. LNCS, vol. 11207, pp. 36–54. Springer, Cham (2018). https://doi.org/10.1007/978-3-030-01219-9_3
9. Gao, R., Grauman, K.: 2.5D visual sound. In: Proceedings of the IEEE Conference on Computer Vision and Pattern Recognition, pp. 324–333 (2019)
10. Gao, R., Grauman, K.: Co-separating sounds of visual objects. In: The IEEE International Conference on Computer Vision (ICCV), October 2019
11. Gemmeke, J.F., et al.: Audio set: an ontology and human-labeled dataset for audio events. In: 2017 IEEE International Conference on Acoustics, Speech and Signal Processing (ICASSP), pp. 776–780, March 2017. https://doi.org/10.1109/ICASSP.2017.7952261

12. Hadsell, R., Chopra, S., LeCun, Y.: Dimensionality reduction by learning an invariant mapping. In: 2006 IEEE Computer Society Conference on Computer Vision and Pattern Recognition (CVPR 2006), vol. 2, pp. 1735–1742, June 2006. https://doi.org/10.1109/CVPR.2006.100

13. He, K., Zhang, X., Ren, S., Sun, J.: Deep residual learning for image recognition. In: The IEEE Conference on Computer Vision and Pattern Recognition (CVPR), June 2016

14. Hershey, S., et al.: CNN architectures for large-scale audio classification. In: 2017 IEEE International Conference on Acoustics, Speech and Signal Processing (ICASSP), pp. 131–135, March 2017. https://doi.org/10.1109/ICASSP.2017.7952132

15. Hu, D., Nie, F., Li, X.: Deep multimodal clustering for unsupervised audiovisual learning. In: The IEEE Conference on Computer Vision and Pattern Recognition (CVPR), June 2019

16. Hu, D., Wang, Z., Xiong, H., Wang, D., Nie, F., Dou, D.: Curriculum audiovisual learning. arXiv preprint arXiv:2001.09414 (2020)

17. Korbar, B., Tran, D., Torresani, L.: Co-training of audio and video representations from self-supervised temporal synchronization. arXiv:1807.00230 (2018)

18. Owens, A., Efros, A.A.: Audio-visual scene analysis with self-supervised multisensory features. In: Ferrari, V., Hebert, M., Sminchisescu, C., Weiss, Y. (eds.) ECCV 2018. LNCS, vol. 11210, pp. 639–658. Springer, Cham (2018). https://doi.org/10.1007/978-3-030-01231-1_39

19. Owens, A., Wu, J., McDermott, J.H., Freeman, W.T., Torralba, A.: Ambient sound provides supervision for visual learning. In: Leibe, B., Matas, J., Sebe, N., Welling, M. (eds.) ECCV 2016. LNCS, vol. 9905, pp. 801–816. Springer, Cham (2016). https://doi.org/10.1007/978-3-319-46448-0_48

20. Pennington, J., Socher, R., Manning, C.D.: GloVe: global vectors for word representation. In: Empirical Methods in Natural Language Processing (EMNLP), pp. 1532–1543 (2014). http://www.aclweb.org/anthology/D14-1162

21. Ronneberger, O., Fischer, P., Brox, T.: U-Net: convolutional networks for biomedical image segmentation. In: Navab, N., Hornegger, J., Wells, W.M., Frangi, A.F. (eds.) MICCAI 2015. LNCS, vol. 9351, pp. 234–241. Springer, Cham (2015). https://doi.org/10.1007/978-3-319-24574-4_28

22. Rouditchenko, A., Zhao, H., Gan, C., McDermott, J., Torralba, A.: Self-supervised audio-visual co-segmentation. In: ICASSP 2019–2019 IEEE International Conference on Acoustics, Speech and Signal Processing (ICASSP), pp. 2357–2361. IEEE (2019)

23. Selvaraju, R.R., Cogswell, M., Das, A., Vedantam, R., Parikh, D., Batra, D.: Grad-CAM: visual explanations from deep networks via gradient-based localization. In: The IEEE International Conference on Computer Vision (ICCV), October 2017

24. Senocak, A., Oh, T.H., Kim, J., Yang, M.H., So Kweon, I.: Learning to localize sound source in visual scenes. In: The IEEE Conference on Computer Vision and Pattern Recognition (CVPR), June 2018

25. Shi, B., Bai, X., Yao, C.: An end-to-end trainable neural network for image-based sequence recognition and its application to scene text recognition. IEEE Trans. Pattern Anal. Mach. Intell. **39**(11), 2298–2304 (2017). https://doi.org/10.1109/TPAMI.2016.2646371

26. Spiertz, M., Gnann, V.: Source-filter based clustering for monaural blind source separation. In: Proceedings of the 12th International Conference on Digital Audio Effects (2009)

27. Tian, Y., Shi, J., Li, B., Duan, Z., Xu, C.: Audio-visual event localization in unconstrained videos. In: Ferrari, V., Hebert, M., Sminchisescu, C., Weiss, Y. (eds.) ECCV 2018. LNCS, vol. 11206, pp. 252–268. Springer, Cham (2018). https://doi.org/10.1007/978-3-030-01216-8_16
28. Zhao, H., Gan, C., Ma, W.C., Torralba, A.: The sound of motions. In: The IEEE International Conference on Computer Vision (ICCV), October 2019
29. Zhao, H., Gan, C., Rouditchenko, A., Vondrick, C., McDermott, J., Torralba, A.: The sound of pixels. In: Ferrari, V., Hebert, M., Sminchisescu, C., Weiss, Y. (eds.) ECCV 2018. LNCS, vol. 11205, pp. 587–604. Springer, Cham (2018). https://doi.org/10.1007/978-3-030-01246-5_35
30. Zhou, B., Khosla, A., Lapedriza, A., Oliva, A., Torralba, A.: Learning deep features for discriminative localization. In: The IEEE Conference on Computer Vision and Pattern Recognition (CVPR), June 2016
31. Zhou, H., Xu, X., Lin, D., Wang, X., Liu, Z.: Sep-stereo: visually guided stereophonic audio generation by associating source separation. In: Vedaldi, A., Bischof, H., Brox, T., Frahm, J.-M. (eds.) ECCV 2020. LNCS, vol. 12357, pp. 52–69. Springer, Cham (2020). https://doi.org/10.1007/978-3-030-58610-2_4

Task-Aware Quantization Network for JPEG Image Compression

Jinyoung Choi and Bohyung Han[✉]

Department of ECE and ASRI, Seoul National University, Seoul, Korea
{jin0.choi,bhhan}@snu.ac.kr

Abstract. We propose to learn a deep neural network for JPEG image compression, which predicts image-specific optimized quantization tables fully compatible with the standard JPEG encoder and decoder. Moreover, our approach provides the capability to learn task-specific quantization tables in a principled way by adjusting the objective function of the network. The main challenge to realize this idea is that there exist non-differentiable components in the encoder such as run-length encoding and Huffman coding and it is not straightforward to predict the probability distribution of the quantized image representations. We address these issues by learning a differentiable loss function that approximates bitrates using simple network blocks—two MLPs and an LSTM. We evaluate the proposed algorithm using multiple task-specific losses— two for semantic image understanding and another two for conventional image compression—and demonstrate the effectiveness of our approach to the individual tasks.

Keywords: JPEG image compression · Adaptive quantization · Bitrate approximation

1 Introduction

Image compression is a classical task to reduce the file size of an input image while minimizing the loss of visual quality. This task has two categories—lossy and lossless compression. Lossless compression algorithms preserve the contents of input images perfectly even after compression, but their compression rates are typically low. On the other hand, lossy compression techniques allow the degradation of the original images by quantization and reduce the file size significantly compared to lossless counterparts. Note that the rate-distortion trade-off [6] in lossy compression characterizes the relationship between image file size and its visual quality.

JPEG [30] is the most widely accepted image compression standard. The encoder and decoder of JPEG have several building blocks for the subtasks

Electronic supplementary material The online version of this chapter (https:// doi.org/10.1007/978-3-030-58565-5_19) contains supplementary material, which is available to authorized users.

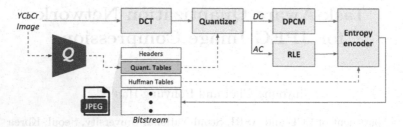

Fig. 1. The application example of the proposed approach incorporated into general JPEG encoding pipeline. Every compoents remain the same apart from that the recommendable quantization table is inferred by the pretrained quantization network (Q) before encoded. This quantization table can be specified as coding parameters of JPEG encoder and reused at decoding process from the header file.

including transform coding, chroma subsampling, quantization and entropy coding, where each component provides options for further optimization and customization. JPEG2000 [34] and BPG have been proposed after JPEG to improve the performance of image compression, yet they are not as accepted universally as JPEG that benefits from high compatibility and low complexity. Despite the popularity of JPEG for decades, its standard configuration is rather suboptimal.

Recently, there have been huge advances in learned image compression using deep neural networks. One of the most common approaches is to use autoencoders, where the intermediate bottleneck representation is used as the compressed code for an input image. Some approaches have reached to outperform the traditional compression algorithms by introducing novel deep neural network architectures with non-linear operations [1,4,5,17,21,23,26,28,36,37]. Although learned image compression algorithms are more flexible to integrate diverse objective functions to improve image quality and extend to the images in other domains, their applicability is still limited because they require dedicated decoders trained with encoders jointly and high-performance hardware.

To address the limitations, we propose a novel framework for JPEG image compression based on deep neural networks. Figure 1 illustrates the JPEG image compression pipeline accompanying with the proposed quantization network. Our method incorporates a learning-based approach into the JPEG compression standard and estimates the data-driven quantization tables perfectly compatible with the off-the-shelf JPEG encoder and decoder. Moreover, contrary to the conventional image compression methods that focus only on low-level image quality measures, our framework also allows to optimize performance of arbitrary high-level image understanding tasks, *e.g.*, image classification and image captioning, by introducing proper loss functions. As the proposed framework requires bitrate loss calculations which involve non-differentiable coding algorithms, we instead devise a deep neural network model that directly estimates the code length given JPEG DCT representations.

The main contributions of the proposed approach are summarized as follows:

- We propose a novel task-aware JPEG image compression framework based on deep neural networks, which optimizes for performance of high-level target tasks, *e.g.*, image recognition, in addition to visual quality of a decoded image.
- The proposed approach learns a quantization network to estimate image-specific quantization tables fully compatible with the standard JPEG Codec.
- To simulate the JPEG's coding algorithm, we design a code length prediction network of JPEG DCT representations, which empowers differentiable learning and accurate inference on a bitrate.

The rest of the paper is organized as follows. Section 2 and 3 briefly discuss the related work and the background of JPEG, respectively. The proposed approach is presented in Sect. 4. Section 5 describes the modeling of bitrate prediction in detail. The experimental results with analysis are in Sect. 6.

2   Related Work

The optimal quantization table may differ image by image and also depend on bitrate constraints and image quality standards. Since finding an explicit solution of the optimal quantization table under the exact distribution of images is infeasible, various techniques with different error metrics have been studied to find the optimal quantization table.

A rate-distortion (RD) optimization method based on an MSE measure uses the statistics of DCT coefficients to compute bitrate and distortion for each frequency [31] and identifies the optimal quantization table. While the distortion metric based on MSE makes the algorithm efficient, the models driven by human visual system (HVS) [3, 16, 41] often show empirically better performance. Note that the default JPEG quantization tables are also derived by exploiting HVS properties in an image-agnostic manner. Heuristics such as genetic algorithm and simulated annealing are also employed to search for improved quantization tables in [13, 29]. Especially, Hopkins *et al.* [13] propose new baseline tables for a subset of chosen quality factors by perturbing standard tables via simulated annealing with respect to FSIM [43] measure.

Recently, the errors given by deep neural networks have arisen as new metrics for image quality assessment. Dodge and Karam [7] studied how image quality affects classification accuracy, where JPEG compression is employed as an image quality degradation factor. Liu *et al.* [24] suggested a heuristic image compression framework that optimizes performance of a target task, by analyzing the importance of each frequency and the statistics for better quantization.

3   JPEG Compression

This section presents the standard procedure in the JPEG encoder and decoder. Before processing described in Sect. 3.1, color components of an image are transformed to YCbCr color space and chrominace channels are optionally subsampled. Then the image is split into 8×8 blocks for each channel. Encoding and decoding procedures are performed on each 8×8 block independently.

3.1 Encoder

Discrete Cosine Transform (DCT). A frequency domain representation including DCT has the capability to capture spatial redundancy and represent raw data with a small number of coefficients. JPEG encoder transforms the pixels in an 8×8 block by DCT [2] (2D DCT Type 2) to a coefficient matrix in the same size, denoted by $\mathbf{f} = (f_{i,j})$. The coefficient matrix is arranged in the order of DCT bases, where the first coefficient $f_{0,0}$ represents the DC component, the average value of all pixel data within the block, while the rest of 63 coefficients are the AC components. Note that JPEG DCT coefficients take integers in the range of $[-2^{10}, 2^{10})$.

Quantization. The elements in the DCT coefficient matrix are divided by the corresponding entries in a quantization matrix $\mathbf{q} = (q_{i,j})$ preset in the bitstream and rounded up to the nearest integers. The quantized DCT is represented by $\hat{\mathbf{f}} = (\hat{f}_{i,j})$, where $\hat{f}_{i,j} = \lceil f_{i,j}/q_{i,j} \rceil$. The performance of compression is determined mostly in this step.

Symbol Coding. The quantized DCT coefficients are reordered in a zigzag manner, forming a vector, and then coded into intermediate symbols. The reshaped vector is denoted by $\hat{\mathbf{f}} = (\hat{f}_0, \hat{f}_1, \ldots, \hat{f}_{63})$, where $\hat{f}_0$ is the quantized DC coefficient. From this point, DC and AC coefficients are treated separately as follows. First, the encoder applies differential pulse code modulation (DPCM) to DC coefficients of a whole image in the raster-scan order. In other words, by letting $\hat{f}_0^j$ be the DC coefficient in the jth block, the encoded symbol δ_j is given by $\delta_j = \hat{f}_0^j - \hat{f}_0^{j-1}$ for $j \neq 0$ while $\delta_0 = \hat{f}_0^0$. Second, it performs run-length encoding (RLE) using AC coefficients, which scans the elements in $\hat{\mathbf{f}}_{-0} = (\hat{f}_1, \ldots, \hat{f}_{63})$ and assigns a tuple symbol (r_i, s_i) to each of nonzero coefficients, $\hat{f}_i (\neq 0)$. Note that r_i and s_i denote the run-length of zero that immediately precedes $\hat{f}_i$ and the number of bits needed to encode $\hat{f}_i$, respectively. There is an exception that symbols are generated for $\hat{f}_i = 0$; when total length of consecutive zeros exceedes 16 before encountering a nonzero, every succession of 16 zeros are coded into $(r_i, s_i) = (15, 0)$. If the remaining coefficients are all zeros, we mark a special symbol, $(r_i, s_i) = (0, 0)$, which denotes end-of-block (EOB). Note that the EOB symbol is not necessary when $\hat{f}_{63} \neq 0$ since it is redundant to clarify the case. Finally, a sequence of generated symbols for $\hat{\mathbf{f}}_{-0}$ after RLE looks like

$$(r_{i_1}, s_{i_1})\hat{f}_{i_1}; (r_{i_2}, s_{i_2})\hat{f}_{i_2}; \cdots ; (r_{i_K}, s_{i_K})\hat{f}_{i_K}$$

where $\{i_k\}_{k=1}^K$ are the selected indices in an increasing order for which symbols are generated.

Entropy Coding. Each symbol is entropy-coded by the Huffman coding or the arithmetic coding. Our work adopts the Huffman coding, the most common method, based on the Huffman tables for DC and AC specified in the bitstream.

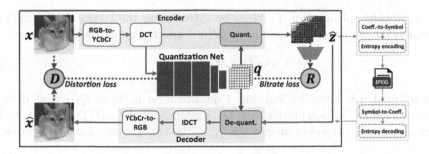

Fig. 2. The overall training framework of our method. The blue dashed lines are for the loss calculation whose gradients update our quantization network. The blue bold arrows indicate that the output of the quantization network is used as a quantization table for encoding/decoding processes. Bitrate loss is drawn from the pretrained network (colored grey). The grey dashed operations on the right-hand side are not involved in the training procedure. (Color figure online)

3.2   Decoder

The decoding procedure is given by the inverse operations of the encoder. Note that, as quantization step involves rounding operations, the inverse quantization, which is given by an element-wise product of the quantized DCT coefficient and the quantization table, leads to inevitable loss of information within the original image.

4   Quantization Network

We discuss how to predict a quantization table for task-specific image compression using the proposed quantization network.

4.1   Framework

Let $\mathcal{X}$ and $\mathcal{Z}$ be a set of training images and a set of quantized representations, respectively. Each image $\mathbf{x} \in \mathcal{X}$ is mapped to $\hat{\mathbf{z}} \in \mathcal{Z}$ by a JPEG encoder, *i.e.*, $\hat{\mathbf{z}} = \text{Enc}(\mathbf{x}, \mathbf{q})$, where $\mathbf{q}$ denotes a set of coding parameters. *i.e.*, a quantization table. The bitrate $R(\cdot)$ of $\hat{\mathbf{z}}$, which is proportional to the number of bits required to express $\hat{\mathbf{z}}$, is predicted by an approximation model and expected to be under a target value. On the other hand, a JPEG decoder (Dec) reconstructs an image by $\hat{\mathbf{x}} = \text{Dec}(\hat{\mathbf{z}}, \mathbf{q})$ while incurring some distortion due to its lossy properties. Note that we can bypass symbol coding and entropy coding functions, *e.g.*, the Huffman encoding and decoding for training because they are performed outside the pipeline of the network. The objective of the proposed compression algorithm is to minimize distortion between an input and output pair given a constraint $R \leq R_{\text{target}}$ by identifying the optimal $\mathbf{q}$ for each $\mathbf{x}$. This is reformulated as an unconstrained optimization problem by introducing the Lagrange multiplier λ that depends on the distortion metric $D(\cdot, \cdot)$ and the regulairzer R_{target} as

$$\min_{\mathbf{q}} D(\hat{\mathbf{x}}, \mathbf{x}) + \lambda R(\hat{\mathbf{z}}). \tag{1}$$

The optimal $\mathbf{q}$ is given by learning a quantization network $Q(\cdot)$ that directly estimates a quantization matrix from DCT coefficients $\mathbf{F}(= (\mathbf{f}^j))$, $i.e.$, $\mathbf{q} = Q(\mathbf{F})$. Then, for given n training images, $\{\mathbf{x}^i\}_{i=1}^n$, the training loss for $Q(\cdot)$ becomes

$$\mathcal{L}_Q = \sum_{i=1}^n D(\text{Dec}(\hat{\mathbf{z}}^i, \mathbf{q}^i), \mathbf{x}^i) + \lambda R(\text{Enc}(\mathbf{x}^i, \mathbf{q}^i)), \tag{2}$$

where $\mathbf{z}^i = \text{Enc}(\mathbf{x}^i, \mathbf{q}^i)$ and $\mathbf{q}^i = Q(\mathbf{F}^i)$. Figure 2 illustrates the overall scheme of our algorithm, where the distortion loss can be given by perceptual image quality or task-specific error.

Although we make a mathematical formulation of the objective function in (2), there exist multiple non-differentiable components in the loss. In particular, it is not straightforward to define a differentiable bitrate loss function or its surrogate. To handle this challenge, we design a deep neural network for estimating a proper bitrate in (2) that is trainable via the standard error backpropagation. We present the details of our model for bitrate approximation in Sect. 5. Before that, we discuss how to make JPEG encoding and decoding procedure differentiable.

Differentiable JPEG Encoder and Decoder. The original JPEG encoder and decoder contain non-differentiable components such as rounding operations during DCT transformation and quantization, which hampers training via the standard backpropagation. This issue is resolved by adopting a differentiable alternative introduced in [36], which simply replaces the derivative of a rounding function with an identity. This technique essentially changes only the derivative of the non-differentiable function without modifying the function itself. In other words, rounding functions are performed as normal in the forward pass while the backpropagation simply bypasses them.

4.2   Network Architecture

The quantization network of our framework takes DCT coefficients as an input and outputs two quantization tables, one for luminance and the other for chrominance, per image. Our base architecture consists of several convolutional layers and fully-connected (FC) layers. The role expected from the convolutional layers is to convey useful information in spatial and frequency domains while FC layers are to predict the appropriate quantization levels considering the absolute values of input coefficients and relative importance within an entire image for each frequency. Learning importance map for image compression appears frequently in recent deep learning based approaches [17, 21, 23, 26]. They typically intend to

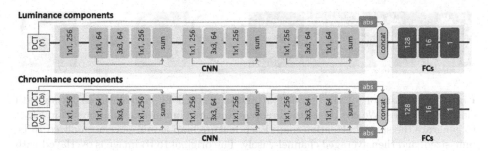

Fig. 3. The network architecture of the quantization network. The notation $K \times K, C$ in convolutional layers denotes that $K \times K$ kernels and C filters are applied. The concat operation before FC layers means the channel-wise concatenation. Batch normalization followed by ReLU activation comes right after each convolutional layer, though omitted in the figure for simplicity. The numbers in FC layers refer to the size of output sample.

allocate different number of bits depending on the complexity and the context of an image. We also adopt the same concept to control the quantization coefficients for each frequency using the features from a convolutional neural network (CNN).

The internal flow of our quantization network is depicted in Fig. 3. Before being passed to the network, a DCT coefficient matrix obtained from an image is reshaped to a 3D tensor whose channels represent individual DCT frequency; this process is similar to a reverse operation of the sub-pixel convolution (pixel shuffle) [33]. We expect that the salient regions in the informative channels have higher activations. Figure 4 visualizes the output of the convolutional layers in the quantization network, which learns attention-like representations implicitly. The attention-like features are then augmented with the original DCT representations after applying the absolute value function. Finally, the FC layers produce quantization values for each of 64 DCT frequency bases, which forms a 8×8 quantization table. We construct two independent quantization tables, one for luminance and the other for chrominance. Note that the two channels in the chrominance channels share convolutional parameters and are eventually merged before the FC layers. Figure 3 demonstrates the architectural difference between the two channels. We borrow a bottleneck skip connection block from ResNet50 [11], with only minor changes in order to match the channel sizes. Our model assumes no chroma subsampling (4:4:4 mode), which means that luminance and chrominance channels have the same resolution; it is possible to apply various ratios of chroma subsampling, which is handled merely by adding convolutional layers that reduce the spatial dimensions of chrominance components.

There are several prior works that learn deep neural networks using DCT coefficients in recent years [10,25,38]. Gueguen *et al.* [10] empirically show that DCT coefficients from JPEG are compatible with the standard convolutional neural network architectures designed for image classification tasks in RGB space. Although we have a different goal from those works, they give us an

Fig. 4. Visualization of the implicit attention learned by convolutional layers with classification loss. We use the learned representation of luminance components in Fig. 3 to generate the spatial attention map. Each feature map is min-max normalized to be unit-sized, and then averaged channel-wisely. The original RGB image is overlayed with the upsampled attention map.

intuition that we can take advantage of the standard convolutional layers for DCT coefficient inputs to learn the features in the frequency domain.

5   Approximation of Bitrate Measure

Predicting a code length given by the Huffman coding algorithm from DCT coefficients is complicated task. This is mainly because the length of AC symbols from RLE are irregular and the behavior of encoder thus becomes difficult to analyze. Motivated by this fact, we develop an approximate model of the bitrate measure $R(\cdot)$ using a deep neural network instead of an explicit analytic function. Since $R(\cdot)$ is exactly proportional to the length of bitstream that results from a sequence of discrete algorithms in JPEG entropy encoder, we design our network model to predict the final code length given the quantized vector considering the mechanism of JPEG encoder.

Several existing works [14,22,27] have studied on the approximation capabilities of a neural network theoretically by assuming certain criteria. Recently, advance of deep learning models based on various structures and components empower deep neural networks to break through complicated tasks. This direction is feasible to our case because the input of the bitrate measure R is bounded and a large number of synthetic examples can be sampled on our own.

Since JPEG operates the same processes over 8×8 basic blocks, we reduce our problem defined on a fixed dimension of domain, an 8×8 matrix. If an image is divided into n_B blocks, the bitrate measure is redefined as $R(\hat{\mathbf{z}}) = \sum_{j=1}^{n_B} R(\hat{\mathbf{z}}_j)$. The approximation of $R(\hat{\mathbf{z}}_j)$ is realized through several networks to embrace the encoding rules more accurately. The constituent networks are an intermediate symbol predictor for AC coefficients (S_{ac}) and a code length predictors for DC and AC coefficients (H_{dc} and H_{ac}, respectively). The predicted code length, which is proportional to our bitrate loss of an input image, is given by combining the three components together as

$$R(\hat{\mathbf{z}}) = \sum_{j=1}^{n_B} \mathrm{H}_{dc}(\delta_j) + \mathrm{H}_{ac}(\mathrm{S}_{ac}(\hat{\mathbf{f}}_{-0}^{j})), \tag{3}$$

where δ_j is a DC symbol and $\hat{\mathbf{f}}_{-0}^{j}$ is an AC vector from $\hat{\mathbf{z}}_j$. The followings are design procedures and implementation details of the three networks.

5.1 Symbol Prediction from RLE Model

Symbol coding process of JPEG encoding involves counting numbers in a serial order and several exception rules described in Sect. 3.1. We adopt an RNN model for the network S_{ac}, which mimics encoding rule during scanning a sequence and outputs a logit of symbol labels. The task can be formulated as a fully supervised classification using randomly generated inputs.

Our model learns the run-length size r_{i_k} for input coefficient f_{i_k} in a symbol, $(r_{i_k}, s_{i_k}) \hat{f}_{i_k}$. For the coefficients with no corresponding symbol, $i.e.$, $i \notin \{i_1, \ldots, i_K\}$, we assign a dummy symbol r_{NIL} to facilitate training. In this correspond, an input AC coefficient sequence derives a symbol sequence $\mathbf{r} = (r_1, \ldots, r_{63})$ of the same dimension. Since the number of possible symbols are confined to 16 (integers in $[0, 15]$, see Sect. 3.1), the network learns to generate the logit representing the probability of symbols given a sequence of AC coefficients. We choose a bidirectional LSTM as our RNN model and let $g : \mathbb{R} \mapsto \mathbb{R}^{16}$ be a function that produces symbol probability vector. Then, our predicted symbol $\hat{r}_i$ is given by the result of the following classification task:

$$\ell^* = \arg\max g(\mathrm{BiLSTM}(f_i)), \tag{4}$$

$i.e.$, $\hat{r}_i = \ell^*$. Now we can train this model by generating a training set, $\{(\hat{\mathbf{f}}_{-0}, \mathbf{r})\}$, from a random sequence in $\mathcal{Z}$. We adopt a single-layer bidirectional LSTM with 16 hidden states. However, since (4) is non-differentiable, we approximate $\hat{r}_i$ to $\tilde{r}_i$ using a Gumbel-softmax function as proposed in [15], which results in the final predicted symbols $\tilde{\mathbf{r}} = (\tilde{r}_1, \ldots, \tilde{r}_{63})$, inputs for the next regression step.

5.2 Regression Model for Final Code Length

We train two MLP models for DC and AC to predict the final code length based on the Huffman tables. We convert each element of DC symbols and AC vectors into the logarithmic scale, $i.e.$, f_i to $\log_2(|f_i| + 1)$, since the lengths of codewords are clustered tightly in that scale. This adjustment makes our training more efficient and accurate by providing training examples more focused to frequently observed input patterns.

The networks are trained in a supervised manner based on the Huber loss using randomly generated vectors whose elements are sampled from $[-10, 10]$. Modifying the input scale in (3), the approximate code length of an image becomes

$$R(\hat{\mathbf{z}}) = \sum_{j=1}^{n_B} \{ \mathrm{H}_{dc}(\log_2(|\delta_j| + 1)) + \sum_{i=1}^{63} \mathrm{H}_{ac}(\log_2(|f_i^j| + 1), \tilde{r}_i^j) \}. \tag{5}$$

Note that all three models in (3) are trained jointly. Our final regression model achieves $5.30\% \pm 1.60$ on SMAPE (symmetric mean absolute percentage error) [9] when tested over 5,000 images sampled from the ImageNet validation set, where each image is JPEG compressed with random quality factor. SMAPE is a common evaluation metric for regression problem that provides a reasonable judgment on relative errors.

In theory, one can further optimize a Huffman coding by using custom Huffman tables or adaptive Huffman coding algorithms, which dynamically updates code tables according to the change of distributions of input symbols [19]. Lakhani [20] reports that variants of the standard compression algorithm have limited benefits considering the additional cost in space and time. In this work, we pursue the method that keeps the standard codec intact and choose to follow the standard Huffman coding. Meanwhile, the proposed method that approximates the bitrate is still applicable to any extensions of Huffman coding.

6 Experiments

Dataset. We train the quantization network on the ImageNet [32] dataset, which has 1,000 class labels. We constructed a test set for classification by sampling 5,000 images in 1,000 classes from the ImageNet validation set. We also used Caltech101 [8] for cross-dataset evaluation, where 406 randomly selected images are set aside for a test set. Flickr8k [12] and Kodak PhotoCD[1] datasets are additionally used for various assessments of our method.

Training. We use the Adam [18] optimizer to learn models in all experiments. The learning rate starts from 0.001 and decreases by 0.1 for every 2k iterations. Each model is trained until the objective function converges.

Comparison. The baseline dataset is generated by varying the JPEG quality factor scaled from 1 to 100 with the standard tables for each image. In all cases, including ours, 4:4:4 chroma subsampling mode is applied to test and evaluation. We compare two compressed images given by our algorithm and the standard JPEG by identifying the image in the baseline dataset with the (almost) same file size as ours. For each rate constraint parameter, we measure average bitrate and distortion (or performance) on test dataset to obtain a single point on the rate-distortion curve. To compute bitrate, we compute the actual bpp (bits per pixel) by applying the symbol coding and Huffman coding to the quantized representations.

Image Classification Accuracy. For classification task, we employed Inception-v3 [35] for distortion metric. We adopted the pretrained model available in PyTorch. Figure 5(a) presents that our quantization improves classification accuracy consistently, especially with aggressive compression rates. In our evaluation setting, the classification accuracy drops dramatically from around 0.4bpp and decent classification accuracy is achieved at higher bitrate. It is

---

[1] http://r0k.us/graphics/kodak/.

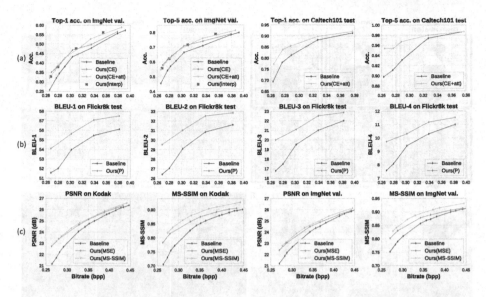

Fig. 5. Comparion by rate-distortion(/performance) curves. (a) Experiments with cross entropy loss of Inception-v3. Ours (CE+att) have the same architecture as ours(CE) except the attention module at the end of CNN. Classification accuracies(top-1/top-5) on original datasets are 0.76/0.93 for ImageNet and 0.96/0.99 for Caltech101. Ours(interp) are interpolated results from the models of ours (CE+att). (b) Experiments with Inception-v3 perceptual loss (ours(P)) for image captioning. Original test set records 61, 36, 26 and 14 on BLEU-1 to BLEU-4 scores. (c) Experiments with MSE loss and MS-SSIM loss.

therefore natural that the proposed algorithm has relatively low gain on high bitrate range. In effect, our quantization network alleviates the failure of the classifier at low bitrates. Further, the results on Caltech101 imply the promising cross-dataset generalization performance as well.

Quality of Image Captioning. To demonstrate the applicability of our method to various tasks, we run an experiment for image captioning, which requires more advanced semantic understanding than image classification. We choose Inception-v3 perceptual loss as a distortion metric. We train the image captioning model introduced in [39] on Flickr8k dataset using Inception-v3 feature extractor. BLEU scores are computed on generated captions as presented in Fig. 5(b). Our quantization method seems to benefit high-level tasks by preserving more semantic information in the images.

Percieved Quality. We also trained the proposed quantization network using conventional distortion metrics such as pixel-wise MSE loss and MS-SSIM [40] loss. We evaluate the results on ImageNet and Kodak test dataset in terms of PSNR and MS-SSIM index because they are widely used as an approximation to

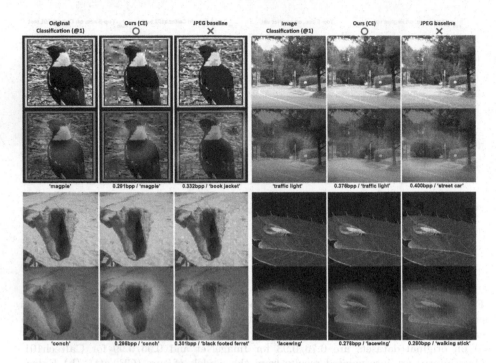

Fig. 6. Examples of classification results on experiment with Inception-v3 loss on ImageNet. Bitrates and predicted classes are shown below the images with CAM visualizations.

human perception of visual quality. Figure 5(c) shows that our methods surpass the baseline on both metrics, especially on MS-SSIM.

Effect of Attention Module. To examine whether the architecture of our quantization network can further improve the compression performance, we added a simple attention module at the end of the original convolution layers in Fig. 3. Our attention module is identical to CBAM [42] except that we omit max-pooled features and spatial attention is drawn ahead of channel attention. Figure 5(a) illustrates that our quantization network benefits from the attention module, which implies the potential improvement of our method by introducing better attention mechanisms or CNN architectures.

Interpolation Using Multiple Models. We present that the interpolation of quantization tables from multiple quantization networks is valid for the bitrate control. As shown in ImageNet plots in Fig. 5(a), interpolated results based on two models still surpass the baseline and also aligned well to the curve given by our algorithm without interpolation. This implies that we can realize an arbitrary bitrate by learning several landmark quantization networks and interpolating the resulting quantization tables for JPEG encoding.

Fig. 7. Comparison on the captions generated by the RNN based caption generator on Flickr8k dataset. (a) Left: Only baseline results commit errors. Right: Both ours and baselines contain mistakes. (b) Ours outperform the baseline results. Errors are colored red and extra descriptions captured only by ours are colored blue. (Color figure online)

Qualitative Results. Figure 6 presents qualitative comparisons between the JPEG baseline and our algorithm, where the JPEG baseline predicts wrong labels while ours approach is correct even with lower bitrates. In addition, we visualize class activation mappings (CAM) [44] for top-1 class on each image. The localized regions in the images support the proposed method on the classification task. We provide more examples with CAM localizations in the supplementary document.

Figure 7 shows the qualitative results of generated captions. We observe that the captions on our compressed images contain fewer mistakes than those on baselines and often grasp detailed information of images missed in the baselines. When our images have a slightly higher bitrate than the baselines, the proposed approach obtains appealing improvements on captions that are hardly seen in the counterpart.

Fig. 8. Comparison on the selectively cropped samples from the Kodak dataset. Bitrate, PSNR and MS-SSIM values are notated below each image.

Some qualitative results on Kodak dataset are shown in Fig. 8. Generally, our quantization yields more natural outputs with lower bitrates; color changes are smoother in monotonous regions and complex structures are less blurred. Unlike the default quantizations, which normally quantize chrominance components more than luminance components, our approach seems to perform more balanced bitrate optimization, which, in turn, produces better visual quality.

7   Conclusion

We proposed a framework for data-driven and task-aware JPEG quantization, which has not been studied intensively. To facilitate our training, we designed a differentiable code length prediction technique given quantized representations based on deep neural networks. The proposed quantization network has been incorporated into the standard JPEG algorithm and improved compression performance substantially. Especially, it is highly effective when the bitrate is very low, where JPEG suffers from severe degradation. The proposed method is indeed practical since it is compatible with any JPEG Codecs with no additional cost for decoding. We believe that our method can be explored further jointly with various options of JPEG compression and for more powerful network architectures.

Acknowledgments. This work was partly supported by Kakao and Kakao Brain Corporation, and IITP grant funded by the Korea government (MSIT) (2016-0-00563, 2017-0-01779). We also thank Hyeonwoo Noh for fruitful discussions.

References

1. Agustsson, E., et al.: Soft-to-hard vector quantization for end-to-end learning compressible representations. In: NeurIPS (2017)
2. Ahmed, N., Natarajan, T., Rao, K.R.: Discrete cosine transform. IEEE Trans. Comput. **100**(1), 90–93 (1974)
3. Ahumada Jr, A.J., Peterson, H.A.: Luminance-model-based DCT quantization for color image compression. In: SPIE (1992)
4. Ballé, J., Laparra, V., Simoncelli, E.P.: End-to-end optimized image compression. In: ICLR (2017)
5. Ballé, J., Minnen, D., Singh, S., Hwang, S.J., Johnston, N.: Variational image compression with a scale hyperprior. In: ICLR (2018)
6. Davisson, L.D.: Rate-distortion theory and application. Proc. IEEE **60**(7), 800–808 (1972)
7. Dodge, S., Karam, L.: Understanding how image quality affects deep neural networks. In: QoMEX (2016)
8. Fei-Fei, L., Fergus, R., Perona, P.: Learning generative visual models from few training examples: an incremental Bayesian approach tested on 101 object categories. In: CVPRW (2004)
9. Flores, B.E.: A pragmatic view of accuracy measurement in forecasting. Omega **14**(2), 93–98 (1986)
10. Gueguen, L., Sergeev, A., Kadlec, B., Liu, R., Yosinski, J.: Faster neural networks straight from JPEG. In: NeurIPS (2018)
11. He, K., Zhang, X., Ren, S., Sun, J.: Deep residual learning for image recognition. In: CVPR (2016)
12. Hodosh, M., Young, P., Hockenmaier, J.: Framing image description as a ranking task: data, models and evaluation metrics. J. Artif. Intell. Res. **47**, 853–899 (2013)
13. Hopkins, M., Mitzenmacher, M., Wagner-Carena, S.: Simulated annealing for JPEG quantization. In: DCC (2018)
14. Hornik, K., Stinchcombe, M., White, H.: Multilayer feedforward networks are universal approximators. Neural Netw. **2**(5), 359–366 (1989)
15. Jang, E., Gu, S., Poole, B.: Categorical reparameterization with gumbel-softmax. In: ICLR (2017)
16. Jayant, N., Johnston, J., Safranek, R.: Signal compression based on models of human perception. Proc. IEEE **81**(10), 1385–1422 (1993)
17. Johnston, N., et al.: Improved Lossy image compression with priming and spatially adaptive bit rates for recurrent networks. In: CVPR (2018)
18. Kingma, D.P., Ba, J.: Adam: a method for stochastic optimization. In: ICLR (2015)
19. Knuth, D.E.: Dynamic Huffman coding. J. Algorithms **6**(2), 163–180 (1985)
20. Lakhani, G.: Optimal Huffman coding of DCT blocks. IEEE Trans. Circuits Syst. Video Technol. **14**(4), 522–527 (2004)
21. Lee, J., Cho, S., Beack, S.K.: Context-adaptive entropy model for end-to-end optimized image compression. In: ICLR (2019)
22. Leshno, M., Lin, V.Y., Pinkus, A., Schocken, S.: Multilayer feedforward networks with a nonpolynomial activation function can approximate any function. Neural Netw. **6**(6), 861–867 (1993)
23. Li, M., Zuo, W., Gu, S., Zhao, D., Zhang, D.: Learning convolutional networks for content-weighted image compression. In: CVPR (2018)
24. Liu, Z., et al.: DeepN-JPEG: a deep neural network favorable JPEG-based image compression framework. In: DAC (2018)

25. Lo, S.Y., Hang, H.M.: Exploring semantic segmentation on the DCT representation. In: MMAsia (2019)
26. Mentzer, F., Agustsson, E., Tschannen, M., Timofte, R., Van Gool, L.: Conditional probability models for deep image compression. In: CVPR (2018)
27. Mhaskar, H.N., Micchelli, C.A.: Approximation by superposition of sigmoidal and radial basis functions. Adv. Appl. Math. **13**(3), 350–373 (1992)
28. Minnen, D., Ballé, J., Toderici, G.D.: Joint autoregressive and hierarchical priors for learned image compression. In: NeurIPS (2018)
29. Monro, D.M., Sherlock, B.G.: Optimum DCT quantization. In: DCC (1993)
30. Pennebaker, W.B., Mitchell, J.L.: JPEG: Still Image Data Compression Standard. Springer Science and Business Media, New York (1992)
31. Ratnakar, V., Livny, M.: RD-OPT: an efficient algorithm for optimizing DCT quantization tables. In: DCC (1995)
32. Russakovsky, O., et al.: Imagenet large scale visual recognition challenge. Int. J. Comput. Vision **115**(3), 211–252 (2015)
33. Shi, W., et al.: Real-time single image and video super-resolution using an efficient sub-pixel convolutional neural network. In: CVPR (2016)
34. Skodras, A., Christopoulos, C., Ebrahimi, T.: The JPEG 2000 still image compression standard. IEEE Signal Process. Mag. **18**(5), 36–58 (2001)
35. Szegedy, C., Vanhoucke, V., Ioffe, S., Shlens, J., Wojna, Z.: Rethinking the inception architecture for computer vision. In: CVPR (2016)
36. Theis, L., Shi, W., Cunningham, A., Huszár, F.: Lossy image compression with compressive autoencoders. In: ICLR (2017)
37. Toderici, G., et al.: Full resolution image compression with recurrent neural networks. In: CVPR (2017)
38. Verma, V., Agarwal, N., Khanna, N.: DCT-domain deep convolutional neural networks for multiple JPEG compression classification. Sig. Process. Image Commun. **67**, 22–33 (2018)
39. Vinyals, O., Toshev, A., Bengio, S., Erhan, D.: Show and tell: a neural image caption generator. In: CVPR (2015)
40. Wang, Z., Simoncelli, E.P., Bovik, A.C.: Multiscale structural similarity for image quality assessment. In: ACSSC (2003)
41. Watson, A.B.: Visually optimal DCT quantization matrices for individual images. In: DCC (1993)
42. Woo, S., Park, J., Lee, J.Y., Kweon, I.S.: CBAM: convolutional block attention module. In: ECCV (2018)
43. Zhang, L., Zhang, L., Mou, X., Zhang, D.: FSIM: a feature similarity index for image quality assessment. IEEE Trans. Image Process. **20**(8), 2378–2386 (2011)
44. Zhou, B., Khosla, A., Lapedriza, A., Oliva, A., Torralba, A.: Learning deep features for discriminative localization. In: CVPR (2016)

Energy-Based Models for Deep Probabilistic Regression

Fredrik K. Gustafsson[1]([✉]), Martin Danelljan[2], Goutam Bhat[2], and Thomas B. Schön[1]

[1] Department of Information Technology, Uppsala University, Uppsala, Sweden
fredrik.gustafsson@it.uu.se
[2] Computer Vision Lab, ETH Zürich, Zürich, Switzerland

Abstract. While deep learning-based classification is generally tackled using standardized approaches, a wide variety of techniques are employed for regression. In computer vision, one particularly popular such technique is that of confidence-based regression, which entails predicting a confidence value for each input-target pair (x, y). While this approach has demonstrated impressive results, it requires important task-dependent design choices, and the predicted confidences lack a natural probabilistic meaning. We address these issues by proposing a general and conceptually simple regression method with a clear probabilistic interpretation. In our proposed approach, we create an energy-based model of the conditional target density $p(y|x)$, using a deep neural network to predict the un-normalized density from (x, y). This model of $p(y|x)$ is trained by directly minimizing the associated negative log-likelihood, approximated using Monte Carlo sampling. We perform comprehensive experiments on four computer vision regression tasks. Our approach outperforms direct regression, as well as other probabilistic and confidence-based methods. Notably, our model achieves a 2.2% AP improvement over Faster-RCNN for object detection on the COCO dataset, and sets a new state-of-the-art on visual tracking when applied for bounding box estimation. In contrast to confidence-based methods, our approach is also shown to be directly applicable to more general tasks such as age and head-pose estimation. Code is available at https://github.com/fregu856/ebms_regression.

1 Introduction

Supervised regression entails learning a model capable of predicting a continuous target value y from an input x, given a set of paired training examples. It is a fundamental machine learning problem with many important applications within computer vision and other domains. Common regression tasks within computer vision include object detection [23,28,47,63], head- and body-pose estimation [5,52,57,59], age estimation [4,42,48], visual tracking [8,31,38,64]

Electronic supplementary material The online version of this chapter (https://doi.org/10.1007/978-3-030-58565-5_20) contains supplementary material, which is available to authorized users.

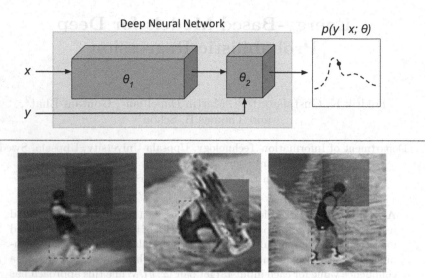

Fig. 1. An overview of the proposed regression method (top). We train an energy-based model $p(y|x;\theta) \propto e^{f_\theta(x,y)}$ of the conditional target density $p(y|x)$, using a DNN f_θ to predict the un-normalized density directly from the input-target pair (x,y). Our approach is capable of predicting highly flexible densities and produce highly accurate estimates. This is demonstrated for the problem of bounding box regression (bottom), visualizing the marginal density for the top right box corner as a heatmap.

and medical image registration [6,39], just to mention a few. Today, such regression problems are commonly tackled using Deep Neural Networks (DNNs), due to their ability to learn powerful feature representations directly from data.

While classification is generally addressed using standardized losses and output representations, a wide variety of different techniques are employed for regression. The most conventional strategy is to train a DNN to directly predict a target y given an input x [27]. In such *direct regression* approaches, the model parameters of the DNN are learned by minimizing a loss function, for example the L^2 or L^1 loss, penalizing discrepancy between the predicted and ground truth target values. From a probabilistic perspective, this approach corresponds to creating a simple parametric model of the conditional target density $p(y|x)$, and minimizing the associated negative log-likelihood. The L^2 loss, for example, corresponds to a fixed-variance Gaussian model. More recent work [7,15,24,26,45,54] has also explored learning more expressive models of $p(y|x)$, by letting a DNN instead output the full set of parameters of a certain family of probability distributions. To allow for straightforward implementation and training, many of these *probabilistic regression* approaches however restrict the parametric model to unimodal distributions such as Gaussian [7,26] or Laplace [15,22,24], still severely limiting the expressiveness of the learned conditional target density. While these methods benefit from a clear probabilistic interpretation, they thus fail to fully exploit the predictive power of the DNN.

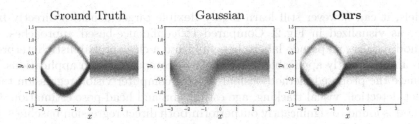

Fig. 2. An illustrative 1D regression problem. The training data $\mathcal{D} = \{(x_i, y_i)\}_{i=1}^{2000}$ is generated by the ground truth conditional target density $p(y|x)$. Our energy-based model $p(y|x; \theta) \propto e^{f_\theta(x,y)}$ of $p(y|x)$ is trained by directly minimizing the associated negative log-likelihood, approximated using Monte Carlo importance sampling. In contrast to the Gaussian model $p(y|x; \theta) = \mathcal{N}(y; \mu_\theta(x), \sigma_\theta^2(x))$, our energy-based model can learn multimodal and complex conditional target densities directly from data.

The quest for improved regression accuracy has also led to the development of more specialized methods, designed for a specific set of tasks. In computer vision, one particularly popular approach is that of *confidence-based regression*. Here, a DNN instead predicts a scalar confidence value for input-target pairs (x, y). The confidence can then be maximized w.r.t. y to obtain a target prediction for a given input x. This approach is commonly employed for image-coordinate regression tasks within e.g. human pose estimation [5,52,57] and object detection [28,63], where a 2D heatmap over image pixel coordinates y is predicted. Recently, the approach was also applied to the problem of bounding box regression by Jiang et al. [23]. Their proposed method, IoU-Net, obtained state-of-the-art accuracy on object detection, and was later also successfully applied to the task of visual tracking [8]. The training of such confidence-based regression methods does however entail generating additional pseudo ground truth labels, e.g. by employing a Gaussian kernel [55,57], and selecting an appropriate loss function. This both requires numerous design choices to be made, and limits the general applicability of the methods. Moreover, confidence-based regression methods do not allow for a natural probabilistic interpretation in terms of the conditional target density $p(y|x)$. In this work, we therefore set out to develop a method combining the general applicability and the clear interpretation of probabilistic regression with the predictive power of the confidence-based approaches.

Contributions. We propose a general and conceptually simple regression method with a clear probabilistic interpretation. Our method employs an energy-based model [30] to predict the un-normalized conditional target density $p(y|x)$ from the input-target pair (x, y). It is trained by directly minimizing the associated negative log-likelihood, exploiting tailored Monte Carlo approximations. At test time, targets are predicted by maximizing the conditional target density $p(y|x)$ through gradient-based refinement. Our energy-based model is straightforward both to implement and train. Unlike commonly used probabilistic models, it can however still learn highly flexible target densities directly from data, as visualized in Fig. 2. Compared to confidence-based approaches, our method requires no pseudo labels, benefits from a clear probabilistic interpretation, and is directly applicable to a variety of computer vision applications. We evaluate the proposed method on four diverse computer vision regression tasks: object detection, visual tracking, age estimation and head-pose estimation. Our method is found to significantly outperform both direct regression baselines, and popular probabilistic and confidence-based alternatives, including the state-of-the-art IoU-Net [23]. Notably, our method achieves a 2.2% AP improvement over FPN Faster-RCNN [32] when applied for object detection on COCO [33], and sets a new state-of-the-art on standard benchmarks [36,37] when applied for bounding box estimation in the recent ATOM [8] visual tracker. Our method is also shown to be directly applicable to the more general tasks of age and head-pose estimation, consistently improving performance of a variety of baselines.

2   Background and Related Work

In supervised regression, the task is to learn to predict a target value $y^\star \in \mathcal{Y}$ from a corresponding input $x^\star \in \mathcal{X}$, given a training set of i.i.d. input-target examples, $\mathcal{D} = \{(x_i, y_i)\}_{i=1}^N$, $(x_i, y_i) \sim p(x, y)$. As opposed to classification, the target space $\mathcal{Y}$ is a continuous set, e.g. $\mathcal{Y} = \mathbb{R}^K$. In computer vision, the input space $\mathcal{X}$ often corresponds to the space of images, whereas the output space $\mathcal{Y}$ depends on the task at hand. Common examples include $\mathcal{Y} = \mathbb{R}^2$ in image-coordinate regression [28,57], $\mathcal{Y} = \mathbb{R}_+$ in age estimation [42,48], and $\mathcal{Y} = \mathbb{R}^4$ in object bounding box regression [23,47]. A variety of techniques have previously been applied to supervised regression tasks. In order to motivate and provide intuition for our proposed method, we here describe a few popular approaches.

Direct Regression. Over the last decade, DNNs have been shown to excel at a wide variety of regression problems. Here, a DNN is viewed as a function $f_\theta : \mathcal{U} \to \mathcal{O}$, parameterized by a set of learnable weights $\theta \in \mathbb{R}^P$. The most conventional regression approach is to train a DNN to directly predict the targets, $y^\star = f_\theta(x^\star)$, called *direct regression*. The model parameters θ are learned by minimizing a loss $\ell(f_\theta(x_i), y_i)$ that penalizes discrepancy between the prediction $f_\theta(x_i)$ and the ground truth target value y_i on training examples (x_i, y_i). Common choices include the L^2 loss, $\ell(\hat{y}, y) = \|\hat{y} - y\|_2^2$, the L^1 loss, $\ell(\hat{y}, y) = \|\hat{y} - y\|_1$, and their close relatives [21,27]. From a probabilistic perspective, the choice of loss corresponds to minimizing the negative log-likelihood $-\log p(y|x; \theta)$ for a specific model $p(y|x; \theta)$ of the conditional target density. For example, the L^2 loss is derived from a fixed-variance Gaussian model, $p(y|x; \theta) = \mathcal{N}(y; f_\theta(x), \sigma^2)$.

Probabilistic Regression. More recent work [7,15,22,24,26,34,54] has explicitly taken advantage of this probabilistic perspective to achieve more flexible parametric models $p(y|x; \theta) = p(y; \phi_\theta(x))$, by letting the DNN output the parameters ϕ of a family of probability distributions $p(y; \phi)$. For example, a general 1D Gaussian model can be realized as $p(y|x; \theta) = \mathcal{N}(y; \mu_\theta(x), \sigma_\theta^2(x))$, where the DNN outputs the mean and log-variance as $f_\theta(x) = \phi_\theta(x) = [\mu_\theta(x) \log \sigma_\theta^2(x)]^\mathsf{T} \in \mathbb{R}^2$. The model parameters θ are learned by minimizing the negative log-likelihood $-\sum_{i=1}^N \log p(y_i|x_i; \theta)$ over the training set $\mathcal{D}$. At test time, a target estimate $y^\star$ is obtained by first predicting the density parameter values $\phi_\theta(x^\star)$ and then, for instance, taking the expected value of $p(y; \phi_\theta(x))$. Previous work has applied simple Gaussian and Laplace models on computer vision tasks such as object detection [13,19] and optical flow estimation [15,22], usually aiming to not only achieve accurate predictions, but also to provide an estimate of aleatoric uncertainty [17,24]. To allow for multimodal models $p(y; \phi_\theta(x))$, mixture density networks (MDNs) [3] have also been applied [34,54]. The DNN then outputs weights for K mixture components along with K sets of parameters, e.g. K sets of means and log-variances for a mixture of Gaussians. Previous work has also applied *infinite* mixture models by utilizing the conditional VAE (cVAE) framework [45,51]. A latent variable model $p(y|x; \theta) = \int p(y; \phi_\theta(x, z))p(z; \phi_\theta(x))dz$ is then employed, where $p(y; \phi_\theta(x, z))$ and $p(z; \phi_\theta(x))$ typically are Gaussian distributions. Our proposed method also entails predicting a conditional target density $p(y|x; \theta)$ and minimizing the associated negative log-likelihood. However, our energy-based model $p(y|x; \theta)$ is not limited to the functional form of any specific probability density (e.g. Gaussian or Laplace), but is instead directly defined via a learned scalar function of (x, y). In contrast to MDNs and cVAEs, our model $p(y|x; \theta)$ is not even limited to densities which are simple to generate samples from. This puts *minimal restricting assumptions* on the true $p(y|x)$, allowing it to be efficiently learned directly from data.

Confidence-Based Regression. Another category of approaches reformulates the regression problem as $y^\star = \arg\max_y f_\theta(x, y)$, where $f_\theta(x, y) \in \mathbb{R}$ is a scalar confidence value predicted by the DNN. The idea is thus to predict a quantity $f_\theta(x, y)$, depending on both input x and target y, that can be maximized over y to obtain the final prediction $y^\star$. This maximization-based formulation is inherent in Structural SVMs [53], but has also been adopted for DNNs. We term this family of approaches *confidence-based regression*. Compared to direct regression, the predicted confidence $f_\theta(x, y)$ can encapsulate multiple hypotheses and other ambiguities. Confidence-based regression has been shown particularly suitable for image-coordinate regression tasks, such as hand keypoint localization [50] and body-part detection [44,55,57]. In these cases, a CNN is trained to output a 2D heatmap over the image pixel coordinates y, thus taking full advantage of the translational invariance of the problem. In computer vision, confidence prediction has also been successfully employed for tasks other than pure image-coordinate regression. Jiang et al. [23] proposed the IoU-Net for bounding box regression in object detection, where a bounding box $y \in \mathbb{R}^4$ and image x are both input to the DNN to predict a confidence $f_\theta(x, y)$. It employs a pooling-based architecture that is differentiable w.r.t. the bounding box y, allowing efficient gradient-based maximization to obtain the final estimate $y^* = \arg\max_y f_\theta(x, y)$. IoU-Net was later also successfully applied to target object estimation in visual tracking [8].

In general, confidence-based approaches are trained using a set of *pseudo label* confidences $c(x_i, y_i, y)$ generated for each training example (x_i, y_i), and by employing a loss $\ell\big(f_\theta(x_i, y), c(x_i, y_i, y)\big)$. One strategy [28,44] is to treat the confidence prediction as a binary classification problem, where $c(x_i, y_i, y)$ represents either the class, $c \in \{0, 1\}$, or its probability, $c \in [0, 1]$, and employ cross-entropy based losses ℓ. The other approach is to treat the confidence prediction as a direct regression problem itself by applying standard regression losses, such as L^2 [8,50,55] or the Huber loss [23]. In these cases, the pseudo label confidences c can be constructed using a similarity measure S in the target space, $c(x_i, y_i, y) = S(y, y_i)$, for example defined as the Intersection over Union (IoU) between two bounding boxes [23] or simply by a Gaussian kernel [52,55,57].

While these methods have demonstrated impressive results, confidence-based approaches thus require important design choices. In particular, the strategy for constructing the pseudo labels c and the choice of loss ℓ are often crucial for performance and highly *task-dependent*, limiting general applicability. Moreover, the predicted confidence $f_\theta(x, y)$ can be difficult to interpret, since it has no natural connection to the conditional target density $p(y|x)$. In contrast, our approach is directly trained to predict $p(y|x)$ itself, and importantly it does *not* require generation of pseudo label confidences or choosing a specific loss.

Regression-by-Classification. A regression problem can also be treated as a classification problem by first discretizing the target space $\mathcal{Y}$ into a finite set of C classes. Standard techniques from classification, such as softmax and the cross-entropy loss, can then be employed. This approach has previously been applied to both age estimation [42,48,60] and head-pose estimation [49,59]. The discretization of the target space $\mathcal{Y}$ however complicates exploiting its inherent neighborhood structure, an issue that has been addressed by exploring ordinal regression methods for 1D problems [4,10]. While our energy-based approach can be seen as a generalization of the softmax model for classification to the continuous target space $\mathcal{Y}$, it does not suffer from the aforementioned drawbacks of regression-by-classification. On the contrary, our model naturally allows the network to exploit the full structure of the continuous target space $\mathcal{Y}$.

Energy-Based Models. Our approach is of course also related to the theoretical framework of energy-based models, which often has been employed for machine learning problems in the past [20,30,35]. It involves learning an energy function $\mathcal{E}_\theta(x) \in \mathbb{R}$ that assigns low energy to observed data x_i and high energy to other values of x. Recently, energy-based models have been used primarily for unsupervised learning problems within computer vision [11,14,29,40,58], where DNNs are directly used to predict $\mathcal{E}_\theta(x)$. These models are commonly trained by minimizing the negative log-likelihood, stemming from the probabilistic model $p(x; \theta) = e^{-\mathcal{E}_\theta(x)} / \int e^{-\mathcal{E}_\theta(x)} dx$, for example by generating approximate image samples from $p(x; \theta)$ using Markov Chain Monte Carlo [11,14,40]. In contrast, we study the application of energy-based models for $p(y|x)$ in *supervised* regression, a mostly overlooked research direction in recent years, and obtain state-of-the-art performance on four diverse computer vision regression tasks.

3 Proposed Regression Method

We propose a general and conceptually simple regression method with a clear probabilistic interpretation. Our method employs an energy-based model within a probabilistic regression formulation, defined in Sect. 3.1. In Sect. 3.2, we introduce our training strategy which is designed to be simple, yet highly effective and applicable to a wide variety of regression tasks within computer vision. Lastly, we describe our prediction strategy for high accuracy in Sect. 3.3.

3.1 Formulation

We take the probabilistic view of regression by creating a model $p(y|x; \theta)$ of the conditional target density $p(y|x)$, in which θ is learned by minimizing the associated negative log-likelihood. Instead of defining $p(y|x; \theta)$ by letting a DNN predict the parameters of a certain family of probability distributions (e.g. Gaussian or Laplace), we construct a versatile energy-based model that can better leverage the predictive power of DNNs. To that end, we take inspiration from confidence-based regression approaches and let a DNN directly predict a scalar value for any input-target pair (x, y). Unlike confidence-based methods however, this prediction has a clear probabilistic interpretation. Specifically, we view a DNN as a function $f_\theta : \mathcal{X} \times \mathcal{Y} \to \mathbb{R}$, parameterized by $\theta \in \mathbb{R}^P$, that maps an input-target pair $(x, y) \in \mathcal{X} \times \mathcal{Y}$ to a scalar value $f_\theta(x, y) \in \mathbb{R}$. Our model $p(y|x; \theta)$ of the conditional target density $p(y|x)$ is then defined according to,

$$p(y|x; \theta) = \frac{e^{f_\theta(x,y)}}{Z(x,\theta)}, \qquad Z(x,\theta) = \int e^{f_\theta(x,\tilde{y})} d\tilde{y}, \qquad (1)$$

where $Z(x,\theta)$ is the input-dependent normalizing partition function. We train this energy-based model (1) by directly minimizing the negative log-likelihood $-\log p(\{y_i\}_i | \{x_i\}_i; \theta) = \sum_{i=1}^{N} -\log p(y_i|x_i; \theta)$, where each term is given by,

$$-\log p(y_i|x_i; \theta) = \log \left(\int e^{f_\theta(x_i,y)} dy \right) - f_\theta(x_i, y_i). \qquad (2)$$

This direct and straightforward training approach thus requires the evaluation of the generally intractable $Z(x,\theta) = \int e^{f_\theta(x,y)} dy$. Many fundamental computer vision tasks, such as object detection, keypoint estimation and pose estimation, however rely on regression problems with a low-dimensional target space $\mathcal{Y}$. In such cases, effective finite approximations of $Z(x,\theta)$ can be applied. In some tasks, such as image-coordinate regression, this is naturally performed by a grid approximation, utilizing the dense prediction obtained by fully-convolutional networks. In this work, we however investigate a more *generally applicable* technique, namely Monte Carlo approximations with importance sampling. This procedure, when employed for training the network, is detailed in Sect. 3.2.

At test time, given an input x^*, our model in (1) allows evaluating the conditional target density $p(y|x^*; \theta)$ for any target y by first approximating $Z(x^*, \theta)$, and then predicting the scalar $f_\theta(x^*, y)$ using the DNN. This enables the computation of, e.g., the mean and variance of the target value y. In this work, we take inspiration from confidence-based regression and focus on finding the most likely prediction, $y^* = \arg\max_y p(y|x^*; \theta) = \arg\max_y f_\theta(x^*, y)$, which does not require the evaluation of $Z(x^*, \theta)$ during inference. Thanks to the auto-differentiation capabilities of modern deep learning frameworks, we can apply gradient-based techniques to find the final prediction by simply maximizing the network output $f_\theta(x^*, y)$ w.r.t. y. We elaborate on this procedure for prediction in Sect. 3.3.

3.2 Training

Our model $p(y|x; \theta) = e^{f_\theta(x,y)}/Z(x, \theta)$ of the conditional target density is trained by directly minimizing the negative log-likelihood $\sum_{i=1}^{N} - \log p(y_i|x_i; \theta)$. To evaluate the integral in (2), we employ Monte Carlo importance sampling. Each term $- \log p(y_i|x_i; \theta)$ is therefore approximated by sampling values $\{y^{(k)}\}_{k=1}^{M}$ from a proposal distribution $q(y|y_i)$ that depends on the ground truth target value y_i,

$$- \log p(y_i|x_i; \theta) \approx \log \left(\frac{1}{M} \sum_{k=1}^{M} \frac{e^{f_\theta(x_i, y^{(k)})}}{q(y^{(k)}|y_i)} \right) - f_\theta(x_i, y_i). \tag{3}$$

The final loss $J(\theta)$ used to train the DNN f_θ is then obtained by averaging over all training examples $\{(x_i, y_i)\}_{i=1}^{n}$ in the current mini-batch,

$$J(\theta) = \frac{1}{n} \sum_{i=1}^{n} \log \left(\frac{1}{M} \sum_{m=1}^{M} \frac{e^{f_\theta(x_i, y^{(i,m)})}}{q(y^{(i,m)}|y_i)} \right) - f_\theta(x_i, y_i), \tag{4}$$

where $\{y^{(i,m)}\}_{m=1}^{M}$ are M samples drawn from $q(y|y_i)$. Qualitatively, minimizing $J(\theta)$ encourages the DNN to output large values $f_\theta(x_i, y_i)$ for the ground truth target y_i, while minimizing the predicted value $f_\theta(x_i, y)$ at all other targets y. In ambiguous or uncertain cases, the DNN can output small values everywhere or large values at multiple hypotheses, but at the cost of a higher loss.

As can be seen in (4), the DNN f_θ is applied both to the input-target pair (x_i, y_i), and all input-sample pairs $\{(x_i, y^{(i,m)})\}_{m=1}^{M}$ during training. While this can seem inefficient, most applications in computer vision employ network architectures that first extract a deep feature representation for the input x_i. The DNN f_θ can thus be designed to combine this input feature with the target y at a late stage, as visualized in Fig. 1. The input feature extraction process, which becomes the main computational bottleneck, therefore needs to be performed only once for each x_i. In practice, we found our training strategy to not add any significant overhead compared to the direct regression baselines, and the computational cost to be *identical* to that of the confidence-based methods.

Compared to confidence-based regression, a significant advantage of our approach is however that there is no need for generating task-dependent pseudo label confidences or choosing between different losses. The *only* design choice of our training method is the proposal distribution $q(y|y_i)$. Note however that since the loss $J(\theta)$ in (4) explicitly adapts to $q(y|y_i)$, this choice has no effect on the overall behaviour of the loss, only on the quality of the sampled approximation. We found a mixture of a few equally weighted Gaussian components, all centered at the target label y_i, to consistently perform well in our experiments across all four diverse computer vision applications. Specifically, $q(y|y_i)$ is set to,

$$q(y|y_i) = \frac{1}{L} \sum_{l=1}^{L} \mathcal{N}(y; y_i, \sigma_l^2 I), \tag{5}$$

where the standard deviations $\{\sigma_l\}_{l=1}^{L}$ are hyperparameters selected based on a validation set for each experiment. We only considered the simple Gaussian proposal in (5), as this was found sufficient to obtain state-of-the-art experimental results. Full ablation studies for the number of components L and $\{\sigma_l\}_{l=1}^{L}$ are provided in the supplementary material. Figure 2 illustrates that our model $p(y|x;\theta)$ can learn complex conditional target densities, containing both multimodalities and asymmetry, directly from data using the described training procedure. In this illustrative example, we use (5) with $L = 2$ and $\sigma_1 = 0.1$, $\sigma_2 = 0.8$.

3.3   Prediction

Given an input $x^\star$ at test time, the trained DNN f_θ can be used to evaluate the full conditional target density $p(y|x^\star; \theta) = e^{f_\theta(x^\star, y)}/Z(x^\star, \theta)$, by employing the aforementioned techniques to approximate the constant $Z(x^\star, \theta)$. In many applications, the most likely prediction $y^\star = \arg\max_y p(y|x^\star; \theta)$ is however the single desired output. For our energy-based model, this is obtained by directly maximizing the DNN output, $y^\star = \arg\max_y f_\theta(x^\star, y)$, thus not requiring $Z(x^\star, \theta)$ to be evaluated. By taking inspiration from IoU-Net [23] and designing the DNN f_θ to be differentiable w.r.t. the target y, the gradient $\nabla_y f_\theta(x^\star, y)$ can be efficiently evaluated using the auto-differentiation tools implemented in modern deep learning frameworks. An estimate of $y^\star = \arg\max_y f_\theta(x^\star, y)$ can therefore be obtained by performing gradient ascent to find a local maximum of $f_\theta(x^\star, y)$.

The gradient ascent refinement is performed either on a single initial estimate $\hat{y}$, or on a set of random initializations $\{\hat{y}_k\}_{k=1}^{K}$ to obtain a final accurate prediction $y^\star$. Starting at $y = \hat{y}_k$, we thus run T gradient ascent iterations, $y \leftarrow y + \lambda \nabla_y f_\theta(x^\star, y)$, with step-length λ. In our experiments, we fix T (typically, $T = 10$) and select λ using grid search on a validation set. As noted in Sect. 3.2, this prediction procedure can be made highly efficient by extracting the feature representation for $x^\star$ only once. Back-propagation is then performed only through a few final layers of the DNN to evaluate the gradient $\nabla_y f_\theta(x^\star, y)$. The gradient computation for a set of candidates $\{\hat{y}_k\}_{k=1}^{K}$ can also be parallelized on the GPU by simple batching, requiring no significant overhead. Overall, the

Table 1. Impact of L and $\{\sigma_l\}_{l=1}^{L}$ in the proposal distribution $q(y|y_i)$ (5), for the object detection task on the *2017 val* split of the COCO [33] dataset. For $L = 2$, $\sigma_1 = \sigma_2/4$. For $L = 3$, $\sigma_1 = \sigma_3/4$ and $\sigma_2 = \sigma_3/2$. $L = 3$ with $\sigma_L = 0.15$ is selected.

Number of components L	1			2			3		
Base proposal st. dev. σ_L	0.02	0.04	0.08	0.1	0.15	0.2	0.1	0.15	0.2
AP (%)	38.1	38.5	37.5	39.0	**39.1**	39.0	39.0	**39.1**	38.8

Table 2. Results for the object detection task on the *2017 test-dev* split of the COCO [33] dataset. Our proposed method significantly outperforms the baseline FPN Faster-RCNN [32] and the state-of-the-art confidence-based IoU-Net [23].

Formulation	Direct	Gaussian	Gaussian	Gaussian	Gaussian	Gaussian	Laplace	Confidence	Confidence	
Approach	Faster-RCNN		Mixt. 2	Mixt. 4	Mixt. 8	cVAE		IoU-Net	IoU-Net*	**Ours**
AP (%)	37.2	36.7	37.1	37.0	36.8	37.2	37.1	38.3	38.2	**39.4**
AP$_{50}$(%)	**59.2**	58.7	59.1	59.1	59.1	**59.2**	59.1	58.3	58.4	58.6
AP$_{75}$(%)	40.3	39.6	40.0	39.9	39.7	40.0	40.2	41.4	41.4	**42.1**
FPS	**12.2**	**12.2**	**12.2**	12.1	12.1	9.6	**12.2**	5.3	5.3	5.3

inference speed is somewhat decreased compared to direct regression baselines, but is *identical* to confidence-based methods such as IoU-Net [23]. An algorithm detailing this prediction procedure is found in the supplementary material.

4   Experiments

We perform comprehensive experiments on four different computer vision regression tasks: object detection, visual tracking, age estimation and head-pose estimation. Our proposed approach is compared both to baseline regression methods and to state-of-the-art models. Notably, our method significantly outperforms the confidence-based IoU-Net [23] method for bounding box regression in direct comparisons, both when applied for object detection on the COCO dataset [33] and for target object estimation in the recent ATOM [8] visual tracker. On age and head-pose estimation, our approach is shown to consistently improve performance of a variety of baselines. All experiments are implemented in PyTorch [43]. For all tasks, further details are also provided in the supplementary material.

4.1   Object Detection

We first perform experiments on object detection, the task of classifying and estimating a bounding box for each object in a given image. Specifically, we compare our regression method to other techniques for the task of bounding box regression, by integrating them into an existing object detection pipeline. To this end, we use the Faster-RCNN [47] framework, which serves as a popular

Table 3. Results for the visual tracking task on the two common datasets TrackingNet [37] and UAV123 [36]. The symbol † indicates an approximate value (± 1), taken from the plot in the corresponding paper. Our proposed method significantly outperforms the baseline ATOM and other recent state-of-the-art trackers.

Dataset	Metric	ECO [9]	SiamFC [1]	MDNet [38]	UPDT [2]	DaSiamRPN [64]	SiamRPN++ [31]	ATOM [8]	ATOM*	Ours
TrackingNet	Precision (%)	49.2	53.3	56.5	55.7	59.1	69.4	64.8	66.6	**69.7**
	Norm. Prec. (%)	61.8	66.6	70.5	70.2	73.3	80.0	77.1	78.4	**80.1**
	Success (%)	55.4	57.1	60.6	61.1	63.8	73.3	70.3	72.0	**74.5**
UAV123	$OP_{0.50}$ (%)	64.0	-	-	66.8	73.6	$75^\dagger$	78.9	79.0	**80.8**
	$OP_{0.75}$ (%)	32.8	-	-	32.9	41.1	$56^\dagger$	55.7	56.5	**60.2**
	AUC (%)	53.7	-	52.8	55.0	58.4	61.3	65.0	64.9	**67.2**

baseline in the object detection field due to its strong state-of-the-art performance. It employs one network head for classification and one head for regressing the bounding box using the direct regression approach. We also include various probabilistic regression baselines and compare with simple Gaussian and Laplace models, by modifying the Faster-RCNN regression head to predict both the mean and log-variance of the distribution, and adopting the associated negative log-likelihood loss. Similarly, we compare with mixtures of $K = \{2, 4, 8\}$ Gaussians by duplicating the modified regression head K times and adding a network head for predicting K component weights. Moreover, we compare with an infinite mixture of Gaussians by training a cVAE. Finally, we also compare our approach to the state-of-the-art confidence-based IoU-Net [23]. It extends Faster-RCNN with an additional branch that predicts the IoU overlap between a target bounding box y and the ground truth. The IoU prediction branch uses differentiable region pooling [23], allowing the initial bounding box predicted by the Faster-RCNN to be refined using gradient-based maximization of the predicted IoU confidence.

For our approach, we employ an *identical architecture* as used in IoU-Net for a fair comparison. Instead of training the network to output the IoU, we predict the exponent $f_\theta(x, y)$ in (1), trained by minimizing the negative log-likelihood in (4). We parametrize the bounding box as $y = (c_x/w_0, c_y/h_0, \log w, \log h) \in \mathbb{R}^4$, where (c_x, c_y) and (w, h) denote the center coordinate and size, respectively. The reference size (w_0, h_0) is set to that of the ground truth during training and the initial box during prediction. Based on the ablation study found in Table 1, we employ $L = 3$ isotropic Gaussians with standard deviation $\sigma_l = 0.0375 \cdot 2^{l-1}$ for the proposal distribution (5). In addition to the standard IoU-Net, we compare with a version (denoted IoU-Net*) employing the same proposal distribution and inference settings as in our approach. For both our method and IoU-Net*, we set the refinement step-length λ using grid search on a separate validation set.

Our experiments are performed on the large-scale COCO benchmark [33]. We use the *2017 train* split ($\approx 118\,000$ images) for training and the *2017 val* split ($\approx 5\,000$ images) for setting our hyperparameters. The results are reported on the *2017 test-dev* split ($\approx 20\,000$ images), in terms of the standard COCO metrics AP, AP_{50} and AP_{75}. We also report the inference speed in terms of frames-per-second (FPS) on a single NVIDIA TITAN Xp GPU. We initialize all networks in our comparison with the pre-trained Faster-RCNN weights, using the ResNet50-FPN [32] backbone, and re-train *only* the newly added layers for a fair

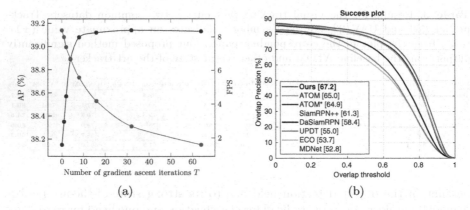

Fig. 3. (a) Impact of the number of gradient ascent iterations T on performance (AP) and inference speed (FPS), for the object detection task on the *2017 val* split of the COCO [33] dataset. (b) Success plot on the UAV123 [36] visual tracking dataset, showing the overlap precision OP_H as a function of the overlap threshold H.

comparison. The results are shown in Table 2. Our proposed method obtains the best results, significantly outperforming Faster-RCNN and IoU-Net by 2.2% and 1.1% in AP, respectively. The Gaussian model is outperformed by the mixture of 2 Gaussians, but note that adding more components does *not* further improve the performance. In comparison, the cVAE achieves somewhat improved performance, but is still clearly outperformed by our method. Compared to the probabilistic baselines, we believe that our energy-based model offers a more direct and effective representation of the underlying density via the scalar DNN output $f_\theta(x,y)$. The inference speed of our method is somewhat lower than that of Faster-RCNN, but identical to IoU-Net. How the number of iterations T in the gradient-based refinement affects inference speed and performance is analyzed in Fig. 3a, showing that our choice $T = 10$ provides a reasonable trade-off.

4.2   Visual Tracking

Next, we evaluate our approach on the problem of generic visual object tracking. The task is to estimate the bounding box of a target object in every frame of a video. The target object is defined by a given box in the first video frame. We employ the recently introduced ATOM [8] tracker as our baseline. Given the first-frame annotation, ATOM trains a classifier to first roughly localize the target in a new frame. The target bounding box is then determined using an IoU-Net-based module, which is also conditioned on the first-frame target appearance using a modulation-based architecture. We train our network to predict the conditional target density through $f_\theta(x,y)$ in (1), using a network architecture *identical* to the baseline ATOM tracker. In particular, we employ the same bounding box parameterization as for object detection (Sect. 4.1) and sample $M = 128$ boxes during training from a proposal distribution (5) generated by $L = 2$ Gaussians

Table 4. Results for the age estimation task on the UTKFace [62] dataset. Gradient-based refinement using our proposed method consistently improves MAE (lower is better) for the age predictions produced by a variety of different baselines.

+Refine	Niu et al. [41]	Cao et al. [4]	Direct	Gaussian	Laplace	Softmax (CE, L^2)	Softmax (CE, L^2, Var)
	5.74 ± 0.05	5.47 ± 0.01	4.81 ± 0.02	4.79 ± 0.06	4.85 ± 0.04	4.78 ± 0.05	4.81 ± 0.03
✓	-	-	4.65 ± 0.02	4.66 ± 0.04	4.81 ± 0.04	4.65 ± 0.04	4.69 ± 0.03

with standard deviations $\sigma_1 = 0.05$, $\sigma_2 = 0.5$. During tracking, we follow the same procedure as in ATOM, sampling 10 boxes in each frame followed by gradient ascent to refine the estimate generated by the classification module. The inference speed of our approach is thus identical to ATOM, running at over 30 FPS on a single NVIDIA GT-1080 GPU.

We demonstrate results on two standard tracking benchmarks: TrackingNet [37] and UAV123 [36]. TrackingNet contains challenging videos sampled from YouTube, with a test set of 511 videos. The main metric is the Success, defined as the average IoU overlap with the ground truth. UAV123 contains 123 videos captured from a UAV, and includes small and fast-moving objects. We report the overlap precision metric (OP_H), defined as the percentage of frames having bounding box IoU overlap larger than a threshold H. The final AUC score is computed as the average OP over all thresholds $H \in [0, 1]$. Hyperparameters are set on the OTB [56] and NFS [25] datasets, containing 100 videos each. Due to the significant challenges imposed by the limited supervision and generic nature of the tracking problem, there are no competitive baselines employing direct bounding box regression. Current state-of-the-art employ either confidence-based regression, as in ATOM, or anchor-based bounding box regression techniques [31,64]. We therefore only compare with the ATOM baseline and include other recent state-of-the-art methods in the comparison. As in Sect. 4.1, we also compare with a version (denoted ATOM*) of the IoU-Net-based ATOM employing the same training and inference settings as our final approach. The results are shown in Table 3, and the success plot on UAV123 is shown in Fig. 3b. Our approach achieves a significant 2.5% and 2.2% absolute improvement over ATOM on the overall metric on TrackingNet and UAV123, respectively. Note that the improvements are most prominent for high-accuracy boxes, as indicated by $OP_{0.75}$. Our approach also outperforms the recent SiamRPN++ [31], which employs anchor-based bounding box regression [46,47] and a much deeper backbone network (ResNet50) compared to ours (ResNet18). Figure 1 (bottom) visualizes an illustrative example of the target density $p(y|x; \theta) \propto e^{f_\theta(x,y)}$ predicted by our approach during tracking. As illustrated, it predicts flexible densities which qualitatively capture meaningful uncertainty in challenging cases.

4.3   Age Estimation

To demonstrate the general applicability of our proposed method, we also perform experiments on regression tasks not involving bounding boxes. In age estimation, we are given a cropped image $x \in \mathbb{R}^{h \times w \times 3}$ of a person's face, and the

Table 5. Results for the head-pose estimation task on the BIWI [12] dataset. Gradient-based refinement using our proposed method consistently improves the average MAE (lower is better) for yaw, pitch and roll for the predicted pose produced by our baselines.

+Refine	Gu et al. [16]	Yang et al. [59]	Direct	Gaussian	Laplace	Softmax (CE, L^2)	Softmax (CE, L^2, Var)
	3.66	3.60	3.09 ± 0.07	3.12 ± 0.08	3.21 ± 0.06	3.04 ± 0.08	3.15 ± 0.07
✓	-	-	3.07 ± 0.07	3.11 ± 0.07	3.19 ± 0.06	$\mathbf{3.01 \pm 0.07}$	3.11 ± 0.06

task is to predict his/her age $y \in \mathbb{R}_+$. We utilize the UTKFace [62] dataset, specifically the subset of 16 434 images used by Cao et al. [4]. We also utilize the dataset split employed in [4], with 3 287 test images and 11 503 images for training. Additionally, we use 1 644 of the training images for validation. Methods are evaluated in terms of the Mean Absolute Error (MAE). The DNN architecture $f_\theta(x, y)$ of our model first extracts ResNet50 [18] features $g_x \in \mathbb{R}^{2048}$ from the input image x. The age y is processed by four fully-connected layers, generating $g_y \in \mathbb{R}^{128}$. The two feature vectors are then concatenated and processed by two fully-connected layers, outputting $f_\theta(x, y) \in \mathbb{R}$. We apply our proposed method to refine the age predicted by baseline models, using the gradient ascent maximization of $f_\theta(x, y)$ detailed in Sect. 3.3. All baseline DNN models employ a similar architecture, including an identical ResNet50 for feature extraction and the same number of fully-connected layers to output either the age $y \in \mathbb{R}$ (*Direct*), mean and variance parameters for Gaussian and Laplace distributions, or to output logits for C discretized classes (*Softmax*). The results are found in Table 4. We observe that age refinement provided by our method consistently improves the accuracy of the predictions generated by the baselines. For *Direct*, e.g., this refinement marginally decreases inference speed from 49 to 36 FPS.

4.4 Head-Pose Estimation

Lastly, we evaluate our method on the task of head-pose estimation. In this case, we are given an image $x \in \mathbb{R}^{h \times w \times 3}$ of a person, and the aim is to predict the orientation $y \in \mathbb{R}^3$ of his/her head, where y is the yaw, pitch and roll angles. We utilize the BIWI [12] dataset, specifically the processed dataset provided by Yang et al. [59], in which the images have been cropped to faces detected using MTCNN [61]. We also employ protocol 2 as defined in [59], with 10 613 images for training and 5 065 images for testing. Additionally, we use 1 010 training images for validation. The methods are evaluated in terms of the average MAE for yaw, pitch and roll. The network architecture of the DNN $f_\theta(x, y)$ defining our model takes the image $x \in \mathbb{R}^{h \times w \times 3}$ and orientation $y \in \mathbb{R}^3$ as inputs, but is otherwise identical to the age estimation case (Sect. 4.3). Our model is again evaluated by applying the gradient-based refinement to the predicted orientation $y \in \mathbb{R}^3$ produced by a number of baseline models. We use the same baselines as for age estimation, and apart from minor changes required to increase the output dimension from 1 to 3, identical network architectures are also used. The results are found in Table 5, and also in this case we observe that refinement using our proposed method consistently improves upon the baselines.

5 Conclusion

We proposed a general and conceptually simple regression method with a clear probabilistic interpretation. It models the conditional target density $p(y|x)$ by predicting the un-normalized density through a DNN $f_\theta(x, y)$, taking the input-target pair (x, y) as input. This energy-based model $p(y|x; \theta) = e^{f_\theta(x,y)}/Z(x, \theta)$ of $p(y|x)$ is trained by directly minimizing the associated negative log-likelihood, employing Monte Carlo importance sampling to approximate the partition function $Z(x, \theta)$. At test time, targets are predicted by maximizing the DNN output $f_\theta(x, y)$ w.r.t. y via gradient-based refinement. Extensive experiments performed on four diverse computer vision tasks demonstrate the high accuracy and wide applicability of our method. Future directions include exploring improved architectural designs, studying other regression applications, and investigating our proposed method's potential for aleatoric uncertainty estimation.

Acknowledgments. This research was supported by the Swedish Foundation for Strategic Research via *ASSEMBLE*, the Swedish Research Council via *Learning flexible models for nonlinear dynamics*, the ETH Zürich Fund (OK), a Huawei Technologies Oy (Finland) project, an Amazon AWS grant, and Nvidia.

References

1. Bertinetto, L., Valmadre, J., Henriques, J.F., Vedaldi, A., Torr, P.H.S.: Fully-convolutional siamese networks for object tracking. In: Hua, G., Jégou, H. (eds.) ECCV 2016. LNCS, vol. 9914, pp. 850–865. Springer, Cham (2016). https://doi.org/10.1007/978-3-319-48881-3_56
2. Bhat, G., Johnander, J., Danelljan, M., Khan, F.S., Felsberg, M.: Unveiling the power of deep tracking. In: Proceedings of the European Conference on Computer Vision (ECCV), pp. 483–498 (2018)
3. Bishop, C.M.: Mixture density networks (1994)
4. Cao, W., Mirjalili, V., Raschka, S.: Rank-consistent ordinal regression for neural networks. arXiv preprint arXiv:1901.07884 (2019)
5. Cao, Z., Simon, T., Wei, S.E., Sheikh, Y.: Realtime multi-person 2D pose estimation using part affinity fields. In: Proceedings of the IEEE Conference on Computer Vision and Pattern Recognition (CVPR), pp. 7291–7299 (2017)
6. Chou, C.R., Frederick, B., Mageras, G., Chang, S., Pizer, S.: 2D/3D image registration using regression learning. Comput. Vis. Image Underst. **117**(9), 1095–1106 (2013)
7. Chua, K., Calandra, R., McAllister, R., Levine, S.: Deep reinforcement learning in a handful of trials using probabilistic dynamics models. In: Advances in Neural Information Processing Systems (NeurIPS), pp. 4759–4770 (2018)
8. Danelljan, M., Bhat, G., Khan, F.S., Felsberg, M.: ATOM: accurate tracking by overlap maximization. In: Proceedings of the IEEE Conference on Computer Vision and Pattern Recognition (CVPR), pp. 4660–4669 (2019)
9. Danelljan, M., Bhat, G., Khan, F.S., Felsberg, M.: ECO: efficient convolution operators for tracking. In: Proceedings of the IEEE Conference on Computer Vision and Pattern Recognition (CVPR), pp. 6638–6646 (2017)

10. Diaz, R., Marathe, A.: Soft labels for ordinal regression. In: Proceedings of the IEEE Conference on Computer Vision and Pattern Recognition (CVPR) (2019)
11. Du, Y., Mordatch, I.: Implicit generation and modeling with energy based models. In: Advances in Neural Information Processing Systems (NeurIPS) (2019)
12. Fanelli, G., Dantone, M., Gall, J., Fossati, A., Van Gool, L.: Random forests for real time 3D face analysis. Int. J. Comput. Vis. (IJCV) **101**(3), 437–458 (2013)
13. Feng, D., Rosenbaum, L., Timm, F., Dietmayer, K.: Leveraging heteroscedastic aleatoric uncertainties for robust real-time Lidar 3D object detection. In: 2019 IEEE Intelligent Vehicles Symposium (IV), pp. 1280–1287. IEEE (2019)
14. Gao, R., Lu, Y., Zhou, J., Zhu, S.C., Wu, Y.N.: Learning generative ConvNets via multi-grid modeling and sampling. In: Proceedings of the IEEE Conference on Computer Vision and Pattern Recognition (CVPR), pp. 9155–9164 (2018)
15. Gast, J., Roth, S.: Lightweight probabilistic deep networks. In: Proceedings of the IEEE Conference on Computer Vision and Pattern Recognition (CVPR), pp. 3369–3378 (2018)
16. Gu, J., Yang, X., De Mello, S., Kautz, J.: Dynamic facial analysis: from Bayesian filtering to recurrent neural network. In: Proceedings of the IEEE Conference on Computer Vision and Pattern Recognition (CVPR), pp. 1548–1557 (2017)
17. Gustafsson, F.K., Danelljan, M., Schön, T.B.: Evaluating scalable Bayesian deep learning methods for robust computer vision. In: Proceedings of the IEEE/CVF Conference on Computer Vision and Pattern Recognition (CVPR) Workshops (2020)
18. He, K., Zhang, X., Ren, S., Sun, J.: Deep residual learning for image recognition. In: Proceedings of the IEEE Conference on Computer Vision and Pattern Recognition (CVPR), pp. 770–778 (2016)
19. He, Y., Zhu, C., Wang, J., Savvides, M., Zhang, X.: Bounding box regression with uncertainty for accurate object detection. In: Proceedings of the IEEE Conference on Computer Vision and Pattern Recognition (CVPR), pp. 2888–2897 (2019)
20. Hinton, G., Osindero, S., Welling, M., Teh, Y.W.: Unsupervised discovery of nonlinear structure using contrastive backpropagation. Cogn. Sci. **30**(4), 725–731 (2006)
21. Huber, P.J.: Robust estimation of a location parameter. Ann. Math. Stat. 73–101 (1964)
22. Ilg, E., et al.: Uncertainty estimates and multi-hypotheses networks for optical flow. In: Proceedings of the European Conference on Computer Vision (ECCV), pp. 652–667 (2018)
23. Jiang, B., Luo, R., Mao, J., Xiao, T., Jiang, Y.: Acquisition of localization confidence for accurate object detection. In: Proceedings of the European Conference on Computer Vision (ECCV), pp. 784–799 (2018)
24. Kendall, A., Gal, Y.: What uncertainties do we need in Bayesian deep learning for computer vision? In: Advances in Neural Information Processing Systems (NeurIPS), pp. 5574–5584 (2017)
25. Galoogahi, H.K., Fagg, A., Huang, C., Ramanan, D., Lucey, S.: Need for speed: a benchmark for higher frame rate object tracking. In: Proceedings of the IEEE International Conference on Computer Vision (ICCV), pp. 1125–1134 (2017)
26. Lakshminarayanan, B., Pritzel, A., Blundell, C.: Simple and scalable predictive uncertainty estimation using deep ensembles. In: Advances in Neural Information Processing Systems (NeurIPS), pp. 6402–6413 (2017)
27. Lathuilière, S., Mesejo, P., Alameda-Pineda, X., Horaud, R.: A comprehensive analysis of deep regression. IEEE Trans. Pattern Anal. Mach. Intell. (TPAMI) **42**(9), 2065–2081 (2019)

28. Law, H., Deng, J.: CornerNet: detecting objects as paired keypoints. In: Proceedings of the European Conference on Computer Vision (ECCV), pp. 734–750 (2018)
29. Lawson, D., Tucker, G., Dai, B., Ranganath, R.: Energy-inspired models: learning with sampler-induced distributions. In: Advances in Neural Information Processing Systems (NeurIPS) (2019)
30. LeCun, Y., Chopra, S., Hadsell, R., Ranzato, M., Huang, F.: A tutorial on energy-based learning. Predicting Struct. Data 1 (2006)
31. Li, B., Wu, W., Wang, Q., Zhang, F., Xing, J., Yan, J.: SiamRPN++: evolution of Siamese visual tracking with very deep networks. In: Proceedings of the IEEE Conference on Computer Vision and Pattern Recognition (CVPR), pp. 4282–4291 (2019)
32. Lin, T.Y., Dollár, P., Girshick, R., He, K., Hariharan, B., Belongie, S.: Feature pyramid networks for object detection. In: Proceedings of the IEEE Conference on Computer Vision and Pattern Recognition (CVPR), pp. 2117–2125 (2017)
33. Lin, T.Y., et al.: Microsoft COCO: common objects in context. In: Proceedings of the European Conference on Computer Vision (ECCV), pp. 740–755 (2014)
34. Makansi, O., Ilg, E., Cicek, O., Brox, T.: Overcoming limitations of mixture density networks: a sampling and fitting framework for multimodal future prediction. In: Proceedings of the IEEE Conference on Computer Vision and Pattern Recognition (CVPR), pp. 7144–7153 (2019)
35. Mnih, A., Hinton, G.: Learning nonlinear constraints with contrastive backpropagation. In: Proceedings of the IEEE International Joint Conference on Neural Networks, vol. 2, pp. 1302–1307. IEEE (2005)
36. Mueller, M., Smith, N., Ghanem, B.: A benchmark and simulator for UAV tracking. In: Proceedings of the European Conference on Computer Vision (ECCV), pp. 445–461 (2016)
37. Muller, M., Bibi, A., Giancola, S., Alsubaihi, S., Ghanem, B.: TrackingNet: a large-scale dataset and benchmark for object tracking in the wild. In: Proceedings of the European Conference on Computer Vision (ECCV), pp. 300–317 (2018)
38. Nam, H., Han, B.: Learning multi-domain convolutional neural networks for visual tracking. In: Proceedings of the IEEE Conference on Computer Vision and Pattern Recognition (CVPR), pp. 4293–4302 (2016)
39. Niethammer, M., Huang, Y., Vialard, F.-X.: Geodesic regression for image time-series. In: Fichtinger, G., Martel, A., Peters, T. (eds.) MICCAI 2011. LNCS, vol. 6892, pp. 655–662. Springer, Heidelberg (2011). https://doi.org/10.1007/978-3-642-23629-7_80
40. Nijkamp, E., Hill, M., Han, T., Zhu, S.C., Wu, Y.N.: On the anatomy of MCMC-based maximum likelihood learning of energy-based models. In: Thirty-Fourth AAAI Conference on Artificial Intelligence (2020)
41. Niu, Z., Zhou, M., Wang, L., Gao, X., Hua, G.: Ordinal regression with multi-ple output CNN for age estimation. In: Proceedings of the IEEE Conference on Computer Vision and Pattern Recognition (CVPR), pp. 4920–4928 (2016)
42. Pan, H., Han, H., Shan, S., Chen, X.: Mean-variance loss for deep age estimation from a face. In: Proceedings of the IEEE Conference on Computer Vision and Pattern Recognition (CVPR), pp. 5285–5294 (2018)
43. Paszke, A., et al.: PyTorch: an imperative style, high-performance deep learning library. In: Advances in Neural Information Processing Systems (NeurIPS), pp. 8024–8035 (2019)
44. Pishchulin, L., et al.: DeepCut: joint subset partition and labeling for multi person pose estimation. In: Proceedings of the IEEE Conference on Computer Vision and Pattern Recognition (CVPR), pp. 4929–4937 (2016)

45. Prokudin, S., Gehler, P., Nowozin, S.: Deep directional statistics: Pose estimation with uncertainty quantification. In: Proceedings of the European Conference on Computer Vision (ECCV), pp. 534–551 (2018)

46. Redmon, J., Farhadi, A.: YOLO9000: better, faster, stronger. In: Proceedings of the IEEE Conference on Computer Vision and Pattern Recognition (CVPR), pp. 7263–7271 (2017)

47. Ren, S., He, K., Girshick, R.B., Sun, J.: Faster R-CNN: towards real-time object detection with region proposal networks. IEEE Trans. Pattern Anal. Mach. Intell. (TPAMI) **39**, 1137–1149 (2015)

48. Rothe, R., Timofte, R., Van Gool, L.: Deep expectation of real and apparent age from a single image without facial landmarks. Int. J. Comput. Vis. (IJCV) **126**(2–4), 144–157 (2016)

49. Ruiz, N., Chong, E., Rehg, J.M.: Fine-grained head pose estimation without keypoints. In: Proceedings of the IEEE Conference on Computer Vision and Pattern Recognition (CVPR) Workshops, pp. 2074–2083 (2018)

50. Simon, T., Joo, H., Matthews, I., Sheikh, Y.: Hand keypoint detection in single images using multiview bootstrapping. In: Proceedings of the IEEE conference on Computer Vision and Pattern Recognition (CVPR), pp. 1145–1153 (2017)

51. Sohn, K., Lee, H., Yan, X.: Learning structured output representation using deep conditional generative models. In: Advances in Neural Information Processing Systems (NeurIPS), pp. 3483–3491 (2015)

52. Sun, K., Xiao, B., Liu, D., Wang, J.: Deep high-resolution representation learning for human pose estimation. In: Proceedings of the IEEE Conference on Computer Vision and Pattern Recognition (CVPR), pp. 5693–5703 (2019)

53. Tsochantaridis, I., Joachims, T., Hofmann, T., Altun, Y.: Large margin methods for structured and interdependent output variables. J. Mach. Learn. Res. (JMLR) **6**, 1453–1484 (2005)

54. Varamesh, A., Tuytelaars, T.: Mixture dense regression for object detection and human pose estimation. In: Proceedings of the IEEE/CVF Conference on Computer Vision and Pattern Recognition (CVPR), pp. 13086–13095 (2020)

55. Wei, S.E., Ramakrishna, V., Kanade, T., Sheikh, Y.: Convolutional pose machines. In: Proceedings of the IEEE Conference on Computer Vision and Pattern Recognition (CVPR), pp. 4724–4732 (2016)

56. Wu, Y., Lim, J., Yang, M.H.: Object tracking benchmark. IEEE Trans. Pattern Anal. Mach. Intell. (TPAMI) **37**(9), 1834–1848 (2015)

57. Xiao, B., Wu, H., Wei, Y.: Simple baselines for human pose estimation and tracking. In: Proceedings of the European Conference on Computer Vision (ECCV), pp. 466–481 (2018)

58. Xie, J., Lu, Y., Zhu, S.C., Wu, Y.: A theory of generative ConvNet. In: International Conference on Machine Learning (ICML), pp. 2635–2644 (2016)

59. Yang, T.Y., Chen, Y.T., Lin, Y.Y., Chuang, Y.Y.: FSA-Net: learning fine-grained structure aggregation for head pose estimation from a single image. In: Proceedings of the IEEE Conference on Computer Vision and Pattern Recognition (CVPR), pp. 1087–1096 (2019)

60. Yang, T.Y., Huang, Y.H., Lin, Y.Y., Hsiu, P.C., Chuang, Y.Y.: SSR-Net: a compact soft stagewise regression network for age estimation. In: Proceedings of the International Joint Conference on Artificial Intelligence (IJCAI) (2018)

61. Zhang, K., Zhang, Z., Li, Z., Qiao, Y.: Joint face detection and alignment using multitask cascaded convolutional networks. IEEE Signal Process. Lett. **23**(10), 1499–1503 (2016)

62. Zhang, Z., Song, Y., Qi, H.: Age progression/regression by conditional adversarial autoencoder. In: Proceedings of the IEEE Conference on Computer Vision and Pattern Recognition (CVPR), pp. 5810–5818 (2017). https://susanqq.github.io/UTKFace/

63. Zhou, X., Zhuo, J., Krahenbuhl, P.: Bottom-up object detection by grouping extreme and center points. In: Proceedings of the IEEE Conference on Computer Vision and Pattern Recognition (CVPR), pp. 850–859 (2019)

64. Zhu, Z., Wang, Q., Li, B., Wu, W., Yan, J., Hu, W.: Distractor-aware Siamese networks for visual object tracking. In: Proceedings of the European Conference on Computer Vision (ECCV), pp. 101–117 (2018)

CLOTH3D: Clothed 3D Humans

Hugo Bertiche[1,2](✉) ⓘ, Meysam Madadi[1,2] ⓘ, and Sergio Escalera[1,2] ⓘ

[1] Universitat de Barcelona, Barcelona, Spain
hugo_bertiche@hotmail.com
[2] Computer Vision Center, Barcelona, Spain

Abstract. We present CLOTH3D, the first big scale synthetic dataset of 3D clothed human sequences. CLOTH3D contains a large variability on garment type, topology, shape, size, tightness and fabric. Clothes are simulated on top of thousands of different pose sequences and body shapes, generating realistic cloth dynamics. We provide the dataset with a generative model for cloth generation. We propose a Conditional Variational Auto-Encoder (CVAE) based on graph convolutions (GCVAE) to learn garment latent spaces. This allows for realistic generation of 3D garments on top of SMPL model for any pose and shape.

Keywords: 3D · Human · Garment · Cloth · Dataset · Generative model

1 Introduction

The modelling, recovery and generation of 3D clothes will allow for enhanced virtual try-ons experience, reducing designers and animators workload, or understanding of physics simulations through deep learning, just to mention a few. However, current literature in the modelling, recovery and generation of clothes is almost focused on 2D data [8,13,23,27]. This is because of two factors. First, deep learning approaches are data-hungry, and nowadays not enough 3D cloth data is available (see Table 1). Second, garments present a huge variability in terms of shape, sizes, topologies, fabrics, or textures, among others, increasing the complexity of representative 3D garment generation.

One could define three main strategies in order to produce data of 3D dressed humans: 3D scans, 3D-from-RGB, and synthetic generation. In the case of 3D scans, they are costly, and at most they can produce a single mesh (human + garments). Alternatively, datasets that infer 3D geometry of clothes from RGB images are inaccurate and cannot properly model cloth dynamics. Finally, synthetic data is easy to generate and is ground truth error free. Synthetic data has proved to be helpful to train deep learning models to be used in real applications [20,25,28].

Electronic supplementary material The online version of this chapter (https://doi.org/10.1007/978-3-030-58565-5_21) contains supplementary material, which is available to authorized users.

© Springer Nature Switzerland AG 2020
A. Vedaldi et al. (Eds.): ECCV 2020, LNCS 12365, pp. 344–359, 2020.
https://doi.org/10.1007/978-3-030-58565-5_21

Fig. 1. Left: CLOTH3D is the first big scale dataset of animated clothed humans. It contains thousands of different outfits and subjects, high variability of poses and rich cloth dynamics. Right: generated 3D garments with proposed GCVAE. (http:// chalearnlap.cvc.uab.es/dataset/38/description/.)

Table 1. CLOTH3D vs. available 3D cloth datasets. [1]: 3D data includes depth, normal and scene flow maps, but not 3D models. [2]: 3DPW contains 18 clothed models that can be shaped as SMPL. [3]: garments of [29] are shaped to different sizes. [4]: Garment variability not specified, nonetheless, authors propose a generation pipeline that can modify template garments into many different sizes. [5]: poses are strongly related to number of frames, and in [29] most samples share the same static pose.

Dataset	3DPW [18]	BUFF [35]	Untitled [29]	3DPeople [24]	TailorNet [21]	CLOTH3D
Resolution	2.5 cm	0.4 cm	1 cm	$-^1$	1 cm	1 cm
Missing	x	✓	x	x	x	x
Dynamics	x	✓	x	x	x	✓
Garments	18^2	10–20	3^3	High[4]	20	11.3K
Fabrics	x	x	x	x	x	✓
Poses[5]	Low	Low	Very low	Low	1782	High
Subjects	18^2	6	2K	80	9	8.5K
Layered	x	x	✓	$-^1$	✓	✓
#samples	51k	11K	24K	2.5M	55.8k	2.1M
Type	Real	Real	Synth	Synth	Synth	Synth.
RGB	✓	x	✓	✓	x	x
GT error	26 mm	1.5–3 mm	None	None	None	None

In this work, we present CLOTH3D, the first synthetic dataset composed of thousands of sequences of humans dressed with high resolution 3D clothes, see Fig. 1. CLOTH3D is unique in terms of garment, shape, and pose variability, including more than 2 million 3D samples. We developed a generation pipeline that creates a unique outfit for each sequence in terms of garment type, topology, shape, size, tightness and fabric. While other datasets contain just a few different garments, ours has thousands of different ones. On Table 1 we summarize features of existing datasets and CLOTH3D.

Additionally, we provide a baseline model able to generate dressed human models. Similar to [2,17,32] we encode garments as offsets connecting skin to cloth, using SMPL [15] as human body model. This yields an homogeneous dimensionality on the data. As in [22], we use a segmentation mask to extract the garment by removing body vertices. In our case, the mask is predicted by the network. We propose a Conditional Variational Auto-Encoder (CVAE) based on graph convolutions [6,7,17,19,31,34] (GCVAE) to learn garment latent spaces. This later allows for the generation of 3D garments on top of SMPL model for any pose and shape (right on Fig. 1).

2   Related Work

3D Garment Datasets. Current literature on 3D garment lacks on large public available datasets. One strategy to capture 3D data is through **3D scans**. The BUFF dataset [35] provides high resolution 3D scans, but few number of subjects, poses and garments. Furthermore, scanning techniques cannot provide layered models (one mesh for the body and one for each garment) and often one can find regions occluded at scanning time, meaning missing vertices or corrupted shapes. The work of [22] proposed a methodology to segment scans to obtain layered models. Authors of [33] combined 3D scans with cloth simulation fitting at each frame to deal with missing vertices. Similarly, [5] provided a dataset from 3D scans. However, the amount of samples is in the order of a few hundreds. The 3DPW dataset [18] is not focused on garments, but rather on pose and shape in-the-wild. The authors proposed a modified SMPL **parameterized model** for each outfit (18 clothed models), which, as SMPL, can be shaped and posed. Nevertheless, resolution is low and posing is through rigid rotations. Therefore, cloth dynamics are not represented. The dataset of [29] is synthetically created through **physics simulation**, with three different garment types: tshirt, skirt and kimono. They propose an automatic garment resizing based on real patterns, but provide only static samples on few different poses. The work of [21] also includes a synthetic dataset obtained through simulation of 20 combinations of different garment styles and body shapes into 1782 static poses. Finally, 3DPeople dataset [24] is the most comparable to ours in terms of scale, but has significant differences w.r.t. CLOTH3D. On one hand, this dataset has been designed specifically for computer vision. Data are given as **multi-view images** (RGB, depth, normal and scene flow), there are no 3D models. On the other hand, the garments are rigged models, so there is no proper cloth dynamics. And lastly, source pose data is sparse, 70 pose sequences with an average length of 110 frames. Our CLOTH3D dataset aims to overcome previous datasets issues. We automatically generate garments to obtain a huge variability on garment type, topology, shape, size, tightness and fabric. Afterwards, we simulate clothes on top of thousands of different pose sequences and body shapes. Table 1 shows a comparison of features for existing datasets and ours. In CLOTH3D we focus on sample variability (garments, poses, shapes), containing realistic cloth dynamics. 3DPW and 3DPeople sequences are based on rotations on rigged models, datasets of [21,29] contain static poses only, and BUFF has very few and short sequences. Moreover, none other provides metadata about fabrics, which has a strong influence on cloth behaviour. Similarly, the scarcity of these datasets implies low variability on garments, poses and subjects. Finally, note how only synthetic datasets provide with layered models and have no annotation error.

3D Garment Generation. Current works in 3D clothing focus on the generation of dressed humans. We split related work into non-deep and deep-learning approaches. Regarding **non-deep learning**, the authors of [10] proposed a data-driven model that learns deformations from template garment to garment fitted to the human body, shaped and posed. They factorize deformations into shape-dependant and pose-dependant by training on rest pose data first, and later on posed bodies. Transformations are learnt per triangle, and thus it yields inconsistent meshes that need to be reconstructed. The data-driven model of [22] is able to recover and retarget garments from 4D scan sequences relying on masks to separate body and cloth. Authors propose an energy optimization process to identify underlying body shape and garment geometry, later, cloth displacements w.r.t. body are computed and applied to new body shapes. This means information such as wrinkles is "copied" to new bodies, which produces valid samples but cannot properly generate its variability. Regarding **deep learning** strategies, the work of [11] deals with body and garments as different point clouds through different streams of a network, which are later fused. They also use skin-cloth correspondences for computing local-features and losses through nearest neighbour. The works of [2, 17, 21, 32] consider encoding clothes as offsets from SMPL body model with different goals. In [17] authors propose a combination of graph VAE and GAN to model SMPL offsets into clothing. Similarly, in [21], authors propose encoding garments as SMPL offsets and topology as a subset of SMPL vertices, later, they learn two models for low and high frequency details which effectively generate realistic wrinkles on the garments. In [29, 32] a PCA decomposition is used to reduce clothing space. In [3, 12], authors register garments to low resolution meshes (garment templates and SMPL respectively), to later use UV normal maps to represent high-frequency cloth details (wrinkles). Authors of [26] propose learning Pose Space Deformation models for template garments by training deep models instead of SVD (as SMPL). The work of [30] presents a template garment autoencoder where latent spaces are disentangled into motion and static properties to realistically interpolate into 3D keyframes. Similar to previous approaches, our proposed methodology also encodes clothes as SMPL offsets. Nevertheless, the assumption that garments follow body topology does not hold for skirts and dresses. In this sense, we propose a novel body topology specific for those cases. Additionally, our model predicts garment mask along offsets to generate layered models.

3   Dataset

CLOTH3D is the first big scale dataset of 3D clothed humans. The dataset is composed of 3D sequences of animated human bodies wearing different garments. Figure 1 depicts a sequence (first row) and randomly sampled frames from different sequences. Samples are layered, meaning each garment and body are represented by different 3D meshes. Garments are automatically generated for

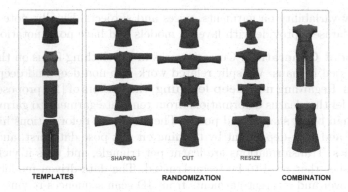

Fig. 2. Unique outfit generation pipeline. First, one upper-body and lower-body garment template is selected. Then, garments are individually shaped, cut and resized. Finally, garments might be combined into a single one.

each sequence with randomized shape, tightness, topology and fabric, and resized to target human shape. This process yields a unique outfit for each sequence. It contains over 7000 non-overlapping sequences of 300 frames each at 30fps, yielding a total of 2.1M samples. As seen in Table 1, garment and pose variability is scarce in available datasets, and CLOTH3D aims to fill that gap. To ensure garment type balance, given that females present higher garment variability, we balance gender as 2:1 (female:male). Finally, for validation purposes, we split the data in 80% sequences as training and 20% as test. Splitting by sequences ensures no garment, shape or pose is repeated in training and test.

The data generation pipeline starts with sequences of human bodies in 3D. Human pose data source is [1], later transformed to volumetric bodies through SMPL [15]. These sequences might present body self-collisions which will hinder cloth simulation, not only on affected regions, but also in global garment dynamics. We automatically solve collisions or reject these samples. Human generation process is described in Subsect. 3.1. Later, we generate unique outfits for each sequence. We start from a few template meshes which are randomly shaped, cut and resized to generate a unique pair of garments for each sample, with the possibility to be combined into a single full-body garment. Figure 2 shows the generation process, which is also detailed in Subsect. 3.2. Finally, once human sequence and outfit are done, we use a physics based simulation to obtain the garment 3D sequences. Simulation details are described in Subsect. 3.3.

3.1   Human 3D Sequences

SMPL. It is a parametric human body model which takes as input shape $\beta \in \mathbb{R}^{10}$ and pose $\theta \in \mathbb{R}^{24 \times 3}$ to generate the corresponding mesh with 6890 vertices. We use this model to generate animated human 3D sequences. We refer to [16] for SMPL details. To generate animated bodies, we need a source of valid sequences of SMPL pose parameters $\theta \in \mathbb{R}^{f \times 24 \times 3}$. We take such data from

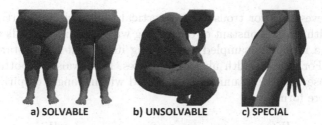

a) SOLVABLE   b) UNSOLVABLE   c) SPECIAL

Fig. 3. Types of self-collision: a) collided vertices can be linearly separated with the aid of a body part segmentation, b) no trivial solution, we reject this kind of sample, c) correct simulation might be possible if forearm is removed.

the work of [28], where pose is inferred from CMU MoCap data [1] following the methodology proposed at [14]. These pose data come from around 2600 sequences of 23 different actions (dancing, playing, running, walking, jumping, climbing, etc.) performed by over 100 different subjects. SMPL shape deformations are linearly modeled through PCA. To obtain a balanced dataset we uniformly sample shape within range $[-3, 3]$ for each sequence.

Self-collision. Body collides with itself for certain combinations of pose and shape parameters. Intersection volumes create regions where simulated repel forces are inconsistent, corrupting global cloth dynamics. We classify these collisions in three generic cases. Solvable Fig. 3(a): small intersection volumes near joints, specially armpits and crotch. We use SMPL body parts segmentation to linearly separate the collided vertices to permit a correct simulation. Separation space is 4mm so that a folded cloth can fit. Unsolvable Fig. 3(b): big intersection volumes or incompatible intersections (e.g.: arm vs. leg). We reject or re-simulate with thinner body. Special cases Fig. 3(c): removing hands, forearms or arms for short-sleeved upper-body and lower-body garments significantly increases the amount of valid samples. This requires manual supervision. Self-collision solution is not stored, hence, if collided vertices change significantly, garments might present interpenetration w.r.t. unsolved body. Only small intersected volumes are corrected and the rest are rejected (or simulated with thinner body). The goal of self-collision solving is to avoid invalid cloth dynamics. Accurate, realistic solving of soft-body self-collision is out of the scope of this work.

3.2   Garment Generation

Garment Templates. Generation starts with a few template garments for each gender. Garments can be classified in upper-body and lower-body. Lower-body can be further split into trousers and skirts. These three categories, and combinations between them, encompass almost any day-to-day garment. Template garments have been manually created by designers from real patterns and are: t-shirt, top, trousers and skirt.

Shaping. On sleeves, legs and skirt, we find a significant shape variability. It is possible to define them as cylinders of variable width around certain axes: along arms for sleeves, legs for trousers and vertical body axis for skirt. For sleeves and legs, width will be constant or decreasing while moving towards wrist/ankle, and beyond a randomly sampled point along its axis, it might start increasing (widening). For skirts, width always increases, from waist to bottom. Rate of width decrease/increase is uniformly sampled within ranges empirically set per garment. More formally:

$$W(x) = \alpha_1 x + \alpha_2 \max(0, x - x_{offset}) + W_0, \tag{1}$$

where x is position along axis (0 at shoulder/hips), $W(x)$ is width at position x, W_0 is width at $x = 0$, x_{offset} is a uniformly sampled point along the axis and α_1 and α_2 are constants empirically defined for each garment. For t-shirts and trousers, $\alpha_1 < 0 < \alpha_2$. For skirts, $\alpha_1 > \alpha_2 = 0$.

Cut. Template garments cover most of the body (long sleeves, legs and skirt). At this generation step, garments are cut to increase variability on length and topology. Cuts are along arms, legs and torso. Plus, upper-body garments have specific cuts to generate different types of garments (e.g., t-shirt, shirt, polo).

Resizing. Garments are resized to random body shapes. It is safe to assume that size variability on garments is similar to body shape variability. Following this reasoning, SMPL shape displacements are transferred to garments by nearest neighbour. Nevertheless, this process is noisy and human body details are transferred to garment. To address these issues, an iterative Laplacian smoothing is applied to shape displacements, removing noise and filtering high frequency body details, while preserving the geometry of the original garment. On SMPL, first and second shape parameters correspond to global human size and overall fatness. Knowing this, garments are resized to a different target shape. This new shape has two offsets at first and second parameters, the garment tightness $\gamma \in \mathbb{R}^2$. These offsets on garment resizing will generate loose or tight variability. As tighter garments present less dynamics and complexity, we bias the generator towards loose clothes by sampling tightness on the range $[-1.5, 0.5]$.

Jumpsuits and Dresses. Full-body garments can be generated by combining upper-body and lower-body garments. After generating the clothes individually, a final step automatically sews them together.

3.3   Simulation

Cloth simulation is performed on Blender, an open source 3D creation suite. Blender's cloth physics, as it is in version 2.8, has been implemented with state-of-the-art algorithms based on mass-spring model. The simulation performs $420-$ -600 steps per second, depending on the complexity of the garment.

Fabrics. Changing the parameters of the mass-spring model allows simulation of different fabrics. Blender provides different presets for *cotton, leather, silk* and *denim*, among others. These four fabrics have been used for the creation of the dataset. Upper-body garments might be cotton or silk, while the rest of the

Table 2. CLOTH3D statistics per action label.

Walk	Animal	Fight	Jump	Run	Sing	Wait	Swim	Story	Sports	Dance	Yoga	Spin
27.49%	10.79%	4.38%	2.78%	2.49%	2.38%	2.31%	1.97%	1.70%	1.63%	1.37%	1.01%	0.90%

Exercise	Climb	Carry	Stand	Wash	Balancing	Trick	Sit	Interact	Drink	Pose	Others
0.84%	0.71%	0.67%	0.66%	0.63%	0.54%	0.51%	0.28%	0.20%	0.14%	0.14%	33.48%

garment types can be any of those fabrics. Different fabrics produce different dynamics and wrinkles on simulation time.

Elastics. At simulation time, sleeves and legs have a 50% chance each of presenting an elastic behaviour at their ends, also at waist on full-body garments.

3.4 Additional Dataset Statistics

Table 2 shows the CLOTH3D statistics in terms of action labels by grouping them into generic categories. Note that original data action label is very heterogeneous, specific and incomplete. These labels are gathered from CMU MoCap dataset. We observe a high density on *Walk*, but it is important to note that this gathers many different sub-actions (walk backwards, zombie walk, walk stealthily, ...) as many other action labels do. Additionally, most of these actions were performed by different subjects, which implies an increase in intra-class variability. The label 'others' contains all action labels that cannot be included in any of the categories plus all the missing action labels.

4   Dressed Human Generation

This section presents the methodology for deep garment generation. As [2,17, 21,32], data dimensionality and topology is fixed by encoding it as body offsets. In addition, by masking body vertices we represent different garment types and separate them from the body, e.g. in a similar fashion to [21,22]. To compute ground truth offsets, a body-to-garment matching is needed. A dedicated algorithm for this task should be able to correctly register skirt-like garments which have a different topology than the body. In Sect. 4.1 we explain details of our data pre-processing. Our proposed model is a Graph Conditional Variational Auto-Encoder (GCVAE). By conditioning on available metadata (pose, shape and tightness), we learn a latent space encoding specific information about garment type and its dynamics (details are given in Sect. 4.3). Figure 5 illustrates the proposed model.

4.1   Data Pre-processing

In order to match among garment and body, we apply non-rigid ICP [4]. Registration is performed once per sequence in rest pose. Due to SMPL low vertex resolution, garment details could be lost. For this reason we subdivide the mesh

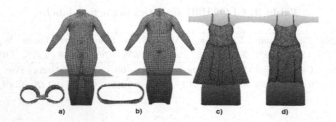

Fig. 4. Dual topology and registration. a) New additional proposed topology, where inner legs are connected. This topology is used for graph convolutions as well. b) Result of Laplacian smoothing of inner leg vertices. It is used only for skirt/dress registration. We show top view of meshes around an imaginary red cutting plane. c) Garment in rest pose. d) Garment registered to body model. (Color figure online)

(and corresponding SMPL model parameters). Head, hands and feet are not used to find correspondences and removing them halves input dimensionality. This yields a final mesh with $N = 14475$ vertices. Finally, note that skirt-like garments do not follow the same topology as SMPL mesh. For this task we introduce a novel topology explained on the subsection below. An example of the registration is shown in Fig. 4. Finally, body to cloth correspondences and garment mask are extracted by nearest neighbor matching.

4.2   SMPL-Skirt Topology

From SMPL body mesh, a 'column' of inner faces of each leg is removed and a new set of faces is created by connecting vertices from both legs, see Fig. 4a. New faces are highly stretched, producing noisy garment registrations if used as is, NR-ICP yields optimal results for homogeneous meshes (in garment domain). Because of this, we apply an iterative Laplacian smoothing to vertices belonging to the inner parts of each leg, see Fig. 4b for the result. This process is repeated before registration with the corresponding shape of the subject in the sequence in T-pose. This gives a matching between garment and body vertices to compute offsets. For encoding garments as offsets we use body mesh without smoothing, as this process will misbehave for posed bodies. Finally, for graph convolutions, we use the Laplacian matrix corresponding to this new topology for garments of type Dress and Skirt. This ensures that vertex deep features are aggregated with the correct neighbourhood. Afterwards, we transfer body topology to the predicted garment, and it is therefore crucial to use the correct topology for each garment type.

4.3   Network

As shown in Fig. 5, our network is based on a VAE generative model. The goal is to learn a meaningful latent space associated to the garments of any type, shape or with wrinkles which is used to generate realistic draped garments. Garment

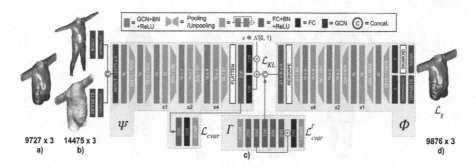

Fig. 5. Model pipeline. a) Input garment b) body and offsets w.r.t. body (Sect. 4.1). Model input is the concatenation of body and offsets. c) Network architecture. Conditional variables (CVAR) are processed by an AutoEncoder. To improve latent space factorization, CVAR are also regressed from the first encoder FC layer. Decoder outputs are offsets and mask. d) Reconstruction of the garment by adding offsets to body and removing body vertices according to mask. We set N as 128.

type and shape are associated to the static state of the garment while wrinkles belong to the dynamics of the garments. Here, we disentangle the latent space between statics and dynamics of the garments, and refer to learnt latent codes as garment code ($z_s \in \mathbb{R}^{128}$) and wrinkle code ($z_d \in \mathbb{R}^{128}$), respectively. To do so, we build two separate networks, one trained on static garments (so called SVAE) and one trained on dynamic garments (so called DVAE). To factorize the latent space from irrelevant parameters to the garment type and shape, we condition SVAE on body shape ($\beta \in \mathbb{R}^{11}$)[1] and garment tightness ($\gamma \in \mathbb{R}^2$). Likewise, DVAE is conditioned on β, γ, body pose ($\theta \in \mathbb{R}^{f \times 72}$) and z_s, where f is the number of frames in a temporal sequence. Let $cvar_s$ and $cvar_d$ be the stacking of conditioning variables of SVAE and DVAE in a single vector. It is worth noting that θ is constant in SVAE so that we do not include it in $cvar_s$. We implement graph convolutions as in [6,7,17,19,31,34]. We also include skip connections throughout the whole network.

Architecture. Let $X_s \in \mathbb{R}^{V_T \times 3}$ and $X_d \in \mathbb{R}^{V_T \times 3}$ be offsets computed on static and dynamic samples, respectively. From now on we use subscript s and d for static and dynamic variables and discard them for general cases. SVAE and DVAE have a similar structure with three main modules: encoder $\{cvar^z, z\} = \Psi(\bar{X}, \bar{T})$, conditioning $\{cvar, cvar^z\} = \Gamma(cvar)$ and decoder $\{\bar{X}, M\} = \Phi(z, cvar^z)$, where $M \in \mathbb{R}^{V_T \times 1}$ is the garment mask. Conditioning network Γ is an autoencoder with one skip connection and $cvar^z$ is its middle layer features. The goal of this network is to provide a trade-off between $cvar$ and z. The architecture details are shown in Fig. 5. Note that all GCN layer features (except first and last layers) are doubled in DVAE vs. SVAE. We refer the reader to the supplementary material for more details on the network architecture.

---

[1] We include gender as an additional dimension to the shape parameters.

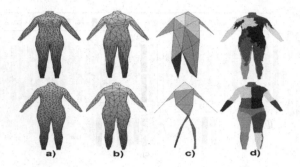

Fig. 6. Mesh hierarchy for pooling. Upper: default [9]. Lower: proposed. a), b) and c) depict the mesh hierarchy used for graph pooling through the model. Observe the difference on spatial distribution at a) and b). c) shows how lowest pooling is more meaningful regarding the segments (one vertex per segment). d) is the visualization of correspondences (receptive field) between highest and lowest hierarchy levels. The proposed pooling yields more meaningful pooling receptive fields w.r.t. body parts.

Pooling. We resort to a mesh simplification algorithm [9] to create a hierarchy of meshes with decreasing detail in order to implement the pooling operator. We follow [34] to have vertices uniformly distributed in the graph coarsening. However, this approach does not guarantee a uniform or meaningful receptive field on a high resolution mesh. To achieve a homogeneous distribution of correspondences throughout the body between pooling layers, we define a segmentation (Fig. 6(d)) and forbid the algorithm from contracting edges connecting vertices of different segments. Segmentation contains 21 segments and it is designed such that regions of the body with highest offset variability have smaller segments. Thus, more capacity of the network is available to model those parts. See Fig. 6. Our mesh hierarchy is formed by 6 different levels. The dimensionality of those meshes is: $14475 \rightarrow 3618 \rightarrow 904 \rightarrow 226 \rightarrow 56 \rightarrow 21$, leaving a single node for each segment on the last pooling layer. We use max-pooling in the proposed hierarchy. For unpooling, features are copied to all corresponding vertices of the immediate higher mesh.

Loss. We train conditioning network Γ independently using L1 loss and freeze its weights while training VAE. S/DVAE loss is a combination of a garment related term, a *cvar* term and KL-divergence:

$$\mathcal{L} = \mathcal{L}_g + \mathcal{L}_{cvar} + \lambda_{KL} D_{KL}(q(z|X, cvar)||p(z|cvar)), \tag{2}$$

Garment related term handles offsets, mask (if available), smoothness and collisions:

$$\mathcal{L}_g = \mathcal{L}_o + \lambda_n \mathcal{L}_n + \lambda_m \mathcal{L}_m + \lambda_c \mathcal{L}_c, \tag{3}$$

where $\mathcal{L}_o$ is an L1-norm applied to output offsets. $\mathcal{L}_n$ is the smoothness term based on L1-norm on normals. We found that regular Laplacian loss ensures smoothness at the cost of losing high frequency geometric details, while a normal loss makes output geometry consistent w.r.t. the input. $\mathcal{L}_m$ consists on L1-norm

Table 3. (a) Ablation results on the static dataset for all clothes. (b) Ablation results (full model) on the static dataset for each cloth category. Surface and normal errors are shown in mm and radians, respectively.

	Surface	Normals	Mask	KL loss		Surface	Normals	Mask	KL loss
All	14.3	1.04	0.9518	0.9820	Top	11.9	1.20	0.9035	0.9536
No normals	22.8	1.07	0.9472	0.5966	T-shirt	15.5	1.21	0.9565	1.1701
No mask	92.7	1.19	-	0.8799	Trousers	10.9	0.84	0.9475	0.9008
No collision	14.7	1.02	0.9522	0.9414	Skirt	21.4	0.79	0.9520	1.0255
No CVAR	14.8	1.02	0.9520	1.1009	Jumpsuit	13.3	1.07	0.9637	0.8788
Default pooling	14.9	1.03	0.9390	0.7623	Dress	16.7	1.06	0.9662	0.9995

Table 4. Ablation results (full model) on the dynamic dataset conditioning on different number of frames. Left: surface error (mm)/Right: normals error (radians).

# frames	Top	T-shirt	Trousers	Skirt	Jumpsuit	Dress	Avg.
1	21.8/1.24	28.8/1.29	20.7/0.89	37.6/0.92	28.2/1.15	35.5/1.13	29.0/1.10
4	20.1/1.23	28.0/1.28	18.5/0.86	33.2/0.89	26.1/1.09	32.2/1.11	26.1/1.08

on mask. Finally, $\mathcal{L}_c$ is the collision loss. Given that garments are represented as offsets, we design this loss as:

$$\mathcal{L}_c = max(0, -o \cdot V_N), \tag{4}$$

where o are the output offsets and V_N are the body normals at the corresponding vertices, this penalizes offsets that go within the body. $\mathcal{L}_{cvar}$ is $L1$ loss on encoder $cvar^z$ regressor.

5   Experiments

First, we detail the metrics chosen to analyze the results.

Surface. Given that input and prediction have the same dimensionality and order, we use standard euclidean norm (in mm.).

Normals. Measure of surface quality. We compute normals error based on mesh face normals by their angle difference (in radians) to ground truth normals.

Mask. Garment mask is evaluated by the intersection over union (IoU).

KL Loss. We use KL loss as a measure of quality of latent code factorization and meaningfulness of the latent space.

5.1   Ablation Study

We trained SVAE on an additional dataset of static samples (in rest pose) with 30 K samples. 20% of the data is kept for evaluation and the rest for training. The results are shown in Table 3a and 3b.

Normals. Looking at the second row of Table 3a we observe that enforcing a reconstruction consistent with normals significantly reduces surface error and, as expected normals error. However, including normals has a negative impact on KL loss comparing to first row.

Mask. As seen in third row of Table 3a, both, surface and normals error are significantly higher without mask prediction (comparing to first row).

Collision. Fourth row of Table 3a shows how collision loss helps to improve vertex location by pushing collided vertices to their correct position. On the other hand, it is observable a non-significant increase on other losses.

CVARs. As explained in Sect. 4.3, conditional variables are regressed from the first FC layer of the encoder to improve latent space factorization. On fifth row of Table 3a we can see that, while surface or normals error have no significant differences, KL loss improves.

Pooling. On Sect. 4.3 we discussed different approaches for tackling the pooling on a graph neural network. To do this, we built a mesh hierarchy. We compared default mesh simplification algorithm versus our proposed modification. Results are shown in the last row of Table 3a. While improvement on surface and normals errors is marginal, this new pooling benefits mask prediction.

Per Garment Category Error. Results per garment are shown in Table 3b. Skirts present the highest surface error, as its vertices are further away from the body compared to other garments. Following this reasoning, we find trousers having the less surface error. If we look at normals error, we find an opposite behaviour for skirts, as their geometry is the simplest one. On the other hand we see that upper-body garments present more complex geometries, and therefore, higher normals error. Looking at mask error, we see that garments that cover most of the body have the lowest error. This is due to IoU metric nature, the lower the number of points, the more impact shall have each wrong prediction. Finally, looking at KL loss, we observe the model has difficulties to obtain meaningful spaces for T-shirts. As explained on Sect. 3.2, T-shirts category includes open shirts as well, which highly increases class variability. We also see that trousers and jumpsuits have the lowest KL loss.

Learned Latent Space. In Fig. 7a, we show distribution of 5K random static samples computed by t-SNE algorithm. As one can see, the proposed GCVAE network can group garments in a meaningful space. Interestingly, dress and jumpsuit that share more vertices also share the same latent space. Additionally, we show garment transitions in this space in Fig. 7b. One can see how garments transit between two different topologies (3rd row) or among different genders and shapes (4th row).

We study DVAE model in Table 4. We condition DVAE on pose for a single frame vs. four frames. Four frames are selected every 3 frames, resulting in a 12-frame clip. Training the model on a sequence of frames leads to better results in all garment categories (3 mm improvement in average). This is while we do not include any temporal information in the encoder nor any specific sequence

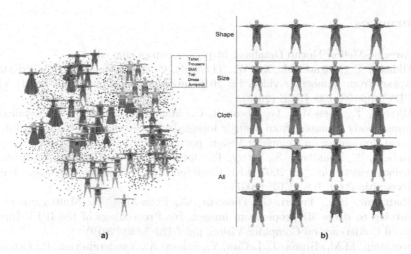

Fig. 7. a) Visualization of the learned latent space for static samples using t-SNE algorithm. b) Transitions of static samples. First three rows: conditioning on shape, tightness or cloth while the rest are fixed. Last two rows: transition of all variables. Variables are linearly graduated.

Fig. 8. Garment reconstruction for sequences. Note that the model has not been trained to keep temporal consistency.

prediction loss. DVAE qualitative results for single frames and sequences are shown in Fig. 1(right) and Fig. 8, respectively.

6   Conclusions

We presented CLOTH3D, the first large scale synthetic dataset of 3D clothed humans. It has a large data variability in terms of body shape and pose, garment type, topology, shape, tightness and fabric. Generated garments also show complex dynamics, providing with a challenging corpus for 3D garment generation. We developed a baseline method using a graph convolutional network trained as a variational autoencoder, and proposed a new pooling grid. Evaluation of the proposed GCVAE on CLOTH3D showed realistic garment generation.

Acknowledgments. This work is partially supported by ICREA under the ICREA Academia programme, and by the Spanish project PID2019-105093GB-I00 (MINECO / FEDER, UE) and CERCA Programme / Generalitat de Catalunya.

References

1. Carnegie-Mellon Mocap Database. http://mocap.cs.cmu.edu/
2. Alldieck, T., Magnor, M., Xu, W., Theobalt, C., Pons-Moll, G.: Detailed human avatars from monocular video. In: 2018 International Conference on 3D Vision (3DV), pp. 98–109. IEEE (2018)
3. Alldieck, T., Pons-Moll, G., Theobalt, C., Magnor, M.: Tex2Shape: detailed full human body geometry from a single image. In: Proceedings of the IEEE International Conference on Computer Vision, pp. 2293–2303 (2019)
4. Amberg, B., Romdhani, S., Vetter, T.: Optimal step nonrigid ICP algorithms for surface registration. In: 2007 IEEE Conference on Computer Vision and Pattern Recognition, pp. 1–8. IEEE (2007)
5. Bhatnagar, B.L., Tiwari, G., Theobalt, C., Pons-Moll, G.: Multi-garment net: learning to dress 3D people from images. In: Proceedings of the IEEE International Conference on Computer Vision, pp. 5420–5430 (2019)
6. Bronstein, M.M., Bruna, J., LeCun, Y., Szlam, A., Vandergheynst, P.: Geometric deep learning: going beyond euclidean data. IEEE Sig. Process. Mag. **34**(4), 18–42 (2017)
7. Defferrard, M., Bresson, X., Vandergheynst, P.: Convolutional neural networks on graphs with fast localized spectral filtering. In: Advances in neural information processing systems, pp. 3844–3852 (2016)
8. Dong, Q., Gong, S., Zhu, X.: Multi-task curriculum transfer deep learning of clothing attributes. In: 2017 IEEE Winter Conference on Applications of Computer Vision (WACV), pp. 520–529. IEEE (2017)
9. Garland, M., Heckbert, P.S.: Surface simplification using quadric error metrics. In: Proceedings of the 24th Annual Conference on Computer Graphics and Interactive Techniques, pp. 209–216. ACM Press/Addison-Wesley Publishing Co. (1997)
10. Guan, P., Reiss, L., Hirshberg, D.A., Weiss, A., Black, M.J.: Drape: dressing any person. ACM Trans. Graph. **31**(4), 35:1–35:10 (2012)
11. Gundogdu, E., Constantin, V., Seifoddini, A., Dang, M., Salzmann, M., Fua, P.: GarNet: a two-stream network for fast and accurate 3D cloth draping. In: IEEE International Conference on Computer Vision (ICCV). IEEE, October 2019
12. Lahner, Z., Cremers, D., Tung, T.: DeepWrinkles: accurate and realistic clothing modeling. In: Proceedings of the European Conference on Computer Vision (ECCV), pp. 667–684 (2018)
13. Lin, K., Yang, H.F., Liu, K.H., Hsiao, J.H., Chen, C.S.: Rapid clothing retrieval via deep learning of binary codes and hierarchical search. In: Proceedings of the 5th ACM on International Conference on Multimedia Retrieval, pp. 499–502. ACM (2015)
14. Loper, M., Mahmood, N., Black, M.J.: Mosh: motion and shape capture from sparse markers. ACM Trans. Graph. (TOG) **33**(6), 220 (2014)
15. Loper, M., Mahmood, N., Romero, J., Pons-Moll, G., Black, M.J.: SMPL: a skinned multi-person linear model. ACM Trans. Graph. (Proc. SIGGRAPH Asia) **34**(6), 248:1–248:16 (2015)
16. Loper, M., Mahmood, N., Romero, J., Pons-Moll, G., Black, M.J.: SMPL: a skinned multi-person linear model. ACM Trans. Graph. (TOG) **34**(6), 248 (2015)
17. Ma, Q., Tang, S., Pujades, S., Pons-Moll, G., Ranjan, A., Black, M.J.: Dressing 3D humans using a conditional Mesh-VAE-GAN. arXiv preprint arXiv:1907.13615 (2019)

18. von Marcard, T., Henschel, R., Black, M., Rosenhahn, B., Pons-Moll, G.: Recovering accurate 3D human pose in the wild using IMUs and a moving camera. In: European Conference on Computer Vision (ECCV), September 2018
19. Niepert, M., Ahmed, M., Kutzkov, K.: Learning convolutional neural networks for graphs. In: International Conference on Machine Learning, pp. 2014–2023 (2016)
20. Nikolenko, S.I.: Synthetic data for deep learning. arXiv abs/1909.11512 (2019)
21. Patel, C., Liao, Z., Pons-Moll, G.: TailorNet: predicting clothing in 3D as a function of human pose, shape and garment style. In: Proceedings of the IEEE/CVF Conference on Computer Vision and Pattern Recognition, pp. 7365–7375 (2020)
22. Pons-Moll, G., Pujades, S., Hu, S., Black, M.J.: ClothCap: seamless 4D clothing capture and retargeting. ACM Trans. Graph. (TOG) **36**(4), 73 (2017)
23. Pumarola, A., Goswami, V., Vicente, F., De la Torre, F., Moreno-Noguer, F.: Unsupervised image-to-video clothing transfer. In: The IEEE International Conference on Computer Vision (ICCV) Workshops, October 2019
24. Pumarola, A., Sanchez-Riera, J., Choi, G., Sanfeliu, A., Moreno-Noguer, F.: 3Dpeople: modeling the geometry of dressed humans. In: Proceedings of the IEEE International Conference on Computer Vision, pp. 2242–2251 (2019)
25. Ros, G., Sellart, L., Materzynska, J., Vazquez, D., Lopez, A.M.: The SYNTHIA dataset: a large collection of synthetic images for semantic segmentation of urban scenes. In: The IEEE Conference on Computer Vision and Pattern Recognition (CVPR), June 2016
26. Santesteban, I., Otaduy, M.A., Casas, D.: Learning-based animation of clothing for virtual try-on. In: Computer Graphics Forum, vol. 38, pp. 355–366. Wiley Online Library (2019)
27. Shin, D., Chen, Y.: Deep garment image matting for a virtual try-on system. In: The IEEE International Conference on Computer Vision (ICCV) Workshops, October 2019
28. Varol, G., et al.: Learning from synthetic humans. In: Proceedings of the IEEE Conference on Computer Vision and Pattern Recognition, pp. 109–117 (2017)
29. Wang, T.Y., Ceylan, D., Popovic, J., Mitra, N.J.: Learning a shared shape space for multimodal garment design. arXiv preprint arXiv:1806.11335 (2018)
30. Wang, T.Y., Shao, T., Fu, K., Mitra, N.J.: Learning an intrinsic garment space for interactive authoring of garment animation. ACM Trans. Graph. (TOG) **38**(6), 1–12 (2019)
31. Wu, Z., Pan, S., Chen, F., Long, G., Zhang, C., Yu, P.S.: A comprehensive survey on graph neural networks. arXiv preprint arXiv:1901.00596 (2019)
32. Yang, J., Franco, J.S., Hétroy-Wheeler, F., Wuhrer, S.: Analyzing clothing layer deformation statistics of 3D human motions. In: Proceedings of the European Conference on Computer Vision (ECCV), pp. 237–253 (2018)
33. Yu, T., et al.: SimulCap: single-view human performance capture with cloth simulation. arXiv preprint arXiv:1903.06323 (2019)
34. Yuan, Y.J., Lai, Y.K., Yang, J., Fu, H., Gao, L.: Mesh variational autoencoders with edge contraction pooling. arXiv preprint arXiv:1908.02507 (2019)
35. Zhang, C., Pujades, S., Black, M.J., Pons-Moll, G.: Detailed, accurate, human shape estimation from clothed 3D scan sequences. In: Proceedings of the IEEE Conference on Computer Vision and Pattern Recognition, pp. 4191–4200 (2017)

Encoding Structure-Texture Relation with P-Net for Anomaly Detection in Retinal Images

Kang Zhou[1], Yuting Xiao[1], Jianlong Yang[2], Jun Cheng[3], Wen Liu[1],
Weixin Luo[1], Zaiwang Gu[3], Jiang Liu[2,4], and Shenghua Gao[1,5(✉)]

[1] School of Information Science and Technology, ShanghaiTech University,
Shanghai, China
{zhoukang,xiaoyt,liuwen,luowx,gaoshh}@shanghaitech.edu.cn
[2] Cixi Institute of Biomedical Engineering, Chinese Academy of Sciences,
Beijing, China
yangjianlong@nimte.ac.cn
[3] UBTech Research, Shenzhen, China
juncheng@ieee.org, guzaiwang01@gmail.com
[4] Southern University of Science and Technology, Shenzhen, China
liuj@sustech.edu.cn
[5] Shanghai Engineering Research Center of Intelligent Vision and Imaging,
Shanghai, China

Abstract. Anomaly detection in retinal image refers to the identification of abnormality caused by various retinal diseases/lesions, by only leveraging normal images in training phase. Normal images from healthy subjects often have regular structures (e.g., the structured blood vessels in the fundus image, or structured anatomy in optical coherence tomography image). On the contrary, the diseases and lesions often destroy these structures. Motivated by this, we propose to leverage the relation between the image texture and structure to design a deep neural network for anomaly detection. Specifically, we first extract the structure of the retinal images, then we combine both the structure features and the last layer features extracted from original health image to reconstruct the original input healthy image. The image feature provides the texture information and guarantees the uniqueness of the image recovered from the structure. In the end, we further utilize the reconstructed image to extract the structure and measure the difference between structure extracted from original and the reconstructed image. On the one hand, minimizing the reconstruction difference behaves like a regularizer to guarantee that the image is corrected reconstructed. On the other hand, such structure difference can also be used as a metric for normality measurement. The whole network is termed as P-Net because it has a "P"

K. Zhou and Y. Xiao—Equally contribute to this work.

Electronic supplementary material The online version of this chapter (https://doi.org/10.1007/978-3-030-58565-5_22) contains supplementary material, which is available to authorized users.

shape. Extensive experiments on RESC dataset and iSee dataset validate the effectiveness of our approach for anomaly detection in retinal images. Further, our method also generalizes well to novel class discovery in retinal images and anomaly detection in real-world images.

Keywords: Structure-texture relation · Anomaly detection · Novel class discovery

1 Introduction

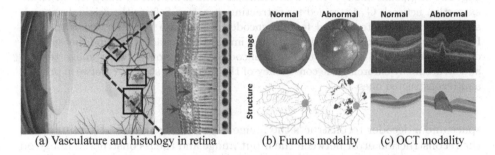

(a) Vasculature and histology in retina   (b) Fundus modality   (c) OCT modality

Fig. 1. The motivation of leveraging structure information for anomaly detection. The normal medical images are highly structured, while the regular structure is broken in abnormal images. For example, the lesions (denoted by black bounding box and red arrow in (a) of diabetic retinopathy destroy the blood vessel and histology layer in retina. Thus, in the abnormal retinal fundus image and optical coherence tomography (OCT) image, the lesions (denoted by red color in (b) and (c)) broke the structure. Moreover, this phenomenon agrees with the cognition of doctors. Motivated by this clinical observation, we suggest utilizing the structure information in anomaly detection. The figure (a) is adopted from the website of American Academy of Ophthalmology [1]. (Color figure online)

Deep convolutional neural networks (CNNs) have achieved many breakthroughs in medical image analysis [2–7]. However, these methods usually depend on large-scale balanced data in medical image domain, and the data acquisition of diseased images is extremely expensive because of the privacy issues of patients. Furthermore, sometimes the incidence of some diseases is extremely rare. In contrast, it is relatively easier to collect the normal (healthy) data. Human can distinguish those images with diseases from normal healthy data, and it is important for an intelligent system to mimic the behavior of the human for detecting those images with diseases by only leveraging the normal training data, and such task is defined as anomaly detection [8] in medical image analysis domain.

Typical anomaly detection methods are usually based on image reconstruction [9–14] which means given an image, an encoder maps the image to feature

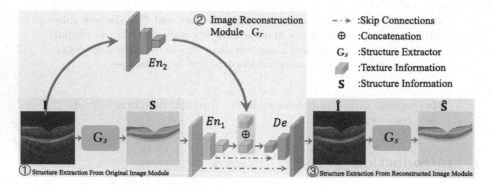

Fig. 2. The pipeline of our P-Net, which consists of three modules. Firstly, the structure extraction network $\mathbf{G}_s$ is trained for extracting structure $\mathbf{S}$ from the original image $\mathbf{I}$, and then the extracted $\mathbf{S}$ and feature encoded from $\mathbf{I}$ are fused for reconstruction. Finally, we further utilize the reconstructed image $\hat{\mathbf{I}}$ to extract the $\hat{\mathbf{S}}$ and measure the difference between $\mathbf{S}$ and $\hat{\mathbf{S}}$. Our P-Net encodes the relation between image texture and structure by enforcing the consistency of the image and structure between original and reconstructed ones.

space and a decoder reconstructs the image based on the feature. By minimizing the reconstruction error between the input image and the reconstructed image on the normal training data, the encoder and decoder are trained for image reconstruction. In the testing phase, an image can be classified as normal or abnormal by measuring the reconstruction error [12,13]. To guarantee the fidelity of the reconstructed image on the normal training data, generative adversarial networks (GAN) [15] based solutions have been introduced [9,10], which guide the generator to synthesize more realistic images with a discriminator. Further, GANomaly [16] and f-AnoGAN [11] are proposed, which append an additional encoder to the generator to further encode the reconstructed image. Then the reconstruction errors corresponding both images and features to measure the anomaly. However, all these existing methods directly feed the image into the CNNs for anomaly detection without leveraging any prior information. When doctors make diagnosis, besides the textures of the organ in the image, the structures (here **we treat the semantically meaningful edges in an image as the structure**, e.g., vessel topological structure in fundus images, the anatomic layer structure in OCT images, *etc.*) also help them to make the decision [17–19]. As shown in Fig. 1, for eye images with diseases, the normal structures are destroyed. For normal (healthy) images, the structure can be extracted, and the extracted structure also provides a cue about texture distribution. Since both texture and structure helps anomaly detection, then a question is naturally raised: *How to encode the structure-texture relation with CNNs for anomaly detection?* Towards this end, we propose to leverage the dependencies between structure and image texture for image and structure reconstruction circularly, and use the reconstruction error for both structure and image as normality measurement.

Specifically, we first propose to extract the structure from the original image, then we map the structure to the reconstructed image. However, the mapping from the structure to the reconstructed image is ill-posed. Thus we propose to fuse the last layer image feature with structure feature to reconstruct the image. We further use the reconstructed image to extract the structure, which also serves as a regularizer and helps improve the image reconstruction in previous stage. Meanwhile, the structure difference between the structure extracted from original image and that from the reconstructed image also helps us to measure the anomaly score. As shown in Fig. 2, since the whole network architecture is like a "P", we term it as P-Net.

In the training phase, since the structure of retinal image are usually not given for anomaly detection, we propose to use the vessel segmentation datasets and OCT layer segmentation datasets to train the structure extraction module of our network with a domain adaption method [20]. By minimizing the error between the input image and its reconstructed version (referred to as contents error), and the error between the structure extracted from original image and that extracted from the reconstructed image (referred to as structure error), our P-Net can be trained. In the inference stage, by measuring the contents error and structure error, each image can be classified as normal/abnormal accordingly. It is worth noting that our retinal image anomaly detection approach is a general framework, it can be readily applied to anomaly detection for general object images and novel class discovery for retinal images where testing data contains data falling out of the distribution of the training data[1]. For example, training data contains some given types of diseases while testing data contains a new type of disease. The reason for the success of our P-Net in these cases is that our network can capture the consistency between the structure and image contents, and the structure and image contents relation is different from the training ones for those new diseases.

The main **contributions** of this work are summarized as follows: i) we propose to utilize the structure information for anomaly detection in the retinal image. Our solution agrees with the cognition of clinicians that the normal retinal images usually have regular structures, and the irregular structure hints the incidence of some diseases. To the best of our knowledge, this is the first work that infuses structure information into CNNs for anomaly detection; ii) we propose a novel P-Net that encodes the relation between structure and textures for anomaly detection by using the cycle reconstruction between the image contents and structure. In the inference stage, both image reconstruction error and structure difference are utilized for anomaly score measurement; iii) since the structures are not given on almost all anomaly detection datasets for retinal images, we employ a domain adaptation method to extract structure by leveraging other datasets annotated with structure; iv) extensive experiments validate the effectiveness of our method for anomaly detection in both fundus modality and OCT modality for retinal images. Further, our method can be well

---

[1] These tasks are also termed as general anomaly detection in computer vision.

generalized to novel class discovery for retinal images and anomaly detection for general object images.

2 Related Work

2.1 Anomaly Detection

Anomaly detection is a vital field in the machine learning. An intuitive assumption is that the anomalies are out of the distribution of normal samples. Based on this hypothesis, it is natural to learn a discriminative hyperplane to separate the abnormal samples from the normal ones. One-class support vector machine (OCSVM) [21] was one of the classical methods, and its derived deep one-class SVDD [22] constrained the normal samples in a hypersphere so that the potential anomalies are the outliers being far away from the center of the hypersphere. Besides, Gaussian Mixture Models (GMM) tends to model the distribution of normal samples, and the outliers out of the distribution might result in a high probability of being abnormal.

Schlegl *et al.* [8] initially introduced Generative Adversarial Networks (GANs) [15] for anomaly detection that termed AnoGAN. The AnoGAN generates images from a Gaussian latent space, and samples are recognized as anomalies when the corresponding latent code is out of the distribution. Similar to AnoGAN, GANomaly [16] also involved representation learning in latent space. Compared with AnoGAN, GANomaly does not seek the latent code in the manifold by gradient descent in the test phase. David *et al.* [13] proposed the context-encoding Variational Auto-Encoder in brain MRI images, which combines reconstruction with density-based anomaly scoring. Schlegl *et al.* [11] proposed to utilize a generator [15] to map latent space to normal retinal OCT image, and use an encoder to learn the mapping from retinal OCT image to latent space. Pramuditha *et al.* [23] proposed OCGAN to make all the samples in a closed latent space. It reconstructs all samples to the normal ones. Also, the memory-augmented network such as [24] provided a fascinating idea to map the latent code of each sample to the nearest item in a learned dictionary with only normal patterns.

As discussed before, for normal healthy images, the structure and image texture are closely related. However, these existing methods fail to encode the structure-texture relation.

2.2 Structure-Texture Relation Encoding Networks

The texture and structure in an image are complementary to each other [25], and image structure has been successful used for image inpainting [26,27]. Nazeri *et al.* [27] proposed a two-stage network, which took the edge information as the structure. The model [27] first predicts the full edge map of incomplete image by the edge generator. Then the predicted edge map and incomplete image are passed to an image completion network to compute the full image. Since the distribution of edge map is significantly different from the distribution of the color image, Ren *et al.* [26] proposed to employ edge-preserved smooth images to represents the structure of the color images. The network proposed in [26] consists of a structure reconstructor to predict the image structure and a texture generator to complete the image texture. The relation of structure-texture can be encoded in the 'image-structure-image' pipeline, and this motivates us to infuse the normal structure into deep neural networks for anomaly detection. In our work, we further encode the relation between normal image and structure by enforcing the consistency of normal image, and the consistency between the structure extracted from normal image and that extracted from the reconstructed image.

3   Method

For healthy populations, the distribution of vasculature and histology of the retinal layers is regular. On the contrary, for subjects with diseases, the lesion of diseases will destroy the regularity of vasculature and histology. For example, the blood vessel and histology layer in retina will be destroyed by diabetic retinopathy (DR). The layer-wise structure in OCT will also be destroyed by various lesions such as pigment epithelium detachment (PED), subretinal fluid (SRF) [28], *etc.*

Based on these clinical observations, we define the retinal blood vessels in fundus images and the retinal layers in OCT as structure. Besides the anomalies in texture, the anomalies of structure would also help ophthalmologists and clinicians to make the diagnosis decision [17,19]. Motivated by the functionality of structure in retinal disease diagnosis, we propose to leverage the structure as an additional cue for anomaly detection. Further, for healthy images, structure extracted from the image provides a cue about texture distribution. By leveraging the relation between structure and texture in retinal images, we propose a P-Net for anomaly detection, and P-Net encodes the dependencies between structure and relation.

Specifically, our network architecture consists of three modules: 1) structure extraction from original image module, denoted as $\mathbf{G}_s$, which extracts structure $\mathbf{S}$ from original image $\mathbf{I}$; 2) image reconstruction module, denoted as $\mathbf{G}_r$, which leverages the last layer image encoder feature and structure to reconstruct the input image. We denote the reconstructed image as $\hat{\mathbf{I}}$. By minimizing the difference between $\mathbf{I}$ and $\hat{\mathbf{I}}$, the relation between texture and structure is encoded into the network. Thus we use image reconstruction error ($\|\mathbf{I} - \hat{\mathbf{I}}\|_1$) as a normality measurement; 3) structure extraction from reconstructed image module, which further extracts structure from the reconstructed image $\hat{\mathbf{I}}$. We denote the structure extracted from $\hat{\mathbf{I}}$ as $\hat{\mathbf{S}}$. By minimizing the difference between $\mathbf{S}$ and $\hat{\mathbf{S}}$, this module enforces the original image to be correctly reconstructed by $\mathbf{G}_r$. Further, the structure difference $\|\mathbf{S} - \hat{\mathbf{S}}\|_1$) can also be used to measure the normality of the image. The network architecture of P-Net is shown in Fig. 2. The detailed architecture of each module can be found in the supplementary (Section S1).

3.1   Structure Extraction from Original Image Module

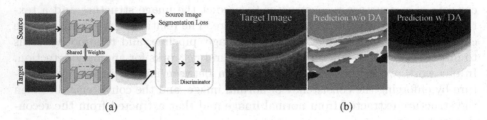

(a)   (b)

Fig. 3. (a) Structure extraction network with domain adaptation (DA). (b) The qualitative results of DA for OCT images. The structure of target image cannot be extracted well without DA.

The datasets used in previous retinal image anomaly detection work [8,11] are not publicly available, therefore we propose to use the Retinal Edema Segmentation Challenge Dataset (RESC, a OCT image dataset) [28], and a fundus multi-disease diagnosis dataset (iSee dataset [29]) collected in a local hospital for performance evaluation. However, the structure in both datasets are not provided. Manually annotating the structure, including vessels in fundus and layer segmentation in OCT, is extremely time consuming. Fortunately, there are many publicly available datasets for vessel segmentation in fundus images and layer segmentation in OCT images [30,31]. To get structure without tedious manual annotation, we utilize existing datasets to train a network for structure extraction. However, retinal images in different datasets are captured by various devices, consequently, different datasets have different noises and data distribution. To tackle this problem, we leverage AdaSeg [32], a domain adaptation based image segmentation method to learn the structure extractor $\mathbf{G}_s$. Specifically, we map images in different datasets but with the same modality to their corresponding structures with a U-Net [33], and add a discriminator to make the segmentation results from source and target datasets indistinguishable. The network architecture is shown in Fig. 3(a). For RESC, we use the Topcon dataset [34] as the source; while for iSee, we use the DRIVE dataset [31] as the source. The training loss in this module is as follows:

$$\mathcal{L}_{\text{seg}}(I_{\text{src}}) = -\sum S_{\text{src}} \log(\mathbf{G}_s(I_{\text{src}})) \tag{1}$$

$$\mathcal{L}_{\text{seg}}(I_{\text{tar}}) = \mathbb{E}[\log(1 - D(\mathbf{G}_s(I_{\text{tar}})))] + \mathbb{E}[\log D(\mathbf{G}_s(I_{\text{src}}))] \tag{2}$$

where I_{src} and S_{src} denote the source image and its ground truth, respectively. I_{tar} denotes the target image, and D denotes the discriminator. Once the structure extraction module is trained, we fix the module to simplify the optimization of the other modules in our P-Net.

3.2   Image Reconstruction Module

Since the structure is represented by vessels in fundus or layer section in OCT, and the ambiguity exists for the direct mapping from structure to original image [26,35], we propose to combine structure information and image texture information to reconstruct the original image. We define the texture as complementary information of the structure, and the texture provides the details over the local regions.

Specifically, we encode the original image and its structure with En_1 and En_2, respectively. Then we concatenate the two features and feed them into a decoder (De) to reconstruct the original image. Skip connections are introduced between the structure encoder and decoder for features at the same level, which avoid the information loss caused by downsampling pooling in structures, while there is no skip connection between the image encoder and decoder. The reason is that if we introduce the skip connection between them, then it is possible that we learn an identity mapping between the image and reconstructed image, which leads that there is no information flowed from structure to the original image, which is not desirable because identity mapping also makes abnormal images well reconstructed in the testing phase [36], where anomaly detection is impossible. It is expected that only information related to texture is encoded in the original encoder and passed to decoder to help the image reconstruction, therefore probably the last layer feature in the image encoder is enough for this purpose.

Following [16,35], we use L_1 norm to measure the difference between the reconstructed image and the original image.

$$\mathcal{L}_{rec}(\mathbf{I}) = \|\mathbf{I} - \hat{\mathbf{I}}\|_1 \tag{3}$$

To improve the quality of the reconstructed image, we apply PatchGAN [35] to penalize the reconstruction error for the reconstructed image $\hat{\mathbf{I}}$. Formally, let $\mathbf{D}$ be the discriminator, the adversarial loss $\mathcal{L}_{adv}$ for training reconstruction network is shown as follows:

$$\mathcal{L}_{adv}(\mathbf{I}) = \mathbb{E}[\log(1 - \mathbf{D}(\mathbf{G}_r(\mathbf{I}, \mathbf{S})))] + \mathbb{E}[\log \mathbf{D}(\mathbf{I})] \tag{4}$$

3.3   Structure Extraction from Reconstructed Image Module

We further append the structure extractor $\mathbf{G}_r$ to the reconstructed image. There are two purposes: 1) by enforcing the structure extracted from original image and that from reconstructed image to be the same, the original image can better reconstructed. In this sense, image reconstruction from reconstructed image module behaves like a regularizer; 2) some lesions are more discriminative in structure, then we extract structure from original image and reconstructed image, respectively, and use their difference for normality measurement. The loss function in this module is defined as follows:

$$\mathcal{L}_{str}(\mathbf{I}) = \|\mathbf{S} - \hat{\mathbf{S}}\|_1 \tag{5}$$

3.4 Objective Function

We fix the structure extractor $\mathbf{G}_s$ in the training of image reconstruction module $\mathbf{G}_r$. Therefore, we arrive at the objective function of our P-Net:

$$\mathcal{L} = \lambda_1 \mathcal{L}_{\text{adv}} + \lambda_2 \mathcal{L}_{\text{rec}} + \lambda_s \mathcal{L}_{\text{str}} \tag{6}$$

where $\lambda_1, \lambda_2, \lambda_s$ are the hyper-parameters. Empirically, we set $\lambda_1 = 0.1, \lambda_2 = 1, \lambda_s = 0.5$ on all datasets in our experiments.

3.5 Anomaly Detection for Testing Data

We combine image reconstruction error with structure difference for anomaly score $(\mathcal{A}(\mathbf{I}))$ measurement:

$$\mathcal{A}(\mathbf{I}) = (1 - \lambda_f)\|\mathbf{I} - \hat{\mathbf{I}}\|_1 + \lambda_f \|\mathbf{S} - \hat{\mathbf{S}}\|_1 \tag{7}$$

where λ_f is a weight used to balance the image difference and structure difference. A higher anomaly score indicates that the image is more likely to be abnormal.

4 Experiments

4.1 Implementation

To train the network, the input image size is 224×224, and the batch size is 8. The optimizer for the generator and the discriminator are both Adam, and the learning rate is 0.001. We train our model for 800 epochs. We implement our method with the PyTorch on a NVIDIA TITAN V GPU. The codes are released in https://github.com/ClancyZhou/P_Net_Anomaly_Detection.

4.2 Evaluation Metric

Following previous work [14,37,38], we calculate the Area Under Receiver Operation Characteristic (AUC) by gradually changing the threshold of $\mathcal{A}(\mathbf{I})$ for normal/abnormal classification. A higher AUC indicates that the performance of the method is better.

4.3 Anomaly Detection in Retinal Images

A. Datasets. Since the datasets used in previous retinal image anomaly detection work [8,11] are not released, we evaluate our proposed method with a publicly available dataset [28] and a local hospital dataset [29].

Retinal Edema Segmentation Challenge Dataset (RESC) [28]. Retinal edema is a retinal disease, which causes blurry vision and affects the patient's life quality. Optical coherence tomography (OCT) images can be used to assist

Table 1. Performance comparison on different datasets.

Method	RESC (OCT)	ISee (fundus)
Deep SVDD [22]	0.7440	0.6059
Auto-Encoder [12]	0.8207	0.6127
VAE-GAN [9]	0.9064	0.6969
Pix2Pix [35]	0.7934	0.6722
GANomaly [16]	0.9196	0.7015
Cycle-GAN [41]	0.8739	0.6699
Our Method	**0.9288**	**0.7245**

clinicians in diagnosing retinal edema. Thus the RESC dataset is proposed for OCT based retinal edema segmentation. As discussed previously, retinal edema damages the normal layer structure in OCT, thus we leverage this dataset for performance evaluation. This dataset contains the standard training/validating split. We use the normal images in the original training set as our training images to train the model, and use all testing images for performance evaluation.

Fundus Multi-disease Diagnosis Dataset (iSee) [29]. Previous retinal fundus datasets usually only contain one or two types of disease [39,40], but in clinical diagnosis, many eye diseases can be observed in the fundus image. Thus we collect a dataset from a local hospital, which comprises of 10000 fundus images. Eye diseases in this dataset include age-related macular degeneration (AMD), pathological myopia (PM), glaucoma, diabetic retinopathy (DR), and some other types of eye diseases. To validate the effectiveness of P-Net for different retinal diseases, we use 4000 normal images as the training set, and we use the remaining 3000 normal images, 700 images with AMD, 800 images with PM, 420 images with glaucoma, 480 images with DR, and 600 images with other types of eye diseases, as our testing set.

B. Performance Evaluation
Baselines. We compare our method with AnoGAN [10] proposed for retinal OCT images, VAE-GAN [9] proposed for Brain MRI images, GANomaly [16] for X-ray security images, and Auto-Encoder based anomaly detection [12]. As our work consists of the translation between image to the structure. Therefore we also compare P-Net with image-to-image translation networks, including Pix2Pix [35] and Cycle-GAN [41]. For Pix2Pix [35] and Cycle-GAN [41], we use the original image and structures extracted with domain adaptation method to train the network, and use the same measurement as ours for anomaly detection.

As shown in Table 1, our method outperforms all baseline methods on both datasets, which verifies the effectiveness of our method for retinal images with different modalities.

Table 2. The results of sub-class on iSee dataset.

Method	AMD	PM	Glaucoma	DR	Other
Auto-Encoder [12]	0.5463	0.7479	0.5604	0.6002	0.5479
AnoGAN [8]	0.5630	0.7499	0.5731	0.5704	0.6412
VAE-GAN [9]	0.5593	0.8412	**0.6149**	0.6590	0.7961
GANomaly [16]	**0.5713**	0.8336	0.6056	0.6627	0.8013
Our Method	0.5688	**0.8726**	0.6103	**0.6830**	**0.8069**

We further report the AUC of our method for five sub-classes in the iSee dataset, i.e., AMD, PM, glaucoma, DR, and other disease classes, and show the results in Table 2, As the lesions of PM and DR are related to blood vessel structure, and our method encodes the relation between vessels and texture, our method performs well for these diseases. While the lesions of AMD and glaucoma are associated with the macular area and the optic disc, respectively, and the structures we used cannot cover these areas in our current implementation, therefore our solution doesn't perform very well for these diseases.

C. Ablation Study

Domain Adaptation (DA). As shown in Fig. 3(b) since there is domain discrepancy between source images and target images, if we train a segmentation model without domain adaptation, the quality of structure is not good enough for image reconstruction. The quantitative results are listed in Table 3 (row 1 vs. row 4). We can see that our method benefits from DA on both datasets.

The Input of G_r. Our P-Net takes both the structure map and the original image as input for reconstruction. To investigate the effectiveness of this design, we conduct qualitative and quantitative experiments. The results are shown in Fig. 4 and Table 3 (row 2, 3, and 4), respectively. As shown in Table 3, our P-Net solution is better than single input based image reconstruction strategy. Further, from Fig. 4, we can observe that: i) if G_r only takes the structure as input, the image texture such as the optic disc area will be poorly reconstructed; ii) if G_r only takes the image as input, the blood vessel and macular area will be poorly reconstructed, for example, the macular area is reconstructed as the blood vessel, which is obviously incorrect.

Structure Consistency Loss. The $\mathcal{L}_{str}$ constrains the consistency between $\hat{S}$ and S, which behaves like a regularizer to enforce the consistency between $\hat{I}$ and I. The results in Table 3 (row 2 vs. row 5, row 3 vs. row 6, and row 4 vs. row 7) validate the effectiveness of the $\mathcal{L}_{str}$.

D. Evaluation of λ_f

In the testing phase, we use Eq. (7) to measure the anomaly score. $\lambda_f = 0$ denotes that only image difference $\|I - \hat{I}\|_1$ is used for anomaly detection, and $\lambda_f = 1$ means only structure difference $\|S - \hat{S}\|_1$ is used for anomaly detection. We vary λ_f and show the results in Table 4. We can see that the performance of

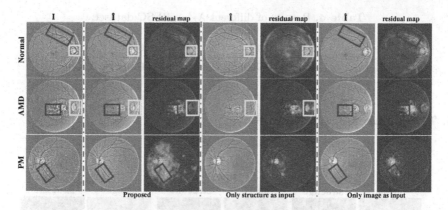

Fig. 4. The qualitative results of different input of $\mathbf{G}_r$ show that **both image and structure are necessary for anomaly detection**. On the one hand, when the input is only structure, we can observe that optical disc (yellow box) cannot be reconstructed precisely. The reason is the lack of texture information of optical disc region. On the other hand, when the input is only image, the lack of structure (blood vessel) information results in the vessel information loss (red box of normal and PM), and the lesion region is reconstructed incorrectly as the vessel (red box of AMD). (Color figure online)

Table 3. Ablation study in different datasets. DA and $\mathcal{L}_{str}$ denote domain adaptation, and structure consistency loss respectively.

Index	DA	Input of $\mathbf{G}_r$		$\mathcal{L}_{str}$	AUC	
		Image	Structure		RESC	ISee
1		✓	✓		0.8152	0.5914
2	✓	✓			0.8219	0.6487
3	✓		✓		0.8277	0.6914
4	✓	✓	✓		0.8518	0.7196
5	✓	✓		✓	0.8835	0.6574
6	✓		✓	✓	0.8821	0.6993
Ours	✓	✓	✓	✓	**0.9288**	**0.7245**

image difference only based anomaly detection is worse than structure difference only based method. The possible reason is that the structure is more evident for anomaly detection, which agrees with practice of clinicians. If we combine both, then it leads to a better performance. Further, the model is robust to different λ_f's. When $\lambda_f = 0.8$, our proposed method achieves the best performance, thus we set $\lambda_f = 0.8$ in all the experiments.

Table 4. Results of different λ_f on RESC dataset.

λ_f	0.0	0.2	0.4	0.5	0.6	**0.8**	1.0
AUC	0.8481	0.9010	0.9226	0.9232	0.9234	**0.9288**	0.9084

E. The Number of Cycles in P-Net

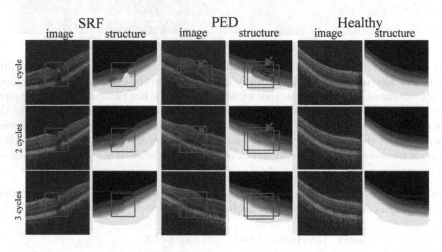

Fig. 5. The qualitative results with different number of cycles. It can be observed that the texture and the layer-wise structure between original and reconstructed ones in the healthy sample are consistent, while the consistency in abnormal samples is broken.

The lesion areas cannot be well reconstructed, and we found that these reconstructed lesion areas are very similar to normal areas. Thus, the results of appending our framework several times are different from that with only one cycle. We show the distribution of reconstruction errors for both normal images and abnormal images with multiple cycles reconstruction. It shows that more cycles in testing phase improve the performance, while more cycles in training phase reduce the performance. The poor performance of more cycles in training phase is probably because more loss terms make the optimization more difficult.

In Fig. 5, we further show the qualitative effect of more cycles in testing phase, where the images correspond to pigment epithelium detachment (PED), subretinal fluid (SRF), and healthy image, respectively. In the multiple cycles in testing phase, the abnormal lesion becomes more and more similar to normal patterns, which is a little like "anomalies repairing". Such phenomenon is more obvious in the structure map. For the healthy image, both the image and structure map remain the same even after multiple cycles. Thus more cycles would enlarge the reconstruction error for abnormal images, and retain the same reconstruction error for normal ones, which explains the phenomenon that more cycles in testing phase improve the anomaly detection (Table 5).

Table 5. The results of different number of cycle for training and testing on RESC dataset.

Cycle number in test	1	2	3	4	5
1 cycle in train	0.9288	0.9304	0.9361	0.9380	0.9374
2 cycles in train	0.8935	0.8962	0.9022	0.8973	0.9015

4.4 Anomaly Detection in Real World Images

We also apply our method on the MVTec AD dataset [42], which is a very challenging and comprehensive anomaly detection dataset for general object and texture images. This dataset contains 5 texture categories and 10 object categories. Since the structure is not annotated on these real-world images, we simply take the edges detected by Canny edge detection as the structure. We compare our method with Auto-Encoder with L2 loss or SSIM loss [42], CNN Feature Dictionary (CFD) [43], Texture Inspection (TI) [44], AnoGAN [8], Deep SVDD [22], Cycle-GAN [41], VAE-GAN [9] and GANomaly [16]. The quantitative results are shown in Table 6, and qualitative results are provided in the supplementary (Fig. S1).

We utilize AUC and region overlap as evaluation metrics to evaluate the performance of our model on MVTec AD dataset. Following [42], we define a minimum defect area for normal class data. Then we segment the difference map of normal class samples with increased threshold. This process is not stopped until the area of anomaly region is just below the defect area we defined and this threshold is utilized for segmentation anomaly region in testing phase.

We can see our method achieves the best performance in terms of the average AUC and average anomaly region overlap on all categories. Further, our method is effective for object images and less effective for some type of texture images. The possible reason is that we use the edge as structure. For object images, such edges usually correspond to shapes, which is closely related to the image contents. Thus the mapping between image and structure is relatively easy, which consequently helps the anomaly detection. For abnormal object images, usually some parts are broken or missing, which would leads to a large reconstruction error. However, since there are too many edges in texture images and the edges are very noisy, the texture image is hard to reconstruct, consequently reduces the performance of anomaly detection.

The experimental results of novel class discovery are provided in the supplementary (Section S3).

Table 6. For each category, the top row is the anomaly region **overlap** which is the same as the evaluation metric in [42] and the bottom row is **AUC**. The 5 categories at the top of the table are textures image and the other 10 categories at the bottom of the table is objects image. The results of AE (SSIM), AE (L2), AnoGAN [8], CFD [43], and TI [44] are adopted from MVTec AD [42] dataset directly.

Categories	AE (SSIM)	AE (L2)	Ano GAN	CFD	Deep SVDD	Cycle GAN	VAE- GAN	GAN omaly	TI	Our Method
Carpet	**0.69**	0.38	0.34	0.20	-	0.04	0.01	0.23	0.29	0.14
	0.87	0.59	0.54	0.72	0.54	0.46	0.35	0.55	**0.88**	0.57
Grid	**0.88**	0.83	0.04	0.02	-	0.36	0.04	0.41	0.01	0.59
	0.94	0.90	0.58	0.59	0.59	0.86	0.76	0.80	0.72	**0.98**
Leather	0.71	0.67	0.34	0.74	-	0.09	0.12	0.31	**0.98**	0.52
	0.78	0.75	0.64	0.87	0.73	0.65	0.64	0.77	**0.97**	0.89
Tile	0.04	0.23	0.08	0.14	-	0.14	0.09	0.19	0.11	**0.23**
	0.59	0.51	0.50	0.93	0.81	0.64	0.70	0.69	0.41	**0.97**
Wood	0.36	0.29	0.14	**0.47**	-	0.19	0.11	0.32	0.51	0.37
	0.73	0.73	0.62	0.91	0.87	0.95	0.77	0.91	0.78	**0.98**
Bottle	0.15	0.22	0.05	0.07	-	0.09	0.11	0.13	-	**0.43**
	0.93	0.86	0.86	0.78	0.86	0.76	0.73	0.82	-	**0.99**
Cable	0.01	0.05	0.01	0.13	-	0.02	0.05	0.14	-	**0.16**
	0.82	**0.86**	0.78	0.79	0.71	0.61	0.60	0.83	-	0.70
Capsule	0.09	0.11	0.04	0.00	-	0.04	0.19	0.51	-	**0.64**
	0.94	0.88	0.84	0.84	0.69	0.61	0.59	0.72	-	0.84
Hazelnut	0.00	0.41	0.02	0.00	-	0.33	0.34	0.37	-	**0.66**
	0.97	0.95	0.87	0.72	0.71	0.87	0.75	0.86	-	**0.97**
Metal Nut	0.01	**0.26**	0.00	0.13	-	0.04	0.01	0.18	-	0.24
	0.89	0.86	0.76	0.82	0.75	0.43	0.46	0.69	-	0.79
Pill	0.07	0.25	0.17	0.00	-	0.29	0.01	0.17	-	**0.58**
	0.91	0.85	0.87	0.68	0.77	0.80	0.62	0.76	-	**0.91**
Screw	0.03	**0.34**	0.01	0.00	-	0.17	0.02	0.24	-	0.32
	0.96	0.96	0.80	0.87	0.64	0.95	0.97	0.72	-	**1.00**
Toothbrush	0.08	0.51	0.07	0.00	-	0.13	0.10	0.48	-	**0.63**
	0.92	0.93	0.90	0.77	0.70	0.70	0.67	0.82	-	**0.99**
Transistor	0.01	0.22	0.08	0.03	-	0.20	0.05	0.15	-	**0.24**
	0.90	0.86	0.80	0.66	0.65	0.72	0.78	0.79	-	0.82
Zipper	0.10	0.13	0.01	0.00	-	0.05	0.04	0.21	-	**0.34**
	0.88	0.77	0.78	0.76	0.74	0.63	0.60	0.84	-	**0.90**
Mean	0.22	0.33	0.09	0.13	-	0.15	0.09	0.27	-	**0.41**
	0.87	0.82	0.74	0.78	0.72	0.71	0.66	0.77	-	**0.89**

5   Conclusion

In this work, we propose a novel P-Net for retina image anomaly detection. The motivation of our method is the correlation between structure and texture in healthy retinal images. Our model extracts structure from original images first, and then reconstructs the original images by using both structure information and texture information. At last, we extract the structure from the reconstructed images, and minimizing the difference between the structures extracted from original image and that from reconstructed image. Then we combine the image reconstruction error and structure difference as a measurement for anomaly detection. Extensive experiments validate the effectiveness of our approach.

Acknowledge. The work was supported by National Key R&D Program of China (2018AAA0100704), NSFC #61932020, Guangdong Provincial Key Laboratory (2020B121201001), ShanghaiTech-Megavii Joint Lab, and ShanghaiTech-UnitedImaging Joint Lab.

References

1. Boyd, K.: What is diabetic retinopathy. https://www.aao.org/eye-health/diseases/what-is-diabetic-retinopathy (2019)
2. Litjens, G., et al.: A survey on deep learning in medical image analysis. Med. Image Anal. **42**, 60–88 (2017)
3. Xing, F., Xie, Y., Su, H., Liu, F., Yang, L.: Deep learning in microscopy image analysis: a survey. IEEE Trans. Neural Netw. Learn. Syst. **29**(10), 4550–4568 (2017)
4. Zhou, S.K., Greenspan, H., Shen, D.: Deep Learning for Medical Image Analysis. Academic Press, Cambridge (2017)
5. Zhou, K., et al.: Multi-cell multi-task convolutional neural networks for diabetic retinopathy grading. In: 2018 40th Annual International Conference of the IEEE Engineering in Medicine and Biology Society (EMBC), pp. 2724–2727. IEEE (2018)
6. Fu, H., Cheng, J., Xu, Y., Wong, D.W.K., Liu, J., Cao, X.: Joint optic disc and cup segmentation based on multi-label deep network and polar transformation. IEEE Trans. Med. Imaging **37**(7), 1597–1605 (2018)
7. Zhang, S., et al.: Attention guided network for retinal image segmentation. In: Shen, D., et al. (eds.) MICCAI 2019. LNCS, vol. 11764, pp. 797–805. Springer, Cham (2019). https://doi.org/10.1007/978-3-030-32239-7_88
8. Schlegl, T., Seeböck, P., Waldstein, S.M., Schmidt-Erfurth, U., Langs, G.: Unsupervised anomaly detection with generative adversarial networks to guide marker discovery. In: Niethammer, M., et al. (eds.) IPMI 2017. LNCS, vol. 10265, pp. 146–157. Springer, Cham (2017). https://doi.org/10.1007/978-3-319-59050-9_12
9. Baur, C., Wiestler, B., Albarqouni, S., Navab, N.: Deep autoencoding models for unsupervised anomaly segmentation in brain MR images. In: Crimi, A., Bakas, S., Kuijf, H., Keyvan, F., Reyes, M., van Walsum, T. (eds.) BrainLes 2018. LNCS, vol. 11383, pp. 161–169. Springer, Cham (2019). https://doi.org/10.1007/978-3-030-11723-8_16
10. Chen, X., Konukoglu, E.: Unsupervised detection of lesions in brain MRI using constrained adversarial auto-encoders. arXiv preprint arXiv:1806.04972 (2018)
11. Schlegl, T., Seeböck, P., Waldstein, S.M., Langs, G., Schmidt-Erfurth, U.: f-anogan: fast unsupervised anomaly detection with generative adversarial networks. Med. Image Anal. **54**, 30–44 (2019)
12. Zhou, C., Paffenroth, R.C.: Anomaly detection with robust deep auto encoders. In: Proceedings of the 23rd ACM SIGKDD International Conference on Knowledge Discovery and Data Mining, pp. 665–674. ACM (2017)
13. Zimmerer, D., Kohl, S.A., Petersen, J., Isensee, F., Maier-Hein, K.H.: Context-encoding variational auto encoder for unsupervised anomaly detection. arXiv preprint arXiv:1812.05941 (2018)
14. Zhou, K., et al.: Sparse-gan: sparsity-constrained generative adversarial network for anomaly detection in retinal oct image. In: 2020 IEEE 17th International Symposium on Biomedical Imaging(ISBI), pp. 1227–1231. IEEE (2020)
15. Goodfellow, I., et al.: Generative adversarial nets. In: Advances in Neural Information Processing Systems, pp. 2672–2680 (2014)

16. Akcay, S., Atapour-Abarghouei, A., Breckon, T.P.: GANomaly: semi-supervised anomaly detection via adversarial training. In: Jawahar, C.V., Li, H., Mori, G., Schindler, K. (eds.) ACCV 2018. LNCS, vol. 11363, pp. 622–637. Springer, Cham (2019). https://doi.org/10.1007/978-3-030-20893-6_39
17. Puliafito, C.A., et al.: Imaging of macular diseases with optical coherence tomography. Ophthalmology **102**(2), 217–229 (1995)
18. Zinreich, S.J., et al.: Fungal sinusitis: diagnosis with ct and mr imaging. Radiology **169**(2), 439–444 (1988)
19. Hartnett, M.E., Weiter, J.J., Staurenghi, G., Elsner, A.E.: Deep retinal vascular anomalous complexes in advanced age-related macular degeneration. Ophthalmology **103**(12), 2042–2053 (1996)
20. Chai, Z., et al.: Perceptual-assisted adversarial adaptation for choroid segmentation in optical coherence tomography. In: 2020 IEEE 17th International Symposium on Biomedical Imaging(ISBI), pp. 1966–1970. IEEE (2020)
21. Schölkopf, B., Williamson, R.C., Smola, A.J., Shawe-Taylor, J., Platt, J.C.: Support vector method for novelty detection. In: Advances in Neural Information Processing Systems, pp. 582–588 (2000)
22. Ruff, L., et al.: Deep one-class classification. In: International Conference on Machine Learning, pp. 4393–4402 (2018)
23. Perera, P., Nallapati, R., Xiang, B.: Ocgan: one-class novelty detection using gans with constrained latent representations. In: Proceedings of the IEEE Conference on Computer Vision and Pattern Recognition, pp. 2898–2906 (2019)
24. Gong, D., et al.: Memorizing normality to detect anomaly: memory-augmented deep auto encoder for unsupervised anomaly detection. arXiv preprint arXiv:1904.02639 (2019)
25. Aujol, J.F., Gilboa, G., Chan, T., Osher, S.: Structure-texture image decomposition–modeling, algorithms, and parameter selection. Int. J. Comput. Vis. **67**(1), 111–136 (2006)
26. Ren, Y., Yu, X., Zhang, R., Li, T.H., Liu, S., Li, G.: Structure flow: image in painting via structure-aware appearance flow. In: The IEEE International Conference on Computer Vision (ICCV), October 2019
27. Nazeri, K., Ng, E., Joseph, T., Qureshi, F., Ebrahimi, M.: Edge connect: structure guided image in painting using edge prediction. In: The IEEE International Conference on Computer Vision (ICCV) Workshops, Oct 2019
28. Hu, J., Chen, Y., Yi, Z.: Automated segmentation of macular edema in oct using deep neural networks. Med. Image Anal. **55**, 216–227 (2019)
29. Yan, Y., et al.: Oversampling for imbalanced data via optimal transport. Proc. AAAI Conf. Artif. Intell. **33**, 5605–5612 (2019)
30. Hoover, A., Kouznetsova, V., Goldbaum, M.: Locating blood vessels in retinal images by piecewise threshold probing of a matched filter response. IEEE Trans. Med. Imaging **19**(3), 203–210 (2000)
31. Staal, J., Abràmoff, M.D., Niemeijer, M., Viergever, M.A., Van Ginneken, B.: Ridge-based vessel segmentation in color images of the retina. IEEE Trans. Med. Imaging **23**(4), 501–509 (2004)
32. Tsai, Y.H., Hung, W.C., Schulter, S., Sohn, K., Yang, M.H., Chandraker, M.: Learning to adapt structured output space for semantic segmentation. In: Proceedings of the IEEE Conference on Computer Vision and Pattern Recognition, pp. 7472–7481 (2018)

33. Ronneberger, O., Fischer, P., Brox, T.: U-Net: convolutional networks for biomedical image segmentation. In: Navab, N., Hornegger, J., Wells, W.M., Frangi, A.F. (eds.) MICCAI 2015. LNCS, vol. 9351, pp. 234–241. Springer, Cham (2015). https://doi.org/10.1007/978-3-319-24574-4_28

34. Cheng, J., et al.: Speckle reduction in 3d optical coherence tomography of retina by a-scan reconstruction. IEEE Trans. Med. Imaging **35**(10), 2270–2279 (2016)

35. Isola, P., Zhu, J.Y., Zhou, T., Efros, A.A.: Image-to-image translation with conditional adversarial networks. In: Proceedings of the IEEE Conference on Computer Vision and Pattern Recognition, pp. 1125–1134 (2017)

36. Chen, X., Pawlowski, N., Rajchl, M., Glocker, B., Konukoglu, E.: Deep generative models in the real-world: an open challenge from medical imaging. arXiv preprint arXiv:1806.05452 (2018)

37. Luo, W., Liu, W., Gao, S.: A revisit of sparse coding based anomaly detection in stacked rnn framework. In: Proceedings of the IEEE International Conference on Computer Vision, pp. 341–349 (2017)

38. Luo, W., et al.: Video anomaly detection with sparse coding inspired deep neural networks. IEEE Trans. Pattern Anal. Mach. Intell. (2019)

39. Porwal, P., et al.: Idrid: diabetic retinopathy-segmentation and grading challenge. Med. Image Anal. **59**, 101561 (2019)

40. Orlando, J.I., et al.: Refuge challenge: a unified framework for evaluating automated methods for glaucoma assessment from fundus photographs. Med. Image Anal. **59**, 101570 (2020)

41. Zhu, J.Y., Park, T., Isola, P., Efros, A.A.: Unpaired image-to-image translation using cycle-consistent adversarial networks. In: Proceedings of the IEEE International Conference on Computer Vision, pp. 2223–2232 (2017)

42. Bergmann, P., Fauser, M., Sattlegger, D., Steger, C.: Mvtec ad-a comprehensive real-world dataset for unsupervised anomaly detection. In: Proceedings of the IEEE Conference on Computer Vision and Pattern Recognition, pp. 9592–9600 (2019)

43. Napoletano, P., Piccoli, F., Schettini, R.: Anomaly detection in nanofibrous materials by cnn-based self-similarity. Sensors **18**(1), 209 (2018)

44. Böttger, T., Ulrich, M.: Real-time texture error detection on textured surfaces with compressed sensing. Pattern Recognit. Image Anal. **26**(1), 88–94 (2016). https://doi.org/10.1134/S1054661816010053

CLNet: A Compact Latent Network for Fast Adjusting Siamese Trackers

Xingping Dong[1][iD], Jianbing Shen[1(✉)][iD], Ling Shao[1,2][iD], and Fatih Porikli[3][iD]

[1] Inception Institute of Artificial Intelligence, Abu Dhabi, UAE
shenjianbingcg@gmail.com
[2] Mohamed bin Zayed University of Artificial Intelligence, Abu Dhabi, UAE
[3] Australian National University, Canberra, Australia

Abstract. In this paper, we provide a deep analysis for Siamese-based trackers and find that the one core reason for their failure on challenging cases can be attributed to the problem of *decisive samples missing* during offline training. Furthermore, we notice that the samples given in the first frame can be viewed as the decisive samples for the sequence since they contain rich sequence-specific information. To make full use of these sequence-specific samples, we propose a compact latent network to quickly adjust the tracking model to adapt to new scenes. A statistic-based compact latent feature is proposed to efficiently capture the sequence-specific information for the fast adjustment. In addition, we design a new training approach based on a diverse sample mining strategy to further improve the discrimination ability of our compact latent network. To evaluate the effectiveness of our method, we apply it to adjust a recent state-of-the-art tracker, SiamRPN++. Extensive experimental results on five recent benchmarks demonstrate that the adjusted tracker achieves promising improvement in terms of tracking accuracy, with almost the same speed. The code and models are available at https://github.com/xingpingdong/CLNet-tracking.

Keywords: Siamese tracker · Latent feature · Sequence-specific · Sample mining · Fast adjustment

1 Introduction

Recently, Siamese-based trackers [3,30,31] have attracted significant attention in the tracking community, since they successfully incorporated data-driven deep learning with real-time visual tracking, and achieved impressive tracking accuracy. However, these trackers are still unable to address more challenging situations, such as similar distractors or huge deformation as shown in Fig. 1. To analyze the core reason for these failures, we simplify the Siamese model to a linear binary-classifier and transfer the tracking task to a classification problem. We find that the issues can be attributed to the problem of *decisive samples missing*, i.e. some key samples, such as the ones in the above challenging cases,

© Springer Nature Switzerland AG 2020
A. Vedaldi et al. (Eds.): ECCV 2020, LNCS 12365, pp. 378–395, 2020.
https://doi.org/10.1007/978-3-030-58565-5_23

SiamRPN++ ▬▬▬   Ours ▬▬▬

Fig. 1. Sample results of our compact latent network incorporated into the state-of-the-art tracker, SiamRPN++ [30]. By only adjusting the base model (SiamRPN++) with the sequence-specific samples from the first frame, we significantly improve its discrimination ability under the challenging cases, such as similar distractors (top) or huge deformation (bottom).

are rare or unseen during offline training. This results in the trained model having poor discrimination ability for these challenging samples. This is a normal problem for most data-driven models since they cannot capture all data for training. In contrast, in the tracking task, annotated bounding boxes are given in the first frame of each sequence, which can provide sequence-specific samples to improve the discrimination ability of the model, since these samples are similar to the ones in the other frames of the same sequence. In addition, most Siamese-based methods ignore the rich context information, only applying the annotations to extract templates. Thus, the ignored context information can be used to adjust these Siamese-based models and improve the discrimination ability for all samples in the sequence. As shown in Fig. 1, the model, adjusted by the sequence-specific supervision information in the first frame, achieves significant improvement compared with the original model.

Making full use of the sequence-specific information to adjust the offline trained model is not a trivial task, especially for real-time tracking, because of the limitation of computational load. A simple solution is to directly retrain the Siamese-based model using an optimization method, such as stochastic gradient descent (SGD) [42], ride regression [6], or Lagrange multipliers [24]. However, these methods are often time-consuming and not practicable for tracking.

To meet real-time requirements and extract effective information from sequence-specific samples, we propose a Compact Latent Network (CLNet) to adjust recent Siamese-based trackers. Our CLNet contains an feature-adjusting sub-network, latent encoder, and prediction sub-network. The first provides the adjusting feature for each sequence-specific sample, using three 1×1 convolutional layers for efficiency. The core module, the latent encoder, produces a compact feature representation for the entire set of sequence-specific samples, by computing the statistical information inside the positive and negative adjusting feature sets, respectively. Then, the latent feature is fed into the last sub-network (a three-layer perceptron), to predict the adjusting parameters.

It is worth mentioning that our latent feature is compact, with only a few thousand parameters, and more robust than the normal features, since statistics-based features contain uncertainty information in the distribution, which is beneficial for better classification performance [26]. In addition, we propose a new training method based on diverse sample mining to further enhance the training performance. In contrast to the training method of Siamese models, we sample image-pairs from a sequence for each batch to effectively extract the sequence-specific information for the latent feature. We also incorporate diverse sample mining to benefit the adjustment network training. These diverse samples improve the discrimination ability of the adjustment network enabling to address similar distractors and significant appearance changes.

To evaluate the effectiveness of the proposed approach, we take the state-of-the-art tracker, SiamRPN++ [30], as our basic model. To maintain the generalization ability of this model, we use the proposed CLNet to adjust the last layers in the classification and regression branches. For fast adjustment, we only run CLNet once in the first frame and omit it in the following frames. A thorough evaluation on five popular benchmarks (seen in Sect. 4) clearly demonstrates the advantage of our algorithm.

2   Related Work

Although many techniques have been successfully applied to visual object tracking, such as the correlation filter [5,7,21], regression model [20,37], and sparse coding [39,40], here, we only focus on the recent Siamese network based trackers [3,31], which are mainstream in the tracking community, and meta-learning approaches [22,50], which are related to our latent feature.

2.1   Siamese Network Based Trackers

The pioneering work, SiamFC [3], provided a new paradigm based on the Siamese network to fully exploit the increasing number of labeled video datasets. After this work, several researchers tried to further mine the potentiality of the offline tracking model by designing different Siamese architectures [12,19,60,67], using the powerful training loss [8], learning efficient Siamese networks [36], and so on [51,63,64]. Some focus on improving the performance of the online updating method through various strategies, such as incorporating a correlation filter [58], learning a dynamic network [18], utilizing deep reinforcement learning [10,11,25]. Among these Siamese-based trackers, the recent SiamRPN [31], which introduces the region proposal network after the Siamese network, achieves very high speed and impressive tracking accuracy on the popular VOT benchmark [29]. The following works [14,30,68,69] also obtain state-of-the-art performance on this benchmark. For example, Zhu et al. [69] proposed a distractor-aware data augmentation approach and an incremental learning method to enhance the offline model and online tracking mechanism, respectively. In consequence, more attention is paid to improving the generalization of the base network by using more discriminative network structures, such as cascaded RPN [14], deeper networks [30], and wider networks [68]. These state-of-the-art trackers prefer to provide a more powerful offline model that can use more training data. However, they do not fully exploit the supervised information in the first frame

2.2 Meta-Learning

Meta-learning can be interpolated as the inception of *fast weights* [2,22], or *learning-to-learn* [1,23,50,57], and is usually applied to few-shot classification, specifically for the image recognition task. There are three major categories of recent meta-learning approaches, including 1) metric-based methods [27,55,59], which focus on learning powerful similarity metrics to discriminate samples from the same class; 2) memory-based methods [44,49], which explore the storage of critical training examples with effective memory architectures or encoding fast adaptation methods, and 3) optimization-based methods [15,16], which search for adaptive parameters to quickly adjust the model for new tasks.

Although meta-learning has been widely applied for few-shot classification [15,32,48], there exist few related works in the community of visual object tracking [4,43]. Park *et al.* [43] proposed an optimization-based meta-learner, analogous to MAML [15], to learn an adaptive step for gradient-based online updating. This method has been applied to two trackers based on online training [42,56] for acceleration, by reducing the number of training iterations. However, it cannot be directly used for offline training models, like Siamese-based trackers. Recently, a meta-learner network [4] and gradient-guided network [33] were proposed to update the Siamese network based tracker online, by utilizing the gradients to extract target-specific information. In contrast, our approach explores a new direction to capture the sequence-specific information, by using a statistic-based latent feature. Besides, we only adjust the basic model in the first frame, rather than using online updating. Thus, the time cost for our adjustment is almost negligible.

3 Siamese Tracker with Compact Latent Network

SiamRPN++ [30], a recent representative Siamese tracker, is adopted as our basic tracker. Thus, we briefly introduce the framework of this tracker in §3.1. Then, we conduct a deep analysis into the issue of *decisive samples missing* in Siamese-based trackers (see §3.2). To overcome this issue, we propose an efficient Compact Latent Network (CLNet) in §3.3, to adjust the basic model, and provide a diverse sample mining strategy to boost training performance in §3.4. Fig. 2 shows the framework of our method.

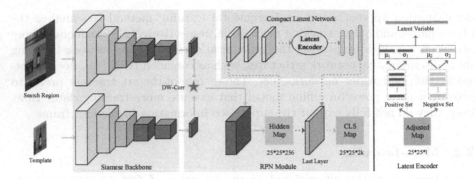

Fig. 2. The framework of Compact Latent Network (CLNet) for adjusting SiamRPN++ [30]. For clarity, we only show the classification branch. Given an Annotated Bounding Box (AB-Box) in the first frame, the proposed CLNet predicts the weights in the last layer of SiamRPN++. At this time, the hidden map is fed into CLNet, not the last layer (i.e. the red arrow is removed). In the following frames, we remove the CLNet to reduce computational requirements and use the adjusted model for tracking. The latent encoder module is shown on the right, where μ and σ present the mean and standard deviation of a sample set. The positive and negative sets are produced using the AB-Box. (Color figure online)

3.1 Revisiting SiamRPN for Tracking

In the early Siamese network based tracking algorithm, SiamFC [3], the tracking task is formulated as a nearest neighbor searching problem in a semantic embedding space. Given a target patch provided in the first frame of a sequence, the goal of SiamFC is to seek the most similar patch from the search region in the subsequent frames. To extract representative semantic features, SiamFC [3] build a fully-convolutional Siamese network ϕ, which contains a template branch for representing the target patch $\mathbf{z}$, and an instance branch for representing the search region $\mathbf{x}$. Then the cross-correlation (convolution) operation is applied on these semantic features to produce the final similarity map $\mathbf{S}$, which is formulated as $\mathbf{S}(\mathbf{z}, \mathbf{x}) = \phi(\mathbf{z}) * \phi(\mathbf{x}) + b$, where b is the offset of the similarity value, and $*$ represents the cross-correlation operation. $\mathbf{S} \in \mathbb{R}^{w \times h}$ measures the similarity between the template and instances in the search region, where w and h are the width and height of this map. Then the peak of $\mathbf{S}$ corresponds to the target location in the search region.

To avoid multi-scale estimation, SimRPN [31] extends SiamFC by incorporating an additional Region Proposal Network (RPN). The outputs of SiamRPN include one classification branch and one regression branch to regress the target bounding box (b-box) for both position and scale estimation. A multi-anchors technique [46] is further used for better performance. Combined with the Siamese network, SiamRPN produces $w \times h \times k$ anchors, where k is the anchor number for each searching position on instances feature map $\phi(\mathbf{x})$. For each anchor, the regression and classification branches obtain a proposal (b-box) and corresponding score, respectively. The corresponding outputs are formulated as follows,

$$\mathbf{A}^{cls} = con_{cls}^{fea}(\phi(\mathbf{x})) * con_{cls}^{ker}(\phi(\mathbf{z})), \mathbf{A}^{loc} = con_{loc}^{fea}(\phi(\mathbf{x})) * con_{loc}^{ker}(\phi(\mathbf{z})), \quad (1)$$

where con indicates the convolutional network obtaining new feature maps. Then the final target b-box is the regression output on the anchor with the highest classification score. Furthermore, Li $et\ al.$ [30] proposed SiamRPN++ to utilize the asymmetrical depth-wise cross correlation to reduce the number of parameters in the RPN block, providing efficient computation and solving the problem caused by the differences between the classification and regression branches. The new RPN block is formulated as follows,

$$\mathbf{A}^{cls} = h^{cls}\left(\alpha_{cls}^{fea}(\phi(\mathbf{x})) \star \alpha_{cls}^{ker}(\phi(\mathbf{z}))\right), \mathbf{A}^{loc} = h^{loc}\left(\alpha_{loc}^{fea}(\phi(\mathbf{x})) \star \alpha_{loc}^{ker}(\phi(\mathbf{z}))\right), \quad (2)$$

where α is an adjust (1×1 convolutional) layer, $\star$ is the depth-wise cross correlation, and h^s denotes the head block for predicting the classification and regression map.

3.2   Analysis for Siamese-Based Training Method

Siamese-based trackers take advantage of large numbers of image pairs to train a network from labeled video datasets (e.g., VID [47]) which can provide richer training samples. These numerous training samples can effectively enhance the generalization of tracking models for most testing sequences. However, this training strategy does not utilize sequence-specific information, provided by the annotation in the first frame of each testing sequence. Here, we introduce a simple binary-classification case to intuitively illustrate the underlying problem caused by using the general training method. In fact, SiamFC [3] can also be viewed as a binary-classification problem, where the template is the classifier discriminating the instance patch in the search region. Thus, the following analysis is suitable for most methods based on SiamFC [3] or SiamRPN [31].

Without loss of generality, we can assume that there are various positive and negative samples that come from different videos during the training phase, which is consistent with the Siamese-based training method. As shown in Fig. 3, we use a group of positive samples (the big blue ellipse) as well as negative samples (the big green ellipse) for training. The optimal decision hyperplane should be located in the middle of the two groups of samples to maintain the largest margin between the boundary samples and itself. Then, we can assume w^1 is the ideal decision hyperplane based on these two groups of training data in Fig. 3. During the testing phase, the positive and negative samples have no overlap with the training samples (i.e., we apply the learned tracker on unseen videos), and the number of testing samples is usually far less than that of the training phase. Thus, we use small ellipses to represent the testing samples and assume the challenging samples lie near the decision hyperplane. As shown in Fig. 3, some challenging samples may pass through the decision hyperplane into the wrong region, which means the trained classifier is invalid.

In the general classification task, an error will occur if any negative sample's score is larger than some positive sample. In contrast, a tracking error occurs only when the classification score of one negative sample is larger than all positive samples' scores. However, the tracking task still suffers from the issue of an unsuitable decision hyperplane (like w^1). For example, in Fig. 3, we can assume that the testing data points are sampled from a search region. The red triangle is the point with the largest distance from the decision boundary w^1 among all negative samples, which means it has the

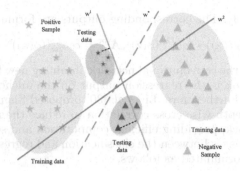

Fig. 3. Illustration of issue on binary-classification with the general training method. w^1 and w^2 are the ideal decision hyperplanes based on training and testing sets, respectively. w^* is the decision boundary considering both two sets.

highest positive classification score. Similarly, the red star has the highest score among all positive samples. Obviously, the score of the red triangle is larger than that of the red star; thus, the red triangle is regarded as the target, resulting in tracking faults.

In this paper, we focus on alleviating this issue and find a reasonable decision hyperplane for the tracking task. We find that the target ground-truth b-box, given in the first frame of a sequence, can provide rich supervision information to enhance the model discrimination ability for this sequence which helps to find a reasonable decision hyperplane. However, most Siamese-based trackers only use this b-box to extract the template feature and ignore the discriminative context information in the first frame. Effectively utilizing the supervision information is vital for the tracking model (classifier) learning. One simple solution is to finetune the tracking model with the positive and negative samples (testing data in Fig. 3) in the first frame. This is time-consuming since the model finetuning may converge after numerous iterations with normal gradient descent optimization [42]. Furthermore, the limited samples generated in the first frame easily lead to over-fitting. As shown in Fig. 3, if we only consider the testing data, the optimal decision hyperplane is w^2. However, this is not suitable for some training samples, and provides wrong labels for them. In fact, the ideal decision hyperplane for both training and testing data is w^*, which is not easily found. In the next section, we try to find an ideal tracking model which is suitable for both training data (large-scale labeled videos) and testing data (samples in the first frame), by using a compact latent network.

3.3   Compact Latent Network

To demonstrate the effectiveness of our compact latent network, we select the recent state-of-the-art Siamese-based model, SiamRPN++ [30], as our base tracker. To maintain the generality of the original tracking model, we fix all layers except the last one in the classification and regression branches. Here, we only show how to incorporate our compact latent network into the classification branches, and a similar process is also applied to the regression branches. For simplicity, we omit the notation *cls* in the following description. Firstly, we reformulate the base model to better explain the new proposed module. As mentioned in Sect. 3.1, the last head block in SiamRPN++ contains two convolutional layers. We decompose the head block into two components, i.e. $h = h_1(h_0)$. Denoting all layers except the last one in the classification branch as a function f, the classification map in Eq. (2) can be reformulated as follows:

$$A = h_1(f(\mathbf{x}, \mathbf{z}); \theta_1), \qquad (3)$$

where $f(\mathbf{x}, \mathbf{z}) = h_0 \left(\alpha^{fea}(\phi(\mathbf{x})) \star \alpha^{ker}(\phi(\mathbf{z})) \right)$. In fact, $f(\mathbf{x}, \mathbf{z}) \in \mathbb{R}^{w \times h \times c}$ is viewed as a $w \times h$ feature map $\mathbf{M}$ with c channels, and θ_1 is the parameter in h_1.

To better exploit the feature map $\mathbf{M}$, we provide a compact feature representation by utilizing the statistical information inside it. Firstly, this feature map $\mathbf{M}$ can be regarded as a set including the hidden vectors corresponding to the template-instance pair, i.e., $\mathbf{M} = \{\mathbf{m}_1, \mathbf{m}_2, \cdots, \mathbf{m}_{wh}\}$. Furthermore, according to the classification labels, this set can be split into two groups, the positive set $\mathcal{P} = \{\mathbf{m}_1^+, \mathbf{m}_2^+, \cdots, \mathbf{m}_{n+}^+\}$ and negative set $\mathcal{N} = \{\mathbf{m}_1^-, \mathbf{m}_2^-, \cdots, \mathbf{m}_{n-}^-\}$. Given these two sets, we capture the statistical information by computing the mean μ and standard deviation σ as follows,

$$\mu^\rho = \frac{1}{n^\rho} \sum\nolimits_{i=1}^{n^\rho} g_a(\mathbf{m}_i^\rho), \sigma^\rho = \sqrt{\frac{1}{n^\rho} \sum\nolimits_{i=1}^{n^\rho} (g_a(\mathbf{m}_i^\rho) - \mu^\rho)^2}, \qquad (4)$$

where $\mu \in \mathbb{R}^l$, $\sigma \in \mathbb{R}+^l$, $\rho \in \{+, -\}$, and g_a is a feature-adjusting sub-network containing three 1×1 convolutional layers, which is used to reduce the channel number of the latent vector from c to l. Here, we set $l \leq 2c$ to avoid a too high computational burden. Then, the final latent compact feature $\mathbf{c}$ for the original $\mathbf{m}$ is constructed by concatenation, i.e., $\mathbf{c} = concat(\mu^+, \sigma^+, \mu^-, \sigma^-)$.

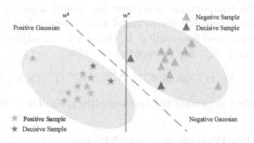

Fig. 4. Comparison of binary-classification based on normal samples and Gaussian distributions. w^n and w^g are the corresponding ideal decision hyperplanes.

In practice, the proposed statistic-based feature is more robust than the original features. We give an intuitive example in Fig. 4 to demonstrate the powerful representative ability of the statistic-based feature. Assume the positive (blue stars) and negative (green triangles) samples are respectively drawn from two Gaussian distributions (the blue and green ellipses). As shown in Fig. 4, we can easily find the 'ideal' decision hyperplane w^n according to the rule of the largest margin. However, the true decision hyperplane should be w^g, since the true sample boundaries are the edges of the two ellipses. The incorrect decision hyperplane is caused by *decisive samples missing*, i.e. the key samples (red star and triangle) are not drawn. Usually, the critical samples are difficult to capture, but we can provide the mean and standard deviation of each sample set to re-shape the Gaussian distribution. Then the distributions can be used to find the ideal decision hyperplane and achieve better classification performance, by utilizing some uncertainty-based optimization methods [26]. Notice that a Gaussian distribution only depends on its mean and standard deviation, which indicates that these contain enough information to represent the distribution. Thus, we use the mean and standard deviation as the compact feature to alleviate the issue of *decisive samples missing*, by utilizing the underlying distribution.

The proposed compact representation brings two advantages: firstly, it has fewer parameters than the original feature. Notice that l is kept in the same order of magnitude as c. Thus, in practice, the parameter number $4 \times l$ of the compact feature $\mathbf{c}$ is less than the original one $w \times h \times c$. Secondly, the compact feature $\mathbf{c}$ is number-free, in other words, we can use a different number of positive and negative samples to construct this feature. This is very suitable for SiamRPN-based tracking models, since the number of positive or negative samples changes with the different input image-pairs [31].

After obtaining the latent compact feature $\mathbf{c}$, a multi-layer perceptron is used as the prediction sub-network to produce a deviation for the weights of the last head layer:

$$\Delta\theta_1 = g_\Delta(\mathbf{c}), \tag{5}$$

where g_Δ is the weight deviation predictor containing three fully connected layers. These deviations are added into the corresponding weights to adjust the model for different sequences, which is formulated as:

$$\theta_a = \theta_1 + \Delta\theta_1. \tag{6}$$

Finally, the adjusted weight θ_a is used to produce the classification map. For the regression branch, the computation procedure for weight adjustment is similar except that we use the positive sample set to build the compact latent feature, since only the positive samples are used for training. In summary, the adjusted classification map $\mathbf{A}_a^{cls}$ and regression map $\mathbf{A}_a^{loc}$ are formulated as follow:

$$\mathbf{A}_a^{cls} = h_1^{cls}(f^{cls}(\mathbf{x}, \mathbf{z}); \theta_a^{cls}), \mathbf{A}_a^{loc} = h_1^{loc}(f^{loc}(\mathbf{x}, \mathbf{z}); \theta_a^{loc}). \tag{7}$$

These maps are applied to predict the tracked object, similar to SiamRPN++ [30].

3.4   Training with Diverse Sample Mining

To train the proposed compact latent networks, we fix all parameters in the original model, and use the same softmax loss L^{cls} and smooth-L1 loss L^{loc} in SiamRPN++ [30] for the adjusted classification and regression maps, respectively. The final loss is formulated as follows,

$$L = L^{cls}(\mathbf{A}_a^{cls}, y^{cls}) + \lambda L^{loc}(\mathbf{A}_a^{loc}, y^{loc}), \tag{8}$$

where y^{cls} and y^{loc} are the classification and regression ground-truth, respectively, and λ is the trade-off parameter between the two losses, which is set as 1.2 in our experiments. In SiamRPN++, the image-pairs are sampled from different sequences in one training batch to achieve a more discriminative feature, which is not suitable for training our adjustment network. This is because the goal of our adjustment network is to predict the adjusted weights for each specific sequence rather than the whole videos. During training, we need to capture the important information inside a specific sequence not the general information across the sequences. Besides, our statistic-based latent feature also requires the local statistical information in a sequence not the global statistical information across sequences. Thus, in each training batch, we randomly sample several image-pairs from the same sequence and feed them into the network.

To enhance the training performance, we propose a diverse sample mining strategy, by ranking the classification scores of unused negative samples. SiamRPN++ [30] adopts the IoU between the anchor and ground-truth b-box to select the positive and negative samples. The negative ones are the anchors with $IoU < 0.3$, and the positive samples are those with $IoU > 0.6$. Only at most 16 positive samples and a total of 64 samples are used for one training pair. The unused negative samples may contain some diverse samples, which are helpful for enhancing the model discrimination ability. To mine these diverse samples, we first compute the original score map $\mathbf{A}^{cls}$. Then, we sort the unused negative samples in descending order according to the positive scores in $\mathbf{A}^{cls}$. The first 16 negative samples are regarded as the diverse samples and appended into the training samples. Thus, a total of 80 samples are used for one training pair. The newly proposed diverse samples, near the decision hyperplane of the original model, are more likely to be the decisive samples, such as the ones in Fig. 4. As the analysis in Sect. 3.3, these samples are helpful to find the ideal decision hyperplane and build a more robust compact latent feature.

4   Experimental Results

Our approach is implemented in Python 3 using Pytorch 0.4.0 and evaluated on a single Nvidia RTX 2080Ti GPU. We compare our tracker and the base tracker with several representative trackers on NFS [17], DTB70 [34], UAV123 [41], VOT2019 [28], and LaSOT [13] benchmarks. The tracking speed of our method is about 45.6 fps, closing to the base tracker SiamRPN++ [30] (46.9 fps). We evaluate the base model with its official code in our machine for fair comparison.

4.1   Implementation Details

Architecture. Our Compact Latent Network (CLNet) has two sub-networks g_a and g_δ. In our experiments, g_a contains three convolutional blocks constructed by a 1×1 convolution, batch-norm, and ReLU layer. For the classification branch, the output channel number of each convolutional layer is set as 256, and that of the regression branch is set as 512. This ensures the compact latent features are the same size in both two branches. Sub-network g_δ contains three fully connected layers, the first two layers of which are followed by a ReLU layer and the last of which is followed a $Tanh$ layer. For the classification branch, the output numbers of the three layers are $[128, 128, n_{\theta_1^{cls}}]$, where $n_{\theta_1^{cls}}$ is the parameter number of θ_1^{cls} to be adjusted. Similarly, the numbers in the regression branch are set as $[128, 128, n_{\theta_1^{loc}}]$. Here, we adopt the SiamRPN++ [30] with three layer-wise features aggregation as the base model. Since the output feature maps in these three layers have the same size, we can use the adjustment network with the same structure for each feature map.

Training. We follow the training protocol of SiamRPN++ [30], using the same training datasets (COCO [35], DET [47], VID [47], and YouTubeBB [45]). Synchronized stochastic gradient descent is used for training over four GPUs with a total of 64 pairs per minibatch (16 pairs per GPU). We train over 20 epochs, each of which contains

60,000 training pairs. We use a step learning rate from 0.001 to 0.005 for the first five epochs as a warmup training. In the last 15 epochs, the learning rate is exponentially decayed from 0.005 to 0.0005. The other hyper-parameters are the same as SiamRPN++.

4.2   Comparison with Other Trackers

NFS30 Dataset. Need for Speed (NFS) [17] includes 100 challenging sequences with fast-moving objects. We evaluate the proposed method on the 30 FPS version (NFS30) by comparing the trackers in [17]. As shown in Fig. 5, our tracker achieves a precision and AUC 21.8% and 24.2% higher than MDNet [42], which is the best tracker reported in the original paper. Compared with the baseline SiamRPN++, we also achieve the significant relative gains of 8.2% in terms of both precision and AUC.

DTB70 Dataset. Our method is also evaluated on the Drone Tracking Benchmark [34], which includes 70 videos captured by drone cameras. We report the precision and AUC plots in Fig. 6 in comparison to the recent SiamFC-v2 [58], and other trackers reported in DTB70. Specifically, our tracker significantly outperforms the second-best tracker, SiamRPN++, by large gains of 5.5% and 6.8% in terms of precision and AUC. We attribute the performance promotion to the proposed compact latent network.

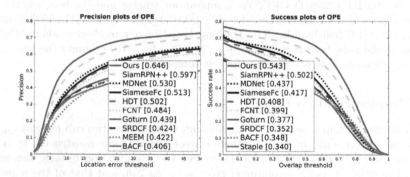

Fig. 5. Precision and success plots on the NFS30 dataset [17].

UAV123 Dataset. UAV123 [41] includes 123 low altitude aerial sequences captured from an aerial viewpoint, with an average sequence length of 915 frames. Besides the recent methods in UAV123, we add SiamFC-v2 [58] into the comparison. Figure 7 shows the precision and AUC plots for the top ten trackers. Among the compared methods, SiamRPN++ obtains the best precision and AUC scores of 0.804 and 0.611, respectively. However, our approach outperforms this with a precision score of 0.830 and an AUC score of 0.633, which further demonstrates the effectiveness of our method.

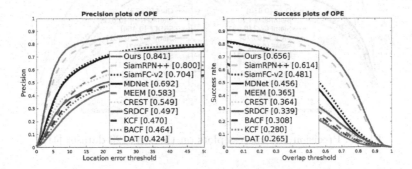

Fig. 6. Precision and success plots on the DTB70 dataset [34].

Table 1. Evaluation of the real-time challenge in VOT2019 [28] by EAO, ACC, and ROB. The best scores are highlighted in red.

	SiamCRF_RT	SiamMask	ARTCS	SiamDW_ST	DCFST	DiMP	SiamFCOT	SiamMargin	SiamRPN++	Ours
EAO ↑	0.262	0.287	0.287	0.299	0.317	0.321	0.350	0.366	0.285	0.313
ACC ↑	0.549	0.594	0.602	0.600	0.585	0.582	0.601	0.585	0.599	0.606
ROB ↓	0.346	0.461	0.482	0.467	0.376	0.371	0.386	0.321	0.482	0.461

Table 2. Comparison on the LaSOT dataset [13] by the success (AUC), precision (P), and normalized precision (P_{norm}). The best scores are highlighted in red.

	StrSiam [67]	SiamFC [3]	VITAL [56]	MDNet [42]	MLT [4]	GradNet [33]	SiamDW [68]	C-RPN [14]	SiamRPN++ [30]	Ours
P (%)	34	34.1	37.2	37.4	–	35.1	–	44.3	48.5	49.4
P_{norm} (%)	44.3	44.9	48.4	48.1	–	–	–	54.2	56.5	57.4
AUC (%)	35.6	35.8	41.2	41.3	34.5	36.5	38.4	45.5	49.3	49.9

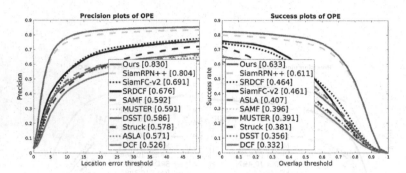

Fig. 7. Precision and success plots on the UAV123 dataset [41].

VOT2019 Dataset. We also evaluate our CLNet on the real-time challenge of the VOT2019 Dataset [28], which contains 60 public sequences with different challenging factors. This dataset performs re-initialization of a tracker when it fails to track the target, to order to measure its short-term tracking performance. According to the evaluation protocol of VOT2019, we adopt the Expected Average Overlap (EAO), Accuracy (ACC) and Robustness (ROB) to compare different trackers, including the top nine algorithms ranked by EAO in the real-time challenge. As shown in Table 1, our approach obtains the best score in terms of ACC. Compared with our baseline SiamRPN++, the proposed method achieves a significant performance improvement of 9.8% in terms of EAO, and also boosts the ACC and ROB scores. This demonstrates our approach can effectively improve the short-term tracking ability of the base model.

LaSOT Dataset. The recent LaSOT [13] provides high-quality manual annotations for a large-scale dataset, which includes a total 1,400 sequences with an average sequence length of 2,512 frames. To further validate the proposed approach on a larger and longer dataset, we conduct experiments on the testing set of LaSOT with 280 sequences, comparing the recent MLT [4], GradNet [33], SiamDW [68], and C-RPN [14], as well as the trackers from LaSOT. Following [13], three metrics are used for evaluation, including the success (AUC), precision (P), and normalized precision (P_{norm}). As shown in Table 2, our tracker achieves the best results in terms of all three metrics, which clearly demonstrates the generalization ability of our approach for the large-scale dataset.

4.3 Ablation Study

Extensive experiments are performed to analyze the main components of the proposed compact latent network. We conduct these experiments on a combined dataset including the whole DTB70 [34], NFS30 (30 FPS version) [17] and UAV123 [41] datasets. This new combined dataset contains 293 diverse videos for thorough analysis. The variants of our method and the baseline are evaluated using the precision (P) and AUC metrics [65].

We retrain our base tracker (**BT**) SiamRPN++ initialized with its original parameters using our training method and test it on the combined dataset. The results show that the retrained tracker (**RT**) improves the precision (**BT**: 73.3% vs **RT**: 74.3%)

Table 3. Comparison of key components in terms of precision (P) and AUC scores on the combined DTB70 [34], NFS30 [17], and UAV123 [41] dataset. SiamRPN++ [30] is the base tracker (**BT**). **RT** means the retrained base tracker. The critical components include an adjustment network (**+AN**), latent encoder (**+LE**), one sequence for training (**+OS**), and diverse sample mining (**+DM**).

	RT	BT	+AN	+LE	+OS	+DM
P (%)	74.3	73.3	73.8	75.5	76.6	77.2
AUC (%)	57.4	57.7	58.2	60.1	60.2	61.1

but reduces the AUC (**BT**: 57.6% vs **RT**: 57.4%), which indicates that the additional training on the original model does not provide significant gains. To analyze the impact of key components in the proposed framework, we add them to the base tracker (**BT**) one by one. All results are shown in Table 3. We first train a adjustment network without the latent encoder to adjust the base model (**+MN**). The performance gains in terms of P (0.5%) and AUC (0.5%) scores indicate that the base model benefits from the sequence-specific information, extracted by the adjustment network. By adding the latent encoder (**+LE**), CLNet achieves a major improvement with a P gain of 1.7% and AUC gain of 1.9%. This demonstrates the advantages of the latent encoder in providing a compact and effective feature for the sequence-specific information. Furthermore, we sample the image-pairs from one sequence in each training batch (**+OS**), to provide a more robust latent feature. This yields a further improvement, with 1.1% and 0.1% gains in terms of P and AUC scores, respectively. Finally, the diverse sample mining technique (**+DM**) improves the P and AUC score by another 0.6% and 0.9%. In summary, compared with our baseline, the final version (**+DM**) achieves significant relative gains of 5.3% and 5.9% in terms of the P and AUC scores.

5 Conclusion

This paper provided an in-depth analysis into the performance degradation of Siamese-based trackers and found that an important factor is *decisive samples missing* during training. To alleviate this problem, we proposed a Compact Latent Network (CLNet), which can efficiently extract the sequence-specific information in the first frame, to adjust the Siamese-based model. To further facilitate the adjustment network training, we proposed a new training strategy based on diverse sample mining to enhance the discrimination ability of CLNet. Since we only carry out one forward computation for the adjustment in each sequence, the time cost is almost negligible. Extensive evaluations on SiamRPN++ have clearly demonstrated the effectiveness of the proposed CLNet. In the future, we will apply our method to other vision tasks, such as multi-object tracking [52,66], segmentation [9,38], deblurring [53,54], and saliency detection [61,62].

References

1. Andrychowicz, M., et al.: Learning to learn by gradient descent by gradient descent. In: NeurIPS (2016)

2. Ba, J., Hinton, G.E., Mnih, V., Leibo, J.Z., Ionescu, C.: Using fast weights to attend to the recent past. In: NeurIPS (2016)
3. Bertinetto, L., Valmadre, J., Henriques, J.F., Vedaldi, A., Torr, P.H.S.: Fully-convolutional siamese networks for object tracking. In: Hua, G., Jégou, H. (eds.) ECCV 2016. LNCS, vol. 9914, pp. 850–865. Springer, Cham (2016). https://doi.org/10.1007/978-3-319-48881-3_56
4. Choi, J., Kwon, J., Lee, K.M.: Deep meta learning for real-time target-aware visual tracking. In: ICCV (2019)
5. Danelljan, M., Bhat, G., Khan, F.S., Felsberg, M., et al.: Eco: efficient convolution operators for tracking. In: CVPR (2017)
6. Danelljan, M., Robinson, A., Shahbaz Khan, F., Felsberg, M.: Beyond correlation filters: learning continuous convolution operators for visual tracking. In: Leibe, B., Matas, J., Sebe, N., Welling, M. (eds.) ECCV 2016. LNCS, vol. 9909, pp. 472–488. Springer, Cham (2016). https://doi.org/10.1007/978-3-319-46454-1_29
7. Dong, X., Shen, J., Yu, D., Wang, W., Liu, J., Huang, H.: Occlusion-aware real-time object tracking. IEEE TMM 19, 763–771 (2017)
8. Dong, X., Shen, J.: Triplet loss in Siamese network for object tracking. In: ECCV (2018)
9. Dong, X., Shen, J., Shao, L., Van Gool, L.: Sub-Markov random walk for image segmentation. IEEE TIP 25, 516–527 (2015)
10. Dong, X., Shen, J., Wang, W., Liu, Y., Shao, L., Porikli, F.: Hyperparameter optimization for tracking with continuous deep q-learning. In: CVPR (2018)
11. Dong, X., Shen, J., Wang, W., Shao, L., Ling, H., Porikli, F.: Dynamical hyper-parameter optimization via deep reinforcement learning in tracking. IEEE TPAMI (2019)
12. Dong, X., Shen, J., Wu, D., Guo, K., Jin, X., Porikli, F.: Quadruplet network with one-shot learning for fast visual object tracking. IEEE TIP 28, 3516–3527 (2019)
13. Fan, H., et al.: Lasot: a high-quality benchmark for large-scale single object tracking. In: CVPR (2019)
14. Fan, H., Ling, H.: Siamese cascaded region proposal networks for real-time visual tracking. In: CVPR (2019)
15. Finn, C., Abbeel, P., Levine, S.: Model-agnostic meta-learning for fast adaptation of deep networks. In: ICML (2017)
16. Finn, C., Xu, K., Levine, S.: Probabilistic model-agnostic meta-learning. In: NeurIPS (2018)
17. Galoogahi, H.K., Fagg, A., Huang, C., Ramanan, D., Lucey, S.: Need for speed: A benchmark for higher frame rate object tracking. In: ICCV (2017)
18. Guo, Q., Feng, W., Zhou, C., Huang, R., Wan, L., Wang, S.: Learning dynamic siamese network for visual object tracking. In: ICCV (2017)
19. He, A., Luo, C., Tian, X., Zeng, W.: A twofold siamese network for real-time object tracking. In: CVPR (2018)
20. Held, D., Thrun, S., Savarese, S.: Learning to track at 100 FPS with deep regression networks. In: Leibe, B., Matas, J., Sebe, N., Welling, M. (eds.) ECCV 2016. LNCS, vol. 9905, pp. 749–765. Springer, Cham (2016). https://doi.org/10.1007/978-3-319-46448-0_45
21. Henriques, J.F., Rui, C., Martins, P., Batista, J.: High-speed tracking with kernelized correlation filters. IEEE TPAMI 37, 583–596 (2015)
22. Hinton, G.E., Plaut, D.C.: Using fast weights to deblur old memories. In: CCSS (1987)

23. Hochreiter, S., Younger, A.S., Conwell, P.R.: Learning to learn using gradient descent. In: Dorffner, G., Bischof, H., Hornik, K. (eds.) ICANN 2001. LNCS, vol. 2130, pp. 87–94. Springer, Heidelberg (2001). https://doi.org/10.1007/3-540-44668-0_13

24. Hong, S., You, T., Kwak, S., Han, B.: Online tracking by learning discriminative saliency map with convolutional neural network. In: ICML (2015)

25. Huang, C., Lucey, S., Ramanan, D.: Learning policies for adaptive tracking with deep feature cascades. In: ICCV (2017)

26. Khan, S., Hayat, M., Zamir, S.W., Shen, J., Shao, L.: Striking the right balance with uncertainty. In: CVPR (2019)

27. Koch, G., Zemel, R., Salakhutdinov, R.: Siamese neural networks for one-shot image recognition. In: ICML deep learning workshop (2015)

28. Kristan, M., et al.: The seventh visual object tracking vot2019 challenge results (2019)

29. Kristan, M., et al.: A novel performance evaluation methodology for single-target trackers. IEEE TPAMI **38**, 2137–2155 (2016)

30. Li, B., Wu, W., Wang, Q., Zhang, F., Xing, J., Yan, J.: Siamrpn++: evolution of siamese visual tracking with very deep networks. In: CVPR (2019)

31. Li, B., Yan, J., Wu, W., Zhu, Z., Hu, X.: High performance visual tracking with siamese region proposal network. In: CVPR (2018)

32. Li, H., Dong, W., Mei, X., Ma, C., Huang, F., Hu, B.G.: Lgm-net: learning to generate matching networks for few-shot learning. In: ICML (2019)

33. Li, P., Chen, B., Ouyang, W., Wang, D., Yang, X., Lu, H.: Gradnet: gradient-guided network for visual object tracking. In: ICCV (2019)

34. Li, S., Yeung, D.Y.: Visual object tracking for unmanned aerial vehicles: a benchmark and new motion models. In: AAAI (2017)

35. Lin, T.Y., et al.: Microsoft COCO: common objects in context. In: Fleet, D., Pajdla, T., Schiele, B., Tuytelaars, T. (eds.) ECCV 2014. LNCS, vol. 8693, pp. 740–755. Springer, Cham (2014). https://doi.org/10.1007/978-3-319-10602-1_48

36. Liu, Y., Dong, X., Lu, X., Khan, F.S., Shen, J., Hoi, S.: Teacher-Students Knowledge Distillation for Siamese Trackers. arXiv (2019)

37. Lu, X., Ma, C., Ni, B., Yang, X., Reid, I., Yang, M.H.: Deep regression tracking with shrinkage loss. In: ECCV (2018)

38. Lu, X., Wang, W., Shen, J., Tai, Y.W., Crandall, D.J., Hoi, S.C.: Learning video object segmentation from unlabeled videos. In: CVPR (2020)

39. Ma, B., Hu, H., Shen, J., Zhang, Y., Porikli, F.: Linearization to nonlinear learning for visual tracking. In: ICCV (2015)

40. Ma, B., Shen, J., Liu, Y., Hu, H., Shao, L., Li, X.: Visual tracking using strong classifier and structural local sparse descriptors. IEEE TMM **17**, 1818–1828 (2015)

41. Mueller, M., Smith, N., Ghanem, B.: A benchmark and simulator for UAV tracking. In: Leibe, B., Matas, J., Sebe, N., Welling, M. (eds.) ECCV 2016. LNCS, vol. 9905, pp. 445–461. Springer, Cham (2016). https://doi.org/10.1007/978-3-319-46448-0_27

42. Nam, H., Han, B.: Learning multi-domain convolutional neural networks for visual tracking. In: CVPR (2016)

43. Park, E., Berg, A.C.: Meta-tracker: fast and robust online adaptation for visual object trackers. In: ECCV (2018)

44. Ravi, S., Larochelle, H.: Optimization as a model for few-shot learning. In: ICLR (2017)

45. Real, E., Shlens, J., Mazzocchi, S., Pan, X., Vanhoucke, V.: Youtube-boundingboxes: a large high-precision human-annotated data set for object detection in video. In: CVPR (2017)
46. Ren, S., He, K., Girshick, R., Sun, J.: Faster r-cnn: towards real-time object detection with region proposal networks. In: NeurIPS (2015)
47. Russakovsky, O., et al.: ImageNet large scale visual recognition challenge. IJCV 115, 211–252 (2015). https://doi.org/10.1007/s11263-015-0816-y
48. Rusu, A.A., et al.: Meta-learning with latent embedding optimization. In: ICLR (2019)
49. Santoro, A., Bartunov, S., Botvinick, M., Wierstra, D., Lillicrap, T.: Meta-learning with memory-augmented neural networks. In: ICML (2016)
50. Schmidhuber, J.: Evolutionary principles in self-referential learning, or on learning how to learn: the meta-meta-... hook. Ph.D. thesis, Technische Universität München (1987)
51. Shen, J., Tang, X., Dong, X., Shao, L.: Visual object tracking by hierarchical attention siamese network. IEEE TCYB 50, 3068–3080 (2020)
52. Shen, J., Yu, D., Deng, L., Dong, X.: Fast online tracking with detection refinement. IEEE TITS 19, 162–173 (2017)
53. Shen, Z., Lai, W.S., Xu, T., Kautz, J., Yang, M.H.: Exploiting semantics for face image deblurring. IJCV 128, 1829–1846 (2020). https://doi.org/10.1007/s11263-019-01288-9
54. Shen, Z., et al.: Human-aware motion deblurring. In: ICCV (2019)
55. Snell, J., Swersky, K., Zemel, R.: Prototypical networks for few-shot learning. In: NeurIPS (2017)
56. Song, Y., et al.: Vital: visual tracking via adversarial learning. In: CVPR (2018)
57. Thrun, S., Pratt, L.: Learning to learn: introduction and overview. In: Thrun, S., Pratt, L. (eds.) Learning to learn, pp. 3–17. Springer, Boston (1998). https://doi.org/10.1007/978-1-4615-5529-2_1
58. Valmadre, J., Bertinetto, L., Henriques, J.F., Vedaldi, A., Torr, P.H.: End-to-end representation learning for correlation filter based tracking. In: CVPR (2017)
59. Vinyals, O., Blundell, C., Lillicrap, T., Wierstra, D., et al.: Matching networks for one shot learning. In: NeurIPS (2016)
60. Wang, Q., Teng, Z., Xing, J., Gao, J., Hu, W., Maybank, S.: Learning attentions: residual attentional siamese network for high performance online visual tracking. In: CVPR (2018)
61. Wang, W., Shen, J., Dong, X., Borji, A.: Salient object detection driven by fixation prediction. In: CVPR (2018)
62. Wang, W., Shen, J., Dong, X., Borji, A., Yang, R.: Inferring salient objects from human fixations. IEEE TPAMI 42, 1913–1927 (2019)
63. Wang, X., Li, C., Luo, B., Tang, J.: Sint++: robust visual tracking via adversarial positive instance generation. In: CVPR (2018)
64. Yang, T., Chan, A.B.: Learning dynamic memory networks for object tracking. In: ECCV (2018)
65. Yi, W., Jongwoo, L., Yang, M.H.: Object tracking benchmark. IEEE TPAMI (2015)
66. Yin, J., Wang, W., Meng, Q., Yang, R., Shen, J.: A unified object motion and affinity model for online multi-object tracking. In: CVPR (2020)
67. Zhang, Y., Wang, L., Qi, J., Wang, D., Feng, M., Lu, H.: Structured siamese network for real-time visual tracking. In: ECCV (2018)

68. Zhang, Z., Peng, H.: Deeper and wider siamese networks for real-time visual tracking. In: CVPR (2019)
69. Zhu, Z., Wang, Q., Li, B., Wu, W., Yan, J., Hu, W.: Distractor-aware siamese networks for visual object tracking. In: ECCV (2018)

Occlusion-Aware Siamese Network for Human Pose Estimation

Lu Zhou[1,2]([⊠]), Yingying Chen[1,2,3], Yunze Gao[1,2], Jinqiao Wang[1,2,4], and Hanqing Lu[1,2]

[1] National Laboratory of Pattern Recognition, Institute of Automation, Chinese Academy of Sciences, Beijing 100190, China
{lu.zhou,yingying.chen,yunze.gao,jqwang,luhq}@nlpr.ia.ac.cn
[2] School of Artificial Intelligence, University of Chinese Academy of Sciences, Beijing 100049, China
[3] ObjectEye Inc., Beijing, China
[4] NEXWISE Co., Ltd., Guangzhou, China

Abstract. Pose estimation usually suffers from varying degrees of performance degeneration owing to occlusion. To conquer this dilemma, we propose an occlusion-aware siamese network to improve the performance. Specifically, we introduce scheme of feature erasing and reconstruction. Firstly, we utilize attention mechanism to predict the occlusion-aware attention map which is explicitly supervised and clean the feature map which is contaminated by different types of occlusions. Nevertheless, the cleaning procedure not only removes the useless information but also erases some valuable details. To overcome the defects caused by the erasing operation, we perform feature reconstruction to recover the information destroyed by occlusion and details lost in cleaning procedure. To make reconstructed features more precise and informative, we adopt siamese network equipped with OT divergence to guide the features of occluded images towards those of the un-occluded images. Algorithm is validated on MPII, LSP and COCO benchmarks and we achieve promising results.

Keywords: Siamese network · Occlusion · Human pose estimation

1 Introduction

2D human pose estimation has enjoyed great success in recent years owing to the development of deep neural networks. It aims at predicting the positions of human joints given a single RGB image and serves as a significant basis for several vision tasks such as action recognition [26,38], person re-identification [27] and human-computer interaction [20]. Nevertheless, it is still confronted with a lot of challenges such as view changes, complex human gestures, human joints scale changes and occlusion. Among these troublesome factors, occlusion shown in Fig. 1 poses great degradation to the performance of human pose

© Springer Nature Switzerland AG 2020
A. Vedaldi et al. (Eds.): ECCV 2020, LNCS 12365, pp. 396–412, 2020.
https://doi.org/10.1007/978-3-030-58565-5_24

Fig. 1. Illustration of the results on some occluded images of MPII datasets.

estimation. In general, presentation of occlusions leads to contamination of deep features and confuses the network to make incorrect decisions.

Previous methods based on deep neural networks [3,21,28,36] mainly focused on searching more efficient and powerful architectures of the deep neural networks. [8] utilized CRF-based attention to settle the occlusion problem. [4] proposed an adversarial posenet to tackle this issue. However, attention used in [8] leads to large increases of the parameters and computation cost while adversarial network in [4] is usually hard to converge. In this paper, an occlusion-aware siamese network is proposed to conquer the dilemma caused by occlusion and surpasses these mentioned methods based on the same backbone.

We leverage the attention mechanism to exclude the interference of occlusions. Among those popular human pose estimation benchmarks, COCO keypoint detection dataset [16], MPII dataset [1], usually, occlusion flag is offered as another labeling information. Here, we employ the occlusion flag which is seldom excavated before to predict corresponding occlusion circumstances and obtain occlusion-aware attention map. Compared with previous attention mechanisms [8,42] used in human pose estimation, attention map employed here is learned explicitly via intermediate supervision, which is more purposeful and can predict occlusion more precisely. The obtained attention map serves as a solid foundation for feature erasing and reconstruction.

Feature erasing means erasing the contaminated feature map and provides cleaner representation. Guided by explicitly learned occlusion-aware attention map, we can remove the ambiguities caused by occlusion and obtain relatively cleaner feature map.

However, cleaned feature map cannot provide precise and holistic description of the whole human skeleton due to the missing semantic information. The erasing procedure not only deletes tremendous incorrect expressions but also mistakenly gets rid of some informative cues especially under the circumstances of self-occlusion. Hence, feature reconstruction is necessary for obtaining more powerful and informative feature representations. On one hand, feature reconstruction attains refreshed information to replace those occluded features in the case that semantics are destroyed by occlusion. On the other hand, feature reconstruction is able to recover the wrongly removed semantics when useful information is mistakenly erased. Here, we design a feature reconstruction submodule which can capture information from surrounding areas without occlusion to facilitate the recovering.

To provide ample prior guidance for reconstruction, here, we advance a siamese framework to facilitate this process. The siamese network possesses two branches overall where model weights are shared between them. The second branch takes images without artificial occlusion as input to extract the clean feature representation. In contrast, the first branch takes occluded images which contain the same content as the second branch except for the appearance of the occlusion as input. The occlusion appearing in the first branch is manually created. Purpose of the siamese structure is to make the occluded branch imitate the behavior of the branch without occlusion. How to pull these two branches more closely in high-dimension feature space is challenging. In this paper, we employ optimal transport (OT) divergence [18,25] with additional mask as deluxe regularization instead of correspondence-based approaches to achieve this purpose. Branch without occlusion encodes more confident information whilst the other branch is less confident somehow. The introduction of OT divergence enables the less confident feature to be aligned with the more confident one.

Integrating submodules aforementioned together forms our occlusion-aware siamese network and whole framework is named as OASNet which aims at settling the occlusion problem. The main contributions are three folds:

- We propose a feature erasing and reconstruction submodule to obtain cleaner feature representation and reconstruct the erased feature. Different from previous methods, attention map which is occlusion-aware is put forward to remove the ambiguities caused by different types of occlusion.
- To make the occluded feature mimic the behavior of feature without occlusion, siamese network equipped with erasing and reconstruction submodule is put forward.
- Instead of utilizing correspondence-based methods to narrow the discrepancy of these two sets features, we adopt the optimal transport to fulfill this task. Our model makes the first attempt to perform human pose estimation under the primal form of optimal transport algorithm and proves effective.

2   Related Work

Human Pose Estimation. Recent years human pose estimation has achieved promising progress due to the application of deep neural networks. DeepPose [34] made the first attempt to integrate human pose estimation and deep neural network together. Pose estimation was regarded as a regression task and coordinates of human joints were predicted directly as model output. Nevertheless, directly regressing human joints was somewhat difficult and heatmap regression methods [3,6,8,13,21,30,36,37,39] emerged as a new fashion. Among these methods, [11,19,32,33] were devoted to reducing the false positive predictions via different types of Markov Random Field (MRF). [7] concentrated on building the spatial relationships of different human joints features with the Conditional Random Field (CRF). In addition to these deep graphical models, searching more efficient network structures yielded state-of-the-art performance. [36] proposed the concept of deep convolutional pose machines to enlarge the respective field

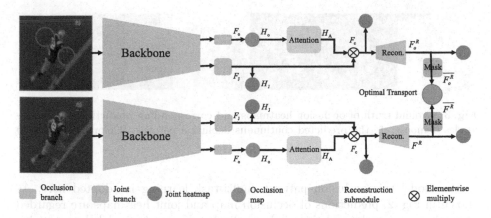

Fig. 2. Illustration of proposed occlusion-aware siamese network. There exist two branches where the first branch takes the artificially occluded image as input and the second branch takes the primal image as input.

and refined initial predictions via cascaded design. Hourglass [21], also called conv-deconv structure, adopted the cascaded design as well to refine previously generated results step by step. Subsequent works such as [8,13,22,29,30,39,40] all took hourglass as their backbone to extract efficient feature representations and implemented their ideas. [28] proposed HRNet which aimed at maintaining high resolution features across all stages of the network and achieved state-of-the-art performance across several human pose benchmarks.

3 Method

Overview of the proposed framework can be found in Fig. 2. In this section, we will detail the proposed occlusion-aware siamese network in three aspects, feature erasing and reconstruction, siamese framework and optimal transport divergence.

3.1 Feature Erasing and Feature Reconstruction

Occlusion poses great threat to human pose estimation due to missing semantics of corresponding human joints and contamination of the features. Existence of the occlusion confuses the network to make right decisions and hesitate around the area of occlusion. Hence, predicting occlusion flag serves as a necessary task to perceive the occlusion and provides essential cues for subsequent recognition and location. Previous methods generally take use of auto-learned attention to highlight the informative patches yet occluded regions are also picked out. It is difficult to perform the cleaning schedule in this case. In this paper, we exploit the occlusion flag which is additionally labeled to learn the attention explicitly. Previous works seldom leverage this labeling resource and ignore this valuable cue.

Fig. 3. Ground truth of occlusion heatmaps and corresponding predictions. Red rectangles demonstrate the predicted continuous occlusion patches. (Color figure online)

To model this occlusion pattern, multi-task learning is adopted here. As shown in Fig. 2, predictions of occlusion map and joint heatmaps are regarded as two separate tasks and the whole prediction process is modeled as a multi-task learning framework. Hard sharing mechanism where backbone for feature extraction is shared is adopted here.

We try two different approaches to perform the multi-task learning. For the first one, we regard the prediction of occlusion status as a classification task,

$$L_o = -\sum_{i=1}^{N} \sum_{c=0}^{C'-1} p^{i,c} log(p^{i,c}), \tag{1}$$

where cross entropy loss is utilized, N represents the number of human joints and C' indicates class numbers. Value of C' is 3 where class 0 indicates "not labeled", 1 indicates "labeled but not visible" and 2 indicates "labeled and visible".

In addition, we also try modeling the occlusion prediction as a heatmap regression task. Supervision for heatmap regression is formulated as shown in Fig. 3. We sum the occluded joint heatmaps up and the resulted heatmap is clamped to $[0, 1]$. Loss for this branch is denoted as

$$L_o = ||H_o - \hat{H}_o||_2^2, \tag{2}$$

where H_o is the predicted occlusion map and $\hat{H}_o$ represents corresponding ground truth. From Fig. 3 we can observe that predicted occlusion heatmaps are capable of predicting the continuous occlusion patch especially under extremely severe occluded situations. Prediction manner shown in Eq. 1 brings in performance drop and we abandon the utilization of it. Directly classifying occlusion flag seems to be a hard task. Loss for human joints regression is expressed as

$$L_J = \sum_{i=1}^{N} ||H_J^i - \hat{H}_J^i||_2^2, \tag{3}$$

where N represents the number of human joints. Overall loss for this multi-task learning framework is denoted as

$$L = L_J + \lambda_o L_o, \tag{4}$$

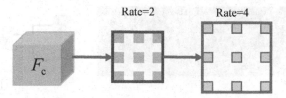

Fig. 4. Design of the reconstruction submodule. Two consecutive dilated convolution operations are adopted.

where λ_o is a hyper-parameter which modulates the proportion of losses with respect to these two tasks.

We convert the resulted occlusion heatmap to corresponding attention map via

$$H_A = 1 - H_o, \tag{5}$$

where $H_A \in R^{1 \times H \times W}$ represents the occlusion-aware attention map. Operation of feature cleaning can be denoted as

$$F_c = F_J \odot H_A, \tag{6}$$

where feature map $F_J \in R^{C \times H \times W}$ is weighted by H_A. However, the missing information may deteriorate the overall performance. It is critical for the network to learn an automatic resuming mechanism and reconstruct the missing knowledge.

To obtain enough semantic information from surrounding areas of the occluded patches, two consecutive dilated convolutions with kernel 3×3 are adopted to ensure ample spatial coverage and enlarge respective field of the submodule. Dilation rates are 2 and 4 respectively. Maybe more complex design can exhibit better performance, however, it is not the main concern of this paper and the submodule here has shown promising advantage. Concrete demonstrations can be found in Fig. 4.

3.2 Siamese Framework

Feature reconstruction submodule reconstructs the erased features without any instruction. Though it takes advantage of context from neighboring regions, it still cannot recover the missing information precisely owing to the lack of prior guidance. The information recovered may not be adequate for final locating and still carries enormous distractive information. It is critical to provide a precise mentor for the reconstruction submodule to make the reestablishment process more reasonable. Perfect reestablishment may be the reproduction of the features of the images without occlusion. The reconstructed feature in this case can encode the same context as the un-occluded image.

It is intuitive to think of the teacher-student mode to perform the guidance procedure, i.e., distillation. Pre-trained model which takes the un-occluded

Fig. 5. (a) Illustrations of mask mechanism. (b) Illustrations of optimal transport submodule.

images as input serves as the teacher and the model to be trained with occluded images acts as the student. Teacher model carrying more reliable sets of information provides more confident supervision for the student model. Nevertheless, the features and parameters of pre-trained teacher model differ largely from the student and they are totally two different models. Directly executing the distillation over these two feature sets from two completely different models is challenging and not that adequate for our task.

In this paper, we abandon the usage of distillation and propose a novel siamese framework to conduct the mimicking process. As depicted in Fig. 2, siamese training is utilized to fulfill the mission of the similarity learning. The first branch takes the image with artificial occlusions as input and encodes the less confident information. The second branch takes the primal images without artificial occlusions and offers more confident information. The self-supervised training mechanism executes another form of teacher-student guidance and outperforms the distillation technique mentioned above.

To enforce artificial occlusions on primal images, we follow the same pasting operation as [13]. Random numbers of occlusion patches are chosen on each image with different scales to enrich the occlusion types. However, some primal images may have been endowed with some natural occlusions and it is non-trivial to perform the mimicking with mask to exclude the interference of the natural occlusions. The masked mimicking learning can effectively narrow the gap across the two branches of siamese network.

3.3 Optimal Transport Divergence

The most straightforward manner for reducing the gap between the two branches of siamese network is to narrow the corresponding pixel discrepancy. Various evaluation losses can be adapted into this kind of framework. Distinct from these methods, matching the distributions of these two branches acts as another substitute. In contrast, matching corresponding distributions demonstrates more superior advantages than correspondence-based techniques especially over the space of high dimension. In this section, we will detail the feature mimicking losses we explore.

Correspondence-Based Approaches. Correspondence-based methods seek to measure the discrepancy between these two branches by means of pixel correspondence. We denote the feature after reconstruction of the first branch as $F_o^R \in R^{C \times H \times W}$, and the feature of the second branch is expressed as $F^R \in R^{C \times H \times W}$. Since there might exist some natural occlusions, it is necessary to exclude the guidance from these areas. In these areas, features from the second branch suffer from contamination as well and reconstruction may not be better than the first branch. We add a mask which excludes the mimicking of the areas with natural occlusions and is denoted as $\overline{M} \in R^{1 \times H \times W}$. Illustrations can be found in Fig. 5(a). Feature map decorated by mask can be obtained via

$$\overline{F^R} = F^R \odot \overline{M},$$
$$\overline{F_o^R} = F_o^R \odot \overline{M}, \tag{7}$$

where $\overline{F^R}, \overline{F_o^R} \in R^{C \times H \times W}$ indicate masked feature maps. To minimize corresponding distinctions, $L2$ loss is adopted as follows:

$$L_{mimic} = \sum_{i=1}^{N} ||\overline{F^R}(i) - \overline{F_o^R}(i)||_2^2, \tag{8}$$

where i means the ith location and N is $H \times W$. Cosine similarity can be implemented following the similar way.

Distribution-Based Approaches. Aligning the distributions of these two groups features serves as another variant to eliminate the existing discrepancy. Usually KL divergence and JS divergence are two common measurements to assess the divergence between two distinct distributions. However, the comparison of these two distributions is still carried out on high-dimension space. To settle this dilemma, optimal transport divergence is adopted to compare the two distributions in a low-dimension feature space and relieves the difficulty.

Optimal transport seeks to find the optimal transportation strategy γ_0 to perform the mass moving from distribution u to distribution v and minimizes the transport cost. Usually, discretized version of optimal transport is adopted,

$$\gamma_0 = \arg\min_{\gamma \in \Pi(u,v)} \langle \gamma, M \rangle_F,$$
$$\Pi(u, v) \stackrel{def.}{=} \{\gamma \in R_+^{m_1 \times m_2} : \gamma 1_{m_2} = u, \gamma^T 1_{m_1} = v\}, \tag{9}$$

where $\langle .,. \rangle_F$ indicates the Frobenius dot product, $1_m := (1/m, ..., 1/m) \in R_+^m$. $M \in R_+^{m_1 \times m_2}$ indicates the cost matrix.

Algorithm 1. Iterative implementation of Sinkhorn divergence.

Input: Input masked feature maps $\overline{F^R}$ and $\overline{F_o^R}$, critic module D
Output: Sinkhorn loss $W_M(\overline{F^R}, \overline{F_o^R})$
1: Feature $\overline{F^R}$ and $\overline{F_o^R}$ are both sent into the critic, $\widetilde{F^R} = D(\overline{F^R})$ and $\widetilde{F_o^R} = D(\overline{F_o^R})$
2: $\forall (i,j)$ in $\widetilde{F^R}, \widetilde{F_o^R}$, $M_{ij} \stackrel{def.}{=} cos\_dis(\widetilde{F^R}(i), \widetilde{F_o^R}(j))$ and $M \in R^{C \times C}$
3: Initialize $b^{(0)} \leftarrow 1_C$
4: Compute Gibbs Kernel $K_{i,j} = exp(-M_{i,j}/\varepsilon)$
5:

   for $r = 0; r < R; r++$ **do**
       $a^{r+1} := \frac{1_C}{K^T b^r}, b^{r+1} := \frac{1_C}{K a^r}$
   end for
6: Matrix P^R can be obtained via $diag(b^R) \cdot K \cdot diag(a^R)$
7: W_M can be obtained via: $\langle M, P \rangle$
8: return W_M

Given the two sets of features F^R, F_o^R shown in Fig. 2, masked features are denoted as $\overline{F^R}, \overline{F_o^R}$ as well. Optimal transport divergence problem can be formulated as

$$L_{mimic} = OT(\overline{F^R}, \overline{F_o^R})$$
$$= W_M(\overline{F^R}, \overline{F_o^R}) \tag{10}$$
$$\stackrel{def.}{=} \min_{\gamma \in \Pi(u,v)} \langle \gamma, M \rangle_F,$$

where $OT(\overline{F^R}, \overline{F_o^R})$ evaluates the distance between these two distributions. The channel number of $\overline{F^R}$ and $\overline{F_o^R}$ is denoted as C. At first, a critic which attempts to down-sample these two groups features from $C \times H \times W$ to $C \times H' \times W'$ with only one convolution layer is utilized and channel dimension is kept unchanged. The changed features are denoted as $\widetilde{F^R}, \widetilde{F_o^R}$. Concrete illustrations can be found in Fig. 5(b). $\widetilde{F^R}, \widetilde{F_o^R}$ are then reshaped into $C \times k$ and $k = H' \times W'$. When it comes to the computation of W_M, we take the same policy as [9,15] in an iterative manner. Sinkhorn divergence is hence implemented and reduces the computational complexity. Cost M_{ij} is defined as the cosine distance. Illustrations of the algorithm can be found in Algorithm 1. Coefficient ε in Algorithm 1 is set to 0.1 and iteration number R is set to 5 finally.

Compared with correspondence-based manners, OT divergence overcomes the defect of sensitivity to the disturbances from outliers. Compared with KL divergence, for one hand, OT divergence conducts the similarity comparison in a low-dimension feature space. On the other hand, OT divergence relieves the issue of "vanishing gradient" under the circumstances of non-overlapped [2,35] distributions and enforces more strict constraints. The optimal transport assures that distributions between F^R and F_o^R become closer and facilitates the mimicking process.

3.4   Training and Inference

Effectiveness of the algorithm is validated on two backbones Hourglass [21] and HRNet [28]. Erasing and reconstruction submodule is appended at the end of both two backbones.

Loss of the framework can be separated into three parts and denoted as follows:

$$L = L_J + \lambda_o L_o + \lambda_{mimic} L_{mimic}, \tag{11}$$

where $\lambda_o, \lambda_{mimic}$ represent the balancing factors to regulate the proportion of these losses and L_{mimic} represents all the feature mimicking losses mentioned in Sect. 3.2. L_J and L_o take advantages of MSE loss which is a common scheme in human pose estimation. Here, λ_o is taken as 1. Value of λ_{mimic} depends on the loss type. When L2 distance, cosine distance, and OT divergence are accepted, it is endowed with value 0.001. When KL divergence is taken, it is endowed with 100 to achieve better balance.

During inference, heatmaps fetched from the last stack of hourglass and the end of the HRNet are evaluated.

4   Experiments

4.1   Datasets

We evaluate our approach on three widely applied benchmarks, MPII [1], LSP [12] and COCO datasets [16]. MPII dataset contains 25k images with around 40k poses. LSP dataset consists of primal LSP split which contains 2k samples and LSP-extended split which possesses 10k samples. Usually, 1k samples out of the primal LSP dataset are used for test purpose and the other 11k samples are employed for training. COCO serves as one of the largest human pose benchmarks where 200k images are involved with 250k person instances labeled. In our implementation, 150k images with around 150k person instances are included during the training process. The proposed method is evaluated on the validation split where 5000 images are engaged.

4.2   Implementations

Data Augmentation. The experiments conducted on the MPII and LSP dataset take utilization of the same data augmentations scheme as previous works [8,39]. During training, random rotation (±30), color jittering, random scaling and random flipping are adopted. Input resolution is 256 × 256. Experiments on COCO dataset take advantage of completely the same data augmentations as [28] for fair comparison.

Training Schedule. All the experiments are conducted on the platform of Pytorch. For hourglass-based model, we employ RMSProp [31] to optimize the network. Learning rate is initialized with 5.0×10^{-4} and dropped by 10 at the epoch of 150, 170, and 200 with overall 220 epochs. For HRNet-based model, training

Table 1. Evaluation results using PCKh@0.5 as measurement on the MPII test set

Method	Head	Sho.	Elb.	Wri.	Hip	Knee	Ank.	Mean
Insafutdinov et al. [10]	96.8	95.2	89.3	84.4	88.4	83.4	78.0	88.5
Wei et al. [36]	97.8	95.0	88.7	84.0	88.4	82.8	79.4	88.5
Newell et al. [21]	98.2	96.3	91.2	87.1	90.1	87.4	83.6	90.9
Ning et al. [23]	98.1	96.3	92.2	87.8	90.6	87.6	82.7	91.2
Chu et al. [8]	98.5	96.3	91.9	88.1	90.6	88.0	85.0	91.5
Liu et al. [17]	98.4	96.4	92.0	87.9	90.7	88.3	85.3	91.6
Chou et al. [5]	98.2	96.8	92.2	88.0	91.3	89.1	84.9	91.8
Yang et al. [39]	98.5	96.7	92.5	88.7	91.1	88.6	86.0	92.0
Ke et al. [13]	98.5	96.8	92.7	88.4	90.6	89.3	86.3	92.1
Tang et al. [30]	98.4	96.9	92.6	88.7	91.8	89.4	86.2	92.3
Sun et al. [28]	98.6	96.9	92.8	89.0	91.5	89.0	85.7	92.3
Zhou et al. [41]	98.5	96.9	92.8	89.3	91.8	89.5	86.4	92.5
Tang et al. [29]	98.7	97.1	93.1	89.4	91.9	90.1	86.7	92.7
Ours (hg)	98.5	97.0	93.0	89.4	91.7	**90.3**	86.5	92.7
Ours (HRNet-W32)	**98.8**	97.0	92.9	89.1	91.3	89.3	85.8	92.4

Table 2. Performance of our model based on HRNet-w32 over MPII validation split.

Method	Head	Sho.	Elb.	Wri.	Hip	Knee	Ank.	Mean
HRNet	97.03	96.02	90.73	86.62	89.41	86.66	82.45	90.33
HRNet+Ours	97.24	96.50	91.07	86.81	89.55	87.08	83.63	90.71

schedule follows [28]. Learning rate for HRNet-based model is initialized with 1.0×10^{-3} and decayed by 10 at the epoch of 170 and 200. Adam optimizer [14] is adopted in HRNet-based model.

Test Schedule. Test over the MPII, LSP dataset follows [8,30,39] and takes use of six-scale pyramid pattern with flipping. Test over the COCO dataset follows the same procedure as [28] and bounding boxes used are kept the same as [28] as well.

4.3   Benchmark Results

MPII Dataset. Results on the MPII test set can be found in Table 1. Hourglass-based model (8 stacks) is used for test. We can observe that our approach achieves promising results compared with previous state-of-the-art methods. Final PCKh score is 92.7 and the improvement over baseline reaches up to 1.8%.

To validate the effectiveness of the algorithm, we try different backbones and results of HRNet-based methods over MPII validation split can be found in Table 2. For HRNet-based methods, we test on the MPII validation split with

Table 3. Evaluation results using PCK@0.2 as measurement on the LSP dataset

Method	Head	Sho.	Elb.	Wri.	Hip	Knee	Ank.	Mean
Rafi et al. [24]	95.8	86.2	79.3	75.0	86.6	83.8	79.8	83.8
Insafutdinov et al. [10]	97.4	92.7	87.5	84.4	91.5	89.9	87.2	90.1
Wei et al. [36]	97.8	92.5	87.0	83.9	91.5	90.8	89.9	90.5
Chu et al. [8]	98.1	93.7	89.3	86.9	93.4	94.0	92.5	92.6
Liu et al. [17]	98.1	94.0	91.0	89.0	93.4	95.2	94.4	93.6
Yang et al. [39]	98.3	94.5	92.2	88.9	94.4	95.0	93.7	93.9
Chou et al. [5]	98.2	94.9	92.2	89.5	94.2	95.0	94.1	94.0
Tang et al. [29]	98.6	95.4	93.3	89.8	94.3	95.7	94.4	94.5
Ours (hg)	**98.8**	95.2	92.3	89.8	**95.2**	95.5	**94.7**	94.5

Table 4. Results on the COCO validation set.

Method	Backbone	Pretrain	Input Size	Params	GFLOPs	AP	AP^{50}	AP^{75}	AP^M	AP^L	AR
HRNet-W32 [28]	HRNet-W32	N	256 × 192	28.5M	7.10	73.4	89.5	80.7	70.2	80.1	78.9
HRNet-W32 [28]	HRNet-W32	Y	256 × 192	28.5M	7.10	74.4	90.5	81.9	70.8	81.0	79.8
HRNet-W48 [28]	HRNet-W48	Y	256 × 192	63.6M	14.6	75.1	90.6	82.2	71.5	81.8	80.4
Ours	HRNet-W32	Y	256 × 192	29.9M	9.0	75.0	90.4	81.8	71.5	81.9	80.4
Ours	HRNet-W48	Y	256 × 192	66.0M	17.3	75.5	90.7	82.4	72.0	82.4	80.7

flipping and omit the six-scale pyramid testing for fair comparison. Compared with original HRNet which achieves 90.33 PCKh@0.5 score (We re-implement HRNet and the results is almost consistent with the results from official website.), our new algorithm achieves 90.71 PCKh@0.5 score and surpasses primal version by 0.38%. The occlusion-aware siamese network can still improve the performance even based on a strong baseline. Results over test split with 6-scale pyramid test can be found in Table 1, which achieve 92.4 PCKh score.

LSP Dataset. Results of the LSP dataset can be found in Table 3. When training LSP dataset, MPII dataset is included following previous works [8,39]. However, occlusion flag for LSP-extended split is omitted somehow and cannot provide precise supervision for LSP training. To obtain corresponding supervision for occlusion attention map, attention map from model pre-trained on MPII dataset is employed as the ground truth which serves as an approximation. From Table 3, we can observe that our model achieves promising results compared with previous state-of-the-art methods.

COCO Dataset. For COCO dataset, evaluation results on the validation set are illustrated in Table 4. The model is based on primal HRNet and input size is set to 256 × 192. The results displayed of the other works are fetched from [28]. Following completely the same training and testing strategy as HRNet, our HRNet-w32 surpasses the baseline by 0.6 mAP and HRNet-w48 surpasses the baseline by 0.4 mAP.

Table 5. Evaluation results using PCKh@0.5 as measurement on the MPII validation set with respect to the occluded joints and un-occluded joints

Method	Occluded	Un-occluded	Method	Occluded	Un-occluded
Hourglass	72.59	92.06	HRNet	76.21	94.00
Hourglass (ours)	74.31	93.18	HRNet (ours)	77.72	94.19

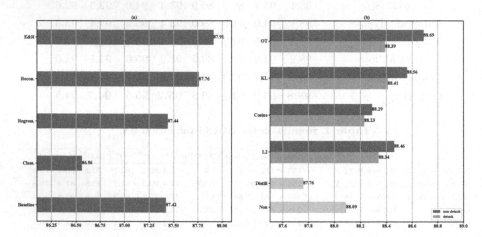

Fig. 6. (a) Effectiveness of the erasing and reconstruction submodule. "Class." means predicting occlusion flag via classification-based methods, "Regress." means predicting occlusion flag leveraging regression-based methods, "Recon." means the reconstruction without cleaning. "E&R" means cooperation of erasing and reconstruction. (b) Effectiveness of different losses of the feature mimicking. "L2", "Cosine", "KL", "OT" are four different losses we adopted in our paper. "Non" represents the omitting of the mimicking loss. "detach" indicates operation of detachment of the un-occluded branch, whilst "non-detach" indicates the omitting of the detachment.

Improvement Over Occluded and Un-occluded Human Joints. Table 5 demonstrates the overall improvement over occluded and un-occluded human joints. The models are based on 2-stack hourglass model and HRNet. Improvement over occluded joints based on hourglass model is 1.72. The algorithm improves the performance over occluded joints. In contrast, the improvements over un-occluded joints is 1.12. These improvements can be ascribed to the reconstruction model which also benefits the un-occluded joints due to the capturing of more semantics. When utilizing HRNet as backbone, we can observe that improvement over occluded human joints makes the main contribution to the performance boosting. Progress over occluded human joints reaches about 1.51 PCKh score while progress over un-occluded human joints is only 0.19. From Table 5, we can observe that the algorithm improves the performance of occluded human joints across different backbones.

4.4   Ablation Study

We conduct the ablation study on the validation split of the MPII dataset and take 2-stack hourglass model whose result serves as the baseline as backbone. All the evaluation results are tested with single scale image and flipping operation is not involved.

Effectiveness of the E&R Submodule. Different forms of the multi-task learning of occlusion prediction cause distinct effects. For classification-based methods shown in Eq. 1, performance drops obviously compared with baseline. In contrast, regression-based approach shown in Fig. 3 maintains the performance and causes non-deterioration. The disparity may primarily come from the large gap of different types losses and we adopt the regression-based methods in the end. The effectiveness of the erasing and reconstruction submodule can be found in Fig. 6(a). We can note that reconstruction without cleaning improves the performance by 0.34%. The improvement mainly originates from the enrichment of context and enlargement of respective field, which confirms the rationality of the reconstructing design. When erasing operation is involved, the improvement promotes further. The erasing procedure excludes enormous interferences and thus benefits reconstruction process.

Effectiveness of the OT Divergence. Effectiveness of different losses of the feature mimicking can be found in Fig. 6(b). For each loss listed in Fig. 6(b), we investigate two different formats of the mimicking. The first format means the feature of the un-occluded branch is detached to provide supervision for the occluded branch, yet the second format which is denoted as "non-detach" means that feature of the un-occluded branch is not detached and back propagated together with occluded branch to update the parameters of the network.

If L2 loss is adopted, PCKh score of the whole framework reaches up to 88.46 without "detach" operation and 88.34 with "detach" operation. If we utilize cosine distance, PCKh score reaches up to 88.23 with "detach" operation and 88.46 without "detach" operation. Both of these two methods improve the performance, which verifies the effectiveness of mimicking mechanism.

When KL divergence is applied as loss to narrow the gap between distributions, performance can be improved to 88.41 PCKh score with "detach" operation and 88.56 without "detach" operation. If optimal transport divergence is involved, performance can be further boosted up to 88.39 PCKh score with "detach" operation and 88.69 PCKh score without "detach" operation.

We can notice that distribution-based methods outperform correspondence-based approaches overall, which confirms our conjecture that narrowing the correspondence discrepancy over high-dimension feature space seems less efficient. From Fig. 6(b), variants without "detach" operation generally exceed those with "detach" operation. This can be ascribed to the unprecise supervised signal at the early stage. Among these approaches, OT without "detach" operation achieves the best performance and certifies the effectiveness. If we omit the feature mimicking loss and retrain model, which is displayed as "Non" in Fig. 6(b), PCKh score of this variant reaches 88.09 and the improvement over the E&R submodule mainly comes from the data augmentation. However, it is not the main concern of this work. If we utilize distillation to replace the siamese framework, we can notice that distillation-based approach results in no improvement at all. For visualization, we provide several examples shown in Fig. 1. Predictions under severe occlusions get improved via our approach.

5   Conclusion

The paper proposes an occlusion-aware siamese network for human pose estimation. Firstly, erasing and reconstruction submodule is utilized to erase and reconstruct the occluded features. Secondly, to improve the quality of reconstruction, we propose the siamese framework which enforces the occluded branch to mimic the behavior of the occluded branch. Finally, we employ optimal transport divergence to narrow the distribution discrepancy of these two branches. We conduct our method on three widely used human pose benchmarks and achieve promising results.

Acknowledgements. This work was supported by the Research and Development Projects in the Key Areas of Guangdong Province (No.2019B010153001), National Natural Science Foundation of China under Grants 61772527, 61976520 and 61806200. This work was also supported by the Technology Cooperation Project of Application Laboratory, Huawei Technologies Co., Ltd. (FA2018111061-2019SOW05).

References

1. Andriluka, M., Pishchulin, L., Gehler, P., Schiele, B.: 2D human pose estimation: new benchmark and state of the art analysis. In: Proceedings of the IEEE Conference on computer Vision and Pattern Recognition, pp. 3686–3693 (2014)
2. Chen, L., et al.: Symmetric variational autoencoder and connections to adversarial learning. In: International Conference on Artificial Intelligence and Statistics, pp. 661–669 (2018)
3. Chen, Y., Wang, Z., Peng, Y., Zhang, Z., Yu, G., Sun, J.: Cascaded pyramid network for multi-person pose estimation. In: Proceedings of the IEEE Conference on Computer Vision and Pattern Recognition, pp. 7103–7112 (2018)
4. Chen, Y., Shen, C., Wei, X.S., Liu, L., Yang, J.: Adversarial PoseNet: a structure-aware convolutional network for human pose estimation. In: Proceedings of the IEEE International Conference on Computer Vision, pp. 1212–1221 (2017)
5. Chou, C.J., Chien, J.T., Chen, H.T.: Self adversarial training for human pose estimation. arXiv preprint arXiv:1707.02439 (2017)
6. Chu, X., Ouyang, W., Li, H., Wang, X.: Structured feature learning for pose estimation. In: Proceedings of the IEEE Conference on Computer Vision and Pattern Recognition, pp. 4715–4723 (2016)
7. Chu, X., Ouyang, W., Wang, X., et al.: CRF-CNN: modeling structured information in human pose estimation. In: Advances in Neural Information Processing Systems, pp. 316–324 (2016)
8. Chu, X., Yang, W., Ouyang, W., Ma, C., Yuille, A.L., Wang, X.: Multi-context attention for human pose estimation. In: Proceedings of the IEEE Conference on Computer Vision and Pattern Recognition, pp. 1831–1840 (2017)

9. Genevay, A., Peyré, G., Cuturi, M.: Learning generative models with Sinkhorn divergences. arXiv preprint arXiv:1706.00292 (2017)

10. Insafutdinov, E., Pishchulin, L., Andres, B., Andriluka, M., Schiele, B.: DeeperCut: a deeper, stronger, and faster multi-person pose estimation model. In: Leibe, B., Matas, J., Sebe, N., Welling, M. (eds.) ECCV 2016. LNCS, vol. 9910, pp. 34–50. Springer, Cham (2016). https://doi.org/10.1007/978-3-319-46466-4_3

11. Jain, A., Tompson, J., Andriluka, M., Taylor, G.W., Bregler, C.: Learning human pose estimation features with convolutional networks. arXiv preprint arXiv:1312.7302 (2013)

12. Johnson, S., Everingham, M.: Clustered pose and nonlinear appearance models for human pose estimation. In: BMVC, vol. 2, p. 5. Citeseer (2010)

13. Ke, L., Chang, M.-C., Qi, H., Lyu, S.: Multi-scale structure-aware network for human pose estimation. In: Ferrari, V., Hebert, M., Sminchisescu, C., Weiss, Y. (eds.) ECCV 2018. LNCS, vol. 11206, pp. 731–746. Springer, Cham (2018). https://doi.org/10.1007/978-3-030-01216-8_44

14. Kingma, D.P., Ba, J.: Adam: a method for stochastic optimization. arXiv preprint arXiv:1412.6980 (2014)

15. Li, H., Dai, B., Shi, S., Ouyang, W., Wang, X.: Feature intertwiner for object detection. In: International Conference on Learning Representations (2018)

16. Lin, T.-Y., et al.: Microsoft COCO: common objects in context. In: Fleet, D., Pajdla, T., Schiele, B., Tuytelaars, T. (eds.) ECCV 2014. LNCS, vol. 8693, pp. 740–755. Springer, Cham (2014). https://doi.org/10.1007/978-3-319-10602-1_48

17. Liu, W., Chen, J., Li, C., Qian, C., Chu, X., Hu, X.: A cascaded inception of inception network with attention modulated feature fusion for human pose estimation. In: AAAI (2018)

18. Lu, Y., Chen, L., Saidi, A.: Optimal transport for deep joint transfer learning. arXiv preprint arXiv:1709.02995 (2017)

19. Marras, I., Palasek, P., Patras, I.: Deep globally constrained MRFs for human pose estimation. In: Proceedings of the IEEE International Conference on Computer Vision, pp. 3466–3475 (2017)

20. Moeslund, T.B., Granum, E.: A survey of computer vision-based human motion capture. Comput. Vis. Image Underst. **81**(3), 231–268 (2001)

21. Newell, A., Yang, K., Deng, J.: Stacked hourglass networks for human pose estimation. In: Leibe, B., Matas, J., Sebe, N., Welling, M. (eds.) ECCV 2016. LNCS, vol. 9912, pp. 483–499. Springer, Cham (2016). https://doi.org/10.1007/978-3-319-46484-8_29

22. Nie, X., Feng, J., Zuo, Y., Yan, S.: Human pose estimation with parsing induced learner. In: Proceedings of the IEEE Conference on Computer Vision and Pattern Recognition, pp. 2100–2108 (2018)

23. Ning, G., Zhang, Z., He, Z.: Knowledge-guided deep fractal neural networks for human pose estimation. IEEE Trans. Multimedia **20**(5), 1246–1259 (2018)

24. Rafi, U., Leibe, B., Gall, J., Kostrikov, I.: An efficient convolutional network for human pose estimation. In: BMVC, vol. 1, p. 2 (2016)

25. Salimans, T., Zhang, H., Radford, A., Metaxas, D.: Improving GANs using optimal transport. arXiv preprint arXiv:1803.05573 (2018)

26. Shi, L., Zhang, Y., Cheng, J., Lu, H.: Skeleton-based action recognition with directed graph neural networks. In: Proceedings of the IEEE Conference on Computer Vision and Pattern Recognition, pp. 7912–7921 (2019)

27. Su, C., Li, J., Zhang, S., Xing, J., Gao, W., Tian, Q.: Pose-driven deep convolutional model for person re-identification. In: Proceedings of the IEEE International Conference on Computer Vision, pp. 3960–3969 (2017)

28. Sun, K., Xiao, B., Liu, D., Wang, J.: Deep high-resolution representation learning for human pose estimation. In: Proceedings of the IEEE Conference on Computer Vision and Pattern Recognition, pp. 5693–5703 (2019)

29. Tang, W., Wu, Y.: Does learning specific features for related parts help human pose estimation? In: Proceedings of the IEEE Conference on Computer Vision and Pattern Recognition, pp. 1107–1116 (2019)

30. Tang, W., Yu, P., Wu, Y.: Deeply learned compositional models for human pose estimation. In: Ferrari, V., Hebert, M., Sminchisescu, C., Weiss, Y. (eds.) ECCV 2018. LNCS, vol. 11207, pp. 197–214. Springer, Cham (2018). https://doi.org/10.1007/978-3-030-01219-9_12

31. Tieleman, T., Hinton, G.: Lecture 6.5-RMSprop: divide the gradient by a running average of its recent magnitude. COURSERA Neural Netw. Mach. Learn. **4**(2), 26–31 (2012)

32. Tompson, J., Goroshin, R., Jain, A., LeCun, Y., Bregler, C.: Efficient object localization using convolutional networks. In: Proceedings of the IEEE Conference on Computer Vision and Pattern Recognition, pp. 648–656 (2015)

33. Tompson, J.J., Jain, A., LeCun, Y., Bregler, C.: Joint training of a convolutional network and a graphical model for human pose estimation. In: Advances in Neural Information Processing Systems, pp. 1799–1807 (2014)

34. Toshev, A., Szegedy, C.: DeepPose: human pose estimation via deep neural networks. In: Proceedings of the IEEE Conference on Computer Vision and Pattern Recognition, pp. 1653–1660 (2014)

35. Wang, W., Xu, H., Wang, G., Wang, W., Carin, L.: An optimal transport framework for zero-shot learning. arXiv preprint arXiv:1910.09057 (2019)

36. Wei, S.E., Ramakrishna, V., Kanade, T., Sheikh, Y.: Convolutional pose machines. In: Proceedings of the IEEE Conference on Computer Vision and Pattern Recognition, pp. 4724–4732 (2016)

37. Xiao, B., Wu, H., Wei, Y.: Simple baselines for human pose estimation and tracking. In: Ferrari, V., Hebert, M., Sminchisescu, C., Weiss, Y. (eds.) ECCV 2018. LNCS, vol. 11210, pp. 472–487. Springer, Cham (2018). https://doi.org/10.1007/978-3-030-01231-1_29

38. Yan, S., Xiong, Y., Lin, D.: Spatial temporal graph convolutional networks for skeleton-based action recognition. In: Thirty-Second AAAI Conference on Artificial Intelligence (2018)

39. Yang, W., Li, S., Ouyang, W., Li, H., Wang, X.: Learning feature pyramids for human pose estimation. In: 2017 IEEE International Conference on Computer Vision (ICCV), pp. 1290–1299. IEEE (2017)

40. Zhang, H., et al.: Human pose estimation with spatial contextual information. arXiv preprint arXiv:1901.01760 (2019)

41. Zhou, L., Chen, Y., Wang, J., Lu, H.: Progressive bi-c3d pose grammar for human pose estimation. In: AAAI, pp. 13033–13040 (2020)

42. Zhou, L., Chen, Y., Wang, J., Tang, M., Lu, H.: Bi-directional message passing based scanet for human pose estimation. In: 2019 IEEE International Conference on Multimedia and Expo (ICME), pp. 1048–1053. IEEE (2019)

Learning to Predict Salient Faces:
A Novel Visual-Audio Saliency Model

Yufan Liu[1,2], Minglang Qiao[4], Mai Xu[4(✉)], Bing Li[1(✉)], Weiming Hu[1,2,3], and Ali Borji[5]

[1] National Laboratory of Pattern Recognition, CASIA, Beijing, China
bli@nlpr.ia.ac.cn
[2] AI School, University of Chinese Academy of Sciences, Beijing, China
[3] CEBSIT, Beijing, China
[4] The School of Electronic and Information Engineering and Hangzhou Innovation Institute, Beihang University, Beijing, China
maixu@buaa.edu.cn
[5] MarkableAI Inc., New York, USA

Abstract. Recently, video streams have occupied a large proportion of Internet traffic, most of which contain human faces. Hence, it is necessary to predict saliency on multiple-face videos, which can provide attention cues for many content based applications. However, most of multiple-face saliency prediction works only consider visual information and ignore audio, which is not consistent with the naturalistic scenarios. Several behavioral studies have established that sound influences human attention, especially during the speech turn-taking in multiple-face videos. In this paper, we thoroughly investigate such influences by establishing a large-scale eye-tracking database of Multiple-face Video in Visual-Audio condition (MVVA). Inspired by the findings of our investigation, we propose a novel multi-modal video saliency model consisting of three branches: visual, audio and face. The visual branch takes the RGB frames as the input and encodes them into visual feature maps. The audio and face branches encode the audio signal and multiple cropped faces, respectively. A fusion module is introduced to integrate the information from three modalities, and to generate the final saliency map. Experimental results show that the proposed method outperforms 11 state-of-the-art saliency prediction works. It performs closer to human multi-modal attention.

Keywords: Visual-audio · Saliency prediction · Multiple-face video.

Y. Liu, B. Li, W. Hu are with National Laboratory of Pattern Recognition, Institution of Automation, Chinese Academy of Sciences (CASIA), the School of Artificial Intelligence (AI), University of Chinese Academy of Sciences (UCAS) and CAS Center for Excellence in Brain Science and Intelligence Technology (CEBSIT).
Y. Liu and M. Qiao—Equal contribution.

Electronic supplementary material The online version of this chapter (https://doi.org/10.1007/978-3-030-58565-5_25) contains supplementary material, which is available to authorized users.

A. Vedaldi et al. (Eds.): ECCV 2020, LNCS 12365, pp. 413–429, 2020.
https://doi.org/10.1007/978-3-030-58565-5_25

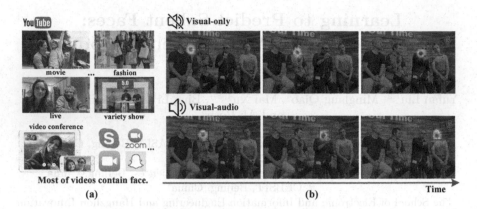

Fig. 1. (a) Thumbnails of various videos over the Internet. Most contain faces. (b) Example of visual attention on a multiple-face video. Four persons are speaking in a sequence from the left to the right. The first row ("visual-only") represents the condition when subjects view only mute frames. The second row ("visual-audio") shows the condition when both visual and audio information is present.

1   Introduction

Saliency prediction [2] is an effective way to model the deployment of possible attention on visual inputs in biological vision system. In the recent years, a surge of interest in video saliency prediction has emerged, partly because of a large number of its applications in various areas. Besides, it can be also found that most videos over the Internet contain faces, as shown in Fig. 1(a). In particular, video conference applications (e.g., Skype and Zoom) have become popular recently, in which almost every frame has human faces. It has been reported [35] that Zoom Video Communications achieved over 39 billion annualized meeting minutes in 2018. Thus, it is necessary to predict saliency on multiple-face videos, since saliency can be used as attention cues for the content based applications, including perceptual video coding [30], quality assessment [17] and panoramic video processing [31].

Most of the video saliency works focus on the visual information and few works have taken auditory information into account. Previous works barely mention soundtracks or explicitly discard them during the eye-tracking experiments. In practice, videos are always played with sound and the world we live in always contains multi-modal information. Human attention is driven by several factors. Two most important ones include visual and auditory cues. As shown in Fig. 1(b), humans focus on different regions in visual-only condition vs. visual-audio condition. They fixate at the salient face and transit to another faster when sound is available. Without sound, people can only rely on visual cue (e.g. motion) to locate the speaking person, leading to slower attention transition. Thus, only considering visual information is not enough to predict where people look.

Table 1. The information of the existing visual-audio eye-tracking databases.

Database	Video Num.	Resolution	Duration	Subject	Details
Coutrot I [5]	60	720 × 576	10–24.8 s	20 (10 per auditory condition)	French; Scenes: one MO (Moving Object), several MO, conversation and landscapes.
Coutrot II [7]	15	720 × 576	12–30 s	72 (18 per auditory condition)	French; Scenes: Conversation
Coutrot III [8]	15	1232 × 504	20–80 s	40	English; Scenes: 4 persons meeting
Pierre et al. [19]	148 (from Coutrot dbs & Hollywood)			averaged 44 each experiment	Scenes: MO, conversation and landscapes
Ours	300	≥ 1280 × 720	10–30 s	34	Chinese & English; 6 kinds of scenes

To address the above shortcomings, we first create a large-scale eye-tracking database dubbed Multiple-face Videos in Visual-Audio condition (MVVA). It includes fixations of 34 subjects viewing 300 videos with diverse content. To the best of our knowledge, so far this is the largest dataset of its kind. During the eye-tracking experiment, both video and audio have been presented to the viewers. Through analysis on our database, we find that faces indeed explain the majority of fixations. We further confirm that audio influences the fixation distribution on faces and attention transition across faces. In particular, human attention in visual-audio condition significantly differs from visual-only condition, when turn-taking takes place. Inspired by these findings, we propose a novel multi-modal network to predict fixations on videos in the visual-audio condition. Our work takes faces, global visual content and audio information into consideration. It consists of three branches, namely visual, audio and face branches, to process these information respectively. Specifically, the visual branch constructs a two-stream architecture to model spatial-temporal visual saliency representation. Without other information, the output of the visual branch can be seen as the saliency map under the visual-only condition. The audio branch encodes the 1D audio signal into a 2D feature map sequence. Additionally, the face branch processes multiple cropped faces and explore the relationship between them. And then it generates a face saliency map. After that, a fusion module is introduced to integrate the three modalities, and to generate the final saliency map. We study the impact of each of these cues individually.

To summarize, our main contributions include:

- We introduce a large-scale eye-tracking database including multiple-face videos with sound, to facilitate the research on visual-audio saliency prediction.
- We present a thorough analysis on our database and study how human attention is affected by multiple factors including face and sound.
- We propose a novel multi-modal network, which fuses visual, face and audio information to obtain effective features for accurate saliency prediction.

2   Related Work

Visual Saliency Prediction. Visual saliency models have been widely developed to predict where people look in images [4,13,21,27,33] or videos [1,12,15,18,20,28,32]. Recently, DNNs have achieved a great success in visual saliency prediction. Over images, some deep saliency models [13,27] use multi-scale visual information to predict saliency. Over videos, most works [15,18,28] combine a CNN and an LSTM to learn spatial and temporal visual features. Bak et al. [1] proposed a two-stream CNN architecture. RGB frames and optical flow sequences were fed to the two streams. Zanca et al. [32] leveraged various visual features, such as face and motion, to predict the fixation scanpath. Recently, some works have focused on predicting saliency over multiple-face videos. Liu et al. [18] presented an architecture which combined a CNN and a multiple-stream LSTM to learn face features. None of the methods above take audio modality into account. In contrast, our approach utilizes both audio and video modalities.

Visual-Audio Saliency Prediction. Only a few methods take the auditory information into account. Early saliency models adopted hand-crafted features. For instance, in [6], low-level features (e.g., luminance information) and faces are used as visual information. Audio is fed into a speaker diarization algorithm to locate the speaking person. A saliency map is then generated by integrating the two modalities. [8] improved this method by taking the body into consideration. These methods rely heavily on the detection algorithms, which limits their performance and usability. Recent works tend to make use of learning-based methods. Tsiami et al. [26] combined a visual saliency model [14] and an audio saliency model [16]. But it only considers the scenario that a simple stimuli moving in clustered images. More recently, [25] used a two-stream 3D-CNN to encode visual and audio information into feature vectors, which are then concatenated to learn the final prediction.

Visual-Audio Databases. Few datasets have been collected for studying visual-audio attention as shown in Table 1. They have three main drawbacks. Firstly, they usually have a small scale. The number of videos in these datasets are typically under 100. Secondly, they contain only one or a few scenes. For example, Coutrot II [7] and Coutrot III [8] only consider eye-tracking events in a specific scene. Thirdly, their videos have low resolution. Coutrot I [5] and Coutrot II [7] contain videos with a 720×576 resolution. Consequently, the existing visual-audio saliency prediction methods are designed under specific conditions (e.g. under a certain scene or a low resolution). The efficiency and generalization of these models need further verification. Driven by these motivations, here we propose a dataset of 300 videos with the resolution of at least 1280×720 over 6 different scenes. Further, we analyze our dataset to reveal the impact of audio on human attention, and give some inspirations for saliency prediction.

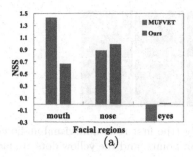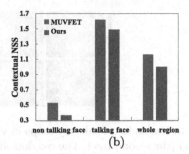

Fig. 2. (a) NSS of saliency on different facial landmarks in visual-only (MUFVET)/visual-audio (Ours) conditions. (b) Contextual NSS of optical flow maps over different face regions.

3 The Proposed Dataset

In this section, we introduce a large-scale eye-tracking database called Multiple-face Video in Visual-Audio condition (MVVA). The proposed dataset contains eye-tracking fixations when both audio and video were presented. To the best of our knowledge, our dataset is the first public eye-tracking database that has multiple-face videos with audio. In addition to saliency, it can be used in other research areas such as sound localization, since the faces of speakers are manually marked in our dataset. Our dataset is publicly available in https://github.com/MinglangQiao/MVVA-Database.

3.1 Data Collection

Stimuli. A total number of 300 videos with 146,529 frames, containing both images and audio, were collected. Among them, 143 videos were selected from MUFVET [18] and other 157 videos were selected from YouTube, with the criterion that the videos should contain obvious faces and audio. All of them were encoded by H.264 with duration varying from 10 to 30 s. Note that these videos are either indoor or outdoor scenes, and can be classified into 6 categories: TV play/movie, interview, video conference, variety show, music and group discussion. The audio content covers different scenarios including quiet scenes (e.g., news broadcasting) and noisy scenes (e.g., interview at subway).

Apparatus. For monitoring the binocular eye movements, an eye tracker, Eye-Link 1000 Plus [24], was used in our experiment. EyeLink1000 Plus is an integrated eye tracker with a 23.8" TFT monitor at screen resolution of 1280×720. During the experiment, EyeLink1000 Plus captured gaze data 500 Hz. According to [24], the gaze accuracy can reach 0.25–0.5 visual degrees in the head free-to-move mode. For more details on EyeLink1000 Plus, see [24].

Participants. 34 participants (21 males and 13 females), aging from 20 to 54 (24 in average), were recruited to participate in the eye-tracking experiment. All

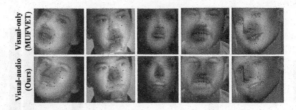

Fig. 3. Examples of saliency maps in visual-only (the first row) and visual-audio condition (the second row). The red dots are fixation points, and the yellow dots are facial landmarks. (Color figure online)

participants had normal or corrected-to-normal vision. It is worth pointing out that only subjects who passed the eye tracking calibration were quantified for the experiment. As a result, 34 subjects (out of 39) were selected in our experiment.

Procedure. During the eye tracking experiment, all subjects were required to sit on a comfortable chair with the viewing distance of ~ 55 cm from the screen. Before viewing the videos, each subject was required to perform a 9-point calibration for the eye tracker. Afterwards, videos were shown in a random order and subjects were asked to view them freely. Note that the audio and video stimuli were presented simultaneously during the experiment. In order to avoid eye fatigue, the 300 videos were equally divided into 6 sessions, and there was a 5-min rest after viewing each session. Besides, a 5-s blank period with a black screen was inserted between each two successive videos for a short break. In total we collected 5,013,980 fixations over all 34 subjects and the 300 videos.

3.2 Database Analysis

Here, we thoroughly analyze our data. To annotate faces and face landmarks in video frame, we used [34] and [22], respectively, and then corrected the predictions manually. The talking/non-talking faces are manually annotated.

Finding 1: Audio Influences the Fixation Distribution on Faces. With the presence of audio, fixation distribution is different from that of visual-only scenario. First, we find that the face saliency distribution in visual-audio condition is slightly more dispersed than that in visual-only condition. We compute the averaged entropy and dispersion [9,19] of each face saliency map, and obtain 10.58 and 44.06 on our MVVA (visual-audio condition), larger than 10.16 and 39.34 of MUVFET (visual-only condition). It may be because people need to focus on mouth to identify the talking face without audio, but do not need that when audio is available. Second, as shown in Fig. 3, in the visual-audio condition, human attention tends to fixate at the center of the face (i.e., near the nose), while people tend to focus on mouth in the visual-only condition. We calculate the Normalized Scanpath Saliency (NSS) between saliency map and different facial landmarks to quantify the correlation between salient regions and facial

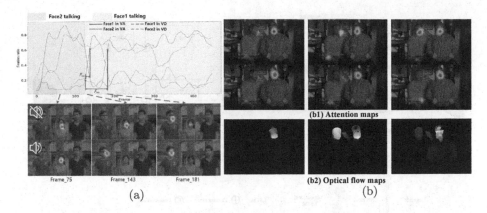

Fig. 4. (a) An example of attention transition in Visual-Only (VO, the first row of heat maps) and Visual-Audio condition (VA, the second row of heat maps). (b1) One video example showing the saliency difference between visual-only condition (the first row) and visual-audio condition (the second row). The person at the right is talking while the other is turning his head. (b2) The corresponding optical flow maps of each frame.

regions in Fig. 2(a). It depicts that saliency maps in our database have the highest NSS values on nose, while on MUFVET the salient region is on mouth. This may be because people do not need to concentrate on the mouth motion, when they can clearly hear the sound. Third, attention transits from mouth/nose to eyes when face becomes larger. We compute NSS of saliency map on facial landmarks, and calculate the Pearson correlation coefficient between the NSS and the normalized face size. We find that the Pearson correlation coefficients between face size and NSS on {eyes, mouth, nose} in order are {0.29, −0.44, −0.12} in our dataset, and {0.54, −0.49, 0.14} in MUFVET. Positive correlation between face size and NSS on eyes reflects more attention on eyes when subjects are viewing larger faces.

Finding 2: In the Turn-Taking Scenes, the Transition of Fixations Across Faces Is Largely Influenced by Audio. Figure 4(a) shows an example of attention transition in the turn-taking scenes. It can be observed that human fixations transit and follow the talking face faster in the visual-audio condition than that in the visual-only condition. Figure 1 also shows the similar observation. For quantitative analysis, we compare the attention transition time in visual-audio and visual-only conditions. We define the attention transition time by the average number of frames that fixations transit to the talking face, when turn-taking happens. Here, F_{va} and F_{vo} denote the attention transition time in MVVA (visual-audio condition) and MUVFET (visual-only condition), respectively. The results of F_{va} and F_{vo} are 30 and 24 frames. Thus, the attention transition time in visual-audio condition is shorter than that in visual-only condition by 25%. From the above results, we can conclude that the fixations transit across faces are largely influenced by audio.

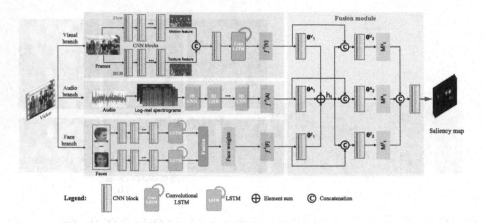

Fig. 5. Overall framework of the proposed method.

Finding 3: Human Attention Is More Influenced by Motion in the Absence of Audio. It is intuitive that people are guided by the visual cues (e.g., motion) more in the visual-only condition, compared to the visual-audio condition. This is because people can only rely on the visual cues to figure out what is going on in the video under the visual-only condition. For instance, in Fig. 4(b), in visual-only condition attention is mostly attracted to the person on the left who is turning his head, while in the visual-audio condition, subjects concentrate on the right speaking person. To quantify the relationship between motion and saliency, we computed the contextual NSS [25] of the optical flow maps on fixations. Figure 2(b) illustrates that human attention correlates more with motion in the visual-only condition.

4   The Proposed Method

According to the findings above, visual information, audio and faces are all important factors that influence human attention. In this section, we introduce our multi-modal saliency method that utilizes these information for predicting fixations over multiple-face videos. Figure 5 summarizes the overall framework of the proposed method. A three-branch neural network is used to integrate multiple information cues and to generate a saliency map. Particularly, a video segment $Video = \{\mathbf{V}, \mathbf{A}, \mathbf{F}\}$, comprising visual frames $\mathbf{V} = \{V_t\}_{t=1}^{T}$, audio signals $\mathbf{A} = \{A_t\}_{t=1}^{T}$ and faces $\mathbf{F} = \{F_t\}_{t=1}^{T}$, is first fed into our multi-modal neural network. Each component of the video segment is conveyed to the corresponding branch of the network. The predicted saliency maps $\mathbf{S} = \{S_t\}_{t=1}^{T}$ are then computed as:

$$\mathbf{S} = f(\mathbf{V}, \mathbf{A}, \mathbf{F}) = \Phi(f^V(\mathbf{V}), f^A(\mathbf{A}), f^F(\mathbf{F})), \tag{1}$$

where $f(\cdot)$ is the proposed model, and $f^V(\cdot), f^A(\cdot), f^F(\cdot)$ are the three branches for visual, audio and face cues, respectively. Besides, $\Phi(\cdot)$ is the fusion module to integrate the three modalities and to generate the final saliency maps.

4.1 Architecture

Visual Branch. Figure 5 shows visual branch constructs a two-stream CNN & convolutional LSTM architecture to model spatial-temporal visual representation. In detail, on the one hand, the frames $\mathbf{V}$ are fed to an RGB sub-branch to obtain the features of texture. On the other hand, frames are fed to a flow sub-branch to get the features of motion. Note that the flow sub-branch is initialized by FlowNet [10] so that it can obtain motion-oriented features. Then, these extracted features are concatenated (denoted as $C(\cdot)$) and are fed to a two-layer convolutional LSTM [29], which is leveraged to process spatial-temporal information. After that, feature maps $f^V(\mathbf{V})$ are obtained as:

$$f^V(\mathbf{V}) = \mathrm{LSTM}(\mathrm{C}(g_1(\mathbf{V}), g_2(\mathbf{V}))). \tag{2}$$

Note that $g_1(\cdot)$ represents the RGB sub-branch, consisting of four CNN blocks of VGG-16 [23]. And $g_2(\cdot)$ denotes the flow sub-branch, which comprises three CNN blocks and one deconvolutional layer of FlowNet.

Audio Branch. In audio branch, a frequency domain based 3D-CNN is designed to convolute 1D audio signal by converting it to 2D spectrum. As such, the spectrum can be better integrated with 2D image features. In detail, the audio signal is first re-sampled to $22\,\mathrm{kHz}$ and is then transformed to log-mel spectrogram using Short-Time Fourier Transform (STFT) and mel-mapping [11], with a hop length of 512. To be consistent with the visual frame, the log-mel spectrogram is converted into a sequence of successive overlapping frames, and is cropped in a $(-230, 230]$ ms window. After that, 4-layer 3D-CNNs $g_{3d}(\cdot)$ are embedded to encode the log-mel spectrogram sequence and to obtain the audio feature maps:

$$f^A(\mathbf{A}) = g_{3d}(\mathrm{STFT}(\mathbf{A})). \tag{3}$$

Face Branch. In face branch, a dynamic multi-stream spatial-temporal LSTM model is designed for exploring relationship between multi-faces with features interacting with each other. Figure 6(a) gives a detailed illustration of the face branch. Firstly, given a sequence of video frames, the MTCNN face detector [34] is leveraged to detect and crop faces. Secondly, N cropped faces are fed into N parameter-shared sub-branches containing an 13-layer CNNs and a 2-layer LSTM, and are transformed to N feature vectors. After that, these features are fused by the fusion part of face branch, which helps face features to capture the correlation and competition with each other. Hence, each face sub-branch perceives the sufficient information and we can obtain N face saliency weights: $\mathbf{w}_1 = \{w_{1,t}\}_{t=1}^T, \mathbf{w}_2, ..., \mathbf{w}_N$. Larger weight for a face means that it is more salient.

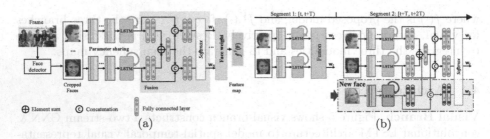

Fig. 6. (a) Structure of face branch. (b) An example of face branch processing variant face numbers.

Finally, we calculate the face feature map $f^F(F_t)$ at the t-th frame as follows,

$$f^F(F_t) = \sum_{n=1}^{N} w_{n,t} \cdot \mathcal{N}_{n,t}. \tag{4}$$

Here, we follow [18] to regard saliency on the n-th face as a Gaussian distribution $\mathcal{N}_{n,t}(\mu_{n,t}, \Sigma_{n,t})$[1].

The parameter-sharing architecture can process videos with different face numbers. As shown in Fig. 6(b), a new CNN-LSTM stream is instantiated when there is a new face appearing in the video. To be specific, we use PyTorch to instantiate CNN-LSTM streams with different number at each iteration.

In the training process, firstly we pre-train the face branch. The fixation proportion of the n-th face to all faces at frame t (denoted as $w_{n,t}$) is taken as the Ground Truth (GT) weight to supervise the predicted face saliency weight (denoted as $\hat{w}_{n,t}$). Hence, the optimization can be formulated as

$$\min \sum_{t=1}^{T} \sum_{n=1}^{N} ||\hat{w}_{n,t} - w_{n,t}||_2^2, \quad s.t. \sum_{n=1}^{N} \hat{w}_{n,t} = 1. \tag{5}$$

Fusion. After encoding each video modality to feature maps, the proposed model integrates visual, audio and face feature maps together to learn a joint representation. We propose a fusion module depicted in Fig. 5, instead of direct concatenation. Given visual, audio and face feature maps $\{f^F(V_t), f^F(A_t), f^F(F_t)\}$, the fusion module performs the computations below:

$$\begin{aligned}
\mathrm{M}_t^V &= \Theta_2^V * \mathrm{C}(h_t, f^V(V_t)), \\
\mathrm{M}_t^A &= \Theta_2^A * \mathrm{C}(h_t, f^A(A_t)), \\
\mathrm{M}_t^F &= \Theta_2^F * \mathrm{C}(h_t, f^F(F_t)), \\
s.t. \quad h_t &= \Theta_1^V * f^F(V_t) + \Theta_1^A * f^F(A_t) + \Theta_1^F * f^F(F_t).
\end{aligned} \tag{6}$$

Note that the Θs are the parameters of different CNN blocks, which align multimodal features with different scales and receptive fields (e.g., visual branch outputs global features while face branch outputs local features). And '$*$' denotes

---

[1] $\mathcal{N}_{n,t}(\mathbf{x}) = \exp\{-\frac{1}{2}(\mathbf{x} - \mu_{n,t})^T \Sigma_{n,t}^{-1}(\mathbf{x} - \mu_{n,t})\}$.

Table 2. Accuracy of saliency prediction by our method and 11 competing methods over different datasets.

		Ours	TASED	SAM_res	SAM_vgg	Liu	ACLNet	DeepVS	SalGAN	Coutrot	SALICON	OBDL	BMS	G-Eymol
MVVA	AUC	**0.905**	0.905	0.897	0.896	0.893	0.889	0.890	0.891	0.869	0.866	0.786	0.765	0.615
	NSS	**3.976**	3.319	3.495	3.466	3.279	3.437	3.270	2.650	2.604	2.523	1.342	0.936	0.551
	CC	**0.722**	0.653	0.634	0.634	0.625	0.639	0.615	0.539	0.509	0.477	0.273	0.193	0.125
	KL	**0.823**	0.970	1.004	1.012	1.098	1.044	1.117	1.234	1.557	1.447	1.995	2.051	4.253
Coutrot II [7]	AUC	**0.922**	0.877	0.905	0.849	0.908	0.848	0.896	0.900	0.883	0.865	0.723	0.751	0.698
	NSS	**3.568**	2.731	3.446	3.306	2.833	3.127	3.058	2.286	3.033	2.408	0.730	0.739	0.884
	CC	**0.639**	0.545	0.607	0.593	0.585	0.521	0.556	0.553	0.606	0.433	0.181	0.153	0.162
	KL	**0.915**	1.271	1.031	1.093	1.035	1.357	1.209	1.717	1.428	1.514	2.228	2.073	2.932

convolution operator and $C(\cdot)$ is the concatenation operation. With help of the fusion module, the three branches can share information and preserve original characteristics of themselves.

4.2 Optimization

To train and optimize the proposed multi-modal network, we use the GT fixation map $\mathbf{G}$, obtained from the fixation density map, to supervise the predicted saliency map $\mathbf{S}$. The loss function is the Kullback-Leibler (KL) divergence between the two maps,

$$\mathbf{L} = \sum_{t=1}^{T} KL(G_t||S_t) = \sum_{t=1}^{T} \sum_{i \in \mathbf{I}} G_t(i) \log \frac{G_t(i)}{S_t(i)}, \tag{7}$$

in which i denotes a position in the 2D saliency map. Note that KL divergence is chosen because Huang et al. [13] have proven that the KL divergence is more effective than other metrics in training DNNs for predicting saliency. To make the convergence speed faster, we pre-train the three branches. In particular, the visual and face branches are pre-trained on MVVA separately. For the visual branch, the RGB sub-branch is initialized with VGG parameters on ImageNet, while the Flow sub-branch is initialized with FlowNet parameters. The face branch is also initialized with VGG. Then, the audio branch is pre-trained jointly with the visual branch, since only audio cannot locate salient faces.

5   Experiments and Results

5.1   Settings

In our experiment, 300 videos in our MVVA are randomly divided into training (240 videos) and test (60 videos) sets. Specifically, for the visual branch, RGB frames are resized to 256×256. To train the convolutional LSTM, we temporally segment 240 training videos into 9,806 clips, all of which have $T = 12$ frames. For the audio branch, we use the 16-frame segmented log-mel spectrograms which are also resized to 256×256. For the face branch, the resolution of N input faces

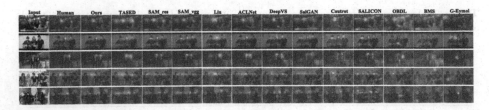

Fig. 7. Saliency maps of 5 videos randomly selected from the test set of our eye-tracking database.

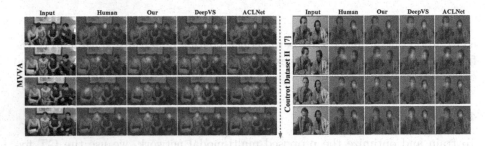

Fig. 8. Saliency maps for different frames of two video sequences, selected from our MVVA and Coutrot II [7].

is 128 × 128. The parameters of the proposed network are updated by using the Stochastic Gradient Descent (SGD) algorithm with Adam optimizer. The initial learning rate is set to be 1e-4.

To evaluate our method, we adopt four metrics: Area Under the receiver operating Characteristic curve (AUC), NSS, Correlation Coefficient (CC), and KL divergence [2]. Note that the larger values for AUC, NSS or CC indicate more accurate saliency prediction. The opposite holds for the KL divergence. Please see [3] for more details on these metrics. All experiments are conducted on a computer with Intel(R) Core(TM) i7-8700 CPU@3.20 GHz, 62.8 GB RAM and 2 Nvidia GeForce GTX 1080 Ti GPUs.

5.2   Performance Comparison

We compare the performance of our multi-modal method with 11 state-of-the-art saliency prediction methods, including TASED [20], SAM [4], Liu [18], ACLNet [28], DeepVS [15], SalGAN [21], SALICON [13], Coutrot [8], OBDL [12], BMS [33] and G-Eymol [32]. Among them, SalGAN, SALICON, SAM and BMS are state-of-the-art saliency prediction methods over images, and others are for videos. SAM has two versions, including SAM_res with ResNet backbone and SAM_vgg with VGGNet backbone. Note that Coutrot and Liu focus on multiple-face videos. In Coutrot, static saliency map, dynamic saliency map, speaker map and center bias map are weighted with estimated weights, and merged into the final saliency map. To eliminate the influence of the feature extraction algo-

Table 3. Performance of different modules in our model.

	Models	CC	KL	NSS	AUC
Different modules	Visual (RGB only)	0.527	1.324	2.728	0.860
	Visual (Flow only)	0.510	1.354	2.631	0.869
	Visual (RGB+flow)	0.632	1.043	3.358	0.893
	Visual (RGB+flow+LSTM)	0.671	0.971	3.548	0.896
	Visual+audio	0.712	0.843	3.838	0.907
	Face only	0.569	1.292	2.766	0.872
	Face+audio	0.609	1.116	3.211	0.878
	Visual+audio+face	**0.722**	**0.823**	**3.976**	**0.905**

rithm (e.g., face/speaking detection), we re-implement Coutrot *et al.* method with manual annotated features and treat the performance as the upper bound of Coutrot *et al.* Liu is the latest DL based method for multiple-face videos, but it ignores the audio information. Besides, face is also considered in G-Eymol as a semantic-based feature. To effectively assess the power of our method, we test it on different databases as follows.

Evaluation on Our Dataset. Table 2 presents AUC, NSS, CC and KL divergence for the proposed method versus 11 competing methods. Scores are averaged over 60 test videos in our eye-tracking database. As shown in this table, the proposed method performs significantly better than all other methods over all 4 metrics. Specifically, compared with the best competing result, our method achieves over 0.481, 0.069 and 0.147 improvements in NSS, CC and KL, respectively. The main reasons for this result are: 1) Most of state-of-the-art methods do not consider audio information, while our method does utilize audio cue for saliency prediction, 2) The face temporal subnet of our method learns detailed face features to predict salient faces, and 3) Our fusion module effectively integrates the multi-modal information.

Next, we compare models qualitatively. Figure 7 demonstrates saliency maps over 5 randomly selected videos in the test set, predicted by the proposed method and 11 other methods. As is shown, our method is capable of locating the salient faces. Its prediction is much closer to the GT. Besides, the proposed method shows excellent performance on predicting attention transition, as depicted in Fig. 8. In contrast, most of the other methods fail to accurately predict the regions that attract human attention, perhaps because these methods do not consider extra information such as sound and face.

Evaluation on Generalization Ability. To evaluate the generalization capability of the proposed method, we further evaluate our method and 11 other methods on the Coutrot II database [7]. Table 2 compares the average AUC, NSS, CC and KL scores. As shown in this table, the proposed method again outperforms all the competing methods. In particular, there are at least 0.032 and 0.116 improvements in CC and KL, respectively. Such improvements are

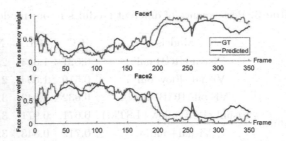

Fig. 9. Face saliency weights across frames for a randomly selected video.

comparable to those in our MVVA. Qualitative results, shown in Fig. 8, shows the proposed method predicts attention transition accurately, while other methods miss salient faces. These results demonstrate the generalization capability of our method in video saliency prediction.

5.3   Ablation Analysis

Here, we thoroughly analyze the effectiveness of each module in our method.

Visual Branch. Visual branch uses basic visual information, i.e., texture, motion and temporal cues, to predict saliency. We evaluate the visual branch of the proposed network and report the results in Table 3. It shows that visual branch reaches to CC of 0.632 and KL of 1.043, which is better than many methods and comparable with the best competing method TASED. When adding convolutional LSTM to fuse the temporal cues, the performance reaches to 0.671 in CC and 0.971 in KL. Hence, the entire visual branch and its components are all useful to saliency prediction. Moreover, as shown in Table 3, combination of face and audio results in lower performance than combining all cues (i.e., the whole network, visual+audio+face) by a large margin. It further manifests the effectiveness of visual branch. We add visual branch, because there are still some other regions drawing attention, besides faces.

Audio Branch. Besides visual branch, we add audio branch to the framework. With the help of the audio branch, the visual-audio model achieves 0.712 in CC and 0.843 in KL, much better than the visual branch. In addition, the combination of face and audio branches improves the performance of the single face branch, by 0.040 in CC and 0.176 in KL. Thus, these results manifest the contribution of audio information and the effectiveness of the proposed audio branch.

Face Branch. Finally, the face branch is added to complete the whole network. From Table 3, CC of 0.722 and KL of 0.823 are reached, after combining face branch with visual-audio model. It is worth mentioning that the single face branch can only achieve a fair performance, which is inferior to other combinations. Hence, single face branch cannot reach the best accuracy, even most attention is attracted by faces. In addition, since the face branch aims at predicting saliency weight of faces across the video frames, we plot the face saliency weights of the proposed face branch and GT in Fig. 9. In this figure, the curve of the face branch fits close to the curve of GT. It can be concluded that the face branch accurately predicts the salient face and further enhances the performance of the proposed model.

In summary, the ablation analysis manifests the necessity of different cues for saliency prediction, and verifies the effectiveness of each part in our model. More details can be found in the supplementary document.

6 Conclusion

In this paper, we explored how audio influences human attention in multiple-face videos. Various findings have been verified by the statistical analysis on our new eye-tracking database. To predict multiple-face video saliency, we presented a novel multi-modal network consisting of visual, audio and face branches. The three branches encode visual frames, audio spectrograms and faces into feature maps, respectively. A fusion module was designed to integrate the three modalities, and to generate the final saliency map. Finally, experimental results shown that our method outperforms 11 state-of-the-art methods over several datasets.

Acknowledgement. This work is supported by Beijing Natural Science Foundation (Grant No. L172051, JQ18018), the Natural Science Foundation of China (Grant No. 61902401, 61972071, 61751212, 61721004, 61876013, 61922009, 61573037 and U1803119), the NSFC-general technology collaborative Fund for basic research (Grant No. U1636218, U1936204), CAS Key Research Program of Frontier Sciences (Grant No. QYZDJ-SSW-JSC040), CAS External cooperation key project, and NSF of Guangdong (No. 2018B030311046). Bing Li is also supported by CAS Youth Innovation Promotion Association.

References

1. Bak, C., Kocak, A., Erdem, E., Erdem, A.: Spatio-temporal saliency networks for dynamic saliency prediction. IEEE Trans. Multimedia **20**(7), 1688–1698 (2017)
2. Borji, A.: Saliency prediction in the deep learning era: an empirical investigation. arXiv preprint arXiv:1810.03716 (2018)
3. Bylinskii, Z., Judd, T., Oliva, A., Torralba, A., Durand, F.: What do different evaluation metrics tell us about saliency models? IEEE Trans. Pattern Anal. Mach. Intell. (2018)
4. Cornia, M., Baraldi, L., Serra, G., Cucchiara, R.: Predicting human eye fixations via an LSTM-based saliency attentive model. IEEE Trans. Image Process. **27**(10), 5142–5154 (2018)
5. Coutrot, A., Guyader, N.: Toward the introduction of auditory information in dynamic visual attention models. In: International Workshop on Image Analysis for Multimedia Interactive Services, pp. 1–4. IEEE (2013)
6. Coutrot, A., Guyader, N.: An audiovisual attention model for natural conversation scenes. In: IEEE International Conference on Image Processing, pp. 1100–1104. IEEE (2014)

7. Coutrot, A., Guyader, N.: How saliency, faces, and sound influence gaze in dynamic social scenes. J. Vis. **14**(8), 5 (2014)
8. Coutrot, A., Guyader, N.: An efficient audiovisual saliency model to predict eye positions when looking at conversations. In: European Signal Processing Conference, pp. 1531–1535. IEEE (2015)
9. Coutrot, A., Guyader, N., Ionescu, G., Caplier, A.: Influence of soundtrack on eye movements during video exploration. J. Eye Mov. Res. **5**(4), 2 (2012)
10. Dosovitskiy, A., et al.: FlowNet: learning optical flow with convolutional networks. In: IEEE International Conference on Computer Vision, pp. 2758–2766 (2015)
11. Hershey, S., et al.: CNN architectures for large-scale audio classification. In: IEEE International Conference on Acoustics, Speech and Signal Processing, pp. 131–135. IEEE (2017)
12. Hossein Khatoonabadi, S., Vasconcelos, N., Bajic, I.V., Shan, Y.: How many bits does it take for a stimulus to be salient? In: IEEE Conference on Computer Vision and Pattern (2015)
13. Huang, X., Shen, C., Boix, X., Zhao, Q.: SALICON: reducing the semantic gap in saliency prediction by adapting deep neural networks. In: IEEE International Conference on Computer Vision (2015)
14. Itti, L., Koch, C., Niebur, E.: A model of saliency-based visual attention for rapid scene analysis. IEEE Trans. Pattern Anal. Mach. Intell. **11**, 1254–1259 (1998)
15. Jiang, L., Xu, M., Liu, T., Qiao, M., Wang, Z.: DeepVS: a deep learning based video saliency prediction approach. In: Ferrari, V., Hebert, M., Sminchisescu, C., Weiss, Y. (eds.) Computer Vision – ECCV 2018. LNCS, vol. 11218, pp. 625–642. Springer, Cham (2018). https://doi.org/10.1007/978-3-030-01264-9_37
16. Kayser, C., Petkov, C.I., Lippert, M., Logothetis, N.K.: Mechanisms for allocating auditory attention: an auditory saliency map. Curr. Biol. **15**(21), 1943–1947 (2005)
17. Li, C., Xu, M., Du, X., Wang, Z.: Bridge the gap between VQA and human behavior on omnidirectional video: a large-scale dataset and a deep learning model. In: ACM International Conference on Multimedia, pp. 932–940 (2018)
18. Liu, Y., Zhang, S., Xu, M., He, X.: Predicting salient face in multiple-face videos. In: IEEE Conference on Computer Vision and Pattern Recognition, pp. 4420–4428 (2017)
19. Marighetto, P., et al.: Audio-visual attention: eye-tracking dataset and analysis toolbox. In: IEEE International Conference on Image Processing, pp. 1802–1806. IEEE (2017)
20. Min, K., Corso, J.J.: TASED-Net: temporally-aggregating spatial encoder-decoder network for video saliency detection (2019)
21. Pan, J., Ferrer, C.C., McGuinness, K., O'Connor, N.E., Torres, J., Sayrol, E., Giro-iNieto, X.: Salgan: Visual saliency prediction with generative adversarial networks. arXiv preprint arXiv:1701.01081 (2017)
22. Ren, S., Cao, X., Wei, Y., Sun, J.: Face alignment at 3000 fps via regressing local binary features. In: IEEE Conference on Computer Vision and Pattern Recognition, pp. 1685–1692 (2014)
23. Simonyan, K., Zisserman, A.: Very deep convolutional networks for large-scale image recognition. arXiv preprint arXiv:1409.1556 (2014)
24. SR-Research: Eyelink 1000 plus. https://www.sr-research.com/products/eyelink-1000-plus/
25. Tavakoli, H.R., Borji, A., Rahtu, E., Kannala, J.: DAVE: a deep audio-visual embedding for dynamic saliency prediction. arXiv preprint arXiv:1905.10693 (2019)

26. Tsiami, A., Katsamanis, A., Maragos, P., Vatakis, A.: Towards a behaviorally-validated computational audiovisual saliency model. In: IEEE International Conference on Acoustics, Speech and Signal Processing, pp. 2847–2851. IEEE (2016)
27. Wang, W., Shen, J.: Deep visual attention prediction. IEEE Trans. Image Process. 27(5), 2368–2378 (2017)
28. Wang, W., Shen, J., Guo, F., Cheng, M.M., Borji, A.: Revisiting video saliency: a large-scale benchmark and a new model. In: IEEE Conference on Computer Vision and Pattern Recognition, pp. 4894–4903 (2018)
29. Xingjian, S., Chen, Z., Wang, H., Yeung, D.Y., Wong, W.K., Woo, W.C.: Convolutional LSTM network: a machine learning approach for precipitation nowcasting. In: Advances in Neural Information Processing Systems, pp. 802–810 (2015)
30. Xu, M., Liu, Y., Hu, R., He, F.: Find who to look at: turning from action to saliency. IEEE Trans. Image Process. 27(9), 4529–4544 (2018)
31. Xu, M., Song, Y., Wang, J., Qiao, M., Huo, L., Wang, Z.: Predicting head movement in panoramic video: a deep reinforcement learning approach. IEEE Trans. Pattern Anal. Mach. Intell. 41(11), 2693–2708 (2019)
32. Zanca, D., Melacci, S., Gori, M.: Gravitational laws of focus of attention. IEEE (2019)
33. Zhang, J., Sclaroff, S.: Exploiting surroundedness for saliency detection: a boolean map approach. IEEE Trans. Pattern Anal. Mach. Intell., 889–902 (2016)
34. Zhang, K., Zhang, Z., Li, Z., Qiao, Y.: Joint face detection and alignment using multitask cascaded convolutional networks. IEEE Signal Process. Lett. 23(10), 1499–1503 (2016)
35. Zoom: Zoom announces lineup of global technology and thought leaders for zoomtopia 2018. https://blog.zoom.us/wordpress/2018/07/11/zoom-announces-lineup-of-global-technology-and-thought-leaders-for-zoomtopia-2018/

NormalGAN: Learning Detailed 3D Human from a Single RGB-D Image

Lizhen Wang⑩, Xiaochen Zhao⑩, Tao Yu⑩, Songtao Wang⑩,
and Yebin Liu⁽⊠⁾⑩

Tsinghua University, Beijing, China
liuyebin@mail.tsinghua.edu.cn

Abstract. We propose NormalGAN, a fast adversarial learning-based method to reconstruct the complete and detailed 3D human from a single RGB-D image. Given a single front-view RGB-D image, NormalGAN performs two steps: front-view RGB-D rectification and back-view RGB-D inference. The final model was then generated by simply combining the front-view and back-view RGB-D information. However, inferring back-view RGB-D image with high-quality geometric details and plausible texture is not trivial. Our key observation is: Normal maps generally encode much more information of 3D surface details than RGB and depth images. Therefore, learning geometric details from normal maps is superior than other representations. In NormalGAN, an adversarial learning framework conditioned by normal maps is introduced, which is used to not only improve the front-view depth denoising performance, but also infer the back-view depth image with surprisingly geometric details. Moreover, for texture recovery, we remove shading information from the front-view RGB image based on the refined normal map, which further improves the quality of the back-view color inference. Results and experiments on both testing data set and real captured data demonstrate the superior performance of our approach. Given a consumer RGB-D sensor, NormalGAN can generate the complete and detailed 3D human reconstruction results in 20 fps, which further enables convenient interactive experiences in telepresence, AR/VR and gaming scenarios.

Keywords: 3D human reconstruction · Single-view 3D reconstruction · Single-image 3D reconstruction · Generation and adversarial networks.

1 Introduction

Reconstructing 3D human from RGB or RGB-D images is a popular research topic with a long history in computer vision and computer graphics for the

Electronic supplementary material The online version of this chapter (https://doi.org/10.1007/978-3-030-58565-5_26) contains supplementary material, which is available to authorized users.

reason of its wide applications in image/video editing, movie industries, VR/AR content creation, etc.

The recent trend of using a single depth camera has enabled many applications especially in 3D dynamic scenes and objects reconstruction [15,34,35]. Using depth images, the depth ambiguity of monocular inputs is resolved as it is straight-forward to calculate the 3D coordinate of each pixel. However, in order to obtain a complete model, traditional reconstruction approaches [6,34] using depth cameras usually require multi-frame information with tedious capture procedures. Moreover, 3D models of the subjects have to maintain a fixed geometric topology in the whole sequence in current fusion-based methods, which limits the ability to handle topology changes during capture. Finally, the tracking-based methods [35] need to fuse multi-frame RGB-D information which will result in over-smoothed geometry and texture.

On the other end of the spectrum, recent progress has shown impressive capability of using learning-based techniques to reconstruct 3D human from a single RGB image [4,21,28,38]. However, current learning-based methods pay more attention on learning shapes but not surface details of the subject, which makes them struggle from recovering 3D models with complete geometric details when comparing with multi-view or multi-image-based methods [2,15]. Furthermore, due to the inherent depth ambiguity of a single RGB image, the generated 3D model can not describe the real world scale of the subject. Finally, due to the heavy network and the complicated 3D representation used in current works, it is hard for current learning-based methods to achieve real-time reconstruction performance.

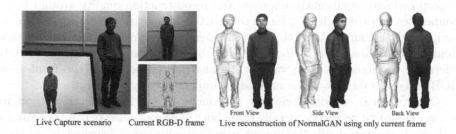

Live Capture scenario   Current RGB-D frame   Front View   Side View   Back View

Live reconstruction of NormalGAN using only current frame

Fig. 1. System setup and live reconstruction result of the current frame. We use a single Kinect V2 sensor for data capture.

The most related work to our method is Moulding Humans [4], which uses a single front-view RGB image to infer front-and-back-view-depth images. Although moulding human generates plausible 3D human reconstruction results, the final output models are over smoothed, lacking geometric details even in the visible regions. Moreover, texture recovery is not considered in Moulding Humans, as well as the real world size of the subject. To overcome the challenges in Moulding Humans, we incorporate depth information into our method, and use front-view RGB-D image as input to infer the back-view RGB-D image.

Although the incorporation of the front-view depth image eliminates the depth ambiguities and provides real world scales, using a single front-view RGB-D image to infer a complete and detailed 3D human model remains challenging. The reasons include: 1) RGB-D images captured by consumer RGB-D sensors always contain severe depth noise, which makes it extremely difficult to extract sharp geometric details while smoothing severe noise, and texture copy artifacts are inevitable even using the most recent learning based depth denoising methods [32]; 2) Although GAN-based methods have shown the capability of inferring the invisible area, they can only generate a reasonably over-smoothed results without any details. Moreover, even with a noise-free depth image, it remains challenging to learn geometric details from depth values directly. Compared with the depth variance on the global body shape, the depth variance around local geometric details is too subtle to "learn" for the deep neural networks. 3) The performance of inferring back-view RGB from front-view RGB is unstable due to the various shading effects coupled in the RGB images.

To tackle the above problems, we propose NormalGAN, a novel adversarial framework conditioned by normal maps. The proposed method can generate high-quality geometry with complete details given a single front-view RGB-D image. Different from previous methods that directly constrain each pixel on the depth maps, NormalGAN also focuses on constraining the adjacent relations of each pixel. Specifically, we use normal maps, in which pixel values change drastically around geometric details, instead of depth images to condition a GAN, and enable the generation of more reasonable and realistic geometric details for both front-view depth denoising and back-view depth inference. Moreover, an RGB-D rectification module based on orthographic projection and neural networks is proposed and significantly improves the reconstruction quality around body boundaries and extremities. The rectified RGB-D images achieve more regular sampling of the human body than the raw perspective projected RGB-D images from sensors. Finally, to further improve the performance of back-view RGB inference, we decompose the various shading information from the front-view RGB images to factor out the misleading impacts of shading variations.

Our technical contributions can be concluded as: 1) A novel method to recover complete geometric details from both the front-view depth (denoising) and the back-view depth (inference) using an adversarial learning framework conditioned by normal maps. 2) An RGB-D rectification module based on orthographic projection and neural networks to enable regular RGB-D sampling of the human body. 3) A method for back-view RGB inference in the intrinsic domain, which further improves the texture inference quality in the invisible area.

2   Related Work

3D Human from RGBD Sequences. For 3D human body modeling, the most intuitive method is to get enough RGB or depth observations from different viewpoints first, and then fuse them together. KinectFusion [9] is the pioneer work in this direction which combines rigid alignment with volumetric depth fusion in an incremental manner. Subsequent works [1,27,36] combined KinectFusion with non-rigid bundling for more accurate reconstruction. Moreover, to handle dynamic scenes, DynamicFusion [15] contributes the first method for real-time non-rigid volumetric fusion. Follow up works keep improving the performance of DynamicFusion by incorporating non-rigid deformation constraints [8,23,24], articulated motion prior [12,34], appearance information [6], and parametric body shape prior [35]. Due to the incremental fusion strategy used in current fusion-based methods, subjects are required to maintain a fixed geometry topology in the whole sequence, which limits the usage of such methods for more general scenarios.

Human Body Reconstruction from a Single Image. Rencent studies focusing on reconstructing a 3D human model from a single image adopt various representations including the parametric human model, depth map, silhouette and implicit function. Primitive approaches require strong priors of parametric human models, which are widely used for human shape and pose estimation [5,13,16,19]. BodyNet [28] first shows the capability of reconstructing a 3D human from only a single image employing SMPL [13] as a constraint. Follow up approaches [11,17] improve the robustness of parameters estimation for challenging images. DeepHuman [38] employs SMPL [13] as a volumetric initialization and achieves stable results for complex poses. The geometric details like clothes folds, hair and facial features are mostly ignored. Recently, Gabeur et al. [4] proposed a novel moulding representation, which divides the whole person into two parts. Employing two depth maps, they transfer the complicated 3D problem to an image-to-image translation problem, which significantly improves efficiency. SiCloPe [14] generates fully textured 3D meshes using a silhouette-based representation. Saito et al. [21] presents PIFu, which recovers high-resolution 3D textured surfaces. PIFu achieves state-of-the-art results by encoding the whole image into a feature map, from which the implicit function infers a textured 3D model. Besides, FACSIMILE [25] reconstructs detailed 3D naked body by directly constraining normal maps, which helps to recover the geometric details of naked bodies. However, the inherent depth ambiguities of 2D-to-3D estimation from RGB images is inevitable.

Depth Denoising. Depth images are widely used in various applications, but consumer depth cameras suffer from heavy noise due to complex lighting conditions, the interference of light and so on. As RGB images usually have higher quality than depth images, many methods focus on enhancing depth images with the support of RGB images. Some methods leverage RGB images by investigating lighting conditions. Shape-from-shading techniques can extract geometric details from RGB images [18,37]. Recent progress has shown that shading information helps to recover geometric details even in uncontrolled lighting conditions, with a depth camera [7,33], or multi-view cameras [30,31]. However, recovering geometric details is still very challenging for traditional schemes due to the unknown reflectance. More recently, Yan et al. [32] proposes DDR-Net to handle this problem with a learning-based framework, which can effectively remove the noise while recovering geometric details in a data-driven way.

Afterwards, Sterzentsenko et al. [26] improves the denoising qualities with multi-view RGB-D images. Despite the efforts, extracting accurate geometric information from RGB images is still a challenge. Our approach tackles this problem by constraining the normal maps in an adversarial network architecture.

3   Overveiw

The overview of our method is shown in Fig. 2. Our method takes a front-view RGB-D image (including a color image C_{pers} and a depth image D_{pers}) as input, where the subscript $_{pers}$ indicates the input RGB-D image was captured using the perspective projection model. We then perform front-view rectification and back-view inference sequentially to get the rectified front-view RGB-D image (output1 and output2 in Fig. 2) and the inferred back-view RGB-D image (output3 and output4 in Fig. 2).

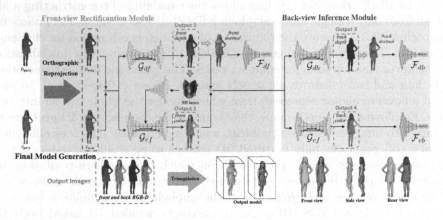

Fig. 2. The overview of our approach.

For the front-view rectification, in order to avoid the artifacts caused by the irregular sampling property of the perspective projection, we first transform the RGB-D image into a colored 3D point cloud, and then render a new RGB-D image using the orthographic projection, which brings a pair of incomplete images, C_{orth} and D_{orth}. To further refine D_{orth}, we use a UNet $\mathcal{G}_{df}$ to inpaint the missing areas after orthographic re-projection, and, more importantly, to remove the severe depth noise. Note that it is difficult to prevent the traditional CNN-based depth denoising networks from over-smoothing the geometric details on the depth map. So we incorporate a discriminator $\mathcal{F}_{df}$, which is conditioned by normal maps, to enforce the adjacency relation of each point on the refined depth map, and finally guides $\mathcal{G}_{df}$ to generate the refined front-view depth (output1) with high-quality geometric details. Finally, to refine C_{orth}, we use the network $\mathcal{G}_{cf}$ and the shading information calculated from the refined depth maps [31] for color inpainting and shading decomposition, and finally get the refined (intrinsic) front-view color image (output2).

For back-view RGB-D inference, we use two CNNs $\mathcal{G}_{db}$ and $\mathcal{G}_{cb}$ combined with two discriminators ($\mathcal{F}_{db}$ and $\mathcal{F}_{cb}$) to infer the back-view depth and color image (output3 and output 4 in Fig. 2), respectively. The discriminator $\mathcal{F}_{db}$ is also conditioned by normal maps as in $\mathcal{F}_{df}$, which helps to generate reasonable and realistic geometric details on the back-view depth image. Moreover, the discriminator $\mathcal{F}_{cb}$ is conditioned by ground truth color, which enforces more plausible back-view color generation.

After getting the front-view and back-view RGB-D image pair (output 1, 2, 3 and 4 in Fig. 2) from our networks, we directly triangulate the resulting 3D points into a complete mesh with vertex color for final model generation (as shown in the bottom of Fig. 2). Note that the final model is relighting-ready benefiting from the intrinsic-domain-color-inference.

4 Method

4.1 Dataset Generation

To generate our training and testing dataset, we use 1000 static 3D scans of clothed people purchased from twindom[1]. 800 of them are used in train-dataset and the other 200 are used to test. While rendering, 800 3D scans are randomly rotated in the range between $-30°$ and $30°$ to enrich our training dataset. To obtain the supervised data of our networks, we first collect a dataset of RGB-D images (C_{pers}, D_{pers}) in the perspective view, together with corresponding ground-truth RGB-D images (C_{gt}, D_{gt}) in the orthographic view. All images are rendered with the resolution of 424×512, which is the same as that of depth maps captured by Kinect v2 sensors. The training code and pre-trained models will be public available. And please note that we cannot release the full training dataset due to business constraints.

In order to make our networks applicable to real data, data augmentation is necessary. Firstly, we simulate the typical noise distribution of Kinect v2 depth cameras (see the left images in Fig. 3). Noticing that real noise distribution has local correlation rather than pixel-wise independence, we apply multiple 2D Gauss kernels on D_{pers}. The standard deviation of Gauss kernels are set as constant and the position of Gauss kernels are uniformly distributed over the image. To simulate the different noise levels of Kinect depth maps, we calculate the amplitude of the above Gauss kernel with the formulation proposed by Péter et al. [3]. Our networks trained on the simulated depth images show stability in Kinect v2 depth images (see the middle images in Fig. 3). Secondly, we render the models with random illuminations to get the more realistic color images, an example can be see in Fig. 3. Finally, we get a training set with 5,600 groups of images and a testing set with 1,400 groups of images in total.

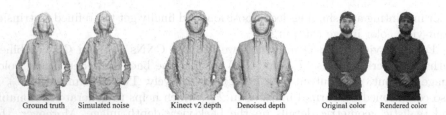

Ground truth   Simulated noise   Kinect v2 depth   Denoised depth   Original color   Rendered color

Fig. 3. Left: we add simulated noise to the ground truth depth map. Middle: the networks trained on our simulated depth images show stability in denoising Kinect v2 depth images. Right: We render the models with random illuminations.

4.2 Front-View RGB-D Rectification

Our method adopts a double-sided representation for human bodies similar to Moulding Humans [4], which facilitates the subsequent processing and is able to speed up with lightweight networks. The representation is based on the assumption of dividing a person into a visible front-view map and an invisible back-view map. However, in the perspective-view images, the visible part is actually smaller than a "half" of a person, which will cause the irregular sampling property. In order to solve the above problem, we first transform the perspective-view RGB-D images (C_{pers} and D_{pers}) into 3D colored point clouds, then re-project them into the orthographic view. And the missing areas in the generated orthographic-view RGB-D images (C_{orth} and D_{orth}) will be filled by the following networks.

To get the complete and denoised front-view depth images, we use a generator $\mathcal{G}_{df}$. The basic structure of $\mathcal{G}_{df}$ is UNet [20], which is commonly used for image-to-image translation tasks. However, it is difficult for a simple UNet to denoise the depth images while preserving the geometric details. So we incorporate a discriminator $\mathcal{F}_{df}$ and use the GAN architecture to enhance the denoising ablity of $\mathcal{G}_{df}$. As the shading information of the input color images indicates the geometric information, we take the color images C_{orth} as input to support the refinement of D_{orth}. However, while training $\mathcal{G}_{df}$ with only depth maps, the output depth images usually become over-smooth and complex textures usually lead to wrong geometric details as the network can not distinguish the geometric details from the texture changes. Even if we use the GAN structure, there is no noticeable change. This is because the depth variance around local geometric details is too subtle compared with the depth variance on the global body, which is also demonstrated by FACSIMILE [25]. However, FACSIMILE mainly focuses on A-pose naked body recovery by directly constraining normal maps with L1 loss, and this can not be used to handle the clothed bodies directly without GAN loss. Therefore, we apply GAN on normal maps to recover geometric details of the clothed bodies. The normal map can be described as

$$\mathbf{N}_i = Norm(\sum_{j,k} Norm((\mathbf{P}_j - \mathbf{P}_i) \times (\mathbf{P}_k - \mathbf{P}_i))) \tag{1}$$

where $\mathbf{N}_i$ is the normal vector of point i, and $\mathbf{P}_i$ is the 3D coordinate of point i. The function $Norm(\cdot)$ normalizes the input vector. Point j is in the clockwise direction of point k relative to point i and both of them belong to the neighborhood of point i.

Obviously, normal maps have noticeable changes around the geometric details compared with depth maps. Additionally, normal maps show the adjacency relations of each point on the depth map, which are important for generating the geometric details. However, note that it is not straightforward to use the normal information as the drastically changing normal values may cause numerical crash during the training process. Therefore, we add additional loss terms for the GAN structure (See Sect. 4.4) and pretrain $\mathcal{G}_{df}$ before joint training. Finally, $\mathcal{F}_{df}$ conditioned by normal maps guides $\mathcal{G}_{df}$ to generate denoised depth maps with geometric details preserved.

Then, to get high-quality textures of human bodies, we use another UNet $\mathcal{G}_{cf}$ to remove the shading from the input C_{orth}. For the color images captured in real-world scenes, various shading effects are coupled in the RGB images, which have great influence on inferring the invisible textures. In order to remove the shading effects, we encode the shading information calculated by the spherical harmonics function [31] from the refined depth images and concatenate it with the tensor of $\mathcal{G}_{cf}$ (See the green network in Fig. 2). Finally, the trained $\mathcal{G}_{cf}$ shows good capability on shading removal and brings the refined (intrinsic) front-view color images.

4.3   Back-View RGB-D Infernence

Obtaining the rectified front RGB-D images, we need to infer the invisible back-view RGB-D images with reasonable details. As it is difficult for traditional CNN-based methods to infer the details, we also use the GAN structure to enhance the inference of our generators. Specifically, for the bakc-view depth inference networks (the generator $\mathcal{G}_{db}$ and the discriminator $\mathcal{F}_{db}$), we still use normal maps to condition the $\mathcal{F}_{db}$ which helps to generate reasonable geometric details. As shown in Fig. 4, our GAN conditioned by normal maps shows great superiority in inferring the geometric details on the back side. Furthermore, the different details of NormalGAN and ground truth eliminate the possibility of over-fitting. For the back-view color inference networks $\mathcal{G}_{db}$ and $\mathcal{F}_{cb}$, we condition the GAN by the ground truth color images, which helps to infer more plausible textures. Moreover, the shading removal of front-view color images shows great influence on the back-view color inference (See Fig. 9). Additionally, due to the orthographic re-projection, the front-view images and the back-view images share the same silhouette, which makes the inference simple but reasonable. Finally, plausible and realistic inferred details are generated in the back-view RGB-D images by our networks.

In the end, after getting the colored 3D point clouds from the front-view and the back-view RGB-D images, we triangulate the points by directly connecting the adjacent points and get the 3D meshes of the human bodies. However, there still remains a gap between front-view and back-view depth boundaries for mesh

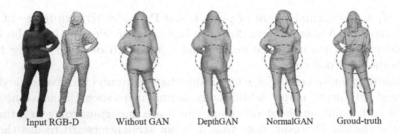

Input RGB-D   Without GAN   DepthGAN   NormalGAN   Groud-truth

Fig. 4. Results of our method without GAN, DepthGAN (GAN conditioned by depth maps) and NormalGAN.

reconstruction. To fill this gap, we first interpolate three points between each boundary pairs (the same pixel on the boundary of front-view and back-view depth images), and then stitch the adjacent points.

4.4   Loss Functions

To ensure the convergence of the above networks, we put independent constraints on each network. First of all, L1-norm term is necessary for typical supervised training process. The L1 loss of the output $\mathbf{X}_{pred}$ and the ground-truth $\mathbf{X}_{gt}$ can be expressed as

$$\mathcal{L}_{L1}(\mathbf{X}) = \|\mathbf{X}_{pred} - \mathbf{X}_{gt}\|_1 \tag{2}$$

To generate more sharp details for color images, we also use the perceptual loss [10]. Here, we use the pretrained VGG19 [22] to extract the features from the color images. Denoting the activations of the ith layer in the VGG network as ϕ_i and representing the weights of the ith loss term with λ_i, the perceptual loss can be expressed as

$$\mathcal{L}_{Perc}(\mathbf{X}) = \sum_i \lambda_i \|\phi_i(\mathbf{X}_{pred}) - \phi_i(\mathbf{X}_{gt})\|_1 \tag{3}$$

For the adversarial parts, the typical GAN loss:

$$\mathcal{L}_{GAN}(\mathbf{X}) = \mathbb{E}_{\mathbf{X}_{gt}}[log\mathcal{F}(\mathbf{X}_{gt})] + \mathbb{E}_{\mathbf{X}_{pred}}[log(1 - \mathcal{F}(\mathbf{X}_{pred}))] \tag{4}$$

is necessary, where the discriminator $\mathcal{F}$ tries to maximize the objective function to distinguish the inferred images from the ground-truth images. By contrast, the generator $\mathcal{G}$ aims to minimize the loss to make the inferred images similar to the ground-truth images.

Trained only with the GAN loss, our GANs usually fail to converge due to the dramatic numerical changes caused by normal maps. So we introduce the feature matching loss inspired by pix2pixHD [29] to further constrain the discriminators. Specifically, we calculate the loss of multi-scale feature maps extracted from the layers of a discriminator. The feature matching loss can effectively stabilize the parameters of the discriminator. We denote the kth-layer feature map of the discriminator as $D_{[k]}$ and the total number of layers as N. The loss can be expressed as:

$$\mathcal{L}_{FM}(\mathbf{X}) = \sum_{k=2}^{T-1} \|D_{[k]}(\mathbf{X}_{pred}) - D_{[k]}(\mathbf{X}_{gt})\|_1 \tag{5}$$

Finally, the loss functions for each network are formulated as

$$\begin{aligned}
\mathcal{L}_{\mathcal{G}_{df}} &= \mathcal{L}_{L1}(D_{front}) + \mathcal{L}_{Perc}(N_{front}) + \mathcal{L}_{FM}(N_{front}) + \mathcal{L}_{GAN}(N_{front}) \\
\mathcal{L}_{\mathcal{G}_{cf}} &= \mathcal{L}_{L1}(C_{front}) + \mathcal{L}_{Perc}(C_{front}) \\
\mathcal{L}_{\mathcal{G}_{db}} &= \mathcal{L}_{L1}(D_{back}) + \mathcal{L}_{FM}(N_{back}) + \mathcal{L}_{GAN}(N_{back}) \\
\mathcal{L}_{\mathcal{G}_{cb}} &= \mathcal{L}_{L1}(C_{back}) + \mathcal{L}_{FM}(C_{back}) + \mathcal{L}_{GAN}(C_{back}) \\
\mathcal{L}_{\mathcal{F}_{df}} &= -\mathcal{L}_{GAN}(N_{front}) \\
\mathcal{L}_{\mathcal{F}_{db}} &= -\mathcal{L}_{GAN}(N_{back}) \\
\mathcal{L}_{\mathcal{F}_{cb}} &= -\mathcal{L}_{GAN}(C_{back})
\end{aligned} \tag{6}$$

5 Experiments

5.1 Ablation Study

The Validity of Data Augmentation. To demonstrate the validity of data augmentation in Sect. 4.1, we train a reference model using the unprocessed dataset for comparison. As shown in Fig. 5, without our simulated noise, the reference network can not clearly remove the noise from the real-captured depth image and the back-view inference becomes unstable. In contrast, the data augmentation solves these problems and significantly improves our applicability for images captured in real scenes.

The Capability of Depth Denoising and Details Preserving. Using normal maps with the GAN structure, the capability of our networks to generate geometric details is significantly improved. For comparison, we train the state-of-the-art depth denoising network, DDRNet [32], on our dataset. As shown in Fig. 6, all the networks achieve effective results in depth denoising. However, from the first row in Fig. 6, we can see that DDRNet, our network without

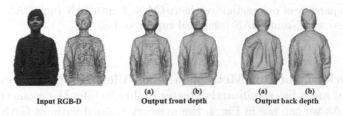

Input RGB-D   (a)   (b)   (a)   (b)
            Output front depth   Output back depth

Fig. 5. (a): Results without using data augmentation. (b): Results using data augmentation. The input RGB-D was captured by a Kinect v2 camera.

Table 1. Quantitative comparisons of depth denoising on our testing set.

Error Metric	MAE	RMSE
Input	7.09	18.70
DDRNet [32]	5.00	7.49
Ours without GAN	4.75	7.38
Our DepthGAN	5.02	7.43
Ours	**4.63**	**7.18**

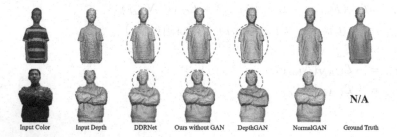

Input Color   Input Depth   DDRNet   Ours without GAN   DepthGAN   NormalGAN   Ground Truth

Fig. 6. Validation of depth denoising on both testing data and real captured data.

GAN, and our GAN conditioned by depth maps (DepthGAN) all suffer from texture-copy artifacts (copying texture changes as geometric details). Besides, the second row shows the ability of our method to preserve more accurate details like facial expressions and wrinkles on the cloth. Finally, Table 1 gives the quantitative comparison on depth denoising accuracy, which further validates the effectiveness of our proposed method.

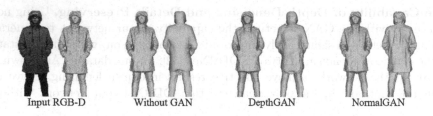

Input RGB-D   Without GAN   DepthGAN   NormalGAN

Fig. 7. Comparsion of our method without GAN, DepthGAN (our GAN input with depth images) and NormalGAN using real captured data.

The Superiority of Our Method in Back-View Depth Inference. GAN with normal maps has significantly greater ability to infer the geometry of invisible areas. As we can see in Fig. 4, the network trained without GAN and even DepthGAN can only generate over-smoothed results for reducing the L1 losses. However, using normal maps, the proposed NormalGAN can produce realistic and reasonable results despite the differences between the inferred details and the corresponding ground truth. Our method with normal maps also achieves more detailed results for images captured in real scenes as shown in Fig. 7.

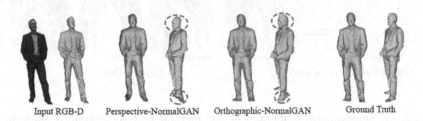

Input RGB-D   Perspective-NormalGAN   Orthographic-NormalGAN   Ground Truth

Fig. 8. Comparison of NormalGAN trained on the perspective-view dataset and the orthographic-view dataset.

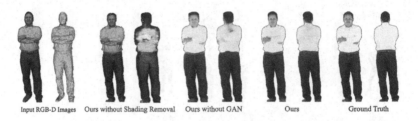

Input RGB-D Images   Ours without Shading Removal   Ours without GAN   Ours   Ground Truth

Fig. 9. Texture results of our method with/without GAN.

Orthographic Reprojection. The orthographic projection helps our method to reconstruct more plausible results around the boundary areas and body extremities. As we can see in Fig. 8, the performance of networks trained under the perspective view decreases around body extremities like hair and feet.

The Effectiveness of Shading Removal. To remove shading from input color images, we encode the geometric information using the SH (spherical harmonics) bases. This module improves the applicability for real captured images. As shown in Fig. 9, the network without shading removal fails to handle the complicated shading caused by cloth wrinkles. Additionally, the shading removal helps to enhance the back-view color inference.

More detailed experiments are presented in the supplementary materials.

5.2   Comparison

Single-image methods. As previous single-image methods to reconstruct the human bodies all take color images as their input, we retrain the methods

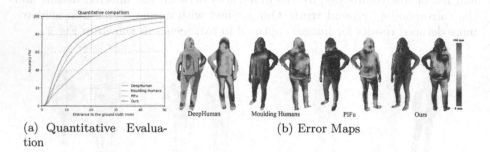

(a) Quantitative Evaluation

(b) Error Maps

Fig. 10. (a) Quantitative evaluation of our method and the retrained single-image methods. (b) Error maps of our method and the retrained single-image methods on one of the testing models. Errors above 100 mm are shown in red. (Color figure online)

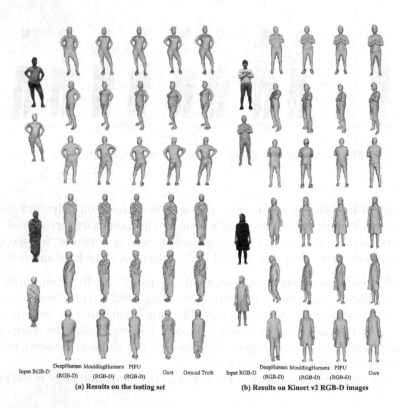

(a) Results on the testing set

(b) Results on Kinect v2 RGB-D images

Fig. 11. We evaluate our approach with the retrained DeepHuman (RGBD) [38], Moulding Humans (RGBD) [4] and PIFu (RGBD) [21] on testing dataset (the first three columns) and images captured by a Kinect v2 depth camera (the last two columns).

on our dataset with RGB-D images. Specifically, for DeepHuman [38], we use depth images to fit more accurate SMPL models as its initialization model. For PIFU [21] and Moulding Humans [4], we retrain the networks with our dataset by concatenating the RGB image and the depth image into a 4-channel RGB-D image as the new input for Moulding Humans and PIFu, which is exactly the same input as ours. Besides, the results of the above methods using RGB only are also presented in our supplementary materials.

As shown in Fig. 11, our approach generate results with more geometric details, which indicates our capability to reconstruct details human models with the support of normal maps. The comparisons on images captured by a Kienct v2 depth camera demonstrate our capability to reconstruct the persons in real scenes. Then, we select 12 models in common poses from our testing set which all methods can generate correct 3D models. As shown in Fig. 10(a), our method also achieve the best result in the quantitative evaluation. Besides, the error maps in Fig. 10(b) also demonstrate the superiority of our method.

Multi-frame RBG-D Methods. We extensively evaluate our method with the volumetric fusion methods DoubleFusion [35] and Guo et al. [6]. The results are presented in the supplementary materials.

5.3 Training Details and Runtime Performance

During the training procedure, we first train the four generators separately to accelerate the convergence. Then, after the convergence of each network, we train them together with the discriminators. The input images are cropped to the resolution of 424×424. All networks converge after 60 epochs of our training set. The training procedure takes about 8 h on four GTX 1080Ti graphics cards. As the discriminators will not calculate in the testing procedure, our testing procedure occupies 3.5-GB GPU memory. Generating a 3D human model takes 50 ms on average using a RTX Titan.

6 Conclusion

In this paper, we have presented NormalGAN, an adversarial learning-based method to reconstruct a complete and detailed 3D human from a single RGB-D image. By *learning details from normal maps*, our method can not only achieve high-quality depth denoising performance, but also infer the back-view depth image with much more realistic geometric details. Moreover, the proposed RGB-D rectification module based on orthographic projection is effective for generating reasonable boundaries, and can be used in other related topics. Finally, with the support of shading removal in the front-view RGB images, we can improve the quality of back-view color inference. A live capture system was implemented and can robustly run at 20 fps, which further demonstrates the effectiveness of our method.

Similar to Moulding Humans [4], NormalGAN is based on the basic assumption of dividing a person into a front-and-back-view image pair. So we can not handle severe self-occlusions. However, this might be solved by combining other representations which are strong on body shape and pose prediction (like the implicit function used in PIFU [21] and the parametric model used in DeepHuman [38]), and our NormalGAN can act as a detail layer generation module to guarantee fully detailed reconstruction. Another direction to tackle this limitation is that using temporal information in RGB-D sequence to recover detailed geometries for current occluded body parts. We believe our method will stimulate future researches on 3D human reconstruction as well as enable more real-scene applications.

Acknowledgement. This paper is supported by the National Key Research and Development Program of China [2018YFB2100500] and the NSFC No.61827805 and No.61861166002.

References

1. Cui, Y., Chang, W., Nöll, T., Stricker, D.: KinectAvatar: fully automatic body capture using a single kinect. In: Park, J.-I., Kim, J. (eds.) ACCV 2012. LNCS, vol. 7729, pp. 133–147. Springer, Heidelberg (2013). https://doi.org/10.1007/978-3-642-37484-5_12

2. Dou, M., et al.: Fusion4D: real-time performance capture of challenging scenes. ACM Trans. Graph. **35**(4) (2016). https://doi.org/10.1145/2897824.2925969

3. Fankhauser, P., Bloesch, M., Rodriguez, D., Kaestner, R., Hutter, M., Siegwart, R.: Kinect v2 for mobile robot navigation: Evaluation and modeling. In: 2015 International Conference on Advanced Robotics (ICAR), pp. 388–394. IEEE (2015)

4. Gabeur, V., Franco, J., Martin, X., Schmid, C., Rogez, G.: Moulding humans: nonparametric 3D human shape estimation from single images. CoRR abs/1908.00439 (2019). http://arxiv.org/abs/1908.00439

5. Guan, P., Weiss, A., Balan, A., Black, M.J.: Estimating human shape and pose from a single image. In: International Conference on Computer Vision, ICCV, pp. 1381–1388 (2009)

6. Guo, K., Xu, F., Yu, T., Liu, X., Dai, Q., Liu, Y.: Real-time geometry, albedo, and motion reconstruction using a single RGB-D camera. ACM Trans. Graph. **36**(3), 32:1–32:13 (2017). https://doi.org/10.1145/3083722

7. Han, Y., Lee, J., Kweon, I.S.: High quality shape from a single RGB-D image under uncalibrated natural illumination. In: International Conference on Computer Vision, pp. 1617–1624 (2013)

8. Innmann, M., Zollhöfer, M., Nießner, M., Theobalt, C., Stamminger, M.: VolumeDeform: real-time volumetric non-rigid reconstruction. In: Leibe, B., Matas, J., Sebe, N., Welling, M. (eds.) ECCV 2016. LNCS, vol. 9912, pp. 362–379. Springer, Cham (2016). https://doi.org/10.1007/978-3-319-46484-8_22

9. Izadi, S., et al.: KinectFusion: real-time 3D reconstruction and interaction using a moving depth camera. In: Proceedings UIST, pp. 559–568. ACM (2011)

10. Johnson, J., Alahi, A., Feifei, L.: Perceptual losses for real-time style transfer and super-resolution. In: Computer Vision and Pattern Recognition (2016)

11. Kanazawa, A., Black, M.J., Jacobs, D.W., Malik, J.: End-to-end recovery of human shape and pose. In: Computer Vision and Pattern Recognition, pp. 7122–7131 (2018)

12. Li, C., Zhao, Z., Guo, X.: ArticulatedFusion: real-time reconstruction of motion, geometry and segmentation using a single depth camera. In: Ferrari, V., Hebert, M., Sminchisescu, C., Weiss, Y. (eds.) ECCV 2018. LNCS, vol. 11212, pp. 324–340. Springer, Cham (2018). https://doi.org/10.1007/978-3-030-01237-3_20

13. Loper, M., Mahmood, N., Romero, J., Pons-Moll, G., Black, M.J.: SMPL: a skinned multi-person linear model. ACM Trans. Graphics (Proc. SIGGRAPH Asia) **34**(6), 248:1–248:16 (2015)

14. Natsume, R., et al.: SiCloPe: silhouette-based clothed people. In: Computer Vision and Pattern Recognition, pp. 4480–4490 (2019)

15. Newcombe, R.A., Fox, D., Seitz, S.M.: DynamicFusion: reconstruction and tracking of non-rigid scenes in real-time. In: IEEE Conference on Computer Vision and Pattern Recognition (CVPR), pp. 343–352. IEEE, Boston (2015)

16. Pavlakos, G., et al.: Expressive body capture: 3D hands, face, and body from a single image. In: Proceedings IEEE Conference on Computer Vision and Pattern Recognition (CVPR), June 2019. http://smpl-x.is.tue.mpg.de

17. Pavlakos, G., Zhu, L., Zhou, X., Daniilidis, K.: Learning to estimate 3D human pose and shape from a single color image. In: Computer Vision and Pattern Recognition, pp. 459–468 (2018)

18. Petrov, A.P.: On obtaining shape from color shading. Color Res. Appl. **18**(6), 375–379 (1993)

19. Rhodin, H., Robertini, N., Casas, D., Richardt, C., Seidel, H., Theobalt, C.: General automatic human shape and motion capture using volumetric contour cues. In: Computer Vision and Pattern Recognition (2016)

20. Ronneberger, O., Fischer, P., Brox, T.: U-Net: convolutional networks for biomedical image segmentation. In: Computer Vision and Pattern Recognition (2015)

21. Saito, S., Huang, Z., Natsume, R., Morishima, S., Kanazawa, A., Li, H.: PIFU: pixel-aligned implicit function for high-resolution clothed human digitization. CoRR abs/1905.05172 (2019). http://arxiv.org/abs/1905.05172

22. Simonyan, K., Zisserman, A.: Very deep convolutional networks for large-scale image recognition. In: Computer Vision and Pattern Recognition (2014)

23. Slavcheva, M., Baust, M., Cremers, D., Ilic, S.: KillingFusion: non-rigid 3D reconstruction without correspondences. In: IEEE Conference on Computer Vision and Pattern Recognition (CVPR), pp. 5474–5483. IEEE, Honolulu (2017)

24. Slavcheva, M., Baust, M., Ilic, S.: SobolevFusion: 3D reconstruction of scenes undergoing free non-rigid motion. In: The IEEE Conference on Computer Vision and Pattern Recognition (CVPR), pp. 2646–2655. IEEE, Salt Lake City, June 2018

25. Smith, D., Loper, M., Hu, X., Mavroidis, P., Romero, J.: FACSIMILE: fast and accurate scans from an image in less than a second. In: The IEEE International Conference on Computer Vision (ICCV), pp. 5330–5339 (2019)

26. Sterzentsenko, V., et al.: Self-supervised deep depth denoising. arXiv: Computer Vision and Pattern Recognition (2019)

27. Tong, J., Zhou, J., Liu, L., Pan, Z., Yan, H.: Scanning 3D full human bodies using Kinects. IEEE Trans. Visual Comput. Graphics **18**(4), 643–650 (2012)

28. Varol, G., et al.: BodyNet: volumetric inference of 3d human body shapes. In: Computer Vision and Pattern Recognition (2018)

29. Wang, T.C., Liu, M.Y., Zhu, J.Y., Tao, A., Kautz, J., Catanzaro, B.: High-resolution image synthesis and semantic manipulation with conditional GANs. In: Proceedings of the IEEE Conference on Computer Vision and Pattern Recognition, pp. 8798–8807 (2018)

30. Wu, C., Varanasi, K., Liu, Y., Seidel, H., Theobalt, C.: Shading-based dynamic shape refinement from multi-view video under general illumination. In: 2011 International Conference on Computer Vision, pp. 1108–1115, November 2011. https://doi.org/10.1109/ICCV.2011.6126358

31. Wu, C., Stoll, C., Valgaerts, L., Theobalt, C.: On-set performance capture of multiple actors with a stereo camera. ACM Trans. Graph. **32**, 1–11 (2013). https://doi.org/10.1145/2508363.2508418

32. Yan, S., et al.: DDRNet: depth map denoising and refinement for consumer depth cameras using cascaded CNNs. In: Ferrari, V., Hebert, M., Sminchisescu, C., Weiss, Y. (eds.) ECCV 2018. LNCS, vol. 11214, pp. 155–171. Springer, Cham (2018). https://doi.org/10.1007/978-3-030-01249-6_10

33. Yu, L., Yeung, S., Tai, Y., Lin, S.: Shading-based shape refinement of RGB-D images. In: Computer Vision and Pattern Recognition, pp. 1415–1422 (2013)

34. Yu, T., et al.: BodyFusion: real-time capture of human motion and surface geometry using a single depth camera. In: IEEE International Conference on Computer Vision (ICCV), pp. 910–919. IEEE, Venice (2017)

35. Yu, T., et al.: DoubleFusion: real-time capture of human performances with inner body shapes from a single depth sensor. In: 2018 IEEE Conference on Computer Vision and Pattern Recognition, CVPR 2018, Salt Lake City, UT, USA, 18–22 June 2018, pp. 7287–7296 (2018)

36. Zeng, M., Zheng, J., Cheng, X., Liu, X.: Templateless quasi-rigid shape modeling with implicit loop-closure. In: The IEEE Conference on Computer Vision and Pattern Recognition (CVPR), June 2013

37. Zhang, R., Tsai, P., Cryer, J.E., Shah, M.: Shape-from-shading: a survey. IEEE Trans. Pattern Anal. Mach. Intell. **21**(8), 690–706 (1999)

38. Zheng, Z., Yu, T., Wei, Y., Dai, Q., Liu, Y.: DeepHuman: 3D human reconstruction from a single image. CoRR abs/1903.06473 (2019). http://arxiv.org/abs/1903.06473

Model-Based Occlusion Disentanglement
for Image-to-Image Translation

Fabio Pizzati[1,2], Pietro Cerri[2], and Raoul de Charette[1(✉)]

[1] Inria, Paris, France
{fabio.pizzati,raoul.de-charette}@inria.fr
[2] VisLab, Parma, Italy
pcerri@ambarella.com

Abstract. Image-to-image translation is affected by entanglement phenomena, which may occur in case of target data encompassing occlusions such as raindrops, dirt, etc. Our unsupervised model-based learning disentangles scene and occlusions, while benefiting from an adversarial pipeline to regress physical parameters of the occlusion model. The experiments demonstrate our method is able to handle varying types of occlusions and generate highly realistic translations, qualitatively and quantitatively outperforming the state-of-the-art on multiple datasets.

Keywords: GAN · Image-to-image translation · Occlusions ·
Raindrop · Soil

| Target sample | Source | MUNIT [14] | Ours disentangled | Ours w/ focus drops |

Fig. 1. Our method learns to disentangle scene from occlusions using unsupervised adversarial disentanglement with guided injection of a differentiable occlusion model. Here, we separate unfocused drops from rainy scene and show that, opposed to existing baselines, we learn a fully disentangled translation without drops and can re-inject occlusions with unseen parameters (e.g. in-focus drops).

1   Introduction

Image-to-image (i2i) translation GANs are able to learn the source $\mapsto$ target style mapping of paintings, photographs, etc. [16,20,54]. In particular, synthetic to real [4] or weather translation [27,29,38] attracted many works as they are

Electronic supplementary material The online version of this chapter (https://doi.org/10.1007/978-3-030-58565-5_27) contains supplementary material, which is available to authorized users.

alternatives to the menial labeling task, and allow domain adaptation or finetuning to boost performance on unlabeled domains. However, GANs notoriously fail to learn the underlying physics [45]. This is evident when *target* data encompass occlusions (such as raindrop, dirt, etc.) as the network will learn an entangled representation of the scene with occlusions. For example, with clear ↦ rain the GAN translation will tend to have too many drops occlusions, often where the translation is complex as it is an easy way to fool the discriminator.

We propose an unsupervised model-based adversarial disentanglement to separate target and occlusions. Among other benefits, it enables accurate translation to the target domain and permits proper re-injection of occlusions. More importantly, occlusions with different physical parameters can be re-injected, which is crucial since the appearance of occlusions varies greatly with the camera setup. For example, drops occlusions appear different when imaged in-focus or out-of-focus. There are obvious benefits for occlusion-invariant outdoor vision like mobile robotics or autonomous driving. A comparison showcasing standard i2i (that partially entangles unrealistic drops) and our framework capabilities is available in Fig. 1. Our method builds on top of existing GAN architectures enabling unsupervised adversarial disentanglement with the only prior of the occlusion model. Parameters of the occlusion model are regressed on the target data and used when training to re-inject occlusions further driven by our disentanglement guide. We demonstrate our method is the only one able to learn an accurate translation in the context of occlusions, outperforming the literature on all tested metrics, and leading to better transfer learning on semantic segmentation. Our method is able to cope with various occlusion models such as drops, dirt, watermark, or else, among which raindrop is thoroughly studied. Our contributions may be summarized as follows:

- we propose the first unsupervised model-based disentanglement framework,
- our adversarial parameter estimation strategy allows estimating and replicating target occlusions with great precision and physical realism,
- our disentanglement guidance helps the learning process without losing generative capabilities in the translation task,
- we conducted exhaustive experiments on raindrops occlusions proving we outperform the literature, boost transfer learning, and provide a focus agnostic framework of high interest for autonomous driving applications.

2   Related Work

Image-to-Image Translation. Seminal works on image-to-image translation (i2i) was conducted by Isola et al. [16] and Zhu et al. [54] for paired and unpaired data respectively, where the later introduced the cycle consistency loss extended in [48,55]. Liu et al. [20] further proposed using Variational Auto Encoders to learn a shared latent space. A common practice to increase accuracy is to learn scene-aware translation exploiting additional supervision from semantic [6,19,30,41], instance [25] or objects [38]. Furthermore, a recent trend is to use attention-guided translation [17,22,24,40] to preserve important features.

Regarding disentangled representations, MUNIT [14] and DRIT [18] decouple image content and style to enable multi-modal i2i, similar in spirit to our goal, while FUNIT [21] uses disentangled representations for few-shot learning. FineGAN [39] disentangles background and foreground using bounding boxes supervision. Multi-domain i2i also opens new directions to control elements at the image level [3,7,15,32,47], since it may be used to represent elements learned from various datasets. Attribute-based image generation [43,44,51] follows a similar scheme, explicitly controlling features. Nonetheless, these methods require attributes annotations or multiple datasets – hardly compatible with occlusions. Finally, Yang et al. [46] exploit a disentangled physical model for dehazing.

Lens Occlusion Generation (drops, dirt, soiling, etc.). Two strategies co-exist in the literature: physics-based rendering or generative networks. Early works on geometrical modeling showcased accurate rendering of raindrops via ray-tracing and 3D surface modeling [13,34,35], sometimes accounting for complex liquid dynamics [50] or focus blur [13,35]. A general photometric model was also proposed in [10] for thin occluders, while recent works use displacement maps to approximate the raindrops refraction behavior [2,28]. Generative networks were also recently leveraged to learn general dirt generation [42] but using semantic soiling annotations. To the best of our knowledge, there are no approaches that simultaneously handle occlusions and scene-based modifications with i2i. Note that we intentionally do not review the exhaustive list of works on de-raining or equivalent as it is quite different from disentanglement in the i2i context.

3   Model-Based Disentanglement

We aim to learn the disentangled representation of a target domain and occlusions. For example, when translating clear to rain images having raindrops on the lens, standard image-to-image (i2i) fails to learn an accurate mapping as the target entangles the scene and the drops on the lens. We depart from the literature by learning a disentangled representation of the target domain from the injection of an occlusion model, in which physical parameters are estimated from the target dataset. Not only does it allows us to learn the disentangled representation of the scene (e.g. target image without any occlusions) but also to re-inject the occlusion model either with the estimated parameters or with different parameters (e.g. target image with drops in focus).

Our method handles any sort of occlusions such as raindrops, soil, dirt, watermark, etc. but for clarity we focus on raindrops as it of high interest and exhibits complex visual appearance. Figure 2 shows an overview of our training pipeline, which is fully unsupervised and only exploits the prior of occlusion type. To learn adversarial disentanglement by injecting occlusions (Sect. 3.1), we first pretrain a baseline to regress the model parameters (Sect. 3.2) and estimate domain shifts to further guide the disentanglement learning process (Sect. 3.3).

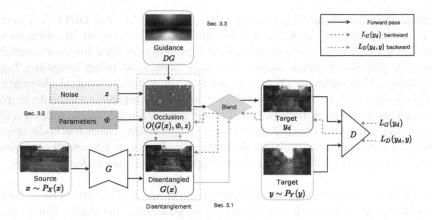

Fig. 2. To disentangle the i2i translation process in an unsupervised manner, we inject occlusions $O(.)$ with estimated parameters $\hat{w}$ before forwarding the generated image $G(x)$ through the discriminator D. The Disentanglement Guidance (DG) avoids losing translation capabilities in low domain shift areas. *Fake* and *real* data are drawn red and green, respectively. (Color figure online)

3.1   Adversarial Disentanglement

Let X and Y be the domains of a *source* and a *target* dataset, respectively. In an i2i setup, the task is to learn the $X \mapsto Y$ mapping translating source to target. Now, if the target dataset has occlusions of any sort, Y encompasses two domains: the scene domain $_S$, and the occlusion domain $_O$. Formally, as in [27] we introduce a disentangled representation of domains such that $Y = \{Y_S, Y_O\}$ and $X = \{X_S\}$. In adversarial training strategies, the generator is led to approximate P_X and P_Y, the probability distributions associated with the domains stochastic process, defined as

$$\forall x \in X, x \sim P_X(x),$$
$$\forall y \in Y, y \sim P_Y(y). \tag{1}$$

Having occlusions, the target domain Y is interpreted as the composition of two subdomains, and we seek to estimate $P_{Y_S,Y_O}(y_S, y_O)$ corresponding to the scene and occlusion domain. To address this, let's make the *naive* assumption that marginals $P_{Y_S}(y_S)$ and $P_{Y_O}(y_O)$ are independent from each other. Thus, exploiting the definition of joint probability distribution, $P_Y(y)$ becomes

$$P_Y(y) = P_{Y_S,Y_O}(y_S, y_O) = P_{Y_S}(y_S)P_{Y_O}(y_O), \tag{2}$$

and it appears that knowing one of the marginals would enable learning disentangled i2i translations between subdomains. In particular, if $P_{Y_O}(y_O)$ is known it is intuitively possible to learn $X_S \mapsto Y_S$, satisfying our initial requirement.

In reality, transparent occlusions - such as raindrops - are not fully disentangled from the scene, as their appearance is varying with scene content (see ablation in Sect. 4.4). However, the physical properties of occlusions may be seen as quite independent. As an example, while the appearance of drops on the lens varies greatly with scene background, their physics (e.g. size, shape, etc.) is little- or un- related to the scene. Fortunately, there is extensive literature providing appearance models for different types of occlusions (drop, dirt, etc.) given their physical parameters, which we use to estimate $P_{Y_O}(y_O)$. We thus formalize occlusion models as $O(s, w, z)$ parametrized by the scene s, the set of disentangled physical properties w, and a random noise vector z. The latter is used to map characteristics that can not be regressed as they are stochastic in nature. This is the case for raindrops positions for example. Assuming we know the type of occlusion such as drop, dirt, etc., we rely on existing models (described in Sect. 4) to render the visual appearance of occlusions.

Ultimately, as depicted in Fig. 2, we add occlusions rendered with a known model on generated images before forwarding them to the discriminator. Assuming sufficiently accurate occlusion models, the generator G is pushed to estimate the disentangled P_{Y_S}, thus learning to translate only scene-related features. As a comparison to a standard LSGAN [23] training which enforces a zero-sum game by minimizing

$$y_d = G(x),$$
$$L_{gen} = L_G(y_d) = \mathbb{E}_{x \sim P_X(x)}[(D(y_d) - 1)^2], \qquad (3)$$
$$L_{disc} = L_D(y_d, y) = \mathbb{E}_{x \sim P_X(x)}[(D(y_d))^2] + \mathbb{E}_{y \sim P_Y(y)}[(D(y) - 1)^2],$$

with L_{gen} and L_{disc} being respectively the tasks of the generator G and discriminator D, we instead learn the desired disentangled mapping by injecting occlusions $O(.)$ on the translated image. Hence, we newly define y_d as the disentangled composition of translated scene and injected occlusions, that is

$$y_d = \alpha G(x) + (1 - \alpha)O(G(x), \tilde{w}, z), \qquad (4)$$

where α is a pixel-wise measure of the occlusion transparency. Opaque occlusions will locally set $\alpha = 1$ while a pixel with transparent occlusions has $\alpha < 1$. Because physical parameters greatly influence the appearance of occlusions (e.g. drop in focus or out of focus), we render occlusions in Eq. 4 using $\tilde{w}$, the optimal set of physical parameters to model occlusions in Y.

3.2   Adversarial Parameters Estimation

We estimate the set of physical parameters $\tilde{w}$ from Y in an unsupervised manner, benefiting from the entanglement of scene and occlusion in the target domain. We build here upon Eq. 2. Assuming a naive i2i baseline being trained on source and target data, *without* disentanglement, the discriminator learned to distinguished examples from source and target by discriminating $P_X = P_{X_S}$ from $P_Y = P_{Y_S}(y_S)P_{Y_O}(y_O)$. Let's consider the trivial case where a generator G' performs identity (i.e. $G'(x) = x$) then we get $P_{Y_S}(y_S) = P_{X_S}(x_S)$ and it is now possible to estimate the optimal $\tilde{w}$ as it corresponds to the distance minimization of P_Y and P_X. Intuitively, as the domain gap results of both occlusion and

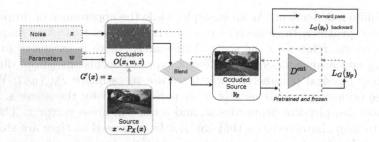

Fig. 3. We estimate the optimal parameters to use for the disentanglement adding occlusions on *source* images and optimizing the parameters of the physical model in order to fool the discriminator. Since we are not using a generator network, the gradient, represented as red arrows, flows only in the occlusion model direction. (Color figure online)

scene domain (which is fixed), reducing the source and target domain gap implies reducing the occlusion domain gap, in extenso regressing w.

Figure 3 illustrates the estimation process. In practice, we pretrain a simple i2i baseline (e.g. MUNIT[14]) to learn $X \mapsto Y$ in a naive - entangled - manner, by training a generator and discriminator. We then freeze the naive discriminator denoted D^{ent} and solve the following optimization objective

$$y_p = \alpha G'(x) + (1 - \alpha)O(G'(x), w, z),$$
$$\min_w L_G(y_p),$$
(5)

by backpropagating the gradient flow through the derivable occlusion model. For most occlusions where transparency depends on the model, we in fact consider the blending mask $\alpha = \alpha(w, z)$. Note that it is required to freeze the discriminator otherwise we would lose any feedback capabilities on the images of the target domain. For simplicity in Fig. 3, we omit the generator G' during parameter estimation since $G'(x) = x$. Training until convergence, we extract the optimal parameter set $\tilde{w}$. In Sect. 4.2 we evaluate our parameters estimation on synthetic and real data.

Alternately, $\tilde{w}$ could also be tuned manually but at the cost of menial labor and obvious approximation. Still, one may note than an inaccurate estimation of $\tilde{w}$ would lead to a poor disentanglement of P_{Y_S} and P_{Y_O}.

3.3   Disentanglement Guidance

We highlight now an easy pitfall in the disentangled GAN training, since an unwanted optimum is reached if the generator simply adds occlusions. Indeed because occlusions are visually simple and constitute a strong discriminative signal for the discriminator, it may be easier for the generator to entangle occlusions rather than to learn the underlying scene mapping. Specifically, occlusions will be entangled where source and target differ the least, since it is an easy way to minimize L_{gen} as even with a perfect i2i *there* the discriminator will provide relatively uncertain feedback. For example, we noticed that drops were entangled over trees or buildings as both exhibit little visual differences in the clear and rainy domains.

To avoid such undesirable behavior, we spatially guide the disentanglement to prevent the i2i task from entangling occlusions in the scene representation. The so-called *disentanglement guide* is computed through the estimation of the domains gap database-wide. Specifically, we use GradCAM [37] which relies on gradient flow through the discriminator to identify which regions contribute to the *fake* classification, and thus exhibit a large domain gap. Similar to the parameter estimation (Sect. 3.2), we pretrain a simple i2i baseline and exploit the discriminator. To preserve resolution, we upscale and average the response of GradCAM for each discriminator layer and further average responses over the dataset[1]. Formally, using LSGAN we extract *Disentanglement Guidance (DG)*

$$DG = \mathbb{E}_{x \sim P_X(x)}[\mathbb{E}_{l \in L}[\text{GradCAM}_l(D(x))]], \qquad (6)$$

with L being the discriminator layers. During training of our method, the guide serves to inject occlusions only where domain gaps are low, that is where $DG < \beta$, with $\beta \in [0,1]$ a hyperparameter. While this may seem counter-intuitive, explicitly injecting drops in low domain shift areas mimics the GAN intended behavior lowering the domain shift with drops. This logically prevents entanglement phenomena since they are simulated by the injection of occlusions. We refer to Fig. 8b in the ablation study for a visual understanding of this phenomenon.

4   Experiments

We validate the performances of our method on various real occlusions, leveraging recent real datasets such as nuScenes [5], RobotCar [28], Cityscapes [9] or WoodScape [49], and synthetic data such as Synthia [33]. Our most comprehensive results focus on the harder raindrops occlusion (Sect. 4.2), but we also extend to soil/dirt and other general occlusions such as watermark, fence, etc. (Sect. 4.3). For each type of occlusion we detail the model used and report qualitative and quantitative results against recent works: DRIT [18], U-GAT-IT [17], AttentionGAN [40], CycleGAN [54], and MUNIT [14]. Because the literature does not account for disentanglement, we report both the disentangled underlying domain (*Ours disentangled*) and the disentangled domain *with* injection of *target* occlusions (*Ours target*). Note that while still images are already significantly better with our method, the full extent is better sensed on the supplementary video as disentangling domains implicitly enforces temporal consistency.

---

[1] Note that averaging through the dataset implies similar image aspects and viewpoints. Image-wise guidance could be envisaged at the cost of less reliable guidance.

4.1 Training Setup

Our method is trained in a three stages unsupervised fashion, with the only prior that the occlusion model is known (e.g. drop, dirt, watermark, etc.). First, we train an i2i baseline to learn the entangled source $\mapsto$ target and extract D^{ent}. Second, the occlusion model parameters are regressed as in Sect. 3.2 and DG is estimated with the same pre-trained discriminator following Sect. 3.3. While being not mandatory for disentanglement, DG often improves visual results. Third, the disentangled pipeline described in Sect. 3.1 is trained from scratch injecting the occlusion model only where the Disentanglement Guidance allows it. We refer to the supplementary for more details.

We use MUNIT [14] for its multi-modal capacity and train with LSGAN [23]. Occlusion models are implemented in a differentiable manner with Kornia [31].

4.2 Raindrops

We now evaluate our method on the complex task of raindrops disentanglement when learning the i2i clear $\mapsto$ rain task. Because of their refractive and semi-transparent appearance, raindrops occlusions are fairly complex.

Occlusion Model. To model raindrops, we use the recent model of Alletto *et al.* [2] which provides a good realism/simplicity trade-off. Following [2], we approximate drop shapes with simple trigonometric functions and add random noise to increase variability as in [1]. The photometry of drops is approached with a displacement map (U, V) encoding the 2D coordinate mapping in the target image, such that drop at (u, v) with thickness ρ has its pixel (u_i, v_i) mapped to

$$\big(u + \mathrm{U}(u_i, v_i) \cdot \rho, v + \mathrm{V}(u_i, v_i) \cdot \rho\big). \tag{7}$$

Intuitively, this approximates light refractive properties of raindrops. Technically, $(\mathrm{U}, \mathrm{V}, \rho)$ is conveniently encoded as a 3-channels image. We refer to [2] for details. We also account for the imaging focus, as it has been highlighted that drops with different focus have dramatically different appearance [2,8,12]. We approximate focus blur with a Gaussian point spread function [26] which variance σ is learned, thus $w = \{\sigma\}$. I.e., our method handles drops occlusions with any type of focus. During training, drops are uniformly distributed in the image space, with size being a hyperparameter which we study later, and defocus σ is regressed with our parameters estimation (Sect. 3.2). During inference, drops are generated at random position with p_r probability, which somehow controls the rain intensity. Figure 4 illustrates our drop occlusion model with variable shapes and focus blur.

Datasets. We evaluate using 2 recent datasets providing clear/rain images.

nuScenes [5] is an urban driving dataset recorded in the US and Singapore with coarse frame-wise weather annotation. Using the latter, we split the validation

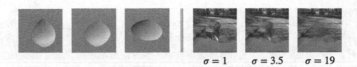

$\sigma = 1$ $\sigma = 3.5$ $\sigma = 19$

Fig. 4. Raindrop occlusion model. Left are schematic views of our model where the shape is modeled as trigonometric functions and photometry as displacement maps (cf. Eq. 7), encoded here as RGB. Right demonstrates our ability to handle the high variability of drops appearance with a different focus (σ).

into clear/rain and obtain 114251/29463 for training and 25798/5637 for testing. *RobotCar* [28] provides pairs of clear/rain images acquired with binocular specialized hardware where one camera is continuously sprayed with water. The clear images are warped to the rainy image space using calibration data, and we use a clear/rain split of 3816/3816 for training and 1000/1000 for validation.

Qualitative Evaluation. Outputs of the clear $\mapsto$ rain i2i task are shown in Fig. 5 against the above cited [14,17,18,40,54]. At first sight, it is evident that drops are entangled in other methods, which is expected as they are *not* taught to disentangle drops. To allow fair comparison we thus provide our disentangled estimation (*Ours disentangled*) but also add drops occlusions to it, modeled with the physical parameters $\tilde{w}$ estimated from target domain (*Ours target*).

Looking at *Ours disentangled*, the i2i successfully learned the appearance of a rainy scene (e.g. reflections or sky) with sharp pleasant translation to rain, without any drops. Other methods noticeably entangle drops, often at fixed positions to avoid learning i2i translation. This is easily noticed in the 4th column where all methods generated drops on the leftmost tree. Conversely, we benefit from our disentangled representation to render scenes with drops occlusions (row *Ours target*) fairly matching the appearance of the target domain (1st row), subsequently demonstrating the efficiency of our adversarial parameter estimation.

What is more, we inject drops with different sets of parameters $\{w, z\}$ arbitrary mimicking dashcam sequences (Fig. 5, last 2 rows). The quality of the dashcam translations, despite the absence of similar data during training, proves the benefit of disentanglement and the adequacy of the occlusion model. Note that with any set of parameters, our occlusion (last 3 rows) respect the refractive properties of raindrops showing the scene up-side-down in each drop, while other baselines simply model white and blurry occlusions.

Quantitative Evaluation

GAN Metrics. Table 1a reports metrics on the nuScenes clear $\mapsto$ rain task. Each metric encompasses different meanings: Inception Score (IS) [36] evaluates quality/diversity against target, LPIPS distance [52] evaluates translation diversity thus avoiding mode-collapse, and Conditional Inception Score [14] single-image translations diversity for multi-modal baselines. Note that we evaluate against

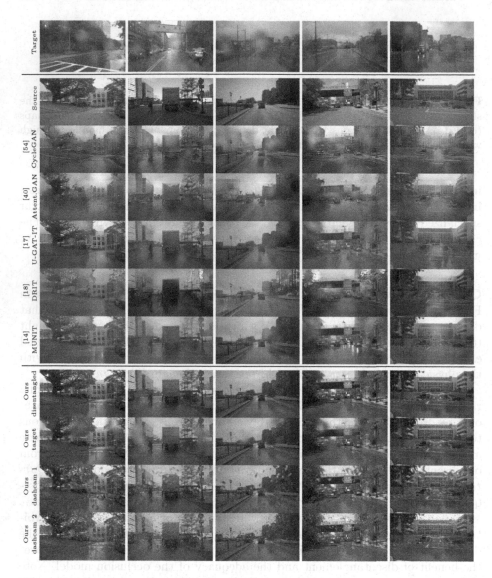

Fig. 5. Qualitative comparison against recent baselines on the clear ↦ rain task with drops occlusions. Target samples are displayed in the first row for reference. Other rows show the source image (2nd row) and all its subsequent translations below. Our method efficiently disentangled drops occlusion from the scene (row *Ours disentangled*) and subsequently allows the generation of realistic drops matching target style (row *Ours target*) or any arbitrary style (last 2 rows).

our disentangled + target drops occlusion *Ours target*, since baselines are neither supposed to disentangle the occlusion layer nor to generate different kinds of drop. On all metrics, our method outperforms the state of the art by a com-

Table 1. Quantitative evaluation of clear ↦ rain effectiveness on nuScenes [5] (for all higher is better). (a) shows GAN metrics of ours i2i translation with target drop inclusion (i.e. *Ours Target*) against i2i baselines. Our method outperforms literature on all metrics which is imputed to the variability and realism that come with the disentanglement. Note that CIS is multi-modal. (b) Evaluation of the Average Precision (AP) of semantic segmentation when finetuning PSPNet [53] and evaluating on a subset of nuScenes with semantic labels from [11].

Network	IS↑	LPIPS↑	CIS↑
CycleGAN [54]	1.151	0.473	-
AttentionGAN [40]	1.406	0.464	-
U-GAT-IT [17]	1.038	0.489	-
DRIT [18]	1.189	0.492	1.120
MUNIT [14]	1.211	0.495	1.030
Ours target	**1.532**	**0.515**	**1.148**

(a) GAN metrics

Method	AP↑
Original (from [11])	18.7
Finetuned w/ Halder *et al.* [11]	25.6
Finetuned w/ Ours target	**27.7**

(b) Semantic segmentation

fortable margin. This is easily ascribable to our output being both more realistic, since we are evaluating with drops with the physical parameters extracted from target dataset, and more variable, since we do not suffer from entanglement phenomena that greatly limit the drops visual stochasticity. This is also evident when comparing against [14] which we use as the backbone in our framework. Technically, IS is computed over the whole validation set, CIS on 100 translations of 100 random images (as in [14]), and LPIPS on 1900 random pairs of 100 translations. The InceptionV3 for IS/CIS was finetuned on source/target as [14].

Semantic Segmentation. Because GAN metrics are reportedly noisy [52] we aim at providing a different perspective for quantitative evaluation, and thus measure the usefulness of our translated images for semantic segmentation. To that aim, following the practice of Halder et al. [11] we use *Ours target* (i.e. trained on rainy nuScenes) to infer a rainy version of the popular Cityscapes [9] dataset and use it to finetune PSPNet [53]. The evaluation on the small subset of 25 semantic labeled images of rainy nuScenes provided by [11] is reported in Table 1b. It showcases finetuning with our rainy images is better than with [11], which uses physics-based rendering to generate rain. Note that both finetune *Original* weights, and that the low numbers results of the fairly large Cityscapes-nuScenes gap (recall that nuScenes has no semantic labels to train on).

Parameter Estimation. We verify the validity of our parameter estimation strategy (Sect. 3.2) using the RobotCar dataset, which provides real *clear/rain* pairs of images. As the viewpoints are warped together (cf. Datasets details above), there is no underlying domain shift in the clear/rain images so we set $G(x) = x$ and directly train on discriminator to regress physical parameters (we

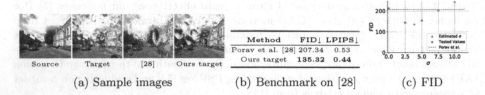

(a) Sample images   (b) Benchmark on [28]   (c) FID

Method	FID↓	LPIPS↓
Porav et al. [28]	207.34	0.53
Ours target	**135.32**	**0.44**

Fig. 6. Parameter estimation using real clear/rainy pairs of images from RobotCar [28]. Visually, *Ours target* is fairly closer to the *Target* sample regardless of drops position/size (a), while quantitatively lower FID and LPIPS distance is obtained (b). With FID measures at different defocus sigma in (c), we demonstrate our estimated parameters ($\sigma = 3.87$) successfully led to the best parameters.

get $\sigma = 3.87$) and render rain with it on clear images. We can then measure the distance of the translated and real rainy images, with FID and LPIPS distances reported in Fig. 6b. Unlike before, LPIPS measures distance (not diversity) so lower is better. For both we significantly outperform [28], which is visually interpretable in Fig. 6a, where drops rendered with our parameter estimation looks more similar to *Target* than those of [28] (regardless of their size/position).

To further assess the accuracy of our estimation, we plot in Fig. 6c the FID for different defocus blurs ($\sigma \in \{0.0, 2.5, 5.0, 7.5, 10\}$). It shows our estimated defocus ($\sigma = 3.87$) leads to the minimum FID of all tested values, further demonstrating the accuracy of our adversarial estimation. We quantify the precision by training on clear images with synthetic injection of drops having $\sigma \in [5, 25]$, and we measured an average error of 1.02% (std. 1.95%).

4.3   Extension to Other Occlusion Models

To showcase the generality of our method, we demonstrate its performance on two generally encountered types of occlusions: Dirt and General occlusion.

Dirt. We rely on the recent WoodScape dataset [49] and a simple occlusion model to learn the disentangled representation.

Datasets. WoodScape [49] provides a large amount of driving fish-eye images, and comes with metadata indicating the presence of dirt/soil[2]. Different from rain sequences having rainy scenes+drops occlusions, apart from soiling there isn't any domain shift in the clean/dirt images provided. Hence, to study disentanglement we introduce an additional shift by converting clean images to grayscale and refer to them as *clean_gray*. We train our method on non-paired clean_gray/dirt images with 5117/4873 for training and 500/500 for validation.

Occlusion Model. To generate synthetic soiling, we use a modified version of our drop model with random trigonometric functions and larger varying sizes. Displacement maps are not used since we consider dirt to be opaque and randomly

---

[2] Note that WoodScape provides soiling mask which we do *not* use.

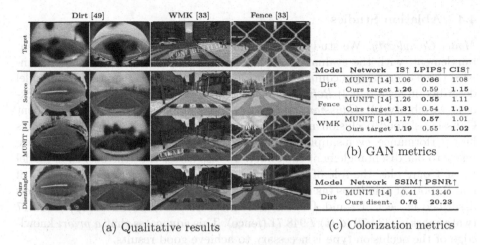

(a) Qualitative results

(b) GAN metrics

Model	Network	IS↑	LPIPS↑	CIS↑
Dirt	MUNIT [14]	1.06	0.66	1.08
	Ours target	1.26	0.59	1.15
Fence	MUNIT [14]	1.26	0.55	1.11
	Ours target	1.31	0.54	1.19
WMK	MUNIT [14]	1.17	0.57	1.01
	Ours target	1.19	0.55	1.02

(c) Colorization metrics

Model	Network	SSIM↑	PSNR↑
Dirt	MUNIT [14]	0.41	13.40
	Ours disent.	0.76	20.23

Fig. 7. Various occlusions disentanglement. We seek to learn disentangled representation of clean_gray ↦ clean_color on WoodScape [49] (real) and clear ↦ snow on Synthia [33] (synthetic). For all, MUNIT [14] partly entangles occlusions in the translation, often occluding hard-to-translate areas, while our method learned correctly the color mapping and the snow mapping despite complex occlusions (7a). Quantitative evaluation with GAN metrics (7b) confirms the increase in image quality for all occlusions models and with colorization metrics for dirt (7c) exploiting our unpaired disentanglement framework.

brownish, with apparent semi-transparency only as a result of the high defocus. As for drops, the defocus σ is regressed so again $w = \{\sigma\}$.

Performance. Figure 7a (left) shows sample results where the task consists of disentangling the color characteristics from the dirt occlusion (since color is only in the dirt data). Comparing to MUNIT [14], *Ours disentangled* successfully learned color without dirt entanglement, while [14] failed to learn accurate colorization due to entanglement. Performances are validated quantitatively in Table 7b–7c.

General Occlusions (synthetic). In Fig. 7a (right) we also demonstrate the ability to disentangle general occlusion, in the sense of an alpha-blended layer on an image (watermarks, logos, etc.). We used synthetic Synthia [33] clear/snow data, and augmented only snow either with a "confidential" watermark (WMK) or a fence image, both randomly shifted. Our i2i takes 3634/3739 clear/snow images for training, and 901/947 for validation. The occlusion model is the ground truth composite alpha-blended model, with random translation, and without any regressed parameters (i.e. $w = \emptyset$). From Fig. 7a, our method learned a disentangled representation, while MUNIT [14] partially entangled the occlusion model. In Table 7b, CIS/IS confirm the higher quality visual results.

4.4 Ablation Studies

Model Complexity. We study here how much model complexity impacts disentanglement, with the evaluation on the nuScenes clear $\mapsto$ rain task. We compare three decreasingly complex occlusion models: 1) *Ours*, the raindrop model described in Sect. 4.2; 2) *Refract*, which is our model without any shape or thickness variability; 3) *Gaussian*, where drops are modeled as scene-independent Gaussian-shaped occlusion maps following [10]. From Fig. 8a, while *Ours* has best performance, even simpler models lead to better image translation which we relate to our disentanglement capability. To also assess that the occlusion model doesn't only play the role of an adversarial attack, we also compare the FID of real RobotCar raindrops (as in Sect. 4.2) when training with either of the models described in Sect. 4.2 and 4.3. The FID measured are **135.32** (drop) / 329.17 (watermark) / 334.76 (dirt) / 948.71 (fence). This advocates that *a priori* knowledge of the occlusion type is necessary to achieve good results.

Disentanglement Guidance (DG). We study the effects of guidance (Eq. 6) on the nuScenes clear $\mapsto$ rain task, by varying the β threshold used to inject occlusion where $DG < \beta$. From Fig. 8b, with conservative guidance ($\beta = 0$, i.e. no occlusions injected) it behaves similar to MUNIT baseline entangling drops in the translation, while deactivating guidance ($\beta = 1$) correctly achieves a disentangled representation but at the cost of losing translation in high domain shifts areas (note the lack of road reflections). Appropriate guidance ($\beta = 0.75$) helps learning target characteristics while preserving from entanglement.

Model	IS↑	LPIPS↑	CIS↑
N/A ([14])	1.21	0.50	1.03
Gaussian	1.35	0.51	1.13
Refract	1.46	0.50	1.12
Ours	**1.53**	**0.52**	1.15

Source $\beta = 0$ (i.e. [14]) $\beta = 0.75$ (ours) $\beta = 1$

(a) Model complexity   (b) Disentanglement guidance

Fig. 8. Ablation of model complexity and disentanglement guidance for the clear $\mapsto$ rain task on nuScenes. In (a), our disentanglement performs better than baseline [14] with all occlusion models. In (b), studying the influence of β we note that without guidance ($\beta = 1$) the translation lacks important rainy features (reflections, glares, etc.) while with appropriate guidance ($\beta = 0.75$) it learns correct rainy characteristics without entanglement.

5   Conclusion

We propose the first unsupervised method for model-based disentanglement in i2i translation, relying on guided injection of occlusions with parameters regressed from target and assuming only prior knowledge of the occlusion model. Our method outperformed the literature visually and on all tested metrics, and the applicability was shown on various occlusions models (raindrop, dirt, watermark, etc.). Our strategy of adversarial parameter estimation copes with drops of any focus, which is of high interest for any outdoor system as demonstrated in the experiments.

References

1. Rain drops on screen. https://www.shadertoy.com/view/ldSBWW
2. Alletto, S., Carlin, C., Rigazio, L., Ishii, Y., Tsukizawa, S.: Adherent raindrop removal with self-supervised attention maps and spatio-temporal generative adversarial networks. In: ICCV Workshops (2019)
3. Anoosheh, A., Agustsson, E., Timofte, R., Van Gool, L.: ComboGAN: unrestrained scalability for image domain translation. In: CVPR Workshops (2018)
4. Bi, S., Sunkavalli, K., Perazzi, F., Shechtman, E., Kim, V.G., Ramamoorthi, R.: Deep CG2Real: Synthetic-to-real translation via image disentanglement. In: ICCV (2019)
5. Caesar, H., et al.: nuScenes: a multimodal dataset for autonomous driving. In: CVPR (2020)
6. Cherian, A., Sullivan, A.: Sem-GAN: semantically-consistent image-to-image translation. In: WACV (2019)
7. Choi, Y., Choi, M., Kim, M., Ha, J.W., Kim, S., Choo, J.: StarGAN: unified generative adversarial networks for multi-domain image-to-image translation. In: CVPR (2018)
8. Cord, A., Aubert, D.: Towards rain detection through use of in-vehicle multipurpose cameras. In: IV (2011)
9. Cordts, M., et al.: The cityscapes dataset for semantic urban scene understanding. In: CVPR (2016)
10. Gu, J., Ramamoorthi, R., Belhumeur, P., Nayar, S.: Removing image artifacts due to dirty camera lenses and thin occluders. In: SIGGRAPH Asia (2009)
11. Halder, S.S., Lalonde, J.F., de Charette, R.: Physics-based rendering for improving robustness to rain. In: ICCV (2019)
12. Halimeh, J.C., Roser, M.: Raindrop detection on car windshields using geometric-photometric environment construction and intensity-based correlation. In: IV (2009)
13. Hao, Z., You, S., Li, Y., Li, K., Lu, F.: Learning from synthetic photorealistic raindrop for single image raindrop removal. In: ICCV Workshops (2019)
14. Huang, X., Liu, M.-Y., Belongie, S., Kautz, J.: Multimodal unsupervised image-to-image translation. In: Ferrari, V., Hebert, M., Sminchisescu, C., Weiss, Y. (eds.) ECCV 2018. LNCS, vol. 11207, pp. 179–196. Springer, Cham (2018). https://doi.org/10.1007/978-3-030-01219-9_11
15. Hui, L., Li, X., Chen, J., He, H., Yang, J.: Unsupervised multi-domain image translation with domain-specific encoders/decoders. In: ICPR (2018)
16. Isola, P., Zhu, J.Y., Zhou, T., Efros, A.A.: Image-to-image translation with conditional adversarial networks. In: CVPR (2017)
17. Kim, J., Kim, M., Kang, H., Lee, K.: U-GAT-IT: unsupervised generative attentional networks with adaptive layer-instance normalization for image-to-image translation. In: ICLR (2020)
18. Lee, H.Y., et al.: DRIT++: diverse image-to-image translation via disentangled representations. arXiv preprint arXiv:1905.01270 (2019)

19. Li, P., Liang, X., Jia, D., Xing, E.P.: Semantic-aware grad-GAN for virtual-to-real urban scene adaption. BMVC (2018)
20. Liu, M.Y., Breuel, T., Kautz, J.: Unsupervised image-to-image translation networks. In: NeurIPS (2017)
21. Liu, M.Y., et al.: Few-shot unsupervised image-to-image translation. In: ICCV (2019)
22. Ma, S., Fu, J., Wen Chen, C., Mei, T.: DA-GAN: instance-level image translation by deep attention generative adversarial networks. In: CVPR (2018)
23. Mao, X., Li, Q., Xie, H., Lau, R.Y., Wang, Z., Paul Smolley, S.: Least squares generative adversarial networks. In: ICCV (2017)
24. Mejjati, Y.A., Richardt, C., Tompkin, J., Cosker, D., Kim, K.I.: Unsupervised attention-guided image-to-image translation. In: NeurIPS (2018)
25. Mo, S., Cho, M., Shin, J.: InstaGAN: instance-aware image-to-image translation. In: ICLR (2019)
26. Pentland, A.P.: A new sense for depth of field. T-PAMI (1987)
27. Pizzati, F., de Charette, R., Zaccaria, M., Cerri, P.: Domain bridge for unpaired image-to-image translation and unsupervised domain adaptation. In: WACV (2020)
28. Porav, H., Bruls, T., Newman, P.: I can see clearly now: image restoration via de-raining. In: ICRA (2019)
29. Qu, Y., Chen, Y., Huang, J., Xie, Y.: Enhanced pix2pix dehazing network. In: CVPR (2019)
30. Ramirez, P.Z., Tonioni, A., Di Stefano, L.: Exploiting semantics in adversarial training for image-level domain adaptation. In: IPAS (2018)
31. Riba, E., Mishkin, D., Ponsa, D., Rublee, E., Bradski, G.: Kornia: an open source differentiable computer vision library for PyTorch. In: WACV (2020)
32. Romero, A., Arbeláez, P., Van Gool, L., Timofte, R.: SMIT: stochastic multi-label image-to-image translation. In: ICCV Workshops (2019)
33. Ros, G., Sellart, L., Materzynska, J., Vazquez, D., Lopez, A.M.: The SYNTHIA dataset: a large collection of synthetic images for semantic segmentation of urban scenes. In: CVPR (2016)
34. Roser, M., Geiger, A.: Video-based raindrop detection for improved image registration. In: ICCV Workshops (2009)
35. Roser, M., Kurz, J., Geiger, A.: Realistic modeling of water droplets for monocular adherent raindrop recognition using Bezier curves. In: ACCV (2010)
36. Salimans, T., Goodfellow, I., Zaremba, W., Cheung, V., Radford, A., Chen, X.: Improved techniques for training GANs. In: NeurIPS (2016)
37. Selvaraju, R.R., Cogswell, M., Das, A., Vedantam, R., Parikh, D., Batra, D.: Grad-CAM: visual explanations from deep networks via gradient-based localization. In: ICCV (2017)
38. Shen, Z., Huang, M., Shi, J., Xue, X., Huang, T.S.: Towards instance-level image-to-image translation. In: CVPR (2019)
39. Singh, K.K., Ojha, U., Lee, Y.J.: FineGAN: unsupervised hierarchical disentanglement for fine-grained object generation and discovery. In: CVPR (2019)
40. Tang, H., Xu, D., Sebe, N., Yan, Y.: Attention-guided generative adversarial networks for unsupervised image-to-image translation. In: International Joint Conference on Neural Networks (IJCNN) (2019)
41. Tang, H., Xu, D., Yan, Y., Corso, J.J., Torr, P.H., Sebe, N.: Multi-channel attention selection GANs for guided image-to-image translation. In: CVPR (2019)

42. Uricar, M., et al.: Let's get dirty: GAN based data augmentation for soiling and adverse weather classification in autonomous driving. arXiv preprint arXiv:1912.02249 (2019)

43. Xiao, T., Hong, J., Ma, J.: DNA-GAN: learning disentangled representations from multi-attribute images. In: ICLR Workshops (2018)

44. Xiao, T., Hong, J., Ma, J.: ELEGANT: exchanging latent encodings with GAN for transferring multiple face attributes. In: Ferrari, V., Hebert, M., Sminchisescu, C., Weiss, Y. (eds.) ECCV 2018. LNCS, vol. 11214, pp. 172–187. Springer, Cham (2018). https://doi.org/10.1007/978-3-030-01249-6_11

45. Xie, Y., Franz, E., Chu, M., Thuerey, N.: tempoGAN: a temporally coherent, volumetric GAN for super-resolution fluid flow. In: SIGGRAPH (2018)

46. Yang, X., Xu, Z., Luo, J.: Towards perceptual image dehazing by physics-based disentanglement and adversarial training. In: AAAI (2018)

47. Yang, X., Xie, D., Wang, X.: Crossing-domain generative adversarial networks for unsupervised multi-domain image-to-image translation. In: MM (2018)

48. Yi, Z., Zhang, H., Tan, P., Gong, M.: DualGAN: unsupervised dual learning for image-to-image translation. In: ICCV (2017)

49. Yogamani, S., et al.: WoodScape: a multi-task, multi-camera fisheye dataset for autonomous driving. In: ICCV (2019)

50. You, S., Tan, R.T., Kawakami, R., Mukaigawa, Y., Ikeuchi, K.: Adherent raindrop modeling, detectionand removal in video. T-PAMI (2015)

51. Zhang, J., Huang, Y., Li, Y., Zhao, W., Zhang, L.: Multi-attribute transfer via disentangled representation. In: AAAI (2019)

52. Zhang, R., Isola, P., Efros, A.A., Shechtman, E., Wang, O.: The unreasonable effectiveness of deep features as a perceptual metric. In: CVPR (2018)

53. Zhao, H., Shi, J., Qi, X., Wang, X., Jia, J.: Pyramid scene parsing network. In: CVPR (2017)

54. Zhu, J.Y., Park, T., Isola, P., Efros, A.A.: Unpaired image-to-image translation using cycle-consistent adversarial networks. In: CVPR (2017)

55. Zhu, J.Y., et al.: Toward multimodal image-to-image translation. In: NeurIPS (2017)

Rotation-Robust Intersection over Union for 3D Object Detection

Yu Zheng[1,2,3], Danyang Zhang[1], Sinan Xie[1], Jiwen Lu[1,2,3(✉)],
and Jie Zhou[1,2,3,4]

[1] Department of Automation, Tsinghua University, Beijing, China
{zhengyu19,zhang-dy16,xsn18}@mails.tsinghua.edu.cn,
{lujiwen,jzhou}@tsinghua.edu.cn
[2] State Key Lab of Intelligent Technologies and Systems,
Beijing, China
[3] Beijing National Research Center for Information Science and Technology,
Beijing, China
[4] Tsinghua Shenzhen International Graduate School, Tsinghua University,
Beijing, China

Abstract. In this paper, we propose a Rotation-robust Intersection over Union ($RIoU$) for 3D object detection, which aims to learn the overlap of rotated bounding boxes. In most existing 3D object detection methods, the norm-based loss is adopted to individually regress the parameters of bounding boxes, which may suffer from the loss-metric mismatch due to the scaling problem. Motivated by the IoU loss in the axis-aligned 2D object detection which is invariant to the scale, our method jointly optimizes the parameters via the $RIoU$ loss. To tackle the uncertainty of convex caused by rotation, a projection operation is defined to estimate the intersection area. The calculation process of $RIoU$ and its loss function is robust to the rotation condition and feasible for back-propagation, which only comprises basic numerical operations. By incorporating the $RIoU$ loss with the conventional norm-based loss function, we enforce the network to directly optimize the $RIoU$. Experimental results on the KITTI, nuScenes and SUN RGB-D datasets validate the effectiveness of our proposed method. Moreover, we show that our method is suitable for the detection task of 2D rotated objects, such as text boxes and cluttered targets in the aerial images.

Keywords: 3D object detection · Loss function · Rotation-robust

1 Introduction

Recent years have witnessed the advances in 2D object detection [11,25,37] along with the breakthrough of deep learning methods. However, detection of

Electronic supplementary material The online version of this chapter (https://doi.org/10.1007/978-3-030-58565-5_28) contains supplementary material, which is available to authorized users.

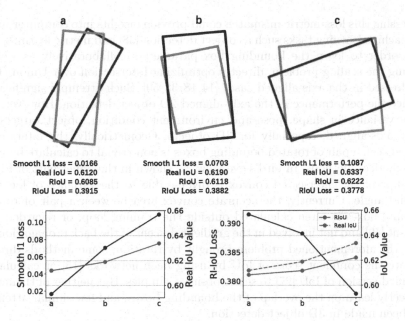

Fig. 1. Examples of inconsistency between the smooth-$\ell 1$ loss and real IoU. From left to right, the $\ell 1$ difference of bounding box parameters is becoming larger, while the overlap is becoming closer. The consistency is preserved between our proposed *RIoU* loss and real IoU in this example. The result is calculated from numerical simulation. (*best viewed in color pdf file*) (Color figure online)

3D objects, such as outdoor vehicles and pedestrians [1,10], remains a challenging issue. The detection algorithms are designed to regress the translation, scale and yaw angle of the bounding boxes. Compared to the axis-aligned 2D targets, more attributes of 3D object are obtained attributed to the sufficient spatial information provided by the mounted lidar scanners [1]. Directly consuming lidar points as the detection input has drawn more attention recently [22,39,54]. State-of-the-art 3D object detection methods project the point cloud to a certain viewpoint [7,52] for convolutional feature extraction in the 2D plane, or voxelize the point cloud and apply 3D convolution [30,54]. Recently two-stage RCNN methods [8,39] are proposed to better leverage the point-wise information. Compared to the monocular [2,4,20,28,45] or stereo [6,23,24,36] methods, the attributes of 3D object are obtained from the lidar points with fewer stages, which makes it possible for real-time detection usage.

To regress the parameters of rotated bounding boxes, existing approaches of 3D object detection regress the translation, scale and yaw angle individually by using the smooth-$\ell 1$ loss [11,37], which is based on the $\ell 1$-norm of parameter distance. While each parameter (i.e., height) might be normalized by the anchor parameters [21,54], the size of the anchor is a pre-defined scalar. Therefore, the value of the $\ell 1$-norm is still sensitive to the scale of the bounding box [38]. As shown in Fig. 1, the conventional loss and evaluation metric are inconsistent.

Addressing this loss-metric mismatch could provide insights into computer vision and machine learning tasks such as object detection [38] and metric learning [13].

In order to learn the bounding box parameters collaboratively as well as avoiding the scaling problem, directly optimizing Intersection over Union (IoU) is addressed in the axis-aligned cases [14,18,38,50]. Such attempts significantly enhance the performance in the axis-aligned 2D object detection. However, due to the variance in shape, pose and environment condition, object targets are hardly axis-aligned, especially for 3D objects. Geometrically, the intersection area between a pair of rotated bounding boxes is non-trivial to calculate by using the numerical methods. In bird's eye view, as shown in the upper part of Fig. 1, the shape of the intersected convex is diverse due to the variance of location, size and angle. Currently, the accurate convex area between a pair of rotated bounding boxes is often calculated outside the training loop, or regarded as a constant [49] and not involved in the gradient descent of the back propagation. To tackle the aforementioned problem brought by rotation, some methods directly estimate the confident score of IoU by using deep networks [15] or calculate a simplified version of IoU [27] to select positive samples. But neither of them tries to directly learn on the overlap of the bounding boxes, and few similar attempts have been made in 3D object detection.

In this paper, we propose an IoU for 3D object detection called Rotation-robust Intersection over Union ($RIoU$) with its loss function format ($\mathcal{L}_{RIoU}$), and incorporate it into the conventional $\ell 1$ loss. Specifically, we define a pair of projected rectangles to calculate the intersection in the 2D plane. It is suitable for bounding box regression in arbitrary angles. Besides, it only comprises basic arithmetic operations and the min / max function, which is feasible for back propagation during training. We also extend $RIoU$ to the volume and recent Generalized Intersection over Union [38] format. Experimental results on the KITTI [10] and nuScenes [1] datasets show that combined with our $\mathcal{L}_{RIoU}$, the performance of 3D object detection is improved by a large margin. Moreover, we test our method on the 2D rotated object detection to validate its applicability.

2   Related Work

Point-Based 3D Object Detection: While 3D oriented objects can be detected from monocular [2,4,20,28,45] or stereo [6,23,24,36] images, the spatial information is better preserved in point cloud data collected by the lidar scanners. It provides multiple projection viewpoints for feature aggregation [7]. Most state-of-the-art approaches consume raw lidar data as input. Early works directly apply 3D convolution to process the point cloud [9,22]. Several methods group point cloud into stacked 3D voxels [30,54] to generate more structured data, and [21] restricts the grouping operation within the ground plane to achieve real time detection. As for two-stage pipelines, some methods adopt detection results of 2D images to crop ROI regions in the 3D space [33,43,46], or fuse the image and point cloud feature to reduce the missing instances in the first stage [19]. Recently proposed RCNN methods [8,39] adopt PointNet-based [34] module for better extracting and aggregating the point-wise feature. Similar to object detection in 2D images, all those methods adopt the $\ell 1$ regression loss [11,37], which focuses on the difference of individual bounding box parameters.

Intersection over Union: Intersection over Union (IoU) is widely adopted as the evaluation metric in many visual tasks, such as object detection [5,11,25, 37], segmentation [3,34,35] and visual tracking [31]. Generally, it is calculated outside the training loop and not involved in the process of back-propagation. For example, it is adopted as a metric to discriminate between the positive and negative samples [18,54]. Attempts towards directly learning IoU have been made in the scenario of axis-aligned 2D object detection, since IoU is invariant to the scale of the problem [38]. Instead of calculating IoU between the detected and ground-truth bounding boxes, [15] predicts the IoU as a metric in non-maximum suppression (NMS). IoU loss is adopted for axis-aligned face detection [50], visual tracking [18] and lumbar region localization [14]. [42] designs Intersection over Ground-truth (IoG) to penalize the wrongly matched detections. [38] proposes Generalized IoU (GIoU) to penalize poor detection instances. In the context of rotation-free bounding box regression, [29,53] optimize axis-aligned IoU loss and angle loss seperately for text localization. [27] proposes a surrogate IoU, called Angle related IoU (ArIoU), to select prior boxes as positive samples for aerial image detection. More recently, [28] proposes *FQNet* to directly predict 3D IoU between samples and objects in monocular data, which is similar to [15]. The accurate 3D IoU loss is firstly proposed in [51], where the intersection can be calculated through traversing the vertices of the overlap area, which requires the sophisticated design of the forward and backward computation. It demonstrates superior performance over the $\ell 1$-based loss function. Another alternative is to regard the accurate IoU as a constant coefficient [49], where the calculation of IoU is not involved in the back propagation of the training process.

3   Approach

In this section, we formulate the proposed approach in the bird's eye view of 3D space, which corresponds to the general 2D cases and can be easily extended to the 3D cuboid formulation.

3.1   Rotation-Robust Intersection over Union

In the 3D space, a rotated bounding box B is defined by (x, y, z, l, h, w, r), where (x, y, z), (l, h, w) and r represent center coordinates, box size and rotation around z axis (yaw) respectively. As shown in (1), Intersection over Union (IoU) is calculated as an evaluation metric in object detection task generally.

$$IoU = \frac{B_1 \cap B_2}{B_1 + B_2 - B_1 \cap B_2}. \tag{1}$$

It is introduced as an optimized target in several conventional 2D cases [38, 41]. However, when extended to 3D or other cases, where the bounding box is

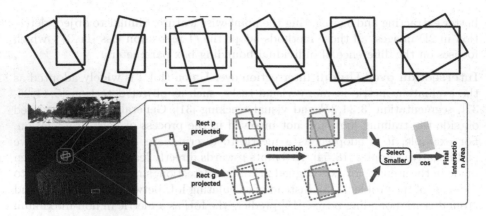

Fig. 2. Upper: Some of the overlapped situations between two rotated bounding boxes. **Bottom**: The calculation of Rotation-robust Intersection of rotated bounding box p and g corresponding to one of the upper situations, which is sampled from the KITTI [10] dataset. The projected rectangle p' (dotted) is defined in the canonical coordinate system built around g. And vice versa for g'. The smaller of $p' \cap g$ and $g' \cap p$ is preserved and multiplied by a cosine coefficient to get the final intersection, which is the numerator of $RIoU(p,g)$. (*best viewed in color pdf file*) (Color figure online)

rotatable, the calculation of the intersection area becomes non-trivial. The shape of the intersection polygon depends largely on the location, size and yaw angle of 2 bounding boxes. As shown in the upper part of Fig. 2, the polygon can be triangle, parallelogram, trapezoid or even pentagon, etc.

In bird's eye view or general 2D cases, a rotated bounding box is defined by (x, y, l, w, r). With the shape of 2×4, the coordinates of the bounding box corners C can be obtained from the parameters above. Given a pair of predicted bounding box $B_p(C_p)$ and ground-truth bounding box $B_g(C_g)$, a canonical coordinate system is firstly built around the center of B_g. In this system, B_g is axis-aligned and can be represented as $(0, 0, l_g, w_g, 0)$. Then we define a projected rectangle of B_p by satisfying the following properties: Firstly, B_p is inside the projected rectangle. Secondly, The projected rectangle is aligned to the axes of the new canonical coordinate system, i.e., the axes of B_g. Thirdly, The area of the projected rectangle is minimum. An example of defining such rectangles is shown in the bottom part of Fig. 2. As shown in (2), we first calculate the corner coordinates of B_p in the canonical coordinate system of B_g as $C_{p,a}$, including shifting the origin and rotating the axes. Here we denote the coordinate of i-th corner of predicted box as C_p^i. "$*$" denotes the matrix multiplication.

$$
\begin{aligned}
C_p^i &= C_p^i - [x_g, y_g]^T, i \in 1, 2, 3, 4 \\
C_{p,a} &= \begin{bmatrix} \cos r_g & \sin r_g \\ -\sin r_g & \cos r_g \end{bmatrix} * C_p.
\end{aligned}
\tag{2}
$$

In the canonical coordinate system of B_g, the corners of the projected rectangle can be easily defined by extracting the min / max coordinate value of corners. For example, $C_{p'}^1$, the top left coordinate of $B_{p'}$ is extracted as follows:

$$C_{p'}^1 = [\min_x C_{p,a}, \max_y C_{p,a}]^T \tag{3}$$

$B_{p'}$ is axis-aligned in the canonical coordinate system of B_g. It is easy to calculate a pair of $(I1, Un1)$ from $B_{p'}$ and B_g, which corresponds to the area of intersection and the smallest enclosing box of $B_{p'}$ and B_g.

By swapping B_g and B_p and then repeating (2) and (3), we can get another pair of $(I2, Un2)$. The smaller intersection value is preserved and multiplied by a cosine coefficient to get the final intersection area. The final intersection and union area is calculated as follows:

$$
\begin{aligned}
I_{RIoU} &= \min(I1, I2) \cdot |\cos(2 \cdot (r_g - r_p))|, \\
U_{RIoU} &= \max(I_{RIoU}, l_g \cdot w_g + l_p \cdot w_p - I_{RIoU}), \\
RIoU &= \frac{I_{RIoU}}{U_{RIoU}}.
\end{aligned} \tag{4}
$$

As shown in bottom part of Fig. 2, the area of $p' \cap g$ ($I1$) or $g' \cap p$ ($I2$) is larger than $g \cap p$. To remedy this error, we preserve the minimum area of $p' \cap g$ and $g' \cap p$. Besides, we set the angle coefficient of cosine as 2. Therefore, the calculated area decreases more sharply as the angle difference becomes larger. Note that RIoU equals zero when the angle difference is 45 degree. However, the partial derivative of $\mathcal{L}_{RIoU}$ with regard to all parameters except the rotation angle is zero, which pushes the angle difference down to zero. And our $RIoU$ degrades to the conventional axis-aligned IoU when the boxes are parallel or orthogonal. We choose the cosine function in (4) based on its following properties: It decreases as the angle deviates from zero, which penalizes the fluctuation of angle difference. Moreover, it is periodic, which corresponds to the periodic orientation of objects. Please refer to the supplementary pages for more design details.

Apart from $RIoU$, we also implement its Generalized Intersection over Union ($GIoU$) format proposed in [38]. It is designed specifically to reveal and penalize the low intersection between 2 bounding boxes:

$$
\begin{aligned}
Un_{RIoU} &= \max(Un1, Un2), \\
RGIoU &= RIoU - \frac{Un_{RIoU} - U_{RIoU}}{Un_{RIoU}}.
\end{aligned} \tag{5}
$$

The complete process of calculation is summarized in Algorithm 1. The algorithm only comprises basic arithmetic operations and the min / max function, which is feasible for back propagation during training.

As the $RIoU$ above is implemented in bird's eye view, it can be easily extended to 3D IoU format by introducing another axis-aligned z dimension, as shown in (6). Here we denote the upper/lower z coordinate of ground-truth and predicted bounding box as $z_{g,u}/z_{g,l}$ and $z_{p,u}/z_{p,l}$. But in the experiment section we show that, the incorporation of $\mathcal{L}_{RIoU}$ implemented in the 2D plane enhances the performance of both 2D and 3D target detection.

$$\delta z = \min(z_{g,u}, z_{p,u}) - \max(z_{g,l}, z_{p,l})$$
$$RIoU(v) = \max(0, \delta z) \cdot RIoU \qquad (6)$$

Algorithm 1: *RIoU, RGIoU* and their loss function.

---

    input : Bounding box B_g, B_p and their corners.
    output: *RIoU, RGIoU*, $\mathcal{L}_{RIoU}$, $\mathcal{L}_{RGIoU}$.

1 Function Project(B_1, B_2):
2   In the canonical coordinate system of B_1, set new the origin and corner coordinates for B_2 using (2);
3   Locate B_2', the projected rectangle of B_2 using (3);
4   Calculate *Intersection* $B_1 \cap B_2'$ as I;
5   Calculate *Universal* of B_1 and B_2' as Un;
6   **return** I, Un

7 1 Calculate 2 pairs of intersection and universal:
8 $I1, Un1 = $ **Project** (B_g, B_p);
9 $I2, Un2 = $ **Project** (B_p, B_g);
10 2 Calculate *RIoU* and *RGIoU* using (4) and (5);
11 3 $\mathcal{L}_{RIoU} = 1 - RIoU$, $\mathcal{L}_{RGIoU} = 1 - RGIoU$.

Our $\mathcal{L}_{RIoU}$ and $\mathcal{L}_{RGIoU}$ is bounded in terms of stability. The final intersection area of $RIoU$ is the minimum value of a subset of p and a subset of g. Hence I_{RIoU} is always smaller than the area of p or g, thus smaller than U_{RIoU} in (4). Therefore, the $RIoU$ and $\mathcal{L}_{RIoU}$ are both bounded in $[0, 1]$. As for $RGIoU$ and $\mathcal{L}_{RGIoU}$, since Un_{RIoU} is always larger than U_{RIoU} in (4), $RGIoU$ is bounded in $[-1, 1]$. And $\mathcal{L}_{RGIoU}$ is bounded in $[0, 2]$.

3.2 Discussion

Comparison of RIoU Loss and the Smooth-$\ell 1$ Loss. When rotation is introduced in the detection task, the smooth-$\ell 1$ loss [11,37] is often adopted as the regression target, which focuses on the element-wise difference of the bounding box parameters. A typical set of element-wise difference in 3D cases is defined in (7) [21,54], where gt and a denote the parameter of a ground-truth bounding box and its matched anchor box respectively.

$$\Delta x = \frac{x^{gt} - x^a}{d^a}, \Delta y = \frac{y^{gt} - y^a}{d^a}, \Delta z = \frac{z^{gt} - z^a}{h^a},$$
$$\Delta w = \log \frac{w^{gt}}{w^a}, \Delta l = \log \frac{l^{gt}}{l^a}, \Delta h = \log \frac{h^{gt}}{h^a}, \qquad (7)$$
$$\Delta \theta = \sin \left(\theta^{gt} - \theta^a\right).$$

Smooth-$\ell 1$ loss shares with $\ell 1$-norm difference the drawback demonstrated in [38]. As each parameter is optimized independently, smaller parameter difference can not guarantee bigger IoU (see Fig. 1). The normalization brought by the pre-defined anchor parameters d_a and h_a is not fully effective, because the size parameters of anchors are usually pre-defined scalars. Consequently, the $\ell 1$ difference is sensitive to the scale of the bounding box. Therefore, an approximate function that directly optimizes IoU may further enhance the performance.

Comparison of RIoU and Other IoUs. Our RIoU shares the non-negativity, identity of indiscernibles and commutativity with the accurate IoU. The closest to our work is the angle-related IoU ($ArIoU$) proposed in [27]:

$$ArIoU_{180}(A, B) = \frac{area(\hat{A} \cap B)}{area(\hat{A} \cup B)} \cdot |cos(\theta_A - \theta_B)|. \tag{8}$$

$ArIoU$ is used for selecting positive anchors at the training period. $\hat{A}$ shares the parameters with A except that its rotation is the same with B. $RIoU$ and $ArIoU$ both take the angle difference into consideration. But $ArIoU$ is a non-communicative function, which means $ArIoU(A, B) \neq ArIoU(B, A)$. Besides, the area of $\hat{A} \cup B$ might be smaller than $A \cup B$. The cosine part further decays the intersection area, which makes the estimation even worse.

Recently [51] proposes to replace the $\ell 1$ loss with the accurate IoU loss function, which does not suffer from the approximation error. The forward computation of IoU and the backward propagation of the error are firstly implemented manually in this work. However, our proposed $RIoU$ can be easily implemented into the existing framework, and does not require the traversal of the vertices.

4   Experiment

To evaluate our $RIoU$ loss and its variant for rotated 3D object detection, we used the popular KITTI dataset [10] and the newly proposed challenging nuScenes [1] dataset. We plugged $\mathcal{L}_{RIoU}$ and $\mathcal{L}_{RGIoU}$ into the loss function of Frustum-PointNet v1 [33,34], Frustum-PointNet v2 [33,35], PointPillars [21] and VoteNet [32]. The weights for the $\ell 1$ loss and the proposed loss are the same. Here we denote the raw $\ell 1$ based regression function baseline as $\ell 1$, baseline incorporated with our proposed $\mathcal{L}_{RIoU}$ or $\mathcal{L}_{RGIoU}$ as $\ell 1 + iou$ or $\ell 1 + giou$.

4.1   Datasets and Settings

KITTI: The KITTI dataset [10] contains 7481 training and 7518 testing samples for 3D object detection benchmark. The evaluation is classified into Easy, Moderate or Hard according to the object size, occlusion and truncation. We followed [7] to split the training set into 3712 training samples and 3769 validation samples. As for input modality of the KITTI dataset, We took raw point cloud [21] and fusion [33] into consideration.

We reported the experiment results on the KITTI validation set. The evaluation took 3D average precision as the metric. The threshold for car, pedestrian and cyclist is 0.7, 0.5 and 0.5 respectively.

Table 1. Comparisons of different loss settings on car category of the KITTI validation set. The baseline model is Frustum-PointNet [33] (F-PointNet). The backbone network is PointNet [34] (v1) and PointNet++ [35] (v2) respectively. The results are reported on the task of **3D object localization** (Loc.) and **3D object detection** (Det.).

Method		Easy		Moderate		Hard	
		v1	v2	v1	v2	v1	v2
Loc.	$\ell 1$ (baseline)	87.67	88.16	82.68	84.02	74.74	76.44
	$\ell 1$+ArIoU	**88.36**	88.17	82.81	84.12	74.23	76.39
	$\ell 1$+$RIoU$	88.01	88.56	82.83	**85.07**	75.45	**77.02**
	$\ell 1$+$RGIoU$	88.10	**88.67**	**82.93**	84.83	**75.65**	76.81
Det.	$\ell 1$ (baseline)	83.47	83.76	69.52	70.92	62.86	63.65
	$\ell 1$+ARIoU	83.00	84.07	68.94	71.12	60.96	63.71
	$\ell 1$+$RIoU$	84.45	**84.83**	71.20	**72.13**	63.61	**64.35**
	$\ell 1$+$RGIoU$	**84.72**	84.10	**71.46**	71.71	**63.75**	64.00

NuScenes: The nuScenes dataset [1] contains 1k scenes, 1.4M camera images, 400k LIDAR sweeps, 1.4M RADAR sweeps and 40k key frames, which has 7x as many annotations as the KITTI dataset. Each key frame is annotated with 35 3D boxes on average, which is 2.6x as many as the KITTI dataset. The annotation of each instance comprises semantic category, parameters of 3D bounding box, velocity and attribute (parked, stopped, moving, etc.). Each scene is captured continuously for 20 s. The whole dataset is categorized into 23 semantic categories (car, pedestrian, truck, etc.) and 8 attributes.

For the nuScenes 3D object detection evaluation, we followed the evaluation protocol proposed along with the dataset [1]. While the average precision (AP) was calculated as final metric, 2D box center distance on the ground plane instead of IoU was used as threshold. We also evaluated the result following the KITTI protocol. The instance was regarded as easy, moderate or hard according to the number of points inside the bounding box.

SUN RGB-D: The challenging SUN RGB-D[40] dataset for scene understanding contains 10k RGB-D images, 5,285 for training and 5,050 for testing. It's densely annotated with 64k oriented 3D bounding boxes. The whole dataset is categorized into 37 indoor object classes (bed, chair, desk, etc.). The standard evaluation protocol reports the performance on the 10 most common categories.

4.2 Results and Analysis

Frustum-PointNet: The training process took 200 epochs. We used the 2D object detections of the training and validation set provided by the authors[1]. As shown in Table 1, when the backbone network of F-PointNet is Point-Net [34], $\mathcal{L}_{RIoU}$ outperforms these compared methods in both 2D localization

---

[1] github.com/charlesq34/frustum-pointnets/.

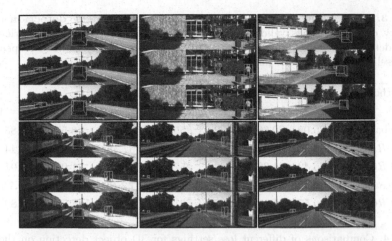

Fig. 3. Visualization of 6 predicted samples on the KITTI validation set (predictions in blue, ground-truths in pink). In each sample, we compare the baseline (**upper**) with the incorporation of $\mathcal{L}_{RIoU}$ (**middle**) or $\mathcal{L}_{RGIoU}$ (**lower**). (Color figure online)

Table 2. Comparisons of different loss settings for **3D object detection** and **3D object localization** on car category of the KITTI validation set. The baseline model is PointPillars [21].

Method	3D detection			3D localization		
	Easy	Moderate	Hard	Easy	Moderate	Hard
$\ell 1$ (baseline)	87.29	76.99	70.84	89.92	87.88	86.72
IoU [51]	87.88	**77.92**	**75.70**	90.21	**88.25**	**87.56**
$\ell 1 + RIoU$	**88.02**	77.37	74.04	**90.45**	87.98	85.83

and 3D detection. The $\mathcal{L}_{RGIoU}$ further improves the detection performances. This is because the predicted boxes are generated from anchors in different sizes and angles but the same center, which could not guarantee the positive match between anchor and ground-truth. Then those negative matches are penalized more by $\mathcal{L}_{RGIoU}$ than $\mathcal{L}_{RIoU}$. For the experimental results of the *cyclist* and *pedestrian* categories, please refer to the supplementary pages.

Several visualization results are shown in Fig. 3. We projected the bounding boxes with confidence score larger than 0.3 into the raw images. In each of the 6 samples, the inaccuracy of localization exists in the **upper** baseline results. When incorporated with $\mathcal{L}_{RGIoU}$ (**middle**) or $\mathcal{L}_{RIoU}$ (**bottom**), the localization is notably improved. The results are from Frustum PointNet v2.

PointPillars: We used the SECOND [47] implementation[2] for the nuScenes and KITTI. We experimented car-only detection on both KITTI and nuScenes, using SECOND v1.5. The training process took 600k iterations for both datasets. And

---

[2] github.com/traveller59/second.pytorch

Table 3. Comparisons of different loss settings for **3D object detection** on car category of the nuScenes validation set. The Average Precision (AP) metric of 3D object detection is based on the matching of center distance(D) and IoU respectively. The baseline model is PointPillars [21].

Method	3D detection (IoU)			3D detection (D)			
	Easy	Moderate	Hard	D = 0.5	D = 1.0	D = 2.0	D = 4.0
$\ell 1$ (baseline)	86.02	80.66	62.03	55.30	64.79	68.55	71.85
$\ell 1 + RIoU$	86.30	81.24	62.53	57.26	67.18	70.47	73.44
$\ell 1 + RGIoU$	86.42	81.03	62.65	57.9	67.75	71.07	73.91
$\ell 1 + RIoU$(v)	**86.82**	**82.97**	**65.15**	**61.87**	**72.89**	**75.76**	**77.73**
$\ell 1 + RGIoU$(v)	86.57	81.13	63.79	61.29	71.87	74.75	76.89

Table 4. Comparisons of different loss settings for 3D object detection on the SUN RGB-D dataset. The baseline model is VoteNet [32].

Method	bathtub	bed	bookshelf	chair	desk	dresser	nightstand	sofa	table	toilet	mAP	mAR
votenet	73.7	81.6	28.5	73.5	24.4	27.9	62.5	65.2	50.0	**90.1**	57.7	83.9
votenet+RIoU	73.5	**84.6**	31.6	**74.6**	24.8	**30.0**	**62.7**	**65.9**	**50.7**	89.3	**58.8**	**86.9**
votenent+RGIoU	**78.7**	84.1	**32.2**	73.5	**25.8**	29.4	60.4	65.5	49.5	88.6	**58.8**	85.4

we also evaluated a 9-class subset on the nuScenes using the proposed loss, which can be seen in the supplementary pages. The results are summarized in Table 2 and Table 3. All trials were evaluated on the whole validation set. While $\mathcal{L}_{RIoU}$ and $\mathcal{L}_{RGIoU}$ both improve the detection performance by an obvious margin, the enhancement by $\mathcal{L}_{RGIoU}$ is not superior to $\mathcal{L}_{RIoU}$. In Table 2, the combination of $\ell 1$ loss and the RIoU loss achieves the competitive performance in the easy mode, compared to the IoU loss which computes the accurate IoU. Note that our proposed RIoU saves the sophisticated forward and backward computation.

VoteNet: We followed the official implementation[3] of VoteNet [32]. The training process took 180 epochs. The learning rate was decayed at epoch 40 and epoch 80 respectively. As shown in Table 4, both $\mathcal{L}_{RIoU}$ and $\mathcal{L}_{RGIoU}$ enhance the performance in terms of mAP and mAR, where $\mathcal{L}_{RIoU}$ achieves the best results. Besides, as for the AP of the individual categories, the baseline method only achieves the best result in the "toilet" category. Especially in the "bathtub" category, the $\mathcal{L}_{RGIoU}$ improves upon the baseline method by 5 AP.

Compared with ArIoU: We also implemented the loss format of angle-related IoU [27] (ArIoU) as $1 - ArIoU$, and incorporated it into regression loss function just like $\mathcal{L}_{RIoU}$. The experiment results on Frustum PointNet [33] is presented in Table 1. When incorporated with $\mathcal{L}_{ArIoU}$, about half of the detection metrics of Frustum PointNet even drop compared with baseline. Compared with $RIoU$ loss function, ArIoU is not beneficial to the detection performance. Besides, during

---

[3] github.com/facebookresearch/votenet.

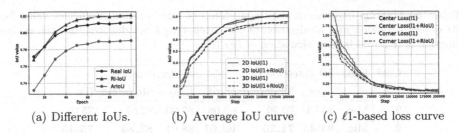

(a) Different IoUs. (b) Average IoU curve (c) ℓ1-based loss curve

Fig. 4. (a): The average real IoU, $ArIoU$ and our $RIoU$ of sampled bird's eye view prediction and ground-truth pairs. (b): The average IoU curve with regard to training steps. (c): The center loss and corner loss curve w.r.t. training steps.

first 100 epochs before convergence, we collected the predicted bounding boxes and their corresponding ground-truths. We randomly picked 50k sample pairs with the interval of 10 epochs, and calculated the average real IoU, $ArIoU$ and our $RIoU$. The result in Fig. 4(a) shows that our $RIoU$ approximates better than $ArIoU$, especially during first 40 epochs.

3D Assisted by 2D: While we implemented the $RIoU$ in 2D bird's eye view, it benefits 2D localization and 3D detection performance simultaneously. Specifically, our $RIoU$ improves 2D bird's eye view IoU (Fig. 4(b)), 3D IoU (Fig. 4(b)), center loss (Fig. 4(c)) and corner loss optimization (Fig. 4(c)) jointly. Note that the center loss and corner loss are both in ℓ1 format, which means our loss can in tern benefit the traditional ℓ1 based regression loss. When incorporated with our $\mathcal{L}_{RIoU}$, the overlap between the prediction and ground-truth is higher. The detection network also learns bounding box parameters more efficiently. The data was collected from the experiment on Frustum PointNet v2 [33].

Given the $RIoU$ in bird's eye view, we implemented the volume format of our $RIoU$ by introducing the z axis. The calculation process is the same with the axis-aligned 3D IoU. Following the setting, the training process took 40k iterations. We denote the volume format as ℓ1+$RIoU$(v) or ℓ1+$RGIoU$(v). As shown in the last 2 rows of Table 3, the volume format further enhanced the detection performance based on the localization improvement. When incorporated with the volume format of $\mathcal{L}_{RIoU}$, the network achieves the best detection performance.

4.3 Ablation Study

The goal of the ablation study is to verify the heuristic design of our $RIoU$. We did the ablation experiments on the 3D car detection task of the KITTI [10] dataset. We chose F-PointNet v1 [33] as the baseline method.

The Minimum of Intersection Areas: While min, max and *mean* function all hold the stability for the proposed method, we choose the min function in (4) to mitigate the estimation error of $Interseciton1$ and $Intersection2$. In the ablation experiment, we replaced the min function with max or *mean*. As shown

Table 5. Ablation experiment results on different function and coefficient value for 3D object detection and localization of car category. "w.o." denotes that the cosine function is removed in the calculation of I_{RIoU}.

Coef	Func	3D detection			3D localization		
		Easy	Moderate	Hard	Easy	Moderate	Hard
2	Max	83.53	70.79	63.08	87.90	82.67	75.01
2	Min	**84.45**	**71.20**	**63.61**	88.01	**82.83**	**75.45**
2	Avg	83.11	69.68	62.85	**88.09**	82.82	74.94
1	Min	83.86	70.73	63.22	87.96	82.53	74.67
2	Min	**84.45**	**71.20**	**63.61**	88.01	**82.83**	**75.45**
3	Min	83.79	70.10	63.11	87.83	82.31	74.93
4	Min	83.23	70.88	63.45	**88.33**	82.26	75.31
5	Min	82.90	70.39	63.08	87.67	82.27	74.22
w.o	Min	82.41	69.02	61.13	87.87	82.67	75.01

in Table 5, except for the easy mode in 3D object localization, the min function gave the best detection result.

The Cosine Coefficient: The ablation study on the cosine coefficient in (4) focuses on 2 issues: the necessity of the cosine coefficient and the angle coefficient value within the cosine function. As shown in the lower part of Table 5, F-PointNet achieved the best detection performance when the cosine coefficient was preserved and the angle coefficient was 2. Note that the other 2 categories also achieved the best performance with Min function and coefficient 2, which is not shown in the table to save space. After we removed the cosine coefficient from the calculation of I_{RIoU} in (4), or modified the angle coefficient value, the detection performance dropped by an obvious margin. Note that F-PointNet gave the best 3D object localization performance under the easy mode when the angle coefficient value was 4. This might be due to similar degradation property when the 2 boxes are parallel or orthogonal. Besides, the larger angle coefficient value penalizes the angle difference more.

4.4 Applications in 2D Object Detection

As mentioned above, the proposed $RIoU$ loss function improves the 3D object detection performance by an obvious margin. To further verify its effectiveness in various rotated object detection tasks, we validated it on several 2D detection benchmarks, such as text localization and aerial image detection. The details of the latter are presented in the supplementary pages.

Datasets and Settings: The ICDAR 2015 text localization benchmark [16] contains 1000 images for training and 500 images for testing. Each annotated text region is represented by 4 quadrangle corners. We chose EAST [53] as our baseline method, which optimizes the axis-aligned IoU and angle seperately. We

Table 6. Text localization results, evaluated on the ICDAR 2015 test set. The 2013 and 2015 stand for the ICDAR 2013 and ICDAR 2015 dataset respectively.

Method	Trained on		Metric		
	2013	2015	Recall	Precision	F-Score
$\ell1$ (baseline)		✓	83.80	76.46	79.96
$\ell1$ (baseline)[a]	✓	✓	84.66	77.32	80.83
$\ell1+RGIoU$		✓	82.86	77.52	80.10
$\ell1+RIoU$		✓	**86.20**	**78.48**	**82.16**

[a] Reported on the ICDAR 2015 benchmark website.

used the implementation with RBOX and adopted ResNet-50 [12] as the feature extractor. Note that the network was trained and evaluated on the single ICDAR 2015 dataset when incorporated with the proposed loss. One of the baseline networks was also tuned on the ICDAR 2013 dataset [17], which contains 229 training images with horizontal text annotations.

Results: The text localization results are reported in 3 metrics: recall, precision and F-score. As shown in Table 6, when incorporated with $\mathcal{L}_{RGIoU}$ and trained only on the ICDAR 2015 dataset, the detection performance outperforms the baseline in terms of Precision and F-score. Especially when incorporated with $\mathcal{L}_{RIoU}$, all the 3 metrics even surpass the jointly-trained baseline by an obvious margin. The $RIoU$ helps to propose the text boxes more adequately and locate them more accurately, which demonstrates the effectiveness of our proposed loss function. The illustration is shown in the supplementary pages.

From the experiment results in text localization and detection in aerial images, we can see that the proposed loss function could significantly improve the detection performance of the rotated 2D targets. Apart from the 3D cuboids, it is also suitable for detection targets in the shape of narrow rectangle and large numbers of small, cluttered rotated targets in an image.

5 Conclusion

In this paper, we have proposed a loss function called Rotation-robust Intersection over Union ($RIoU$) for robust object detection. It is designed for bounding boxes in arbitrary rotation conditions. The implementation only comprises basic operations, and is feasible for back-propagation. It is suitable for both 2D target localization and 3D object detection. Incorporated into traditional $\ell1$-based regression loss function, the proposed loss function achieves notable improvement over several state-of-the-art baselines. In the future, we will focus on the invariance of IoU with regard to the rotation. We will also explore its application in more abundant cases, such as object detection in indoor scenes.

Acknowledgement. This work was supported in part by the National Key Research and Development Program of China under Grant 2017YFA0700802, in part by the

National Natural Science Foundation of China under Grant 61822603, Grant U1813218, Grant U1713214, and Grant 61672306, in part by Beijing Academy of Artificial Intelligence (BAAI), in part by a grant from the Institute for Guo Qiang, Tsinghua University, in part by the Shenzhen Fundamental Research Fund (Subject Arrangement) under Grant JCYJ20170412170602564, and in part by Tsinghua University Initiative Scientific Research Program.

References

1. Caesar, H., et al.: nuScenes: a multimodal dataset for autonomous driving. arXiv preprint arXiv:1903.11027 (2019)
2. Chabot, F., Chaouch, M., Rabarisoa, J., Teuliere, C., Chateau, T.: Deep Manta: a coarse-to-fine many-task network for joint 2D and 3D vehicle analysis from monocular image. In: CVPR, pp. 2040–2049 (2017)
3. Chen, L.C., Papandreou, G., Kokkinos, I., Murphy, K., Yuille, A.L.: DeepLab: Semantic image segmentation with deep convolutional nets, atrous convolution, and fully connected CRFs. TPAMI **40**(4), 834–848 (2017)
4. Chen, X., Kundu, K., Zhang, Z., Ma, H., Fidler, S., Urtasun, R.: Monocular 3D object detection for autonomous driving. In: CVPR, pp. 2147–2156 (2016)
5. Chen, X., Kundu, K., Zhu, Y., Berneshawi, A.G., Ma, H., Fidler, S., Urtasun, R.: 3D object proposals for accurate object class detection. In: NIPS, pp. 424–432 (2015)
6. Chen, X., Kundu, K., Zhu, Y., Ma, H., Fidler, S., Urtasun, R.: 3D object proposals using stereo imagery for accurate object class detection. TPAMI **40**(5), 1259–1272 (2017)
7. Chen, X., Ma, H., Wan, J., Li, B., Xia, T.: Multi-view 3D object detection network for autonomous driving. In: CVPR, pp. 1907–1915 (2017)
8. Chen, Y., Liu, S., Shen, X., Jia, J.: Fast point R-CNN. In: ICCV, pp. 9775–9784 (2019)
9. Engelcke, M., Rao, D., Wang, D.Z., Tong, C.H., Posner, I.: Vote3Deep: fast object detection in 3D point clouds using efficient convolutional neural networks. In: ICRA, pp. 1355–1361 (2017)
10. Geiger, A., Lenz, P., Urtasun, R.: Are we ready for autonomous driving? The KITTI vision benchmark suite. In: CVPR, pp. 3354–3361 (2012)
11. Girshick, R.: Fast R-CNN. In: ICCV, pp. 1440–1448 (2015)
12. He, K., Zhang, X., Ren, S., Sun, J.: Deep residual learning for image recognition. In: CVPR, pp. 770–778 (2016)
13. Huang, C., Zhai, S., Talbott, W., Bautista, M.A., Sun, S.Y., Guestrin, C., Susskind, J.: Addressing the loss-metric mismatch with adaptive loss alignment. In: ICML (2019)
14. Janssens, R., Zeng, G., Zheng, G.: Fully automatic segmentation of lumbar vertebrae from CT images using cascaded 3D fully convolutional networks. In: ISBI, pp. 893–897 (2018)
15. Jiang, B., Luo, R., Mao, J., Xiao, T., Jiang, Y.: Acquisition of localization confidence for accurate object detection. In: Ferrari, V., Hebert, M., Sminchisescu, C., Weiss, Y. (eds.) Computer Vision – ECCV 2018. LNCS, vol. 11218, pp. 816–832. Springer, Cham (2018). https://doi.org/10.1007/978-3-030-01264-9_48
16. Karatzas, D., et al.: ICDAR 2015 competition on robust reading. In: ICDAR, pp. 1156–1160 (2015)

17. Karatzas, D., et al.: ICDAR 2013 robust reading competition. In: ICDAR, pp. 1484–1493 (2013)
18. Kosiorek, A., Bewley, A., Posner, I.: Hierarchical attentive recurrent tracking. In: NIPS, pp. 3053–3061 (2017)
19. Ku, J., Mozifian, M., Lee, J., Harakeh, A., Waslander, S.L.: Joint 3D proposal generation and object detection from view aggregation. In: IROS, pp. 1–8 (2018)
20. Ku, J., Pon, A.D., Waslander, S.L.: Monocular 3D object detection leveraging accurate proposals and shape reconstruction. In: CVPR, pp. 11867–11876 (2019)
21. Lang, A.H., Vora, S., Caesar, H., Zhou, L., Yang, J., Beijbom, O.: PointPillars: fast encoders for object detection from point clouds. In: CVPR, pp. 12697–12705 (2019)
22. Li, B.: 3D fully convolutional network for vehicle detection in point cloud. In: IROS, pp. 1513–1518 (2017)
23. Li, P., Chen, X., Shen, S.: Stereo R-CNN based 3D object detection for autonomous driving. In: CVPR, pp. 7644–7652 (2019)
24. Li, P., Qin, T., et al.: Stereo vision-based semantic 3D object and ego-motion tracking for autonomous driving. In: ECCV, pp. 646–661 (2018)
25. Lin, T.Y., Dollár, P., Girshick, R., He, K., Hariharan, B., Belongie, S.: Feature pyramid networks for object detection. In: CVPR, pp. 2117–2125 (2017)
26. Lin, T.Y., Goyal, P., Girshick, R., He, K., Dollár, P.: Focal loss for dense object detection. In: ICCV, pp. 2980–2988 (2017)
27. Liu, L., Pan, Z., Lei, B.: Learning a rotation invariant detector with rotatable bounding box. arXiv preprint arXiv:1711.09405 (2017)
28. Liu, L., Lu, J., Xu, C., Tian, Q., Zhou, J.: Deep fitting degree scoring network for monocular 3D object detection. In: CVPR, pp. 1057–1066 (2019)
29. Liu, X., Liang, D., Yan, S., Chen, D., Qiao, Y., Yan, J.: FOTS: fast oriented text spotting with a unified network. In: CVPR, pp. 5676–5685 (2018)
30. Maturana, D., Scherer, S.: VoxNet: a 3D convolutional neural network for real-time object recognition. In: IROS, pp. 922–928 (2015)
31. Nam, H., Han, B.: Learning multi-domain convolutional neural networks for visual tracking. In: CVPR, pp. 4293–4302 (2016)
32. Qi, C.R., Litany, O., He, K., Guibas, L.J.: Deep hough voting for 3D object detection in point clouds. In: Proceedings of the IEEE International Conference on Computer Vision, pp. 9277–9286 (2019)
33. Qi, C.R., Liu, W., Wu, C., Su, H., Guibas, L.J.: Frustum PointNets for 3D object detection from RGB-D data. In: CVPR, pp. 918–927 (2018)
34. Qi, C.R., Su, H., Mo, K., Guibas, L.J.: PointNet: deep learning on point sets for 3D classification and segmentation. In: CVPR, pp. 652–660 (2017)
35. Qi, C.R., Yi, L., Su, H., Guibas, L.J.: PointNet++: deep hierarchical feature learning on point sets in a metric space. In: NIPS, pp. 5099–5108 (2017)
36. Qin, Z., Wang, J., Lu, Y.: Triangulation learning network: from monocular to stereo 3D object detection. In: CVPR, pp. 11867–11876 (2019)
37. Ren, S., He, K., Girshick, R., Sun, J.: Faster R-CNN: towards real-time object detection with region proposal networks. In: NIPS, pp. 91–99 (2015)
38. Rezatofighi, H., Tsoi, N., Gwak, J., Sadeghian, A., Reid, I., Savarese, S.: Generalized intersection over union: a metric and a loss for bounding box regression. In: CVPR, pp. 658–666 (2019)
39. Shi, S., Wang, X., Li, H.: PointRCNN: 3D object proposal generation and detection from point cloud. In: CVPR, pp. 770–779 (2019)

40. Song, S., Lichtenberg, S.P., Xiao, J.: Sun RGB-D: a RGB-D scene understanding benchmark suite. In: Proceedings of the IEEE Conference on Computer Vision and Pattern Recognition, pp. 567–576 (2015)
41. Tychsen-Smith, L., Petersson, L.: Improving object localization with fitness NMS and bounded IoU loss. In: CVPR, pp. 6877–6885 (2018)
42. Wang, X., Xiao, T., Jiang, Y., Shao, S., Sun, J., Shen, C.: Repulsion loss: detecting pedestrians in a crowd. In: CVPR, pp. 7774–7783 (2018)
43. Wang, Z., Jia, K.: Frustum convNet: sliding frustums to aggregate local point-wise features for a modal 3D object detection. arXiv preprint arXiv:1903.01864 (2019)
44. Xia, G.S., et al.: DOTA: a large-scale dataset for object detection in aerial images. In: CVPR, pp. 3974–3983 (2018)
45. Xu, B., Chen, Z.: Multi-level fusion based 3D object detection from monocular images. In: CVPR, pp. 2345–2353 (2018)
46. Xu, D., Anguelov, D., Jain, A.: PointFusion: deep sensor fusion for 3D bounding box estimation. In: CVPR, pp. 244–253 (2018)
47. Yan, Y., Mao, Y., Li, B.: Second: sparsely embedded convolutional detection. Sensors 18(10), 3337 (2018)
48. Yang, X., Liu, Q., Yan, J., Li, A.: R3Det: refined single-stage detector with feature refinement for rotating object. arXiv preprint arXiv:1908.05612 (2019)
49. Yang, X., et al.: SCRDet: towards more robust detection for small, cluttered and rotated objects. In: ICCV, pp. 8232–8241 (2019)
50. Yu, J., Jiang, Y., Wang, Z., Cao, Z., Huang, T.: UnitBox: an advanced object detection network. In: ACM MM, pp. 516–520 (2016)
51. Zhou, D., et al.: IoU loss for 2D/3D object detection. In: 3DV, pp. 85–94 (2019)
52. Zhou, J., Lu, X., Tan, X., Shao, Z., Ding, S., Ma, L.: FVNet: 3D front-view proposal generation for real-time object detection from point clouds. arXiv preprint arXiv:1903.10750 (2019)
53. Zhou, X., et al.: East: an efficient and accurate scene text detector. In: CVPR, pp. 5551–5560 (2017)
54. Zhou, Y., Tuzel, O.: VoxelNet: end-to-end learning for point cloud based 3D object detection. In: CVPR, pp. 4490–4499 (2018)

New Threats Against Object Detector with Non-local Block

Yi Huang$^{(\boxtimes)}$, Fan Wang , Adams Wai-Kin Kong , and Kwok-Yan Lam

Nanyang Technological University, Singapore, Singapore
{S160042,fan005}@e.ntu.edu.sg, {adamskong,kwokyan.lam}@ntu.edu.sg

Abstract. The introduction of non-local blocks to the traditional CNN architecture enhances its performance for various computer vision tasks by improving its capabilities of capturing long-range dependencies. However, the usage of non-local blocks may also introduce new threats to computer vision systems. Therefore, it is important to study the threats caused by non-local blocks before directly applying them on commercial systems. In this paper, two new threats named disappearing attack and appearing attack against object detectors with a non-local block are investigated. The former aims at misleading an object detector with a non-local block such that it is unable to detect a target object category while the latter aims at misleading the object detector such that it detects a predefined object category, which is not present in images. Different from the existing attacks against object detectors, these threats are able to be performed in long range cases. This means that the target object and the universal adversarial patches learned from the proposed algorithms can have long distance between them. To examine the threats, digital and physical experiments are conducted on Faster R-CNN with a non-local block and 6331 images from 56 videos. The experiments show that the universal patches are able to mislead the detector with greater probabilities. To explain the threats from non-local blocks, the reception fields of CNN models with and without non-local blocks are studied empirically and theoretically.

Keywords: Non-local block · Adversarial examples · Object detection

1 Introduction

Convolutional neural networks (CNNs) have been becoming an essential component in computer vision systems where many of them have been deployed commercially. Traditional CNNs are built on local operators, such as convolution and pooling. In order to extract information in a wide area, the local operators

Electronic supplementary material The online version of this chapter (https://doi.org/10.1007/978-3-030-58565-5_29) contains supplementary material, which is available to authorized users.

© Springer Nature Switzerland AG 2020
A. Vedaldi et al. (Eds.): ECCV 2020, LNCS 12365, pp. 481–497, 2020.
https://doi.org/10.1007/978-3-030-58565-5_29

are stacked, resulting in larger receptive fields in theory. However, Luo *et al.* pinpointed that the effective receptive fields of CNNs are much smaller than their theoretical receptive fields [20]. Furthermore, stacking the local operators, especially convolution, would dramatically increase the computational cost and cause optimization difficulties [8]. To address these issues, Wang *et al.* generalized the classical non-local mean operator for image denoising [1] and proposed non-local blocks [31] in 2018. Since the non-local blocks can be easily inserted into many existing architectures and combined with other operators, they have been taken as a generic family of building blocks in CNNs for capturing long-range dependencies. In fact, the non-local neural network has raised a new trend in computer vision with an outstanding performance in object detection [13,25,29,35], as well as other various techniques on this basis, such as action recognition [9,24] and person re-identification [16]. There are nearly 200 related articles published in top computer vision venues during the past two years. Non-local blocks have also been applied on other research fields, such as computer-assisted radiology and surgery, bioinformatics, electronic and automation control, speech processing, *etc.* With it being a heated topic, and its potentials, it has also drawn attention from industry and companies, including Facebook [31], Microsoft [2], Baidu [36], Tencent [6,28], Huawei [5], Face++ [3], *etc.*

However, massively applying the non-local blocks in commercial systems without studying their threats would be risky. Traditional CNNs are well-known in suffering from adversarial examples. Researchers have demonstrated that using carefully crafted adversarial examples, they can mislead different CNNs designed for various computer vision problems. These include image and video classification, segmentation and object detection [4,10,11,27,34,37]. To mislead object detectors, the current attacks either modify pixels inside target objects [4,17,26] or put the adversarial patches very close to target objects [10,11]. Though non-local blocks have been applied to a lot of computer vision problems, object detection is selected for this study because it is an essential component in many cyber-physical systems, *e.g.*, autonomous vehicles. In order to investigate whether the non-local blocks would bring new threats to object detectors, two types of attacks are studied in this paper—appearing and disappearing attacks. The former aims at misleading object detector such that it is unable to detect a target object category, *e.g.*, stop sign, and the latter aims at misleading object detector such that it detects a predefined object category which is not present in images. If an adversarial patch is similar to a target object, the object detector would detect it as a target object. However, this is not the goal of appearing attack where wrongly detected target objects should appear beyond the adversarial patch itself. Different from the previous adversarial examples against object detectors, in these attacks, the adversarial patches are required neither to put very close to the target objects [10,11] nor to overlap with them [4,17,26].

To study the threats caused by non-local block, a non-local block is added into a Faster R-CNN and algorithms are designed to craft adversarial examples for carrying out these two types of attacks. By comparing the experimental results of the adversarial examples on the Faster R-CNN with non-local block and the original Faster R-CNN as a control, new threats from non-local blocks can be identified. To further explain the threats, the reception fields of non-local blocks are studied empirically and theoretically.

The rest of the paper is organized as follows. Section 2 summarizes the related works. Section 3 presents the algorithms designed to craft adversarial examples for appearing and disappearing attacks. Section 4 reports digital attack experiments on 4073 images from 36 in-car videos and physical attack experiments on 2258 images from 20 videos. Section 5 offers an analysis to explain the experimental findings. Section 6 gives some conclusive remarks.

2   Related Work

2.1   Non-local Neural Networks

Capturing long-range dependencies is of great importance in many computer vision tasks such as video classification, semantic segmentation, and object detection. However, traditional CNNs are ineffective on it. Inspired by non-local means in [1], Wang et al. [31] proposed non-local blocks to capture long-range dependencies. The response of a non-local block at a particular position is the weighted sum of the features at all positions in the feature maps. Wang et al. [31] described four different non-local blocks: Gaussian, embedded Gaussian, dot product and concatenation and found that they perform similarly and are able to consistently enhance the performance of CNNs in different computer vision tasks. The non-local blocks can be easily inserted into other existing architectures, which makes them widely adopted by other researchers. Zhen et al. [39] embedded a pyramid sampling module into non-local blocks to capture semantic statistics in different scales with only a minor computational budget while maintaining the excellent performance as the original non-local modules in semantic segmentation. Yue et al. [36] generalized the non-local blocks and took the correlations between the positions of any two channels into account to improve their representation power. They proposed a compact representation for different kernel functions employed in the non-local blocks and used Taylor expansion to reduce their computational demand. Zhang et al. [38] extended the non-local blocks and designed a residual non-local attention network for image restoration.

The non-local blocks have also been applied to various applications. Ma et al. [21] used the non-local operator in a framework that restores reasonable and realistic images by globally modeling the correlation among different regions. Shokri et al. [25] applied non-local neural networks to capture long-range dependencies and to determine the salient objects. Xia et al. [33] proposed a novel mechanism for person re-identification that directly captures long-range relationships via second-order feature statistics based on non-local blocks. In medical applications, Chen et al. [3] used a non-local spatial feature learning block to learn long-range correlations of the liver pixel position for a better liver segmentation. Besides, non-local neural networks are also applied in image de-raining [14], video captioning [12], cloth detection [15], text recognition [19], building extraction [30], and road extraction [32].

2.2 Adversarial Examples

Adversarial examples have drawn great attention since the discovery by Szgedy *et al.* [27]. They found that the state-of-the-art image classifiers would classify an image with deliberately designed noise to an incorrect label and the image with the noise looks almost the same as the original image for naked eyes. Thereafter, different attacks against image classifiers are investigated [7,22,23] and the risks in other computer vision methods are also studied. Object detector, a critical component in many computer vision systems, has a lot of real-world applications, *e.g.*, autonomous driving car. To study its potential security risk, researchers developed attacks against object detectors digitally and physically. In 2017, Xie *et al.* [34] and Lu *et al.* [18] proposed methods to digitally attack Faster R-CNN and YOLO respectively. Their attacks are implemented by inserting noise into whole images. These attacks are not able to be carried out in the physical world. Lu *et al.* [17] designed an adversarial stop sign by adding noise to the stop sign in order to fool Faster R-CNN in both digital and physical worlds. Different from the adversarial examples against image classifiers, the adversarial stop sign looks very different from a normal stop sign. To make the adversarial stop sign more realistic, Chen *et al.* [4] proposed a method to change every pixel inside the stop sign, except for those inside the 'STOP' word region. Song *et al.* [26] further limited the attack region and produced an adversarial sticker that can mislead an object detector digitally and physically by putting it on a target stop sign. Different from the previous attacks, Huang *et al.* [10,11] attempted to mislead an object detector by placing adversarial examples outside the target object. However, their adversarial examples need to be placed very close to the target object. These works show that attacking object detectors is relatively hard, especially in the physical world when attackers have no access to target objects and their surrounding area. All these studies were performed on traditional object detectors without non-local blocks. To the best of the authors' knowledge, there are no recorded studies on threats against object detectors with non-local block.

3 Methodology

3.1 Faster R-CNN and Non-local Block

To study the threats caused by the non-local blocks, adversarial patches are designed for carrying out disappearing and appearing attacks. In this study, Faster R-CNN with a ResNet-101 as its backbone and a non-local block is used to train the adversarial patches. The Faster R-CNN is selected on the account of its popularity and that many detectors are relying on the Faster R-CNN architecture. For a clear presentation, the original Faster R-CNN without the non-local block is first described. It consists of three major components: a backbone network, a region proposal network (RPN) and a detection network. The backbone network computes features for both RPN and detection network. The RPN takes the features and produces region proposals that have high probability with objects. The detection network takes the features and the region proposals as inputs. Its box regression layer refines the bounding box coordinates provided by RPN and its classification layer outputs a probability matrix, P, each of whose row and column respectively corresponds to one region proposal and one class label. The element in the ith row and the jth column of P representing the probability of the ith region proposal belonging to the jth class is denoted as p_{ij} and the ith row and the jth column of P are denoted $p_{i.}$ and $p_{.j}$ respectively. Faster R-CNN applies a threshold and non-maximum suppression to determine final object classes and their bounding boxes.

For this study, a non-local block is inserted between the 3rd and 4th residual blocks in the ResNet-101. It is inserted at the same location as Wang et $al.$ [31], and inserting at a lower layers would require a lot of memory and computation power when training a non-local block. For the sake of convenience, the term Faster R-CNN-WN is used to refer to the Faster R-CNN with the non-local block. Several types of non-local blocks have been proposed. The embedded Gaussian non-local block is employed in this study because different types of non-local blocks have very similar effect [31] and embedded Gaussian non-local block is the most popular one among them. Formally, a non-local block is defined as

$$z_k = W_z y_k + x_k \tag{1}$$

where x_k is a feature vector at the kth spatial location of the previous layer, W_z is a matrix optimized through training and

$$y_k = \frac{1}{C(x)} \sum\nolimits_{\forall m} f(x_k, x_m) g(x_m). \tag{2}$$

In embedded Gaussian non-local block,

$$f(x_k, x_m) = c^{\theta(x_k)^T \phi(x_m)} \tag{3}$$

where $\theta(x_k) = W_\theta x_k, \phi(x_m) = W_\phi x_m$, the normalize factor is set as $C(x) = \sum_{\forall m} f(x_k) f(x_m)$ and $g(x_m) = W_g x_m$.

3.2   Disappearing Attack

Let T be a target object category, I be a training image and $B_{gT}(I)$ be the ground truth bounding box of a target object in I with a size of $w_{gt} \times h_{gt}$ pixels. To carry out disappearing attack, an adversarial patch Λ with a size of $w \times h$ pixels is constructed to minimize all the probabilities of the target object category in P, i.e., $p_{.T}$. Let $p_{jT} = F_N(I, j)$, where F_N represents the operations in the Faster R-CNN-WN computing the probability of the jth region proposal belonging to the target class. To enhance the robustness of the adversarial patch for target objects in different images taken from different viewpoints and illumination conditions, Λ is trained on images from k videos, each of which contains at least one target object. The entire training set is denoted as Q. To properly model the variations of zoom factors and the distance between camera and target object in different images, Λ is resized according to the target object. More precisely, Λ is resized to $\alpha w_{gt} \times \beta h_{gt}$, where α and β are parameters controlling the size of Λ in the image. In the training, Λ is placed below $B_{gT}(I)$ with a distance. If the training image has more than one target object, one of them is randomly selected and Λ is placed below it. Though the relative location between Λ and the target object is fixed in training, in testing, Λ can be placed in different locations to perform the attack. Section 5 will explain why the difference between training and testing locations is not important. Let $f(I, \Lambda, B_{gT}(I))$ be a training image with the rescaled adversarial patch. In the training, Λ is trained to minimize the sum of $p_{jT}, \forall j$. The objective function

$$\Lambda = \underset{\Lambda}{\operatorname{argmin}} \sum_{I \in Q} \sum_{\forall j} F_N(f(I, \Lambda, B_{gT}(I)), j) \tag{4}$$

is used to perform this minimization.

3.3 Appearing Attack

In this sub-section, we use the same notations as in the previous sub-section. As with the previous attack, an adversarial patch Λ with a size of $w \times h$ is inserted into a training image I, according to the location of a reference object and its size. The size of the rescaled Λ is set to $\alpha w_{ht} \times \beta h_{ht}$ pixels and Λ is placed below the reference object with a distance. In the experiments, stop sign is used as a reference object for placing and rescaling Λ in the appearing attack. The image with the rescaled Λ is denoted as $f(I, \Lambda, B_{gT}(I))$. To carry out this attack, a target label T is selected and the adversarial patch Λ is trained to minimize the negative $\log p_{jT}$ for the region proposal not overlapping with Λ. To avoid the appearing objects overlapping with Λ, the objective function also minimizes the negative $\log p_{jB}$ for region proposals overlapping with Λ, where p_{jB} is the background probability of the jth region proposals. Mathematically, the objective function below is used to train Λ,

$$\Lambda = \underset{\Lambda}{\operatorname{argmin}} \sum_{I \in Q} \sum_{j \in \phi^C} -\varepsilon \log F_N(f(I, \Lambda, B_{gT}(I)), j)$$
$$- \sum_{j \in \phi} (1 - \varepsilon) \log F_{NB}(f(I, \Lambda, B_{gT}(I)), j) \tag{5}$$

where ε is a parameter balancing the two terms, F_{NB} represents the operations of the Faster R-CNN-WN computing p_{jB}, ϕ is a set storing indexes of the region proposals overlapping with Λ and ϕ^C is its complement storing indexes of the region proposals not overlapping with Λ.

In this objective function, the first term is to mislead the region proposals that are not intersecting with Λ and make them target objects. The second term is designed to keep the proposals intersecting with Λ to be the background. It is noticed that the appearing attack will be weak when ε is too small, and bounding boxes will appear around or inside Λ when ε is too large (Fig. 3c).

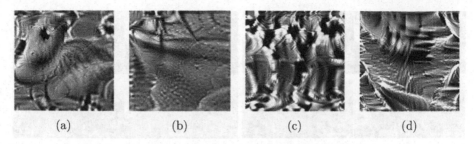

Fig. 1. Adversarial patches for the (a) disappearing attacks and (b) appearing attacks against the Faster R-CNN-WN. Adversarial patches for the (c) disappearing attacks and (d) appearing attacks against the Faster R-CNN.

4 Experiments

To evaluate the threats caused by non-local block, appearing and disappearing attacks are performed on the Faster R-CNN with the non-local block (Faster R-CNN-WN). The attacks are also performed on the original Faster R-CNN without the non-local block, as a control experiment. The two Faster R-CNNs are trained on the COCO dataset (2017 training images) and their backbone networks are ResNet-101. In the disappearing attacks, stop sign is selected as a target object and also a reference object for resizing and placing the adversarial patches in the images. In the appearing attacks, stop sign is selected as a reference object, because it is a common target object in the previous adversarial example studies [4,11,17,26] and an important object for autonomous vehicles. In the appearing attacks, boat is selected as a target object because none of the training and testing videos has boat and it would make the evaluation easier. In the experiments, 721 images sampled every other frame from five in-car videos are used as a training set. The image sizes are 406×720 pixels or 1080×720 pixels. Four adversarial patches with a size of 200×200 pixels are generated. Figure 1 shows the four adversarial patches. These adversarial patches are used to evaluate the threats caused by the non-local block in both digital and physical worlds.

4.1 Digital Attack

In digital attack, 4073 images sampled from 36 Internet in-car videos are taken as a testing set. The sizes of the images are 1080×1920 pixels and the sizes of the stop signs range from 21×22 pixels to 660×633 pixels. The original detection rates of the Faster R-CNN-WN and the Faster R-CNN are 80.6% and 78.6%, respectively. These results match with Wang et al.'s findings [31] that non-local block can improve detection performance. The adversarial patches are scaled and then placed below the detected stop signs with a certain distance away from it. In theory, the attack rate would be higher with a larger adversarial patch. In the disappearing attack experiments, we would like to keep the size of adversarial

(a)   (b)

Fig. 2. Disappearing attack results. (a) The detection results of stop sign from the original Faster R-CNN and (b) the detection results of stop sign from the Faster R-CNN-WN. The first column is the original detection results without the adversarial patches and the second column is the detection results with the adversarial patches.

patch similar to that of the traffic signs in the real world. Thus, α and β are set to 1.5. When at least one detectable stop sign in an original image is missing due to the adversarial patches, the attack is considered a success. Denote the number of original images with at least one detectable stop sign as Det_{imgs}. The successful disappearing attack rate D_{ar} defined as:

$$D_{ar} = \frac{\text{number of sucessful attacks}}{Det_{imgs}} \tag{6}$$

is used as a performance index. Table 1 lists the original detection rate (DR_{org}) and the successful disappearing attack rates of the two detectors. It indicates that the impact of the disappearing attacks is much greater on the Faster R-CNN-WN than the original Faster R-CNN. Figure 2 shows typical detection results from these two detectors.

In the appearing attack experiments, boat and stop sign are respectively selected as a target object and a reference object. Similar to disappearing attack, α and β are set to 2 and ε in Eq. 5 is set to 0.4. Note that without the adversarial patches, the detectors would still have the probability of wrongly detecting other objects or background as a boat. When the detector has wrong detections in absence of the adversarial patches, only the case where the intersection over union of these detected boxes and the predictions for boats is smaller than 0.6 will be considered as a result of the appearing attack. The adversarial patches may cause the detectors to wrongly detecting multiple boats. The wrongly detected boats with no intersection with the adversarial patches are considered as a clear success (Fig. 3a). In some cases, the wrongly detected boats are very large and have some overlap with the adversarial patches (Fig. 3b). Hence, the intersection of the detected boat and the adversarial patch over the detected boat (IOD) is used to define successful attack. If there is no intersection, IOD will be zero and if the detected boat is completely inside the adversarial patch, IOD will be one. When IOD is smaller than a threshold, it is considered as a successful attack.

Table 1. Successful disappearing attack rates (%)

	Original Faster R-CNN	Faster R-CNN-WN
DR_{org}	78.6	80.6
D_{ar}	7.6	52.7

Table 2. The successful appearing attack rates (%) under different IOD thresholds.

	Original Faster R-CNN	Faster R-CNN-WN
IOD $= 0$	0	53.5
IOD < 0.1	0.6	55
IOD < 0.2	1.4	55.2
IOD < 0.3	3.1	55.4
IOD < 0.4	6.6	55.4

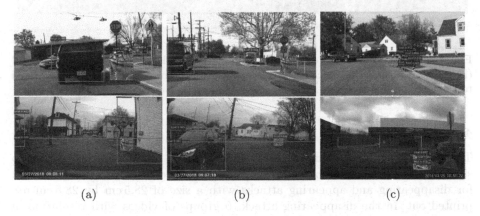

(a)   (b)   (c)

Fig. 3. Appearing attack results, where boat is a target object. (a)–(b) The detection results of boat from the Faster R-CNN-WN. (c) The detection results of boat from the original Faster R-CNN.

The successful appearing attack rate A_{ar} is defined as

$$A_{ar} = \frac{\text{number of images with at least one successful attack}}{\text{number of testing images}} \tag{7}$$

Table 2 gives the successful appearing attack rates from the two detectors and Fig. 3 shows some typical detection results from Faster R-CNN-WN and original Faster R-CNN. The Faster R-CNN can only detect the adversarial patch or it sub-region as the target object (Fig. 3c). However, the Faster R-CNN-WN is misled by the adversarial patch and detects large areas as boat. Since the original Faster R-CNN is insensitive to the disappearing and appearing attacks in the digital world, it is not included in the following physical experiments.

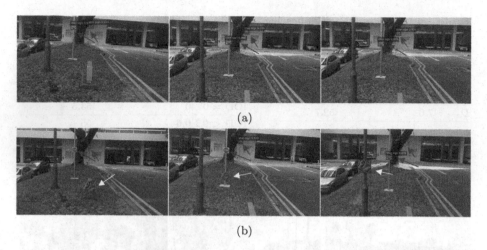

(a)

(b)

Fig. 4. The detection results of stop sign from the Faster R-CNN-WN (a) without and (b) with the adversarial patch in disappearing attack. Note that the stop sign closed to the tree is a real stop sign.

4.2 Physical Attack

To examine the threats caused by non-local block in the physical world, a stop sign with a size of 19.3 cm by 19.3 cm and the adversarial patches generated for disappearing and appearing attacks with a size of 28.5 cm by 28.5 cm are printed out. In the disappearing attack, 6 groups of videos with resolution of 1080×1920 or 1920×1080 pixels are taken from outdoor environments by a smartphone camera. In each group, there are 2 videos taken from the same location and roughly the same viewpoint. One video has the stop sign only; one video has the stop sign and the adversarial patch for disappearing attack. The adversarial patch is placed below or in front of the stop sign without a fixed distance (Fig. 4b). On average, 110 frames are sampled from each video for testing. As in the digital experiment, every other frame is sampled. In the digital disappearing attacks, the successful disappearing attack rate is used as a performance index. However, it is not applicable to physical attack because the videos with and without adversarial patches are neither collected from the exact same viewpoint nor at the same time, and have different numbers of frames. Thus, the detection rates with and without the influence from the adversarial patch are used to evaluate the impact and provided in Table 3. In some videos, there is also a real stop sign, so the detection rate here is defined as the number of detected stop signs divided by the number of stop signs in the images. Table 3 shows that for the Faster R-CNN-WN, the adversarial patch reduces the average detection rates from 87.2% to 48.0%. Figure 4 shows some example results of the physical disappearing attack.

In the digital appearing attacks, stop sign is just used as a reference object for resizing and placing the adversarial patch. Since it is impossible to resize the adversarial patch in physical attack and in fact, it is not necessary, stop sign is

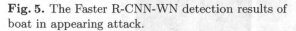

Fig. 5. The Faster R-CNN-WN detection results of boat in appearing attack.

Fig. 6. Two sample images with the grids.

not used as a reference object. For examining appearing attacks in the physical world, 4 groups of videos, with resolution of 1080 × 1920 pixels are taken in 4 locations. In each group, there are 2 videos with and without the adversarial patch for appearing attack taken from the same location and roughly the same viewpoint. The videos are sampled in every other frame. On average, 118 frames per video are used for testing. The appearing rate here is defined as the number of frames detected with the target object divided by the total number of the frames. Table 4 shows that for the Faster R-CNN-WN, the adversarial patch increases the average appearing rates of boat from 0.8% to 31.3%. Figure 4 shows some example results from the physical appearing attack.

4.3   Effective Attack Regions

In the previous disappearing attack experiments, the relative locations between the target object i.e., stop sign and the adversarial patches are fixed. More precisely, in both training and testing of the digital attacks, the adversarial patches are placed 1.5 h_t pixels below the stop sign, where h_t is the detected height of the stop sign in the image. In this experiment, the adversarial patches trained in the fixed relative position are placed in different locations. 831 images are sampled from every 5 frames from the 36 testing videos in the digital experiments. From them, 670 and 645 images are detected with stop sign by the Faster R-CNN-WN and the Faster R-CNN, respectively. Only the images with detected stop signs are employed in the following evaluation. Each image is divided by a grid and the size of each block in the grid is $1.5 h_t \times 1.5 w_t$. Note that the number of blocks in different images is different. Figure 6 shows images with the grids. In total 11 × 11 positions are tested. The adversarial patches (Figs. 1a and 1c) are rescaled based on the stop signs and put in the centers of the blocks. If the detector cannot detect the stop sign, it is considered as a successful attack. Note that the size and the location of the stop sign in each image are different. To compute the successful attack rates at different relative locations, the grids are rescaled and aligned. Figure 7 shows the successful attack rates from both Faster R-CNN-WN and

Table 3. The detection rate of stop sign in disappearing attacks in the physical world.

Detection rate	Faster R-CNN-WN
Without attack	89.9
With attack	47.6

Table 4. The appearing rate of boat in appearing attacks in the physical world.

Appearing rate	Faster R-CNN-WN
Without attack	0.8
With attack	31.3

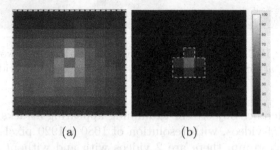

(a)   (b)

Fig. 7. Successful attack rates in different locations, (a) Faster R-CNN-WN and (b) Faster R-CNN. The red boxes indicate the locations of the stop signs and the yellow lines indicate successful attack rates greater than 10%. (Color figure online)

Faster R-CNN. The red boxes indicate the locations of the aligned stop signs. Note that the successful attack rates at different locations are computed from different numbers of images, because some stop signs are close to image boundary. Figure 7a shows that the effective attack region for the Faster R-CNN-WN covers the entire grid and most of the successful attack rates are higher than 30%. The region close to the target object has much higher successful attack rates and the upper, lower and right borders have relatively lower successful attack rates. The rest of the region has similar successful attack rates. Without the non-local block, the successful attack rates become very low (Fig. 7b), except for the region very close to the center. These results indicate that disappearing attacks can be applied in long-distance and the difference between training and testing location is not a matter.

5   Analysis of the Effective Attack Regions

The experiments in Sect. 4.3 expose several properties of the effective attack regions of the two detectors. To discuss the properties observed in Fig. 7 systematically, in this section, an effective attack region is defined as where the successful attack rate is higher than 10%, which is highlighted by the yellow color boundaries. To understand these properties, analysis and discussion are provided in this section. The effective attack region of the Faster R-CNN is first discussed and then an analysis for the effective attack region of the Faster R-CNN-WN is provided. Since they are in fact the same, except for the non-local block in the backbone networks, the analysis below focuses on the reception fields of the backbone networks.

The effective attack region of the Faster R-CNN is very small and very concentrated on the center. Luo *et al.* [20] points out that the output neurons of deep CNNs, like ResNet-101 has a small effective receptive field with a Gaussian shape, which is much smaller than its theoretical receptive field. Thus, the adversarial patch can only affect its surrounding region and the successful attack rate decays exponentially when the distance between the target object and the adversarial patch increases (see Fig. 7b). Also because of the Gaussian shape effective receptive field, Fig. 7b has a roughly circular shape.

The effective attack region of the Faster R-CNN-WN (Fig. 7a) is very different. It covers the entire Fig. 7a with high successful attack rates. The region around the center has a very high successful attack rate and the successful attack rate in the rest of the region is roughly the same, except for the boundaries. It implies that the non-local block extends the effective receptive field to entire images. We would like to mathematically quantify how the receptive field has been changed after adding the non-local block on top of the convolution neural network. Here we only consider single-channel case for every layer and dot-product form of non-local block for simplicity. The result can be derived similarly for multi-channel cases by considering inter-channel correlations, and extended to other versions of non-local block by replacing the pairwise function f.

Following Luo *et al.*'s effective receptive field analysis [20], we compute the gradient of a single output neuron with respect to all input pixels. What we are interested here is the gradient of a single output pixel with respect to all input pixels, *i.e.*, $\partial y_i / \partial a_m$ for all $m \in \{1, \ldots, N^2\}$, where y is the output of non-local block, and a is an $N \times N$ input image. The output of the CNN block, also the input of non-local block, is denoted by x. Without the loss of generality, we assume that x_i's are uniformly distributed. The gradient can be decomposed to $\partial y_i / \partial a_m = \sum_k \partial y_i / \partial x_k \cdot \partial x_k / \partial a_m$ using chain rule, which is further divided into the following two cases,

$$\frac{\partial y_i}{\partial a_m} = \begin{cases} \sum_{k \neq i} \dfrac{\partial y_i}{\partial x_k} \cdot \dfrac{\partial x_k}{\partial a_m} + \dfrac{\partial y_i}{\partial x_i} \cdot \dfrac{\partial x_i}{\partial a_i}, & m = i \\ \sum_{k \neq m} \dfrac{\partial y_i}{\partial x_k} \cdot \dfrac{\partial x_k}{\partial a_m} + \dfrac{\partial y_i}{\partial x_m} \dfrac{\partial x_m}{\partial a_m}, & m \neq i \end{cases} \tag{8}$$

Recall that the dot-product version non-local operator follows the function $z_i = W_z y_i + x_i$, where

$$y_i = \frac{1}{C(x)} \sum_{\forall j} f(x_i, x_j) g(x_j) = \frac{1}{N} \sum_{\forall j} x_i x_j W_g x_j \tag{9}$$

Thus, the gradient signal on x, $\partial y_i / \partial x_m$, can also be computed by considering the cases when $m = i$ and $m \neq i$,

$$\frac{\partial y_i}{\partial x_m} = \frac{1}{N} W_g \times \begin{cases} \sum_{j \neq m} x_j^2 + 3x_m^2, & m = i \\ 2x_i x_m, & m \neq i \end{cases} \tag{10}$$

It is presented by the previous work [20] that $\partial x_k / \partial a_m$ for all m forms a Gaussian shape, which diminishes fast at its tails. Thus, the summation terms in both cases of Eq. 8 are negligible since $\partial x_k / \partial a_m$ is close to zero when $|k - m|$ becomes larger. Moreover, we noticed in Eq. 10 that the gradient when $m = i$ is strictly greater than that when $m \neq i$ since $\sum_{j \neq m} x_j^2 + 3x_m^2 - 2x_i x_m$ is strictly positive, when not all x_i's are zeros, and $\partial x_i / \partial a_i$ for all i is the value of a Gaussian density function taken at its mean, which is assumed to be equal for all i. We then conclude that the gradient $\partial y_i / \partial a_m$ when $m = i$ is greater than that when $m \neq i$. Besides, since not all x_i's are zeros, the gradients $\partial y_i / \partial a_m$ is also non-zeros for all $m \neq i$.

This gives us an intuition of analyzing the receptive field by considering the non-local block. Different from the effective receptive field of CNNs without non-local block, which has non-zero gradient values in the neighborhood of the center pixel and zero gradients further away, the receptive field of CNNs with non-local block covers the whole input space. More specifically, the gradient of a single output pixel with respect to the corresponding pixel, $\partial y_i / \partial a_m$, is non-zero everywhere. It also proved that the gradient with respect to center pixel ($\partial y_i / \partial a_i$) is the maximum. With the consideration of the skip connection in the non-local block, which is the sum of x_j over all j in computing z_i, the neighborhood region of the center would have higher gradients because of its Gaussian shape receptive field [20]. The gradients of other regions are strictly smaller and have similar values.

The analysis above does not explain why the successful attack rate is lower at the boundary. When the adversarial patch is put in the image border, it would affect lesser number of neurons in the input layer of the non-local block, x. Therefore, the attack would be weaker as illustrated in Fig. 7. The experimental results also show that the adversarial patch trained at a fixed relative location with respect to the target object is effective in other locations. Because CNNs without a fully connected layer is roughly translation invariant, putting the adversarial patch in two different locations, p and q, their corresponding neuron outputs x_p and x_q should be roughly the same. Since the non-local block (Eq. 1) considers all $x_i, \forall i$, the adversarial patch can attack on other locations, different from the training location.

6   Conclusion

To overcome the weaknesses of traditional deep neural networks, which are ineffective to capture long-range dependency, researchers developed non-local blocks and demonstrated their effectiveness on various computer vision tasks. However, without understanding the threats caused by the non-local blocks and applying them to critical systems is risky. In this paper, two types of attacks, disappearing and appearing attacks against object detectors are studied. Different from the previous attacks against object detectors, these attacks are performed in long distance. The digital and physical experimental results show that the universal adversarial patches obtained by the proposed algorithms can mislead the Faster

R-CNN with a non-local block to classify stop sign as background and to wrongly detect boats that are not in the images. To understand the effective attack region and its properties, the reception field of the non-local block is analysed.

Acknowledgements. This work is partially supported by the Ministry of Education, Singapore through Academic Research Fund Tier 1, RG30/17.

References

1. Buades, A., Coll, B., Morel, J.M.: A non-local algorithm for image denoising. In: 2005 IEEE Computer Society Conference on Computer Vision and Pattern Recognition (CVPR 2005), vol. 2, pp. 60–65. IEEE (2005)
2. Cao, Y., Xu, J., Lin, S., Wei, F., Hu, H.: GCNet: non-local networks meet squeeze-excitation networks and beyond. In: Proceedings of the IEEE International Conference on Computer Vision Workshops (2019)
3. Chen, L., Song, H., Li, Q., Cui, Y., Yang, J., Hu, X.T.: Liver segmentation in CT images using a non-local fully convolutional neural network. In: 2019 IEEE International Conference on Bioinformatics and Biomedicine (BIBM), pp. 639–642. IEEE (2019)
4. Chen, S.T., Cornelius, C., Martin, J., Chau, D.H.: ShapeShifter: robust physical adversarial attack on faster R-CNN object detector. In: ECML/PKDD (2018)
5. Chi, L., Tian, G., Mu, Y., Xie, L., Tian, Q.: Fast non-local neural networks with spectral residual learning. In: Proceedings of the 27th ACM International Conference on Multimedia, pp. 2142–2151 (2019)
6. Fu, C., et al.: Non-local recurrent neural memory for supervised sequence modeling. In: Proceedings of the IEEE International Conference on Computer Vision, pp. 6311–6320 (2019)
7. Goodfellow, I., Shlens, J., Szegedy, C.: Explaining and harnessing adversarial examples. In: International Conference on Learning Representations (2015). http://arxiv.org/abs/1412.6572
8. He, K., Zhang, X., Ren, S., Sun, J.: Deep residual learning for image recognition. In: Proceedings of the IEEE Conference on Computer Vision and Pattern Recognition, pp. 770–778 (2016)
9. Hu, G., Cui, B., Yu, S.: Skeleton-based action recognition with synchronous local and non-local spatio-temporal learning and frequency attention. In: 2019 IEEE International Conference on Multimedia and Expo (ICME), pp. 1216–1221. IEEE (2019)
10. Huang, Y., Kong, A.W.K., Lam, K.Y.: Adversarial signboard against object detector. In: Proceedings of the British Machine Vision Conference (BMVC) (2019)
11. Huang, Y., Kong, A.W.-K., Lam, K.-Y.: Attacking object detectors without changing the target object. In: Nayak, A.C., Sharma, A. (eds.) PRICAI 2019. LNCS (LNAI), vol. 11672, pp. 3–15. Springer, Cham (2019). https://doi.org/10.1007/978-3-030-29894-4_1
12. Lee, J., Kim, J.: Improving video captioning with non-local neural networks. In: 2018 IEEE International Conference on Consumer Electronics - Asia (ICCE-Asia), pp. 206–212 (2018)
13. Levi, H., Ullman, S.: Efficient coarse-to-fine non-local module for the detection of small objects. arXiv preprint arXiv:1811.12152 (2018)

14. Li, G., He, X., Zhang, W., Chang, H., Dong, L., Lin, L.: Non-locally enhanced encoder-decoder network for single image de-raining. arXiv preprint arXiv:1808.01491 (2018)
15. Li, Y., Tang, S., Ye, Y., Ma, J.: Spatial-aware non-local attention for fashion landmark detection. In: 2019 IEEE International Conference on Multimedia and Expo (ICME), pp. 820–825. IEEE (2019)
16. Liao, X., He, L., Yang, Z., Zhang, C.: Video-based person re-identification via 3D convolutional networks and non-local attention. In: Jawahar, C.V., Li, H., Mori, G., Schindler, K. (eds.) ACCV 2018. LNCS, vol. 11366, pp. 620–634. Springer, Cham (2019). https://doi.org/10.1007/978-3-030-20876-9_39
17. Lu, J., Sibai, H., Fabry, E.: Adversarial examples that fool detectors. CoRR abs/1712.02494 (2017)
18. Lu, J., Sibai, H., Fabry, E., Forsyth, D.A.: No need to worry about adversarial examples in object detection in autonomous vehicles. CoRR abs/1707.03501 (2017)
19. Lu, N., Yu, W., Qi, X., Chen, Y., Gong, P., Xiao, R.: MASTER: multi-aspect non-local network for scene text recognition. arXiv preprint arXiv:1910.02562 (2019)
20. Luo, W., Li, Y., Urtasun, R., Zemel, R.: Understanding the effective receptive field in deep convolutional neural networks. In: Advances in Neural Information Processing Systems, pp. 4898–4906 (2016)
21. Ma, Y., Liu, X., Bai, S., Wang, L., He, D., Liu, A.: Coarse-to-fine image inpainting via region-wise convolutions and non-local correlation. In: Proceedings of the 28th International Joint Conference on Artificial Intelligence, pp. 3123–3129. AAAI Press (2019)
22. Moosavi-Dezfooli, S.M., Fawzi, A., Frossard, P.: DeepFool: a simple and accurate method to fool deep neural networks. In: 2016 IEEE Conference on Computer Vision and Pattern Recognition (CVPR), pp. 2574–2582 (2016)
23. Papernot, N., McDaniel, P.D., Jha, S., Fredrikson, M., Celik, Z.B., Swami, A.: The limitations of deep learning in adversarial settings. In: 2016 IEEE European Symposium on Security and Privacy (EuroS&P), pp. 372–387 (2016)
24. Shi, L., Zhang, Y., Cheng, J., Lu, H.: Non-local graph convolutional networks for skeleton-based action recognition. arXiv preprint arXiv:1805.07694 (2018)
25. Shokri, M., Harati, A., Taba, K.: Salient object detection in video using deep non-local neural networks. arXiv preprint arXiv:1810.07097 (2018)
26. Song, D., et al.: Physical adversarial examples for object detectors. In: 12th USENIX Workshop on Offensive Technologies (WOOT 2018) (2018)
27. Szegedy, C., et al.: Intriguing properties of neural networks. In: International Conference on Learning Representations (2014). http://arxiv.org/abs/1312.6199
28. Tang, Y., Zhang, X., Wang, J., Chen, S., Ma, L., Jiang, Y.-G.: Non-local NetVLAD encoding for video classification. In: Leal-Taixé, L., Roth, S. (eds.) ECCV 2018. LNCS, vol. 11132, pp. 219–228. Springer, Cham (2019). https://doi.org/10.1007/978-3-030-11018-5_20
29. Tu, Z., Ma, Y., Li, C., Tang, J., Luo, B.: Edge-guided non-local fully convolutional network for salient object detection. arXiv preprint arXiv:1908.02460 (2019)
30. Wang, S., Hou, X., Zhao, X.: Automatic building extraction from high-resolution aerial imagery via fully convolutional encoder-decoder network with non-local block. IEEE Access 8, 7313–7322 (2020)
31. Wang, X., Girshick, R., Gupta, A., He, K.: Non-local neural networks. In: Proceedings of the IEEE Conference on Computer Vision and Pattern Recognition, pp. 7794–7803 (2018)
32. Wang, Y., Seo, J., Jeon, T.: NL-LinkNet: toward lighter but more accurate road extraction with non-local operations. arXiv preprint arXiv:1908.08223 (2019)

33. Xia, B.N., Gong, Y., Zhang, Y., Poellabauer, C.: Second-order non-local attention networks for person re-identification. In: Proceedings of the IEEE International Conference on Computer Vision, pp. 3760–3769 (2019)
34. Xie, C., Wang, J., Zhang, Z., Zhou, Y., Xie, L., Yuille, A.L.: Adversarial examples for semantic segmentation and object detection. In: 2017 IEEE International Conference on Computer Vision (ICCV), pp. 1378–1387 (2017)
35. Xu, X., Wang, J.: Extended non-local feature for visual saliency detection in low contrast images. In: Leal-Taixé, L., Roth, S. (eds.) ECCV 2018. LNCS, vol. 11132, pp. 580–592. Springer, Cham (2019). https://doi.org/10.1007/978-3-030-11018-5_46
36. Yue, K., Sun, M., Yuan, Y., Zhou, F., Ding, E., Xu, F.: Compact generalized non-local network. In: Advances in Neural Information Processing Systems, pp. 6510–6519 (2018)
37. Zajac, M., Zołna, K., Rostamzadeh, N., Pinheiro, P.O.: Adversarial framing for image and video classification. In: Proceedings of the AAAI Conference on Artificial Intelligence, vol. 33, pp. 10077–10078 (2019)
38. Zhang, Y., Li, K., Li, K., Zhong, B., Fu, Y.: Residual non-local attention networks for image restoration. arXiv preprint arXiv:1903.10082 (2019)
39. Zhu, Z., Xu, M., Bai, S., Huang, T., Bai, X.: Asymmetric non-local neural networks for semantic segmentation. In: Proceedings of the IEEE International Conference on Computer Vision, pp. 593–602 (2019)

Self-Supervised CycleGAN
for Object-Preserving Image-to-Image
Domain Adaptation

Xinpeng Xie[1], Jiawei Chen[2], Yuexiang Li[2(✉)], Linlin Shen[1], Kai Ma[2],
and Yefeng Zheng[2]

[1] Computer Vision Institute, Shenzhen University, Shenzhen, China
xiexinpeng2017@email.szu.edu.cn,llshen@szu.edu.cn
[2] Tencent Jarvis Lab, Shenzhen, China
{jiaweichen,vicyxli,kylekma,yefengzheng}@tencent.com

Abstract. Recent generative adversarial network (GAN) based methods (e.g., CycleGAN) are prone to fail at preserving image-objects in image-to-image translation, which reduces their practicality on tasks such as domain adaptation. Some frameworks have been proposed to adopt a segmentation network as the auxiliary regularization to prevent the content distortion. However, all of them require extra pixel-wise annotations, which is difficult to fulfill in practical applications. In this paper, we propose a novel GAN (namely OP-GAN) to address the problem, which involves a self-supervised module to enforce the image content consistency during image-to-image translations without any extra annotations. We evaluate the proposed OP-GAN on three publicly available datasets. The experimental results demonstrate that our OP-GAN can yield visually plausible translated images and significantly improve the semantic segmentation accuracy in different domain adaptation scenarios with off-the-shelf deep learning networks such as PSPNet and U-Net.

Keywords: Image-to-image translation · Domain adaptation ·
Semantic segmentation

1 Introduction

Deep learning networks have shown impressive successes on various computer vision tasks such as image classification [9,19,28] and semantic segmentation [2,11,33]. However, most of current deep learning based approaches easily suffer from the problem of domain shift—the models trained on a dataset (source) seldom maintain the same performance on other datasets (target) obtained under

---

X. Xie and J. Chen—The first two authors are equal contribution.

Electronic supplementary material The online version of this chapter (https://doi.org/10.1007/978-3-030-58565-5_30) contains supplementary material, which is available to authorized users.

© Springer Nature Switzerland AG 2020
A. Vedaldi et al. (Eds.): ECCV 2020, LNCS 12365, pp. 498–513, 2020.
https://doi.org/10.1007/978-3-030-58565-5_30

different conditions. Image-to-image (I2I) translation is one of the potential solutions to address the problem by enforcing the input data distributions of two domains to be similar. Due to the recent success of generative adversarial network (GAN) [8] on generating high-quality synthetic images, many studies adopted GANs for the I2I domain adaptation [12,36], which authentically convert an input image to a corresponding output image by constructing a pixel-to-pixel mapping. As a representative method, Pix2Pix [12] shows a strategy to learn such adaptation mapping with a conditional setting to capture structure information. However, it requires paired cross-domain images as training data, which are often difficult to acquire.

To loose the requirement of pairwise training images, GAN-based unpaired I2I domain adaptation methods, e.g., CycleGAN [36], DiscoGAN [13], and Dual-GAN [32] were recently proposed, where a cycle consistency constraint was applied to encourage bidirectional image translations with regularized structural output. Although these GANs present realistic visual results on several I2I translation tasks, the corruptions of image content are frequently observed in the translated images, which is unacceptable for the domain adaptation scenarios, requiring rigorous preservation of image content. Some researchers [10,34] spent efforts to address the problem of content distortions. They employed additional segmentation branches to embed the semantic information to the generators, which enforced the CycleGAN to perform an content-aware image translation. Nevertheless, the obvious drawback of these methods is the demand of pixel-wise annotations.

Inspired by the recent study [3], using a self-supervised loss to retain the benefit of conditional GAN, we explore the potential of self-supervised task for improving CycleGAN's capacity of image content preservation without the demand of pixel-wise annotations. In this paper, we propose an object-preserving I2I domain adaptation network, namely OP-GAN, with the specific capability to address the problem of content distortion occurred in the typical CycleGAN. To be more specific, the newly introduced self-supervised task disentangles the features of image content from the disturbance of domain differences, so as to bring additional regularization for maintaining the consistency of image-objects. The proposed OP-GAN is evaluated on three publicly available datasets. The experimental results show that our OP-GAN can produce satisfactory cross-domain images, while impeccably preserving the image content. The quantitative results demonstrate that the proposed OP-GAN can significantly increase the performance of semantic segmentation networks such as PSPNet [35] and U-Net [24], so as to close the performance gap between different domains.

2   Related Work

In this section, we briefly review previous works on self-supervised learning and unpaired I2I translation.

2.1 Self-supervised Learning

To deal with the deficiency of annotated data, researchers attempted to exploit useful information from unlabeled data without direct supervision information. The self-supervised learning, as a new paradigm of unsupervised learning, attracts increasing attentions from the community. The typical self-supervised learning framework defines a proxy task to enforce neural networks to deeply mine useful information from the unlabeled raw data, which can boost the accuracy of the subsequent target task with limited training data. Various proxy tasks have been proposed, which include grayscale image colorization [15], jigsaw puzzles [23] and object motion estimation [16]. More recently, researchers began to adopt the idea of self-supervised learning to address some key issues of deep learning. For example, Chen et al. [3] introduced an auxiliary self-supervised loss to the typical conditional GAN to address the problem of discriminator forgetting during training. Gidaris et al. [7] integrated the self-supervised learning task to the few-shot learning framework for exploiting richer and more transferable visual representations from few annotated samples.

2.2 Unpaired Image-to-image Translation

Witnessing the success of cycle-consistency-based approaches [13,32,36], an increasing number of researchers [4,6,22,25] made their effort to the area of unpaired I2I translation. For example, UNIT [21], a recently proposed model, assumes that there exists a shared-latent space in which a pair of corresponding images from different domains could be mapped to the same latent representation. Through such latent representation, the I2I cross-domain translation can be achieved. To further increase the output diversity, Lee et al. [17] proposed a disentangled representation framework, namely DRIT, with unpaired training data. DRIT embedded images into two spaces—a domain-invariant content space capturing shared information across domains, and a domain-specific attribute space to achieve diversity of the translated results. However, none of those approaches explicitly takes the image content preservation into account during translation, which may result in content distortion of the translated images and limit their practicality for the task requiring rigorous preservation of image-objects such as domain adaptation.

3   Revisiting the Problem of CycleGAN

CycleGAN has two paired generator-discriminator modules, which are capable of learning two mappings, i.e., from domain A to domain B $\{G_{AB}, D_B\}$ and the inverse B to A $\{G_{BA}, D_A\}$. The generators (G_{AB}, G_{BA}) translate images between the source and target domains, while the discriminators (D_A, D_B) aim to distinguish the original data from the translated ones. Thereby, the generators and discriminators are gradually updated during this adversarial competition.

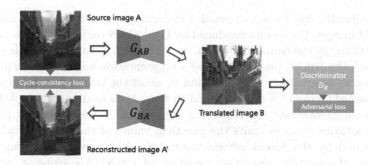

Fig. 1. The overview of CycleGAN [36]. Taking the translation from domain A to domain B as an example, the framework consists of generators (G_{AB} and G_{BA}) and discriminator (D_B), which are supervised by cycle-consistency and adversarial losses, respectively. Due to the bijective geometric transformation (e.g., translation, rotation, scaling, or even nonrigid transformation) and its inverse (i.e., T and T^{-1}), an obvious content distortion is observed in the translated image B, which limits the application of CycleGAN for the tasks required rigorous image-object preservation such as domain adaptation.

As shown in Fig. 1, the original CycleGAN is supervised by two losses, i.e., adversarial loss $\mathcal{L}_{adv}$ and cycle-consistency loss $\mathcal{L}_{cyc}$. The adversarial loss encourages local realism of the translated data. Taking the translation from domain A to domain B as an example, the adversarial loss can be written as:

$$
\begin{aligned}
\mathcal{L}_{adv}(G_{AB}, D_B) =& \mathbb{E}_{x_B \sim p_{x_B}} \left[(D_B(x_B) - 1)^2 \right] \\
&+ \mathbb{E}_{x_A \sim p_{x_A}} \left[(D_B(G_{AB}(x_A)))^2 \right]
\end{aligned}
\tag{1}
$$

where p_{x_A} and p_{x_B} denote the sample distributions of domain A and B, respectively; x_A and x_B are samples from domain A and B, respectively.

The cycle-consistency loss $\mathcal{L}_{cyc}$ relieves the requirement of paired training data. The idea behind the cycle-consistency loss is that the translated data from the target domain can be exactly converted back to the source domain, which can be expressed as:

$$
\begin{aligned}
\mathcal{L}_{cyc}(G_{AB}, G_{BA}) =& \mathbb{E}_{x_A \sim p_{x_A}} \left[\| G_{BA}(G_{AB}(x_A)) - x_A \|_1 \right] \\
&+ \mathbb{E}_{x_B \sim p_{x_B}} \left[\| G_{AB}(G_{BA}(x_B)) - x_B \|_1 \right].
\end{aligned}
\tag{2}
$$

With these two losses, CycleGAN can perform I2I translation using unpaired training data. However, recent study [34] found that the cycle-consistency has an intrinsic ambiguity with respect to geometric transformations. Let T be a bijective geometric transformation (e.g., translation, rotation, scaling, or even nonrigid transformation) with inverse transformation T^{-1}, the following generators G'_{AB} and G'_{BA} are also cycle consistent.

$$
G'_{AB} = G_{AB}T, \ G'_{BA} = G_{BA}T^{-1}.
\tag{3}
$$

Consequently, due to lack of penalty in content disparity between source and translated images, the results produced by CycleGAN may suffer from geometrical distortions, as the translated result shown in Fig. 1. To address this problem, existing studies [10,34] proposed to use a segmentation sub-task with pixel-wise annotation as an auxiliary regularization to assist the training of the generators, which enabled CycleGAN to be applied to tasks such as domain adaptation [34] and data augmentation [10]. However, the expensive and laborious pixel-wise image annotation process limits the practical values of those frameworks.

Motivated by the recent advancements of self-supervised learning, we try to address the content distortion problem of CycleGAN using a novel self-supervised task. The proposed self-supervised task disentangles the content information from the domain variations and accordingly optimizes the generators of CycleGAN without any extra annotations.

4   OP-GAN

In this section, we introduce the proposed OP-GAN in details. Similar to the original CycleGAN, our OP-GAN involves the adversarial and cycle-consistency losses to achieve unpaired I2I translation. In addition, a multi-task self-supervised siamese network (S) is integrated in our OP-GAN, which takes the source and translated images as input, to preserve image content during the I2I image translation.

4.1   Multi-task Self-supervised Learning

We formulate two self-supervised learning tasks, the content registration and domain classification, to disentangle the features of image content and domain information. We introduce the proposed multi-task self-supervised learning framework in the following section.

Self-supervision Formulation. As no preexistent label information is available for the self-supervised siamese network, the supervision is derived from the image data itself. We first divide both the source and translated images into a grid of 3×3.[1] As shown in Fig. 2, letting A and B represent the source and translated images respectively, the generated patches (P) can be written as $P \in \{A_1, ..., A_9\} \cup \{B_1, ..., B_9\}$. There are four scenes if we randomly select two patches from the patch pool, as listed in Table 1. Note that, the $\{A_1, A_5, B_1, B_5\}$ in Fig. 2 are examples for the illustration purpose. During the training stage, the framework randomly selects two patches from the patch pool as the paired input of the siamese network.

Based on the design of the self-supervision, we propose two assumptions to formulate the object-aware domain adaptation: 1) the patches from the same position of source and translated images (C_1) should have consistent content;

---

[1] The analysis of grid size can be found in *Appendix*.

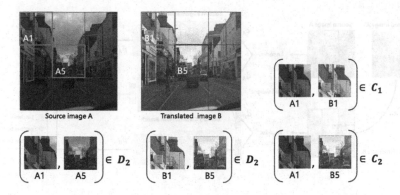

Fig. 2. The supervision signals for the proposed multi-task self-supervised learning framework. The relative position of two patches are used to supervise the content registration, while the domain classification is formulated as a 1-of-K classification task. The A_1, A_5, B_1, B_5 are examples for illustration. The framework randomly selects two patches from the source and translated images as the paired input of the siamese network.

Table 1. Scenes for random patch selection

Scenes
D_1: Two patches are both from the source image
D_2: Two patches are both from the translated image
C_1: Two patches are respectively from the source and translated images on the same position of the grid
C_2: Two patches are respectively from the different positions of source and translated images

2) the patches from the same image (D_1, D_2) should contain similar domain information (e.g., illumination). Accordingly, the relative position of two patches can be used to supervise the proxy task that extracts features with content information, while the provenance information of the patches can be used to formulate the proxy task as a domain classification.

Network Architecture. The architecture of the proposed siamese network is presented in Fig. 3, which consists of two shared-weight encoders,[2] a content registration branch, and a domain classification branch. The blue, orange, red, and cyan rectangles represent the convolutional, interpolation, global average pooling (GAP), and concatenation layers, respectively.

---

[2] The network architecture of the shared-weight encoder is presented in *Appendix*.

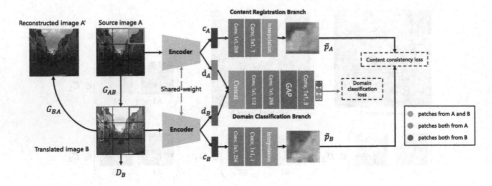

Fig. 3. The architecture of our siamese network. Here, we use the scene with two patches from the same position of two domains as an example. Our siamese network involves three components—two shared-weight encoders, a content registration branch, and a domain classification branch. There are two losses (i.e., content consistency loss and domain classification loss) used for the optimization. The shared-weight encoders embed the two patches into a latent feature space and produce four $11 \times 11 \times 512$ feature maps (c_A, d_A, c_B, d_B) for content registration and domain classification branches.

The shared-weight encoders embed the input patches (P) into a latent feature space (Z) and disentangle the features that contain the content and domain information, respectively. Taking the source (A) and translated (B) images as an example, the feature embedding process can be defined as:

$$E_A : P_A \rightarrow Z(c_A, d_A), \ E_B : P_B \rightarrow Z(c_B, d_B) \tag{4}$$

where c_A and c_B are the disentangled content features; d_A and d_B are the features containing domain information. The size of the four disentangled features is $11 \times 11 \times 512$. Afterwards, c_A and c_B are compacted with 1×1 convolutional layers and interpolated to the original size of the input patch for the computation of content consistency loss, while d_A and d_B are concatenated and fed to the domain classification branch to distill domain information from the features.

Content Registration. The content registration branch aims to maintain the patch content during the I2I domain adaptation process. As shown in Fig. 3, the content features are separately processed to produce the content attention maps $(\tilde{p})$, which represent the shape and position of image-objects. As minimum content distortion is a mandatory requirement in our domain adaptation task, the image-objects in source and translated images should be geometrically consistent (i.e., maintaining the shape and position of objects). Hence, we formulate the content consistency loss $(\mathcal{L}_{cc})$ using the two content attention maps $(\tilde{p})$ in L2 norm:

$$\mathcal{L}_{cc} = \frac{1}{M \times N} \sum_{x=1}^{M} \sum_{y=1}^{N} (\tilde{p}_{x,y}^A - \tilde{p}_{x,y}^B)^2 \tag{5}$$

where M and N are the width and height of the patch under processing, respectively, and (x, y) is the coordinate of pixel in the attention map.[3]

The content consistency loss produces the pixel-wise penalty for any content disparity between the source and translated images, which enables our OP-GAN to synthesize a realistic result without distortions. The relative position of two input patches is also taken into consideration for the calculation of $\mathcal{L}_{cc}$, i.e., the loss is calculated and optimized only for the scene C_1, and set to 0 otherwise.

Domain Classification. As aforementioned, the scenes for random patch selection are adopted as the supervision signals for the domain classification task. It is formulated as a 1-of-K classification, which consists of three classes—D_1, D_2 and C ($C = \{C_1, C_2\}$). The domain features (d_A and d_B) are first fused using concatenation, which results in a $11 \times 11 \times 1024$ discriminative feature map. The feature map is then transformed and downsampled to a $1 \times 1 \times 3$ vector by convolutional and global average pooling layers for the following scene prediction. The cross-entropy loss (denoted as $\mathcal{L}_{dc}$) is adopted in this task for optimization, which can be defined as:

$$\mathcal{L}_{dc} = - \sum_i log(\frac{e^{p_{g_i}}}{\sum_j e^{p_j}}) \tag{6}$$

where p_j denotes the jth element ($j \in [1, K]$, K is the number of classes) of vector of class scores, and g_i is the label of ith input sample. The domain classification branch mainly distills domain information from the features, which leads to a better disentanglement of content features.

4.2 Generator and Discriminator

In consistent with the standard CycleGAN, the proposed OP-GAN has cyclic generators (G_{AB}, G_{BA}) and corresponding discriminators (D_B, D_A), which have the same architectures as described in [36]. The generators employ the instance normalization [29] to produce elegant image translation results, aiming to fool the discriminators, while the discriminators adopt PatchGAN [12,18] to provide patch-wise predictions of given image being real or fake, rather than classifying the whole image.

4.3 Objective Function

Given the definitions of content consistency loss and domain classification loss, we define the self-supervised loss ($\mathcal{L}_S$) as: $\mathcal{L}_S = \mathcal{L}_{cc} + \mathcal{L}_{dc}$.[4] Therefore, the full

---

[3] After excluding the domain specific information, the content features $\tilde{p}$ from different domains are directly comparable. So, we use the simple mean squared error to measure the difference.

[4] The detailed training process with self-supervised loss can be found in *Appendix*.

objective function of our OP-GAN can be written as:

$$\mathcal{L}(G_{AB}, G_{BA}, D_A, D_B, S) = \mathcal{L}_{adv}(G_{BA}, D_A) + \mathcal{L}_{adv}(G_{AB}, D_B) \\ + \alpha\mathcal{L}_{cyc}(G_{AB}, G_{BA}) + \beta\mathcal{L}_S(G_{AB}, G_{BA}, S) \quad (7)$$

where α and β are loss weights (we heuristically set $\alpha = 10$ and $\beta = 1$ in our experiments).

The optimization of $\mathcal{L}_S$ is performed in the same manner of $\mathcal{L}_{adv}$—fixing the siamese network (S) and D_A/D_B to optimize G_{BA}/G_{AB} first, and then optimize S and D_A/D_B respectively, with G_{BA}/G_{AB} fixed. Therefore, similar to the discriminators, our siamese network can directly pass the knowledge of image-objects to the generators, which helps to improve the quality of their translated results in terms of object preservation.

5   Experiments

Given two domains (A, B), our goal is to narrow down their gap not only in terms of visual perception i.e., plausible adaptation results, but also feature representations, i.e., improved model robustness. We visualize the I2I domain adaptation results to qualitatively evaluate the former factor. For the latter one, we evaluate the OP-GAN in a similar transfer learning scenario as [27]. Let domain A be in good image condition (e.g., daylight scene with proper exposure), while domain B is unsatisfactory (e.g., image is dark, losing detailed information). In this case, the models trained on domain A usually fail to generalize well to the data from domain B, due to the cross-domain variations. To alleviate the problem, we try different I2I translation frameworks to adapt the domain B data to domain A for testing.

5.1   Experiment Settings

Datasets. Experiments are conducted on three publicly available datasets to demonstrate the effectiveness of our OP-GAN.

CamVid [1]: It contains driving videos under different weathers, e.g., cloudy and sunny. The task adapting cloudy videos to sunny ones in terms of illumination and color distribution is very challenging, as the cloudy videos are often very dark, which lose much detailed information. We conduct experiments on the cloudy-to-sunny adaptation to evaluate our OP-GAN.

SYNTHIA [38]: It consists of photo-realistic frames rendered from a virtual city. The night-to-day adaptation is a more difficult task than the cloudy-to-sunny, since the night domain suffers from severe loss of context information. We examine how the proposed OP-GAN performs on the night-to-day adaptation task using two sub-sequences (i.e., winter-day and winter-night) from the Old European Town, which is a subset of SYNTHIA.

Colonoscopic Datasets: Medical images from multicentres often have different imaging conditions, e.g., color and illumination, which make the model trained on one centre difficult to generalize to another. Our OP-GAN tries to address the problem. Two publicly available colonoscopic datasets (i.e., CVC-Clinic [30] and ETIS-Larib [26]) are used as two domains for the multicentre adaptation.

Evaluation Criterion. To evaluate the performance of domain adaptation, the mean of class-wise intersection over union (mIoU) [35] is used to evaluate the improvement achieved by our OP-GAN on the semantic segmentation tasks for CamVid and SYNTHIA datasets. For medical image segmentation, the widely-used F1 score [20], which measures the spatial overlap index between the segmentation result and ground truth, is adopted as the metric to assess the accuracy of colorectal ployp segmentation on the colonoscopic datasets.

Baseline Overview. Several unpaired I2I domain adaptation frameworks, including CycleGAN [36], UNIT [21], and DRIT [17] are taken as baselines for the performance evaluation. The direct transfer approach, which takes the target domain data for testing without any adaptation, is also involved for comparison. Note that the recent proposed GANs for image-based adaptation, e.g., SPGAN [5], PTGAN [31], and AugGAN [10], are not involved for comparison, due to the strong prior-knowledge used in those approaches. SPGAN, which was proposed for person re-identification task, used the prior-knowledge of the personal ID sets of different domains. PTGAN required coarse segmentation results to distinguish foreground and background areas. AugGAN added a segmentation subtask to the CycleGAN-based framework, which requires pixel-wise annotations. The use of prior-knowledge degrades the generalization of those GANs, which are only suitable for the domains fulfilling the specific requirements.

Training Details. The proposed OP-GAN is implemented using PyTorch. The generator, discriminator, and siamese network are iteratively trained for 200 epochs with the Adam solver [14]. The baselines involved in this study adopt the same training protocol.

5.2 Visualization of Adaptation Results

The adaptation results for the three tasks generated by different I2I domain adaptation frameworks are presented in Fig. 4, which illustrate the main problem of existing approaches (UNIT [21], DRIT [17], and CycleGAN [36])—image content corruptions. Due to the lack of penalty in content disparity between the source and translated images, the existing I2I adaptation frameworks intend to excessively edit the image content such as changing the shape and colors of image-objects, referring to the distorted road and building in the CamVid and SYNTHIA translated images. Furthermore, the polyps in colonoscopy images are essential clue for the screening of colorectal cancer. However, few of the existing

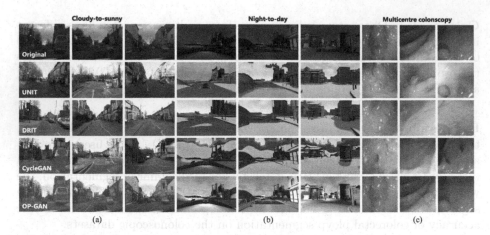

(a)   (b)   (c)

Fig. 4. Comparison of translated images with different approaches. The image-based adaptation performance is evaluated on three tasks: (a) cloudy-to-sunny, (b) night-to-day, and (c) multicentres. The original images, adaptation results produced by UNIT [21], DRIT [17], CycleGAN [36], and our OP-GAN are presented.

Table 2. Semantic segmentation IoU (%) of the cloudy images from CamVid with different I2I domain adaptation frameworks. (val.—validation)

	Bicyclist	Building	Car	Pole	Fence	Pedestrian	Road	Sidewalk	Sign	Sky	Tree	mIoU
Sunny (val.)	84.03	86.30	90.91	18.36	74.91	63.09	94.07	89.75	7.49	94.00	91.48	70.38
Cloudy (test)												
Direct transfer	48.70	40.29	51.15	21.59	4.95	**43.84**	71.64	60.69	21.29	40.59	63.90	41.86
UNIT [21]	0.67	49.28	6.99	6.10	1.54	0.79	45.05	15.16	0.00	62.61	39.34	19.94
DRIT [17]	0.34	40.00	0.31	0.33	0.83	0.23	48.27	26.81	0.00	64.85	23.73	18.20
CycleGAN [36]	6.16	56.64	10.76	8.61	0.01	4.06	50.49	30.21	8.67	75.97	45.62	26.26
OP-GAN (Ours)	**51.28**	**73.10**	**74.19**	**25.84**	**12.42**	42.75	70.48	51.74	14.71	**81.09**	**72.40**	**51.40**

frameworks successfully maintain the shape and texture of polyps during multicentre adaptation, which is unacceptable and limits their practical values in medical-related applications. On the contrary, the proposed OP-GAN can excellently perform cross-domain adaptation, while preserving the image-objects.

5.3   Cloudy-to-sunny Adaptation on CamVid

The CamVid dataset contains four sunny videos (577 frames in total) and one cloudy video (124 frames). Each frame of the videos is manually annotated, which associate each pixel with one of the 32 semantic classes. Based on the widely-accepted protocol [37], we focus on 11 classes including bicyclist, building, car, pole, fence, pedestrian, road, sidewalk, sign, sky, and tree. To evaluate the domain adaptation performance yielded by our OP-GAN, a semantic

Table 3. Semantic segmentation IoU (%) of the night images from SYNTHIA with different I2I domain adaptation frameworks. (Veg.—Vegetation, Ped.—Pedestrian, l.-m.—lane-marking, val.—validation)

	Sky	Building	Road	Sidewalk	Fence	Veg.	Pole	Car	Sign	Ped.	Bicycle	l.-m.	mIoU
Day (val.)	94.84	93.71	96.49	92.09	27.99	50.06	54.04	91.35	46.31	69.21	54.46	77.18	70.02
Night (test)													
Direct transfer	0.04	61.45	70.41	78.22	**11.35**	37.76	34.67	80.88	26.62	53.51	54.33	38.42	44.49
UNIT [21]	**63.52**	**72.69**	65.80	47.44	0.93	48.76	28.11	37.54	9.71	28.10	26.76	9.87	34.97
DRIT [17]	33.63	43.96	50.35	13.10	0.03	17.92	0.41	2.69	0.06	0.38	0.03	0.62	12.66
CycleGAN [36]	37.73	51.79	55.48	36.37	0.71	44.23	14.60	17.94	1.57	8.19	10.67	11.89	22.88
OP-GAN (Ours)	21.90	66.22	**86.78**	**79.05**	7.70	**54.86**	**39.11**	**85.09**	**31.40**	**55.77**	**54.54**	**47.61**	**50.86**

segmentation network (PSPNet[5] [35]) is trained with the sunny frames and tested on the original cloudy frames and the translated ones. In the experiment, the sunny frames are separated into training (three videos) and validation (one video) sets. The evaluation results are shown in Table 2.

Due to the loss of detailed information, it can be observed from Table 2 that the performance of PSPNet trained with sunny images dramatically drops to 41.86% while tested on the original cloudy images. As the existing I2I domain adaptation approaches encounter the content distortion problem, the segmentation mIoU of PSPNet further degrades to 26.26%, 19.94% and 18.20% using the CycleGAN, UNIT and DRIT, respectively. In contrast, the proposed OP-GAN achieves a significant improvement (+9.54%) compared to the direct transfer, which demonstrates that our OP-GAN can narrow down the gap between the cloudy and sunny domains while excellently preserving the image-objects. The proposed OP-GAN significantly boosts the IoU of some object-related classes such as building, car, and fence (i.e., +32.81%, +23.04%, and +7.47%, respectively). Specifically, AugGAN [10], using pixel-wise annotations for image-object preservation, achieves a mIoU of 55.31% in our experiment, which can be regarded as the upper bound for our approach.

5.4 Night-to-day Adaptation on SYNTHIA

We adopt two sub-sequences (winter-day and winter-night) from SYNTHIA to perform night-to-day adaptation. The winter-day and winter-night sequences contain 947 and 785 frames, respectively. SYNTHIA dataset provides pixel-wise semantic annotations for each frame, which can be categoried to 13 classes (12 semantic classes and background). The partition of training, validation, and test sets complies with the same protocol to that of the CamVid dataset—the day images are separated into training and validation sets according to the ratio of 70:30, while all the night images are used as the test set. The fully convolutional

---

[5] The top-1 solution (without extra training data) on the leaderboard of semantic segmentation on CamVid: https://paperswithcode.com/sota/semantic-segmentation-on-camvid.

Table 4. Ablation study of OP-GAN for the semantic segmentation task on CamVid (%). (D. T.—Direct Transfer)

	–	A	B	C	D
Setup	D. T.	Original CycleGAN	$A + L_{cc}$	$A + L_{dc}$	$A + L_{cc} + L_{dc}$
mIoU	41.86	26.26	45.63	45.86	51.40

network (PSPNet [35]) is also adopted in this experiment to perform semantic segmentation.

The segmentation mIoUs yielded by different testing strategies are shown in Table 3. Similar to the cloudy images, the PSPNet trained with day images fails to propoerly process the night images—an mIoU of 44.49%, due to the loss of information. The night-to-day adaptation on SYNTHIA is a more challenging task compared to the cloudy-to-sunny adaptation on CamVid, since a large portion of the night images is dark, where the image-objects (e.g., buildings) are difficult to recognize. Refer to Fig. 4, existing I2I domain adaptation frameworks used to create extra contents to fill the extremely dark areas, which consequently corrupts the original image-objects. Due to these distortions, the images translated by UNIT, CycleGAN and DRIT further decrease the mIoU of PSPNet to 34.97%, 22.88% and 12.66%, respectively. Our OP-GAN can excellently prevent image-object corruptions during night-to-day adaptation (as shown in Fig. 4) and achieves the best mIoU (50.86%) for the night images, which is +6.37% higher than the direct transfer.

5.5 Multicentre Colonoscopy Adaptation

Due to the limitation of paper length, the experimental results on multicentre colonoscopy adaptation are presented in *Appendix*.

5.6 Ablation Study

An ablation study is conducted on the cloudy-to-sunny adaptation task on CamVid to evaluate the contribution produced by each component of our OP-GAN. The result of ablation study is presented in Table 4. Due to the capacity of feature distillation, the content registration and domain classification branches can respectively improve the mIoU of original CycleGAN with +19.37% and +19.6%. The combination of these two branches lead to a better disentanglement of content and domain information, which results in the highest improvement (+25.14%). To validate the effectiveness of the proposed self-supervised learning tasks, we visualize the knowledge learned by different branches and analyze their contributions for image-object preservation.

Content Registration. The content registration branch aims to maintain the shape and texture of image-objects before and after domain adaptation. We visualize two pairs of attention maps ($\tilde{p}$) generated by content registration branches

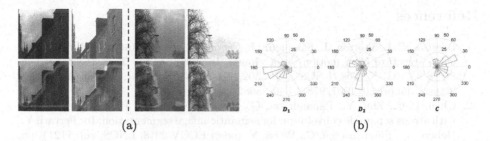

(a)   (b)

Fig. 5. Validation of self-supervised proxy tasks. (a) Visualization of attention maps produced by content registration branch. For an object-preserving I2I domain adaptation, the patches on the same position of source and translated images should have similar content attention maps ($\tilde{p}$). (b) The activation patterns of different classes (D_1, D_2, and C) in domain classification.

to validate whether they have the 'object'-related concept. The attention maps are presented in Fig. 5 (a), which shows that the content registration branch prefers to activate the areas containing image-objects (e.g., buildings and trees) and ignore those containing more domain information such as sky. As a result, this branch penalizes the generator if the translated image-objects have large distortions, which encourages the OP-GAN to perform object-aware translation.

Domain Classification. To ensure the scene classification is a learnable proxy task, we plot the $1 \times 1 \times 256$ averaged activation patterns for different classes (D_1, D_2, C) produced by the global average pooling layer of domain classification branch in Fig. 5 (b). It can be observed that different neurons are activated when processing paired patches from different scenes, which demonstrates that the scenes defined in Table 1 indeed contain specific domain information for the classifier to distinguish each other.

6   Conclusion

In this paper, we proposed a novel GAN (namely OP-GAN) to perform object-preserving image-to-image domain adaptation without supervision from manual labels. Extensive experiments have been conducted on three publicly available datasets. The experimental results demonstrated the effectiveness of our OP-GAN—performing excellent cross-domain translation while preserving image-objects.

Acknowledge. This work is supported by the Natural Science Foundation of China (No. 91959108 and 61702339), the Key Area Research and Development Program of Guangdong Province, China (No. 2018B010111001), National Key Research and Development Project (2018YFC2000702) and Science and Technology Program of Shenzhen, China (No. ZDSYS201802021814180).

References

1. Brostow, G.J., Shotton, J., Fauqueur, J., Cipolla, R.: Segmentation and recognition using structure from motion point clouds. In: Forsyth, D., Torr, P., Zisserman, A. (eds.) ECCV 2008. LNCS, vol. 5302, pp. 44–57. Springer, Heidelberg (2008). https://doi.org/10.1007/978-3-540-88682-2_5
2. Chen, L.-C., Zhu, Y., Papandreou, G., Schroff, F., Adam, H.: Encoder-decoder with atrous separable convolution for semantic image segmentation. In: Ferrari, V., Hebert, M., Sminchisescu, C., Weiss, Y. (eds.) ECCV 2018. LNCS, vol. 11211, pp. 833–851. Springer, Cham (2018). https://doi.org/10.1007/978-3-030-01234-2_49
3. Chen, T., Zhai, X., Ritter, M., Lucic, M., Houlsby, N.: Self-supervised GANs via auxiliary rotation loss. In: CVPR (2019)
4. Chen, Y., Lai, Y.K., Liu, Y.J.: CartoonGAN: generative adversarial networks for photo cartoonization. In: CVPR (2018)
5. Deng, W., Zheng, L., Ye, Q., Kang, G., Yang, Y., Jiao, J.: Image-image domain adaptation with preserved self-similarity and domain-dissimilarity for person re-identification. In: CVPR (2018)
6. Fu, H., Gong, M., Wang, C., Batmanghelich, K., Zhang, K., Tao, D.: Geometry-consistent generative adversarial networks for one-sided unsupervised domain mapping. In: CVPR (2019)
7. Gidaris, S., Bursuc, A., Komodakis, N., Pérez, P., Cord, M.: Boosting few-shot visual learning with self-supervision. In: ICCV (2019)
8. Goodfellow, I., et al.: Generative adversarial nets. In: NeurIPS (2014)
9. Hu, J., Shen, L., Sun, G.: Squeeze-and-excitation networks. In: CVPR (2018)
10. Huang, S.-W., Lin, C.-T., Chen, S.-P., Wu, Y.-Y., Hsu, P.-H., Lai, S.-H.: Aug-GAN: cross domain adaptation with GAN-based data augmentation. In: Ferrari, V., Hebert, M., Sminchisescu, C., Weiss, Y. (eds.) ECCV 2018. LNCS, vol. 11213, pp. 731–744. Springer, Cham (2018). https://doi.org/10.1007/978-3-030-01240-3_44
11. Huang, Z., Wang, X., Huang, L., Huang, C., Wei, Y., Liu, W.: CCNet: criss-cross attention for semantic segmentation. In: ICCV (2019)
12. Isola, P., Zhu, J.Y., Zhou, T., Efros, A.A.: Image-to-image translation with conditional adversarial networks. In: CVPR (2017)
13. Kim, T., Cha, M., Kim, H., Lee, J., Kim, J.: Learning to discover cross-domain relations with generative adversarial networks. In: ICML (2017)
14. Kingma, D.P., Ba, J.: Adam: a method for stochastic optimization. arXiv preprint arXiv:1412.6980 (2014)
15. Larsson, G., Maire, M., Shakhnarovich, G.: Colorization as a proxy task for visual understanding. In: CVPR (2017)
16. Lee, H.Y., Huang, J.B., Singh, M., Yang, M.H.: Unsupervised representation learning by sorting sequences. In: ICCV (2017)
17. Lee, H.-Y., Tseng, H.-Y., Huang, J.-B., Singh, M., Yang, M.-H.: Diverse image-to-image translation via disentangled representations. In: Ferrari, V., Hebert, M., Sminchisescu, C., Weiss, Y. (eds.) ECCV 2018. LNCS, vol. 11205, pp. 36–52. Springer, Cham (2018). https://doi.org/10.1007/978-3-030-01246-5_3
18. Li, C., Wand, M.: Precomputed real-time texture synthesis with Markovian generative adversarial networks. In: Leibe, B., Matas, J., Sebe, N., Welling, M. (eds.) ECCV 2016. LNCS, vol. 9907, pp. 702–716. Springer, Cham (2016). https://doi.org/10.1007/978-3-319-46487-9_43
19. Li, X., Wang, W., Hu, X., Yang, J.: Selective kernel networks. In: CVPR (2019)

20. Li, Y., Xie, X., Liu, S., Li, X., Shen, L.: GT-Net: A deep learning network for gastric tumor diagnosis. In: ICTAI (2018)
21. Liu, M.Y., Breuel, T., Kautz, J.: Unsupervised image-to-image translation networks. In: NeurIPS (2017)
22. Ma, S., Fu, J., Wen Chen, C., Mei, T.: DA-GAN: instance-level image translation by deep attention generative adversarial networks. In: CVPR (2018)
23. Noroozi, M., Vinjimoor, A., Favaro, P., Pirsiavash, H.: Boosting self-supervised learning via knowledge transfer. In: CVPR (2018)
24. Ronneberger, O., Fischer, P., Brox, T.: U-Net: convolutional networks for biomedical image segmentation. In: International Conference on Medical Image Computing & Computer Assisted Intervention (2015)
25. Shrivastava, A., Pfister, T., Tuzel, O., Susskind, J., Wang, W., Webb, R.: Learning from simulated and unsupervised images through adversarial training. In: CVPR (2017)
26. Silva, J., Histace, A., Romain, O., Dray, X., Granado, B.: Toward embedded detection of polyps in WCE images for early diagnosis of colorectal cancer. Int. J. Comput. Assist. Radiol. Surg. **9**(2), 283–293 (2013). https://doi.org/10.1007/s11548-013-0926-3
27. Sun, L., Wang, K., Yang, K., Xiang, K.: See clearer at night: towards robust nighttime semantic segmentation through day-night image conversion. arXiv preprint arXiv:1908.05868 (2019)
28. Szegedy, C., Ioffe, S., Vanhoucke, V., Alemi, A.A.: Inception-v4, inception-ResNet and the impact of residual connections on learning. In: AAAI (2017)
29. Ulyanov, D., Vedaldi, A., Lempitsky, V.: Instance normalization: the missing ingredient for fast stylization. arXiv preprint arXiv:1607.08022 (2016)
30. Vázquez, D., et al.: A benchmark for endoluminal scene segmentation of colonoscopy images. J. Healthc. Eng. **2017**, 9 (2017)
31. Wei, L., Zhang, S., Gao, W., Tian, Q.: Person transfer GAN to bridge domain gap for person re-identification. In: CVPR (2018)
32. Yi, Z., Zhang, H., Tan, P., Gong, M.: DualGAN: unsupervised dual learning for image-to-image translation. In: ICCV (2017)
33. Yu, C., Wang, J., Peng, C., Gao, C., Yu, G., Sang, N.: Learning a discriminative feature network for semantic segmentation. In: CVPR (2018)
34. Zhang, Z., Yang, L., Zheng, Y.: Translating and segmenting multimodal medical volumes with cycle- and shape-consistency generative adversarial network. In: CVPR (2018)
35. Zhao, H., Shi, J., Qi, X., Wang, X., Jia, J.: Pyramid scene parsing network. In: CVPR (2017)
36. Zhu, J., Park, T., Isola, P., Efros, A.A.: Unpaired image-to-image translation using cycle-consistent adversarial networks. In: ICCV (2017)
37. Zhu, Y., et al.: Improving semantic segmentation via video propagation and label relaxation. In: CVPR (2019)
38. Zolfaghari Bengar, J., et al.: Temporal coherence for active learning in videos. arXiv preprint arXiv:1908.11757 (2019)

On the Usage of the Trifocal Tensor in Motion Segmentation

Federica Arrigoni[1(✉)], Luca Magri[2], and Tomas Pajdla[3]

[1] DISI, University of Trento, Trento, Italy
federica.arrigoni@unitn.it
[2] DEIB, Politecnico di Milano, Milan, Italy
luca.magri@polimi.it
[3] Czech Institute of Informatics, Robotics and Cybernetics (CIIRC),
Czech Technical University in Prague, Prague, Czech Republic
pajdla@cvut.cz

Abstract. Motion segmentation, i.e., the problem of clustering data in multiple images based on different 3D motions, is an important task for reconstructing and understanding dynamic scenes. In this paper we address motion segmentation in multiple images by combining partial results coming from triplets of images, which are obtained by fitting a number of trifocal tensors to correspondences. We exploit the fact that the trifocal tensor is a stronger model than the fundamental matrix, as it provides fewer but more reliable matches over three images than fundamental matrices provide over the two. We also consider an alternative solution which merges partial results coming from both triplets and pairs of images, showing the strength of three-frame segmentation in a combination with two-frame segmentation. Our real experiments on standard as well as new datasets demonstrate the superior accuracy of the proposed approaches when compared to previous techniques.

Keywords: Motion segmentation · Structure from motion · Multi-model fitting · Trifocal tensor

1 Introduction

Motion segmentation, i.e., the problem of clustering data in multiple images based on different 3D motions, has attracted a lot of attention in Computer Vision. Existing techniques can be divided into three categories, according to the type of data that is being clustered and the assumptions that are made about the input.

The first category, which accounts for the majority of works in the literature, assumes that a set of points is tracked through multiple images, and the task is to

Electronic supplementary material The online version of this chapter (https://doi.org/10.1007/978-3-030-58565-5_31) contains supplementary material, which is available to authorized users.

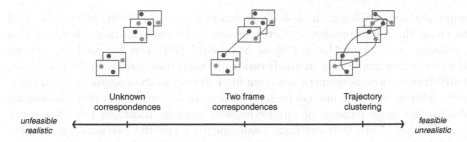

Fig. 1. The proposed taxonomy divides existing approaches into three categories: trajectory clustering; segmentation with two-frame correspondences; segmentation with unknown correspondences. When moving from right to left the problem becomes more difficult to solve since assumptions are weaker (but more realistic). This paper comes under the middle category.

cluster those trajectories (i.e., *multi-frame* correspondences) into different groups based on the moving object they belong to. Methods performing subspace separation (e.g., [7,17,25,33,44,48]) and multi-model fitting (e.g., [4–6,14,28,39]) belong to this category. Other solutions include [22,23,30,35,37,47]. The typical scenario consists in videos where there are small motions between consecutive frames (e.g., the Hopkins benchmark [42]). This involves several applications such as surveillance [19], scene understanding [34] and autonomous driving [9]. We name this category "trajectory clustering" (see Fig. 1).

The second category considers the problem of clustering image points (e.g., SIFT keypoints [26]) into different motions, assuming that matches between pairs of images (i.e., *two-frame* correspondences) are available only. This task is poorly studied and there are only a few works addressing it [2,3]. The typical scenario involves unstructured/unordered image sets where there are large motions between different frames (e.g., the indoor scenes used in [2,3]). This finds application in multi-body structure from motion [36], where the objective is to reconstruct a 3D scene containing multiple moving objects. This category is represented in the middle of Fig. 1.

The third category, shown in the left part of Fig. 1, assumes that a set of image points (e.g., SIFT keypoints) is given and considers the case of *unknown* correspondences. This problem is addressed in [15,46] only, where the authors aim at computing multi-frame correspondences while at the same time classifying those trajectories into different groups. However, such approaches are not suitable for practical applications: only sequences with (at most) 200 tracks are analyzed in [15,46] due to algorithmic complexity.

In the first case, multi-frame correspondences are needed *before* motion segmentation. Note that recovering trajectories in the presence of multiple moving objects is a hard task [16]. To overcome such a difficulty, correspondences are usually cleaned with manual operations (see, e.g., the Hopkins benchmark), hence they are not realistic at all. In the second case, multi-frame correspondences are not computed explicitly. However, they could be recovered *after* motion segmentation as follows: single-body techniques (e.g., RANSAC [8]) can be used to clean the input two-frame correspondences for each motion; then, existing solutions (e.g., QuickMatch [43] or StableSfM [29]) can be used for getting tracks starting from those (refined) two-frame correspondences. In the third case, multi-frame correspondences are computed *during* motion segmentation. However, addressing segmentation under such a weak assumption is very challenging due to the large number of unknowns, and existing solutions [15,46] are not practical yet. Note that methods belonging to a specific category are, in general, sub-optimal when applied to the task associated with another category. To sum up, the second category lies at the middle between the first one and the third one, hence it can be viewed as a good trade-off between making realistic assumptions and addressing a feasible/practical task. This motivates our interest in those methods, which are reviewed in Sect. 1.1.

1.1   Related Work

The most related work [2,3] address motion segmentation in two steps:

1. motion segmentation is solved independently on different image pairs;
2. such partial results are combined in order to get a multi-frame segmentation.

Concerning the first step, multiple fundamental matrices are fitted to corresponding points via Robust Preference Analysis (RPA) [27]. Concerning the second step, different techniques are proposed.

In [2] all the two-frame segmentations produced by Step 1 are represented as binary matrices, and they are collected in a big block-matrix. Then, the unknown multi-frame segmentation is recovered from the spectral decomposition of such a matrix, followed by a rounding procedure. This method – named SYNCH– can be viewed as a "synchronization" of binary matrices [1] or as a special case of "spectral clustering" [45].

In [3] it is observed that all the two-frame segmentations involving a fixed image provide – up to a permutation of the motions – a possible solution for clustering points in that image. In order to resolve such ambiguity, *permutation synchronization* [31] is performed. Then, each point is assigned to the most frequent label (i.e., the mode) among all the possible solutions coming from different two-frame segmentations. For this reason the method is named MODE.

1.2   Contribution

In this paper we propose two methods that tackle motion segmentation by exploiting the trifocal tensor, motivated by the fact that the latter constitutes a stronger model than the fundamental matrix. Indeed, it is well known that the trifocal tensor can be used to determine the exact position of a point in a third image (given its position in the other two images), hence there are fewer mismatches over three images than there are over two [11]. In the case of the fundamental matrix, instead, there is only the weaker constraint of an epipolar line against which to verify a possible correspondence.

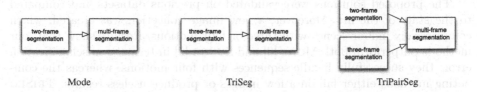

Fig. 2. The method developed in [3] and our approaches combine segmentation results independently obtained from subsets of images: MODE [3] considers pairs of images (i.e., the fundamental matrix); TRISEG considers triplets of images (i.e., the trifocal tensor); TRIPAIRSEG considers both pairs and triplets of images (i.e., both the fundamental matrix and the trifocal tensor).

Our methods are outlined in Fig. 2. They belong to the second category (i.e., the case of two-frame correspondences represented in the middle of Fig. 1) and are inspired by [3]. The first approach – named TRISEG– addresses motion segmentation in two steps:

1. motion segmentation is solved independently on different triplets of images;
2. such partial results are combined in order to get a multi-frame segmentation.

Concerning Step 1, we exploit RPA [27] in order to fit multiple trifocal tensors to correspondences. Concerning Step 2, we adapt the method proposed in [3] – which was developed for merging results coming from pairs of images – in order to deal with triplets of images. The relevance of the trifocal tensor for addressing motion segmentation in *three* images was already observed in some early works [10,40,41]. However, this is the first paper where the trifocal tensor is exploited in order to solve motion segmentation in *multiple* images.

The second approach – named TRIPAIRSEG– is made of three steps:

1. motion segmentation is solved independently on different pairs of images;
2. motion segmentation is solved independently on different triplets of images;
3. the partial results derived in the first two steps are combined in order to get a multi-frame segmentation.

Concerning Step 1, multiple fundamental matrices are fitted to corresponding points via RPA, as done in [3]. Concerning Step 2, multiple trifocal tensors are fitted to correspondences via RPA, as done by TRISEG. Concerning Step 3, we explain how TRISEG can be easily adapted in order to deal with both pairs and triplets of images. The idea of merging results coming from different models is also present in [47], where the authors consider both the homography, the fundamental matrix and the affine subspace. Such approach, however, differs from ours in three respects. First of all, it addresses a different task for it belongs to the first category of methods. Secondly, the analysed models are not used one at a time to provide a possible segmentation involving a subset of images – as happens for our method – but they are used all together to build an accumulated affinity matrix. Finally, the trifocal tensor is not used in [47].

The proposed solutions were validated on previous datasets and compared to the state of the art. Moreover, a new image collection was created, which comprises six indoor scenes with three or four motions. Results show that: our methods outperform both MODE [3] and SYNCH [2] in terms of misclassification error; they successfully handle sequences with four motions, whereas the competing methods either fail on a few images or produce useless results; TRISEG usually classifies less points than TRIPAIRSEG with higher accuracy.

The paper is organized as follows. Section 2 is devoted to our solutions to motion segmentation: Sect. 2.1 describes TRISEG whereas Sect. 2.2 presents TRIPAIRSEG. Experimental results are reported in Sect. 3 and Sect. 3.1 explains how the RPA algorithm can be used in order to fit multiple trifocal tensors. The conclusion is drawn in Sect. 4.

2 Proposed Methods

Let us introduce some useful notation. Let n denote the number of images and let d denote the number of motions, which is known by assumption. Similarly to [2,3], we assume that a set of points is given in all the images and correspondences between points in image pairs have been established (using SIFT [26] for instance). Let p_i denote the number of points in image i, and let $p = \sum_{i=1}^{n} p_i$ denote the total amount of points over all the images. Let $\mathbf{s}_i \in \{0, 1, \ldots, d\}^{p_i}$ be a vector – named the *total segmentation* of image i – representing the labels of points in image i. Labels from 1 to d identify the membership to a specific motion, while the zero label identifies those points (also known as *unclassified* points) whose cluster can not be established due to high corruption in the correspondences. The goal here is to estimate $\mathbf{s}_i$ for all $i = 1, \ldots, n$. Two approaches are developed to accomplish such a task, which are presented in Sect. 2.1 and 2.2.

2.1 TRISEG

Let $\alpha = (i, j, k)$ be a triplet of images and let $\mathbf{t}_\alpha \in \{0, 1, \ldots, d\}^{m_\alpha}$ be a vector – named the *partial segmentation* of triplet α – representing the labels of corresponding points in images i, j and k, where $m_\alpha \leq \min\{p_i, p_j, p_k\}$ denotes the number of correspondences in the triplet. Hereafter Greek letters are used to denote triplets of images. In practice each partial segmentation is computed by fitting multiple trifocal tensors to correspondences with RPA [27], as explained in Sect. 3.1, where points labelled as outlier (if any) are given the zero label. Note that the usage of the trifocal tensor is a relevant difference with respect to [3], where fundamental matrices are used. Such difference brings significant improvement in performance, as shown in Sect. 3. The goal here is to estimate the total segmentations starting from a redundant set of partial segmentations, as shown in Fig. 3. In this respect, two issues have to be addressed:

- each partial segmentation considers its own labelling of the motions, i.e., the same motion may be given a different label in different triplets;

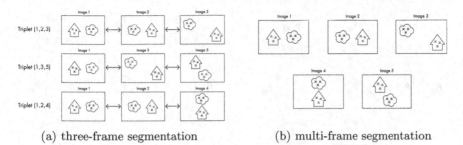

(a) three-frame segmentation   (b) multi-frame segmentation

Fig. 3. The task of TRISEG is to assign a label (blue or red) to each point in multiple images based on the moving object (house or cloud) it belongs to. The starting point is a set of partial results obtained by solving motion segmentation on different triplets. Observe that such results may contain errors and they are not absolute: the house is given the red label in the first triplet but it is given the blue label in the second triplet (Color figure online)

– each partial segmentation may contain some errors, which can be caused either by wrong correspondences or by failure of the RPA algorithm.

We now explain how to address the first challenge. Note that $\mathbf{t}_\alpha \in \{0, 1, \ldots, d\}^{m_\alpha}$ gives rise to three vectors

$$
\begin{aligned}
\mathbf{s}_i^\alpha &\in \{0, 1, \ldots, d\}^{p_i} \\
\mathbf{s}_j^\alpha &\in \{0, 1, \ldots, d\}^{p_j} \\
\mathbf{s}_k^\alpha &\in \{0, 1, \ldots, d\}^{p_k}
\end{aligned}
\tag{1}
$$

which contain labels of corresponding points in images i, j and k, where missing correspondences are given the zero label. Observe that the superscript in Eq. (1) refers to the triplet whereas subscripts refer to the images in the triplet. Let us construct a graph $\mathcal{G} = (\mathcal{V}, \mathcal{E})$ with vertex set $\mathcal{V}$ and edge set $\mathcal{E}$ as follows:

– each vertex corresponds to one triplet;
– an edge is drawn between two vertices each time the associated triplets have one image in common.

Note that $\mathcal{G}$ is a *multigraph*, i.e., a graph with multiple edges: in the case where two triplets share two images there will be two edges between the corresponding vertices, as shown in Fig. 4a. Observe that a multigraph is not constructed in [3], since different pairs can not share two images but (at most) one.

Each vertex in the multigraph is associated with an *unknown* permutation and each edge is associated with a *known* permutation[1]. Let P_α denote the $d \times d$ permutation matrix associated with vertex α, which corresponds to triplet α. The interpretation is that – after applying P_α to the partial segmentation $\mathbf{t}_\alpha$ – the ambiguity in the local labelling of motions is fixed, i.e., the same motion

---

[1] Observe that these permutations are represented as *square* matrices since we are assuming that the number of motions is known and constant over all the frames.

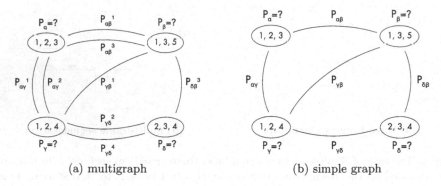

(a) multigraph   (b) simple graph

Fig. 4. The relations between different triplets of images can be represented as multigraph or a simple graph. In both cases each vertex corresponds to one triplet. In the multigraph an edge connects two triplets all the times they share one image. Triplets $(1, 2, 3)$ and $(1, 3, 5)$, for instance, are linked by two edges since they have two common images. In the simple graph, instead, one (single) edge is drawn between two triplets if and only if they share (at least) one image. Vertices correspond to unknown permutations and edges correspond to known permutations, as explained in the text.

has the same label in different triplets. Let k denote a common image between triplets α and β (i.e., $k \in \alpha \cap \beta$) and let $P_{\alpha\beta}^k$ denote the $d \times d$ permutation matrix associated with the k-th edge between vertices α and β. Such a matrix represents the permutation that best maps the vector $\mathbf{s}_k^\alpha$ (i.e., labels of image k in triplet α) into the vector $\mathbf{s}_k^\beta$ (i.e., labels of image k in triplet β):

$$P_{\alpha\beta}^k = \text{bestMap} \, (\mathbf{s}_k^\alpha, \mathbf{s}_k^\beta). \tag{2}$$

Recall that $\mathbf{s}_k^\alpha$ and $\mathbf{s}_k^\beta$ are recovered from $\mathbf{t}_\alpha$ and $\mathbf{t}_\beta$ respectively, as stated by Eq. (1). Finding $P_{\alpha\beta}^k$ is a *linear assignment* problem, which can be solved with the Hungarian algorithm [21].

Now we turn $\mathcal{G}$ into a *simple graph* (i.e., a graph without multiple edges) in order to have (at most) one single measure between each pair of vertices (instead of multiple measures), as shown in Fig. 4b. Thus the task is to find a permutation $P_{\alpha\beta}$ associated with edge (α, β) that best represents (or, in other words, that "averages") the set $\{P_{\alpha\beta}^k \text{ s.t. } k \in \alpha \cap \beta\}$:

$$P_{\alpha\beta} = \text{mean}\{P_{\alpha\beta}^k \text{ s.t. } k \in \alpha \cap \beta\}. \tag{3}$$

Finding $P_{\alpha\beta}$ can be cast to a linear assignment problem, as explained in the supplementary material, which can be solved with the Hungarian algorithm [21].

Now we have to face the problem of computing an unknown permutation P_α for each vertex $\alpha \in \mathcal{V}$ starting from a redundant set of permutations $P_{\alpha\beta}$ with $(\alpha, \beta) \in \mathcal{E}$, where $\mathcal{G} = (\mathcal{V}, \mathcal{E})$ is a simple graph. It can be seen that such matrices satisfy the following consistency relation

$$P_{\alpha\beta} = P_\alpha P_\beta^\mathsf{T} \tag{4}$$

which defines a *permutation synchronization* problem [31]. Equation (4) can be solved via spectral decomposition (see [31,38] for more details). At this point the permutation P_α is applied to the partial segmentation $\mathbf{t}_\alpha$ for each triplet α. This has the effect of (possibly) reshuffling the labels of motions in individual triplets so that the permutation ambiguity is fixed, i.e., the same motion has the same label in different triplets.

We now explain how to deal with errors in individual partial segmentations, thus addressing the second challenge mentioned above. Recall that Eq. (1) means that each partial segmentation provides a possible solution for the total segmentation of the three images involved in the triplet. Hence, for a given image, several estimates are available for its total segmentation. If $\mathcal{T}_i$ denotes the set of triplets involving image i, then such estimates are given by $\{\mathbf{s}_i^\alpha \text{ s.t. } \alpha \in \mathcal{T}_i\}$. In order to assign a unique label to each point, the following criterion [3] is used

$$\mathbf{s}_i[r] = \text{mode} \{\mathbf{s}_i^\alpha[r] \text{ s.t. } \alpha \in \mathcal{T}_i, \ \mathbf{s}_i^\alpha[r] \neq 0\} \tag{5}$$

with $r = 1,\ldots,p_i$ and $i = 1,\ldots,n$. The idea is that the most frequent label (i.e. the *mode*) is, in general, correct in the presence of moderate noise. The condition $\mathbf{s}_i^\alpha[r] \neq 0$ means that both missing correspondences and points labelled as outlier (if any) by RPA are ignored, and the mode is computed over remaining points. We set $\mathbf{s}_i[r] = 0$ (i.e., point r in image i is labelled as unknown) in the case where $\mathbf{s}_i^\alpha[r] = 0$ for all $\alpha \in \mathcal{T}_i$, meaning that the point is either missing or deemed as outlier in *all* the triplets. For the sake of robustness, we further require that the mode is equal to (at least) two measures, otherwise the point is labelled as unknown.

To summarize, our method – named TRISEG– is made of the following steps:

i) for each triplet α, the partial segmentation $\mathbf{t}_\alpha$ is computed by fitting multiple trifocal tensors with RPA (see Sect. 3.1); the three vectors in Eq. (1) are derived from $\mathbf{t}_\alpha$;

ii) for each pair (α, β) of triplets with some images in common, the following operations are performed: first, the permutation matrix $P_{\alpha\beta}^k$ is computed from Eq. (2) for all $k \in \alpha \cap \beta$ (linear assignment problem); then, the permutation matrix $P_{\alpha\beta}$ is computed from Eq. (3) (linear assignment problem – see supplementary material);

iii) the permutation matrices $P_\alpha,\ldots,P_\beta$ are computed simultaneously for all the triplets from Eq. (4) (permutation synchronization);

iv) for each triplet α, the permutation matrix P_α is applied to the partial segmentation $\mathbf{t}_\alpha$; the three vectors in Eq. (1) are derived from $\mathbf{t}_\alpha$;

v) for each image i, the total segmentation $\mathbf{s}_i$ is derived from Eq. (5).

Step i) is a pre-processing phase where motion segmentation is solved on triplets of images. Steps ii)-iv) aim at expressing all such partial/local results with respect to the same numbering of motions (see the first challenge mentioned at the beginning of this section). Step v) explains how to robustly assign a unique label to each point starting from multiple measures possibly corrupted by noise (see the second challenge mentioned at the beginning of this section).

2.2 TRIPAIRSEG

We introduce here another technique – named TRIPAIRSEG– which computes the total segmentations starting from partial segmentations of two different types, as shown in Fig. 2. Such partial results are derived by fitting either fundamental matrices (in the case of image pairs) or trifocal tensors (in the case of triplets of images) via RPA. The idea is that, by using models of two different types, the advantages of both are inherited, as shown in Sect. 3.

It is straightforward to see that the approach developed in Sect. 2.1 applies equally well to this case, with the provision that the multigraph $\mathcal{G} = (\mathcal{V}, \mathcal{E})$ is now constructed as follows: each vertex can be either an image pair or a triplet of images; an edge is present between two pairs if and only if they share one image (i.e., there are no multiple edges between two pairs); an edge is present between a triplet and a pair (or between two triplets) each time they have one image in common. After constructing the multigraph, TRIPAIRSEG proceeds in the same way as TRISEG: it first solves linear assignment problems, it then performs permutation synchronization and it finally computes the mode.

3 Experiments

In this section we report experimental results on both existing datasets and new image collections. We implemented TRISEG and TRIPAIRSEG in Matlab and we made our code publicly available.[2] We compared our approaches to previous techniques belonging to the same category (see Fig. 1), namely methods working under the mild assumption of two-frame correspondences (MODE [3] and SYNCH [2]), whose implementation is available online.[3] All the analysed techniques assumed that the number of motions d was known.

3.1 Implementation Details

Given a set of two-frame correspondences, we proceed as follows in order to compute the partial segmentations, which constitute the input to TRISEG. First, triplets of images are identified: for the smallest sequences (i.e., $n < 10$) all the possible triplets are considered; in the remaining cases, a fixed number of triplets is sampled [32]. Such number is set equal to twice the number of image pairs. Then, for each triplet, a set of trajectories is computed by chaining two-frame correspondences. Note that these are *not* multi-frame correspondences, for they involve three images at a time. Moreover, observe that they are, in general, much noisier than the input two-frame correspondences: a mismatch between two images in the triplet propagates also to the third one. Finally, motion segmentation is solved in each triplet by fitting multiple trifocal tensors to those trajectories via RPA [27].

---

[2] https://github.com/federica-arrigoni/ECCV_20.
[3] https://github.com/federica-arrigoni/ICCV_19.

Robust Preference Analysis (RPA) is a general technique[4] for fitting multiple instances of a model to data corrupted by noise and outliers. Three main steps can be singled out. First, points are described in a conceptual space as vectors of "preferences", which measure how well they are fitted by a pool of provisional models instantiated via random sampling. Specifically, model hypotheses are instantiated from a minimal sample set (i.e., the minimum number of points necessary to fit a model), residuals are computed for every model, and the preference a point grants to a model is expressed in terms of its residual using the Cauchy weight function [13]. Vectors are hence collected in a matrix that is segmented leveraging on robust principal component analysis [24] and symmetric non negative factorization [20]. A model is fitted to every cluster using robust statistics and the segmentation is accordingly refined. Possible applications of RPA include fitting geometric primitives (e.g., lines or circles) to points in the plane and fitting geometric models (e.g., fundamental matrices or homographies) to correspondences in an image pair. However, fitting trifocal tensors (and hence, performing motion segmentation in three images) has not been explored in [27]. In order to use RPA for such a task, we proceed as follows:

- we randomly sample subsets of 7 points and use them to instantiate a tentative trifocal tensor via linear estimation [12];
- residuals between points and a tensor are expressed using the reprojection error, as explained in [11];
- the final models are refined using Gauss-Helmert optimization with Ressl parametrization[5], as suggested in [18];
- the parameter σ_n (representing the standard deviation of the residuals of the inliers [27]) is set equal to 0.1 in all the experiments.[6]

Concerning TRIPAIRSEG, partial segmentations of two different types are required as input: the ones associated with triplets of images are computed by fitting trifocal tensors with RPA, as explained above; the ones associated with pairs of images are obtained by fitting fundamental matrices with RPA (using default values for the algorithmic parameters specified in [27]).

3.2   Existing Datasets

We considered the benchmark provided in [2,3] consisting of 12 indoor scenes with two or three motions counting from 6 to 10 images. Image points (with ground-truth labels) and noisy two-frame correspondences are available in this dataset. As done in [2,3], we computed the *misclassification error* – defined as

---

[4] http://www.diegm.uniud.it/fusiello/demo/rpa/.

[5] https://github.com/LauraFJulia/TFT_vs_Fund.

[6] This value was optimally determined on a small subset of sequences (Penguin, Flowers, Pencils and Bag [3]). As for the remaining parameters of RPA (e.g. the number of sampled hypotheses), we used default values provided in the code by the authors.

Table 1. Misclassification error [%] (the lower the better) and classified points [%] (the higher the better) for several methods on the data used in [2,3]. The number of motions d, the number of images n, and the total number of image points p are also reported for each sequence. The best results are highlighted in boldface. *In this experiment all the correspondences are used.*

Dataset	d	n	p	TriSeg		TriPairSeg		Mode [3]		Synch [2]	
				Error	Classified	Error	Classified	Error	Classified	Error	Classified
Pen [2]	2	6	4550	**0.15**	60.51	0.55	79.56	0.58	80.07	0.82	83.23
Pouch [2]	2	6	4971	**1.07**	33.86	3.09	67.09	3.79	65.34	4.15	69.89
Needlecraft [2]	2	6	6617	**0.53**	45.40	0.84	73.76	0.83	72.81	1.04	76.76
Biscuits [2]	2	6	13158	**0.04**	63.59	0.35	85.72	0.47	84.47	0.51	87.28
Cups [2]	2	10	14664	**0.07**	50.31	0.49	66.37	0.56	65.42	1.01	69.82
Tea [2]	2	10	32612	**0.01**	61.69	0.23	82.37	0.29	81.70	28.12	52.21
Food [2]	2	10	36723	**0.01**	52.87	0.26	77.17	0.36	76.19	0.56	80.66
Penguin [3]	2	6	5865	0.75	34.31	**0.73**	69.70	0.76	69.17	44.21	46.97
Flowers [3]	2	6	7743	**0.05**	51.62	0.86	75.00	1.23	73.65	1.62	77.28
Pencils [3]	2	6	2982	5.04	35.28	**3.73**	65.56	3.80	65.33	27.53	40.44
Bag [3]	2	7	6114	1.40	40.97	**1.37**	64.26	1.52	57.95	25.92	54.27
Bears [3]	3	10	15888	**2.84**	41.21	4.38	74.31	4.82	73.65	38.95	74.59

Table 2. Misclassification error [%] (the lower the better) and classified points [%] (the higher the better) for several methods on the data used in [2,3]. The number of motions d, the number of images n, and the total number of image points p are also reported for each sequence. The best results are highlighted in boldface. *In this experiment all the trajectories of length two are removed.*

Dataset	d	n	p	TriSeg		TriPairSeg		Mode [3]		Synch [2]	
				Error	Classified	Error	Classified	Error	Classified	Error	Classified
Pen [2]	2	6	3208	**0.15**	83.98	0.17	88.29	0.24	88.77	0.42	93.47
Pouch [2]	2	6	2227	1.07	75.57	**0.65**	76.29	1.94	74.14	3.16	79.48
Needlecraft [2]	2	6	3733	0.53	80.47	**0.45**	82.67	0.56	81.94	1.21	88.51
Biscuits [2]	2	6	9306	0.04	89.91	**0**	91.91	0.07	91.15	0.20	94.87
Cups [2]	2	10	10452	**0.07**	70.58	0.21	78.10	0.26	77.58	0.84	83.31
Tea [2]	2	10	26134	**0.01**	76.98	0.09	88.22	0.15	88.02	24.48	63.08
Food [2]	2	10	27021	**0.01**	71.86	0.03	83.61	0.10	83.24	0.34	88.75
Penguin [3]	2	6	3035	0.75	66.29	**0.61**	81.58	0.73	81.29	35.29	51.73
Flowers [3]	2	6	4813	0.05	83.05	**0**	84.50	0.15	83.94	0.52	88.61
Pencils [3]	2	6	1424	5.04	73.88	**1.04**	74.44	1.58	75.49	34.72	45.72
Bag [3]	2	7	3108	1.40	80.60	**0.92**	80.57	1.24	72.52	2.10	82.82
Bears [3]	3	10	9998	2.84	65.48	**2.56**	81.73	3.08	81.13	29.08	65.18

the percentage of misclassified points over the total amount of *classified* points[7] – and we also considered the percentage of points labelled by each method.

---

[7] This choice is motivated by the fact that, in the presence of high corruption among the correspondences, one may not expect to classify *all* the points, as explained in [3]. Observe also that this error metric reports the fraction of wrong labelled data, that one wants to minimize in practice.

Results are reported in Table 1, showing that TRISEG achievest the lowest misclassification error in 9 out of 12 sequences, outperforming the competing techniques. This clearly shows the benefit of using the trifocal tensor, which is more robust to mismatches than the fundamental matrix. TRIPAIRSEG is slightly better than MODE and significantly better than SYNCH in terms of accuracy. Note that the latter fails in 5 cases. Concerning the amount of classified data, the best results are achieved by SYNCH in all the cases where it does not fail. The amount of point labelled by TRIPAIRSEG is slightly better than MODE. The lowest amount is given by TRISEG, which, however, is not surprising: this method actually ignores all the points that have only one correspondence (points that are visible in 3 images are required to estimate the trifocal tensor).

In order to enrich the evaluation, we considered another scenario, reported in Table 2. Starting from the data used in [2,3], the input correspondences were then filtered as follows: all the points that are matched in just one other image were removed. In other words, only correspondences involving (at least) 3 images were kept. In this way the performance of TRISEG remains unchanged in terms of misclassification error, but it is not penalized when counting the percentage of classified data. The output of the remaining methods, instead, generally improves. Observe that the lowest misclassification error is achieved either by TRISEG or TRIPAIRSEG, outperforming the competing techniques, and SYNCH fails in 4 out of 12 cases. There is no significative difference between all the analysed methods in terms of amount of classified points in this experiment.

3.3   Novel Benchmark

In order to study a more challenging scenario, we created a new dataset consisting of six indoor image collections with three or four motions. The benchmark created in [2,3], instead, counts several sequences with two motions and only one sequence with three motions. Two frame correspondences were obtained with SIFT [26] without any cleaning procedure, and ground-truth labels of image points were obtained by manual operations. More information about the dataset is provided in the supplementary material.

Results are collected in Table 3, which reports the misclassification error and the percentage of classified data for all the analysed techniques. SYNCH presents poor performances on most cases, thus it is not a practical solution to motion segmentation, confirming the outcome of the experiments in Sect. 3.2. Some interesting observations can be made about the remaining methods, which share the same framework but they are based on different models: MODE uses the fundamental matrix; TRISEG uses the trifocal tensor; TRIPAIRSEG uses both the fundamental matrix and the trifocal tensor. Using only the fundamental matrix as underlying model is not enough to segment the most difficult scenes. This aspect can be appreciated from the poor performance of MODE on the sequences with four motions. It is remarkable that TRISEG achieves very good results on all the sequences, outperforming all the analysed techniques. This is due to the usage of the trifocal tensor, which constitutes a stronger model than the fundamental matrix. The percentage of points classified by TRISEG is, in general, lower than

Table 3. Misclassification error [%] (the lower the better) and classified points [%] (the higher the better) for several methods on our dataset. The number of motions d, the number of images n, and the total number of image points p are also reported for each sequence. The best results are highlighted in boldface.

Dataset	d	n	p	TRISEG		TRIPAIRSEG		MODE [3]		SYNCH [2]	
				Error	Classified	Error	Classified	Error	Classified	Error	Classified
stuffed_animals1	4	7	11507	**1.82**	64.99	4.73	86.95	8.92	83.98	40.79	56.88
stuffed_animals2	4	7	11159	**3.05**	61.78	6.92	83.87	17.56	79.29	9.96	49.95
stuffed_animals3	4	7	10989	**2.20**	59.07	7.39	83.78	15.03	81.49	27.58	73.53
stuffed_animals4	4	7	8079	**3.33**	55.80	6.96	78.79	13.37	76.57	32.97	62.02
stuffed_animals5	3	7	13851	**0.72**	60.19	2.00	88.10	2.56	87.04	2.20	89.26
stuffed_animals6	3	7	12170	**0.60**	58.89	4.68	84.77	5.43	84.80	15.60	65.46

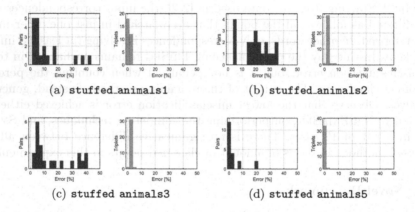

(a) stuffed_animals1   (b) stuffed_animals2

(c) stuffed animals3   (d) stuffed animals5

Fig. 5. Histograms of misclassification error achieved by RPA on sample sequences from our dataset. Each point in the horizontal axis corresponds to a possible misclassification error in an individual pair/triplet of images. Each point in the vertical axis corresponds to the number of pairs/triplets where a given error is reached.

the other approaches but it is still acceptable. TRIPAIRSEG achieves reasonably good results (although not comparable to TRISEG) and it is better than MODE both in terms of misclassification error and amount of classified points. Note that TRIPAIRSEG inherits the advantages of both models: on one side, it provides a good segmentation thanks to the presence of the trifocal tensor; on the other side, it classifies a high amount of points thanks to the presence of the fundamental matrix, which does not discard trajectories of length two.

The fact that the trifocal tensor usually provides a better segmentation than the fundamental matrix can also be appreciated in Fig. 5, which shows the distribution of the misclassification error achieved by RPA on all the triplets/pairs. This gives an idea about the quality of the input partial segmentations used by different approaches. It is clear that those produced by trifocal tensor fitting are the most accurate, since the blu light histograms are concentrated to the left. Those produced by fundamental matrix fitting, instead, are very noisy: note

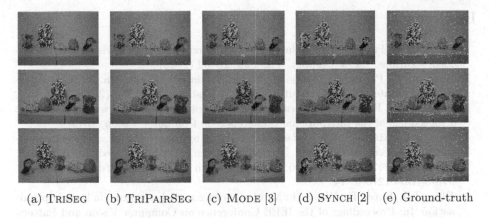

(a) TRISEG   (b) TRIPAIRSEG   (c) MODE [3]   (d) SYNCH [2]   (e) Ground-truth

Fig. 6. Segmentation results are reported on sample images from `stuffed_animals4` for several methods. Different colours correspond to different motions. For better visualization, unclassified points are not drawn. Ground-truth segmentation is also reported.

that RPA can even reach a misclassification error larger than 30% in some pairs related to `stuffed_animals1` (see the purple histogram in Fig.5a).

Some qualitative results are reported in Fig. 6 and further analysis is given in the supplementary material. Note that both SYNCH and MODE presents difficulties in segmenting this scene: the former produces useless results whereas the latter switches two motions in the middle image. TRISEG and TRIPAIRSEG, instead, report good performances.

4   Conclusion

We presented two novel solutions to motion segmentation that combine local results independently obtained from subsets of images: TRISEG considers triplets of images whereas TRIPAIRSEG considers both triplets and image pairs. In order to tackle segmentation in a triplet, multiple trifocal tensors were fitted to correspondences via robust preference analysis. The usage of the trifocal tensor within motion segmentation was the key to success for our methods, for it is more robust to wrong correspondences than the fundamental matrix. The proposed solutions outperform previous techniques on existing datasets as well as on a new image collection, and they can handle scenes with four motions. The choice of one method between TRISEG– which classifies less points with higher accuracy – and TRIPAIRSEG depends on the task and is left to the reader.

Acknowledgements. This research was supported by the European Regional Development Fund under IMPACT No. CZ.02.1.01/0.0/0.0/15 003/0000468, R4I 4.0 No. CZ.02.1.01/0.0/0.0/15 003/0000470, EU H2020 ARtwin No. 856994, and EU H2020 SPRING No. 871245 Projects.

References

1. Arrigoni, F., Fusiello, A.: Synchronization problems in computer vision with closed-form solutions. Int. J. Comput. Vis. **128**, 26–52 (2020)
2. Arrigoni, F., Pajdla, T.: Motion segmentation via synchronization. In: IEEE International Conference on Computer Vision Workshops (ICCVW) (2019)
3. Arrigoni, F., Pajdla, T.: Robust motion segmentation from pairwise matches. In: Proceedings of the International Conference on Computer Vision (2019)
4. Barath, D., Matas, J.: Multi-class model fitting by energy minimization and mode-seeking. In: Ferrari, V., Hebert, M., Sminchisescu, C., Weiss, Y. (eds.) ECCV 2018. LNCS, vol. 11220, pp. 229–245. Springer, Cham (2018). https://doi.org/10.1007/978-3-030-01270-0_14
5. Chin, T.J., Suter, D., Wang, H.: Multi-structure model selection via kernel optimisation. In: Proceedings of the IEEE Conference on Computer Vision and Pattern Recognition, pp. 3586–3593 (2010)
6. Delong, A., Osokin, A., Isack, H.N., Boykov, Y.: Fast approximate energy minimization with label costs. Int. J. Comput. Vis. **96**(1), 1–27 (2012)
7. Elhamifar, E., Vidal, R.: Sparse subspace clustering: algorithm, theory, and applications. IEEE Trans. Pattern Anal. Mach. Intell. **35**(11), 2765–2781 (2013)
8. Fischler, M., Bolles, R.: Random sample consensus: a paradigm for model fitting with applications to image analysis and automated cartography. Morgan Kaufmann Readings Ser. **24**, 726–740 (1987)
9. Geiger, A., Lenz, P., Urtasun, R.: Are we ready for autonomous driving? The KITTI vision benchmark suite. In: Proceedings of the IEEE Conference on Computer Vision and Pattern Recognition (2012)
10. Hartley, R., Vidal, R.: The multibody trifocal tensor: motion segmentation from 3 perspective views. In: Proceedings of the IEEE Conference on Computer Vision and Pattern Recognition, vol. 1, pp. I-769-I-775, June 2004. https://doi.org/10.1109/CVPR.2004.1315109
11. Hartley, R.I., Zisserman, A.: Multiple View Geometry in Computer Vision, 2nd edn. Cambridge University Press, Cambridge (2004)
12. Hartley, R.: Lines and points in three views and the trifocal tensor. Int. J. Comput. Vis. **22**(2), 125–140 (1997)
13. Holland, P.W., Welsch, R.E.: Robust regression using iteratively reweighted least-squares. Commun. Stat. Theory Methods **6**(9), 813–827 (1977)
14. Isack, H., Boykov, Y.: Energy-based geometric multi-model fitting. Int. J. Comput. Vis. **97**(2), 123–147 (2012)
15. Ji, P., Li, H., Salzmann, M., Dai, Y.: Robust motion segmentation with unknown correspondences. In: Fleet, D., Pajdla, T., Schiele, B., Tuytelaars, T. (eds.) ECCV 2014. LNCS, vol. 8694, pp. 204–219. Springer, Cham (2014). https://doi.org/10.1007/978-3-319-10599-4_14
16. Ji, P., Li, H., Salzmann, M., Zhong, Y.: Robust multi-body feature tracker: a segmentation-free approach. In: Proceedings of the IEEE Conference on Computer Vision and Pattern Recognition (2016)
17. Ji, P., Salzmann, M., Li, H.: Shape interaction matrix revisited and robustified: efficient subspace clustering with corrupted and incomplete data. In: Proceedings of the International Conference on Computer Vision, pp. 4687–4695 (2015)
18. Julià, L.F., Monasse, P.: A critical review of the trifocal tensor estimation. In: Paul, M., Hitoshi, C., Huang, Q. (eds.) PSIVT 2017. LNCS, vol. 10749, pp. 337–349. Springer, Cham (2018). https://doi.org/10.1007/978-3-319-75786-5_28

19. Kim, J.B., Kim, H.J.: Efficient region-based motion segmentation for a video monitoring system. Pattern Recogn. Lett. **24**(1), 113–128 (2003)
20. Kuang, D., Yun, S., Park, H.: SymNMF: nonnegative low-rank approximation of a similarity matrix for graph clustering. J. Global Optim. **62**(3), 545–574 (2014). https://doi.org/10.1007/s10898-014-0247-2
21. Kuhn, H.W.: The Hungarian method for the assignment problem. Naval Res. Logistics Q. **2**(2), 83–97 (1955)
22. Lai, T., Wang, H., Yan, Y., Chin, T.J., Zhao, W.L.: Motion segmentation via a sparsity constraint. IEEE Trans. Intell. Transp. Syst. **18**(4), 973–983 (2017)
23. Li, Z., Guo, J., Cheong, L.F., Zhou, S.Z.: Perspective motion segmentation via collaborative clustering. In: Proceedings of the International Conference on Computer Vision, pp. 1369–1376 (2013)
24. Lin, Z., Chen, M., Ma, Y.: The augmented Lagrange multiplier method for exact recovery of corrupted low-rank matrices. eprint arXiv:1009.5055 (2010)
25. Liu, G., Lin, Z., Yan, S., Sun, J., Yu, Y., Ma, Y.: Robust recovery of subspace structures by low-rank representation. IEEE Trans. Pattern Anal. Mach. Intel. **26**(5), 171–184 (2013)
26. Lowe, D.G.: Distinctive image features from scale-invariant keypoints. Int. J. Comput. Vis. **60**(2), 91–110 (2004). https://doi.org/10.1023/B:VISI.0000029664.99615. 94
27. Magri, L., Fusiello, A.: Robust multiple model fitting with preference analysis and low-rank approximation. In: Proceedings of the British Machine Vision Conference, pp. 20.1-20.12. BMVA Press, September 2015
28. Magri, L., Fusiello, A.: Multiple models fitting as a set coverage problem. In: Proceedings of the IEEE Conference on Computer Vision and Pattern Recognition, pp. 3318–3326, June 2016
29. Olsson, C., Enqvist, O.: Stable structure from motion for unordered image collections. In: Heyden, A., Kahl, F. (eds.) SCIA 2011. LNCS, vol. 6688, pp. 524–535. Springer, Heidelberg (2011). https://doi.org/10.1007/978-3-642-21227-7_49
30. Ozden, K.E., Schindler, K., Van Gool, L.: Multibody structure-from-motion in practice. IEEE Trans. Pattern Anal. Mach. Intell. **32**(6), 1134–1141 (2010)
31. Pachauri, D., Kondor, R., Singh, V.: Solving the multi-way matching problem by permutation synchronization. In: Advances in Neural Information Processing Systems 26, pp. 1860–1868. Curran Associates, Inc. (2013)
32. Pavan, A., Tangwongsan, K., Tirthapura, S., Wu, K.L.: Counting and sampling triangles from a graph stream. Proc. VLDB Endowment **6**(14), 1870–1881 (2013)
33. Rao, S., Tron, R., Vidal, R., Ma, Y.: Motion segmentation in the presence of outlying, incomplete, or corrupted trajectories. Pattern Anal. Mach. Intell. **32**(10), 1832–1845 (2010)
34. Rubino, C., Del Bue, A., Chin, T.J.: Practical motion segmentation for urban street view scenes. In: Proceedings of the IEEE International Conference on Robotics and Automation (2018)
35. Sabzevari, R., Scaramuzza, D.: Monocular simultaneous multi-body motion segmentation and reconstruction from perspective views. In: Proceedings of the IEEE International Conference on Robotics and Automation, pp. 23–30 (2014)
36. Saputra, M.R.U., Markham, A., Trigoni, N.: Visual SLAM and structure from motion in dynamic environments: a survey. ACM Comput. Surveys **51**(2), 37:1–37:36 (2018)
37. Schindler, K., Suter, D., Wang, H.: A model-selection framework for multibody structure-and-motion of image sequences. Int. J. Comput. Vis. **79**(2), 159–177 (2008)

530   F. Arrigoni et al.

38. Shen, Y., Huang, Q., Srebro, N., Sanghavi, S.: Normalized spectral map synchronization. In: Advances in Neural Information Processing Systems 29, pp. 4925–4933. Curran Associates, Inc. (2016)
39. Toldo, R., Fusiello, A.: Robust multiple structures estimation with J-Linkage. In: Proceedings of the European Conference on Computer Vision, pp. 537–547 (2008)
40. Torr, P.H.S., Zisserman, A.: Concerning Bayesian motion segmentation, model averaging, matching and the trifocal tensor. In: Burkhardt, H., Neumann, B. (eds.) ECCV 1998. LNCS, vol. 1406, pp. 511–527. Springer, Heidelberg (1998). https://doi.org/10.1007/BFb0055687
41. Torr, P.H.S., Zisserman, A., Murray, D.W.: Motion clustering using the trilinear constraint over three views. In: Europe-China Workshop on Geometric Modelling and Invariants for Computer Vision, pp. 118–125. Springer (1995)
42. Tron, R., Vidal, R.: A benchmark for the comparison of 3-D motion segmentation algorithms. In: Proceedings of the IEEE Conference on Computer Vision and Pattern Recognition, pp. 1–8. IEEE (2007)
43. Tron, R., Zhou, X., Esteves, C., Daniilidis, K.: Fast multi-image matching via density-based clustering. In: Proceedings of the International Conference on Computer Vision, pp. 4077–4086 (2017)
44. Vidal, R., Ma, Y., Sastry, S.: Generalized principal component analysis (GPCA). IEEE Trans. Pattern Anal. Mach. Intell. 27(12), 1945–1959 (2005)
45. Von Luxburg, U.: A tutorial on spectral clustering. Stat. Comput. 17(4), 395–416 (2007)
46. Wang, Y., Liu, Y., Blasch, E., Ling, H.: Simultaneous trajectory association and clustering for motion segmentation. IEEE Signal Process. Lett. 25(1), 145–149 (2018)
47. Xu, X., Cheong, L.F., Li, Z.: Motion segmentation by exploiting complementary geometric models. In: Proceedings of the IEEE Conference on Computer Vision and Pattern Recognition, pp. 2859–2867 (2018)
48. Yan, J., Pollefeys, M.: A general framework for motion segmentation: independent, articulated, rigid, non-rigid, degenerate and nondegenerate. In: Proceedings of the European Conference on Computer Vision, pp. 94–106 (2006)

3D-Rotation-Equivariant Quaternion Neural Networks

Wen Shen[2], Binbin Zhang[2], Shikun Huang[2], Zhihua Wei[2],
and Quanshi Zhang[1(✉)]

[1] Shanghai Jiao Tong University, Shanghai, China
zqs1022@sjtu.edu.cn
[2] Tongji University, Shanghai, China
{wen_shen,0206zbb,hsk,zhihua_wei}@tongji.edu.cn

Abstract. This paper proposes a set of rules to revise various neural networks for 3D point cloud processing to rotation-equivariant quaternion neural networks (REQNNs). We find that when a neural network uses quaternion features, the network feature naturally has the rotation-equivariance property. Rotation equivariance means that applying a specific rotation transformation to the input point cloud is equivalent to applying the same rotation transformation to all intermediate-layer quaternion features. Besides, the REQNN also ensures that the intermediate-layer features are invariant to the permutation of input points. Compared with the original neural network, the REQNN exhibits higher rotation robustness.

Keywords: Rotation equivariance · Permutation invariance · 3D point cloud processing · Quaternion

1 Introduction

3D point cloud processing has attracted increasing research attention in recent years. Unlike images with rich color information, 3D point clouds mainly use spatial contexts for feature extraction. Therefore, the rotation is not supposed to have essential impacts on 3D tasks, such as 3D shape classification and reconstruction. Besides, reordering input points should not have crucial effects on these tasks as well, which is termed the permutation-invariance property.

In this study, we focus on the problem of learning neural networks for 3D point cloud processing with rotation equivariance and permutation invariance.

- **Rotation equivariance:** Rotation equivariance has been discussed in recent research [6]. In this study, we define rotation equivariance for neural networks

---

W. Shen, B. Zhang and S. Huang—Have equal contributions.

Electronic supplementary material The online version of this chapter (https://doi.org/10.1007/978-3-030-58565-5_32) contains supplementary material, which is available to authorized users.

A. Vedaldi et al. (Eds.): ECCV 2020, LNCS 12365, pp. 531–547, 2020.
https://doi.org/10.1007/978-3-030-58565-5_32

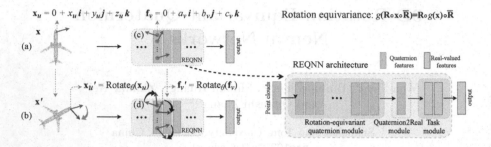

Fig. 1. Overview. In the REQNN, both input point clouds and intermediate-layer features are represented by quaternion features (blue). In this paper, the rotation equivariance is defined as follows. When we rotate the input point cloud **x** (a) with a specific angle (*e.g.* 60°) to obtain the same point cloud **x'** (b) with a different orientation, then the intermediate-layer feature (d) generated by the REQNN is equivalent to applying the transformation *w.r.t.* the same rotation to the feature (c) of the original point cloud. *I.e.* the rotation equivariance is defined as $g(\text{Rotate}_\theta(\mathbf{x})) = \text{Rotate}_\theta(g(\mathbf{x}))$. REQNNs exhibit significantly higher rotation robustness than traditional neural networks.

as follows. If an input point cloud is rotated by a specific angle, then the feature generated by the network is equivalent to applying the transformation *w.r.t.* the same rotation to the feature of the original point cloud (see Fig. 1 (left)). In this way, we can use the feature of a specific point cloud to synthesize features of the same point cloud with different orientations. Specifically, we can apply the transformation of a specific rotation to the current feature to synthesize the target feature.

- **Permutation invariance:** Permutation invariance measures whether intermediate-layer features essentially keep unchanged when we reorder input 3D points. Fortunately, we find that quaternion features in a neural network naturally satisfy the rotation-equivariance property under certain conditions (details will be introduced later). Therefore, we propose a set of rules to revise most existing neural networks to rotation-equivariant quaternion neural networks (REQNNs). Given a specific neural network for 3D point cloud processing (*e.g.* PointNet [21], PointNet++ [22], DGCNN [33], PointConv [37], etc., which are learned for various tasks, such as 3D shape classification and reconstruction), our rules can help revise the network to a REQNN with both properties of rotation equivariance and permutation invariance.

To revise a neural network to a REQNN with rotation equivariance, we transform both the input and intermediate-layer features of the original neural network into quaternion features (*i.e.* vectors/matrices/tensors, in which each element is a quaternion). A quaternion is a hyper-complex number with three imaginary parts ($\boldsymbol{i}, \boldsymbol{j}$, and $\boldsymbol{k}$) [11]. 3D rotations can be represented using quaternions. *I.e.* rotating a quaternion $\mathbf{q} \in \mathbb{H}$ with an angle $\theta \in [0, 2\pi)$ around an axis $\mathbf{o} = 0 + o_1\boldsymbol{i} + o_2\boldsymbol{j} + o_3\boldsymbol{k} \in \mathbb{H}$ ($o_1, o_2, o_3 \in \mathbb{R}$) can be represented as $\mathbf{Rq\overline{R}}$, where $\mathbf{R} = e^{\mathbf{o}\frac{\theta}{2}} \in \mathbb{H}; \overline{\mathbf{R}} = e^{-\mathbf{o}\frac{\theta}{2}} \in \mathbb{H}$ is the conjugation of $\mathbf{R}$.

In this way, the rotation equivariance of a REQNN is defined as follows. When we apply a specific rotation to the input $\mathbf{x} \in \mathbb{H}^n$, $i.e.$ $\mathbf{x'} = \mathbf{R} \circ \mathbf{x} \circ \overline{\mathbf{R}}$, the network will generate an intermediate-layer quaternion feature $g(\mathbf{x'}) \in \mathbb{H}^d$, where ∘ denotes the element-wise multiplication. The rotation equivariance ensures that $g(\mathbf{x'}) = \mathbf{R} \circ g(\mathbf{x}) \circ \overline{\mathbf{R}}$. Note that the input and the feature here can be vectors/matrices/tensors, in which each element is a quaternion.

Therefore, we revise a number of layerwise operations in the original neural network to make them rotation-equivariant, such as operations of the convolution, ReLU, batch-normalization, max-pooling, 3D coordinates weighting [37], etc., in order to ensure the rotation-equivariance property.

Note that most tasks, such as the shape classification, require outputs composed of real numbers. However, the REQNN's features consist of quaternions. Therefore, for real applications, we revise quaternion features of a specific high layer of the REQNN into ordinary features, in which each element is a real number. We transform quaternion features into real numbers by using the square of the norm of each quaternion element in the feature to replace the corresponding feature element. We put the revised real-valued features into the last few layers to generate real-valued outputs, as Fig. 1 (right) shows. Such revision ensures that the last few layerwise operations are rotation invariant. We will introduce this revision in Sect. 3.5.

Besides the rotation-equivariance property, the REQNN is also supposed to have the permutation-invariance property as follows. When we reorder 3D points in the input point cloud $\mathbf{x}$ to obtain the same point cloud $\mathbf{x}^{\text{reorder}}$ with a different order, the network will generate the same feature, $i.e.$ $g(\mathbf{x}^{\text{reorder}}) = g(\mathbf{x})$. Therefore, we revise a few operations in the original neural network to be permutation invariant, $e.g.$ the farthest point sampling [22] and the ball-query-search-based grouping [22], to ensure the permutation-invariance property of the REQNN.

In this study, we do not limit our attention to a specific architecture. Our method can be applied to various neural networks for different tasks. Experimental results proved that REQNNs exhibited superior performance than the original networks in terms of rotation robustness.

Contributions of our study are summarized as follows. We propose a set of generic rules to revise various neural networks to REQNNs with both properties of rotation equivariance and permutation invariance. The proposed rules can be broadly applied to different neural networks for different tasks, such as 3D shape classification and point cloud reconstruction. Experiments have demonstrated the effectiveness of our method that REQNNs exhibit higher rotation robustness than traditional neural networks.

2   Related Work

Deep Learning for 3D Point Cloud Processing: Recently, a series of studies have focused on deep neural networks (DNNs) for 3D point cloud processing and have achieved superior performance in various 3D tasks [21,25,27,28,32,41]. As a pioneer of using DNNs for 3D point cloud processing, PointNet [21] aggregated all individual point features into a global feature using a max-pooling operation. In order to further extract contextual information of 3D point clouds, existing studies have made lots of efforts. PointNet++ [22] hierarchically used PointNet as a local descriptor. KC-Net [24] proposed kernel correlation to measure the similarity between two point sets, so as to represent local geometric structures around each point. PointSIFT [14] proposed a SIFT-like operation to encode contextual information of different orientations for each point. Point2Sequence [18] employed an RNN-based encoder-decoder structure to capture correlations between different areas in a local region by aggregating multi-scale areas of each local region with attention.

Unlike images, 3D point clouds cannot be processed by traditional convolution operators. To address this problem, Kd-network [16] built a kd-tree on subdivisions of the point cloud, and used such kd-tree structure to mimics the convolution operator to extract and aggregate features according to the subdivisions. PointCNN [17] proposed an $\mathcal{X}$-Conv operator to aggregate features from neighborhoods into fewer representative points. Pointwise CNN [12] binned nearest neighbors into kernel cells of each point and convolved them with kernel weights. PointConv [37] treated convolution kernels as nonlinear functions that were learned from local coordinates of 3D points and their densities, respectively. Besides, some studies introduced graph convolutional neural networks for the extraction of geodesic information [27,33]. Some studies focused on the use of spatial relations between neighboring points [19,44]. In this study, we aim to learn DNNs with properties of rotation equivariance and permutation invariance.

3D Rotation Robustness: The most widely used method to improve the rotation robustness was data augmentation [31]. However, data augmentation significantly boosted the computational cost. Spatial Transformer Networks (STNs) [13] allowed spatial manipulations of data and features within the network, which improved the rotation robustness.

Some studies went beyond rotation robustness and focused on rotation invariance. The rotation-invariance property means that the output always keeps unchanged when we rotate the input. One intuitive way to achieve rotation invariance was to project 3D points onto a sphere [23,40,42] and constructed spherical CNNs [5] to extract rotation-invariant features. Other studies learned rotation-invariant representations that discarded orientation information of input point clouds [4,8,43].

However, such rotation-invariant methods directly discarded rotation information, so the rotation equivariance is proposed as a more promising property of feature representations. Rotation-equivariant methods both encode rotation information and disentangle rotation-independent information from the point cloud. To the best of our knowledge, there were very few studies in this direction. Previous studies developed specific network architectures [45] or designed specific operations [29] to achieve rotation equivariance. In comparison, we aim to propose a set of generic rules to revise most existing neural networks to achieve the rotation-equivariance property. Unlike [29,45], our method can be applied to various neural networks for different tasks.

Complex and Quaternion Networks: Recently, besides neural networks using real-valued features, neural networks using complex-valued features or quaternion-valued [11] features have been developed [2,7,9,10,15,20,30,35,36, 39,46]. In this study, we use quaternions to represent intermediate-layer features and 3D rotations to achieve 3D rotation-equivariance property.

3 Approach

3.1 Quaternion Features in Neural Networks and Rotations

> **Quaternion:** A quaternion [11] $\mathbf{q} = q_0 + q_1 i + q_2 j + q_3 k \in \mathbb{H}$ is a hyper-complex number with a real part (q_0) and three imaginary parts $(q_1 i, q_2 j, q_3 k)$, where $q_0, q_1, q_2, q_3 \in \mathbb{R}$; $\mathbb{H}$ denotes the algebra of quaternions. If the real part of $\mathbf{q}$ is 0, then $\mathbf{q}$ is a **pure quaternion**. If the norm of a quaternion $\|\mathbf{q}\| = \sqrt{q_0^2 + q_1^2 + q_2^2 + q_3^2} = 1$, then $\mathbf{q}$ is a **unit quaternion**. The **conjugation** of $\mathbf{q}$ is $\overline{\mathbf{q}} = q_0 - q_1 i - q_2 j - q_3 k$.
>
> The products of basis elements i, j, and k are defined by $i^2 = j^2 = k^2 = ijk = -1$ and $ij = k, jk = i, ki = j, ji = -k, kj = -i$, and $ik = -j$. Note that the multiplication of two quaternions is non-commutative, *i.e.* $ij \neq ji, jk \neq kj$, and $ki \neq ik$.
>
> Each quaternion has a **polar decomposition**. In this study, we only focus on the polar decomposition of a unit quaternion in the form of $\mathbf{q} = \cos\frac{\theta}{2} + \sin\frac{\theta}{2}(o_1 i + o_2 j + o_3 k)$, $\sqrt{o_1^2 + o_2^2 + o_3^2} = 1$. The polar decomposition of such a unit quaternion is $\mathbf{q} = e^{\mathbf{o}\frac{\theta}{2}}$, where $\mathbf{o} = o_1 i + o_2 j + o_3 k$. As aforementioned, multiplication of two quaternions is non-commutative, therefore, $e^{\mathbf{o}\frac{\theta}{2}} \mathbf{p} e^{-\mathbf{o}\frac{\theta}{2}} \neq \mathbf{p}$.

For a traditional neural network, inputs, features, and parameters are vectors/matrices/tensors, in which each element is a real number. However, in a REQNN, inputs and features are vectors/matrices/tensors composed of quaternions; parameters are still vectors/matrices/tensors composed of real numbers.

Quaternion Inputs and Features: In a REQNN, each u-th point $([x_u, y_u, z_u]^\top \in \mathbb{R}^3)$ in a 3D point cloud is represented as a pure quaternion $\mathbf{x}_u = 0 + x_u i + y_u j + z_u k$. Each v-th element of the intermediate-layer feature is also a pure quaternion $\mathbf{f}_v = 0 + a_v i + b_v j + c_v k$, where $a_v, b_v, c_v \in \mathbb{R}$.

Quaternion Rotations: Each element of a feature, $\mathbf{f}_v = 0 + a_v i + b_v j + c_v k$, can be considered to have an orientation, *i.e.* $[a_v, b_v, c_v]^\top$. In this way, 3D rotations can be represented using quaternions. Suppose we rotate $\mathbf{f}_v$ around an axis $\mathbf{o} = 0 + o_1 i + o_2 j + o_3 k$ (where $o_1, o_2, o_3 \in \mathbb{R}$, $\|\mathbf{o}\| = 1$) with an angle $\theta \in [0, 2\pi)$ to get $\mathbf{f}_v'$. Such a rotation can be represented using a unit quaternion $\mathbf{R} = \cos\frac{\theta}{2} + \sin\frac{\theta}{2}(o_1 i + o_2 j + o_3 k) = e^{\mathbf{o}\frac{\theta}{2}}$ and its conjugation $\overline{\mathbf{R}}$, as follows.

$$\mathbf{f}_v' = \mathbf{R}\mathbf{f}_v\overline{\mathbf{R}}. \tag{1}$$

Note that $\mathbf{f}'_v = \mathbf{R}\mathbf{f}_v\overline{\mathbf{R}} \neq \mathbf{f}_v$. The advantage of using quaternions to represent rotations is that quaternions do not suffer from the singularity problem, but the Euler Angle [34] and the Rodrigues parameters [26] do. Besides, although the redundancy ratio of quaternions is two, the redundancy does not affect the rotation equivariance property of the REQNN.

To ensure that all quaternion features are rotation equivariant, all imaginary parts (*i.e.* $\boldsymbol{i}$, $\boldsymbol{j}$, and $\boldsymbol{k}$) of a quaternion element share the same **real-valued** parameter w. Take the convolution operation $\otimes$ as an example, $w \otimes \mathbf{f} = w \otimes (0 + a\boldsymbol{i} + b\boldsymbol{j} + c\boldsymbol{k}) = 0 + (w \otimes a)\boldsymbol{i} + (w \otimes b)\boldsymbol{j} + (w \otimes c)\boldsymbol{k}$, where w is the **real-valued** parameter; $\mathbf{f}$ is the quaternion feature; a, b, and c are **real-valued** tensors of the same size for the convolution operation in this example.

3.2 Rotation Equivariance

In order to recursively achieve the rotation-equivariance property for a REQNN, we should ensure that each layerwise operation of the REQNN has the rotation-equivariance property. In a REQNN, the rotation equivariance is defined as follows. Let $\mathbf{x} \in \mathbb{H}^n$ and $\mathbf{y} = \boldsymbol{\Phi}(\mathbf{x}) \in \mathbb{H}^C$ denote the input and the output of the REQNN, respectively. Note that outputs for most tasks are traditional vectors/matrices/tensors, in which each element is a real number. In this way, we learn rotation-equivariant quaternion features in most layers, and then transform these features into ordinary real-valued rotation-invariant features in the last few layers, as shown in Fig. 1 (right). We will introduce details for such revision in Sect. 3.5.

For each rotation $\mathbf{R} = e^{\mathbf{o}\frac{\theta}{2}}$ and its conjugation $\overline{\mathbf{R}}$, the rotation equivariance of a REQNN is defined as follows.

$$\boldsymbol{\Phi}(\mathbf{x}^{(\theta)}) = \mathbf{R} \circ \boldsymbol{\Phi}(\mathbf{x}) \circ \overline{\mathbf{R}}, \quad \text{s.t.} \quad \mathbf{x}^{(\theta)} \triangleq \mathbf{R} \circ \mathbf{x} \circ \overline{\mathbf{R}}, \tag{2}$$

where $\circ$ denotes the element-wise multiplication (*e.g.* $\mathbf{x}^{(\theta)} \triangleq \mathbf{R} \circ \mathbf{x} \circ \overline{\mathbf{R}}$ can also be formulated as $\mathbf{x}_u^{(\theta)} \triangleq \mathbf{R}\mathbf{x}_u\overline{\mathbf{R}}, u = 1, 2, ..., n$). As discussed in the previous paragraph, outputs for most tasks are real-valued features. Therefore, Eq. (2) does not hold for all layers in the neural network. Instead, we transform features in last few layers to be real-valued rotation-invariant features.

To achieve the above rotation equivariance, we must ensure the layerwise rotation equivariance. Let $\boldsymbol{\Phi}(\mathbf{x}) = \boldsymbol{\Phi}_L(\boldsymbol{\Phi}_{L-1}(\cdots\boldsymbol{\Phi}_1(\mathbf{x})))$ represent the cascaded functions of multiple layers of a neural network, where $\boldsymbol{\Phi}_l(\cdot)$ denotes the function of the l-th layer. Let $\mathbf{f}_l = \boldsymbol{\Phi}_l(\mathbf{f}_{l-1}) \in \mathbb{H}^d$ denote the output of the l-th layer. The layerwise rotation equivariance is given as follows.

$$\boldsymbol{\Phi}_l(\mathbf{f}_{l-1}^{(\theta)}) = \mathbf{R} \circ \boldsymbol{\Phi}_l(\mathbf{f}_{l-1}) \circ \overline{\mathbf{R}}, \quad \text{s.t.} \quad \mathbf{f}_{l-1}^{(\theta)} \triangleq \mathbf{R} \circ \mathbf{f}_{l-1} \circ \overline{\mathbf{R}}. \tag{3}$$

This equation recursively ensures the rotation-equivariance property of the REQNN. Let us take a neural network with three layers as a toy example. $\boldsymbol{\Phi}(\mathbf{x}^\theta) = \boldsymbol{\Phi}_3(\boldsymbol{\Phi}_2(\boldsymbol{\Phi}_1(\mathbf{R} \circ \mathbf{x} \circ \overline{\mathbf{R}}))) = \boldsymbol{\Phi}_3(\boldsymbol{\Phi}_2(\mathbf{R} \circ \boldsymbol{\Phi}_1(\mathbf{x}) \circ \overline{\mathbf{R}})) = \boldsymbol{\Phi}_3(\mathbf{R} \circ \boldsymbol{\Phi}_2(\boldsymbol{\Phi}_1(\mathbf{x})) \circ \overline{\mathbf{R}}) = \mathbf{R} \circ \boldsymbol{\Phi}_3(\boldsymbol{\Phi}_2(\boldsymbol{\Phi}_1(\mathbf{x}))) \circ \overline{\mathbf{R}} = \mathbf{R} \circ \boldsymbol{\Phi}(\mathbf{x}) \circ \overline{\mathbf{R}}$. Please see supplementary materials for more discussion.

Table 1. Rotation-equivariance and permutation-invariance properties of layerwise operations in the original neural network. "×" denotes that the operation does not have the property, "✓" denotes that the operation naturally has the property, and "–" denotes that the layerwise operation is naturally unrelated to the property (which will be discussed in the last paragraph of Sect. 3.4). Please see Sect. 3.3 and Sect. 3.4 for rules of revising layerwise operations to be rotation-equivariant and permutation-invariant, respectively.

Operation	Rotation equivariance	Permutation invariance	Operation	Rotation equivariance	Permutation invariance
Convolution	×	–	Grouping (k-NN) [37]	✓	✓
ReLU	×	–	Grouping (ball query) [22]	✓	×
Batch-normalization	×	–	Density estimation [37]	✓	✓
Max-pooling	×	–	3D coordinates weighting [37]	×	✓
Dropout	×	–	Graph construction [33]	✓	✓
Farthest point sampling [22]	✓	×			

3.3 Rules for Rotation Equivariance

We propose a set of rules to revise layerwise operations in the original neural network to make them rotation-equivariant, *i.e.* satisfying Eq. (3). Table 1 shows the list of layerwise operations in the original neural network with the rotation-equivariance property, and those without the rotation-equivariance property. *The rotation-equivariance property of the revised layerwise operations has been proved in supplementary materials.*

Convolution: We revise the operation of the convolution layer, $Conv(\mathbf{f}) = w \otimes \mathbf{f} + b$, to be rotation-equivariant by removing the bias term b, where w is the real-valued parameter and $\mathbf{f}$ is the quaternion feature.

ReLU: We revise the ReLU operation as follows to make it rotation-equivariant.

$$ReLU(\mathbf{f}_v) = \frac{\|\mathbf{f}_v\|}{\max\{\|\mathbf{f}_v\|, c\}} \mathbf{f}_v, \tag{4}$$

where $\mathbf{f}_v \in \mathbb{H}$ denotes the v-th element in the feature $\mathbf{f} \in \mathbb{H}^d$; c is a positive constant, which can be implemented as $c = \frac{1}{d} \sum_{v=1}^{d} \|\mathbf{f}_v\|$.

Batch-Normalization: We revise the batch-normalization operation to be rotation-equivariant, as follows.

$$norm(\mathbf{f}_v^{(i)}) = \frac{\mathbf{f}_v^{(i)}}{\sqrt{\mathbb{E}_j[\|\mathbf{f}_v^{(j)}\|^2] + \epsilon}}, \tag{5}$$

where $\mathbf{f}^{(i)} \in \mathbb{H}^d$ denotes the feature of the i-th sample in the batch; ϵ is a tiny positive constant to avoid dividing by 0.

Max-Pooling: We revise the max-pooling operation, as follows.

$$maxPool(\mathbf{f}) = \mathbf{f}_{\hat{v}} \quad \text{s.t.} \quad \hat{v} = \arg\max_{v=1,\ldots,d}[\|\mathbf{f}_v\|]. \tag{6}$$

Note that for 3D point cloud processing, a special element-wise max-pooling operation designed in [21] is widely used. The revision for this special max-pooling operation can be decomposed to a group of operations as Eq. (6) defined. Please see our supplementary materials for revision details of this operation.

Dropout: For the dropout operation, we randomly drop out a number of quaternion elements from the feature. For each dropped element, both the real and imaginary parts are set to zero. Such revision naturally satisfies the rotation-equivariance property in Eq. (3).

3D Coordinates Weighting: The 3D coordinates weighting designed in [37] focuses on the use of 3D coordinates' information to reweight intermediate-layer features. This operation is not rotation-equivariant, because the rotation changes coordinates of points. To make this operation rotation-equivariant, we use the Principal Components Analysis (PCA) to transform 3D points to a new local reference frame (LRF). Specifically, we choose eigenvectors corresponding to the first three principal components as new axes x, y, and z of the new LRF. In this way, the coordinate system rotates together with input points, so the transformed new coordinates are not changed. Note that contrary to [45] relying on the LRF, our research only uses LRF to revise the 3D coordinates weighting operation, so as to ensure the specific neural network designed in [37] to be rotation equivariant.

The following five layerwise operations in the original neural network, which are implemented based on distances between points, are naturally rotation-equivariant, including the farthest point sampling [22], the k-NN-search-based grouping [33,37], the ball-query-search-based grouping [22], the density estimation [37], and the graph construction [33] operations.

3.4   Rules for Permutation Invariance

As shown in Table 1, the farthest point sampling [22], and the ball-query-search-based grouping [22] are not permutation-invariant. Therefore, we revise these two operations to be permutation-invariant as follows.

Farthest Point Sampling: The farthest point sampling (FPS) is an operation for selecting a subset of points from the input point cloud, in order to extract local features [22]. Suppose that we aim to select n points from the input point cloud, if $i - 1$ points have already been selected, *i.e.* $S_{i-1} = \{x_1, x_2, \ldots, x_{i-1}\}$, then the next selected point x_i is the farthest point from S_{i-1}. The FPS is not permutation-invariant, because the subset selected by this operation depends on which point is selected first. To revise the FPS to be permutation-invariant, we always use the centroid of a point cloud, which is a virtual point, as the first selected point. In this way, the FPS would be permutation-invariant.

Grouping (ball query): The ball-query-search-based grouping is used to find K neighboring points within a radius for each given center point, in order to extract contextual information [22]. This operation is not permutation-invariant, because when there are more than K points within the radius, the top K points will be selected according to the order of points. To revise this operation to be permutation-invariant, we replace the ball query search by k-NN search when the number of points within the radius exceeds the required number.

Other operations that implemented based on distances between points are permutation-invariant, because reordering input points has no effects on distances between points, including the k-NN-search-based grouping [33,37], the density estimation [37], the 3D coordinates weighting [37], and the graph construction [33] operations.

Note that there is no need to discuss the permutation invariance of the convolution, the ReLU, the batch-normalization, the max-pooling, and the dropout operations. It is because the permutation invariance of these operations depends on receptive fields. *I.e.* if the receptive field of each neural unit keeps the same when we reorder input points, then the operation is permutation-invariant. Whereas receptive fields are determined by other operations (*e.g.* the FPS and grouping).

3.5 Overview of the REQNN

Although using quaternions to represent intermediate-layer features helps achieve the rotation-equivariance property, most existing tasks (*e.g.* the shape classification) require outputs of real numbers. Thus, we need to transform quaternion features into ordinary real-valued features, in which each element is a real number. Note that for the point cloud reconstruction task, features of the entire neural network are quaternions. It is because outputs required by the point cloud reconstruction task are 3D coordinates, which can be represented by quaternions.

Therefore, as Fig. 1 shows, the REQNN consists of (a) rotation-equivariant quaternion module, (b) Quaternion2Real module, and (c) task module.

Rotation-Equivariant Quaternion Module: Except for very few layers on the top of the REQNN, other layers in the REQNN comprise the rotation-equivariant quaternion module. This module is used to extract rotation-equivariant quaternion features. We use rules proposed in Sect. 3.3 to revise layerwise operations in the original neural network to be rotation-equivariant, so as to obtain the rotation-equivariant quaternion module. We also use rules in Sect. 3.4 to revise these layerwise operations to be permutation invariant.

Quaternion2Real Module: The Quaternion2Real module is located after the rotation-equivariant quaternion module. The Quaternion2Real module is used to transform quaternion features into real-valued vectors/matrices/tensors as features. Specifically, we use an element-wise operation to compute the square of the norm of each quaternion element as the real-valued feature element. *I.e.* for each v-th element of a quaternion feature, $\mathbf{f}_v = 0 + a_v \mathbf{i} + b_v \mathbf{j} + c_v \mathbf{k}$, we compute the square of the norm $\|\mathbf{f}_v\|^2 = a_v^2 + b_v^2 + c_v^2$ as the corresponding element of the real-valued feature. Note that the transformed features are rotation-invariant.

Task Module: The task module is composed of the last few layers of the REQNN. The task module is used to obtain ordinary real-valued outputs, which are required by the task of 3D shape classification. As aforementioned, the

Table 2. Comparisons of the number of floating-point operations (FLOPs) and the number of parameters (#Params) of original neural networks and REQNNs. All neural networks were tested on the ModelNet40 dataset.

	PointNet++ (see footnote 1) [22]		DGCNN (see footnote 2) [33]		PointConv [37]		PointNet [21]	
	FLOPs(G)	#Params(M)	FLOPs(G)	#Params(M)	FLOPs(G)	Params(M)	FLOPs(G)	#Params(M)
Ori	0.87	1.48	3.53	2.86	1.44	19.57	0.30	0.29
REQNN	2.51	1.47	8.24	2.86	4.22	20.61	0.88	0.28

Table 3. Layerwise operations of different neural networks. "✓" denotes that the network contains the layerwise operation.

Layerwise operation	PointNet++ [22]	DGCNN [33]	PointConv [37]	PointNet [21]
Convolution	✓	✓	✓	✓
ReLU	✓	✓	✓	✓
Batch-normalization	✓	✓	✓	✓
Max-pooling	✓	✓		✓
Dropout	✓	✓	✓	✓
Farthest point sampling	✓		✓	
Grouping (k-NN)		✓	✓	
Grouping (ball query) [22]	✓			
Density estimation [37]			✓	
3D coordinates weighting [37]			✓	
Graph construction [33]		✓		

Quaternion2Real module transforms quaternion features into real-valued vectors/matrices/tensors as features. In this way, the task module (*i.e.* the last few layers) in the REQNN implements various tasks just like traditional neural networks.

Complexity of the REQNN: The REQNN's parameter number is no more than that of the original neural network. The REQNN's operation number is theoretically less than three times of that of the original neural network. We have compared numbers of operations and numbers of parameters of original neural networks and REQNNs in Table 2.

3.6 Revisions of Traditional Neural Networks into REQNNs

In this study, we revise the following four neural networks to REQNNs, including PointNet++ [22], DGCNN [33], PointConv [33], and PointNet [21].

Model 1, PointNet++: As Table 3 shows, the PointNet++ [22] for shape classification includes seven types of layerwise operations. To revise the PointNet++ for shape classification[1] to a REQNN, we take the last three

---

[1] The PointNet++ for shape classification used in this paper is slightly revised by concatenating 3D coordinates to input features of the 1-st and 4-th convolution layers, in order to enrich the input information. For fair comparisons, both the REQNN and the original PointNet++ are revised in this way.

fully-connected (FC) layers as the task module and take other layers as the rotation-equivariant quaternion module. We add a Quaternion2Real module between these two modules. We use rules proposed in Sect. 3.3 to revise four types of layerwise operations to be rotation-equivariant, including the convolution, ReLU, batch-normalization, and max-pooling operations. We also use rules proposed in Sect. 3.4 to revise farthest point sampling and ball-query-search-based grouping operations in the original PointNet++ to be permutation-invariant.

Model 2, DGCNN: As Table 3 shows, the DGCNN [33] for shape classification contains seven types of layerwise operations. To revise the DGCNN for shape classification to a REQNN, we take the last three FC layers as the task module and take other layers as the rotation-equivariant quaternion module. The Quaternion2Real module[2] is added between these two modules. We revise four types of layerwise operations to be rotation-equivariant, including the convolution, ReLU, batch-normalization, and max-pooling operations. All layerwise operations in the original DGCNN are naturally permutation-invariant. Therefore, there is no revision for permutation invariance here.

Model 3, PointConv: As Table 3 shows, the PointConv [37] for shape classification includes eight types of layerwise operations. To revise the PointConv for shape classification to a REQNN, we take the last three FC layers as the task module and take other layers as the rotation-equivariant quaternion module. The Quaternion2Real module is added between these two modules. We revise the following four types of layerwise operations to be rotation-equivariant, *i.e.* the convolution, ReLU, batch-normalization, and 3D coordinates weighting operations. We also revise all farthest point sampling operations in the original PointConv to be permutation-invariant.

Model 4, PointNet: In order to construct a REQNN for shape reconstruction, we slightly revise the architecture of the PointNet [21] for shape classification. As Table 3 shows, the PointNet for shape classification contains five types of layerwise operations. We take all remaining layers in the PointNet as the rotation-equivariant quaternion module except for the max-pooling and Spatial Transformer Network (STN) [13]. The STN discards all spatial information (including the rotation information) of the input point cloud. Therefore, in order to encode rotation information, we remove the STN from the original PointNet.

Note that there is no the Quaternion2Real module or the task module in this REQNN, so that all features in the REQNN for reconstruction are quaternion features. We revise the following four types of layerwise operations to be rotation-equivariant, *i.e.* the convolution, the ReLU, the batch-normalization, and the dropout operations.

---

[2] We add one more convolution layer in the Quaternion2Real module in the REQNN revised from DGCNN, in order to obtain reliable real-valued features considering that the DGCNN has no downsampling operations. For fair comparisons, we add the same convolution layer to the same location of the original DGCNN.

Table 4. Accuracy of 3D shape classification on the ModelNet40 and the 3D MNIST datasets. "Baseline w/o rotations" indicates the original neural network learned without rotations. "Baseline w/ rotations" indicates the original neural network learned with the z-axis rotations (data augmentation with the z-axis rotations has been widely applied in [22,33,37]). "REQNN" indicates the REQNN learned without rotations. Note that the accuracy of shape classification reported in [22,33,37] was obtained under the test without rotations. The accuracy reported here was obtained under the test with rotations. Therefore, it is normal that the accuracy in this paper is lower than the accuracy in those papers.

Method	ModelNet40 dataset			3D MNIST dataset		
	Baseline w/o rotations	Baseline w/ rotations	REQNN	Baseline w/o rotations	Baseline w/ rotations	REQNN
PointNet++ (see footnote 1) [22]	23.57 (see footnote 3)	26.43	**63.95**	44.15	51.16	**68.99**
DGCNN (see footnote 3) [33]	30.05 (see footnote 3)	31.34	**83.03**	45.37	49.25	**82.09**
PointConv [37]	21.93	23.72	**78.14**	44.63	50.95	**78.59**

Table 5. Comparisons of 3D shape classification accuracy between different methods on the ModelNet40 dataset. **NR/NR** denotes that neural networks were learned and tested with **No Rotations**. **NR/AR** denotes that neural networks were learned with **No Rotations** and tested with **Arbitrary Rotations**. Experimental results show that the REQNN exhibited the highest rotation robustness. Note that the classification accuracy of the REQNN in scenarios of NR/NR and NR/AR was the same due to the rotation-equivariance property of the REQNN.

Method	NR/NR (do **not** Consider rotation in testing)	NR/AR (consider rotation in testing)
PointNet [21]	88.45	12.47
PointNet++ [22]	89.82	21.35 (see footnote 3)
Point2Sequence [18]	92.60	10.53
KD-Network [16]	86.20	8.49
RS-CNN [19]	92.38	22.49
DGCNN [33]	**92.90**	29.74 (see footnote 3)
PRIN [40]	80.13	68.85
QE-Capsule network [45]	74.73	74.07
REQNN (revised from DGCNN (see footnote 2))	83.03 =	**83.03**

4   Experiments

Properties of the rotation equivariance and the permutation invariance of REQNNs could be proved theoretically, please see our supplementary materials for details. In order to demonstrate other advantages of REQNNs, we conducted the following experiments. We revised three widely used neural networks to REQNNs for the shape classification task, including PointNet++ [22], DGCNN [33], and PointConv [37]. We revised the PointNet [21] to a REQNN for the point cloud reconstruction task. In all experiments, we set $c = 1$ in Eq. (4) and set $\epsilon = 10^{-5}$ in Eq. (5).

3D Shape Classification: We used the ModelNet40 [38] dataset (in this study, we used corresponding point clouds provided by PointNet [21]) and the 3D MNIST [1] dataset for shape classification. The ModelNet40 dataset consisted of 40 categories; and the 3D MNIST dataset consisted of 10 categories. Each shape consisted of 1024 points. In this experiment, we conducted experiments on three types of baseline neural networks, including (1) the original neural network learned without rotations, (2) the original neural network learned with the z-axis rotations (the z-axis rotations were widely used in [22,33,37] for data augmentation), and (3) the REQNN learned without rotations (the REQNN naturally had the rotation-equivariance property, so it did not require any rotation augmentation). The testing set was generated by arbitrarily rotating each sample ten times. We will release this testing set when this paper is accepted.

As Table 4[3] shows, the REQNN always outperformed all baseline neural networks learned with or without rotations. We achieved the highest accuracy of 83.03% using the REQNN revised from DGCNN (see footnote 2). Baseline neural networks that were learned without rotations exhibited very low accuracy (21.93%–31.34% on the ModelNet40 dataset and 44.15%–51.16% on the 3D MNIST dataset). In comparison, baseline neural networks that were learned with z-axis rotations had little improvement in rotation robustness.

Besides, we compared the REQNN with several state-of-the-art methods for 3D point cloud processing in two scenarios, including neural networks learned with **No Rotations** and tested with **No Rotations**, and neural networks learned with **No Rotations** and tested with **Arbitrary Rotations**, as Table 5 shows. Note that the classification accuracy of the REQNN in the scenario of NR/NR was the same as that of NR/AR, because the REQNN was rigorously rotation equivariant. The best REQNN in this paper (*i.e.* the REQNN revised from the DGCNN(see footnote 2)) achieved the highest accuracy of 83.03% in the scenario of NR/AR, which indicated the significantly high rotation robustness of the REQNN. Traditional methods, including PointNet [21], PointNet++ [22], Point2Sequence [18], KD-Network [16], RS-CNN [19], and DGCNN [33], achieved high accuracy in the scenario of NR/NR. However, these methods performed poor in the scenario of NR/AR, because they could not deal with point clouds with unseen orientations. Compared with these methods, PRIN [40] and QE-Capsule network [45] made some progress in handling point clouds with unseen orientations. Our REQNN outperformed them by 14.18% and 8.96%, respectively, in the scenario of NR/AR.

3D Point Cloud Reconstruction: In this experiment, we aimed to prove that we could rotate intermediate-layer quaternion features of the original point cloud to synthesize new point clouds with target orientations. Therefore, we learned a REQNN revised from the PointNet [21] for point cloud reconstruction

---

[3] The classification accuracy in the scenario of NR/AR in Table 4 and Table 5 was slightly different for PointNet++ [22] (23.57% *vs.* 21.35%) and DGCNN [33] (30.05% *vs.* 29.74%). It was because architectures of PointNet++ (see footnote 1) and DGCNN (see footnote 2) examined in Table 4 and Table 5 were slightly different. Nevertheless, this did not essentially change our conclusions.

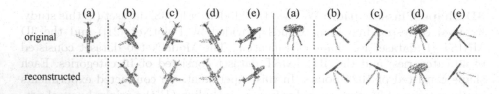

Fig. 2. Manual manipulation of intermediate-layer features to control the object rotation in 3D point cloud reconstruction. The experiment was conducted to prove that point clouds reconstructed using the synthesized quaternion features had the same orientations as point clouds generated by directly rotating the original point cloud. Here we displayed results of four random orientations for each point cloud. Point clouds ("original" (b–e)) were generated by directly rotating the original point cloud ("original" (a)) around axis $[0.46, 0.68, 0.56]^\top$ with angle $\frac{\pi}{3}$, around axis $[-0.44, -0.61, 0.66]^\top$ with angle $\frac{\pi}{4}$, around axis $[0.34, 0.94, 0.00]^\top$ with angle $\frac{\pi}{6}$, and around axis $[0.16, 0.83, 0.53]^\top$ with angle $\frac{2\pi}{3}$, respectively. Given a specific intermediate-layer quaternion feature of the original point cloud ("original" (a)), we rotated the quaternion feature with the same angles to obtain quaternion features with different orientations, which were used to reconstruct point clouds ("reconstructed" (b–e)).

on the ShapeNet [3] dataset. Each point cloud consisted of 1024 points in our implementation. We took the output quaternion feature of the top fourth linear transformation layer of the REQNN to synthesize quaternion features with different orientations. Such synthesized quaternion features were used to reconstruct point clouds with target orientations.

As Fig. 2 shows, for each given point cloud (Fig. 2 "original" (a)), we directly rotated it with different angles (Fig. 2 "original" (b–e)). For comparison, we rotated the corresponding quaternion feature of the original point cloud with the same angles to synthesize quaternion features. These generated quaternion features were used to reconstruct point clouds (Fig. 2 "reconstructed" (b–e)). We observed that these reconstructed point clouds had the same orientations with those of point clouds generated by directly rotating the original point cloud.

5   Conclusion

In this paper, we have proposed a set of generic rules to revise various neural networks for 3D point cloud processing to REQNNs. We have theoretically proven that the proposed rules can ensure each layerwise operation in the neural network is rotation equivariant and permutation invariant. Experiments on various tasks have shown the rotation robustness of REQNNs.

We admit that revising a neural network to a REQNN has some negative effects on its representation capacity. Besides, it is challenging to revise all layerwise operations in all neural networks for 3D point cloud processing.

Acknowledgments. The work is partially supported by the National Key Research and Development Project (No. 213), the National Nature Science Foundation of China (No. 61976160, U19B2043, and 61906120), the Special Project of the Ministry of Public Security (No. 20170004), and the Key Lab of Information Network Security, Ministry of Public Security (No.C18608).

References

1. https://www.kaggle.com/daavoo/3d-mnist/version/13
2. Arjovsky, M., Shah, A., Bengio, Y.: Unitary evolution recurrent neural networks. In: International Conference on Machine Learning, pp. 1120–1128 (2016)
3. Chang, A.X., et al.: ShapeNet: An information-rich 3D model repository. arXiv preprint arXiv:1512.03012 (2015)
4. Chen, C., Li, G., Xu, R., Chen, T., Wang, M., Lin, L.: ClusterNet: deep hierarchical cluster network with rigorously rotation-invariant representation for point cloud analysis. In: Proceedings of the IEEE Conference on Computer Vision and Pattern Recognition, pp. 4994–5002 (2019)
5. Cohen, T.S., Geiger, M., Köhler, J., Welling, M.: Spherical CNNs. In: International Conference on Learning Representations (2018). https://openreview.net/forum?id=Hkbd5xZRb
6. Cohen, T.S., Welling, M.: Steerable CNNs. arXiv preprint arXiv:1612.08498 (2016)
7. Danihelka, I., Wayne, G., Uria, B., Kalchbrenner, N., Graves, A.: Associative long short-term memory. arXiv preprint arXiv:1602.03032 (2016)
8. Deng, H., Birdal, T., Ilic, S.: PPF-FoldNet: unsupervised learning of rotation invariant 3D local descriptors. In: Ferrari, V., Hebert, M., Sminchisescu, C., Weiss, Y. (eds.) ECCV 2018. LNCS, vol. 11209, pp. 620–638. Springer, Cham (2018). https://doi.org/10.1007/978-3-030-01228-1_37
9. Gaudet, C.J., Maida, A.S.: Deep quaternion networks. In: 2018 International Joint Conference on Neural Networks (IJCNN), pp. 1–8. IEEE (2018)
10. Guberman, N.: On complex valued convolutional neural networks. arXiv preprint arXiv:1602.09046 (2016)
11. Hamilton, W.R.: On quaternions; or on a new system of imaginaries in algebra. Lond. Edinb. Dublin Philos. Mag. J. Sci. **33**(219), 58–60 (1848)
12. Hua, B.S., Tran, M.K., Yeung, S.K.: Pointwise convolutional neural networks. In: Proceedings of the IEEE Conference on Computer Vision and Pattern Recognition, pp. 984–993 (2018)
13. Jaderberg, M., Simonyan, K., Zisserman, A., et al.: Spatial transformer networks. In: Advances in Neural Information Processing Systems, pp. 2017–2025 (2015)
14. Jiang, M., Wu, Y., Zhao, T., Zhao, Z., Lu, C.: PointSIFT: a SIFT-like network module for 3D point cloud semantic segmentation. arXiv preprint arXiv:1807.00652 (2018)
15. Kendall, A., Grimes, M., Cipolla, R.: PoseNet: a convolutional network for real-time 6-DOF camera relocalization. In: Proceedings of the IEEE International Conference on Computer Vision, pp. 2938–2946 (2015)
16. Klokov, R., Lempitsky, V.: Escape from cells: deep kd-networks for the recognition of 3D point cloud models. In: Proceedings of the IEEE International Conference on Computer Vision, pp. 863–872 (2017)
17. Li, Y., Bu, R., Sun, M., Wu, W., Di, X., Chen, B.: PointCNN: convolution on x-transformed points. In: Advances in Neural Information Processing Systems, pp. 820–830 (2018)

18. Liu, X., Han, Z., Liu, Y.S., Zwicker, M.: Point2Sequence: learning the shape representation of 3D point clouds with an attention-based sequence to sequence network. In: Proceedings of the AAAI Conference on Artificial Intelligence, vol. 33, pp. 8778–8785 (2019)

19. Liu, Y., Fan, B., Xiang, S., Pan, C.: Relation-shape convolutional neural network for point cloud analysis. In: Proceedings of the IEEE Conference on Computer Vision and Pattern Recognition, pp. 8895–8904 (2019)

20. Parcollet, T., et al.: Quaternion convolutional neural networks for end-to-end automatic speech recognition. In: Interspeech 2018, 19th Annual Conference of the International Speech Communication Association, pp. 22–26 (2018)

21. Qi, C.R., Su, H., Mo, K., Guibas, L.J.: PointNet: deep learning on point sets for 3D classification and segmentation. In: Proceedings of the IEEE Conference on Computer Vision and Pattern Recognition, pp. 652–660 (2017)

22. Qi, C.R., Yi, L., Su, H., Guibas, L.J.: Pointnet++: deep hierarchical feature learning on point sets in a metric space. In: Advances in Neural Information Processing Systems, pp. 5099–5108 (2017)

23. Rao, Y., Lu, J., Zhou, J.: Spherical fractal convolutional neural networks for point cloud recognition. In: Proceedings of the IEEE Conference on Computer Vision and Pattern Recognition, pp. 452–460 (2019)

24. Shen, Y., Feng, C., Yang, Y., Tian, D.: Mining point cloud local structures by kernel correlation and graph pooling. In: Proceedings of the IEEE Conference on Computer Vision and Pattern Recognition, pp. 4548–4557 (2018)

25. Shi, S., Wang, X., Li, H.: PointRCNN: 3D object proposal generation and detection from point cloud. In: Proceedings of the IEEE Conference on Computer Vision and Pattern Recognition, pp. 770–779 (2019)

26. Shuster, M.D., et al.: A survey of attitude representations. Navigation **8**(9), 439–517 (1993)

27. Simonovsky, M., Komodakis, N.: Dynamic edge-conditioned filters in convolutional neural networks on graphs. In: Proceedings of the IEEE Conference on Computer Vision and Pattern Recognition, pp. 3693–3702 (2017)

28. Su, H., et al.: SPLATNet: sparse lattice networks for point cloud processing. In: Proceedings of the IEEE Conference on Computer Vision and Pattern Recognition, pp. 2530–2539 (2018)

29. Thomas, N., et al.: Tensor field networks: rotation-and translation-equivariant neural networks for 3D point clouds. arXiv preprint arXiv:1802.08219 (2018)

30. Trabelsi, C., et al.: Deep complex networks. arXiv preprint arXiv:1705.09792 (2017)

31. Van Dyk, D.A., Meng, X.L.: The art of data augmentation. J. Comput. Graph. Stat. **10**(1), 1–50 (2001)

32. Wang, W., Yu, R., Huang, Q., Neumann, U.: SGPN: similarity group proposal network for 3D point cloud instance segmentation. In: Proceedings of the IEEE Conference on Computer Vision and Pattern Recognition, pp. 2569–2578 (2018)

33. Wang, Y., Sun, Y., Liu, Z., Sarma, S.E., Bronstein, M.M., Solomon, J.M.: Dynamic graph CNN for learning on point clouds. arXiv preprint arXiv:1801.07829 (2018)

34. Weisstein, E.W.: Euler angles (2009)

35. Wisdom, S., Powers, T., Hershey, J., Le Roux, J., Atlas, L.: Full-capacity unitary recurrent neural networks. In: Advances in Neural Information Processing Systems, pp. 4880–4888 (2016)

36. Wolter, M., Yao, A.: Complex gated recurrent neural networks. In: Advances in Neural Information Processing Systems, pp. 10536–10546 (2018)

37. Wu, W., Qi, Z., Fuxin, L.: PointConv: deep convolutional networks on 3D point clouds. In: Proceedings of the IEEE Conference on Computer Vision and Pattern Recognition, pp. 9621–9630 (2019)

38. Wu, Z., et al.: 3D ShapeNets: a deep representation for volumetric shapes. In: Proceedings of the IEEE Conference on Computer Vision and Pattern Recognition, pp. 1912–1920 (2015)

39. Xiang, L., Ma, H., Zhang, H., Zhang, Y., Zhang, Q.: Complex-valued neural networks for privacy protection. arXiv preprint arXiv:1901.09546 (2019)

40. You, Y., et al.: PRIN: pointwise rotation-invariant network. arXiv preprint arXiv:1811.09361 (2018)

41. Yu, L., Li, X., Fu, C.W., Cohen-Or, D., Heng, P.A.: PU-Net: point cloud upsampling network. In: Proceedings of the IEEE Conference on Computer Vision and Pattern Recognition, pp. 2790–2799 (2018)

42. Zhang, Y., Lu, Z., Xue, J.H., Liao, Q.: A new rotation-invariant deep network for 3D object recognition. In: 2019 IEEE International Conference on Multimedia and Expo (ICME), pp. 1606–1611. IEEE (2019)

43. Zhang, Z., Hua, B.S., Rosen, D.W., Yeung, S.K.: Rotation invariant convolutions for 3D point clouds deep learning. In: 2019 International Conference on 3D Vision (3DV), pp. 204–213. IEEE (2019)

44. Zhao, H., Jiang, L., Fu, C.W., Jia, J.: PointWeb: enhancing local neighborhood features for point cloud processing. In: Proceedings of the IEEE Conference on Computer Vision and Pattern Recognition, pp. 5565–5573 (2019)

45. Zhao, Y., Birdal, T., Lenssen, J.E., Menegatti, E., Guibas, L., Tombari, F.: Quaternion equivariant capsule networks for 3D point clouds. arXiv preprint arXiv:1912.12098 (2019)

46. Zhu, X., Xu, Y., Xu, H., Chen, C.: Quaternion convolutional neural networks. In: Ferrari, V., Hebert, M., Sminchisescu, C., Weiss, Y. (eds.) ECCV 2018. LNCS, vol. 11212, pp. 645–661. Springer, Cham (2018). https://doi.org/10.1007/978-3-030-01237-3_39

InterHand2.6M: A Dataset and Baseline for 3D Interacting Hand Pose Estimation from a Single RGB Image

Gyeongsik Moon[1], Shoou-I Yu[2], He Wen[2], Takaaki Shiratori[2],
and Kyoung Mu Lee[1(✉)]

[1] ECE & ASRI, Seoul National University, Seoul, Korea
{mks0601,kyoungmu}@snu.ac.kr
[2] Facebook Reality Labs, Pittsburgh, USA
{shoou-i.yu,hewen,tshiratori}@fb.com

Abstract. Analysis of hand-hand interactions is a crucial step towards better understanding human behavior. However, most researches in 3D hand pose estimation have focused on the isolated single hand case. Therefore, we firstly propose (1) a large-scale dataset, InterHand2.6M, and (2) a baseline network, InterNet, for 3D interacting hand pose estimation from a single RGB image. The proposed InterHand2.6M consists of **2.6 M labeled single and interacting hand frames** under various poses from multiple subjects. Our InterNet simultaneously performs 3D single and interacting hand pose estimation. In our experiments, we demonstrate big gains in 3D interacting hand pose estimation accuracy when leveraging the interacting hand data in InterHand2.6M. We also report the accuracy of InterNet on InterHand2.6M, which serves as a strong baseline for this new dataset. Finally, we show 3D interacting hand pose estimation results from general images. Our code and dataset are available (https://mks0601.github.io/InterHand2.6M/).

1 Introduction

The goal of 3D hand pose estimation is to localize semantic keypoints (*i.e.*, joints) of a human hand in 3D space. It is an essential technique for human behavior understanding and human-computer interaction. Recently, many methods [6,11, 15,38,46] utilize deep convolutional neural networks (CNNs) and have achieved noticeable performance improvement on public datasets [29,33,36,43,46].

Most of the previous 3D hand pose estimation methods [6,11,15,38,46] are designed for single hand cases. Given a cropped single hand image, models estimate the 3D locations of each hand keypoint. However, single hand scenarios have limitations in covering all realistic human hand postures because human hands often interact with each other to interact with other people and objects.

Electronic supplementary material The online version of this chapter (https:// doi.org/10.1007/978-3-030-58565-5_33) contains supplementary material, which is available to authorized users.

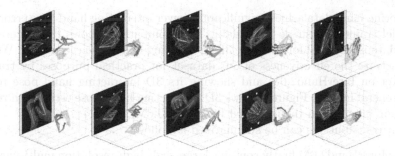

Fig. 1. Qualitative 3D interacting hand pose estimation results from our InterNet on the proposed InterHand2.6M.

To address this issue, we firstly propose a large-scale dataset, *InterHand2.6M*, and a baseline, *InterNet*, for 3D interacting hand pose estimation.

Our newly constructed InterHand2.6M is the first large-scale real (*i.e.*, non-synthetic) RGB-based 3D hand pose dataset that includes both single and interacting hand sequences under various poses from multiple subjects. Each hand sequence contains a single hand or interacting right and left hands of a single person. InterHand2.6M is captured in a precisely calibrated multi-view studio with 80 to 140 high-resolution cameras. For 3D keypoint coordinate annotation, we use a semi-automatic approach, which is a combination of manual human annotation and automatic machine annotation. This approach makes annotation procedure much more efficient compared with full manual annotation while achieving similar annotation accuracy as the fully manual one.

The proposed InterNet simultaneously estimates 3D single and interacting hand pose from a single RGB image. For this, we design InterNet to predict handedness, 2.5D right and left hand pose, and right hand-relative left hand depth. The handedness can tell whether right or left hands are included in the input image; therefore InterNet can exclude the pose of a hand that does not exist in the testing stage. The 2.5D hand pose consists of 2D pose in x- and y-axis and root joint (*i.e.*, wrist)-relative depth in z-axis, widely used in state-of-the-art 3D human body [16] and hand [11] pose estimation from a single RGB image. It provides high accuracy because of its image-aligned property and ability to model the uncertainty of the prediction. To lift 2.5D right and left hand pose to 3D space, we obtain an absolute depth of the root joint from RootNet [16]. However, as obtaining absolute depth from a single RGB image is highly ambiguous, RootNet outputs unreliable depth in some cases. To resolve this, we design Inter-Net to predict right hand-relative left hand depth by leveraging the appearance of the interacting hand from the input image. This relative depth can be used instead of the output of the RootNet when both right and left hands are visible in the input image.

To demonstrate the benefit of the newly captured interacting hand data, we compare the performance of models trained on only single hand data, on only interacting hand data, and on both. We observed that models trained on interacting hand data achieve significantly lower interacting hand pose error than a model trained on single hand data. This comparison shows that interacting hand data is essential for accurate 3D interacting hand pose estimation. We also demonstrate the effectiveness of our dataset for practical purposes by training InterNet on InterHand2.6M and showing its 3D interacting hand pose results from general images. Figure 1 shows 3D interacting hand pose estimation results from our InterNet on the proposed InterHand2.6M.

Our contributions can be summarized as follows.

- Our InterHand2.6M firstly contains large-scale high-resolution multi-view single and interacting hand sequences. By using a semi-automatic approach, we obtained accurate 3D keypoint coordinate annotations efficiently.
- We propose InterNet for 3D single and interacting hand pose estimation. Our InterNet estimates handedness, 2.5D hand pose, and right hand-relative left hand depth from a single RGB image.
- We show that single hand data is not enough, and interacting hand data is essential for accurate 3D interacting hand pose estimation.

2   Related Works

Depth-Based 3D Single Hand Pose Estimation. Early depth-based 3D hand pose estimation methods are mainly based on a generative approach. They fit a pre-defined hand model to the input depth image by minimizing hand-crafted cost functions [25,34]. Particle swarm optimization [25], iterative closest point [31], and their combination [22] are the common algorithms used to obtain optimal hand poses.

Recent deep neural network-based methods are mainly based on a discriminative approach, which directly localizes hand joints from an input depth map. Tompson et al. [36] firstly utilized the deep neural network to localize hand keypoints by estimating 2D heatmaps for each hand joint. Ge et al. [5] extended this method by estimating multi-view 2D heatmaps. Guo et al. [7] proposed a region ensemble network to estimate the 3D coordinates of hand keypoints accurately. Moon et al. [15] designed a 3D CNN model that takes voxel input and outputs a 3D heatmap for each keypoint. Wan et al. [38] proposed a self-supervised system, which can be trained only from an input depth map.

RGB-Based 3D Single Hand Pose Estimation. Pioneering works [13,39] estimate hand pose from RGB image sequences. Gorce et al. [13] proposed a model that estimates 3D hand pose, texture, and illuminant dynamically. Recently, deep learning-based methods show noticeable improvement. Zimmermann et al. [46] proposed a deep neural network that learns a network-implicit 3D articulation prior. Mueller et al. [17] used an image-to-image translation model to generate a realistic hand pose dataset from a synthetic dataset. Cai et al. [2] and Iqbal et al. [11] implicitly reconstruct depth map and estimate 3D hand keypoint coordinates from it. Spurr et al. [27] and Yang et al. [41] proposed deep generative models to learn latent space for hand.

Table 1. Comparison of existing 3D hand pose estimation datasets and the proposed InterHand2.6M. For the RGBD-based datasets, we report their RGB resolution. For the multi-view captured datasets, we consider each image from different views as different images when reporting the number of frames. InterHand2.6M was initially captured at 4096 × 2668 resolution, but to protect fingerprint privacy, the released set has resolution 512 × 334.

Dataset	Source	Resolution	Annotation	Sub.	Fr.	Int. hand
ICVL [33]	real depth	320 × 240	track	10	18K	✗
NYU [36]	real depth	640 × 480	track	2	243K	✗
MSRA [29]	real depth	320 × 240	track	9	76K	✗
BigHand2.2M [44]	real depth	640 × 480	marker	10	2.2M	✗
FPHA [4][a]	real RGBD	1920 × 1080	marker	6	105K	✗
Dexter+Object [28]	real RGBD	640 × 480	manual	1	3K	✗
EgoDexter [19]	real RGBD	640 × 480	manual	4	3K	✗
STB [45]	real RGBD	640 × 480	manual	1	36K	✗
FreiHAND [47]	real RGB	224 × 224	semi-auto.	32	134K	✗
RHP [46]	synth. RGBD	320 × 320	synth	20	44K	✗
Tzionas et al. [37]	real RGBD	640 × 480	manual	n/a	36K	✓
Mueller et al. [18]	synth. depth	n/a	synth	5	80K	✓
Simon et al. [26]	real RGB	1920 × 1080	semi-auto	n/a	15K	✓
InterHand2.6M (ours)	real RGB	**512 × 334** (**4096 × 2668**)	semi-auto	**27**	**2.6 M**	✓

[a] There are markers on hands in the RGB sequence.

3D Interacting Hand Pose Estimation.

There are few works that tried to solve the 3D interacting hand pose estimation. Oikonomidis et al. [20] firstly attempted to address this problem using particle swarm optimization from an RGBD sequence. Ballan et al. [1] presented a framework that outputs 3D hand pose and mesh from multi-view RGB sequences. They combined a generative model with discriminatively trained salient points to achieve a low tracking error. Tzionas et al. [37] extended Ballan et al. [1] by incorporating a physical model. Taylor et al. [35] proposed to perform joint optimization over both the hand model pose and the correspondences between observed data points and the hand model surface. Simon et al. [26] performed 2D hand pose estimation from multi-view images and triangulated them into the 3D space. Mueller et al. [18] proposed a model that estimates a correspondence map and hand segmentation map from a single depth map. The correspondence map provides a correlation between mesh vertices and image pixels, and the segmentation map separates right and left hand. They fit a hand model [23] to the estimated maps.

However, all of the above methods have limitations to be used for 3D single and interacting hand pose estimation from a single RGB image. Tzionas et al. [37] and Simon et al. [26] require additional depth map or multi-view images. The model of Mueller et al. [18] takes a single depth map and not a single RGB image. In contrast, our proposed InterNet can perform 3D single and interacting hand pose estimation simultaneously from a single RGB image.

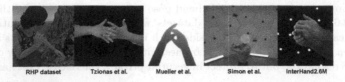

RHP dataset   Tzionas et al.   Mueller et al.   Simon et al.   InterHand2.6M

Fig. 2. Comparisons of interacting hand images from RHP [46], Tzionas et al. [37], Mueller et al. [18], Simon et al. [26], and the proposed InterHand2.6M.

3D Hand Pose Estimation Datasets. Table 1 shows specification of existing 3D hand pose datasets and the proposed InterHand2.6M. Compared with depth-based 3D hand pose estimation datasets [4,29,33,36,44], existing RGB-based datasets [19,28,45,46] have very limited number of frames and subjects because obtaining accurate 3D annotation from RGB images is difficult. Recently, Zimmermann et al. [47] captured a large-scale single hand pose and mesh dataset.

Several datasets contain two or interacting hand sequences, and Fig. 2 shows example images of the datasets. RHP [46] contains two isolated hand data. However, their images are far from real because they are synthesized by animating 3D human models using commercial software. In addition, in most of their two hand images, right and left hands perform separate actions and are not interacting with each other. The dataset of Tzionas et al. [37] is the most similar dataset with ours in that it is constructed to analyze RGB interacting hand-focused sequences. It contains RGBD interacting hand sequences, however only 2D joint coordinates annotations are available instead of the 3D coordinates. In addition, the scale of the dataset is much smaller compared with that of our dataset. The dataset of Mueller et al. [18] mainly consists of synthesized depth maps, which are not very realistic. Although some depth maps of their dataset are real-captured ones, 3D keypoint coordinate annotations of them are not available. The dataset of Simon et al. [26] is not large-scale, and their annotations from a machine annotator are unstable because the resolution of the hand area of their dataset is low.

Compared with them, our InterHand2.6M consists of large-scale real-captured RGB images and includes more variety of sequences. In addition, our strong machine annotator provides accurate and less jittering 3D hand joints coordinates annotations because of our strong semi-automatic annotation and high-resolution hand area. Our dataset can be used when the hand is a central subject in the input image, for example, capturing the hand by a head-mounted device for virtual/augmented reality.

3   InterHand2.6M

3.1   Data Capture

InterHand2.6M is captured in a multi-camera studio consisting of 80–140 cameras capturing at 30–90 frames-per-second (fps), and 350–450 directional LED point lights directed at the hand to promote uniform illumination[1]. The cameras captured at image resolution 4096 × 2668. The multi-view system was calibrated with a 3D calibration target [8] and achieved pixel root mean square error ranging from 0.42 to 0.48.

We captured a total of 36 recordings consisting of 26 unique subjects, where 19 of them are males, and other 7 are females. There are two types of hand sequences[2]. First, peak pose (PP) is a short transition from neutral pose to pre-defined hand poses (e.g., fist) and then transition back to neutral pose. The pre-defined hand poses include various sign languages that are frequently used in daily life and extreme poses where each finger is maximally bent or extended. There are 40 pre-defined hand poses for each right and left hand, and 13 for the interacting hand. In the neutral pose, hands are in front of the person's chest, fingers do not touch, and palms face the side. The second type is a range of motion (ROM), which represents conversational gestures with minimal instructions. For example, subjects are instructed to wave their hands as if telling someone to come over. There are 15 conversational gestures for each right and left hand, and 17 for the interacting hand. The hand poses from PP and ROM in our dataset are chosen to sample a variety of poses and conversational gestures while being easy to follow by capture participants. The proposed InterHand2.6M is meant to cover a reasonable and general range of hand poses instead of choosing an optimal hand pose set for specific applications.

3.2 Annotation

To annotate keypoints of hands, we directly extend the commonly used 21 keypoints per hand annotation scheme [46] to both hands, thus leading to a total of 42 unique points. For each finger, we annotate the fingertip and the rotation centers of three joints. In addition to the 20 keypoints per hand, the wrist rotation center is also annotated.

Annotating rotation centers is challenging because the rotation center of a joint is occluded by the skin. The annotations become more challenging when the fingers are occluded by other fingers, or viewed from an oblique angle. Therefore, we developed a 3D rotation center annotation tool which allows the annotator to view and annotate 6 images simultaneously[3]. These 6 images are captured at the same time, but viewing the hand from different angles. When the annotator annotates a joint in two views, the tool will automatically perform triangulation and re-project the point to all other views, thus enabling the annotator to verify that the annotations are consistent in 3D space.

Despite having the annotation tool, manually annotating large amounts of images is still very labor-intensive. Thus, we adopted a two-stage procedure to

---

[1] There were two settings. Setting 1: on average 34 RGB and 46 monochrome cameras (80 cameras total), 350 lights, and 90fps. Setting 2: on average 139 color cameras, 450 lights, and 30fps. Due to camera failures, not all cameras were operational; thus, each capture would have slightly different number of cameras.

[2] The examples of hand sequences are described in supplementary material.

[3] The human annotation procedure is described in supplementary material.

annotate the images following Simon et al. [26]. In the first stage, we rely on human annotators. The annotators leveraged our annotation tool and manually annotated 94,914 2D images from 9,036 unique time instants where 1,880 of them had two hand annotations. These 2D annotations are triangulated to get 3D positions of joints, which are subsequently projected to all roughly 80 views to get 2D annotations for each view. The unique time steps are sampled to cover many hand poses of our recording scripts. At the end of this stage, a total of 698,922 images are labeled with 2D keypoints.

In the second stage, we utilize an automatic machine annotator. For this, we trained a state-of-the-art 2D keypoint detector [14] from the images annotated in the previous stage. EfficientNet [32] is used as a backbone of the keypoint detector for computational efficiency. The detector was then run through unlabeled images, and the 3D keypoints were obtained by triangulation with RANSAC. As our InterHand2.6M is captured from a large number of high-resolution cameras, this machine-based annotation gives highly accurate estimations. We tested this method on the held-out evaluation set, and the error is 2.78 mm. The final dataset is an integration of human annotations from the first stage and machine annotations from the second stage. Simon et al. [26] performed iterative bootstrap because their initial machine annotator does not provide accurate annotations, and the hand area of their dataset has low resolution. In contrast, our strong machine annotator on high-resolution hand images achieves significantly low error (2.78 mm); therefore, we did not perform iterative bootstrap.

3.3   Dataset Release

The captured hand sequences will be released under two configurations: downsized 512×334 image resolution at 5 fps, and downsized 512×334 resolution at 30 fps. Downsizing is to protect fingerprint privacy. The annotation file includes camera type, subject index, camera index, bounding box, handedness, camera parameters, and 3D joint coordinates. All reported frame numbers and experimental results in the paper are from the 5 fps configuration.

4   InterNet

Our InterNet takes a single RGB image $\mathbf{I}$ as an input and extracts the image feature $\mathbf{F}$ using ResNet [9] whose fully-connected layers are trimmed. We prepare $\mathbf{I}$ by cropping the hand region from an image and resizing it to uniform resolution. From $\mathbf{F}$, InterNet simultaneously predicts handedness, 2.5D right and left hand pose, and right hand-relative left hand depth, which will be described in the following subsections. We do not normalize the hand scale for the 2.5D hand pose estimation. Figure 3 shows overall pipeline of InterNet.

4.1   Handedness Estimation

To decide which hand is included in the input image, we design our InterNet to estimate the probability of the existence of the right and left hand $\mathbf{h} = (h^{\mathrm{R}}, h^{\mathrm{L}}) \in$

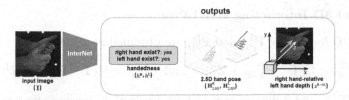

Fig. 3. Three outputs of the proposed InterNet.

$\mathbb{R}^2$ in the input image. For this, we build two fully-connected layers, which take the image feature $\mathbf{F}$ and estimates the probabilities $\mathbf{h}$. The hidden activation size of the fully-connected layers is 512. Each fully-connected layer is followed by the ReLU activation function except for the last one. We apply a sigmoid activation function at the last layer to get the probabilities.

4.2 2.5D Right and Left Hand Pose Estimation

To estimate 2.5D right and left hand pose, denoted as $\mathbf{P}^{R}_{2.5D} \in \mathbb{R}^{J \times 3}$ and $\mathbf{P}^{L}_{2.5D} \in \mathbb{R}^{J \times 3}$, respectively, we construct two upsamplers for each right and left hand. Each upsampler consists of three deconvolutional and one convolutional layers, and each deconvolutional layer is followed by batch normalization layers [10] and ReLU activation functions, therefore it upsamples the input feature map 2^3 times. The upsamplers take $\mathbf{F}$ and output 3D Gaussian heatmaps of the right and left hand joints, denoted as $\mathbf{H}^{R}_{2.5D}$ and $\mathbf{H}^{L}_{2.5D}$ following Moon et al. [16], where they have the same dimension $\mathbb{R}^{J \times D \times H \times W}$. D, H, and W denote depth discretization size, height, and width of the heatmaps, respectively. x- and y-axis of $\mathbf{H}^{R}_{2.5D}$ and $\mathbf{H}^{L}_{2.5D}$ are in image space, and z-axis of them are in root joint (*i.e.*, wrist)-relative depth space. To obtain a 3D Gaussian heatmap from the 2D feature map, we reshape the output of the upsampler by a reshaping function $\psi : \mathbb{R}^{JD \times H \times W} \rightarrow \mathbb{R}^{J \times D \times H \times W}$. Each voxel of the 3D Gaussian heatmap of the joint j represents the likelihood of the existence of a hand joint j in that position.

4.3 Right Hand-Relative Left Hand Depth Estimation

The depth of each hand is defined as that of the hand root joint. We construct two fully-connected layers and the ReLU activation function after each fully connected layer except for the last layer. The hidden activation size of the fully-connected layers is 512. It takes $\mathbf{F}$ and outputs 1D heatmap $\mathbf{d}^{R \rightarrow L} \in \mathbb{R}^{64}$. Then, soft-argmax [30] is applied to $\mathbf{d}^{R \rightarrow L}$ and output the relative depth value $z^{R \rightarrow L}$. We observed that estimating the 1D heatmap followed by soft-argmax operation provides a more accurate relative depth value compared with directly regressing it, which is a similar spirit to Moon et al. [15].

4.4   Final 3D Interacting Hand Pose

The final 3D hand pose $\mathbf{P}_{3D}^R$ and $\mathbf{P}_{3D}^L$ are obtained as follows:

$$\mathbf{P}_{3D}^R = \Pi(\mathbf{T}^{-1}\mathbf{P}_{2.5D}^R + \mathbf{Z}^R), \quad \text{and} \quad \mathbf{P}_{3D}^L = \Pi(\mathbf{T}^{-1}\mathbf{P}_{2.5D}^L + \mathbf{Z}^L),$$

where Π, $\mathbf{T}^{-1}$, and $\emptyset$ denote camera back-projection, inverse affine transformation (*i.e.*, 2D crop and resize), and empty pose set, respectively. We use normalized camera intrinsic parameters if not available following Moon et al. [16]. $\mathbf{Z}^R \in \mathbb{R}^{1\times 3}$ and $\mathbf{Z}^L \in \mathbb{R}^{1\times 3}$ are defined as follows:

$$\mathbf{Z}^R = [(0),(0),(z^R)], \qquad \mathbf{Z}^L = \begin{cases} [(0),(0),(z^L)], & \text{if } h^R < 0.5 \\ [(0),(0),(z^R + z^{R\to L})], & \text{otherwise,} \end{cases}$$

where z^R and z^L denote the absolute depth of the root joint of right and left hand, respectively. We use RootNet [16] to obtain them.

4.5   Loss Functions

To train our InterNet, we use three loss functions.

Handedness Loss. For the handedness estimation, we use binary cross-entropy loss function as defined as follows: $L_h = -\frac{1}{2}\sum_{\mathcal{Q}\in(R,L)}(\delta^{\mathcal{Q}}\log h^{\mathcal{Q}}+(1-\delta^{\mathcal{Q}})\log(1-h^{\mathcal{Q}}))$, where $\delta^{\mathcal{Q}}$ is a binary value which represents existence of the $\mathcal{Q}$ hand in an input image.

2.5D Hand Pose Loss. For the 2.5D hand pose estimation, we use $L2$ loss as defined as follows: $L_{pose} = \sum_{\mathcal{Q}\in(R,L)}\|\mathbf{H}_{2.5D}^{\mathcal{Q}} - \mathbf{H}_{2.5D}^{\mathcal{Q}*}\|_2$, where $*$ denotes groundtruth. If one of the right or left hand is not included in the input image, we set the loss from it zero. The groundtruth 3D Gaussian heatmap is computed using a Gaussian blob [15] as follows:

$$\mathbf{H}_{2.5D}^{\mathcal{Q}*}(j,z,x,y) = \exp\left(-\frac{(x-x_j^{\mathcal{Q}})^2+(y-y_j^{\mathcal{Q}})^2+(z-z_j^{\mathcal{Q}})^2}{2\sigma^2}\right), \text{ where } x_j^{\mathcal{Q}}, y_j^{\mathcal{Q}}, \text{ and } z_j^{\mathcal{Q}} \text{ are}$$

jth joint coordinates of $\mathcal{Q}$ hand from $\mathbf{P}_{2.5D}^{\mathcal{Q}}$.

Right Hand-Relative Left Hand Depth Loss. For the right hand-relative left hand localization, we use $L1$ loss as defined as follows: $L_{rel} = |z^{R\to L}-z^{R\to L*}|$, where $*$ denotes groundtruth. The loss becomes zero when only a single hand is included in the input image.

We train our model in an end-to-end manner using all the three loss functions as follows: $L = L_h + L_{pose} + L_{rel}$.

5   Implementation Details

PyTorch [21] is used for implementation. The backbone part is initialized with the publicly released ResNet-50 [9] pre-trained on the ImageNet dataset [24], and the weights of the remaining part are initialized by Gaussian distribution

Table 2. Training, validation, and test set split of the proposed InterHand2.6M. H and M denote human annotation and machine annotation, respectively. SH and IH denote single and interacting hand, respectively.

Split	Sequence	Subjects	Frames (SH)	Frames (IH)	Frames (All)
Train (H)	PP+ROM	16	142 K	386 K	528 K
Train (M)	PP+ROM	9	594 K	315 K	909 K
Train (H+M)	PP+ROM	21	688 K	674 K	**1361 K**
Val (M)	ROM	1	234 K	146 K	**380 K**
Test (H)	PP+ROM	6	34 K	88 K	122 K
Test (M)	ROM	2	455 K	272 K	728 K
Test (H+M)	PP+ROM	8	489 K	360 K	**849 K**

with $\sigma = 0.001$. The weights are updated by the Adam optimizer [12] with a mini-batch size of 64. To crop the hand region from the input image, we use groundtruth bounding box in both of training and testing stages. The cropped hand image is resized to 256×256; thus the spatial size of the heatmap is $H \times W = 64 \times 64$. We set $D = 64$. Data augmentations including translation ($\pm 15\%$), scaling ($\pm 25\%$), rotation ($\pm 90°$), horizontal flip, and color jittering ($\pm 20\%$) is performed in training. The initial learning rate is set to 10^{-4} and reduced by a factor of 10 at the 15th and 17th epoch. We train our model for 20 epochs with four NVIDIA TitanV GPUs, which takes 48 hours when training on our InterHand2.6M. Our InterNet runs at a speed of 53 fps.

6   Experiment

6.1   Dataset and Evaluation Metric

STB. STB [45] includes 6 pairs of stereo sequences of diverse poses with different backgrounds from a single person. For evaluation, end point error (EPE) is widely used, which is defined as a mean Euclidean distance (mm) between the predicted and ground-truth 3D hand pose after root joint alignment.

RHP. RHP [46] has a large number of synthesized images. They used 3D human models of 20 different subjects to synthesize 39 actions. For the evaluation metric, EPE is used.

InterHand2.6M. InterHand2.6M is our newly captured 3D hand pose dataset. We split our InterHand2.6M into training, validation, and test set, as shown in Table 2. Val (M) and Test (M) contain many unseen hand poses and only subjects not seen in Train (H+M). Also, Val (M) and Test (M) only consists of ROM, which includes longer and more diverse sequences than that of Train (H+M). This can make Val (M) and Test (M) more similar to real-world scenarios. Test (H) contains many seen hand poses, and half of the subjects are seen in Train

Table 3. Single and interacting hand
MPJPE comparison from models trained
on the different training sets. SH and 1H
denote single and interacting hand, respectively.

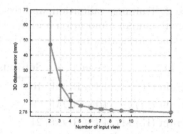

Training set	SH MPJPE	IH MPJPE
SH only	13.08	51.19
IH only	13.70	16.86
SH+IH (ours)	**12.16**	**16.02**

Fig. 4. The 3D distance error of our
machine annotation on the Test (H).

(H). There are duplicated frames and annotations in Train (H) and Train (M),
and we overwrite them with Train (H).

For the evaluation, we introduce three metrics. First, we use the average precision of handedness estimation (AP_h) to measure the accuracy of handedness
estimation. Second, the mean per joint position error (MPJPE) is defined as
a Euclidean distance (mm) between predicted and groundtruth 3D joint locations after root joint alignment. The root joint alignment is performed for each
left and right hand separately. This metric measures how accurately the root-
relative 3D hand pose estimation is performed. Last, mean relative-root position
error (MRRPE) is defined as a Euclidean distance (mm) between predicted and
groundtruth right hand root-relative left hand root position. It measures how
right hand-relative left hand localization is accurately performed.

6.2   Ablation Study

Benefit of the Interacting Hand Data. To investigate the benefit of the
interacting hand data for 3D interacting hand pose estimation, we compare single
and interacting hand MPJPE of our InterNet trained with and without interacting hand data in Table 3. For all settings, we used the same RootNet trained on
both single and interacting hand data. As the table shows, a model trained only
on interacting hand provides significantly lower interacting hand pose error than
a model trained only on single hand data. This shows existing 3D single hand
pose estimation datasets are not enough for accurate 3D interacting hand pose
estimation. In addition, we trained a model on combined single and interacting
hand data, which is our InterHand2.6M. We observed that additional interacting
hand data improves not only interacting hand pose estimation performance, but
also single hand pose estimation. These comparisons clearly show the benefit of
our newly introduced interacting hand data for 3D single and interacting hand
pose estimation.

Accuracy of the Machine Annotation. To show the accuracy of our machine
annotation model, we train our annotation model on Train (H) and test on Test
(H). Figure 4 shows 3D distance error (mm) on Test (H) according to the number
of input views. For each number of input views, the vertical line represents a

Table 4. Single and interacting hand MPJPE comparison from models trained on the different training sets. The numbers on the left of the slash are single hand, and the ones on the right are interacting hand MPJPE.

Training set	Val (M)	Test (H)	Test (M)	Test (H+M)
Train (H)	15.02/19.70	10.42/13.05	12.74/18.10	12.58/17.16
Train (M)	15.36/20.13	10.64/14.26	12.56/18.59	12.43/17.79
Train (H+M)	**14.65/18.58**	**9.85/12.29**	**12.32/16.88**	**12.16/16.02**

standard deviation, which shows performance variation due to view selection. In the testing time, the model takes randomly selected v views and performs 2D hand pose estimation, followed by triangulation. To cover various combinations of selecting v views from all V views, we repeat the same testing procedure 100 times for each v views. The figure shows that as the number of input views increases, both the error and standard deviation becomes smaller, and finally, the error becomes *2.78 mm* when all 90 views are used. This shows our annotation method is highly accurate by utilizing state-of-the-art 2D keypoint detection network and a large number of views for triangulation.

Benefit of Machine-Generated Annotation. To show the benefit of the automatically obtained machine annotations, we compare the accuracy of models trained without and with Train (M) in Table 4. As the table shows, a model trained on Train (Ĥ) achieves better performance than a model trained on Train (M). We hypothesize that although our machine annotator has very low 3D distance error, human annotation is still more accurate, which makes a model trained on Train (H) performs better. However, as the machine provides annotation more efficiently than a human, it can annotate many frames easily that may not be included in Train (H). Therefore, this machine-generated annotations can have better coverage of hand pose space, which can be a benefit in the training stage. To utilize this better coverage, we add machine annotation to the human annotation. The last row of the table shows that a model trained on the combined dataset achieves the best accuracy. This comparison clearly shows the benefit of adding the machine-generated annotation to the human annotation. We provide more analysis of human and machine annotation in the supplementary material.

Benefit of Using $z^{R \to L}$. To show the benefit of using $z^{R \to L}$ when right hand is visible (*i.e.*, $h^R \geq 0.5$) instead of always using z^L, we compare MRRPE between the two cases. We checked that MRRPE of always using z^L is 92.14 mm, while that of using $z^{R \to L}$ when $h^R \geq 0.5$ is 32.57 mm. This is because estimating z^L from a cropped single image inherently involves high depth ambiguity because the camera position is not provided in the cropped input image. In contrast, estimating $z^{R \to L}$ from a cropped image involves less depth ambiguity because both hands are visible in the cropped input image.

Table 5. EPE comparison with previous state-of-the-art methods on STB and RHP. The checkmark denotes a method use groundtruth information during inference time. S and H denote scale and handness, respectively.

Methods	GT S	GT H	EPE (STB)	EPE (RHP)
Zimm. et al. [46]	✓	✓	8.68	30.42
Chen et al. [3]	✓	✓	10.95	24.20
Yang et al. [41]	✓	✓	8.66	19.95
Spurr et al. [27]	✓	✓	8.56	19.73
Spurr et al. [27]	✗	✗	9.49	22.53
InterNet (ours)	✗	✗	**7.95**	**20.89**

6.3   Comparison with State-of-the-Art Methods

We compare the performance of our InterNet with previous state-of-the-art 3D hand pose estimation methods on the STB and RHP in Table 5. The table shows the proposed InterNet outperforms previous methods without relying on ground-truth information during inference time. Our InterNet estimates 3D heatmap of each joint, while other methods directly estimate 3D joint coordinates. As shown in Moon et al. [15], directly regressing 3D joint coordinates from an input image is a highly non-linear mapping. In contrast, our InterNet estimates per-voxel likelihoods, which makes learning easier and provides state-of-the-art performance.

6.4   Evaluation on InterHand2.6M

Table 4 shows 3D errors of InterNet on InterHand2.6M. Table 3 shows that Inter-Net trained on both single and interacting hand data yields the 32% larger error on interacting hand sequences than single hand sequences. This comparison tells us that interacting hand sequences are harder to analyze than single hand cases. To analyze the difficulty of InterHand2.6M, we compare our error with 3D hand pose error of current state-of-the-art depth map-based 3D hand pose estimation methods [15,40] on the large-scale depth map 3D hand pose datasets [42,44]. They achieved 8–9 mm error on large scale depth map dataset [42,44], which is far less than 3D interacting hand pose estimation error of our InterNet (*i.e.*, 16.02 mm). Considering our InterNet achieves state-of-the-art performance on publicly available datasets [45,46], we can conclude that 3D interacting hand pose estimation from a single RGB image is far from solved. Our InterNet achieves 99.09 AP_h and 32.57 MRRPE on Test (H+M).

6.5   3D Interacting Hand Pose Estimation from General Images

We show 3D interacting hand pose estimation results from general images in Fig. 5. For this, we additionally utilize the dataset of Tzionas et al. [37], which is captured from the general environment but only provides the 2D groundtruth

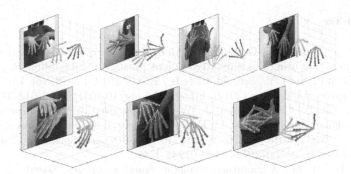

Fig. 5. Qualitative results on the dataset of Tzionas et al. [37], which is captured from a general environment.

joints coordinates. We randomly split the dataset of Tzionas et al. [37] at a 9:1 ratio as a training and testing set, respectively. During the training, a mini-batch consists of half-InterHand2.6M and half-dataset of Tzionas et al. [37]. For the simultaneous 3D and 2D supervision from our dataset and that of Tzionas et al. [37], respectively, we perform soft-argmax [30] on the estimated heatmaps $\mathbf{H}^R$ and $\mathbf{H}^L$ to extract the 3D coordinates in a differentiable way. Then, we modify L_{pose} to a $L1$ distance between the extracted 3D coordinates and the groundtruth. We set a loss of z-axis coordinate to zero when the input image is from the dataset of Tzionas et al. [37]. The figure shows our InterNet successfully produces 3D interacting hand pose results from general images from the dataset of Tzionas et al. [37], although the 3D supervision is only applied to the data from our InterHand2.6M.

7 Conclusion

We propose a baseline, InterNet, and dataset, InterHand2.6M, for 3D interacting hand pose estimation from a single RGB image. The proposed InterHand2.6M is the first large-scale 3D hand pose dataset that includes various single and interacting hand sequences from multiple subjects. As InterHand2.6M only provides 3D hand joint coordinates, fitting 3D hand model [23] to our dataset for the 3D rotation and mesh data of interacting hand can be interesting future work.

Acknowledgments. We would like to thank Alexander Hypes, David Whitewolf, Eric Brockmeyer, Kevyn McPhail, Mark Pitts, Matt Stewart, Michal Perdoch, Scott Ardisson, Steven Krenn, and Timothy Godisart for building the capture system, Autumn Trimble, Danielle Belko, Junko Saragih, Laura Millerschoen, Lucas Evans, Rohan Bali, Taylor Koska, and Xiaomin Luo for the data capture and annotation efforts, and Chenglei Wu, Jason Saragih, Tomas Simon, and Yaser Sheikh for constructive feedback on data collection and the paper. This work was partially supported by the Next-Generation Information Computing Development Program (NRF-2017M3C4A7069369) and the Visual Turing Test project (IITP-2017-0-01780) funded by the Ministry of Science and ICT of Korea.

References

1. Ballan, L., Taneja, A., Gall, J., Van Gool, L., Pollefeys, M.: Motion capture of hands in action using discriminative salient points. In: Fitzgibbon, A., Lazebnik, S., Perona, P., Sato, Y., Schmid, C. (eds.) ECCV 2012. LNCS, vol. 7577, pp. 640–653. Springer, Heidelberg (2012). https://doi.org/10.1007/978-3-642-33783-3_46
2. Cai, Y., Ge, L., Cai, J., Yuan, J.: Weakly-supervised 3D hand pose estimation from monocular RGB images. In: Ferrari, V., Hebert, M., Sminchisescu, C., Weiss, Y. (eds.) ECCV 2018. LNCS, vol. 11210, pp. 678–694. Springer, Cham (2018). https://doi.org/10.1007/978-3-030-01231-1_41
3. Chen, L., et al.: Generating realistic training images based on tonality-alignment generative adversarial networks for hand pose estimation. arXiv preprint arXiv:1811.09916 (2018)
4. Arrabales, R., Ledezma, A., Sanchis, A.: ConsScale: a pragmatic scale for measuring the level of consciousness in artificial agents. J. Conscious. Stud. **17**(3–4), 131–164 (2010)
5. Ge, L., Liang, H., Yuan, J., Thalmann, D.: Robust 3D hand pose estimation in single depth images: from single-view CNN to multi-view CNNs. In: CVPR (2016)
6. Ge, L., Liang, H., Yuan, J., Thalmann, D.: 3D convolutional neural networks for efficient and robust hand pose estimation from single depth images. In: CVPR (2017)
7. Guo, H., Wang, G., Chen, X., Zhang, C., Qiao, F., Yand, H.: Region ensemble network: improving convolutional network for hand pose estimation. ICIP (2017)
8. Ha, H., Perdoch, M., Alismail, H., So Kweon, I., Sheikh, Y.: Deltille grids for geometric camera calibration. In: CVPR (2017)
9. He, K., Zhang, X., Ren, S., Sun, J.: Deep residual learning for image recognition. In: CVPR (2016)
10. Ioffe, S., Szegedy, C.: Batch normalization: accelerating deep network training by reducing internal covariate shift. In: ICML (2015)
11. Iqbal, U., Molchanov, P., Breuel, T., Gall, J., Kautz, J.: Hand pose estimation via latent 2.5D heatmap regression. In: Ferrari, V., Hebert, M., Sminchisescu, C., Weiss, Y. (eds.) ECCV 2018. LNCS, vol. 11215, pp. 125–143. Springer, Cham (2018). https://doi.org/10.1007/978-3-030-01252-6_8
12. Kingma, D.P., Ba, J.: Adam: a method for stochastic optimization. In: ICLR (2014)
13. de La Gorce, M., Fleet, D.J., Paragios, N.: Model-based 3D hand pose estimation from monocular video. In: IEEE TPAMI (2011)
14. Li, W., et al.: Rethinking on multi-stage networks for human pose estimation. arXiv preprint arXiv:1901.00148 (2019)
15. Moon, G., Ju, Y.C., Lee, K.M.: V2V-PoseNet: voxel-to-voxel prediction network for accurate 3D hand and human pose estimation from a single depth map. In: CVPR (2018)
16. Moon, G., Ju, Y.C., Lee, K.M.: Camera distance-aware top-down approach for 3D multi-person pose estimation from a single RGB image. In: ICCV (2019)
17. Mueller, F., et al.: GANerated hands for real-time 3D hand tracking from monocular RGB. In: CVPR (2018)
18. Mueller, F., et al.: Real-time pose and shape reconstruction of two interacting hands with a single depth camera. In: ACM TOG (2019)
19. Mueller, F., Mehta, D., Sotnychenko, O., Sridhar, S., Casas, D., Theobalt, C.: Real-time hand tracking under occlusion from an egocentric RGB-D sensor. In: ICCV (2017)

20. Oikonomidis, I., Kyriazis, N., Argyros, A.A.: Tracking the articulated motion of two strongly interacting hands. In: CVPR (2012)
21. Paszke, A., et al.: Automatic differentiation in pytorch (2017)
22. Qian, C., Sun, X., Wei, Y., Tang, X., Sun, J.: Realtime and robust hand tracking from depth. In: CVPR (2014)
23. Romero, J., Tzionas, D., Black, M.J.: Embodied hands: modeling and capturing hands and bodies together. In: ACM TOG (2017)
24. Russakovsky, O., et al.: ImageNet large scale visual recognition challenge. IJCV (2015)
25. Sharp, T., et al.: Accurate, robust, and flexible real-time hand tracking. In: ACM Conference on Human Factors in Computing Systems (2015)
26. Simon, T., Joo, H., Matthews, I., Sheikh, Y.: Hand keypoint detection in single images using multiview bootstrapping. In: CVPR (2017)
27. Spurr, A., Song, J., Park, S., Hilliges, O.: Cross-modal deep variational hand pose estimation. In: CVPR (2018)
28. Sridhar, S., Mueller, F., Zollhöfer, M., Casas, D., Oulasvirta, A., Theobalt, C.: Real-time joint tracking of a hand manipulating an object from RGB-D input. In: Leibe, B., Matas, J., Sebe, N., Welling, M. (eds.) ECCV 2016. LNCS, vol. 9906, pp. 294–310. Springer, Cham (2016). https://doi.org/10.1007/978-3-319-46475-6_19
29. Sun, X., Wei, Y., Liang, S., Tang, X., Sun, J.: Cascaded hand pose regression. In: CVPR (2015)
30. Sun, X., Xiao, B., Wei, F., Liang, S., Wei, Y.: Integral human pose regression. In: Ferrari, V., Hebert, M., Sminchisescu, C., Weiss, Y. (eds.) ECCV 2018. LNCS, vol. 11210, pp. 536–553. Springer, Cham (2018). https://doi.org/10.1007/978-3-030-01231-1_33
31. Tagliasacchi, A., Schröder, M., Tkach, A., Bouaziz, S., Botsch, M., Pauly, M.: Robust articulated-ICP for real-time hand tracking. In: Computer Graphics Forum (2015)
32. Tan, M., Le, Q.V.: EfficientNet: rethinking model scaling for convolutional neural networks. In: ICML (2019)
33. Tang, D., Jin Chang, H., Tejani, A., Kim, T.K.: Latent regression forest: structured estimation of 3D articulated hand posture. In: CVPR (2014)
34. Tang, D., Taylor, J., Kohli, P., Keskin, C., Kim, T.K., Shotton, J.: Opening the black box: hierarchical sampling optimization for estimating human hand pose. In: ICCV (2015)
35. Taylor, J., et al.: Efficient and precise interactive hand tracking through joint, continuous optimization of pose and correspondences. ACM Trans. Graph. (TOG) **35**, 143 (2016)
36. Tompson, J., Stein, M., Lecun, Y., Perlin, K.: Real-time continuous pose recovery of human hands using convolutional networks. ACM TOG (2014)
37. Tzionas, D., Ballan, L., Srikantha, A., Aponte, P., Pollefeys, M., Gall, J.: Capturing hands in action using discriminative salient points and physics simulation. IJCV (2016)
38. Wan, C., Probst, T., Gool, L.V., Yao, A.: Self-supervised 3D hand pose estimation through training by fitting. In: CVPR (2019)
39. Wu, Y., Lin, J., Huang, T.S.: Analyzing and capturing articulated hand motion in image sequences. IEEE TPAMI (2005)
40. Xiong, F., et al.: A2J: anchor-to-joint regression network for 3D articulated pose estimation from a single depth image. In: ICCV (2019)
41. Yang, L., Yao, A.: Disentangling latent hands for image synthesis and pose estimation. In: CVPR (2019)

42. Yuan, S., et al.: Depth-based 3D hand pose estimation: from current achievements to future goals. In: CVPR (2018)
43. Yuan, S., Ye, Q., Garcia-Hernando, G., Kim, T.K.: The 2017 hands in the million challenge on 3D hand pose estimation. arXiv preprint arXiv:1707.02237 (2017)
44. Yuan, S., Ye, Q., Stenger, B., Jain, S., Kim, T.K.: BigHand2.2M benchmark: hand pose dataset and state of the art analysis. In: CVPR (2017)
45. Zhang, J., Jiao, J., Chen, M., Qu, L., Xu, X., Yang, Q.: 3D hand pose tracking and estimation using stereo matching. arXiv preprint arXiv:1610.07214 (2016)
46. Zimmermann, C., Brox, T.: Learning to estimate 3D hand pose from single RGB images. In: ICCV (2017)
47. Zimmermann, C., Ceylan, D., Yang, J., Russell, B., Argus, M., Brox, T.: FreiHand: a dataset for markerless capture of hand pose and shape from single RGB images. In: ICCV (2019)

Active Crowd Counting with Limited Supervision

Zhen Zhao[1], Miaojing Shi[2], Xiaoxiao Zhao[1], and Li Li[1,3(✉)]

[1] College of Electronic and Information Engineering, Tongji University,
Shanghai, China
zhenzhao0917@gmail.com, lili@tongji.edu.cn
[2] King's College London, London, UK
miaojing.shi@kcl.ac.uk
[3] Institute of Intelligent Science and Technology, Tongji University, Shanghai, China

Abstract. To learn a reliable people counter from crowd images, head center annotations are normally required. Annotating head centers is however a laborious and tedious process in dense crowds. In this paper, we present an active learning framework which enables accurate crowd counting with limited supervision: given a small labeling budget, instead of randomly selecting images to annotate, we first introduce an active labeling strategy to annotate the most informative images in the dataset and learn the counting model upon them. The process is repeated such that in every cycle we select the samples that are diverse in crowd density and dissimilar to previous selections. In the last cycle when the labeling budget is met, the large amount of unlabeled data are also utilized: a distribution classifier is introduced to align the labeled data with unlabeled data; furthermore, we propose to mix up the distribution labels and latent representations of data in the network to particularly improve the distribution alignment in-between training samples. We follow the popular density estimation pipeline for crowd counting. Extensive experiments are conducted on standard benchmarks i.e. ShanghaiTech, UCF_CC_50, MAll, TRANCOS, and DCC. By annotating limited number of images (e.g. 10% of the dataset), our method reaches levels of performance not far from the state of the art which utilize full annotations of the dataset.

1 Introduction

The task of crowd counting in computer vision is to automatically count people numbers in images/videos. With the rapid growth of world's population, crowd gathering becomes more frequent than ever. To help with crowd control and public safety, accurate crowd counting is demanded.

Z. Zhao and M. Shi—Contributed equally.

Electronic supplementary material The online version of this chapter (https:// doi.org/10.1007/978-3-030-58565-5_34) contains supplementary material, which is available to authorized users.

© Springer Nature Switzerland AG 2020
A. Vedaldi et al. (Eds.): ECCV 2020, LNCS 12365, pp. 565–581, 2020.
https://doi.org/10.1007/978-3-030-58565-5_34

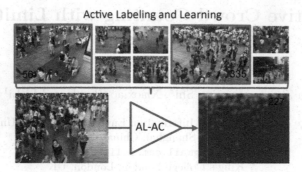

Fig. 1. Given a crowd counting dataset, we propose an active learning framework (AL-AC) which actively labels only a small proportion of the dataset and learns an accurate density estimation network using both labeled and unlabeled data.

Early methods count crowds via the detection of individuals [2,34,49]. They suffer from heavy occlusions in dense crowds. More importantly, learning such people detectors normally requires bounding box or instance mask annotations for individuals, which often makes it undesirable in large-scale applications. Modern methods mainly conduct crowd counting via density estimation [20,21,26,32,37,44,54,60]. Counting is realized by estimating a density map of an image whose integral over the image gives the total people count. Given a training image, its density map is obtained via Gaussian blurring at every head center. Head centers are the required annotations for training. Thanks to the powerful deep neural networks (DNNs) [17], density estimation based methods show a great success in recent progress [20,25,35,39,42,43,54,60].

Despite above, annotating head centers in dense crowds is still a laborious and tedious process. For instance, it can take up to 10 min for our annotators to annotate a single image with 500 persons; while the popular counting dataset ShanghaiTech PartA [60] has 300 training images with an average of 501 persons per image! To substantially reduce the annotation cost, we study the crowd density estimation in a semi-supervised setting where only handful images are labeled while the rest are unlabeled. This setting has not been largely explored in crowd counting: [4,61] propose to actively annotate the most informative video frames for semi-supervised crowd counting, yet the algorithms are not deep learning based and rely on frame consecutiveness. Recently, some deep learning works propose to leverage additional web data [23,24] or synthetic data [51] for crowd counting; images in existing dataset are still assumed annotated, or at least many of them. The model transferability is also evaluated in some works [12,54] where a network is trained on a source dataset with full annotations and tested on a target dataset with no/few annotations.

Given an existing dataset and a power DNN, we find that 1) learning from only a small subset, the performance can vary a lot depending on the subset selection; 2) for the specific subset that covers diverse crowd densities, the performance can be quite good (see results in Sect. 4.2). This motivates us to study crowd counting with very limited annotations yet producing very competitive precision. To achieve this goal, we propose an Active Learning framework for Accurate crowd Counting (AL-AC) as illustrated in Fig. 1: given a labeling budget, instead of randomly selecting images to annotate, we first introduce an active labelling strategy to iteratively annotate the most informative images in the dataset and learn the counting model on them. In each cycle we select samples that cover different crowd densities and also dissimilar to previous selections. Eventually, the large amount of unlabeled data are also included into the network training: we design a classifier with gradient reversal layer [7] to align the intrinsic distributions of labeled and unlabeled data. Since all training samples contain the same object class, e.g. person, we propose to further align distributions in-between training samples by mixing up the latent representations and distribution labels among labeled and unlabeled data in the network. With very limited labeled data, our model produces very competitive counting result.

To summarize, several new elements are offered:

- We introduce an active learning framework for accurate crowd counting with limited supervision.
- We propose a partition-based sample selection with weights (PSSW) strategy to actively select and annotate both diverse and dissimilar samples for network training.
- We design a distribution alignment branch with latent MixUp to align the distribution between the labeled data and large amount of unlabeled data in the network.

Extensive experiments are conducted on standard counting benchmarks, i.e. ShanghaiTech [60], UCF_CC_50 [13], Mall [5], TRANCOS [9], and DCC [28]. Results demonstrate that, with a small number of labeled data, our AL-AC reaches levels of performance not far from state of the art fully-supervised methods.

2   Related Works

In this section, we mainly survey deep learning based crowd counting methods and discuss semi-supervised learning and active learning in crowd counting.

2.1   Crowd Counting

The prevailed crowd counting solution is to estimate a density map of a crowd image, whose integral of the density map gives the total person count of that image [60]. A density map encodes spatial information of an image, regressing it in a DNN is demonstrated to be more robust than simply regressing a global crowd count [26,58]. Due to the commonly occurred heavy occlusions and perspective distortions in crowd images, multi-scale or multi-resolution architectures are often exploited in DNNs: Ranjan et al. [35] propose an iterative crowd counting network which produces the low-resolution density map and uses it to generate the high-resolution density map. Cao et al. [3] propose a novel encoder-decoder network, where the encoder extracts multi-scale features with scale aggregation modules and the decoder generates high-resolution density maps by using a set of transposed convolutions. Furthermore, Jiang et al. [15] develop a trellis encoder-decoder network that incorporates multiple decoding paths to hierarchically aggregate features at different encoding stages. In order to better utilize multi-scale features in the network, the attention [21,43], context [22,44], or perspective [42,55] information in crowd images is often leveraged into the network. Our work is a density estimation based approach.

2.2 Semi-supervised Learning

Semi-supervised learning [29] refers to learning with a small amount of labeled data and a large amount of unlabeled data, and has been a popular paradigm in deep learning [18,36,52,57]. It is traditionally studied for classification, where a label represents a class per image [10,18,19,36]. In this work, we focus on semi-supervised learning in crowd counting, where the label of an image means the people count, with individual head points available in most cases. The common semi-supervised crowd counting solution is to leverage both labeled and unlabeled data into the learning procedure: Tan et al. [46] propose a semi-supervised elastic net regression method by utilizing sequential information between unlabeled samples and their temporally neighboring samples as a regularization term; Loy et al. [4] further improve it by utilizing both the spatial and temporal regularization in a semi-supervised kernel ridge regression problem; finally, in [61], graph Laplacian regularization and spatiotemporal constraints are incorporated into the semi-supervised regression. All these are not deep learning works and rely on temporal information among video frames.

Recently, Olmschenk et al. [30,31] employ a generative adversarial network (GAN) in DNN to allow the usage of unlabeled data in crowd counting. Sam et al. [38] introduce an almost unsupervised learning method that only a tiny proportion of model parameters is trained with labeled data while vast parameters are trained with unlabeled data. Liu et al. [23,24] propose to learn from unlabeled crowd data via a self-supervised ranking loss in the network. In [23,24], they mainly assume the existence of a labeled dataset and add extra data from the web; in contrast, our AL-AC seeks a solution for accurate crowd counting with limited labeled data. Our method is also similar to [30,31] in spirit of the distribution alignment between labeled and unlabeled data. While in [30,31] they need to generate fake images to learn the discriminator in GAN which makes it hard to learn and converge. Our AL-AC instead mixes representations of labeled and unlabeled data in the network and learns the discriminator against them.

2.3 Active Learning

Active learning defines a strategy determining data samples that, when added to the training set, improve a previously trained model most effectively [40].

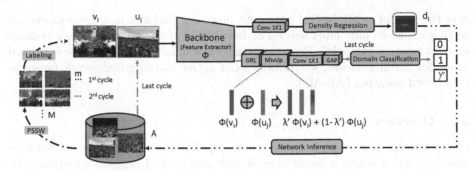

Fig. 2. Overview of our active learning framework for accurate crowd counting (AL-AC). GRL: gradient reversal layer; GAP: global average pooling. PSSW: Partition-based sample selection with weights; Conv 1×1: output channel is 1.

Although it is not possible to obtain an universally good active learning strategy [6], there exist many heuristics [41], which have been proved to be effective in practice. Active learning has been explored in many applications such as image classification [16,45] and object detection [8], while in this paper we focus on crowd counting. Methods in this context normally assumes the availability of the whole counting set and choose samples from it, which is the so-called pool-based active learning [56]. [4] and [61] employ the graph-based approach to build adjacency matrix of all crowd images in the pool, sample selection is therefore cast as a matrix partitioning problem. Our work is also pool-based active learning.

Lately, Liu et al. [23] apply active learning in DNN where they measure the informativeness of unlabeled samples via mistakes made by the network on a self-supervised proxy task. The method is conducted iteratively and in each cycle it selects a group of images based their uncertainties to the model. The diversity of selected images is however not carefully taken care in their uncertainty measure, which might result in a biased selection within some specific count range. Our work instead interprets uncertainty from two perspectives: selected samples are diverse in crowd density and dissimilar to previous selection in each learning cycle. It should also be noted that [23] mainly focuses on adding extra unlabeled data to an existing labeled dataset, while our AL-AC seeks for the limited data to be labeled within a given dataset.

3   Method

3.1   Problem

We follow *crowd density estimation* in deep learning context where density maps are pixel-wise regressed in a DNN [20,60]. A ground truth density map is generated by convolving Gaussian kernels at head centers in an image [60]. The network is optimized through a loss function minimizing the prediction error over the ground truth. In this paper, we place our problem in a *semi-supervised* setting where we only label several or few dozens of images while the rest large amount remains unlabeled. Both the labeled and unlabeled data will be exploited in model learning. Below, we introduce our active learning framework for accurate crowd counting (AL-AC).

3.2 Overview

Our algorithm follows an active learning pipeline in general. It is an iterative process where a model is learnt in each cycle and a set of samples is chosen to be labeled from a pool of unlabeled samples [41]. In classic setting, only one single sample is chosen in each cycle. This is however not feasible for DNNs because it is infeasible to train as many models as the number of samples since many practical problems of interest are very large-scale [40]. Hence, the commonly used strategy is batch mode selection [23,50] where a subset is selected and labeled in each cycle. This subset is added into the labeled set to update the model and repeat the selection in next cycle. The procedure continues until a predefined criterion is met, e.g. a fixed budget.

Our method is illustrated in Fig. 2: given a dataset $\mathcal{A}$ with labeling budget M (number of images as in [23,38]), we start by labeling m samples uniformly at random from $\mathcal{A}$. For each labeled sample v_i, we generate its count label c_i and density map d_i based on the annotated head points in v_i. We denote $\mathcal{V}^1 = \{v_i, c_i, d_i\}$ and $\mathcal{U}^1 = \{u_j\}$ as the labeled and unlabeled set in cycle 1, respectively. A DNN regressor R^1 is trained on $\mathcal{V}^1$ for crowd density estimation. Based on R^1's estimation of density maps on $\mathcal{U}^1$, we propose a partition-based sample selection with weights strategy to select and annotate m samples from $\mathcal{U}^1$. These samples are added to $\mathcal{V}^1$ so we have the updated labeled and unlabeled set $\mathcal{V}^2$ and $\mathcal{U}^2$ in 2rd cycle. Model R^1 is further trained on $\mathcal{V}^2$ and updated as R^2. The prediction of R^2 is better than R^1 as it uses more labeled data, we use the new prediction on $\mathcal{U}^2$ to again select m samples and add them to $\mathcal{V}^2$. The process moves on until the labeling budget M is met. The unlabeled set $\mathcal{U}$ is also employed in network training through our proposed distribution alignment with latent MixUp. We only use $\mathcal{U}$ ($\mathcal{U}^T$) in the last learning cycle T as we observe that adding it in every cycle does not bring us accumulative benefits but rather additional training cost.

The backbone network is not specified in Fig. 2 as it can be any standard backbone. We will detail our selection of backbone, M, m and R in Sect. 4. Below we introduce our partition-based sample selection with weights and distribution alignment with latent MixUp. Overall loss function is given in this end.

3.3 Partition-Based Sample Selection with Weights (PSSW)

In each learning cycle, we want to annotate the most informative/uncertain samples and add them to the network. The *informativeness/uncertainty* of samples is evaluated from two perspectives: *diverse* in density and *dissimilar* to previous selections. It is observed that crowd data often forms a well structured manifold where different crowd densities normally distribute smoothly within the manifold space [4]; the diversity is to select crowd samples that cover different crowd densities in the manifold. This is realized by separating the unlabeled set into different density partitions for diverse selection. Within each partition, we want to select those samples that are dissimilar to previous labeled samples, such that the model has not seen them. The dissimilarity is measured considering both local crowd density and global crowd count: we introduce a grid-based dissimilarity measure (GDSIM) for this purpose. Below, we formulate our partition-based sample selection with weights.

Formally, given the model R^t, unlabeled set $\mathcal{U}^t$ and labeled set $\mathcal{V}^t$ in t^{th} cycle, we denote by $\tilde{c}_j$ the predicted crowd count by R^t for an unlabeled image u_j. The histogram of all $\tilde{c}_j$ on $\mathcal{U}^t$ discloses the overall density distribution. For the sake of diversity, we want to partition the histogram into m parts and select one sample from each. Since the crowd counts are not evenly distributed (see Fig. 3: Left), sampling images evenly from the histogram can end up with a biased view of the original distribution. We therefore employ the Jenks natural breaks optimization [14] to partition the histogram. Jenks minimizes the variation within each range, so the partitions between ranges reflect the natural breaks of the histogram (Fig. 3).

Within each partition P_k, inspired by grid average mean absolute error (GAME) [9], we propose a grid-based dissimilarity from an unlabeled sample to labeled samples. Given an image i, GAME is originally introduced as an evaluation measure for density estimation,

$$\text{GAME}(L) = \sum_{l=1}^{4^L} |\tilde{c}_i^l - c_i^l|, \tag{1}$$

where $\tilde{c}_i^l$ is the estimated count in region l of image i. It can be obtained via the integration over the density d_i^l of that region l; c_i^l is the corresponding ground truth count. Given a specific level L, GAME(L) subdivides the image using a grid of 4^L non-overlaping regions which cover the full image (Fig. 3); the difference between the prediction and ground truth is the sum of the mean absolute error (MAE) in each of these regions. With different L, GAME indeed offers moderate ways to compute the dissimilarity between two density maps, taking care of both global counts and local details. Building on GAME, we introduce grid-based dissimilarity measure GDSIM as,

$$\text{GDSIM}(u_j, L_A) = \min_{\substack{i, v_i \in \mathcal{P}_k \\ u_j \in \mathcal{P}_k}} \left(\sum_{L=0}^{L_A} \sum_{l=1}^{4^L} |\tilde{c}_j^l - c_i^l| \right), \tag{2}$$

where u_j and v_i are from the unlabeled set $\mathcal{U}^t$ and labeled set $\mathcal{V}^t$, respectively; they both fall into the $\mathcal{P}_k$-th partition. $\tilde{c}_i^l$ and c_i^l are crowd counts in region l as in formula (1) but for different images u_j and v_i (see Fig. 3: Right). Given the level L_A, unlike GAME, we compute the dissimilarity between u_j and v_i by traversing all levels from 0 to L_A (Fig. 3). In this way, the dissimilarity is computed based

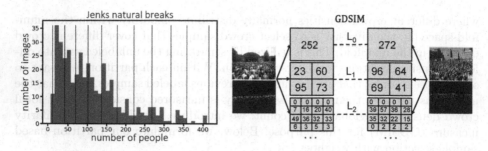

Fig. 3. Illustration of Jenks natural breaks (Left) and grid-based dissimilarity measure (GDSIM, Right). We take the histogram of crowd count on SHB.

on both global count ($L = 0$) and local density ($L = L_A$) differences. Afterwards, instead of averaging the dissimilarity scores from u_j to all the v_i in $\mathcal{P}_k$, we use min to indicate if u_j is closer to any one of the labeled images, it is regarded as a familiar sample to the model. Ideally, we should choose the most dissimilar sample from each partition; nevertheless, the crowd count $\widetilde{c}_j^l$ in formula (2) is not ground truth. We convert the GDSIM scores to probabilities and adopt weighted random selection to label one sample from each partition.

3.4   Distribution Alignment with Latent MixUp

Since labeled data only represents partial crowd manifold, particularly when they are limited, distribution alignment with large amount of unlabeled data becomes necessary even within the same domain. In order for the model to learn a proper subspace representation of the entire set, we introduce distribution alignment with latent MixUp.

We assign labeled data with distribution labels 0 while unlabeled data with labels 1. A distribution classifier branched off from the deep extractor (ϕ in Fig. 2) is designed: it is composed of a gradient reversal layer (GRL) [7], 1×1 convolution layer and global average pooling (GAP) layer. The GRL multiplies the gradient by a certain negative constant (-1 in this paper) during the network back propagation; it enforces that the feature distributions over the labeled and unlabeled data are made as indistinguishable as possible for the distribution classifier, thus aligning them together.

The hard distribution labels create hard boundaries between labeled and unlabeled data. To further merge the distributions and particularly align in-between training samples, we adapt the idea from MixUp [59]. MixUp normally trains a model on random convex combinations of raw inputs and their corresponding labels. It encourages the model to behave linearly "between" training samples, as this linear behavior reduces the amount of undesirable oscillations when predicting outside the training samples. It has been popularly employed in several semi-supervised classification works [1,47,48,59]. In this work, we integrate it into our distribution alignment branch for semi-supervised crowd counting. We find that mixing raw input images does not work for our problem. Instead we propose to mix their latent representations in the network: supposedly we have two images, x_1, x_2, and their distribution labels y_1, y_2, respectively. The latent representations of x_1 and x_2 are produced by the deep extractor ϕ as two tensors ($\phi(x_1)$ and $\phi(x_2)$) from the last convolutional layer of the backbone. We mix up ($\phi(x_1)$, y_1), ($\phi(x_2)$, y_2) with a weight λ' as

$$z' = \lambda'\phi(x_1) + (1 - \lambda')\phi(x_2)$$
$$y' = \lambda' \times y_1 + (1 - \lambda') \times y_2. \tag{3}$$

where (z', y') denotes the mixed latent representation and label. λ' is generated in the same way with [1]: $\lambda' = max(\lambda, 1 - \lambda)$, $\lambda \sim \text{Beta}(\alpha, \alpha)$; α is a hyperparameter set to 0.5. Both labeled and unlabeled data can be mixed. For two samples with the same label, their mixed label remains. We balance the number of labeled and unlabeled data with data augmentation (see Sec. 4.1) so a mixed pair can be composed of labeled or unlabeled data with (almost) the same probability. MixUp enriches the distribution in-between training samples. Together with GRL, it allows the network to elaborately knit the distributions of labeled and unlabeled data. The alignment is only carried out in the last active learning cycle as an efficient practice. The network training proceeds with a multi-task optimization that minimizes the density regression loss on labeled data and the distribution classification loss for all data including mixed ones, specified below.

3.5 Loss Function

For density regression, we adopt the commonly used pixel-wise MSE loss $\mathcal{L}_{reg}$:

$$\mathcal{L}_{reg} = \frac{1}{2K} \sum_{k=1}^{K} \|d_k^e - d_k^g\|_2^2 \tag{4}$$

d_k^e and d_k^g denote the density map prediction and ground truth of image k, respectively. K is the number of labeled images. For the distribution classification, since distribution labels for mixed samples can be non-integers, we adopt the binary cross entropy with logits loss $\mathcal{L}_{dc}$, which combines a Sigmoid layer with the binary cross entropy loss. Given an image pair, $\mathcal{L}_{dc}$ is computed on each individual as well as their mixed representations (see Fig. 2). The overall multi-task loss function is given by

$$\mathcal{L} = \mathcal{L}_{reg} + \beta\mathcal{L}_{dc} \tag{5}$$

4   Experiments

We conduct our experiments on three counting datasets: ShanghaiTech [60], UCF_CC_50 [13], Mall [5]. In the supplementary material, we offer more results not only in the three datasets for people counting, but also in the TRANCOS [9] and DCC [28] datasets for vehicle and cell counting, respectively.

Table 1. Ablation study of the proposed partition-based sample selection with weights (PSSW) strategy. Left: comparison against random selection (RS). Right: comparison to some variants of PSSW; Even Partition means evenly splitting on the histogram of crowd count; Global Diff refers to using global count difference for dissimilarity. MAE is reported on SHA and SHB.

Dataset	SHA		SHB	
Method	PSSW	RS	PSSW	RS
M= 10, m = 10	121.2 ± 9.3	121.2 ± 9.3	20.5 ± 4.8	20.5 ± 4.8
M = 20, m = 10	96.7 ± 7.3	111.5 ± 7.4	17.0 ± 1.9	19.3 ± 2.2
M = 30, m = 10	93.5 ± 2.9	102.1 ± 7.0	15.7 ± 1.5	19.9 ± 3.1
M = 40, m = 10	**85.4 ± 2.5**	**93.8 ± 5.6**	**14.6 ± 1.3**	**17.9 ± 1.9**
M = 30, m = 5	92.6 ± 3.1	102.1 ± 7.0	15.1 ± 1.5	19.9 ± 3.1
M = 40, m = 5	**84.4 ± 2.6**	**93.8 ± 5.6**	**14.4 ± 1.2**	**17.9 ± 1.9**

M = 40, m = 10	SHA	SHB
RS (Baseline)	93.8	17.9
Even partition	89.6	16.2
Global diff	86.6	15.3
PSSW	**84.4**	**14.4**

4.1   Experimental Setup

Datasets. *ShanghaiTech* [60] consists of 1,198 annotated images with a total of 330,165 people with head center annotations. This dataset is split into SHA and SHB. The average crowd counts are 123.6 and 501.4, respectively. Following [60], we use 300 images for training and 182 images for testing in SHA; 400 images for training and 316 images for testing in SHB. *UCF_CC_50* [13] has 50 images with 63,974 head center annotations in total. The head counts range between 94 and 4,543 per image. The small dataset size and large variance make this a very challenging counting dataset. We call it UCF for short. Following [13], we perform 5-fold cross validations to report the average test performance. *Mall* [5] contains 2000 frames collected in a shopping mall. Each frame on average has only 31 persons. The first 800 frames are used as the training set and the rest 1200 frames as the test set.

Implementation Details. The backbone (ϕ) design follows [20]: VGGnet with 10 convolutional and 6 dilated convolutional layers, it is pretrained on ILSVRC classification task. We follow the setting in [20] to generate ground truth density maps. To have a strong baseline, the training set is augmented by randomly cropping patches of 1/4 size of each image. We set a reference number 1200, both labeled and unlabeled data in each dataset are augmented up to this number to have a balanced distribution. For instance, if we have 30 labeled images, we need to crop 40 patches from each image to augment it to 1200. We feed the network with a minibatch of two image patches each time. In order to have the same size of two patches, we further crop them to keep the shorter width and height of the two. We set the learning rate as 1e−7, momentum 0.95 and weight decay 5e−4. We train 100 epochs with SGD optimizer for each active learning cycle and before the last cycle, the network is trained with only labeled data. In the last cycle, it is trained with both labeled and unlabeled data. In all experiments, L_A is 3 for GDSIM (2) and β is 3 for loss weight (5).

Evaluation Protocol. We evaluate the counting performance via the commonly used mean absolute error (MAE) and mean square error (MSE) [21,39,44] which measures the difference between the counts of ground truth and estimation. For active learning, we choose to label around 10% images of the entire set, which goes along with our setting of limited supervision. m is chosen not too small so that we can normally reach the labeling budget in about 2–4 active learning cycles. Sect. 5 gives a discussion on the time complexity. M and m are by default 30/40 and 10 on SHA and SHB, 10 and 3 on UCF (initial number is 4), 80 and 20 on Mall, respectively. We also evaluate different M and m to show the effectiveness of our method. The baseline is to randomly label M images and train a regression model using the same backbone with our AL-AC but without distribution alignment. As in [4,61], taken the randomness into account, we repeat each experiment with 10 trials for both mean and standard deviation, to show the improvement of our method over baseline.

4.2 ShanghaiTech

Ablation Study. The proposed partition-based sample selection with weights and distribution alignment with latent MixUp are ablated.

Labeling Budget M and m. As mentioned in Sect. 4.1, we set $M = 30/40$ and $m = 10$ by default. Comparable experiments are offered in two ways. First, keeping $m = 10$, we vary M from 10 to 40. The results are shown in Table 1. We compare our partition-based sample selection with weights (PSSW) with random selection (RS); distribution alignment is not added in this experiment. For PSSW, its MAE on SHA is gradually decreased from 121.2 with $M = 10$ to 85.4 with $M = 40$, the standard deviation is also decreased from 9.3 to 2.5. The MAE result is in general 10 points lower than RS. With different M, PSSW also produces lower MAE than RS on SHB. For example, with $M = 40$, PSSW yields an MAE of 14.6 v.s. 17.9 for RS.

Second, by keeping $M = 30/40$, we decrease m from 10 to 5 and repeat the experiment. Results show that having a small m indeed works slightly better: for instance, PSSW with $M = 30$ and $m = 5$ reduces MAE by 1.0 on SHA compared to PSSW with $M = 30$ and $m = 10$. On the other hand, m can not be too small as discussed in Sects. 3.2 and 5. In practice, we still keep $m = 10$ for both efficiency and effectiveness.

Variants of PSSW. Our PSSW has two components: the Jenks-based partition for diversity, and the GDSIM for dissimilarity (Sect. 3). In order to show the effectiveness of each, we present two variants of PSSW: Even Partition and Global Diff. Even Partition means that Jenks-based partition is replaced by evenly splitting the ranges on the histogram of crowd count while GSDIM remains; Global Diff means that GDSIM is replaced by using the global count difference to measure the dissimilarity while Jenks-based partition remains. We report MAE on SHA and SHB in Table 1: Right. It can be seen that Even Partition produces MAE 89.6 on SHA and 16.2 on SHB, while Global Diff produces 86.6 and 15.3. Both are clearly inferior to PSSW (84.4 and 14.4). This suggests the importance of the proposed diversity and dissimilarity measure.

Table 2. Ablation study of the proposed distribution alignment with latent MixUp. Left: analysis on latent MixUp (MX) and gradient reversal layer (GRL). Right: comparison against RS plus GRL and MX. MAE is reported in the right table.

Dataset	SHA		SHB	
M = 30, m = 10	MAE	MSE	MAE	MSE
PSSW	93.5 ± 2.9	151.0 ± 15.1	15.7 ± 1.5	28.3 ± 3.4
PSSW+GRL	90.8 ± 2.7	144.9 ± 14.5	14.7 ± 1.3	27.8 ± 2.9
PSSW+GRL+MX	**87.9 ± 2.3**	**139.5 ± 12.7**	**13.9 ± 1.2**	**26.2 ± 2.5**
M = 40, m = 10	MAE	MSE	MAE	MSE
PSSW	85.4 ± 2.5	144.7 ± 10.7	14.6 ± 1.3	24.6 ± 3.0
PSSW+GRL	82.7 ± 2.4	140.9 ± 11.3	13.7 ± 1.3	23.5 ± 2.2
PSSW+GRL+MX	**80.4 ± 2.4**	**138.8 ± 10.1**	**12.7 ± 1.1**	**20.4 ± 2.1**

M = 40, m = 10	SHA	SHB
RS (Baseline)	93.8	17.9
RS+GRL+MX	87.3	15.1
PSSW	84.4	14.4
PSSW+GRL+MX	**80.4**	**12.7**

Distribution Alignment with Latent MixUp. Our proposed distribution alignment with latent MixUp is composed of two elements: distribution classifer with GRL and latent MixUp (Sect. 3.4). To demonstrate their effectiveness, we present the result of PSSW plus GRL classifer (denoted as PSSW + GRL), and latent MixUp (denoted as PSSW + GRL + MX) in Table 2. We take $M = 40$ as an example, adding GRL and MX to PSSW contributes to 5.0 points MAE decrease on SHA and 1.9 points decrease on SHB. Specifically, The MX contributes to 2.3 and 1.0 points decrease on SHA and SHB, respectively. The same observation goes for MSE: by adding GRL and MX, it decreases from 144.7 to 138.8 on SHA, from 24.6 to 20.4 on SHB.

To make a further comparison, we also add the proposed distribution alignment with latent MixUp to RS in Table 2: Right, where we achieve MAE 87.3 on SHA and 15.1 on SHB. Adding GRL+MX to RS also improves the baseline: the performance difference between PSSW and RS becomes smaller; yet, the absolute value of the difference is still big, which justifies our PSSW. Notice PSSW + GRL + MX is the final version of our AL-AC hereafter.

Comparison with Fully-Supervised Methods. We compare our work with those prior arts [20,27,35,39,42,43,60]. All these approaches are fully-supervised methods which utilize annotations of the entire dataset (300 in SHA and 400 in SHB). While in our setting, we label only 30/40 images, 10% of the entire set. It can be seen that our method outperforms the representative methods [39,60] a few years ago, and are not far from other recent arts, i.e. [20,27,35,42,43]. A direct comparison to ours is CSRNet [20], we share the same backbone. With about 10% labeled data, our AL-AC retains 85% accuracy on SHA (68.2/80.4), 83% accuracy on SHB (10.6/12.7). Compared to our baseline (denoted as RS in Table 1), AL-AC in general produces significantly lower MAE, e.g. 87.9 v.s. 102.1 on SHA with $M = 30$; 17.9 v.s. 12.7 on SHB with $M = 40$.

Despite that we only label 10% data, our distribution alignment with latent MixUp indeed enables us to make use of more unlabeled data across datasets: for instance, a simple implementation with M = 40 on SHA, if we add SHB as unlabeled data to AL-AC for distribution alignment, we obtain an even lower MAE 78.6 v.s. 80.4 in Table 3.

Table 3. Comparison of AL-AC to the state of the art on SHA and SHB.

Dataset	SHA		SHB	
Measures	MAE	MSE	MAE	MSE
MCNN [60]	110.2	173.2	26.4	41.3
Switching CNN [39]	90.4	135.0	21.6	33.4
CSRNet [20]	68.2	115.0	10.6	16.0
ic-CNN [35]	68.5	116.2	10.7	16.0
PACNN [42]	**62.4**	102.0	7.6	11.8
CFF [43]	65.2	109.4	**7.2**	11.2
BAYESIAN+ [27]	62.8	**101.8**	7.7	12.7
Baseline (M = 30)	102.1	164.0	19.9	30.6
AL-AC (M = 30)	**87.9**	**139.5**	**13.9**	**26.2**
Baseline (M = 40)	93.8	150.9	17.9	27.3
AL-AC (M = 40)	**80.4**	**138.8**	**12.7**	**20.4**

Table 4. Comparison of AL-AC with state of the art on UCF.

Counting	UCF	
Measures	MAE	MSE
MCNN [60]	377.6	509.1
Switching CNN [39]	318.1	439.2
CP-CNN [44]	295.8	320.9
CSRNet [20]	266.1	397.5
ic-CNN [35]	260.0	365.5
PACNN [42]	241.7	320.7
BAYESIAN+ [27]	**229.3**	**308.2**
Baseline (M = 10, m = 3)	444.7 ± 25.9	600.3 ± 32.7
AL-AC (M = 10, m = 3)	351.4 ± 19.2	448.1 ± 24.5
Baseline (M = 20, m = 10)	417.2 ± 29.8	550.1 ± 25.5
AL-AC (M = 20, m = 10)	**318.7 ± 23.0**	**421.6 ± 24.1**

Fig. 4. Examples of AL-AC on SHA, SHB, UCF, TRANCOS, and DCC. Ground truth counts are in the original images while predicted counts in the estimated density maps.

Comparison with Semi-supervised Methods. There are also some semi-supervised crowd counting methods [23,31,38][1]. For instance in [31,38], with $M = 50$ they produce MAE 170.0 and 136.9 on SHA, respectively. These are much higher MAE than ours. Since [31,38] use different architectures from AL-AC, they are not straightforward comparisons. For [23], it uses about 50% labeled data on SHA (Fig. 7 in [23]) to reach the similar performance of our AL-AC with 10% labeled data. We both adopt the VGGnet yet [23] utilizes extra web data for ranking loss while we only use unlabeled data within SHA, we use dilated convolutions while [23] does not. To make them more comparable, we instead use the same backbone of [23] and repeat AL-AC on SHA (implementation details still follow Sect. 4.1), the mean MAE with M=30, m=10 on SHA becomes 91.4 (v.s. 87.9 in Table 3), which is still much better than that of [23].

In the supplementary material, we also provide the result by gradually increasing M till 280 on SHA, where we show that by labelling about 80–100 labeled data (nearly 30% of the dataset), AL-AC already reaches the performance close to the fully-supervised method, as in [20] (Table 3).

---

[1] Results of [23,38] can be estimated from their curve plots.

Table 5. Comparison of AL-AC with state of the art on Mall ($M = 80$, m = 20).

Mall	Baseline	AL-AC	Count Forest [33]	ConvLSTM [53]	DecideNet [21]	E3D [62]	SAAN [11]
MAE	$5.9_{\pm 0.9}$	$3.8_{\pm 0.5}$	4.4	2.1	1.5	1.6	1.3
MSE	$6.3_{\pm 1.1}$	$5.4_{\pm 0.8}$	2.4	7.6	1.9	2.1	1.7

4.3 UCF_CC_50

It has 40 training images in total. We show in Table 4 that, labeling ten of them ($M = 10, m = 3$) already produces a very competitive result: the MAE is 351.4 while the MSE is 448.1. The MAE and MSE are significantly lower (93.3 and 152.2 points) than baseline. We analyzed the result and found that our AL-AC is able to select those hard samples with thousands of persons and label them for training, while this is not guaranteed in random selection. Compared to fully supervised method, e.g. [20], our MAE is not far. We also present the result of $M = 20, m = 10$: MAE/MSE is further reduced.

4.4 Mall

Different from ShanghaiTech and UCF datasets, Mall contains images with much sparser crowds, 31 persons on average per image. Following our setup, we label 80 out of 800 images and compare our AL-AC with both baseline and other fully-supervised methods [11,21,33,53,62] in Table 5. With 10% labeled data, we achieve MAE 3.8 superior to the baseline and [33], MSE 5.4 superior to the baseline and [53]. This shows the effectiveness of our method on sparse crowds.

5 Discussion

We present an active learning framework for accurate crowd counting with limited supervision. Given a counting dataset, instead of annotating every image, we introduce a partition-based sample selection with weights to label only a few most informative images and learn a crowd regression network upon them. This process is iterated till the labeling budget is reached. Next, rather than learning from only labeled data, the abundant unlabeled data are also exploited: we introduce a distribution alignment branch with latent MixUp in the network. Experiments conducted on standard benchmarks show that labeling only 10% of the entire set, our method already performs close to recent state-of-the-art.

By choosing an appropriate m, we normally reach the labeling budget in three active learning cycles. In our setting, training data in each dataset are augmented to a fixed number. We run our experiments with GPU GTX1080. It takes around three hours to complete each active learning cycle. The total training hours are more or less the same to fully-supervised training, as in each learning cycle we train much fewer epochs with limited number of labeled data. More importantly, compared to the annotation cost for an entire dataset (see Sect. 1 for an estimation on SHA), ours is substantially reduced!

Acknowledgement. This work was supported by the National Natural Science Foundation of China (NSFC) under Grant No. 61828602 and 51475334; as well as National Key Research and Development Program of Science and Technology of China under Grant No. 2018YFB1305304, Shanghai Science and Technology Pilot Project under Grant No. 19511132100.

References

1. Berthelot, D., Carlini, N., Goodfellow, I., Papernot, N., Oliver, A., Raffel, C.: MixMatch: a holistic approach to semi-supervised learning. arXiv preprint arXiv:1905.02249 (2019)
2. Brostow, G.J., Cipolla, R.: Unsupervised Bayesian detection of independent motion in crowds. In: CVPR (2006)
3. Cao, X., Wang, Z., Zhao, Y., Su, F.: Scale aggregation network for accurate and efficient crowd counting. In: Ferrari, V., Hebert, M., Sminchisescu, C., Weiss, Y. (eds.) ECCV 2018. LNCS, vol. 11209, pp. 757–773. Springer, Cham (2018). https://doi.org/10.1007/978-3-030-01228-1_45
4. Change Loy, C., Gong, S., Xiang, T.: From semi-supervised to transfer counting of crowds. In: CVPR (2013)
5. Chen, K., Loy, C.C., Gong, S., Xiang, T.: Feature mining for localised crowd counting. In: BMVC (2012)
6. Dasgupta, S.: Analysis of a greedy active learning strategy. In: NIPS (2005)
7. Ganin, Y., Lempitsky, V.: Unsupervised domain adaptation by backpropagation. In: JMLR (2015)
8. Gonzalez-Garcia, A., Vezhnevets, A., Ferrari, V.: An active search strategy for efficient object class detection. In: CVPR (2015)
9. Guerrero-Gómez-Olmedo, R., Torre-Jiménez, B., López-Sastre, R., Maldonado-Bascón, S., Onoro-Rubio, D.: Extremely overlapping vehicle counting. In: Iberian Conference on Pattern Recognition and Image Analysis (2015)
10. Hoffer, E., Ailon, N.: Semi-supervised deep learning by metric embedding. arXiv preprint arXiv:1611.01449 (2016)
11. Hossain, M., Hosseinzadeh, M., Chanda, O., Wang, Y.: Crowd counting using scale-aware attention networks. In: WACV (2019)
12. Hossain, M.A., Kumar, M., Hosseinzadeh, M., Chanda, O., Wang, Y.: One-shot scene-specific crowd counting. In: BMVC (2019)
13. Idrees, H., Saleemi, I., Seibert, C., Shah, M.: Multi-source multi-scale counting in extremely dense crowd images. In: CVPR (2013)
14. Jenks, G.F.: The data model concept in statistical mapping. Int. Yearb. Cartography **7**, 186–190 (1967)
15. Jiang, X., Xiao, Z., Zhang, B., Zhen, X., Cao, X., Doermann, D., Shao, L.: Crowd counting and density estimation by trellis encoder-decoder networks. In: CVPR (2019)
16. Joshi, A.J., Porikli, F., Papanikolopoulos, N.: Multi-class active learning for image classification. In: CVPR (2009)
17. Krizhevsky, A., Sutskever, I., Hinton, G.E.: ImageNet classification with deep convolutional neural networks. In: NIPS (2012)
18. Laine, S., Aila, T.: Temporal ensembling for semi-supervised learning. In: ICLR (2016)
19. Lee, D.H.: Pseudo-label: the simple and efficient semi-supervised learning method for deep neural networks. In: ICMLW (2013)

20. Li, Y., Zhang, X., Chen, D.: CSRNet: dilated convolutional neural networks for understanding the highly congested scenes. In: CVPR (2018)
21. Liu, J., Gao, C., Meng, D., G. Hauptmann, A.: DecideNet: counting varying density crowds through attention guided detection and density estimation. In: CVPR (2018)
22. Liu, W., Salzmann, M., Fua, P.: Context-aware crowd counting. In: CVPR (2019)
23. Liu, X., Van De Weijer, J., Bagdanov, A.D.: Exploiting unlabeled data in CNNs by self-supervised learning to rank. IEEE Trans. Pattern Anal. Mach. Intell. **41**, 1862–1878 (2019)
24. Liu, X., Weijer, J., Bagdanov, A.D.: Leveraging unlabeled data for crowd counting by learning to rank. In: CVPR (2018)
25. Liu, Y., Shi, M., Zhao, Q., Wang, X.: Point in, box out: beyond counting persons in crowds. In: CVPR (2019)
26. Lu, Z., Shi, M., Chen, Q.: Crowd counting via scale-adaptive convolutional neural network. In: WACV (2018)
27. Ma, Z., Wei, X., Hong, X., Gong, Y.: Bayesian loss for crowd count estimation with point supervision. In: ICCV (2019)
28. Marsden, M., McGuinness, K., Little, S., Keogh, C.E., O'Connor, N.E.: People, penguins and petri dishes: adapting object counting models to new visual domains and object types without forgetting. In: CVPR (2018)
29. Olivier, C., Bernhard, S., Alexander, Z.: Semi-supervised learning. IEEE Trans. Neural Networks **20**, 542–542 (2006)
30. Olmschenk, G., Tang, H., Zhu, Z.: Crowd counting with minimal data using generative adversarial networks for multiple target regression. In: WACV (2018)
31. Olmschenk, G., Zhu, Z., Tang, H.: Generalizing semi-supervised generative adversarial networks to regression using feature contrasting. Computer Vision and Image Understanding (2019)
32. Oñoro-Rubio, D., López-Sastre, R.J.: Towards perspective-free object counting with deep learning. In: Leibe, B., Matas, J., Sebe, N., Welling, M. (eds.) ECCV 2016. LNCS, vol. 9911, pp. 615–629. Springer, Cham (2016). https://doi.org/10.1007/978-3-319-46478-7_38
33. Pham, V.Q., Kozakaya, T., Yamaguchi, O., Okada, R.: Count forest: co-voting uncertain number of targets using random forest for crowd density estimation. In: ICCV (2015)
34. Rabaud, V., Belongie, S.: Counting crowded moving objects. In: CVPR (2006)
35. Ranjan, V., Le, H., Hoai, M.: Iterative crowd counting. In: Ferrari, V., Hebert, M., Sminchisescu, C., Weiss, Y. (eds.) ECCV 2018. LNCS, vol. 11211, pp. 278–293. Springer, Cham (2018). https://doi.org/10.1007/978-3-030-01234-2_17
36. Rasmus, A., Berglund, M., Honkala, M., Valpola, H., Raiko, T.: Semi-supervised learning with ladder networks. In: NIPS (2015)
37. Sam, D.B., Babu, R.V.: Top-down feedback for crowd counting convolutional neural network. In: AAAI (2018)
38. Sam, D.B., Sajjan, N.N., Maurya, H., Babu, R.V.: Almost unsupervised learning for dense crowd counting. In: AAAI (2019)
39. Sam, D.B., Surya, S., Babu, R.V.: Switching convolutional neural network for crowd counting. In: CVPR (2017)
40. Sener, O., Savarese, S.: Active learning for convolutional neural networks: a core-set approach. In: ICLR (2018)
41. Settles, B.: Active learning literature survey. Technical report, University of Wisconsin-Madison Department of Computer Sciences (2009)

42. Shi, M., Yang, Z., Xu, C., Chen, Q.: Revisiting perspective information for efficient crowd counting. In: CVPR (2019)

43. Shi, Z., Mettes, P., Snoek, C.G.: Counting with focus for free. In: ICCV (2019)

44. Sindagi, V.A., Patel, V.M.: Generating high-quality crowd density maps using contextual pyramid CNNs. In: ICCV (2017)

45. Sinha, S., Ebrahimi, S., Darrell, T.: Variational adversarial active learning. In: ICCV (2019)

46. Tan, B., Zhang, J., Wang, L.: Semi-supervised elastic net for pedestrian counting. Pattern Recogn. 44(10–11), 2297–2304 (2011)

47. Verma, V., et al.: Manifold mixup: better representations by interpolating hidden states. In: ICML (2019)

48. Verma, V., Lamb, A., Kannala, J., Bengio, Y., Lopez-Paz, D.: Interpolation consistency training for semi-supervised learning. arXiv preprint arXiv:1903.03825 (2019)

49. Viola, P., Jones, M.J., Snow, D.: Detecting pedestrians using patterns of motion and appearance. IJCV 63(2), 153–161 (2003)

50. Wang, K., Zhang, D., Li, Y., Zhang, R., Lin, L.: Cost-effective active learning for deep image classification. IEEE Trans. Circuits Syst. Video Technol. 27(12), 2591–2600 (2016)

51. Wang, Q., Gao, J., Lin, W., Yuan, Y.: Learning from synthetic data for crowd counting in the wild. In: CVPR (2019)

52. Weston, J., Ratle, F., Mobahi, H., Collobert, R.: Deep learning via semi-supervised embedding. In: Montavon, G., Orr, G.B., Müller, K.-R. (eds.) Neural Networks: Tricks of the Trade. LNCS, vol. 7700, pp. 639–655. Springer, Heidelberg (2012). https://doi.org/10.1007/978-3-642-35289-8_34

53. Xiong, F., Shi, X., Yeung, D.Y.: Spatiotemporal modeling for crowd counting in videos. In: ICCV (2017)

54. Xu, C., Qiu, K., Fu, J., Bai, S., Xu, Y., Bai, X.: Learn to scale: Generating multipolar normalized density map for crowd counting. In: ICCV (2019)

55. Yan, Z., Yuan, Y., Zuo, W., Tan, X., Wang, Y., Wen, S., Ding, E.: Perspective-guided convolution networks for crowd counting. In: ICCV (2019)

56. Yang, Y., Ma, Z., Nie, F., Chang, X., Hauptmann, A.G.: Multi-class active learning by uncertainty sampling with diversity maximization. Int. J. Comput. Vision 113(2), 113–127 (2015)

57. Yang, Z., Shi, M., Avrithis, Y., Xu, C., Ferrari, V.: Training object detectors from few weakly-labeled and many unlabeled images. arXiv preprint arXiv:1912.00384 (2019)

58. Zhang, C., Li, H., Wang, X., Yang, X.: Cross-scene crowd counting via deep convolutional neural networks. In: CVPR (2015)

59. Zhang, H., Cisse, M., Dauphin, Y.N., Lopez-Paz, D.: Mixup: beyond empirical risk minimization. In: ICLR (2018)

60. Zhang, Y., Zhou, D., Chen, S., Gao, S., Ma, Y.: Single-image crowd counting via multi-column convolutional neural network. In: CVPR (2016)

61. Zhou, Q., Zhang, J., Che, L., Shan, H., Wang, J.Z.: Crowd counting with limited labeling through submodular frame selection. IEEE Trans. Intell. Transp. Syst. 20(5), 1728–1738 (2018)

62. Zou, Z., Shao, H., Qu, X., Wei, W., Zhou, P.: Enhanced 3D convolutional networks for crowd counting. In: BMVC (2019)

Self-supervised Monocular Depth Estimation: Solving the Dynamic Object Problem by Semantic Guidance

Marvin Klingner[✉], Jan-Aike Termöhlen, Jonas Mikolajczyk,
and Tim Fingscheidt

Technische Universität Braunschweig, Braunschweig, Germany
{m.klingner,j.termoehlen,j.mikolajczykt.fingscheidt}@tu-bs.de

Abstract. Self-supervised monocular depth estimation presents a powerful method to obtain 3D scene information from single camera images, which is trainable on arbitrary image sequences without requiring depth labels, e.g., from a LiDAR sensor. In this work we present a new self-supervised semantically-guided depth estimation (SGDepth) method to deal with moving dynamic-class (DC) objects, such as moving cars and pedestrians, which violate the static-world assumptions typically made during training of such models. Specifically, we propose (i) mutually beneficial cross-domain training of (supervised) semantic segmentation and self-supervised depth estimation with task-specific network heads, (ii) a semantic masking scheme providing guidance to prevent moving DC objects from contaminating the photometric loss, and (iii) a detection method for frames with non-moving DC objects, from which the depth of DC objects can be learned. We demonstrate the performance of our method on several benchmarks, in particular on the Eigen split, where we exceed all baselines without test-time refinement.

1 Introduction

The accurate estimation of depth information from a scene is essential for applications requiring a 3D environment model such as autonomous driving or virtual reality. Therefore, a long-standing research field of computer vision is the prediction of depth maps from camera images. Classical model-based algorithms can predict depth from stereo images [26] or from image sequences (videos) [1], limited by the quality of the model. Deep learning enables the prediction of depth from single monocular images by supervision from LiDAR or RGB-D camera measurements [11,12,14]. More recently, self-supervised approaches [16,18] were introduced which solely rely on geometric image projection models and optimize the depth by minimizing photometric errors without the need of any labels. While these self-supervised monocular depth estimation approaches

Electronic supplementary material The online version of this chapter (https://doi.org/10.1007/978-3-030-58565-5_35) contains supplementary material, which is available to authorized users.

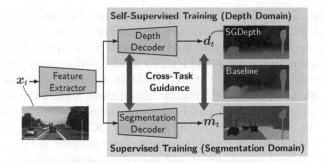

Fig. 1. Overview over our framework for the combined prediction of semantic segmentation m_t and depth d_t from a single image x_t at time instant t. By combining **supervised training of semantic segmentation** in a source domain with **self-supervised training of depth** in a target domain, the segmentation masks guide the self-supervised monocular depth estimation inside the target domain.

require only a single image as input during inference, they rely either on stereo images [16], or on sequential images from a video [71] during training.

For self-supervised monocular depth estimation from video data, the assumptions made during the geometric projections (which are required to calculate the photometric error) impose several problems: Firstly, occlusions can occur inducing artifacts in the photometric error. Secondly, consecutive more or less identical frames caused by a lack of ego-motion present a problem as without any movement between the frames no structure can be inferred. Thirdly, moving dynamic-class (DC) objects such as cars, trucks and pedestrians violate the static world assumption. Early approaches [38,71] did not address these problems. A current state-of-the-art approach by Godard et al. [20] approaches the first two problems by a minimum reprojection loss and an auto-masking technique, which we adopt (same as [5,23,24]). The third problem was left open in [5,20,23,24].

Starting to approach this dynamic object problem, we first need to identify dynamic-class (DC) objects pixel-wise by incorporating an image segmentation technique. For this purpose previous approaches either rely on pre-trained segmentation networks [5,6,24,39], which are not available for arbitrary datasets, or an implicit binary segmentation trained as part of the image projection model [37,49,63], thereby coupled and limited to the projection quality. Our solution is somewhat related to Chen et al. [7]: We jointly optimize depth estimation and semantic segmentation, still keeping the depth estimation self-supervised by training the supervised semantic segmentation in a different domain (Fig. 1). However, as [7] is limited to training on stereo images and proposes a unified decoder head for both tasks, we transfer it to the *monocular* case and utilize gradient scaling described by [15] to enable cross-domain training with *task-specific decoder heads*. This yields optimally learned task-specific weights inside the respective decoders and the *possibility to generalize the concept* to even more tasks.

While we expect the depth estimation to take profit from sharper edges at object boundaries provided by semantic segmentation, the DC objects have to be handled once identified by the segmentation. In contrast to most other approaches [5,37,39,49,63], we do not extend the image projection model to include DC objects, but simply exclude the pixels belonging to DC objects from the loss. However, this alone would lead to a poor performance, as the depth of DC objects would not be learned at all. Therefore, we propose a detection method for frames with *non-moving* DC objects. From these frames the depth of (non-moving) DC objects can be learned with the normal (valid) image projection model, while in the other frames, the (moving) DC objects are excluded from the loss. Here, our approach presents a significantly simpler, yet powerful method to handle DC objects in self-supervised monocular depth estimation.

To sum up, our contribution to the field is threefold. Firstly, we generalize the mutually beneficial cross-domain training of self-supervised depth estimation and supervised semantic segmentation to a more general setting with task-specific network heads. Secondly, we introduce a solution to the dynamic object problem by using a novel semantically-masked photometric loss. Thirdly, we introduce a novel method of detecting *moving* DC objects, which can then be excluded from the training loss computation, while *non-moving* DC objects should still contribute. We demonstrate the effectiveness of our approach on the KITTI Eigen split, where we exceed all baselines without test-time refinement, as well as on two further KITTI benchmarks.[1]

2   Related Work

Here, we give an overview about current methods for self-supervised depth estimation trained on sequential images. Afterwards we review how the dynamic object problem has been approached in multi-task learning settings.

Depth Estimation: Before the emergence of neural networks, stereo algorithms [26,52] and structure from motion [1,48] were used to infer depth from stereo image pairs or a series of images, respectively. Employing neural networks, Eigen et al. [12] introduced the estimation of depth from a single image by training a network on sparse labels provided by LiDAR scans. Rapidly, the idea was further developed to improved architectures [11,32] and training techniques [31, 34]. Nowadays, many benchmarks [40,56] in depth estimation are dominated by algorithms based on neural networks [14,66].

Self-supervised Depth Estimation: More recently, self-supervised monocular depth estimation was proposed modeling depth as the geometric property of an image projection transformation between stereo image pairs [16,18], thereby optimizing a network based on the photometric error between the projected image and the actual image. Following, Zhou et al. [71] showed that it is possible to jointly optimize networks for the simultaneous prediction of depth and relative pose between two video frames. Since then this idea was complemented by improved loss functions [2,38], specialized network architectures [23,58,70], a hybrid approach utilizing video and stereo data [65], and refinement strategies

---

[1] Code is available at https://github.com/ifnspaml/SGDepth.

[5,6] to optimize the network or the prediction at test time. A state-of-the-art algorithm is presented by Godard et al. [20], who propose a minimum repro-jection loss to handle occlusions between different frames. For general image data it was proposed to additionally learn camera calibration parameters [22] or utilize additional depth labels from synthetic data [4]. Other approaches employ teacher-student learning [45], Generative Adversarial Networks (GANs) [2,10,46], proxy labels from traditional stereo algorithms [54], or recurrent neu-ral networks [59,67]. However, as the used geometric projection relies on the assumption of a static world, current stand-alone algorithms for self-supervised monocular depth estimation trained on video are still not able to robustly handle moving DC objects.

Multi-task Learning: Multi-task learning has shown improvements in many research fields, e.g., domain adaptation [3,41,69], depth estimation [11,47,68] and semantic segmentation [28,30]. Yang et al. [62] incorporated a semantic seg-mentation cue into the self-supervised depth estimation with stereo images as input, thus computing the cross-entropy loss between the predicted and respec-tively warped segmentation output scores of a network and corresponding ground truth labels. Chen et al. [7] further develop this idea to single images at infer-ence (still training on stereo images), and also compute losses between output scores of two stereo frames to supplement the photometric error, while supervis-ing the semantic segmentation in another domain. However, their approach relies on a unified decoder structure for both tasks, whereas our approach generalizes cross-domain training to separate decoder heads and thereby better task-specific learned weights through the application of gradient scaling from [15]. Also we train on image sequences while [7] trains on stereo image pairs.

Handling Dynamic-Class (DC) Objects: In the following, we review other approaches to the dynamic object problem in self-supervised monocular depth estimation. Most existing works follow the classical way in considering optical flow, which can also be predicted in an unsupervised fashion [36,50]. By simul-taneously predicting optical flow and depth, existing works impose losses for cross-task consistency [35,37,60,63], geometric constraints [8,49], and modified reconstruction of the warped image [8,64], all approaches extending the image projection model to moving DC objects. For example, Yang et al. [63] predict a binary segmentation mask to identify moving DC objects and design loss func-tions for rigid and dynamic motion separately.

Our method is also related to approaches that rely on state-of-the-art seg-mentation techniques [5,6,39,55,57], which either give these as an additional input to the network [39] or use it to predict the relative pose between the same DC object in two consecutive frames [5,6,57], using this information to apply an additional separate rigid transformation for each DC object. Note, that all dis-cussed related approaches add complexity to the geometric projection model in order to handle moving DC objects whereas our approach simply excludes DC objects from the loss, utilizing segmentation masks which are simultaneously and independently optimized by supervision from another domain. Finally, Li et al. [33] propose to design a *dataset* that consists solely of non-moving DC

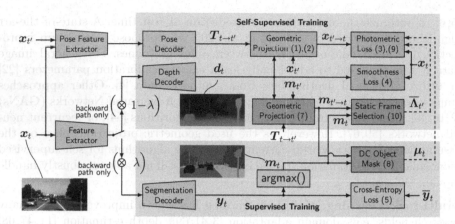

Fig. 2. Overview over our **proposed framework** for **joint prediction of depth and semantic segmentation**. The grey blocks correspond to neural networks, the blue blocks correspond to the plain self-supervised depth estimation, the orange blocks correspond to the plain supervised semantic segmentation, and the red blocks correspond to semantic cross-task guidance between the two tasks. The numbers inside the blocks refer to the corresponding equations.

objects. Our method differs as we provide a *detection method* for frames containing non-moving DC objects, from which the depth of DC objects can indeed be learned.

3   Method

In this part we will describe our framework (Fig. 2). We first describe both predicted tasks independently. Afterwards we define our approach for solving the dynamic object problem by multi-task learning across domains and our novel semantic masking technique.

3.1   Self-supervised Monocular Depth Estimation

Self-supervised monocular depth estimation defines the task of assigning depth values to camera image pixels without using any ground truth labels. Instead, the predicted depth is used as a geometric property to warp the frame at discrete time instance $t+1$ to the previous frame at time t with the photometric error between projected image and target image as the optimization objective.

Inference Setting: During inference, the neural network takes only a single RGB image $\boldsymbol{x}_t \in \mathbb{G}^{H \times W \times C}$ as input, where $\mathbb{G}$ is defined as the set of gray values $\mathbb{G} = \{0, 1, ..., 255\}$ of an image and H, W, and $C = 3$ define the height, the width, and the number of color channels, respectively. The output of the neural network is a dense depth map $\boldsymbol{d}_t \in \mathbb{D}^{H \times W}$ which assigns a depth to each pixel.

The interval of possible depth values $\mathbb{D} = [d_{\min}, d_{\max}]$ is defined by a lower bound $d_{\min}$ and an upper bound $d_{\max}$.

Training Setting: During training, the network utilizes preceding and succeeding frames $x_{t'}$, with $t' \in \mathcal{T}' = \{t{-}1, t{+}1\}$, which are warped into the current frame at time t. This geometric transformation requires knowledge of the intrinsic camera parameter matrix $K \in \mathbb{R}^{3 \times 3}$, which we assume to be constant throughout one dataset and known in advance as in [20]. Additionally, we require the prediction of the two relative poses $T_{t \to t'} \in SE(3)$ between x_t and $x_{t'}$, $t' \in \mathcal{T}'$, performed by the pose decoder in Fig. 2. The special Euclidean group $SE(3)$ defines the set of all possible rotations and translations [53]. While any such transformation is usually represented by a 4×4 matrix $T_{t \to t'}$, we follow [71] in predicting only the six degrees of freedom. To predict the warped images $x_{t' \to t}$, the image pixel coordinates $u_t \in \mathcal{U}^{H \times W} = \left\{ (h, w, 1)^{\mathrm{T}} \mid h \in \{0, ..., H{-}1\}, w \in \{0, ..., W{-}1\} \right\}$ are transformed to the pixel coordinate system at time t', yielding coordinates $u_{t \to t'}$, where $(\cdot)^{\mathrm{T}}$ denotes the vector transpose. Here, $\mathcal{U}^{H \times W}$ defines the set of pixel positions inside the image. For a single pixel coordinate $u_{t,i} = (h_i, w_i, 1)^{\mathrm{T}} \in \mathcal{U}$ with corresponding depth $d_{t,i} \in \mathcal{D}$ and $i \in \mathcal{I} = \{1, ..., HW\}$, the transformation can be written as [8]

$$
u_{t \to t', i} = \underbrace{[K|0]\, T_{t \to t'}}_{\substack{\text{transformation} \\ \text{to frame } t'}} \underbrace{\left[\begin{pmatrix} d_{t,i} K^{-1} u_{t,i} \\ 1 \end{pmatrix} \right]}_{\substack{\text{projection to} \\ \text{3D point cloud}}}, \tag{1}
$$

with 0 being a three-dimensional zero vector. From right to left, the three parts can be interpreted as follows: First, the pixel with coordinate $u_{t,i} \in \mathcal{U}$ is projected to the 3D space, afterwards the coordinate system is shifted by the relative pose $T_{t \to t'}$, and finally the pixel is reprojected to the image at time $t' \in \mathcal{T}'$. We apply bilinear sampling bil() [27] to assign gray values to each pixel coordinate, as the projected coordinates $u_{t \to t'}$ do not coincide with the pixel coordinates $u_{t'} \in \mathcal{U}^{H \times W}$. In conclusion, the two warped images $x_{t' \to t}$ are calculated as:

$$
x_{t' \to t} = \mathrm{bil}\left(x_{t'}, u_{t \to t'}, u_{t'} \right), t' \in \mathcal{T}'. \tag{2}
$$

Minimum Reprojection Loss: We follow common practice in choosing a mixture of absolute difference and structural similarity (SSIM) difference [61] to compute the photometric loss J_t^{ph} between x_t and both $x_{t' \to t}$, $t' \in \mathcal{T}'$, with a weighting factor $\alpha = 0.85$ as in [5,38,64]. Adopting the *per-pixel minimum* photometric loss [20], we get

$$
J_t^{\mathrm{ph}} = \left\langle \min_{t' \in \mathcal{T}'} \left(\frac{\alpha}{2} \left(1 - \mathbf{SSIM}\left(x_t, x_{t' \to t} \right) \right) + (1 - \alpha) \left| x_t - x_{t' \to t} \right| \right) \right\rangle, \tag{3}
$$

with 1 being a $H \times W$ matrix containing only ones, $\min(\cdot)$ of a matrix applying individually to each element (pixel position), $|\cdot|$ of a matrix delivering a matrix

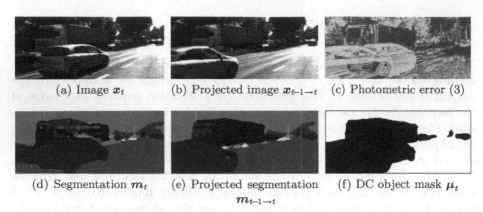

(a) Image $\boldsymbol{x}_t$ (b) Projected image $\boldsymbol{x}_{t-1 \to t}$ (c) Photometric error (3)

(d) Segmentation $\boldsymbol{m}_t$ (e) Projected segmentation   (f) DC object mask $\boldsymbol{\mu}_t$
$\boldsymbol{m}_{t-1 \to t}$

Fig. 3. Example on how **moving DC objects can contaminate the photometric error**. Due to the movement of the car, the projected view in (b) is not valid, leading to unfavorable contributions for the photometric loss from (3) as depicted in (c). This is addressed by masking the regions with potentially moving DC objects by calculating the DC object mask $\boldsymbol{\mu}_t$ (f) as in (8) from the segmentation masks (d) and (e).

with its absolute elements, and $\langle \cdot \rangle$ representing the mean over all pixels. Note that $\mathbf{SSIM}(\cdot) \in \mathbb{I}^{H \times W}, \mathbb{I} = [0, 1]$, is calculated on 3×3 patches of the image.

Smoothness Loss: Encouraging pixels at nearby positions to have similar depths, we adapt the smoothness loss J^{sm} [18,20] on the mean-normalized inverse depth $\overline{\boldsymbol{\rho}}_t \in \mathbb{R}^{H \times W}$, which is pixel-wise defined by $\rho_{t,i} = \frac{1}{d_{t,i}}$, and $\overline{\boldsymbol{\rho}}_t = \frac{\rho_t}{\langle \rho_t \rangle}$. The loss function is defined by

$$J_t^{\mathrm{sm}} = \langle |\partial_h \overline{\boldsymbol{\rho}}_t| \exp\left(-|\partial_h \boldsymbol{x}_t|\right) + |\partial_w \overline{\boldsymbol{\rho}}_t| \exp\left(-|\partial_w \boldsymbol{x}_t|\right) \rangle, \tag{4}$$

where ∂_h and ∂_w signify the one-dimensional difference quotient at each pixel position $\boldsymbol{u}_{t,i} \in \mathcal{U}$ with respect to the height and width direction of the image, respectively.[2] The smoothness loss allows large differences in depth only in regions with large differences between the gray values.

3.2   Supervised Semantic Segmentation

The task of semantic segmentation is defined as assigning a label $m_{t,i} \in \mathcal{S}$ from a set of classes $\mathcal{S} = \{1, 2, ..., S\}$ to each pixel $\boldsymbol{x}_{t,i}$, which is achieved by a neural network that implements a non-linear mapping between the input image and output scores $\boldsymbol{y}_t \in \mathbb{I}^{H \times W \times S}$ for each pixel index i and class $s \in \mathcal{S}$. Each element $y_{t,i,s}$ of the output scores $\boldsymbol{y}_t$ can be thought of as a posterior probability that the pixel $\boldsymbol{x}_{t,i}$ belongs to the class s. A segmentation mask $\boldsymbol{m}_t \in \mathcal{S}^{H \times W}$ can be obtained by computing $m_{t,i} = \mathrm{argmax}_{s \in \mathcal{S}} \, y_{t,i,s}$ and thus assigning a class to each

---

[2] As an example, $\partial_w \overline{\rho}_{t,i} = \overline{\rho}_{t,i+1} - \overline{\rho}_{t,i}$, under the condition that pixel index $i+1$ is in the same image row as i.

pixel. The network is trained by imposing a weighted cross-entropy loss between the posterior probabilities of the network y_t and the ground truth labels $\overline{y}_t$ with class weights w_s [43]. Finally, again averaging over all pixels, the loss function for the image's posterior probabilities $y_{t,s} \in \mathbb{I}^{H \times W}$ of class s is defined as

$$J_t^{ce} = - \left\langle \sum_{s \in \mathcal{S}} w_s \overline{y}_{t,s} \odot \log (y_{t,s}) \right\rangle, \tag{5}$$

with $\log(\cdot)$ applied to each element of $\overline{y}_{t,s}$, and $\odot$ standing for the element-wise multiplication between two matrices.

3.3 Semantic Guidance

Now we describe our method to complement the depth estimation by a semantic masking strategy, which aims at resolving the problem of moving DC objects.

Multi-task Training Across Domains: We employ a single encoder with two decoder heads, one for the depth and one for the segmentation (see Fig. 2). The decoder for the segmentation is trained in a source domain supervised by $\overline{y}_{t,s}$, using (5), while the decoder for the depth is trained in a target domain under self-supervision according to (3) and (4). However, for mini-batches containing data from two domains, the question arises how to propagate the gradients from the separate decoders into the shared encoder. Other approaches weigh the loss functions by a factor [38,71] inducing the downside that the gradients inside the decoders are also scaled. Instead, we choose to follow [15] in scaling the gradients when they reach the encoder, see Fig. 2. Let g^{depth} and g^{seg} be the gradients which are calculated according to the two decoders, then the total gradient g^{total} propagated back to the encoder is calculated by:

$$g^{total} = (1 - \lambda) g^{depth} + \lambda g^{seg}. \tag{6}$$

Masking Out All DC Objects: Motivated by the fact that moving DC objects contaminate the photometric error as shown in Fig. 3(c), we want to mask out all DC objects that are present in the current frame x_t (Fig. 3(a)), as well as the wrongfully projected DC objects inside both projected frames $x_{t' \to t}$, $t' \in \mathcal{T}'$, (Fig. 3(b)). Accordingly, we need to calculate both projected semantic masks $m_{t' \to t}$, $t' \in \mathcal{T}'$, (Fig. 3(e)). To this end we apply nearest-neighbor sampling near $(\cdot)$, where the interpolation strategy for the calculation of all pixels $x_{t' \to t,i}$ from the bilinear sampling bil $(\cdot)$ of [27] is replaced by assigning the value of the closest pixel inside of $m_{t'}$ to the pixels of $m_{t' \to t,i}$, $i \in \mathcal{I}$. Consequently, the projected semantic mask can be calculated as:

$$m_{t' \to t} = \text{near} (m_{t'}, u_{t \to t'}, u_{t'}). \tag{7}$$

By defining DC object classes $\mathcal{S}_{DC} \subset \mathcal{S}$, the DC object mask $\mu_t \in \{0, 1\}^{H \times W}$ is defined by its pixel elements:

$$\mu_{t,i} = \begin{cases} 1, & m_{t,i} \notin \mathcal{S}_{DC} \wedge m_{t' \to t,i} \notin \mathcal{S}_{DC} \mid t' \in \mathcal{T}' \\ 0, & \text{else.} \end{cases} \tag{8}$$

The mask contains 0 at each pixel position i belonging to a DC object in one of the three frames, and 1 otherwise. Having obtained the DC object mask $\boldsymbol{\mu}_t$, we can define a semantically-masked photometric loss adapting (3)

$$J_t^{\text{phm}} = \left\langle \boldsymbol{\mu}_t \odot \min_{t' \in \mathcal{T}'} \left(\frac{\alpha}{2} \left(1 - \text{SSIM}\left(\boldsymbol{x}_t, \boldsymbol{x}_{t' \to t} \right) \right) + (1 - \alpha) \left| \boldsymbol{x}_t - \boldsymbol{x}_{t' \to t} \right| \right) \right\rangle, \quad (9)$$

which only considers non-DC pixels. We also consider the mask from the auto-masking technique [20, 23, 24], which is omitted in (3) and (9) for simplicity.

Detecting Non-moving DC Objects: Inspired by [33], we do not want to exclude the DC objects completely, instead we only learn from them, when they are not in motion. Accordingly, we need a measure to decide whether a DC object is in motion or not. The idea is based on the fact that if a DC object was observed to be in motion, the warped semantic mask in the target image $\boldsymbol{m}_{t' \to t}$ has a low consistency with the semantic mask $\boldsymbol{m}_t$ inside the target image, as shown in Fig. 4. Accordingly, we can measure the intersection over union for dynamic object classes between $\boldsymbol{m}_{t' \to t}$ and $\boldsymbol{m}_t$ by:

$$\Lambda_{t,t'} = \frac{\sum_{i \in \mathcal{I}} \kappa_{t,t',i}}{\sum_{i \in \mathcal{I}} \nu_{t,t',i}}, \text{ with } \quad \kappa_{t,t',i} = \begin{cases} 1, & m_{t,i} \in \mathcal{S}_{\text{DC}} \ \wedge \ m_{t' \to t,i} \in \mathcal{S}_{\text{DC}} \\ 0, & \text{else}, \end{cases} \quad (10)$$

$$\nu_{t,t',i} = \begin{cases} 1, & m_{t,i} \in \mathcal{S}_{\text{DC}} \ \vee \ m_{t' \to t,i} \in \mathcal{S}_{\text{DC}} \\ 0, & \text{else}. \end{cases}$$

The indicator $\Lambda_{t,t'} \in [0, 1]$ signals perfect alignment and no moving DC objects if it equals 1, while a value of 0 indicates a high share of moving DC objects. If two frames at times $t' \in \mathcal{T}' = \{t-1, t+1\}$ are considered, the mean value $\overline{\Lambda}_t$ of all $\Lambda_{t,t'}$ is to be taken. We define the threshold $\theta_\Lambda \in [0, 1]$, above which an image is considered as static, see Fig. 4.

Learning from Non-moving DC Objects: Having a measure that can indicate after each epoch whether an image is static or dynamic, we calculate $\overline{\Lambda}_t$ for each image of the dataset and choose the threshold θ_Λ such that a fraction $\epsilon \in [0, 1]$ of the images is trained without the semantically-masked photometric loss. The final loss is a combination of the photometric losses (9) and (3), the smoothness loss (4), and the cross-entropy loss (5), given by:

$$J_t^{\text{total}} = J_t^{\text{ce}} + \beta J_t^{\text{sm}} + \begin{cases} J_t^{\text{phm}}, & \overline{\Lambda}_t < \theta_\Lambda \\ J_t^{\text{ph}}, & \text{else}. \end{cases} \quad (11)$$

Note that J_t^{ph}, J_t^{phm} and J_t^{sm} are computed only on images used for training of the depth, while J_t^{ce} is only computed in the domain of the segmentation, see Fig. 2. Also note that in (11) the segmentation and depth losses are not weighted against each other, as this weighting takes place in the midst of the backward pass guided by (6).

Target image

Projected image

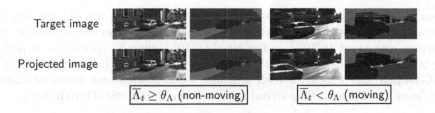

$\overline{\Lambda}_t \geq \theta_\Lambda$ (non-moving) $\overline{\Lambda}_t < \theta_\Lambda$ (moving)

Fig. 4. Concept of the threshold θ_Λ **in** (11). For non-moving DC objects, target and projected segmentation mask are very similar (left), while they differ a lot for moving DC objects (right).

4   Experimental Setup

In this section we describe the network topological aspects followed by the training details of our `PyTorch` [44] implementation. Afterwards, we describe the datasets and metrics used throughout our experimental evaluation.

Network Topology: Our topology is based on [20], where an encoder-decoder architecture with skip connections is employed. To ensure comparability to existing work [5,20,24,58], we choose an `Imagenet` [51] pretrained `ResNet18` encoder [25]. The depth head has a sigmoid output $\sigma_{t,i}$, which is converted to a depth map by $\frac{1}{a\sigma_{t,i}+b}$, where a and b constrain the depth values to the range $[0.1, 100]$. For simplicity, the segmentation decoder uses the same architecture as the depth decoder, except for the last layer having S feature maps, whose elements are converted to class probabilities by a softmax function. The pose network's architecture is the same as in [20].

Training Aspects: For the training of the depth estimation, we resize all images to a resolution of 640×192 (416×128 and 1280×384 are also evaluated), if not mentioned otherwise, while for the semantic segmentation, the images are randomly cropped to the same resolution. We adopt the zero-mean normalization for the RGB images used during training of the `ResNet` encoder. For input images we use augmentations including horizontal flipping, random brightness (± 0.2), contrast (± 0.2), saturation (± 0.2) and hue (± 0.1), while the photometric losses (3, 9) are calculated on images without color augmentations. We compute the loss on four scales as in [20].

We apply the gradient scaling from (6) at all connections between encoder and decoder with an empirically found optimal scale factor of $\lambda = 0.1$. The fraction ϵ of images, whose photometric loss is *not masked* according to (9) is set to 0 after 30 epochs and increased linearly, such that inside the last epoch the loss is calculated only according to (3). This follows the idea that after removing the DC objects completely from the loss, the network is encouraged to learn from the frames with non-moving DC objects. We define DC object classes $\mathcal{S}_{\mathrm{DC}}$ as all classes belonging to the human and vehicle categories [9] (cf. Supp. A.2).

We train our models for 40 epochs with the Adam [29] optimizer and batch sizes of 12 and 6 for the single- and multi-task models, respectively. The batches from the two task-specific datasets are first concatenated, passed through the encoder, then disconnected and passed through the respective decoders. The learning rate is set to 10^{-4} and reduced to 10^{-5} after 30 epochs, as in [20]. If we train only the depth estimation (with the architecture from [20]), we dub it "**SGDepth** only depth", if both semantic segmentation and depth estimation are being trained according to our approach, we dub it "**SGDepth** full".

Databases: We always utilize one dataset to train the semantic segmentation and another one for self-supervised training of the depth estimation of our SGDepth model. For training the semantic segmentation we utilize the *Cityscapes* dataset [9] while at the same time we use different subsets of the KITTI dataset [17] for training the depth estimation. Similar to other state-of-the-art approaches we compare our depth estimation results by training and evaluating on the *Eigen split* [12] of the KITTI dataset, following [71] in removing static scenes from the training subset. We also train and evaluate on the single image depth prediction *Benchmark split* from KITTI [56]. To evaluate the joint prediction of depth and segmentation we utilize the *KITTI split* defined by [18] whose test set is the official training set of the KITTI Stereo 2015 dataset [40]. The number of training images deviates slightly from the original definitions, as we need a preceding and a succeeding image *to train* the depth estimation. The sizes of all data subsets are given in Table 4 of the appendix.

Evaluation Metrics: To evaluate the depth estimation we follow other works [38,71] in computing four error metrics between predicted and ground truth depth as defined in [12], namely the absolute relative error (Abs Rel), the squared relative error (Sq Rel), the root mean squared error (RMSE), and the logarithmic root mean squared error (RMSE log). Additionally, we compute three accuracy metrics, which give the fraction δ of predicted depth values inside an image whose ratio and inverse ratio with the ground truth is below the thresholds 1.25, 1.25^2 and 1.25^3. On the Benchmark split we evaluate using the scale-invariant logarithmic RMSE from [12] and the RMSE of the inverse depth (iRMSE). We follow [71] by applying median scaling to the predicted depths. The semantic segmentation is evaluated using the mean intersection over union (mIoU) [13], which is computed considering the classes as defined in [9].

5   Evaluation and Discussion

In this section we start by a comparison to multiple state-of-the-art approaches, followed by an analysis how the single components of our method improve the results over our depth estimation and semantic segmentation baselines.

5.1   Depth Evaluation w.r.t. the Baselines

The main evaluation is done on the *Eigen split*, with the achieved results in Table 1. *Our full SGDepth approach outperforms all comparable baselines,* where we compare to methods which use only image sequences as supervision on the target dataset (KITTI) and report results for the evaluation on single images at test-time. As we noted a high dependency of the results on the input resolution, we report our results on three resolutions. *Note that at each resolution we outperform the baselines.* Furthermore, we provide results for our model, trained only with self-supervision for the depth estimation (SGDepth only depth), and show that the full SGDepth model is significantly better. Due to fairness, we do not compare against results with test-time refinement (e.g., in [5]) or results employing a significantly larger network architecture (e.g., in [23]), as such techniques anyway can improve each of the methods further.

Table 1. Evaluation of our new **self-supervised semantically-guided depth estimation** (SGDepth full) on the **KITTI Eigen split**. Baseline results are taken from the cited publications. For a fair comparison, we report results at 3 resolutions and **do not compare to methods with test-time refinement or significantly larger network architectures**. Additionally, we provide results for our model trained only for the depth estimation task (SGDepth only depth). CS indicates training of the depth estimation on Cityscapes, K training on the KITTI Eigen split, and (CS) training of the segmentation branch on Cityscapes. **Best results** at each resolution are written in **boldface** (the `ResNet50` model is out of competition).

Method	Resolution	Dataset	Lower is better				Higher is better		
			Abs Rel	Sq Rel	RMSE	RMSE log	$\delta < 1.25$	$\delta < 1.25^2$	$\delta < 1.25^3$
Zhou et al. [71]	416 × 128	CS + K	0.198	1.836	6.565	0.275	0.718	0.901	0.960
Mahjourian et al. [38]	416 × 128	CS + K	0.159	1.231	5.912	0.243	0.784	0.923	0.970
Yin and Shi [64]	416 × 128	CS + K	0.153	1.328	5.737	0.232	0.802	0.934	0.972
Wang et al. [58]	416 × 128	CS + K	0.148	1.187	5.583	0.228	0.810	0.936	0.975
Casser et al. [5,6]	416 × 128	K	0.141	1.026	5.291	0.215	0.816	0.945	0.979
Meng et al. [39]	416 × 128	K	0.139	0.949	5.227	0.214	0.818	0.945	**0.980**
Godard et al. [19]	416 × 128	K	0.128	1.087	5.171	0.204	0.855	0.953	0.978
SGDepth only depth	416 × 128	K	0.128	1.003	5.085	0.206	0.853	0.951	0.978
SGDepth full	416 × 128	(CS) + K	**0.121**	**0.920**	**4.935**	**0.199**	**0.863**	**0.955**	**0.980**
Guizilini et al. [24]	640 × 192	K	0.117	0.854	4.714	**0.191**	0.873	**0.963**	**0.981**
Godard et al. [19,20]	640 × 192	K	0.115	0.903	4.863	0.193	0.877	0.959	**0.981**
SGDepth only depth	640 × 192	K	0.117	0.907	4.844	0.196	0.875	0.958	0.980
SGDepth full	640 × 192	(CS) + K	**0.113**	**0.835**	**4.693**	**0.191**	**0.879**	0.961	**0.981**
SGDepth full, ResNet50	640 × 192	(CS) + K	0.112	0.833	4.688	0.190	0.884	0.961	0.981
Luo et al. [37]	832 × 256	K	0.141	1.029	5.350	0.216	0.816	0.941	0.976
Ranjan et al. [49]	832 × 256	CS + K	0.139	1.032	5.199	0.213	0.827	0.943	0.977
Zhou et al. [70]	1248 × 384	K	0.121	0.837	4.945	0.197	0.853	0.955	**0.982**
Godard et al. [19,20]	1024 × 320	K	0.115	0.882	4.701	0.190	0.879	0.961	**0.982**
SGDepth only depth	1280 × 384	K	0.113	0.880	4.695	0.192	0.884	0.961	0.981
SGDepth full	1280 × 384	(CS) + K	**0.107**	**0.768**	**4.468**	**0.186**	**0.891**	**0.963**	**0.982**

Furthermore, in Table 2 we provide results on the *Benchmark split* for our full SGDepth model, which were computed on the KITTI online evaluation server. As

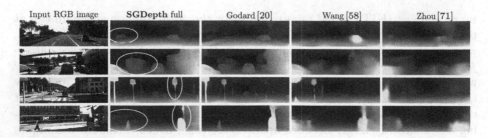

Fig. 5. Qualitative examples of our full SGDepth method. Note: Boundaries of **DC objects are sharpened**, and in contrast to previous methods, **small objects** (e.g., traffic signs, third row) **are better detected/distinguished** by SGDepth full.

Table 2. Results on the **KITTI depth prediction benchmark** (Benchmark split).

Method	Lower is better			
	SILog	Abs Rel [%]	Sq Rel [%]	iRMSE
Fu et al. [14] (supervised)	11.77	2.23	8.78	12.98
Ochs et al. [41] (supervised)	14.68	3.90	12.31	15.96
SGDepth full, ResNet50 (self-supervised)	15.30	5.00	13.29	15.80
SGDepth full (self-supervised)	15.49	4.78	13.33	16.07
Goldman et al. [21] (self-supervised)	17.92	6.88	14.04	17.62

we cannot use median scaling, we calculate a global scale factor on the validation split, which is applied before submitting the results for evaluation. Table 2 shows that we outperform the only other listed self-supervised approach [21], thereby reducing the gap to supervised methods [14,41].

Qualitatively, we observe in Fig. 5 that the depth estimation has clearly shaped DC objects compared to the baselines. Furthermore, our SGDepth method is able to detect small objects such as traffic signs, where other methods fail.

5.2   Ablation Studies

To show the effectiveness of our proposed improvements, we show results on the *Kitti split* in Table 3, starting from our baselines and individually adding our contributions up to our full method. Starting with our baselines trained only on the depth or the segmentation task, we observed depth estimation improvement when training both together in a multi-task fashion, where we simply add up the depth and segmentation losses from (3), (4), and (5). Note that the multi-task prediction of depth and segmentation is only done during training of our SGDepth models, while evaluation can be done separately for each task, inducing no additional complexity at test-time. Adding gradient scaling (6) improves on top, but particularly the semantic segmentation. In a first attempt to improve the depth estimation for DC objects, we masked out all DC objects that potentially contaminate the loss as described by (8) and (9). Obviously, now the network does not get any objective on how to reconstruct the depth of DC objects, which

Table 3. Evaluation of the **combined prediction of depth and semantic segmentation** on the **KITTI split** according to the standard protocol: We show how the single components of our approach improve the self-supervised depth estimation and how they compare to a stereo baseline. Note that in contrast to the stereo baseline all methods make use of median scaling. The values for mIoU scores on Cityscapes are obtained on the validation set. **Best results** overall and for monocular-trained methods are written in **boldface** (the ResNet50 model is out of competition).

Method	Higher is better		Lower is better				Higher is better		
	mIoU$_K$	mIoU$_{CS}$	Abs Rel	Sq Rel	RMSE	RMSE log	$\delta < 1.25$	$\delta < 1.25^2$	$\delta < 1.25^3$
Ramirez et al. [47] (stereo)	-	-	0.143	2.161	6.526	0.222	0.850	0.939	0.972
Chen et al. [7] (stereo)	37.7	47.8	0.102	**0.890**	**5.203**	0.183	0.863	0.955	0.984
Yang et al. [63] (mono)	-	-	0.131	1.254	6.117	0.220	0.826	0.931	0.973
Liu et al. [35] (mono)	-	-	0.108	1.020	**5.528**	0.195	0.863	0.948	0.980
Oršić et al. [42]	-	**75.5**	-	-	-	-	-	-	-
SGDepth only segmentation	43.1	63.3	-	-	-	-	-	-	-
SGDepth only depth	-	-	0.108	1.101	6.379	0.171	0.878	0.967	0.988
SGDepth add multi-task training	42.6	55.6	0.105	1.052	6.298	0.168	0.882	0.971	0.990
SGDepth add scaled gradients	48.6	67.7	0.102	1.023	6.183	0.164	0.889	0.972	**0.991**
SGDepth add semantic mask	48.3	67.6	0.106	1.113	6.337	0.169	0.884	0.970	0.989
SGDepth add threshold	**51.6**	68.2	0.099	1.012	6.120	**0.160**	0.894	**0.973**	0.990
SGDepth full	50.1	67.7	**0.097**	**0.983**	6.173	**0.160**	**0.898**	0.972	0.990
SGDepth full, ResNet50	54.2	70.7	0.098	0.940	5.841	0.156	0.900	0.976	0.991

leads to a decrease in performance. Therefore, we introduced the *threshold* θ_Λ to learn the depth of DC objects from a fraction ϵ of images containing non-moving DC objects as described by (10) and (11). For further improvement, we added a scheduling for the fraction ϵ, to first learn the depth from the best samples, while afterwards allowing more and more "noisy" samples. *Our final SGDepth model outperforms the Liu et al. [35] mono approach in 6 out of 7 measures and even outperforms the stereo approach of Chen et al. [7] in 5 out of 7 measures.*

5.3   Semantics Evaluation

The multi-task training of depth estimation and semantic segmentation not only achieves top results on the depth estimation, but also mutually improves the semantic segmentation in the source domain (Cityscapes), the semantic segmentation in the target domain (KITTI), and the depth estimation in the target domain (KITTI), as shown in Table 3. We achieve a notable improvement from 43.1% to 51.6% on KITTI (mIoU$_K$) and from 63.3% to 68.2% on Cityscapes

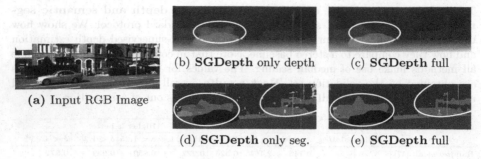

(a) Input RGB Image

(b) SGDepth only depth   (c) SGDepth full

(d) SGDepth only seg.   (e) SGDepth full

Fig. 6. Qualitative comparison between our **depth-** and **segmentation-only base-lines** and our **full training approach**. Notice, how the depth boundaries are sharpened, while the artifacts inside the segmentation mask are reduced.

(mIoU$_{CS}$) for our best performing model on the segmentation task, denoted as "**SGDepth** add threshold". Our results are further improved when employing a larger `ResNet50` feature extractor. Additionally, Fig. 6 shows that not only the depth boundaries of DC objects are sharpened but also the domain shift artifacts inside the semantic segmentation are significantly reduced.

6   Conclusion

In this work, we show how two tasks benefit from each other inside a multi-task cross-domain setting and develop a novel semantic masking technique to improve self-supervised monocular depth estimation for moving objects. We show superior performance on the KITTI Eigen split, exceeding all baselines without test-time refinement. We also demonstrate the effectiveness of each of our contributions on the KITTI split, where we outperform previous mono approaches in 6 out of 7 and even a stereo approach in 5 out of 7 measures.

Our approach is advantageous as long as the dataset used for training of our method contains some frames with non-moving dynamic-class (DC) objects belonging to the pre-defined semantic classes, e.g., parked vehicles, from which the depth of DC objects can be learned.

References

1. Akhter, I., Sheikh, Y., Khan, S., Kanade, T.: Nonrigid structure from motion in trajectory space. In: Proceedings of NIPS, Vancouver, BC, Canada, pp. 41–48, December 2009
2. Aleotti, F., Tosi, F., Poggi, M., Mattoccia, S.: Generative adversarial networks for unsupervised monocular depth prediction. In: Leal-Taixé, L., Roth, S. (eds.) ECCV 2018. LNCS, vol. 11129, pp. 337–354. Springer, Cham (2019). https://doi.org/10.1007/978-3-030-11009-3_20
3. Bolte, J.A., et al.: Unsupervised domain adaptation to improve image segmentation quality both in the source and target domain. In: Proceedings of CVPR - Workshops, Long Beach, CA, USA, pp. 1–10, June 2019

4. Bozorgtabar, B., Rad, M.S., Mahapatra, D., Thiran, J.P.: SynDeMo: synergistic deep feature alignment for joint learning of depth and ego-motion. In: Proceedings of ICCV, Seoul, Korea, pp. 4210–4219, October 2019
5. Casser, V., Pirk, S., Mahjourian, R., Angelova, A.: Depth prediction without the sensors: leveraging structure for unsupervised learning from monocular videos. In: Proceedings of AAAI, Honolulu, HI, USA, January 2019
6. Casser, V., Pirk, S., Mahjourian, R., Angelova, A.: Unsupervised monocular depth and ego-motion learning with structure and semantics. In: Proceedings of CVPR - Workshops, Long Beach, CA, USA, June 2019
7. Chen, P.Y., Liu, A.H., Liu, Y.C., Wang, Y.C.F.: Towards Scene Understanding: unsupervised monocular depth estimation with semantic-aware representation. In: Proceedings of CVPR, Long Beach, CA, USA, June 2019
8. Chen, Y., Schmid, C., Sminchisescu, C.: Self-supervised learning with geometric constraints in monocular video connecting flow, depth, and camera. In: Proceedings of ICCV, Seoul, Korea, pp. 7063–7072, October 2019
9. Cordts, M., et al.: The cityscapes dataset for semantic urban scene understanding. In: Proceedings of CVPR, Las Vegas, NV, USA, pp. 3213–3223, June 2016
10. CS Kumar, A., Bhandarkar, S.M., Prasad, M.: Monocular depth prediction using generative adversarial networks. In: Proceedings of CVPR - Workshops, Salt Lake City, UT, USA, pp. 1–9, June 2018
11. Eigen, D., Fergus, R.: Predicting depth, surface normals and semantic labels with a common multi-scale convolutional architecture. In: Proceedings of ICCV, Santiago, Chile, pp. 2650–2658, December 2015
12. Eigen, D., Puhrsch, C., Fergus, R.: Depth map prediction from a single image using a multi-scale deep network. In: Proceedings of NIPS, Montréal, QC, Canada, pp. 2366–2374, December 2014
13. Everingham, M., Van Gool, L., Williams, C.K.I., Winn, J., Zisserman, A.: The Pascal visual object classes challenge: a retrospective. Int. J. Comput. Vis. (IJCV) 111(1), 98–136 (2015)
14. Fu, H., Gong, M., Wang, C., Batmanghelich, K., Tao, D.: Deep ordinal regression network for monocular depth estimation. In: Proceedings of CVPR, Salt Lake City, UT, USA, pp. 2002–2011, June 2018
15. Ganin, Y., Lempitsky, V.: Unsupervised domain adaptation by backpropagation. In: Proceedings of ICML, Lille, France, pp. 1180–1189, July 2015
16. Garg, R., B.G., V.K., Carneiro, G., Reid, I.: Unsupervised CNN for single view depth estimation: geometry to the rescue. In: Leibe, B., Matas, J., Sebe, N., Welling, M. (eds.) ECCV 2016. LNCS, vol. 9912, pp. 740–756. Springer, Cham (2016). https://doi.org/10.1007/978-3-319-46484-8_45
17. Geiger, A., Lenz, P., Stiller, C., Urtasun, R.: Vision meets robotics: the KITTI dataset. Int. J. Robot. Res. (IJRR) 32(11), 1231–1237 (2013)
18. Godard, C., Mac Aodha, O., Brostow, G.J.: Unsupervised monocular depth estimation with left-right consistency. In: Proceedings of CVPR, Honolulu, HI, USA, pp. 270–279, July 2017
19. Godard, C., Mac Aodha, O., Firman, M., Brostow, G.J.: Digging into self-supervised monocular depth estimation. arXiv arXiv:1806.01260v4, June 2018
20. Godard, C., Mac Aodha, O., Firman, M., Brostow, G.J.: Digging into self-supervised monocular depth estimation. In: Proceedings of ICCV, Seoul, Korea, pp. 3828–3838, October 2019
21. Goldman, M., Hassner, T., Avidan, S.: Learn stereo, infer mono: siamese networks for self-supervised, monocular, depth estimation. In: Proceedings of CVPR - Workshops, Long Beach, CA, USA, pp. 1–10, June 2019

22. Gordon, A., Li, H., Jonschkowski, R., Angelova, A.: Depth from videos in the wild: unsupervised monocular depth learning from unknown cameras. In: Proceedings of ICCV, Seoul, Korea, pp. 8977–8986, October 2019
23. Guizilini, V., Ambrus, R., Pillai, S., Gaidon, A.: 3D packing for self-supervised monocular depth estimation. In: Proceedings of CVPR, Seattle, WA, USA, pp. 2485–2494, June 2020
24. Guizilini, V., Hou, R., Li, J., Ambrus, R., Gaidon, A.: Semantically-guided representation learning for self-supervised monocular depth. In: Proceedings of ICLR, Addis Ababa, Ethiopia, pp. 1–14, April 2020
25. He, K., Zhang, X., Ren, S., Sun, J.: Deep residual learning for image recognition. In: Proceedings of CVPR, Las Vegas, NV, USA, pp. 770–778, June 2016
26. Hirschmüller, H.: Stereo processing by semi-global matching and mutual information. IEEE Trans. Pattern Anal. Mach. Intell. (TPAMI) 30(2), 328–341 (2008)
27. Jaderberg, M., Simonyan, K., Zisserman, A., Kayukcuoglu, K.: Spatial transformer networks. In: Proceedings of NIPS, Montréal, QC, Canada, pp. 2017–2025, December 2015
28. Kendall, A., Gal, Y., Cipolla, R.: Multi-task learning using uncertainty to weigh losses for scene geometry and semantics. In: Proceedings of CVPR, Salt Lake City, UT, USA, pp. 7482–7491, June 2018
29. Kingma, D.P., Ba, J.: Adam: a method for stochastic optimization. In: Proceedings of ICLR, San Diego, CA, USA, pp. 1–15, May 2015
30. Kirillov, A., Girshick, R., He, K., Dollár, P.: Panoptic feature pyramid networks. In: Proceedings of CVPR, Long Beach, CA, USA, pp. 6399–6408, June 2019
31. Kuznietsov, Y., Stuckler, J., Leibe, B.: Semi-supervised deep learning for monocular depth map prediction. In: Proceedings of CVPR, Honolulu, HI, USA, pp. 6647–6655, July 2017
32. Laina, I., Rupprecht, C., Belagiannis, V., Tombari, F., Navab, N.: Deeper depth prediction with fully convolutional residual networks. In: Proceedings of 3DV, Stanford, CA, USA, pp. 239–248, October 2017
33. Li, Z., et al.: Learning the depths of moving people by watching frozen people. In: Proceedings of CVPR, Long Beach, CA, USA, pp. 4521–4530, June 2019
34. Liu, F., Shen, C., Lin, G., Reid, I.: Learning depth from single monocular images using deep convolutional neural fields. IEEE Trans. Pattern Anal. Mach. Intelli. (TPAMI) 38(10), 2024–2039 (2016)
35. Liu, L., Zhai, G., Ye, W., Liu, Y.: Unsupervised learning of scene flow estimation fusing with local rigidity. In: Proceedings of IJCAI, Macao, China, pp. 876–882, August 2019
36. Liu, P., Lyu, M., King, I., Xu, J.: SelFlow: self-supervised learning of optical flow. In: Proceedings of CVPR, Long Beach, CA, USA, pp. 4571–4580, June 2019
37. Luo, C., et al.: Every pixel counts++: joint learning of geometry and motion with 3D holistic understanding. arXiv arXiv:1810.06125, July 2019
38. Mahjourian, R., Wicke, M., Angelova, A.: Unsupervised learning of depth and ego-motion from monocular video using 3D geometric constraints. In: Proceedings of CVPR, Salt Lake City, UT, USA, pp. 5667–5675, June 2018
39. Meng, Y., et al.: SIGNet: semantic instance aided unsupervised 3D geometry perception. In: Proceedings of CVPR, Long Beach, CA, USA, pp. 9810–9820, June 2019
40. Menze, M., Geiger, A.: Object scene flow for autonomous vehicles. In: Proceedings of CVPR, Boston, MA, USA, pp. 3061–3070, June 2015

41. Ochs, M., Kretz, A., Mester, R.: SDNet: semantically guided depth estimation network. In: Proceedings of GCPR, Dortmund, Germany, pp. 288–302, September 2019

42. Oršić, M., Krešo, I., Bevandić, P., Šegvić, S.. In defense of pre-trained imagenet architectures for real-time semantic segmentation of road-driving images. In: Proceedings of CVPR, Long Beach, CA, USA, pp. 12607–12616, June 2019

43. Paszke, A., Chaurasia, A., Kim, S., Culurciello, E.: ENet: a deep neural network architecture for real-time semantic segmentation. arXiv arXiv:1606.02147, June 2016

44. Paszke, A., et al.: PyTorch: an imperative style, high-performance deep learning library. In: Proceedings of NeurIPS, Vancouver, BC, Canada, pp. 8024–8035, December 2019

45. Pilzer, A., Lathuiliere, S., Sebe, N., Ricci, E.: Refine and distill: exploiting cycle-inconsistency and knowledge distillation for unsupervised monocular depth estimation. In: Proceedings of CVPR, Long Beach, CA, USA, pp. 9768–9777, June 2019

46. Pilzer, A., Xu, D., Puscas, M., Ricci, E., Sebe, N.: Unsupervised adversarial depth estimation using cycled generative networks. In: Proceedings of 3DV, Verona, Italy, pp. 587–595, September 2018

47. Zama Ramirez, P., Poggi, M., Tosi, F., Mattoccia, S., Di Stefano, L.: Geometry meets semantics for semi-supervised monocular depth estimation. In: Jawahar, C.V., Li, H., Mori, G., Schindler, K. (eds.) ACCV 2018. Geometry Meets Semantics for Semi-Supervised Monocular Depth Estimation, vol. 11363, pp. 298–313. Springer, Cham (2019). https://doi.org/10.1007/978-3-030-20893-6_19

48. Ranftl, R., Vineet, V., Chen, Q., Koltun, V.: Dense monocular depth estimation in complex dynamic scenes. In: Proceedings of CVPR, Las Vegas, NV, USA, pp. 4058–4066, June 2016

49. Ranjan, A., et al.: Competitive collaboration: joint unsupervised learning of depth, camera motion, optical flow and motion segmentation. In: Proceedings of CVPR, Long Beach, CA, USA, pp. 12240–12249, June 2019

50. Ren, Z., Yan, J., Ni, B., Liu, B., Yang, X., Zha, H.: Unsupervised deep learning for optical flow estimation. In: Proceedings of AAAI, San Francisco, CA, USA, pp. 1495–1501, February 2017

51. Russakovsky, O., et al.: ImageNet large scale visual recognition challenge. Int. J. Comput. Vis. (IJCV) 115(3), 211–252 (2015)

52. Sun, J., Li, Y., Kang, S.B., Shum, H.Y.: Symmetric stereo matching for occlusion handling. In: Proceedings of CVPR, San Diego, CA, USA, pp. 399–406, June 2005

53. Szeliski, R.: Computer Vision: Algorithms and Applications. Springer, London (2010). https://doi.org/10.1007/978-1-84882-935-0

54. Tosi, F., Aleotti, F., Poggi, M., Mattoccia, S.: Learning monocular depth estimation infusing traditional stereo knowledge. In: Proceedings of CVPR, Long Beach, CA, USA, pp. 9799–9809, June 2019

55. Tosi, F., et al.: Distilled semantics for comprehensive scene understanding from videos. In: Proceedings of CVPR, Seattle, WA, USA, pp. 4654–4665, June 2020

56. Uhrig, J., Schneider, N., Schneider, L., Franke, U., Brox, T., Geiger, A.: Sparsity invariant CNNs. In: Proceedings of 3DV, Verona, Italy, pp. 11–20, October 2017

57. Vijayanarasimhan, S., Ricco, S., Schmid, C., Sukthankar, R., Fragkiadaki, K.: SfM-Net: learning of structure and motion from video. arXiv arXiv:1704.0780, April 2017

58. Wang, C., Miguel Buenaposada, J., Zhu, R., Lucey, S.: Learning depth from monocular videos using direct methods. In: Proceedings of CVPR, Salt Lake City, UT, USA, pp. 2022–2030, June 2018
59. Wang, R., Pizer, S.M., Frahm, J.M.: Recurrent neural network for (un-)supervised learning of monocular video visual odometry and depth. In: Proceedings of CVPR, Long Beach, CA, USA, pp. 5555–5564, June 2019
60. Wang, Y., Wang, P., Yang, Z., Luo, C., Yang, Y., Xu, W.: UnOS: unified unsupervised optical-flow and stereo-depth estimation by watching videos. In: Proceedings of CVPR, Long Beach, CA, USA, pp. 8071–8081, June 2019
61. Wang, Z., Bovik, A.C., Sheikh, H.R., Simoncelli, E.P.: Image quality assessment: from error visibility to structural similarity. IEEE Trans. Image Process. **13**(4), 600–612 (2004)
62. Yang, G., Zhao, H., Shi, J., Deng, Z., Jia, J.: SegStereo: exploiting semantic information for disparity estimation. In: Ferrari, V., Hebert, M., Sminchisescu, C., Weiss, Y. (eds.) ECCV 2018. LNCS, vol. 11211, pp. 660–676. Springer, Cham (2018). https://doi.org/10.1007/978-3-030-01234-2_39
63. Yang, Z., Wang, P., Wang, Y., Xu, W., Nevatia, R.: Every pixel counts: unsupervised geometry learning with holistic 3D motion understanding. In: Leal-Taixé, L., Roth, S. (eds.) ECCV 2018. LNCS, vol. 11133, pp. 691–709. Springer, Cham (2019). https://doi.org/10.1007/978-3-030-11021-5_43
64. Yin, Z., Shi, J.: GeoNet: unsupervised learning of dense depth, optical flow and camera pose. In: Proceedings of CVPR, Salt Lake City, UT, USA, pp. 1983–1992, June 2018
65. Zhan, H., Garg, R., Saroj Weerasekera, C., Li, K., Agarwal, H., Reid, I.: Unsupervised learning of monocular depth estimation and visual odometry with deep feature reconstruction. In: Proceedings of CVPR, Salt Lake City, UT, USA, pp. 340–349, June 2018
66. Zhang, F., Prisacariu, V., Yang, R., Torr, P.H.S.: GA-Net: guided aggregation net for end-to-end stereo matching. In: Proceedings of CVPR, Long Beach, CA, USA, pp. 185–194, June 2019
67. Zhang, H., Shen, C., Li, Y., Cao, Y., Liu, Y., Yan, Y.: Exploiting temporal consistency for real-time video depth estimation. In: Proceedings of ICCV, Seoul, Korea. pp. 1725–1734, October 2019
68. Zhang, Z., Cui, Z., Xu, C., Yan, Y., Sebe, N., Yang, J.: Pattern-affinitive propagation across depth, surface normal and semantic segmentation. In: Proceedings of CVPR, Long Beach, CA, USA, pp. 4106–4115, June 2019
69. Zhao, S., Fu, H., Gong, M., Tao, D.: Geometry-aware symmetric domain adaptation for monocular depth estimation. In: Proceedings of CVPR, Long Beach, CA, USA, June 2019
70. Zhou, J., Wang, Y., Qin, K., Zeng, W.: Unsupervised high-resolution depth learning from videos with dual networks. In: Proceedings of ICCV, Seoul, Korea, pp. 6872–6881, October 2019
71. Zhou, T., Brown, M., Snavely, N., Lowe, D.G.: Unsupervised learning of depth and ego-motion from video. In: Proceedings of CVPR, Honolulu, HI, USA, pp. 1851–1860, July 2017

Hierarchical Visual-Textual Graph for Temporal Activity Localization via Language

Shaoxiang Chen and Yu-Gang Jiang[(⊠)]

Shanghai Key Lab of Intelligent Information Processing,
School of Computer Science, Fudan University, Shanghai, China
{sxchen13,ygj}@fudan.edu.cn

Abstract. Temporal Activity Localization via Language (TALL) in video is a recently proposed challenging vision task, and tackling it requires fine-grained understanding of the video content, however, this is overlooked by most of the existing works. In this paper, we propose a novel TALL method which builds a Hierarchical Visual-Textual Graph to model interactions between the objects and words as well as among the objects to jointly understand the video contents and the language. We also design a convolutional network with cross-channel communication mechanism to further encourage the information passing between the visual and textual modalities. Finally, we propose a loss function that enforces alignment of the visual representation of the localized activity and the sentence representation, so that the model can predict more accurate temporal boundaries. We evaluated our proposed method on two popular benchmark datasets: Charades-STA and ActivityNet Captions, and achieved state-of-the-art performances on both datasets. Code is available at https://github.com/forwchen/HVTG.

Keywords: Temporal Activity Localization via Language · Hierarchical Visual-Textual Graph · Visual-textual alignment

1 Introduction

Localizing temporal region-of-interest in video is a popular research topic in computer vision. Human actions have been the main target for temporal localization in video, and significant progresses are made [4,10,23,27,34,35,55] during the past few years thanks to the development of deep learning. However, actions that are categorized to a limited number of classes are not sufficient for understanding the events in videos. Recently, Gao *et al.* [12] and Hendricks *et al.* [16] proposed to localize complex activities in videos via free-form language queries (*i.e.*, sentence descriptions), and the task is named Temporal Activity Localization via

Electronic supplementary material The online version of this chapter (https://doi.org/10.1007/978-3-030-58565-5_36) contains supplementary material, which is available to authorized users.

© Springer Nature Switzerland AG 2020
A. Vedaldi et al. (Eds.): ECCV 2020, LNCS 12365, pp. 601–618, 2020.
https://doi.org/10.1007/978-3-030-58565-5_36

Sentence: A person takes a bottle of water from the refrigerator.

Localized segment: 1.4s ⟵――――――――――――――――――――――⟶ 8.4s

Fig. 1. Demonstration of the Temporal Activity Localization via Language task. The motivation for our work is that the objects and their interactions must be explicitly modeled while jointly considering the sentence content. In this example, the model should understand the interactions among the key objects from the query: bottle, person, and refrigerator, so that it is aware of when the refrigerator is opened/closed and the bottle is taken out of the refrigerator.

Language (TALL). An example of TALL is shown in Fig. 1. The main difference between TALL and action localization is that an activity can be a composition of multiple actions or sub-activities (*e.g.*, opening refrigerator, taking bottle, and closing refrigerator), and an activity involves frequent interactions among persons and objects. Moreover, some actions or sub-activities are not explicitly described by the sentence. Thus, one key to tackling this challenging task is the fine-grained joint understanding of the video's visual content and the sentence's textual content.

TALL has recently attracted attention from both the computer vision and natural language processing communities. Early approaches for solving TALL are inspired by action localization methods and are mainly based on sliding window proposals. In [24,25,37], candidate temporal regions are first generated by sliding windows of fixed scales over the video, then each candidate and the sentence are separately processed by visual and textual encoding modules, and they are finally fed to a cross-modal processing module to generate a ranking score and boundary offsets. These sliding window candidates are query-irrelevant, so some works [7,48] try to generate learned query-guided proposals by leveraging sentence semantics to assign weights to temporal regions. Proposal-based methods generate a large amount of candidate regions in order to achieve a high recall, thus they suffer from high computational cost in both the training and testing phases. Moreover, proposal-based methods are two-stage and cannot be optimized in an end-to-end manner. Similar to the efficient action localization method [4], a group of works [6,42] adopt anchor-based network structure that can generate multi-scale region predictions for all time steps in one pass. Anchor-based methods are end-to-end trainable and can address the efficiency problem, however, they still rely on heuristic rules such as the candidate region scales and strides, which are usually dependent on the dataset statistics. Most recently, some works [26,53] try to discard proposals and directly predict the start and end boundaries of an activity. Although this type of approaches cannot generate multiple proposals, they are computationally more efficient and do not rely on the dataset statistics to design heuristic rules. To summarize, most existing methods focus on generating and refining temporal proposals and improving efficiency, but rarely explore the modeling of fine-grained object interactions.

We argue that while actions can be well captured by their motion patterns [5], understanding activities requires fine-grained modeling of the relations among the objects/persons in videos. As shown in Fig. 1, the main motivation for this work is that object interactions should be modeled jointly with the sentence content for better localization. Existing methods mostly use pretrained action recognition network (such as C3D [39]) to extract global feature representations for video frames, but such representations do not preserve the object-level information inside frames. To address this issue, we extract object-level features in each video frame via an object detection network, and then use a Hierarchical Visual-Textual Graph (HVTG) to encode the features. In the HVTG, objects and words in the sentence are all considered graph nodes. In the first level, the object features first connect and interact with word representations to gather textual information that's relevant to themselves. This achieves a fine-grained understanding of the sentence query based on the video's contents. Next, a fully-connected object graph models the object-object interactions inside each frame, and each node (object) absorbs information from its neighbors. To further aggregate the object graph to obtain a compact representation, a sentence-guided node aggregation is applied to each frame's object features and then bidirectional temporal relation is built via LSTMs. Following the HVTG, we design a convolutional localizer with cross-channel communication [51] between visual and textual modalities (which can be regarded as a more fine-grained visual-textual graph) to predict each frame's relatedness with the sentence. Finally, in order to further close the gap between the visual and textual modalities, an auxiliary loss function is used to align the visual representation of the localized activity and the textual representation. We abbreviate our method as HVTG.

Our contributions in this work are summarized as follows:

- We propose Hierarchical Visual-Textual Graph (HVTG), a novel model for the Temporal Activity Localization via Language (TALL) task. HVTG performs visual-textual interaction in both the object and channel levels, and is among the first methods that consider fine-grained object interactions for the TALL task.
- We propose a novel loss function for the TALL task which aligns the visual representation of the localized activity and the sentence representation, and can effectively improve the localization performance.
- We demonstrate the effectiveness of our HVTG through extensive ablation studies and experiments on two challenging benchmark datasets: Charades-STA and ActivityNet Captions. Our HVTG outperformed recent state-of-the-art methods on both datasets.

2 Related Work

Temporal Action Localization and Proposals. Temporal action localization is closely related to TALL and has been extensively studied in the computer vision literature. The current state-of-the-art methods can be divided into two groups: proposal-based methods and anchor based methods, according to how they generate proposals (candidate temporal segments). Proposal-based methods first generate a set of candidate temporal segments of the target action and then produce classification scores and boundary refinements for the proposals. Representative methods such as SCNN [35] and TCN [9] generate proposals with simple multi-sale sliding-window strategy, and then exhaustively evaluate the video segments using CNNs. Based on the SCNN proposals, Shou et al. [34] further design a more powerful 3D CNN to model the spatio-temporal structure in raw videos and produce fine-grained predictions for temporal boundary refinement. Another direction for improvement is designing more effective proposal generation strategy. Zhao et al. [57] propose the Temporal Actionness Grouping (TAG) method for merging high actionness snippets into a proposal using a grouping scheme similar to [32]. Proposal-based methods are not efficient due to their exhaustive evaluation of all the proposals. Anchor-based methods such as DAP [10], SS-TAD [3], and SST [4] overcome this efficiency problem by using RNN (GRU [8] and LSTM [17]) to process videos in one pass and generate a set of fixed-length proposals with confidence scores at every time step. Another line of work adopts CNN architectures to process videos. SSAD [23] applies multiple 2D convolutions to multi-scale video feature maps and predicts action categories and locations at multiple layers. R-C3D [47] extends the ROI-pooling method in object detection, and it applies 3D ROI-pooling to proposals' feature maps from 3D CNN, and the ROI-pooling produces fixed-size features for predicting temporal boundaries and action scores. The proposal generation strategies in most TALL methods are similar to those used in temporal action localization. However, actions are restricted to a predefined categories and can often be captured by their motion patterns. Thus, localizing activities via language is more flexible and challenging.

Video/Image-Text Retrieval. Video/image-text retrieval is also a closely related topic. State-of-the-art methods mainly focus on either learning a visual-semantic common space or encoding techniques for video and text. In [30], video and text (sentence) are respectively encoded with CNN and RNN in parallel and then projected into a common space where embeddings of relevant videos and texts are pulled close. Faghri et al. [11] propose VSE++ which improves the visual-semantic common space learning objective by utilizing hard negative image-text pairs. Miech et al. [28] design a Mixture of Embedding Experts (MEE) model which computes similarity scores between text and video as a weighted combination of multiple expert embeddings, where the weights are estimated from the aggregated word representations. Wray et al. [45] propose to learn separate embeddings for each part-of-speech in a sentence, such as verbs and nouns for retrieving fine-grained actions in videos. The importance of sentence structure is also noted by methods that focus on the encoding techniques. Xu et al. [50] and Lin et al. [22] both parse a sentence into a parse tree to obtain the syntactic role of each word during sentence encoding. Information fusion is also important when encoding the video or text. Mithun et al. [29] utilize multimodal cues in video, such as motion, audio, and object features. JSFusion [52] deeply fuses text and video representations by constructing a pairwise joint representation of word and frame sequences using a soft-attention mechanism. A recent work [54] explores video retrieval with multiple sentences by encoding and aligning video and text hierarchically. Our method draws inspiration from video-text retrieval to perform feature alignment of the localized activity and sentence in a common space.

Temporal Activity Localization via Language. A large body of TALL methods are proposal-based [12,13,18,24,25,37], which adopt a sliding-window proposal generation strategy and evaluate each proposal using visual-textual cross-modal processing models. Xu *et al.* [49] use the temporal segment proposal network in R-C3D [47], however, R-C3D is designed for action localization and there is a discrepancy between action and activity. Some methods also incorporate semantic information of the sentence into the proposal generation process. The QSPN [48] method uses a query-guided segment proposal network which incorporates sentence embeddings to derive attention weights and re-weight the video features for proposal generation. SAP [7] computes frame-wise visual-semantic correlation scores by extracting concepts from video frames and sentence, then uses a score grouping method to form proposal regions. TGN [6], CBP [42], and MAN [56] use the one-shot proposal generation strategy similar to the one in SST [4], the visual and textual features are fused using RNN or CNN to generate a set of proposals at each time step. Recently, ABLR [53] and DEBUG [26] discard proposals and directly predict a (start, end) time pair, which is more efficient. Although there are a few works that use object-level features [18], we emphasize that fine-grained interaction between visual and textual modalities is rarely considered for the TALL task.

3 Proposed Approach

As shown in Fig. 2, our method can be divided into two parts: the HVTG for encoding the video, and the sentence localizer for generating predictions. In Sect. 3.1, we first describe how our HVTG models the interaction between objects and sentence and among the objects. In Sect. 3.2, we then present our convolutional sentence localizer with the cross-channel communication mechanism to further encourage information passing between the visual and textual modalities. In Sect. 3.3, we formulate the set of losses for training our proposed model, among which the visual-textual alignment loss is critical.

3.1 Hierarchical Visual-Textual Graph

Given a video, we first uniformly sample N frames and extract object-level features for each frame: $O_n = \{o_n^1, o_n^2, ..., o_n^M\}$, where $n \in [1, N]$ is the frame index, M is the number of object features, and $o_n \in \mathbb{R}^{d_{obj}}$ is a feature vector. The sentence is represented by a sequence of words $S = \{w^1, w^2, ..., w^Q\}$, where $w \in \mathbb{R}^{d_{word}}$ is a word vector produced by the GloVe [31] word embedding. Note that the sentence is zero-padded or truncated to a fixed length Q. The goal of

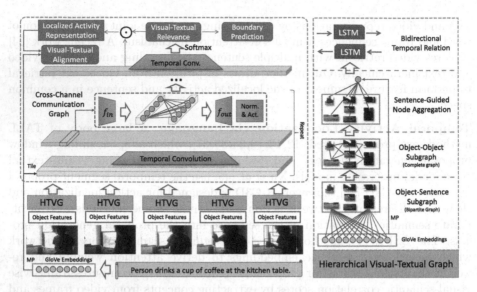

Fig. 2. Overview of our approach. The object features are extracted from each frame, and then processed by the Hierarchical Visual-Textual Graph (HVTG) in four stages: Object-Sentence Subgraph (Eq. (1), (2)), Object-Object Subgraph (Eq. (3), (4)), Sentence-Guided Node Aggregation (Eq. (5), (6)), and Bidirectional Temporal Relation (Eq. (7)). The aggregated visual representation for each frame is processed by multi-layer temporal convolutions with the channel interaction mechanism (Eq. (9), (10)), where f_{in} and f_{out} are linear transformations. Finally, boundary prediction and localized activity representation are obtained based on the visual-textual relevance scores.

Hierarchical Visual-Textual Graph is to aggregate object-level visual features to obtain a compact representation for each frame, and simultaneously capture the interaction between objects and sentence and among the objects. As Fig. 2 shows, the HVTG processes the video frame by frame with shared parameters.

Object-Sentence Subgraph (OSS). As Fig. 2 shows, the OSS is a bipartite graph, in which the nodes are divided into two disjoint and independent sets (objects and words) and every edge connects an interacting pair of object and word. We compute the weight of the edge connecting o_n^i and w^j as

$$I_n^{ij} = \mathbf{1}^T\big((o_n^i \boldsymbol{W}_O) \odot (w^j \boldsymbol{W}_S)\big), \tag{1}$$

where $\boldsymbol{W}_O \in \mathbb{R}^{d_{obj} \times d}$ and $\boldsymbol{W}_S \in \mathbb{R}^{d_{word} \times d}$ are projection matrices for projecting the object and word features into a common space, $\odot$ denotes element-wise multiplication, and $\mathbf{1}$ is a vector of ones. We then normalize the edge weights for each object node i, and use them to gather textual information from the whole sentence:

$$\hat{\boldsymbol{I}}_n^{ij} = \mathrm{Softmax}_j(\boldsymbol{I}_n^{ij}), \quad \overline{\boldsymbol{o}}_n^i = \sum_{j=1}^{Q} \hat{\boldsymbol{I}}_n^{ij}(w^j \boldsymbol{U}_S), \tag{2}$$

where $\text{Softmax}_j(\cdot)$ represents column-wise Softmax normalization of a matrix, and $U_S \in \mathbb{R}^{d_{word} \times d_{obj}}$ projects word feature vectors into the object feature space. The resulting object feature $\overline{o}_n^i$ now carries textual information that's relevant to itself. We also introduce a residual connection from the object feature o_n^i to $\overline{o}_n^i$ to preserve the original object information. Then a Layer Normalization [2] and an object-wise feed-forward network are used to transform the outputs into a lower-dimensional space. The outputs are the sentence-aware object features for the n-th frame, and they are denoted by $\hat{O}_n = \{\hat{o}_n^1, ..., \hat{o}_n^M\}$.

Object-Object Subgraph (OOS). Since the basic elements of an activity are object-object interactions, we build a complete (fully-connected) subgraph inside each frame. The object features from the OSS are the graph nodes, and the edge weight between two arbitrary objects $\hat{o}_n^i$ and $\hat{o}_n^j$ is computed as

$$e_n^{ij} = g(\hat{o}_n^i || \hat{o}_n^j). \tag{3}$$

Since the object features are already in the same feature space, we use a single-layer feed-forward neural network for $g(\cdot)$ as in [41], and it linearly transforms the concatenation of $\hat{o}_n^i$ and $\hat{o}_n^j$ into a scalar, and it has a LeakyReLU [46] activation. Again, the edge weights for each node i are then normalized and used to gather information from all its neighbors:

$$\hat{e}_n^{ij} = \text{Softmax}_j(e^{ij}), \quad \tilde{o}_n^i = \sum_{j=1}^{M} \hat{e}_n^{ij} \hat{o}_n^j. \tag{4}$$

The resulting object features $\widetilde{O}_n = \{\tilde{o}_n^1, ..., \tilde{o}_n^M\}$ now carry object-object interactions between all pairs of objects inside each frame.

Sentence-Guided Node Aggregation. The object-object subgraph needs to be further aggregated in order to reduce computational cost for subsequent steps. Unlike the previous work [44], which aggregates all the nodes of a graph using mean-pooling, we instead use a sentence-guided attention to assign sentence relevance scores to the objects:

$$u = \tanh(\overline{S}W_S + \widetilde{O}_nW_O + b_O), \quad \hat{u} = \text{Softmax}(uW_r + b_r), \tag{5}$$

where $\overline{S}$ is the mean-pooled sentence feature used to guide the attention, and $W_S \in \mathbb{R}^{d_{word} \times d_{rel}}, W_O \in \mathbb{R}^{d_{obj} \times d_{rel}}, b_O \in \mathbb{R}^{d_{rel}}, W_r \in \mathbb{R}^{d_{rel} \times 1}$, and $b_r \in \mathbb{R}^1$ are the learnable parameters. The normalized sentence relevance scores $\hat{u} \in \mathbb{R}^M$ are then used to re-weight the object features to obtain an aggregated visual representation for each frame:

$$v_n = \sum_{i=1}^{M} \hat{u}^i \tilde{o}_n^i. \tag{6}$$

Note that the operations in Eq. (1)–(6) are performed for each frame with shared parameters.

Bidirectional Temporal Relation. Finally, we establish temporal relations among the frames with a bidirectional LSTM network:

$$\widetilde{V} = f(\overrightarrow{\text{LSTM}}(\{v_1, ..., v_N\}) || \overleftarrow{\text{LSTM}}(\{v_N, ..., v_1\})), \qquad (7)$$

where $\overrightarrow{\text{LSTM}}$ and $\overleftarrow{\text{LSTM}}$ are the LSTM cells that take the visual representation sequence and produce outputs by aggregating information temporally in forward and backward directions, respectively. We then use a single-layer feedforward neural network with ReLU activation denoted by $f(\cdot)$ to transform the concatenated LSTM outputs. The final outputs of HVTG, $\widetilde{V} \in \mathbb{R}^{N \times d_{vis}}$, have aggregated the visual information both spatially (in the object level) and temporally, and textual information is also incorporated during the process.

3.2 Sentence Localizer

Given the encoded visual representation $\widetilde{V}$, the sentence localizer's goal is to compute the position-wise visual-textual relevance scores of each frame with the sentence, and then make boundary predictions based on the relevance scores. For this purpose, we first encode the sentence (word sequence) using a bidirectional LSTM like in Eq. (7), and then mean-pool over the LSTM outputs, resulting in an aggregated sentence representation $\widetilde{S} \in \mathbb{R}^{d_{sent}}$. Since computing the frame-wise visual-textual relevance should focus more on the local structure of the visual representation, we use an L-layer temporal convolutional network to process $\widetilde{V}$. Basically, the l-th convolutional layer can be formulated as

$$C^l = \text{Conv}^l(\widetilde{V}^{l-1} || \widetilde{S}; (k^l, c^l)), \qquad (8)$$

where $\widetilde{V}^{l-1}$ is the output from the previous layer ($\widetilde{V}^0 = \widetilde{V}$), $\widetilde{S}$ is tiled along the temporal dimension, and $||$ is tensor concatenation along the channel axis. The convolutional operation has two main hyper-parameters: kernel size k^l and number of output channels c^l.

Cross-Channel Communication Graph. We add one key component to the convolutional network, which is a cross-channel communication mechanism [51] that encourages information passing across feature channels in the same layer. By building a cross-channel communication graph (C^3G) on the convolutional outputs of the channel-concatenated visual and textual features, more complementary cross-modal representations can be learned in addition to the HVTG.

Firstly, $C^l \in \mathbb{R}^{N \times c^l}$ is linearly projected to a lower dimensional space to reduce computational cost for the C^3G, resulting in $P^l \in \mathbb{R}^{N \times d^l}$. Then the edge weight for each pair of channels is computed as (the layer index l is omitted)

$$T_n^{ij} = -(P_n^i - P_n^j)^2, \qquad (9)$$

where the subscript n stands for index of temporal location (frame), and the superscripts i, j are channel indices. The edge weights for channel i are normalized and averaged across all temporal locations to increase robustness, and then used to aggregate information from all channels:

$$\hat{T}^{ij} = \frac{1}{N} \sum_{n=1}^{N} \text{Softmax}_j(T_n^{ij}), \quad \hat{P}^i = \sum_{j=1}^{d^l} P_n^j \hat{T}^{ij}, \tag{10}$$

where $\hat{P}_n^i$ is the i-th channel output. In linear transformations (such as convolution), each output channel's computation is independent from the others. By concatenating visual and textual features along the channel axis and then connecting the channels via this C^3G, fine-grained cross-modal information will be captured. Finally, $\hat{P}_n^i$ is projected back to the original c^l-dimensional space, resulting in $\hat{C}^l \in \mathbb{R}^{N \times c^l}$. Residual connection, Instance Normalization [40], and LeakyReLU [46] activation are sequentially applied to $\hat{C}^l$, producing the output for the l-th convolutional layer:

$$\tilde{V}^l = \text{LeakyReLU}(\text{InstanceNorm}(\hat{C}^l + C^l)). \tag{11}$$

Prediction. Note that the L-th (last) layer is the prediction layer, which has 1 output channel. The visual-textual relevance scores are obtained by applying Softmax to $\tilde{V}^L$, and we make boundary predictions based on the scores:

$$d = \text{Softmax}(\tilde{V}^L), \quad r = \text{ReLU}(dW_d + b_d), \tag{12}$$

where $d \in \mathbb{R}^N$ represents the relevance scores for all the temporal locations (frames) in the video, and $r \in \mathbb{R}^2$ are two scalars representing the predicted start and end time of the localized sentence.

3.3 Losses

The training is done in a mini-batch optimization manner. We denote the batch predictions by $D = \{d_1, ..., d_B\}$ and $R = \{r_1, ..., r_B\}$. The ground-truth labels are denoted by $\hat{R} = \{\hat{r}_1, ..., \hat{r}_B\}$, where $\hat{r}_i \in \mathbb{R}^2$ is the human-annotated start and end times. We first use two basic objectives for the boundary and relevance score predictions.

Boundary Loss. We simply use the Huber loss for boundary prediction:

$$\text{Loss}_b = \sum_{i=1}^{B} \text{Huber}(r_i - \hat{r}_i). \tag{13}$$

Relevance Loss. Based on the ground-truth temporal boundaries, we construct the position-wise relevance masks $\hat{D} = \{\hat{d}_1, ..., \hat{d}_B\}$, where $\hat{d}_i \in \mathbb{R}^N$ is constructed as

$$\hat{d}_i[n] = \begin{cases} 1 & \hat{r}_i[0] \leq n \leq \hat{r}_i[1], \\ 0 & \text{otherwise}, \end{cases} \tag{14}$$

where $[\cdot]$ is the indexing operator along the first axis. Then the relevance loss is computed as

$$\text{Loss}_r = -\sum_{i=1}^{B} \frac{\hat{d}_i \cdot \log(d_i)}{\sum_n \hat{d}_i[n]}, \tag{15}$$

where $\cdot$ represents vector dot-product. This loss encourages the visual-textual relevance scores to be high at the ground-truth locations.

Visual-Textual Alignment Loss. Based on the predicted visual-textual relevance scores, we can obtain the representation for the localized activity by a weighted-sum of the visual representation (convolutional outputs prior to the prediction layer) using the relevance scores as the weights:

$$\overline{V}_i = \sum_{n=1}^{N} d_i[n] \widetilde{V}_i^{L-1}[n]. \tag{16}$$

Then the visual-textual alignment is performed across the mini-batch:

$$\text{Loss}_a = \frac{1}{B^2}(\sum_{i=1}^{B} \log(1 + \exp(-\text{sim}_{i,i})) + \frac{1}{B}\sum_{i=1}^{B}\sum_{\substack{j=1 \\ j \neq i}}^{B} \log(1 + \exp(\text{sim}_{i,j}))). \tag{17}$$

where $\text{sim}_{i,j}$ is the similarity function (*e.g.*, negative ℓ_2 distance) between the visual representation $\overline{V}_i$ and the textual representation $\widetilde{S}_j$ in a mini-batch. The representations of the matching video segment and sentence are pulled close in the feature space by this loss, and otherwise their representations are pushed away. Note that this loss supervises not only the learning of the visual and textual representations, but also the relevance score predictions, since the gradients back-propagate through $\overline{V}$, $\widetilde{S}$, and also d.

Feature Normalization Loss. To regularize the feature learning for visual-textual alignment and make the model focus more on predicting better visual-textual relevance scores, we further apply a learnable feature normalization [58] to the $(L-1)$-th convolutional layer's outputs:

$$\text{Loss}_n = \sum_{i=1}^{B}\sum_{n=1}^{N}(||\widetilde{V}_i^{L-1}[n]||_2 - F)^2, \tag{18}$$

where $|| \cdot ||_2$ is the ℓ_2-norm of a vector, and F is a learnable parameter. Finally, the above losses are combined with constant weights to balance their scales:

$$\text{Loss} = \lambda_b \text{Loss}_b + \lambda_r \text{Loss}_r + \lambda_a \text{Loss}_a + \lambda_n \text{Loss}_n. \tag{19}$$

4 Experiments

In this section, we conduct extensive ablation studies to validate the design choices for the different components of our model, and we also present performance comparisons with state-of-the-art methods on the benchmark datasets.

4.1 Datasets and Experimental Settings

Charades-STA. The Charades-STA dataset [12] is built based on the Charades dataset [36], which contains around 10k videos with temporal action (157 classes) annotations and video-level descriptions for indoor activities. Charades-STA is built by semi-automatically constructing temporal sentence annotations for the activities, and the annotations are human-checked. There are 12,408 and 3,720 sentence-video pairs for training and testing, respectively. The average video duration is 30 s, and the average sentence length is 6.2 words.

ActivityNet Captions. The ActivityNet Captions dataset [20] contains around 20k videos with temporal sentence annotation. The dataset is originally split into 10,024, 4,926, and 5,044 videos for training, validation, and testing, respectively. Since the testing set is not publicly available, we follow previous works to use the validation set for testing. ActivityNet Captions is the largest dataset for TALL, and it also has the most diverse activities. The average video duration is 117 s, and the average sentence length is 13.5 words.

Evaluation Metrics. We measure the average recall of our predictions of N sentence-video pairs at different temporal IoU thresholds, and this is the same as previous works [12,53]. Formally, Recall $= \frac{1}{N} \sum_{i=1}^{N} R(s_i, a_i, m)$, where $R(s_i, a_i, m) = 1$ if the temporal IoU between our prediction s_i and annotation a_i is greater than m, otherwise $R(s_i, a_i, m) = 0$. We also choose the same IoU thresholds $\{0.3, 0.5, 0.7\}$ as previous works.

Implementation Details. The video frames are temporally down-sampled with a rate of 1/4 and 1/32 for Charades-STA and ActivityNet Captions, respectively. For each frame, we extract 16 object regions (bounding boxes) with the object detection network [1,33] trained on Visual Genome [21], and then we perform ROIAlign [15] on the InceptionResnet V2 [38] feature maps to obtain object features. The sentences are truncated or padded to a maximum length of 12 words and 30 words for Charades-STA and ActivityNet Captions, respectively. Then the words are initialized with the 300d GloVe [31] embeddings, and all word vectors are fixed during training. The temporal boundaries for each sentence are normalized to be in $[0, 1]$. In the HVTG, we employ 8 attention heads as [41] in the object-sentence subgraph to learn more diverse representations. We use 4 convolutional layers for the sentence localizer, whose output channel numbers are $[512, 256, 256, 1]$ and kernel sizes are set to 5 or 3. The learnable parameter F for the feature normalization loss is initialized to 10. We use the Adam optimizer [19] with a learning rate of 0.0001 and a batch size of 32 to optimize the loss in Eq. (19). The loss weights λ_b, λ_r, λ_a, and λ_n are empirically set to 1, 5, 1, and 0.001, respectively.

4.2 Ablation Study

To demonstrate the effectiveness of our proposed approach, we first examine the effects of each important component by performing ablation studies[1].

Table 1. Performances of our model variants with different HVTG configurations. OSS means object-sentence subgraph, OOS means object-object subgraph, and SGNA means sentence-guided node aggregation.

#	OSS	OOS	SGNA	IoU = 0.3	IoU = 0.5	IoU = 0.7
0	✗	✗	✗	55.56	40.38	19.49
1	✓	✗	✗	58.36	44.97	21.77
2	✗	✓	✗	57.42	42.31	19.97
3	✗	✗	✓	58.46	42.93	20.86
4	✓	✓	✓	61.37	47.27	23.30

Table 2. Performances of our model variants with Cross-Channel Communication Graph (C^3G) and alignment loss enabled/disabled. Note that the experiments are done with all the HVTG components of Table 1 enabled.

#	C^3G	Alignment Loss	IoU = 0.3	IoU = 0.5	IoU = 0.7
0	✗	✗	58.18	43.23	20.77
1	✗	✓	60.36	45.51	22.31
2	✓	✗	59.27	44.65	22.42
3	✓	✓	61.37	47.27	23.30

Effects of Hierarchical Visual-Textual Graph Components. As shown in Table 1, for the HVTG, we mainly focus on the effects of the object-sentence subgraph (OSS), object-object subgraph (OOS), and sentence-guided node aggregation (SGNA). When all the three components are removed from our model, the objects do not connect and interact with the sentence and their features are simply mean-pooled and fed to the bi-LSTM, which is the case of setting 0 in Table 1 and is used as the baseline here. And note that disabling SGNA also means the object features are just mean-pooled, and the sentence localizer used here is the same as in our full model. Comparing settings 1, 2, and 3 with the baseline, we can see that each of the three components can effectively improve the performances. The average improvements brought by OSS, OOS, and SGNA are 9.5%, 3.7%, and 6.3%, respectively. This demonstrates that the visual-textual interaction in the HVTG is crucial for TALL. Combining all the three components consistently yields better performances, which indicates that our HVTG can benefit from the these interactions to better understand the video content and sentence query.

Effects of Cross-Channel Communication Graph. C^3G is the critical component of our convolutional localizer. As shown in Table 2, enabling it leads to a significant performance boost (comparing Settings 0 and 2, or 1 and 3). This means that visual-textual interaction at the object-sentence level is not enough,

---

[1] Due to the space limit, more experiments are placed in the Supplementary Material.

Table 3. Performance comparison on the Charades-STA dataset.

Method	IoU = 0.3	IoU = 0.5	IoU = 0.7
MCN [16]	32.59	11.67	2.63
ACRN [24]	38.06	20.26	7.64
ROLE [25]	37.68	21.74	7.82
SLTA [18]	38.96	22.81	8.25
CTRL [12]	–	23.63	8.89
VAL [37]	–	23.12	9.16
ACL [13]	–	30.48	12.20
SAP [7]	–	27.42	13.36
SM-RL [43]	–	24.36	11.17
TripNet [14]	51.33	36.61	14.50
QSPN [48]	54.7	35.6	15.8
CBP [42]	–	36.80	18.87
MAN [56]	–	46.53	22.72
ABLR [53]	51.55	35.43	15.05
DEBUG [26]	54.95	37.39	17.69
HVTG	**61.37**	**47.27**	**23.30**

Table 4. Performance comparison on the ActivityNet Captions dataset.

QSPN [48]	45.3	27.7	13.6
TGN [6]	43.81	27.93	–
TripNet [14]	48.42	32.19	13.93
CBP [42]	54.30	35.76	17.80
ABLR [53]	55.67	36.79	–
DEBUG [26]	55.91	39.72	–
HVTG	**57.60**	**40.15**	**18.27**

and channel-level interaction is an effective way to further encourage the messaging passing between the two modalities, and the local associations between video frames and sentence are better captured with C^3G.

Effects of Alignment Loss. Comparing settings 0 and 1 (or 2 and 3) in Table 2, it is clear that the alignment loss is beneficial for the TALL task, which validates our design of encouraging the localized activity and the sentence to be close in the feature space.

4.3 Comparison with State-of-the-Art Methods

Compared Methods. The state-of-the-art TALL methods we compared with are categorized as follows:

- Sliding-window proposal methods: TALL [12], ACRN [24], MAC [13], ROLE [25], SLTA [18], and VAL [37].
- Learned proposal generation methods: QSPN [48], EF+Cap [49], and SAP [7].
- Anchor-based methods: TGN [6], CBP [42], and MAN [56].
- Direct boundary prediction methods: ABLR [53] and DEBUG [26].
- Reinforcement Learning-based methods: SM-RL [43] and TripNet [14].

Results on Charades-STA. Table 3 shows the performance comparison on the Charades-STA dataset, which is more commonly used. As can be observed, our HVTG outperforms all the compared methods in all three evaluation metrics.

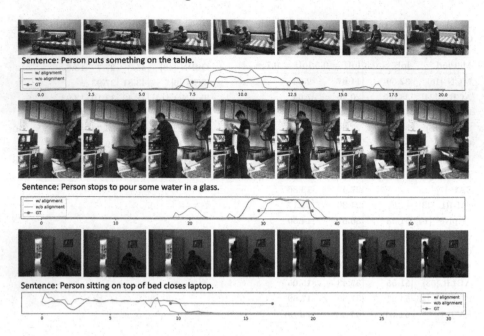

Fig. 3. Example results with the visual-textual relevance scores visualized. The last one is a failed case where the relevance scores do not match the ground-truth well.

Especially when comparing with methods that also adopt the direct boundary prediction strategy, ABLR [53] and DEBUG [26], the advantages of our HVTG is significant, which demonstrates the effectiveness of modeling visual-textual interaction and alignment for the TALL task.

Results on ActivityNet Captions. The video contents of the ActivityNet dataset and the Charades-STA dataset are quite different, because ActivityNet contains not only indoor activities and the duration of its videos are generally longer. Moreover, the language queries in ActivityNet Captions are more complex than Charades-STA. Thus, strong adaptivity is required for TALL methods to work well on both datasets. There are less state-of-the-art methods that have reported results on ActivityNet Captions. As shown in Table 4, our HVTG also outperforms the compared methods, demonstrating the superiority of HVTG. It is worth noting that limited by the GPU memory, the ActivityNet videos are temporally down-sampled with a larger stride, which may have affected the performances of our method.

4.4 Result Visualizations

In Fig. 3, we provide some examples with visualization of the visual-textual relevance scores. As can be observed in the first two examples (top and middle), when the visual-textual alignment is enabled, our model predicts better relevance scores which are more concentrated in the ground-truth region. We also show a failed example (bottom), where the "closes laptop" activity is not accurately localized. We conjecture the reason is that the poor lighting affects the quality of the captured visual information in the object features.

5   Conclusions

We presented a novel method named Hierarchical Visual-Textual Graph (HVTG) for tackling the Temporal Activity Localization via Language (TALL) task, which is challenging since it requires fine-grained understanding of visual contents while jointly considering the language query. To tackle the challenge, our HVTG method builds a hierarchical graph structure to perform interactions between the object and sentence and among the objects. We also adopt a cross-channel communication graph to encourage more fine-grained information passing between the visual and textual modalities. Finally, visual-textual alignment is enforced to encourage the localized activity to be close to the corresponding language query in the feature space. We achieved state-of-the-art performances on two challenging datasets: Charades-STA and ActivityNet Captions. Future work includes incorporating temporal relation modeling into the object subgraphs and improving the interpretability of visual-textual interactions inside the graph.

References

1. Anderson, P., et al.: Bottom-up and top-down attention for image captioning and visual question answering. In: CVPR (2018)
2. Ba, L.J., Kiros, J.R., Hinton, G.E.: Layer normalization. arXiv preprint arXiv:1607.06450 (2016)
3. Buch, S., Escorcia, V., Ghanem, B., Fei-Fei, L., Niebles, J.C.: End-to-end, single-stream temporal action detection in untrimmed videos. In: BMVC (2017)
4. Buch, S., Escorcia, V., Shen, C., Ghanem, B., Niebles, J.C.: SST: single-stream temporal action proposals. In: CVPR (2017)
5. Carreira, J., Zisserman, A.: Quo vadis, action recognition? A new model and the kinetics dataset. In: CVPR (2017)
6. Chen, J., Chen, X., Ma, L., Jie, Z., Chua, T.: Temporally grounding natural sentence in video. In: EMNLP (2018)
7. Chen, S., Jiang, Y.: Semantic proposal for activity localization in videos via sentence query. In: AAAI (2019)
8. Chung, J., Gulcehre, C., Cho, K., Bengio, Y.: Empirical evaluation of gated recurrent neural networks on sequence modeling. In: NIPS Workshop on Deep Learning (2014)
9. Dai, X., Singh, B., Zhang, G., Davis, L.S., Chen, Y.Q.: Temporal context network for activity localization in videos. In: ICCV (2017)
10. Escorcia, V., Caba Heilbron, F., Niebles, J.C., Ghanem, B.: DAPs: deep action proposals for action understanding. In: Leibe, B., Matas, J., Sebe, N., Welling, M. (eds.) ECCV 2016. LNCS, vol. 9907, pp. 768–784. Springer, Cham (2016). https://doi.org/10.1007/978-3-319-46487-9_47

11. Faghri, F., Fleet, D.J., Kiros, J.R., Fidler, S.: VSE++: improving visual-semantic embeddings with hard negatives. In: BMVC (2018)
12. Gao, J., Sun, C., Yang, Z., Nevatia, R.: TALL: temporal activity localization via language query. In: ICCV (2017)
13. Ge, R., Gao, J., Chen, K., Nevatia, R.: MAC: mining activity concepts for language-based temporal localization. In: WACV (2019)
14. Hahn, M., Kadav, A., Rehg, J.M., Graf, H.P.: Tripping through time: efficient localization of activities in videos. arXiv preprint arXiv:1904.09936 (2019)
15. He, K., Gkioxari, G., Dollár, P., Girshick, R.B.: Mask R-CNN. In: ICCV (2017)
16. Hendricks, L.A., Wang, O., Shechtman, E., Sivic, J., Darrell, T., Russell, B.C.: Localizing moments in video with natural language. In: ICCV (2017)
17. Hochreiter, S., Schmidhuber, J.: Long short-term memory. Neural Comput. **9**(8), 1735–1780 (1997)
18. Jiang, B., Huang, X., Yang, C., Yuan, J.: Cross-modal video moment retrieval with spatial and language-temporal attention. In: ICMR (2019)
19. Kingma, D.P., Ba, J.: Adam: a method for stochastic optimization. In: ICLR (2015)
20. Krishna, R., Hata, K., Ren, F., Fei-Fei, L., Niebles, J.C.: Dense-captioning events in videos. In: ICCV (2017)
21. Krishna, R., et al.: Visual genome: connecting language and vision using crowd-sourced dense image annotations. Int. J. Comput. Vis. **123**(1), 32–73 (2017). https://doi.org/10.1007/s11263-016-0981-7
22. Lin, D., Fidler, S., Kong, C., Urtasun, R.: Visual semantic search: retrieving videos via complex textual queries. In: CVPR (2014)
23. Lin, T., Zhao, X., Shou, Z.: Single shot temporal action detection. In: ACM MM (2017)
24. Liu, M., Wang, X., Nie, L., He, X., Chen, B., Chua, T.: Attentive moment retrieval in videos. In: ACM SIGIR (2018)
25. Liu, M., Wang, X., Nie, L., Tian, Q., Chen, B., Chua, T.: Cross-modal moment localization in videos. In: ACM MM (2018)
26. Lu, C., Chen, L., Tan, C., Li, X., Xiao, J.: DEBUG: a dense bottom-up grounding approach for natural language video localization. In: EMNLP-IJCNLP (2019)
27. Mettes, P., van Gemert, J.C., Cappallo, S., Mensink, T., Snoek, C.G.M.: Bag-of-fragments: selecting and encoding video fragments for event detection and recounting. In: ICMR (2015)
28. Miech, A., Laptev, I., Sivic, J.: Learning a text-video embedding from incomplete and heterogeneous data. arXiv preprint arXiv:1804.02516 (2018)
29. Mithun, N.C., Li, J., Metze, F., Roy-Chowdhury, A.K.: Learning joint embedding with multimodal cues for cross-modal video-text retrieval. In: ICMR (2018)
30. Otani, M., Nakashima, Y., Rahtu, E., Heikkilä, J., Yokoya, N.: Learning joint representations of videos and sentences with web image search. In: Hua, G., Jégou, H. (eds.) ECCV 2016. LNCS, vol. 9913, pp. 651–667. Springer, Cham (2016). https://doi.org/10.1007/978-3-319-46604-0_46
31. Pennington, J., Socher, R., Manning, C.D.: GloVe: global vectors for word representation. In: EMNLP (2014)
32. Pont-Tuset, J., Arbelaez, P., Barron, J.T., Marqués, F., Malik, J.: Multiscale combinatorial grouping for image segmentation and object proposal generation. IEEE TPAMI **39**(1), 128–140 (2017)
33. Ren, S., He, K., Girshick, R.B., Sun, J.: Faster R-CNN: towards real-time object detection with region proposal networks. In: NIPS (2015)

34. Shou, Z., Chan, J., Zareian, A., Miyazawa, K., Chang, S.: CDC: convolutional-de-convolutional networks for precise temporal action localization in untrimmed videos. In: CVPR (2017)
35. Shou, Z., Wang, D., Chang, S.: Temporal action localization in untrimmed videos via multi-stage CNNs. In: CVPR (2016)
36. Sigurdsson, G.A., Varol, G., Wang, X., Farhadi, A., Laptev, I., Gupta, A.: Hollywood in homes: crowdsourcing data collection for activity understanding. In: Leibe, B., Matas, J., Sebe, N., Welling, M. (eds.) ECCV 2016. LNCS, vol. 9905, pp. 510–526. Springer, Cham (2016). https://doi.org/10.1007/978-3-319-46448-0_31
37. Song, X., Han, Y.: VAL: visual-attention action localizer. In: PCM (2018)
38. Szegedy, C., Ioffe, S., Vanhoucke, V., Alemi, A.A.: Inception-v4, inception-ResNet and the impact of residual connections on learning. In: AAAI (2017)
39. Tran, D., Bourdev, L.D., Fergus, R., Torresani, L., Paluri, M.: Learning spatiotemporal features with 3D convolutional networks. In: ICCV (2015)
40. Ulyanov, D., Vedaldi, A., Lempitsky, V.S.: Instance normalization: the missing ingredient for fast stylization. arXiv preprint arXiv:1607.08022 (2016)
41. Velickovic, P., Cucurull, G., Casanova, A., Romero, A., Liò, P., Bengio, Y.: Graph attention networks. In: ICLR (2018)
42. Wang, J., Ma, L., Jiang, W.: Temporally grounding language queries in videos by contextual boundary-aware prediction. In: AAAI (2020)
43. Wang, W., Huang, Y., Wang, L.: Language-driven temporal activity localization: a semantic matching reinforcement learning model. In: CVPR (2019)
44. Wang, X., Gupta, A.: Videos as space-time region graphs. In: Ferrari, V., Hebert, M., Sminchisescu, C., Weiss, Y. (eds.) ECCV 2018. LNCS, vol. 11209, pp. 413–431. Springer, Cham (2018). https://doi.org/10.1007/978-3-030-01228-1_25
45. Wray, M., Larlus, D., Csurka, G., Damen, D.: Fine-grained action retrieval through multiple parts-of-speech embeddings. arXiv preprint arXiv:1908.03477 (2019)
46. Xu, B., Wang, N., Chen, T., Li, M.: Empirical evaluation of rectified activations in convolutional network. arXiv preprint arXiv:1505.00853 (2015)
47. Xu, H., Das, A., Saenko, K.: R-C3D: region convolutional 3D network for temporal activity detection. In: ICCV (2017)
48. Xu, H., He, K., Plummer, B.A., Sigal, L., Sclaroff, S., Saenko, K.: Multilevel language and vision integration for text-to-clip retrieval. In: AAAI (2019)
49. Xu, H., He, K., Sigal, L., Sclaroff, S., Saenko, K.: Text-to-clip video retrieval with early fusion and re-captioning. arXiv preprint arXiv:1804.05113 (2018)
50. Xu, R., Xiong, C., Chen, W., Corso, J.J.: Jointly modeling deep video and compositional text to bridge vision and language in a unified framework. In: AAAI (2015)
51. Yang, J., Ren, Z., Gan, C., Zhu, H., Parikh, D.: Cross-channel communication networks. In: NeurIPS (2019)
52. Yu, Y., Kim, J., Kim, G.: A joint sequence fusion model for video question answering and retrieval. In: Ferrari, V., Hebert, M., Sminchisescu, C., Weiss, Y. (eds.) ECCV 2018. LNCS, vol. 11211, pp. 487–503. Springer, Cham (2018). https://doi.org/10.1007/978-3-030-01234-2_29
53. Yuan, Y., Mei, T., Zhu, W.: To find where you talk: temporal sentence localization in video with attention based location regression. In: AAAI (2019)
54. Zhang, B., Hu, H., Sha, F.: Cross-modal and hierarchical modeling of video and text. In: Ferrari, V., Hebert, M., Sminchisescu, C., Weiss, Y. (eds.) ECCV 2018. LNCS, vol. 11217, pp. 385–401. Springer, Cham (2018). https://doi.org/10.1007/978-3-030-01261-8_23

618   S. Chen and Y.-G. Jiang

55. Zhang, D., Dai, X., Wang, X., Wang, Y.: S3D: single shot multi-span detector via fully 3D convolutional networks. In: BMVC (2018)
56. Zhang, D., Dai, X., Wang, X., Wang, Y., Davis, L.S.: MAN: moment alignment network for natural language moment retrieval via iterative graph adjustment. In: CVPR (2019)
57. Zhao, Y., Xiong, Y., Wang, L., Wu, Z., Tang, X., Lin, D.: Temporal action detection with structured segment networks. In: ICCV (2017)
58. Zheng, Y., Pal, D.K., Savvides, M.: Ring loss: convex feature normalization for face recognition. In: CVPR (2018)

Do Not Mask What You Do Not Need to Mask: A Parser-Free Virtual Try-On

Thibaut Issenhuth$^{(\boxtimes)}$, Jérémie Mary, and Clément Calauzènes

Criteo AI Lab, Paris, France
{t.issenhuth,j.mary,c.calauzenes}@criteo.com

Abstract. The 2D virtual try-on task has recently attracted a great interest from the research community, for its direct potential applications in online shopping as well as for its inherent and non-addressed scientific challenges. This task requires fitting an in-shop cloth image on the image of a person, which is highly challenging because it involves cloth warping, image compositing, and synthesizing. Casting virtual try-on into a supervised task faces a difficulty: available datasets are composed of pairs of pictures (cloth, person wearing the cloth). Thus, we have no access to ground-truth when the cloth on the person changes. State-of-the-art models solve this by masking the cloth information on the person with both a human parser and a pose estimator. Then, image synthesis modules are trained to reconstruct the person image from the masked person image and the cloth image. This procedure has several caveats: firstly, human parsers are prone to errors; secondly, it is a costly preprocessing step, which also has to be applied at inference time; finally, it makes the task harder than it is since the mask covers information that should be kept such as hands or accessories. In this paper, we propose a novel student-teacher paradigm where the teacher is trained in the standard way (reconstruction) before guiding the student to focus on the initial task (changing the cloth). The student additionally learns from an adversarial loss, which pushes it to follow the distribution of the real images. Consequently, the student exploits information that is masked to the teacher. A student trained without the adversarial loss would not use this information. Also, getting rid of both human parser and pose estimator at inference time allows obtaining a real-time virtual try-on.

Keywords: Virtual try-on · Teacher-student · Model distillation

1 Introduction

A photo-realistic virtual try-on system would provide a significant improvement for online shopping. Whether used to create catalogs of new products or to propose an immersive environment for shoppers, it could impact e-commerce and open the door for automated image-editing possibilities.

Electronic supplementary material The online version of this chapter (https://doi.org/10.1007/978-3-030-58565-5_37) contains supplementary material, which is available to authorized users.

© Springer Nature Switzerland AG 2020
A. Vedaldi et al. (Eds.): ECCV 2020, LNCS 12365, pp. 619–635, 2020.
https://doi.org/10.1007/978-3-030-58565-5_37

| Reference
person | Target
cloth | Human
parsing | CP-VTON | T-WUTON
(ours) | S-WUTON
(ours) |

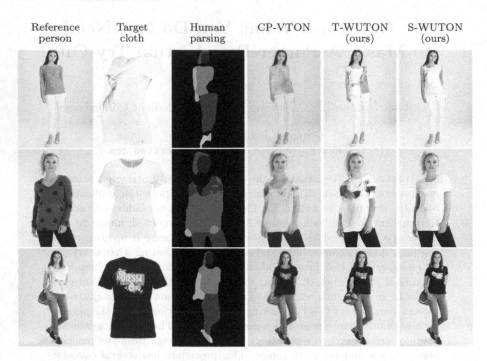

Fig. 1. Typical failure cases of the human parser. On the two first rows, it does not segment the person properly. On the third row, it masks the handbag which we would like to preserve in a virtual try-on. CP-VTON and our T-WUTON, which rely on the parsing information, are not robust to a bad parsing. However, the student model S-WUTON which is distilled from the human parser, pose estimator and T-WUTON, can preserve the person's attributes and does not rely on the parsing information.

Earlier work addresses this challenge using 3D measurements and model-based methods [9,11,28]. However, these are, by nature, computationally intensive and require expensive material, which would not be acceptable at scale for shops. Recent works aim to leverage deep generative models to tackle the virtual try-on problem [6,13,19,38]. CAGAN [19] is a U-net based Cycle-GAN [17] approach. However, this method fails to generate realistic results since such networks cannot handle large spatial deformations. In VITON [13], the authors recast the virtual try-on as a supervised task. They propose to use a human parser and a pose estimator to mask the cloth in the person image and construct an agnostic person representation $p^\star$. The human parser allows segmenting the upper-body and the cloth, while the pose estimator locates the keypoints (*i.e.* shoulders, wrists, etc.) of the person. Then, with $p^\star$ and the image of the original cloth c on a white background, they train a model in a fully supervised fashion to reconstruct p. Namely, they propose a coarse-to-fine synthesis strategy with shape context matching algorithm [3] to warp the cloth on the target person. To improve this model, CP-VTON [38] incorporates a convolutional geometric matcher [31], which learns geometric deformations (*i.e.* thin-plate spline transform [4]) that align the cloth with the person. State-of-the-art models are based on the supervised formulation of the virtual try-on task, which has some drawbacks. Human parsers and pose estimators are trained on other datasets and thus fail in some situations (see Fig. 1, two first rows). Retraining them on fashion datasets would require similar labels of semantic segmentation or unsupervised domain adaptation methods. Even though they would still be imperfect. Moreover, for a virtual try-on, one wants to preserve person's attributes like handbags or jewels. When constructing p^*, these person's attributes are masked and can not be preserved, such as the partially masked handbag on the third row of Fig. 1. Finally, the human parsing and pose estimation are the wall clock bottleneck of the pipeline.

In our work, we distill [15] the standard pipeline of virtual try-on composed of human parser, pose estimator, and synthesis modules in the synthesis modules. Namely, we train a student synthesizer with the outputs of a pre-trained standard virtual try-on pipeline. To force the student to use information that is masked to the teacher, we also train the student with an adversarial loss. The distillation process allows us to remove the need for human parsing and pose estimation at inference time, which improves image quality and speeds up the computations from 6FPS to 77FPS. In Fig. 1, we show visual results of a baseline CP-VTON, our teacher model T-WUTON and our student model S-WUTON. Since S-WUTON does not rely on human parsing, it is robust to parsing errors and preserves a person's attributes such as fingers or handbags.

Additionally, to build an efficient teacher model, we propose an improved architecture for virtual try-on, a Warping U-Net for a Virtual Try-On (WUTON). Our architecture is composed of two modules: a convolutional geometric matcher [31] and a U-net generator with a siamese encoder, where the former warps the feature maps of the latter. The architecture is trained end-to-end, which leads to high-quality synthesized images.

We demonstrate the benefit of our method with several experiments on a virtual try-on dataset, with quantitative and visual results, and a user study.

2   Problem Statement and Related Work

Given the 2D images $p \in \mathbb{R}^{h \times w \times 3}$ of a person and $c \in \mathbb{R}^{h \times w \times 3}$ of a clothing item, we want to generate the image $\tilde{p} \in \mathbb{R}^{h \times w \times 3}$ where a person p wears the cloth c. The task can be separated in two parts: the geometric deformation T required to align c with p, and the refinement that fits the aligned cloth $\tilde{c} = T(c)$ on p. These two sub-tasks can be modelled with learnable neural networks, $i.e.$ spatial transformers networks STN [18,31] that output parameters $\theta = STN(p, c)$ of geometric deformations, and conditional generative networks G that give $\tilde{p} = G(p, c, \theta)$.

Because it would be costly to construct a dataset with $\{(p, c), \tilde{p}\}$ triplets, previous works [13,38] propose to use an agnostic person representation $p^* \in \mathbb{R}^{h \times w \times c}$ where the clothing items in p are hidden but identity and shape of the persons are preserved. p^* is built with pre-trained human parsers and pose estimators: $p^* = h(p)$. These triplets $\{(p^*, c), p\}$ allow to train for reconstruction.

$(p^\star, c)$ are the inputs, $\tilde{p}$ the output and p the ground-truth. We finally have the conditional generative process:

$$\tilde{p} = G(\underbrace{h(p)}_{\text{agnostic person}}, \underbrace{c}_{\text{cloth}}, \underbrace{STN(h(p), c)}_{\text{geometric transform}}) \tag{1}$$

Although it eases the training of G, h is a bottleneck in the virtual try-on pipeline. We will show that we can train a student model with synthetic triplets $\{(p, c), \tilde{p}\}$, where $\tilde{p}$ comes from our pre-trained teacher generative model in Eq. 1. This allows to remove the need for h at inference time for the student model:

$$\hat{p} = G_s(\underbrace{p}_{\text{original person}}, \underbrace{c}_{\text{cloth}}, \underbrace{STN_s(p, c)}_{\text{geometric transform}}) \tag{2}$$

where G_s and STN_s are the student modules and $\hat{p}$ the generated image.

Conditional Image Generation. Generative models for image synthesis have shown impressive results with adversarial training [8]. Combined with deep networks [29], this approach has been extended to conditional image generation in [27] and performs increasingly well on a wide range of tasks, from image-to-image translation [17,45] to video editing [34]. However, as noted in [26], these models cannot handle large spatial deformations and fail to modify the shape of objects, which is necessary for a virtual try-on.

Appearance Transfer. Close to the virtual try-on task, some research focus on human appearance transfer. Given two images of different persons, the goal is to transfer the appearance of a part of the person A on the person B. Approaches using pose and appearance disentanglement [24,25] fit this task but others are specifically designed for it. SwapNet [30] is a dual path network which generates a new human parsing of the reference person and region of interest pooling to transfer the texture. In [40], the method relies on DensePose information [1], which provides a 3D surface estimation of a human body, to perform a warping and align the two persons. The transfer is then done with segmentation masks and refinement networks. However, the warping relies on matching source and target pose, which is not feasible for the virtual try-on task.

Virtual Try-On. Most of the approaches for a virtual try-on system come from computer graphics and rely on 3D measurements or representations. Drape [9] learns a deformation model to render clothes on 3D bodies of different shapes. In [11], Hahn et al. use subspace methods to accelerate physics-based simulations and generate realistic wrinkles. ClothCap [28] aligns a 3D cloth-template to each frame of a sequence of 3D scans of a person in motion. However, the use of 3D scans is expensive and thus not doable for online users.

The task we are interested in is the one introduced in CAGAN [19] and further studied by VITON [13] and CP-VTON [38], which we defined in the problem statement. In CAGAN [19], Jetchev et al. propose a cycle-GAN approach that requires three images as input: the reference person, the cloth worn by the person and the target in-shop cloth. Thus, it limits its practical uses. To facilitate the task, VITON [13] introduces the supervised formulation of the virtual try-on, as described above. Their pipeline separates the task in sub-tasks: constructing the agnostic person representation (*i.e.* mask the area to replace but preserve body shape), warping the cloth and compositing the final image. Based on the agnostic person representation p^* and the cloth image c, the VITON model performs a generative composition between the warped cloth and a coarse result. The warping is done with a non-parametric geometric transform [3]. To improve this model, CP-VTON [38] incorporates a learnable geometric matcher STN [31]. The STN is trained to align c on p with a L1 loss on paired images. However, the L1 loss is overwhelmed with the white background and the solid color parts of clothes. Thus, it faces difficulties to align patterns and to preserve inner structure of the cloth. In VTNFP [42] and ClothFlow [12], a module generating the new human parsing is added. It allows to better preserve body parts and edges, but at an increased computational cost. Moreover, ClothFlow [12] replaces the TPS warping by a dense flow from the target cloth to the person. All these recent works [12,13,38,42] rely on pre-trained human parser and pose estimator.

Recent work MG-VTON [6] extends the task to a multi-pose virtual try-on system, where they also change the pose of the reference person. Similarly to [5,6,42], they add a module generating the new human parsing, based on input and target pose information.

3   Our Approach

Our task is to build a virtual try-on system that is able to fit a given in-shop cloth on a reference person. In this work, we build a virtual try-on that does not rely on a human parser nor a pose estimator for inference. To do so, we use a teacher-student approach to distill the standard virtual try-on pipeline composed of human parser, pose estimator, and synthesis module in the synthesis module.

In Sect. 3.1, we detail the architecture of our synthesis module WUTON. It is trainable end-to-end and composed of two existing modules: a convolutional geometric matcher STN [31] and a U-net [32] with siamese encoder whose skip connections from the cloth encoder to the decoder are deformed by STN. We then explain its training procedure in the standard supervised setting, which gives the teacher T-WUTON.

We finally explain our distillation process. Once the first generative model is trained, the pipeline $\{h, \text{T-WUTON}\}$ becomes a teacher model for a student model S-WUTON by constructing synthetic triplets $\{(p, c), \tilde{p}\}$. These serve to supervise the training of S-WUTON, which hence does not need a human parser to pre-process the image and construct the agnostic person representation. Importantly, S-WUTON also learns from an adversarial loss so it does not only follow the teacher's distribution and it can learn to preserve a person's attributes.

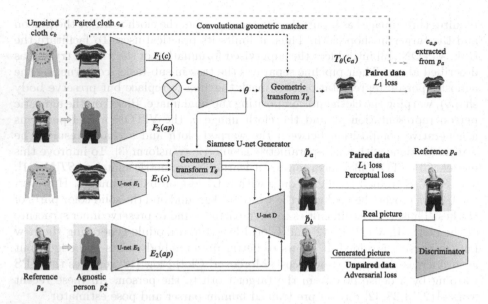

Fig. 2. The teacher T-WUTON: our proposed end-to-end warping U-net architecture. Dotted arrows correspond to the forward pass only performed during training. Green arrows are the human parser, red ones are the loss functions. The geometric transforms share the same parameters but do not operate on the same spaces. The different training procedure for paired and unpaired pictures is explained in Sect. 3.2.

3.1   WUTON Architecture

Our warping U-net is composed of two connected modules, as shown in Fig. 2. The first one is a convolutional geometric matcher, which has a similar architecture as [31,38]. It outputs the parameters θ of a geometric transformation, a TPS transform in our case. This geometric transformation aligns the in-shop cloth image with the reference person. However, in contrast to previous work [6,13,38], we use the geometric transformation on the feature maps of the generator rather than at a pixel-level. Thus, we learn to deform the feature maps that pass through the skip connections of the second module, a U-net [32] generator which synthesizes the output image $\tilde{p}$.

The architecture of the convolutional geometric matcher is taken from CP-VTON [38], which reuses the generic geometric matcher from [31]. It is composed of two feature extractors F_1 and F_2, which are standard convolutional neural networks. The local vectors of feature maps $F_1(c)$ and $F_2(p^\star)$ are then L2-normalized and a correlation map C is computed as follows:

$$C_{ijk} = F_{1_{i,j}}(c) \cdot F_{2_{m,n}}(p^\star) \tag{3}$$

where k is the index for the position (m, n). This correlation map captures dependencies between distant locations of the two feature maps, which is useful to align the two images. C is the input of a regression network, which outputs the parameters θ and allows to perform the geometric transformation T_θ. We use TPS transformations [4], which generate smooth sampling grids given control points. Each scale of the U-net is transformed with the same parameters θ.

The input of the U-net generator is also the tuple of pictures $(p^\star, c)$. Since these two images are not spatially aligned, we cannot simply concatenate them and feed a standard U-net. To alleviate this, we use two different encoders E_1 and E_2 processing each image independently and with non-shared parameters. Then, the feature maps of the in-shop cloth $E_1(c)$ are transformed at each scale i: $E_1^i(c) = T_\theta(E_1^i(c))$. Then, the feature maps of the two encoders are concatenated and feed the decoder at each scale. With aligned feature maps, the generator is able to compose them and to produce realistic results. Feature maps warping was also proposed in [5,35]. We use instance normalization in the U-net generator, which is more effective than batch normalization [16] for image generation [37].

3.2   Training Procedure of the Teacher Model

We will now detail the training procedure of T-WUTON, *i.e.* the data representation and the different loss functions of the teacher model.

While previous works use a rich person representation with more than 20 channels representing human pose, body shape and the RGB image of the head, we only mask the upper-body of the reference person. Our agnostic person representation $p^\star$ is thus a 3-channel RGB image with a masked area. We compute the upper-body mask from pose and body parsing information provided by a pretrained neural network from [23]. Precisely, we mask the areas corresponding to the arms, the upper-body cloth and a bounding box around the neck.

Using the dataset from [6], we have pairs of in-shop cloth image c_a and a person wearing the same cloth p_a. Using a human parser and a human pose estimator, we generate $p_a^\star$. From the parsing information, we can also isolate the cloth on the image p_a and get $c_{a,p}$, the cloth worn by the reference person. Moreover, we get the image of another in-shop cloth c_b. The inputs of our network are the two tuples $(p_a^\star, c_a)$ and $(p_a^\star, c_b)$. The outputs are respectively $(\tilde{p}_a, \theta_a)$ and $(\tilde{p}_b, \theta_b)$.

The cloth worn by the person $c_{a,p}$ allows us to guide directly the geometric matcher with a L_1 loss:

$$L_{warp} = \|T_{\theta_a}(c_a) - c_{a,p}\|_1 \tag{4}$$

The image p_a of the reference person provides a supervision for the whole pipeline. Similarly to CP-VTON [38], we use two different losses to guide the generation of the final image $\tilde{p}_a$, the pixel-level L_1 loss $\|\tilde{p}_a - p_a\|_1$ and the perceptual loss [20]. We focus on L_1 losses since they are known to generate less blur than L_2 for image generation [44]. The latter consists of using the features extracted with a pre-trained neural network, VGG [36] in our case. Specifically, our perceptual loss is:

$$L_{perceptual} = \sum_{i=1}^{5} \|\phi_i(\tilde{p}_a) - \phi_i(p_a)\|_1 \tag{5}$$

where $\phi_i(I)$ are the feature maps of an image I extracted at the i-th layer of the VGG network. Furthermore, we exploit adversarial training to train the network to fit c_b on the same agnostic person representation $p_a^\star$, which is extracted from a person wearing c_a. This is only feasible with an adversarial loss, since there is no available ground-truth for this pair $(p_a^\star, c_b)$. Thus, we feed the discriminator with the synthesized image $\tilde{p}_b$ and real images of persons from the dataset. This adversarial loss is also back-propagated to the convolutional geometric matcher, which allows to generate much more realistic spatial transformations. We use the relativistic adversarial loss [21] with gradient-penalty [2,10], which trains the discriminator to predict relative realness of real images compared to synthesized ones. Finally, we optimize with Adam [22] the following objective function:

$$L = \lambda_w L_{warp} + \lambda_p L_{perceptual} + \lambda_{L_1} L_1 + \lambda_{adv} L_{adv} \tag{6}$$

3.3 Training Procedure of the Student Model

We propose to use a teacher-student approach to distill the pipeline composed of $\{h, \text{T-WUTON}\}$ in a single student WUTON (S-WUTON). Indeed, our pre-trained T-WUTON is able to generate realistic images and geometric deformations of clothes on images pre-processed by h. We leverage it and use it as a way to construct generated triplets $\{(p_a, c_b), \tilde{p}_b\}$, where $\tilde{p}_b$ is the image synthesized by T-WUTON. With this pre-trained model, we can supervise the training of a student model S-WUTON. This allows to train the student model on the initial task of changing the cloth rather than reconstructing the upper-body. The student model has the exact same architecture than T-WUTON but different inputs and ground-truth. Hence, its inputs are (p_a, c_b), where p_a is the non-masked

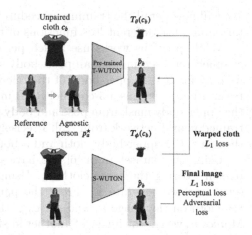

Fig. 3. S-WUTON: our training scheme allowing to remove the need for a human parser at inference time. We use human parser and pre-trained T-WUTON to generate synthetic ground-truth for a student model S-WUTON.

image of a person. Having this non-masked image as input, the student model does not need a human parser for pre-processing images. The ground-truth of S-WUTON are the outputs of T-WUTON, for both the warped cloth $T_\theta(c_b)$ and the final synthesized image $\tilde{p}_b$. The training scheme of the student model S-WUTON is shown in Fig. 3.

More precisely, let us define the inputs-outputs of the teacher and student model: $(\hat{p}_b, \phi) = \text{S-WUTON}(p_a, c_b)$ and $(\tilde{p}_b, \theta) = \text{T-WUTON}(h(p_a), c_b)$. Then, the loss functions of S-WUTON are:

$$L_{warp} = \|T_\phi(c_b) - T_\theta(c_b)\|_1 \tag{7}$$

$$L_{perceptual} = \sum_{i=1}^{5} \|\phi_i(\hat{p}_b) - \phi_i(\tilde{p}_b)\|_1 \tag{8}$$

$$L_1 = \|\hat{p}_b - \tilde{p}_b\|_1 \tag{9}$$

Finally, the total loss of the student model is:

$$L = \lambda_w L_{warp} + \lambda_p L_{perceptual} + \lambda_{L_1} L_1 + \lambda_{adv} L_{adv} \tag{10}$$

The adversarial loss L_{adv} is independent from T-WUTON. Here, we also use the relativistic loss with gradient penalty on the discriminator. The real data consists of images of persons from the dataset p_a, and the fake data corresponds to the synthesized images $\hat{p}_b$. Notice that without the adversarial loss, it would be a standard teacher-student setting, where the student is only guided by the outputs of the teacher. In our case, the discriminator (*i.e.* L_{adv}) helps S-WUTON to be close to the real data distribution, and not only to the teacher's distribution. As shown by the ablation study in Sect. 4.6, it is an important component and is necessary to make S-WUTON exploit the components that are masked from T-WUTON (*e.g.* hands).

4   Experiments and Analysis

We first describe the dataset. We then compare our approach with CP-VTON [38], a current state-of-the-art for the virtual try-on task. We present visual and quantitative results proving that S-WUTON achieves state-of-the-art results, and that the distillation process allows to improve image quality. We show that this stands for several metrics, and with a user study. We then provide a comparison of the runtime of virtual try-on algorithms on a Tesla NVIDIA V100 GPU. The teacher-student distillation allows to decrease the runtime by an order of magnitude. Finally, we outline the importance of the adversarial loss in our teacher-student setting.

We also show some visual comparisons with recent work VTNFP [42]. Images are taken from their paper. However, since their model is not available, we could not compute the other metrics. We provide more visual comparisons with VTNFP and ClothFlow [12] in supplementary material.

4.1   Dataset

For copyright issues, we can not use the dataset from VITON [13] and CP-VTON [38]. Instead, we leverage the *Image-based Multi-pose Virtual try-on* dataset. This dataset contains 35,687/13,524 person/cloth images at 256 × 192 resolution.

Ref. person	Target cloth	CP- VTON	T-WUT- ON(ours)	S-WUTON (ours)	Ref. person	Target cloth	CP- VTON	VTNFP	S-WUTON (ours)

Fig. 4. On the left side, comparison of our method with CP-VTON [38]. For fairness, the two methods are trained on the same dataset and on the same agnostic person representation $p^\star$. More examples are provided in supplementary material. On the right side, comparison with recent work VTNFP. Except for S-WUTON's column, images are taken from their paper.

4175 pairs are kept for test so the cloth was not seen during training. A random shuffle of these pairs produces the unpaired person/cloth images. For each in-shop cloth image, there are multiple images of a model wearing the given cloth from different views and in different poses. We remove images tagged as back images since the in-shop cloth image is only from the front. We process the images with a neural human parser and pose estimator, specifically the joint body parsing and pose estimation network [7,23].

4.2   Visual Results

Visual results of our method and CP-VTON are shown in Fig. 4. On the left side, images are computed from models trained on MG-VTON dataset, with $p^\star_{t-wuton}$ representation for T-WUTON and CP-VTON for fairness. On the right side, images are taken from VTNFP paper [42]. There, CP-VTON and VTNFP were trained on the original dataset from VITON, and CP-VTON uses $p^\star_{cp-vton}$. More images from S-WUTON are provided in Fig. 1 and Fig. 6.

CP-VTON has trouble to realistically deform and render complex patterns like stripes or flowers. Control points of the T_θ transform are visible and lead to unrealistic curves and deformations on the clothes. Also, the edges of cloth patterns and body contours are blurred.

Firstly, our proposed T-WUTON architecture allows to improve the baseline CP-VTON. Indeed, our method generates spatial transformations of a much higher visual quality, which is specifically visible for stripes (1st row). It is able to preserve complex visual patterns of clothes and produces sharper images than CP-VTON and VTNFP on the edges. Secondly, we can observe the importance of our distillation process with the visual results from S-WUTON. Since it has a non-masked image as input, it is able to preserve body details, especially the hands. Moreover, as shown in Fig. 1, S-WUTON is robust to a bad parsing and preserves a person's attributes that are important for the virtual try-on task.

Generally, our method generates results of high visual quality while preserving the characteristics of the target cloth and of the person. However, VTNFP can surpass S-WUTON when models are crossing arms (4th row, right side), which is sometimes a failure case of our method. Note that this is not general, since on (3rd row, right side) and (4th row, left side) in Fig. 4 and on the two last columns in Fig. 5, models are crossing arms and S-WUTON manages to nicely compose the arms with the occluded cloth.

4.3 Quantitative Results

Table 1. Quantitative results on paired setting (LPIPS and SSIM) and on unpaired setting (IS and FID). For LPIPS and FID, the lower is the better. For SSIM and IS, the higher is the better. ± reports std. dev. The two last lines (methods with *) are the results presented in ACGPN [41]. However, it has to be taken carefully since the experiments are performed on another dataset.

Method	LPIPS	SSIM	IS	FID
Real data	0	1	3.135	0
CP-VTON on $p^{\star}_{cp-vton}$	0.182 ± 0.049	0.679 ± 0.073	2.684	37.237
CP-VTON on $p^{\star}_{t-wuton}$	0.131 ± 0.058	0.773 ± 0.088	2.938	16.843
T-WUTON	$\mathbf{0.101 \pm 0.047}$	$\mathbf{0.799 \pm 0.089}$	3.114	9.877
S-WUTON	NA	NA	**3.154**	**7.927**
VTNFP*	NA	0.803	2.784	NA
ACGPN*	NA	0.845	2.829	NA

To further evaluate our method, we use four different metrics. Two are designed for the paired setting, that does not allow us to evaluate S-WUTON (because the input image is not masked), and one is for the unpaired setting. The first one for the paired setting is the linear perceptual image patch similarity (LPIPS) developed in [43], a state-of-the-art metric for comparing pairs of images. It is very similar to the perceptual loss we use in training (see Sect. 3.2) since the idea is to use the feature maps extracted by a pre-trained neural network to quantify the perceptual difference between two images. Different from the basic perceptual loss, they first unit-normalize each layer in the channel dimension and then learn a rescaling that match human perception.

Such as previous works, we also use the structural similarity (SSIM) [39] in the paired setting, inception score (IS) [33] and Fréchet Inception Distance (FID) [14] in the unpaired setting. We evaluate CP-VTON [38] on their agnostic person representation $p^\star_{cp-vton}$ (20 channels with RGB image of head and shape/pose information) and on $p^\star_{t-wuton}$. Results are reported in Table 1.

4.4   User Study

We perform A/B tests on 7 users. Each one has to vote 100 times between CP-VTON and S-WUTON synthesized images, given reference person and target cloth. The user is asked to choose for the most realistic image, that preserves both person and target cloth details. The selected 100 images are a random subset of the test set in the unpaired setting. This subset is sampled for each user and is thus different for each user. There is no time limit for the users.

Let us denote p the probability that an image from S-WUTON is preferable to an image from CP-VTON. The users choose our method 88% of the time. In terms of statistical significance, it means that we can say $p > 0.85$ with a confidence level of 98.7%.

ClothFlow and VTNFP also performed user studies where they compare to CP-VTON. The authors respectively report that users prefer their method 81.2% and 77.4% of the time. Note that the experiment was not performed in the same setting (dataset, number of users, number of pictures per user).

4.5   Runtime Analysis

Table 2. Comparison of runtime of state-of-the-art architectures for virtual try-on. The time is computed on a NVIDIA Tesla V100 GPU.

	CP-VTON	VTNFP	ClothFlow	T-WUTON	S-WUTON
Parsing + pose	168 ms	168 ms	168 ms	168 ms	**0 ms**
Try-on	**9 ms**	>9 ms	>0 ms	13 ms	13 ms
Total	177 ms	>177 ms	>168 ms	181 ms	**13 ms**

In Table 2, we compare the runtime of our method to CP-VTON, ClothFlow and VTNFP. Note that the running times are estimated on a NVIDIA V100 GPU. For the human parsing and pose estimation networks, we use state-of-the-art models from [7,23]. These are based on shared neural backbones for the two tasks, which accelerates the computations.

The try-on architecture of T-WUTON and S-WUTON is slightly slower than that of CP-VTON, due to the non-shared encoder and the warping at each scale of the U-Net. However, with S-WUTON we remove the wall clock bottleneck of virtual try-on system, which is the human parsing and pose estimation. Doing so, we decrease by an order of magnitude the runtime of virtual try-on algorithms, from 6FPS to 77FPS.

We include comparisons with VTNFP and ClothFlow in the Table 2. Indeed, both models use human parsing and pose estimation. For VTNFP, they add a module on top of CP-VTON architecture, so their try-on architecture takes at least 9 ms per image. For ClothFlow, the use of human parser and pose estimator gives a lower bound on the total runtime.

4.6   The Impact of Adversarial Loss in the Teacher-Student Setting

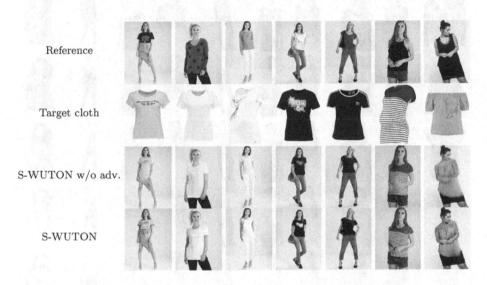

Fig. 5. Visual comparison of the student model with and without the adversarial loss. Interestingly, the student model without the adversarial loss can not exploit information that is masked to the teacher, *e.g.* arms and hands.

We show the impact of the adversarial loss on S-WUTON. We train a variant student model S-WUTON without the adversarial loss. We provide a comparison of synthesized images in Fig. 5, and IS and FID scores in Table 3. The adversarial loss on the student model is a constraint to make

Table 3. Comparison of IS and FID scores of S-WUTON and S-WUTON without the adversarial loss.

	S-WUTON w/o adv.	S-WUTON
IS	2.912	**3.154**
FID	12.620	**7.927**

the student model closer to the real data distribution and to not only follow the teacher's distribution. Without the adversarial loss, the student model does not preserve person's attributes, even though they are not masked.

Fig. 6. Our student model S-WUTON generates high-quality images and preserves both person's and cloth's attributes.

5 Conclusion

In this work, we propose a teacher-student setting to distill the standard virtual try-on pipeline and refocus on the initial task: changing the cloth of a non-masked person. This leads to a significant computational speed-up and largely improves image quality. Importantly, this allows to preserve person's attributes such as hands or accessories, which is necessary for a virtual try-on.

Acknowledgements. The authors thank David Picard and Marie-Morgane Paumard for their helpful advices.

References

1. Alp Güler, R., Neverova, N., Kokkinos, I.: DensePose: dense human pose estimation in the wild. In: Proceedings of the IEEE Conference on Computer Vision and Pattern Recognition, pp. 7297–7306 (2018)
2. Arjovsky, M., Chintala, S., Bottou, L.: Wasserstein generative adversarial networks. In: International Conference on Machine Learning, pp. 214–223 (2017)
3. Belongie, S., Malik, J., Puzicha, J.: Shape matching and object recognition using shape contexts. IEEE Trans. Pattern Anal. Mach. Intell. **24**(4), 509–522 (2002)
4. Bookstein, F.L.: Principal warps: thin-plate splines and the decomposition of deformations. IEEE Trans. Pattern Anal. Mach. Intell. **11**(6), 567–585 (1989)
5. Dong, H., Liang, X., Gong, K., Lai, H., Zhu, J., Yin, J.: Soft-gated warping-GAN for pose-guided person image synthesis. In: Advances in Neural Information Processing Systems, pp. 472–482 (2018)
6. Dong, H., Liang, X., Wang, B., Lai, H., Zhu, J., Yin, J.: Towards multi-pose guided virtual try-on network. In: The IEEE International Conference on Computer Vision (ICCV), October 2019
7. Gong, K., Liang, X., Zhang, D., Shen, X., Lin, L.: Look into person: self-supervised structure-sensitive learning and a new benchmark for human parsing. In: Proceedings of the IEEE Conference on Computer Vision and Pattern Recognition, pp. 932–940 (2017)
8. Goodfellow, I., et al.: Generative adversarial nets. In: Advances in Neural Information Processing Systems, pp. 2672–2680 (2014)
9. Guan, P., Reiss, L., Hirshberg, D.A., Weiss, A., Black, M.J.: DRAPE: dressing any person. ACM Trans. Graph. **31**(4), 35–41 (2012)
10. Gulrajani, I., Ahmed, F., Arjovsky, M., Dumoulin, V., Courville, A.C.: Improved training of wasserstein GANs. In: Advances in Neural Information Processing Systems, pp. 5767–5777 (2017)
11. Hahn, F., et al.: Subspace clothing simulation using adaptive bases. ACM Trans. Graph. (TOG) **33**(4), 105 (2014)
12. Han, X., Hu, X., Huang, W., Scott, M.R.: ClothFlow: a flow-based model for clothed person generation. In: The IEEE International Conference on Computer Vision (ICCV), October 2019
13. Han, X., Wu, Z., Wu, Z., Yu, R., Davis, L.S.: VITON: an image-based virtual try-on network. In: Proceedings of the IEEE Conference on Computer Vision and Pattern Recognition, pp. 7543–7552 (2018)

14. Heusel, M., Ramsauer, H., Unterthiner, T., Nessler, B., Hochreiter, S.: GANs trained by a two time-scale update rule converge to a local nash equilibrium. In: Advances in Neural Information Processing Systems, pp. 6626–6637 (2017)

15. Hinton, G., Vinyals, O., Dean, J.: Distilling the knowledge in a neural network. arXiv preprint arXiv:1503.02531 (2015)

16. Ioffe, S., Szegedy, C.: Batch normalization: accelerating deep network training by reducing internal covariate shift. In: International Conference on Machine Learning, pp. 448–456 (2015)

17. Isola, P., Zhu, J.-Y., Zhou, T., Efros, A.A.: Image-to-image translation with conditional adversarial networks. In: Proceedings of the IEEE Conference on Computer Vision and Pattern Recognition, pp. 1125–1134 (2017)

18. Jaderberg, M., Simonyan, K., Zisserman, A., et al.: Spatial transformer networks. In: Advances in Neural Information Processing Systems, pp. 2017–2025 (2015)

19. Jetchev, N., Bergmann, U.: The conditional analogy GAN: swapping fashion articles on people images. In: Proceedings of the IEEE International Conference on Computer Vision, pp. 2287–2292 (2017)

20. Johnson, J., Alahi, A., Fei-Fei, L.: Perceptual losses for real-time style transfer and super-resolution. In: Leibe, B., Matas, J., Sebe, N., Welling, M. (eds.) ECCV 2016. LNCS, vol. 9906, pp. 694–711. Springer, Cham (2016). https://doi.org/10.1007/978-3-319-46475-6_43

21. Jolicoeur-Martineau, A.: The relativistic discriminator: a key element missing from standard GAN. In: International Conference on Learning Representations (2019)

22. Kingma, D.P., Ba, J.: Adam: a method for stochastic optimization. In: International Conference on Learning Representations (2015)

23. Liang, X., Gong, K., Shen, X., Lin, L.: Look into person: joint body parsing & pose estimation network and a new benchmark. IEEE Trans. Pattern Anal. Mach. Intell. **41**(4), 871–885 (2019)

24. Lorenz, D., Bereska, L., Milbich, T., Ommer, B.: Unsupervised part-based disentangling of object shape and appearance. In: Proceedings of the IEEE Conference on Computer Vision and Pattern Recognition (2019)

25. Ma, L., Sun, Q., Georgoulis, S., Van Gool, L., Schiele, B., Fritz, M.: Disentangled person image generation. In: Proceedings of the IEEE Conference on Computer Vision and Pattern Recognition, pp. 99–108 (2018)

26. Mejjati, Y.A., Richardt, C., Tompkin, J., Cosker, D., In Kim, K.: Unsupervised attention-guided image-to-image translation. In: Advances in Neural Information Processing Systems, pp. 3693–3703 (2018)

27. Mirza, M., Osindero, S.: Conditional generative adversarial nets. arXiv preprint arXiv:1411.1784 (2014)

28. Pons-Moll, G., Pujades, S., Hu, S., Black, M.J.: ClothCap: seamless 4D clothing capture and retargeting. ACM Trans. Graph. (TOG) **36**(4), 73 (2017)

29. Radford, A., Metz, L., Chintala, S.: Unsupervised representation learning with deep convolutional generative adversarial networks. In: International Conference on Learning Representations (2016)

30. Raj, A., Sangkloy, P., Chang, H., Hays, J., Ceylan, D., Lu, J.: SwapNet: image based garment transfer. In: Ferrari, V., Hebert, M., Sminchisescu, C., Weiss, Y. (eds.) ECCV 2018. LNCS, vol. 11216, pp. 679–695. Springer, Cham (2018). https://doi.org/10.1007/978-3-030-01258-8_41

31. Rocco, I., Arandjelovic, R., Sivic, J.: Convolutional neural network architecture for geometric matching. In: Proceedings of the IEEE Conference on Computer Vision and Pattern Recognition, pp. 6148–6157 (2017)

32. Ronneberger, O., Fischer, P., Brox, T.: U-Net: convolutional networks for biomedical image segmentation. In: Navab, N., Hornegger, J., Wells, W.M., Frangi, A.F. (eds.) MICCAI 2015. LNCS, vol. 9351, pp. 234–241. Springer, Cham (2015). https://doi.org/10.1007/978-3-319-24574-4_28

33. Salimans, T., Goodfellow, I., Zaremba, W., Cheung, V., Radford, A., Chen, X.: Improved techniques for training GANs. In: Advances in Neural Information Processing Systems, pp. 2234–2242 (2016)

34. Shetty, R.R., Fritz, M., Schiele, B.: Adversarial scene editing: automatic object removal from weak supervision. In: Advances in Neural Information Processing Systems, pp. 7717–7727 (2018)

35. Siarohin, A., Sangineto, E., Lathuilière, S., Sebe, N.: Deformable GANs for pose-based human image generation. In: Proceedings of the IEEE Conference on Computer Vision and Pattern Recognition, pp. 3408–3416 (2018)

36. Simonyan, K., Zisserman, A.: Very deep convolutional networks for large-scale image recognition. In: International Conference on Learning Representations (2015)

37. Ulyanov, D., Vedaldi, A., Lempitsky, V.: Improved texture networks: maximizing quality and diversity in feed-forward stylization and texture synthesis. In: Proceedings of the IEEE Conference on Computer Vision and Pattern Recognition, pp. 6924–6932 (2017)

38. Wang, B., Zheng, H., Liang, X., Chen, Y., Lin, L., Yang, M.: Toward characteristic-preserving image-based virtual try-on network. In: Ferrari, V., Hebert, M., Sminchisescu, C., Weiss, Y. (eds.) ECCV 2018. LNCS, vol. 11217, pp. 607–623. Springer, Cham (2018). https://doi.org/10.1007/978-3-030-01261-8_36

39. Wang, Z., Bovik, A.C., Sheikh, H.R., Simoncelli, E.P.: Image quality assessment: from error visibility to structural similarity. IEEE trans. Image Process. 13(4), 600–612 (2004)

40. Wu, Z., Lin, G., Tao, Q., Cai, J.: M2e-try on net: fashion from model to everyone. arXiv preprint arXiv:1811.08599 (2018)

41. Yang, H., Zhang, R., Guo, X., Liu, W., Zuo, W., Luo, P.: Towards photo-realistic virtual try-on by adaptively generating-preserving image content. In: Proceedings of the IEEE/CVF Conference on Computer Vision and Pattern Recognition, pp. 7850–7859 (2020)

42. Yu, R., Wang, X., Xie, X.: VTNFP: an image-based virtual try-on network with body and clothing feature preservation. In: The IEEE International Conference on Computer Vision (ICCV), October 2019

43. Zhang, R., Isola, P., Efros, A.A., Shechtman, E., Wang, O.: The unreasonable effectiveness of deep features as a perceptual metric. In: Proceedings of the IEEE Conference on Computer Vision and Pattern Recognition, pp. 586–595 (2018)

44. Zhao, H., Gallo, O., Frosio, I., Kautz, J.: Loss functions for image restoration with neural networks. IEEE Trans. Comput. Imaging 3(1), 47–57 (2016)

45. Zhu, J.-Y., Park, T., Isola, P., Efros, A.A.: Unpaired image-to-image translation using cycle-consistent adversarial networks. In: Proceedings of the IEEE International Conference on Computer Vision, pp. 2223–2232 (2017)

NODIS: Neural Ordinary Differential Scene Understanding

Yuren Cong[1], Hanno Ackermann[1], Wentong Liao[1], Michael Ying Yang[2(✉)], and Bodo Rosenhahn[1]

[1] Institute of Information Processing, Leibniz University, Hannover, Germany
{cong,ackermann,liao,rosenhahn}@tnt.uni-hanover.de
[2] Scene Understanding Group, University of Twente, Enschede, The Netherlands
michael.yang@utwente.nl

Abstract. Semantic image understanding is a challenging topic in computer vision. It requires to detect all objects in an image, but also to identify all the relations between them. Detected objects, their labels and the discovered relations can be used to construct a scene graph which provides an abstract semantic interpretation of an image. In previous works, relations were identified by solving an assignment problem formulated as (Mixed-)Integer Linear Programs. In this work, we interpret that formulation as Ordinary Differential Equation (ODE). The proposed architecture performs scene graph inference by solving a neural variant of an ODE by end-to-end learning. The connection between (Mixed-)Integer Linear Program and ODEs in combination with the end-to-end training amounts to learning how to solve assignment problems with image-specific objective functions. Intuitive, visual explanations are provided for the role of the single free variable of the ODE modules which are associated with time in many natural processes. The proposed model achieves results equal to or above state-of-the-art on all three benchmark tasks: scene graph generation (SGGEN), classification (SGCLS) and visual relationship detection (PREDCLS) on Visual Genome benchmark. The strong results on scene graph classification support the claim that assignment problems can indeed be solved by neural ODEs.

Keywords: Semantic image understanding · Scene graph · Visual relationship detection

1 Introduction

This paper investigates the problem of semantic image understanding. Given an image, the objective is to detect objects within, label them and infer the relations

Electronic supplementary material The online version of this chapter (https://doi.org/10.1007/978-3-030-58565-5_38) contains supplementary material, which is available to authorized users.

© Springer Nature Switzerland AG 2020
A. Vedaldi et al. (Eds.): ECCV 2020, LNCS 12365, pp. 636–653, 2020.
https://doi.org/10.1007/978-3-030-58565-5_38

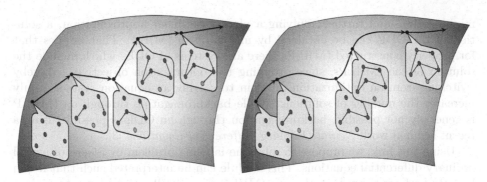

Fig. 1. Visualization of the main contributions made in this work. *Left*: state-of-the-art works rely on multiple embedding layers which amounts to an evenly-spaced, discrete sampling. *Right*: the proposed module relies on ordinary differential equations (ODE), thus it learns a continuous approximation of the trajectory onto the embedding manifolds.

which might exist between objects. These data provide rich semantic information about the image content. So called scene graphs contain all these information and constitute abstract representations of images [15]. Nodes of a scene graph represent objects detected in an image, while edges represent relationships between objects. Applications range from image retrieval [15] to high-level vision tasks such as visual question answering [39], image captioning [44,47] and visual reasoning [35]. The community has been very active in the past years to investigate these problems. Results on public benchmarks such as the Visual Genome database [20] have improved drastically within the past few years [2,41,49].

A naive approach to infer scene graphs is to use a standard object detector, classify the objects, and use a separate network to label the relationships between the objects. This, however, ignores the conditional information shared between the objects. It has therefore become standard practice to also use relationship information for object classification [13,25,28].

Scene graph estimation relies on two classification problems, both for objects and for relationships. Classification, or more generally, assignment problems can be solved by (Mixed) Integer Linear Programs, (M)ILP, for instance in [36]. Powerful solvers are able to even infer globally optimal solutions for many types of problems. A drawback of (M)ILPs is that the optimization objective and all constraints must be defined in advance. Objective functions usually include multiple terms and weights per term. Furthermore, backpropagation through an (M)ILP solver is not possible, thus such pipelines cannot adapt to data.

For many other problems in which adaption to data is less important, (M)ILPs have been successfully employed. In [8], network flows and transport problem are modeled by Partial Differential Equations (PDEs). The arising systems of PDEs are transformed to systems of Ordinary Differential Equations (ODEs) by finite differences. Adding constraints such as minimal or maximal capacities, integral constraints and an objective, for instance energy minimization, and further applying a piece-wise linear approximation, a solution of the ODE can be obtained by means of an (M)ILP. That implies that for properly constructed (M)ILPs there are systems of ODEs which include the solution of the (M)ILPs, since dropping the optimization objective – thereby switching from an optimization problem to solving an equation system – only increases the number of solutions. While backpropagating through an (M)ILP is generally not possible, backpropagation through an ODE is possible using a recent seminal work *Neural Ordinary Differential Equations* [3].

Using this link, we propose to solve the labeling problem by means of neural ordinary differential equations. This module can be interpreted such that it can learn to perform the same task as an (M)ILP. Since it allows end-to-end training, it adapts to the data, thus it learns a near-optimal objective per image. A further question is which role the time-variable of the ODE plays in our architecture. We will provide visual explanations of that variable, namely that it controls how many objects are classified and how many relationships are classified (cf. Figs. 1 and 4). In our experimental evaluation, we demonstrate results that are equal to state-of-the-art or above in all three benchmark problems: scene graph generation (SGGEN), scene graph classification (SGCLS) and visual relationship prediction (PREDCLS).

The **contributions** made in this work can be summarized as follows: (1) We propose to use ODE modules for scene graph generation. (2) It can be interpreted that it learns the optimal assignment function per image. (3) Intuitive, visual explanations are provided for the role of the single free variable of the ODE modules which are associated with time in many natural processes. (4) The proposed method achieves state-of-the-art results. Our code is published on GitHub[1].

2   Related Work

Context for Visual Reasoning: Context has been used in semantic image understanding [7,13,22,27,28,46]. For scene graph generation, context information has been recently proposed and is still being investigated. Message passing has been used to include object context in images in several works, for instance by graphical models [24,42], by recurrent neural networks (RNN) [40,49], or by an iterative refinement process [19,41]. Context from language priors [30] has been proved to be helpful for visual relationships detection and scene graph generation [25,29,48].

Scene Graph Generation: Scene graphs are proposed in [15] for the task of image retrieval and also potential for many applications [17,18,32]. They consist of not only detected objects but also the object classes and the relationships between the detected objects. The estimation of scene graphs from images is attracting more and more attention in computer vision [6,14,24–26,40,49,51].

---

[1] https://github.com/yrcong/NODIS.

Several of these methods use message passing to capture the context of the two related objects [23,40,49], or of the objects and their relationships [24,25,41,42]. The general pipeline for message passing is to train some shared matrices to transform the source features into a semantic domain and then to assemble them to update the target features. In some works, an attention mechanism is implemented to weight the propagated information to achieve further improvement [9,12,24,42]. Graph CNNs [16] have been used to propagate information between object and relationship nodes [4,42]. Some works also introduce generative models for scene understanding [5,10].

Contrastive Training: Contrastive losses [1] have been applied for scene understanding [50]. They have also been applied for image captioning, visual question answering (VQA) and vector embeddings [31,34,45]. They are based on the idea that it can be easier to randomly select similar and dissimilar samples. Such losses can then be used even if no label information is available.

Losses: In Visual Genome [20], many semantically meaningful relations are not labeled. Furthermore, relations that can have multiple labels, for instance on and sit, are usually labeled only once. Networks for visual relationship detection which use cross-entropy as training loss may encounter difficulties during training, since almost identical pairs of objects can have either label, or even none at all. To overcome the problem of such contradicting label information, margin-based [21] and contrastive [50] losses have been proposed.

Support Inference: Inferring physical support, i.e. which structures for instance carry others, e.g. floor → table, was investigated for object segmentation [36], instance segmentation [52], and also for scene graph inference [43].

Proposed Model: The proposed model uses neither iterations, except for LSTM-cells, nor message passing, nor a Graph CNN. As most recent works do, language priors are included. We further use a standard loss based on cross-entropy. Unlike most state-of-the-art algorithms, we propose to use a new module which has never before been used for semantic image analysis. The ODE module [3] can be interpreted as learning a deep residual model. In contrast to residual networks, the ODE-module *continuously* models its solutions according to a pre-defined, problem-specific precision.

This idea is motivated by works on gas, water, energy and transport networks which need to be modeled by systems of Partial Differential Equations (PDE). In [8], it was proposed to simplify such systems to obtain systems of Ordinary Differential Equations (ODE), add one or multiple optimization objectives and then use a Mixed-Integer Linear Program to compute the solution. That implies that, given an (M)ILP, we can always find a system of ODEs that can generate the same solution among others. Using a neural ODE [3], we can thus learn a function of the system of ODEs. Due to the end-to-end training, that system further encodes near-optimal assignment functions per image.

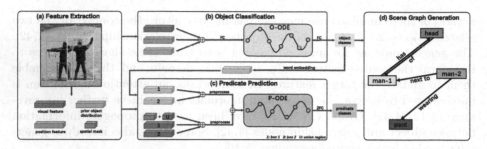

Fig. 2. Overview of the proposed method: (a) given an image, many object regions are proposed, (b) those regions are classified by an Object ODE (O-ODE), (c) after pre-processing the features of object pairs, a Predicate ODE (P-ODE) is applied to predict predicates, (d) a scene graph is generated.

3   Method

In this section, we first define scene graphs, then we define straight-forward ILP models for object and relationship classification in Sect. 3.2. Neural Ordinary Differential Equations [3] are briefly explained in Sect. 3.3. Both models are combined in Sects. 3.4 and 3.5.

3.1   Scene Graphs

A scene graph [15] is an abstract semantic representation of all objects in an image and the relationships between them. The set of objects consists of a set of bounding boxes along with a label for each object. The relationships between two objects, also known as predicates, consists of bounding boxes which usually cover both object bounding boxes, and labels for each relation. As in [49], we include a particular predicate to indicate that there is no relation between two objects.

3.2   Models for Object and Relationship Detection

Assume a graph $G_{obj} = (U_{obj}, E_{obj})$ whose nodes represent the detected yet unlabeled objects in an image. Each node is further assigned to a label $l \in \mathcal{L}_{obj}$. Each label l is associated with a score $\alpha_{u,l}$ with $u \in U$. That score can represent an agreement with some given feature map. The integer variables $x_{u,l} \in \{0,1\}$ indicate that node u is given label l. We assume that each object can only belong to a single class.

We further include a term $\beta_{u,u',l,l'}$ which models statistical prior knowledge about co-occurrences of object pairs u and u', $u \neq u'$, and their corresponding labels l and l'. We then arrive at the following Integer Linear Problem (ILP) for object classification

$$\max \sum_{u \in U_{obj}} \sum_{l \in \mathcal{L}_{obj}} \alpha_{u,l} x_{u,l} + w_{obj} \sum_{u,\,u' \in U_{obj}} \sum_{l,\,l'} \beta_{u,u',l,l'} x_{u,l} x_{u',l'} \tag{1a}$$

$$s.t. \quad x_{u,l} \in \{0,1\}, \quad \sum_{l \in \mathcal{L}_{obj}} x_{u,l} \le 1 \tag{1b}$$

where w_{obj} is a scalar weight which balances the two terms. How to exactly determine the scores $\alpha_{u,l}$, $\beta_{u,u',l,l'}$ and the weight w_{obj} constitutes a hyper-parameter search. The large search space makes this problem by itself challenging. Some of the parameters remain invariant for all images.

Assume a further graph $G_{pred} = (V_{pred}, E_{pred})$ whose nodes represent all possible subject-object pairs. Each node is assigned to a label $k \in \mathcal{L}_{pred}$. Each label k is associated with a score $\alpha_{v,k}$ with $v \in V_{pred}$. The integer variables $x_{v,k} \in \{0,1\}$ indicate that node v is given label k, for instance the subject-object pair *dog-street* with a label *sit* or *walk*. The number of labels per node is limited by T_v, and the total number of labels by K. The latter arises from the *recall-at-K* metric commonly used in visual relationship detection and scene graph estimation tasks.

Here, we also include a term $\beta_{v,v',k,k'}$ which models statistical prior knowledge about co-occurrences of subject-object pairs v with pairs v', $v \ne v'$, and their corresponding relationship labels k and k'. We then arrive at the following Integer Linear Problem (ILP) for relationship classification

$$\max \sum_{v \in V_{pred}} \sum_{k \in \mathcal{L}_{pred}} \alpha_{v,k} x_{v,k} + w_{pred} \sum_{v,\,v' \in V_{pred}} \sum_{k,\,k'} \beta_{v,v',k,k'} x_{v,k} x_{v',k'} \tag{2a}$$

$$s.t. \quad x_{v,k} \in \{0,1\}, \quad \sum_{k \in \mathcal{L}} x_{v,k} \le T_v, \quad \sum_{v \in V_{pred}} \sum_{k \in \mathcal{L}_{pred}} x_{v,k} \le K, \tag{2b}$$

where w_{pred} is a scalar weight which balances the two terms.

Denote by $\alpha(t)$ the *function* in the single variable t that assigns *continuous* scalar weights which express label strengths. The values that the label weights take on vary with t. Likewise, let $\beta(t)$ be a function in t that assigns scalar weights according to co-occurrence. From [8], we can see that the optimization problems defined by Eqs. 1 and 2 correspond to ordinary differential equation (ODE) models defined by

$$\frac{d}{dt} f = f(x(t), t). \tag{3}$$

In other words, we can use Eqs. 1 and 2 to obtain a solution of problem (3) subject to several constraints. A disadvantage of the optimization problem in Eqs. 1 and 2 is that it is not possible to backpropagate through the ILPs. Thus, feature-generating neural networks cannot be trained to adapt to given data when using the ILPs.

3.3   Neural Ordinary Differential Equations [3]

For many problems it is hard to explicitly define functions $\alpha(t)$ and $\beta(t)$. In [3], it was proposed to parameterize $f(t)$ by a function $f_\theta(t)$ based on neural network with parameters θ. The idea is then to use $f_\theta(t)$ to solve an ODE. Thus, starting with an input $x(0)$ at time $t = 0$, the output at time T can be computed by a standard ODE-solver

$$\frac{d}{dt} f_\theta = f_\theta\left(x(t), t\right). \tag{4}$$

The dynamics of the system can thereby be approximated up to the required precision. Importantly, model states at times $0 < t < T$ need not be evenly spaced.

For back-propagation, the derivatives for the adjoint $a(t) = -\partial L / \partial x(t)$

$$\frac{d}{dt} a = -a(t)^\top \frac{\partial}{\partial t} f\left(x(t), t, \theta\right) \tag{5}$$

and

$$\frac{d}{d\theta} L = \int_T^0 a(t)^\top \frac{\partial}{\partial\theta} f\left(x(t), t, \theta\right) dt \tag{6}$$

have to be computed for loss L. This computation, along with the reverse computation of $x(t)$ starting at time T can be done by a single call of the ODE-solver backwards in time.

3.4   Assignments by Neural Ordinary Differential Equations

While Eqs. 1 and 2 can be used to obtain solutions of problem (3), this does not allow to train previous modules if used in a neural network. Furthermore, the hyper-parameters of the ILP must be determined in advance and cannot be easily adapted to the data. On the other hand, we can construct an ODE from Eqs. 1 or 2, respectively. Since a manual construction would be hard, we can use a neural ODE layer to learn the optimal assignment function. In contrast to an ILP, the neural ODE both allows to train a feature generating network in front of it, and can adapt to each image. The latter implies that the hyper-parameters of the corresponding, yet unknown ILP vary with each image.

ODEs involve the variable t which is usually associated with time in many natural processes. Here, we are posed with the question what this variable represents for object or relationship classification. It will be demonstrated in Sect. 4.4 that the two variables of two neural ODE layers control how many objects and relationships are classified correctly (cf. Fig. 4). In other words, specifying particular values of the variable of the relationship module determines the connectivity of estimated scene graph, whereas such values of the object layer determine if too few or too many objects are correctly labeled.

As outlined in Fig. 2, we use two separate ODE layers. The visual features of detected objects, their positional features and the prior object distributions are concatenated into a vector x_v and processed by an ODE layer in the object classifier

$$\frac{d}{dt_1} f_{\theta_u} = f_{\theta_u}\left(x_u(t_1), t_1\right). \tag{7}$$

In the following, this ODE layer will be denoted by O-ODE.

The word embedding resulting from the object classifier, the spatial mask with the union box and the visual features of two detected and classified object are concatenated and pre-processed to yield vector $x_{v,v'}$ before being processed by an ODE layer for predicate classification ($P\text{-}ODE$)

$$\frac{d}{dt_2} f_{\theta_v} = f_{\theta_v}\left(x_{v,v'}(t_2),\, t_2 \right).$$ (8)

The variables t_1 and t_2 in Eqs. (7) and (8) control how many objects or relations are labeled. In other words, graphs constructed using different t and t', either for Eq. (7) or (8), result in scene graphs with differently many objects or relations correctly labeled.

3.5   Architecture

Our model is built on Faster-RCNN [33] which provides proposal boxes, feature maps and primary object distributions. There are two fundamental modules in the model: object classifier and predicate classifier. Each of them contains a neural ordinary differential equation layer, Object ODE (O-ODE) and Predicate ODE (P-ODE). For both of them we use bidirectional LSTMs as the approximate function in the ODE solver. The data in the model are organized as sequences with random order.

In the object classifier, the feature maps, bounding box information and primary object distribution from Faster-RCNN are concatenated and fed through a fully connection layer. The object class scores are computed by the O-ODE and a following linear layer. The predicate classifier uses feature maps, spatial and semantic information of object pairs to predict the predicate categories. The spatial masks are forwarded into a group of convolution layers so that the output has the same size as the feature maps of the union box $(512 \cdot 7 \cdot 7)$ and can be added per element. Global average pooling is applied on the feature maps of the subject box, object box and union box. The features of the subject, object, and union boxes are concatenated as $(3 \cdot 512)$-dimensional visual vectors. Two 200-dimensional semantic embedding vectors are generated from the subject and object classes predicted by the object classifier and concatenated as 400-dimensional semantic vectors.

The visual vectors and semantic vectors of object pairs can be pre-processed by three methods before the P-ODE: *FC-Layer:* The $(3 \cdot 512)$-dimensional visual vectors and 400-dimensional semantic vectors are forwarded into two independent fully connection layers that both have 512 neurons. Then, the outputs are concatenated together as 1024-dimensional representation vectors for the P-ODE. *GCNN:* The visual vectors and semantic vectors are first concatenated. Then, we use a graph convolutional neural network (GCNN) to infer information about context. Since the number of object pairs in each image is variable, we set each element on the diagonal of the adjacency matrix to 0.8. The weight of 0.2 is uniformly distributed among the remaining entries of each row. The output vectors of the GCNN are passed into the P-ODE. *LSTM:* Similar as for the first variant, the $(3 \cdot 512)$-dimensional visual vectors and 400-dimensional semantic vectors are fed into two single layer LSTMs. Both of them have the output dimension 512. We concatenate the two outputs for the P-ODE.

The final class scores of the relations are computed by the P-ODE followed by two linear layers.

4   Experiments

In this section, we firstly clarify the experimental settings and implementation details. Then, we show quantitative and qualitative results on the Visual Genome (VG) benchmark dataset [20] in terms of scene graph generation.

4.1   Dataset, Settings, and Evaluation

Dataset. We validated our methods on the VG benchmark dataset [20] for the task of scene graph generation. However, there are varying data pre-processing strategies and dataset splits in different works. For fair comparison, we adopted the data split as described in [41] which is the most widely used. According to the data pre-processing strategy, the most-frequent 150 object categories and 50 predicate types are selected. The training set has 75651 images while the test set has 32422 images.

Settings. For comparison with prior works, we use Faster R-CNN [33] with VGG16 [37] as the backbone network for proposing object candidates and extracting visual features. We adopted the code base and a pre-trained model provided by [49]. As in NeuralMotifs [49], the input image is resized to 592×592, bounding box scales and dimension ratios are scaled, and a ROIAlign layer [11] is used to extract features within the boxes of object proposals and the union boxes of object pairs from the shared feature maps.

Evaluation. There are three standard experiment settings for evaluating the performance of scene graph generation: (1) **Predicate classification** (PRED-CLS): predict relationship labels of object pairs given ground truth bounding boxes and labels of objects. (2) **Scene graph classification** (SGCLS): given ground truth bounding boxes of objects, predict object labels and relationship labels. (3) **Scene graph detection** (SGGEN): predict boxes, labels of object proposals and relation labels of object pairs given an image. Only when the labels of the subject, relation, and object are correctly classified, and the boxes of subject and object have more than 50% intersection-over-union (IoU) with the ground truth, it is counted as a correctly detected entity. The most widely adopted recall@K metrics ($K = [20, 50, 100]$) for relations are used to evaluate the system performance.

Table 1. Comparison on VG test set [41] **using graph constraints**. All numbers in %. We use the same object detection backbone provided by [49] for fair comparison. Bold blue numbers indicate results better than competitors by >0.5. Regarding GCL [50], cf. to the text. Methods in the lower part use the same data split as [41]. Results for MSDN⋆ [25] are from [49].

Data Split	Method	SGGEN			SGCLS			PREDCLS		
		R@20	R@50	R@100	R@20	R@50	R@100	R@20	R@50	R@100
[25]	MSDN⋆ [25]	–	11.7	14.0	–	20.9	24.0	–	42.3	48.2
	FacNet [24]	–	13.1	16.5	–	22.8	28.6	–	–	–
[41] split	VRD [29]		0.3	0.5		11.8	14.1		27.9	35.0
	IMP [41]	14.6	20.7	24.6	31.7	34.6	35.4	52.7	59.3	61.3
	Graph R-CNN [42]	–	11.4	13.7	–	29.6	31.6	–	54.2	59.1
	Mem [40]	7.7	11.4	13.9	23.3	27.8	29.5	42.1	53.2	57.9
	MotifNet [49]	21.4	27.2	30.3	32.9	35.8	36.5	58.5	65.2	67.1
	MotifNet-Freq	20.1	26.2	30.1	29.3	32.3	32.6	53.6	60.6	62.2
	GCL [50]	21.1	28.3	32.7	36.1	36.8	36.8	66.9	68.4	68.4
	VCTREE [38]	22.0	27.9	31.3	35.2	38.1	38.8	60.1	66.4	68.1
	CMAT [2]	22.1	27.9	31.2	35.9	39.0	39.8	60.2	66.4	68.1
	Ours-FC	21.5	27.5	30.9	**37.7**	**41.7**	**42.8**	58.6	66.1	68.1
	Ours-GCNN	21.4	27.1	30.6	33.2	38.2	39.7	52.0	60.9	63.8
	Ours-LSTM	21.6	27.7	31.0	**37.9**	**41.9**	**42.9**	58.9	66.0	67.9

Training. We train our model with the sum of the cross entropy losses for objects and predicates. We collect all annotated relationships in the image and add negative relationships so that the relation sequences in the batch have identical length if there are sufficiently many ground truth boxes. We randomly select one if the object pairs are annotated with multiple relationships. For SGCLS and SGGEN, ground truth object labels are provided to the semantic part at the training stage. For fair comparison we use the same pre-trained Faster-RCNN as [49] and freeze its parameters. An ADAM optimizer was used with batch size 6, initial learning rate 10^{-4}, and cross-entropy as loss both for object and relationship classification. We choose *dopri5* as ODE solver and set the absolute tolerance $atol = 0.01$ and the relative tolerance $rtol = 0.01$. The integral time t_{end} is set to 1.5 (cf. Sect. 4.4). Please confer to the supplementary for a more detailed explanation of our model architecture.

4.2 Quantitative Results and Comparison

Our results **using graph constraints** are shown in Table 1. The middle block indicates methods that all use the same data split that is used in [41]. Two methods that use different splits are listed in the top section of the table. For MSD-net [25] in this part, we show the results reported in [49].

We used bold blue numbers to indicate the best result in any column that was at least 0.5% larger than the next best competing method. Since GCL [50] used a different VGG backbone than other works, and also larger input images than all other methods (1024 × 1024 compared to 592 × 592), results cannot be fairly compared with other methods, so we did not highlight best results in this row (SGGEN-R@100 and PREDCLS-R@20).

The bottom part of Table 1 shows results of the proposed ODE layers using three different front-ends: (1) One in which the function used inside the ODE layer is taken to be a linear layer (**ours-FC**), (2) the second in which a Graph-CNN is used (**ours-GCNN**), (3) and the third in which a bidirectional LSTM is used (**ours-LSTM**).

As can be seen from Table 1, most recent methods (MotifNet [49], VCTREE [38] and CMAT [2]) including ours are very similar in performance with respect to the scores in SGGEN and PREDCLS. The only exception among state-of-the-art works is GCL [50] in two out of nine scores, yet by using a more powerful front-end.

For SGCLS, however, the proposed ODE layer turns out to be very effective. Apparently both the version using a linear layer inside the ODE layer (**ours-FC**) and the one using the bidirectional LSTM (**ours-LSTM**) perform very similar. Their scores improve state-of-the-art (CMAT [2]) between ≈ 2% (SGCLS-R@20), ≈ 3% (SGCLS-R@50) and ≈ 3% (SGCLS-R@100). Compared with GCL [50] our results improve by up to 5% (SGCLS-R@100) although our VGG was trained on coarser images. This demonstrates the effectiveness of the proposed ODE layer. It is sufficient to use a simple linear layer, since the ODE layer is so powerful that it produces similar outputs to those of a function based upon a more complicated and slower bidirectional LSTM.

4.3   Ablation Studies

For ablation studies, we consider several variants of the proposed network architecture. Results are shown in Table 2. For model-1 (first row), we removed the ODE networks and directly classified the output of the feature generating networks. This measures the impact of both ODE modules. In model-2 (second row), we removed only the ODE layer for object classification (O-ODE) in the proposed network. The third model shows the results when the relationship ODE (P-ODE) is removed. Finally, the fourth rows shows the results if both ODE modules are present.

Table 2. Ablation study demonstrating the effect if both ODE layers are removed (first row), only the layer for object classification (second row), only the layer for predicate classification (third row), or if both are present (last row).

Model	O-ODE	P-ODE	SGGEN		SGCLS		PREDCLS	
			R@50	R@100	R@50	R@100	R@50	R@100
1	–	–	27.1	30.4	35.3	36.1	65.4	67.4
2	–	✓	27.3	30.6	35.9	36.6	65.9	67.9
3	✓	–	27.3	30.7	41.4	42.5	65.4	67.5
4	✓	✓	27.7	31.0	41.9	42.9	66.0	67.9

As can be seen, removing the ODE layer for predicate classification has a negligible effect since the PREDCLS scores hardly change. Removing the ODE layer for object classification has a strong, negative effect, however. This study shows that the ODE module can have a very positive impact. It further confirms our main claim that classification/assignment problems can be solved by means of neural ODEs.

Regarding the scores on PREDCLS, we conjecture that the noise in VG (missing relationship labels, incorrect labels) is so strong that scores cannot improve anymore. This hypothesis is supported by the fact that results in the past two years have not improved since [49].

4.4   Neural ODE Analysis

We propose two neural ordinary differential equations: Object ODE (O-ODE) and Predicate ODE (P-ODE) in the object classifier and predicate classifier respectively. Here, we tune the hyper-parameter, integral time t_{end} in the ODE solver, to understand how that variables influences neural ordinary differential equations and final performance. Moreover, we extract the hidden states at different points in time and generate the scene graph to visualize how features are refined in the ODE space.

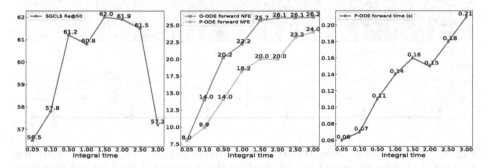

Fig. 3. The effect of integral time in the ODE solver on SGCLS Re@50, average forward NFE (number of function evaluation) and average forward running time per image of O-ODE and P-ODE. Because of different number of objects in different images the experimental results are based on 5000 samples from the training set.

Since the O-ODE and P-ODE both work in the setting SGCLS, SGCLS Re@50 is used as performance indicator. Because different images contain different number of objects, we randomly sample 5000 images from the training set to compute the average number of function evaluation (NFE) for a forward pass and the computation time per image. This experiment is implemented on a single GTX 1080Ti GPU. We vary the integral time t_{end} from 0.05 to 3.00 (x-axes).

According to the left plot in Fig. 3, SGCLS Re@50 increases gradually from 56.5 to 62.0 until $T = 1.50$ and then decreases; (middle plot) the average forward

NFE of O-ODE increases from 8.0 to 26.2 and from 8.0 to 24.0 for P-ODE; (right plot) the average forward time of the P-ODE layer increases from 0.06 s to 0.21 s whereas the average forward time of the O-ODE layer is negligibly small ($<10^{-4}$ s), thus we omit these measurements. The P-ODE requires much more time than the O-ODE due to the large amount of object pairs. Considering the above points, we set $t_{end} = 1.5$ for all other experiments.

To provide an intuitive interpretation of the parameters t_1 and t_2 in the O-ODE and the P-ODE, respectively, we use a model trained on SGGEN with the hyper-parameter $t_{end} = 1.5$ and evaluate it using different latent vectors corresponding to different points between 0 and 2.5. The hidden states at $t = 2.0$ and $t = 2.5$ imply extrapolation. The detection results and scene graphs generated by the different hidden states are shown in Fig. 4. The features are more and more refined by the neural ODE layers if t_1 and t_2 increase, hence more objects and relationships are correctly classified. After $t_{end} = 1.5$, increasingly many relationships are misclassified due to the extrapolation.

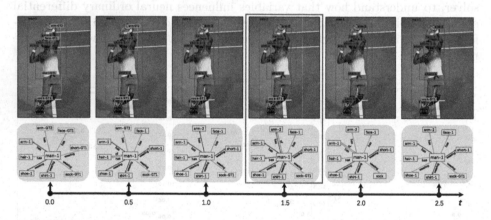

Fig. 4. We evaluate the model trained with the hyper-parameter $t_{end} = 1.5$, i.e. during training the hidden vector at $t = 1.5$ is used for classifications. The upper row visualizes detection results while the lower row shows the corresponding scene graphs. The red box indicates the state corresponding to $t = 1.5$. The orange boxes and edges indicate the objects and predicates in the ground truth that are not detected, purple that the objects and predicates are predicted correctly. Blue edges show false positives. (Color figure online)

4.5 Qualitative Results

Qualitative results for scene graph generation (SGGEN) are shown in Fig. 5. The images include object detections. The purple color indicates correctly detected and classified objects and relations, whereas orange means failure. The blue color indicates false negatives, i.e. relationships that are not in the ground truth.

Most of the errors stem from the object detection stage. Whenever an object is not detected, relationships connecting this object are also not present in the

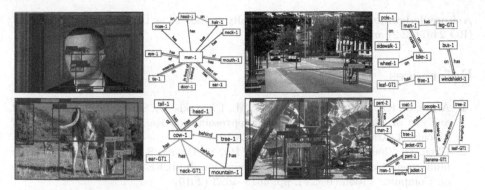

Fig. 5. Qualitative results from our model in the scene graph generation setting. Purple boxes denote correctly detected objects while orange boxes denote ground truth objects that are not detected. Purple edges correspond to correctly classified relationships at the R@20 setting while orange edges denote ground truth relationships that are not detected. Blue edges denote detected relationships that do not exist in ground truth annotations (false positives). (Color figure online)

scene graph. The cause of these errors is the Faster R-CNN detector which is used in all previous works.

There are a few false positives (blue links) which are semantically meaningful, for instance `eye-of-man` in the upper left example. In other words, the ground truth lacks this particular relationship in such cases. Several false positives result from semantically indistinguishable classes, for instance `has` and `of` in the lower left example.

5 Conclusions

We presented Neural Ordinary Differential Equations for Scene Understanding (NODIS). The idea of this work is based on the fact that Mixed-Integer Linear Programs can be used to solve problems defined by ordinary differential equations; therefore, given a particular (M)ILP, we can find a system of ODEs that can produce the solution of the (M)ILP within a time series. Since it is not possible to manually define the system of ODE to solve, we draw on recent advances in machine learning and use a trainable function approximator instead of an explicitly defined system of ODEs. In other words, the proposed network *learns* the optimal function to solve the assignment problem, whereas previous works manually define modules to do so.

We use this newly defined module for object classification and relationship classification. The proposed model using ODE layers shows large improvements on SGCLS, between 2% and 3% compared with the best SOTA in that category. We believe that ODE layers can be valuable improvements for neural architectures in semantic image understanding.

Acknowledgement. This work was partially supported by the DFG grant COVMAP (RO 2497/12-2) and EXC 2122.

References

1. Arora, S., Khandeparkar, H., Khodak, M., Plevrakis, O., Saunshi, N.: A theoretical analysis of contrastive unsupervised representation learning. In: Proceedings of Machine Learning Research (PMLR) (2019)
2. Chen, L., Zhang, H., Xiao, J., He, X., Pu, S., Chang, S.F.: Counterfactual critic multi-agent training for scene graph generation. In: IEEE International Conference on Computer Vision (ICCV), pp. 4613–4623 (2019)
3. Chen, T.Q., Rubanova, Y., Bettencourt, J., Duvenaud, D.: Neural ordinary differential equations. In: Neural Information Processing Systems (NeurIPS), pp. 6571–6583 (2018)
4. Chen, T., Yu, W., Chen, R., Lin, L.: Knowledge-embedded routing network for scene graph generation. In: Proceedings of the IEEE Conference on Computer Vision and Pattern Recognition, pp. 6163–6171 (2019)
5. Chen, V.S., Varma, P., Krishna, R., Bernstein, M., Re, C., Fei-Fei, L.: Scene graph prediction with limited labels. In: Proceedings of the IEEE International Conference on Computer Vision, pp. 2580–2590 (2019)
6. Dai, B., Zhang, Y., Lin, D.: Detecting visual relationships with deep relational networks. In: IEEE Conference on Computer Vision and Pattern Recognition (CVPR), pp. 3076–3086 (2017)
7. Divvala, S.K., Hoiem, D., Hays, J.H., Efros, A.A., Hebert, M.: An empirical study of context in object detection. In: IEEE Conference on Computer Vision and Pattern Recognition (CVPR), pp. 1271–1278 (2009)
8. Fügenschuh, A., Herty, M., Klar, A., Martin, A.: Combinatorial and continuous models for the optimization of traffic flows on networks. SIAM J. Optim. **16**(4), 1155–1176 (2006)
9. Gkanatsios, N., Pitsikalis, V., Koutras, P., Maragos, P.: Attention-translation-relation network for scalable scene graph generation. In: Proceedings of the IEEE International Conference on Computer Vision Workshops (2019)
10. Gu, J., Zhao, H., Lin, Z., Li, S., Cai, J., Ling, M.: Scene graph generation with external knowledge and image reconstruction. In: Proceedings of the IEEE Conference on Computer Vision and Pattern Recognition, pp. 1969–1978 (2019)
11. He, K., Georgia, G., Dollár, P., Girshick, R.: Mask R-CNN. In: IEEE International Conference on Computer Vision (ICCV), pp. 2961–2969 (2017)
12. Herzig, R., Raboh, M., Chechik, G., Berant, J., Globerson, A.: Mapping images to scene graphs with permutation-invariant structured prediction. In: Advances in Neural Information Processing Systems, pp. 7211–7221 (2018)
13. Hu, H., Gu, J., Zhang, Z., Dai, J., Wei, Y.: Relation networks for object detection. In: IEEE Conference on Computer Vision and Pattern Recognition (CVPR), pp. 3588–3597 (2018)
14. Hu, T., Liao, W., Yang, M.Y., Rosenhahn, B.: Exploiting attention for visual relationship detection. In: Fink, G.A., Frintrop, S., Jiang, X. (eds.) DAGM GCPR 2019. LNCS, vol. 11824, pp. 331–344. Springer, Cham (2019). https://doi.org/10.1007/978-3-030-33676-9_23
15. Johnson, J., et al.: Image retrieval using scene graphs. In: IEEE Conference on Computer Vision and Pattern Recognition (CVPR), pp. 3668–3678 (2015)

16. Kipf, T.N., Welling, M.: Semi-supervised classification with graph convolutional networks. In: International Conference on Learning Representations (ICLR) (2016)
17. Kluger, F., Ackermann, H., Yang, M.Y., Rosenhahn, B.: Temporally consistent horizon lines. In: ICRA (2020)
18. Kluger, F., Brachmann, E., Ackermann, H., Rother, C., Yang, M.Y., Rosenhahn, B.: CONSAC: robust multi-model fitting by conditional sample consensus. In: IEEE/CVF Conference on Computer Vision and Pattern Recognition, pp. 4634–4643 (2020)
19. Krishna, R., Chami, I., Bernstein, M., Fei-Fei, L.: Referring relationships. In: IEEE Conference on Computer Vision and Pattern Recognition (CVPR) (2018)
20. Krishna, R., et al.: Visual genome: connecting language and vision using crowd-sourced dense image annotations. Int. J. Comput. Vis. (IJCV) **123**(1), 32–73 (2017). https://doi.org/10.1007/s11263-016-0981-7
21. Krishnaswamy, N., Friedman, S., Pustejovsky, J.: Combining deep learning and qualitative spatial reasoning to learn complex structures from sparse examples with noise. Association for the Advancement of Artificial Intelligence (AAAI), vol. 33, pp. 2911–2918 (2019)
22. Ladicky, L., Russell, C., Kohli, P., Torr, P.H.S.: Graph cut based inference with co-occurrence statistics. In: Daniilidis, K., Maragos, P., Paragios, N. (eds.) ECCV 2010. LNCS, vol. 6315, pp. 239–253. Springer, Heidelberg (2010). https://doi.org/10.1007/978-3-642-15555-0_18
23. Li, Y., Ouyang, W., Wang, X.: Vip-CNN: visual phrase guided convolutional neural network. In: IEEE Conference on Computer Vision and Pattern Recognition (CVPR), pp. 1347–1356 (2017)
24. Li, Y., Ouyang, W., Zhou, B., Shi, J., Zhang, C., Wang, X.: Factorizable net: an efficient subgraph-based framework for scene graph generation. In: Ferrari, V., Hebert, M., Sminchisescu, C., Weiss, Y. (eds.) ECCV 2018. LNCS, vol. 11205, pp. 346–363. Springer, Cham (2018). https://doi.org/10.1007/978-3-030-01246-5_21
25. Li, Y., Ouyang, W., Zhou, B., Wang, K., Wang, X.: Scene graph generation from objects, phrases and region captions. In: IEEE International Conference on Computer Vision (ICCV), pp. 1261–1270 (2017)
26. Liang, X., Lee, L., Xing, E.P.: Deep variation-structured reinforcement learning for visual relationship and attribute detection. In: IEEE International Conference on Computer Vision (ICCV), pp. 848–857 (2017)
27. Liao, W., Rosenhahn, B., Shuai, L., Yang, M.Y.: Natural language guided visual relationship detection. In: IEEE/CVF Conference on Computer Vision and Pattern Recognition (CVPR) Workshops (2019)
28. Liu, Y., Wang, R., Shan, S., Chen, X.: Structure inference net: object detection using scene-level context and instance-level relationships. In: IEEE Conference on Computer Vision and Pattern Recognition (CVPR), pp. 6985–6994 (2018)
29. Lu, C., Krishna, R., Bernstein, M., Fei-Fei, L.: Visual relationship detection with language priors. In: Leibe, B., Matas, J., Sebe, N., Welling, M. (eds.) ECCV 2016. LNCS, vol. 9905, pp. 852–869. Springer, Cham (2016). https://doi.org/10.1007/978-3-319-46448-0_51
30. Mikolov, T., Chen, K., Corrado, G., Dean, J.: Efficient estimation of word representations in vector space. arXiv:1301.3781 (2013)
31. Nagaraja, V.K., Morariu, V.I., Davis, L.S.: Modeling context between objects for referring expression understanding. In: Leibe, B., Matas, J., Sebe, N., Welling, M. (eds.) ECCV 2016. LNCS, vol. 9908, pp. 792–807. Springer, Cham (2016). https://doi.org/10.1007/978-3-319-46493-0_48

32. Reinders, C., Ackermann, H., Yang, M.Y., Rosenhahn, B.: Learning convolutional neural networks for object detection with very little training data. In: Multimodal Scene Understanding, pp. 65–100. Elsevier (2019)

33. Ren, S., He, K., Girshick, R., Sun, J.: Faster R-CNN: towards real-time object detection with region proposal networks. In: Neural Information Processing Systems (NeurIPS), pp. 91–99 (2015)

34. Rohrbach, A., Rohrbach, M., Hu, R., Darrell, T., Schiele, B.: Grounding of textual phrases in images by reconstruction. In: Leibe, B., Matas, J., Sebe, N., Welling, M. (eds.) ECCV 2016. LNCS, vol. 9905, pp. 817–834. Springer, Cham (2016). https://doi.org/10.1007/978-3-319-46448-0_49

35. Shi, J., Zhang, H., Li, J.: Explainable and explicit visual reasoning over scene graphs. In: IEEE Conference on Computer Vision and Pattern Recognition (CVPR), pp. 8376–8384 (2019)

36. Silberman, N., Hoiem, D., Kohli, P., Fergus, R.: Indoor segmentation and support inference from RGBD images. In: Fitzgibbon, A., Lazebnik, S., Perona, P., Sato, Y., Schmid, C. (eds.) ECCV 2012. LNCS, vol. 7576, pp. 746–760. Springer, Heidelberg (2012). https://doi.org/10.1007/978-3-642-33715-4_54

37. Simonyan, K., Zisserman, A.: Very deep convolutional networks for large-scale image recognition. arXiv:1409.1556 (2014)

38. Tang, K., Zhang, H., Wu, B., Luo, W., Liu, W.: Learning to compose dynamic tree structures for visual contexts. In: IEEE Conference on Computer Vision and Pattern Recognition (CVPR), June 2019

39. Teney, D., Liu, L., van den Hengel, A.: Graph-structured representations for visual question answering. In: IEEE Conference on Computer Vision and Pattern Recognition (CVPR), pp. 3233–3241 (2017)

40. Wang, W., Wang, R., Shan, S., Chen, X.: Exploring context and visual pattern of relationship for scene graph generation. In: IEEE Conference on Computer Vision and Pattern Recognition (CVPR), pp. 8188–8197 (2019)

41. Xu, D., Zhu, Y., Choy, C.B., Fei-Fei, L.: Scene graph generation by iterative message passing. In: IEEE Conference on Computer Vision and Pattern Recognition (CVPR), pp. 5410–5419 (2017)

42. Yang, J., Lu, J., Lee, S., Batra, D., Parikh, D.: Graph R-CNN for scene graph generation. In: Ferrari, V., Hebert, M., Sminchisescu, C., Weiss, Y. (eds.) ECCV 2018. LNCS, vol. 11205, pp. 690–706. Springer, Cham (2018). https://doi.org/10.1007/978-3-030-01246-5_41

43. Yang, M.Y., Liao, W., Ackermann, H., Rosenhahn, B.: On support relations and semantic scene graphs. ISPRS J. Photogram. Remote Sens. (ISPRS) **131**, 15–25 (2017)

44. Yang, X., Tang, K., Zhang, H., Cai, J.: Auto-encoding scene graphs for image captioning. In: IEEE Conference on Computer Vision and Pattern Recognition (CVPR), pp. 10685–10694 (2019)

45. Yang, X., Zhang, H., Cai, J.: Shuffle-then-assemble: learning object-agnostic visual relationship features. In: Ferrari, V., Hebert, M., Sminchisescu, C., Weiss, Y. (eds.) ECCV 2018. LNCS, vol. 11216, pp. 38–54. Springer, Cham (2018). https://doi.org/10.1007/978-3-030-01258-8_3

46. Yao, B., Fei-Fei, L.: Modeling mutual context of object and human pose in human-object interaction activities. In: IEEE Conference on Computer Vision and Pattern Recognition (CVPR), pp. 17–24 (2010)

47. Yao, T., Pan, Y., Li, Y., Mei, T.: Exploring visual relationship for image captioning. In: Ferrari, V., Hebert, M., Sminchisescu, C., Weiss, Y. (eds.) Computer Vision – ECCV 2018. LNCS, vol. 11218, pp. 711–727. Springer, Cham (2018). https://doi.org/10.1007/978-3-030-01264-9_42

48. Yu, R., Li, A., Morariu, V.I., Davis, L.S.: Visual relationship detection with internal and external linguistic knowledge distillation. In: IEEE International Conference on Computer Vision (ICCV), pp. 1974–1982 (2017)

49. Zellers, R., Yatskar, M., Thomson, S., Choi, Y.: Neural motifs: Scene graph parsing with global context. In: IEEE Conference on Computer Vision and Pattern Recognition (CVPR), pp. 5831–5840 (2018)

50. Zhang, J., Shih, K.J., Elgammal, A., Tao, A., Catanzaro, B.: Graphical contrastive losses for scene graph parsing. In: IEEE Conference on Computer Vision and Pattern Recognition (CVPR) (2019)

51. Zhuang, B., Liu, L., Shen, C., Reid, I.: Towards context-aware interaction recognition for visual relationship detection. In: IEEE International Conference on Computer Vision (ICCV), pp. 589–598 (2017)

52. Zhuo, W., Salzmann, M., He, X., Liu, M.: Indoor scene parsing with instance segmentation, semantic labeling and support relationship inference. In: IEEE Conference on Computer Vision and Pattern Recognition (CVPR), pp. 5429–5437 (2017)

AssembleNet++: Assembling Modality Representations via Attention Connections

Michael S. Ryoo[1,2]([✉]), A. J. Piergiovanni[1], Juhana Kangaspunta[1], and Anelia Angelova[1]

[1] Robotics at Google, Mountain View, USA
{mryoo,ajpiergi,juhana,anelia}@google.com
[2] Stony Brook University, New York, USA

Abstract. We create a family of powerful video models which are able to: (i) learn interactions between semantic object information and raw appearance and motion features, and (ii) deploy attention in order to better learn the importance of features at each convolutional block of the network. A new network component named *peer-attention* is introduced, which dynamically learns the attention weights using another block or input modality. Even without pre-training, our models outperform the previous work on standard public activity recognition datasets with continuous videos, establishing new state-of-the-art. We also confirm that our findings of having neural connections from the object modality and the use of peer-attention is generally applicable for different existing architectures, improving their performances. We name our model explicitly as AssembleNet++. The code will be available at: https://sites. google.com/corp/view/assemblenet/.

Keywords: Video understanding · Activity recognition · Attention

1 Introduction

Video understanding is a fundamental problem in vision with many novel approaches proposed recently. While many advanced neural architectures have been used for video understanding [4,43], including two-stream and multi-stream ones [4,9,34], learning of interactions between raw input modalities (e.g., RGB and motion) and semantic input modalities such as objects in the scene (e.g., persons and objects) have been limited.

Inspired by previous work, e.g. AssembleNet architectures for videos [34] and RandWire architectures for images [53] which proposed random or targeted connectivity between layers in a neural network, we create a family of powerful

Electronic supplementary material The online version of this chapter (https:// doi.org/10.1007/978-3-030-58565-5_39) contains supplementary material, which is available to authorized users.

video models that explicitly learn interactions between spatial object-specific information and raw appearance and motion features. In particular, inter-block attention connectivity is searched for to best capture the interplay between different modality representations.

The main technical contributions of this paper include:

1. Optimizing neural architecture connectivity for object modality fusion. We discover that models with 'omnipresent' connectivity from object input allows the best multi-modal fusion.
2. Learning of video models with *peer-attention* on the connections. We newly introduce an one-shot model formulation to efficiently search for architectures with better peer-attention connectivity.

We test the approach extensively on challenging video understanding datasets, showing notable improvements: compared to the baseline backbone architecture we use, our new one-shot attention search model with object modality obtains +12.6% on Charades classification task and +6.22% on Toyota Smarthome dataset. Our approach also outperforms reported numbers of existing approaches on both datasets, establishing new state-of-the-art.

2   Previous Work

Video CNNs. Convolutional neural network (CNNs) for videos [4,8,9,18,31, 38,42,43,46,54] are a popular approach to video understanding, for example, solutions, such as 3D Video CNNs [4,12,17,40–42], (2+1)D CNNs [43] or even novel architecture searched models [27,28,34] are widely used. Action recognition has also been the topic of intense research [11,45].

Action Recognition with Objects. Action recognition with objects has been traditionally studied years back [26]. The presence of specific objects in video frames, has been shown to be important for video recognition, even in the context of advanced feature learned by deep neural models, e.g., Sigurdsson et al. [37]; they are useful even if provided as a single label per frame. This is not surprising as many of the activities, e.g. 'speaking on the phone', or 'reading a book' are primarily determined by the objects themselves. Furthermore, clues about the location of persons, e.g., by 2D human pose has also been shown to be beneficial [5]. Recent video CNNs have also tried to integrate object-related information, from segmentation [2,32] or pre-training from image datasets [6]. One-time late (or intermediate) fusion of object representation with RGB and flow representations has been widely used (e.g., [24]). Ji et al. [16] modeled scene relations on top of video CNNs using graph neural networks, for better usage of object information. However, we are not aware of any prior work that 'learns' the connectivity between among input modalities including object information, as we do in this paper.

Attention. Use of attention within CNNs have been widely studied. Vaswani et al. [44] investigated different forms and applications of attention while focusing on self-attention. Hu et al. [14] introduced Squeeze-and-Excitation, which is a form of channel-wise self-attention. Researchers also developed other forms of channel-wise self-attention [10,15,19,47,50], often together with spatial self-attention. Attention was also applied to video CNN models [5,22,29]. However, we are not aware of prior work explicitly searching for inter-block attention connectivity (i.e., peer-attention) as we do in this paper.

Neural Architecture Search. Neural Architecture Search (NAS) is the concept of automatically finding superior architectures based on training data [20,33,39,58,59]. Multiple different strategies including learning of reinforcement learning controller (e.g., [58,59] as well as evolutionary algorithms (e.g., [33]) have been developed for NAS. In particular, one-shot differentiable architecture search [3,21] has been successful as it does not require a massive amount of model training. RandWire network [53] could also be interpreted as a form of differentiable architecture search, as it learns weights of (random) connections to minimize the classification loss.

However, architecture search for neural attention connectivity has been very limited. Ahmed and Torresani [1] searched for layer connectivity and Ryoo et al. [34] searched for multi-stream connectivity for video CNNs, but they were without any attention learning which becomes a crucial component when we have a mixture of input modalities. We believe this paper is the first paper to search for models with attention connectivity.

3   Approach

3.1   Preliminaries

This section describes the video CNN architecture framework, which will be used as a base for developing our approach.

We here adopt a multi-stream, multi-block architecture design from AssembleNet [34]. AssembleNet design allows learning of connections between modalities and their intermediate features. This architecture is similar to other two-stream models [4,9], but is more flexible in two ways: 1) it allows the use of more than two streams, and 2) it allows connections to be formed (and potentially learned) between individual blocks of the neural architecture.

More specifically, the architecture we use has multiple input blocks, each corresponding to an input modality. The network blocks have a structure inspired by ResNet architectures [13]. Each input block is composed of a small number of pooling and convolutional layers attached directly on top of the input. The input blocks are then connected to network blocks at the next level. We follow the (2+1)D ResNet block structure from [43], where each module is composed of one 1D temporal conv., one 2D spatial conv., and one 1 × 1 conv. layer. A block is formed by repeating the (2+1)D residual module multiple times. This allows a fair and direct comparison between our approach and previous models using the same module and block [9,34,43].

Each network block (or block for short) can be connected to any block from any modality at the next level, including its own. Blocks are organized at levels so that connections do not form cycles. Connections can also be formed to skip levels. We note that since many connections between blocks are formed early, the neural blocks themselves will often contain information from many input modalities as early as the first level of the network.

Figure 4(a) shows one example architecture, where the structure of the network and example connectivity can be seen.

3.2 Input Modalities and Semantics

In addition to the standard raw RGB video input, motion information is added as a separate modality. More specifically, optical flow, either pre-computed for the dataset [55], or trained on the fly [7,30], has been shown to be a crucial input for achieving better accuracy across the board [4].

We here propose to use object segmentation information as a separate 'object' modality. Objects and their locations provide semantics information which conveys useful information about activities in a video. Crucially here, semantic information is incorporated in the full architecture so that it is able to interact with other modalities and the intermediate features from them (as described more in Sects. 3.3 to 3.5), to maximize its utilization for the best representation.

Input Block Details. We construct an input block for each input modality. Each input block is composed of one pooling and up to two convolutional layers for raw RGB and optical flow inputs, and just one pooling layer for semantic object inputs applied directly on top of the inputs. In the object input block, a segmentation mask having an integer class value per pixel is converted into a HxWxC_O tensor using one-hot operation, where C_O is the number of object classes. The segmentation masks are obtained from a model trained on a non-related image-based dataset.

3.3 Learning Weighted Connections

Blocks in the network can potentially form connections with one or more blocks. While connectivity and the strength of the connectivity could also be hand-coded, we formulate our networks so that they are learnable.

Let G be the connectivity graph of the network where (j, i) specifies that there is a connection from the jth block to ith block. We allow each block to receive its inputs from multiple different input blocks as well as intermediate convolutional blocks, and generates an output. Specifically, we formulate the input of the block as a weighted summation over multiple connections where we learn one weight for each connection.

$$x_i^{in} = \sum_{(j,i) \in G} \sigma(w_{ji}) \cdot x_j^{out} \tag{1}$$

where i and j are block indexes, x_i^{in} corresponds on the final input to the ith block, and x_i^{out} corresponds to the output of the block. σ is a sigmoid function.

Learning of the connection weights together with the other convolutional layer parameters with the standard back propagation allows the network to optimize itself on which connections to use and which to not based on the training data. In our approach, this is done by initially connecting every possible blocks in the graph while using the block levels to avoid cycles, and then learning them. We consider every connection (j, i) from the jth block to ith block as valid as long as $L(j) < L(i)$ where $L(i)$ indicates the level of the block.

3.4   Attention Connectivity and Peer-Attention

In addition to having and learning static weights per connection, we use attention to dynamically control the behavior of each connection. The intuition is that objects and activities are correlated, and using attention allows the model to focus on important objects based on motion context and vice versa. For instance, motion features of 'drinking' could suggest another network stream to focus more on objects related to such motion (e.g., 'cups' and 'bottles').

We formulate our connectivity graph G to have one more component for each edge: $((j, i), k)$, where k is the convolutional block influencing the connection (j, i) via attention. A channel-wise attention is used to implement this behavior. Let C_i be the size of the input channel of block i. For each connection (j, i), the attention vector of size C_i is computed per frame as:

$$A_i(x) = [a_1, \ldots, a_{C_i}] = \sigma(f(\text{GAP}(x))) \tag{2}$$

where f is a function (one fully connected layer in our case) mapping a vector to a vector of size C. GAP is the global average pooling over spatial resolution in the input tensor, making $\text{GAP}(x)$ to have a form of a vector per frame.

Using $A_i(x)$, the input for each block i is computed by combining every connection (j, i) while considering its attention from block k:

$$x_i^{in} = \sum_{((j,i),k) \in G} \sigma(w_{ji}) \cdot (A_i(x_k^{out}) \cdot x_j^{out}). \tag{3}$$

The simplest special case of our attention is self-attention, which is done by making x_k and x_j to be identical. In this form, the usage of attention becomes similar to Squeeze-and-Excitation [14].

Importantly, in our approach, we learn to select different x_k where $x_k \neq x_j$, which we discuss more in the following subsection. Attention with $x_k \neq x_j$ implies that the channels to use for the connection is dynamically decided based on another input modality and peer blocks. We more explicitly name this approach as *peer-attention*. In principle, we define a 'peer' as any block p that could potentially be connected to i. In our formulation where the convolutional blocks are organized into multiple levels (to avoid cycles), the set of peers P for a connection (j, i) is computed as $P_{(j,i)} = \{p \mid L(p) < L(i)\}$ where $L(p)$ indicates

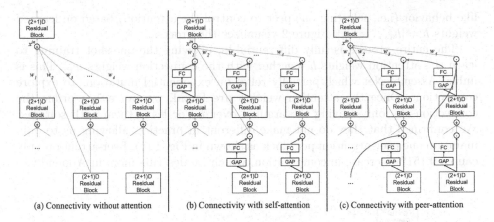

(a) Connectivity without attention   (b) Connectivity with self-attention   (c) Connectivity with peer-attention

Fig. 1. Examples of convolutional block connectivity (a) without attention, (b) with self-attention, and (c) with peer-attention. Red lines indicate weighted connections from Sect. 3.3. Blue curves specify the attention connectivity. GAP is global average pooling and, FC is a fully connected layer. Our attention is channel-wise attention, and it is applied per frame. (Color figure online)

the level of the block p. We consider the attention connection $((j,i),k)$ to be valid as long as $k \in P_{(j,i)}$.

Figure 1 compares connectivity without attention and connectivity with self- and peer-attention.

3.5   One-Shot Attention Search Model

Given a set of convolutional blocks, instead of hand-designing peer-attention connections, we search for the attention connectivity. Our new one-shot attention search model is introduced, which optimizes the model's peer-attention configuration directly based on training data.

Our one-shot attention search model is formulated by combining attention from all possible peer blocks for each connection with learnable weights. The idea is to enable the model to soft-select the best peer for each block by learning differentiable weights, maximizing the recognition performance. All possible attention connectivity is considered as a consequence, and the searching is done solely based on the standard backpropagation.

For each pair of blocks (j,i) where $L(j) < L(i)$, we place a weight for every $k \in P_{(j,i)}$. Let h be a weight vector of size $m = |P_{(j,i)}|$, and $X_P^{out} = [x_1^{out}, \ldots, x_m^{out}]$ be the tensor concatenating x_k^{out} of every possible peer k in P. Then, we reformulate Eq. 3 as:

$$x_i^{in} = \sum_{(j,i) \in G} \sigma(w_{ji}) \cdot (A(x) \cdot x_j^{out}) \quad \text{where} \quad x = \mathbf{1}^T \left(\text{softmax}(h) \cdot X_{P_{(j,i)}}^{out} \right). \quad (4)$$

$\mathbf{1}$ is a vector of size m having 1 as all its element values, making x to be a weighted sum of peer block outputs x_k^{out}. Use of softmax function allows one-hot like behavior (i.e., selecting one peer to control the attention) based on learned weights $h = [h_1, \ldots, h_m]$. Figure 2 visualizes the process.

The entire process is fully differentiable, allowing the one-shot training to learn the attention weights h together with the connection weights w_{ji}. This is unlike AssembleNet which partially relies on exponential mutations to explore connections. Once the attention weights are found, we can either prune the connections by only leaving the argmax over h_k or leave them with softmax. We confirmed that they do not make different in practice, allowing us to only maintain one peer-attention per block as shown in Fig. 1 (c). Peer-attention only causes 0.151% increase in computation, which we describe more in Appendix.

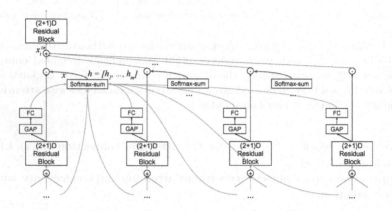

Fig. 2. Visualization of our one-shot attention search model. Magenta connections illustrate weights for the attention connection h. The softmax-sum module in the illustration corresponds to Eq. 4, fusing attentions from different blocks. These weights are fully differentiable and are learned together with convolutional filters, enabling the one-shot connectivity search.

3.6 Model Implementation Details

In order to provide fair comparison to previous work, we comply with the same block structure as AssembleNet [34], which by itself is comparable to (2+1)D ResNet-50.

We build two RGB input blocks (whose temporal resolutions are searched), two optical flow input blocks, and one object input block. RGB blocks and optical flow blocks have the same number of channels and layers as AssembleNet, while the object input block only has one max spatial pooling layer which does not increase the number of parameters of the model.

The object input block obtains its input from a fixed object segmentation model trained independently with the ADE-20K object segmentation dataset [57]. We treat this module as a blackbox and do not propagate gradients into it.

Because this is an off-the-shelf segmentation module and was not trained on any video dataset, its outputs become noisy when directly applied to video datasets as shown in Fig. 3.

Our model has convolutional blocks of four levels (five levels if we count input blocks). The sum of channel sizes are held as a constant at each level (regardless the number of blocks), in order to maintain the total number of parameters. The total channels are 128 at input level, and 128, 256, 512, and 512 at levels 1 to 4 following the ResNet module and block formulation. As a result, all models have equivalent number of parameters to standard two-stream CNNs with (2+1)D residual modules.

Each convolutional block was implemented by alternating 2-D residual modules and (2+1)D residual modules as was done in [34,43]. (2+1)D module is composed of 1D temporal convolution layer followed by 2D spatial convolution layer, followed by 1×1 convolution layer. The temporal resolution of each block is controlled using temporally dilated 1-D convolution, avoiding hard frame downsampling. More details of the blocks are in the supplementary material.

Although the number of blocks at each level could be hand-designed, we use AssembleNet architecture search (with an evolutionary algorithm) to find the optimal combination of convolutional blocks and their temporal resolutions. Once we have the blocks, we connect blocks with weighted connections (doing weighted summation) following Sect. 3.3. Finally, the one-shot attention search model obtained by implementing our peer-attention with softmax-weighted-sum, as described in Sect. 3.5.

Approach Summary. The overall process could be summarized as follows:

1. Prepare blocks. We use AssembleNet evolution to find convolutional blocks, roughly connected.
2. Initialize our one-shot search model by including all possible block connections as well as new attention connections, as described in Sects. 3.3–3.5.

Fig. 3. Examples of the segmentation CNN applied directly on Charades video frames with in-home activities. These noisy masks serve as an input to the object input block, suggesting that our video model is required to learn to handle such noisy input.

3. Train the one-shot model, learning the attention connectivity weights.
4. Prune low weight connections to make the model more compact. We maintain only one peer-attention per block.

We name our final approach specifically as AssembleNet++.

4   Experimental Results

We conduct experiments on popular video recognition datasets: multi-class multi-label Charades [36], and also the recent Toyota Smarthome dataset [5], which records natural person activities in their homes.

We note that we report results **without any pre-training** on a large-scale video dataset, which is unlike most of previous work. Regardless of that, AssembleNet++ outperforms prior work. We conduct multiple ablation experiments to confirm the benefit of our multi-modal model formulation with peer-attention and our one-shot attention search.

Charades Dataset. The Charades dataset [36] is composed of continuous videos of humans interacting with objects. This dataset is a multi-class multi-label video dataset with a total of 66,500 annotations. The videos in the dataset involve motion of small objects in real-world home environments, making it a very challenging dataset. Example video frames of the Charades dataset could be found in Fig. 3. We follow the standard v1 classification setting of the dataset, reporting mAP %. We use Charades as our main dataset for ablations, as it is a realistic dataset explicitly requiring modeling of interactions between object information and other raw inputs such as RGB.

Toyota Smarthomes Dataset. The Toyota Smarthomes dataset [5] consists of real-world activities of humans in their daily lives, such as reading, watching TV, making coffee or breakfast, etc. Humans often interact with objects in this dataset (e.g., 'drink from a can' and 'cook-cut'). The dataset contains 16,115 videos of 31 action classes, and the videos are taken from 7 different camera viewpoints. We only use RGB frames from this dataset, although depth and skeleton inputs are also present in the dataset.

Baselines. As a baseline model, we use AssembleNet architecture backbone [34] which consists of multiple configurable (2+1)D ResNet blocks. Ablations, including our models without the object input block and without peer-attention, are also implemented and compared.

In our ablation experiments which compare different aspects of the proposed approach (Sects. 4.1, 4.2, 4.4, and 4.5), we train the models 50K iterations with cosine decay for the Charades dataset. When using the Toyota dataset, we train our models 15K iterations with cosine decay as this is a smaller dataset than Charades (66,500 annotations in Charades vs. 16,115 segmented videos in Toyota

Smarthome). Further, when comparing against the state-of-the-art, we use the learning rate following a cosine decay function with 'warm-restart' [23], which we discuss more in Sect. 4.3.

Since the model is a one-shot architecture search to discover the attention connectivity, training is efficient and takes only 20–30 h.

4.1 Using Object Modality

In this ablation experiment, we explore the importance of the object input. For this study, our model learns the block connectivity from the Charades training, while not using any attention (i.e., they look like Fig. 1(a)).

Figure 4(a) shows the best connectivity the one-shot model discovered. This is obtained by (i) evolving the blocks with 100 rounds of architecture evolution, (ii) connecting all blocks, (iii) training the weights in one-shot, and then (iv) pruning the low-weight connections. The connections weights w_{ji} with values higher than 0.2 are visualized. Interestingly, the best model is obtained by connecting the object input block to every possible block. The model with this 'omnipresent' object connectivity obtains 50.43 mAP on Charades compared to 47.18 mAP of the model without any object connections, which attests the usefulness of the object modality. The learned weights of each object connection is more than 0.7, suggesting the strong usage of it.

Motivated by the finding that the usage of object information at every block is beneficial (i.e., omnipresent object modality connectivity), we ran an experiment to investigate how performance changes with respect to the best models found with different number of object connections. Fig. 4(b) shows the Charades classification performances of our best found models with full vs. restricted object input usage. X-axis of the graph corresponds to how often the model uses the direct input from the object input block. 0 means that it does not use object information at all, and 1 means it fuses the object information at every block. We are able to clearly observe that the performance increases proportionally to the usage of the object information.

4.2 Attention Search

Next, we confirm the effectiveness of our proposed AssembleNet++ with attention search. Table 1 illustrates how much performance gain we get by using attention connections as opposed to the standard weighted connections.

In addition to attention connectivity with self-attention (Fig. 1(b)) and peer-attention (Fig. 1(c)), we implemented and tested 'static attention'. This is when learning fixed weights not influenced by any input. We are able to observe that our approach of one-shot attention search (with peer-attention) greatly improves the performance. The benefit was even higher (i.e., by ∼6% mAP) when using the object input.

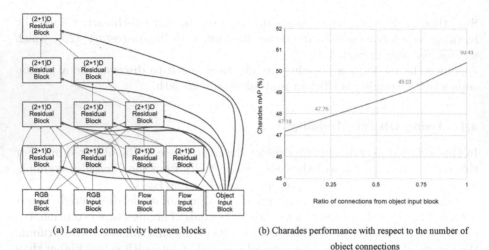

(a) Learned connectivity between blocks

(b) Charades performance with respect to the number of object connections

Fig. 4. (a) Learned connectivity graph of the model and (b) Charades classification performance per object connection ratio. The highlighted blue edges correspond to the direct connections from the object input block. (Color figure online)

Table 1. Comparison between performance with and without attention connections on Charades (mAP). The models were trained 50K iterations.

Attention	Without object	With object
None	47.18	50.43
Static	48.82	51.15
Self	51.91	55.40
Peer	52.39	**56.38**

4.3   Comparison to the State-of-the-Art

In this section, we compare the performance of our AssembleNet++ model with the previous state-of-the-art approaches. We use the model with optimal peer-attention found using our one-shot attention search, and compare it against the results reported by previous work. Unlike most of the existing methods benefiting from pre-training with a large-scale video dataset, we demonstrate that we are able to outperform state-of-the-art **without such pre-training**. Below, we show our results on Charades and Toyota Smarthome datasets.

We also note that the proposed learned attention mechanisms are very powerful, as also seen in the ablation experiments in Sect. 4.2, and even without object information and without pre-training can outperform, or be competitive to, the state-of-the-art.

Charades Dataset. Table 2 shows the results of our method on the Charades dataset. Notice that we are establishing a new state-of-the-art number on this dataset, outperforming previous approaches relying on pre-training. Further, we emphasize that our model is organized to have a maximum of 50 convolutional layers as its depth, explicitly denoting it as 'AssembleNet++ 50'. Our model performs, without pre-training, even superior to AssembleNet with the depth of 101 layers that uses a significantly larger number of parameters. We also note that the use of object modality and attention mechanism proposed here, improves the corresponding AssembleNet baseline by +12.6%.

For this experiment, we use the learning rate with 'warm-restart' [23]. More specifically, we use a cosine decay function that restarts to a provided initial learning rate at every cycle. The motivation is to train our models with an identical amount of training iterations compared to the other state-of-the-art. We 100K training iterations with 50K cycles while only using Charades videos, in contrast to previous work (e.g., AssembleNet [34] and SlowFast [9]) that 50K pre-training with another dataset and 50K fine-tuning with Charades on top of it. We note that the results of our model without 'warm-restart' and without pre-training (as seen in the ablation results in Table 1) at 56.38 are also very competitive to the state-of-the-art.

Table 2. Classification performance on the Charades dataset (mAP).

Method	Pre-training	mAP
Two-stream [35]	UCF101	18.6
CoViAR [52] (Compressed)	ImageNet	21.9
Asyn-TF [35]	UCF101	22.4
MultiScale TRN [56] (RGB)	ImageNet	25.2
I3D [4] (RGB-only)	Kinetics	32.9
I3D from [48] (RGB-only)	Kinetics	35.5
I3D + Non-local [48] (RGB-only)	Kinetics	37.5
EvaNet [28] (RGB-only)	Kinetics	38.1
STRG [49] (RGB-only)	Kinetics	39.7
LFB-101 [51] (RGB-only)	Kinetics	42.5
SGFB-101 [16] (RGB-only)	Kinetics	44.3
SlowFast-101 [9] (RGB+RGB)	Kinetics	45.2
Two-stream (2+1)D ResNet-101	Kinetics	50.6
AssembleNet-50 [34]	MiT	53.0
AssembleNet-50 [34]	Kinetics	56.6
AssembleNet-101 [34]	Kinetics	58.6
AssembleNet-50 [34]	None	47.2
AssembleNet++ 50 (ours) without object	None	54.98
AssembleNet++ 50 (ours)	None	**59.8**

Toyota Smarthome Dataset. We follow the dataset's Cross-Subject (CS) evaluation setting, and measure performance in terms of two standard metrics of the dataset [5]: (1) activity classification accuracy (%) and (2) 'mean per-class accuracies' (%). Table 3 reports our results. Compared to [5], which benefits from Kinetics pre-training and additional 3D skeleton joint information, we obtain superior performance while training the model from scratch and without skeletons. We believe we are establishing new state-of-the-art numbers on this dataset.

Table 3. Performance on the Toyota Smarthome dataset. Classification % and mean per-class accuracy % are reported. Note that our models are being trained from scratch without any pre-training, while the previous work (e.g., [5]) relies on Kinetics pre-training.

Method	Classification %	Mean per-class
LSTM [25]	–	42.5
I3D (with Kinetics pre-training)	72.0	53.4
I3D (pre-trained) + NL [48]	–	53.6
I3D (pre-trained) + separable STA [5]	75.3	54.2
Baseline AssembleNet-50	77.77	57.42
Baseline + self-attention	77.59	57.84
Ours (object + self-attention)	79.08	62.30
Ours (object + peer-attention)	**80.64**	**63.64**

Table 4. Comparing AssembleNet++ using peer-attention vs. a modification using 1×1 convolutional layer instead of attention. They use an identical number of parameters. Charades classification accuracy (mAP) and Toyota mean per-class accuracy (%) are reported.

Model	Charades	Toyota
Base	50.43	59.16
Base + 1×1 conv	50.24	59.44
Random peer-attention	53.40	60.23
Our peer-attention	**56.38**	**63.64**

4.4 Ablation

In this experiment, we explicitly compare AssembleNet++ using peer-attention with its modifications using the same number of parameters. Specifically, we compare our model against (i) the model using 1×1 convolutional layers instead of attention and (ii) the model using peer-attention but with random attention connectivity. For (i), we make the number of 1×1 convolutional layer parameters identical to the number of parameters in FC layers for attention. Table 4 compares the accuracies of these models on Charades and Toyota Smarthome datasets. While using the identical number of parameters, our one-shot peer-attention search model obtains superior results.

4.5   General Applicability of the Findings

Based on the findings that (1) having 'omnipresent' neural connectivity from the object modality and (2) using attention connectivity are beneficial, we investigate further whether such findings are generally applicable for many different CNN models. We add object modality connections and attention to (i) standard R(2+1)D network, (ii) two-stream R(2+1)D network, (iii) original AssembleNet, and (iv) our Charades-searched network (without object connectivity and attention), and observe how their recognition accuracy changes compared to the original models. Our model without object and attention is obtained by manually removing connections from the object input block.

Table 5 shows the results tested on Charades. We are able to confirm that our findings are applicable to other manually designed, as well as, architecture searched architectures. The increase in accuracy is significant for all architectures. Note that our architecture itself is not significantly superior to AssembleNet without object. However, since its connectivity was searched together the object input block (i.e., Sect. 3.5), we are able to observe that our model better takes advantage of the object input via peer attention. 50K training iterations with cosine decay was used for this comparison.

Table 5. Comparison between original CNN models (without object modality and without attention) and their modifications based on our attention connectivity and object modality. The value corresponding to 'AssembleNet++' for the column 'base' is obtained by manually removing connections from the object input block and removing attention from our final one-shot attention search model. Measured with Charades classification (mAP, higher is better), trained from scratch for 50k iterations.

CNN model	Base	+ object + attention
RGB R(2+1)D	36.51	**45.30**
Two-stream R(2+1)D	39.93	**47.74**
AssembleNet	47.18	**53.48**
AssembleNet++	47.62	**56.38**

5   Conclusion

We present a family of novel video models which are designed to learn interactions between the object modality input and the other raw inputs: AssembleNet++. We propose connectivity search to fuse new object input into the model, and introduce the concept of peer-attention to best capture the interplay between different modality representations. The concept of peer-attention generalizes previous channel-wise self-attention by allowing the attention weights to be computed based on other intermediate representations. An efficient differentiable one-shot attention search model is proposed to optimize the attention connectivity. Experimental results confirm that (i) our approach is able to appropriately take advantage of the object modality input (by learning connectivity to the object modality consistently) and that (ii) our searched peer-attention greatly benefits the final recognition. The method outperforms all existing approaches on two very challenging video datasets with daily human activities. Furthermore, we confirm that our proposed approach and the strategy are not just specific to one particular model but is generally applicable for different video CNN models, improving their performance notably.

References

1. Ahmed, K., Torresani, L.: Connectivity learning in multi-branch networks. In: Workshop on Meta-Learning (MetaLearn), NeurIPS (2017)
2. Baradel, F., Neverova, N., Wolf, C., Mille, J., Mori, G.: Object level visual reasoning in videos. In: Ferrari, V., Hebert, M., Sminchisescu, C., Weiss, Y. (eds.) ECCV 2018. LNCS, vol. 11217, pp. 106–122. Springer, Cham (2018). https://doi.org/10.1007/978-3-030-01261-8_7
3. Bender, G., Kindermans, P.J., Zoph, B., Vasudevan, V., Le, Q.: Understanding and simplifying one-shot architecture search. In: International Conference on Machine Learning (ICML) (2018)
4. Carreira, J., Zisserman, A.: Quo vadis, action recognition? A new model and the kinetics dataset. In: Proceedings of the IEEE Conference on Computer Vision and Pattern Recognition (CVPR) (2017)
5. Das, S., et al.: Toyota smarthome: real-world activities of daily living. In: Proceedings of the IEEE International Conference on Computer Vision (ICCV) (2019)
6. Diba, A., et al.: Holistic large scale video understanding. arxiv.org/pdf/1904.11451 (2019)
7. Fan, L., Huang, W., Gan, C., Ermon, S., Gong, B., Huang, J.: End-to-end learning of motion representation for video understanding. In: Proceedings of the IEEE Conference on Computer Vision and Pattern Recognition (CVPR) (2018)
8. Feichtenhofer, C., Pinz, A., Wildes, R.: Spatiotemporal residual networks for video action recognition. In: Advances in Neural Information Processing Systems (NeurIPS) (2016)
9. Feichtenhofer, C., Fan, H., Malik, J., He, K.: Slowfast networks for video recognition. In: Proceedings of the IEEE International Conference on Computer Vision (ICCV) (2019)
10. Fu, J., et al.: Dual attention network for scene segmentation. In: Proceedings of the IEEE Conference on Computer Vision and Pattern Recognition (CVPR) (2019)
11. Girdhar, R., Ramanan, D., Gupta, A., Sivic, J., Russell, B.: ActionVLAD: learning spatio-temporal aggregation for action classification. In: Proceedings of the IEEE Conference on Computer Vision and Pattern Recognition (CVPR), pp. 971–980 (2017)

12. Hara, K., Kataoka, H., Satoh, Y.: Learning spatio-temporal features with 3D residual networks for action recognition. In: Proceedings of the ICCV Workshop on Action, Gesture, and Emotion Recognition, vol. 2, p. 4 (2017)

13. He, K., Zhang, X., Ren, S., Sun, J.: Deep residual learning for image recognition. In: Proceedings of the IEEE Conference on Computer Vision and Pattern Recognition (CVPR) (2016)

14. Hu, J., Shen, L., Albanie, S., Sun, G., Wu, E.: Squeeze-and-excitation networks. In: Proceedings of the IEEE Conference on Computer Vision and Pattern Recognition (CVPR) (2018)

15. Huang, Z., Wang, X., Huang, L., Huang, C., Wei, Y., Liu, W.: CCNet: criss-cross attention for semantic segmentation. In: Proceedings of the IEEE International Conference on Computer Vision (ICCV) (2019)

16. Ji, J., Krishna, R., Fei-Fei, L., Niebles, J.C.: Action genome: actions as composition of spatio-temporal scene graphs. In: Proceedings of the IEEE Conference on Computer Vision and Pattern Recognition (CVPR) (2020)

17. Ji, S., Xu, W., Yang, M., Yu, K.: 3D convolutional neural networks for human action recognition. IEEE Trans. Pattern Anal. Mach. Intell. **35**(1), 221–231 (2013)

18. Kay, W., et al.: The kinetics human action video dataset. arXiv preprint arXiv:1705.06950 (2017)

19. Li, X., Zhong, Z., Wu, J., Yang, Y., Lin, Z., Liu, H.: Expectation-maximization attention networks for semantic segmentation. In: Proceedings of the IEEE International Conference on Computer Vision (ICCV) (2019)

20. Liu, C., et al.: Progressive neural architecture search. In: Ferrari, V., Hebert, M., Sminchisescu, C., Weiss, Y. (eds.) ECCV 2018. LNCS, vol. 11205, pp. 19–35. Springer, Cham (2018). https://doi.org/10.1007/978-3-030-01246-5_2

21. Liu, H., Simonyan, K., Yang, Y.: DARTS: differentiable architecture search. In: International Conference on Learning Representations (ICLR) (2019)

22. Long, X., Gan, C., de Melo, G., Wu, J., Liu, X., Wen, S.: Attention clusters: purely attention based local feature integration for video classification. In: Proceedings of the IEEE Conference on Computer Vision and Pattern Recognition (CVPR), pp. 7834–7843 (2018)

23. Loshchilov, I., Hutter, F.: SGDR: stochastic gradient descent with warm restarts. In: International Conference on Learning Representations (ICLR) (2017)

24. Ma, M., Fan, H., Kitani, K.M.: Going deeper into first-person activity recognition. In: Proceedings of the IEEE Conference on Computer Vision and Pattern Recognition (CVPR) (2016)

25. Mahasseni, B., Todorovic, S.: Regularizing long short term memory with 3D human-skeleton sequences for action recognition. In: Proceedings of the IEEE Conference on Computer Vision and Pattern Recognition (CVPR) (2016)

26. Moore, D.J., Essa, I.A., HayesIII, M.H.: Exploiting human actions and object context for recognition tasks. In: Proceedings of the IEEE Conference on Computer Vision and Pattern Recognition (CVPR) (1999)

27. Nekrasov, V., Chen, H., Shen, C., Reid, I.: Architecture search of dynamic cells for semantic video segmentation. CoRR:1904.02371 (2019)

28. Piergiovanni, A., Angelova, A., Toshev, A., Ryoo, M.S.: Evolving space-time neural architectures for videos (2019)

29. Piergiovanni, A., Fan, C., Ryoo, M.S.: Learning latent sub-events in activity videos using temporal attention filters. In: Proceedings of AAAI Conference on Artificial Intelligence (AAAI) (2017)

30. Piergiovanni, A., Ryoo, M.S.: Representation flow for action recognition. In: Proceedings of the IEEE Conference on Computer Vision and Pattern Recognition (CVPR) (2019)
31. Qiu, Z., Yao, T., Mei, T.: Learning spatio-temporal representation with pseudo-3D residual networks. In: Proceedings of the IEEE International Conference on Computer Vision (ICCV), pp. 5533–5541 (2017)
32. Ray, J., et al.: Scenes-objects-actions: a multi-task, multi-label video dataset. In: Ferrari, V., Hebert, M., Sminchisescu, C., Weiss, Y. (eds.) Computer Vision – ECCV 2018. LNCS, vol. 11218, pp. 660–676. Springer, Cham (2018). https://doi.org/10.1007/978-3-030-01264-9_39
33. Real, E., Aggarwal, A., Huang, Y., Le, Q.V.: Regularized evolution for image classifier architecture search. In: Proceedings of AAAI Conference on Artificial Intelligence (AAAI) (2019)
34. Ryoo, M., Piergiovanni, A., Tan, M., Angelova, A.: AssembleNet: searching for multi-stream neural connectivity in video architectures. In: International Conference on Learning Representations (ICLR) (2020)
35. Sigurdsson, G.A., Divvala, S., Farhadi, A., Gupta, A.: Asynchronous temporal fields for action recognition. In: Proceedings of the IEEE Conference on Computer Vision and Pattern Recognition (CVPR) (2017)
36. Sigurdsson, G.A., Gupta, A., Schmid, C., Farhadi, A., Alahari, K.: Charades-ego: a large-scale dataset of paired third and first person videos. arXiv preprint arXiv:1804.09626 (2018)
37. Sigurdsson, G.A., Russakovsky, O., Gupta, A.: What actions are needed for understanding human actions in videos? In: Proceedings of the IEEE International Conference on Computer Vision (ICCV) (2017)
38. Simonyan, K., Zisserman, A.: Two-stream convolutional networks for action recognition in videos. In: Advances in Neural Information Processing Systems (NeurIPS), pp. 568–576 (2014)
39. Tan, M., Le, Q.: EfficientNet: rethinking model scaling for convolutional neural networks. In: International Conference on Machine Learning (ICML) (2019)
40. Taylor, G.W., Fergus, R., LeCun, Y., Bregler, C.: Convolutional learning of spatio-temporal features. In: Daniilidis, K., Maragos, P., Paragios, N. (eds.) ECCV 2010. LNCS, vol. 6316, pp. 140–153. Springer, Heidelberg (2010). https://doi.org/10.1007/978-3-642-15567-3_11
41. Tran, D., Bourdev, L., Fergus, R., Torresani, L., Paluri, M.: Learning spatiotemporal features with 3D convolutional networks. In: Proceedings of the IEEE International Conference on Computer Vision (ICCV) (2015)
42. Tran, D., Bourdev, L.D., Fergus, R., Torresani, L., Paluri, M.: C3D: generic features for video analysis. CoRR, abs/1412.0767, vol. 2, no. 7, p. 8 (2014)
43. Tran, D., Wang, H., Torresani, L., Ray, J., LeCun, Y., Paluri, M.: A closer look at spatiotemporal convolutions for action recognition. In: Proceedings of the IEEE Conference on Computer Vision and Pattern Recognition (CVPR), pp. 6450–6459 (2018)
44. Vaswani, A., et al.: Attention is all you need. In: Advances in Neural Information Processing Systems (NeurIPS) (2017)
45. Wang, H., Kläser, A., Schmid, C., Liu, C.L.: Action recognition by dense trajectories. In: Proceedings of the IEEE Conference on Computer Vision and Pattern Recognition (CVPR), pp. 3169–3176. IEEE (2011)
46. Wang, L., Li, W., Li, W., Gool, L.V.: Appearance-and-relation networks for video classification. In: Proceedings of the IEEE Conference on Computer Vision and Pattern Recognition (CVPR) (2018)

47. Wang, Q., Wu, B., Zhu, P., Li, P., Zuo, W., Hu, Q.: ECA-Net: efficient channel attention for deep convolutional neural networks. arXiv:1910.03151 (2019)
48. Wang, X., Girshick, R., Gupta, A., He, K.: Non-local neural networks. In: Proceedings of the IEEE Conference on Computer Vision and Pattern Recognition (CVPR), pp. 7794–7803 (2018)
49. Wang, X., Gupta, A.: Videos as space-time region graphs. In: Ferrari, V., Hebert, M., Sminchisescu, C., Weiss, Y. (eds.) ECCV 2018. LNCS, vol. 11209, pp. 413–431. Springer, Cham (2018). https://doi.org/10.1007/978-3-030-01228-1_25
50. Woo, S., Park, J., Lee, J.-Y., Kweon, I.S.: CBAM: convolutional block attention module. In: Ferrari, V., Hebert, M., Sminchisescu, C., Weiss, Y. (eds.) ECCV 2018. LNCS, vol. 11211, pp. 3–19. Springer, Cham (2018). https://doi.org/10.1007/978-3-030-01234-2_1
51. Wu, C.Y., Feichtenhofer, C., Fan, H., He, K., Krähenbühl, P., Girshick, R.: Long-term feature banks for detailed video understanding. arXiv preprint arXiv:1812.05038 (2018)
52. Wu, C.Y., Zaheer, M., Hu, H., Manmatha, R., Smola, A.J., Krähenbühl, P.: Compressed video action recognition. In: Proceedings of the IEEE Conference on Computer Vision and Pattern Recognition (CVPR), pp. 6026–6035 (2018)
53. Xie, S., Kirillov, A., Girshick, R., He, K.: Exploring randomly wired neural networks for image recognition. In: Proceedings of the IEEE International Conference on Computer Vision (ICCV), pp. 1284–1293 (2019)
54. Xie, S., Sun, C., Huang, J., Tu, Z., Murphy, K.: Rethinking spatiotemporal feature learning: speed-accuracy trade-offs in video classification. In: Ferrari, V., Hebert, M., Sminchisescu, C., Weiss, Y. (eds.) ECCV 2018. LNCS, vol. 11219, pp. 318–335. Springer, Cham (2018). https://doi.org/10.1007/978-3-030-01267-0_19
55. Zach, C., Pock, T., Bischof, H.: A duality based approach for realtime TV-L_1 optical flow. In: Hamprecht, F.A., Schnörr, C., Jähne, B. (eds.) DAGM 2007. LNCS, vol. 4713, pp. 214–223. Springer, Heidelberg (2007). https://doi.org/10.1007/978-3-540-74936-3_22
56. Zhou, B., Andonian, A., Oliva, A., Torralba, A.: Temporal relational reasoning in videos. In: Ferrari, V., Hebert, M., Sminchisescu, C., Weiss, Y. (eds.) ECCV 2018. LNCS, vol. 11205, pp. 831–846. Springer, Cham (2018). https://doi.org/10.1007/978-3-030-01246-5_49
57. Zhou, B., Zhao, H., Puig, X., Fidler, S., Barriuso, A., Torralba, A.: Scene parsing through ADE20K dataset. In: Proceedings of the IEEE Conference on Computer Vision and Pattern Recognition (CVPR) (2017)
58. Zoph, B., Le, Q.: Neural architecture search with reinforcement learning. In: International Conference on Learning Representations (ICLR) (2017)
59. Zoph, B., Vasudevan, V., Shlens, J., Le, Q.V.: Learning transferable architectures for scalable image recognition. In: Proceedings of the IEEE Conference on Computer Vision and Pattern Recognition (CVPR) (2018)

Learning Propagation Rules
for Attribution Map Generation

Yiding Yang[1], Jiayan Qiu[2], Mingli Song[3], Dacheng Tao[2],
and Xinchao Wang[1(✉)]

[1] Stevens Institute of Technology, Hoboken, NJ 07030, USA
{yyang99,xinchao.wang}@stevens.edu
[2] UBTECH Sydney AI Centre, School of Computer Science, Faculty of Engineering,
The University of Sydney, Darlington, NSW 2008, Australia
jqiu3225@uni.sydney.edu.au, dacheng.tao@sydney.edu.au
[3] College of Computer Science and Technology, Zhejiang University,
Hangzhou, China
brooksong@zju.edu.cn

Abstract. Prior gradient-based attribution-map methods rely on hand-crafted propagation rules for the non-linear/activation layers during the backward pass, so as to produce gradients of the input and then the attribution map. Despite the promising results achieved, such methods are sensitive to the non-informative high-frequency components and lack adaptability for various models and samples. In this paper, we propose a dedicated method to generate attribution maps that allow us to learn the propagation rules automatically, overcoming the flaws of the hand-crafted ones. Specifically, we introduce a learnable plugin module, which enables adaptive propagation rules for each pixel, to the non-linear layers during the backward pass for mask generating. The masked input image is then fed into the model again to obtain new output that can be used as a guidance when combined with the original one. The introduced learnable module can be trained under any auto-grad framework with higher-order differential support. As demonstrated on five datasets and six network architectures, the proposed method yields state-of-the-art results and gives cleaner and more visually plausible attribution maps.

Keywords: Propagation rules · Attributions maps · Learnable module

1 Introduction

Deep learning has made encouraging progress and yielded state-of-the-art performances in almost all vision and language tasks. The gratifying results, however, come at cost of huge amount of training effort as well as the often uninterpretable

Electronic supplementary material The online version of this chapter (https://doi.org/10.1007/978-3-030-58565-5_40) contains supplementary material, which is available to authorized users.

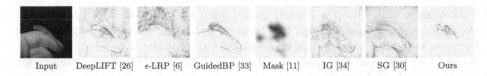

Input   DeepLIFT [26]   ε-LRP [6]   GuidedBP [33]   Mask [11]   IG [34]   SG [30]   Ours

Fig. 1. What makes this image a *newt*? This figure shows the attribution maps generated by different methods. Existing gradient-based methods fail even in this simple case. For example, IG and GuidedBP focus on non-relevant regions, such as the boundary of the hand. Our method, on the other hand, produces cleaner and more focused attribution map.

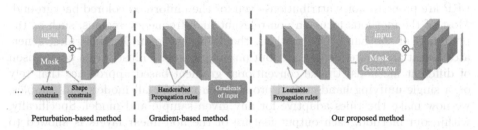

Fig. 2. Comparing the perturbation-based method, gradient-based method, and our proposed method for generating attribution maps. Different from the perturbation-based method that introduces various constraints to the mask, we generate the mask by making use of the gradients of the input; Moreover, unlike the gradient-based method that handcrafts the propagation rules, we make them learnable.

behaviors, making deep networks less dependable under some circumstances such as medical image processing. Recently, interpreting deep networks has aroused more and more attention from researchers [1,2,4,7,9,12,22,25,36–40,42]. Among the many endeavors, estimating the *attribution map* has become a mainstream direction. The main goal of producing an attribution map is to generate a mapping between the pixels and their corresponding contributions to the prediction, so that the supports of the prediction can be discovered. The work of [31,32] have also demonstrated that attention maps can be utilized in estimating task transferability.

Existing attribution-map generation methods can be divided into three categories: optimization-based, perturbation-based, and gradient-based methods. Optimization-based methods produce attribution maps using conventional optimization methods like signal estimation [16], and local function approximation [21]. Such optimizers, however, often require a large number of samples, making them data-dependent and time-consuming. Perturbation-based methods, on the other hand, produce attribution maps by modifying the input image according to a mask and then recording the change of output. However, they ignore the original gradients of the input. Gradient-based methods explicitly utilize gradients of the input for attribution map generation, and therefore encode the interaction across different pixels, yielding more informative attribution maps [19]. Given a trained model with fixed parameters, gradients of the input are obtained through loss back-propagation, where existing methods focus on designing hand-crafted propagation rules for the non-linear/activation layers [3,6]. However, such pre-defined and thus fixed rules lack adaptability for various models and samples.

In this paper, we propose a new method to generate the attribution map that makes the propagation rules for the non-linear layers *learnable*, and optimize the rules using supervision from the model and the input image themselves. In Fig. 1, we compare our produced attribution map with those obtained from the state-of-the-art methods. Conventional gradient-based methods such as DeepLIFT and ϵ-LRP are prone to noisy attributions even for the uniformed-colored background. Most of the methods focus on non-relevant high-frequency regions, such as the boundary of the hand. Our method, thanks to the more flexible rules, generates a neat and more focused attribution map. Figure 2 illustrates a comparison of different methods. Unlike conventional gradient-based approaches that rely on a single unifying hand-crafted propagation rule for all models and samples, we now make the rules adaptive for any given sample and model. Specifically, within our method, each output feature of the non-linear layers is allowed to behave differently during the backward pass, making it possible to learn more flexible and advisable propagation rules for the attribution map. As a result, the non-informative regions, e.g. the high-frequency ones, are suppressed under the supervision, leading to a cleaner attribution map.

To learn the propagation rules, a new optimization scheme is proposed as shown in Fig. 3. The input image is first fed into a trained neural network with fixed parameters to obtain the original prediction. Then, gradients of the input can be obtained during the backward pass, in which process, a *learnable plugin module*, e.g. neural network, is introduced to control the propagation rules of the non-linear layers. After obtained the gradients of the input, we compute the attribution map and then generate masks for the input. The input image will then be masked and fed into the trained network for deriving the difference with respect to the original prediction. Such difference is adopted as a supervision to optimize the learnable plugin module through a new backward pass. Since the computation of second-order gradients is required, an auto-grad framework with higher-order differential support is used to implement the proposed optimization scheme.

Our contribution is therefore, to our best knowledge, the first dedicated approach that enables the learning of the propagation rules for the non-linear layers to generate attribution maps. Unlike the hand-crafted rules, our method makes it possible to find adaptive propagation rules for any given model and sample. The learning of the rule is achieved via a novel optimization scheme: the learnable module we introduced can be optimized under any auto-grad framework with higher-order differential support. We conduct experiments on three different datasets and six models with different architectures. Our proposed method yields state-of-the-art results and produces a cleaner attribution map.

2   Related Work

Here we give a brief description of the related work. We start by reviewing the attribution-map methods of three categories: optimization-based, gradient-based, and perturbation-based methods. We then discuss the higher-order differential algorithms for implementing our proposed method. Note that the proposed method differs from all three categories of attribution-map methods. Specifically, compared with optimization-based methods, our proposed method depends only on given samples; compared with gradient-based methods, our proposed method enables the learning of the propagation rules; compared with perturbation-based methods, our proposed method involves the gradients of inputs as the condition to generate the mask rather than the human designed constraints.

Optimization-Based Methods. These methods adopt conventional optimization scheme to generate an attribution map. For example, PatternNet [16] designs a signal detector to filter out the non-informative components. Then, a quality measurement criterion is introduced to optimize the attribution map generation. Instance feature selector [8] learns a feature selector by maximizing the mutual information between the selected features and the model's response. Another method, LIME [21], locally approximates a non-linear model with a linear function on the given sample, and then generates the attribution map from the linear function. However, these methods are data-dependent and time-consuming.

Gradient-Based Methods. Such methods utilize gradients of the input to generate an attribution map. For example, Deep saliency [28] generates the attribution map by backwarding the loss with respect to the input and taking the absolute value of the gradients. Moreover, the element-wise multiplication between the input and its gradients improves the performance [27]. Another method, Guided backpropagation [33], shows that ignoring the negative gradients helps to distinguish the contribution of each pixel. As for DeepLIFT [26], reference features are added to the non-linear layers to reduce the influence from baseline. However, the fixed propagation rules of these methods lack adaptability for various models and samples.

Perturbation-Based Methods. Methods along this line make the assumption that removing important pixels will degrade the prediction accuracy, and generate the mask based on some constraints. One of the methods, Occlusion [41], generates the attribution map by systematically occluding different parts of the input image and then recording the change of output. Moreover, it is also possible to obtain an occlusion mask by learning [11] rather than brute force searching. sMask [10] introduce predefined area constrain and smooth constrain.

Higher-Order Differential Algorithms. High-order differential algorithms make the second-order gradients computation possible [13,18], and are thus essential for our proposed attribution-map method. Most of the current deep learning libraries implement these algorithms. In Pytorch, for example, gradients of a variable remains a variable, which enables the computation of higher-order

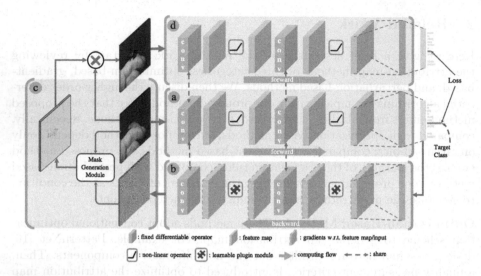

Fig. 3. Illustration of our proposed optimization scheme. Step *a* forwards the input image through the trained model to obtain the original activation and its loss. Specifically, we use the pre-softmax/pre-sigmoid output as the activation of the model. Step *b* then backwards the gradients of input image with respect to the prediction loss, in which we introduce the *Learnable Plugin Module*. The attribution map is obtained by the element-wise multiplication between the input image and its gradients. Next, step *c* generates the masks with the attribution map. Finally, step *d* masks the input image and then forwards the masked image through the trained model to get a new activation. The difference between the new activation and the original one of the target class serves as the loss, which is used to optimize the learnable plugin module.

gradients by recursively computing the first-order gradients. These implementations serve as the backbone of our proposed optimization scheme.

3   Method

Propagation rules for the non-linear layers during the backward pass can be treated as a pixel-to-pixel mapping between gradients of the adjacent feature maps. For gradient-based attribution-map methods, they are proven to be unified and distinguished only on the propagation rules of the non-linear layers [3]. However, existing gradient-based methods formulate the gradient computation as hand-crafted rules, which are hard to fit all models and samples. For example, a method may work well for images with clean backgrounds but fail on those with complex backgrounds.

To this end, we propose a novel method, which makes the rules learnable. The rules will be optimized individually under the supervision of every combination of the input image and the trained neural network, making it adaptive for given models and samples. Figure 3 illustrates the proposed optimization scheme, which is also based on the gradient-descent optimization method. There are four steps in a single optimization iteration for attribution map generation. In Step 1, we forward the input image throughout the network; in Step 2, we backward gradients of the input through our learnable plugin module for attribution map generation; in Step 3, we generate the mask with the attribution map; in Step 4, we forward the masked input image to obtain the loss by computing the difference of activations between the original input and the masked one, where the activation is referred as the pre-softmax/pre-sigmoid output of the model.

3.1 Step 1: Forwarding the Input Image

In this step, the input image is fed into a trained neural network model to obtain the activation. Once the target class to be interpreted is chosen, we set the gradient of the activation to one for target class and zero for the others which is commonly used in gradient-based methods [6,27,33]. We then pass the gradient to the next step.

3.2 Step 2: Backwarding the Gradients of the Input

Given the gradient of the model's activation from previous step, the gradients of the input image can be computed through the back-propagation algorithm. During this process, we implement our proposed learnable plugin module to learn the propagation rules for non-linear layers, instead of modifying the hand-crafted function.

Specifically, after feeding a feature map f_{in} into a non-linear function g, we will have the output $f_{out} = g(f_{in})$. Let $\mathcal{L}$ denotes the training loss during the backward pass. The gradient of f_{out} is the partial derivatives of $\mathcal{L}$ with respect to the output feature map that be expressed as $\frac{\partial \mathcal{L}}{\partial f_{out}}$.

Then, following the chain rule of the back-propagation algorithm, the partial derivatives of $\mathcal{L}$ with respect to f_{out}, can be computed as

$$\frac{\partial \mathcal{L}}{\partial f_{in}} = \frac{\partial \mathcal{L}}{\partial f_{out}} \cdot \frac{\partial g(x)}{\partial f_{in}} = \frac{\partial \mathcal{L}}{\partial f_{out}} \cdot \frac{\partial g(f_{in})}{\partial f_{in}}, \tag{1}$$

where $\frac{\partial g(x)}{\partial x}$ denotes the derivation of non-linear function g with respect to it's input.

In existing gradient-based methods, $\frac{\partial g(x)}{\partial x}$ is manually modified for different purposes, such as ignoring the neurons that suppress the target output [33]. Although numerous hand-crafted propagation rules are proposed, none of them is optimal for all scenarios. For example, some hand-crafted rules are unresponsive to certain target class, while others may be too sensitive to ignore non-relevant high-frequency components.

Therefore, instead of using a fixed hand-crafted $\frac{\partial g(x)}{\partial x}$, we introduce a learnable plugin module, denoted as G, as the basic modules. This module takes the gradients of feature map $\frac{\partial \mathcal{L}}{\partial f_{out}}$ from the upper layer and computes $\frac{\partial \mathcal{L}}{\partial f_{in}}$ as

$$\frac{\partial \mathcal{L}}{\partial f_{in}} = G(\frac{\partial \mathcal{L}}{\partial f_{out}}) \tag{2}$$

where G can be plug-and-play without modifying the original architecture of the given trained neural network. We provide two architectures for G, For the first architecture, we have C parameters per layer, where C is the number of channels. The operation of G is similar to a standard convolutional operation without the sum operation, which shares parameters across different positions within a same layer. For the second architecture, we do not share parameters across different positions, leading to more flexible control of the rules at cost of more parameters. Once the gradients of the input are obtained, the attribution map can be computed as

$$\mathcal{A} = \frac{\partial \mathcal{L}}{\partial I} \circ I, \tag{3}$$

where $\mathcal{A}$, I, and $\frac{\partial \mathcal{L}}{\partial I}$ denote the attribution map, input image, its gradients respectively, and $\circ$ is Hadamard product. The pros and cons of multiplying the generated gradient with the input have been discussed in [30]. In this paper, this multiplication is adopted across all experiments.

3.3 Step 3: Mask Generation

Given the attribution map, a mask can be generated to segment out the image parts that contribute most to the target-class recognition. Since the distribution of attribution map varies a lot, we propose a *Mask Generation Module* for generating suitable masks here.

It can be seen from Fig. 4 that the attribution map is first scaled to $[0, 1]$ and then shifted to a fixed center. Finally, we implement the mask generation using a sigmoid function. We write,

$$\mathcal{M}^p = 1 - \frac{1}{1 + e^{(-\gamma * (\mathcal{A} - \alpha))}}, \tag{4}$$

$$\mathcal{M}^n = \frac{1}{1 + e^{(-\gamma * (\mathcal{A} - \beta))}}, \tag{5}$$

where $\mathcal{M}^p$ denotes the positive mask that segments pixels with positive contribution, $\mathcal{M}^n$ denotes the negative mask that segments pixels with negative contribution, α, β denote the fixed centers and γ denotes the scale factor for sharpening the mask.

Notice that many other mask generation strategies can be directly adopted here, leading to different properties of the generated attribution map. For example, in order to generate smoother mask, a Gaussian smooth function can be replaced for the previous mask generation functions, which can be written as:

$$\mathcal{M}^p = \frac{\sum_{v \in \mathcal{A}} \mathcal{S}_\sigma(u - v)\mathcal{A}(v)}{\sum_{v \in \mathcal{A}} \mathcal{S}_\sigma(u - v)}, \mathcal{S}_\sigma(u) = e^{-\frac{\|u\|^2}{2\sigma^2}} \tag{6}$$

where $\mathcal{A}$ is the generation attribution map, u, v is the index of values in $\mathcal{A}$ and $\mathcal{S}$ is the smooth function.

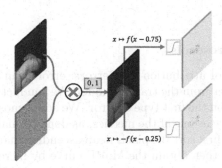

Fig. 4. Illustration of the mask generation module. First, the attribution map is generated by element-wise multiplication between the input image and its gradients. Then, the two masks are computed by feeding the shifted and scaled attribution map into a sigmoid function.

3.4   Step 4: Forwarding the Masked Image

Based on the generated masks, pixels with special contributions will be segmented out from the input image to form the masked image. We then forward the masked image through the trained model to obtain the difference between the activation of input image and masked image, which is used as the loss to train the learnable plugin module.

Some pixels in the masked image contribute to correct prediction while some pixels degrade the accuracy. Therefore, instead of measuring the contribution according to the sign of gradients, we propose a *sign-aware loss* to distinguish the pixels.

There are two terms in the sign-aware loss, a positive term and a negative one. The positive term $\mathcal{L}^p$ considers the positively contributed components of the input image:

$$\mathcal{L}^p = F_t(I \circ \mathcal{M}^p) - F_t(I), \tag{7}$$

where F denotes the trained model, t denotes the index of the target class, and $F_t(I)$ denotes the predicted possibility of I to be class t. By the same token, the negative term is defined as

$$\mathcal{L}^n = F_t(I) - F_t(I \circ \mathcal{M}^n). \tag{8}$$

This term is defined as the difference of predictions between the input image and the negatively masked image, because deleting the negatively contributed pixels should improve the prediction accuracy.

To avoid the trivial solutions like an all-zero mask or an all-one mask, we introduce mask loss to constrain the strength of the generated masks:

$$\mathcal{L}^m = |\mathbf{1} - \mathcal{M}^p| + |\mathbf{1} - \mathcal{M}^n|, \tag{9}$$

where $|\bullet|$ denotes the L_1-Norm, $\mathbf{1}$ denotes matrix with all ones. We thus have the final loss function:

$$\mathcal{L} = (\mathcal{L}^p + \mathcal{L}^n) + \lambda \cdot \mathcal{L}^m, \tag{10}$$

where λ is the hyper-parameter for loss balancing.

4 Experiments

4.1 Evaluation Protocols

There are two kinds of attribution-map errors: error from the attribution-map method itself and error from the trained model. We conduct objective evaluation which focuses purely on the first type of error. We adopt most important relevant features (MoRF) curve as one of the metrics, as done by many other methods [5, 6,23]. Specifically, we first sort the pixels in an ascending manner according to the attribution map, and then obtain the MoRF curve by incrementally computing the correlation between the different ratios of the activation and the ratios of masked pixels. We also adopt least important relevant features (LeRF) curve as one objective evaluation metric. LeRF is of the same setting as MoRF except it first sorts the pixels in a descending manner. For all objective evaluations, we set the upper limit of the number of masked pixels to be 5% of the entire input image. We derive the MoRF curve by averaging 1,000 random samples for stability.

ROAR [15] is another metric to evaluate the performance of attribution map. ROAR first replaces fraction of the pixels that are estimated by the attribution map as the most important ones with uninformative value. Then, the modified data are used to retrain the same model from scratch and test it on the modified test set. It claims that a good attribution map should lead to a sharp degradation of the performance on the modified dataset.

4.2 Implementation Details

Attribution-Map Framework. We build a PyTorch-based attribution-map toolbox, which implements the proposed optimization scheme and some of the compared methods. In our toolbox, the gradient-based methods are unified by sharing the forward and backward hook functions. In the objective experiments, since our only concern is about the model interpretation, the class with the highest prediction possibility is set as the ground truth. We then adopt the negative log likelihood function as the loss function. The running time of our method for an ImageNet-like input with a VGG-16 model is about 3s using an Nvidia 1080Ti GPU.

Learnable Plugin Module. For the objective experiments, we use the second architecture of *learnable plugin module*. Specifically, we set the parameter matrices of learnable plugin module to be of the same size as the input feature map. For every non-linear layers in the model, learnable plugin module first computes the Hadamard product between its parameter matrix and the input feature map, then follows a tanh activation function, We also conduct some experiments of the first architecture of the learnable plugin module which is similar as the convolution without summation and shares parameters within one layer. Although the structure is concise, it leads to a significant improvement of the performance. The learnable plugin module is optimized with Adam [17]. Similar to sMask [10], we train the plugin module separately for each sample. The plugin modules within different layers do not share parameters and are placed in every nonlinear layer within two convolution layers.

Reference Baseline. In order to improve the flexibility of learnable plugin module, we adopt the reference baseline from DeepLIFT [26]. Specifically, an additional all-zero input is added in the forward pass to obtain the reference feature maps. Then, all the original features are modified by subtracting their corresponding reference feature map.

Hyper-parameters Settings. We adopt same hyper-parameters to all experiments, with λ set to be 0.1, α set to be 0.75, β set to be 0.25, and γ set to be 10. For the Adam optimizer, we set the learning rate to be 0.2. No weight decay is used. The performance with respect to these hyper-parameters are stable within a large value range, and the analysis will be presented in the sensitivity analysis section.

4.3 Compared Methods

Here, we give a brief description of the compared methods.

- **Gradient-based methods.** GradientXInput (GradXIn) [27] and Deep-Saliency (Saliency) [28] generate attribution maps from the gradients of the input. Specifically, DeepSaliency utilizes the gradients only, while GradXIn uses both the input and its gradients. ϵ-LRP [5], and DeepLIFT [26], on the other hand, focus on designing hand-crafted fixed propagation rules to enhance performances. SQ_SG [15] is an improvement over smooth grad method by averaging the squared gradients. Integrated Gradients (IG) [34] and Smooth Gradients (SG) [30] compute the average gradients of multiple inputs by introducing integration paths and adding noises, respectively.
- **Perturbation-based methods.** Mask [11] treats the attribution map as a mask and learns it from a designed framework. sMask [10] adds more constraints to the mask. RISE [20] generates random masks and obtains the attribution map by linear combining these masks according to outputs of masked images.

The Mask method is tested on ImageNet dataset only, because it is designed for ImageNet-similar images. The hyper-parameters of Mask are set according to their published work. For the SmoothGrad method, the number of random noised images is set to 50. As for the IntegratedGrad method, the number of integrated images along the integral path from zero baseline to the original input is set to 50. The tolerance of pointing game is set to 15 for all compared methods.

4.4 Experimental Results

In this section, we first analyze the comparison results between our proposed method and the compared methods in the aspects of MoRF, LeRF, and ROAR. Then, we present the case study, the sensitivity analysis of hyper-parameters, and the ablation study to completely evaluate our proposed method.

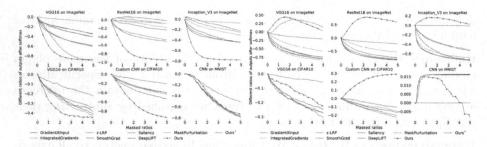

Fig. 5. MoRF (left) and LeRF (right) curves. The x-axis represents the masked ratio of the entire image and the y-axis represents the difference ratio of the activation after masking the input. Our method produces consistently steeper curves, especially for complex models and samples. Note that for the LeRF metric, our method provides the correct negative attributions, which will lead to an increase of the prediction accuracy when removing them. All other methods, as a comparison, fail and still generate positive attributions.

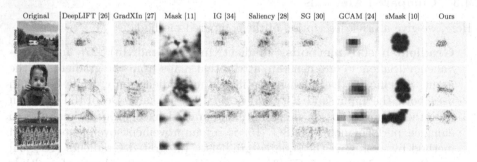

Fig. 6. Visualization of the attribution maps generated by different methods on ImageNet dataset. The attribution maps generated by our method are cleaner and more visually plausible. For gradient-based methods, some of them are too sensitive to ignore the non-relevant high-frequency components while others are not responsive enough to the target class (e.g. the last line). More visualization results will be presented in the supplemental material.

MoRF/LeRF Result Analysis. Figure 5 compares the MoRF and LeRF curves of our proposed method and the compared methods. We conduct the objective experiments on three widely used datasets, MNIST, CIFAR-10, and ImageNet. ∗ means the plugin module with the first architecture which shares parameters across different positions. The analysis of the results on the three datasets is as follows:

– **MNIST** is a relative small and simple dataset, in which the images contain only unit digits with clean background. We test on it using a customized CNN model with two convolutional layers. It can be seen that all methods lead to similar performances on both the MoRF and LeRF curves. This can be in part explained by the fact that, simple images cannot distinguish the potentials of these methods.

- **CIFAR-10** is a larger dataset, in which the images contain common objects but with low resolution. We test two CNN models on this dataset, a custom CNN model with four convolutional layers and a VGG-16 model [29]. It can be seen that our proposed method performs the best on both the MoRF and LeRF curves.
- **ImageNet** is one of the largest and most complex datasets, in which the images come from the real-world scenes. We test all methods with three state-of-the-art models on this dataset, a VGG-16 model, a ResNet18 model [14], and a Inception-V3 model [35]. It can be seen that our method performs the best on the MoRF curve consistently by a large margin. As for the LeRF cure, thanks to the sign-aware loss, our method gives the correct negative attributions while all compared methods fail.

Table 1. Evaluation of ROAR on the CIFAR10 dataset with the custom CNN model. Our method consistently performs better that others especially when the fraction of removed pixels are large. We report the test accuracy on the modified dataset (lower is better).

Fraction	Original	Random	SQ_SG	Ours
40%	80.73%	73.65%	74.90%	71.83%
50%	80.73%	72.46%	72.97%	69.81%
60%	80.73%	70.89%	70.79%	67.32%
70%	80.73%	68.98%	68.33%	63.80%
80%	80.73%	65.85%	65.19%	59.08%
90%	80.73%	59.58%	57.47%	50.72%

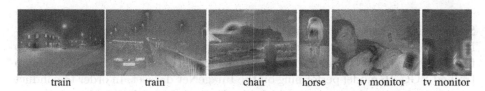

train   train   chair   horse   tv monitor   tv monitor

Fig. 7. Illustration of some misclassified images and their corresponding attribution maps. The predictions of these images are train, train, chair, horse, tv monitor and tv monitor respectively. Red color highlights the supports of the predictions. Note that although the attribution map does not align well with the human perception, masking the image according to the attribution map still lead to a significant drop of the wrong prediction. (Color figure online)

We visualize the attribution maps on ImageNet dataset with a trained VGG-16 model in Fig. 6. It can be seen that some compared methods are too sensitive to ignore the non-relevant high-frequency components (e.g. the grass and the boundary of trees). Other methods, unfortunately, fail to localize the most contributed areas to the prediction (e.g. the results in the last line). As a comparison, our method provides consistently cleaner and more focused attribution maps.

ROAR Result Analysis. Table 1 shows the ROAR result. We change the fraction of removed pixels from 40% to 90% and retrain the model on the modified dataset. The test accuracy is reported and lower is better. Our method consistently leads to a lower accuracy on the modified test set.

Case Study. We first conduct a case study of some misclassified images shown in Fig. 7. It can be seen that even the generated attribution map does not align well with the human perception, masking the input according to the attribution map stills lead to a significant drop of the wrong prediction. We also conduct a case study on a composite image. It contains two objects from different classes. Our method is truly responsive to the target class, as can be seen from Fig. 8, and focuses on the most informative areas while many gradient-based methods are not sensitive to the target class or even give the opposite signs (like DeepLIFT).

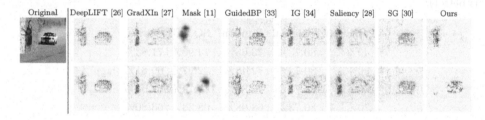

Fig. 8. Visualization of a composite image with two different objects. The target name of the first line is Rhinoceros beetle while the target name of the second line is Land Rover. Many gradient-based methods are not sensitive to the target class.

Sensitivity Analysis. Here, we conduct experiments for analyzing the sensitivity of the four hyper-parameters in our method including the scale factor γ, two fixed centers α and β, and λ for loss balancing. All results are obtained using a trained VGG-16 model performing on the ImageNet dataset. In order to conduct a more comprehensive analysis, we also evaluate the sensitivity of learning rates and optimization iterations. The performance is measured by Area Under The Curve (AUC) of the MoRF curve, for which a lower value indicates a better result. We present all the results in Table 2, where intensities of the color are associated with the AUC values. It can be seen that the performance of our method is not sensitive to λ. For other hyper-parameters, the performance stays stable when they are set in a reasonable range.

Ablation Studies. We conduct ablation studies to analyze the effect of two terms, including the sign-aware loss and the reference baseline. The comparison results between the full model and models without one of two terms are

Table 2. Results of sensitivity analysis for the hyper-parameters. AUC is the area under MoRF curve and lower is better. The performance is not sensitive to λ and stays stable when choosing reasonable values for other hyper-parameters.

γ	1	7.5	14	21	27	34	40	47	53.5	60
AUC	0.40	0.27	0.16	0.13	0.14	0.15	0.17	0.18	0.20	0.22
Iters	1	8	14	21	27	34	40	47	54	60
AUC	0.86	0.29	0.27	0.27	0.26	0.24	0.23	0.23	0.22	0.23
λ	0.1	0.2	0.3	0.4	0.5	0.6	0.7	0.8	0.9	1
AUC	0.23	0.22	0.22	0.22	0.22	0.22	0.21	0.22	0.21	0.22
lr	0.01	0.06	0.12	0.17	0.23	0.28	0.34	0.39	0.45	0.5
AUC	0.40	0.33	0.29	0.26	0.25	0.25	0.21	0.21	0.20	0.21
α	0.55	0.59	0.64	0.68	0.73	0.77	0.82	0.86	0.90	0.95
AUC	0.47	0.37	0.30	0.26	0.23	0.21	0.19	0.18	0.18	0.21

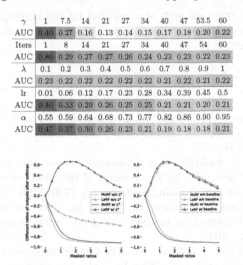

Fig. 9. Ablation studies of the sign-aware loss and the reference baseline. The sign-aware loss dramatically improves the performance on LeRF curve while the baseline reference has a little influence on the performance.

presented in Fig. 9. It can be seen that the sign-aware loss improves the performance on LeRF curve by a significant margin with cost of a little affect on the performance of MoRF. The intuition behind is that the sign-aware loss, which contains two branches, will generate the guided supervisions for two types of mask separately. As for the reference baseline, it influences the performance of the proposed method on both LeRF and MoRF curves slightly, implying that the learnable plugin module is already flexible enough even without the cues provided by the added reference features. We also tried to use the standard convolution as the plugin module but fail to generate a meaningful attribution map. This can be partially explained by that, the standard convolution operation does a substantial change to the gradients, leading to a pointless attribution map that is unrelated to the model anymore.

5   Conclusion

In this paper, we propose a dedicated attribution-map method that enables the propagation rules learnable for the non-linear layers, so as to overcome the drawbacks of existing gradient-base methods. The propagation rules are controlled by the plugin module and can be optimized by the proposed optimization scheme under any auto-grad framework with higher-order differential support. The learnable rules are adaptive, thanks to the supervision from the model and the input themselves. As demonstrated on several datasets and models, our method yields state-of-the-art results and produces cleaner and more focused attribution maps.

Acknowledgments. This research is supported by the startup funding of Stevens Institute of Technology and Australian Research Council Projects FL-170100117, DP-180103424, IC-190100031.

References

1. Adebayo, J., Gilmer, J., Muelly, M., Goodfellow, I., Hardt, M., Kim, B.: Sanity checks for saliency maps. In: Advances in Neural Information Processing Systems, pp. 9505–9515 (2018)
2. Alvarez-Melis, D., Jaakkola, T.S.: Towards robust interpretability with self-explaining neural networks. In: Proceedings of the 32nd International Conference on Neural Information Processing Systems, pp. 7786–7795 (2018)
3. Ancona, M., Ceolini, E., Öztireli, C., Gross, M.: Towards better understanding of gradient-based attribution methods for deep neural networks. arXiv preprint arXiv:1711.06104 (2017)
4. Ancona, M., Öztireli, C., Gross, M.: Explaining deep neural networks with a polynomial time algorithm for Shapley values approximation. arXiv preprint arXiv:1903.10992 (2019)
5. Bach, S., Binder, A., Montavon, G., Klauschen, F., Müller, K.R., Samek, W.: On pixel-wise explanations for non-linear classifier decisions by layer-wise relevance propagation. PLoS ONE **10**(7), e0130140 (2015)
6. Binder, A., Montavon, G., Lapuschkin, S., Müller, K.-R., Samek, W.: Layer-wise relevance propagation for neural networks with local renormalization layers. In: Villa, A.E.P., Masulli, P., Pons Rivero, A.J. (eds.) ICANN 2016. LNCS, vol. 9887, pp. 63–71. Springer, Cham (2016). https://doi.org/10.1007/978-3-319-44781-0_8
7. Chen, H., et al.: Data-free learning of student networks. In: Proceedings of the IEEE International Conference on Computer Vision, pp. 3514–3522 (2019)
8. Chen, J., Song, L., Wainwright, M.J., Jordan, M.I.: Learning to explain: an information-theoretic perspective on model interpretation. arXiv preprint arXiv:1802.07814 (2018)
9. Feng, Z., Wang, X., Ke, C., Zeng, A.X., Tao, D., Song, M.: Dual swap disentangling. In: Advances in Neural Information Processing Systems 31 (2018)
10. Fong, R., Patrick, M., Vedaldi, A.: Understanding deep networks via extremal perturbations and smooth masks. In: Proceedings of the IEEE International Conference on Computer Vision, pp. 2950–2958 (2019)
11. Fong, R.C., Vedaldi, A.: Interpretable explanations of black boxes by meaningful perturbation. In: Proceedings of the IEEE International Conference on Computer Vision, pp. 3429–3437 (2017)
12. Ghorbani, A., Abid, A., Zou, J.: Interpretation of neural networks is fragile. In: Proceedings of the AAAI Conference on Artificial Intelligence, vol. 33, pp. 3681–3688 (2019)
13. Griewank, A., Walther, A.: Evaluating Derivatives: Principles and Techniques of Algorithmic Differentiation, vol. 105. SIAM, Philadelphia (2008)
14. He, K., Zhang, X., Ren, S., Sun, J.: Deep residual learning for image recognition. In: Proceedings of the IEEE Conference on Computer Vision and Pattern Recognition, pp. 770–778 (2016)

15. Hooker, S., Erhan, D., Kindermans, P.J., Kim, B.: A benchmark for interpretability methods in deep neural networks. In: Advances in Neural Information Processing Systems, pp. 9737–9748 (2019)
16. Kindermans, P.J., et al.: Learning how to explain neural networks: PatternNet and PatternAttribution. arXiv preprint arXiv:1705.05598 (2017)
17. Kingma, D.P., Ba, J.: Adam: a method for stochastic optimization. arXiv preprint arXiv:1412.6980 (2014)
18. Maclaurin, D.: Modeling, inference and optimization with composable differentiable procedures. Ph.D. thesis (2016)
19. Montavon, G., Lapuschkin, S., Binder, A., Samek, W., Müller, K.R.: Explaining nonlinear classification decisions with deep Taylor decomposition. Pattern Recogn. **65**, 211–222 (2017)
20. Petsiuk, V., Das, A., Saenko, K.: RISE: randomized input sampling for explanation of black-box models. arXiv preprint arXiv:1806.07421 (2018)
21. Ribeiro, M.T., Singh, S., Guestrin, C.: Why should I trust you?: Explaining the predictions of any classifier. In: Proceedings of the 22nd ACM SIGKDD International Conference on Knowledge Discovery and Data Mining, pp. 1135–1144 (2016)
22. Ribeiro, M.T., Singh, S., Guestrin, C.: Anchors: high-precision model-agnostic explanations. In: Thirty-Second AAAI Conference on Artificial Intelligence (2018)
23. Samek, W., Binder, A., Montavon, G., Lapuschkin, S., Müller, K.R.: Evaluating the visualization of what a deep neural network has learned. IEEE Trans. Neural Netw. Learn. Syst. **28**(11), 2660–2673 (2016)
24. Selvaraju, R.R., Cogswell, M., Das, A., Vedantam, R., Parikh, D., Batra, D.: Grad-CAM: visual explanations from deep networks via gradient-based localization. In: Proceedings of the IEEE International Conference on Computer Vision, pp. 618–626 (2017)
25. Shen, C., Wang, X., Song, J., Sun, L., Song, M.: Amalgamating knowledge towards comprehensive classification. In: Proceedings of the AAAI Conference on Artificial Intelligence (AAAI) (2019)
26. Shrikumar, A., Greenside, P., Kundaje, A.: Learning important features through propagating activation differences. In: Proceedings of the 34th International Conference on Machine Learning Volume 70, pp. 3145–3153 (2017)
27. Shrikumar, A., Greenside, P., Shcherbina, A., Kundaje, A.: Not just a black box: learning important features through propagating activation differences. arXiv preprint arXiv:1605.01713 (2016)
28. Simonyan, K., Vedaldi, A., Zisserman, A.: Deep inside convolutional networks: visualising image classification models and saliency maps. arXiv preprint arXiv:1312.6034 (2013)
29. Simonyan, K., Zisserman, A.: Very deep convolutional networks for large-scale image recognition. arXiv preprint arXiv:1409.1556 (2014)
30. Smilkov, D., Thorat, N., Kim, B., Viégas, F., Wattenberg, M.: SmoothGrad: removing noise by adding noise. arXiv preprint arXiv:1706.03825 (2017)
31. Song, J., Chen, Y., Wang, X., Shen, C., Song, M.: Deep model transferability from attribution maps. In: Advances in Neural Information Processing Systems 32 (2019)
32. Song, J., et al.: DEPARA: deep attribution graph for deep knowledge transferability. In: The IEEE Conference on Computer Vision and Pattern Recognition (CVPR) (2020)
33. Springenberg, J.T., Dosovitskiy, A., Brox, T., Riedmiller, M.: Striving for simplicity: the all convolutional net. arXiv preprint arXiv:1412.6806 (2014)

34. Sundararajan, M., Taly, A., Yan, Q.: Axiomatic attribution for deep networks. In: Proceedings of the 34th International Conference on Machine Learning-Volume 70, pp. 3319–3328 (2017)
35. Szegedy, C., Vanhoucke, V., Ioffe, S., Shlens, J., Wojna, Z.: Rethinking the inception architecture for computer vision. In: IEEE Conference on Computer Vision and Pattern Recognition, June 2016
36. Wang, Y., Xu, C., Xu, C., Tao, D.: Adversarial learning of portable student networks. In: Thirty-Second AAAI Conference on Artificial Intelligence (2018)
37. Yang, Y., Qiu, J., Song, M., Tao, D., Wang, X.: Distilling knowledge from graph convolutional networks. In: The IEEE Conference on Computer Vision and Pattern Recognition (CVPR) (2020)
38. Ye, J., Ji, Y., Wang, X., Gao, X., Song, M.: Data-free knowledge amalgamation via group-stack dual-GAN. In: The IEEE Conference on Computer Vision and Pattern Recognition (CVPR) (2020)
39. Ye, J., Ji, Y., Wang, X., Ou, K., Tao, D., Song, M.: Student becoming the master: knowledge amalgamation for joint scene parsing, depth estimation, and more. In: The IEEE Conference on Computer Vision and Pattern Recognition (CVPR) (2019)
40. Yu, X., Liu, T., Wang, X., Tao, D.: On compressing deep models by low rank and sparse decomposition. In: Proceedings of the IEEE Conference on Computer Vision and Pattern Recognition (CVPR) (2017)
41. Zeiler, M.D., Fergus, R.: Visualizing and understanding convolutional networks. In: Fleet, D., Pajdla, T., Schiele, B., Tuytelaars, T. (eds.) ECCV 2014. LNCS, vol. 8689, pp. 818–833. Springer, Cham (2014). https://doi.org/10.1007/978-3-319-10590-1_53
42. Zhang, Q., Cao, R., Shi, F., Wu, Y.N., Zhu, S.C.: Interpreting CNN knowledge via an explanatory graph. In: Thirty-Second AAAI Conference on Artificial Intelligence (2018)

Reparameterizing Convolutions for Incremental Multi-Task Learning Without Task Interference

Menelaos Kanakis[1(✉)], David Bruggemann[1], Suman Saha[1],
Stamatios Georgoulis[1], Anton Obukhov[1], and Luc Van Gool[1,2]

[1] ETH Zurich, Zurich, Switzerland
menelaos.kanakis@vision.ee.ethz.ch
[2] KU Leuven, Leuven, Belgium

Abstract. Multi-task networks are commonly utilized to alleviate the need for a large number of highly specialized single-task networks. However, two common challenges in developing multi-task models are often overlooked in literature. First, enabling the model to be inherently incremental, continuously incorporating information from new tasks without forgetting the previously learned ones (incremental learning). Second, eliminating adverse interactions amongst tasks, which has been shown to significantly degrade the single-task performance in a multi-task setup (task interference). In this paper, we show that both can be achieved simply by reparameterizing the convolutions of standard neural network architectures into a non-trainable shared part (filter bank) and task-specific parts (modulators), where each modulator has a fraction of the filter bank parameters. Thus, our reparameterization enables the model to learn new tasks without adversely affecting the performance of existing ones. The results of our ablation study attest the efficacy of the proposed reparameterization. Moreover, our method achieves state-of-the-art on two challenging multi-task learning benchmarks, PASCAL-Context and NYUD, and also demonstrates superior incremental learning capability as compared to its close competitors. The code and models are made publicly available (https://github.com/menelaoskanakis/RCM).

Keywords: Multi-task learning · Incremental learning · Task interference

1 Introduction

Over the last decade, convolutional neural networks (CNNs) have been established as the standard approach for many computer vision tasks, like image classification [17,25,54], object detection [15,32,48], semantic segmentation [3,33,63],

Electronic supplementary material The online version of this chapter (https://doi.org/10.1007/978-3-030-58565-5_41) contains supplementary material, which is available to authorized users.

© Springer Nature Switzerland AG 2020
A. Vedaldi et al. (Eds.): ECCV 2020, LNCS 12365, pp. 689–707, 2020.
https://doi.org/10.1007/978-3-030-58565-5_41

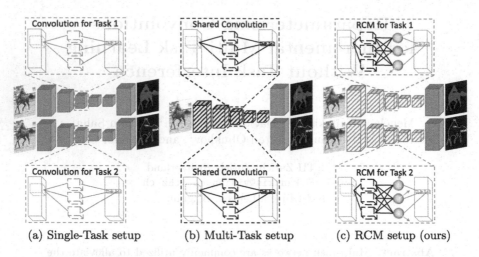

(a) Single-Task setup   (b) Multi-Task setup   (c) RCM setup (ours)

Fig. 1. (a) Optimizing independent models per task allows for the easy addition of new tasks, at the expense of a multiplicative increase in the total number of parameters with respect to a single model (green and blue denote task-specific parameters). **(b)** A single backbone for multiple tasks must be meaningful to all, thus, all tasks interact with the said backbone (black indicates common parameters). **(c)** Our proposed setup, RCM (Reparameterized Convolutions for Multi-task learning), uses a pre-trained filter bank (denoted in black) and independently optimized task-specific modulators (denoted in colour) to adapt the filter bank on a per-task basis. New task addition is accomplished by training the task-specific modulators, thus explicitly addressing task interference while parameters scale at a slower rate than having independent models per task. (Color figure online)

and monocular depth estimation [12, 26]. Typically, these tasks are handled by CNNs independently, i.e., a separate model is optimized for each task, resulting in several task-specific models (Fig. 1a). However, real-world problems are more complex and require models to perform multiple tasks on-demand without significantly compromising each task's performance. For example, an interactive advertisement system tasked with displaying targeted content to its audience should be able to detect the presence of humans in its viewpoint effectively, estimate their gender and age group, recognize their head pose, etc. At the same time, there is a need for flexible models able to gradually add more tasks to their knowledge, without forgetting previously known tasks or having to re-train the whole model from scratch. For instance, a car originally deployed with lane and pedestrian detection functionalities can be extended with depth estimation capabilities post-production.

When it comes to learning multiple tasks under a single model, multi-task learning (MTL) techniques [2, 50] have been employed in the literature. On the one hand, encoder-focused approaches [1, 10, 24, 31, 34, 38, 40, 57] emphasize learning feature representations from multi-task supervisory signals by employing architectures that encode shared and task-specific information. On the other hand, decoder-focused approaches [58,59,61,62] utilize the multi-task feature representations learned at the encoding stage to distill cross-task information at the decoding stage, thus refining the original feature representations. In both cases, however, the joint learning from multiple supervisory signals (i.e., tasks) can hinder the individual task performance if the associated tasks point to conflicting gradient directions during the update step of the shared feature representations (Fig. 1b). Formally this is known as *task interference* or *negative transfer* and has been well documented in the literature [24,36,65]. To suppress negative transfer, several approaches [6,16,21,36,52,55,65] dynamically re-weight each task's loss function or re-order the task learning, to find a 'sweet spot' where individual task performance does not degrade significantly. Arguably, such approaches mainly focus on mitigating the negative transfer problem in the MTL architectures above, rather than eliminating it (see Sect. 3.2). At the same time, existing works seem to disregard the fact that MTL models are commonly desired to be incremental, i.e., information from new tasks should be continuously incorporated while existing task knowledge is preserved. In existing works, the MTL model has to be re-trained from scratch if the task dictionary changes; this is arguably sub-optimal.

Recently, task-conditional networks [36] emerged as an alternative for MTL, inspired by work in multi-domain learning [45,46]. That is, performing separate forward passes within an MTL model, one for each task, every time activating a set of task-specific residual responses on top of the shared responses. Note that, this is useful for many real-world setups (e.g., an MTL model deployed in a mobile phone with limited resources that adapts its responses according to the task at hand), and particularly for incremental learning (e.g., a scenario where the low-level tasks should be learned before the high-level ones). However, the proposed architecture in [36] is prone to task interference due to the inherent presence of shared modules, which is why the authors introduced an adversarial learning scheme on the gradients to minimize the performance degradation. Moreover, the model needs to be trained from scratch if the task dictionary changes.

All given, existing works primarily focus on either improving the multi-task performance or reducing the number of parameters and computations in the MTL model. In this paper, we take a different route and explicitly tackle the problems of incremental learning and task interference in MTL. We show that both problems can be addressed simply by reparameterizing the convolutional operations of a neural network. In particular, building upon the task-conditional MTL direction, we propose to decompose each convolution into a shared part that acts as a filter bank encoding common knowledge, and task-specific modulators that adapt this common knowledge uniquely for each task. Figure 1c illustrates our approach, RCM (Reparameterized Convolutions for Multi-task learning). Unlike existing works, the shared part in our case is not trainable to explicitly avoid negative transfer. Most notably, as any number of task-specific modulators can be introduced in each convolution, our model can incrementally solve more tasks without interfering with the previously learned ones. Our results demonstrate that the proposed RCM can outperform state-of-the-art methods in multi-task (Sect. 4.6) and incremental learning (Sect. 4.7) experiments. At the same time, we address the common multi-task challenge of task interference by construction, by ensuring tasks can only update task-specific components and cannot interact with each other.

2 Related Work

Multi-Task Learning (MTL) aims at developing models that can solve a multitude of tasks [2,50]. In computer vision, MTL approaches can roughly be divided into encoder-focused and decoder-focused ones. Encoder-focused approaches primarily emphasize on architectures that can encode multi-purpose feature representations through supervision from multiple tasks. Such encoding is typically achieved, for example, via feature fusion [38], branching [24,34,40,57], self-supervision [10], attention [31], or filter grouping [1]. Decoder-focused approaches start from the feature representations learned at the encoding stage, and further refine them at the decoding stage by distilling information across tasks in a one-off [59], sequential [61], recursive [62], or even multi-scale [58] manner. Due to the inherent layer sharing, the approaches above typically suffer from task interference. Several works proposed to dynamically re-weight the loss function of each task [6,21,52,55], sort the order of task learning [16], or adapt the feature sharing between 'related' and 'unrelated' tasks [65], to mitigate the effect of negative transfer. In general, existing MTL approaches have primarily focused on improving multi-task performance or reducing the network parameters and computations. Instead, in this paper, we look at the largely unexplored problems of incremental learning and negative transfer in MTL models and propose a principled way to tackle them.

Incremental Learning (IL) is a paradigm that attempts to augment the existing knowledge by learning from new data. IL is often used, for example, when aiming to add new classes [47] to an existing model, or learn new domains [30]. It aims to mitigate 'catastrophic forgetting' [14], the phenomenon of forgetting old tasks as new ones are learned. To minimize the loss of existing knowledge, Li and Hoiem [30] optimized the new task while preserving the old task's responses. Other works [23,28] constrained the optimization process to minimize the effect learning has on weights important for older tasks. Rebuffi et al. [47] utilized exemplars that best approximate the mean of the learned classes in the feature space to preserve performance. Note that the performance of such techniques is commonly upper bounded by the joint training of all tasks. More relevant to our work, in a multi-domain setting, a few approaches [35,45,46,49] utilize a pre-trained network that remains untouched and instead learn domain-specific components that adapt the behavior of the network to address the performance drop common in IL techniques. Inspired by this research direction, we investigate the training of parts of the network, while keeping the remaining components constant from initialization amongst all tasks. This technique not only addresses catastrophic forgetting but also task interference, which is crucial in MTL.

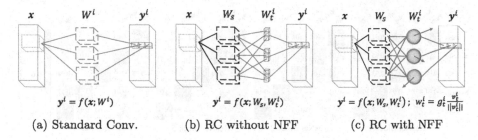

$$y^i = f(x; W^i)$$

(a) Standard Conv.

$$y^i = f(x; W_s, W_t^i)$$

(b) RC without NFF

$$y^i = f(x; W_s, W_t^i) \; ; \; w_t^i = g_t^i \frac{v_t^i}{||v_t^i||}$$

(c) RC with NFF

Fig. 2. (a) A standard convolutional module for a given task i, with task-specific weights W^i in orange. (b) A reparameterized convolution (RC) consisting of a shared filter bank W_s in black, and task-specific modulator W_t^i in orange. (c) An RC with Normalized Feature Fusion (NFF), consisting of a shared filter bank W_s in black, and task-specific modulator W_t^i in orange. Each row w_t^i of W_t^i is reparameterized as $g_t^i \cdot v_t^i / \| v_t^i \|$.

Decomposition of filters and tensors within CNNs has been explored in the literature. In particular, filter-wise decomposition into a product of low-rank filters [20], filter groups [44], a basis of filter groups [29], etc. have been utilized. In contrast, tensor-wise examples include SVD decomposition [9,60], CP-decomposition [27], Tucker decomposition [22], Tensor-Train decomposition [42], Tensor-Ring decomposition [64], T-Basis [41], etc. These techniques have been successfully used for compressing neural networks or reducing their inference time. Instead, in this paper, we utilize decomposition differently. We decompose each convolutional operation into two components: a shared and a task-specific part. Note that although we utilize the SVD decomposition for simplicity, the same principles hold for other decomposition types too.

3   Reparameterizing CNNs for Multi-Task Learning

In this section, we present techniques to adapt a CNN architecture, such that it can increasingly learn new tasks in an MTL setting while scaling more efficiently than simply adding single-task models. Section 3.1 introduces the problem formulation. Section 3.2 demonstrates the effect of task interference in MTL and motivates the importance of CNN reparameterization. Section 3.3 presents techniques to reparameterize CNNs and limit the parameter increase with respect to task-specific models.

3.1   Problem Formulation

Given P tasks and input tensor x, we aim to learn a function $f(x; W_s, W_t^i) = y^i$ that holds for task $i = 1, 2, \ldots P$, where W_s and W_t^i are the shared and task-specific parameters respectively. Unlike existing approaches [34,38] which learn such functions $f(\cdot)$ on the layer level of the network, i.e., explicitly designing

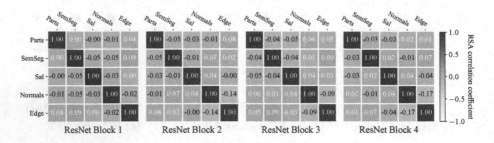

Fig. 3. Visualization of the Representation Similarity Analysis (RSA) on the task-specific gradients at different depths of a ResNet-26 model [36]. The analysis was conducted on: human parts segmentation (Parts), semantic segmentation (SemSeg), saliency estimation (Sal), normals estimation (Normals), and edge detection (Edge).

shared and task-specific layers, we aim to learn f on a block-level by *reparameterizing* the convolutional operation, and adapting its behaviour conditioned on the task i, as depicted in Fig. 2b and Fig. 2c. By doing so, we can explicitly address the task interference and catastrophic forgetting problems within an MTL setting.

3.2 Task Interference

To motivate the importance of addressing task interference by construction, we analyze the task-specific gradient directions on the shared modules of a state-of-the-art MTL model. Specifically, we utilize the work of [36], who used a discriminator to enforce indistinguishable gradients amongst tasks.

We acquire the gradients from the training dataset of PASCAL-Context [39] for each task, using minibatches of size 128, yielding 40 minibatches. We then use the Representation Similarity Analysis (RSA), proposed in [11] for transfer learning, as a means to quantify the correlation of the gradients amongst the different tasks. Figure 3 depicts the task gradient correlations at different depths of a ResNet-26 model [17], trained to have indistinguishable gradients in the output layer [36]. It can be seen that there is a limited gradient correlation amongst the tasks, demonstrating that addressing task interference indirectly (here with the use of adversarial learning on the gradients) is a very challenging problem. We instead follow a different direction and propose to utilize reparameterizations with shared components amongst different tasks that are untouched during the training process, and each task being able to optimize only its parameters. As such, task interference is eliminated by construction.

3.3 Reparameterizing Convolutions

We define a convolutional operation $f(\boldsymbol{x}; \boldsymbol{w}) = y$ for the single-task learning setup, Fig. 2a. $\boldsymbol{w} \in \mathbb{R}^{k^2 c_{in}}$ denotes the parameters of a single convolutional layer (we omit the bias to simplify notation) for a kernel size k and c_{in} channels.

$x \in \mathbb{R}^{k^2 c_{in}}$ is the input tensor volume at a given spatial location (x and w are expressed in vector notation), and y is the scalar response. Assuming c_{out} such filters, the convolutional operator can be rewritten in matrix notation as $f(x; W) = y$, where $y \in \mathbb{R}^{c_{out}}$ provides c_{out} responses, and $W \in \mathbb{R}^{c_{out} \times k^2 c_{in}}$. In a single-task setup:

$$f(x; W^1) = y^1, \quad \ldots, \quad f(x; W^P) = y^P \tag{1}$$

where W^i and y^i are the task-specific parameters and responses for a given convolutional layer, respectively. The total number of parameters for this setup is $\mathcal{O}(Pk^2 c_{in} c_{out})$. Our goal is to reparameterize $f(\cdot)$ in Eq. 1 as:

$$f(x; W^i) = h(x; W_s, W_t^i), \quad \forall i = 1, \ldots, P \tag{2}$$

using a set of shared ($W_s \in \mathbb{R}^{c_{out} \times k^2 c_{in}}$) and task-specific ($W_t^i \in \mathbb{R}^{c_{out} \times c_{out}}$) parameters for each convolutional layer of the backbone. Our formulation aims to retain the prediction performance of the original convolutional layer (Eq. 1), while simultaneously reducing the rate in which the total number of parameters grows. The complexity now becomes $\mathcal{O}((k^2 c_{in} + P c_{out}) c_{out})$, which is less than $\mathcal{O}(Pk^2 c_{in} c_{out})$ for standard layers. We argue that this reparameterization is necessary for coping with task interference and incremental learning in an MTL setup, in which we only optimize for task-specific parameters W_t^i, while keeping the shared parameters W_s intact. Note that, when adding a new task $i = \omega$, we do not need to train the entire network from scratch as in [36]. We only optimize W_t^ω for each layer of the reparameterized CNN.

We denote our reparameterized convolutional layer as a matrix multiplication between the two sets of parameters: $W_t^i W_s$. In order to find a set of parameters $W_t^i W_s$ that approximates the single-task weights W^i a natural choice is to minimize the Frobenius norm $\|W_t^i W_s - W^i\|_F$ directly. Even though direct minimization of this metric is appealing due to its simplicity, it poses some major caveats. (i) It assumes that all directions in the parameter space affect the final performance for task i in the same way and are thus penalized uniformly. However, two different solutions for W_t^i with the same Frobenius norm can yield drastically different losses. (ii) This approximation is performed independently for each convolutional layer, neglecting the chain effect an inaccurate prediction in one layer can have in the succeeding layers. In the remainder of this section, we propose different techniques to address these limitations.

Reparameterized Convolution. We implement the Reparameterized Convolution (RC) $W_t^i W_s$ as a stack of two 2D convolutional layers without non-linearity in between, with W_s having a spatial filter size k and W_t^i being a 1×1 convolution (Fig. 2b)[1]. We optimize only W_t^i directly on the task-specific loss function using stochastic gradient descent while keeping the shared weights W_s constant.

---

[1] To ensure compliance with ImageNet [8] initialization, the new architecture is first pre-trained on ImageNet using the publicly available training script from PyTorch [43].

This ensures that training for one task is independent of other tasks, ruling out interference amongst tasks while optimizing the metric of interest.

Normalized Feature Fusion. One can view w_t^i, a row in matrix W_t^i, as a soft filter adaptation mechanism, i.e., a modulator which generates new task-specific filters from a given filter bank W_s, depicted in Fig. 2b. However, instead of training the vector w_t^i directly, we propose its reparameterization into two terms, a vector term $v_t^i \in \mathbb{R}^{c_{out}}$, and a scalar term g_t^i as:

$$w_t^i = g_t^i \frac{v_t^i}{\| v_t^i \|}, \tag{3}$$

where $\| \cdot \|$ denotes the Euclidean norm. We refer to this reparameterization as Normalized Feature Fusion (NFF), depicted in Fig. 2c. NFF provides an easier optimization process in comparison to an unconstrained w_t^i. This reparametrization enforces $v_t^i / \| v_t^i \|$ to be unit length and point in the direction which best merges the filter bank. The vector norm $\| w_t^i \| = g_t^i$ learns independently the appropriate scale of the newly generated filters, and thus the scale of the activation. Directly optimizing w_t^i attempts to learn both jointly, which is a harder optimization problem. Normalizing weight tensors has been generally explored for speeding up the convergence of the optimization process [7,51,56]. In our work, we use it differently and demonstrate empirically (see Sect. 4.5) that such a reparameterization in series with a filter bank also improves performance in the MTL setting. As seen in Eq. 3, additional learnable parameters are introduced in the training process (g_t^i and v_t^i), however, w_t^i can be computed after training and used directly for deployment, eliminating additional overhead.

Response Initialization. We build upon the findings of matrix/tensor decomposition literature [9,60] that network weights/responses lie on a low dimensional subspace. We further assume that such a subspace can be beneficial for multiple tasks, and thus good for network initialization under a MTL setup. To this end, we identify a meaningful subspace of the responses for the generation of a better filter bank W_s when compared to that directly learned by pre-training W_s on ImageNet. More formally, let $y = f(x; W^m)$ be the responses for input tensor x, where $W^m \in \mathbb{R}^{c_{out} \times k^2 c_{in}}$ are the pre-trained ImageNet weights. We define $Y \in \mathbb{R}^{c_{out} \times n}$ as a matrix containing n responses of y with the mean vector $\bar{y}$ subtracted. We compute the eigen-decomposition of the covariance matrix $YY^T = USU^T$ (using Singular Value Decomposition, SVD), where $U \in \mathbb{R}^{c_{out} \times c_{out}}$ is an orthogonal matrix with the eigenvectors on the columns, and S is a diagonal matrix of the corresponding eigenvalues. We can now initialize the shared convolution parameters W_s with $U^T W^m$, and the task-specific W_t^i with U. We refer to this initialization methodology as Response Initialization (RI). We point the reader to the supplementary material for more details.

4   Experiments

4.1   Datasets

We focus our evaluation on dense prediction tasks, making use of two datasets. We conduct the majority of the experiments on PASCAL [13], and more specifically, PASCAL-Context [39]. We address edge detection (Edge), semantic segmentation (SemSeg), human parts segmentation (Parts), surface normals estimation (Normals), and saliency (Sal). We evaluate single-task performance using optimal dataset F-measure (odsF) [37] for edge detection, mean intersection over union (mIoU) for semantic segmentation, human parts and saliency, and finally mean error (mErr) for surface normals. Labels for human parts segmentation are acquired from [5], while for saliency and surface normals from [36].

We further evaluate the proposed method on the smaller NYUD dataset [53], comprised of indoor scenes, on edge detection (Edge), semantic segmentation (SemSeg), surface normals estimation (Normals), and depth (Depth). The evaluation metrics for edge detection, semantic segmentation, and surface normals estimation are identical to those for PASCAL-Context, while for depth we use root mean squared error (RMSE).

4.2   Architecture

All of our experiments make use of the DeepLabv3+ architecture [4], originally designed for semantic segmentation, which performs competitively for all tasks of interest as demonstrated in [36]. DeepLabv3+ encodes multi-scale contextual information by utilizing a ResNet [17] encoder with a-trous convolutions [3] and an a-trous spatial pyramid pooling (ASPP) module, while a decoder with a skip connection refines the predictions. Unless otherwise stated, we use a ResNet-18 (R-18) based DeepLabv3+, and report the mean performance of five runs for each experiment[2].

4.3   Evaluation Metric

We follow standard practice [36,58] and quantify the performance of a model m as the average per-task performance drop with respect to the corresponding single-task baseline b:

$$\Delta_m = \frac{1}{P} \sum_{i=1}^{P} (-1)^{l_i} \frac{M_{m,i} - M_{b,i}}{M_{b,i}} \tag{4}$$

where l_i is either 1 or 0 if a lower or a greater value indicates better performance, respectively, for a performance measure M. P indicates the total number of tasks.

---

[2] Baseline comparisons to competing methods, as well as additional backbone experiments, can be found in the supplementary material.

Table 1. Performance analysis of task-specific modules. We report the effect network modules (Convs and BNs) have on the performance of PASCAL-Context.

Method	Convs	BNs	Edge ↑	SemSeg ↑	Parts ↑	Normals ↓	Sal ↑	Δ_m% ↓
Freeze encoder			67.32	60.37	47.86	17.40	58.39	14.98
Task-specific BNs		✓	69.80	63.93	53.22	14.78	64.44	5.76
Task-specific Convs	✓		71.72	66.00	59.05	13.78	66.31	0.62
Single-task	✓	✓	71.88	66.22	59.69	13.64	66.62	–

4.4 Analysis of Network Module Sharing

We investigate the level of task-specific adaptation required for a common backbone to perform competitively to single-task models, while additionally eliminating negative transfer. In other words, the necessity for task-specific modules, i.e., convolutions (Convs) and batch normalizations (BNs) [19]. Specifically, we optimize for task-specific Convs, BNs, or both along the network's depth. Modules that are not being optimized maintain their ImageNet pre-trained parameters. Table 1 presents the effect on performance, while Fig. 4 depicts the total number of parameters with respect to the number of tasks. Experiments vary from common Convs and BNs (Freeze encoder) to task-specific Convs and BNs (Single-task), and anything in-between.

The model utilizing a common backbone pre-trained on ImageNet (Freeze encoder), as expected, is unable to perform competitively to the single-task counterpart, with a performance drop of 14.98%. Task-specific BNs significantly improve performance with a percentage drop of 5.76%, at a minimal increase in parameters (Fig. 4). The optimization of Convs is essential for competitive performance to single-task, with a percentage drop of 0.62%. However, the increase in parameters is comparable to single-task, which is undesirable (Fig. 4).

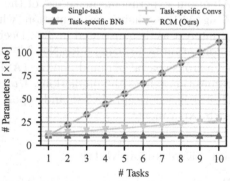

Fig. 4. Backbone parameter scaling. Total number of parameters with respect to the number of tasks for R-18 backbone.

4.5 Ablation Study

To validate the proposed methodology from Sect. 3, we conduct an ablation study, presented in Table 2. We additionally report the performance of a model trained jointly on all tasks, consisting of a fully shared encoder and task-specific decoders (Multi-task). This multi-task model is not trained in an IL setup but

Table 2. Ablation study of the proposed RCM. We present ablation experiments for the proposed Reparameterized Convolution (RC), Response Initialization (RI), Normalized Feature Fusion (NFF) on PASCAL-Context dataset.

Method	NFF	RI	Edge ↑	SemSeg ↑	Parts ↑	Normals ↓	Sal ↑	Δ_m% ↓
Single-task			71.88	66.22	59.69	13.64	66.62	–
Multi-task			70.74	62.43	57.89	14.43	66.31	3.32
RC			71.10	64.56	56.87	13.91	66.37	2.13
RC+NFF	✓		71.12	64.71	56.91	13.90	66.33	2.07
RC+RI		✓	71.36	65.58	57.99	13.70	66.21	1.12
RC+RI+NFF	✓	✓	71.34	65.70	58.12	13.70	66.38	0.99

merely serves as a reference to the traditional multi-tasking techniques. We report a performance drop of 3.32% with respect to the single-task setup.

Reparameterized Convolution. We first develop a new baseline for our proposed reparameterization, where we replace every convolution with the RC (Sect. 3.3) counterpart. As seen in Table 2, RC achieves a performance drop of 2.13%, outperforming the 3.32% drop of the multi-task baseline, as well as the Task-specific BNs (Table 1) that achieved a performance drop of 5.76%. This observation corroborates the claim made in Sect. 4.4 that task-specific adaptation of the convolutions is essential for a model to perform competitively for all tasks. Additionally, we demonstrate that even without training entirely task-specific convolutions, as in Table 1 (Task-specific Convs), a performance boost can still be observed at a smaller magnitude, while the total number of parameters scales at a slower rate (Fig. 4). RCM in Fig. 4 depicts the parameter scaling of all the RC-based methods introduced in Table 2, described in this section. As such, improvements in performance from this baseline do not stem from an increase in network capacity.

Response Initialization. We investigate the effect on the performance of a more meaningful filter bank, RI (Sect. 3.3), against the filter bank learned by directly pre-training the RC architecture on ImageNet. In Table 2 we report the performance of our proposed model when directly pre-trained on ImageNet (Table 2-RC), and with the RI based filter bank (Table 2-RC+RI). Compared to the RC model, the performance significantly improves from a 2.13% drop to a 1.12% drop with the RC+RI model. This observation clearly demonstrates that the filter bank generated using our proposed RI approach is beneficial for better weight initialization.

Normalized Feature Fusion. We replace the unconstrained task-specific components of RC with the proposed NFF (Sect. 3.3). We demonstrate in Table 2 that NFF improves the performance no matter the initialization of the filter bank. RC improves from a 2.13% drop to a 2.07% in RC+NFF, while RC+RI improved from a 1.12% drop to 0.99% for RC+RI+NFF.

Table 3. Comparison with state-of-the-art methods on PASCAL-Context.

Method	Edge ↑	SemSeg ↑	Parts ↑	Normals ↓	Sal ↑	Δ_m% ↓
Single-task	71.88	66.22	59.69	13.64	66.62	–
ASTMT (R-18 w/o SE) [36]	71.20	64.31	57.79	15.06	66.59	3.49
ASTMT (R-26 w SE) [36]	71.00	64.61	57.25	15.00	64.70	4.12
Series RA [45]	70.62	65.99	55.32	14.27	66.08	2.97
Parallel RA [46]	70.84	66.51	56.56	14.16	66.36	2.09
RCM (ours)	71.34	65.70	58.12	13.70	66.38	**0.99**

Table 4. Comparison with state-of-the-art methods on NYUD.

Method	Edge ↑	SemSeg ↑	Normals ↓	Depth ↓	Δ_m% ↓
Single-task	68.83	35.45	22.20	0.56	–
ASTMT (R-18 w/o SE) [36]	68.60	30.69	23.94	0.60	6.96
ASTMT (R-26 w SE) [36]	73.50	30.07	24.32	0.63	7.56
Series RA [45]	67.56	31.87	23.35	0.60	5.88
Parallel RA [46]	68.02	32.13	23.20	0.59	5.02
RCM (ours)	68.44	34.20	22.41	0.57	**1.48**

The architecture used for the remaining experiments is the Reparameterized Convolution (RC) with Normalized Feature Fusion (NFF), initialized using the Response Initialization (RI) methodology. This architecture is denoted as RCM.

4.6   Comparison to State-of-the-Art

In this work, we focus on comparing to task-conditional methods that can address MTL. We compare the performance of our method to Series Residual Adapter (Series RA) [45] and Parallel RA [46]. Series and Parallel RAs learn multiple visual domains by optimizing domain-specific residual adaptation modules (rather than using RCM as in our work, Fig. 2c) on an ImageNet pre-trained backbone. Since both methods were developed for multi-domain settings, we optimize them using our own pipeline, ensuring a fair comparison amongst the methods while additionally benchmarking the capabilities of multi-domain methods in a multi-task setup. We further report the performance of ASTMT [36], which utilizes an architecture resembling that of Parallel RA [46] with Squeeze-and-Excitation (SE) blocks [18] and adversarial task disentanglement of gradients. Specifically, we report the performance of the models using a ResNet-26 (R-26) DeepLab-V3+ with SE as reported in [36], and also optimize with the use of their codebase a ResNet-18 model without SE. The latter model uses an architecture resembling more closely that of the other methods since SE can be additionally incorporated in the others as well. We report the average performance drop with respect to our single-task baseline.

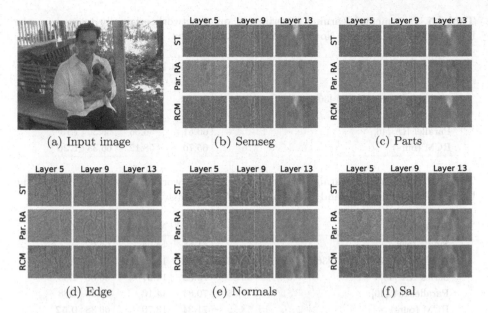

Fig. 5. Feature visualizations. We visualize the features of the input image (a) for the tasks of PASCAL-Context. The first row of each sub-figure corresponds to the responses of the single-task model (ST), the second row those of Parallel RA (Par. RA) [46] and the final row of our proposed method (RCM). For all tasks and depths of the network, the responses of RCM closely resemble those of ST, in contrast to the responses of Par. RA. This is made apparent from the colours utilized by the different methods. The RGB values were identified from a common PCA basis across the three methods in order to highlight similarities and differences between them.

The results for PASCAL-Context (Table 3) and NYUD (Table 4) demonstrate that our method achieves the best performance, outperforming the other methods that make use of RA modules. This demonstrates that although the RA can perform competitively in multi-domain settings, placing the convolution in series without non-linearity is a more promising direction for the drastic adaptations required for different tasks in a multi-task learning setup.

We visualize in Fig. 5 the learned representations of single-task, Parallel RA [46], and RCM across tasks and network depths. For each task and layer combination, we compute a common PCA basis for the methods above and depict the first three principal components as RGB values. For all tasks and layers of the network, the representations of RCM closely resemble those of the single-task models. Simultaneously, Parallel RA is unable to adapt the convolution behavior to the extent required to be comparable to single-task models.

4.7 Incremental Learning for Multi-tasking

We further evaluate the methods from Sect. 4.6 in the incremental learning (IL) setup. In other words, we investigate the capabilities of the models to learn

Table 5. Incremental learning experiments on a network originally trained on the low-level tasks (Edge and Normals) of PASCAL-Context.

Method	Edge ↑	Normals ↓	SemSeg ↑	Parts ↑	Sal ↑	Δ_m% ↓
Single-task	71.88	13.64	66.22	59.69	66.62	–
ASTMT (R-18 w/o SE) [36]	70.70	14.84	55.32	50.49	64.34	11.77
Series RA [45]	70.62	14.27	65.99	55.32	66.08	2.83
Parallel RA [46]	70.84	14.16	66.51	56.56	66.36	1.73
RCM (ours)	71.34	13.70	65.70	58.12	66.38	**1.26**

Table 6. Incremental learning experiments on a network originally trained on the high-level tasks (SemSeg and Parts) of PASCAL-Context.

Method	SemSeg ↑	Parts ↑	Edge ↑	Normals ↓	Sal ↑	Δ_m% ↓
Single-task	66.22	59.69	71.88	13.64	66.62	–
ASTMT (R-18 w/o SE) [36]	63.91	57.33	68.67	14.12	64.43	3.76
Series RA [45]	65.99	55.32	70.62	14.27	66.08	2.39
Parallel RA [46]	66.51	56.56	70.84	14.16	66.36	1.88
RCM (ours)	65.70	58.12	71.34	13.70	66.38	**0.52**

new tasks without the need to be completely retrained on the entire task dictionary. We divide the tasks of PASCAL-Context into three groups, **(i)** edge detection and surface normals (low-level tasks), **(ii)** saliency (mid-level task) and **(iii)** semantic segmentation and human parts segmentation (high-level tasks). IL experiments are conducted by allowing the base network to initially use knowledge from either (i) or (iii), and reporting the capability for the optimized model to learn additional tasks without affecting the performance of the already learned tasks (the performance drop is calculated over the new tasks that were not used in the initial training). In the IL setup, ASTMT [36] is initially trained using an R-18 backbone without SE (a comparable backbone to the competing methods for a fair comparison) on the subset of the tasks (either i or iii). New tasks can be incorporated by training their task-specific modules independently. On the other hand, Series RA, Parallel RA, and RCM, were designed to be inherently incremental due to directly optimizing only the task-specific modules. Consequently, their task-specific performance in the IL setup is identical to that reported in Sect. 4.6.

In Tables 5 and 6 we report the performance of tasks that are utilized to generate the initial knowledge of the model in grey (important for ASTMT [36]), while in black the performance of the incrementally learned tasks. As shown in both tables, and in particular Table 5, ASTMT does not perform competitively in the IL experiments. This observation further demonstrates the importance of utilizing generic filter banks that can be adapted based on the task-specific needs, in particular for IL setups. We consider research in generic multi-task filter banks to be a promising direction.

5 Conclusion

We have presented a novel method of a convolutional operation reparameterization and its application to training multi-task learning architectures. These reparameterized architectures can be applied on a multitude of different tasks, and allow the CNN to be inherently incremental, while additionally eliminating task interference, all by construction. We evaluate our model on two datasets and multiple tasks, and show experimentally that it outperforms competing baselines that address similar challenges. We further demonstrate its efficacy when compared to the state-of-the-art task-conditional multi-task method, which is unable to tackle incremental learning.

Acknowledgments. This work was sponsored by Advertima AG and co-financed by Innosuisse. We thank the anonymous reviewers for their valuable feedback.

References

1. Bragman, F.J., Tanno, R., Ourselin, S., Alexander, D.C., Cardoso, J.: Stochastic filter groups for multi-task CNNs: learning specialist and generalist convolution kernels. In: Proceedings of the IEEE International Conference on Computer Vision, pp. 1385–1394 (2019)
2. Caruana, R.: Multitask learning. Mach. Learn. **28**(1), 41–75 (1997). https://doi.org/10.1023/A:1007379606734
3. Chen, L.C., Papandreou, G., Kokkinos, I., Murphy, K., Yuille, A.L.: DeepLab: semantic image segmentation with deep convolutional nets, atrous convolution, and fully connected CRFs. IEEE Trans. Pattern Anal. Mach. Intell. **40**(4), 834–848 (2017)
4. Chen, L.-C., Zhu, Y., Papandreou, G., Schroff, F., Adam, H.: Encoder-decoder with atrous separable convolution for semantic image segmentation. In: Ferrari, V., Hebert, M., Sminchisescu, C., Weiss, Y. (eds.) ECCV 2018. LNCS, vol. 11211, pp. 833–851. Springer, Cham (2018). https://doi.org/10.1007/978-3-030-01234-2_49
5. Chen, X., Mottaghi, R., Liu, X., Fidler, S., Urtasun, R., Yuille, A.: Detect what you can: detecting and representing objects using holistic models and body parts. In: Proceedings of the IEEE Conference on Computer Vision and Pattern Recognition, pp. 1971–1978 (2014)
6. Chen, Z., Badrinarayanan, V., Lee, C.Y., Rabinovich, A.: GradNorm: gradient normalization for adaptive loss balancing in deep multitask networks. arXiv preprint arXiv:1711.02257 (2017)
7. Dauphin, Y.N., Fan, A., Auli, M., Grangier, D.: Language modeling with gated convolutional networks. In: Proceedings of the 34th International Conference on Machine Learning-Volume 70, pp. 933–941. JMLR.org (2017)
8. Deng, J., Dong, W., Socher, R., Li, L.J., Li, K., Fei-Fei, L.: ImageNet: a large-scale hierarchical image database. In: 2009 IEEE Conference on Computer Vision and Pattern Recognition, pp. 248–255. IEEE (2009)
9. Denton, E.L., Zaremba, W., Bruna, J., LeCun, Y., Fergus, R.: Exploiting linear structure within convolutional networks for efficient evaluation. In: Advances in Neural Information Processing Systems, pp. 1269–1277 (2014)

10. Doersch, C., Zisserman, A.: Multi-task self-supervised visual learning. In: Proceedings of the IEEE International Conference on Computer Vision, pp. 2051–2060 (2017)

11. Dwivedi, K., Roig, G.: Representation similarity analysis for efficient task taxonomy & transfer learning. In: Proceedings of the IEEE Conference on Computer Vision and Pattern Recognition, pp. 12387–12396 (2019)

12. Eigen, D., Puhrsch, C., Fergus, R.: Depth map prediction from a single image using a multi-scale deep network. In: Advances in Neural Information Processing Systems, pp. 2366–2374 (2014)

13. Everingham, M., Van Gool, L., Williams, C.K.I., Winn, J., Zisserman, A.: The pascal visual object classes (VOC) challenge. Int. J. Comput. Vis. **88**(2), 303–338 (2010). https://doi.org/10.1007/s11263-009-0275-4

14. French, R.M.: Catastrophic forgetting in connectionist networks. Trends Cogn. Sci. **3**(4), 128–135 (1999)

15. Girshick, R., Donahue, J., Darrell, T., Malik, J.: Rich feature hierarchies for accurate object detection and semantic segmentation. In: Proceedings of the IEEE Conference on Computer Vision and Pattern Recognition, pp. 580–587 (2014)

16. Guo, M., Haque, A., Huang, D.-A., Yeung, S., Fei-Fei, L.: Dynamic task prioritization for multitask learning. In: Ferrari, V., Hebert, M., Sminchisescu, C., Weiss, Y. (eds.) ECCV 2018. LNCS, vol. 11220, pp. 282–299. Springer, Cham (2018). https://doi.org/10.1007/978-3-030-01270-0_17

17. He, K., Zhang, X., Ren, S., Sun, J.: Deep residual learning for image recognition. In: Proceedings of the IEEE Conference on Computer Vision and Pattern Recognition, pp. 770–778 (2016)

18. Hu, J., Shen, L., Sun, G.: Squeeze-and-excitation networks. In: Proceedings of the IEEE Conference on Computer Vision and Pattern Recognition, pp. 7132–7141 (2018)

19. Ioffe, S., Szegedy, C.: Batch normalization: accelerating deep network training by reducing internal covariate shift. In: International Conference on Machine Learning, pp. 448–456 (2015)

20. Jaderberg, M., Vedaldi, A., Zisserman, A.: Speeding up convolutional neural networks with low rank expansions. arXiv preprint arXiv:1405.3866 (2014)

21. Kendall, A., Gal, Y., Cipolla, R.: Multi-task learning using uncertainty to weigh losses for scene geometry and semantics. In: Proceedings of the IEEE Conference on Computer Vision and Pattern Recognition, pp. 7482–7491 (2018)

22. Kim, Y.D., Park, E., Yoo, S., Choi, T., Yang, L., Shin, D.: Compression of deep convolutional neural networks for fast and low power mobile applications. arXiv preprint arXiv:1511.06530 (2015)

23. Kirkpatrick, J., et al.: Overcoming catastrophic forgetting in neural networks. Proc. Natl. Acad. Sci. **114**(13), 3521–3526 (2017)

24. Kokkinos, I.: UberNet: training a universal convolutional neural network for low-, mid-, and high-level vision using diverse datasets and limited memory. In: Proceedings of the IEEE Conference on Computer Vision and Pattern Recognition, pp. 6129–6138 (2017)

25. Krizhevsky, A., Sutskever, I., Hinton, G.E.: ImageNet classification with deep convolutional neural networks. In: Advances in Neural Information Processing Systems, pp. 1097–1105 (2012)

26. Laina, I., Rupprecht, C., Belagiannis, V., Tombari, F., Navab, N.: Deeper depth prediction with fully convolutional residual networks. In: 2016 Fourth International Conference on 3D Vision (3DV), pp. 239–248. IEEE (2016)

27. Lebedev, V., Ganin, Y., Rakhuba, M., Oseledets, I., Lempitsky, V.: Speeding-up convolutional neural networks using fine-tuned CP-decomposition. arXiv preprint arXiv:1412.6553 (2014)
28. Lee, S.W., Kim, J.H., Jun, J., Ha, J.W., Zhang, B.T.: Overcoming catastrophic forgetting by incremental moment matching. In: Advances in Neural Information Processing Systems, pp. 4652–4662 (2017)
29. Li, Y., Gu, S., Gool, L.V., Timofte, R.: Learning filter basis for convolutional neural network compression. In: Proceedings of the IEEE International Conference on Computer Vision, pp. 5623–5632 (2019)
30. Li, Z., Hoiem, D.: Learning without forgetting. IEEE Trans. Pattern Anal. Mach. Intell. **40**(12), 2935–2947 (2017)
31. Liu, S., Johns, E., Davison, A.J.: End-to-end multi-task learning with attention. In: Proceedings of the IEEE Conference on Computer Vision and Pattern Recognition, pp. 1871–1880 (2019)
32. Liu, W., et al.: SSD: single shot multibox detector. In: Leibe, B., Matas, J., Sebe, N., Welling, M. (eds.) ECCV 2016. LNCS, vol. 9905, pp. 21–37. Springer, Cham (2016). https://doi.org/10.1007/978-3-319-46448-0_2
33. Long, J., Shelhamer, E., Darrell, T.: Fully convolutional networks for semantic segmentation. In: Proceedings of the IEEE Conference on Computer Vision and Pattern Recognition, pp. 3431–3440 (2015)
34. Lu, Y., Kumar, A., Zhai, S., Cheng, Y., Javidi, T., Feris, R.: Fully-adaptive feature sharing in multi-task networks with applications in person attribute classification. In: Proceedings of the IEEE Conference on Computer Vision and Pattern Recognition, pp. 5334–5343 (2017)
35. Mallya, A., Davis, D., Lazebnik, S.: Piggyback: adapting a single network to multiple tasks by learning to mask weights. In: Ferrari, V., Hebert, M., Sminchisescu, C., Weiss, Y. (eds.) ECCV 2018. LNCS, vol. 11208, pp. 72–88. Springer, Cham (2018). https://doi.org/10.1007/978-3-030-01225-0_5
36. Maninis, K.K., Radosavovic, I., Kokkinos, I.: Attentive single-tasking of multiple tasks. In: Proceedings of the IEEE Conference on Computer Vision and Pattern Recognition, pp. 1851–1860 (2019)
37. Martin, D.R., Fowlkes, C.C., Malik, J.: Learning to detect natural image boundaries using local brightness, color, and texture cues. IEEE Trans. Pattern Anal. Mach. Intell. **26**(5), 530–549 (2004)
38. Misra, I., Shrivastava, A., Gupta, A., Hebert, M.: Cross-stitch networks for multi-task learning. In: Proceedings of the IEEE Conference on Computer Vision and Pattern Recognition, pp. 3994–4003 (2016)
39. Mottaghi, R., et al.: The role of context for object detection and semantic segmentation in the wild. In: Proceedings of the IEEE Conference on Computer Vision and Pattern Recognition, pp. 891–898 (2014)
40. Neven, D., De Brabandere, B., Georgoulis, S., Proesmans, M., Van Gool, L.: Fast scene understanding for autonomous driving. arXiv preprint arXiv:1708.02550 (2017)
41. Obukhov, A., Rakhuba, M., Georgoulis, S., Kanakis, M., Dai, D., Van Gool, L.: T-basis: a compact representation for neural networks. In: Proceedings of Machine Learning and Systems 2020, pp. 8889–8901 (2020)
42. Oseledets, I.V.: Tensor-train decomposition. SIAM J. Sci. Comput. **33**(5), 2295–2317 (2011)
43. Paszke, A., et al.: PyTorch: an imperative style, high-performance deep learning library. In: Advances in Neural Information Processing Systems, pp. 8024–8035 (2019)

44. Peng, B., Tan, W., Li, Z., Zhang, S., Xie, D., Pu, S.: Extreme network compression via filter group approximation. In: Ferrari, V., Hebert, M., Sminchisescu, C., Weiss, Y. (eds.) ECCV 2018. LNCS, vol. 11212, pp. 307–323. Springer, Cham (2018). https://doi.org/10.1007/978-3-030-01237-3_19

45. Rebuffi, S.A., Bilen, H., Vedaldi, A.: Learning multiple visual domains with residual adapters. In: Advances in Neural Information Processing Systems, pp. 506–516 (2017)

46. Rebuffi, S.A., Bilen, H., Vedaldi, A.: Efficient parametrization of multi-domain deep neural networks. In: Proceedings of the IEEE Conference on Computer Vision and Pattern Recognition, pp. 8119–8127 (2018)

47. Rebuffi, S.A., Kolesnikov, A., Sperl, G., Lampert, C.H.: iCaRL: incremental classifier and representation learning. In: Proceedings of the IEEE Conference on Computer Vision and Pattern Recognition, pp. 2001–2010 (2017)

48. Redmon, J., Divvala, S., Girshick, R., Farhadi, A.: You only look once: unified, real-time object detection. In: Proceedings of the IEEE Conference on Computer Vision and Pattern Recognition, pp. 779–788 (2016)

49. Rosenfeld, A., Tsotsos, J.K.: Incremental learning through deep adaptation. IEEE Trans. Pattern Anal. Mach. Intell. (2018)

50. Ruder, S.: An overview of multi-task learning in deep neural networks. arXiv preprint arXiv:1706.05098 (2017)

51. Salimans, T., Kingma, D.P.: Weight normalization: a simple reparameterization to accelerate training of deep neural networks. In: Advances in Neural Information Processing Systems, pp. 901–909 (2016)

52. Sener, O., Koltun, V.: Multi-task learning as multi-objective optimization. In: Advances in Neural Information Processing Systems, pp. 527–538 (2018)

53. Silberman, N., Hoiem, D., Kohli, P., Fergus, R.: Indoor segmentation and support inference from RGBD images. In: Fitzgibbon, A., Lazebnik, S., Perona, P., Sato, Y., Schmid, C. (eds.) ECCV 2012. LNCS, vol. 7576, pp. 746–760. Springer, Heidelberg (2012). https://doi.org/10.1007/978-3-642-33715-4_54

54. Simonyan, K., Zisserman, A.: Very deep convolutional networks for large-scale image recognition. In: International Conference on Learning Representations (2015)

55. Sinha, A., Chen, Z., Badrinarayanan, V., Rabinovich, A.: Gradient adversarial training of neural networks. arXiv preprint arXiv:1806.08028 (2018)

56. Srebro, N., Shraibman, A.: Rank, trace-norm and max-norm. In: Auer, P., Meir, R. (eds.) COLT 2005. LNCS (LNAI), vol. 3559, pp. 545–560. Springer, Heidelberg (2005). https://doi.org/10.1007/11503415_37

57. Vandenhende, S., Georgoulis, S., De Brabandere, B., Van Gool, L.: Branched multi-task networks: deciding what layers to share. arXiv preprint arXiv:1904.02920 (2019)

58. Vandenhende, S., Georgoulis, S., Van Gool, L.: MTI-Net: multi-scale task interaction networks for multi-task learning. arXiv preprint arXiv:2001.06902 (2020)

59. Xu, D., Ouyang, W., Wang, X., Sebe, N.: PAD-Net: multi-tasks guided prediction-and-distillation network for simultaneous depth estimation and scene parsing. In: Proceedings of the IEEE Conference on Computer Vision and Pattern Recognition, pp. 675–684 (2018)

60. Zhang, X., Zou, J., He, K., Sun, J.: Accelerating very deep convolutional networks for classification and detection. IEEE Trans. Pattern Anal. Mach. Intell. **38**(10), 1943–1955 (2015)

61. Zhang, Z., Cui, Z., Xu, C., Jie, Z., Li, X., Yang, J.: Joint task-recursive learning for semantic segmentation and depth estimation. In: Ferrari, V., Hebert, M., Sminchisescu, C., Weiss, Y. (eds.) ECCV 2018. LNCS, vol. 11214, pp. 238–255. Springer, Cham (2018). https://doi.org/10.1007/978-3-030-01249-6_15
62. Zhang, Z., Cui, Z., Xu, C., Yan, Y., Sebe, N., Yang, J.: Pattern-affinitive propagation across depth, surface normal and semantic segmentation. In: Proceedings of the IEEE Conference on Computer Vision and Pattern Recognition, pp. 4106–4115 (2019)
63. Zhao, H., Shi, J., Qi, X., Wang, X., Jia, J.: Pyramid scene parsing network. In: Proceedings of the IEEE Conference on Computer Vision and Pattern Recognition, pp. 2881–2890 (2017)
64. Zhao, Q., Zhou, G., Xie, S., Zhang, L., Cichocki, A.: Tensor ring decomposition. arXiv preprint arXiv:1606.05535 (2016)
65. Zhao, X., Li, H., Shen, X., Liang, X., Wu, Y.: A modulation module for multi-task learning with applications in image retrieval. In: Ferrari, V., Hebert, M., Sminchisescu, C., Weiss, Y. (eds.) ECCV 2018. LNCS, vol. 11205, pp. 415–432. Springer, Cham (2018). https://doi.org/10.1007/978-3-030-01246-5_25

Learning Predictive Models from Observation and Interaction

Karl Schmeckpeper[1]([✉]) [iD], Annie Xie[3] [iD], Oleh Rybkin[1] [iD], Stephen Tian[2] [iD],
Kostas Daniilidis[1] [iD], Sergey Levine[3] [iD], and Chelsea Finn[2] [iD]

[1] University of Pennsylvania, Philadelphia, PA, USA
karls@seas.upenn.edu
[2] Stanford University, Stanford, CA, USA
[3] University of California, Berkeley, Berkeley, CA, USA

Abstract. Learning predictive models from interaction with the world allows an agent, such as a robot, to learn about how the world works, and then use this learned model to plan coordinated sequences of actions to bring about desired outcomes. However, learning a model that captures the dynamics of complex skills represents a major challenge: if the agent needs a good model to perform these skills, it might never be able to collect the experience on its own that is required to learn these delicate and complex behaviors. Instead, we can imagine augmenting the training set with observational data of other agents, such as humans. Such data is likely more plentiful, but cannot always be combined with data from the original agent. For example, videos of humans might show a robot how to use a tool, but (i) are not annotated with suitable robot actions, and (ii) contain a systematic distributional shift due to the embodiment differences between humans and robots. We address the first challenge by formulating the corresponding graphical model and treating the action as an observed variable for the interaction data and an unobserved variable for the observation data, and the second challenge by using a domain-dependent prior. In addition to interaction data, our method is able to leverage videos of passive observations in a driving dataset and a dataset of robotic manipulation videos to improve video prediction performance. In a real-world tabletop robotic manipulation setting, our method is able to significantly improve control performance by learning a model from both robot data and observations of humans.

Keywords: Video prediction · Visual planning · Action representations · Robotic manipulation

1 Introduction

Humans have the ability to learn skills not just from their own interaction with the world but also by observing others. Consider an infant learning to use tools.

Electronic supplementary material The online version of this chapter (https://doi.org/10.1007/978-3-030-58565-5_42) contains supplementary material, which is available to authorized users.

© Springer Nature Switzerland AG 2020
A. Vedaldi et al. (Eds.): ECCV 2020, LNCS 12365, pp. 708–725, 2020.
https://doi.org/10.1007/978-3-030-58565-5_42

In order to use a tool successfully, it needs to learn how the tool can interact with other objects, as well as how to move the tool to trigger this interaction. Such intuitive notion of physics can be learned by observing how adults use tools. More generally, observation is a powerful source of information about the world and how actions lead to outcomes. However, in the presence of physical differences (such as between an adult body and infant body), leveraging observation is challenging, as there is no direct correspondence between the demonstrator's and observer's actions. Evidence from neuroscience suggests that humans can effectively infer such correspondences and use them to learn from observation [44, 45]. In this paper, we consider this problem: can agents learn to solve tasks using both their own interaction and the passive observation of other agents?

In model-based reinforcement learning, solving tasks is commonly addressed via learning action-conditioned predictive models. However, prior works have learned such predictive models from interaction data alone [16,23,24,28,68]. When using both interaction and observation data, the setup differs in two important ways. First, the actions of the observed agent are not known, and therefore directly learning an action-conditioned predictive model is not possible. Second, the observation data might suffer from a domain shift if the observed agent has a different embodiment, operates at a different skill level, or exists in a different environment. Yet, if we can overcome these differences and effectively leverage observational data, we may be able to unlock a substantial source of broad data containing diverse behaviors and interactions with the world (Fig. 1).

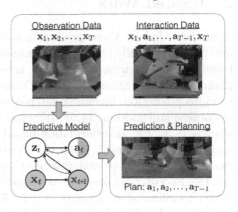

Fig. 1. Our system learns from action-observation sequences collected through interaction, such as robotic manipulation or autonomous vehicle data, as well as action-free observations of another demonstrator agent, such as data from a human or a dashboard camera. By combining interaction and observation data, our model is able to learn to generate predictions for complex tasks and new environments without costly expert demonstrations.

Our main contribution is an approach for learning predictive models that can leverage both videos of an agent annotated with actions and observational data for which actions are not available. We formulate a latent variable model for prediction, in which the actions are observed variables in the first case and unobserved variables in the second case. We further address the domain shift between the observation and interaction data by learning a domain-specific prior over the latent variables. We instantiate the model with deep neural networks and train it with amortized variational inference. In two problem settings – driving and object manipulation – we find that our method is able to effectively leverage observational data from dashboard cameras and humans, respectively, to improve the performance of action-conditioned prediction. Furthermore, we find that the resulting model enables a robot to solve pushing and sweeping tool-use tasks, and achieves significantly greater success than a model that does not use observational data of a human using tools. Finally, we release our dataset of human demonstrations of pushing and sweeping with tools to allow others to study this problem. To the best of our knowledge, this is the first work to demonstrate a method for learning predictive models from both observation and interaction data.

2   Related Work

Predictive Models. Video prediction can be used to learn useful representations and models in a fully unsupervised manner. These representations can be used for tasks such as action recognition [50], action prediction [62], classification [14], and planning [6,16,18–20,23,24,29,30]. Many different approaches have been applied to video prediction, including patch-centric methods [43], compositional models of content and motion [14,58,61], pixel autoregressive models [31], hierarchical models [8,39,40], transformation-based methods [1,3,9,18,33,34,36,37,42,63], and other techniques [5,12,38,67]. We choose to leverage transformation-based models, as they have demonstrated good results on robotic control domains [16,18]. Recent work has also developed stochastic video prediction models for better handling of uncertainty [3,9,13,33,64,69]. We also use a stochastic latent variable, and unlike these prior works, use it to model actions.

Learning action-conditioned visual dynamics models was proposed in [10,18, 41]. Using model predictive control techniques, flow based action-conditioned prediction models have been applied to robotic manipulation [6,16,18,19,29,73]. Other works address video games or physical simulation domains [20,23,24,30,66].

The models have been shown to generalize to unseen tasks and objects while allowing for challenging manipulation of deformable objects, such as rope or clothing [11,65,70]. Unfortunately, large amounts of robotic interaction data containing complex behavior are required to train these models. These models are unable to learn from cheap and abundantly available natural videos of humans as they are trained in *action-conditioned* way, requiring corresponding control data for every video. In contrast, our method can learn from videos without actions, allowing it to leverage videos of agents for which the actions are unknown.

Learning to Control Without Actions. Recent work in imitation learning allows the agent to learn without access to the ground-truth expert actions. One set of approaches learn to translate the states of the expert into actions the agent can execute [55,72]. Action-free data can also be used to learn a set of sub-goals for hierarchical RL [32,48]. Another common approach is to learn a policy in the agent's domain that matches the expert trajectories under some similarity metric. Adversarial training or other metrics have been used to minimize the difference between the states generated by the demonstrated policy and the states generated by the learned policy [51,53,56,57]. Liu et al. transform images from the expert demonstrations into the robot's domain to make calculating the similarity between states generated by different policies in different environments more tractable [35]. Edwards et al. learn a latent policy on action-free data and use action-conditioned data to map the latent policy to real actions [17]. Several works learn state representations that can be used to transfer policies from humans to robots [2,15,47]. Shon et al. learn a mapping between human and robot degrees of freedom to allow the robot to match the human's pose [49]. Sun et al. use partially action-conditioned data to train a generative adversarial network to synthesize the missing action sequences [52]. Unlike these works, which aim to specify a specific task to be solved through expert demonstrations, we aim to learn predictive models that can be used for multiple tasks, as we learn general properties of the real world through model-building.

Recent prior work has considered learning predictive models from an initial dataset that is entirely action-free [46], learning a mapping from actions to latent variables post-hoc. However, this approach has been limited to simple simulated settings with no domain shift. Unlike this prior work, we explicitly handle domain shift between the interaction and observational data, and consider challenging real video datasets. Furthermore, our experiments indicate that our approach substantially outperforms the approach of Rybkin et al. [46] on multiple domains.

Domain Adaptation. In order to handle both observational and interaction data, our method must handle the missing actions and bridge the gap between the two domains (e.g., human arms vs. robot arms). Related domain adaptation methods have sought to map samples in one domain into equivalent samples in another domain [4,26,54,75], or learn feature embeddings with domain invariance losses [21,22,59,60,76]. In our setting, regularizing for invariance across domains is insufficient. For example, if the observational data of humans involves complex manipulation (e.g., tool use), while the interaction data involves only simple manipulation, we do not want the model to be invariant to these differences. Therefore, instead of regularizing for invariance across domains, we explicitly model the distributions over (latent) action variables in each of the domains.

Related to our method, DIVA [27] aims to avoid losing this information by proposing a generative model with a partitioned latent space. The latent space is composed of both components that are domain invariant and components that are conditioned on the domain. This allows the model to use domain-specific information while still remaining robust to domain shifts. We find that using an approach similar to DIVA in our model for learning from observation and interaction makes it more robust to the domain shift between interaction and observation data. However, in contrast to DIVA, our method explicitly handles sequence data with missing actions in one of the domains.

3 Learning Predictive Models from Observation and Interaction

In our problem setting, we assume access to observation data of the form $[\mathbf{x}_1, \ldots, \mathbf{x}_T]$ and interaction data of the form $[\mathbf{x}_1, \mathbf{a}_1, \ldots, \mathbf{a}_{T-1}, \mathbf{x}_T]$, where $\mathbf{x}_i$ denotes the ith frame of a video and $\mathbf{a}_i$ denotes the action taken at the ith time step. Domain shift may exist between the two datasets: for example, when learning object manipulation from videos of humans and robotic interaction, as considered in our experiments, there is a shift in the embodiment of the agent. Within this problem setting, our goal is to learn an action-conditioned video prediction model, $p(\mathbf{x}_{c+1:T}|\mathbf{x}_{1:c}, \mathbf{a}_{1:T})$, that predicts future frames conditioned on a set of c context frames and sequence of actions.

To approach this problem, we formulate a probabilistic graphical model underlying the problem setting where actions are only observed in a subset of the data. In particular, in Subsect. 3.1, we introduce a latent variable that explains the transition from the current

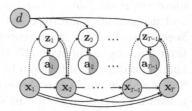

Fig. 2. We learn a predictive model of visual dynamics (in solid lines) that predicts the next frame x_{t+1} conditioned on the current frame x_t and action representation z_t. We optimize the likelihood of the interaction data, for which the actions are available, and observation data, for which the actions are missing. Our model is able to leverage joint training on the two kinds of data by learning a latent representation z that corresponds to the true action.

frame to the next and, in the case of interaction data, encodes the action taken by the agent. We further detail how the latent variable model is learned from both observation and interaction data by amortized variational inference. In Subsect. 3.2, we discuss how we handle domain shift by allowing the latent variables from different datasets to have different prior distributions. Finally, we discuss implementation details in Subsect. 3.3.

3.1 Graphical Model

To leverage both passive observations and active interactions, we formulate the probabilistic graphical model depicted in Fig. 2. To model the action of the agent $\mathbf{a}_t$, we introduce a latent variable $\mathbf{z}_t$, distributed according to a domain-dependent distribution. The latent $\mathbf{z}_t$ generates the action $\mathbf{a}_t$. We further introduce a forward dynamic model that, at each time step t, generates the frame $\mathbf{x}_t$ given the previous frames $\mathbf{x}_{1:t-1}$ and latent variables $\mathbf{z}_{1:t-1}$. The generative model can be summarized as:

$$\mathbf{z}_t \sim p(\mathbf{z}_t|d) \tag{1}$$

$$\mathbf{a}_t \sim p(\mathbf{a}_t|\mathbf{z}_t) \tag{2}$$

$$\mathbf{x}_{t+1} \sim p(\mathbf{x}_{t+1}|\mathbf{x}_{1:t}, \mathbf{z}_{1:t}). \tag{3}$$

The domain-dependent distribution over $\mathbf{z}_t$ is Gaussian with learned mean and variance, described in more detail in Subsect. 3.2, while the *action decoder* $p(\mathbf{a}_t|\mathbf{z}_t)$ and *transition model* $p(\mathbf{x}_{t+1}|\mathbf{x}_{1:t}, \mathbf{z}_{1:t})$ are neural networks with Gaussian distribution outputs, described in Subsect. 3.3.

The transition model takes $\mathbf{z}_t$ as input and thus necessitates the posterior distributions $p(\mathbf{z}_t|\mathbf{a}_t)$ and $p(\mathbf{z}_t|\mathbf{x}_t, \mathbf{x}_{t+1})$. We require $p(\mathbf{z}_t|\mathbf{a}_t)$ to generate latent variables for action-conditioned video prediction, i.e. sampling from

$$p(\mathbf{x}_{t+1}|\mathbf{x}_{1:t}, \mathbf{a}_{1:t}) = \mathbb{E}_{p(\mathbf{z}_{1:t}|\mathbf{a}_{1:t})}\left[p(\mathbf{x}_{t+1}|\mathbf{x}_{1:t}, \mathbf{z}_{1:t})\right].$$

We also require $p(\mathbf{z}_t|\mathbf{x}_t, \mathbf{x}_{t+1})$ since the actions are not available in some trajectories to obtain the first distribution.

The computation of these two posterior distributions is intractable, since the model is highly complex and non-linear, so we introduce the variational distributions $q_{\text{act}}(\mathbf{z}_t|\mathbf{a}_t)$ and $q_{\text{inv}}(\mathbf{z}_t|\mathbf{x}_t, \mathbf{x}_{t+1})$ to approximate $p(\mathbf{z}_t|\mathbf{a}_t)$ and $p(\mathbf{z}_t|\mathbf{x}_t, \mathbf{x}_{t+1})$. The distributions are modeled as Gaussian and the variational parameters are learned by optimizing the evidence lower bound (ELBO), which is constructed by considering two separate cases. In the first, the actions are observed, and we optimize an ELBO on the joint probability of the frames and the actions:

$$\log p(\mathbf{x}_{1:T}, \mathbf{a}_{1:T}) \geq \sum_t \mathbb{E}_{q_{\text{act}}(\mathbf{z}_{1:t}|\mathbf{a}_{1:t})} \left[\log p(\mathbf{x}_{t+1}|\mathbf{x}_{1:t}, \mathbf{z}_{1:t}) + \log p(\mathbf{a}_t|\mathbf{z}_t)\right]$$
$$- \sum_t D_{KL}(q_{\text{act}}(\mathbf{z}_t|\mathbf{a}_t)\|p(\mathbf{z}_t)) = -\mathcal{L}_i(\mathbf{x}_{1:T}, \mathbf{a}_{1:T}). \tag{4}$$

In the second case, the actions are not observed, and we optimize an ELBO on only the probability of the frames:

$$\log p(\mathbf{x}_{1:T}) \geq \sum_t \mathbb{E}_{q_{\text{inv}}(\mathbf{z}_t|\mathbf{x}_t, \mathbf{x}_{t+1})} \left[\log p(\mathbf{x}_{t+1}|\mathbf{x}_t, \mathbf{z}_t)\right]$$
$$- \sum_t D_{KL}(q_{\text{inv}}(\mathbf{z}_t|\mathbf{x}_t, \mathbf{x}_{t+1})\|p(\mathbf{z}_t)) = -\mathcal{L}_o(\mathbf{x}_{1:T}). \tag{5}$$

The full ELBO is the combination of the lower bounds for the interaction data with actions, D^i, and the observation data without actions, D^o:

$$\mathcal{J} = \sum_{(\mathbf{x}_{1:T}, \mathbf{a}_{1:T}) \sim D^i} \mathcal{L}_i(\mathbf{x}_{1:T}, \mathbf{a}_{1:T}) + \sum_{\mathbf{x}_{1:T} \sim D^o} \mathcal{L}_o(\mathbf{x}_{1:T}). \tag{6}$$

We also add an auxiliary loss to align the distributions of $\mathbf{z}$ generated from the encoders $q_{\text{act}}(\mathbf{z}_t|\mathbf{a}_t)$ and $q_{\text{inv}}(\mathbf{z}_t|\mathbf{x}_t, \mathbf{x}_{t+1})$, since the encoding $\mathbf{z}$ should be independent of the distribution it was sampled from. We encourage the two distributions to be similar through the Jensen-Shannon divergence:

$$\mathcal{L}_{JS} = \sum_{(\mathbf{x}_{1:T}, \mathbf{a}_{1:T}) \sim D^i} D_{JS}(q_{\text{act}}(\mathbf{z}_t|\mathbf{a}_t)\|q_{\text{inv}}(\mathbf{z}_t|\mathbf{x}_t, \mathbf{x}_{t+1})). \tag{7}$$

Our final objective combines the evidence lower bound for the entire dataset and the Jensen-Shannon divergence, computed for the interaction data:

$$\mathcal{F} = \mathcal{J} + \alpha \mathcal{L}_{JS}. \tag{8}$$

We refer to our method as prediction from observation and interaction (POI).

3.2   Domain Shift

When learning from both observation and interaction, domain shift may exist between the two datasets. For instance, in the case of a robot learning by observing people, the two agents differ both in their physical appearance, as well as their action spaces. To address these domain shifts, we take inspiration from the domain-invariant approach described in [27]. We divide our latent variable $\mathbf{z}$ into $\mathbf{z}^{\text{shared}}$, which captures the parts of the latent action that are shared between domains, and $\mathbf{z}^{\text{domain}}$, which captures the parts of the latent action that are unique to each domain.

We allow the network to learn the difference between the $\mathbf{z}^{\text{domain}}$ for each dataset by using different prior distributions. The prior $p(\mathbf{z}_t^{\text{shared}})$ is the same for both domains, however, the prior for $\mathbf{z}_t^{\text{domain}}$ is different for the interaction dataset, $p_i(\mathbf{z}_t^{\text{domain}})$, and the observational dataset, $p_o(\mathbf{z}_t^{\text{domain}})$. $p(\mathbf{z}_t^{\text{shared}})$ and $p_a(\mathbf{z}_t^{\text{domain}})$ are both multivariate Gaussian distributions with a learned mean and variance for each dimension. The prior is the same for all timesteps t.

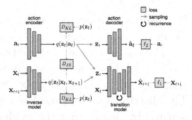

Fig. 3. Network architecture. To optimize the ELBO, we predict the latent action $\mathbf{z}_t$ from $\mathbf{x}_t$ and $\mathbf{x}_{t+1}$ using the inverse model q_{inv}. When the true actions are available, we additionally predict the latent action from the true action $\mathbf{a}_t$ using the action encoder q_{act}, and encourage the predictions from q_{act} and q_{inv} to be similar with a Jensen-Shannon divergence loss. The next frame is predicted from $\mathbf{z}_t$ and $\mathbf{x}_t$.

Unlike the actions for the robot data, which are sampled from the same distribution at each time step, the actions of the human are correlated across time. For the human observation data, the prior $p_o(\mathbf{z}_{1:T}^{\text{domain}}|\mathbf{x}_1)$ models a joint distribution over timesteps, and is parameterized as a long short-term memory (LSTM) network [25]. The input to the LSTM at the first timestep is an encoding of the initial observation, and the LSTM cell produces the parameters of the multivariate Gaussian distribution for each time step.

3.3   Deep Neural Network Implementation

A high-level diagram of our network architecture is shown in Fig. 3. Our action encoder $q_{\text{act}}(\mathbf{z}_t|\mathbf{a}_t)$ is a multi-layer perceptron (MLP) with 3 layers of 64 units to encode the given action $\mathbf{a}_t$ to the means and variances for each dimension of the encoding. Our action decoder predicts the mean of the distribution $p(\mathbf{a}_t|\mathbf{z}_t)$ using an MLP with 3 layers of 64 units each, while using a fixed unit variance.

Our inverse model $q_{\mathrm{inv}}(\mathbf{z}_t|\mathbf{x}_t, \mathbf{x}_{t+1})$ is a convolutional network that predicts the distribution over the action encoding. The network is made up of three convolutional layers with $\{32, 64, 128\}$ features with a kernel size of 4 and a stride of 2. Each convolutional layer is followed by instance normalization and a leaky-ReLU. The output of the final convolutional layer is fed in a fully connected layer, which predicts the means and variances of the action encoding.

We encourage the action encodings generated by the action encoder q_{act} and the inverse model q_{inv} to be similar using the Jensen-Shannon divergence in Eq. 7. Since the Jensen-Shannon divergence does not have a closed form solution, we approximate it by using a mean of the Gaussians instead of a mixture. Our model uses a modified version of the SAVP architecture [33] as the transition model which predicts $\mathbf{x}_{t+1}$ from $\mathbf{x}_t$ and an action encoding $\mathbf{z}$, either sampled from $q_{\mathrm{act}}(\mathbf{z}_t|\mathbf{a}_t)$ or from $q_{\mathrm{inv}}(\mathbf{z}_t|\mathbf{x}_t, \mathbf{x}_{t+1})$. In the case where the actions are observed, we generate two predictions, one from each of q_{inv} and q_{act}, and in the case where actions are not observed, we only generate a prediction from the inverse model, q_{inv}. This architecture has been shown to be a useful transition model for robotic planning in [11, 16].

4   Experiments

We aim to answer the following in our experiments:

1. Do passive observations, when utilized effectively, improve an action-conditioned visual predictive model despite large domain shifts?
2. How does our approach compare to alternative methods for combining passive and interaction data?
3. Do improvements in the model transfer to downstream tasks, such as robotic control?

To answer question 1, we compare our method to a strong action-conditioned prediction method, SAVP [33], which is trained only on interaction data as it is not able to leverage the observation data. To answer question 2, we further compare to CLASP [46], a prior method that infers actions in a post-hoc manner and does not model domain shift. We study questions 1 and 2 in both the driving domain in Subsect. 4.1 and the robotic manipulation domain in Subsect. 4.2 and evaluate the methods on action-conditioned prediction. We evaluate question 3 by controlling the robotic manipulator using our learned model.

4.1   Visual Prediction for Driving

We first evaluate our model on video prediction for driving. Imagine that a self-driving car company has data from a fleet of cars with sensors that record both video and the driver's actions in one city, and a second fleet of cars that only record dashboard video, without actions, in a second city. If the goal is to

Table 1. Action-conditioned prediction results on the Singapore portion of the nuScenes dataset, reporting the mean and standard error of each metric. By leveraging observational driving data from Singapore or from BDD dashboard cameras, our method is able to outperform prior models that cannot leverage such data (i.e. SAVP) and slightly outperform alternative approaches to using such data.

Method	PSNR (↑)	SSIM (↑)	LPIPS [74] (↓)
SAVP [33] (Boston w/ actions)	19.74 ± 0.41	0.5121 ± 0.0164	0.1951 ± 0.0075
CLASP [46] (Boston w/ actions, Singapore w/o actions)	20.57 ± 0.48	0.5431 ± 0.0161	0.1964 ± 0.0076
POI (ours) (Boston w/ actions, BDD100K w/o actions)	**20.88 ± 0.24**	**0.5508 ± 0.0076**	0.2106 ± 0.0089
POI (ours) (Boston w/ actions, Singapore w/o actions)	20.81 ± 0.49	0.5486 ± 0.0164	**0.1933 ± 0.0074**
Oracle: SAVP [33] (Boston w/ actions. Singapore w/ actions)	21.17 ± 0.47	0.5752 ± 0.0156	0.1738 ± 0.0076

train an action-conditioned model that can be utilized to predict the outcomes of steering actions, our method allows us to train such a model using data from both cities, even though only one of them has actions.

We use the nuScenes [7] and BDD100K [71] datasets for our experiments. The nuScenes dataset consists of 1000 driving sequences collected in either Boston or Singapore, while the BDD100K dataset contains only video from dashboard cameras. In nuScenes, we discard all action and state information for the data collected in Singapore, simulating data that could have been collected by a car equipped with only a camera. We train our model with action-conditioned video from Boston and action-free video either from the nuScenes Singapore data or the BDD100K data, and evaluate on action-conditioned prediction on held-out data from Singapore (from nuScenes). Since the action distribution for all datasets is likely very similar as they all contain human driving, we use the same learned means and

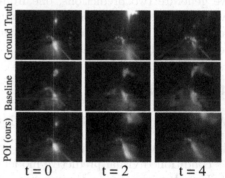

Fig. 4. Example predictions on the Singapore portion of the Nuscenes dataset. This sequence was selected for large MSE difference between the models. More examples are available in the supplementary material. We compare our model to the baseline of the SAVP model trained on the Boston data with actions. Our model is able to maintain the shape of the car in front.

variances for the Gaussian prior over z for both portions of the dataset. We additionally train a our model with the action-conditioned video from Boston and action-free video taken from the BDD100K dataset [71].

We compare our predictions to those generated by the SAVP [33] model trained with only the action-conditioned data from Boston, since SAVP cannot leverage action-free data for action-conditioned prediction. We additionally compare our predictions to those generated by CLASP [46] trained with action-conditioned video from Boston, and action-free video from Singapore. As an upper-bound, we train the SAVP [33] model with action-conditioned data from Boston and action-conditioned data from Singapore.

Comparisons between these methods are shown in Table 1. Qualitative results are shown in Fig. 4. With either form of observational data, BDD2K or nuScenes Singapore, our method significantly outperforms the SAVP model trained with only action-conditioned data from Boston, demonstrating that our model can leverage observation data to improve the quality of its predictions. Further, our method slightly outperforms alternative approaches to learning from observation and interaction.

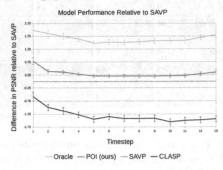

Model Performance Relative to SAVP

Timestep

— Oracle   — POI (ours)   — SAVP   — CLASP

Fig. 5. Frame-by-frame differences in PSNR relative to SAVP, on the robotic domain. Our method consistently outperforms both SAVP and CLASP.

4.2   Robotic Manipulation: Prediction

We evaluate our model on the robotic manipulation domain, which presents a large distributional shift challenge between robot and human videos. In particular, we study a tool-use task and evaluate whether human videos of tool-use can improve predictions of robotic tool-use interactions.

Learning predictive models from interaction with the world allows an agent, such as a robot, to learn about how the world works, and then use this learned model to plan coordinated sequences of actions to bring about desired outcomes.

For our interaction data, we acquired 20,000 random trajectories of a Sawyer robot from the open-source datasets from [16] and [68], which consist of both video and corresponding actions. We then collected 1,000 videos of a human using different tools to push objects as the observation data. By including the human videos, we provide the model with examples of tool-use interactions, which are not available in the random robot data. Our test set is composed of 1,200 kinesthetic demonstrations from [68], in which a human guides the robot to use tools to complete pushing tasks similar to those in the human videos. Kinesthetic demonstrations are time-consuming to collect, encouraging us to build a system that can be trained without them, but they serve as a good

Fig. 6. Example images from the robot (left) and human (right) datasets.

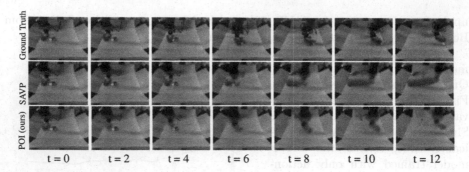

Fig. 7. Example predictions on the robotic dataset. We compare our model to the SAVP model trained with random robot data. This sequence was selected to maximize the MSE difference between the models. More examples are available in the supplementary material. Our model more accurately predicts both the tool and the object it pushes.

proxy for evaluating robot tool-use behavior. Example images from the datasets are shown in Fig. 6.[1] This dataset is especially challenging because of the large domain shift between the robot and human data. The human arm has a different appearance from the robot and moves in a different action space.

We compare to the CLASP model [46] trained with the same data as our model. We also evaluate the SAVP model [33], trained the same robot data, but without the human data, since the SAVP model is unable to leverage action-free data for action-conditioned prediction. For an oracle, we trained the SAVP model [33] on both the random robot trajectories and the kinesthetic demonstrations.

As shown in Table 2, our model is able to leverage information from the human videos to outperform the other models. Our model outperforms the SAVP model trained on only the random robot data, showing that it is possible to leverage passive observation data to improve action-conditioned prediction, even in the presence of the large domain shift between human and robot arms. Figure 5 shows the frame-by-frame differences in PSNR relative to SAVP.

Table 2. Means and standard errors for action-conditioned prediction on the manipulation dataset. By leveraging observational data of human tool use, our model was able to outperform prior models that cannot leverage such data (i.e. SAVP) and slightly outperform alternative approaches to using such data.

Method	PSNR (↑)	SSIM (↑)	LPIPS [74] (↓)
CLASP [46] (random robot, expert human)	22.14 ± 0.11	0.763 ± 0.004	0.0998 ± 0.0023
SAVP [33] (random robot)	23.31 ± 0.10	0.803 ± 0.004	0.0757 ± 0.0022
POI (ours) (random robot, expert human)	$\mathbf{23.79 \pm 0.12}$	$\mathbf{0.813 \pm 0.005}$	$\mathbf{0.0722 \pm 0.0024}$
Oracle: SAVP [33] (random robot, expert kinesthetic)	24.99 ± 0.11	0.858 ± 0.003	0.0486 ± 0.0017

---

[1] Data will be made available at https://sites.google.com/view/lpmfoai.

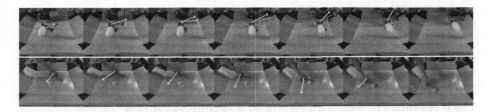

Fig. 8. Action predictions on human and robot data. The sequences of images show the ground truth observations, while the arrows show the action in the (x, y) plane between each pair of frames. The blue arrow is the ground truth action, the green arrow is the action generated from decoding the output of the action encoder, and the red is the action generated by decoding the output of the inverse model. The human data only has actions generated by the inverse model. Our model is able to infer plausible actions for both domains, despite never seeing ground truth human actions. (Color figure online)

Qualitative results are shown in Fig. 7. Our model is able to generate more accurate predictions than the baseline SAVP model that was trained with only the robotic interaction data. In addition to predicting future states, our model is able to predict the action that occurred between two states. Examples for both robot and human demonstrations are shown in Fig. 8. Our inverse model is able to generate reasonable actions for both the robot and the human data despite having never been trained on human data with actions. Our model can reconstruct the actions with an average percent error of 14.3, while CLASP reconstructs the actions with an average percent error of 70.4. Our model maps human and robot actions to a similar space, allowing it to exploit their similarities to improve prediction performance on robotic tasks.

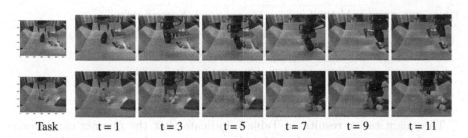

| Task | t = 1 | t = 3 | t = 5 | t = 7 | t = 9 | t = 11 |

Fig. 9. Examples of a robot using our model to successfully complete tool use tasks. The robot must move the objects specified by the red symbols to the locations of the corresponding green symbols. The robot uses a tool to simultaneously move several objects to their goal locations. (Color figure online)

4.3 Robotic Manipulation: Planning and Control

To study the third and final research question, we evaluate the efficacy of our visual dynamics model in a set of robotic control experiments. We evaluate each predictive model's ability to control the robot on a baseline task [68] by integrating the model with an existing visual model predictive control pipeline, which optimizes actions with respect to a user-provided task [16,19].

To evaluate the importance of the human data, we focus on control tasks that involve moving multiple objects, which would be difficult to complete without using a tool. While [16,19] only evaluated on simple one-step planning tasks, we want to see whether our model can be used to successfully solve more complex tasks by incorporating observational data of humans. Therefore, for testing our model, we position the objects such that it is not possible to solve the task greedily by moving directly towards the goal, following the evaluation setup for pushing and sweeping tool use tasks from Xie et al. [68]. In each task setting, several objects, as well as a tool that the robot could potentially use to complete the task, are placed in the scene. Tasks are specified by designating a pixel corresponding to an object and the goal position for the object, following [16,19, 68]. We specify moving multiple objects by selecting multiple pairs of pixels. We quantitatively evaluate each model on 15 tasks with tools seen during training and 15 tasks with previously unseen tools. In Fig. 9, we show qualitative examples of the robot completing tool-use tasks.

Table 3. Robotic control results, measuring the success rate and standard error for three object manipulation tasks. "random" denotes random robot data, "human" denotes human interaction data, and "kinesthetic" is an oracle dataset of expert robot trajectories. POI performs comparably to the oracle, and successfully leverages the observational videos to improve over SAVP.

Method	Success rate
SAVP [33] (random)	$23.3 \pm 7.7\%$
POI (ours) (random, human)	$\mathbf{40.0 \pm 8.9\%}$
Oracle (random, kinesthetic)	$36.7 \pm 8.8\%$

The quantitative results, in Table 3, indicate that the planner can leverage our model to execute more successful plans relative to the baseline SAVP model, which was trained only using random robot trajectories. In our evaluation, a trial is successful if the average distance between the objects and their respective goal positions at the final time step is less than or equal to 10 cm. Using our model, the robot achieves similar performance to the oracle model trained on kinesthetic demonstrations with action labels. This suggests that our model's improvements on prediction leads to a corresponding improvements on control.

5   Conclusion

We present a method for learning predictive models from both passive observation and active interactions. Active interactions are usually more expensive and less readily-available than passive observation: for example, consider the amount of observational data of human activities on the internet. Active interaction, on the other hand, is especially difficult when the agent is trying to collect information about regions of the state-space which are difficult to reach. Without an existing policy that can guide the agent to those regions, time consuming on-policy exploration, expert teleoperated or kinesthetic demonstrations are often required, bringing additional costs.

By learning a latent variable over the semi-observed actions, our approach is able to leverage passive observational data to improve action-conditioned predictive models, even in the presence of domain shift between observation and interaction data. Our experiments illustrate these benefits in two problem settings: driving and object manipulation, and find improvements both in prediction quality and in control performance when using these models for planning.

Overall, we hope that this work represents a first step towards enabling the use of broad, large-scale observational data when learning about the world. However, limitations and open questions remain. Our experiments studied a limited aspect of this broader problem where the observational data was either a different embodiment in the same environment (i.e. humans manipulating objects) or a different environment within the same underlying dataset (i.e. driving in Boston and Singapore). In practice, many source of passive observations will exhibit more substantial domain shift than those considered in this work. Hence, an important consideration for future work is to increase robustness to domain shift to realize greater benefits from using more large and diverse observational datasets. Finally, we focused our study on learning predictive models; an exciting direction for future work is to study how to incorporate similar forms of observational data in representation learning and reinforcement learning.

Acknowledgements. We thank Karl Pertsch, Drew Jaegle, Marvin Zhang, and Kenneth Chaney. This work was supported by the NSF GRFP, ARL RCTA W911NF-10-2-0016, ARL DCIST CRA W911NF-17-2-0181, and by Honda Research Institute.

References

1. van Amersfoort, J., Kannan, A., Ranzato, M., Szlam, A., Tran, D., Chintala, S.: Transformation-based models of video sequences. arXiv preprint, January 2017. http://arxiv.org/abs/1701.08435
2. Aytar, Y., Pfaff, T., Budden, D., Paine, T., Wang, Z., de Freitas, N.: Playing hard exploration games by watching YouTube. In: Advances in Neural Information Processing Systems 31 (2018). http://papers.nips.cc/paper/7557-playing-hard-exploration-games-by-watching-youtube.pdf
3. Babaeizadeh, M., Finn, C., Erhan, D., Campbell, R.H., Levine, S.: Stochastic variational video prediction. In: International Conference on Learning Representations (2018)

4. Bousmalis, K., Silberman, N., Dohan, D., Erhan, D., Krishnan, D.: Unsupervised pixel-level domain adaptation with generative adversarial networks. In: Proceedings of the IEEE Conference on Computer Vision and Pattern Recognition (2017)
5. Byeon, W., Wang, Q., Srivastava, R.K., Koumoutsakos, P.: ContextVP: fully context-aware video prediction. In: Ferrari, V., Hebert, M., Sminchisescu, C., Weiss, Y. (eds.) ECCV 2018. LNCS, vol. 11220, pp. 781–797. Springer, Cham (2018). https://doi.org/10.1007/978-3-030-01270-0_46
6. Byravan, A., Leeb, F., Meier, F., Fox, D.: SE3-Pose-Nets: structured deep dynamics models for visuomotor control. In: IEEE International Conference on Robotics and Automation (ICRA), pp. 1–8. IEEE (2018)
7. Caesar, H., et al.: nuScenes: a multimodal dataset for autonomous driving. arXiv preprint arXiv:1903.11027 (2019)
8. Castrejon, L., Ballas, N., Courville, A.: Improved conditional VRNNs for video prediction. arXiv preprint, April 2019. http://arxiv.org/abs/1904.12165
9. Chen, B., Wang, W., Wang, J., Chen, X.: Video imagination from a single image with transformation generation. arXiv preprint, June 2017. http://arxiv.org/abs/1706.04124
10. Chiappa, S., Racanière, S., Wierstra, D., Mohamed, S.: Recurrent environment simulators. In: International Conference on Learning Representations (2017)
11. Dasari, S., et al.: RoboNet: large-scale multi-robot learning. In: Conference on Robot Learning, October 2019. http://arxiv.org/abs/1910.11215
12. De Brabandere, B., Jia, X., Tuytelaars, T., Van Gool, L.: Dynamic filter networks. In: Neural Information Processing Systems, May 2016. http://arxiv.org/abs/1605.09673
13. Denton, E., Fergus, R.: Stochastic video generation with a learned prior. In: International Conference on Machine Learning (ICML) (2018)
14. Denton, E., Birodkar, V.: Unsupervised learning of disentangled representations from video. In: Neural Information Processing Systems, pp. 4417–4426 (2017)
15. Dwibedi, D., Tompson, J., Lynch, C., Sermanet, P.: Learning actionable representations from visual observations. In: 2018 IEEE/RSJ International Conference on Intelligent Robots and Systems (IROS), pp. 1577–1584. IEEE (2018). https://arxiv.org/abs/1808.00928
16. Ebert, F., Finn, C., Dasari, S., Xie, A., Lee, A., Levine, S.: Visual foresight: model-based deep reinforcement learning for vision-based robotic control. arXiv:1812.00568 (2018)
17. Edwards, A.D., Sahni, H., Schroecker, Y., Isbell, C.L.: Imitating latent policies from observation. In: International Conference on Machine Learning, May 2019. http://arxiv.org/abs/1805.07914
18. Finn, C., Goodfellow, I., Levine, S.: Unsupervised learning for physical interaction through video prediction. In: Neural Information Processing Systems (2016)
19. Finn, C., Levine, S.: Deep visual foresight for planning robot motion. In: Proceedings of International Conference in Robotics and Automation (ICRA) (2017)
20. Fragkiadaki, K., Agrawal, P., Levine, S., Malik, J.: Learning visual predictive models of physics for playing billiards. In: International Conference on Learning Representations, November 2016. http://arxiv.org/abs/1511.07404
21. Ganin, Y., Lempitsky, V.: Unsupervised domain adaptation by backpropagation. In: International Conference on Machine Learning, pp. 1180–1189. PMLR (2015)
22. Ganin, Y., et al.: Domain-adversarial training of neural networks. J. Mach. Learn. Res. 17(1), 2096–2030 (2016)
23. Ha, D., Schmidhuber, J.: Recurrent world models facilitate policy evolution. In: Neural Information Processing Systems (2018)

24. Hafner, D., et al.: Learning latent dynamics for planning from pixels. In: International Conference on Machine Learning, pp. 2555–2565. PMLR (2019)
25. Hochreiter, S., Schmidhuber, J.: Long short-term memory. Neural Comput. **9**(8), 1735–1780 (1997)
26. Hoffman, J., et al.: CyCADA: cycle-consistent adversarial domain adaptation. In: International Conference on Machine Learning (ICML), November 2018. http://arxiv.org/abs/1711.03213
27. Ilse, M., Tomczak, J.M., Louizos, C., Welling, M.: DIVA: domain invariant variational autoencoders. arXiv preprint, May 2019. http://arxiv.org/abs/1905.10427
28. Janner, M., Fu, J., Zhang, M., Levine, S.: When to trust your model: model-based policy optimization. In: NeurIPS (2019)
29. Janner, M., Levine, S., Freeman, W.T., Tenenbaum, J.B., Finn, C., Wu, J.: Reasoning about physical interactions with object-oriented prediction and planning. In: International Conference on Learning Representations, December 2019. http://arxiv.org/abs/1812.10972
30. Kaiser, L., et al.: Model-based reinforcement learning for Atari. In: International Conference on Learning Representations (2019)
31. Kalchbrenner, N., et al.: Video pixel networks. arXiv preprint, October 2016. http://arxiv.org/abs/1610.00527
32. Kumar, A., Gupta, S., Malik, J.: Learning navigation subroutines by watching videos. CoRR abs/1905.12612 (2019). http://arxiv.org/abs/1905.12612
33. Lee, A.X., Zhang, R., Ebert, F., Abbeel, P., Finn, C., Levine, S.: Stochastic adversarial video prediction. arXiv:1804.01523 abs/1804.01523 (2018)
34. Liang, X., Lee, L., Dai, W., Xing, E.P.: Dual motion GAN for future-flow embedded video prediction. In: International Conference on Computer Vision, August 2017. http://arxiv.org/abs/1708.00284
35. Liu, Y., Gupta, A., Abbeel, P., Levine, S.: Imitation from observation: learning to imitate behaviors from raw video via context translation. Ph.D. thesis, University of California, Berkeley, July 2018. http://arxiv.org/abs/1707.03374
36. Liu, Z., Yeh, R.A., Tang, X., Liu, Y., Agarwala, A.: Video frame synthesis using deep voxel flow. In: Proceedings of the IEEE International Conference on Computer Vision, pp. 4463–4471 (2017)
37. Lotter, W., Kreiman, G., Cox, D.: Deep predictive coding networks for video prediction and unsupervised learning. arXiv preprint, May 2016. http://arxiv.org/abs/1605.08104
38. Lu, C., Hirsch, M., Scholkoph, B.: Flexible spatio-temporal networks for video prediction. In: Computer Vision and Pattern Recognition (2017)
39. Luc, P., Neverova, N., Couprie, C., Verbeek, J., LeCun, Y.: Predicting deeper into the future of semantic segmentation. In: International Conference on Computer Vision, March 2017. http://arxiv.org/abs/1703.07684
40. Mathieu, M., Couprie, C., LeCun, Y.: Deep multi-scale video prediction beyond mean square error. In: International Conference on Learning Representations (2016)
41. Oh, J., Guo, X., Lee, H., Lewis, R., Singh, S.: Action-conditional video prediction using deep networks in atari games. In: Neural Information Processing Systems (2015)
42. Patraucean, V., Handa, A., Cipolla, R.: Spatio-temporal video autoencoder with differentiable memory. arXiv preprint, November 2015. http://arxiv.org/abs/1511.06309

43. Ranzato, M., Szlam, A., Bruna, J., Mathieu, M., Collobert, R., Chopra, S.: Video (language) modeling: a baseline for generative models of natural videos. arXiv preprint arXiv:1412.6604 (2014)
44. Rizzolatti, G., Craighero, L.: The mirror-neuron system. Annu. Rev. Neurosci. **27**, 169–192 (2004)
45. Rizzolatti, G., Fadiga, L., Gallese, V., Fogassi, L.: Premotor cortex and the recognition of motor actions. Cogn. Brain. Res. **3**(2), 131–141 (1996)
46. Rybkin, O., Pertsch, K., Derpanis, K.G., Daniilidis, K., Jaegle, A.: Learning what you can do before doing anything. In: International Conference on Learning Representations (2019). https://openreview.net/forum?id=SylPMnR9Ym
47. Sermanet, P., et al.: Time-contrastive networks: self-supervised learning from video. In: Proceedings of International Conference in Robotics and Automation (ICRA) (2018). http://arxiv.org/abs/1704.06888
48. Sharma, P., Pathak, D., Gupta, A.: Third-person visual imitation learning via decoupled hierarchical controller. In: Neural Information Processing Systems (2019)
49. Shon, A.P., Grochow, K., Hertzmann, A., Rao, R.P.: Learning shared latent structure for image synthesis and robotic imitation. In: Advances in Neural Information Processing Systems, pp. 1233–1240 (2005)
50. Srivastava, N., Mansimov, E., Salakhudinov, R.: Unsupervised learning of video representations using LSTMs. In: International Conference on Machine Learning (ICML) (2015)
51. Stadie, B.C., Abbeel, P., Sutskever, I.: Third-person imitation learning. arXiv preprint arXiv:1703.01703 (2017)
52. Sun, M., Ma, X.: Adversarial imitation learning from incomplete demonstrations. In: International Joint Conference on Artificial Intelligence, May 2019. http://arxiv.org/abs/1905.12310
53. Sun, W., Vemula, A., Boots, B., Bagnell, J.A.: Provably efficient imitation learning from observation alone. In: International Conference on Machine Learning, May 2019. http://arxiv.org/abs/1905.10948
54. Taigman, Y., Polyak, A., Wolf, L.: Unsupervised cross-domain image generation. In: International Conference on Learning Representations, November 2017. https://arxiv.org/abs/1611.02200
55. Torabi, F., Warnell, G., Stone, P.: Behavioral cloning from observation. In: International Joint Conference on Artificial Intelligence, May 2018. http://arxiv.org/abs/1805.01954
56. Torabi, F., Warnell, G., Stone, P.: Generative adversarial imitation from observation. arXiv preprint, July 2018. http://arxiv.org/abs/1807.06158
57. Torabi, F., Warnell, G., Stone, P.: Imitation learning from video by leveraging proprioception. In: International Joint Conference on Artificial Intelligence, May 2019. http://arxiv.org/abs/1905.09335
58. Tulyakov, S., Liu, M.Y., Yang, X., Kautz, J.: MoCoGAN: decomposing motion and content for video generation. In: Computer Vision and Pattern Recognition (2018)
59. Tzeng, E., Hoffman, J., Saenko, K., Darrell, T.: Adversarial discriminative domain adaptation. In: Computer Vision and Pattern Recognition, February 2017. http://arxiv.org/abs/1702.05464
60. Tzeng, E., Hoffman, J., Zhang, N., Saenko, K., Darrell, T.: Deep domain confusion: maximizing for domain invariance. arXiv preprint, December 2014. http://arxiv.org/abs/1412.3474

61. Villegas, R., Yang, J., Hong, S., Lin, X., Lee, H.: Decomposing motion and content for natural video sequence prediction. In: International Conference on Learning Representations (2017)
62. Vondrick, C., Pirsiavash, H., Torralba, A.: Anticipating visual representations from unlabeled video. In: Computer Vision and Pattern Recognition (2016)
63. Vondrick, C., Torralba, A.: Generating the future with adversarial transformers. In: Conference on Vision and Pattern Recognition (2017)
64. Walker, J., Doersch, C., Gupta, A., Hebert, M.: An uncertain future: forecasting from static images using variational autoencoders. In: Leibe, B., Matas, J., Sebe, N., Welling, M. (eds.) ECCV 2016. LNCS, vol. 9911, pp. 835–851. Springer, Cham (2016). https://doi.org/10.1007/978-3-319-46478-7_51. http://arxiv.org/abs/1606.07873
65. Wang, A., Kurutach, T., Tamar, A., Abbeel, P.: Learning robotic manipulation through visual planning and acting. In: Robotics: Science and Systems (2019)
66. Watter, M., Springenberg, J.T., Boedecker, J., Riedmiller, M.: Embed to control: a locally linear latent dynamics model for control from raw images. In: Neural Information Processing Systems (2015)
67. Wichers, N., Villegas, R., Erhan, D., Lee, H.: Hierarchical long-term video prediction without supervision. In: ICML (2018)
68. Xie, A., Ebert, F., Levine, S., Finn, C.: Improvisation through physical understanding: using novel objects as tools with visual foresight. In: Robotics: Science and Systems, April 2019. http://arxiv.org/abs/1904.05538
69. Xue, T., Wu, J., Bouman, K.L., Freeman, W.T.: Visual dynamics: probabilistic future frame synthesis via cross convolutional networks. IEEE Trans. Pattern Anal. Mach. Intell. (2016). http://arxiv.org/abs/1607.02586
70. Yen-Chen, L., Bauza, M., Isola, P.: Experience-embedded visual foresight. In: Conference on Robot Learning, November 2019. http://arxiv.org/abs/1911.05071
71. Yu, F., et al.: BDD100K: a diverse driving video database with scalable annotation tooling. arXiv preprint, May 2018. http://arxiv.org/abs/1805.04687
72. Yu, T., et al.: One-shot imitation from observing humans via domain-adaptive meta-learning. In: Robotics: Science and Systems, February 2018. http://arxiv.org/abs/1802.01557
73. Zhang, M., Vikram, S., Smith, L., Abbeel, P., Johnson, M.J., Levine, S.: SOLAR: deep structured representations for model-based reinforcement learning. In: International Conference on Machine Learning, August 2018. http://arxiv.org/abs/1808.09105
74. Zhang, R., Isola, P., Efros, A.A., Shechtman, E., Wang, O.: The unreasonable effectiveness of deep features as a perceptual metric. In: Computer Vision and Pattern Recognition (2018)
75. Zhu, J.Y., Park, T., Isola, P., Efros, A.A.: Unpaired image-to-image translation using cycle-consistent adversarial networks. In: 2017 IEEE International Conference on Computer Vision (ICCV) (2017)
76. Zhuang, F., Cheng, X., Luo, P., Pan, S.J., He, Q.: Supervised representation learning with double encoding-layer autoencoder for transfer learning. In: International Joint Conference on Artificial Intelligence (2015). https://doi.org/10.1145/3108257

Unifying Deep Local and Global Features for Image Search

Bingyi Cao, André Araujo[✉], and Jack Sim

Google Research, Mountain View, USA
bingyi@google.com, andrearaujo@google.com, jacksim@google.com

Abstract. Image retrieval is the problem of searching an image database for items that are similar to a query image. To address this task, two main types of image representations have been studied: global and local image features. In this work, our key contribution is to unify global and local features into a single deep model, enabling accurate retrieval with efficient feature extraction. We refer to the new model as DELG, standing for DEep Local and Global features. We leverage lessons from recent feature learning work and propose a model that combines generalized mean pooling for global features and attentive selection for local features. The entire network can be learned end-to-end by carefully balancing the gradient flow between two heads – requiring only image-level labels. We also introduce an autoencoder-based dimensionality reduction technique for local features, which is integrated into the model, improving training efficiency and matching performance. Comprehensive experiments show that our model achieves state-of-the-art image retrieval on the Revisited Oxford and Paris datasets, and state-of-the-art single-model instance-level recognition on the Google Landmarks dataset v2. Code and models are available at https://github.com/tensorflow/models/tree/master/research/delf.

Keywords: Deep features · Image retrieval · Unified model

1 Introduction

Large-scale image retrieval is a long-standing problem in computer vision, which saw promising results [26,38,43,44] even before deep learning revolutionized the field. Central to this problem are the representations used to describe images and their similarities.

B. Cao and A. Araujo—Contributed equally to this work.

Electronic supplementary material The online version of this chapter (https://doi.org/10.1007/978-3-030-58565-5_43) contains supplementary material, which is available to authorized users.

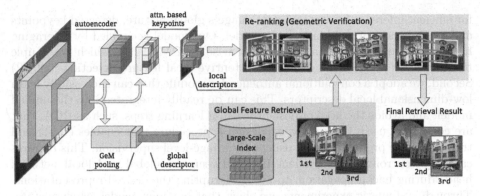

Fig. 1. Our proposed **DELG (DEep Local and Global features)** model (left) jointly extracts deep local and global features. Global features can be used in the first stage of a retrieval system, to efficiently select the most similar images (bottom). Local features can then be employed to re-rank top results (top-right), increasing precision of the system. The unified model leverages hierarchical representations induced by convolutional neural networks to learn local and global features, combined with recent advances in global pooling and attentive local feature detection.

Two types of image representations are necessary for high image retrieval performance: global and local features. A global feature [1,17,26,46,47], also commonly referred to as "global descriptor" or "embedding", summarizes the contents of an image, often leading to a compact representation; information about spatial arrangement of visual elements is lost. Local features [7,28,34,39,62], on the other hand, comprise descriptors and geometry information about specific image regions; they are especially useful to match images depicting rigid objects. Generally speaking, global features are better at recall, while local features are better at precision. Global features can learn similarity across very different poses where local features would not be able to find correspondences; in contrast, the score provided by local feature-based geometric verification usually reflects image similarity well, being more reliable than global feature distance. A common retrieval system setup is to first search by global features, then re-rank the top database images using local feature matching – to get the best of both worlds. Such a hybrid approach gained popularity in visual localization [49,54] and instance-level recognition problems [42,61].

Today, most systems that rely on both these types of features need to separately extract each of them, using different models. This is undesirable since it may lead to high memory usage and increased latency, e.g., if both models require specialized and limited hardware such as GPUs. Besides, in many cases similar types of computation are performed for both, resulting in redundant processing and unnecessary complexity.

Contributions. (1) Our first contribution is a unified model to represent both local and global features, using a convolutional neural network (CNN), referred to as DELG (DEep Local and Global features) – illustrated in Fig. 1. This allows for efficient inference by extracting an image's global feature, detected keypoints and local descriptors within a single model. Our model is enabled by leveraging hierarchical image representations that arise in CNNs [64], which we couple to generalized mean pooling [46] and attentive local feature detection [39]. (2) Second, we adopt a convolutional autoencoder module that can successfully learn low-dimensional local descriptors. This can be readily integrated into the unified model, and avoids the need of post-processing learning steps, such as PCA, that are commonly used. (3) Finally, we design a procedure that enables end-to-end training of the proposed model using only image-level supervision. This requires carefully controlling the gradient flow between the global and local network heads during backpropagation, to avoid disrupting the desired representations. Through systematic experiments, we show that our joint model achieves state-of-the-art performance on the Revisited Oxford, Revisited Paris and Google Landmarks v2 datasets.

2   Related Work

We review relevant work in local and global features, focusing mainly on approaches related to image retrieval.

Local Features. Hand-crafted techniques such as SIFT [28] and SURF [7] have been widely used for retrieval problems. Early systems [28,32,40] worked by searching for query local descriptors against a large database of local descriptors, followed by geometrically verifying database images with sufficient number of correspondences. Bag-of-Words [53] and related methods [24,43,44] followed, by relying on visual words obtained via local descriptor clustering, coupled to TF-IDF scoring. The key advantage of local features over global ones for retrieval is the ability to perform spatial matching, often employing RANSAC [15]. This has been widely used [3,43,44], as it produces reliable and interpretable scores. Recently, several deep learning-based local features have been proposed [6,14,29, 33,34,39,41,48,62]. The one most related to our work is DELF [39]; our proposed unified model incorporates DELF's attention module, but with a much simpler training pipeline, besides also enabling global feature extraction.

Global Features excel at delivering high image retrieval performance with compact representations. Before deep learning was popular in computer vision, they were developed mainly by aggregating hand-crafted local descriptors [25–27, 57]. Today, most high-performing global features are based on deep convolutional neural networks [1,4,5,17,46,47,58], which are trained with ranking-based [9,19, 50] or classification losses [11,60]. Our work leverages recent learned lessons in global feature design, by adopting GeM pooling [46] and ArcFace loss [11]. This leads to improved global feature retrieval performance compared to previous techniques, which is further boosted by geometric re-ranking with local features obtained from the same model.

Joint Local and Global CNN Features. Previous work considered neural networks for joint extraction of global and local features. For indoor localization,

Taira et al. [54] used NetVLAD [1] to extract global features for candidate pose retrieval, followed by dense local feature matching using feature maps from the same network. Simeoni et al.'s DSM [52] detected keypoints in activation maps from global feature models using MSER [30]; activation channels are interpreted as visual words, in order to propose correspondences between a pair of images. Our work differs substantially from [52,54], since they only post-process pre-trained global feature models to produce local features, while we jointly train local and global. Sarlin et al. [49] distill pre-trained local [12] and global [1] features into a single model, targeting localization applications. In contrast, our model is trained end-to-end for image retrieval, and is not limited to mimicking separate pre-trained local and global models. To the best of our knowledge, ours is the first work to learn a non-distilled model producing both local and global features.

Dimensionality Reduction for Image Retrieval. PCA and whitening are widely used for dimensionality reduction of local and global features in image retrieval [4,39,47,58]. As discussed in [23], whitening downweights co-occurrences of local features, which is generally beneficial for retrieval applications. Mukundan et al. [35] further introduce a shrinkage parameter that controls the extent of applied whitening. If supervision in the form of matching pairs or category labels is available, more sophisticated methods [18,31] can be used. More recently, Gordo et al. [16] propose to replace PCA/whitening by a fully-connected layer, that is learned together with the global descriptor.

In this paper, our goal is to compose a system that can be learned end-to-end, using only image-level labels and without requiring post-processing stages that make training more complex. Also, since we extract local features from feature maps of common CNN backbones, they tend to be very high-dimensional and infeasible for large-scale problems. All above-mentioned approaches would either require a separate post-processing step to reduce the dimensionality of features, or supervision at the level of local patches – making them unsuitable to our needs. We thus introduce an autoencoder in our model, which can be jointly and efficiently learned with the rest of the network. It requires no extra supervision as it can be trained with a reconstruction loss.

3 DELG

3.1 Design Considerations

For optimal performance, image retrieval requires semantic understanding of the types of objects that a user may be interested in, such that the system can distinguish between relevant objects versus clutter/background. Both local and global features should thus focus only on the most discriminative information within the image. However, there are substantial differences in terms of the desired behavior for these two feature modalities, posing a considerable challenge to jointly learn them.

Global features should be similar for images depicting the same object of interest, and dissimilar otherwise. This requires high-level, abstract representations that are invariant to viewpoint and photometric transformations. Local features, on the other hand, need to encode representations that are grounded to specific image regions; in particular, the keypoint detector should be equivariant with respect to viewpoint, and the keypoint descriptor needs to encode localized visual information. This is crucial to enable geometric consistency checks between query and database images, which are widely used in image retrieval systems.

Besides, our goal is to design a model that can be learned end-to-end, with local and global features, without requiring additional learning stages. This simplifies the training pipeline, allowing faster iterations and wider applicability. In comparison, it is common for previous feature learning work to require several learning stages: attentive deep local feature learning [39] requires 3 learning stages (fine-tuning, attention, PCA); deep global features usually require two stages, e.g., region proposal and Siamese training [17], or Siamese training and supervised whitening [46], or ranking loss training and PCA [47].

3.2 Model

We design our DELG model, illustrated in Fig. 1, to fulfill the requirements outlined above. We propose to leverage hierarchical representations from CNNs [64] in order to represent the different types of features to be learned. While global features can be associated with deep layers representing high-level cues, local features are more suitable to intermediate layers that encode localized information.

Given an image, we apply a convolutional neural network backbone to obtain two feature maps: $S \in \mathcal{R}^{H_S \times W_S \times C_S}$ and $D \in \mathcal{R}^{H_D \times W_D \times C_D}$, representing shallower and deeper activations respectively, where H, W, C correspond to the height, width and number of channels in each case. For common convolutional networks, $H_D \leq H_S$, $W_D \leq W_S$ and $C_D \geq C_S$; deeper layers have spatially smaller maps, with a larger number of channels. Let $s_{h,w} \in \mathcal{R}^{C_S}$ and $d_{h,w} \in \mathcal{R}^{C_D}$ denote features at location h, w in these maps. For common network designs, these features are non-negative since they are obtained after the ReLU non-linearity, which is the case in our method.

In order to aggregate deep activations into a global feature, we adopt generalized mean pooling (GeM) [46], which effectively weights the contributions of each feature. Another key component of global feature learning is to whiten the aggregated representation; we integrate this into our model with a fully-connected layer $F \in \mathcal{R}^{C_F \times C_D}$, with learned bias $b_F \in \mathcal{R}^{C_F}$, similar to [17]. These two components produce a global feature $g \in \mathcal{R}^{C_F}$ that summarizes the discriminative contents of the whole image:

$$g = F \times \left(\frac{1}{H_D W_D} \sum_{h,w} d_{h,w}^p \right)^{1/p} + b_F \tag{1}$$

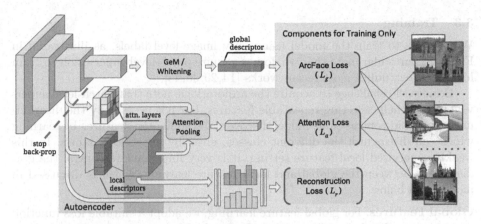

Fig. 2. Illustration of our **training pipeline**. The components highlighted in green are used solely during training. There are two classification losses: ArcFace for global feature learning (L_g), and softmax for attention learning (L_a). In both cases, the classification objective is to distinguish different landmarks (an instance-level recognition problem). The autoencoder (purple) is further trained with a reconstruction loss (L_r). The whole model is learned end-to-end, and benefits substantially from stopping gradient back-propagation from L_a and L_r into the CNN backbone. (Color figure online)

where p denotes the generalized mean power parameter, and the exponentiation $d_{h,w}^p$ is applied elementwise.

Regarding local features, it is important to select only the relevant regions for matching. This can be achieved by adopting an attention module M [39], whose goal is to predict which among the extracted local features are discriminative for the objects of interest. This is performed as $\mathcal{A} = M(\mathcal{S})$, where M is a small convolutional network and $\mathcal{A} \in \mathcal{R}^{H_S \times W_S}$ denotes the attention score map associated to the features from $\mathcal{S}$.

Furthermore, since hundreds to thousands of local features are commonly used, they must be represented compactly. To do so, we propose to integrate a small convolutional autoencoder (AE) module [21], which is responsible for learning a suitable low-dimensional representation. The local descriptors are obtained as $\mathcal{L} = T(\mathcal{S})$, where $\mathcal{L} \in \mathcal{R}^{H_S \times W_S \times C_T}$, and T is the encoding part of the autoencoder, corresponding to a 1×1 convolutional layer with C_T filters. Note that, contrary to $\mathcal{S}$, the local descriptors $\mathcal{L}$ are not restricted to be non-negative.

Each extracted local feature at position h, w is thus represented with a local descriptor $l_{h,w} \in \mathcal{L}$ and its corresponding keypoint detection score $a_{h,w} \in \mathcal{A}$. Their locations in the input image are set to corresponding receptive field centers, which can be computed using the parameters of the network [2].

The global and local descriptors are L_2-normalized into $\hat{g}$ and $\hat{l}_{h,w}$, respectively.

3.3 Training

We propose to train the model using only image-level labels, as illustrated in Fig. 2. In particular, note that we do not require patch-level supervision to train local features, unlike most recent works [14,29,36,48].

Besides the challenge to acquire the annotations, note that patch-level supervision could help selecting repeatable features, but not necessarily the discriminative ones; in contrast, our model discovers discriminative features by learning which can distinguish the different classes, given by image-level labels. In this weakly-supervised local feature setting, it is very important to control the gradient flow between the global and local feature learning, which is discussed in more detail below.

Global Features. For global feature learning, we adopt a suitable loss function with L_2-normalized classifier weights $\hat{\mathcal{W}}$, followed by scaled softmax normalization and cross-entropy loss [59]; this is sometimes referred to as "cosine classifier". Additionally, we adopt the ArcFace margin [11], which has shown excellent results for global feature learning by inducing smaller intra-class variance. Concretely, given $\hat{g}$, we first compute the cosine similarity against $\hat{\mathcal{W}}$, adjusted by the ArcFace margin. The ArcFace-adjusted cosine similarity can be expressed as $\mathrm{AF}(u, c)$:

$$\mathrm{AF}(u, c) = \begin{cases} \cos(\mathrm{acos}(u) + m), & \text{if } c = 1 \\ u, & \text{if } c = 0 \end{cases} \tag{2}$$

where u is the cosine similarity, m is the ArcFace margin and c is a binary value indicating if this is the ground-truth class. The cross-entropy loss, computed using softmax normalization can be expressed in this case as:

$$L_g(\hat{g}, y) = -\log\left(\frac{\exp(\gamma \times \mathrm{AF}(\hat{w}_k^T \hat{g}, 1))}{\sum_n \exp(\gamma \times \mathrm{AF}(\hat{w}_n^T \hat{g}, y_n))} \right) \tag{3}$$

where γ is a learnable scalar, $\hat{w}_i$ refers to the L_2-normalized classifier weights for class i, y is the one-hot label vector and k is the index of the ground-truth class ($y_k = 1$).

Local Features. To train the local features, we use two losses. First, a mean-squared error regression loss that measures how well the autoencoder can reconstruct $\mathcal{S}$. Denote $\mathcal{S}' = T'(\mathcal{L})$ as the reconstructed version of $\mathcal{S}$, with same dimensions, where T' is a 1×1 convolutional layer with C_S filters, followed by ReLU. The loss can be expressed as:

$$L_r(\mathcal{S}', \mathcal{S}) = \frac{1}{H_S W_S C_S} \sum_{h,w} \|s'_{h,w} - s_{h,w}\|^2 \tag{4}$$

Second, a cross-entropy classification loss that incentivizes the attention module to select discriminative local features. This is done by first pooling the reconstructed features $\mathcal{S}'$ with attention weights $a_{h,w}$:

$$a' = \sum_{h,w} a_{h,w} s'_{h,w} \tag{5}$$

Then using a standard softmax-cross-entropy loss:

$$L_a(a', k) = -\log\left(\frac{\exp(v_k^T a' + b_k)}{\sum_n \exp(v_n^T a' + b_n)}\right) \tag{6}$$

where v_i, b_i refer to the classifier weights and biases for class i and k is the index of the ground-truth class; this tends to make the attention weights large for the discriminative features. The total loss is given by $L_g + \lambda L_r + \beta L_a$.

Controlling Gradients. Naively optimizing the above-mentioned total loss experimentally leads to suboptimal results, because the reconstruction and attention loss terms significantly disturb the hierarchical feature representation which is usually obtained when training deep models. In particular, both tend to induce the shallower features S to be more semantic and less localizable, which end up being sparser. Sparser features can more easily optimize L_r, and more semantic features may help optimizing L_a; this, as a result, leads to underperforming local features.

We avoid this issue by stopping gradient back-propagation from L_r and L_a to the network backbone, i.e., to S. This means that the network backbone is optimized solely based on L_g, and will tend to produce the desired hierarchical feature representation. This is further discussed in the experimental section that follows.

4   Experiments

4.1   Experimental Setup

Model Backbone and Implementation. Our model is implemented using TensorFlow, leveraging the Slim model library [51]. We use ResNet-50 (R50) and ResNet-101 (R101) [20]; R50 is used for ablation experiments. We obtain the shallower feature map S from the *conv4* output, and the deeper feature map D from the *conv5* output. Note that the Slim implementation moves the *conv5* stride into the last unit from *conv4*, which we also adopt – helping reduce the spatial resolution of S. The number of channels in D is $C_D = 2048$; GeM pooling [46] is applied with parameter $p = 3$, which is not learned. The whitening fully-connected layer, applied after pooling, produces a global feature with dimensionality $C_F = 2048$. The number of channels in S is $C_S = 1024$; the autoencoder module learns a reduced dimensionality for this feature map with $C_T = 128$. The attention network M follows the setup from [39], with 2 convolutional layers, without stride, using kernel sizes of 1; as activation functions, the first layer uses ReLU and the second uses Softplus [13].

Training Details. We use the training set of the Google Landmarks dataset (GLD) [39], containing 1.2M images from 15k landmarks, and divide it into two subsets 'train'/'val' with 80%/20% split. The 'train' split is used for the actual learning, and the 'val' split is used for validating the learned classifier as training progresses. Models are initialized from pre-trained ImageNet weights. The images first undergo augmentation, by randomly cropping/distorting the aspect ratio; then, they are resized to 512×512 resolution. We use a batch size of 16, and train using 21 Tesla P100 GPUs asynchronously, for 1.5M steps (corresponding to approximately 25 epochs of the 'train' split). The model is optimized using SGD with momentum of 0.9, and a linearly decaying learning rate that reaches zero once the desired number of steps is reached. We experiment with initial learning rates within $[3 \times 10^{-4}, 10^{-2}]$ and report results for the best performing one. We set the ArcFace margin $m = 0.1$, the weight for L_a to $\beta = 1$, and the weight for L_r to $\lambda = 10$. The learnable scalar for the global loss L_g is initialized to $\gamma = \sqrt{C_F} = 45.25$.

Evaluation Datasets. To evaluate our model, we use several datasets. First, Oxford [43] and Paris [44], with revisited annotations [45], referred to as $\mathcal{R}$Oxf and $\mathcal{R}$Par, respectively. There are 4993 (6322) database images in the $\mathcal{R}$Oxf ($\mathcal{R}$Par) dataset, and a different query set for each, both with 70 images. Performance is measured using mean average precision (mAP). Large-scale results are further reported with the $\mathcal{R}$1M distractor set [45], which contains 1M images. As in previous papers [37,47,55], parameters are tuned in $\mathcal{R}$Oxf/$\mathcal{R}$Par, then kept fixed for the large-scale experiments. Second, we report large-scale instance-level retrieval and recognition results on the Google Landmarks dataset v2 (GLDv2) [61], using the latest ground-truth version (2.1). GLDv2-retrieval has 1129 queries (379 validation and 750 testing) and 762k database images; performance is measured using mAP@100. GLDv2-recognition has 118k test (41k validation and 77k testing) and 4M training images from 203k landmarks; the training images are only used to retrieve images and their scores/labels are used to form the class prediction; performance is measured using μAP@1. We perform minimal parameter tuning based on the validation split, and report results on the testing split.

Feature Extraction and Matching. We follow the convention from previous work [17,39,46] and use an image pyramid at inference time to produce multi-scale representations. For global features, we use 3 scales, $\{\frac{1}{\sqrt{2}}, 1, \sqrt{2}\}$; L_2 normalization is applied for each scale independently, then the three global features are average-pooled, followed by another L_2 normalization step. For local features, we experiment with the same 3 scales, but also with the more expensive setting from [39] using 7 image scales in total, with range from 0.25 to 2.0 (this latter setting is used unless otherwise noted). Local features are selected based on their attention scores $\mathcal{A}$; a maximum of 1k local features are allowed, with a minimum attention score τ, where we set τ to the median attention score in the last iteration of training, unless otherwise noted. For local feature matching, we use RANSAC [15] with an affine model. When re-ranking global feature retrieval results with local feature-based matching, the top 100 ranked images from the first stage are considered. For retrieval datasets, the final ranking is based on the number of inliers, then breaking ties using the global feature distance; for the recognition dataset, we follow the exact protocol from the GLDv2 paper [61] to combine local and global scores, aggregating scores for different classes based on the top-ranked images. Our focus is on improving global and local features for

Table 1. Local feature ablation. Comparison of local features, trained separately or jointly, with different methods for dimensionality reduction (DR). We report average precision (AP) results of matching image pairs from the Google Landmarks dataset (GLD).

DR method	λ	Jointly trained	Stop gradients	GLD-pairs AP (%)
PCA [39]	-	✗	-	51.48
FC	-			52.67
AE [ours]	0	✗	-	49.95
	1			51.28
	5			52.26
	10			54.21
	20			53.51
	10	✓	✗	37.05
	10		✓	53.73

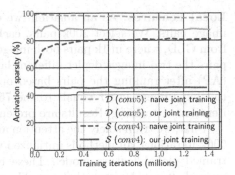

Fig. 3. Evolution of **activation sparsity** over training iterations for $\mathcal{D}$ (conv5) and $\mathcal{S}$ (conv4), comparing the naive joint training method and our improved version that controls gradient propagation. The naive method leads to much sparser feature maps.

Table 2. Global feature ablation. Comparison of global features, trained separately or jointly, with different pooling methods (SPoC, GeM) and loss functions (Softmax, ArcFace). We report mean average precision (mAP %) on the $\mathcal{R}$Oxf and $\mathcal{R}$Par datasets.

		Jointly trained	Stop gradients	Medium		Hard	
Pooling	Loss			$\mathcal{R}$Oxf	$\mathcal{R}$Par	$\mathcal{R}$Oxf	$\mathcal{R}$Par
SPoC	Softmax	✗	–	51.2	72.0	26.3	47.7
SPoC	ArcFace	✗	–	59.8	80.8	35.6	61.7
GeM	ArcFace	✗	–	69.3	**82.2**	44.4	**64.0**
GeM	ArcFace	✓	✗	68.8	78.9	42.4	58.3
GeM	ArcFace	✓	✓	**69.7**	81.6	**45.1**	63.4

retrieval/recognition, so we do not consider techniques that post-process results such as query expansion [10, 46] or diffusion/graph traversal [8, 22]. These are expensive due to requiring additional passes over the database, but if desired could be integrated to our system and produce stronger performance.

4.2 Results

First, we present ablation experiments, to compare features produced by our joint model against their counterparts which are separately trained, and also to discuss the effect of controlling the gradient propagation. For a fair comparison, our jointly trained features are evaluated against equivalent separately-trained models, with the same hyperparameters as much as possible. Then, we compare our models against state-of-the-art techniques. See also the appendices for more details, visualizations and discussions.

Local Features. As an ablation, we evaluate our local features by matching image pairs. We select 200k pairs, each composed of a test and a train image from GLD, where in 1k pairs both images depict the same landmark, and in 199k pairs the two images depict different landmarks. We compute average precision (AP) after ranking the pairs based on the number of inliers. All variants for this experiment use τ equals to the 75th percentile attention score in the last iteration of training. Results are presented in Table 1.

First, we train solely the attention and dimensionality reduction modules, for 500k iterations, all methods initialized with the same weights from a separately-trained global feature model. These results are marked as not being jointly trained. It can be seen that our AE outperforms PCA and a simpler method using only a single fully-connected (FC) layer. Performance improves for the AE as λ increases from 0 to 10, decreasing with 20. Then, we jointly train the unified model; in this case, the variant that does not stop gradients to the backbone suffers a large drop in performance, while the variant that stops gradients obtains similar results as in the separately-trained case.

The poor performance of the naive jointly trained model is due to the degradation of the hierarchical feature representation. This can be assessed by observing the evolution of activation sparsity in S ($conv4$) and D ($conv5$), as shown in Fig. 3. Generally, layers representing more abstract and high-level semantic properties (usually deeper layers) have high levels of sparsity, while shallower layers representing low-level and more localizable patterns are dense. As a reference, the ImageNet pre-trained model presents on average 45% and 82% sparsity for these two feature maps, respectively, when run over GLD images. For the naive joint training case, the activations of both layers quickly become much sparser, reaching 80% and 97% at the end of training; in comparison, our proposed training scheme preserves similar sparsity as the ImageNet model: 45% and 88%. This suggests that the $conv4$ features in the naive case degrade for the purposes of local feature matching; controlling the gradient effectively resolves this issue.

Global Features. Table 2 compares global feature training methods. The first three rows present global features trained with different loss and pooling techniques. We experiment with standard Softmax Cross-Entropy and ArcFace [11] losses; for pooling, we consider standard average pooling (equivalent to SPoC [4]) and GeM [46]. ArcFace brings an improvement of up to 14%, and GeM of up to 9.5%. GeM pooling and ArcFace loss are adopted in our final model. Naively training a joint model, without controlling gradients, underperforms when compared to the baseline separately-trained global feature, with mAP decrease of up to 5.7%. Once gradient stopping is employed, the performance can be recovered to be on par with the separately-trained version (a little better on $\mathcal{R}$Oxf, a little worse on $\mathcal{R}$Par). This is expected, since the global feature in this case is optimized by itself, without influence from the local feature head.

Comparison to Retrieval State-of-the-Art. Table 3 compares our model against the retrieval state-of-the-art. Three settings are presented: (A) local feature aggregation and re-ranking (previous work); (B) global feature similarity

Table 3. Comparison to retrieval state-of-the-art. Results (% mAP) on the $\mathcal{R}$Oxf/$\mathcal{R}$Par datasets (and their large-scale versions $\mathcal{R}$Oxf+1M/$\mathcal{R}$Par+1M), with both Medium and Hard evaluation protocols. The top set of rows (A) presents previous work's results using local feature aggregation and re-ranking. Other sets of rows present results using (B) global features only, or (C) global features for initial search then re-ranking using local features. DELG* refers to a version of DELG where the local features are binarized. DELG and DELG* outperform previous work in setups (B) and (C) substantially. DELG also outperforms methods from setting (A) in 7 out of 8 cases.

Method	Medium				Hard			
	$\mathcal{R}$Oxf	+1M	$\mathcal{R}$Par	+1M	$\mathcal{R}$Oxf	+1M	$\mathcal{R}$Par	+1M
(A) Local feature aggregation + re-ranking								
HesAff-rSIFT-ASMK*+SP [57]	60.6	46.8	61.4	42.3	36.7	26.9	35.0	16.8
HesAff-HardNet-ASMK*+SP [34]	65.6	–	65.2	–	41.1	–	38.5	–
DELF-ASMK* +SP [39,45]	67.8	53.8	76.9	57.3	43.1	31.2	55.4	26.4
DELF-R-ASMK*+SP (GLD) [55]	**76.0**	**64.0**	**80.2**	**59.7**	**52.4**	**38.1**	**58.6**	**29.4**
(B) Global features								
AlexNet-GeM [46]	43.3	24.2	58.0	29.9	17.1	9.4	29.7	8.4
VGG16-GeM [46]	61.9	42.6	69.3	45.4	33.7	19.0	44.3	19.1
R101-R-MAC [17]	60.9	39.3	78.9	54.8	32.4	12.5	59.4	28.0
R101-GeM [46]	64.7	45.2	77.2	52.3	38.5	19.9	56.3	24.7
R101-GeM↑ [52]	65.3	46.1	77.3	52.6	39.6	22.2	56.6	24.8
R101-GeM-AP [47]	67.5	47.5	80.1	52.5	42.8	23.2	60.5	25.1
R101-GeM-AP (GLD) [47]	66.3	–	80.2	–	42.5	–	60.8	–
R152-GeM (GLD) [46]	68.7	–	79.7	–	44.2	–	60.3	–
R101-GeM+SOLAR (GLD) [37]	69.9	53.5	81.6	59.2	47.9	29.9	64.5	33.4
R50-DELG **[ours]**	69.7	**55.0**	81.6	59.7	45.1	27.8	63.4	34.1
R101-DELG **[ours]**	**73.2**	54.8	**82.4**	**61.8**	**51.2**	**30.3**	**64.7**	**35.5**
(C) Global features + Local feature re-ranking								
R101-GeM↑+DSM [52]	65.3	47.6	77.4	52.8	39.2	23.2	56.2	25.0
R50-DELG* **[ours]**	–	60.4	–	60.3	–	35.3	–	34.1
R101-DELG (3 scales global & local) **[ours]**	77.2	61.7	82.4	62.3	55.4	37.5	62.7	35.3
R101-DELG* (3 scales global & local) **[ours]**	–	61.2	–	62.2	–	36.4	–	35.4
R101-DELG **[ours]**	**78.5**	**62.7**	**82.6**	**62.5**	**58.6**	**39.2**	**63.9**	**36.3**
R101-DELG* **[ours]**	–	62.2	–	62.4	–	38.3	–	36.1

search; (C) global feature search followed by re-ranking with local feature matching and spatial verification (SP).

In setting (B), the DELG global feature variants strongly outperform previous work for all cases (most noticeably in the large-scale setting), as well as outperforming concurrent work [37]. Compared to previous work, we see 7.1% improvement in $\mathcal{R}$Oxf+1M-Hard and 7.5% in $\mathcal{R}$Par+1M-Hard. Note that we obtain strong improvements even when using the ResNet-50 backbone, while the previous state-of-the-art used ResNet-101/152, which are much more

Table 4. GLDv2 evaluation. Results on the GLDv2 dataset, for the retrieval and recognition tasks, on the "testing" split of the query set. For a fair comparison, all methods are trained on GLD.

Method	Retrieval mAP (%)	Recognition μAP (%)
DELF-R-ASMK*+SP [55]	18.8	–
R101-GeM+ArcFace [61]	20.7	33.3
R101-GeM+CosFace [63]	21.4	–
DELF-KD-tree [39]	–	44.8
R50-DELG (global-only) [ours]	20.4	32.4
R101-DELG (global-only) [ours]	21.7	32.0
R50-DELG [ours]	22.3	56.8
R101-DELG [ours]	**24.3**	**58.8**

Table 5. Re-ranking experiment. Comparison of DELG against other recent local features; results (% mAP) on the $\mathcal{R}$Oxf dataset.

Method	Hard	Medium
R50-DELG (global-only)	45.1	69.7
Local feature re-ranking		
SIFT [28]	44.4	69.8
SOSNet [56]	45.5	69.9
D2-Net [14]	47.2	70.4
R50-DELG [ours]	**53.7**	**75.4**

complex (2X/3X the number of floating point operations, respectively). To ensure a fair comparison, we present results from [46,47] which specifically use the same training set as ours, marked as "(GLD)" – the results are obtained from the authors' official codebases. In particular, note that "R152-GeM (GLD) [46]" uses not only the same training set, but also the same exact scales in the image pyramid; even if our method is much cheaper, it consistently outperforms others.

For setup (C), we use both global and local features. For large-scale databases, it may be impractical to store all raw local features in memory; to alleviate such requirement, we also present a variant, DELG*, where we store local features in binarized format, by simply applying an elementwise function: $b(x) = +1$ if $x > 0$, -1 otherwise.

Local feature re-ranking boosts performance substantially for DELG, compared to only searching with global features, especially in large-scale cases: gains of up to 8.9% (in $\mathcal{R}$Oxf+1M-Hard). We also present results where local feature extraction is performed with 3 scales only, the same ones used for global features. The large-scale results are similar, providing a boost of up to 7.2%. Results for DELG* also provide large improvements, but with performance that is slightly lower than the corresponding unbinarized versions. Our retrieval results also outperform DSM [52] significantly, by more than 10% in several cases. Different from our proposed technique, the gain from spatial verification reported in their work is small, of at most 1.5% absolute. DELG also outperforms local feature aggregation results from setup (A) in 7 out of 8 cases, establishing a new state-of-the-art across the board.

GLDv2 Evaluation. Table 4 compares DELG against previous GLDv2 results, where for a fair comparison we report methods trained on GLD. DELG achieves top performance in both retrieval and recognition tasks, with local feature re-ranking providing significant boost in both cases – especially on the recognition task (26.8% absolute improvement). Note that recent work has reported even higher performance on the retrieval task, by learning on GLDv2's training set and using query expansion techniques [63]/ensembling [61]. On the other hand, DELG's performance on the recognition task is so far the best reported single-model result, outperforming many ensemble-based methods (by itself, it would have been ranked top-5 in the 2019 challenge) [61]. We expect that our results could be further improved by re-training on GLDv2's training set.

Re-ranking Experiment. Table 5 further compares local features for re-ranking purposes. R50-DELG is compared against SIFT [28], SOSNet [56] (HPatches model, DoG keypoints) and D2-Net [14] (trained, multiscale). All methods are given the same retrieval short list of 100 images for re-ranking (based on R50-DELG-global retrieval); for a fair comparison, all methods use 1k features and 1k RANSAC iterations. We tuned matching parameters separately for each method: whether to use ratio test or distance threshold for selecting correspondences (and their associated thresholds); RANSAC residual threshold; minimum number of inliers (below which we declare no match). SIFT and SOS-Net provide little improvement over the global feature, due to suboptimal feature detection based on our observation (i.e., any blob-like feature is detected, which may not correspond to landmarks). D2-Net improves over the global feature, benefiting from a better feature detector. DELG outperforms other methods by a large margin.

Latency and Memory, Qualitative Results. Please refer to the appendices for a comparison of latency and memory requirements for different methods, and for qualitative results.

5   Conclusions

Our main contribution is a unified model that enables joint extraction of local and global image features, referred to as DELG. The model is based on a ResNet backbone, leveraging generalized mean pooling to produce global features and attention-based keypoint detection to produce local features. We also introduce an effective dimensionality reduction technique that can be integrated into the same model, based on an autoencoder. The entire network can be trained end-to-end using image-level labels and does not require any additional post-processing steps. For best performance, we show that it is crucial to stop gradients from the attention and autoencoder branches into the network backbone, otherwise a suboptimal representation is obtained. We demonstrate the effectiveness of our method with comprehensive experiments, achieving state-of-the-art performance on the Revisited Oxford, Revisited Paris and Google Landmarks v2 datasets.

References

1. Arandjelović, R., Gronat, P., Torii, A., Pajdla, T., Sivic, J.: NetVLAD: CNN architecture for weakly supervised place recognition. In: Proceedings of the CVPR (2016)

2. Araujo, A., Norris, W., Sim, J.: Computing receptive fields of convolutional neural networks. Distill (2019). https://distill.pub/2019/computing-receptive-fields
3. Avrithis, Y., Tolias, G.: Hough pyramid matching: speeded-up geometry re-ranking for large scale image retrieval. Int. J. Comput. Vision 107(1), 1–19 (2013). https://doi.org/10.1007/s11263-013-0659-3
4. Babenko, A., Lempitsky, V.: Aggregating local deep features for image retrieval. In: Proceedings of the ICCV (2015)
5. Babenko, A., Slesarev, A., Chigorin, A., Lempitsky, V.: Neural codes for image retrieval. In: Fleet, D., Pajdla, T., Schiele, B., Tuytelaars, T. (eds.) ECCV 2014. LNCS, vol. 8689, pp. 584–599. Springer, Cham (2014). https://doi.org/10.1007/978-3-319-10590-1_38
6. Barroso-Laguna, A., Riba, E., Ponsa, D., Mikolajczyk, K.: Key.Net: keypoint detection by handcrafted and learned CNN filters. In: Proceedings of the ICCV (2019)
7. Bay, H., Ess, A., Tuytelaars, T., Van Gool, L.: Speeded-up robust features (SURF). CVIU 110(3), 346–359 (2008)
8. Chang, C., Yu, G., Liu, C., Volkovs, M.: Explore-exploit graph traversal for image retrieval. In: Proceedings of the CVPR (2019)
9. Chopra, S., Hadsell, R., LeCun, Y.: Learning a dimilarity metric discriminatively, with application to face verification. In: Proceedings of the CVPR (2005)
10. Chum, O., Philbin, J., Sivic, J., Isard, M., Zisserman, A.: Total recall: automatic query expansion with a generative feature model for object retrieval. In: Proceedings of the ICCV (2007)
11. Deng, J., Guo, J., Xue, N., Zafeiriou, S.: ArcFace: additive angular margin loss for deep face recognition. In: Proceedings of the CVPR (2019)
12. DeTone, D., Malisiewicz, T., Rabinovich, A.: SuperPoint: self-supervised interest point detection and description. In: Proceedings of the CVPR Workshops (2018)
13. Dugas, C., Bengio, Y., Nadeau, C., Garcia, R.: Incorporating second-order functional knowledge for better option pricing. In: Proceedings of the NIPS (2001)
14. Dusmanu, M., et al.: D2-Net: a trainable CNN for joint detection and description of local features. In: Proceedings of the CVPR (2019)
15. Fischler, M., Bolles, R.: Random sample consensus: a paradigm for model fitting with applications to image analysis and automated cartography. Commun. ACM 24(6), 381–395 (1981)
16. Gordo, A., Almazán, J., Revaud, J., Larlus, D.: Deep image retrieval: learning global representations for image search. In: Leibe, B., Matas, J., Sebe, N., Welling, M. (eds.) ECCV 2016. LNCS, vol. 9910, pp. 241–257. Springer, Cham (2016). https://doi.org/10.1007/978-3-319-46466-4_15
17. Gordo, A., Almazán, J., Revaud, J., Larlus, D.: End-to-end learning of deep visual representations for image retrieval. Int. J. Comput. Vision 124(2), 237–254 (2017). https://doi.org/10.1007/s11263-017-1016-8
18. Gordo, A., Rodriguez-Serrano, J.A., Perronin, F., Valveny, E.: Leveraging category-level labels for instance-level image retrieval. In: Proceedings of the CVPR (2012)
19. He, K., Lu, Y., Sclaroff, S.: Local descriptors optimized for average precision. In: Proceedings of the CVPR (2018)
20. He, K., Zhang, X., Ren, S., Sun, J.: Deep residual learning for image recognition. In: Proceedings of the CVPR (2016)
21. Hinton, G.: Connectionist learning procedures. Artif. Intell. 40(1–3), 185–234 (1989)
22. Iscen, A., Tolias, G., Avrithis, Y., Furon, T., Chum, O.: Efficient diffusion on region manifolds: recovering small objects with compact CNN representations. In: Proceedings of the CVPR (2017)

23. Jégou, H., Chum, O.: Negative evidences and co-occurences in image retrieval: the benefit of PCA and whitening. In: Fitzgibbon, A., Lazebnik, S., Perona, P., Sato, Y., Schmid, C. (eds.) ECCV 2012. LNCS, vol. 7573, pp. 774–787. Springer, Heidelberg (2012). https://doi.org/10.1007/978-3-642-33709-3_55
24. Jegou, H., Douze, M., Schmid, C.: Hamming embedding and weak geometric consistency for large scale image search. In: Forsyth, D., Torr, P., Zisserman, A. (eds.) ECCV 2008. LNCS, vol. 5302, pp. 304–317. Springer, Heidelberg (2008). https://doi.org/10.1007/978-3-540-88682-2_24
25. Jégou, H., Douze, M., Schmidt, C., Perez, P.: Aggregating local descriptors into a compact image representation. In: Proceedings of the CVPR (2010)
26. Jégou, H., Perronnin, F., Douze, M., Sanchez, J., Perez, P., Schmid, C.: Aggregating local image descriptors into compact codes. IEEE Trans. Pattern Anal. Mach. Intell. **34**(9), 1704–1716 (2012)
27. Jegou, H., Zisserman, A.: Triangulation embedding and democratic aggregation for image search. In: Proceedings of the CVPR (2014)
28. Lowe, D.G.: Distinctive image features from scale-invariant keypoints. Int. J. Comput. Vision **60**, 91–110 (2004). https://doi.org/10.1023/B:VISI.0000029664.99615.94
29. Luo, Z., et al.: ContextDesc: local descriptor augmentation with cross-modality context. In: Proceedings of the CVPR (2019)
30. Matas, J., Chum, O., Urban, M., Pajdla, T.: Robust wide-baseline stereo from maximally stable extremal regions. Image Vis. Comput. **22**(10), 761–767 (2004)
31. Mikolajczyk, K., Matas, J.: Improving descriptors for fast tree matching by optimal linear projection. In: Proceedings of the ICCV (2007)
32. Mikolajczyk, K., Schmid, C.: An affine invariant interest point detector. In: Heyden, A., Sparr, G., Nielsen, M., Johansen, P. (eds.) ECCV 2002. LNCS, vol. 2350, pp. 128–142. Springer, Heidelberg (2002). https://doi.org/10.1007/3-540-47969-4_9
33. Mishchuk, A., Mishkin, D., Radenovic, F., Matas, J.: Working hard to know your neighbor's margins: local descriptor learning loss. In: Proceedings of the NIPS (2017)
34. Mishkin, D., Radenović, F., Matas, J.: Repeatability is not enough: learning affine regions via discriminability. In: Ferrari, V., Hebert, M., Sminchisescu, C., Weiss, Y. (eds.) ECCV 2018. LNCS, vol. 11213, pp. 287–304. Springer, Cham (2018). https://doi.org/10.1007/978-3-030-01240-3_18
35. Mukundan, A., Tolias, G., Bursuc, A., Jégou, H., Chum, O.: Understanding and improving kernel local descriptors. Int. J. Comput. Vision **127**(11), 1723–1737 (2018). https://doi.org/10.1007/s11263-018-1137-8
36. Mukundan, A., Tolias, G., Chum, O.: Explicit spatial encoding for deep local descriptors. In: Proceedings of the CVPR (2019)
37. Ng, T., Balntas, V., Tian, Y., Mikolajczyk, K.: SOLAR: second-order loss and attention for image retrieval. In: Proceedings of the ECCV (2020)
38. Nistér, D., Stewenius, H.: Scalable recognition with a vocabulary tree. In: Proceedings of the CVPR (2006)
39. Noh, H., Araujo, A., Sim, J., Weyand, T., Han, B.: Large-scale image retrieval with attentive deep local features. In: Proceedings of the ICCV (2017)
40. Obdrzalek, S., Matas, J.: Sub-linear indexing for large scale object recognition. In: Proceedings of the BMVC (2005)
41. Ono, Y., Trulls, E., Fua, P., Yi, K.M.: LF-Net: learning local features from images. In: Proceedings of the NIPS (2018)
42. Ozaki, K., Yokoo, S.: Large-scale landmark retrieval/recognition under a noisy and diverse dataset. arXiv:1906.04087 (2019)

43. Philbin, J., Chum, O., Isard, M., Sivic, J., Zisserman, A.: Object retrieval with large vocabularies and fast spatial matching. In: Proceedings of the CVPR (2007)
44. Philbin, J., Chum, O., Isard, M., Sivic, J., Zisserman, A.: Lost in quantization: improving particular object retrieval in large scale image databases. In: Proceedings of the CVPR (2008)
45. Radenović, F., Iscen, A., Tolias, G., Avrithis, Y., Chum, O.: Revisiting Oxford and Paris: large-scale image retrieval benchmarking. In: Proceedings of the CVPR (2018)
46. Radenović, F., Tolias, G., Chum, O.: Fine-tuning CNN image retrieval with no human annotation. IEEE Trans. Pattern Anal. Mach. Intell. **41**(7), 1655–1668 (2018)
47. Revaud, J., Almazan, J., de Rezende, R.S., de Souza, C.R.: Learning with average precision: training image retrieval with a listwise loss. In: Proceedings of the ICCV (2019)
48. Revaud, J., Souze, C.D., Weinzaepfel, P., Humenberger, M.: R2D2: repeatable and reliable detector and descriptor. In: Proceedings of the NeurIPS (2019)
49. Sarlin, P.E., Cadena, C., Siegwart, R., Dymczyk, M.: From coarse to fine: robust hierarchical localization at large scale. In: Proceedings of the CVPR (2019)
50. Schroff, F., Kalenichenko, D., Philbin, J.: FaceNet: a unified embedding for face recognition and clustering. In: Proceedings of the CVPR (2015)
51. Silberman, N., Guadarrama, S.: TensorFlow-Slim Image Classification Model Library (2016). https://github.com/tensorflow/models/tree/master/research/slim
52. Simeoni, O., Avrithis, Y., Chum, O.: Local features and visual words emerge in activations. In: Proceedings of the CVPR (2019)
53. Sivic, J., Zisserman, A.: Video Google: a text retrieval approach to object matching in videos. In: Proceedings of the ICCV (2003)
54. Taira, H., et al.: InLoc: indoor visual localization with dense matching and view synthesis. In: Proceedings of the CVPR (2018)
55. Teichmann, M., Araujo, A., Zhu, M., Sim, J.: Detect-to-retrieve: efficient regional aggregation for image search. In: Proceedings of the CVPR (2019)
56. Tian, Y., Yu, X., Fan, B., Wu, F., Heijnen, H., Balntas, V.: SOSNet: second order similarity regularization for local descriptor learning. In: Proceedings of the CVPR (2019)
57. Tolias, G., Avrithis, Y., Jégou, H.: Image search with selective match kernels: aggregation across single and multiple images. Int. J. Comput. Vis. **116**, 247–261 (2016). https://doi.org/10.1007/s11263-015-0810-4
58. Tolias, G., Sicre, R., Jégou, H.: Particular object retrieval with integral max-pooling of CNN activations. In: Proceeedings of the ICLR (2015)
59. Wang, F., Xiang, X., Cheng, J., Yuille, A.: NormFace: L2 hypersphere embedding for face verification. In: Proceedings of the ACM MM (2017)
60. Wang, H., et al.: CosFace: large margin cosine loss for deep dace recognition. In: Proceedings of the CVPR (2018)
61. Weyand, T., Araujo, A., Cao, B., Sim, J.: Google landmarks dataset v2 - a large-scale benchmark for instance-level recognition and retrieval. In: Proceedings of the CVPR (2020)
62. Yi, K.M., Trulls, E., Lepetit, V., Fua, P.: LIFT: learned invariant feature transform. In: Leibe, B., Matas, J., Sebe, N., Welling, M. (eds.) ECCV 2016. LNCS, vol. 9910, pp. 467–483. Springer, Cham (2016). https://doi.org/10.1007/978-3-319-46466-4_28

63. Yokoo, S., Ozaki, K., Simo-Serra, E., Iizuka, S.: Two-stage discriminative re-ranking for large-scale landmark retrieval. In: Proceedings of the CVPR Workshops (2020)
64. Zeiler, M.D., Fergus, R.: Visualizing and understanding convolutional networks. In: Fleet, D., Pajdla, T., Schiele, B., Tuytelaars, T. (eds.) ECCV 2014. LNCS, vol. 8689, pp. 818–833. Springer, Cham (2014). https://doi.org/10.1007/978-3-319-10590-1_53

Human Body Model Fitting by Learned Gradient Descent

Jie Song[1(✉)], Xu Chen[1,2], and Otmar Hilliges[1]

[1] ETH Zürich, Zürich, Switzerland
jsong@inf.ethz.ch
[2] Max Planck ETH Center for Learning Systems, Zürich, Switzerland

Abstract. We propose a novel algorithm for the fitting of 3D human shape to images. Combining the accuracy and refinement capabilities of iterative gradient-based optimization techniques with the robustness of deep neural networks, we propose a gradient descent algorithm that leverages a neural network to predict the parameter update rule for each iteration. This per-parameter and state-aware update guides the optimizer towards a good solution in very few steps, converging in typically few steps. During training our approach only requires MoCap data of human poses, parametrized via SMPL. From this data the network learns a subspace of valid poses and shapes in which optimization is performed much more efficiently. The approach does not require any hard to acquire image-to-3D correspondences. At test time we only optimize the 2D joint re-projection error without the need for any further priors or regularization terms. We show empirically that this algorithm is fast (avg. 120ms convergence), robust to initialization and dataset, and achieves state-of-the-art results on public evaluation datasets including the challenging 3DPW in-the-wild benchmark (improvement over SMPLify (45%) and also approaches using image-to-3D correspondences).

Keywords: Human body fitting · 3D human pose · Inverse problem

1 Introduction

Recovering the 3D human pose and its shape from a single image is a long standing problem in computer vision with many downstream applications. To solve the problem, one has to reconstruct the parameters that characterize human pose and shape from indirect, low-dimensional image observations. Thus, this falls into the category of inverse problems which are generally ill-posed [12].

In recent years, the computer vision community has wholeheartedly embraced deep-learning based approaches to such problems. For the case of human shape

---

J. Song and X. Chen—Equal contribution.

Electronic supplementary material The online version of this chapter (https://doi.org/10.1007/978-3-030-58565-5_44) contains supplementary material, which is available to authorized users.

A. Vedaldi et al. (Eds.): ECCV 2020, LNCS 12365, pp. 744–760, 2020.
https://doi.org/10.1007/978-3-030-58565-5_44

Ours (green)

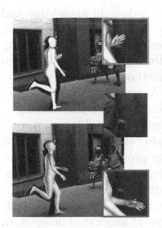

SOTA (red)

Fig. 1. textbfFitting by Learned Gradient Descent: We propose a gradient-based iterative optimization technique that combines the refinement capabilities of optimization techniques with the speed and robustness of deep-learning. The approach achieves state-of-the art performance in the most challenging in-the-wild setting, despite not having seen any image data at training time. Compared to the recent SoA regression-based method [18] (bottom), *ours* (top) can register fine details such as the lower extremities more precisely and is more robust to visual clutter, such as the pedestrians in the background. (Color figure online)

recovery from monocular images, deep neural networks have been successfully leveraged to regress the parameters of a generative human body model, such as SMPL [22], directly from pixel inputs [16,18,28,35]. Since it is hard to accurately annotate 3D shapes, very little training data for direct 3D supervision exists (the largest in-the-wild dataset consists of only 60 short sequences [24]). Hence, many approaches like [16] attempt to leverage large-scale 2D keypoint annotations of in-the-wild images via proxy-objectives such as minimizing the distance between ground-truth 2D joint positions and the re-projection of the network predictions.

Recent work [18] proposes to deploy iterative optimization in-the-loop to generate 3D pseudo-labels for further training. While improving over direct regression, the scalability of this approach is limited since the iterative optimization has to be run until convergence for each training sample. Furthermore, the accuracy of these pseudo-labels remains bounded by the existing optimization method.

In contrast, iterative gradient descent-based optimization methods search for the unknown parameters of the model that best match the available measurements. In the case of human shape recovery, this also often involves minimizing the 2D re-projection error of the rendered human shape with learned priors [7,10,15,20,29]. These approaches suffer from the non-linear, non-convex, and large-scale nature of the inversion. In consequence, the optimization process tends to be slow and finding good solutions remains very challenging. One reason can be seen in the reliance on multiple regularization and prior terms which have to be traded-off against each other, leading to many possible sub-optimal minima. Furthermore, improving results typically requires domain knowledge and incorporation of heuristics which impact generality. Despite these difficulties, iterative optimization has many appealing properties such as: 1) not requiring any images with 3D annotation for training, 2) better registration of details to 2D observations compared to end-to-end regression methods via iterative refinement, and 3) no overfitting to a specific dataset. A well tuned optimization algorithm should perform consistently well on different datasets and domains.

In this paper, we take motivation from the optimization and learning communities [1,2,4,9] and propose a learning-based update rule for a gradient-based iterative algorithm to fit a human model to 2D. The proposed technique combines the accurate refinement capabilities of optimization techniques with the robustness of learning-based methods when training data is well distributed. Our goal is to make iterative optimization competitive when compared to state-of-the-art regression methods that rely on large amounts of annotated image data (Fig. 1).

More specifically, we replace the hand-crafted gradient descent update rule with a deep network that has been trained to predict per-parameter, state dependent parameter updates. We show that this allows for very efficient optimization. Intuitively, our approach can be seen as joint learning of i) a model prior, ii) regularization terms and iii) gradient prediction. That is, the network learns to generate parameter updates that allow the fitting algorithm to stay on the manifold of natural poses and shape as well as to recover from local minima. Hence, the optimizer can take larger, parameter-specific steps compared to standard gradient descent, leading to convergence in just a few iterations (typically ≤ 4 which on the same hardware equates to a speed-up of 500x compared to SMPLify [7], see Fig. 4). Importantly, at training time the method only requires a dataset of human poses and shapes (e.g., AMASS [23]) and does not use images during training. At inference, the algorithm optimizes the 2D re-projection error directly and does not require any further priors or regularization in order to converge. In summary we contribute:

- A novel iterative algorithm to fit the parameters of a human model to 2D observations via learned gradient descent.
- A data efficient way to learn the gradient mapping network, requiring only 3D Mocap data and no image-to-pose correspondences.
- Empirical evidence that demonstrates the method is fast, accurate and robust, achieving state-of-the-art results, especially on the most challenging in-the-wild setting (i.e., 3DPW dataset [24]).

2   Related Work

Our work is related to a large body of research in optimization, machine learning and vision-based pose estimation. Here we briefly review the most related works in human shape estimation and those at the intersection of learning and iterative gradient based optimization.

Human Shape Recovery from Natural Images

Deep neural networks have significantly advanced skeleton-based 3D human pose estimation from single images [25,26,33,41]. In order to obtain more fine-grained representations of the human body, parametric body models such as SCAPE [5] or SMPL [22] have been introduced to capture the 3D body pose (the skeleton) and its shape (the surface). More expressive models, including hands, feet and face, have recently been proposed [29,38]. Iterative optimization-based approaches have been leveraged for model-based human pose estimation. Early works in the area [10,13,32] proposed to estimate the parameters of the human model by leveraging silhouettes or 2D keypoints. In these approaches good correspondences are necessary which are sometimes provided via manual user intervention. More recently, the first fully automatic approach, SMPLify, was introduced by Bogo et al. [7]. Applying an off-the-shelf 2D keypoint detector [31], SMPLify iteratively fit the SMPL parameters to the detected 2D keypoints and several strong priors were employed to regularize the optimization process. Lassner et al. [20] leveraged hand-curated results from SMPLify to first train a denser keypoint detector and subsequently incorporate silhouette cues into the fitting procedure. In [29], a deep variational autoencoder was proposed as replacement for Gaussian mixtures as pose prior. [36] proposed to fit SMPL on the regressed volumetric representation obtained from deep networks. Generally speaking, the above model-fitting approaches are not real-time and require about one minute per image or longer. The solutions to the optimization problem are also very sensitive to the choice of the initialization and usually strong regularizing assumptions have to be made in such multi-step optimization pipelines, which can result in difficulty to tune algorithms.

On the other hand, direct parameter regression via neural networks has been explored as alternative means to the problem of 3D human pose and shape estimation [11,16,28,34,35,37,39,40]. Given a single RGB image, a deep network is used to regress the human model parameters. Due to the lack of datasets that contain images with full 3D shape ground truth annotations, these methods have focused on alternative supervision signals to guide the training. These include 2D keypoints, silhouettes, or part segmentation masks. However, such approaches still suffer from coarse estimation in terms of image-model alignment. At the same time, acquiring large amounts of data with image to 3D human shape ground truth correspondences is an extremely hard and cost intensive process. Recent work [18] proposes to include iterative optimization in the learning loop to automatically augment the dataset via pseudo-labelling. While demonstrating the promise of combining learning- and optimization-based approaches, the scalability of the approach remains bounded by the run-time speed and the accuracy of the existing optimization method itself. For each training iteration, the pseudo ground truth label is obtained by running the SMPLify method, which itself is slow and may get trapped in local minima even with good initialization.

Learned Gradient Descent for Inverse Problem

Recently research in different domains has suggested to interpret iterative optimization algorithms as unrolled neural networks with a set of inference and

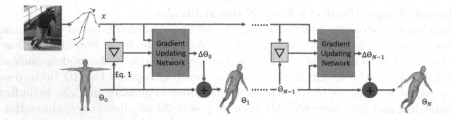

Fig. 2. Inference pipeline. Given a human image, the target 2D keypoints x are obtained from a joint detector. Θ_0 is initialized with zero values. After re-projection via Eq. 1, the error between predicted and observed measurements $\mathcal{L}(\Theta_0)$ is calculated, followed by computation of the partial derivative $\frac{\partial \mathcal{L}(\Theta_0)}{\partial \Theta_0}$, denoted by ∇. Together with the current state of Θ_0 and target x, the gradient ∇ is passed into the Gradient Updating Network to obtain the update term $\Delta\Theta_0$. Adding $\Delta\Theta_0$ to Θ_0, yields Θ_1. The whole process will continue until the last iteration N to attain an estimate Θ_N.

model parameters that can be learned jointly via back-propagation [1,2,4,9]. Andrychowicz et al. [4] proposed to leverage learned gradients in the context of classification tasks. In follow-up work [1,2] the concept has been advanced into a partially learned gradient scheme, applied to a non-linear tomographic inversion problem with simulated data. Most recently, Flynn et al. [9] introduced a CNN based framework for the task of novel view synthesis based on multi-plane images. Leveraging learned gradients this approach improves performance on challenging scene features such as object boundaries, thin structures, and scenes with high depth complexity. In this work, we adopt a hybrid approach that incorporates learning of the parameter update into an iterative model fitting algorithm. We model human shape generation as an inverse problem to be solved using a learned gradient descent algorithm. At inference time (see Fig. 2), this algorithm iteratively computes gradients of the current human model with regard to the input 2D detections. A network takes these partial derivatives together with the current parameter set as input and generates a per-parameter update rule for the human shape model. We empirically demonstrate that the neural network learns to generate parameter updates that allow the optimization method to stay on the manifold of natural poses and shapes and also to take large steps, thus requiring only a few iterations for convergence.

3   Method

Problem Setting

Our task is to reconstruct the full 3D mesh of human bodies from 2D observations (e.g. 2D keypoints extracted from images). The 3D human mesh is encoded by the statistical SMPL body model [22], which is a differentiable function that outputs a triangulated mesh $M(\theta, \beta)$ that takes as input the pose parameters $\theta \in \mathbb{R}^{23 \times 3}$ and the shape parameters $\beta \in \mathbb{R}^{10}$. Specifically, the template body vertices are first conditioned on β and θ, then the bones are articulated according to the joint rotations θ via forward kinematics, and finally the surface is deformed with linear blend skinning to return the body mesh $M \in \mathbb{R}^{N \times 3}$, with $N = 6890$ vertices. Conveniently, the 3D body joints $X \in \mathbb{R}^{k \times 3}$ of the model can be defined as a linear combination of the mesh vertices. A linear regressor W is usually pre-trained to map the vertices to k joints of interest, defined as $X = WM$. To re-project 3D joints to 2D, a weak-perspective camera model is employed. The camera model is parameterized by the global rotation $R \in \mathbb{R}^{3 \times 3}$ in axis-angle representation, translation $t \in \mathbb{R}^2$ and scale $s \in \mathbb{R}$. Thus the set of parameters that represent the reconstruction of a human body is expressed as a vector $\Theta = \{\theta, \beta, R, t, s\}$. Given Θ, the projection of 3D joints X to 2D is:

$$\hat{x} = s\Pi(RX(\theta, \beta)) + t, \tag{1}$$

where Π is an orthographic projection.

In this paper, we seek to solve the inverse problem associated with Eq. 1. That is, we wish to compute a set of parameters $\Theta = \{\theta, \beta, R, t, s\}$ that match the observed 2D keypoints x. Since the number of model parameters Θ is typically larger than the number of 2D measurements, this inverse problem is ill-posed and solving it usually requires additional priors and strong regularizers. Here we seek a method that finds good solutions without requiring such auxilliary measures.

Iterative Optimization with Explicit Regularization
In most inverse problems a closed-form map from observations to signal is intractable. Inverse problems are often solved via iterative optimization by minimization, e.g.:

$$\underset{\Theta}{\operatorname{argmin}} = \mathcal{L}(\Theta) + \Phi(\Theta), \tag{2}$$

where $\mathcal{L}(\Theta) = L_{reproj}(\hat{x}, x)$ is the data term measuring the agreement between predicted and observed measurements. More specifically, in our context, $\hat{x}$ are the projected 2D joints from SMPL parameters computed by Eq. 1. $\Phi(\Theta)$ is a prior term on Θ to regularize the optimization process via maximum a posteriori. Such non-linear optimization problems can be solved via iterative methods such as stochastic gradient descent. The update rule (with step size λ) is given by:

$$\Theta_{n+1} = \Theta_n + \lambda[\frac{\partial \mathcal{L}(\Theta_n)}{\partial \Theta_n} + \frac{\partial \Phi(\Theta_n)}{\partial \Theta_n}] \tag{3}$$

For example, in the seminal work of SMPLify by Bogo et al. [7] $\Phi(\Theta)$ corresponds to several prior terms defined on both θ and β. The priors are usually seperately pre-trained on fitted MoCap data and serve the purpose of penalizing implausible poses and shapes such as unnatural bends and physically impossible interpenetrations. The first step of SMPLify involves an optimization over the camera translation and body orientation, while keeping the model pose and shape fixed. After estimating the camera pose, SMPLify attempts to minimize Eq. 2 with a four-stage fitting procedure via a quasi-newton method. However, this whole process is very slow and remains prone to local minima. It is noteworthy that, the update step size λ is usually subject to either a manual schedule or obtained through a deterministic algorithm such as line search. That implies that the step sizes are always chosen according to a predefined routine.

Learned Gradient Descent for Human Shape Recovery

While finding good solutions with existing iterative optimization algorithms is challenging, they *can* produce very good registrations to unseen data *if* bad local minima are avoided. This is partially due to the iterative refinement and the absence of overfitting that can be problematic for regression methods. Motivated by recent ideas that connect the optimization and learning communities [1,2,4,9], we propose to replace the standard gradient descent rule with a learned per-parameter update:

$$\Theta_{n+1} = \Theta_n + \mathcal{N}_w(\frac{\partial \mathcal{L}(\Theta_n)}{\partial \Theta_n}, \Theta_n, x) \tag{4}$$

where $\mathcal{N}_w$ is a deep network parameterized by a set of weights w. The network processes the gradients and the current state of the model parameters to generate an update. Notice that λ and $\Phi(\Theta)$ have been merged into $\mathcal{N}_w$ to jointly learn parameter prior, regularization terms and gradient update rule. This enables $\mathcal{N}_w$ to generate adaptive, parameter-specific updates that allow the fitting algorithm to stay on the manifold of natural poses and shape and to recover from local minima. Furthermore, this process allows the optimization method to take large steps and hence to converge more quickly.

The inference process is illustrated in Fig. 2. Given a monocular image as input, an off-the-shelf body joint detector is run to attain the estimated target 2D keypoints x. For the first iteration, we initialize Θ_0 with zero values. After applying the re-projection process via Eq. 1, the error between predicted and observed measurements $\mathcal{L}(\Theta_0) = L_{reproj}(\hat{x}_0, x)$ is calculated. We then compute the partial derivative of the loss wrt the model parameters $\frac{\partial \mathcal{L}(\Theta_0)}{\partial \Theta_0}$. Together with the current state of Θ_0 and target x, the gradient $\frac{\partial \mathcal{L}(\Theta_0)}{\partial \Theta_0}$ is passed into the Gradient Updating Network to obtain the update term $\Delta\Theta_0$. Finally, Θ_0 is updated to Θ_1 by adding $\Delta\Theta_0$. The whole process will continue until the last iteration N to attain the estimated Θ_N. N is usually less than four iterations.

Training

For training, the *only* source of data we use is a large dataset of 3D meshes of human bodies of varying shape and in different poses [23]. The SMPL parameters are obtained by running MOSH [21] on different MoCap datasets. In order to ensure a fair comparison with other methods, we use the same subset as reported in [16,29]. Please refer to supplementary materials for details.

The training algorithm for a single sample is given in pseudo-code in Algorithm 1 and illustrated in Fig. 3. During training, we randomly sample the pose θ_{gt} and shape β_{gt} pair from the dataset, and re-project them with randomly generated camera extrinsics in order to obtain corresponding ground-truth 2D keypoints x_{gt}. For illustration purposes we unroll the N-iteration process in Fig. 3,

Algorithm 1 - Training scheme

$\theta_{gt}, \beta_{gt} \leftarrow$ sample from database
$R_{gt}, t_{gt}, s_{gt} \leftarrow$ randomly sample within feasible range
$\Theta_{gt} \leftarrow \{\theta_{gt}, \beta_{gt}, R_{gt}, t_{gt}, s_{gt}\}$
$X_{gt} \leftarrow WM(\theta_{gt}, \beta_{gt})$
$x_{gt} \leftarrow s_{gt}\Pi(R_{gt}X_{gt}(\theta_{gt}, \beta_{gt})) + t_{gt}$
$\Theta_0 \leftarrow \{\theta_0, \beta_0, R_0, t_0, s_0\} \leftarrow 0$
for $n = 0, ..., N - 1$ **do**
    $X_n \leftarrow WM(\theta_n, \beta_n)$
    $\hat{x}_n \leftarrow s_n\Pi(R_nX_n(\theta_n, \beta_n)) + t_n$
    $\mathcal{L}(\Theta_n) \leftarrow L_{reproj}(\hat{x}_n, x_{gt})$
    $\Delta\Theta_n \leftarrow \mathcal{N}_w(\frac{\partial\mathcal{L}(\Theta_n)}{\partial\Theta_n}, \Theta_n, x_{gt})$
    $\Theta_{n+1} \leftarrow \Theta_n + \Delta\Theta_n$
    $L_{\Theta_n} \leftarrow ||\Theta_n - \Theta_{gt}||_1$
end for

obtaining the full training architecture. More specifically, for each batch of training samples, we initialize Θ_0 with zero values. After re-projection Eq. 1, the error between predicted and ground-truth 2D measurements $\mathcal{L}(\Theta_0) = L_{reproj}(\hat{x}_0, x_{gt})$ is calculated. The partial derivative $\frac{\partial\mathcal{L}(\Theta_0)}{\partial\Theta_0}$ is then computed and fed as input to the Gradient Updating Network. The other inputs are the current state of Θ_0 and the target 2D measurements x. Once the gradient update term $\Delta\Theta_0$ is obtained, Θ is updated to Θ_1 by adding it to Θ_0. The whole process will continue until convergence to get Θ_N.

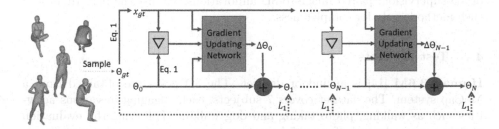

Fig. 3. Training scheme. For training, the *only* source of data we use is a pool of 3D meshes of human bodies of varying shape and pose. To generate a batch of training samples, we randomly sample the pose θ_{gt} and shape β_{gt} pair from the dataset. For each pair of θ_{gt} and β_{gt}, A camera poses (s_{gt}, R_{gt}, t_{gt}) is randomly sampled within feasible range. For the sample Θ_{gt}, its corresponding ground-truth 2D keypoints x_{gt} is obtained via re-projection Eq. 1. Θ_0 is initialized with zero values. After applying the re-projection Eq. 1, the partial gradient ∇_0 wrt Θ_0 is calculated based on the re-projection loss. Once the gradient update term $\Delta\Theta_0$ is obtained from Gradient Updating Network, by adding to Θ_0, Θ is updated to Θ_1. The whole process will continue till the last iteration N to get the Θ_N. The training loss is only based on the error between true Θ_{gt} and estimated Θ_n.

The training loss is only based on the error between true Θ_{gt} and estimated Θ_n. During training, in order to bridge the gap between perfect 2D joints x_{gt} obtained via re-projection to noisy 2D detections with missing joints from the CNN-based off-the-shelf detector, we randomly dropout some joints of x_{gt}. Importantly, we do not leverage any image data for training and the only form of supervision stems from MoCap data processed via MOSH [21].

4   Experiments

4.1   Training Data Comparison

For training, we *only* use a dataset of 3D meshes of human bodies of varying shape and in different poses [23]. For clarity, we emphasize that our primary goal is to boost the robustness and effectiveness of iterative optimization due to their importance to register SMPL meshes to new, entirely unseen data (e.g., to produce new datasets). Therefore, the most related method is SMPLify [7]. SMPLify leverages a learned prior and uses exactly the same MoCap data to train it. Thus, a direct comparison is fair. Note that our method can additionally be used as a standalone pose estimator and hence we compare to learning-based regression methods. All learning methods require stronger 3D supervision and much more data. For example, the current state-of-art approaches [16,18] utilize 6 additional datasets with 2D pose annotation (5.1M samples in total) and 2 additional datasets (4.9M samples in total) with 3D annotation. Since neither SMPLify nor ours leverages any image data at training or inference time, these can only be compared directly to methods that do not require the strongest form of 3D supervision: paired image-to-3D annotations. We list the performance of such methods only for completeness.

4.2   Test Datasets

Human 3.6M [14] is an indoor dataset. The 3D poses are obtained from a MoCap system. The dataset covers 7 subjects, each engaging in various activities such as walking, photo taking and dog walking. Following the evaluation protocol, we evaluate 1 of every 5 frames and only on the frontal camera (camera 3). We report the reconstruction error (MPJPE after procrustes alignment). Similar to other optimization based methods, we obtain 2D pose estimates from a CNN based pose detector (a stacked hourglass network [27] trained on MPI [3] and fine-tuned on the Human 3.6M training set).

3DPW [24] is a challenging outdoor dataset which provides 3D pose and shape ground-truth obtained by fusing information of IMU and 2D keypoint detections. It covers complex natural poses in-the-wild and is currently the best benchmark for real-world performance. Note that this dataset is *not* used for training and a pure hold-out test set for all methods. We report the 3D pose reconstruction error on the test set. Frames in which less than 6 joints are detected are discarded as in [17]. We use the 2D keypoints included in the dataset (from openpose [8]).

EHF [29]. The expressive hands and faces dataset (EHF) has 100 images with vertex level annotation of the whole human body. They are obtained first by fitting the SMPL-X model and then manually curated by an expert annotator. The dataset can be considered as dense pseudo ground-truth, according to its alignment quality. The pseudo ground-truth meshes allow to use a stricter vertex to-vertex (v2v) error metric, in contrast to the common paradigm of reporting 3D joint error, which does neither capture misalignment of the surface itself nor rotations along the bones. To the best of our knowledge, EHF is the only available real-world dataset with direct shape measurements (from 3D scans).

Table 1. Ablation on gradient components. Each entry represents an experiment including the gradient components labeled as target 2D pose (x), current estimated $\hat{\Theta}$, and unmapped gradient ($\nabla \hat{\Theta}$).

Input			Rec. Error
x	-	-	67.7
x	-	$\nabla \hat{\Theta}$	64.2
x	$\hat{\Theta}$	-	61.9
-	$\hat{\Theta}$	$\nabla \hat{\Theta}$	60.5
x	$\hat{\Theta}$	$\nabla \hat{\Theta}$	56.4

Table 2. Ablation on number of iterations. We also measure the effect of varying the number of iterations from 1 to 5 for training. The optimization converges around 4 iterations on average.

#Iterations	Rec. Error
1	66.3
2	62.1
3	57.2
4	56.6
5	56.4

4.3 Ablation and Iteration Studies

Inputs to the Gradient Update Network. In this experiment, we evaluate the importance of each of the input components for the Gradient Update Network. To this end we discard one or more of the components and measure the influence in terms of final accuracy. The experiment is conducted on the Human 3.6M test set. Results are shown in Table 1. When using only the target 2D pose x as input, the network is equivalent to a residual network that operates by directly lifting Θ from 2D keypoints. As expected, in this configuration the model performs poorly since no prior knowledge on the human model is incorporated. Adding additional inputs gradually increases performance with the best performance is achieved when all gradient update components are used. In the following experiments, we fix our setting to use all three input components.

Number of Iterations During Training. In Table 2 we measure the effect of varying the number of update iterations from 1 to 5 for each training sample. The experiment is also conducted on the Human 3.6M test set. Not surprisingly, the results improve as the number of iterations increases. We note that after four iterations there is no further improvement (we use four iterations in our experiments). Note that extrapolation beyond this training window is possible within reason (cf. Fig. 4).

Comparison with Direct Lifting from 2D Pose. We also compare to the baseline method proposed in [25], i.e., directly lifting 2D pose to 3D pose. The main difference is that direct lifting is non-iterative and does not take gradients as input. Its reconstruction error is 67.8, which is 15% worse than ours. This suggests that gradient-based refinement indeed leads to better and more detailed registration compared to simple lifting.

4.4   Comparison with Other Methods

We compare results with other state-of-art methods on the three datasets as introduced in Sect. 4.2.

Table 3. Evaluation on H3.6M. Mean reconstruction errors in mm. We compare with approaches that output a mesh of the human body. The lower half of the table contains methods that do not require image-to-3D annotations (such as ours). We achieve state-of-the-art performance.

Method	Image + 3D annotation	Rec. Error
Lasssner *et al.* [20]	Yes	93.9
Pavlakos *et al.* [30]	Yes	75.9
NBF [28]	Yes	59.9
HMR (with additional 3D data) [16]	Yes	56.8
SPIN (with additional 3D data) [18]	Yes	41.1
SMPLify [7]	No	82.3
SMPLify-X (with SMPL Body model) [29]	No	75.9
SMPLify (with GT 2D) [7]	No	71.1
HMR [16]	No	66.5
SPIN [18]	No	62.0
Ours	No	**56.4**

Human 3.6M [14]. We report the reconstruction error on Protocol 2 following [7]. Since our method does not use images for 3D fitting, it is only possible to directly compare to methods which output SMPL parameters from a single image and *do not* require image-to-3D paired data for training. As shown in Table 3, we outperform SMPLify [7] by a large margin, even when they fit to ground truth 2D keypoints. Figure 4 shows two representative examples of the progression of the reconstruction error as function of iterations. Compared to SMPLify, *ours* converges much quicker and more stable. The images in the inset provide insights into why this is the case. Our approach jointly manipulates global and body pose and arrives at a good solution in few steps. Note that the

steps in light blue indicate steps beyond the training window (N = 4). While the SMPLify (red) shows clear signs of the adaptive weighting of different loss terms, which can also be seen in the intermediate states, where first the global pose is adjusted and body pose is only optimized later (cf. Fig. 4, insets). Figure 4, right illustrates a case where SMPLify gets stuck in a bad local minima and fails to recover from it.

Ours also achieves a lower reconstruction error than state-of-the-art regression methods [16,18] if compared fairly to ours. That is we directly compare the setting in which these methods do not use image-to-3D paired information since our method does not have access to this additional data. We use the same 3D MoCap data that [16,18] use to train their pose priors. While we outperform HMR even in the paired setting, SPIN performs better when allowed to use additional data. However, we note that H3.6M is a controlled and relatively small dataset and is known to be prone to overfitting. Qualitative results shown

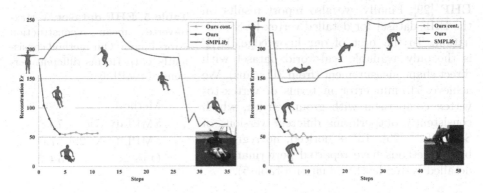

Fig. 4. Reconstruction error as function of iteration count. Two examples of fitting progression on the H3.6m test set. Compared to SMPLify (red), our inference converges quicker and is more stable. SMPLify either converges slowly or fails to avoid local minima. Insets show intermediate pose configurations. (Color figure online)

Table 4. Evaluation on 3DPW. Mean reconstruction errors in mm. Our method outperforms SMPLify by a significant margin. We achieve the state-of-art performance even compared with image based methods that use additional datasets with expensive image-to-3D annotations and 3D pseudo-labels in the case of [18].

Method	Image + 3D annotation	Rec. Error
HMR (with additional 3D data) [16]	Yes	81.3
Kanazawa *et al.* [17]	Yes	72.6
Arnab *et al.* [6]	Yes	72.2
Kolotorous *et al.* [19]	Yes	70.2
SPIN (with additional 3D data) [18]	Yes	59.2
SbMPLify [7]	No	106.1
Ours	No	**55.9**

in Fig. 5 show that regression methods are sensitive to scene clutter close to the person. Our results align better after iterative refinement.

3DPW [24]. This in-the-wild dataset is used solely for testing, hence a better indicator of real-world performance. While direct regression methods (HMR, SPIN) use the same MoCap data as ours *and* large amounts of additional annotated data, these methods exhibit a clear performance decrease on this dataset compared to H3.6M (see Table 4). In this challenging setting, we significantly outperform optimization methods that use the same data as ours (45% over SMPLify [7]). Furthermore, our method outperforms regression based methods (e.g., by 29% over HMR [16]), even in the setting where they are allowed to use additional 3D supervision. We also outperform the current state-of-art [18], which not only employs several datasets with image-to-3D labels but also leverages SMPLify to obtain pseudo 3D labels on a large scale dataset with 2D annotations.

EHF [29]. Finally, we also report results on the EHF dataset for detailed vertex level evaluation. To the best of our knowledge, EHF is the only available real-world dataset with direct shape measurement (from 3D scans). We achieve 54.7 mm error in terms of vertex-to-vertex comparison with ground truth, which consistently outperforms different versions of SMPLify [7,29]. To be noticed, no regression based methods have reported performance on detailed vertex level evaluation (Table 5).

Table 5. EHF dataset. Vertex-to-vertex mean reconstruction errors in mm. Our method consistently outperforms different versions of SMPLify.

Method	v-v
SMPLify [7]	73.8
SMPLify-X [29]	57.6
Ours	**54.7**

4.5 Qualitative Results

Figure 5 shows comparisons to regression based methods. The highlight depicts instances where iterative refinement (ours) better aligns details such as the lower limbs. Figure 6 shows more qualitative results of our approach from different datasets, demonstrating consistent behavior irrespective of the dataset.

4.6 Speed and Model Size

On the same hardware, our method converges on average in 120 ms, whereas SMPLify generally takes 1 to 2 min. This 500x speed-up is due to: **i)** fewer iterations (5 vs. 100) and **ii)** requiring only first order derivatives while SMPLify relies on second order methods. Our gradient updating network is lightweight, with 4.3M parameters and 8M FLOPs (0.008G) (Fig. 6).

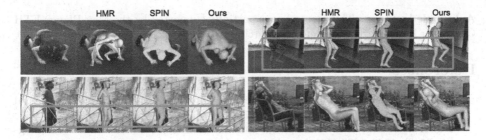

Fig. 5. Qualitative comparison with other methods. Our results align better with the 2D observations thanks to our iterative update scheme.

Fig. 6. Qualitative results. Human 3.6M (row 1), 3DPW (row 2), and EHF (row 3). The last row is the fitting results for a dancing video from the internet. We can see our algorithm generalizes well on random input sources.

5   Conclusion

We propose a novel optimization algorithm for 3D human body model fitting. We replace the normal gradient descent update rule, which depends on a hand-tuned step-size, with a deep network to predict per-parameter, state dependent updates. Our method significantly improves over the closest state-of-art, formed by non-convex optimization methods such as SMPLify, in terms of convergence, speed, and accuracy when using the same MoCap data. Accurately annotating 3D human shape in unconstrained natural environments is extremely challenging and will remain so for a long time. Hence, improved optimization based methods have the potential to provide more training data by fitting 2D annotated images.

Acknowledgement. This research was partially supported by the Max Planck ETH Center for Learning Systems and a research gift from NVIDIA.

References

1. Adler, J., Öktem, O.: Solving ill-posed inverse problems using iterative deep neural networks. Inverse Prob. **33**(12), 124007 (2017)
2. Adler, J., Öktem, O.: Learned primal-dual reconstruction. IEEE Trans. Med. Imaging **37**(6), 1322–1332 (2018)
3. Andriluka, M., Pishchulin, L., Gehler, P., Schiele, B.: 2D human pose estimation: new benchmark and state of the art analysis. In: Proceedings of the IEEE Conference on Computer Vision and Pattern Recognition, pp. 3686–3693 (2014)
4. Andrychowicz, M., et al.: Learning to learn by gradient descent by gradient descent. In: Advances in Neural Information Processing Systems, pp. 3981–3989 (2016)
5. Anguelov, D., Srinivasan, P., Koller, D., Thrun, S., Rodgers, J., Davis, J.: SCAPE: shape completion and animation of people. ACM Trans. Graph. (TOG) **24**, 408–416 (2005)
6. Arnab, A., Doersch, C., Zisserman, A.: Exploiting temporal context for 3D human pose estimation in the wild. In: Proceedings of the IEEE Conference on Computer Vision and Pattern Recognition, pp. 3395–3404 (2019)
7. Bogo, F., Kanazawa, A., Lassner, C., Gehler, P., Romero, J., Black, M.J.: Keep it SMPL: automatic estimation of 3D human pose and shape from a single image. In: Leibe, B., Matas, J., Sebe, N., Welling, M. (eds.) ECCV 2016. LNCS, vol. 9909, pp. 561–578. Springer, Cham (2016). https://doi.org/10.1007/978-3-319-46454-1_34
8. Cao, Z., Hidalgo, G., Simon, T., Wei, S.E., Sheikh, Y.: OpenPose: real-time multi-person 2D pose estimation using part affinity fields. arXiv preprint arXiv:1812.08008 (2018)
9. Flynn, J., et al.: DeepView: view synthesis with learned gradient descent. arXiv preprint arXiv:1906.07316 (2019)
10. Guan, P., Weiss, A., Balan, A.O., Black, M.J.: Estimating human shape and pose from a single image. In: 2009 IEEE 12th International Conference on Computer Vision, pp. 1381–1388. IEEE (2009)
11. Guler, R.A., Kokkinos, I.: HoloPose: holistic 3D human reconstruction in-the-wild. In: Proceedings of the IEEE Conference on Computer Vision and Pattern Recognition, pp. 10884–10894 (2019)
12. Hadamard, J.: Sur les problèmes aux dérivées partielles et leur signification physique. Princeton University Bulletin, pp. 49–52 (1902)
13. Hasler, N., Ackermann, H., Rosenhahn, B., Thormählen, T., Seidel, H.P.: Multilinear pose and body shape estimation of dressed subjects from image sets. In: 2010 IEEE Computer Society Conference on Computer Vision and Pattern Recognition, pp. 1823–1830. IEEE (2010)
14. Ionescu, C., Papava, D., Olaru, V., Sminchisescu, C.: Human3.6M: large scale datasets and predictive methods for 3D human sensing in natural environments. IEEE Trans. Pattern Anal. Mach. Intell. **36**(7), 1325–1339 (2013)
15. Joo, H., Simon, T., Sheikh, Y.: Total capture: a 3D deformation model for tracking faces, hands, and bodies. In: Proceedings of the IEEE Conference on Computer Vision and Pattern Recognition, pp. 8320–8329 (2018)
16. Kanazawa, A., Black, M.J., Jacobs, D.W., Malik, J.: End-to-end recovery of human shape and pose. In: Proceedings of the IEEE Conference on Computer Vision and Pattern Recognition, pp. 7122–7131 (2018)

17. Kanazawa, A., Zhang, J.Y., Felsen, P., Malik, J.: Learning 3D human dynamics from video. In: Proceedings of the IEEE Conference on Computer Vision and Pattern Recognition, pp. 5614–5623 (2019)
18. Kolotouros, N., Pavlakos, G., Black, M.J., Daniilidis, K.: Learning to reconstruct 3D human pose and shape via model-fitting in the loop. In: Proceedings of the IEEE International Conference on Computer Vision, pp. 2252–2261 (2019)
19. Kolotouros, N., Pavlakos, G., Daniilidis, K.: Convolutional mesh regression for single-image human shape reconstruction. In: Proceedings of the IEEE Conference on Computer Vision and Pattern Recognition, pp. 4501–4510 (2019)
20. Lassner, C., Romero, J., Kiefel, M., Bogo, F., Black, M.J., Gehler, P.V.: Unite the people: closing the loop between 3D and 2D human representations. In: Proceedings of the IEEE Conference on Computer Vision and Pattern Recognition, pp. 6050–6059 (2017)
21. Loper, M., Mahmood, N., Black, M.J.: MoSH: motion and shape capture from sparse markers. ACM Trans. Graph. (TOG) **33**(6), 220 (2014)
22. Loper, M., Mahmood, N., Romero, J., Pons-Moll, G., Black, M.J.: SMPL: a skinned multi-person linear model. ACM Trans. Graph. (TOG) **34**(6), 248 (2015)
23. Mahmood, N., Ghorbani, N., F. Troje, N., Pons-Moll, G., Black, M.J.: AMASS: archive of motion capture as surface shapes. In: The IEEE International Conference on Computer Vision (ICCV), October 2019. https://amass.is.tue.mpg.de
24. von Marcard, T., Henschel, R., Black, M.J., Rosenhahn, B., Pons-Moll, G.: Recovering accurate 3D human pose in the wild using IMUs and a moving camera. In: Ferrari, V., Hebert, M., Sminchisescu, C., Weiss, Y. (eds.) ECCV 2018. LNCS, vol. 11214, pp. 614–631. Springer, Cham (2018). https://doi.org/10.1007/978-3-030-01249-6_37
25. Martinez, J., Hossain, R., Romero, J., Little, J.J.: A simple yet effective baseline for 3D human pose estimation. In: Proceedings of the IEEE International Conference on Computer Vision, pp. 2640–2649 (2017)
26. Mehta, D., et al.: VNect: real-time 3D human pose estimation with a single RGB camera. ACM Trans. Graph. (TOG) **36**(4), 44 (2017)
27. Newell, A., Yang, K., Deng, J.: Stacked hourglass networks for human pose estimation. In: Leibe, B., Matas, J., Sebe, N., Welling, M. (eds.) ECCV 2016. LNCS, vol. 9912, pp. 483–499. Springer, Cham (2016). https://doi.org/10.1007/978-3-319-46484-8_29
28. Omran, M., Lassner, C., Pons-Moll, G., Gehler, P., Schiele, B.: Neural body fitting: unifying deep learning and model based human pose and shape estimation. In: 2018 International Conference on 3D Vision (3DV), pp. 484–494. IEEE (2018)
29. Pavlakos, G., et al.: Expressive body capture: 3D hands, face, and body from a single image. In: Proceedings of the IEEE Conference on Computer Vision and Pattern Recognition, pp. 10975–10985 (2019)
30. Pavlakos, G., Zhu, L., Zhou, X., Daniilidis, K.: Learning to estimate 3D human pose and shape from a single color image. In: Proceedings of the IEEE Conference on Computer Vision and Pattern Recognition, pp. 459–468 (2018)
31. Pishchulin, L., et al.: DeepCut: joint subset partition and labeling for multi person pose estimation. In: Proceedings of the IEEE Conference on Computer Vision and Pattern Recognition, pp. 4929–4937 (2016)
32. Sigal, L., Balan, A., Black, M.J.: Combined discriminative and generative articulated pose and non-rigid shape estimation. In: Advances in Neural Information Processing Systems, pp. 1337–1344 (2008)

33. Sun, X., Xiao, B., Wei, F., Liang, S., Wei, Y.: Integral human pose regression. In: Ferrari, V., Hebert, M., Sminchisescu, C., Weiss, Y. (eds.) ECCV 2018. LNCS, vol. 11210, pp. 536–553. Springer, Cham (2018). https://doi.org/10.1007/978-3-030-01231-1_33

34. Tan, V., Budvytis, I., Cipolla, R.: Indirect deep structured learning for 3D human body shape and pose prediction (2018)

35. Tung, H.Y., Tung, H.W., Yumer, E., Fragkiadaki, K.: Self-supervised learning of motion capture. In: Advances in Neural Information Processing Systems, pp. 5236–5246 (2017)

36. Varol, G., et al.: BodyNet: volumetric inference of 3D human body shapes. In: Ferrari, V., Hebert, M., Sminchisescu, C., Weiss, Y. (eds.) ECCV 2018. LNCS, vol. 11211, pp. 20–38. Springer, Cham (2018). https://doi.org/10.1007/978-3-030-01234-2_2

37. Varol, G., et al.: Learning from synthetic humans. In: Proceedings of the IEEE Conference on Computer Vision and Pattern Recognition, pp. 109–117 (2017)

38. Xiang, D., Joo, H., Sheikh, Y.: Monocular total capture: posing face, body, and hands in the wild. In: Proceedings of the IEEE Conference on Computer Vision and Pattern Recognition, pp. 10965–10974 (2019)

39. Xu, Y., Zhu, S.C., Tung, T.: DenseRaC: joint 3D pose and shape estimation by dense render-and-compare. In: Proceedings of the IEEE International Conference on Computer Vision, pp. 7760–7770 (2019)

40. Zheng, Z., Yu, T., Wei, Y., Dai, Q., Liu, Y.: DeepHuman: 3D human reconstruction from a single image. In: Proceedings of the IEEE International Conference on Computer Vision, pp. 7739–7749 (2019)

41. Zhou, X., Zhu, M., Leonardos, S., Derpanis, K.G., Daniilidis, K.: Sparseness meets deepness: 3D human pose estimation from monocular video. In: Proceedings of the IEEE Conference on Computer Vision and Pattern Recognition, pp. 4966–4975 (2016)

DDGCN: A Dynamic Directed Graph Convolutional Network for Action Recognition

Matthew Korban and Xin Li[✉]

Louisiana State University, Baton Rouge, USA
{mzadgh1,xinli}@lsu.edu

Abstract. We propose a Dynamic Directed Graph Convolutional Network (DDGCN) to model spatial and temporal features of human actions from their skeletal representations. The DDGCN consists of three new feature modeling modules: (1) Dynamic Convolutional Sampling (DCS), (2) Dynamic Convolutional Weight (DCW) assignment, and (3) Directed Graph Spatial-Temporal (DGST) feature extraction. Comprehensive experiments show that the DDGCN outperforms existing state-of-the-art action recognition approaches in various testing datasets.

Keywords: Action modeling and recognition · Graph Convolutional Network · Dynamic Spatiotemporal Graph

1 Introduction

Human action recognition is an active research topic that attracted great attention in recent years [34]. It has broad applications in video analysis and annotation, content retrieval, human-computer interaction, virtual reality, and so on. However, action recognition remains challenging when the videos have noisy background with complex occlusion or illumination conditions, changing camera view angles, or inconsistency between individuals' motions and their semantics (e.g., different people could perform semantically similar motions differently). The majority of action recognition and analysis algorithms directly model action features on images using deep Convolutional Neural Networks (CNNs) [6]. But image-based approaches are usually sensitive to the aforementioned noisy background, occlusions, and different camera viewpoints. Another modality to model human actions is through human skeletons. The skeleton modality has some advantages over the image modality for its more compact representation, better robustness against occlusion and viewpoint change, and higher expressive power in capturing features in both temporal and spatial domains [18]. An appropriate way to represent human skeletons is using graphs where skeleton joints and

Electronic supplementary material The online version of this chapter (https://doi.org/10.1007/978-3-030-58565-5_45) contains supplementary material, which is available to authorized users.

© Springer Nature Switzerland AG 2020
A. Vedaldi et al. (Eds.): ECCV 2020, LNCS 12365, pp. 761–776, 2020.
https://doi.org/10.1007/978-3-030-58565-5_45

bones are defined as graph nodes and edges respectively. Then to extract features from graphs one can use the Graph Convolutional Network (GCN), whose effectiveness is demonstrated in recent action recognition work [30].

Many GCN-based action recognition approaches use multi-stream networks to process spatial and temporal information of skeleton graphs separately [8, 33], which are usually complex and computationally costly. Recently, the *Spatial-Temporal (ST) graph* is introduced [30] to represent the skeletal graph sequence. A key advantage of using the ST graph is its capability to build a single end-to-end network that comes with better efficiency. Nevertheless, GCN-based action recognition methods still have their own limitations. Our observations are that solving the following two issues could enhance the performance of GCN in action recognition. First, there are spatial-temporal correlations between different parts of a human skeleton. Exploring such correlation patterns helps improve the modeling and recognition of actions. But such correlations are dynamic and varied for different human actions in both spatial and temporal domains. Hence, extracting these correlations effectively is difficult. The standard convolutional operations commonly adopted in traditional GCN [30] are static and only describes spatial correlations between neighboring nodes, thus, cannot capture such dynamic spatial-temporal correlations properly. Second, the spatial hierarchical structure of skeletons and the temporal sequential properties of motions both encode order information that is important in action recognition. But most existing ST graph models [30] describe the actions using undirected graphs, which cannot capture such order information.

To tackle these issues, we propose an end-to-end *Dynamic Directed Graph Convolutional Network* (DDGCN), to recognize human actions on ST graphs. We develop three new modules that can adaptively learn the spatiotemporal correlations and model spatial and temporal order information in actions:

Dynamic Convolutional Sampling (DCS). In action ST graphs, the relationship between spatially or temporally correlated joints provides useful information. We call this relationship *ST correlations* and describe it using a feature vector $f_{ST}(v)$ on each node v. We compute $f_{ST}(v)$ using a convolution of shared kernel weights W on an ST graph node v and its neighboring node set $B(v)$. $B(v)$ includes v's spatiotemporal correlated nodes. We observe that *ST-correlations* among nodes, and hence $B(v)$, are varied for different actions. Hence, unlike existing approaches, we propose to dynamically model such ST-correlations and compute each node's neighboring node set from the data. We design a novel Dynamic Convolutional Sampling (DCS) module (Sect. 3.2) to define B adaptively using ST correlations explored in different actions.

Dynamic Convolutional Weights (DCW). To perform an element-wise ordered convolution within the neighbor $B(v)$ of a node v, we need to assign the learned weights W (of the convolution kernels) to v's neighboring nodes. However, the spatial order of neighboring nodes in a graph is often ambiguous. To make our proposed GCN order-invariant, we develop a Dynamic Convolutional Sampling (DCW) module (Sect. 3.3) to compute the order of weights W in an adaptive and dynamic procedure.

Directed Spatial-Temporal Graph (DSTG) Features. The inputs to DDGCN are ST graphs created by spatial and temporal connections in actions. However, existing ST graphs are usually designed as undirected graphs [30], which cannot capture spatial and temporal order information effectively. However, such order information encodes important attributes of actions. Hence, we propose to use a Directed Spatial-Temporal Graph (DSTG), and develop a DSTG feature extraction module to capture such order information and make the action features more (spatially) structure-aware and (temporally) order-aware.

The main **contributions** of this work are as follows:

- We propose a new Dynamic Directed GCN (DDGCN) architecture to model the spatial and temporal correlations effectively in human actions. Our comprehensive experiments showed that DDGCN outperforms existing state-of-the-art approaches on various public benchmarks.
- We develop two new modules, DCS and DCW, to make DDGCN dynamic and action-adaptive. These new modules can effectively capture ST correlations exhibited among non-adjacent joints.
- We develop a new DSTG feature extraction module to enhance the action feature modeling by including spatial-temporal order information.

2   Related Work

Action recognition algorithms can be classified based on data modalities they run on. The majority of action recognition methods model actions on image sequence directly. Accordingly, they have developed various strategies based on handcrafted features [15,26,31], Convolutional Neural Network (CNN) [2,9,27], or Generative Adversarial Network (GAN) [14,25,29] to perform action recognition. However, using only appearance modality such as RGB images has its limitations including high inference of background, high dimensional inputs, sensitivity to image transformations, and low expressive capability.

To enhance the expressive capability of the appearance modality, some researchers add a new depth dimension to the modality to help extract features from actions. Kamel et al. [8] proposed an Action-Fusion network using both depth maps and posture data based on three CNNs defined on different modalities. Zhang et al. [33] used a multi-stream deep neural network to learn the motion attributes based on depth and joints inputs, and then represented the motions based on the combination of their attributes. However, depth images are sensitive to background inference and local transformations.

Compared with the depth images, motion flows are less sensitive to background inference and has a greater expressive capability. Some recent studies aimed to effectively compute motion flows. Piergiovanni et al. [16] proposed a method to reduce the computational cost of generating optical flows by capturing the flow within the model where the flow parameters are iteratively optimized by jointly learning other CNN model parameters. Sun et al. [22] designed a compact motion representation named Optical Flow guided Feature (OFF) that allows the CNN to extract the spatial-temporal information required for computing the flow between frames. Despite its better reliability, the motion flow is in general expensive to compute and still has limited capability in modeling moving background and dynamic motions.

The skeleton is a compact and expressive modality, and is insensitive to dynamic background and changing camera viewpoint. Li et al. [13] suggested an approach to capture richer motion-specific dependencies by using an encoder-decoder structure. The network automatically creates actional and structural links representing motions where each encoder-decoder block is called as actional-structural graph convolution network. Si et al. [20] proposed a method to extract high-level spatial-temporal features using a novel Attention Enhanced Graph Convolutional LSTM Network. The network captures co-occurrence relationship between spatial and temporal domains where the spatial features extracted by the GCN is fed to the LTSM to extract temporal dependencies.

3   Methodology

3.1   Overview

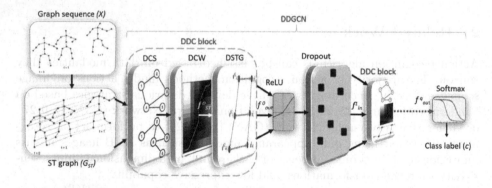

Fig. 1. An overview of the proposed action recognition pipeline.

The main pipeline of our proposed end-to-end action recognition pipeline DDGCN is illustrated in Fig. 1. Given an action sequence X, DDGCN outputs its action class label $c \in \{0, 1, ..., C\}$, C being the number of classes. Let action X be a sequence of skeletal graphs $X = \{G_t, t = 1, 2, ..., T\}$, where each skeletal graph in time t, $G_t = \{V_t, E_t^S\}$ consists of node (joint) set $V_t = \{v_k \in R^3, k = 0, 1, ..., m\}$ and spatial edge (bone) set $E_t^S = \{v_i^t v_j^t | (i, j) \in H\}$, where m is the skeletal node number. Here H is the set of bones (spatial edges) connecting joints (nodes) in a static human body skeleton template; subscripts i and j are the indices of joints, t is the index of the time frame, and T is the length of action sequence.

Spatial-Temporal Graph Construction. From a skeletal graph sequence, we construct an ST graph $G_{ST} = (V, E)$, following the notation given in [30], to store all the skeletal joints and their spatial and temporal relationship. Specifically, nodes $V = \{v\}$ correspond to skeletal joints and are connected by edges E following two rules. (1) Spatially, joints on the same skeleton are connected by spatial edges E^S. (2) Temporally, each node and its counterparts in the previous and next frames are connected by temporal edges, i.e., $\{v_i^t v_i^{t+1}\} \subset E^T$.

Dynamic Directed Convolutional (DDC). The DGCNN takes the ST graph as its input, and builds the feature maps F_{out} using multiple DDC blocks (Fig. 1). Each DDC block consists of (1) two dynamic convolutional modules, namely, *Dynamic Convolutional Sampling (DCS)* and *Dynamic Convolutional Weight (DCW)* assignment, and (2) a *Directed Spatial-Temporal Graph (DSTG)* feature extraction module that captures the spatial-temporal order information. The last, say q-th, DDC block outputs a probability feature vector f_{out}^q, and it is finally converted to a resultant one-hot vector c through a softmax operator.

3.2   Dynamic Convolutional Sampling (DCS)

Adjacent sub-parts of a human body are often correlated in human actions. Meanwhile, in many actions, some non-adjacent sub-parts are also correlated. Figure 2 illustrates an example of running motion, where arm and leg joints exhibit similar spatial-temporal patterns and are correlated. But ST correlations of sub-parts are varied in different actions. So they need to be captured dynamically according to the data. Dai et al. [5] developed a procedure to find the non-local neighbors of a given pixel in an image. Inspired by this, we have generalized this idea to graphs to develop a Dynamic Convolutional Sampling (DCS) module to identify correlated non-adjacent nodes.

DCS runs on a static graph G_0 defined by the given skeleton template. In other words, G_0 is from a specific time frame of the ST-graph G_{ST}. For each node v in a G_0, we first define its *correlative nodes* on edges connecting v and its neighbors. Note that v's neighboring nodes could contain not only its adjacent nodes in G_0, but also other non-adjacent nodes that are correlated (i.e., exhibiting correlated motion patterns). We initiate v's *neighbor list $B(v)$* with its adjacent nodes in the G_0, then the *dynamic convolutional sampling* (DCS) algorithm will update $B(v)$ to include those non-adjacent nodes according to correlated patterns exploited from action X. Specifically, the DCS computes the feature values on each node v_i in two steps. (1) First, we detect all the correlative node pairs $\{(v_i, v_j)\}, v_i, v_j \in G_0$, then we include those non-adjacent nodes to each node v_i's neighboring set $B(v_i)$ accordingly. We connect each v_i and its newly included non-adjacent neighbor v_j using a new edge. The update on $B(v_i)$ is done by performing a dynamic sampling procedure on v_i's non-adjacent correlative nodes. This dynamic procedure adaptively samples v_i's correlative nodes indexes and update their order using an index shift (offset). We use a function p_i to indicate the sampling for v_i, and Δp_i to denote an index shift. So $p_i(B(v_i)) + \Delta p_i(B(v_i))$ orders all the nodes $v_j \in B(v_i)$ and outputs a list of indexes (a permutation of these nodes). We iteratively update the order of v_i's neighboring nodes to find a better ordering, or offsets, such that under the

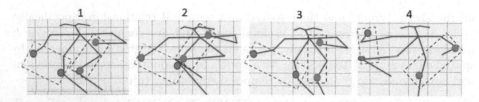

Fig. 2. Sample frames of a running motion, in which correlated patterns can be found on non-adjacent nodes

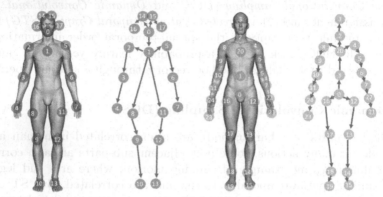

(a) Skeletal graph template from [4] (b) Skeletal graph template of [17]

Fig. 3. Our two (directed) skeletal graph representations, where the joint indexing follows (a) [4] and (b) [17].

new neighbor sampling, the recognition accuracy improves, namely, the recognition loss L decreases. (2) Second, on each edge connecting v_i and its neighbor $v_j \in B(v_i)$, we aggregate the correlative information indicating relative information of node v_i with respect to v_j to get the *correlative features*. Such correlative features can be defined as $f(v_i, p_i(B(v_i)) + \Delta p_i(B(v_i)))$ with respective to node v_i and its neighbor $v_j = p_i(B(v_i)) + \Delta p_i(B(v_i))$.

This **DCS Algorithm** can be summarized as follows.

1) initialize the static graph G_S following a skeleton template, and initialize indexes of all the nodes accordingly;
2) initialize neighbor sampling: for $\forall v_i \in G_S$, create its initial ordered neighboring set $p_i(B(v_i))$ in two steps:
   - create an ordered node set O_i including all the other nodes in the graph sorted by their graph distance to v_i. When two nodes v_j and v_r have the same graph distance (e.g., both are r-hop away from v_i), then sort them based on their initialized indexes;
   - given a kernel size r, pick the first r nodes from O_i, these nodes form the ordered neighboring set in this step $p_i(B(v_i))$;
3) update sampling neighbors: $\forall v_i$, update the index offsets and neighbor sampling by learning optimal offsets Δp_i that reduces recognition loss L.

Finally, on G_{ST}, the feature map f_{ST} is computed through a graph convolution following Eq. (1):

$$f_{ST}(v_i) = \sum_{v_j \in B(v_i)} w(v_i) \cdot (p_i(v_j) + \Delta p_i(v_j)), \qquad (1)$$

where i and j are indices for the central and neighboring sampling nodes respectively, B is the dynamic neighboring sampling nodes set, w is the dynamic weight function, p_i is the dynamic neighboring sampling function and Δp_i is the offset sampling function.

3.3   Dynamic Convolutional Weights

Both CNN and GCN extract features from input data by performing convolutions. On an image, each pixel's neighboring pixels are spatially ordered and the convolution kernel weights are learned following the same order. On a graph, however, each node's adjacent nodes are often unordered, and the number of neighbors could vary. To make our graph convolution order-invariant and valence-insensitive, we develop a DCW weight assignment module to order the computed convolution weights adaptively.

Inspired by [7] that aligns/re-orders weights for each pixel's neighboring pixels on images in CNN's convolutions, we propose a DCW assignment scheme to compute the order/assignment of weights in W on graph nodes. This makes the convolution order-insensitive; and also improves the GCN performance.

Specifically, given a node v and its neighboring nodes $B(v) = \{v_i, i = 1, \ldots, K\}$, where K is the size of neighboring nodes, our DCW assignment re-orders the kernel weights $W = \{w_i \in \mathcal{R}^3, i = 1, \ldots, r\}$ so that w_i is dynamically assigned to the corresponding node v_i. We compute this assignment as a $r \times 2$ matrix $P_v = DTW_{path}(W, B(v))$ that minimizes the distance between the two vectors $B(v)$ and the re-ordered W. The first column in P_v defines the ordered indices of elements in W, and the second column indicates the selected elements and their order in $B(v)$. We compute P_v, using the Dynamic Time Warping (DTW) algorithm [1].

With this dynamically computed P_v, W is adjusted according to $B(v)$, making the GCN convolution order-insensitive, and also, capturing the feature patterns in $B(v)$ more effectively.

The DCW assignment naturally handles the varied size of $B(v)$ through this assignment. While the kernel size r is fixed, the size of $B(v)$, denoted as K could change. Note that K is v's valence plus the size of its non-adjacent correlated vertex set. If K is larger than r, then the top-r significant nodes will be considered (using the DTW algorithm) while the others ignored. This flexibility allows us to use shared fixed-size kernels to have a fully-connected layer without over-adjusting the hyperparemeters [24].

3.4   Directed Spatial-Temporal Graph

We design a Directed Spatial-Temporal Graph (DSTG) feature extraction module to enhance the initial features f_{ST} obtained from the DCS and DCW modules. DSTG considers the spatial and temporal order information of actions which follow hierarchical (spatial) structure of human skeleton and sequential (temporal) properties of human motions respectively. Unlike existing approaches such as [19] that incorporate spatial and temporal order information using 3D joint/bone coordinates, the DSTG uses a high-dimension feature vector pointing from the feature vector of a joint v_i to the feature vector of its correlative joint v_j. The advantage of our method is that it can jointly learn bones and temporal high dimensional features using the spatial-temporal (ST) representation on the ST graph through an end-to-end network. For each node v_i we assign a feature vector $F_i = \{f_i^J, f_i^B, f_i^T\}$ which is the concatenation of three features vectors of joint features f_i^J, bone features f_i^B and temporal features f_i^T.

Directed Spatial Graph. We model the human body skeleton following standard templates. Two widely used skeletal graph templates are from [3] and [17]. Existing ST graphs are developed to be undirected. Based on observations we discussed previously, modeling spatial and temporal information in order is beneficial. Therefore, we change these undirected graphs to directed graphs. We define bone directions following a breadth-first search traversal from the root. The resultant edge directions are illustrated in Fig. 3. The hierarchical structure of skeleton joints is represented as directed bone vectors connecting adjacent joints. Each joint v_i is spatially correlated to its parent node v_{i-1} with a bone $b_i = \overrightarrow{v_{i-1}v_i}$. In this hierarchical structure, movement of a parent joint usually affects its children joints. In the opposite direction, the relationship may not be the same though. Following these bone vectors, we define the **bone features** as $f_i^B = \overrightarrow{f_{i-1}f_i} = f_{i-1} - f_i$, where f_i and f_{i-1} are feature vectors of node v_i and its parent v_{i-1}.

Directed Temporal Graph. Temporal sequence information in actions are important attributes, sometimes referred to as *motion trajectory* [32], in building action features. The temporal sequence order in an ST graph can be defined by directed edges connecting a joint and its counterpart in the next time frame. Such information has not been properly modeled in existing ST graph based approaches. To exploit such information, in ST graphs we calculate the **temporal features** f_i^T for each node v_i by $f_i^T = f_i^t - f_i^{t-1}$ where f_i^t and f_i^{t-1} are feature vectors of the node v_i in the current frame with respect to the previous frame.

3.5   Network Architecture

DDC Block. We compose the DCS, DCW, and DSTG modules to form a DDC block, and build the DDGCN pipeline by integrating multiple DDC blocks, as shown in Fig. 4. The first DDC block DDC_0 takes in an ST skeleton sequence,

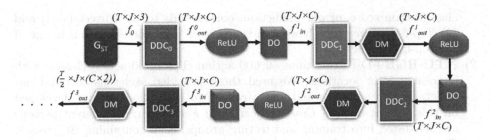

Fig. 4. The DDGCN architecture consisting of DDC blocks, Dropout (DO) layers, Dimension Modifier (DM) and ReLU.

$f_0 \in \mathcal{R}^{T \times J \times 3}$, composed from an ST-graph, where T and J are frame and joint numbers and 3 indicates the 3D coordinates. DDC_0 outputs the feature maps $f_{out}^0 \in \mathcal{R}^{T \times J \times C}$ where C is the channel size. The ST-graph is processed by the DCS to produce dynamic neighboring sets for nodes, upon which the DCW is applied to create ST correlations f_{ST} and then the final features f_{out} are created by the DSTG module. The output features from a DDC block is processed by a ReLU layer then regularized by a DropOut (DO) layer to prevent over-fitting.

Composing Multiple DDC Blocks. We then build our DDGCN pipeline using multiple (9 in the current implementation) DDC blocks, as shown in Fig. 4. Except for the block DDC_0, a subsequent q-th DCC block DDC_q takes in a feature map $f_{in}^q \in \mathcal{R}^{T \times J \times C}$ and outputs a feature map $f_{out}^q \in \mathcal{R}^{T' \times J \times C'}$, where C and C' are the channel sizes. $T' = \frac{T}{2}$ if $q = 3k, k = \{1, 2\}$ and $T' = T$ for other q values, $C' = C \times 2$ if $q = 3k, k = 1, 2, \ldots$ and $C' = C$ for other q values. The dimension of the DCC output is controlled by a Dimension Modifier (DM).

Network Parameters. Our current implementation has 9 DDC blocks. The dimension for $f_{o}^i ut$ for $i = 1, 2, 3$ is $(300, 18, 64)$; for $i = 4, 5, 6$ and $i = 7, 8, 9$, they are $(150, 18, 128)$ and $(75, 18, 256)$, respectively. In our network, the learning rate, dropout probability, and kernel size are 0.01, 0.5 and 3 respectively.

4   Experimental Results

4.1   Datasets and Evaluation Metrics

We evaluated our proposed action recognition algorithm on two public datasets.

1) **Kinect** [10] contains around $300,000$ video clips retrieved from YouTube. The videos cover 400 human action classes and each clip is 30 seconds. The joint locations were extracted from the video clips using the open-source algorithm OpenPose [4]. Following the commonly adopted evaluation in recent action recognition algorithms on this dataset, among these samples we used $240,000$ for training and $20,000$ for testing, and to evaluate the recognition accuracy we used *two metrics*: (1) *Top-1 accuracy* (i.e., how often the highest

classification score, or our prediction, corresponds to the correct label) and (2) *Top-5 accuracy* (i.e., how often the correct label corresponds is in one of the top-five predictions).

2) **NTU-RGB+D** [17] contains 56,000 action clips in 60 action classes, with annotated joint locations. We used these provided skeletons to build our skeletal graph sequence and ST-graphs. Two evaluation metrics developed on this dataset are: (a) *Cross-Subject (CS) Evaluation*: 40 different persons are separated into training and testing groups, each containing 20 persons. The training and testing sets have 40,320 and 16,560 samples, respectively. *Cross-View (CV) Evaluation*: samples from two cameras-views are used for training, and samples from another camera-view are used for testing. The training and testing sets have 37,920 and 18,960 samples, respectively.

Table 1. Comparing action recognition accuracy of our approach with that of other state-of-the-art approaches on NTU-RGB+D [17] dataset.

Metric	DDGCN (ours)	[18]	[20]	[19]	[21]	[23]	[35]	[30]	[11]	[12]
CS	**91.05%**	89.90%	89.20%	88.5%	84.8%	83.5%	81.8%	81.50%	79.6%	83.1%
CV	**97.14%**	96.10%	95.00%	95.1%	92.4%	89.8%	89.0%	88.30%	84.8%	74.3%

Table 2. Comparing action recognition accuracy of our approach with that of other state-of-the-art approaches on Kinect [10] dataset.

Metric	DDGCN (ours)	[18]	[19]	[30]	[12]
top-1	**38.12%**	36.9%	36.1	30.7%	20.3%
top-5	**60.79%**	59.6%	58.7	52.8%	40.0%

4.2   Comparison with Existing Methods on Benchmarks

On the aforementioned benchmarks, we compared our method with existing state-of-the-art methods, including d-GCN (CVPR19) [18], LSTM-GCN (CVPR19) [20], 2S-GCN (CVPR19) [19], ST-TSL (ECCV18) [21], DPRL (CVPR18) [23], Bayesian-GCN (ICCV19) [35], ST-GCN (AAAI18) [30], LSTM-CNN (CVPR17) [11], and T-CNN (CVPR17) [12]. The NTU-RGB+D results are shown in Table 1, and the Kinect results are shown in Table 2. Note that the performance of some approaches is only available on NTU-RGB+D dataset, so Table 2 has a shorter list of compared methods. In both benchmarks, our proposed DDGCN outperforms the existing methods in recognition accuracy.

For qualitative (visual) examination and comparison, we also randomly selected a set of testing action samples from the benchmark (the Kinect dataset) and illustrate the results from DDGCN (ours), ST-GCN [30], d-GCN [18], and 2S-GCN [19] (only these papers released their codes). For example, we picked the videos with indexes number $30 \times k, k = 1, \ldots,$ so actions #30, #60, ... from the Kinect dataset and perform the comparison. Some recognition results are shown in Table 3. Some of these actions are and their recognition results are visualized in Fig. 5, and more are provided in the supplemental video.

Table 3. Comparing our DDGCN with other methods on randomly selected sample actions from the Kinect dataset. The actions with ground truth labels are listed on the left column; each method's results are reported in the table.

Action Sequence	DDGCN	ST-GCN [30]	d-GCN [18]	2S-GCN [19]
class #30 (bookbinding)	**#30**	#30	#30	#137
class #60 (clean and jerk)	**#60**	#60	#60	#60
class #90 (decorating Christmas)	**#90**	#315	#15	#90
class #120 (exercising arm)	**#120**	#224	#217	#372
class #150 (headbanging)	#96	#353	#150	#150
class #180 (krumping)	**#180**	#180	#31	#180

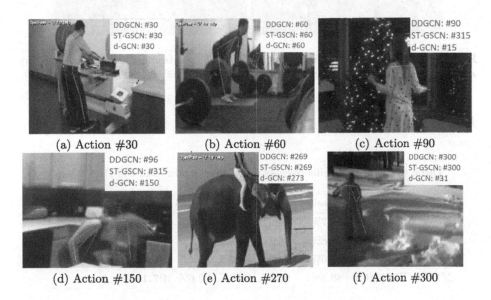

(a) Action #30   (b) Action #60   (c) Action #90

(d) Action #150   (e) Action #270   (f) Action #300

Fig. 5. Recognition of action samples (a) #30 (bookbinding), (b) #60 clean and jerk, (c) #90 (decorating Christmas tree), (d) #150 (headbanging), (e) #270 (riding elephant), and (f) #300 (shoveling snow) from the Kinect dataset [10].

4.3 Real-Time Experiments

We also conducted our real-time experiments by having a volunteer performing actions defined in the Kinect dataset. Some comparison results are illustrated in Fig. 6, and more results are provided in the supplementary video.

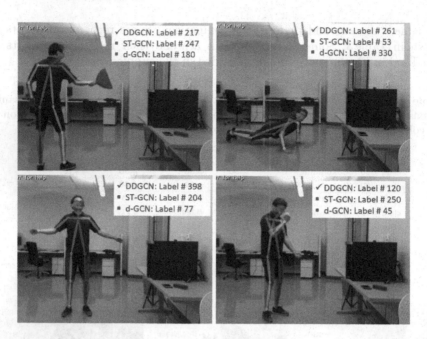

Fig. 6. Recognizing user-performed actions #217 (plastering), #261 (pushing up), #398 (yawning), and #120 (exercising arm), following actions defined in Kinect [10].

4.4   Ablation Study

Table 4. Comparing effectiveness of different modules in the DDC block.

Dataset/Models	Baseline	DCS	DCW	DSTG	DCS + DCW +DSTG
Kinect/top-1	30.7%	34.6%	32.1%	35.5%	**38.12%**
Kinect/top-5	52.8%	55.3%	54.6%	58.1%	**60.79%**
NTU-RGB+D/CS	81.5%	84.5%	81.9%	85.4%	**91.05%**
NTU-RGB+D/CV	88.3%	90.3%	89.4%	92.6%	**97.14%**

We designed an ablation study to evaluate the effectiveness of different components in the DDC block and also their combinations. We choose [30] as the Baseline, where standard convolutional layers and GCN blocks are used. Our proposed DDGCN is designed based on three new modules DCS, DCW, and DSTG. The recognition results are reported in Table 4. From these results, we can see that incorporating DCS, DCW, and DSTG brings 3.9%, 1.4% and 4.8% performance gains respectively for the Kinect/top-1. On other datasets/metrics, these components demonstrate similar performance improvement. Using the full DDC block yields the best accuracy.

4.5   Recognition of Incomplete Actions

Real-world videos often contain incomplete actions. Occlusion, fast motion, changing illumination, or hardware noise could result in blocked body parts, missing frames, or incomplete action sequences [28]. Many existing methods were not designed to address such incomplete action data specifically and cannot recognize them properly. Incomplete actions can sometimes be ambiguous, as similar motion subroutines could exist in different actions, and without a long enough sequence, sometimes they cannot be effectively differentiated. Our DGCNN can enhance the extraction of Spatial-Temporal dependencies and order information. Hence, it could tackle incomplete actions more reliably.

We intentionally removed some frames in the benchmark action videos and conduct experiments to compare our method's recognition performance. We simulated three types of incompleteness: (1) missing frames at the beginning of the motion, (2) missing frames at the end, and (3) random missing frames in the sequence. Different levels of data incompletion are tested on the NTU-RGB+D/CS dataset; each testing experiment run on $16.5k$ action samples.

We compared our algorithm with three other methods d-GCN (CVPR19) [18], 2S-GCN (CVPR19) [19] and ST-GCN (AAAI18) [30], whose source codes were released. The experimental results on the aforementioned three incompleteness types are reported in Tables 5 and 6. The results indicate the better robustness of the DDGCN over the existing approaches, especially when the missing rates are high. In most action sequences, we found a major portion of the features/patterns exists during the beginning of the action, hence, removing frames at the beginning of the sequence makes the recognition harder. This is also demonstrated in the experiments: when the first 30% of frames at the beginning of a sequence are removed, the recognition accuracy drops dramatically; but when a same amount of frames are removed at the end of a video, the recognition is still effective.

Table 5. Recognition of actions with missing frames at the beginning.

Missing Rate	DDGCN	ST-GCN [30]	d-GCN [18]	2S-GCN [19]
0%	**91.5%**	81.5%	89.8%	88.3%
10%	**82.3%**	65.2%	72.5%	71.7%
20%	**43.7%**	28.5%	31.9%	30.9%
30%	**21.1%**	5.9%	9.1%	10.3%

Table 6. Recognition of actions with missing frames, where (1) missing frames are at the end (End), and (2) frames are randomly missing (Rand). The two numbers reported here reflect the recognition accuracy under these two cases, respectively.

Missing Rate	DDGCN	ST-GCN [30]	d-GCN [18]	2S-GCN [19]
0% (End/Rand)	**91.5%/91.5%**	81.5%/81.5%	89.8%/89.8%	88.4%/88.4%
30% (End/Rand)	**91.5%/87.9%**	81.5%/76.0%	89.8%/85.2%	88.3%/85.3%
60% (End/Rand)	**91.2%/79.0%**	80.4%	82.3%	82.5%
70% (End/Rand)	**86.3%/68.8%**	72.5%	76.9%	79.5%
80% (End/Rand)	**65.3%/51.3%**	48.1%	51.1%	55.9%

5   Conclusions

We have developed a Dynamic Directed Graph Convolutional Network (DDGCN) algorithm for action recognition based on skeleton graphs. The DDGCN consists of three new modules: Dynamic Convolutional Sampling (DCS), Dynamic Convolutional Weight (DCW) assignment, and Directed Graph Spatial-Temporal (DGST) features extraction. These new modules help better capture the spatial-temporal dependencies as well as hierarchical and sequential structures for human action modeling and recognition. Experiments demonstrated that DDGCN has outperformed the state-of-the-art algorithms in action recognition accuracy on multiple public benchmarks.

Limitations and Future Work. The recognition accuracy on the Kinect dataset is significantly lower than the NTU dataset. A main reason is that the Kinect data include some videos that have severe occlusion and missing joints. Some failure examples are illustrated in Fig. 5(d,e). In both examples, the skeletons are significantly truncated and incomplete, resulting in incorrect action identifications. Currently, the DDGCN (and other existing methods) has not designed specific module to tackle missing joints. We will explore this for action recognition in unconstrained videos.

References

1. Berndt, D.J., Clifford, J.: Using dynamic time warping to find patterns in time series. In: KDD workshop, Seattle, WA, vol. 10, pp. 359–370 (1994)
2. Bilen, H., Fernando, B., Gavves, E., Vedaldi, A., Gould, S.: Dynamic image networks for action recognition. In: Proceedings of the IEEE Conference on Computer Vision and Pattern Recognition, pp. 3034–3042 (2016)
3. Cao, J., Tagliasacchi, A., Olson, M., Zhang, H., Su, Z.: Point cloud skeletons via laplacian based contraction. In: Shape Modeling International (SMI 2010), pp. 187–197. IEEE (2010)
4. Cao, Z., Simon, T., Wei, S.E., Sheikh, Y.: Realtime multi-person 2D pose estimation using part affinity fields. In: Proceedings of the IEEE Conference on Computer Vision and Pattern Recognition, pp. 7291–7299 (2017)

5. Dai, J., et al.: Deformable convolutional networks. In: Proceedings of the IEEE International Conference on Computer Vision, pp. 764–773 (2017)
6. Herath, S., Harandi, M., Porikli, F.: Going deeper into action recognition: a survey. Image Vis. Comput. **60**, 4–21 (2017)
7. Iwana, B.K., Uchida, S.: Dynamic weight alignment for temporal convolutional neural networks. In: ICASSP 2019–2019 IEEE International Conference on Acoustics, Speech and Signal Processing (ICASSP), pp. 3827–3831. IEEE (2019)
8. Kamel, A., Sheng, B., Yang, P., Li, P., Shen, R., Feng, D.D.: Deep convolutional neural networks for human action recognition using depth maps and postures. IEEE Trans. Syst. Man Cybern. Syst. **49**(9), 1806–1816 (2018)
9. Kar, A., Rai, N., Sikka, K., Sharma, G.: AdaScan: adaptive scan pooling in deep convolutional neural networks for human action recognition in videos. In: Proceedings of the IEEE Conference on Computer Vision and Pattern Recognition, pp. 3376–3385 (2017)
10. Kay, W., et al.: The kinetics human action video dataset. arXiv preprint arXiv:1705.06950 (2017)
11. Ke, Q., Bennamoun, M., An, S., Sohel, F., Boussaid, F.: A new representation of skeleton sequences for 3D action recognition. In: IEEE Conference on Computer Vision and Pattern Recognition (CVPR), pp. 4570–4579 (2017)
12. Kim, T.S., Reiter, A.: Interpretable 3D human action analysis with temporal convolutional networks. In: 2017 IEEE Conference on Computer Vision and Pattern Recognition Workshops (CVPRW), pp. 1623–1631. IEEE (2017)
13. Li, M., Chen, S., Chen, X., Zhang, Y., Wang, Y., Tian, Q.: Actional-structural graph convolutional networks for skeleton-based action recognition. In: Proceedings of the IEEE Conference on Computer Vision and Pattern Recognition, pp. 3595–3603 (2019)
14. Mandal, D., et al.: Out-of-distribution detection for generalized zero-shot action recognition. In: Proceedings of the IEEE Conference on Computer Vision and Pattern Recognition, pp. 9985–9993 (2019)
15. Peng, X., Zou, C., Qiao, Yu., Peng, Q.: Action recognition with stacked fisher vectors. In: Fleet, D., Pajdla, T., Schiele, B., Tuytelaars, T. (eds.) ECCV 2014. LNCS, vol. 8693, pp. 581–595. Springer, Cham (2014). https://doi.org/10.1007/978-3-319-10602-1_38
16. Piergiovanni, A., Ryoo, M.S.: Representation flow for action recognition. In: Proceedings of the IEEE Conference on Computer Vision and Pattern Recognition, pp. 9945–9953 (2019)
17. Shahroudy, A., Liu, J., Ng, T.T., Wang, G.: NTU RGB+ D: a large scale dataset for 3D human activity analysis. In: Proceedings of the IEEE Conference on Computer Vision and Pattern Recognition, pp. 1010–1019 (2016)
18. Shi, L., Zhang, Y., Cheng, J., Lu, H.: Skeleton-based action recognition with directed graph neural networks. In: Proceedings of the IEEE Conference on Computer Vision and Pattern Recognition, pp. 7912–7921 (2019)
19. Shi, L., Zhang, Y., Cheng, J., Lu, H.: Two-stream adaptive graph convolutional networks for skeleton-based action recognition. In: Proceedings of the IEEE Conference on Computer Vision and Pattern Recognition, pp. 12026–12035 (2019)
20. Si, C., Chen, W., Wang, W., Wang, L., Tan, T.: An attention enhanced graph convolutional LSTM network for skeleton-based action recognition. In: Proceedings of the IEEE Conference on Computer Vision and Pattern Recognition, pp. 1227–1236 (2019)

21. Si, C., Jing, Y., Wang, W., Wang, L., Tan, T.: Skeleton-based action recognition with spatial reasoning and temporal stack learning. In: Ferrari, V., Hebert, M., Sminchisescu, C., Weiss, Y. (eds.) ECCV 2018. LNCS, vol. 11205, pp. 106–121. Springer, Cham (2018). https://doi.org/10.1007/978-3-030-01246-5_7

22. Sun, S., Kuang, Z., Sheng, L., Ouyang, W., Zhang, W.: Optical flow guided feature: a fast and robust motion representation for video action recognition. In: Proceedings of the IEEE Conference on Computer Vision and Pattern Recognition, pp. 1390–1399 (2018)

23. Tang, Y., Tian, Y., Lu, J., Li, P., Zhou, J.: Deep progressive reinforcement learning for skeleton-based action recognition. In: Proceedings of the IEEE Conference on Computer Vision and Pattern Recognition, pp. 5323–5332 (2018)

24. Tran, D.V., Navarin, N., Sperduti, A.: On filter size in graph convolutional networks. In: 2018 IEEE Symposium Series on Computational Intelligence (SSCI), pp. 1534–1541. IEEE (2018)

25. Wang, D., Yuan, Y., Wang, Q.: Early action prediction with generative adversarial networks. IEEE Access **7**, 35795–35804 (2019)

26. Wang, H., Schmid, C.: Action recognition with improved trajectories. In: Proceedings of the IEEE International Conference on Computer Vision, pp. 3551–3558 (2013)

27. Wang, J., Jiao, J., Bao, L., He, S., Liu, Y., Liu, W.: Self-supervised spatio-temporal representation learning for videos by predicting motion and appearance statistics. In: Proceedings of the IEEE Conference on Computer Vision and Pattern Recognition, pp. 4006–4015 (2019)

28. Wang, L., Gao, C., Yang, L., Zhao, Y., Zuo, W., Meng, D.: PM-GANs: discriminative representation learning for action recognition using partial-modalities. In: Ferrari, V., Hebert, M., Sminchisescu, C., Weiss, Y. (eds.) ECCV 2018. LNCS, vol. 11210, pp. 389–406. Springer, Cham (2018). https://doi.org/10.1007/978-3-030-01231-1_24

29. Wu, D., Chen, J., Sharma, N., Pan, S., Long, G., Blumenstein, M.: Adversarial action data augmentation for similar gesture action recognition. In: 2019 International Joint Conference on Neural Networks (IJCNN), pp. 1–8. IEEE (2019)

30. Yan, S., Xiong, Y., Lin, D.: Spatial temporal graph convolutional networks for skeleton-based action recognition. In: Thirty-Second AAAI Conference on Artificial Intelligence (2018)

31. Yao, B., Jiang, X., Khosla, A., Lin, A.L., Guibas, L., Fei-Fei, L.: Human action recognition by learning bases of action attributes and parts. In: 2011 International Conference on Computer Vision, pp. 1331–1338. IEEE (2011)

32. Zadghorban, M., Nahvi, M.: An algorithm on sign words extraction and recognition of continuous persian sign language based on motion and shape features of hands. Pattern Anal. Appl. **21**(2), 323–335 (2018)

33. Zhang, C., Tian, Y., Guo, X., Liu, J.: DAAL: deep activation-based attribute learning for action recognition in depth videos. Comput. Vis. Image Underst. **167**, 37–49 (2018)

34. Zhang, H.B., et al.: A comprehensive survey of vision-based human action recognition methods. Sensors **19**(5), 1005 (2019)

35. Zhao, R., Wang, K., Su, H., Ji, Q.: Bayesian graph convolution LSTM for skeleton based action recognition. In: Proceedings of the IEEE International Conference on Computer Vision, pp. 6882–6892 (2019)

Learning Latent Representations Across Multiple Data Domains Using Lifelong VAEGAN

Fei Ye and Adrian G. Bors[⊠]

Department of Computer Science, University of York, York YO10 5GH, UK
adrian.bors@york.ac.uk

Abstract. The problem of catastrophic forgetting occurs in deep learning models trained on multiple databases in a sequential manner. Recently, generative replay mechanisms (GRM) have been proposed to reproduce previously learned knowledge aiming to reduce the forgetting. However, such approaches lack an appropriate inference model and therefore can not provide latent representations of data. In this paper, we propose a novel lifelong learning approach, namely the Lifelong VAEGAN (L-VAEGAN), which not only induces a powerful generative replay network but also learns meaningful latent representations, benefiting representation learning. L-VAEGAN can allow to automatically embed the information associated with different domains into several clusters in the latent space, while also capturing semantically meaningful shared latent variables, across different data domains. The proposed model supports many downstream tasks that traditional generative replay methods can not, including interpolation and inference across different data domains.

Keywords: Lifelong learning · Representation learning · Generative modeling · VAEGAN model.

1 Introduction

The lifelong learning framework describes an intelligent learning process capable of remembering all previously learned knowledge from multiple sources, such as different databases [47]. The ability of continuous, or lifelong learning, is an inherent characteristic of humans and animals, which helps them to adapt to the environment during their entire life. However, such characteristics remain an open challenge for deep learning models. The current state-of-the-art deep learning approaches perform well on many individual databases [18,55], but suffer from catastrophic forgetting when attempting to learn data associated with new tasks [3,13,19,51,62,65]. For example when a deep neural network

Electronic supplementary material The online version of this chapter (https://doi.org/10.1007/978-3-030-58565-5_46) contains supplementary material, which is available to authorized users.

© Springer Nature Switzerland AG 2020
A. Vedaldi et al. (Eds.): ECCV 2020, LNCS 12365, pp. 777–795, 2020.
https://doi.org/10.1007/978-3-030-58565-5_46

is trained on a new database, its parameters are updated in order to learn new information while their previous values are lost. Consequently, their performance on the previously learnt tasks degenerates.

In order to alleviate the catastrophic forgetting problem, memory-based approaches use a buffer to store a small subset of previously seen data samples [2, 4, 8]. However, such approaches cannot be seen as lifelong learning models and they do not scale well when increasing the number of databases defining different tasks. Shin *et al.* [60] proposed a learning model employing the Generative Replay Mechanism (GRM). The idea of the GRM is to train a generative replay network to reproduce previously learnt knowledge by using adversarial learning. A classifier is then trained using jointly generative replay data and data sampled from the current database. This approach was only applied on prediction tasks. Although recent studies, such as the one from [64], have been used to generate images from new classes without forgetting, generative replay approaches do not learn the representation of data and therefore can not be extended to be used in a broad range of tasks. Learning meaningful and disentangled representations of data was shown to benefit many tasks, but they have not been explored so far within the lifelong learning methodology [1, 52]. In this paper, we propose a new lifelong learning model which not only learns a GRM but also induces accurate inference models, benefiting on representation learning.

This research study brings the following contributions:

1) In order to address the drawbacks of generative replay approaches, we propose a novel lifelong learning model aiming to learn informative latent variables over time.
2) We show that the proposed lifelong learning model can be extended for unsupervised, semi-supervised and supervised learning with few modifications.
3) We propose a two-step optimization algorithm to train the proposed model. The latent representation learned by the proposed model can capture both task-specific generative factors and semantic meaningful shared latent variables across different domains over time.
4) We provide a theoretical insight into how GRM models are used for lifelong learning in artificial systems.

2   Related Works

The lifelong learning was approached in previous research studies from three different perspectives: by using regularization, dynamic architectures, and by employing memory replay. Regularization approaches in order to alleviate catastrophic forgetting add an auxiliary term that penalizes changes in the weights when the model is trained on a new task [14, 26, 29, 33, 38, 48, 54, 60]. Dynamic architectures would increase the number of neurons and network layers in order to adapt to learning new information [58]. Most memory replay approaches are using generative models, such as either Generative Adversarial Networks (GANs) [21] or Variational Autoencoders (VAEs) [32]) to replay the previously learnt knowledge. For instance, Wu *et al.* [64] proposed a novel lifelong generative framework, namely Memory Replay GANs (MeRGANs), which mainly generates images from new categories under the lifelong learning setting. The Lifelong GAN [67] employs image to image translation. However, both models from [64,67] lack an image inference procedure and Lifelong GAN would need to load all previously learnt data for the generation task. Approaches employing both generative and inference mechanisms are based on the VAE framework [1,50]. However, these approaches have degenerating performance when learning high-dimensional data, due to lacking a powerful generator.

Hybrid VAE-GAN methods learn an inference model from a GAN model, which can also capture data representations, which is specific to the VAE. Adversarial learning is performed in order to match either the data distribution [36], the latent variables distribution [42], or their joint distributions [10,15,16,37,43,49,61]. These methods perform well only when trained on a single dataset and their performance would degenerate when learning a new task.

This paper is the first research study to propose a novel hybrid lifelong learning model, which not only addresses the drawback of the existing hybrid methods but also provides inference mechanisms for the GRM, benefiting on many downstream tasks across domains under the lifelong learning framework. The approach proposed in this paper also addresses disentangled representation learning [35] in the context of lifelong learning. Many recent approaches would aim to modify the VAE framework in order to learn a meaningful representation of the data by imposing a large penalty on the Kullback-Leibler (KL) divergence term [7,17,25] or on the total correlation latent variables [12,20,28,30]. These approaches perform well on independent and identically distributed data samples from a single domain. However, they are unable to learn the information from piecewise changing stationary data from multiple databases, because they suffer from catastrophic forgetting.

3   The Lifelong VAEGAN

In this section, we introduce the optimization algorithm used for training the proposed model when learning several databases without forgetting.

3.1   Problem Formulation

The lifelong learning problem consists of learning a sequence of K tasks, each characterized by a distinct database, corresponding to the data distributions $p(\mathbf{x}^1), p(\mathbf{x}^2), \ldots, p(\mathbf{x}^K)$. During the k-th database learning, we only access the images sampled from $p(\mathbf{x}^k)$. Most existing lifelong learning approaches focus on prediction or regression tasks. Meanwhile, in this research study we focus on modelling the overall data distribution $p(\mathbf{x})$, by learning latent representations over time:

$$p(\mathbf{x}) := \int \prod_{i=1}^{K} p(\mathbf{x}^i|\mathbf{z})p(\mathbf{z})d\mathbf{z} \tag{1}$$

where $\mathbf{z}$ represents the latent variables defining the information of all previously learnt databases. Besides addressing unsupervised learning, we also incorporate discrete variables into the optimization path in order to capture category discriminating information. Moreover, we also consider the semi-supervised learning problem where we consider that in each dataset we only have some labelled data while the rest are unlabeled.

3.2   Data Generation from Prior Distributions

In the following we aim to learn two separate latent representations for capturing discrete and continuous variations of data. The discrete data are denoted as $\mathbf{c} = \{\mathbf{c}_i | i = 1, \ldots, L\}$ where L is the dimension of the discrete variable space, while the continuous variables $\mathbf{z}$ are sampled from a normal distribution $\mathcal{N}(0, \mathbf{I})$. We also consider the domain variable $\mathbf{a} = \{\mathbf{a}_j | j = 1, \ldots, K\}$, defining each database and aiming to capture the information characterizing its task. The generation process considering the three latent variables $\mathbf{c}$, $\mathbf{z}$ and $\mathbf{a}$ is defined as:

$$
\begin{aligned}
\mathbf{c} &\sim \mathrm{Cat}\left(K = L, p = 1/K\right), \mathbf{z} \sim \mathcal{N}(\mathbf{0}, \mathbf{I}), \\
\mathbf{a} &\sim \mathrm{Cat}\left(p_1, p_2, \ldots, p_K\right), \mathbf{x} \sim p_\theta(\mathbf{x}|\mathbf{z}, \mathbf{a}, \mathbf{c}),
\end{aligned}
\tag{2}
$$

where $\mathrm{Cat}(\cdot)$ is the Categorical distribution, and $p_\theta(\mathbf{x}|\mathbf{z}, \mathbf{a}, \mathbf{c})$ is the distribution characterizing the generator implemented by a neural network with trainable parameters, θ. By incorporating the domain variables $\mathbf{a}$ in the inference model helps to generate images characteristic to a specific task. We consider the Wasserstein GAN (WGAN) [5] loss with the gradient penalty [22], which is defined by:

$$
\begin{aligned}
\min_G \max_D \mathcal{L}_{GAN}^G(\theta, \omega) =\;& \mathbb{E}_{\mathbf{z} \sim p(\mathbf{z}), \mathbf{c} \sim p(\mathbf{c}), \mathbf{a} \sim p(\mathbf{a})}[D(G(\mathbf{c}, \mathbf{z}, \mathbf{a}))] - \\
& \mathbb{E}_{p(\mathbf{x})}[D(\mathbf{x})] + \lambda \mathbb{E}_{\tilde{\mathbf{x}} \sim p(\tilde{\mathbf{x}})}[(\|\nabla_{\tilde{\mathbf{x}}} D(\tilde{\mathbf{x}})\|_2 - 1)^2]
\end{aligned}
\tag{3}
$$

where we introduce a Discriminator D, defined by the trainable parameters ω, $p(\mathbf{x})$ denotes the true data distribution, and the third term is the gradient weighted by the penalty λ. The adversarial loss allows the Generator and Discriminator to be trained alternately such that the Discriminator aims to distinguish real from generated data, while the Generator tends to fool the Discriminator through aiming to generate realistic data [5, 21].

3.3   Training the Inference Model

Most GAN-based lifelong methods [60, 64, 66] do not learn an accurate inference model and therefore can not derive a meaningful data representation. For the model proposed in this paper, we consider three differentiable non-linear functions $f_\varsigma(\cdot)$, $f_\varepsilon(\cdot)$, $f_\delta(\cdot)$, aiming to infer three different types of latent variables $\{\mathbf{z}, \mathbf{c}, \mathbf{a}\}$. We implement $f_\varsigma(\cdot)$ by using the Gaussian distribution $\mathcal{N}(\mu, \sigma)$ where $\mu = \mu_\varsigma(\mathbf{x})$ and $\sigma = \sigma_\varsigma(\mathbf{x})$ are given by the outputs of a neural network with trainable parameters ς. We use the reparameterization trick [32, 56] for sampling

$\mathbf{z} = \mu + \pi \otimes \sigma$, where π is a random noise vector sampled from $\mathcal{N}(0, \mathrm{I})$, in order to ensure end-to-end training.

Discrete Variables. We can not sample the discrete latent variables $\mathbf{a}$ and $\mathbf{c}$ from $f_\varepsilon(\cdot)$ and $f_\delta(\cdot)$, respectively, because the categorical representations are non-differentiable. In order to mitigate this, we use the Gumbel-Max trick [23,41] for achieving the differentiable relaxation of discrete random variables. The Gumbel-softmax trick was also used in [17,27,40,63] and its capability of reducing the variation of gradients was shown in [63].

The sampling process of discrete latent variables is defined as:

$$a_j = \frac{\exp((\log \mathbf{a}'_j + \mathbf{g}_j)/T)}{\sum_{i=1}^{K} \exp((\log \mathbf{a}'_i + \mathbf{g}_i)/T)} \tag{4}$$

where $\mathbf{a}'_i$ is the i-th entry of the probability defined by the softmax layer characterizing $f_\varepsilon(\cdot)$ and $\mathbf{a}_j$ is the continuous relaxation of the domain variable, while $\mathbf{g}_k$ is sampled from the distribution $\mathrm{Gumbel}(0,1)$ and T is the temperature parameter that controls the degree of smoothness. We use the Gumbel softmax trick for sampling both the domain $\mathbf{a}$ and the discrete $\mathbf{c}$ variables.

The Log-Likelihood Objective Function. GANs lack an inference mechanism, preventing them to capture data representations properly. In this paper we propose to maximize the sample log-likelihood for learning the inference models, defined by $p(\mathbf{x}) = \int \int \int p(\mathbf{x}|\mathbf{z}, \mathbf{a}, \mathbf{c})p(\mathbf{z}, \mathbf{a}, \mathbf{c}) \, d\mathbf{z} \, d\mathbf{a} \, d\mathbf{c}$, which is intractable in practice. We therefore derive the following lower bound on the log-likelihood, which is characteristic to VAEs, by introducing variational distributions:

$$\begin{aligned} \mathcal{L}_{\mathrm{VAE}}(\theta, \varsigma, \varepsilon, \delta) = \mathbb{E}_{q_{\varsigma,\varepsilon,\delta}}(\mathbf{z}, \mathbf{a}, \mathbf{c}|\mathbf{x}) \log[p_\theta(\mathbf{x}|\mathbf{z}, \mathbf{a}, \mathbf{c})] - D_{KL}[q_\varsigma(\mathbf{z}|\mathbf{x})\|p(\mathbf{z})] \\ - \mathbb{E}_{q_\varsigma(\mathbf{z}|\mathbf{x})} D_{KL}[q_\varepsilon(\mathbf{a}|\mathbf{x})\|p(\mathbf{a}|\mathbf{z})] - D_{KL}[q_\delta(\mathbf{c}|\mathbf{x})\|p(\mathbf{c})] \end{aligned} \tag{5}$$

where $q_\varsigma(\mathbf{z}|\mathbf{x})$, $q_\varepsilon(\mathbf{a}|\mathbf{z})$, $q_\delta(\mathbf{c}|\mathbf{x})$ are variational distributions modelled by $f_\varsigma(\cdot)$, $f_\varepsilon(\cdot)$, $f_\delta(\cdot)$, respectively. For the third term from (5), we sample from the empirical distribution and then sample $\mathbf{z}$ from $q_\delta(\mathbf{c}|\mathbf{x})$. $p(\mathbf{a}|\mathbf{z})$ is the prior distribution $\mathrm{Cat}(p_1, \ldots, p_K)$, where p_i denotes the probability of the sample belonging to the i-th domain. We consider $q_\varepsilon(\mathbf{a}|\mathbf{z})$ as the task-inference model which aims to infer the task ID for the given data samples.

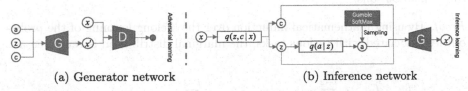

(a) Generator network   (b) Inference network

Fig. 1. The graph structure for the proposed Lifelong VAEGAN (L-VAEGAN) model, where G and D denote the Generator and Discriminator, respectively.

For the supervised learning setting, the auxiliary information such as the class labels can be used to guide the inference model. We minimise the cross-entropy loss $\eta(\cdot, \cdot)$ for $q_\delta(\mathbf{c}|\mathbf{x})$ and $q_\varepsilon(\mathbf{a}|\mathbf{z})$ as:

$$\mathcal{L}_{\mathbf{a}}(\varepsilon) = \mathbb{E}_{(\mathbf{x},\mathbf{a}^*)\sim(\mathbf{X},\mathbf{A}),\mathbf{z}\sim q_\varsigma(\mathbf{z}|\mathbf{x})}\eta(q_\varepsilon(\mathbf{a}|\mathbf{z}),\mathbf{a}^*) \tag{6}$$

$$\mathcal{L}_{\mathbf{c}}(\delta) = \mathbb{E}_{(\mathbf{x},\mathbf{y})\sim(\mathbf{X},\mathbf{Y})}\eta(q_\delta(\mathbf{c}|\mathbf{x}),\mathbf{y}) \tag{7}$$

where $\mathbf{X}$ and $\mathbf{Y}$ represent the empirical data and target distributions, respectively. $\mathbf{a}^*$ is the variable drawn from $\mathbf{A}$ which represents the Categorical distribution $Cat(m_1,\ldots,m_k)$, where m_i is the probability of seeing i-th task, characterizing the corresponding database. The graph structure of the Generator and Inference networks of the proposed Lifelong VAEGAN (L-VAEGAN) is shown in Figs. 1-a and 1-b, respectively, where the variable $\mathbf{a}$ is conditioned on $\mathbf{z}$. The proposed model is flexible to be extended for recognizing new tasks by automatically appending the domain variable $\mathbf{a}$ and optimizing the task-inference model $q_\varepsilon(\mathbf{a}|\mathbf{z})$ when faced with learning a new task.

4   Theoretical Analysis of the GRM

In this section, we analyze the GRM used in lifelong learning.

Definition 1. *We define the distribution modelling the lifelong learned data as $p(\tilde{\mathbf{x}}^t)$, which is encoded through $G_{\gamma_t}(\mathbf{z},\mathbf{c},\mathbf{d})$. The assumption is that the network has learnt the information from all given databases $t = 1,\ldots,K$, and this information is stored, refined and processed across various tasks, where γ_t is the generator parameter updated after the t-th task learning.*

Definition 2. *Let us define*

$$p(\tilde{\mathbf{x}}^t|\tilde{\mathbf{x}}^{t-1},\mathbf{x}^t) = \exp(-\Gamma(p(\tilde{\mathbf{x}}^{t-1},\mathbf{x}^t),p(\tilde{\mathbf{x}}^t))) \tag{8}$$

as the probability of generated data $\tilde{\mathbf{x}}^t$ when observing $\tilde{\mathbf{x}}^{t-1}$ and $\mathbf{x}^t$, where $\Gamma(\cdot)$ is a probabilistic measure of comparison between two distributions, which can be the f-divergence [46], or the Wasserstein distance [5] (Earth-mover distance).

Theorem 1. *By marginalizing over $\tilde{\mathbf{x}}^{t-1}$ and $\mathbf{x}^t$, on $p(\tilde{\mathbf{x}}^t|\tilde{\mathbf{x}}^{t-1},\mathbf{x}^t)$, the resulting marginal distribution $p(\tilde{\mathbf{x}}^t)$ encodes the statistical correlations from all previously learnt distributions.*

Proof. By using mathematical induction over the lifelong learning of the probabilities associated with various tasks, the marginal distribution is rewritten as:

$$p(\tilde{\mathbf{x}}^t) = \int \ldots \int p(\tilde{\mathbf{x}}^1) \prod_{i=0}^{t-2} p(\tilde{\mathbf{x}}^{t-i}|\tilde{\mathbf{x}}^{t-i-1},\mathbf{x}^{t-i}) \prod_{i=0}^{t-2} p(\mathbf{x}^{t-i})d\tilde{\mathbf{x}}^1 \ldots d\tilde{\mathbf{x}}^{t-1}d\mathbf{x}^2 \ldots d\mathbf{x}^t \tag{9}$$

Lemma 1. *The data probability $p(\tilde{\mathbf{x}}^t)$ approximates the true joint distribution $\prod_{i=1}^{t} p(\mathbf{x}^i)$ when all previously learnt distributions are the exact approximations to their target distributions while learning every given task.*

In the following we extend the theoretical analysis on the domain adaptation problem from [53] (Theorem 2) in order to analyze how the knowledge learned by GRMs is lost during the lifelong learning.

Theorem 2. *Let us consider two vector samples, one corresponding to the generated data $\{\nu_{t'} \in \mathbf{R}^s | \nu_{t'} \sim p(\tilde{\mathbf{x}}^t)\}$ and another corresponding to the real data $\{\nu_t \in \mathbf{R}^s | \nu_t \sim p(\mathbf{x}^t)\}$ of sizes n_t and $n_{t'}$. Then let $h^t(\cdot)$ be a new learned model trained on $\nu_{t'}$. For any $s' > s$ and $a' < \sqrt{2}$, there is a constant n_0 depending on s' satisfying that for any $\delta > 0$ and $\min(\nu_t, n_{t'}) \geq n_0 \max(\delta^{-(s'+2)}, 1)$. Then with the probability of at least $1 - \delta$ for all h^t, we have:*

$$E\left(h^t(\nu_t)\right) \leq E\left(h^t(\nu_{t'})\right) + W\left(\nu_t, \nu_{t'}\right) + \sqrt{2\log\left(\frac{1}{\delta}\right)/a'}\left(\sqrt{\frac{1}{n_t}} + \sqrt{\frac{1}{n_{t'}}}\right) + D \tag{10}$$

where $E(h^t(\nu_t)), E(h^t(\nu_{t'}))$ denote the observed risk for ν_t and $\nu_{t'}$, respectively, and $W(\nu_t, \nu_{t'})$ is the Wassenstein distance between ν_t and $\nu_{t'}$. D is the combined error when we find the optimal model $h^{t'} =: \arg\min_{h^t \in \mathcal{H}}(E(h^t(\nu_t)) + E(h^t(\nu_{t'})))$.

This theorem demonstrates that the performance of a model h^t degenerates on the empirical data distribution $p(\mathbf{x}^t)$. From Theorem 2, we conclude that the lifelong learning becomes a special domain adaptation problem in which the target and source domain are empirical data distributions from the current task and the approximation distribution $G_{\gamma_t}(\mathbf{z}, \mathbf{c}, \mathbf{d})$.

Lemma 2. *From Theorem 2 we have a bound on the accumulated errors across tasks during the lifelong learning.*

$$\sum_{i=1}^{K} E\left(h^K(\nu_i)\right) \leq \sum_{i=1}^{K} E\left(h^K(\nu_{i(K)})\right) +$$

$$+ \mathbf{W}\left(\nu_i, \nu_{i(K)}\right) + \sqrt{2\log\left(\frac{1}{\delta}\right)/a'}\left(\sqrt{\frac{1}{n_i}} + \sqrt{\frac{1}{n_{i(K)}}}\right) + D_{(i(K-1), i(K))}, \tag{11}$$

where $E\left(h^K(\nu_{i(K)})\right)$ denotes the observed risks on the probability measure $\nu_{i(K)}$ formed by samples drawn from $p(\tilde{\mathbf{x}}^i)$, after they have been learned across K tasks. $D_{(i(K-1), i(K))}$ is the combined error of an optimal model

$$h^* = \arg\min_{h \in \mathcal{H}}(E\left(h^K(\nu_{i(K-1)})\right) + E\left(h^K(\nu_{i(K)})\right)) \tag{12}$$

Theorem 3. *By having a learning system, acquiring the information from the given databases, we can define $\log p_\theta(\mathbf{x}^t, \tilde{\mathbf{x}}^{t-1})$ as the joint model log-likelihood and $p_\theta(\mathbf{z}^t, \mathbf{z}^{t-1} | \mathbf{x}^t, \tilde{\mathbf{x}}^{t-1})$ as the posterior. $\log p_\theta(\mathbf{x}^t, \tilde{\mathbf{x}}^{t-1})$ can be optimized by maximizing a lower bound.*

Proof. In this case, we consider two underlying generative factors (latent variables) $\mathbf{z}^t$, $\mathbf{z}^{t-1}$ for observing the real data $\mathbf{x}^t$ and generated data $\tilde{\mathbf{x}}^{t-1}$, respectively. We then define the latent variable model $p_\theta(\mathbf{x}^t, \tilde{\mathbf{x}}^{t-1}, \mathbf{z}^t, \mathbf{z}^{t-1}) = p_\theta(\mathbf{x}^t, \tilde{\mathbf{x}}^t | \mathbf{z}^t, \mathbf{z}^{t-1}) p(\mathbf{z}^t) p(\mathbf{z}^{t-1})$ and its marginal log-likelihood is approximated by a lower bound :

$$\log p_\theta(\mathbf{x}^t, \tilde{\mathbf{x}}^{t-1}) \geq \mathbb{E}_{q_\xi(\mathbf{z}^t | \mathbf{x}^t)} \left[\log \frac{p_\theta(\mathbf{x}^t, \mathbf{z}^t)}{q_\xi(\mathbf{z}^t | \mathbf{x}^t)} \right] + \mathbb{E}_{q_\xi(\mathbf{z}^{t-1} | \tilde{\mathbf{x}}^{t-1})} \left[\log \frac{p_\theta(\tilde{\mathbf{x}}^{t-1}, \mathbf{z}^{t-1})}{q_\xi(\mathbf{z}^{t-1} | \tilde{\mathbf{x}}^{t-1})} \right]$$
(13)

We define the above equation as $\mathcal{L}(\theta, \xi; \mathbf{x}^t, \tilde{\mathbf{x}}^{t-1})$.

Lemma 3. *From the Theorems 2 and 3, we can derive a lower bound on the sample log-likelihood at t-th task learning, as expressed by:*

$$\log p_\theta(\mathbf{x}^1, .., \mathbf{x}^t) \geq \mathcal{L}(\theta, \xi; \mathbf{x}^1, .., \mathbf{x}^t) \geq \mathcal{L}(\theta, \xi; \mathbf{x}^t, \tilde{\mathbf{x}}^{t-1})$$
$$- \mathbf{W}(v, v') - \sqrt{2 \log \left(\frac{1}{\delta} \right) / a'} \left(\sqrt{\frac{1}{n}} + \sqrt{\frac{1}{n'}} \right) - D^*$$
(14)

where $\nu \in \mathbf{R}^s, \nu' \in \mathbf{R}^s$ *are formed by n and n' numbers of samples drawn from* $p(\mathbf{x}^t) p(\tilde{\mathbf{x}}^{t-1})$ *and* $\prod_i^t p(\mathbf{x}^i)$, *respectively, where n and n' denote the sample size.*

Lemma 2 provides an explicit way to investigate how information is lost through GRMs during the lifelong learning process. Meanwhile, Lemma 3 derives the evidence lower bound (ELBO) of the sample log-likelihood. All GRM approaches, based on VAE and GAN architectures, can be explained through this theoretical analysis. However, GAN based approaches lack inference mechanisms, such as the one provided in Lemma 3. This motivates us to develop a new lifelong learning approach utilizing the advantages of both GANs and VAEs, enabling the generation of data and the log-likelihood estimation abilities.

5   The Two-Step Latent Variables Optimization over Time

In the following, we introduce a two-step optimization algorithm which combines a powerful generative replay network with inducing latent representations. Our algorithm is different from existing hybrid models which train generator and inference models using a single optimization function [36] or learn an optimal coupling between generator and inference model by using adversarial learning [11,15,16,36,37,42,43,61]. The proposed algorithm contains two independent optimization paths, namely "wake" and "dreaming" phases.

5.1   Supervised Learning

In the "wake" phase, by considering the Definitions 1 and 2, the refined distribution $p(\tilde{\mathbf{x}}^t)$ is trained to approximate $p(\tilde{\mathbf{x}}^{t-1}, \mathbf{x}^t)$ by minimizing the Wasserstein distance:

$$\min_G \max_D \mathcal{L}_{GAN}^G(\theta_t, \omega_t) \triangleq \mathbb{E}_{p(\mathbf{z}), p(\mathbf{c}), p(\mathbf{a})}[D(G(\mathbf{c}, \mathbf{z}, \mathbf{a}))] - \mathbb{E}_{p(\tilde{\mathbf{x}}^{t-1})p(\mathbf{x}^t)}[D(\mathbf{x})], \tag{15}$$

where we omit the penalty term, weighted by λ, for the sake of simplification.

In the "dreaming" phase, we maximize the sample log-likelihood on the joint distribution of the generated data and the empirical data, associated with a given new task, by maximizing the ELBO:

$$\mathcal{L}_{VAE}(\theta_t, \varsigma_t, \varepsilon_t, \delta_t) \triangleq \mathbb{E}_{q_{\varsigma, \varepsilon, \delta}(\mathbf{z}, \mathbf{a}, \mathbf{c}|\mathbf{x}^t)} \left[\log \frac{p_\theta(\mathbf{x}^t|\mathbf{z}, \mathbf{a}, \mathbf{c})}{q_{\varsigma, \varepsilon, \delta}(\mathbf{z}, \mathbf{a}, \mathbf{c}|\mathbf{x}^t)} \right]$$
$$+ \mathbb{E}_{q_{\varsigma, \varepsilon, \delta}(\mathbf{z}, \mathbf{a}, \mathbf{c}|\tilde{\mathbf{x}}^{t-1})} \left[\log \frac{p_\theta(\tilde{\mathbf{x}}^{t-1}|\mathbf{z}, \mathbf{a}, \mathbf{c})}{q_{\varsigma, \varepsilon, \delta}(\mathbf{z}, \mathbf{a}, \mathbf{c}|\tilde{\mathbf{x}}^{t-1})} \right]. \tag{16}$$

This loss function is used to train both Generator and Inference models. After training, the Inference model $q_\delta(\mathbf{c}|\mathbf{x})$ can be used for classification.

5.2   Semi-supervised Learning

Let us consider that we only have a small subset of labelled data from each database, while the rest of data is unlabelled. For the labelled data, we derive the objective function without the inference model $q_\delta(\mathbf{c}|\mathbf{x})$ in the "dreaming" phase as:

$$\mathcal{L}_{VAE}^S(\theta_t, \varsigma_t, \varepsilon_t, \delta_t) \triangleq \sum{}^2 \mathbb{E}_{q_\varsigma(\mathbf{z}|\mathbf{x}), q_\varepsilon(\mathbf{a}|\mathbf{x}), p(\mathbf{y})}[\log p_\theta(\mathbf{x}|\mathbf{z}, \mathbf{a}, \mathbf{y})]$$
$$- D_{KL}[q_\varsigma(\mathbf{z}|\mathbf{x})\|p(\mathbf{z})] - \mathbb{E}_{q_\varsigma(\mathbf{z}|\mathbf{x})} D_{KL}[q_\varepsilon(\mathbf{a}|\mathbf{z})\|p(\mathbf{a}|\mathbf{z})] - D_{KL}[q_\delta(\mathbf{c}|\mathbf{x})\|p(\mathbf{c})], \tag{17}$$

where $\sum^2$ denotes the estimation of ELBO on the joint model log-likelihood. In addition, we model the unlabeled data samples by using $\mathcal{L}_{VAE}(\theta_t, \varsigma_t, \varepsilon_t, \delta_t)$, where the discrete variable $\mathbf{c}$ is sampled from the Gumbel-softmax distribution whose probability vector is obtained by the encoder $q_\delta(\mathbf{c}|\mathbf{x})$. The full semi-supervised loss used to train the hybrid model is defined as:

$$\mathcal{L}_{VAE}^{Semi} \triangleq \mathcal{L}_{VAE}^S + \beta \mathcal{L}_{VAE}, \tag{18}$$

where β is used to control the importance of the unsupervised learning when compared with the component associated with supervised learning. In addition, the entropy loss $\mathcal{L}_c(\delta)$ is also performed with the labeled data samples in order to enhance the prediction ability of $q_\delta(\mathbf{c}|\mathbf{x})$.

5.3   Unsupervised Learning

We also employ the proposed hybrid VAE-GAN model for the lifelong unsupervised learning setting, where we do not have the class labels for each task. Similarly to the supervised learning framework, we minimize the Wasserstein distance between $p(\tilde{\mathbf{x}}^t)$ and $p(\tilde{\mathbf{x}}^{t-1}, \mathbf{x}^t)$:

$$\min_G \max_D \mathcal{L}_{GAN}^U(\theta_t, \omega_t) \triangleq \mathbb{E}_{p(\mathbf{z}), p(\mathbf{a})}[D(G(\mathbf{z}, \mathbf{a}))] - \mathbb{E}_{p(\tilde{\mathbf{x}}^{t-1})p(\mathbf{x}^t)}[D(\mathbf{x})]. \tag{19}$$

In the "dreaming" phase, we train the generator and inference models using:

$$
\begin{aligned}
\mathcal{L}_{VAE}^U(\theta_t, \varsigma_t, \varepsilon_t) \triangleq \sum{}^2 &\mathbb{E}_{q_\varsigma(\mathbf{z}|\mathbf{x}), q_\varepsilon(\mathbf{a}|\mathbf{x})}[\log p_\theta(\mathbf{x}|\mathbf{z}, \mathbf{a})] \\
&- D_{KL}[q_\varsigma(\mathbf{z}|\mathbf{x})||p(\mathbf{z})] - \mathbb{E}_{q_\varsigma(\mathbf{z}|\mathbf{x})} D_{KL}[q_\varepsilon(\mathbf{a}|\mathbf{z})||p(\mathbf{a}|\mathbf{z})],
\end{aligned}
\tag{20}
$$

where the Generator is conditioned on only two variables, $\mathbf{z}$ and $\mathbf{a}$. For learning disentangled representations, we employ the Minimum Description Length (MDL) principle [7,57] and replace the second term from Eq. (20) by $\gamma|D_{KL}[q_\varsigma(\mathbf{z}|\mathbf{x})||p(\mathbf{z})] - C|$, where γ and C are a multiplicative and a linear constant used for controling the degree of disentanglement.

6   Experimental Results

6.1   Lifelong Unsupervised Learning

In this section, we investigate how the proposed Lifelong VAEGAN (L-VAEGAN) model learns meaningful and interpretable representations considering the unsupervised lifelong learning of various image databases.

Reconstruction and Interpolation Results Following Lilfeong Learning. We train the L-VAEGAN model using the loss functions $\mathcal{L}_{GAN}^U$ and $\mathcal{L}_{VAE}^U$ from equations (19) and (20), which contain adversarial and VAE learning terms, respectively, and we consider a learning rate of 0.001. The generation and reconstruction results are presented in Figs. 2a–c, for the lifelong learning of CelebA [39] to CACD [9], and in Figs. 2d–f for CelebA to 3DChair [6]. From these results, the inference model works well for both discrete and continuous latent variables.

   In the following we perform data interpolation experiments under the lifelong learning setting in order to evaluate the manifold continuity. We call lifelong interpolation when the interpolation is performed between multiple data domains, by considering data from different databases, under the lifelong learning setting. We randomly select two images and then infer their discrete $\mathbf{a}$ and continuous $\mathbf{z}$ latent variables by using the inference model. The interpolation results are shown in Fig. 3-a, left and right, for CelebA to CACD and CelebA to 3D-chair lifelong learning, respectively. The first two rows show the interpolation results in images from the same database, while the last two rows show the interpolations of images from two different databases. From the images from the last two rows of Fig. 3-a, from the right side, we observe that a chair is transformed

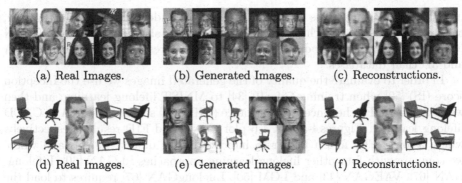

(a) Real Images.   (b) Generated Images.   (c) Reconstructions.

(d) Real Images.   (e) Generated Images.   (f) Reconstructions.

Fig. 2. Images reconstructed and generated by L-VAEGAN following the lifelong learning of CelebA to CACD (top row) and CelebA to 3DChair (bottom row).

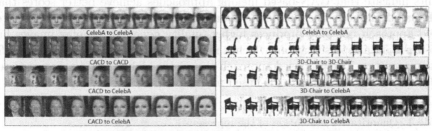

(a) Interpolation results after lifelong learning

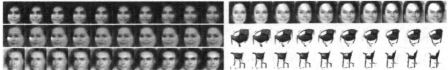

(b) Manipulating latent variables after the CelebA to 3D-chairs lifelong learning. We change a single latent variable from -3.0 to 3.0 while fixing all the others. From left to right and top to bottom, we can see changes in skin, gender, narrowing of the face, chair size, face pose and the style of chairs.

Fig. 3. Interpolation and disentangled results after lifelong learning.

into a human face, where its seat and backside are smoothly changed into the eyes and hair of a person. This shows that L-VAEGAN model can learn the joint latent space of two completely different data configurations.

Lifelong Disentangled Representations. We train the L-VAEGAN model under the CelebA to 3D-Chairs lifelong learning by adapting the loss functions from (19) and (20) in order to achieve unsupervised disentangled representations, as mentioned in Sect. 5.3. We consider the multiplicative parameter $\gamma = 4$, while increasing the linear one C from 0.5 to 25.0 during the training. After the training, we change one dimension of a continuous latent representation $\mathbf{z}$, inferred by using the inference model, for a given input, and then map it back in the visual data space by using the generator. The disentangled results are presented in Fig. 3-b which indicates changes in the skin, gender, narrowing of the face, chair size, face pose and chairs' style. These results show that the L-VAEGAN hybrid model can discover different disentangled representations in both CelebA and 3D chair databases.

In order to evaluate the quality of the generated images we use the Inception score (IS) [59] when training Cifar10 [34] to MNIST lifelong learning, and then we consider the Fréchet Inception Distance (FID) [24] score for CelebA to CACD lifelong learning. Figures 4-a and 4-b plot the IS and FID results, respectively, where a lower FID and a higher IS indicate better quality images and where we compare with four other lifelong learning approaches : LGAN [60], Lifelong-GAN [67], VAEGAN [43] and LGM [50]. LifelongGAN [67] requires to load the previously learnt real data samples in order to prevent forgetting them when is applied in general generation tasks (no conditional images are available). The results indicate that GAN-based lifelong approaches achieve better scores than VAE based methods because VAEs usually generate blurred images. The proposed approach not only produces higher-quality generative replay images but also learns data representations which is not possible with other GAN-based life-long approaches. The proposed approach also yields higher-quality reconstructed and generated images then VAE-based methods.

Table 1. Quantitative evaluation of the representation learning ability.

The lifelong learning of MNIST and Fashion				
Methods	Lifelong	Dataset	Rec	Acc
L-VAEGAN	M-F	MNIST	**4.75**	**92.53**
LGM [50]	M-F	MNIST	7.18	91.26
VAEGAN [43]	M-F	MNIST	6.54	91.87
L-VAEGAN	M-F	Fashion	**17.44**	**67.66**
LGM [50]	M-F	Fashion	18.33	66.17
VAEGAN [43]	M-F	Fashion	17.03	67.23
L-VAEGAN	F-M	MNIST	**4.92**	**93.29**
LGM [50]	F-M	MNIST	7.18	91.26
VAEGAN [43]	F-M	MNIST	5.52	92.16
L-VAEGAN	F-M	Fashion	**13.16**	**66.97**
LGM [50]	F-M	Fashion	18.83	62.53
VAEGAN [43]	F-M	Fashion	16.57	64.98

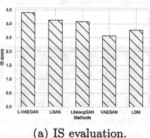

(a) IS evaluation.

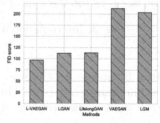

(b) FID evaluation.

Fig. 4. Quality evaluation.

Quantitative Evaluation. In the following we evaluate numerically the image representation ability for the proposed approach. We consider the reconstruction (Rec) as MSE, and the classification accuracy (Acc), as in [67]. The classification accuracy is calculated by a classifier which was trained on the generated images and evaluated on unseen testing samples. We provide the results in Table 1, where L-VAEGAN learns firstly the database MNIST followed by Fashion, denoted as M-F, while F-M represents the learning of the same databases in reversed order. For comparison, we consider LGM [50] and VAEGAN [43], which is one of the best known hybrid models enabled with an inference mechanism. We implement VAEGAN using GRM in order to prevent forgetting. From Table 1 we can see that L-VAEGAN achieves the best results.

Table 2. The classification results for the lifelong learning of MNIST and SVHN.

Dataset	Lifelong	L-VAEGAN	LGAN [60]	LGM [50]	EWC [33]	Transfer	MeRGANs [64]
MNIST	M-S	**96.63**	96.59	96.59	32.63	4.70	96.46
MNIST	S-M	98.55	98.42	98.30	**99.03**	98.45	98.38
SVHN	M-S	81.97	80.77	80.10	89.71	**89.90**	79.67
SVHN	S-M	**80.99**	76.76	80.97	37.69	3.60	80.85

Table 3. Semi-supervised classification error results on MNIST database, under the MNIST to Fashion lifelong learning.

Methods	Lifelong?	Error
L-VAEGAN	Yes	4.34
LGAN [60]	Yes	5.46
Neural networks (NN) [31]	No	10.7
(CNN) [31]	No	6.45
TSVM [31]	No	5.38
CAE [31]	No	4.77
M1+TSVM [31]	No	4.24
M2 [31]	No	3.60
M1+M2 [31]	No	2.40
Semi-VAE [44]	No	2.88

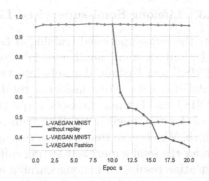

Fig. 5. The accuracy during the semi-supervised training on the testing data samples during the lifelong learning. The model is trained for 10 epochs for each task.

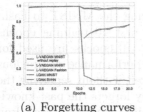 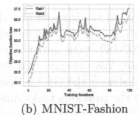 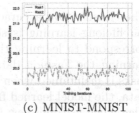

(a) Forgetting curves   (b) MNIST-Fashion   (c) MNIST-MNIST

Fig. 6. Classification accuracy and observed risks during the lifelong learning.

6.2   Lifelong Supervised Learning

We compare L-VAEGAN with various other methods under the lifelong supervised setting. LGAN [60] typically trains a classifier (called Solver) on both the images generated by the GAN and the training data samples from the current task. We also consider an auxiliary classifier for LGM [50] by training it on the mixed dataset consisting of images generated by the LGM and the training samples of the current task.

We train the L-VAEGAN model under the MNIST to SVHN [45] and MNIST to Fashion lifelong learning tasks, respectively. The classification accuracy of various methods is reported in Table 2. We observe that the replay generative images can prevent forgetting and the quality of performing on the previous tasks is depending on the capability of the Generator. For instance, the classification accuracy of previous tasks for LGM is a bit lower than for the other GAN-based methods. The reason for this is that LGM uses VAEs as generators and therefore can not generate high-quality images when compared to GANs. The classification results indicate that the proposed approach yields good results in lifelong supervised learning.

6.3   Lifelong Semi-supervised Learning

For the semi-supervised training of L-VAEGAN, described in Sect. 5.2, we consider only a small number of labelled images from each database. We divide MNIST and Fashion datasets into two subsets each, representing labelled and unlabeled data. We consider a total of 1,000 and 10,000 labelled images for MNIST and Fashion datasets, respectively, with an equal number of data in each class for the labelled set. The semi-supervised learning curves are provided in Fig. 5. We observe that when not using the generative replay samples, the model under the semi-supervised setting suffers from catastrophic forgetting. The classification results for lifelong learning when using L-VAEGAN compared to other semi-supervised learning methods are provided in Table 3. These results show that the proposed approach outperforms LGAN [60], under the semi-supervised learning setting, and achieves competitive results when compared to the state-of-the art models which are not trained using lifelong learning.

6.4   Analysis

The classification accuracy for all testing samples during the MNIST to Fashion lifelong learning is shown in Fig. 6-a, where the first 10 training epochs correspond to learning the MNIST task and the next 10 epochs are used for learning the Fashion database. We observe that the performance of previous tasks is maintained when considering the GRM. However, without replaying the data, the model learned from the previous tasks quickly forgets the past knowledge when learning new tasks, as observed in the significant performance drop from Fig. 6-a. The proposed L-VAEGAN, unlike LGAN [60], is able to provide inference mechanisms, benefiting many downstream tasks, as shown in Fig. 3. In

Fig. 6-b we provide the numerical results for the generalization bounds for GRM, described in Sect. 4, where risk1 and risk2 denote $E(h^1(\mu_1))$ and $E(h^1(\mu_{1'}))$, respectively. We find that $E(h^1(\mu_1))$ is very close to $E(h^1(\mu_{1'}))$ and still a bound on $E(h^1(\mu_{1'}))$ during the training. Figure 6-c provides the numerical results for the observed risks under the MNIST-MNIST lifelong learning. We observe that $E(h^1(\mu_1))$ is still a bound on $E(h^1(\mu_{1'}))$ and this bound is gradually increased during the training. The reason for this is that the model is gradually adapting $p(\tilde{\mathbf{x}}^1)$ and the bound depends on the distance between $p(\tilde{\mathbf{x}}^1)$ and $p(\mathbf{x}^1)$.

7   Conclusion

A novel hybrid model for lifelong representation learning, called Lifelong VAE-GAN (L-VAEGAN) is proposed in this research study. A two-step optimization algorithm, which can also induce higher-quality generative replay samples and learn informative latent representations over time, is used to train L-VAEGAN. The results indicate that L-VAEGAN model is able to discover disentangled representations from multiple domains under the lifelong learning setting. More importantly, L-VAEGAN automatically learns semantic meaningful shared latent variables across different domains, which allows to perform cross-domain interpolation and inference.

References

1. Achille, A., et al.: Life-long disentangled representation learning with cross-domain latent homologies. In: Proceedings of the Advances in Neural Information Processing Systems (NIPS), pp. 9873–9883 (2018)
2. Aljundi, R., et al.: Online continual learning with maximal interfered retrieval. In: Proceedings of the Neural Information Processing Systems (NIPS). arXiv preprint arXiv:1908.04742 (2019)
3. Aljundi, R., Chakravarty, P., Tuytelaars, T.: Expert gate: lifelong learning with a network of experts. In: Proceedings of the IEEE Conference on Computer Vision and Pattern Recognition (CVPR), pp. 3366–3375 (2017)
4. Aljundi, R., Lin, M., Goujaud, B., Bengio, Y.: Gradient based sample selection for online continual learning. In: Proceedings of the Neural Information Processing Systems (NIPS). arXiv preprint arXiv:1903.08671 (2019)
5. Arjovsky, M., Chintala, S., Bottou, L.: Wasserstein generative adversarial networks. In: Proceedings of the International Conference on Machine Learning (ICML), pp. 214–223 (2017)
6. Aubry, M., Maturana, D., Efros, A.A., Russell, B.C., Sivic, J.: Seeing 3D chairs: exemplar part-based 2D–3D alignment using a large dataset of CAD models. In: Proceedings of the IEEE Conference on Computer Vision and Pattern Recognition (CVPR), pp. 3762–3769 (2014)
7. Burgess, C.P., et al.: Understanding disentangling in β-VAE. In: Proceedings of the NIPS Workshop on Learning Disentangled Representation. arXiv preprint arXiv:1804.03599 (2017)
8. Chaudhry, A., et al.: On tiny episodic memories in continual learning. arXiv preprint arXiv:1902.10486 (2019)

9. Chen, B.C., Chen, C.S., Hsu, W.H.: Cross-age reference coding for age-invariant face recognition and retrieval. In: Proceedings of the European Conference on Computer Vision (ECCV), vol. LNCS 8694, pp. 768–783 (2014)

10. Chen, L., Dai, S., Pu, Y., Li, C., Su, Q., Carin, L.: Symmetric variational auto encoder and connections to adversarial learning. In: Proceedings of the International Conference on Artificial Intelligence and Statistics (AISTATS) 2018, vol. PMLR 84, pp. 661–669 (2018)

11. Chen, L., Dai, S., Pu, Y., Li, C., Su, Q., Carin, L.: Symmetric variational auto encoder and connections to adversarial learning. arXiv preprint arXiv:1709.01846 (2017)

12. Chen, T.Q., Li, X., Grosse, R.B., Duvenaud, D.K.: Isolating sources of disentanglement in variational autoencoders. In: Proceedings of the Advances in Neural Information Processing Systems (NIPS), pp. 2615–2625 (2018)

13. Chen, Z., Ma, N., Liu, B.: Lifelong learning for sentiment classification. In: Proceedings of the Annual Meeting of the Association for Comparative Linguistics and International Joint Conference on Natural Language Processing, pp. 750–756 (2015)

14. Dai, W., Yang, Q., Xue, G.R., Yu, Y.: Boosting for transfer learning. In: Proceedings of the International Conference on Machine Learning (ICML), pp. 193–200 (2007)

15. Donahue, J., Krähenbühl, P., Darrell, T.: Adversarial feature learning. In: Proceedings of the International Conference on Learning Representations (ICLR). arXiv preprint arXiv:1605.09782 (2017)

16. Dumoulin, V., et al.: Adversarially learned inference. In: Proceedings of the International Conference on Learning Representations (ICLR). arXiv preprint arXiv:1606.00704 (2017)

17. Dupont, E.: Learning disentangled joint continuous and discrete representations. In: Proceedings of the Advances in Neural Information Processing Systems (NIPS), pp. 710–720 (2018)

18. Erhan, D., Szegedy, C., Toshev, A., Anguelov, D.: Scalable object detection using deep neural networks. In: Proceedings of the IEEE Conference on Computer Vision and Pattern Recognition (CVPR), pp. 2147–2154 (2014)

19. Fagot, J., Cook, R.G.: Evidence for large long-term memory capacities in baboons and pigeons and its implications for learning and the evolution of cognition. Proc. National Acad. Sci. (PNAS) **103**(46), 17564–17567 (2006)

20. Gao, S., Brekelmans, R., ver Steeg, G., Galstyan, A.: Auto-encoding total correlation explanation. In: Proceedings of the International Conference on Artificial Intelligence and Statistics (AISTATS) 2018, vol. PMLR 89, pp. 1157–1166 (2019)

21. Goodfellow, I., et al.: Generative adversarial nets. In: Proceedings of the Advances in Neural Information Processing Systems (NIPS), pp. 2672–2680 (2014)

22. Gulrajani, I., Ahmed, F., Arjovsky, M., Dumoulin, V., Courville, A.C.: Improved training of Wasserstein GANs. In: Proceedings of the Advances in Neural Information Processing Systems (NIPS), pp. 5767–5777 (2017)

23. Gumbel, E.J.: Statistical theory of extreme values and some practical applications: a series of lectures (1954)

24. Heusel, M., Ramsauer, H., Unterthiner, T., Nessler, B., Hochreiter, S.: GANs trained by a two time-scale update rule converge to a local Nash equilibrium. In: Proceedings of the Advances in Neural Information Processing Systems (NIPS), pp. 6626–6637 (2017)

25. Higgins, I., et al.: β-VAE: learning basic visual concepts with a constrained variational framework. In: Proceedings of the International Conference on Learning Representations (ICLR) (2017)
26. Hinton, G., Vinyals, O., Dean, J.: Distilling the knowledge in a neural network. In: Proceedings of the NIPS Deep Learning Workshop. arXiv preprint arXiv:1503.02531 (2014)
27. Jang, E., Gu, S., Poole, B.: Categorical reparameterization with Gumbel-Softmax. In: Proceedings of the International Conference on Learning Representations (ICLR). arXiv preprint arXiv:1611.01144 (2017)
28. Jeong, Y., Song, H.O.: Learning discrete and continuous factors of data via alternating disentanglement. In: Proceedings of the International Conference on Machine Learning (ICML), vol. PMLR 97, pp. 3091–3099 (2019)
29. Jung, H., Ju, J., Jung, M., Kim, J.: Less-forgetting learning in deep neural networks. arXiv preprint arXiv:1607.00122 (2016)
30. Kim, H., Mnih, A.: Disentangling by factorising. In: Proceedings of the International Conference on Machine Learning (ICML), vol. PMLR 80, pp. 2649–2658 (2018)
31. Kingma, D.P., Mohamed, S., Rezende, D.J., Welling, M.: Semi-supervised learning with deep generative models. In: Proceedings of the Advances in Neural Information Processing Systems (NIPS), pp. 3581–3589 (2014)
32. Kingma, D.P., Welling, M.: Auto-encoding variational Bayes. arXiv preprint arXiv:1312.6114 (2013)
33. Kirkpatrick, J., et al.: Overcoming catastrophic forgetting in neural networks. Proc. National Acad. Sci. (PNAS) 114(13), 3521–3526 (2017)
34. Krizhevsky, A., Hinton, G.: Learning multiple layers of features from tiny images. Technical report (2009)
35. Kumar, A., Sattigeri, P., Balakrishnan, A.: Variational inference of disentangled latent concepts from unlabeled observations. In: Proceedings of the International Conference on Learning Representations (ICLR). arXiv preprint arXiv:1711.00848 (2018)
36. Larsen, A.B.L., Sønderby, S.K., Larochelle, H., Winther, O.: Autoencoding beyond pixels using a learned similarity metric. In: Proceedings of the International Conference on Machine Learning (ICML), pp. 1558–1566 (2015)
37. Li, C., et al.: Alice: towards understanding adversarial learning for joint distribution matching. In: Proceedings of the Advances in Neural Information Processing Systems (NIPS), pp. 5495–5503 (2017)
38. Li, Z., Hoiem, D.: Learning without forgetting. IEEE Trans. Pattern Anal. Mach. Intell. 40(12), 2935–2947 (2017)
39. Liu, Z., Luo, P., Wang, X., Tang, X.: Deep learning face attributes in the wild. In: Proceedings of the IEEE International Conference on Computer Vision (ICCV), pp. 3730–3738 (2015)
40. Maddison, C.J., Mnih, A., Teh, Y.W.: The concrete distribution: a continuous relaxation of discrete random variables. In: Proceedings of the International Conference on Learning Representations (ICLR). arXiv preprint arXiv:1611.00712 (2016)
41. Maddison, C.J., Tarlow, D., Minka, T.: A* sampling. In: Proceedings of the Advances in Neural Information Processing Systems (NIPS), pp. 1–10 (2014)
42. Makhzani, A., Shlens, J., Jaitly, N., Goodfellow, I., Frey, B.: Adversarial autoencoders. In: Proceedings of the International Conference on Learning Representations (ICLR). arXiv preprint arXiv:1511.05644 (2016)

43. Mescheder, L., Nowozin, S., Geiger, A.: Adversarial variational bayes: unifying variational autoencoders and generative adversarial networks. In: Proceedings of the International Conference on Machine Learning (ICML), vol. PMLR 70, pp. 2391–2400(2017)

44. Narayanaswamy, S., et al.: Learning disentangled representations with semi-supervised deep generative models. In: Proceedings of the Advances in Neural Information Processing Systems (NIPS), pp. 5925–5935 (2017)

45. Netzer, Y., Wang, T., Coates, A., Bissacco, A., Wu, B., Ng, A.Y.: Reading digits in natural images with unsupervised feature learning. In: NIPS Workshop on Deep Learning and Unsupervised Feature Learning (2011)

46. Nowozin, S., Cseke, B., Tomioka, R.: f-GAN: training generative neural samplers using variational divergence minimization. In: Proceedings of the Advances in Neural Information Processing Systems (NIPS), pp. 271–279 (2016)

47. Parisi, G.I., Kemker, R., Part, J.L., Kanan, C., Wermter, S.: Continual lifelong learning with neural networks: a review. Neural Netw. **113**, 54–71 (2019)

48. Polikar, R., Upda, L., Upda, S.S., Honavar, V.: Learn++: an incremental learning algorithm for supervised neural networks. IEEE Trans. Syst. Man Cybern. Part C **31**(4), 497–508 (2001)

49. Pu, Y., et al.: Adversarial symmetric variational autoencoder. In: Proceedings of the Advances in Neural Information Processing Systems (NIPS), pp. 4333–4342 (2017)

50. Ramapuram, J., Gregorova, M., Kalousis, A.: Lifelong generative modeling. In: Proceedings of the International Conference on Learning Representations (ICLR). arXiv preprint arXiv:1705.09847 (2017)

51. Rannen, A., Aljundi, R., Blaschko, M., Tuytelaars, T.: Encoder based lifelong learning. In: Proceedings of the IEEE International Conference on Computer Vision (ICCV), pp. 1320–1328 (2017)

52. Rao, D., Visin, F., Rusu, A.A., Teh, Y.W., Pascanu, R., Hadsell, R.: Continual unsupervised representation learning. In: Proceedings of the Neural Information Processing Systems (NIPS). arXiv preprint arXiv:1910.14481 (2019)

53. Redko, I., Habrard, A., Sebban, M.: Theoretical analysis of domain adaptation with optimal transport. In: Ceci, M., Hollmén, J., Todorovski, L., Vens, C., Džeroski, S. (eds.) ECML PKDD 2017. LNCS (LNAI), vol. 10535, pp. 737–753. Springer, Cham (2017). https://doi.org/10.1007/978-3-319-71246-8_45

54. Ren, B., Wang, H., Li, J., Gao, H.: Life-long learning based on dynamic combination model. Appl. Soft Comput. **56**, 398–404 (2017)

55. Ren, S., He, K., Girshick, R., Sun, J.: Faster R-CNN: towards real-time object detection with region proposal networks. In: Proceedings of the Advances in Neural Information Processing Systems (NIPS), pp. 91–99 (2015)

56. Rezende, D.J., Mohamed, S., Wierstra, D.: Stochastic backpropagation and approximate inference in deep generative models. In: Proceedings of the International Conference on Machine Learning (ICML), vol. PMLR 32, pp. 1278–1286 (2014)

57. Rissanen, J.: Modeling by shortest data description. Automatica **14**(5), 465–471 (1978)

58. Rusu, A.A., et al.: Progressive neural networks. arXiv preprint arXiv:1606.04671 (2016)

59. Salimans, T., Goodfellow, I., Zaremba, W., Cheung, V., Radford, A., Chen, X.: Improved techniques for training GANs. In: Proceedings of the Advances in Neural Information Processing Systems (NIPS), pp. 2234–2242 (2016)

60. Shin, H., Lee, J.K., Kim, J., Kim, J.: Continual learning with deep generative replay. In: Proceedings of the Advances in Neural Information Processing Systems (NIPS), pp. 2990–2999 (2017)

61. Srivastava, A., Valkov, L., Russell, C., Gutmann, M.U., Sutton, C.: VEEGAN: reducing mode collapse in GANs using implicit variational learning. In: Proceedings of the Advances in Neural Information Processing Systems (NIPS), pp. 3308–3318 (2017)

62. Tessler, C., Givony, S., Zahavy, T., Mankowitz, D.J., Mannor, S.: A deep hierarchical approach to lifelong learning in Minecraft. In: Proceedings of the AAAI Conference on Artificial Intelligence, pp. 1553–1561 (2017)

63. Wang, X., Zhang, R., Sun, Y., Qi, J.: KDGAN: knowledge distillation with generative adversarial networks. In: Proceedings of the Advances in Neural Information Processing Systems (NIPS), pp. 775–786 (2018)

64. Wu, C., Herranz, L., Liu, X., van de Weijer, J., Raducanu, B.: Memory replay GANs: learning to generate new categories without forgetting. In: Proceedings of the Advances in Neural Information Processing Systems (NIPS), pp. 5962–5972 (2018)

65. Yoon, J., Yang, E., Lee, J., Hwang, S.J.: Lifelong learning with dynamically expandable networks. In: Proceedings of the International Conference on Learning Representations (ICLR). arXiv preprint arXiv:1708.01547 (2017)

66. Zhai, M., Chen, L., Tung, F., He, J., Nawhal, M., Mori, G.: Lifelong GAN: continual learning for conditional image generation. arXiv preprint arXiv:1907.10107 (2019)

67. Zhai, M., Chen, L., Tung, F., He, J., Nawhal, M., Mori, G.: Lifelong GAN: continual learning for conditional image generation. In: Proceedings of the IEEE International Conference on Computer Vision (ICCV), pp. 2759–2768 (2019)

Author Index

Printed in the United States
By Bookmasters